To My P.

Edward

The America Invents Act: A Guide to Patent Litigation and Patent Procedure

November 2013 Edition

Edward D. Manzo

THOMSON REUTERS™

For Customer Assistance Call 1-800-328-4880

Mat #41551304

ISBN 978-0-314-62791-9

About the Author

EDWARD D. MANZO practices IP litigation in courts and at the PTAB, client counseling, and IP portfolio development as a partner in the Chicago office of Husch Blackwell LLP. He was voted a Top 100 Super Lawyer® in Illinois several times beginning in 2010 and has been named a Super Lawyer® annually since 2005. In addition to his law practice, he is the creator and editor-in-chief of *Patent Claim Construction in the Federal Circuit* (Thomson West, 2006 et seq.) and *Patent Claim Interpretation-Global Edition* (Thomson West, 2008 et seq.) Mr. Manzo is the lead author of *Patent Reform 2011—The Leahy-Smith America Invents Act: Commentary and Analysis* (Thomson West 2011) and served as the president of the Intellectual Property Law Association of Chicago (IPLAC) for 2010-11. He co-authored the pattern jury instructions (patents) adopted by the Seventh Circuit in 2008 and the local patent rules adopted in 2009 by the U.S. District Court for the Northern District of Illinois. Mr. Manzo is listed in *Best Lawyers in America®* (2010–14), and is a member of the Richard Linn American Inn of Court. He taught the doctrinal course on patent law at the DePaul University College of Law. He also teaches for Patent Resources Group on the America Invents Act and patent claim interpretation. Mr. Manzo holds degrees in physics (Polytechnic Institute of NYU) and law (SUNY-Buffalo) and is admitted to practice in Illinois, New York, and the USPTO. Further information is available at *www.huschblackwell.com*.

Acknowledgements

This monograph follows an earlier publication of Thomson Reuters entitled *Patent Reform 2011—The Leahy Smith America Invents Act: Commentary and Analysis,* by the undersigned together with Erik B. Flom, Samuel Digirolamo, Michael R. Annis, Jon P. Christensen, Glenn Lenzen, Mark E. Stallion, and Daniel S. Cohn. Their earlier work is gratefully acknowledged. While it generally is not repeated here, it provided useful insights. Many thanks to these colleagues for their earlier work.

This work is dedicated with appreciation to the outstanding teachers and lawyers from whom it was my great privilege to learn.

Edward D. Manzo
Dominus illuminateo mea
November 2013

List of Abbreviations

AIA	America Invents Act (2011), Pub. L. 112-29, 125 Stat.284
AIPA	America Inventors Protection Act, Pub. L. 106-113, 113 Stat. 1536 (1999)
Board	Patent Trial and Appeal Board
CBM	Covered Business Method Patent Review
FITF	First Inventor to File
IPR	*Inter Partes* Review
MPEP	Manual of Patent Examining Procedure
PGR	Post-Grant Review
PTAB	Patent Trial and Appeal Board
PTO	United States Patent and Trademark Office
USPTO	United States Patent and Trademark Office

Preface

The America Invents Act makes the most significant changes to the patent law in 60 years. It impacts innovation at all levels, from multinational corporations to individual inventors. The AIA contains 37 separate sections. Some of them address multiple topics or procedures. To assist patent practitioners who need to understand the AIA's changes in the law, attorney-author Edward Manzo has prepared this easy-to-read, well-organized desk book. It is essential reading for every patent practitioner in the United States.

Mr. Manzo's book efficiently explains each of the AIA's modifications to the patent law against the background of existing law and the relevant expressions of congressional intent. The book divides the AIA into five logical parts. Starting with substantive patent law in Part I, the book explains how the AIA changed the U.S. patent system from "first to invent" to "first inventor to file," redefined the concepts of prior art and the grace period, modified the dates for determining what counts as prior art, and made other substantive law changes of which every patent practitioner should be aware. Mr. Manzo intends to provide annual supplements covering important case rulings on these substantive law revisions.

In addition to the AIA's major modifications of substantive law, the AIA has changed the patent litigation process in several ways. For example, it expands the prior user defense, eliminates the best mode defense (but not the best mode requirement), changes the requirements for joining multiple alleged infringers in one action, revokes the public's ability to file *qui tam* actions for false marking, replaces the *qui tam* action with a new cause of action for persons suffering a competitive injury from a false marking violation, legislates on topics including the advice of counsel, state court jurisdiction, the venue for reviewing PTO actions, and the routes for appeal, and makes other provisions to streamline patent litigation. Mr. Manzo covers these points in Part II of the book.

In Part III, the book explains the new administrative trials before the newly established Patent Trial and Appeal Board (PTAB), which the AIA designed to provide, among other things, expeditious determinations on patentability or the right to the patent (in the case of derivation proceedings). Part III also covers the statutes and USPTO rules applicable to these new proceedings, including the PTAB's general procedures and its procedures for post-grant reviews, reviews of covered business method patents, *inter partes* reviews, and derivation proceedings (which have replaced interferences).

Parts IV and V of Mr. Manzo's book focus on the new PTO procedures to handle patent applications. For example, the AIA gives the PTO an important role in "supplemental examination of patents," through which owners of issued patents can present information to the PTO and, subject to some exceptions, can preempt potential inequitable conduct and related issues in future litigation involving the issued patent.

Attorney-author Edward Manzo has done a great service by preparing this comprehensive, essential desk book on the America Invents Act. Everyone interested in the issuance and enforcement of U.S. patents will benefit greatly from reading it, and should keep a copy close at hand as a reference to address the issues that undoubtedly will arise from the application of the AIA in years to come.

James F. Holderman
Chief Judge, United States District Court for the Northern District of Illinois
January 2013

Contents

Introduction and Summary

This monograph is arranged in five parts.

Part I explains the major substantive patent law revisions.

Part II addresses the major changes affecting litigation.

Part III reviews the four trial proceedings at the Patent Trial and Appeal Board ("PTAB").

Part IV addresses the changes to non-trial submissions of prior art and other information to the USPTO, including the new supplementary examination procedure.

Part V focuses on the remaining changes to USPTO practice and miscellaneous provisions in the AIA.

Appendix 1 reproduces excerpts of the House Report on H.R. 1249. There is no Senate report on its bill, S. 23. The House Report explains the reforms that Congress wanted to make to the patent statute.

Appendix 2 provides a copy of the final language of H.R. 1249 as enrolled for the signature of the President.

Appendix 3 provides a copy of the changed USPTO final rules.

Appendix 4 is a copy of a USPTO memorandum re the best mode requirement (Sept. 20, 2011).

Appendix 5 is a copy of a USPTO memorandum re the ban on patenting human organisms (Sept. 20, 2011).

Appendix 6 is a copy of a USPTO memorandum re the patenting of tax strategies (Sept. 20, 2011).

Appendix 7 is a copy of the "Act to Correct and Improve Certain Provisions of the Leahy-Smith America Invents Act and Title 35, United States Code," H.R. 6621 (final, enrolled version).

Appendix 8 is a copy of the PTAB ruling in *Garmin Intl, Inc. v. Cuozzo Speed Technologies LLC*, IPR2012–00001, Paper No. 26 (PTAB March 5, 2013)

This Introduction is divided into three parts. The Executive Summary discusses the most significant aspects of the AIA. Following the Executive Summary is a brief excerpt of the House Report where Congress explained its overall purpose behind the AIA and summarized how it proceeded. This Introduction then concludes with a listing of the 37 section titles of the AIA.

Executive Summary

I. Substantive Patent Law Revisions

First Inventor to File (Sec. 3): Congress completely replaced the old § 102 with a new formulation that redefines prior art and essentially requires absolute novelty subject to a limited grace period. Absent derivation from an earlier inventor who files a patent application, the patent right is awarded to the first inventor to file. However, an inventor who is second to file can overcome certain prior art via the exceptions specified in new § 102(b). Sections 102(c) (abandonment) and 102(f) (did not himself invent) of the prior statute are removed. Section 102(g) (interferences) is replaced with a provision for proving derivation.

Grace Period (Sec. 3): The prior statute allowed a one-year grace period for an inventor to file a patent application despite certain events relative to a disclosure or use. Under the revised statute, the grace period is confined to disclosures by (or via) the actual inventor. Publications or uses by others are not covered by the grace period but instead are prior art unless they are subsequent to a public disclosure of that material by the inventor or unless the disclosing party obtained the subject matter from an inventor or co-inventor.

Prior Art Dates for Patents/Applications (Sec. 3): Under the old statute, a patent or published application speaks as prior art as of its actual U.S. filing date unless it is entitled to an earlier U.S. priority date. Under new § 102(d), if the patent or application is entitled to a foreign priority date under various sections, or an earlier filing date under various sections, then as to any subject matter described in the patent or application, the patent or published application speaks as prior art as of the earliest filing date (including priority date) to which it is entitled. This represents a change in practice under former § 102(e) and *In re Hilmer*.[1] Disclosures appearing in applications and patents are not prior art if the subject matter was obtained from an inventor, is subject to a grace period due to public disclosure by an inventor, or is subject to common ownership or obligation to assign by a certain date. The AIA removes the prior requirement of § 102(e) that the patent document have been published in the English language as a condition to qualifying as prior art.

Definition of Joint Inventor (Sec. 3): The AIA now defines a joint inventor as any of the individuals collectively who invented or discovered the subject matter of a joint invention.

Section 103 (Sec. 3): Consistent with the extensive changes to § 102, § 103 is amended to delete reference to obviousness determinations "at the time the invention was made." Section 103 as revised now calls for determining obviousness "before the effective filing date." The AIA thus removes the statutory basis for determining obviousness *at the date of conception* (or actual reduction to practice) and now focuses on the effective filing date. Additionally, the AIA changes the familiar § 103 language of "subject matter as a whole" to "claimed invention"—just as that phrase is defined in § 100(j) and now used in §§ 102 and 273(b)(1).

Specific Subject Matter Addressed (Sec. 14, 33): The AIA prohibits patents on human "organisms" and places limits on the patentability of tax strategy inventions, declaring that the tax strategy portions of claims are prior art.

Best Mode (Sec. 15): The best mode requirement is retained, but violation of this requirement is not a basis to invalidate an issued patent in federal court for actions commenced after the effective date. Nor can it can be raised in a post-grant review. It remains a requirement of the statute and, as such, examiners can reject claims for failure to disclose the best mode if they have information to support such a rejection.

II. AIA Changes re Patent Litigation

Prior User Defense (Sec. 5): The prior user defense of § 273 is expanded beyond just business methods and now

[1] *In re Hilmer*, 359 F.2d 859, 149 USPQ 480 (C.C.P.A. 1966).

also includes machines, manufactures, or compositions used in manufacturing or other commercial processes. The defense is personal and requires use in the United States at least one year before the effective filing date of the patent being enforced or a pre-filing disclosure, whichever is earlier. The AIA provides an exception for university patents under many circumstances. This defense is for patents granted after enactment, so the provisions of the pre-AIA statute remain in effect for existing patents.

Joinder (Sec. 19): The AIA limits the right to join multiple alleged patent infringers in one action or consolidate actions for trial. Under Rule 20, F.R.Civ.Proc., joinder required meeting a transaction-occurrence limitation and a common question of law or fact limitation. Rule 20 is superseded (as to patent cases) by new 35 U.S.C. § 299 which: (1) specifies that the transaction-occurrence must relate to making, using, importing, offering for sale, or selling the same accused product or process; (2) narrows the "common questions" branch to common questions of fact (common questions of law are not qualifying conditions under § 299); and (3) adds a new, further limitation making it insufficient to plead only that each alleged infringer has infringed the same patent(s)-in-suit.

Patent Marking, Mismarking (Sec. 16): The AIA terminates *qui tam* actions for false marking. Henceforth, only the United States can sue for the false marking penalty (up to $500 per offense). However, a new cause of action is created for persons who suffer a competitive injury from the violation. They may sue in the district court to recover "damages adequate to compensate for the injury." Finally, the failure to modify the patent marking to remove the number of an expired patent "is not a violation...". The AIA also provides for virtual patent marking (using the Internet).

Advice of Counsel (Sec. 17): The AIA forbids using any failure of an infringer to obtain the advice of counsel as evidence of willful infringement or that the actor intended to induce infringement of the patent.

Jurisdiction (Sec. 19): The AIA amends 35 U.S.C. § 1338 to deny expressly any jurisdiction of any State court for claims for relief arising under Acts of Congress relating to patents, plant variety protection, or copyrights. Civil actions may be removed to the district court in which such a claim is made.

Review of USPTO Decisions: Appeals (Sec. 7) and Venue (Sec. 9): The AIA provides that appeals from the Patent Trial and Appeals Board in reexaminations, post grant reviews, and *inter partes* reviews lie with the Federal Circuit. Appeals from derivation proceedings are filed with the Federal Circuit, but a party may opt to proceed under 35 U.S.C. § 146 and commence a civil action. For judicial review of USPTO actions, the AIA places venue in the Eastern District of Virginia instead of the District of Columbia.

Deceptive Intent: The AIA removes deceptive intent from 35 U.S.C. § 288 so that an action for infringement may be maintained as to a valid claim even if another claim in the patent is invalid. Formerly, § 288 indicated that deceptive intent prevented such an action. Deceptive intent is also removed from Sections 116 (correction of inventors in application), 184 (application filed in foreign country), 185 (patent barred for filing without license), 251 (reissue of defective patents), 253 (disclaimer), and 256 (correction of named inventor).

III. Trials at the PTAB

Interferences Replaced by Derivation Proceedings (Sec. 3): Section 135 is rewritten without interferences. Instead, the USPTO may conduct derivation proceedings. If a first-to-file "inventor" derived the invention from a second inventor to file, the Board may conduct a hearing to determine the issue. The Board of Patent Appeals and Interferences is replaced by a Patent Trial and Appeal Board (PTAB) that has responsibilities like those of the old Board, modified to comport with the change in statute. Section 291 is changed from "Interfering Patents" to "Derived Patents" and modified accordingly by Sec. 3(h) of the AIA.

Post-Grant Review (Sec. 6(d)): Anyone except the patent owner may file a petition within 9 months of a patent or reissue grant for a post-grant review ("PGR") based on any ground set forth in 35 U.S.C. § 282(b), para. (2) or (3). The USPTO intends to allow subject matter eligibility challenges also. The petition cannot be granted absent a determination that it is more likely than not that one or more claims is unpatentable or that the petition raises a novel or unsettled legal question that is important to other patents or pending applications. This is an adversarial proceeding where the petitioner and the patent owner participate. The PTAB trial rules (37 C.F.R. §§ 42.1–42.80) apply. The proceeding is heard by the PTAB, with a ruling to occur within 12 months, extendible by 6 months, of the date of notice that the proceeding has been instituted. The burden on the petitioner is a preponderance of the evidence. Various estoppels apply. Appeal is to the Federal Circuit.

Post-Grant Review of Business Method Patents (Sec. 18): A petitioner may seek a PGR to review "covered business method patents" in the USPTO after threats (or the commencement) of litigation. The covered patents must relate to a financial product or service and cannot be patents for "technological inventions." The petition cannot be filed during the 9 months when a regular PGR petition may be filed. The PGR rules apply except on a few points. The estoppel effects of CBM review are not as pervasive as those for PGR and IPR. As with regular PGR, appeal is to the Federal Circuit.

Inter Partes Review (Sec. 6(a)): The AIA replaces *inter partes* reexaminations with *inter partes* review ("IPR"), an adversarial proceeding conducted before the PTAB. All patents are subject to *inter partes* review. Only patents or printed publications can be considered. IPR cannot be initiated until after the 9 month period for PGR expires or, if a PGR involving that patent is underway, until termination of the PGR. The threshold standard for granting IPR is a reasonable likelihood that the petitioner would prevail on at least one claim. The USPTO views this as a lower standard than a preponderance. An IPR cannot be instituted if the petitioner or privies filed a district court action challenging the validity of a claim of a patent. Conversely, if civil litigation is filed upon or after filing a petition for IPR, the civil action must be stayed automatically until certain events occur. The revised statute provides for estoppel. The AIA calls for the IPR to be heard by the PTAB which is to reach a final written determination within 12 months, extendible by 6 months, of "noticing" the review. The AIA permits oral hearings. Appeal is to the Federal Circuit.

IV. Non-Trial Citations of Art & Information to the USPTO; Reexaminations

Pre-Issue Citations by Third Parties (Sec. 8): The AIA adds a new § 122(e) to permit pre-issuance submissions by third parties before a notice of allowance, or the later of 6 months after first publication or the date of a final rejection. This applies to all patent applications, whenever filed.

Post-Issue Submissions (Sec. 6(g)): The AIA expands § 301 so that in addition to citing patents and printed publications, anyone can cite patent owner statements filed in a federal court proceeding or the USPTO where the patent owner took a position on the scope of any claim of a patent. Such statements as to scope can be used by the USPTO to determine the proper scope of a claim. Statements can be submitted in confidence and under anonymity. The patent owner can also submit a written statement explaining how claims differ from any prior art submitted under § 301(a)(1).

Ex Parte Reexamination: The AIA does not change *ex parte* reexaminations. They continue to use the standard of a substantial new question of patentability and continue to be handled by an examiner (rather than by a panel of the PTAB).

Inter Partes Reexamination *Inter partes* reexaminations are replaced by *inter partes* review, as noted above. The change was not immediate, however, and *inter partes* reexaminations remained available during a one-year transition period from Sept.16, 2011 to Sept. 15, 2012. The AIA immediately changed the standard for instituting an *inter partes* reexamination from raising a "substantial new question of patentability" to demonstrating a reasonable likelihood that the petitioner would prevail on at least one challenged claim. As of Sept. 16, 2012, requests for *inter partes* reexamination were no longer entertained. From that date forward, the USPTO will not assign a filing date to such requests.

Supplemental Examination (Sec. 12): A patent owner may request supplemental examination for any information believed to be relevant to the patent. The Director has 3 months to determine whether this presents a substantial new question of patentability. If so, reexamination commences. This allows review of any information that may otherwise have been considered in an inequitable conduct defense.

Standards Mentioned (*passim*):

- Supplemental examination –substantial new question of patentability; 35 U.S.C. § 257
- *Ex parte* reexamination –substantial new question of patentability; 35 U.S.C. § 302
- Pre-issuance and post-issuance submissions –no standard
- *Inter partes* review –reasonable likelihood that the petitioner would prevail re at least one claim; 35 U.S.C. § 314
- Post-Grant review –more likely than not that a challenged claim is unpatentable; 35 U.S.C. § 324

V. Remaining USPTO Practice & Miscellaneous AIA Provisions

Oath and Filing (Sec. 4): Applications need not be filed by the inventors themselves but may be filed by their employers. The name(s) of the individual inventor(s) is (are) still required. Additionally, the prior cumbersome filing requirements for assignees have been relaxed and are more practical to use.

Fees and Micro Entities (Sec. 10-11): The AIA increases most fees modestly and makes special provisions for a new class of customer –the "micro entity" –that has even smaller fees than "small entity" customers. Applicants can obtain prioritized examination for a fee of $4,800.

Correction of Inventorship (Sec. 20(f)): The AIA removes the requirement of having no deceptive intention in order to change the named inventorship on a patent.

Fee Diversion (Sec. 22): One controversial difference between Senate bill S. 23 and House bill H.R. 1249 concerns the diversion of fees collected by the USPTO. The AIA does not provide explicitly for the USPTO to keep all the fees that it collects. Instead, a reserve fund is created within the U.S. Treasury. USPTO access to the reserve fund is dependent on appropriation acts.

Satellite Offices (Sec. 23-24): The AIA requires the establishment of at least 3 branch offices of the USPTO in other locations, starting with Detroit. The AIA set forth considerations for selecting locations, and the USPTO has specified three further satellite offices.

Priority Examination (Sec. 25): The Director is authorized to advance the examination of inventions in certain technologies important to the national economy or national competitiveness.

Small Entities, Individual Inventors: The AIA has several provisions benefiting small entities and individual inventors.

- Sec. 4(l) calls for a study of the effects of removing the use of dates of invention in determining whether an applicant is entitled to a patent. This study is to include examining how the change affects the ability of small business concerns to obtain patents, etc.
- Sec. 10 creates the "micro-entity" which is entitled to large fee reductions.
- Sec. 28 requires the Director to establish a Patent Ombudsman Program, the duties of which must include providing support and services related to patent filings for small business concerns and independent inventors.
- Sec. 30 states that Congress intends to protect rights of small businesses and inventors from predatory behavior that could result in cutting off innovation.
- Sec. 31 requires the Director to conduct a study on how to help small businesses with international patent protection.
- Sec. 32 calls for the Director to work with intellectual property law associations across the United States to establish pro bono programs designed to assist financially under-resourced independent inventors and small businesses.

Historical Development of the America Invents Act

Patent reform has been sought for many years in industry and Congress. The following excerpts from the House Report give a brief overview of the Congressional hearings and efforts:

PURPOSE AND SUMMARY

The Constitution explicitly grants Congress the power to "promote the progress of science and useful arts, by securing for limited times to . . . inventors the exclusive right to their respective . . . discoveries." Congress has responded by authorizing patents to issue to inventors of new and useful inventions or improvements on inventions. The patent law thus accomplishes two objectives, consistent with the authorization granted by the Constitution: first, it encourages inventors by granting them limited, but exclusive rights to their inventions; second, in exchange for the grant of those exclusive rights, the patent law requires disclosure of the invention and terminates the monopoly after a period of years. This disclosure and limited time benefits both society and future inventors by making the details of the invention available to the public immediately, and the right to make use of that invention after the expiration of 20 years from the date the patent application was filed.

Congress has not enacted comprehensive patent law reform in nearly 60 years. The object of the patent law today must remain true to the constitutional command, but its form needs to change, both to correct flaws in the system that have become unbearable, and to accommodate changes in the economy and the litigation practices in the patent realm. The need to update our patent laws has been meticulously documented in 15 hearings before the Committee or its Subcommittee on Courts, the Internet, and Intellectual Property, as well as eight hearings before the United States Senate Committee on the Judiciary. In addition, these legislative findings are augmented by the Federal Trade Commission and the National Academy of Sciences, both of which published authoritative reports on patent reform, and a plethora of academic commentary.

While Congress has considered patent reform legislation over the last four Congresses, the need to modernize our patent laws has found expression in the courts, as well. The Supreme Court has reversed the Federal Circuit in six of the patent-related cases that it has heard since the beginning of the 109th Congress. The Court's decisions have moved in the direction of improving patent quality and making the determination of patent validity more efficient. The decisions reflect a growing sense that questionable patents are too easily obtained and are too difficult to challenge. Recent decisions by the Federal Circuit reflect a similar trend in response to these concerns. But the courts are constrained in their decisions by the text of the statutes at issue. It is time for Congress to act.

The voices heard during the debate over changes to the patent law have been diverse and their proposals have been far from uniform. They have focused the Committee's attention on the value of harmonizing our system for granting patents with the best parts of other major patent systems throughout the industrialized world for the benefit of U.S. patent holders;

improving patent quality and providing a more efficient system for challenging patents that should not have issued; and reducing unwarranted litigation costs and inconsistent damage awards.

The purpose of the "America Invents Act," as reported by the Committee on the Judiciary, is to ensure that the patent system in the 21st century reflects the constitutional imperative. Congress must promote innovation by granting inventors temporally limited monopolies on their inventions in a manner that ultimately benefits the public through the disclosure of the invention to the public. The legislation is designed to establish a more efficient and streamlined patent system that will improve patent quality and limit unnecessary and counterproductive litigation costs.

If the United States is to maintain its competitive edge in the global economy, it needs a system that will support and reward all innovators with high quality patents. The Committee has taken testimony from and its members have held meetings with interested parties that have different and often conflicting perspectives on the patent system. The Committee has taken all of those views into consideration, and drafted and then amended the "America Invents Act" to balance the competing interests. The legislation ordered reported by the Committee on a vote of 32-3 is a consensus approach that will modernize the United States patent system in significant respects.

***

Hearings

The Committee's Subcommittee on Intellectual Property, Competition, and the Internet held 1 day of hearings on H.R. 1249. The hearing took place on March 30, 2011. Testimony was received from the Honorable David Kappos, Under Secretary of Commerce for Intellectual Property and Director of the United States Patent and Trademark Office; Steve Bartlett, President and CEO of The Financial Services Roundtable; Steven Miller, President and General Counsel (Intellectual Property) for Procter & Gamble; Mark Chandler, Senior Vice President, General Counsel, and Secretary for Cisco; and John Vaughn, Executive Vice President of the Association of American Universities.

The Subcommittee also conducted three separate but related hearings on January 25, 2011 ("How an Improved US Patent and Trademark Office Can Create Jobs," Serial No. 112-6), February 11, 2011 ("Crossing the Finish Line on Patent

Reform—What Can and Should be Done," Serial No. 112-8), and March 10, 2011 ("Review of Recent Judicial Decisions on Patent Law," Serial No. 112- 20).

Given that the bill is a 6-year work in progress, the legislative record should also reflect that the Subcommittee conducted related hearings on patent reform in the 109th through 111th Congresses. These hearings include the following: "H.R. 2795, the 'Patent Reform Act of 2005'" (June 19, 2005); "Committee Print Regarding Patent Quality Improvement (Part I)" (April 20, 2005, Serial No. 109-11); "Committee Print Regarding Patent Quality Improvement (Part II)" (April 28, 2005, Serial No. 109-11); "Review of US Patent and Trademark Office Operations" (September 8, 2005, Serial No. 109-48); "Patent Quality Enhancement in the Information-Based Economy" (April 5, 2006, Serial No. 109-99); "Patent Harmonization" (April 26, 2006, Serial No. 109-100); "Patent Trolls: Fact or Fiction?" (June 15, 2006, Serial No. 109-104); "Oversight Hearing on the US Patent and Trademark Office" (February 27, 2008, Serial No. 110-115); "The 'Patent Reform Act of 2007'" (April 26, 2007, Serial No. 110-65); "H.R. 1260, The 'Patent Reform Act of 2009'" (April 30, 2009, Serial No. 111-92); and "The US Patent and Trademark Office" (May 5, 2010, Serial No. 111-135).

Finally, the United States Senate Committee on the Judiciary devoted substantial process to patent reform over the same time period. Beginning in 2005, the Senate Judiciary Committee conducted eight hearings on the subject and reported separate bills in the 110th (S. 1145), 111th (S. 515), and 112th (S. 23) Congresses. The full Senate passed S. 23 on March 8, 2011, by a vote of 95- 5. H.R. 1249 is substantially similar to S. 23.[2]

Contents of the America Invents Act

The America Invents Act includes the following sections:

[2] H. R. Rep. No. 112-98, pt. 1, pp. 38-40, 57 (2011).

Table of Contents

PART I. SUBSTANTIVE PATENT LAW REVISIONS

CHAPTER 1. NEW DEFINITIONS

CHAPTER 2. FIRST INVENTOR TO FILE

CHAPTER 3. BEST MODE AND SECTION 112

CHAPTER 4. UNPATENTABILITY OF "HUMAN ORGANISMS"

CHAPTER 5. LIMITED PATENTABILITY OF TAX STRATEGIES

CHAPTER 6. PATENT MARKING

CHAPTER 7. MISCELLANEOUS SUBSTANTIVE PATENT LAW PROVISIONS

PART II. PATENT ENFORCEMENT ISSUES

CHAPTER 8. THE PRIOR USER DEFENSE

CHAPTER 9. FALSE PATENT MARKING (MISMARKING)

CHAPTER 10. ENHANCED DAMAGES AND ADVICE OF COUNSEL

CHAPTER 11. VENUE FOR REVIEW OF USPTO DECISIONS

CHAPTER 12. JURISDICTION

CHAPTER 13. JOINDER AND CONSOLIDATION

CHAPTER 14. MISCELLANEOUS ENFORCEMENT ISSUES

PART III. USPTO TRIAL PROCEEDINGS

CHAPTER 15. PTAB TRIAL PRACTICE

CHAPTER 16. POST-GRANT REVIEW

CHAPTER 17. REVIEW OF COVERED BUSINESS METHOD PATENTS

CHAPTER 18. INTER PARTES REVIEW

CHAPTER 19. DERIVATION PROCEEDINGS REPLACE INTERFERENCES

PART IV. USPTO NON-TRIAL SUBMISSIONS OF ART OR INFORMATION; REEXAMINATIONS

CHAPTER 20. PRE-ISSUANCE SUBMISSIONS

CHAPTER 21. POST-ISSUANCE SUBMISSIONS

CHAPTER 22. SUPPLEMENTAL EXAMINATION

CHAPTER 23. REEXAMINATIONS (*INTER PARTES* AND *EX PARTE*)

PART V. MISCELLANEOUS PROVISIONS

CHAPTER 24. ASSIGNEE FILING AND INVENTOR'S OATH

CHAPTER 25. PTO FEE SETTING AND FEES

CHAPTER 26. FEE DIVERSION-PTO FUNDING

CHAPTER 27. REMOVAL OF DECEPTIVE INTENT FROM STATUTE

CHAPTER 28. SATELLITE OFFICES

CHAPTER 29. PRIORITIZED EXAMINATION & PRIORITY EXAMINATION FOR IMPORTANT TECHNOLOGIES

CHAPTER 30. PATENT TERM EXTENSION CALCULATION

CHAPTER 31. OTHER AIA PROVISIONS AND PTO PROGRAMS

CHAPTER 32. EFFECTIVE DATES

APPENDICES

Part I

SUBSTANTIVE PATENT LAW REVISIONS

Chapter 1

New Definitions

KeyCite®: Cases and other legal materials listed in KeyCite Scope can be researched through the KeyCite service on Westlaw®. Use KeyCite to check citations for form, parallel references, prior and later history, and comprehensive citator information, including citations to other decisions and secondary materials.

AIA §§ 2, 10
35 U.S.C.A. §§ 100(f)–(j), 123

§ 1:1 Explicit definitions in the AIA

The patent statute prior to the AIA revisions included five definitions in 35 U.S.C. § 100. That section defined (a) "invention," (b) "process," (c) "United States" and "this country," (d) "patentee," and (e) "third-party requester." AIA § 3 adds several new definitions, and other parts of the AIA add still further definitions. The definitions are presented below in alphabetical order rather than their order of appearance in the AIA.

Claimed Invention. New 35 U.S.C. § 100(j) defines a "*claimed invention*" as "the subject matter defined by a claim in a patent or an application for a patent." It may be noted that the definition of "effective filing date" is for "a claimed invention." Since the term "claimed invention" is defined as the subject matter defined in an application claim or patent claim, this means that the effective filing date is defined with respect to each claimed invention rather than the application itself or the issued patent. While in many cases there will be a single date that applies to all claims, this is not necessarily the case. Different claims in a patent or patent application can be entitled to different effective filing dates. This does not represent a change in the law.

Covered Business Method Patent. AIA § 18(d) defines a "*covered business method patent*" as follows:

> (d) DEFINITION.—
>
> (1) IN GENERAL.— For purposes of this section, the term "covered business method patent" means a patent that claims a method or corresponding apparatus for performing data processing or other operations used in the practice, administration, or management of a financial product or service, except that the term does not include patents for technological inventions.

Director. AIA § 2 defines the "Director" as follows:

> (1) DIRECTOR.— The term "Director" means the Under Secretary of Commerce for Intellectual Property and Director of the United States Patent and Trademark Office.

Effective Filing Date. New 35 U.S.C. § 100(i) provides the definition of the "*effective filing date*," which is critical in the first inventor to file system. The new definition provides as follows:

> (i) (1) The term "effective filing date" for a claimed invention in a patent or application for patent means—
>
> (A) if subparagraph (B) does not apply, the actual filing date of the patent or the application for the patent containing a claim to the invention; or
>
> (B) the filing date of the earliest application for which the patent or application is entitled, as to such invention, to a right of priority under section 119, 365(a), or 365(b) or to the benefit of an earlier filing date under section 120, 121, or 365(c).
>
> (2) The effective filing date for a claimed invention in an application for reissue or reissued patent shall be determined by deeming the claim to the invention to have been contained in the patent for which reissue was sought.

Inventor. AIA § 3 adds a new 35 U.S.C. § 100(f) defining the word "*inventor*" as "the individual or, if a joint invention, the individuals collectively who invented or discovered the subject matter of the invention."[1]

Joint Inventor. New 35 U.S.C. § 100(g) is for "*joint inventors*" and states as follows: "the terms 'joint inventor' and 'co-inventor' mean any 1 of the individuals who invented or discovered the subject matter of a joint invention."[2]

Joint Research Agreement. New § 100(h) defines a "*joint research agreement.*" This is important to the revised § 102 and states as follows:

> The term "joint research agreement" means a written contract, grant or cooperative agreement entered into by 2 or more persons or entities for the performance of experimental, developmental or research work in the field of the claimed invention.

This definition came from the Cooperative Research and Technology Enhancement Act of 2004 (CREATE Act) and was previously codified as 35 U.S.C. § 103(c)(3). In the AIA, Congress moved this definition from § 103 into § 100.

Micro entity. AIA § 10 concerns fees and adds a definition codified as 35 U.S.C. § 123 for the new "micro entity" as follows:

> **35 U.S.C. § 123. Micro entity defined**
>
> (a) IN GENERAL.— For purposes of this title, the term 'micro entity' means an applicant who makes a certification that the applicant—
>
> (1) qualifies as a small entity, as defined in regulations issued by the Director;
>
> (2) has not been named as an inventor on more than 4 previously filed patent applications, other than applications filed in another country, provisional applications under section 111(b), or international applications filed under the treaty defined in section 351(a) for which the basic national fee under section 41(a) was not paid;
>
> (3) did not, in the calendar year preceding the calendar year in which the applicable fee is being paid, have a gross income, as defined in section 61(a) of the Internal Revenue Code of 1986, exceeding 3 times the median household income for that preceding calendar year, as most recently reported by the Bureau of the Census; and
>
> (4) has not assigned, granted, or conveyed, and is not under an obligation by contract or law to assign, grant, or

---

[Section 1:1]

[1]Pub. L. No. 112-29, Sec. 3(a), 125 Stat. 284, 285 (2011).

[2]Pub. L. No. 112-29, Sec. 3(a), 125 Stat. 284, 285 (2011).

convey, a license or other ownership interest in the application concerned to an entity that, in the calendar year preceding the calendar year in which the applicable fee is being paid, had a gross income, as defined in section 61(a) of the Internal Revenue Code of 1986, exceeding 3 times the median household income for that preceding calendar year, as most recently reported by the Bureau of the Census.

Office. AIA § 2 specifies, "The term 'Office' means the United States Patent and Trademark Office."

The AIA also defines some other terms that are generally not mentioned in this book but include the terms "Patent Public Advisory Committee," "Trademark Act of 1946," and "Trademark Public Advisory Committee." It should be noted that the provisions as to these committees are amended by H.R. 6621, § 1(l) (2013).

§ 1:2 Definitions missing from the AIA

In the new novelty provisions of Section 102, the AIA uses two differing terms, "publicly disclosed" (§ 102(b)(1)(B)) and "otherwise available to the public" (§ 102(a)(1)). These are *not* defined by the AIA. Judicial explication of these phrases is inevitable.

Chapter 2

First Inventor to File

AIA § 3
35 U.S.C.A. §§ 102, 103

§ 2:1 Introduction

Among the most significant changes to U.S. patent law in the America Invents Act is the change from a first to invent system to a first-inventor-to-file ("FITF") system. Because the U.S. patent system was based on awarding patents to the first inventor, the actual filing date of a patent application was one data point but often was not conclusive. That is, an inventor could obtain a U.S. patent even if he was not the first inventor to file a patent application for the invention. When confronted by an earlier-filed patent application, the inventor has had the opportunity to prove earlier invention and overcome the prior application. This applied to situations where either the earlier-filed application was for the same invention or where the earlier-filed U.S. patent application was being asserted as "prior art" against the inventor's patent or patent application. The inventor had the opportunity to prove priority. This first to invent approach has led to an entire jurisprudence of patent interference law which is unparalleled outside the U.S.

However, the 112th Congress concluded that a change was (1) in the interest of promoting the progress of science and the useful arts, and (2) in the interest of global uniformity of patent laws and certainty in the procedures used for securing patents. Congress stated these findings explicitly in AIA § 3:

> 3. * * *(o) Sense of Congress— It is the sense of the Congress that converting the United States patent system from 'first to invent' to a system of 'first inventor to file' will promote the progress of science and the useful arts by securing for limited times to inventors the exclusive rights to their discoveries and provide inventors with greater certainty regarding the scope of protection provided by the grant of exclusive rights to their discoveries.
>
> (p) Sense of Congress— It is the sense of the Congress that converting the United States patent system from 'first to invent' to a system of 'first inventor to file' will improve the United States patent system and promote harmonization of the United States patent system with the patent systems commonly used in nearly all other countries throughout the world with whom the United States conducts trade and thereby promote greater international uniformity and certainty in the procedures used for securing the exclusive rights of inventors to their discoveries.

§ 2:2 Constitutionality

Congress considered the constitutionality of a FITF system and concluded that this approach is constitutional.[1] The FITF approach does not run afoul of the requirement that a

---

[Section 2:2]

[1]The constitutionality of the FITF system was challenged in *Madstad Engineering, Inc. v. U.S. Patent & Trademark Office*, 2013 WL 3155280 (M.D. Fla. 2013), but the court dismissed the case for lack of standing. Id. at *7. The court noted that the Supreme Court had recently reviewed standing requirements in *Clapper v. Amnesty Intern. USA*, 133 S. Ct. 1138, 185 L. Ed. 2d 264, 41 Media L. Rep. (BNA) 1357 (2013). There,

patent can issue to only an inventor or discoverer. Article I, Section 8, Clause 8 of the U.S. Constitution refers to "inventors"—not to "first inventors." It does not place many limits or conditions on how Congress should determine patent rights. The Constitution permits Congress to protect those who invent or discover, and courts have held that a person who independently invents is an "inventor" even if someone else previously invented the subject matter. Even under § 102 (2006), a valid U.S. patent could issue if the same invention had been previously invented outside the U.S. and placed in public use there before the second inventor's U.S. filing date, assuming the prior inventor does not file in the U.S., publish the invention, place it on sale in the U.S., etc., and the second inventor did not derive or copy.

Under the Constitution, Congress can choose to provide patent protection in a way that Congress believes will best accomplish the constitutional goals. Congress has determined, for various reasons, that it will reward the first inventor to file rather than the first inventor to invent. Congress remarked that the FITF approach returns the U.S. to a system that existed originally in the U.S., namely a first inventor to register system, which prevailed for several decades when the U.S. was first founded.[2]

Other aspects of the AIA have been challenged as unconstitutional. These will be discussed *infra* but concern, for example, challenges that the termination of *qui tam* actions constitutes an unlawful "taking" within the meaning of the Fifth Amendment.

---

plaintiff asserted standing on the basis of added expenditures it undertook to protect itself, but the court explained, "expenditures in anticipation of these conjectural events are controlled entirely by the judgment and discretion of the plaintiffs ([and hence are] 'manufactured' and 'self-inflicted wounds,' 133 S.Ct. at 1151-52)."

[2]H.R. 1249, America Invents Act—Constitutionality (June 2011) at http://judiciary.house.gov/issues/Patent%20Reform%20PDFS/HR%201249%201%20pager%20Constitutionality.pdf. On July 18, 2012, a suit was filed seeking a declaration that the first inventor to file system is unconstitutional. See *Madstad Eng'g., Inc. v. U.S. Patent and Trademark Office,* civil action 8:12-cv-01589-SDM-MAP in the U.S. District Court for the Middle District of Florida.

§ 2:3 The old section 102

Prior to amendments by the AIA, 35 U.S.C. § 102 amalgamated a variety of patent-defeating concepts.[1] In brief, Section 102(a) concerned whether the invention was publicly known before the invention by the applicant. Section 102(b) made a printed publication (globally) or a public use or sale

---

[Section 2:3]

[1]The pre-AIA 35 U.S.C.A. 102 provides as follows: "§ 102. Conditions for patentability; novelty and loss of right to patent. A person shall be entitled to a patent unless—

"(a) the invention was known or used by others in this country, or patented or described in a printed publication in this or a foreign country, before the invention thereof by the applicant for patent, or

"(b) the invention was patented or described in a printed publication in this or a foreign country or in public use or on sale in this country, more than one year prior to the date of the application for patent in the United States, or

"(c) he has abandoned the invention, or

"(d) the invention was first patented or caused to be patented, or was the subject of an inventor's certificate, by the applicant or his legal representatives or assigns in a foreign country prior to the date of the application for patent in this country on an application for patent or inventor's certificate filed more than twelve months before the filing of the application in the United States, or

"(e) the invention was described in—(1) an application for patent, published under section 122(b), by another filed in the United States before the invention by the applicant for patent or (2) a patent granted on an application for patent by another filed in the United States before the invention by the applicant for patent, except that an international application filed under the treaty defined in section 351(a) shall have the effects for the purposes of this subsection of an application filed in the United States only if the international application designated the United States and was published under Article 21(2) of such treaty in the English language; or

"(f) he did not himself invent the subject matter sought to be patented, or

"(g)(1) during the course of an interference conducted under section 135 or section 291, another inventor involved therein establishes, to the extent permitted in section 104, that before such person's invention thereof the invention was made by such other inventor and not abandoned, suppressed, or concealed, or (2) before such person's invention thereof, the invention was made in this country by another inventor who had not abandoned, suppressed, or concealed it. In determining priority of invention under this subsection, there shall be considered not only the respective dates of conception and reduction to practice of the invention, but also the reasonable diligence of one who was first to conceive and last to reduce to practice, from a time prior to conception by the other."

(Amended July 28, 1972, Public Law 92-358, sec. 2, 86 Stat. 501; Nov. 14, 1975, Public Law 94-131, sec. 5, 89 Stat. 691.)

(Subsection (e) amended Nov. 29, 1999, Public Law 106-113, sec. 1000(a)(9), 113 Stat. 1501A-565 (S. 1948 sec. 4505).)

(Subsection (g) amended Nov. 29, 1999, Public Law 106-113, sec. 1000(a)(9), 113 Stat. 1501A-590 (S. 1948 sec. 4806).)

(Subsection (e) amended Nov. 2, 2002, Public Law 107-273, sec. 13205, 116 Stat. 1903.)

in the United States more than one year prior to the U.S. application date an insuperable bar. Section 102(c) concerned abandonment of the invention and did not directly focus on "prior art." Section 102(d) concerned the patenting (or the like) by the applicant in a foreign country based on an application more than 12 months before the U.S. filing date. Section 102(e) concerned treating other applications filed in the United States as prior art. Section 102(f) mandated that the applicant himself had to be the inventor of the subject matter. Finally, Section 102(g) focused on the first to invent and allowed interferences to occur between rival claimants to the same invention.

In shifting away from a "first-to-invent" system to a "first-inventor-to-file" system, Congress generally discarded these provisions and rewrote Section 102 without the substance of former subsections 102(c), (d), (f) and (g).

§ 2:4 Congressional intent

The House Report discusses the differences between a first to invent system and a first to file system and addresses the new "first-inventor-to-file" system as follows:

> *First Inventor to File*
>
> The "America Invents Act" creates a new "first-inventor-to-file" system. Every industrialized nation other than the United States uses a patent priority system commonly referred to as "first-to-file." In a first-to-file system, when more than one application claiming the same invention is filed, the priority of a right to a patent is based on the earlier-filed application. The United States, by contrast, currently uses a "first-to-invent" system, in which priority is established through a proceeding to determine which applicant actually invented the claimed invention first. Differences between the two systems arise in large part from the date that is most relevant to each respective system. In a first-to-file system, the filing date of the application is most relevant;[1] the filing date of an application is an objective date, simple to determine, for it is listed on the face of the patent. In contrast, in a first-to-invent system, the date the invention claimed in the application was actually invented is the determinative date. Unlike the objective date of filing, the date someone invents something is often uncer-

[Section 2:4]

[1]When the term 'filing date' is used herein, it is also meant to include, when appropriate, the effective filing date, *i.e.*, the earliest date the claim in an application-claims priority.

tain, and, when disputed, typically requires corroborating evidence as part of an adjudication.

There are significant, practical differences between the two systems. Among them is the ease of determining the right to a claimed invention in the instance in which two different people file patent applications for the same invention. In a first-to-file system, the application with the earlier filing date prevails and will be awarded the patent, if one issues. In the first-to-invent system, a lengthy, complex and costly administrative proceeding (called an "interference proceeding") must be conducted at the United States Patent and Trademark Office ("USPTO") to determine who actually invented first. Interference proceedings can take years to complete (even if there is no appeal to the United States Court of Appeals for the Federal Circuit), cost hundreds of thousands of dollars, and require extensive discovery. In addition, because it is always possible that an applicant could be involved in an interference proceeding, companies must maintain extensive recording and document retention systems in case they are later required to prove the date they invented the claimed invention.

Another important difference between the two systems is that in some first-to-file systems, prior art can include the inventor's own disclosure of his invention prior to the filing date of his application. Such systems do not provide the inventor any grace period during which time he is allowed to publish his invention without fear of its later being used against him as prior art. The Committee heard from universities and small inventors, in particular, about the importance of maintaining that grace period in our system. They argued that the grace period affords the necessary time to prepare and file applications, and in some instances, to obtain the necessary funding that enables the inventor to prepare adequately the application. In addition, the grace period benefits the public by encouraging early disclosure of new inventions, regardless of whether an application may later be filed for a patent on it.

Numerous organizations, institutions, and companies have advocated that the U.S. adopt a first-to-file system similar to those used in the rest of the world. The National Academy of Sciences made a similar recommendation after an extensive study of the patent system. When the United States patent system was first adopted, inventors did not typically file in other countries. It is now common for inventors and companies to file for protection in several countries at the same time. Thus, United States applicants, who also want to file abroad, are forced to follow and comply with two different filing systems. Maintaining a filing system so different from the rest of the world disadvantages United States applicants who, in most instances, also file in other countries. A change is long overdue.

Drawing on the best aspects of the two existing systems, the

America Invents Act creates a new "first-inventor-to-file" system. This new system provides patent applicants in the United States the efficiency benefits of the first-to-file systems used in the rest of the world by moving the U.S. system much closer to a first-to-file system and making the filing date that which is most relevant in determining whether an application is patentable. The new system continues, however, to provide inventors the benefit of the 1-year grace period. As part of the transition to a simpler, more efficient first-inventor-to-file system, this provision eliminates costly, complex interference proceedings, because priority will be based on the first application. A new administrative proceeding—called a "derivation" proceeding—is created to ensure that the first person to file the application is actually a true inventor. This new proceeding will ensure that a person will not be able to obtain a patent for the invention that he did not actually invent. If a dispute arises as to which of two applicants is a true inventor (as opposed to who invented it first), it will be resolved through an administrative proceeding by the Patent Board. The Act also simplifies how prior art is determined, provides more certainty, and reduces the cost associated with filing and litigating patents.

The Act maintains a 1-year grace period for U.S. applicants. Applicants' own publication or disclosure that occurs within 1 year prior to filing will not act as prior art against their applications. Similarly, disclosure by others during that time based on information obtained (directly or indirectly) from the inventor will not constitute prior art. This 1-year grace period should continue to give U.S. applicants the time they need to prepare and file their applications.

This provision also, and necessarily, modifies the prior-art sections of the patent law. Prior art will be measured from the filing date of the application and will typically include all art that publicly exists prior to the filing date, other than disclosures by the inventor within 1 year of filing. Prior art also will no longer have any geographic limitations. Thus, in section 102 the "in this country" limitation as applied to "public use" and "on sale" is removed, and the phrase "available to the public" is added to clarify the broad scope of relevant prior art, as well as to emphasize the fact that it must be publicly accessible. Prior art based on earlier-filed United States applications is maintained, as is current law's grace period, which will apply to all actions by the patent owner during the year prior to filing that would otherwise create § 102(a) prior art. Sections (and subsections) of the existing statute are renumbered, modified, or deleted consistent with converting to a first-inventor-to-file system. Finally, the intent behind the CREATE Act to promote joint research activities is preserved by including a prior art exception for subject matter invented by parties to a joint research agreement. The Act also provides that its enactment of new section 102(c) of title 35 is done with the same intent to promote joint research activities that was expressed in the Cooperative Research and Technology Enhancement Act of 2004 (Public Law 108-453), and that section 102(c) shall be administered in a manner consistent with such intent.[2]

§ 2:5 Statutory language—35 U.S.C. § 102

The new § 102 is entitled, "§ 102. Conditions for patentability; novelty" and contains subparts (a)–(d). Subparts (a) and (b) recite bars and exceptions to the bars. § 102(a) has two parts: Part (a)(1) names five categories of prior art or bars, and Part (a)(2) recites a further bar similar to former § 102(e). Likewise, § 102(b) has two corresponding parts: Part (b)(1) recites exceptions to Part (a)(1), and Part (b)(2) recites the exceptions to Part (a)(2). The following table shows the statutory language in side-by-side fashion, slightly edited for format:

---

[2] H. R. Rep. No. 112-98, pt. 1, pp. 40-43 (footnotes omitted) (2011).

§ 102(a) bars	§ 102(b) exceptions from the bars
(a) Novelty; Prior Art—A person shall be entitled to a patent unless— (1) the claimed invention was patented, described in a printed publication, or in public use, on sale, or otherwise available to the public before the effective filing date of the claimed invention; or	(b) Exceptions (1) DISCLOSURES MADE 1 YEAR OR LESS BEFORE THE EFFECTIVE FILING DATE OF THE CLAIMED INVENTION— A disclosure made 1 year or less before the effective filing date of a claimed invention shall not be prior art to the claimed invention under subsection (a)(1) if— (A) the disclosure was made by the inventor or joint inventor or by another who obtained the subject matter disclosed directly or indirectly from the inventor or a joint inventor; or (B) the subject matter disclosed had, before such disclosure, been publicly disclosed by the inventor or a joint inventor or another who obtained the subject matter disclosed directly or indirectly from the inventor or a joint inventor.
(2) the claimed invention was described in a patent issued under section 151,[1] or in an application for patent published or deemed published under section 122(b),[2] in which the patent or application, as the case may be, names another inventor and was effectively filed before the effective filing date of the claimed invention.	(2) DISCLOSURES APPEARING IN APPLICATIONS AND PATENTS—A disclosure shall not be prior art to a claimed invention under subsection (a)(2) if— (A) the subject matter disclosed was obtained directly or indirectly from the inventor or a joint inventor; (B) the subject matter disclosed had, before such subject matter was effectively filed under subsection (a)(2), been publicly disclosed by the inventor or a joint inventor or another who obtained the subject matter disclosed directly or indirectly from the inventor or a joint inventor; or (C) the subject matter disclosed and the claimed invention, not later than the effective filing date of the claimed invention, were owned by the same person or subject to an obligation of assignment to the same person.

[Section 2:5]

[1]35 U.S.C.A. § 151 provides, in pertinent part, "If it appears that applicant is entitled to a patent under the law, a written notice of allowance of the application shall be given or mailed to the applicant. * * * Upon payment of this sum the patent shall issue * * *.

[2]35 U.S.C.A. § 122(b) provides, in pertinent part, ". . . each application for a patent shall be published, in accordance with procedures determined by the Director, promptly after the expiration of a period of 18 months from the earliest filing date for which a benefit is sought under this title . . . ."

35 U.S.C.A. § 102 (c) and (d) (2011) provide as follows:

(c) Common Ownership Under Joint Research Agreements.—Subject matter disclosed and a claimed invention shall be deemed to have been owned by the same person or subject to an obligation of assignment to the same person in applying the provisions of subsection (b)(2)(C) if—

(1) the subject matter disclosed was developed and the claimed invention was made by, or on behalf of, 1 or more parties to a joint research agreement that was in effect on or before the effective filing date of the claimed invention;

(2) the claimed invention was made as a result of activities undertaken within the scope of the joint research agreement; and

(3) the application for patent for the claimed invention discloses or is amended to disclose the names of the parties to the joint research agreement.

(d) Patents and Published Applications Effective as Prior Art.—For purposes of determining whether a patent or application for patent is prior art to a claimed invention under subsection (a)(2), such patent or application shall be considered to have been effectively filed, with respect to any subject matter described in the patent or application—

(1) if paragraph (2) does not apply, as of the actual filing date of the patent or the application for patent; or

(2) if the patent or application for patent is entitled to claim a right of priority under section 119, 365 (a), or 365 (b), or to claim the benefit of an earlier filing date under section 120, 121, or 365 (c), based upon 1 or more prior filed applications for patent, as of the filing date of the earliest such application that describes the subject matter.

§ 2:6 The five prior art categories of § 102(a)(1) and the exceptions thereto[1]

Section 102(a) (as amended) is entitled "Novelty; Prior Art." Subsection (a)(1) describes five activities which defeat

---

[Section 2:6]

[1]The prior art under § 102(a)(2) and the exceptions thereto, § 102(b)(2), are discussed in the next section.

novelty: the claimed invention was:

(i) patented,

(ii) described in a printed publication,

(iii) in public use,

(iv) on sale, or

(v) otherwise available to the public before the effective filing date of the claimed invention.

These five activities have no geographic restrictions. This represents a dramatic change as to some of the recited activities which were prior art only if occurring in the U.S.

The exceptions to these five activities are stated in subsection (b)(1) where the AIA provides two specific exceptions as a modified grace period. The statute is quoted in the table above. While subsection (a)(1) identifying the five acts does not refer to any "disclosure" by that exact word, the exceptions in (b)(1) are framed in terms of a "disclosure" or "subject matter disclosed." The statute does not include a definition of "disclosure," but from the context, it appears to be used in a broad sense.[2]

Thus, concerning these five types of prior art, the AIA provides a grace period which continues to be one year. However, the grace period is modified in scope so that it is limited to disclosures by (or via) an actual inventor. Importantly, publications or sufficiently public uses *by others* are generally prior art unless the activity is covered by any of the exceptions. For example, a publication by a third party prior to an applicant's effective filing date is generally prior art under § 102(a)(1) (2011). According to one exception, however, it would not be prior art if (A) that publication had been obtained from the inventor, directly or indirectly. Nor would a publication by a third party, even if completely original, be prior art if the subject matter of the third party's

[2]Though the AIA provides no explicit definition of "disclosure," Section 103 both before and after the AIA uses the phrase "identically disclosed as set forth in Section 102." It would appear that since Section 102(a) which defines prior art does not use the word "disclosed," the usage of "disclosed" in Section 103 must certainly refer to *all* of the prior art under Section 102, and it would be unwarranted to exclude any "prior art" from the obviousness test under Section 103. Thus, Section 103 in using this related word form suggests strongly that "disclosure" is meant to include *all* the prior art of Section 102. Additionally, the introductory language of both Section 102(b)(1) and (2) (2011) refers to "disclosures made . . ." or "disclosures appearing in . . ." Courts would have a solid basis, therefore, to conclude that the word "disclosure" appearing in the Section 102(b) exceptions refers to any of the activities named in Section 102(a).

publication (or other form of disclosure) had already been publicly disclosed by the inventor, a joint inventor, or another who had obtained the subject matter directly or indirectly from the or an inventor. § 102(b)(1)(B).

The USPTO adopted various final rules to implement the FITF provisions of the AIA.[3]In terms of how to prove that an application is entitled to the grace period, two rules apply. For applications that are subject to AIA 35 U.S.C.A. §§ 102 and 103, see 37 C.F.R. § 1.130 ("Affidavit or declaration of attribution or prior public disclosure under the Leahy-Smith America Invents Act").[4] For applications that are not subject

---

[3]See "Changes To Implement and Examination Guidelines for Implementing the First Inventor To File Provisions of the Leahy-Smith America Invents Act; Final Rules," 78 Fed. Reg. 11024-11059 (Feb. 14, 2013) and "Changes To Implement the First Inventor To File Provisions of the Leahy-Smith America Invents Act; Correction," 78 Fed. Reg. 16182 (March 14, 2013) http://www.gpo.gov/fdsys/pkg/FR-2013-03-14/pdf/2013-05815.pdf. See also, "Examination Guidelines for Implementing the First Inventor To File Provisions of the Leahy-Smith America Invents Act" Examination Guidelines for Implementing the First Inventor To File Provisions of the Leahy-Smith America Invents Act, 78 Fed. Reg. 11059 (Feb. 14, 2013), http://www.gpo.gov/fdsys/pkg/FR-2013-02-14/pdf/2013-03450.pdf.

[4]The USPTO rules adopted in light of the AIA are set forth in Appendix 3 hereto, without the USPTO comments on them. In announcing the final version of rule 1.130, the USPTO noted: "The Office is providing for the submission of affidavits or declarations showing that: (1) A disclosure upon which a claim rejection is based was by the inventor or a joint inventor or by another who obtained the subject matter disclosed directly or indirectly from the inventor or a joint inventor; or (2) there was a prior public disclosure by the inventor or a joint inventor or another who obtained the subject matter disclosed directly or indirectly from the inventor or a joint inventor. In response to public comment, the Office has provided a more flexible approach for submission of an affidavit or declaration with evidence of a prior public disclosure. In response to similar comments regarding the prior public disclosure exception provisions, the Office wants to highlight that there is no requirement that the mode of disclosure by an inventor or joint inventor be the same as the mode of disclosure of an intervening disclosure (e.g., inventor discloses his invention at a trade show and the intervening disclosure is in a peer-reviewed journal), as explained in more detail in the examination guidelines. Additionally, there is no requirement that the disclosure by the inventor or a joint inventor be a verbatim or ipsissimis verbis disclosure of an intervening disclosure in order for the exception based on a prior public disclosure of subject matter by the inventor or a joint inventor to apply. The guidelines also clarify that the exception applies to subject matter of the intervening disclosure that is simply a more general description of the subject matter previously publicly disclosed by the inventor or a joint inventor. ***

to FITF regime, see 37 C.F.R. § 1.131 ("Affidavit or declaration of prior invention or to disqualify commonly owned patent or published application as prior art").[5]

a. Questions re Prior Commercial Use

The interpretation by federal courts of "publicly disclosed" within the context of this statute remains to be seen. However, the legislative history emphasizes that availability to the public is the touchstone for determining whether

---

Showing a Prior Disclosure by an Inventor or Another Who Obtained the Subject Matter From an Inventor: The Office proposed setting out the standard for a successful affidavit or declaration where the disclosure is the inventor's own work (i.e., a satisfactory showing that the inventor or a joint inventor is in fact the inventor of the subject matter of the disclosure) and where the disclosure was by another who obtained the subject matter disclosed directly or indirectly from the inventor or a joint inventor (i.e., showing that the inventor or a joint inventor is the inventor of the subject matter disclosed and directly or indirectly communicated the subject matter disclosed to another) in the rules of practice. *See Changes To Implement the First Inventor To File Provisions of the Leahy-Smith America Invents Act*, 77 Fed. Reg. at 43743, 43749-51, and 43758-59. The Office also proposed to require the applicant to file a petition for a derivation proceeding if a rejection is based upon a U.S. patent or U.S. patent application publication of a patented or pending application naming another inventor and the patent or pending application claims an invention that is the same or substantially the same as the applicant's claimed invention. See Changes To Implement the First Inventor To File Provisions of the Leahy-Smith America Invents Act, 77 Fed. Reg. at 43751 and 43759. The Office received a number of comments suggesting that a procedural provision should not set out the standard for a successful affidavit or declaration and suggesting that the Office should not require an applicant to file a petition for a derivation proceeding. The Office is revising the provision in this final rule to simply specify: (1) When an affidavit or declaration of attribution or prior public disclosure may be used to disqualify a disclosure as prior art; and (2) the procedural requirements for such an affidavit or declaration. The Office is also replacing the provision that the Office may require the applicant to file a petition for a derivation proceeding with a provision indicating that such an affidavit or declaration may not be available to overcome a rejection when the affidavit or declaration contends that an inventor named in the U.S. patent or U.S. patent application publication derived the claimed invention from the inventor or a joint inventor named in the application or patent, and that in such a case, an applicant or a patent owner may file a petition for a derivation proceeding." 78 Fed. Reg. 11024, 11027 (Feb. 14, 2013).

[5]As a reminder to USPTO practitioners, § 1.132 also speaks generally to "Affidavits or declarations traversing rejections or objections" and provides, "When any claim of an application or a patent under reexamination is rejected or objected to, any evidence submitted to traverse the rejection or objection on a basis not otherwise provided for must be by way of an oath or declaration under this section."

something is prior art, and secret uses or sales are not intended by Congress to form prior art for patents granted under the new FITF system. It appears to be the intent of Congress to abandon jurisprudence developed over many decades as to uses of an invention that may have been regarded as prior art by courts even when it did not inform the public of the invention.[6]

The Supreme Court cautions against relying on interpretations advanced in legislative statements that are not "anchored in the text of the statute."[7] The authoritative statement "is the statutory text, not the legislative history."[8] However, lower courts have cited the legislative history of the AIA already in recent cases.[9] It remains to be seen whether the specific language chosen by Congress for these exceptions will actually be interpreted by courts to achieve the intent expressed in the House Committee Report and in the Congressional Record. If the word "disclosure" or "subject matter disclosed" within the meaning of new Section 102(b)(1)(A) and (B) is interpreted to include activities such as public uses or sales as opposed to documentary publications or disclosures, then it would seem that placing the invention on sale by the inventor within one year of the inventor's effective filing date would fall within the exception provided in new Section 102(b).

If an inventor places a product on sale and the product itself actually discloses the invention prior to filing a patent application, this activity is clearly within the scope of the new Section 102(a)(1) in that "the claimed invention was . . . in public use, on sale, or otherwise available to the public before the effective filing date of the claimed invention."

---

[6]See the comprehensive review of the legislative history in J. Matal, "A Guide to the Legislative History of the America Invents Act," *The Federal Circuit Bar J.* Vol. 21, No. 3, 435, 467–75 (2011).

[7]*Shannon v. U.S.*, 512 U.S. 573, 583, 114 S. Ct. 2419, 129 L. Ed. 2d 459 (1994), stating "[C]ourts have no authority to enforce [a] principl[e] gleaned solely from legislative history that has no statutory reference point." *Shannon,* 512 U.S. at 584, quoting *International Broth. of Elec. Workers, Local Union No. 474, AFL-CIO v. N.L.R.B.*, 814 F.2d 697, 712, 124 L.R.R.M. (BNA) 2993, 106 Lab. Cas. (CCH) P 12256 (D.C. Cir. 1987).

[8]*Exxon Mobil Corp. v. Allapattah Services, Inc.*, 545 U.S. 546, 568, 125 S. Ct. 2611, 162 L. Ed. 2d 502 (2005).

[9]E.g., *Rogers v. Tristar Products, Inc.*, 102 U.S.P.Q.2d 1722, 2012 WL 1660604, *2 (Fed. Cir. 2012) (non-precedential); *Byrne v. Wood, Herron & Evans, LLP*, 676 F.3d 1024, 1029, 102 U.S.P.Q.2d 1073 (Fed. Cir. 2012) (dissenting opin.).

Congress has said its intent is that an inventor's activity would not be patent defeating so long as the inventor files a patent application within one year. That Committee Report quoted above indicates that the Act maintains a one year grace period for U.S. applicants.[10] That Report states with regard to the grace period that an "Applicants' own publication or disclosure that occurs within 1 year prior to filing will not act as prior art against their applications."[11] Likewise, the next paragraph of the House Report addresses the "public use" and "on sale" provisions. The text accompanying footnotes 19 and 20 states, "Prior art based on earlier-filed United States applications is maintained, as is current law's grace period, which will apply to all actions by the patent owner during the year prior to filing that would otherwise create § 102(a) prior art."[12] Thus, it appears to be Congress' intent that any prior art activity by the inventor is to be protected under the grace period.

If an inventor places a product on sale that does *not* inherently disclose the invention, and the on sale date precedes the effective filing date, it appears to be the intent of Congress through its legislative history that this will not be a bar to the patent. As noted previously, the House Report and other legislative history indicates that *any* activities by the inventor within one year preceding the effective filing date are covered by the grace period. Hence, if the legislative intent corresponds to the scope of the Act as courts may eventually interpret it, then if the on sale activity does inherently disclose the invention, it is covered by the grace period, and if it does not inherently disclose the invention, then it either is not prior art or it is covered by the grace period. Comments by Senator Kyl on September 6, 2011, made in the Senate when it considered the bill that the House had already passed, include the following relevant excerpts as to the definition of "prior art":

> Public uses and sales of an invention will remain prior art, but only if they make the invention available to the public. An

---

[10]The phrase "U.S. applicants" is understood to mean applicants for U.S. patents rather than U.S. citizens who apply for patents. There is no indication that "U.S. applicants" is meant to exclude foreign applicants from the grace period. None of the new definitions for "inventor" or the like include a geographic limitation or qualification on the individuals embraced by the definition.

[11]H. R. Rep. No. 112-98, pt. 1, at 42.

[12]H. R. Rep. No. 112-98, pt. 1, at 43.

> inventor's confidential sale of his invention, his demonstration of its use to a private group, or a third party's unrestricted but private use of the invention will no longer constitute [prior] art. Only the sale or offer for sale of the invention to the relevant public or its use in a way that makes it publicly accessible will constitute prior art.[13]

Further support for this view by Senator Kyl came from his discussion of the cost of discovery in patent litigation and how this new definition would reduce costs:

> The main benefit of the AIA public availability standard of prior art is that it is relatively inexpensive to establish the existence of events that make an invention available to the public. Under current law, depositions and litigation discovery are required in order to identify all of the inventor's private dealings with third parties and determine whether those dealings constitute a secret offer for sale or third party use that invalidates the patent under the current law's forfeiture doctrines. The need for such discovery is eliminated once the definition of "prior art" is limited to those activities that make the [invention] accessible to the public. This will greatly reduce the time and cost of patent litigation and allow the courts and the [USPTO] to operate much more efficiently.[14]

The language of "otherwise available to the public" was added to the definition by the 110th Congress Senate Judiciary Committee. The Senate bill provided that a patent "for a claimed invention may not be obtained if . . . the claimed invention was patented, described in a printed publication or in public use, on sale, or otherwise available to the public."[15]

This particular phrase was the subject of discussion in a 2007 Senate Committee Report where the Report noted that adding this phrase was ". . . to make clear that secret collaborative agreements, which are not available to the public, are not prior art."[16] The 2007 Senate Report also explained that the phrase "available to the public" is added to clarify the broad scope of relevant prior art and emphasize that "it must be publicly available."[17]

Assuming that courts do interpret the revised Section 102 (2011) so that only disclosures that are available to the pub-

---

[13]CFE 157 Cong. Rec. S5319 to S5321 (Daily Ed. September 6, 2011). An apparent transcription error used the "private" in the Record rather than the word "prior."

[14]157 Cong. Rec. S5319 to S5321 at S5120 (daily ed. Sept. 6, 2011).

[15]CS. 1145 Section 2, Section 102(a)(1). (110th Congress).

[16]S. Rep. No. 110-259, at 39 (2008).

[17]S. Rep. No. 110-259, at 9.

lic are prior art, this raises the question of whether an inventor can prolong legal protection through the calculated use of both trade secret law and then patent law. Many cases have held that it is inconsistent with the patent laws for an inventor to practice the invention privately, making sales and benefiting from the invention without actually disclosing the invention, and then when the inventor fears that the secret process or other invention is apt to become known publicly, make application for a patent, thereby seeking a statutory term of protection subsequent to however many years of trade secret protection the invention received during its secret, commercial utilization.[18] Courts will need to evaluate whether the AIA abrogates these cases.

b. Questions re Experimental Use

Another question concerns experimental uses under the new statute. One may weigh the inclusion of "public use" as part of § 102(a)(1) in favor of retention of the exception. Against that inference are the absence of an express experimental use exception in § 102(b)(1) and the new "otherwise available to the public" category in § 102(a)(1).

In *City of Elizabeth v. American Nicholson Pavement Co.*, 97 U.S. 126, 24 L. Ed. 1000, 1877 WL 18449 (1877), an invention relating to pavement was exposed to public use for several years. The Supreme Court explained a distinction, stating, ". . . the public may be incidentally deriving a benefit from [the experimental use]. If it be a grist-mill, or a carding-machine, customers from the surrounding country may enjoy the use of it by having their grain made into flour, or their wool into rolls, and still it will not be in public use, within the meaning of the law."[19] On the other hand, if an inventor allows other persons, either with or without compensation, to use an invented machine and put the resulting products

---

[18]See *Pennock v. Dialogue*, 27 U.S. 1, 7 L. Ed. 327, 1829 WL 3163 (1829) (holding the secret of the invention back from the public for many years and having a first monopoly followed by a second monopoly when competition becomes dangerous and obtaining a patent would retard the progress of science and useful arts; a voluntary act or acquiescence in the public sale and use was an abandonment of the patent right); *Metallizing Engineering Co. v. Kenyon Bearing & Auto Parts Co.*, 153 F.2d 516, 68 U.S.P.Q. 54 (C.C.A. 2d Cir. 1946); *Kewanee Oil Co. v. Bicron Corp.*, 416 U.S. 470, 94 S. Ct. 1879, 40 L. Ed. 2d 315, 181 U.S.P.Q. 673 (1974) (invention ineligible for patent after having been in commercial use for over one year).

[19]*City of Elizabeth*, 97 U.S. at 135.

on sale, "it will be in public use and on public sale, within the meaning of the law."[20] Courts will be asked to reconsider whether experimental uses constitute prior art under the revised statute on the basis that the invention is "otherwise available to the public," regardless of whether the activity would have constituted "public use" or "on sale" activity under the prior statute.

§ 2:7 The patent prior art categories of § 102(a)(2) and exceptions thereto, § 102(d)

The 2011 revision to § 102(a)(2) restates subject matter that had been part of prior § 102(e) (2006) and is specific to U.S. patent documents.

> **(a) Novelty; Prior Art**— A person shall be entitled to a patent unless—* * *(2) the claimed invention was described in a patent issued under section 151, or in an application for patent published or deemed published under section 122(b), in which the patent or application, as the case may be, names another inventor and was effectively filed before the effective filing date of the claimed invention.[1]

This statute omits the prior requirement of 35 U.S.C. § 102(e) that an application must have been published *in the English language* under the International Convention, designating the United States.

The AIA added a further provision to expound on the effective date of patents as prior art:

> **(d) Patents and Published Applications Effective as Prior Art—** For purposes of determining whether a patent or application for patent is prior art to a claimed invention under subsection (a)(2), such patent or application shall be considered to have been effectively filed, with respect to any subject matter described in the patent or application—
>
> (1) if paragraph (2) does not apply, as of the actual filing date of the patent or the application for patent; or
>
> (2) if the patent or application for patent is entitled to claim a right of priority under section 119, 365(a), or 365(b), or to claim the benefit of an earlier filing date under section 120, 121, or 365(c), based upon 1 or more prior filed applications for patent, as of the filing date of the earliest such application that describes the subject

[20]*City of Elizabeth*, 97 U.S. at 135.

[Section 2:7]

[1]35 U.S.C.A. § 102(a)(2) (2011).

matter.[2]

Consequently, this language of new Section 102 expands the scope of patent documents that constitute prior art against a U.S. application or patent. The expansion is with regard to the effective filing date and with regard to the language requirement. As noted, the language is no longer required to be English. As to the effective filing date, this new provision legislatively overrules *In re Hilmer*.[3] Approaching the statute, unless the patent or application "is entitled to claim a right" of priority, then the effective filing date of the patent document is its actual filing date in the U.S., and it speaks as prior art as of that date. However, if the reference is, in fact, "entitled to claim" a right of priority under Sections 119, 365(a), or 365(b), or the benefit of an earlier filing date under Sections 120, 121, or 365(c), based on an earlier filing of a patent application, then the document speaks as prior art as of the earliest application date that describes the subject matter in question. Section 102(d)(2). There is no particular comment on this in the House Report.[4]

The "grace period" or "exceptions" to patent documents are stated in Section 102(b)(2). This exception is not limited to a one year term, unlike the exceptions that apply to the five types of prior art activity. Instead, the disclosures appearing in applications and patents shall not be prior art to a claimed invention under subsection (a)(2) if any of three conditions is met.

The first condition is that the disclosure was obtained from the inventor himself. Hence, a patent document that is issued or published or deemed published which names another inventor and was effectively filed before the effective filing date of the applicant's own claimed invention is not

---

[2]The Federal Circuit noted that "The relevant provisions of § 102(e)(2) were reorganized into newly designated § 102(d)(2) when certain aspects of the Leahy-Smith America Invents Act . . ., Pub.L. No. 112-29, took effect on March 16, 2013." *Taurus IP, LLC v. DaimlerChrysler Corp.*, 2013 WL 4034384, at *33 n.7 (Fed. Cir. 2013).

[3]*Application of Hilmer*, 53 C.C.P.A. 1288, 359 F.2d 859, 149 U.S.P.Q. 480 (1966).

[4]Matal refers to comments on the legislative history of this Section at pp. 489–90, referencing only some statements by Senatory Kyl on March 8, 2011. The section-by-section portion of the House Report simply states that "Section 102(d) defines the effective filing date of a patent or application that is cited as prior art to a claimed invention." H. R. Rep. No. 112-98, pt. 1, at 73.

prior art if the subject matter disclosed by the (earlier application) "was obtained directly or indirectly from the inventor or a joint inventor."[5] Hence, if the applicant of the earlier-filed application or patent obtained the subject matter either directly or indirectly from the inventor or a joint inventor of the later-filed application, then the exception to prior art applies, and the earlier-filed application or patent "shall not be prior art."

The second exception to patent documents concerns an earlier disclosure by the inventor or a joint inventor. Under this section, subject matter disclosed in the earlier-filed application is not prior art under subsection (a)(2) if that subject matter had been "publicly disclosed" by the inventor or a joint inventor (or by a third person who obtained the subject matter directly or indirectly from the inventor or joint inventor). That is to say, if an inventor or joint inventor makes a public disclosure of subject matter he has invented and that public disclosure occurs prior to the effective filing date of an adverse application, then the same subject matter disclosed in the adverse application will not be prior art.

The third exception to patent prior art is the common ownership exception. Under this exception, the subject matter disclosed in an earlier-filed application which would otherwise be prior art under subsection 102(a)(2) is not prior art if both "the subject matter disclosed and the claimed invention, not later than the effective filing date of the claimed invention, were owned by the same person or subject to an obligation of assignment to the same person."[6]

It must be emphasized that the common ownership exception does *not* bear on the five categories of prior art listed in Section 102(a)(1). That is, if an inventor's company places a product on sale that discloses the applicant's invention, if that product is the result of the work of another person who is not the applicant, the common ownership exception does not apply. Likewise, if a co-worker at the same company publishes an article which constitutes prior art under § 102(a)(1), the common ownership exception of § 102(b)(2)(C) is irrelevant. The *only* time the common ownership exception is operative, under the words of the statute, is when the claimed invention was described in a patent issued under Section 151 or an application for a patent published or

[5]35 U.S.C.A. § 102(b)(2)(A) (as amended 2011).

[6]35 U.S.C.A. § 102(b)(2)(C) (as amended 2011).

deemed published under Section 122(b) which names another inventor and has an earlier effective filing date.

Joint research agreements often provide for common ownership, and new Section 102(c) addresses this situation, providing as follows:

> **(c) Common Ownership Under Joint Research Agreements—** Subject matter disclosed and a claimed invention shall be deemed to have been owned by the same person or subject to an obligation of assignment to the same person in applying the provisions of subsection (b)(2)(C) if—
>
> (1) the subject matter disclosed was developed and the claimed invention was made by, or on behalf of, 1 or more parties to a joint research agreement that was in effect on or before the effective filing date of the claimed invention;
>
> (2) the claimed invention was made as a result of activities undertaken within the scope of the joint research agreement; and
>
> (3) the application for patent for the claimed invention discloses or is amended to disclose the names of the parties to the joint research agreement.

§ 2:8 35 U.S.C. § 103 obviousness

The AIA also replaces 35 U.S.C. § 103. Section 103(a) was rewritten, and § 103(b) was deleted. The subject matter of § 103(c) was moved into § 102(c) and § 100(h). Most importantly, the main provision concerning obviousness was amended to read as follows:

New U.S.C. § 103

Sec. 103. Conditions for patentability; non-obvious subject matter

> A patent for a claimed invention may not be obtained, notwithstanding that the claimed invention is not identically disclosed as set forth in section 102, if the differences between the claimed invention and the prior art are such that the claimed invention as a whole would have been obvious before the effective filing date of the claimed invention to a person having ordinary skill in the art to which the claimed invention pertains. Patentability shall not be negated by the manner in which the invention was made.

This revision to § 103 is for consistency. The prior § 103(a) (2006) called for obviousness to be determined as of the time the invention was made. However, the actual date of invention for FITF patents has become substantially irrelevant.[1] What is important under the FITF regime is the effective filing date, an easily-determined fact. Under the new § 103, the relevant date for determining obviousness is "before the effective filing date of the claimed invention."

The following § 103(b) is specific to biotechnology processes and is withdrawn by the AIA:

Repealed 35 U.S.C. § 103(b)

103(b) (1). Notwithstanding subsection (a), and upon timely election by the applicant for patent to proceed under this subsection, a biotechnological process using or resulting in a composition of matter that is novel under section 102 and nonobvious under subsection (a) of this section shall be considered nonobvious if—

(A) claims to the process and the composition of matter are contained in either the same application for patent or in separate applications having the same effective filing date; and

(B) the composition of matter, and the process at the time it was invented, were owned by the same person or subject to an obligation of assignment to the same person.

(2) A patent issued on a process under paragraph (1)—

(A) shall also contain the claims to the composition of matter used in or made by that process, or

(B) shall, if such composition of matter is claimed in another patent, be set to expire on the same date as such other patent, notwithstanding section 154.

(3) For purposes of paragraph (1), the term "biotechnological process" means—

(A) a process of genetically altering or otherwise inducing a single- or multi-celled organism to—

(i) express an exogenous nucleotide sequence,

(ii) inhibit, eliminate, augment, or alter expression

[Section 2:8]

[1]However, even under the FITF regime, the date an invention is "made" is still relevant to whether it is deemed a "university patent" for purposes of the prior user defense under 35 U.S.C.A. § 273 (2011). Such dates may be relevant also to establishing derivation in a derivation proceeding. These appear to be the only times that the date of invention is relevant under the FITF regime. As to derivation proceedings, the date of conception is not something that per se needs to be established, but the petitioner must demonstrate communication of the invention from the petitioner to the deriver. *See* USPTO Rule 42.405(c) and Proposed Rule 1-130.

of an endogenous nucleotide sequence, or

(iii) express a specific physiological characteristic not naturally associated with said organism;

(B) cell fusion procedures yielding a cell line that expresses a specific protein, such as a monoclonal antibody; and

(C) a method of using a product produced by a process defined by subparagraph (A) or (B), or a combination of subparagraphs (A) and (B).

The deletion of § 103(b) required amendment to 35 U.S.C. § 282 (first paragraph), as follows (where strikethrough indicates language deleted by the AIA and underscoring indicates added language):

Amended 35 U.S.C. 282

~~A patent~~ **<u>(a) In general. A patent</u>** shall be presumed valid. Each claim of a patent (whether in independent, dependent, or multiple dependent form) shall be presumed valid independently of the validity of other claims; dependent or multiple dependent claims shall be presumed valid even though dependent upon an invalid claim. ~~Notwithstanding the preceding sentence, if a claim to a composition of matter is held invalid and that claim was the basis of a determination of nonobviousness under section 103(b)(1), the process shall no longer be considered nonobvious solely on the basis of section 103(b)(1).~~ The burden of establishing invalidity of a patent or any claim thereof shall rest on the party asserting such invalidity.

The following § 103(c) is moved to other parts of the patent statute by the AIA:

Former 35 U.S.C. § 103(c)

103(c) (1). Subject matter developed by another person, which qualifies as prior art only under one or more of subsections (e), (f), and (g) of section 102 of this title, shall not preclude patentability under this section where the subject matter and the claimed invention were, at the time the claimed invention was made, owned by the same person or subject to an obligation of assignment to the same person.

(2) For purposes of this subsection, subject matter developed by another person and a claimed invention shall be deemed to have been owned by the same person or subject to an obligation of assignment to the same person if—

(A) the claimed invention was made by or on behalf of parties to a joint research agreement that was in effect on or before the date the claimed invention was made;

(B) the claimed invention was made as a result of activities undertaken within the scope of the joint research agreement; and

(C) the application for patent for the claimed invention discloses or is amended to disclose the names of the parties to the joint research agreement.

(3) For purposes of paragraph (2), the term "joint research agreement" means a written contract, grant, or cooperative agreement entered into by two or more persons or entities for the performance of experimental, developmental, or research work in the field of the claimed invention.

§ 2:9 Effective date and applicability of first inventor to file provisions

AIA § 3(n) generally makes patents with an effective filing date on or after March 16, 2013 subject to the new first-inventor-to-file provisions.

New Statute (AIA Sec. 3(n))

(n) EFFECTIVE DATE—

(1) IN GENERAL— Except as otherwise provided in this section, the amendments made by this section shall take effect upon the expiration of the 18-month period beginning on the date of the enactment of this Act, and shall apply to any application for patent, and to any patent issuing thereon, that contains or contained at any time—

(A) a claim to a claimed invention that has an effective filing date as defined in section 100(i) of title 35, United States Code, that is on or after the effective date described in this paragraph; or

(B) a specific reference under section 120, 121, or 365(c) of title 35, United States Code, to any patent or application that contains or contained at any time such a claim.

(2) INTERFERING PATENTS— The provisions of sections 102(g), 135, and 291 of title 35, United States Code, as in effect on the day before the effective date set forth in paragraph (1) of this subsection, shall apply to each claim of an application for patent, and any patent issued thereon, for which the amendments made by this section also apply, if such application or patent contains or contained at any time—

(A) a claim to an invention having an effective filing date as defined in section 100(i) of title 35, United States Code, that occurs before the effective date set forth in paragraph (1) of this subsection; or

> (B) a specific reference under section 120, 121, or 365(c) of title 35, United States Code, to any patent or application that contains or contained at any time such a claim.

These provisions of the AIA refer to 35 U.S.C. § 100(i) which is one of the definitions to the patent statute:

> (i) (1) The term "effective filing date" for a claimed invention in a patent or application for patent means—
>
> (A) if subparagraph (B) does not apply, the actual filing date of the patent or the application for the patent containing a claim to the invention; or
>
> (B) the filing date of the earliest application for which the patent or application is entitled, as to such invention, to a right of priority under section 119, 365(a), or 365(b) or to the benefit of an earlier filing date under section 120, 121, or 365(c).
>
> (2) The effective filing date for a claimed invention in an application for reissue or reissued patent shall be determined by deeming the claim to the invention to have been contained in the patent for which reissue was sought.

Trigger Date. Section 3(n)(1) refers to the expiration of an 18 month period following the September 16, 2011 enactment of the AIA. It is convenient to call that date the "trigger date." Hence, the trigger date is March 16, 2013. The conditions for applicability of the FITF regime include the relationship of a claim's effective filing date to the trigger date.

Qualification Sweeps in All Claims. AIA § 3(n) has two parts. The first part, § 3(n)(1), is for general applicability, and the second part, § 3(n)(2), is for interfering patents. As to § 3(n)(1), if the qualification is met as to *any* claim, then *all* claims will be treated the same way, even ones not meeting the qualification. § 3(n)(1) states that except as otherwise provided in AIA § 3, the amendments of § 3 "shall apply to any application for patent, and to any patent issuing thereon, that [meets either of conditions (A) or (B)]." As such, meeting either condition (A) or (B) makes AIA § 3 applicable to the whole patent application and resulting patent. Moreover, under § 3(n)(1), if the application *ever* met condition (A) or (B), then the amendments of § 3 apply—even if the application was amended to avoid such conditions.

AIA § 3(n)(2) is more opaque in its language. Under § 3(n)(2), the interference provisions that the AIA is changing or deleting, *i.e.,* 35 U.S.C. §§ 102(g), 135, and 291, "shall apply *to each claim* of an application for patent, and any patent issued thereon, for which the amendments made by this section also apply, if [either of two conditions is met]." It may be noted that the language of § 3(n)(1) is different from that of § 3(n)(2). While § 3(n)(1) states that the amendments apply to an application or patent that qualifies, § 3(n)(2) says that the interference provisions "shall apply to each claim" in an application or resulting patent that qualifies.

The phrase in § 3(n)(2), "for which the amendments made by this section also apply," bears some discussion. As worded, this phrase appears to indicate that if the patent application or patent is within the FITF regime (presumably via meeting the requirements of § 3(n)(1)), then it *also* is governed by the interference provisions, but only if it meets *other* qualifying conditions. The language of § 3(n)(1) and § 3(n)(2) appears not to be mutually exclusive but instead deliberately overlapping. This does not seem self-contradictory. If the application fails to qualify under § 3(n)(1), then it is governed by the prior law including the interference provisions. If it does qualify under § 3(n)(1), but if it also happens to meet the conditions of § 3(n)(2) (which as discussed below deal with claims having an effective filing date prior to the trigger date), then the application and patent are not deprived of the interference provisions but to the contrary the owner will still be entitled to prove prior invention if necessary.[1]

The legislative history explains some of the difficulty in the language. Comments by Senator Kyl explain that an inventor may convert a patent application to a FITF-governed application simply by adding and claiming new matter after the trigger date. This is a one-way street; applicants cannot revert because of the "contains" or "contained at any time" provisions of the Act. Senator Kyl offered the following explanatory comments about AIA § 3(n)(2):

> Paragraph (2) of subsection (o) provides a remedy in situations in which interfering patents are issued, one of which remains subject to first-to-invent rules, and the other of which was filed earlier but has a later date of conception and has transitioned into the first-to-file system. Paragraph (2) subjects the latter patent to the first-to-invent rule, and allows the other patent owner and even third parties to seek invalidation

---

[Section 2:9]

[1]It is not clear how the true inventor will be able to meet the corroboration requirement for communication of the invention, a requirement for petitions for derivation proceedings, when dealing with stolen inventions.

of that later-conceived interfering patent on that basis.[2]

Accordingly, the intent was to be able to invalidate interfering patents by showing prior invention where one patent is under the first-to-invent regime but the other is under the FITF regime.

Relevant Claims for Testing. Both parts of the effective date statute (§ 3(n)) consider all claims now pending, all claims ever pending, and such claims in applications referenced specifically under §§ 120, 121, or 365(c).[3]

The Qualifying Conditions. The qualifying condition under the "General" provisions of AIA § 3(n)(1) is whether any relevant claim has an "effective filing date" *on or after* the trigger date. "Effective filing date" is a newly-defined term in 35 U.S.C. § 100 and is quoted above in § § 2:9 and 1:1.

The qualifying condition under the "Interfering Patents" provisions of § 3(n)(2) is whether any relevant claim has an effective filing date *before* the trigger date. The statute also states a qualification of whether "the amendments made by this section *also* apply." This is discussed above under "Qualification Sweeps in All Claims."

Application. Under § 3(n)(1), if any relevant claim has an effective date on or after the trigger date, then the provisions of AIA § 3 apply to the whole patent or application. This means that the new grace provisions apply, the

[2]157 Cong. Rec. S 1373 (daily ed. Mar. 8, 2011).

[3]35 U.S.C.A. § 365 addresses the Right of priority; benefit of the filing date of a prior application and provides:

(a) In accordance with the conditions and requirements of subsections (a) through (d) of section 119 of this title, a national application shall be entitled to the right of priority based on a prior filed international application which designated at least one country other than the United States.

(b) In accordance with the conditions and requirements of section 119(a) of this title and the treaty and the Regulations, an international application designating the United States shall be entitled to the right of priority based on a prior foreign application, or a prior international application designating at least one country other than the United States.

(c) In accordance with the conditions and requirements of section 120 of this title, an international application designating the United States shall be entitled to the benefit of the filing date of a prior national application or a prior international application designating the United States, and a national application shall be entitled to the benefit of the filing date of a prior international application designating the United States. If any claim for the benefit of an earlier filing date is based on a prior international application which designated but did not originate in the United States, the Director may require the filing in the Patent and Trademark Office of a certified copy of such application together with a translation thereof into the English language, if it was filed in another language.

expanded prior art provisions apply, etc.

Under AIA § 3(n)(2), for "Interfering Patents," if any relevant claim has an effective date before the trigger date, then the pre-AIA interference provisions of the patent statute apply. The enumerated interference provisions are 35 U.S.C. §§ 102(g), 135, and 291.

While an effective filing date of any given claim will be some single date that is either before, on, or after the trigger date, that does not make the AIA effective date provisions mutually exclusive. It is easy to envision a situation where an application or patent contains claims that have different effective filing dates, including one or more claims that are on or after the trigger date and one or more claims that are before the trigger date. In this situation, *both* of the qualifying conditions of the AIA § 3(n) effective date provisions are met. Because at least one relevant claim has an effective filing date on or after the trigger date, then the new § 102 provisions apply to all claims. Additionally, because that is an application or patent "for which the amendments made by this section also apply" (as just explained) and because at least one relevant claim's effective filing date is *before* the trigger date, then the pre-AIAn interference provisions also seem to apply. However, courts have yet to interpret these provisions.

§ 2:10 Prior § 102 can be litigated into the 2040's

The AIA contains many sections stating their own respective dates of effect or applicability. Some of the provisions took effect on September 16, 2011 when President Obama signed the bill into law, some came into effect 12 months later, and others 18 months after signature. Regardless of when a new provision becomes effective, its applicability must be checked also. Some AIA provisions are applicable to all patents that may have already issued and all future patents, while other provisions may be limited. Each portion of the statute should be consulted to determine its applicability.

Section 3(n) of the AIA does not make the new provisions of 35 U.S.C. § 102 retroactive. As such, jurisprudence under the outgoing statute will remain applicable to patents that do not come within the scope of Section 3(n). The "old" section 102 case law will apply to patents based on applications filed before the FITF provisions take effect. That is, absent subsequent modification, an application filed up until March

15, 2013 would not be subject to the new § 102 because it has an effective filing date that is before the trigger date. A resulting patent would have the 20 year term for patents that issue on such applications. That extends the applicability of the old § 102 to at least March 15, 2033 (barring patent term extensions). Moreover, the 20-year expiration of patents granted under the first-to-invent system does not signal the end of § 102's application. Under 35 U.S.C. § 286, a patent owner can file a complaint or counterclaim for infringements occurring up to six years prior. This extends the applicability of the old § 102 to cases filed up to March 15, 2039 on pre-AIA § 3 patents. With patent trials occurring generally at least a year or two after the complaint is filed, and allowing another year for any appeal, it is foreseeable that the old § 102 can be applied well into the 2040s.

Moreover, it is highly likely that by the 2020s, patent litigation will include some patents subject to the new § 102 and other patents subject to the old § 102. Courts will have to deal with the added complexity of having patents governed by different laws in the same civil action.

§ 2:11 Examples of the new section 102 at work

Example 1: First to Invent is Second to File

- A invents subject matter X on January 16, 2013.
- B independently invents X on March 31, 2013.
- B files a patent application for X on April 18, 2013.
- A files a patent application for X on April 19, 2013.

Outcomes: A will be barred; B is not.

As to A: B's application will invalidate A's application after B's application publishes, will be deemed published or issues as a patent because B's application will be prior art to A's application under § 102(a)(2) and no exception applies. However, if B's first-filed application never gets published and never issues (because, illustratively, B might abandon the application by not responding to an Office Action or otherwise withdraw the application, and B may have requested non-publication), then B's application will not be prior art against A's application. Dates of actual invention are irrelevant under the revised statute.

As to B: A's prior invention is not prior art because the applications are filed after the FITF trigger date of March 16, 2013 and contain no claim to earlier priority. A's prior invention is not prior art against B's FITF application for subject matter X. A neither published, patented, placed on sale or in public use, nor otherwise made subject matter X available to the public.

Example 2: Public Disclosure by First to Invent But Second to File

- A invents subject matter X on January 16, 2013.
- A publicly discloses X on January 31, 2013.
- B invents X on March 31, 2013.
- B files an application on April 18, 2013.
- A files an application on April 19, 2013.

Outcomes: A is safe; B is barred.

As to A: B's patent application will become prior art to A's application under § 102(a)(2) if B's application publishes, is deemed published, or issues. However, the operation of § 102(b)(2)(B) saves A because A publicly disclosed his invention prior to B's filing date. A can submit a declaration or affidavit using 37 C.F.R. § 1.130(b) to establish the prior public disclosure.[1] Dates of invention are still irrelevant.

As to B: The January 31, 2013 public disclosure by A bars B under § 102(a)(1).

Example 3: Burglar Files a Derived Application Prior to the First Inventor's Application

---

[Section 2:11]

[1]37 C.F.R. § 1.130 provides in pertinent part: "(b) *Affidavit or declaration of prior public disclosure.* When any claim of an application or a patent under reexamination is rejected, the applicant or patent owner may submit an appropriate affidavit or declaration to disqualify a disclosure as prior art by establishing that the subject matter disclosed had, before such disclosure was made or before such subject matter was effectively filed, been publicly disclosed by the inventor or a joint inventor or another who obtained the subject matter disclosed directly or indirectly from the inventor or a joint inventor. An affidavit or declaration under this paragraph must identify the subject matter publicly disclosed and provide the date such subject matter was publicly disclosed by the inventor or a joint inventor or another who obtained the subject matter disclosed directly or indirectly from the inventor or a joint inventor.

"(1) If the subject matter publicly disclosed on that date was in a printed publication, the affidavit or declaration must be accompanied by a copy of the printed publication.

"(2) If the subject matter publicly disclosed on that date was not in a printed publication, the affidavit or declaration must describe the subject matter with sufficient detail and particularity to determine what subject matter had been publicly disclosed on that date by the inventor or a joint inventor or another who obtained the subject matter disclosed directly or indirectly from the inventor or a joint inventor."

- A invents on January 16, 2013.
- B, an industrial espionage agent, burglarizes A and copies A's materials.
- B files a derived application on April 18, 2013.
- A files an application on April 19, 2013.

Outcomes: Unless A proves the facts, A will lose. B can be awarded a patent but it will be invalid for lack of inventorship.

As to A: After B's application publishes, is deemed published, or issues as a patent, it is prior art against A's application. In order to remove B's filing as a reference, A has to prove derivation under § 102(b)(2)(A). That is because A does not have an earlier disclosure on which to rely. B has no prior art against his application arising from A, so A needs the derivation proof to defeat B. A's invention prior to the theft is relevant to the extent it can be used to prove derivation. If A proves prior invention but not derivation, A does not prevail. A can submit a declaration or affidavit using 37 C.F.R. § 1.130(a) attesting to attribution, but A needs factual evidence in support.[2]

As to B: The patent *ought* not issue to Burglar B, but this part of the statute does not interdict it. B is subject to penalties for having made a false oath or declaration as to inventorship. In a derivation proceeding, if A is successful, the PTAB can change the inventorship on B's application.

Example 4: Same as Ex. 3, but First Inventor Publicly Discloses First

- A invents on January 16, 2013.
- A publicly discloses the invention on January 31, 2013.
- B, an industrial espionage agent, burglarizes A and copies A's materials.
- B files an application on April 18, 2013.
- A files an application on April 19, 2013.

Outcomes: A is safe; B is barred and open to penalties.

As to A: A does not have to prove derivation to prevail or

[2]37 C.F.R. § 1.130 provides in pertinent part: "(a) *Affidavit or declaration of attribution.* When any claim of an application or a patent under reexamination is rejected, the applicant or patent owner may submit an appropriate affidavit or declaration to disqualify a disclosure as prior art by establishing that the disclosure was made by the inventor or a joint inventor, or the subject matter disclosed was obtained directly or indirectly from the inventor or a joint inventor."

obtain a patent because the public disclosure by A removes B's published or deemed published application as prior art to A under § 102(b)(2)(B). Dates of invention are irrelevant.

As to B: B is subject to penalties for having made a false oath or declaration as to inventorship. Also, A's public disclosure before B's filing date destroys novelty for B. B has no applicable exception under § 102(b)(1).

Example 5: Common Ownership; First to Invent is Second to File

- A invents on January 16, 2013.
- B invents on March 31, 2013.
- B files an application on April 18, 2013.
- A files an application on April 19, 2013.
- A and B are each obligated to assign to C.

Outcomes: Both A and B receive patents.

Both applications are fine under § 102(b)(2)(C) because of the common obligation of assignment. Dates of invention are irrelevant, and there are no publications, public uses, etc. to worry about.

Example 6: Same as Ex. 5, but First to Invent Publicly Discloses

Take the same facts as Example 5, but A publicly discloses before B's filing date; there is common ownership. Specifically:

- A invents subject matter X on January 16, 2013.
- B invents subject matter X on March 31, 2013.
- A publicly discloses subject matter X on April 1, 2013.
- B files an application for subject matter X on April 18, 2013.
- A files an application for subject matter X on April 19, 2013.
- A and B are each obligated to assign to C.

Outcomes: A's application is fine; B's application lacks novelty.

As to A: A's application is fine because § 102(b)(2)(C) protects the application from B's earlier-filed application. A is also protected by § 102(b)(2)(B) because A disclosed publicly before B filed an application. Dates of invention are irrelevant.

As to B: The public disclosure of A is prior art to B's application under § 102(a)(1). A's prior disclosure destroys B's novelty because there is no common assignment exception to § 102(a)(1) prior art. The common assignment exception is limited to prior art under § 102(a)(2) relating to patents and applications, but not public disclosures.

Example 7: Common Ownership; Independent Inventors Both Disclose Publicly Before Filing Applications

A is the first to invent and second to file; with common ownership. Specifically:

- A invents subject matter X on January 16, 2013.
- B invents subject matter X on January 31, 2013.
- B publicly discloses X on March 31, 2013.
- A publicly discloses X on April 15, 2013.
- B files an application on April 18, 2013.
- A files an application on April 19, 2013.
- A and B are each obligated to assign to C.

Outcomes: A is barred; B is safe.

As to A: The public disclosure by B before A's filing date destroys the novelty of A's application because there is no obligation of common assignment exception to § 102(a)(1). Also, the exception of § 102(b)(1)(B) does not apply because A did not disclose earlier than B disclosed.

As to B: B's application is fine because A filed after B and because B disclosed before A filed or disclosed. Dates of invention are irrelevant.

In the following examples 8-11, assume that revised Section 102 (2011) is in effect and all applications are filed after March 16, 2013.

Example 8: Second Inventor Files First, Outside U.S.; Common Ownership

- Day 1: A invents X in the U.S.
- Day 2: B invents X in Switzerland.
- Day 3: B files a PCT patent application in Switzerland designating the United States.
- Day 4: A files a U.S. patent application.
- Day X (18 mos. after Day 3): WIPO publishes B's PCT application.
- Day X +1: the USPTO publishes A's patent application.
- Day Y: B timely files a U.S. national application claiming priority to the PCT application filed on Day 3.
- A and B both work for Company C and are obligated to

assign to C.

Outcomes: Neither application is barred in the U.S.

As to A: B's Day 3 application when published becomes prior art to A under § 102(a)(2). However, A benefits from the common ownership exception of § 102(b)(2)(C) under which B's application is not prior art to A's application.

As to B: Although A is first to file in the U.S., B takes advantage of the International Convention and timely files a U.S. application sufficient to obtain the benefit of B's Swiss filing date, giving B an effective filing date of Day 3. 35 U.S.C. § 100(i)(1)(B) (2011). Therefore, the subsequent USPTO publication of A's application on Day X+1 is not prior art and there are no bars against B. B's application is not anticipated by A's application. Dates of invention are irrelevant.

Variation: If all the facts were the same except that A had no obligation to assign to Company C and had not assigned to C by Day 4 (A's effective filing date), then A could not take advantage of the common ownership exception. B's published application would be prior art against A. A, though first to invent, would have the later effective filing date and is not the first inventor to file. A's application would be properly rejected.

Example 9: Second Inventor to File Publishes First; Common Ownership

- Day 1: A invents X in the U.S.
- Day 2: B invents X in the U.S.
- Day 3: A, having been invited to present at a colloquium in his native Switzerland, publishes a paper disclosing subject matter X. Proud of his native language, Rumantsch, a/k/a Romansch, a language of Switzerland used by 1% of the Swiss population, A publishes in that language.
- Day 4: B files a U.S. patent application.
- Day 5: A files a U.S. patent application after B but within 12 months of Day 3.
- A and B are both obligated to assign to C.

Outcomes: B is barred; A is safe.

As to A, the second inventor to file: A's own publication (Day 3) is prior art under § 102(a)(1), but the § 102(b)(1)(A) grace period rescues A. Further, B's application if published will become prior art to A's application under § 102(a)(2) (2011) because B's application has the earlier effective filing date (Day 4). However, both A's earlier public disclosure and the common ownership exception protect A. § 102(b)(2)(B)&(C). A is safe.

As to B, the first inventor to file: A's publication in Switzerland regardless of the language is prior art to B under § 102(a)(1) (2011). The common ownership exception is irrelevant against the prior art of § 102(a)(1). B is barred. Dates of invention are irrelevant.

Variation: Instead of A publishing in Switzerland, a third party deriver D obtains access to A's work. D publishes in Switzerland on Day 3. A is still protected by § 102(b)(1)(A) (2011) because D's disclosure on Day 3 occurs one year or less before A's effective filing date (Day 5), and "the disclosure [by D] was made by . . . another who obtained the subject matter disclosed directly or indirectly from the inventor . . . ."

Example 10: First Inventor to File Publicly Discloses First; Common Ownership

- Day 1: A invents
- Day 2: B invents
- Day 3: B publicly discloses
- Day 4: B files a U.S. patent application within 12 mos. of Day 3
- Day 5: A files a U.S. patent application within 12 mos. of Day 3
- A, B are obligated to assign to C.

Outcomes: A is barred; B is safe.

As to A: B's disclosure (Day 3) ahead of A's effective filing date (Day 5) is prior art to A's application. As A did not publicly disclose his subject matter ahead of Day 3, no exception benefits A. The common ownership exception relates only to U.S. patent art of § 102(a)(2). It is irrelevant to § 102(a)(1) prior art (five kinds).

As to B: B's Day 3 public disclosure is prior art to B's Day 4 application. However, an inventor's own acts less than one year ahead of the effective filing date do not raise a bar. On these facts, B is rescued by the exception of § 102(b)(1)(A). B is safe. Dates of invention are irrelevant.

Example 11: Two Public Disclosures Prior to Filing Dates; Common Ownership

- Day 1: A invents subject matter X.
- Day 2: B invents subject matter X.

- Day 3: B publicly discloses X in a printed publication, places it on sale or in public use, or otherwise makes X available to the public.
- Day 4: A publicly discloses X in a printed publication, on sale, public use, or otherwise makes X available to the public.
- Day 5: B files a U.S. patent application.
- Day 6: A files a U.S. patent application.
- A and B are obligated to assign to C.

Outcomes: A is barred; B is safe.

As to A (second to disclose publicly and second to file): First, consider B's application on Day 5, prior to A's application filed on Day 6. When published, B's application will be prior art to A under § 102(a)(2) (2011). However, A's prior public disclosure on Day 4 protects A against B's application. § 102(b)(2)(B). Also, the common ownership exception is applicable to U.S. patent applications and U.S. patents, and A overcomes that reference via § 102(b)(2)(C).

Next consider B's public disclosure on Day 3. This is prior to A's public disclosure (Day 4) and prior to A's patent application (Day 6). The common ownership exception is irrelevant to prior art under § 102(a)(1) (2011). An inventor can be protected by a public disclosure ahead of the reference. However, A's Day 4 public disclosure occurs *after* B's Day 3 public disclosure, so the grace period of § 102(b)(1)(B) does not protect A. A cannot show that "the subject matter disclosed [X] had, before such disclosure [by B] been publicly disclosed by . . . [A]." Consequently, B's Day 3 disclosure of subject matter X is prior art, and A is barred by the reference.

As to B (first inventor to file and first to disclose): B's public disclosure on Day 3 is prior art against B's application under § 102(a)(1). However, an inventor's own activities less than one year prior to the effective filing date are within the grace period, and under the language of § 102(b)(1)(A), B's own public disclosure less than one year prior to his filing date is not prior art.

Next consider A's public disclosure on Day 4. Since this is prior to B's Day 5 application, it too is prior art. However, B is rescued by § 102(b)(1)(B) because B had made a public disclosure before A did. B is safe. A's disclosure is not prior art. Dates of invention are irrelevant.

Chapter 3

Best Mode and Section 112

AIA §§ 4(c), 15
35 U.S.C.A. §§ 112, 119, 120, 282

§ 3:1 Background

The U.S. patent statute enacted in 1952, like its predecessors, included a requirement that the applicant must include in the patent specification a disclosure of the "best mode" contemplated for practicing the invention:

> 35 U.S.C. 112 Specification.
>
> The specification shall contain a written description of the invention, and of the manner and process of making and using it, in such full, clear, concise, and exact terms as to enable any person skilled in the art to which it pertains, or with which it is most nearly connected, to make and use the same, and shall set forth the **best mode** contemplated by the inventor of carrying out his invention.[1]

This requirement for disclosing the best mode is generally

[Section 3:1]

[1]35 U.S.C.A. § 112 (2006) [emphasis added].

based on the thought that it is part of a reasonable *quid pro quo* for obtaining a right to exclude. Before Congress allows exclusive rights against the public to issue in the form of a patent for an invention, the inventor is required to make full disclosure of the invention so that when the patent rights expire, the public will have the full use of the invention, and before such expiration, the public receives the information about the invention. With such information, others can improve or design around the patented invention. It has been a defense against infringement that the patent fails to enable one to make and use the invention, fails to give a written description of the invention, or fails to disclose the best mode contemplated by the inventor (as of the application filing date) for practicing the invention.[2]

From a global perspective, however, the best mode requirement is unique. Other countries do not have a parallel provision. This has been one objection—that foreign inventors who file outside the U.S. first and later seek U.S. patent rights must prepare their applications to comply with U.S. law even when their native patent statutes lack the best mode requirement.

Second, the best mode requirement has been challenged as being subjective and counterproductive by the time the question is litigated, usually many years after the patent application is first filed.

§ 3:2 Congressional intent[1]

The House Report addresses the best mode requirement at

[2]35 U.S.C.A. § 282 addresses defenses to patent infringement actions and provided, prior to enactment of the AIA, "* * *The following shall be defenses in any action involving the validity or infringement of a patent and shall be pleaded: * * *(2) Invalidity of the patent or any claim in suit on any ground specified in part II of this title as a condition for patentability, (3) Invalidity of the patent or any claim in suit for failure to comply with any requirement of sections 112 or 251 of this title, (4) Any other fact or act made a defense by this title."

[Section 3:2]

[1]The Supreme Court cautions against relying on interpretations advanced in legislative statements that are not "anchored in the text of the statute." *Shannon v. U.S.*, 512 U.S. 573, 583, 114 S. Ct. 2419, 129 L. Ed. 2d 459 (1994), stating "[C]ourts have no authority to enforce [a] principl[e] gleaned solely from legislative history that has no statutory reference point." *Shannon,* 512 U.S. at 584, quoting *International Broth. of Elec. Workers, Local Union No. 474, AFL-CIO v. N.L.R.B.*, 814 F.2d 697, 712, 124 L.R.R.M. (BNA) 2993, 106 Lab. Cas. (CCH) P 12256 (D.C. Cir. 1987). The authoritative statement "is the statutory text, not the

two places, stating as follows:

Best mode requirement

The Act amends § 282(b) to eliminate as a defense to patent infringement the patentee's failure to comply with the best mode requirement of 112. An applicant for a patent must disclose: (1) a written description of the invention; (2) a written description of the manner of making and using the invention, sufficient to enable one skilled in the art to make and use it (known as the "enablement requirement"); and (3) the best mode contemplated by the inventor of carrying out the invention. The disclosures required of an applicant are part of the important tradeoff that underlies the patent laws: the grant of a limited-term monopoly in exchange for disclosure of the invention.[FN53]

FN 53.35 U.S.C. Sec. 112. Section 112 also requires an applicant to disclose a written description of the invention and a written description of the manner of making and using the invention, sufficient to enable one skilled in the art to make and use it.

Under current law, the defense of patent invalidity is available for failure to comply with any requirement of § 112 (specification) or 251 (reissued patents). Further, a defendant in patent litigation may also allege an intentional nondisclosure of the best mode, with intent to deceive the Office, as a basis for an unenforceability defense. Many have argued in recent years that the best mode requirement, which is unique to American patent law, is counterproductive. They argue that challenges to patents based on best mode are inherently subjective and not relevant by the time the patent is in litigation, because the best mode contemplated at the time of the invention may not be the best mode for practicing or using the invention years later.[FN54]

FN 54. Among those who have so argued are the National Academy of Sciences, the Biotechnology Industry Organization, the American Intellectual Property Law Association, the Intellectual Property Owners Association, and Pharmaceutical Research and Manufacturers of America.

In response to these concerns, the Act includes a provision that eliminates best mode as a basis for both invalidity and unenforceability defenses under § 282; other defenses are

---

legislative history." *Exxon Mobil Corp. v. Allapattah Services, Inc.*, 545 U.S. 546, 568, 125 S. Ct. 2611, 162 L. Ed. 2d 502 (2005). However, lower courts have cited the legislative history of the AIA already in recent cases. E.g., *Rogers v. Tristar Products, Inc.*, 102 U.S.P.Q.2d 1722, 2012 WL 1660604, *2 (Fed. Cir. 2012) (non-precedential); *Byrne v. Wood, Herron & Evans, LLP*, 676 F.3d 1024, 1029, 102 U.S.P.Q.2d 1073 (Fed. Cir. 2012) (dissenting opin.).

unaffected.[2]

* * *

Section 15. Best Mode Requirement.

This section amends § 282(b) by removing the failure to disclose the best mode under section 112 as a basis for canceling or holding either invalid or unenforceable a patent claim.[3]

§ 3:3 Changes by the America Invents Act re best mode

The America Invents Act retains the best mode disclosure requirement in § 112 but almost completely removes the consequences for violating the requirement. Section 15 of the AIA amends 35 U.S.C. §§ 112, 119, 120, and 282 paragraph 3 as follows. Preliminarily, AIA § 4(c) amends the six paragraphs of § 112 so they now are separately identified as § 112(a) through (f), respectively:[1]

Revised 35 U.S.C. § 112[2]

§ 112. Specification

---

[2]H. R. Rep. No. 112-98, pt. 1, at 52 (2011).

[3]H. R. Rep. No. 112-98, pt. 1, at 80 (2011).

[Section 3:3]

[1]Amendments to subsequent paragraphs of § 112 do not concern the best mode. Apart from adding paragraph letters, the only substantive amendment is in § 112(b) which previously called for claims "which the applicant regards as his invention." This has been amended to refer to claims "which the inventor or joint inventor regards as the invention." The AIA § 4(c) amendments to the 35 U.S.C.A. § 112, which mentions the best mode requirement, took effect on September 16, 2012—one year after the AIA became law, according to AIA § 4(e). See AIA § 4(c); *In re Bimeda Research & Development Ltd.*, 107 U.S.P.Q.2d 1619, 2013 WL 3821557, at *4 n.3 (Fed. Cir. 2013) (§ 112–1st para.); *Novozymes A/S v. DuPont Nutrition Biosciences APS*, 107 U.S.P.Q.2d 1457, 2013 WL 3779376, at *16 n.3 (Fed. Cir. 2013) (same); *Function Media, L.L.C. v. Google, Inc.*, 708 F.3d 1310, 1317 n.5, 105 U.S.P.Q.2d 1754 (Fed. Cir. 2013) (same); *Cephalon, Inc. v. Watson Pharmaceuticals, Inc.*, 707 F.3d 1330, 1336 n.9, 105 U.S.P.Q.2d 1817 (Fed. Cir. 2013) (same); see also, *Biosig Instruments, Inc. v. Nautilus, Inc.*, 715 F.3d 891, 897 n.3, 106 U.S.P.Q.2d 1554 (Fed. Cir. 2013) (re § 112, 2nd para.); *Ernie Ball, Inc. v. Earvana, LLC*, 502 Fed. Appx. 971, 978 n.4, (Fed. Cir. 2013) (§ 112, 2nd para.); *Saffran v. Johnson & Johnson*, 712 F.3d 549, 557 n.4, 106 U.S.P.Q.2d 1274 (Fed. Cir. 2013) (§ 112, 6th para.); *Power Integrations, Inc. v. Fairchild Semiconductor Intern., Inc.*, 711 F.3d 1348, 1364 n.2, 106 U.S.P.Q.2d 1361 (Fed. Cir. 2013), petition for cert. filed (U.S. Aug. 23, 2013); *In re Avid Identification Systems, Inc.*, 504 Fed. Appx. 885, 891 n.1, (Fed. Cir. 2013) (§ 112, 6th para.).

[2]Revised statutes are shown with underscoring for new language

(a) IN GENERAL.— The specification shall contain a written description of the invention, and of the manner and process of making and using it, in such full, clear, concise, and exact terms as to enable any person skilled in the art to which it pertains, or with which it is most nearly connected, to make and use the same, and shall set forth the best mode contemplated by the inventor ~~of carrying out his invention~~ or joint inventor of carrying out the invention.

Revised 35 U.S.C. § 119

§ 119. Benefit of earlier filing date; right of priority

* * *

(e)(1) An application for patent filed under section 111(a)[3] or section 363[4] ~~of this title~~ for an invention disclosed in the manner provided by ~~the first paragraph of section 112 of this title~~ section 112(a) (other than the requirement to disclose the best mode) in a provisional application filed under section 111(b)[5] ~~of this title~~, by an inventor or inventors named in the provisional application, shall have the same effect, as to such invention, as though filed on the date of the provisional application filed under section 111(b) ~~of this title~~, if the application for patent filed under section 111(a) or section 363 ~~of this title~~ is filed not later than 12 months after the date on which the provisional application was filed and if it contains or is amended to contain a specific reference to the provisional application. * * *

and strikethrough for deleted language.

[3]35 U.S.C.A. § 111(a) concerns nonprovisional applications and provides, in part: "§ 111 Application. (a) In general.—(1) Written application.—An application for patent shall be made, or authorized to be made, by the inventor, except as otherwise provided in this title, in writing to the Director. (2) Contents.—Such application shall include—(A) a specification as prescribed by section 112 of this title; (B) a drawing as prescribed by section 113 of this title; and (C) an oath by the applicant as prescribed by section 115 of this title. * * *" [edited for format]

[4]35 U.S.C.A. § 363 concerns international applications and states: "§ 363. International application designating the United States: Effect. An international application designating the United States shall have the effect, from its international filing date under article 11 of the treaty, of a national application for patent regularly filed in the Patent and Trademark Office except as otherwise provided in section 102(e) of this title."

[5]35 U.S.C.A. § 111(b) concerns provisional applications and provides, in part: "(b) Provisional application.—(1) Authorization.—A provisional application for patent shall be made or authorized to be made by the inventor, except as otherwise provided in this title, in writing to the Director. Such application shall include—(A) a specification as prescribed by the first paragraph of section 112 of this title; and (B) a drawing as prescribed by section 113 of this title. * * *" [edited for format]

Revised 35 U.S.C. § 120

§ 120. Benefit of earlier filing date in the United States

An application for patent for an invention disclosed in the manner provided by ~~the first paragraph of section 112 of this title~~ section 112(a) (other than the requirement to disclose the best mode) in an application previously filed in the United States, or as provided by section 363 ~~of this title~~, ~~which is filed by an inventor or inventors named~~ which names an inventor or joint inventor in the previously filed application shall have the same effect, as to such invention, as though filed on the date of the prior application, if filed before the patenting or abandonment of or termination of proceedings on the first application or on an application similarly entitled to the benefit of the filing date of the first application and if it contains or is amended to contain a specific reference to the earlier filed application. * * *

Revised 35 U.S.C. § 282

§ 282. Presumption of validity; defenses

(a) IN GENERAL.—

(b) DEFENSES.— The following shall be defenses in any action involving the validity or infringement of a patent and shall be pleaded:

(1) Noninfringement, absence of liability for infringement or ~~unenforceability,~~ unenforceability.

(2) Invalidity of the patent or any claim in suit on any ground specified in part II ~~of this title~~ as a condition for ~~patentability,~~ patentability.

~~(3) Invalidity of the patent or any claim in suit for failure to comply with any requirement of sections 112 or 251 of this title,~~

(3) Invalidity of the patent or any claim in suit for failure to comply with—

(A) any requirement of section 112, except that the failure to disclose the best mode shall not be a basis on which any claim of a patent may be canceled or held invalid or otherwise unenforceable; or

(B) any requirement of section 251.

(4) Any other fact or act made a defense by this title.

§ 3:4 Applicable USPTO final rules re best mode

Pursuant to the AIA, the USPTO made changes in its rules concerning the best mode requirement. The applicable final rules state as follows:

§ 1.78. Claiming benefit of earlier filing date and

cross-references to other applications.

(a) (1) A nonprovisional application or international application designating the United States of America may claim an invention disclosed in one or more prior-filed copending nonprovisional applications or international applications designating the United States of America. In order for an application to claim the benefit of a prior-filed copending nonprovisional application or international application designating the United States of America, each prior-filed application must name as an inventor at least one inventor named in the later-filed application and disclose the named inventor's invention claimed in at least one claim of the later-filed application in the manner provided by 35 U.S.C. 112(a), **other than the requirement to disclose the best mode.** In addition, each prior-filed application must be:

* * * * *

(2) * * *

(iii) If the later-filed application is a nonprovisional application, the reference required by this paragraph must be included in an application data sheet (§ 1.76(b)(5)).

* * *

(4) A nonprovisional application, other than for a design patent, or an international application designating the United States of America may claim an invention disclosed in one or more prior-filed provisional applications. In order for an application to claim the benefit of one or more prior-filed provisional applications, each prior-filed provisional application must name as an inventor at least one inventor named in the later-filed application and disclose the named inventor's invention claimed in at least one claim of the later-filed application in the manner provided by 35 U.S.C. 112(a), **other than the requirement to disclose the best mode.** In addition, each prior-filed provisional application must be entitled to a filing date as set forth in § 1.53(c), and the basic filing fee set forth in § 1.16(d) must be paid within the time period set forth in § 1.53(g). * * *

[emphasis added]

§ 3:5 Best mode applicability in patent prosecution

The AIA changes regarding the best mode requirement are a first step toward global harmonization. In the U.S., the best mode *requirement* is retained, but the best mode *defense* is eliminated from litigation. All applicants for U.S. patents, whether they file first in the U.S. or originate new patent applications in foreign countries and later file corresponding applications in the USPTO, are still obligated under the amended patent statute to comply with the best mode requirement. The consequences of not complying are very limited, however.

Nothing in the AIA or the 2012 final rules of the USPTO negates the requirement for disclosing the best mode in a U.S. patent application, and an application for patent can be rejected for failure to disclose the best mode. The Acting Associate Commissioner for Patent Examination Policy at the USPTO issued a memorandum to the Patent Examining Corps on Sept. 20, 2011 (see Appendix 4) instructing the Corps that, *inter alia*:

- the best mode amendment of the AIA "does not alter patent examining practices set forth in MPEP 2165 for evaluation of an application for compliance with the best mode requirement . . ." and "should not noticeably impact patent examining procedure";
- the changes to 35 U.S.C. §§ 119(e) and 120, which are the provisions for claiming the benefit of a provisional application and a nonprovisional application, respectively, will no longer require the earlier application to meet the best mode requirement; and
- the best mode amendment is applicable "only in patent validity or infringement proceedings."[1]

Regarding priority claims, the AIA removes the best mode requirement for the earlier application to support the current application. The right of priority and the benefit of the earlier filing date apply without regard to whether the earlier application complied with the best mode requirement. 35 U.S.C. §§ 119(e)(1), 120 (2011); 37 C.F.R. § 1.78 (2012). This applies also to priority from an international application designating the United States. 35 U.S.C. § 119(e)(1) (2011) and § 363.

With regard to complying with the best mode requirement in filing patent applications, the statute still names *the inventor* (rather than the applicant—which may be an assignee filing the application) as the person whose contemplated best mode must be disclosed. Section 112 (a) states, "The specification . . . shall set forth the best mode contemplated *by the inventor or joint inventor* of carrying out the invention." [emphasis added] It does not name the assignee

[Section 3:5]

[1]See http://www.uspto.gov/aia_implementation/best-mode-memo.pdf visited August 29, 2012. A copy of this 2-page memorandum is included in the appendices.

or the applicant.

§ 3:6 Inapplicability to post-grant review

The prohibitions of AIA § 15 against raising a best mode invalidity defense extend beyond infringement cases at the U.S. District Court and the U.S. International Trade Commission. A best mode challenge cannot be considered in a post-grant review at the USPTO even though the language of § 282 concerns actions where "defenses" are "pleaded." This use of "defenses" and "pleaded" suggests federal court litigation and suggests that changes to the best mode requirement might not impact USPTO proceedings where claims can be canceled.[1]

However, other language closes the door to addressing this issue in post-grant challenges. The AIA legislation for the new "Post-Grant Review" states in new § 321(b) that the grounds for a petition to cancel claims as unpatentable are "any ground that could be raised under paragraph (2) or (3) of § 282(b) (relating to invalidity of the patent or any claim)." In § 282 as now amended, paragraph (2) allows defenses on any ground specified in part II as a condition for patentability. However, paragraph (3) states that a failure to disclose best mode shall *not* be a basis on which a claim may be *canceled*, held invalid, or otherwise unenforceable:

> **§ 282. Presumption of validity; defenses**
>
> * * *
>
> (b) DEFENSES.— The following shall be defenses in any action involving the validity or infringement of a patent and shall be pleaded:
>
> * * *
>
> (3) Invalidity of the patent or any claim in suit for failure to comply with—
>
> (A) any requirement of section 112, *except that the failure to disclose the best mode shall not be a basis on which any claim of a patent may be canceled or held invalid or otherwise unenforceable*; or * * *

[emphasis added] Since a post-grant review is a proceeding

[Section 3:6]

[1]New § 321 establishes post grant reviews. Section (b) provides: "(b) SCOPE.—A petitioner in a post-grant review may request to cancel as unpatentable 1 or more claims of a patent on any ground that could be raised under paragraph (2) or (3) of section 282(b) (relating to invalidity of the patent or any claim)."

in which a claim can be canceled or held invalid, the failure to disclose the best mode is a challenge which § 282 forecloses in post-grant reviews at the USPTO.

§ 3:7 Effective date of best mode amendments

These amendments regarding the best mode requirement took effect immediately on enactment of the AIA and affect all suits filed on or after the date of enactment,[1] *i.e.*, September 16, 2011. The changes are prospective only and apply to lawsuits commenced on or after that date.[2]

[Section 3:7]

[1]AIA § 15(c).

[2]See *In re Cyclobenzaprine Hydrochloride Extended-Release Capsule Patent Litigation*, 676 F.3d 1063, 1084, 102 U.S.P.Q.2d 1760 (Fed. Cir. 2012), petition for cert. filed, 81 U.S.L.W. 3216 (U.S. Oct. 9, 2012); *WesternGeco L.L.C. v. ION Geophysical Corp., 2012 Markman 2450801*, 2012 WL 2450801, *5 (S.D. Tex. 2012), subsequent determination, 2012 WL 2568167 (S.D. Tex. 2012).

Chapter 4

Unpatentability of "Human Organisms"

AIA § 33

§ 4:1 Background and congressional intent re "human organisms"[1]

Since the cloning of "Dolly" the sheep in 1997 by Scottish

[Section 4:1]

[1]The Supreme Court cautions against relying on interpretations advanced in legislative statements that are not "anchored in the text of the statute." *Shannon v. U.S.*, 512 U.S. 573, 583, 114 S. Ct. 2419, 129 L. Ed. 2d 459 (1994), stating "[C]ourts have no authority to enforce [a] principl[e] gleaned solely from legislative history that has no statutory reference point." *Shannon,* 512 U.S. at 584, quoting *International Broth. of Elec. Workers, Local Union No. 474, AFL-CIO v. N.L.R.B.*, 814 F.2d 697, 712, 124 L.R.R.M. (BNA) 2993, 106 Lab. Cas. (CCH) P 12256 (D.C. Cir. 1987). The authoritative statement "is the statutory text, not the legislative history." *Exxon Mobil Corp. v. Allapattah Services, Inc.*, 545 U.S. 546, 568, 125 S. Ct. 2611, 162 L. Ed. 2d 502 (2005). However, lower courts have cited the legislative history of the AIA already in recent cases. E.g., *Rogers v. Tristar Products, Inc.*, 102 U.S.P.Q.2d 1722, 2012 WL 1660604, *2 (Fed. Cir. 2012) (non-precedential); *Byrne v. Wood, Herron & Evans, LLP*, 676 F.3d 1024, 1029, 102 U.S.P.Q.2d 1073 (Fed. Cir. 2012) (dissenting opin.).

scientists at the Roslin Institute, lawmakers and others have been concerned with the scientific and ethical implications of cloning. For several years, Congress has sought to ensure that no U.S. patent would be granted on human beings. This has been the subject of the "Weldon Amendment" (see below) in recent years.

AIA Section 33 forbids patents on "human organisms." The House Report is silent on Section 33. The section-by-section analysis in the House Report extends to only Section 31 of the AIA. However, this is because Section 33 was not added to the AIA until the floor managers' amendment was made in June 2011.[2]

Representative Lamar Smith, House sponsor of H.R. 1249, provided materials in the "Extension Remarks" portion of the Congressional Record in connection with introducing the managers' amendment.[3] This clarifies that AIA Section 33 traces back to the Weldon amendment which Representative Weldon introduced in 2003 that limited the USPTO's ability to issue patents on human beings. Representative Smith's remarks include a "Statement on the codification of the Weldon amendment," a November 2003 letter from the USPTO Director to the Senate, and 2011 information from

---

[2]See J. Matal, "A Guide to the Legislative History of the America Invents Act," *The Federal Circuit Bar J.* Vol. 21, No. 3, 435, 510 (2011) citing 157 Cong. Rec. H4448 to H4451 (daily ed. June 22, 2011).

[3]The Library of Congress in THOMAS provides this explanation of the "Extension of Remarks" portion of the Congressional Record. "The section in each day's Record following the House and Senate proceedings in known as the Extensions of Remarks. This section is now used only by Members of the House to include additional legislative statements not delivered on the House floor as well as extraneous materials such as the text of speeches delivered outside Congress, letters from and tributes to constituents, and newspaper or magazine articles. (Remarks not delivered by Senators that are to be inserted in the Record are usually found in the "Additional Statements" section of the Senate proceedings, effective February 10, 1970.)"

"The Extensions of Remarks and Daily Digest are always the last portion of the daily edition of the Record. Periodically, between them are found various materials to provide useful and diverse information. These include Laws and Rules for Publication of the Record, a listing of Representatives and Senators as well as their office numbers, officers of the House and Senate, the names of the official reporters of debate, committee memberships, and the names of the Justices of the Supreme Court and judges of certain other Federal courts." http://thomas.loc.gov/home/abt.cong.rec.html.

the "Family Research Council," as follows:[4]

AMERICA INVENTS ACT

—

SPEECH OF

HON. LAMAR SMITH

IN THE HOUSE OF REPRESENTATIVES

OF TEXAS

Wednesday, June 22, 2011

The House in Committee of the Whole House on the State of the Union had under consideration the bill (H.R. 1249) to amend title 35, United States Code, to provide for patent reform:

Mr. SMITH of Texas. Madam Chair, I submit: * * * (3) Statement on the codification of the Weldon amendment; * * * (6) November 2003 letter on the Weldon amendment from PTO Director James Rogan; (7) Information on the Weldon amendment from the Family Research Council.

* * *

THE WELDON AMENDMENT

"None of the funds appropriated or otherwise made available by this act may be used to issue patents on claims directed to or encompassing a human organism."

Legislative History:

The legislation prohibits the use of appropriated funds by the Patent and Trademark Office to issue certain types of claims presented in patent applications. The types of patent claims subject to the prohibition are limited precisely to those that the Patent and Trademark Office, pursuant to its policies, has indicated may not be granted (see M.P.E.P 1st rev. 2105). Specifically, this section operates to prohibit the use of appropriated funds to issue a patent containing claim that encompasses a human individual.

The Committee recognizes that the economic viability of the biotechnology industry requires that patents be available for the full spectrum of innovation that may be subject to commercialization. The legislation, accordingly does not limit patent eligibility for any type of biotechnology invention that may be commercialized in the United States.

The Committee also recognizes that continued innovation in

[4]157 Cong. Rec. E1182 to E1185 (daily ed. June 23, 2011) (statement of Rep. L. Smith).

the biomedical and biotechnological fields will lead to new kinds of inventions, and it expects that the overwhelming majority of such inventions will not raise any of the concerns that the present legislation addresses. In particular, nothing in this section should be construed to limit the ability of the PTO to issue a patent containing claims directed to or encompassing:

1. any chemical compound or composition, whether obtained from animals or human beings or produced synthetically, and whether identical to or distinct from a chemical structure as found in an animal or human being, including but not limited to nucleic acids, polypeptides, proteins, antibodies and hormones;

2. cells, tissue, organs or other bodily components produced through human intervention, whether obtained from animals, human beings, or other sources; including but not limited to stem cells, stem cell derived tissues, stem cell lines, and viable synthetic organs;

3. methods for creating, modifying, or treating human organisms, including but not limited to methods for creating embryos through in vitro fertilization, methods of somatic cell nuclear transfer, medical or genetic therapies, methods for enhancing fertility, and methods for implanting embryos;

4. a nonhuman organism incorporating one or more genes taken from a human organism, including but not limited to a transgenic plant or animal, or animal models used for scientific research.

As the legislation addresses only the authority of the PTO to expend funds appropriated by this Act, it concerns patents that may issue on applications filed on or after the date of the legislation. The legislation does not create a claim or give rise to any cause of action to limit the rights associated with, or the enforceability of any patent duly granted by the PTO.

[Nov. 2003 letter]

UNITED STATES PATENT AND TRADEMARK OFFICE, UNDER SECRETARY OF COMMERCE FOR INTELLECTUAL PROPERTY AND DIRECTOR OF THE U.S. PATENT AND TRADEMARK OFFICE,

Alexandria, VA.

Hon. Ted Stevens,

Chairman, Committee on Appropriations, U.S. Senate, Washington, DC.

DEAR MR. CHAIRMAN: Thank you for the opportunity to present the Administration's position on the Weldon amendment adopted by the House during consideration of H.R. 2799, the Commerce-Justice-State Appropriations bill FY 2004, and the effect it would have on the United States Patent and

Trademark Office (USPTO) policy on patenting living subject matter. For the reasons outlined below, we view the Weldon amendment as fully consistent with USPTO's policy on the non-patentability of human life-forms.

The Weldon Amendment would prohibit the U.S. Patent and Trademark Office from issuing any patent "on claims directed to or encompassing a human organism." The USPTO understands the Weldon Amendment to provide unequivocal congressional backing for the long-standing USPTO policy of refusing to grant any patent containing a claim that encompasses any member of the species Homo sapiens at any stage of development. It has long been USPTO practice to reject any claim in a patent application that encompasses a human life-form at any stage of development, including a human embryo or human fetus; hence claims directed to living "organisms" are to be rejected unless they include the adjective "nonhuman."

The USPTO's policy of rejecting patent application claims that encompass human life-forms, which the Weldon Amendment elevates to an unequivocal congressional prohibition, applies regardless of the manner and mechanism used to bring a human organism into existence (e.g., somatic cell nuclear transfer. in vitro fertilization, parthenogenesis). If a patent examiner determines that a claim is directed to a human life-form at any stage of development, the claim is rejected as non-statutory subject matter and will not be issued in a patent as such.

As indicated in Representative Weldon's remarks in the Congressional Record of November 5, 2003, the referenced language precludes the patenting of human organisms, including human embryos. He further indicated that the amendment has "exactly the same scope as the current USPTO policy." which assures that any claim that can be broadly construed as a human being, including a human embryo or fetus, is not patentable subject matter. Therefore, our understanding of the plain language of the Weldon Amendment is fully consistent with the detailed statements that the author of the amendment, Representative Weldon, has made in the Congressional Record regarding the meaning and intent of his amendment.

Given that the scope of Representative Weldon's amendment does not alter the USPTO policy on the non-patentability of human life-forms at any stage of development and is fully consistent with our policy, we support its enactment.

With best personal regards, I remain

Sincerely,

JAMES E. ROGAN,

Under Secretary and Director.

FRCAction,

FAMILY RESEARCH COUNCIL.

CODIFY THE WELDON BAN ON PATENTING HUMANS

CURRENT WELDON PATENT BAN ON HUMANS

The Weldon Amendment is contained in the annual Commerce, Justice and Science Appropriations bills (CJS) and prevents the patenting of humans. Congress has passed it each year since 2004, and it was included most recently as part of the FY2010 Omnibus (Section 518, Title V, Division B, of the FY2010 Consolidated Appropriations Act, 2010 (H.R. 3288, P.L. 111-117)) and extended by the FY2011 Omnibus spending bill (Department of Defense and Full-Year Continuing Appropriations Act, 2011 (H.R. 1473, P.L. 112-10)). Weldon Amendment, Section 518: "None of the friends [*sic*, funds] appropriated or otherwise made available under this Act may be used to issue patents on claims directed to or encompassing a human organism."

CODIFY THE WELDON AMENDMENT—ADD IT TO PATENT REFORM LEGISLATION

Congress has each year since 2004 passed the Weldon Amendment to prevent any profiting from patents on humans. The Weldon Amendment restricts funds under the Commerce, Justice, Science Appropriations bill from being used by the U.S. Patent and Trademark Office (USPTO) to issue patents directed to "human organisms."

The America Invents Act (H.R. 1249) may authorize the USPTO to pay for the issuance of patents with "user fees" instead of with Congressionally appropriated funds. If this funding mechanism becomes law, the Weldon Amendment restriction would not apply since it only covers funds appropriated under the CJS bill. The USPTO could, thereby, issue patents directed to human beings with non-appropriated funds.

Patenting human beings at any stage of development would overturn the long-standing USPTO policy against issuing such patents. As the Quigg Memo stated in 1987 (see below) a grant of a property right in a human being is unconstitutional, and patents on humans are grounds for rejection.

The Weldon restriction can be codified by adding a provision to the America Invents Act to ensure that human beings are not patentable subject matter.

Codifying a ban on patenting of humans would not violate international obligations under the TRIPs agreement with the WTO. The European Union prevents patents on human embryos on the ground that doing so would violate the public order and morality, an exception the TRIPs agreement specifically allows under Article 27, Section 5.

WHAT THE WELDON PATENT AMENDMENT DOES AND DOES NOT AFFECT

The Weldon Amendment does prevent the USPTO from patenting humans at any stage of development, including embryos or fetuses, by preventing patents on claims directed to "human organisms."

The Weldon Amendment's use of the term "human organism" does include human embryos, human fetuses, human-animal chimeras, "she-male" human embryos, or human embryos created with genetic material from more than one embryo.

The Weldon Amendment's use of "human organism" does not include the process of creating human embryos, such as human cloning, nor does it include non-human organisms, *e.g.,* animals.

Then Undersecretary James Rogan wrote to Senate Appropriators on November 20, 2003 stating that the Weldon Amendment gave congressional backing to long-standing USPTO policy against patenting humans stating:

"The Weldon Amendment would prohibit the U.S. Patent and Trademark Office from issuing any patent "on claims directed to or encompassing a human organism." The USPTO understands the Weldon Amendment to provide unequivocal congressional backing for the long-standing USPTO policy of refusing to grant any patent containing a claim that encompasses any member of the species Homo sapiens at any stage of development. It has long been USPTO practice to reject any claim in a patent application that encompasses a human life-form at any stage of development, including a human embryo or human fetus; hence claims directed to living "organisms" are to be rejected unless they include the adjective 'nonhuman."

Secretary Rogan concluded: "The USPTO's policy of rejecting patent application claims that encompass human life-forms, which the Weldon Amendment elevates to an unequivocal congressional prohibition, applies regardless of the manner and mechanism used to bring a human organism into existence (e.g., somatic cell nuclear transfer, in vitro fertilization, parthenogenesis). If a patent examiner determines that a claim is directed to a human life-form at any stage of development, the claim is rejected as non-statutory subject matter and will not be issued in a patent as such."

The Weldon Amendment does not prevent patents on human cells, genes, or other tissues obtained from human embryos or human bodies.

Rep. Dave Weldon submitted a statement to the Congressional Record on December 8, 2003 clarifying that the Weldon Amendment would not prevent patents for non-human organisms even with some human genes. Nor would it affect patents for human cells, tissues or body parts, or for methods of creating human embryos.

Rep. Weldon stated: "This amendment should not be construed to affect claims directed to or encompassing subject matter other than human organisms, including but not limited to claims directed to or encompassing the following: cells, tissues, organs, or other bodily components that are not themselves human organisms (including, but not limited to, stem cells, stem cell lines, genes, and living or synthetic organs); hormones, proteins or other substances produced by human organisms; methods for creating, modifying, or treating human organisms, including but not limited to methods for creating human embryos through in vitro fertilization, somatic cell nuclear transfer, or parthenogensis; drugs or devices (including prosthetic devices) which may be used in or on human organisms."

The Weldon amendment does not ban human stem cell patents, including patents on human embryonic stem cells. "Stem cells" are not "organisms."

On December 2, 1998, several scientists supportive of federal funding of human embryonic stem cell research testified before the Senate Subcommittee on Labor, Health and Human Services, and Education Committee on Appropriations that "stem cells" are not "human organisms." When asked, Dr. James Thomson who first obtained human embryonic stem cells, and has patents on those stem cell lines, responded: "They am not organisms and they are not embryos."

Despite claims in 2003 that the Weldon amendment in 2003 would ban stem cell patents, the USPTO has maintained several embryonic stem cell patents issued previously. The USPTO has also issued several new patents on human embryonic stem cells since 2003, and has issued roughly 300 new patents on pluripotent stout cells. The Weldon amendment only affects patents on human organisms. (Note, the EU recently reaffirmed its rejection of patents on embryonic stem cells, yet, the Weldon amendment does not follow suit.).

HISTORY AND BACKGROUND

Longstanding United States Patent and Trademark Office (USPTO) policy states that human beings at any stage of development are not patentable subject matter under 35 U.S.C. Section 101. In 1980, the U.S. Supreme Court in *Diamond v. Chakrabarty* expanded the scope of patentable subject matter claiming Congress intended statutory subject matter to "include anything under the sun that is made by man." The USPTO eventually issued patents directed to nonhuman organisms, including animals. However, the USPTO rejected patents on humans (see below).

However, as early as 2003 U.S. researchers announced that

they created human male-female embryos and reportedly wanted to patent this research (http:// www.thenewatlantis.com/publications/mymother-the-embryo). The researchers transplanted cells from male embryos into female embryos and allowed them to grow for six days.

Because of the possibility of court challenges to USPTO policy, Rep. Dave Weldon offered an amendment on July 22, 2003 to the CJS Appropriations bill to prevent funding for patents directed to "human organisms."

The Weldon amendment was adopted by voice vote, and was included as Section 634, Title VI of Division B, in the Consolidated Appropriations Act, 2004 (P.L. 108-199). The accompanying report language clarified its scope: "The conferees have included a provision prohibiting funds to process patents of human organisms. The conferees concur with the intent of this provision as expressed in the colloquy between the provisions sponsor in the House and the ranking minority member of the House Committee on Appropriations as occurred on July 22, 2003, with respect to any existing patents on stem cells." (Conference Report 108-401).

The Weldon amendment has been included each year in the CJS appropriations bill since 2004 and reflected the USPTO policy against patenting humans as outlined in 3 USPTO official documents.

First, the USPTO published the "Quigg memo" in its Official Gazette on January 5, 1993, which was written in 1917 [*sic*?] stating: "The Patent and Trademark Office now considers non-naturally occurring non-human multicellular living organisms, including animals, to be patentable subject matter within the scope of 35 U.S.C. 101 . . . . A claim directed to or including within its scope a human being will not be considered patentable subject matter under 35 U.S.C. 101." Furthermore, it "suggests" that that any claim directed to "a non-plant multicellular organism which would include a human being within its scope include the limitation 'nonhuman' to avoid this ground of rejection."

Second, the USPTO policy is also contained in an official media advisory issued on April 2, 1998 in response to news about s patent application directed to a human/nonhuman chimera. USPTO claimed that patents "inventions directed to human/nonhuman chimera could, under certain circumstances, not be patentable because, among other things, they would fail to meet the public policy and morality aspects of the utility requirement."

Third, the USPTO policy is contained in the Manual of Patent Examining Procedure (MPEP) section 2105 under "Patentable Subject Matter." The MPEP states that the USPTO "would now consider nonnaturally occurring, nonhuman multicellular living organisms, including animals, to be patentable subject matter within the scope of 35 U.S.C. 101. If the broadest reasonable interpretation of the claimed invention as a whole encompasses a human being, then a rejection under 35 U.S.C. 101 must be made indicating that the claimed invention is directed to nonstatutory subject matter."

* * *

On the same day, Representative Christopher Smith (New Jersey) also submitted comments on the Weldon Amendment in the Congressional Record Extensions Remarks:[5]

AMERICA INVENTS ACT

SPEECH OF

HON. CHRISTOPHER H. SMITH

OF NEW JERSEY

IN THE HOUSE OF REPRESENTATIVES

Wednesday, June 22, 2011

The House in Committee of the Whole House on the State of the Union had under consideration the bill (H.R. 1249) to amend title 35, United States Code, to provide for patent reform:

Mr. SMITH of New Jersey. Madam Chair, for over two decades, USPTO has had an internal policy that human beings at any stage of development are not patentable subject matter under 35 U.S.C. Section 101. I commend Chairman LAMAR SMITH for including in the manager's amendment to H.R. 1249, the America Invents Act, a provision that will codify an existing pro-life policy rider included in the CJS Appropriations bill since FY2004. This amendment, commonly known as the Weldon amendment, ensures the U.S. Patent and Trade Office, USPTO, does not issue patents that are directed to or encompassing a human organism.

Codifying the Weldon amendment simply continues to put the weight of law behind the USPTO policy.

This amendment and USPTO policy reflect a commonsense understanding that no member of the human species is an "invention," or property to be licensed for financial gain. Patents on human organisms commodify life and allow profiteers to financially gain from the biology and life of another human person.

Codifying a ban on patenting of humans would not violate international obligations under the TRIPs agreement with the WTO, in which member countries can exclude from patent-

---

[5]157 Cong. Rec. E1177 to E1180 (daily ed. June 23, 2011) (statement of Rep. C. Smith).

ability subject matter to prevent commercial exploitation which is "necessary to protect ordre public or morality, [and] to protect human, animal or plant life." (The Agreement on Trade-Related Aspects of Intellectual Property Rights, Article 27, Section 5).

Even the European Union prevents patents on human embryos on the basis of morality and public order without conflicting with the TRIPs agreement. (See Guidelines for Substantive Examination. European Patent Office. Part C, Chapter IV, Section 4.5, iii (Rule 28c).)

4.5 Biotechnological inventions

> In the area of biotechnological inventions, the following list of exceptions to patentability under Art. 53(a) is laid down in Rule 28. The list is illustrative and non-exhaustive and is to be seen as giving concrete form to the concept of "ordre public" and "morality" in this technical field. Under Art. 53(a), in conjunction with Rule 28, European patents are not to be granted in respect of biotechnological inventions which concern: (iii) uses of human embryos for industrial or commercial purposes; The exclusion of the uses of human embryos for industrial or commercial purposes does not affect inventions for therapeutic or diagnostic purposes which are applied to the human embryo and are useful to it (EU Dir.98/44/EC, rec. 42).

I also submit into the RECORD items from previous debate on the Weldon amendment that will add further clarification to the intent of this important provision.

His further extensions remarks included speeches by Rep. Weldon (Florida) on July 22, 2003, November 5, 2003, November 21, 2003, and December 8, 2003,[6] including the following:

SPEECH OF HON. DAVE WELDON OF FLORIDA IN THE HOUSE OF REPRESENTATIVES, JULY 22, 2003

H. Admt. 286

Departments of Commerce, Justice, and State, the Judiciary, and Related Agencies Appropriations Act, 2004—(House of Representatives—July 22, 2003)

AMENDMENT OFFERED BY MR. WELDON OF FLORIDA

* * *

Amendment offered by Mr. WELDON of Florida:

None of the funds appropriated or otherwise made available

[6] 157 Cong. Rec. E1177 to E1180 (daily ed. June 23, 2011) (statement of Rep. C. Smith).

under by the act may be used to issue patents on claims directed to or encompassing a human organism.

Mr. WELDON of Florida. Mr. Chairman, technology proceeds at a rapid rate, bringing great benefits to humankind from treatments of disease to greater wealth and greater knowledge of our world. However, sometimes technology can be used to undermine what is meant to be human, including the exploitation of human nature for the purpose of financial gain.

Several weeks ago, at a meeting of the European Society of Human Reproduction and Embryology in Madrid, Spain, it was reported that scientists had created the first male-female hybrid human embryos. The researchers transplanted cells from male embryos into female embryos and allowed them to grow for 6 days. This research was universally condemned as unnecessary and unethical. Reuters reported that one member of the European Society condemned this research, saying there are very good reasons why this type of research is generally rejected by the international research community. Furthermore, the scientists who created these she-ale embryos reportedly want to patent this research.

It is important that we, as a civilized society, draw the line where some rogue scientists fail to exercise restraint. Just because something can be done does not mean that it should be done. A patent on such human organisms would last for 20 years. We should not allow such researchers to gain financially by granting them an exclusive right to practice such ghoulish research.

Long-standing American patent and trademark policy states that human beings at any stage of development are not patentable, subject to matters under 35 U.S.C. section 101. Though current policy would not issue patents on human embryos, Congress has remained silent on this subject. Though this amendment would not actually ban this practice, it is about time that Congress should simply reaffirm current U.S. patent policy and ensure there is not financial gain or ownership of human beings by those who engage in these activities.

This amendment simply mirrors the current patent policy concerning patenting humans. The Patent Office has, since 1980, issued hundreds of patents on living subject matter, from microorganisms to nonhuman animals. It does not issue patents on human beings nor should it. Congress should reaffirm this policy, and this amendment simply accomplishes this by restricting funds for issuing patents on human embryos, human organisms.

Congress should speak out, and I encourage my colleagues to support this amendment. I would like to add, Mr. Chairman, that this has no bearing on stem cell research or patenting genes, it only affects patenting human organisms, human embryos, human fetuses or human beings.

Mr. OBEY. * * * I think I heard the gentleman say this, but I want it repeated again so it is clear. Is the gentleman saying that this amendment would not interfere in any way with any existing patents with respect to stem cells?

Mr. WELDON of Florida. Reclaiming my time, Mr. Chairman, I would respond that, no, it would not. And I recognize that there are many institutions, particularly in Wisconsin, that have extensive patents on human genes, human stem cells. This would not affect any of those current existing patents. The Patent Office policy is not to issue these patents, and there never has been one. The Congress has been silent on this issue. I am trying to put us on record that we support the Patent Office in this position that human life in any form should not be patentable.

* * *

The CHAIRMAN pro tempore (Mr. TERRY). The question is on the amendment offered by the gentleman from Florida (Mr. WELDON).The amendment was agreed to.[7] * * *

§ 4:2 Patents on "human organisms" banned

New Statute (AIA Sec. 33)

SEC. 33. LIMITATION ON ISSUANCE OF PATENTS.

(a) Limitation.—Notwithstanding any other provision of law, no patent may issue on a claim directed to or encompassing a human organism.

(b) Effective Date.—

(1) In General.—Subsection (a) shall apply to any application for patent that is pending on, or filed on or after, the date of the enactment of this Act.

(2) Prior Applications.—Subsection (a) shall not affect the validity of any patent issued on an application to which paragraph (1) does not apply.

Section 33 of the AIA bars the USPTO from issuing patents "directed to or encompassing a human organism." The AIA did not provide a definition of "human organism" in 35 U.S.C. § 100 or anywhere else. One may ask how broadly "human organism" should be construed and whether AIA Section 33 prohibits a future patent claiming to a human gene, a grown living organ, or other subject matter.

This provision is not codified into Title 35.

§ 4:3 USPTO interpretation re "human organism" ban

The Acting Associate Commissioner for Patent Examina-

[7] 157 Cong. Rec. E1177, 1178 (daily ed. June 23, 2011) (statement of Rep. C. Smith).

tion Policy at the USPTO issued a memorandum to the Patent Examining Corps on September 20, 2011 (see Appendix 5) instructing the Corps on this provision of the AIA.[1] The body of that directive states as follows:

> Section 33(a) of the Leahy-Smith America Invents Act states: "Notwithstanding any other provision of law, no patent may issue on a claim directed to or encompassing a human organism."
>
> This provision of the Leahy-Smith America Invents Act does not change existing law or long-standing USPTO policy that a claim encompassing a human being is not patentable. *See Animals—Patentability,* 1077 *Off. Gaz. Pat. Office* 24 (April 21, 1987) (indicating that human organisms are excluded from the scope of patentable subject matter under 35 U.S.C. 101). This long-standing policy is reflected in MPEP § 2105, which currently provides that:
>
> > If the broadest reasonable interpretation of the claimed invention as a whole encompasses a human being, then a rejection under 35 U.S.C. 101 must be made indicating that the claimed invention is directed to nonstatutory subject matter.
>
> Thus, section 33(a) of the Leahy-Smith America Invents Act codifies existing USPTO policy that human organisms are not patent-eligible subject matter.[2]

§ 4:4 Analysis re human organism ban

AIA Section 33 took effect upon enactment of the AIA on Sept. 16, 2011. Subsection (b)(1) makes the limitation applicable to any patent application pending on or filed on or after that date. By its terms, this limitation does not affect the validity of any patent not described by subsection (b)(1), *i.e.,* patents already granted.

Courts have yet to interpret AIA Section 33. However, the phrase "human organism" has appeared in many judicial rulings, though none of them also mention the America Invents Act. Nevertheless, a concurring opinion of the Federal Circuit in the *Myriad* case on remand from the Supreme Court referred implicitly to the Weldon amend-

---

[Section 4:3]

[1]http://www.uspto.gov/aia_implementation/human-organism-memo.pdf visited August 31, 2012. A copy of this 2-page memorandum is included in the appendices.

[2]http://www.uspto.gov/aia_implementation/human-organism-memo.pdf visited August 31, 2012.

ment and the prohibition on patents on "human organisms."[1] Judge Moore noted various extension remarks of the Congressional Record and noted that "Congress introduced and declined to pass several bills which would put a moratorium on gene patents."[2]

The legislative history explains that Congress thought Section 33 was needed for at least the reason that the Weldon amendment focused on limiting funds from Congressional appropriations, and the America Invents Act would put *other* funds—user fees—at the disposal of the USPTO. Congress added Section 33 to broaden the prohibition on patenting any human being, regardless of where the funding arose for the USPTO.[3]

The Congressional Record extension remarks also suggest that Congress did not intend in Section 33 to limit patent activity in biotechnology. It did not intend to limit obtaining patents on:

- chemical compounds or compositions, even if obtained from human beings;[4]
- cells, tissues, organs (including synthetic organs), or other bodily components produced by human intervention;[5]
- human cells, genes, or other tissues obtained from human embryos or human bodies;[6]
- stem cells, stem cell lines, hormones, proteins or other

[Section 4:4]

[1] *Association for Molecular Pathology v. U.S. Patent and Trademark Office*, 689 F.3d 1303, 103 U.S.P.Q.2d 1681 (Fed. Cir. 2012), certiorari granted in part, 2012 WL 4508118 (U.S. 2012) (concurring opinion of J. Moore)

[2] *Association for Molecular Pathology v. U.S. Patent and Trademark Office*, 689 F.3d 1303, 103 U.S.P.Q.2d 1681 (Fed. Cir. 2012), certiorari granted in part, 2012 WL 4508118 (U.S. 2012) (concurring opinion of J. Moore)

[3] 157 Cong. Rec. E1184 (daily ed. June 23, 2011) (statement of Rep. L. Smith).

[4] 157 Cong. Rec. E1183 (daily ed. June 23, 2011) (statement of Rep. L. Smith).

[5] 157 Cong. Rec. E1183 (daily ed. June 23, 2011) (statement of Rep. L. Smith).

[6] 157 Cong. Rec. E1183, 1185 (daily ed. June 23, 2011) (statement of Rep. L. Smith).

substances produced by human organisms;[7]

- methods or processes, *e.g.*, cloning, for creating embryos via in vitro fertilization or for creating, modifying or treating human organisms;[8] or
- nonhuman organisms.[9]

On the other hand, Congress *did* intend to prohibit any patent having a claim directed to or any of (at least) the encompassing:

- a human being in any form;[10]
- a human organism at any stage of development;[11]
- human embryos;[12]
- human fetuses;[13]
- human-animal chimeras;[14]
- "she-male" human embryos;[15] and
- human embryos created with genetic material from more than one embryo.[16]

If the broadest reasonable interpretation of a claimed invention encompasses a human being, the claim is regarded as non-statutory at the USPTO.[17]

---

[7] 157 Cong. Rec. E1183 (daily ed. June 23, 2011) (statement of Rep. L. Smith).

[8] 157 Cong. Rec. E1183, 1184 (daily ed. June 23, 2011) (statement of Rep. L. Smith).

[9] 157 Cong. Rec. E1183, 1184 (daily ed. June 23, 2011) (statement of Rep. L. Smith).

[10] 157 Cong. Rec. E1184 (daily ed. June 23, 2011) (statement of Rep. L. Smith).

[11] 157 Cong. Rec. E1184 (daily ed. June 23, 2011) (statement of Rep. L. Smith); E1178 (dail ed,. June 23, 2011) (statement of Rep. C. Smith).

[12] 157 Cong. Rec. E1184 (daily ed. June 23, 2011) (statement of Rep. L. Smith).

[13] 157 Cong. Rec. E1184 (daily ed. June 23, 2011) (statement of Rep. L. Smith).

[14] 157 Cong. Rec. E1184 (daily ed. June 23, 2011) (statement of Rep. L. Smith).

[15] 157 Cong. Rec. E1184 (daily ed. June 23, 2011) (statement of Rep. L. Smith).

[16] 157 Cong. Rec. E1184 (daily ed. June 23, 2011) (statement of Rep. L. Smith).

[17] 157 Cong. Rec. E1182, at E1183 (daily ed. June 23, 2011); MPEP (8th ed. Rev. 8, July 2010) § 2105 ("If the broadest reasonable interpretation of the claimed invention as a whole encompasses a human being, then a rejection under 35 U.S.C.A. 101 must be made indicating that the

claimed invention is directed to nonstatutory subject matter.").

Chapter 5

Limited Patentability of Tax Strategies

AIA § 14

§ 5:1 Congressional intent re tax strategies[1]

In recent years, the USPTO has granted patents involving tax strategies; it has even more pending applications pend-

[Section 5:1]

[1]The Supreme Court cautions against relying on interpretations advanced in legislative statements that are not "anchored in the text of the statute." *Shannon v. U.S.*, 512 U.S. 573, 583, 114 S. Ct. 2419, 129 L. Ed. 2d 459 (1994), stating "[C]ourts have no authority to enforce [a] principl[e] gleaned solely from legislative history that has no statutory reference point." Id. at 584, quoting *International Broth. of Elec. Workers, Local Union No. 474, AFL-CIO v. N.L.R.B.*, 814 F.2d 697, 712, 124 L.R.R.M. (BNA) 2993, 106 Lab. Cas. (CCH) P 12256 (D.C. Cir. 1987). The authoritative statement "is the statutory text, not the legislative history." *Exxon Mobil Corp. v. Allapattah Services, Inc.*, 545 U.S. 546, 568, 125 S. Ct. 2611, 162 L. Ed. 2d 502 (2005). However, lower courts have cited the legislative history of the AIA already in recent cases. E.g., *Rogers v. Tristar Products, Inc.*, 102 U.S.P.Q.2d 1722, 2012 WL 1660604, *2 (Fed. Cir. 2012) (non-precedential); *Byrne v. Wood, Herron & Evans, LLP*, 676 F.3d 1024, 1029, 102 U.S.P.Q.2d 1073 (Fed. Cir. 2012) (dissenting opin.).

ing for tax planning methods.[2] Many groups believe that patents ought not be granted covering tax planning or tax strategies. The AIA addressed the issue of tax strategies in AIA § 14.

The House Report comments on the tax strategies legislation as follows:

> *Tax strategies deemed within the prior art*
>
> In recent years, the numbers of patents on tax-strategies have increased. Critics assert that it is not fair to permit patents on techniques used to satisfy a government mandate, such as compliance with the Internal Revenue Code.
>
> Tax preparers, lawyers, and planners have a long history of sharing their knowledge regarding how to file returns, plan estates, and advise clients. The ability to interpret the tax law and implement such interpretations should remain in the public domain, available to all taxpayers and their advisors.
>
> The Act mandates that tax strategies are deemed "insufficient to differentiate a claimed invention from the prior art." In other words, any future tax strategy will be considered indistinguishable from all other publicly available information that is relevant to a patent's claim of originality. Under the Act, however, protection (an exclusion) is made available for software that enables individuals to file their income tax returns or that assists them with managing their finances. The exclusion does not apply to that part of the software related to a tax strategy.[3]
>
> * * *
>
> *Section 14. Tax strategies deemed within the prior art.*
>
> This section provides that strategies for reducing, avoiding, or deferring tax liability shall be deemed insufficient to differentiate an invention from the prior art. In other words, applicants will no longer be able to rely on the novelty or non-obviousness of a tax strategy embodied in their claims in order to distinguish their claims from the prior art under the statutory novelty and non-obviousness requirements of those provisions.
>
> Under the provision, the term "tax liability" refers to any liability for a tax under any Federal, State, or local law, or law of any foreign jurisdiction, including any statute, rule, regulation, or ordinance that levies, imposes, or assesses such tax

[2] A search of the USPTO database as of November 6, 2012 indicates that over 12,000 U.S. patents mention "tax." Further, 180 patents use "tax" in the patent title, and over 560 use "money" in the patent title.

[3] H. R. Rep. No. 112-98, pt. 1, at 51 to 52 (2011).

liability.

The provision is directed to tax strategies, which are a subset of business methods, and is not intended to deny patent protection for an invention that consists of tax preparation software or other tools used solely to enter data on tax or information returns or any other filing required by a tax authority. Thus, a software program that is novel and non-obvious as software would not be affected by this section even though the software is used for a tax purpose. A prior-art software program, however, could not overcome the section 102 and 103 hurdles by implementing a novel and non-obvious strategy for reducing, avoiding, or deferring taxes.

There may be situations in which some aspects of an invention are separable from the tax strategy. In this case, any claim that encompasses a tax strategy will be subject to the provision and the novelty or non-obviousness of the tax strategy will be deemed insufficient to differentiate that claim from the prior art. However, any claim that does not involve a tax strategy would not be within the scope of the provision. In such a case, if the invention includes claims that are separable from the tax strategy, such claims could, if otherwise enforceable, be enforced.

Inventions that fall within the scope of the provision include those especially suitable for use with tax-favored structures that must meet certain requirements, such as employee benefit plans, tax-exempt organizations, or any other entities that must be structured or operated in a particular manner to obtain certain tax consequences. Thus, the provision applies if the effect of an invention is to aid in satisfying the qualification requirements for the desired tax-favored entity status, to take advantage of the specific tax benefits offered in a tax-favored structure, or to allow for tax reduction, avoidance, or deferral not otherwise automatically available in such entity or structure.

In general, the USPTO may seek advice and assistance from Treasury and the IRS to better recognize tax strategies. Such consultations should help ensure that patents do not infringe on the ability of others to interpret the tax law and that implementing such interpretations remains in the public domain, available to all taxpayers and their advisors.[4]

Additional insight may be found in the following statement of Senator Grassley:

Mr. GRASSLEY. Madam President, I understand there are questions about what the tax strategies portion of the bill does and who it impacts. So I want to take a few minutes to address those questions.

In simple terms, a tax strategy is any method for reducing,

[4] H. R. Rep. No. 112-98, pt. 1, at 79 (2011).

avoiding, or deferring tax liability based upon the tax law—including interpretations and applications of the Internal Revenue Code, regulations, and related guidance.

A tax strategy can be as simple as a plan to buy tax-exempt bonds or invest in an IRA to reduce your tax liability or as complex as some sort of sale-leaseback tax shelter involving multiple domestic and foreign corporations and partnerships.

A tax strategy patent, which is what we are talking about in this bill, is just that—a patent on a particular tax strategy.

* * *

Mr. GRASSLEY. Tax strategies are bad because they allow the tax law to be patented. A patent gives the holder the exclusive right to exclude others from using the patented invention. A tax strategy patent makes taxpayers choose between paying more than legally required in taxes or providing a windfall to a tax strategy patent-holder by paying a royalty to comply with the tax law.

Tax strategy patents add another layer of complexity to the tax laws by requiring taxpayers or their advisers to conduct patent searches and exposing them to potential patent infringement lawsuits.

If a tax strategy patent is granted for a tax shelter designed to illegally evade taxes, the fact that a patent was granted may mislead unknowing taxpayers into believing the obvious: That the strategy is valid under the tax law when, in fact, it might not be.

Tax strategies are not like other inventions because everyone wants to pay less tax. Tax strategy patents are on the rise, which then means more and more legal tax strategies are unavailable or, obviously, more expensive for more and more taxpayers.

* * *

However, now, in order to allay the concerns of Intuit, makers of Turbo Tax, I have worked with Senator BAUCUS to make clear that tax preparation software such as Turbo Tax is not a tax strategy. Financial management software, however, is a little murkier. While products such as Quicken and QuickBooks are not tax strategies, tax strategies can be embedded in financial management products and software. The investment banks and the law firms that have patented tax strategies often use software that could be deemed financial management software. The Tax Adviser article I mentioned earlier and got unanimous consent to have printed in the RECORD describes some of these. With financial management software, patent claims that include inventions that are severable from tax strategies may be entitled to patent protection, but the tax strategy itself will remain available to all taxpayers. So it is important to protect intellectual property rights for true tax preparation and financial management software. However, we must be sure to protect the rights of taxpayers to have equal access to legal tax strategies.[5]

§ 5:2 AIA statutory provisions regarding tax strategies and patentability

New Statute (AIA Sec. 14)

(a) IN GENERAL.—For purposes of evaluating an invention under section 102 or 103 of title 35, United States Code, any strategy for reducing, avoiding, or deferring tax liability, whether known or unknown at the time of the invention or application for patent, shall be deemed insufficient to differentiate a claimed invention from the prior art.

(b) DEFINITION.—For purposes of this section, the term "tax liability" refers to any liability for a tax under any Federal, State, or local law, or the law of any foreign jurisdiction, including any statute, rule, regulation, or ordinance that levies, imposes, or assesses such tax liability.

(c) EXCLUSIONS.—This section does not apply to that part of an invention that—

(1) is a method, apparatus, technology, computer program product, or system, that is used solely for preparing a tax or information return or other tax filing, including one that records, transmits, transfers, or organizes data related to such filing; or

(2) is a method, apparatus, technology, computer program product, or system used solely for financial management, to the extent that it is severable from any tax strategy or does not limit the use of any tax strategy by any taxpayer or tax advisor.

(d) RULE OF CONSTRUCTION.—Nothing in this section shall be construed to imply that other business methods are patentable or that other business method patents are valid.

(e) EFFECTIVE DATE; APPLICABILITY.—This section shall take effect on the date of the enactment of this Act and shall apply to any patent application that is pending on, or filed on or after, that date, and to any patent that is issued on or after that date.

§ 5:3 USPTO guidance on AIA section 14 re tax strategies

The USPTO has not issued any rules, preliminary or final, concerning tax strategy claims. However, it has issued two documents regarding AIA § 14. The first is a memorandum (Appendix 6) entitled, "Tax Strategies Are Deemed To Be Within the Prior Art" to the Patent Examining Corps, from

---

[5] 157 Cong. Rec. S1201 (daily ed. Mar. 3, 2001).

Robert Bahr, Acting Associate Commissioner for Patent Examination Policy, dated September 20, 2011.[1] The second is a set of examples.

The memorandum states, in part:

> * * * Applicants will no longer be able to rely on the novelty or non-obviousness of a tax strategy embodied in their claims to distinguish them from the prior art. Section 14 aims to keep the ability to interpret the tax law and to implement such interpretation in the public domain, available to all taxpayers and their advisors.
>
> * * *
>
> There are two exclusions to this provision. The first is that the provision does not apply to that part of an invention that is a method, apparatus, technology, computer program product, or system, that is used solely for preparing a tax of information return or other tax filing, including one that records, transmits, transfers, or organizes data related to such filing.
>
> The second is that the provision does not apply to that part of an invention that is a method, apparatus, technology, computer program product, or system that is used solely for financial management, to the extent that it is severable from any tax strategy or does not limit the use of any tax strategy by any taxpayer or tax advisor.[2]

The memorandum continues with some examination guidance calling for examiners to construe the claim in accordance with MPEP 2111 et seq., analyze the claim for compliance with Sections 101 and 112, identify any limitations relating to a tax strategy, and then . . .

> 4. Evaluate the claim in view of the prior art under 35 U.S.C. §§ 102 and 103, treating any limitations relating to a tax strategy as being within the prior art, and not as a patentable difference between the claim and the prior art." This approach is analogous to the treatment of printed matter limitations in a claim as discussed at MPEP 2112.01 (111).[3]

The memorandum then includes some important guidance as to computer-implemented methods. It states:

> A computer-implemented method that is deemed novel and

[Section 5:3]

[1]See http://www.uspto.gov/aia_implementation/tax-strategies-memo.pdf.

[2]http://www.uspto.gov/aia_implementation/tax-strategies-memo.pdf, at p. 1.

[3]http://www.uspto.gov/aia_implementation/tax-strategies-memo.pdf, at p. 2.

non-obvious would not be affected by this provision even if used for a tax purpose. For example, a novel and non-obvious computer-implemented method for manipulating data would not be affected by this provision, even if the method organized data for a future tax filing. However, the presence of limitations relating to a tax strategy would not cause a claim that is otherwise within the prior art to become novel or non-obvious over the prior art.

Thus, for purposes of applying art to a software-related invention under §§ 102 and 103, claim limitations that are directed solely to enabling individuals to file their income tax returns or assisting them with managing their finances should be given patentable weight, but by contrast, claim limitations directed to a tax strategy should not be given patentable weight[4]

Hence, this September 20, 2011 memorandum to the Patent Examining Corps confirms that the USPTO will issue patents that contain tax strategy in the claims, provided that the patentability over the art resides elsewhere in the claim.

The USPTO also published training examples, as follows:[5]

SECTION 14—TAX STRATEGIES DEEMED TO BE WITHIN THE PRIOR ART

INTRODUCTORY EXAMPLES

Note: The recently signed America Invents Act includes Section 14 which provides that any tax strategy for reducing, avoiding or deferring a tax liability "shall be deemed insufficient to differentiate a claimed invention from the prior art" under 35 U.S.C. § 102 and 103, whether that strategy is known or unknown. In other words, when applying prior art under §§ 102 or 103, your references need not teach any limitations directed to a tax strategy within a claim as these are considered to be within the prior art. Here, a "tax liability" refers to any tax under Federal, state or local law, or even under the law of any foreign jurisdiction.

Issues under Section 14 arise where the claim recites a plan for reducing, avoiding, or deferring a tax liability. The determination of whether a tax strategy is involved is not only a claim-by-claim analysis, but also a limitation-by-limitation analysis within a particular claim and can be very fact specific. Where a claim presents potential Section 14 issues, please

[4]http://www.uspto.gov/aia_implementation/tax-strategies-memo.pdf, at p. 2.

[5]http://www.uspto.gov/aia_implementation/tax-strategies-training-examples.pdf.

consult your SPE to discuss whether any limitations in that claim should be considered within the prior art. Where the scope of the claim is unclear as to whether a tax strategy is claimed, clarification may be sought through 35 U.S.C. 112 in the usual manner.

Section 14 applies regardless of the statutory class of the claim. All claims are to be examined for compliance with 35 U.S.C. §§ 101 and 112 independently of whether Section 14 applies.

Example A—Electronic Tax Return Preparation

Summary: Section 14 does not apply to any part of an invention that is used solely for preparing a tax or information return or other tax filing.

1. An apparatus for collecting and transmitting tax data comprising:

means for collecting tax data from a taxpayer;

means for processing said tax data collected from said taxpayer to obtain processed tax return data;

means for preparing an electronic tax return using said tax return data; and

means for transmitting the electronic tax return to a taxing authority.

Broadest Reasonable Interpretation:

This claim is directed to an apparatus for collecting and processing tax data, then preparing and transmitting an electronic tax return. In light of the specification, the means for collecting tax data is disclosed as a graphical user interface that prompts a user to input tax data; the means for processing collected data is a computer programmed to properly format the collected data for the electronic tax return form; the means for preparing the tax return is the computer further programmed to populate an electronic form with the formatted data; and the means for transmitting is a modem to send out the completed tax return over a communication link.

Analysis / Conclusion:

For the purposes of Sec. 14, even though tax data is handled by the apparatus, the claim falls into the tax filing preparation exclusion. The claimed apparatus merely prepares an electronic tax return by taking input data, formatting it into an electronic form and transmitting it. None of the structure or functionality of the apparatus is concerned with any tax strategy; i.e., a plan for reducing, avoiding, or deferring a tax liability. The claim is directed merely to the internal computer operations necessary to get entered tax data formatted properly and sent out. In other words, no limitations in the claim are directed to a tax strategy for reducing, avoiding or deferring a tax liability as no steps are taken that explicitly or implicitly change any such liability. As a result, since the claimed apparatus is solely for preparing a tax return, it falls into the exclusion specified in Sec. 14(c)(1). Therefore, the entirety of the claim should be evaluated in view of the prior art under §§ 102 and 103.

Example B—Payroll Processing

Summary: Section 14 does not apply to tax-related inventions that are not strategies for reducing, avoiding, or deferring tax liability.

2. A computer implemented method for payroll processing for an employer having employees for whom the payroll is created, comprising:

storing on a first computer, payroll data for each employee including wage information, tax status, and deduction information;

receiving at the first computer the payroll data for the employees;

calculating at the first computer paycheck information for each employee, the paycheck information including wages, tax withholding status, and deductions for the employee;

transmitting from the first computer to a remote computer the calculated paycheck information for direct deposit of paycheck amounts for selected employees, and payment of the employer's tax liabilities; and

printing at the first computer paychecks and direct deposit notices for distribution to the employees of the employer; and entering into an account register a transaction deducting the paid tax liabilities.

Broadest Reasonable Interpretation:

This claim is directed to a computerized payroll accounting method. The broadest reasonable interpretation of the calculating step in light of the specification is merely to do the math to apply pre-determined Federal, state and local tax rates as well as apply pre-determined deductions to the wages. The step of calculation is disclosed to involve only a rote sequence of numerical operations that is performed without regard to any amount of tax liability resulting from the calculation. The storing, receiving, transmitting, printing and entering steps are all directed to data manipulation for financial management purposes.

Analysis / Conclusion:

For the purposes of Sec. 14, even though tax data is handled by the apparatus, the claim falls into the financial management exclusion. Even though tax related data is handled by the method, pre-existing tax liabilities and deductions are merely applied to the wages without concern for any particular tax strategy. The steps merely provide the automated support for payroll and accounting processing. In other words, no limitations of the claim are directed to a tax strategy for reducing, avoiding or deferring tax liability as no steps are taken that explicitly or implicitly change any liability. Thus, the method does not limit the use of any tax strategy by any taxpayer or tax advisor. As a result, since the claimed method is solely for financial management, it falls into the exclusion specified in Sec. 14(c)(2). Therefore, the entirety of the claim should be evaluated in view of the prior art under §§ 102 and 103.

Example C—Tax Deferral

Summary: A claim solely drawn to a plan for deferring tax liability is deemed to be within the prior art per Section 14.

3. A method for deferring federal taxation of corporate profits, said method comprising:

forming a Parent Section 17 Federal Tribal (FT) Corporation;

forming a Subsidiary Section 17 Federal Tribal (FT) Corporation, which is controlled by said Parent Section 17 FT Corporation;

forming at least one pass-through entity, which is linked to the Subsidiary Section 17 FT Corporation, said pass-through entity having federal tax exempt status as a disregarded entity, and equity voting rights and investment basis taxation rights;

wherein said pass-through entity is authorized to sell equity interests therein which are representative of equity capital investments received from non-tribal members; and whereby said business structure provides an opportunity for said non-tribal investors to receive an enhanced return on investment as a consequence of the tax-exempt status of the FT Corporation, and a degree of control over their equity capital investments.

Broadest Reasonable Interpretation:

This claim is directed to a method for deferring federal taxes by forming a particular business structure. Even though one may e.g. form a Federal Tribal Corporation for reasons other than this particular tax strategy, each step of the method is disclosed for the purpose of securing the tax benefits taught regarding the corporate profits.

Analysis / Conclusion:

This claim explicitly recites deferring federal taxation of corporate profits in the preamble, and each of the steps are disclosed for securing the tax deferral benefits taught. Here, the claimed invention recites a plan for satisfying the qualification requirements for a desired tax-favored entity status, and the provisions of Sec. 14 apply. Although the claim stops at merely forming the business structure; i.e., the result of performing the method does not specifically yield any deferral of taxes, the claim recites a plan for deferring taxes (a tax strategy), and the provision of Section 14 applies.

Because each of the steps relates to the tax strategy, the entirety of the claim is "deemed insufficient to differentiate" from the prior art under §§ 102 or 103. Thus, this claim could be rejected under §§ 102 or 103 merely as a matter of law per Sec. 14. As with each of these examples, this claim should be examined for compliance with 35 U.S.C. §§ 101 and 112.

Example D—Tax Reduction

Summary: a claim reciting tax strategy limitations will be examined as if those limitations are present in the prior art.

4. A non-transitory computer readable medium having stored thereon instructions which when executed by a computer perform a method for minimizing the worldwide tax costs of a multinational group of companies, the method comprising:

determining taxable income and calculating a baseline tax exposure for each business entity within a multinational group of companies;

identifying intercompany transactions within the group that have the effect of reducing the tax costs in the countries in which receiving and paying companies are located;

calculating a tax cost of the identified transactions; and

routing and executing the identified transactions among different group entities to reduce the tax cost.

Broadest Reasonable Interpretation:

This claim is directed to a computer readable medium for minimizing worldwide tax costs by identifying transactions that would reduce tax costs and actually executing those transactions among different entities to obtain the tax reduction. The instructions to perform the step of determining taxable income and calculating taxes for each business entity are disclosed as a baseline tax calculation performed without regard to reducing, avoiding, or deferring tax liability. The steps of identifying transactions, calculating cost and routing and executing transactions are disclosed as being performed for the purposes of implementing the disclosed strategy once the baseline data is gathered.

Analysis / Conclusion:

This claim explicitly recites instructions to achieve a reduction in taxes by routing and executing various transactions among the entities in a multinational group of companies. Note that section 14 covers any liability for tax under any Federal, state, or local law, or the law of any foreign jurisdiction and also includes "any statute, rule, regulation, or ordinance that levies, imposes or assesses such tax liability." The determining step does not explicitly or inherently require the performance of any action towards reducing, avoiding, or deterring tax liability, the determining step would not be considered to be within the prior art per Section 14. However, the "identifying", "calculating", "and routing and executing" steps of the claim are explicitly directed to a tax strategy for reducing, avoiding or deferring tax liability. The "minimizing" step in the preamble, to the extent that it would be given patentable weight (if any), would also be considered to be directed to a tax strategy per Section 14.

As indicated in Sec. 14(a), for the purposes of evaluation under 35 U.S.C. §§ 102 or 103, the tax strategy embodied in the last three steps of the claim is "deemed insufficient to differentiate a claimed invention from the prior art." In other words, these steps relating to the tax strategy are considered to be within the prior art and will not contribute to novelty or nonobviousness.

One way to visualize this would be to underline the limitations in the claim that are not "deemed insufficient to differentiate" under Section 14. Here, the instructions for routing and executing clearly generate the tax savings, and the instructions for identifying and calculating are necessarily done in accordance with the tax savings strategy and are thus included in the tax strategy. The initial data gathering step of determining taxable income and calculating taxes, under its broadest reasonable interpretation, is severable from the tax strategy. Thus, the claim can be viewed as:

> 4. <u>A non-transitory computer readable medium having stored thereon instructions which when executed by a computer perform a method for minimizing the worldwide tax costs of a multinational group of companies, the method comprising:</u>
>
> <u>determining taxable income and calculating a baseline tax exposure for each business entity within a multinational group of companies;</u>
>
> identifying intercompany transactions within the group that have the effect of reducing the tax costs in the countries in which receiving and paying companies are located;
>
> calculating a tax cost of the identified transactions; and
>
> routing and executing the identified transactions among different group entities to reduce the tax cost.

As a result, for example, a single reference that taught a non-transitory computer readable medium with instructions thereon to perform the underlined first step above would be sufficient to make a rejection of this claim under 35 U.S.C. § 103.

Where a claim contains tax strategy limitations, and a single prior art reference discloses the claim as a whole except for the tax strategy limitations, a rejection of the claim may be made under 103 over that prior art reference. The language of § 102 requires that the claimed invention be "patented" or "described" in a single patent or printed publication. The language of § 103 states that a patent may not be obtained "if the differences between the claimed invention and the prior art" would have been obvious. Section 14 of the AIA states that any tax strategy "shall be deemed insufficient to differentiate a claimed invention from the prior art." The use of the "differentiate" language suggests that § 103 is a proper statutory basis for rejection over a single prior art reference where the claim differs from the prior art only by tax strategy limitations.

Where a claimed invention differs from a patent or publication only by the tax strategy limitations of the claimed invention, Section 14 causes the tax strategy limitations to be insufficient to differentiate the claimed invention from the patent or publication. Therefore, the differences between the claimed invention and the prior art are such that the claimed invention as a whole would have been obvious. The claim is therefore unpatentable under § 103 over the prior art patent or publication. The following sample rejection illustrates this point.

Sample rejection:

Claim 4 is rejected under 35 U.S.C. 103(a) as obvious over Smith in view of Sec. 14 of the America Invents Act.

The claim limitations *"minimizing the worldwide tax costs of a multinational group of companies"* and *"identifying intercompany transactions within the group that have the effect of reducing the tax costs in the countries in which receiving and paying companies are located; calculating a tax cost of the identified transactions; and routing and executing the identified transactions among different group entities to reduce the tax cost"* are steps which act to reduce tax liability of the group of companies. These steps therefore recite a strategy for reducing, avoiding, or deferring tax liability ("tax strategy") pursuant to Section 14 of the Leahy-Smith America Invents Act. Accordingly, these claim limitations are being treated as being within the prior art and are insufficient to differentiate the invention of claim 4 from the prior art.

Smith teaches a "non-transitory computer readable medium having stored thereon instructions which when executed by a computer perform a method", "the method comprising: determining taxable income and calculating taxes for each business entity within a multinational group of companies." See fig. X and col. Y lines a-b of Smith. While Smith does not specifically teach the "minimizing", "identifying", "calculating", "and routing and executing" limitations identified above as tax strategy limitations, these limitations fail to distinguish the claims from the Smith reference, pursuant to Sec. 14 of the AIA. Thus, the differences between the claimed invention and the invention disclosed by Smith are insufficient to differentiate the claimed invention, and claim 1 is therefore unpatentable under § 103.

See USPTO memo "Tax Strategies Are Deemed To Be Within the Prior Art" dated September 20, 2011, at http://www.uspto.gov/patents/law/exam/memoranda.jsp.

Example E -Manufacturing a Hybrid Vehicle

Summary: a tax strategy per Section 14 requires a plan for reducing, deferring, or avoiding a tax liability.

5. A method of manufacturing a hybrid vehicle, the method comprising:

providing a chassis configured to movably support a plurality of wheels;

providing a drive system comprising a gasoline powered engine coupled to an electrical generator and a battery pack;

coupling the drive system to the chassis at an orientation that positions the generator in front of the engine;

supporting an operator compartment at a forward position along the chassis, wherein the operator compartment is substantially disposed over the generator; and

coupling the generator to at least one electric drive motor powering a wheel of the vehicle.

Broadest Reasonable Interpretation:

This claim is directed to manufacturing a hybrid vehicle. Each step is specifically directed to manipulating the recited physical components to form a vehicle that is powered by a gasoline engine and a generator with a battery pack.

Analysis / Conclusion:

For the purposes of Sec. 14, even though hybrid vehicles currently enjoy certain tax incentives, the claim above is merely directed to manufacturing the hybrid vehicle. None of the steps of the method are [*sic*] concerned with effecting any particular tax strategy as the claim is solely directed to the physical manipulation of the vehicle components during assembly to achieve a technical solution. In other words, no limitations in the claim are directed to a tax strategy for reducing, avoiding or deferring a tax liability as no steps are taken that explicitly or implicitly change any such liability, if a tax liability can even be said to exist. Thus, the method does not limit the use of any tax strategy by any taxpayer or tax advisor and Sec. 14 does not apply.

§ 5:4 Analysis of AIA section 14 re tax strategies

Congress wanted to ensure that "The ability to interpret the tax law and implement such interpretations should remain in the public domain, available to all taxpayers and their advisors."[1] Banning patents for tax strategies was one option that Congress could have used.[2] However, an invention could arise that may include a tax strategy, and Congress did not ban such patents outright.

The phrase, "ban on tax-strategy patents," is an overgeneralization of the statute as actually written and needs to be understood very particularly. It would be correct to say that a (future) patent on a tax strategy is banned only if its claims apart from the tax strategy itself lack novelty or nonobviousness over the prior art. Instead, as is clear from the legislative history, Congress effectively expanded the definition of prior art to be considered under Sections 102 and 103 for tax strategy inventions. Congress intended that any tax strategies per se in an invention should be regarded as indistinguishable over prior art when evaluating patent application claims after the effective date.

The effective date is the date of enactment, September 16, 2011, and applies not only to applications filed on or after that date but also to "any patent application that is pending on . . . that date, and to any patent that is issued on or after that date." AIA § 14(e).

In other words, AIA § 14 does not bar patents that contain tax avoidance strategies but instead declares that a claim including such subject matter must define over prior art under 35 U.S.C. §§ 102, 103 in some manner other than the tax strategy itself in order to be patentable. AIA § 14(a) mandates that "any strategy for reducing, avoiding, or deferring tax liability . . . shall be deemed insufficient to differentiate a claimed invention from the prior art." The statute defines the term "tax liability" in § 14(b). Accordingly, so

---

[Section 5:4]

[1]H. R. Rep. No. 112-98, pt. 1, at 51 (2011).

[2]Matal explains that the 2007 House patent reform bill did indeed propose to amend Section 101. Further, he comments that the present approach was done "Rather than quadrupl[ing] the length of a foundational section of the patent code in order to address a relatively minor matter . . . ." J. Matal, "Guide to the Legislative History of the America Invents Act: Part I of II," *Federal Circuit Bar Journal,* Vol. 21, 435 at 502 (2012).

far as § 14(a) is concerned, a patent claim may include a tax avoidance strategy, but the patentability of such a claim over the prior art must reside outside the tax avoidance strategy. This is shown in the USPTO examples.

Congress intended not to "deny patent protection for an invention that consists of tax preparation software or other tools used solely to enter data on tax or information returns or any other filing required by a tax authority. . . . [A] software program that is novel and non-obvious as software would not be affected by [§ 14] even though the software is used for a tax purpose."[3] As such, § 14(c)(1) provides,

> (c) Exclusions.—This section does not apply to that part of an invention that—(1) * * * is used solely for preparing a tax or information return or other tax filing, including one that records, transmits, transfers, or organizes data related to such filing.

Methods, apparatus, technology, computer program products, and systems that define over the prior art should not be barred from patentability by § 14, provided that the patentability over the art arises from something other than the tax strategy. It is not wholly clear how the wording of this exclusion will be understood. However, Example A of the USPTO examples is for "an example that is used solely for preparing a tax or information return or other tax filing" and, as the USPTO correctly notes, Section 14(c)(1) applies to this situation.

Another exclusion in § 14(c)(2) addresses financial management methods, technology, computer program products, or systems. This exclusion provides:

> (c) Exclusions.—This section does not apply to that part of an invention that * * * (2) is * * * used solely for financial management, to the extent that it is severable from any tax strategy or does not limit the use of any tax strategy by any taxpayer or tax advisor.

This exclusion is not exactly parallel to the exclusion of Section 14(c)(1). First, 14(c)(1) addresses preparing tax and other filings, and 14(c)(2) addresses financial management. Additionally, 14(c)(2) calls for the invention that is "severable from any tax strategy." If it is "severable," or if it "does not limit the use of any tax strategy by a taxpayer or tax advisor," then "section [14] does not apply." The final comments by Senator Grassley quoted above mention the sever-

---

[3] H. R. Rep. No. 112-98, pt. 1, at 79 (2011).

ability issue. The meaning of severability and its application to particular will certainly be the subject of differences of opinion, and one may expect future rulings of the Patent Trial and Appeal Board and the Federal Circuit on this issue.

Regarding this exclusion, the USPTO presents an Example B that avoids the effects of Section 14. The claim is for a tax-related invention that is not a tax strategy for reducing, avoiding, or deferring tax liability. The claim falls into the financial management exclusion even though tax data is handled by the computer-implemented method, as no limitations of the method are directed to tax strategy.

In contrast, USPTO Example C is "solely drawn to a plan for deferring tax liability." Each of the steps relates to the tax strategy. As such, "the entirety of the claim is deemed 'insufficient to differentiate' from the prior art under §§ 102 or 103." Note that the steps in that tax deferral method include forming a certain type of parent corporation and forming a certain type of subsidiary corporation. The USPTO views these steps as *relating to* the tax strategy. It remains to be seen whether courts, and particularly the Federal Circuit, will agree that they could not be considered in assessing patentability over the prior art.

Regarding severability, a claim may have some parts that are excluded from consideration for purposes of defining over prior art (because they relate to or are for a tax strategy), while other parts will be not be excluded. USPTO Example D addresses this. It includes some claim language that the USPTO classifies on one side of the tax strategy line and some claim language on the other side of that line. The USPTO example explains that the determining step would be included in measuring patentability over the art, stating:

> The determining step does not explicitly or inherently require the performance of an action towards reducing, avoiding, or deterring [*sic?,* deferring?] tax liability, [and therefore(?)] the determining step would not be considered to be within the prior art per Section 14.

In contrast, the "identifying," calculating," and "routing and executing" steps fall on the other side of the line according to the USPTO:

> However, the "identifying", "calculating", "and routing and executing" steps of the claim are explicitly directed to a tax strategy for reducing, avoiding or deferring tax liability. The "minimizing" step in the preamble, to the extent that it would be given patentable weight (if any), would also be considered

to be directed to a tax strategy per Section 14.

As indicated in Sec. 14(a), for the purposes of evaluation under 35 U.S.C. §§ 102 or 103, the tax strategy embodied in the last three steps of the claim is "deemed insufficient to differentiate a claimed invention from the prior art." In other words, these steps relating to the tax strategy are considered to be within the prior art and will not contribute to novelty or nonobviousness.

Thus, the USPTO explains in Example D that steps which are explicitly directed to tax strategies carry no patentable weight. In Example C, claim elements that "relate to" a tax strategy also carry no patentable weight. Again, it is likely that differences of opinion will arise in future cases, and further guidance from the PTAB and the Federal Circuit can be expected.

USPTO Example E (manufacturing a hybrid vehicle) does not recite any elements for reducing, deferring, or avoiding a tax liability. Even though hybrid vehicles may enjoy tax incentives, none of the limitations are directed to a tax strategy. Hence, Section 14 does not apply.

It is clear that the applicability of Section 14 must be decided on a claim by claim basis. When it does apply, claims must be considered element by element.

Parenthetically, Section 14(d) adds an admonishment that nothing in § 14 can be construed to imply that other business methods are patentable.

Chapter 6

Patent Marking

KeyCite®: Cases and other legal materials listed in KeyCite Scope can be researched through the KeyCite service on Westlaw®. Use KeyCite to check citations for form, parallel references, prior and later history, and comprehensive citator information, including citations to other decisions and secondary materials.

AIA § 16
35 U.S.C.A. § 287

§ 6:1 Patent marking—Background

Patent marking or actual notice is a requisite to collecting damages for infringement of many patents. 35 U.S.C. § 287. Commenting on the marking/notice provision of the Patent Act of 1952, P.J. Federico explained as follows in his famous *Commentary on the New Patent Act*:

> Section 287 provides that a patentee who makes or sells articles shall not recover damages if he has failed to give notice to the public that the articles made or sold are patented by marking them as specified, unless the infringer was notified of the infringement and continued to infringe thereafter, in which event damages may be recovered only for infringement occurring after such notice the filing of the infringement action constitutes a notice. This section restates the old statute with changes in language and some minor changes or clarifications of substance.[1]

[Section 6:1]

[1]P.J. Federico, *Commentary on the New Patent Act*, at 56 in 35

Thus, while the patent statute allows patent owners or licensees to tout that their products are protected by a U.S. patent, which may provide a marketing advantage, another reason for providing such notice is to avoid forfeiting the right to collect damages from an infringer for past infringement.

Section 287 specifies the mechanism for giving notice to the public that a product is patented. Notice can be given:

> . . . either by fixing thereon the word "patent" or the abbreviation "pat.", together with the number of the patent, or when, from the character of the article, this cannot be done, by fixing to it, or to the package wherein one or more of them is contained, a label containing a like notice.[2]

Some courts have ruled that marking is not required for method patents.[3]

§ 6:2 Congressional intent re patent marking[1]

Congress intended to curtail severely *qui tam* litigation (See Chapter 9) and provide a mechanism to relieve the problems industry faces with changing the markings on products of patent numbers. The House Report commented as follows:

U.S.C.A. (West 1954) *(also available at* http://ipmall.info/hosted_resources/lipa/patents/federico-commentary.asp).

[2]35 U.S.C.A. § 287(a) (1999).

[3]*Devices for Medicine, Inc. v. Boehl*, 822 F.2d 1062, 3 U.S.P.Q.2d 1288 (Fed. Cir. 1987); *Hanson v. Alpine Valley Ski Area, Inc.*, 718 F.2d 1075, 219 U.S.P.Q. 679 (Fed. Cir. 1983).

[Section 6:2]

[1]The Supreme Court cautions against relying on interpretations advanced in legislative statements that are not "anchored in the text of the statute." *Shannon v. U.S.*, 512 U.S. 573, 583, 114 S. Ct. 2419, 129 L. Ed. 2d 459 (1994), stating "[C]ourts have no authority to enforce [a] principl[e] gleaned solely from legislative history that has no statutory reference point." Id. at 584, quoting *International Broth. of Elec. Workers, Local Union No. 474, AFL-CIO v. N.L.R.B.*, 814 F.2d 697, 712, 124 L.R.R.M. (BNA) 2993, 106 Lab. Cas. (CCH) P 12256 (D.C. Cir. 1987). The authoritative statement "is the statutory text, not the legislative history." *Exxon Mobil Corp. v. Allapattah Services, Inc.*, 545 U.S. 546, 568, 125 S. Ct. 2611, 162 L. Ed. 2d 502 (2005). However, lower courts have cited the legislative history of the AIA already in recent cases. E.g., *Rogers v. Tristar Products, Inc.*, 102 U.S.P.Q.2d 1722, 2012 WL 1660604, *2 (Fed. Cir. 2012) (non-precedential); *Byrne v. Wood, Herron & Evans, LLP*, 676 F.3d 1024, 1029, 102 U.S.P.Q.2d 1073 (Fed. Cir. 2012) (dissenting opin.).

Marking

a) Virtual Marking

In general, for patented "articles," a patent holder must give an alleged infringer notice of the claimed infringement, and the infringer must continue to infringe, before the patent holder may succeed in a suit for damages.[FN55] Actual notice requires the affirmative communication of infringement to the defendant, which may include the filing of a lawsuit. Constructive notice is possible by "marking" any patented article that the patent holder (or its licensee) makes, uses, sells or imports. Failure to appropriately mark an article can preclude the recovery of damages until notice is effective.[FN56]

FN 55. *See* 35 U.S.C. Sec. 287.

FN 56. *See* 35 U.S.C. Sec. 287.

The Act permits patent holders to "virtually mark" a product by providing the address of a publicly available website that associates the patented article with the number of the patent. The burden will remain on the patent holder to demonstrate that the marking was effective. This amendment will save costs for producers of products that include technology on which a patent issues after the product is on the market, and will facilitate effective marking on smaller products.[2]

* * *

Section 16. Marking.

Subsection (a) addresses virtual marking. The provision allows a patent holder to satisfy the requirements of § 287 of the Patent Act by affixing to a patented article the word "patent" or the abbreviation "pat." together with an Internet address that the public can access free of charge to determine the status of the patent. The USPTO is also instructed to submit a report to Congress on the effectiveness of virtual marking that is due no later than 3 years after the date of enactment.

Subsection (b) addresses false marking in the following ways: (1) Only the United States may sue for the qui tam penalty under the subsection. (2) A person who has suffered a competitive injury as a result of a violation may still bring a civil action in US district court for compensatory damages. (3) Persons or companies otherwise liable under § 292 (the false marking statute) are protected during a 3-year window beginning on the date the patent at issue expires. Beyond the 3-year window, persons or companies are also protected if they place the word "patent" or "patented", the abbreviation "pat.", or the patent number either on the article or through an Internet

[2] H. R. Rep. No. 112-98, pt. 1, at 52 to 53 (2011).

posting, consistent with the amendments in subsection (a).[3]

§ 6:3 AIA statutory changes re patent marking

AIA § 16(a) is directed to "Virtual Marking" and amends § 287 to provide statutory authority for an alternative method for patent marking. The revised § 287(a) states as follows:

Revised 35 U.S.C. § 287[1]

§ 287. Limitation on damages and other remedies; marking and notice.

(a) Patentees, and persons making, offering for sale, or selling within the United States any patented article for or under them, or importing any patented article into the United States, may give notice to the public that the same is patented, either by fixing thereon the word "patent" or the abbreviation "pat.", together with the number of the patent, ~~or when~~ or by fixing thereon the word "patent" or the abbreviation "pat." together with an address of a posting on the Internet, accessible to the public without charge for accessing the address, that associates the patented article with the number of the patent, or when, from the character of the article, this cannot be done, by fixing to it, or to the package wherein one or more of them is contained, a label containing a like notice. In the event of failure so to mark, no damages shall be recovered by the patentee in any action for infringement, except on proof that the infringer was notified of the infringement and continued to infringe thereafter, in which event damages may be recovered only for infringement occurring after such notice. Filing of an action for infringement shall constitute such notice.

AIA § 16(b) is directed to "False Marking" and is discussed in Chapter 9.

§ 6:4 Effective date

The AIA revision to § 287(a) codifies a method for "virtual patent marking" that has already been in use and which was involved in litigation.[1] In terms of the effective date, the virtual marking provision applies to all cases pending on or

---

[3]H. R. Rep. No. 112-98, pt. 1, at 80 (2011).

[Section 6:3]

[1]In this markup, strikethrough indicates text being removed from the statute, and underscoring indicates text being added to the statute.

[Section 6:4]

[1]*Pequignot v. Solo Cup Co.*, 646 F. Supp. 2d 790, 92 U.S.P.Q.2d 1495 (E.D. Va. 2009), aff'd in part, vacated in part, 608 F.3d 1356, 95 U.S.P.

after Sept. 16, 2011.[2]

§ 6:5 General comments re marking

Virtual marking should be easier for manufacturers to manage, as the notice on the product or product molds need not change. Updating a website to reflect current patent information is much easier than changing labels or molds for products. While this imposes some burden on the public to access the website, it seems a fair assumption that would-be copiers have access to the Internet, as does a very large segment of the population in the U.S.

AIA § 16(a)(3) calls on the Director to report to Congress within 3 years from enactment of the AIA. The report is required to comment on the effectiveness of the permitted virtual marking as an alternative to physical marking. The report also is to analyze whether such virtual marking "has limited or improved the ability of the general public to access information about patents." The Director's Report also must analyze legal issues arising from virtual marking and an analysis of any deficiencies of the virtual marking.

AIA § 16 does not address the question of the requirement, if any, of patent marking and method patents.

Q.2d 1501 (Fed. Cir. 2010).

[2]AIA § 16(a)(2) ("The amendment made by this subsection shall apply to any case that is pending on, or commenced on or after, the date of enactment of this Act.")

Chapter 7

Miscellaneous Substantive Patent Law Provisions

KeyCite®: Cases and other legal materials listed in KeyCite Scope can be researched through the KeyCite service on Westlaw®. Use KeyCite to check citations for form, parallel references, prior and later history, and comprehensive citator information, including citations to other decisions and secondary materials.

AIA § 3(d)(e)
35 U.S.C.A. §§ 104, 157

§ 7:1 Generally

The AIA makes some deletions and changes to substantive provisions beyond those mentioned above.

35 U.S.C. § 104 is repealed by AIA § 3(d). This section was entitled "Invention Made Abroad" and spoke to conditions under which patent applicants could establish a date of invention involving activity in foreign countries. Under the first inventor to file regime, this provision is not necessary.

The statutory invention registration (sometimes called "SIR") provision, 35 U.S.C. § 157, is also repealed by AIA § 3(e)(1). The House Report mentions only in passing that this section is repealed, but it offers no commentary. Under § 157, the USPTO was authorized to publish a document that met the requirements of 35 U.S.C. § 112 but where the applicant waived the right to obtain a patent and paid various fees. During the pendency of an application for an original patent, the applicant had the right to waive the request for a patent and proceed to publication. Such a publication could prevent a future inventor from patenting material disclosed in the SIR.

Part II

PATENT ENFORCEMENT ISSUES

Chapter 8

The Prior User Defense

AIA § 5
35 U.S.C.A. § 273

§ 8:1 Background: the First Inventor's Defense Act of 1999

A manufacturer or other entity may develop or otherwise obtain technology or processes that it uses in production and wishes not to patent. The manufacturer or developer may regard the technology as a trade secret.[1] Such entities run the risk that someone else will invent and patent the same technology. The patent owner might then assert the patent

---

[Section 8:1]

[1]The Supreme Court has acknowledged that trade secret law is compatible with the patent system. *Kewanee Oil Co. v. Bicron Corp.*, 416 U.S. 470, 94 S. Ct. 1879, 40 L. Ed. 2d 315, 181 U.S.P.Q. 673 (1974).

against the prior user. In 1998, the risk of this occurring with respect to financial or business method processes increased with the decision by the U.S. Court of Appeals for the Federal Circuit in *State Street Bank and Trust Co. v. Signature Financial Group, Inc.*,[2] where certain business methods were found to be patent-eligible subject matter. In response, Congress created a limited defense pertaining to business methods. In particular, the First Inventor's Defense Act of 1999, Subtitle C of the American Inventors Protection Act ("AIPA"),[3] amended the patent statute to include a new 35 U.S.C. § 273 providing a defense against infringement in favor of prior users of specific, limited subject matter. The title of that section was "Defense to infringement based on earlier inventor." Until the AIA, this defense had been limited to business method inventions.[4] The prior use must be a commercial one, regardless of whether it was a secret use or not. While the defense has not been sustained in any litigation, it has been the subject of judicial discussion.[5]

The 1999 AIPA imposed various requirements for this defense. Prior to indicating which of these have been retained and which are changed by the AIA, the following discussion identifies the major requirements and limitations of the prior user defense under the AIPA:

Type of Patent Requirement. Under the AIPA (1999), the first inventor defense applied to infringement of business method patents only.[6]

Time Requirement. The defense was available only if the

[2]*State Street Bank & Trust Co. v. Signature Financial Group, Inc*, 149 F.3d 1368, 47 U.S.P.Q.2d 1596 (Fed. Cir. 1998) (abrogated by, *In re Bilski*, 545 F.3d 943, 88 U.S.P.Q.2d 1385, 2008-2 U.S. Tax Cas. (CCH) P 50621 (Fed. Cir. 2008)).

[3]Pub. L. No. 106-113, 113 Stat. 1536 (1999).

[4]35 U.S.C.A. 273(a)(3) (2006) ("the term 'method' means a method of doing or conducting business").

[5]The Supreme Court majority opinion in *Bilski v. Kappos*, 130 S. Ct. 3218, 3222, 177 L. Ed. 2d 792, 95 U.S.P.Q.2d 1001, 2010-1 U.S. Tax Cas. (CCH) P 50481 (2010) cited § 273 as undermining the argument that § 101 categorically excludes business methods. *Sabasta v. Buckaroos, Inc.*, 507 F. Supp. 2d 986 (S.D. Iowa 2007) (granting summary judgment dismissing the defense as inapplicable to a process to manufacture ribbed pipe saddles, even though that may be a business); *cf. PB Farradyne, Inc. v. Peterson*, 2006 WL 132182 (N.D. Cal. 2006) (declined to rule whether "method" includes *any* methods used by a business in doing business, or whether it is limited to internal business methods).

[6]35 U.S.C.A. § 273(b)(3) (2006): "DEFENSE TO INFRINGEMENT.—LIMITATIONS AND QUALIFICATIONS OF DEFENSE.—The defense to infringe-

prior user actually reduced the subject matter to practice at least one year before the effective filing date of a patent sought to be enforced against him.[7]

Good Faith Requirement. The person asserting the defense must have acted in good faith in actually reducing the subject matter to practice.[8]

Domestic Commercial Use Requirement. The defense was available only if the prior user commercially used the subject matter in the United States before the effective filing date of the patent.[9] "Commercial use" was defined to include use of a method in connection with (a) an "internal commercial use" or (b) "an arm's length sale or other arm's length commercial transfer of a useful end result."[10] Under the AIPA, it did not matter whether the subject matter was accessible to "or otherwise known to the public." A further qualifying commercial use was activity during a premarketing regulatory review period in which the safety or efficacy of the subject matter was established.[11]

Yet another "commercial use" under the AIPA was activity

---

ment under this section is subject to the following: (A) PATENT.—A person may not assert the defense under this section unless the invention for which the defense is asserted is for a method." 35 U.S.C.A. § 273(a)(3) provides: "[T]he term 'method' means a method of doing or conducting business."

[7]35 U.S.C.A. § 273(b) (2006): "DEFENSE TO INFRINGEMENT.—(1) IN GENERAL.—It shall be a defense to an action for infringement under section 271 of this title with respect to any subject matter that would otherwise infringe one or more claims for a method in the patent being asserted against a person, if such person had, acting in good faith, actually reduced the subject matter to practice at least 1 year before the effective filing date of such patent, and commercially used the subject matter before the effective filing date of such patent."

[8]35 U.S.C.A. § 273(b) (2006): "DEFENSE TO INFRINGEMENT.—(1) IN GENERAL.—It shall be a defense * * * if such person had, *acting in good faith*, actually reduced the subject matter to practice at least 1 year before the effective filing date of such patent, and commercially used the subject matter before the effective filing date of such patent." [emphasis added]

[9]*See* 35 U.S.C.A. § 273(b)(1) *supra.*

[10]The term "commercially used" was defined in 35 U.S.C.A. § 273(a) (1999) which stated: "DEFINITIONS.—For purposes of this section—(1) the terms 'commercially used' and 'commercial use' mean use of a method in the United States, so long as such use is in connection with an internal commercial use or an actual arm's-length sale or other arm's-length commercial transfer of a useful end result, whether or not the subject matter at issue is accessible to or otherwise known to the public * * *"

[11]35 U.S.C.A. § 273(a) (2006) continues: "DEFINITIONS.—For purposes of this section—(1) * * * the subject matter for which commercial market-

of a nonprofit research laboratory or nonprofit entity such as a university, research center, or hospital. Uses for which the public was the intended beneficiary were considered a "commercial use." However, as to this use, the defense was limited to continued use by and in the laboratory or nonprofit entity. In addition, the defense would not extend to subsequent commercialization or use outside the laboratory or nonprofit entity.[12]

Originality Requirement. The defense was not available to anyone who derived the invention from the inventor.[13]

Proof Requirement. The defense required proof by clear and convincing evidence.[14]

Personal Defense Limitation. The defense was personal to the earlier inventor and not freely assignable.[15]

Location Requirement. The defense carried limitations as to its applicability when the defense was acquired as part of

---

ing or use is subject to a premarketing regulatory review period during which the safety or efficacy of the subject matter is established, including any period specified in section 156(g), shall be deemed 'commercially used' and in 'commercial use' during such regulatory review period";

[12]35 U.S.C.A. § 273(a) (2006) also stated: "DEFINITIONS.—For purposes of this section—* * * (2) in the case of activities performed by a nonprofit research laboratory, or nonprofit entity such as a university, research center, or hospital, a use for which the public is the intended beneficiary shall be considered to be a use described in paragraph (1), except that the use—(A) may be asserted as a defense under this section only for continued use by and in the laboratory or nonprofit entity; and (B) may not be asserted as a defense with respect to any subsequent commercialization or use outside such laboratory or nonprofit entity."

[13]35 U.S.C.A. § 273(b) (2006): "DEFENSE TO INFRINGEMENT.—* * * (3) LIMITATIONS AND QUALIFICATIONS OF DEFENSE.—The defense to infringement under this section is subject to the following: * * * (B) DERIVATION.—A person may not assert the defense under this section if the subject matter on which the defense is based was derived from the patentee or persons in privity with the patentee."

[14]35 U.S.C.A. § 273(b) (2006): "DEFENSE TO INFRINGEMENT.—* * *(4) BURDEN OF PROOF.—A person asserting the defense under this section shall have the burden of establishing the defense by clear and convincing evidence."

[15]35 U.S.C.A. § 273(b) (2006): "DEFENSE TO INFRINGEMENT.—* * *(6) PERSONAL DEFENSE.—The defense under this section may be asserted only by the person who performed the acts necessary to establish the defense and, except for any transfer to the patent owner, the right to assert the defense shall not be licensed or assigned or transferred to another person except as an ancillary and subordinate part of a good faith assignment or transfer for other reasons of the entire enterprise or line of business to which the defense relates."

a *good faith* assignment or transfer of the entire enterprise or the line of business to which the defense relates. In such cases, the defense was limited to specific, previously-used sites where the subject matter was in use as of the *later* of two dates—the effective filing date of the patent or the date of assignment or transfer of the enterprise or the line of business.[16]

The AIPA was silent on whether, absent any good faith transfer, the defense applied to sites added by the prior user after the effective filing date of the patent alleged to be infringed. The general language of the defense in § 273(b)(1) was silent on the sites where the defense applied and any expansion of the allegedly infringing use by the prior user. Limitations to the defense were stated in § 273(b)(3). Those provisions likewise were silent as to the expansion of sites. However, the statute did contemplate changes in volume and improvements to the claimed subject matter.[17]

Continuity Requirement. The defense called for continuous prior use.[18] If there was a gap, continuous use may begin anew. The statute affirmatively prohibited reliance on pre-abandonment activity to establish a defense to later activities.

Sanctions Requirement. The statute mandated a finding that a case would be "exceptional for the purpose of award-

---

[16]35 U.S.C.A. § 273(b) (2006): "DEFENSE TO INFRINGEMENT.—* * *(7) LIMITATION ON SITES.—A defense under this section, when acquired as part of a good faith assignment or transfer of an entire enterprise or line of business to which the defense relates, may only be asserted for uses at sites where the subject matter that would otherwise infringe one or more of the claims is in use before the later of the effective filing date of the patent or the date of the assignment or transfer of such enterprise or line of business."

[17]35 U.S.C.A. § 273(b)(3) (2006): "LIMITATIONS AND QUALIFICATIONS OF DEFENSE.—The defense to infringement under this section is subject to the following: * * * (C) NOT A GENERAL LICENSE.—The defense asserted by a person under this section is not a general license under all claims of the patent at issue, but extends only to the specific subject matter claimed in the patent with respect to which the person can assert a defense under this chapter, except that the defense shall also extend to variations in the quantity or volume of use of the claimed subject matter, and to improvements in the claimed subject matter that do not infringe additional specifically claimed subject matter of the patent."

[18]35 U.S.C.A. § 273(b) (2006): "DEFENSE TO INFRINGEMENT.—* * *(5) ABANDONMENT OF USE.—A person who has abandoned commercial use of subject matter may not rely on activities performed before the date of such abandonment in establishing a defense under this section with respect to actions taken after the date of such abandonment."

ing attorney fees" if the defense were pleaded by a person who was found to infringe and who failed to demonstrate a reasonable basis for asserting the defense.[19]

§ 8:2 Congressional intent re the prior user defense[1]

Congress believed that streamlining the U.S. patent system would help entrepreneurs start new businesses.[2] Congress also was concerned with a "Catch-22" inherent in the U.S. patent system. Specifically, an inventor of a new process or product used in a manufacturing process faced the problem that if he patents the process, he effectively discloses it to competitors. Such patents are difficult to police because manufacturing processes occur in closed factories. It is difficult to detect when competitors simply appropriate the invention in secret and do not pay license fees. "Patenting such manufacturing processes effectively amounts to giving the invention to foreign manufacturers."[3] Senator Kyl explained the other side of the problem was that if the manufacturer opts not to patent the process, someone else may later discover it, obtain a patent, and force the manufacturer to stop using the process. Congress intended to ad-

---

[19]35 U.S.C.A. § 273(b) (2006): "DEFENSE TO INFRINGEMENT.—* * *(8) UNSUCCESSFUL ASSERTION OF DEFENSE.—If the defense under this section is pleaded by a person who is found to infringe the patent and who subsequently fails to demonstrate a reasonable basis for asserting the defense, the court shall find the case exceptional for the purpose of awarding attorney fees under section 285 of this title."

[Section 8:2]

[1]The Supreme Court cautions against relying on interpretations advanced in legislative statements that are not "anchored in the text of the statute." *Shannon v. U.S.*, 512 U.S. 573, 583, 114 S. Ct. 2419, 129 L. Ed. 2d 459 (1994), stating "[C]ourts have no authority to enforce [a] principl[e] gleaned solely from legislative history that has no statutory reference point." *Shannon*, 512 U.S. at 584, quoting *International Broth. of Elec. Workers, Local Union No. 474, AFL-CIO v. N.L.R.B.*, 814 F.2d 697, 712, 124 L.R.R.M. (BNA) 2993, 106 Lab. Cas. (CCH) P 12256 (D.C. Cir. 1987). The authoritative statement "is the statutory text, not the legislative history." *Exxon Mobil Corp. v. Allapattah Services, Inc.*, 545 U.S. 546, 568, 125 S. Ct. 2611, 162 L. Ed. 2d 502 (2005). However, lower courts have cited the legislative history of the AIA already in recent cases. E.g., *Rogers v. Tristar Products, Inc.*, 102 U.S.P.Q.2d 1722, 2012 WL 1660604, *2 (Fed. Cir. 2012) (non-precedential); *Byrne v. Wood, Herron & Evans, LLP*, 676 F.3d 1024, 1029, 102 U.S.P.Q.2d 1073 (Fed. Cir. 2012) (dissenting opin.).

[2]157 Cong. Rec. S5315, 5316 (Daily Ed. September 6, 2011) (statement of Sen. Reid).

[3]Sen. Kyl, 157 Cong. Rec. at S5319 (Daily Ed. September 6, 2011).

dress that problem.

Additional motivation for expanding the prior user defense was that many foreign countries recognize prior user rights, and those rights provide a measure of comfort and predictability for manufacturers who are considering whether to build facilities in those foreign countries. Thus, legislation was needed in the U.S. to "correct[] this imbalance and create[] a strong incentive for businesses to create manufacturing jobs in this country."[4]

The House Report commented on the revisions to this defense as follows:

> *Defense to infringement based on earlier inventor*
>
> Under current law, "prior user rights" may offer a defense to patent infringement when the patent in question is a "business method patent"[5] and its inventor uses the invention, but never files a patent application for it.[6] If the same invention is later patented by another party, the prior user may not be liable for infringement to the new patent holder, although all others may be.
>
> Many counties [*sic*] include a more expansive prior-user rights regime within their first-to-file system. In the United States, this is particularly important to high-tech businesses that prefer not to patent every process or method that is part of their commercial operations. The Act responds to this point by revising US law as follows: First, the prior-use defense may be asserted against any patent (not just method patents), provided the person asserting the defense reduced the subject matter of the patent to practice and commercially used the subject matter at least 1 year before the effective filing date of the patent. Second, the defense cannot be asserted if the subject matter was derived from the patent holder or persons in privity with the patent holder. And third, the defense cannot be asserted unless the prior user both reduced the subject matter of the patent to practice and commercially used it at least 1 year before the effective filing date of the patent or the date that the patentee publicly disclosed the invention and invoked the § 102(b) grace period, whichever is earlier.
>
> This narrow expansion of prior-user rights balances the interests of patent holders, including universities, against the legitimate concerns of businesses that want to avoid infringement suits relating to processes that they developed and used prior to another party acquiring related patents.

---

[4]Sen. Kyl, 157 Cong. Rec. at S5319 (Daily Ed. September 6, 2011).

[5]35 U.S.C.A. Sec. 273(a)(3) states: 'The term 'method' means a method of doing or conducting business.

[6]*See* 35 U.S.C.A. Sec. 273.

* * *

Section 5. Defense to infringement based on earlier inventor.

Section 5 amends § 273 of the Patent Act, which addresses prior user rights, as follows:

The prior-use defense may be asserted against any patent (not just methods), provided the person asserting the defense reduced the subject matter of the patent to practice and commercially used the subject matter at least 1 year before the effective filing date of the patent. However, the defense cannot be asserted if the subject matter was derived from the patent holder or persons in privity with the patent holder. Nor can the defense be asserted unless the and commercially used it at least 1 year before the effective filing date of the patent or the date that the patentee publicly disclosed the invention and invoked the § 102(b) grace period, whichever is earlier.

Section 5 also clarifies that a person may not assert the defense if the subject matter of the patent on which the defense is based was developed pursuant to a funding agreement under Chapter 18 of the Patent Act (patent rights in inventions made with Federal assistance) or by a university or a technology transfer organization affiliated with a university that did not receive private business funding in support of the patent's development.

Finally, Section 5 states that the defense may only be asserted by the person who performed or caused the performance of the acts necessary to establish the defense, as well as any other entity that controls, is controlled by, or is under common control with such person; and except for any transfer to the patent owner, the right to assert the defense cannot be licensed or assigned or transferred to another person except as an ancillary and subordinate part of a good faith assignment or transfer for other reasons of the entire enterprise or line of business to which the defense relates.[7]

This statement does not correspond to the Act as signed. As explained in a comprehensive review of the history of the AIA by Mr. Joe Matal,[8] Section 273 had its genesis in the early 1990s, followed by a bill introduced on August 4, 1995.[9] Mr. Matal notes that bills to establish prior user rights had been introduced in 1967 and 1976. The 1995 bill was not enacted and though similar legislation passed the House in 1997, it was never taken up by the full Senate. In the next Congress, the AIPA included Section 273 and became law in

[7]H. R. Rep. No. 112-98, pt. 1, at 44, 74 to 75.

[8]*See generally*, J. Matal, "A Guide to the Legislative History of the America Invents Act," T*he Federal Circuit Bar J.*, Vol. 21, No. 4, 539, 551 et seq. (2011).

[9]Prior Domestic Use Act of 1995, H.R. 2235, 104th Cong. (1995).

1999 but with the narrow definition of where the defense could be used (business method patents only). A Senate Report in 2007 made note of the "persuasive [*sic,* pervasive?] outcry from university and tech transfer advocates."[10] A compromise was reached in the House in 2011 in respect of university concerns, and Senator Kyl in September of 2011 explained this during the Senate debates on the AIA, stating as follows:

> The compromise reached in the House of Representatives addresses university concerns by requiring a defendant to show that he commercially used the subject matter that infringes the patent at least 1 year before the patent owner filed an application or disclosed the invention to the public. The House compromise also precludes assertion of the defense against most university-owned patents.[11]

§ 8:3 AIA revisions to the prior user defense—The statute

The America Invents Act expands the defense so that it is not confined to business method patents or even method patents. It also exempts many, but not all, university patents from the defense.

Section 5(a) of the AIA repealed the prior 35 U.S.C. § 273 and adopted a new one which reads as follows:

35 U.S.C. § 273 (2011)

§ 273. Defense to infringement based on prior commercial use

(a) IN GENERAL.— A person shall be entitled to a defense under section 282(b) with respect to subject matter consisting of a process, or consisting of a machine, manufacture, or composition of matter used in a manufacturing or other commercial process, that would otherwise infringe a claimed invention being asserted against the person if—

(1) such person, acting in good faith, commercially used the subject matter in the United States, either in connection with an internal commercial use or an actual arm's length sale or other arm's length commercial transfer of a useful end result of such commercial use; and

(2) such commercial use occurred at least 1 year before the earlier of either—

(A) the effective filing date of the claimed invention; or

[10] S. Rep. No. 110-259, at 16 to 17.

[11] 157 Cong. Rec. S5430 (Daily Ed. September 8, 2011) (statement of Sen. Kyl).

(B) the date on which the claimed invention was disclosed to the public in a manner that qualified for the exception from prior art under section 102(b).

(b) Burden of Proof.— A person asserting a defense under this section shall have the burden of establishing the defense by clear and convincing evidence.

(c) Additional Commercial Uses.—

(1) Premarketing Regulatory Review.— Subject matter for which commercial marketing or use is subject to a premarketing regulatory review period during which the safety or efficacy of the subject matter is established, including any period specified in section 156(g), shall be deemed to be commercially used for purposes of subsection (a)(1) during such regulatory review period.

(2) Nonprofit Laboratory Use.— A use of subject matter by a nonprofit research laboratory or other nonprofit entity, such as a university or hospital, for which the public is the intended beneficiary, shall be deemed to be a commercial use for purposes of subsection (a)(1), except that a defense under this section may be asserted pursuant to this paragraph only for continued and noncommercial use by and in the laboratory or other nonprofit entity.

(d) Exhaustion of Rights.— Notwithstanding subsection (e)(1), the sale or other disposition of a useful end result by a person entitled to assert a defense under this section in connection with a patent with respect to that useful end result shall exhaust the patent owner's rights under the patent to the extent that such rights would have been exhausted had such sale or other disposition been made by the patent owner.

(e) Limitations and Exceptions.—

(1) Personal Defense.—

(A) In General.— A defense under this section may be asserted only by the person who performed or directed the performance of the commercial use described in subsection (a), or by an entity that controls, is controlled by, or is under common control with such person.

(B) Transfer of Right.— Except for any transfer to the patent owner, the right to assert a defense under this section shall not be licensed or assigned or transferred to another person except as an ancillary and subordinate part of a good-faith assignment or transfer for other reasons of the entire enterprise or line of business to which the defense relates.

(C) Restriction on Sites.— A defense under this section, when acquired by a person as part of an assignment or transfer described in subparagraph (B), may only be asserted for uses at sites where the subject matter that would otherwise infringe a claimed invention is in use before the later of the effective filing date of the claimed invention or the date of the assignment or transfer of such enterprise or line of business.

(2) DERIVATION.— A person may not assert a defense under this section if the subject matter on which the defense is based was derived from the patentee or persons in privity with the patentee.

(3) NOT A GENERAL LICENSE.—The defense asserted by a person under this section is not a general license under all claims of the patent at issue, but extends only to the specific subject matter for which it has been established that a commercial use that qualifies under this section occurred, except that the defense shall also extend to variations in the quantity or volume of use of the claimed subject matter, and to improvements in the claimed subject matter that do not infringe additional specifically claimed subject matter of the patent.

(4) ABANDONMENT OF USE.— A person who has abandoned commercial use (that qualifies under this section) of subject matter may not rely on activities performed before the date of such abandonment in establishing a defense under this section with respect to actions taken on or after the date of such abandonment.

(5) UNIVERSITY EXCEPTION.—

(A) IN GENERAL.— A person commercially using subject matter to which subsection (a) applies may not assert a defense under this section if the claimed invention with respect to which the defense is asserted was, at the time the invention was made, owned or subject to an obligation of assignment to either an institution of higher education (as defined in section 101(a) of the Higher Education Act of 1965 (20 U.S.C. 1001(a)), or a technology transfer organization whose primary purpose is to facilitate the commercialization of technologies developed by one or more such institutions of higher education.

(B) EXCEPTION.— Subparagraph (A) shall not apply if any of the activities required to reduce to practice the subject matter of the claimed invention could not have been undertaken using funds provided by the Federal Government.

(f) UNREASONABLE ASSERTION OF DEFENSE.— If the defense under this section is pleaded by a person who is found to infringe the patent and who subsequently fails to demonstrate a reasonable basis for asserting the defense, the court shall find the case exceptional for the purpose of awarding attorney fees under section 285.

(g) INVALIDITY.— A patent shall not be deemed to be invalid under section 102 or 103 solely because a defense is raised or established under this section.

Section 5(c) of the AIA states the effective date of the expanded prior user defense as follows: "The amendments made by this section shall apply to any patent issued on or after the date of the enactment of this Act."

§ 8:4 Analysis of the expanded prior use defense

Title of Defense Change. The AIA changes the title of § 273 from "Defense to infringement based on earlier inventor" to "Defense to infringement based on prior commercial use." This change reinforces the fact that the defense does not require a showing of inventorship. As to origination of the subject matter of the defense, one provision of § 273 as discussed below requires that the party asserting the defense cannot have derived the subject matter from the inventor, but otherwise the prior user can assert the defense even if it was not invented by the prior user. On the subject of what is *not* required, the defense also does not require a showing of trade secret status or confidentiality.

Type of Patent Requirement Expanded Beyond Business Methods. The revised statute broadens the defense considerably. Whereas the AIPA (1999) limited this defense to business method patents, the AIA expands the defense to cover patents on methods, machines, manufactures, or compositions used in manufacturing or other commercial processes.[1]

Time Requirement Retained. The AIA retains the one year requirement. That is, the defense is available only if the prior user had a "commercial use" more than one year before the effective filing date of a patent sought to be enforced.[2]

However, if there was a pre-filing disclosure, then the defense requires use at an earlier date. The defense requires use at least one year before the date on which the claimed invention was disclosed to the public in a manner that qualifies for "the exception from prior art under section 102(b)." The AIA specifies that the prior use must precede by at least one year the *earlier* of the two dates, the effective filing date or a public disclosure.

The requirement in § 273(b)(1) of the prior statute for

[Section 8:4]

[1] § 273(a) (2011).

[2] § 273(a)(2) (2011).

actual reduction to practice was not retained explicitly. However, it seems implicit in the requirement of a "commercial" use. Case law regarding "ready for patenting" under *Pfaff*[3] or "offer for sale" under *Group One*[4] and its progeny may guide whether a use was commercial or not.

Good Faith Requirement Retained. Congress retained the "good faith" requirement so that the commercial user must be acting in good faith. § 273(a)(1) (2011).

Domestic Commercial Use Requirement Retained. The prior use must be "in the United States." § 273(a)(1). The statute does not credit prior uses in foreign countries, even if they arise in countries party to WTO, NAFTA, or other international agreements. The use must be in connection with "an internal commercial use," "an actual arm's length sale," or an "arm's length commercial transfer of a useful end result of such commercial use." § 273(a)(1) (2011).

Premarket Regulatory Review Retained. The revised statute qualifies premarketing regulatory reviews of safety or efficacy of the subject matter as commercial uses for purposes of establishing the defense. In the AIPA (1999), this was part of the definition in § 273(a)(1). In the AIA, this use is moved to § 273(c)(1).

Nonprofit Laboratory Use Modified. The America Invents Act treats a use in a nonprofit research laboratory or other nonprofit entity as commercial use for purposes of establishing the defense, thereby to permit continued noncommercial use by the laboratory or other nonprofit entity. § 273(c)(2) (2011). The 1999 statute had a further limitation that is not retained in the AIA. That limitation was that the use for which the public is the intended beneficiary "may not be asserted as a defense with respect to any subsequent commercialization or use outside such laboratory or nonprofit entity." § 273(a)(2)(B) (1999).

University Exception. The AIA immunizes certain patents against the prior user defense. The statute allows university patents to be enforced against otherwise qualified prior users in many circumstances. New § 273(e)(5) denies the defense to persons commercially using the subject matter to which § 273(a) applies if the claimed invention was owned or

[3] *Pfaff v. Wells Electronics, Inc.*, 525 U.S. 55, 66–68, 119 S. Ct. 304, 142 L. Ed. 2d 261, 48 U.S.P.Q.2d 1641 (1998).

[4] *Group One, Ltd. v. Hallmark Cards, Inc.*, 254 F.3d 1041, 1047, 59 U.S.P.Q.2d 1121, 45 U.C.C. Rep. Serv. 2d 88 (Fed. Cir. 2001).

subject to an obligation of assignment to a university (as defined) or a technology transfer organization having the purpose of facilitating the commercialization of technologies developed by such universities.

The statute considers whether this ownership or assignment obligation existed at the time the invention was "made." Subsequent acquisition of title is insufficient. If a university were to acquire an issued patent, it would *not* thereby be made immune to the prior user defense.

Conversely, according to the statute as written, the university exception follows ownership of the patent. If a business corporation or other entity purchases a "university patent," the prior user defense would still apply because the test is ownership at time the invention was "made." The statutory language does not negate the defense to account for transfers after that time.

The apparent policy is to promote university research. Many inventive activities involve collaboration between commercial enterprises and universities. It is not perfectly clear how much ownership the word "owned" contemplates within the meaning of the statute. Certainly if there is 100% ownership of a patent by a university or other appropriate institution at the appropriate time, then the exception applies. Courts will eventually have to decide whether the defense applies to patents that are only partially owned, *e.g.*, 50% owned (or less), by a university. We must await judicial development or further definition from Congress. If the exception does apply to a partially-owned patent, this is motivation to sponsor university research and allow the university to be a co-owner of an undivided interest to a degree sufficient to vest the patent with immunity from the prior user defense.

University Exception Limitation. Not all "university patents" qualify. Even if a patent is a "university patent," the prior user defense is applicable if the activities needed to reduce the subject matter to practice "could not have been undertaken using funds provided by the Federal Government." There is no legislative history in the House Committee Report (2011) on this exclusion. The plain meaning is that if the invention involves subject matter for which federal funding is disallowed, *e.g.,* stem cell research patents, then the university patent exception cannot apply, and the prior user defense is intact.

Non-derivation Requirement Retained. Congress retained

the requirement for no derivation. Section 273(e)(2) (2011) provides, "A person may not assert a defense under this section if the subject matter on which the defense is based was derived from the patentee or persons in privity with the patentee."

- For example, assume that inventor A originates subject matter X. Third party B learns of the subject matter from A and puts it into commercial operation. Assume hypothetically that party B has sufficiently long use to meet the one year requirement. If party A later obtains a patent and sues B, B cannot assert the prior user defense because B derived the subject matter from the inventor A.

Burden of Proof Retained. This requirement of proof of prior use by clear and convincing evidence is retained as § 273(b).

Personal Defense Expanded. Under the AIA, the defense is still a personal one. § 273(e)(1). However, the language of the prior statute said nothing about the company or business enterprise for which the inventor may have worked. Instead, it recited simply that "The defense under this section may be asserted only by the person who performed the acts necessary to establish the defense . . . ." One may ponder whether this meant only the individual(s) who practiced the method, or a broader group, *e.g.*, the company employing them. Under the new Act, the personal defense extends to the entity that controls, is controlled by, or is under common control with the person "who performed or directed the performance of the commercial use . . . ."[5] Thus, the defense is more generally available than before, but it remains a personal defense.

Site Requirement Retained. As with the AIPA (1999), the AIA provisions restrict the locations as to which this defense may be asserted. Specifically, when an acquisition of the line of business or enterprise occurs, the acquiring entity may assert this defense only at sites where the subject matter that would otherwise infringe was in use before the effective filing date of the claimed invention or the date of the assignment or transfer, whichever is *later*. Hence, if the patent application has already been filed, the language of the AIA does not contemplate a manufacturer acquiring an entity or line of business where the prior user defense had been

[5] 35 U.S.C.A. § 273(e) (2011).

established and then expanding that use to new sites and claiming that the defense applies to the new sites. Rather, the sites at which the acquiring entity can practice the subject matter that would otherwise infringe are restricted to those sites where the subject matter was practiced as of the later of the two referenced dates. § 273(e)(1)(C) (2011). If the patent application has not yet been filed, then the new user can expand the locations of use up to the effective filing date of the patent. Note that the AIA does not state a one-year requirement at each site.

Additionally, the AIA retains a requirement of a good faith assignment or transfer of the entire enterprise or line of business to which the defense relates. § 273(e)(1)(B).

Example 1

- 2008: An American automobile manufacturer, F Company, owns a British division J which develops a unique robotic tool and puts it into use in Great Britain for manufacturing motorcars. F Company does not file any patent applications anywhere in the world, nor does it publicize its robotic tool which it uses secretly to produce automobiles that F Company distributes worldwide.
- Feb. 1, 2010: F Company is pleased with the advantages that its J Division obtains from using this robotic tool. F Company obtains and uses more of them in plants belonging to F Company in Michigan and other venues in the U.S. to make other automobiles.
- March 1, 2011: Inventor A applies for a patent in the U.S. A is unrelated to F company.
- March 1, 2012: the USPTO issues the patent to A. The patent contains claims that F Company infringes on account of its use of the robotic tool.
- April 1, 2012: Inventor A sells the patent to H Company, another automobile manufacturer that competes with F Company.
- April 15, 2012: H Company believes that F Company must be using the patented robotic tool to make its automobiles and accuses F Company of infringing the patent.

Analysis of Example 1

The fact that J Division developed the tool in Great Britain is irrelevant. The fact that the patent application was filed prior to the effective date of the America Invents Act is also irrelevant because the effective date provision, AIA § 5(c), focuses on the patent *issue* date. It states that this prior user defense shall apply to any patent issued on or after the date of enactment. Since the patent issued after the September 16, 2011 enactment of the AIA, the revised provisions of Section 273 apply, and the expanded prior user defense is available to F Company.

F Company meets the requirements as to the type of patent because the defense is "with respect to subject matter consisting of a . . . machine . . . used in a manufacturing or other commercial process." § 273(a) (2011).

F Company meets the time requirement of at least one year prior use. Since the effective filing date of the patent is March 1, 2011, the domestic use by F Company prior to March 1, 2010, is sufficient to satisfy the time requirement, assuming that inventor A did not make any earlier public disclosure of the invention. The uses in 2008 and thereafter in Great Britain are immaterial because they are not domestic uses.

F Company also satisfies the good faith requirement, the originality requirement, and all other requirements to sustain the defense unless the patent is subject to the university patents exception. Thus, F Company has a defense at the sites in the U.S. where it used the tool before March 1, 2010.

Example 2

- 2007: Company C begins using a manufacturing process in its plant in Springfield, IL.
- In 2009, a labor union declares a strike against C and walks off the job. The Springfield plant lies fallow for months.
- January 1, 2010: Unable to resolve matters with the labor union, Company C moves its manufacturing plant away from Springfield, Illinois, to a newly constructed plant in the back country of Georgia.
- January 1, 2011: C expands the use of its manufacturing process to a new plant in Dallas, Texas.
- June 1, 2011: C sells this manufacturing division, including the plants in Dallas and in Georgia, to Company D.
- January 1, 2012: D expands the use of the manufacturing process to Denver, Colorado and retains the uses in Georgia and Texas.

- March 1, 2012: inventor A publishes a paper on manufacturing processes. A is unrelated to C and D.
- April 2012: A receives information from a retired employee of C that one process mentioned in A's published paper is not really new, and that the employee had himself seen Company C use that process as far back as 2007. He opined that the process might still be in use by company D. Inventor A consults patent counsel and they determine that the prior use was a secret use that would not bar A from obtaining patent rights.
- May 1, 2012: A files a U.S. patent application and requests prioritized examination pursuant to the America Invents Act.
- July 1, 2012: Company D expands the use of the manufacturing process to North Carolina.
- August 1, 2012: the patent issues to A. A then writes to company D and sends a copy of the patent.
- Company D responds that it has been using this process since it acquired this division on June 1, 2011 from Company C, which had been using it continuously since 2007. Company D declines a license offer from inventor A.
- August 15, 2012: Dismayed, inventor A sells the patent to a patent licensing company L.
- September 1, 2012, L sues D for patent infringement of the patent originally issued to A. In response, D asserts the prior user defense.

Analysis of Example 2

As was the case with Example 1, because the patent issued after September 16, 2011, when the AIA became law, the new provisions of Section 273 apply to this defense.

The time requirement that Company D must satisfy is stated in § 273(a). Company D acted in good faith and made commercial sales at arm's length and meets the requirement of subparagraph (1). Subparagraph (2), however, requires that the commercial use must have occurred at least one year before the earlier of either the effective filing date of the claimed invention (May 1, 2012), or the date on which the claimed invention was disclosed to the public in a manner that qualified for the exception from prior art under Section 102(b). Because inventor A published his paper on March 1, 2012, the defense requires D to have made a domestic commercial use of the subject matter prior to March 1, 2011.

Company D did not yet own this facility, however, and did not practice the invention yet because it did not acquire the assets from Company C until June 1, 2011.

By March 1, 2011, however, Company C had been using the accused process in Illinois, Georgia, and Texas. Under Section 273(e), the prior user defense is a personal defense that C could clearly have asserted and established. One question is whether the defense can be asserted by D, a subsequent purchaser for good faith consideration.

Section 273(e)(1)(B) (2011) entitled "TRANSFER OF RIGHT" addresses this question. Since this transfer was not to the patent owner (which would be specifically excluded by the statute), the transfer appears to be valid as an ancillary and subordinate part of the good faith assignment on June 1, 2011 from Company C to Company D of the entire line of business to which the defense relates. Company D therefore acquired the right to continue to use the process being used at the time of the acquisition. The sites of use at that time were in Dallas and Georgia.

As to whether company D can continue to use the process in its Denver facility (which began January 1, 2012), and North Carolina (which began July 1, 2012), Section 273(e)(1)(C) directed to "RESTRICTION ON SITES" is applicable. That subsection provides that when the defense is acquired as part of an assignment or transfer of the type noted above, it may be asserted for uses only at sites where the otherwise infringing subject matter is in use before the *later* of the effective filing date of the claimed invention or the date of the assignment or transfer of the business. The later of the two dates in question (the assignment of the business and the effective filing date of the claimed invention) is May 1, 2012. Because company D began using the challenged process in Denver on January 1, 2012, *before* May 1, 2012, the use in Denver is protected by the defense. The statutory language does *not* demand that the use in an expanded site, *e.g.*, Denver, must have endured for at least one year.

D's expanded use in North Carolina began on July 1, 2012, two months *after* the effective filing date. Even though the use began prior to the patent issuance on August 1, 2012, the site restriction provision of Section 273 denies the defense to Company D with respect to the use in North Carolina that began subsequent to both (a) the patent application filing date and (b) the acquisition of the business by company D.

Recapitulating, assuming it can sustain the burden of proof, Company D will be successful in establishing the prior user defense with respect to its manufacturing operations in Georgia, Texas and Denver, but not North Carolina where the expansion occurred too late. Plaintiff L may proceed with the suit in respect of those North Carolina activities unless other legal doctrines estop L.

Expansion at Sites. A related question to *where* the use may occur is the question of *how much* use will be permitted. Can the prior user expand the use at a prior site, and if so, to what extent? The AIA addresses this in the "Limitations and Exceptions" section, 35 U.S.C. 273(e), subpart (3):

> (3) Not a General License.— The defense asserted by a person under this section is not a general license under all claims of the patent at issue, but extends only to the specific subject matter for which it has been established that a commercial use that qualifies under this section occurred, except that the defense shall also extend to variations in the quantity or volume of use of the claimed subject matter, and to improvements in the claimed subject matter that do not infringe additional specifically claimed subject matter of the patent.

According to the plain language of this provision, the person who asserts the defense, whether a prior user (who otherwise meets the conditions to establish the defense) or an acquiring entity who meets statutory conditions, may continue to use "the specific subject matter for which . . . a commercial use that qualifies under this section occurred . . . ." This is not absolute: the statute specifically contemplates variations in quantity and volume of use. Hence an otherwise qualified user can expand the use in terms of amount.

Processes and products often improve over time. Another question is whether an otherwise qualified user can improve the existing process and still sustain the defense. The statute addresses this issue also and provides that the user can make improvements in the claimed subject matter "that do not infringe additional specifically claimed subject matter of the patent." From this, it would appear that if a change does not encroach patent claims that were not previously used, the improvement is permitted under the prior user defense. A process, or a machine, manufacture, or composition of matter used in a manufacturing process or other commercial process can be modified and improved by the prior user or qualified successor. However, if the improvement infringes other "specifically claimed subject matter," then the change appears not to be covered by the defense.

Sanctions Requirement Retained. The statute retains the requirement that a court must find the case "exceptional for the purpose of awarding attorney fees" under § 285 if the defense is pleaded by a person who is found to infringe and who fails to demonstrate a reasonable basis for asserting this defense. Naturally, under § 285 the court still "may" award attorney fees in its discretion, or may not.

USPTO Report. Section 3(m) of the AIA directed the USPTO Director to submit a report to the Judiciary Committees of the Senate and of the House of Representatives of findings and recommendations of the Director on the operation of prior user rights in other countries in the industrialized world. That report did issue in January 2012 and is available on the USPTO website.[6] It provides a detailed exposition of prior user rights in foreign countries and shows the various provisions that those countries have adopted.

---

[6]See "Report on the Prior User Rights Defense," by David J. Kappos and Teresa Stanek Rea, available at: http://uspto.gov/aia_implementation/20120113-pur_report.pdf (visited Dec. 26, 2012).

Chapter 9

False Patent Marking (Mismarking)

AIA § 16(b)
35 U.S.C.A. § 292

§ 9:1 False patent marking—Background

As explained in Chapter 6, patent marking or actual notice is a prerequisite to collecting damages for infringement of many patents. 35 U.S.C. § 287. This encourages patent marking. Conversely, *improper* marking is discouraged. To achieve this goal, since 1842, the patent statute has penalized intentional false patent marking. One court recounted the history of false patent marking as follows:

> The False Marking Statute was enacted on August 29, 1842. *See* 5 Stat. 544, § 5. The statute provided for a fine of "not more than $500" for each article a defendant falsely marked as patented "for the purpose of deceiving the public." *Id.* For

over a hundred years, "the fine was levied only once on each scheme to falsely mark, rather than once on each item falsely marked." *Advanced Cartridge Technologies, LLC v. Lexmark International, Inc.,* No. 8:10-cv-486, 2011 WL 6719725, *1 (M.D.Fla. Dec.21, 2011) (citing Odin B. Roberts, *Actions Qui Tam Under the Patent Statutes of the United States,* 10 HARV. L.REV. 265, 272–73 (1896)).

The False Marking Statute's *qui tam* provision "authorize[d] someone to pursue an action on behalf of the government as well as himself." *Stauffer v. Brooks Brothers, Inc.,* 619 F.3d 1321, 1325 (Fed.Cir.2010) (internal quotation mark omitted). According to the Federal Circuit Court of Appeals,

> [f]alse marking can injure the public interest in full and free competition because the act of false marking misleads the public into believing that a patentee controls the article in question (as well as like articles), externalizes the risk of error in the determination, placing it on the public rather than the manufacturer or seller of the article, and increases the cost to the public of ascertaining whether a patentee in fact controls the intellectual property embodied in an article.

Juniper Networks, Inc. v. Shipley, 643 F.3d 1346, 1351 (Fed.Cir.2011) (quoting *Clontech Labs., Inc. v. Invitrogen Corp.,* 406 F.3d 1347, 1356–57 (Fed.Cir.2005)). As an incentive to *qui tam* plaintiffs, the statute enabled "any person to sue for the statutory penalty and retain one-half of the recovery." *Boyd v. Schildkraut Giftware Corp.,* 936 F.2d 76, 79 (2d Cir.1991).

By assigning a portion of the United States' damages claim to "any person," Congress effectively granted *qui tam* plaintiffs Article III standing to sue under the False Marking Statute. *See Stauffer,* 619 F.3d at 1325 (holding that "Congress has, by enacting section 292, defined an injury in fact to the United States . . . . Because the government would have standing to enforce its own law, [a *qui tam* plaintiff], as the government's assignee, also has standing to enforce the [False Marking Statute]"). "[E]ven though a [*qui tam* plaintiff] may suffer no injury himself, a *qui tam* provision operates as a statutory assignment of the United States' rights, and 'the assignee of a claim has standing to assert the injury in fact suffered by the assignor.'" *Id.* (quoting *Vermont Agency of Natural Resources v. United States ex rel. Stevens,* 529 U.S. 765, 773, 120 S.Ct. 1858, 146 L.Ed.2d 836 (2000)). Accordingly, a *qui tam* plaintiff proceeding under the original False Marking Statute did not need to allege injury to himself or injury to competition in order to have standing to sue. *See id.* at 1327.

Despite the provision for *qui tam* suits in the original statute, the False Marking Statute remained largely dormant until 2010, when the effects of the Federal Circuit's decision in *Forest Group, Inc. v. Bon Tool Co.,* 590 F.3d 1295, 1301—04 (Fed.Cir.2009), were realized. *See Berkeley Technology Law Journal Annual Review 2011, Patent Law: Additional Develop-*

ments, 26 BERKELEY TECH. L.J. 367, 368 (2011). The Federal Circuit in *Forest Group, Inc.,* held that a plaintiff bringing suit under the False Marking Statute could recover a distinct fine for each falsely marked item. This holding led to a rapid increase in the number of large false marking awards. *See Advanced Cartridge Technologies, LLC,* 2011 WL 6719725, at *2.[1]

The false marking provision of the patent statute immediately prior to the AIA read as follows:

35 U.S.C. 292 False marking.

(a) Whoever, without the consent of the patentee, marks upon, or affixes to, or uses in advertising in connection with anything made, used, offered for sale, or sold by such person within the United States, or imported by the person into the United States, the name or any imitation of the name of the patentee, the patent number, or the words "patent," "patentee," or the like, with the intent of counterfeiting or imitating the mark of the patentee, or of deceiving the public and inducing them to believe that the thing was made, offered for sale, sold, or imported into the United States by or with the consent of the patentee; or

Whoever marks upon, or affixes to, or uses in advertising in connection with any unpatented article the word "patent" or any word or number importing the same is patented, for the purpose of deceiving the public; or

Whoever marks upon, or affixes to, or uses in advertising in connection with any article the words "patent applied for," "patent pending," or any word importing that an application for patent has been made, when no application for patent has been made, or if made, is not pending, for the purpose of deceiving the public—

Shall be fined not more than $500 for every such offense.

(b) Any person may sue for the penalty, in which event one-half shall go to the person suing and the other to the use of the United States.[2]

This was a "*qui tam*" statute. "*Qui tam*" is short for the Latin phrase "*qui tam pro domino rege quam pro se ipso in hac parte sequitur,*" which means "who pursues this action

---

[Section 9:1]

[1]*Adirondack Cookie Co. Inc. v. Monaco Baking Co.*, 2012 WL 1640565, *2-3 (N.D. N.Y. 2012).

[2]35 U.S.C.A. § 292 (1994). Importantly, applying a wrong patent number is not alone sufficient to establish the offense. Congress did not impose strict liability but instead requires a showing of intent as set forth in the various subparagraphs of § 292(a).

on our Lord the King's behalf as well as his own."[3] These actions were filed by "relators" in federal court, seeking an award of up to $500 for each mismarked product (arguing that each product is a separate "offense").[4] When mismarked products were mass produced, the opportunity arose for "any person" to sue for huge amounts, depending of course on what penalty amount up to $500 the court would deem suitable per product. Even though § 292 (b) of the statute called for one-half of the judgment to be paid to the United States, the opportunity for large awards attracted considerable *qui tam* litigation, especially in 2010 and thereafter.

§ 9:2 Congressional intent re false patent marking[1]

Congress intended to replace *qui tam* litigation for false patent marking with a new approach to balance the problems industry faces with changing markings of patent numbers against the need to deter intentional false patent marking. The House Report commented as follows:

b) False marking

The Federal Circuit's recent decision in *Forest Group, Inc. v.*

[3]*Vermont Agency of Natural Resources v. U.S. ex rel. Stevens*, 529 U.S. 765, 769 n.1, 120 S. Ct. 1858, 146 L. Ed. 2d 836, 50 Env't. Rep. Cas. (BNA) 1545, 16 I.E.R. Cas. (BNA) 417, 30 Envtl. L. Rep. 20622 (2000).

[4]See *Forest Group, Inc. v. Bon Tool Co.*, 590 F.3d 1295, 1301, 93 U.S.P.Q.2d 1097 (Fed. Cir. 2009) (finding error in awarding penalty on a *per decision* (to mismark) basis and stating that the "statute clearly requires that each article that is falsely marked with intent to deceive constitutes an offense").

[Section 9:2]

[1]The Supreme Court cautions against relying on interpretations advanced in legislative statements that are not "anchored in the text of the statute." *Shannon v. U.S.*, 512 U.S. 573, 583, 114 S. Ct. 2419, 129 L. Ed. 2d 459 (1994), stating "[C]ourts have no authority to enforce [a] principl[e] gleaned solely from legislative history that has no statutory reference point." *Shannon*, 512 U.S. at 584, quoting *International Broth. of Elec. Workers, Local Union No. 474, AFL-CIO v. N.L.R.B.*, 814 F.2d 697, 712, 124 L.R.R.M. (BNA) 2993, 106 Lab. Cas. (CCH) P 12256 (D.C. Cir. 1987). The authoritative statement "is the statutory text, not the legislative history." *Exxon Mobil Corp. v. Allapattah Services, Inc.*, 545 U.S. 546, 568, 125 S. Ct. 2611, 162 L. Ed. 2d 502 (2005). However, lower courts have cited the legislative history of the AIA already in recent cases. E.g., *Rogers v. Tristar Products, Inc.*, 102 U.S.P.Q.2d 1722, 2012 WL 1660604, *2 (Fed. Cir. 2012) (non-precedential); *Byrne v. Wood, Herron & Evans, LLP*, 676 F.3d 1024, 1029, 102 U.S.P.Q.2d 1073 (Fed. Cir. 2012) (dissenting opin.).

Bon Tool Co., 590 F.3d 1295 (Fed. Cir. 2009), which held that section 292's $500 fine is assessed for each product that is falsely marked, has created a surge in false-marking qui tam litigation. Though one might assume that section 292 actions are targeted at parties that assert fictitious patents in order to deter competitors, such a scenario is almost wholly unknown to false-marking litigation. False-marking suits are almost always based on allegations that a valid patent that did cover the product has expired, but the manufacturer continued to sell products stamped with the patent; or that an existing patent used to mark products is invalid or unenforceable; or that an existing and valid patent's claims should not be construed to cover the product in question.

Indeed, a recent survey of such suits found that a large majority involved valid patents that covered the products in question but had simply expired. For many products, it is difficult and expensive to change a mold or other means by which a product is marked as patented, and marked products continue to circulate in commerce for some period after the patent expires. It is doubtful that the Congress that originally enacted this section anticipated that it would force manufacturers to immediately remove marked products from commerce once the patent expired, given that the expense to manufacturers of doing so will generally greatly outweigh any conceivable harm of allowing such products to continue to circulate in commerce.

To address the recent surge in litigation, the bill replaces the qui tam remedy for false marking with a new action that allows a party that has suffered a competitive injury as a result of such marking to seek compensatory damages. The United States would be allowed to seek the $500-per-article fine, and competitors may recover in relation to actual injuries that they have suffered as a result of false marking, but the bill would eliminate litigation brought by unrelated, private third parties.[2]

* * *

Section 16. Marking.

* * *

Subsection (b) addresses false marking in the following ways: (1) Only the United States may sue for the qui tam penalty under the subsection. (2) A person who has suffered a competitive injury as a result of a violation may still bring a civil action in US district court for compensatory damages. (3) Persons or companies otherwise liable under § 292 (the false marking statute) are protected during a 3-year window beginning on the date the patent at issue expires. Beyond the 3-year window, persons or companies are also protected if they place

[2] H. R. Rep. No. 112-98, pt. 1, at 53 (2011).

the word "patent" or "patented", the abbreviation "pat.", or the patent number either on the article or through an Internet posting, consistent with the amendments in subsection (a).[3]

§ 9:3 AIA statutory changes re false patent marking

AIA § 16(b) amends 35 U.S.C. § 292 as follows:[1]

35 U.S.C. 292. False marking

(a) Whoever, without the consent of the patentee, marks upon, or affixes to, or uses in advertising in connection with anything made, used, offered for sale, or sold by such person within the United States, or imported by the person into the United States, the name or any imitation of the name of the patentee, the patent number, or the words "patent," "patentee," or the like, with the intent of counterfeiting or imitating the mark of the patentee, or of deceiving the public and inducing them to believe that the thing was made, offered for sale, sold, or imported into the United States by or with the consent of the patentee; or

Whoever marks upon, or affixes to, or uses in advertising in connection with any unpatented article the word "patent" or any word or number importing the same is patented, for the purpose of deceiving the public; or

Whoever marks upon, or affixes to, or uses in advertising in connection with any article the words "patent applied for," "patent pending," or any word importing that an application for patent has been made, when no application for patent has been made, or if made, is not pending, for the purpose of deceiving the public—

Shall be fined not more than $500 for every such offense. Only the United States may sue for the penalty authorized by this subsection.

(b) ~~Any person may sue for the penalty, in which event one-half shall go to the person suing and the other to the use of the United States.~~ A person who has suffered a competitive injury as a result of a violation of this section may file a civil action in a district court of the United States for recovery of damages adequate to compensate for the injury.

(c) The marking of a product, in a manner described in subsection (a), with matter relating to a patent that covered that product but has expired is not a violation of this section.

---

[3] H. R. Rep. No. 112-98, pt. 1, at 80 (2011). The three-year window is not in the statute as enacted.

[Section 9:3]

[1] In this markup, strikethrough indicates text being removed from the statute, and underscoring indicates text being added to the statute.

§ 9:4 Effect on pending litigation

AIA § 16(b) revises 35 U.S.C. § 292(a) and (b) regarding false marking litigation. First, § 16(b)(1) adds language to the end of 35 U.S.C. § 292(a) to state expressly that *only* the United States may sue for the penalty. Accordingly, § 16(b)(2) rewrites § 292(b) to eliminate the *qui tam* provision that previously allowed anyone to sue for the penalty for the violation of § 292(a).

Under AIA § 16(b)(4), these changes are retroactive.[1] They became effective immediately on September 16, 2011 and apply to all cases, regardless of filing date. AIA § 16(b)(4) states,

> EFFECTIVE DATE—The amendments made by this subsection shall apply to all cases, without exception, that are pending on, or commenced on or after, the date of the enactment of this Act.

Some courts dismiss pending litigation or pending claims for false patent marking without prejudice to refiling under the revised statute.[2] Pursuant to this AIA provision, even if a suit is on appeal, the appeal is to be dismissed and remanded to the district court, sometimes with instructions to dismiss[3] and sometimes to "calculate[e] . . . liabilities under the amended statute."[4] It is clear, however, that the new provisions apply to a case on appeal following a judg-

---

[Section 9:4]

[1] See generally *Brooks v. Dunlop Mfg. Inc.*, 702 F.3d 624 (Fed. Cir. 2012); *Presidio Components, Inc. v. American Technical Ceramics Corp.*, 702 F.3d 1351, 1364–65 (Fed. Cir. 2012); *Rogers v. Tristar Products, Inc.*, 102 U.S.P.Q.2d 1722, 2012 WL 1660604, *2 (Fed. Cir. 2012), citing *Boumediene v. Bush*, 553 U.S. 723, 738–39, 128 S. Ct. 2229, 171 L. Ed. 2d 41 (2008); *Lubber, Inc. v. Optari LLC*, 2013 WL 1245679, at*9 n.4 (M.D. Tenn. 2013).

[2] E.g., *Premium Balloon Accessories, Inc. v. Creative Balloons Mfg., Inc.*, 2012 WL 443254 (N.D. Ohio 2012); *West v. Quality Gold, Inc.*, 2012 WL 1067558 (N.D. Cal. 2012) (defendant's motion to dismiss granted with leave to amend the complaint); *Kilts Resources LLC v. Uniden Direct USA, Inc.*, 2011 WL 5320651 (E.D. Tex. 2011) (*sua sponte* dismissal without prejudice to re-file complaint alleging "competitive injury").

[3] *Rogers v. Tristar Products, Inc.*, 449 Fed. Appx. 921 (Fed. Cir. 2011); *FLFMC, LLC v. Wham-O, Inc.*, 444 Fed. Appx. 447, 100 U.S.P.Q.2d 1857 (Fed. Cir. 2011); *Unique Product Solutions, Ltd. v. Hy-Grade Valve, Inc.*, 462 Fed. Appx. 967 (Fed. Cir. 2012).

[4] *Cyclone USA, Inc. v. Sei Kim*, 461 Fed. Appx. 638 (9th Cir. 2011).

ment rendered before the law was enacted.[5]

Plaintiffs may seek to amend their complaints to allege competitive injury in light of the change in the prevailing law brought about by the AIA.[6] In *Pactiv Corp. v. Multisorb*, even though the period for amending the pleadings had passed, an Illinois court allowed amendment for this purpose, finding that "good cause" had been shown under Fed. R. Civ. P. 16(b)(4) and the liberal standard of Rule 15.[7] The court rejected the argument that plaintiff ought to have pleaded a "competitive injury" before passage of the AIA, reasoning that it asks "[too] much of litigants to predict whether pending legislation will pass or what form it might take."[8] Here, plaintiff did not delay seeking to amend once the AIA passed. To remove any prejudice, the court extended discovery and allowed defendant to retake some depositions to focus on the competitive injury. On one occasion, an Ohio court considered whether it would allow the *qui tam* relator to file an amended complaint that would withdraw the false marking claim after the AIA became law, although the court ultimately granted the motion.[9] A New Jersey court ruled that because the AIA deprived plaintiff of standing to file the suit, this deprived the court of jurisdiction and mooted plaintiff's motion to enforce a settlement agreement.[10] A Texas court allowed a *qui tam* relator to amend the complaint to allege competitive injury. After the subsequent amended pleading was successfully challenged as insuf-

[5]*Brooks v. Dunlop Mfg. Inc.*, 2012 WL 6200227, *4 (Fed. Cir. 2012) citing *Plaut v. Spendthrift Farm, Inc.*, 514 U.S. 211, 226, 115 S. Ct. 1447, 131 L. Ed. 2d 328, Fed. Sec. L. Rep. (CCH) P 98,681 (1995); *Presidio Components, Inc. v. American Technical Ceramics Corp.*, 2012 WL 6602786, *10–11 (Fed. Cir. 2012).

[6]*Devicor Medical Products, Inc. v. Biopsy Sciences, LLC*, 2013 WL 1628644, at *1 n.2 (D. Del. 2013) ("While the AIA removed the qui tam provision of 35 U.S.C. § 292, it also amended the statute to permit private suits for false marking where a person 'suffer[s] a competitive injury as a result of a false marking violation.' " (Citing the Leahy-Smith America Invents Act, Pub. L. No. 112-29, § 16(b) (codified at 35 U.S.C.A. § 292(a-b))).

[7]*Pactiv Corp. v. Multisorb Tech. Inc.*, 2011 WL 5244359 (N.D. Ill. 2011).

[8]*Pactiv Corp. v. Multisorb Tech. Inc.*, 2011 WL 5244359, *2 (N.D. Ill. 2011).

[9]*Greene v. Ab Coaster Holdings, Inc.*, 2012 WL 2342927 (S.D. Ohio 2012).

[10]*U.S. ex rel. FLFMC, LLC v. TFH Publications, Inc.*, 855 F. Supp. 2d 300 (D.N.J. 2012).

ficient, the Court declined to allow further amendment of the pleading on this issue.[11]

Most of the *qui tam* cases involved failures of manufacturers to remove from their products the numbers of patents that have expired.[12] Congress addressed that issue specifically with AIA § 16(b)(3), eliminating that liability by adding subsection (3) to § 292: "The marking of a product, in a manner described in subsection (a), with matter relating to a patent that covered that product but has expired is not a violation of this section." Thus, under new § 292(c), if a patent did cover a product and the patent expired, the failure to remove that number is not a violation of § 292. This provision also became effective on September 16, 2011, when President Obama signed the Act into law.

§ 9:5 The meaning of "competitive injury"

Section 292(b) as amended allows anyone who has suffered "a competitive injury as a result of a violation of [§ 292]" to sue the false patent marker for "damages adequate to compensate for the injury."[1] Courts have begun to explore the meaning of "competitive injury." One court noted that the statute does not allow mere consumers to recover under this section, as a competitive injury is "one suffered as a defendant's competitor. . ."[2] The issue has generally arisen thus far in the context of motions to dismiss. Often, such motions challenge the sufficiency of the pleading, which is treated in the next section *infra*, and in the section on standing, treated thereafter. These sections should be reviewed for further relevant discussion on the meaning of "competitive injury."

One recent articulation appears in *Greene v. Ab Coaster*

---

[11] *WE-Flex, LLC v. NBSP, Inc.*, 2012 WL 1440439 (S.D. Tex. 2012).

[12] *Pequignot v. Solo Cup Co.*, 646 F. Supp. 2d 790, 92 U.S.P.Q.2d 1495 (E.D. Va. 2009), aff'd in part, vacated in part, 608 F.3d 1356, 95 U.S.P.Q.2d 1501 (Fed. Cir. 2010).

[Section 9:5]

[1] Based on this amendment, the Federal Circuit has rejected the use of the equitable doctrine of "marking estoppel" in cases of false marking as § 292(b) provides an adequate remedy at law. *Frolow v. Wilson Sporting Goods Co.*, 710 F.3d 1303, 1309-10, 106 U.S.P.Q.2d 1089 (Fed. Cir. 2013).

[2] *Stauffer v. Brooks Bros., Inc.*, 2012 WL 6621374, *4 (S.D. N.Y. 2012)

Holdings, Inc.,[3] where an Ohio court explained:

> "The statute does not define competitive injury, however, 'competitive injury' has been generally defined as '[a] wrongful economic loss at the hands of a commercial rival . . ..' " *U.S. ex rel. FLFMC, LLC v. TFH Publications, Inc.*, No. 10-CV-5477, 2012 WL 1337557, at *4 (D. N.J. Apr 18, 2012) (citing Black's Law Dictionary 302 (8th ed.2004). *See also Rogers v. Conair Corp.*, No. 10-1497, 2012 WL 1443905, at *4 (E.D.Pa. April 25, 2012) ("To establish standing under the [America Invents Act], Plaintiff must allege a tangible economic loss caused by the illegal competitive means (*i.e.*, the false patent marking).") (citing *Advanced Cartridge Tech., LLC v. Lexmark Int'l, Inc.*, No. 10-486, 2011 WL 6719725, at *2, 4 (M.D.Fl. Dec.21, 2011) and *Fisher-Price, Inc. v. Kids II, Inc.*, No. 10-988, 2011 WL 6409665, at *9 (W.D.N.Y. Dec.21, 2011)). "Formulated differently, a competitive injury is a business loss caused by a competitive means, including false patent marking, that the law forbids." *Advanced Cartridge Tech., LLC*, 2011 WL 6719725, at *2 (citation omitted).[4]

In *Advanced Cartridge Technologies, LLC v Lexmark Intl*, a Florida court ruled that plaintiff ("ACT") "incurred no judicially cognizable injury."[5] Defendant urged that ACT sustained no injury of any kind, so it lacked standing to sue. The court discussed the difference between injury in fact and "competitive injury" within the meaning of the AIA. The district court explained that a competitive injury is "a business loss caused by a competitive means, including false patent marking, that the law forbids":

> Lexmark argues that ACT lacks a (statutory) competitive injury but supports the argument with legal authority pertaining to the (constitutional) Article III standing requirement. The result is a jumble. In confusion Lexmark seeks dismissal for lack of subject matter jurisdiction under the Constitution even though Lexmark's argument is effectively that ACT fails to state a claim under the amended False Marking Statute. Further, the competitive injury that Section 292(b) requires differs from the injury-in-fact that Article III requires. *Black's Law Dictionary* 302 (8th ed. 2004) defines a "competitive injury" as "[a] wrongful economic loss at the hands of a commercial rival . . . ." Formulated differently, a competitive injury is a business loss caused by a competitive means, includ-

---

[3] *Greene v. Ab Coaster Holdings, Inc.*, 2012 WL 4442749 (S.D. Ohio 2012).

[4] *Greene v. Ab Coaster Holdings, Inc.*, 2012 WL 4442749, *11 (S.D. Ohio 2012).

[5] *Advanced Cartridge Technologies, LLC v. Lexmark Intern., Inc.*, 2011 WL 6719725 (M.D. Fla. 2011).

ing false patent marking, that the law forbids. *Cf. Ely—Norris Safe Co. v. Mosler Safe Co.,* 7 F.2d 603, 604 (2d Cir.1925) (L.Hand, J.), *rev'd on other grounds,* 273 U.S. 132, 47 S.Ct. 314, 71 L.Ed. 578 (1927). In contrast, the minimum injury-in-fact necessary for standing under Article III is a mere "identifiable trifle." *Common Cause/Georgia v. Billups,* 554 F.3d 1340, 1351 (11th Cir.2009).[6]

A Texas court in *WE-Flex, LLC v. NBSP, Inc.* also cited *Black's Law Dictionary* on the meaning of "competitive injury":

> A "*competitive* injury" is "[a] wrongful economic loss caused by a commercial rival, such as the loss of sales due to unfair competition; a disadvantage in a plaintiff's ability to compete with a defendant, caused by the defendant's unfair competition." *Black's Law Dictionary* (9th ed.2009).[7]

In *Seirus Innovative Accessories, Inc. v. Cabela's Inc.,* a California court declared that under the AIA, the claimant in a false marking suit must show a competitive injury which the court took to mean ". . . predatory pricing, price discrimination, injury to competition, or loss of business opportunities."[8] That court also required the claimant to demonstrate that it is in a competitive relationship with the alleged false patent marker.

In sustaining the adequacy of an amended complaint, an Oregon court in *RB Rubber Products, Inc. v. ECORE Intl, Inc.*[9] considered Ninth Circuit law on this point in another intellectual property law context:

> Although the Ninth Circuit has yet to address the definition of competitive injury in the false marking context, district courts in this circuit have done so and their approaches are instructive. In *McCabe v. Floyd Rose Guitars,* CASE NO. 10CV581 JLS (JMA), 2012 U.S. Dist. LEXIS 56604, at **19–20 (S.D.Cal. Apr. 23, 2012), the court looked to the definition of competitive injury under the Lanham Act for guidance: "Relatedly, however, in the Lanham Act context . . . the Ninth Circuit has defined 'competitive injury' as 'harmful to the

---

[6] *Advanced Cartridge Technologies, LLC v. Lexmark Intern., Inc.*, 2011 WL 6719725, *2 (M.D. Fla. 2011).

[7] *WE-Flex, LLC v. NBSP, Inc.*, 2012 WL 1440439, *7 (S.D. Tex. 2012).

[8] *Seirus Innovative Accessories, Inc. v. Cabela's Inc.*, 100 U.S.P.Q.2d 1953, 2011 WL 6400630, *4 (S.D. Cal. 2011) citing *Volvo Trucks North America, Inc. v. Reeder-Simco GMC, Inc.*, 546 U.S. 164, 176, 126 S. Ct. 860, 163 L. Ed. 2d 663, 2006-1 Trade Cas. (CCH) ¶ 75077 (2006).

[9] *RB Rubber Products, Inc. v. ECORE Intern., Inc.*, 2012 WL 4068557 (D. Or. 2012).

plaintiff's ability to compete with the defendant.' Under this guidance, the Court reads § 292 as requiring that a plaintiff allege the defendant's false marking was harmful to the plaintiff's ability to compete with the defendant." (quoting *Barrus v. Sylvania,* 55 F.3d 468, 470 (9th Cir.1995)) (other citations omitted). And, as with the Lanham Act, competitive injury may be presumed: "While the Ninth Circuit has not yet interpreted 'competitive injury' in the patent marking context, as previously interpreted in the context of a Lanham Act claim, the court imposes a general presumption of a competitive injury whenever the defendant and plaintiff are direct competitors and defendant's misrepresentation has a tendency to mislead consumers." *Ira Green, Inc. v. J.L. Darling Corp.,* CASE NO. 3:11-cv-05796-RJB, 2011 U.S. Dist. LEXIS 139552, at *10 (W.D.Wash. Dec. 5, 2011).[10]

The Oregon court then noted that the legislative history of the AIA had influenced a district court in the Second Circuit so that "the competitive injury requirement was added to the false marking statute to ensure that the claimant was actually an aggrieved party, and not merely an uninvolved third party seeking only to extract damages."[11] Based on these precedents, the Oregon court then defined "competitive injury" as follows:

> The court adopts the approach of the courts cited above that competitive injury exists where the parties are in competition in the relevant market and the alleged false marking harms the plaintiff's ability to compete. Again, courts have analogized this new statute with the Lanham Act which presumes competitive injury where the parties are competitors and the alleged conduct has the tendency to confuse consumers.[12]

Activity that Is *Not* "Competitive Injury." An Illinois court ruled that certain activity cannot constitute "competitive injury," on the basis of new § 292(c). The court held that marking with numbers of expired patent, even for the purpose of seeking competitive advantage by deceiving competitors into believing that they could not manufacture the product without infringing patent rights, could not form the basis of an actionable "competitive injury" under § 292

[10] *RB Rubber Products, Inc. v. ECORE Intern., Inc.*, 2012 WL 4068557, *8 (D. Or. 2012).

[11] *RB Rubber Products, Inc. v. ECORE Intern., Inc.*, 2012 WL 4068557, *9 (D. Or. 2012).

[12] *RB Rubber Products, Inc. v. ECORE Intern., Inc.*, 2012 WL 4068557, *9 (D. Or. 2012).

as amended.[13] The court rejected the argument that the addition of § 292(c) was not intended to protect such violations but only to protect against "a more narrow category," *i.e.*, the failure to *remove* the number of an expired patent, not the addition of a marking for the purpose of competitive advantage. The court did not reach the question of Congressional intent because the language of the statute is clear on its face:

> KI argues that section 292(c) was not intended to protect violations like FFR's but only a more narrow category. It argues that the Leahy—Smith Act's legislative history shows that Congress "was concerned with the cost of removing marked products from commerce or changing the labels after the patent expired." KI Supp. Br. at 4. But courts "need not resort to legislative history when a statute is unambiguous." *Pequignot v. Solo Cup Co.,* 608 F.3d 1356, 1361—62 (Fed.Cir.2010) (refusing to consult legislative history to determine if an earlier version of section 292 covered expired patents). The false marking statute's language, as recently amended, unambiguously provides an exception for any items covered by an expired patent.[14]

§ 9:6 Pleading requirements for false marking "competitive injury"

A complaint for a false marking claim under § 292 must allege three elements: (1) marking an unpatented article, (2) intent to deceive the public, and (3) competitive injury.[1]

Concerning element (1), the failure to plead that the product was not covered by *any* patent at all, whether U.S. or foreign, provided the basis for dismissing the complaint in *Mama Cares Foundation v. Nutriset Société Par Actions*

---

[13] *Fasteners for Retail, Inc. v. Andersen*, 101 U.S.P.Q.2d 1076, 2011 WL 5130445 (N.D. Ill. 2011).

[14] *Fasteners for Retail, Inc. v. Andersen*, 101 U.S.P.Q.2d 1076, 2011 WL 5130445, *3 (N.D. Ill. 2011). See also, *Introsan Dental Products, Inc. v. Dentsply Tulsa Dental, LLC*, 2012 WL 3011830, *3 (D. Md. 2012) (finding "reasonable arguments on both sides of the issue" and, while not reaching the issue due to inadequate pleading, stating that it would find for defendant); *Slack v. Bon Aqua Intern., Inc.*, 2012 WL 1957589 (M.D. N.C. 2012), report and recommendation adopted, 2012 WL 2428255 (M.D. N.C. 2012) (marking with expired patent number fails to state claim for relief).

[Section 9:6]

[1] *RB Rubber Products, Inc. v. ECORE Intern., Inc.*, 2012 WL 4068557, *5 (D. Or. 2012); accord, *WE-Flex, LLC v. NBSP, Inc.*, 2012 WL 1440439, *4 (S.D. Tex. 2012).

Cimplifiée.[2]

Retaining a label of "patent pending" after the patent has issued does not give rise to a claim of false marking, and the failure to plead any competitive injury caused by such a label led to dismissal in *Hall v. Bed Bath & Beyond, Inc.*, 705 F.3d 1357, 1373, 105 U.S.P.Q.2d 1672, 2013-1 Trade Cas. (CCH) ¶ 78244 (Fed. Cir. 2013). With regard to element (2), a heightened pleading requirement has been required for false marking due to the intent elements of the cause of action.[3] Courts have not relaxed this requirement for new causes of action alleging "competitive injury" under Section 292. Indeed, § 292(b) as amended refers to "a competitive injury as a result of violation *of this section* . . . ." [emphasis added] By referring to "this section," Congress referenced all of § 292, and § 292(a) includes language about intent and purpose of the false patent marker. Thus, after enactment of the AIA, courts still apply the heightened pleading requirement as to the intent elements.[4] This means that a plaintiff must show both knowledge that a statement is false and a purpose of deceit.[5]

Turning to element (3), district courts have expressed a

---

[2]*Mama Cares Foundation v. Nutriset Societe Par Actions Cimplifiee*, 825 F. Supp. 2d 178 (D.D.C. 2011).

[3]*In re BP Lubricants USA Inc.*, 637 F.3d 1307, 97 U.S.P.Q.2d 2025, 79 Fed. R. Serv. 3d 325 (Fed. Cir. 2011); *Juniper Networks, Inc. v. Shipley*, 643 F.3d 1346, 1350, 98 U.S.P.Q.2d 1491 (Fed. Cir. 2011); *RB Rubber Products, Inc. v. ECORE Intern., Inc.*, 2012-1 Trade Cas. (CCH) ¶ 77825, 2012 WL 860416, *10-11 (D. Or. 2012) (finding pleading deficient to meet heightened standard); *Promote Innovation LLC v. Ortho-McNeil Pharmaceutical, LLC*, 2011 WL 2837421 (D.N.J. 2011); *Two Moms and a Toy, LLC v. International Playthings, LLC*, 2012 WL 4510686, *2-3 (D. Colo. 2012) (plaintiff failed to meet heightened pleading requirement).

[4]*RB Rubber Products, Inc. v. ECORE Intern., Inc.*, 2012 WL 4068557, *5 (D. Or. 2012). The court addressed the "intent" aspect as follows:

> "Intent to deceive is a state of mind arising when a party acts with sufficient knowledge that what it is saying is not so and consequently that the recipient of its saying will be misled into thinking that the statement is true." A party asserting false marking must show by a preponderance of the evidence that the accused party did not have a reasonable belief that the articles were properly marked. An assertion by a party that it did not intend to deceive, standing alone, "is worthless as proof of no intent to deceive where there is knowledge of falsehood."

(citing *Forest Group, Inc. v. Bon Tool Co.*, 590 F.3d 1295, 1300, 93 U.S.P.Q.2d 1097 (Fed. Cir. 2009) (citing and quoting *Clontech Laboratories, Inc. v. Invitrogen Corp.*, 406 F.3d 1347, 1352–1353, 74 U.S.P.Q.2d 1598 (Fed. Cir. 2005))).

[5]*Two Moms and a Toy, LLC v. International Playthings, LLC*, 2012 WL 4510686, *2-3 (D. Colo. 2012) citing *Pequignot v. Solo Cup Co.*, 608

variety of opinions on what is sufficient to plead a "competitive injury." Considering first the cases where the pleading survived a motion to dismiss, a Nevada court in *Server Technology, Inc. v. American Power Conversion Corp.*[6] noted that the parties competed directly and the false marking benefitted the mismarker because, *e.g.*, consumers were encouraged to buy products with patent markings. The court explained:

> The court has reviewed the documents and pleadings on file in this matter and finds that APC has sufficiently alleged a competitive injury from STI's alleged false marking to survive a motion to dismiss. In its complaint, APC specifically alleged that "APC has suffered competitive injury casually connected to STI's false marking" because: (1) APC and STI are direct competitors in the intelligent power distribution industry; (2) the falsely marked products compete directly with APC's similar products; (3) STI's false marking upset the competitive relationship between the parties as customers were presented with an allegedly patented product design; and (4) STI's false marking created an unfounded image of STI as a product innovator with superior products to its competitors. * * * Further, APC alleges that STI's false marking allowed STI to compete in the market more effectively than APC by encouraging customers to purchase only those products which have patent markings. * * * Thus, based on the allegations in APC's counterclaim, the court finds that APC has sufficiently alleged a competitive injury as a result of STI's false marking. Therefore, the court finds that APC has alleged a claim for false patent marking under 35 U.S.C. § 292 and shall deny STI's motion accordingly. [citations omitted][7]

An Oregon court similarly sustained the pleading of competitive injury in *RB Rubber Products, Inc. v. ECORE Intl, Inc.*,[8] noting *inter alia* that the parties were competitors and that the mismarking allegedly discouraged purchases of products from other sources:

> Here, RB Rubber alleges that it and ECORE are competitors in the "acoustical underlayment market" and that they manufacture similar and competing products. (FAC ¶ 81.) RB Rubber alleges that ECORE intentionally misled RB Rubber, other competitors, and consumers into believing that certain

---

F.3d 1356, 1363, 95 U.S.P.Q.2d 1501 (Fed. Cir. 2010).

[6] *Server Technology, Inc. v. American Power Conversion Corp.*, 2012 WL 3061023 (D. Nev. 2012).

[7] *Server Technology, Inc. v. American Power Conversion Corp.*, 2012 WL 3061023, *2 (D. Nev. 2012).

[8] *RB Rubber Products, Inc. v. ECORE Intern., Inc.*, 2012 WL 4068557 (D. Or. 2012).

of its products were patented, thus unlawfully discouraging competitors from competing with ECORE and discouraging consumers from purchasing non-ECORE products. RB Rubber also alleges that ECORE conducted a campaign of misinformation designed to cause additional confusion, which included sending cease and desist letters to competitors, serving RB Rubber personnel at an industry trade show, and falsely informing competitors that RB Rubber's products were infringing. RB Rubber identified two situations in which ECORE's actions negatively impacted RB Rubber's business interests. First, ECORE sent a letter to a competitor, EJ Welch, informing it that ECORE was suing RB Rubber. Second, ECORE interfered with a business relationship between RB Rubber and Allied Custom Gypsum and, as a result, the contract was cancelled. RB Rubber alleges, by way of explanation, that where two products are substantially similar, a consumer will elect to purchase a patented product in order to avoid involvement in costly patent litigation. Finally, RB Rubber alleges: "As a result of ECORE's actions, i.e. false marking of its products coupled with the intended purpose of deception, RB Rubber has in fact sustained competitive injury through lost profits and sales in the past and future, loss of business relationships, and the loss of the ability to compete in the Relevant Market in the past and future." (FAC ¶ 22.)

These allegations are sufficient to plead competitive injury under the false marking statute. Accordingly, RB Rubber has adequately pleaded its claim for false marking.[9]

In *Fasteners for Retail, Inv. v. Andersen*, an Illinois court concluded that the pleading was sufficient as to competitive injury, where *inter alia* consumers were allegedly deterred from using competing products:

Finally, FFR argues that KI has not alleged that it suffered any competitive injury and that under amended section 292, KI can recover damages only to compensate for a competitive injury. The Court agrees with KI's contention that it has alleged competitive damages by stating that FFR's false marking "is likely to, or at least has the tendency to, discourage and deter persons and companies, such as K International, from commercializing competing products and deters consumers from using competing products." KI 3rd Am. Counterclaim ¶ 35.[10]

Perhaps the most extreme example of a sustained plead-

---

[9] *RB Rubber Products, Inc. v. ECORE Intern., Inc.*, 2012 WL 4068557, *9-10 (D. Or. 2012).

[10] *Fasteners for Retail, Inc. v. Andersen*, 101 U.S.P.Q.2d 1076, 2011 WL 5130445, *6 (N.D. Ill. 2011).

ing occurred in *Lubber, Inc. v. Optari, LLC*[11] where a Tennessee court noted the America Invents Act and its revisions to the false marking statute but declined to dismiss Lubber's false marking claim without ever discussing whether there was a "competitive injury" due to the alleged mismarking.[12] The court did, however, recount particularly egregious facts and substantial injury to Lubber at the hands of defendant.

Courts that have found pleadings insufficient generally focus on the allegation of injury due to the false marking, and they have called for specific nexus between the mismarking and the injury. Thus, a California court in *McCabe v. Floyd Rose Guitars*[13] dismissed a false marking claim, finding that plaintiff's allegations were conclusory and that there was no injury due to the false marking. In its discussion, the court considered Ninth Circuit law and *Black's Law Dictionary* and declared that "a plaintiff must allege that the defendant's false marking was harmful to the plaintiff's ability to compete with the defendant."[14]

A Texas court expressly disagreed with *Fasteners for Retail* in *WE-Flex, LLC v. NBSP, Inc.*,[15] explaining that the allegations assert only potential injuries:

> FN 46. * * * This court disagrees with the Illinois court's decision because the allegations do not assert cognizable injuries but, rather, potential injuries. In its analysis, the Illinois court did not give meaning to the full term "competitive injury." The fact that the parties are in competition and may suffer an injury is not enough to satisfy the new statutory requirement; an injury is necessary.[16]

In *WE-Flex*, the plaintiff alleged competitive injury through competitive advantages improperly obtained by defendant through its false marking, a "corresponding unfair disadvantage" to WE-Flex in the marketplace, an impeded ability to distinguish products from defendant's products, an inhibited ability to increase goodwill and market share, and

---

[11]*Lubber, Inc. v. Optari, LLC*, 66 Collier Bankr. Cas. 2d (MB) 775, 2011 WL 4738264 (M.D. Tenn. 2011).

[12]*Lubber, Inc. v. Optari, LLC*, 66 Collier Bankr. Cas. 2d (MB) 775, 2011 WL 4738264, *9 (M.D. Tenn. 2011).

[13]*McCabe v. Floyd Rose Guitars*, 2012 WL 1409627 (S.D. Cal. 2012).

[14]*McCabe v. Floyd Rose Guitars*, 2012 WL 1409627, *7 (S.D. Cal. 2012).

[15]*WE-Flex, LLC v. NBSP, Inc.*, 2012 WL 1440439 (S.D. Tex. 2012).

[16]*WE-Flex, LLC v. NBSP, Inc.*, 2012 WL 1440439, *7 n.46 (S.D. Tex. 2012).

"competitive harm." While the court was sympathetic to plaintiff's plight, declaring that at "first blush, Plaintiff's allegations of injury appear to have some substance,"[17] it ruled ultimately that no injury was pleaded due to the alleged false marking, explaining as follows:

> Plaintiff alleges that, in marking their products with "patent pending" Pearlessence and NBSP enjoy the recognition of being creative innovators and distinguish themselves from companies lacking patent production. According to Plaintiff, Pearlessence and NBSP receive increased goodwill as a result. Even assuming the truth of those statements, they have everything to do with benefits redounding to Pearlessence and NBSP and nothing to do with injury to Plaintiff.
>
> Paragraphs 44, 45, 60, and 61 all state the same thing: that the goodwill afforded Plaintiff is diminished in comparison to Pearlessence and NBSP because of Plaintiff's inability to distinguish its legitimately marked products from Pearlessence and NBSP's falsely marked products, resulting in an unfair disadvantage to Plaintiff. As a result, Plaintiff alleges, it has been unable to increase its goodwill and market share. These statements occupy the rarified air of theoretical or hypothetical injury. Plaintiff points to no particularized facts indicating ways in which it has actually suffered any diminished goodwill. [footnote omitted] Plaintiff cannot establish injury by merely mentioning the names of several "major players" and alluding to customer confusion without any factual indication that anyone actually has demonstrated or acted on a sense of diminished goodwill toward Plaintiff.[18]

Because WE-Flex offered "no specific instances of either price comparison or of resulting lost sales," WE-Flex had no constitutional standing, and the court lacked subject matter jurisdiction.

A New York court distinguished *Fasteners for Retail* and ruled in *Fisher-Price, Inc. v. Kids II, Inc.*[19] that the pleadings failed to allege a competitive injury. In its decision, the court applied the "plain meaning" of the words in the Act.

> Thus, a competitor is "one that is engaged in selling or buying goods or services in the same market as another." *Id.* "Injury," of course, broadly implies a right of recovery for loss or impairment of a right or damage to property. *Id.* at 1164.

---

[17] *WE-Flex, LLC v. NBSP, Inc.*, 2012 WL 1440439, *6 n.46 (S.D. Tex. 2012).

[18] *WE-Flex, LLC v. NBSP, Inc.*, 2012 WL 1440439, *6 n.46 (S.D. Tex. 2012).

[19] *Fisher-Price, Inc. v. Kids II, Inc.*, 2011 WL 6409665, *9 (W.D. N.Y. 2011).

Accordingly, given the plain meaning of § 292, by reference to its terms, in order to withstand Plaintiffs' motion against Defendant's Third Counterclaim, Defendant must allege sufficient facts to plausibly establish that, as a result of Fisher—Price's mismarking of its cradle swings with the '548 patent, Defendant's ability to compete against Plaintiffs in the marked [*sic*] for purchasers of such products was impaired, resulting in tangible economic loss to Defendant.[FN11] Defendant's allegations, however, fail to do so.[20]

FN11. The court notes that the phrase "competitive injury" has been similarly defined in the context of other market-regulating statutes. *See, e.g., Famous Horse Inc. v. 5th Ave. Photo Inc.*, 624 F.3d 106, 113–14, 96 U.S.P.Q.2d 1963, 2010-2 Trade Cas. (CCH) ¶ 77278 (2d Cir. 2010) (holding allegation that plaintiff clothing retailer lost sales to lower-priced counterfeit garments sold by defendant wholesaler constituted a "competitive injury" for a Lanham Act trademark infringement claim); and *United Magazine Co., Inc. v. Curtis Circulation Co.*, 279 Fed. Appx. 14, 17–18, 2008-1 Trade Cas. (CCH) ¶ 76088 (2d Cir. 2008) (holding plaintiff wholesaler lacked standing to bring claim against national distributor for violation of Robinson—Patman Price Discrimination Act based on defendant distributor's alleged policy favoring plaintiff wholesaler's competitor where wholesaler and alleged competitor, although direct competitors for some bid contracts, were not in head-to-head competition for the subject bid, such that the alleged price discrimination did not substantially affect competition between the two competitors).

The court found the pleading insufficient because it failed to allege that the mismarking had prevented or frustrated defendant's efforts to enter the market and that defendant had not alleged sufficient facts making it plausible to find that the alleged mismarking resulted a competitive injury.[21]

Similarly, in *Greene v. Ab Coaster Holdings, Inc.*,[22] an Ohio court granted a motion to dismiss a false marking claim, rejecting claims that Greene had to incur the expense of reviewing the patents identified falsely on AB Coaster's products. These expenses did not actually deter Greene from

[20] *Fisher-Price, Inc. v. Kids II, Inc.*, 2011 WL 6409665, *9 (W.D. N.Y. 2011).

[21] *Fisher-Price, Inc. v. Kids II, Inc.*, 2011 WL 6409665, *10 (W.D. N.Y. 2011).

[22] *Greene v. Ab Coaster Holdings, Inc.*, 2012 WL 4442749 (S.D. Ohio 2012).

competing.[23] Further, Greene's pleading that it was discouraged from entering the marketplace due to the mismarking could not support "competitive injury" because, in fact, Greene *did* enter the marketplace with alleged counterfeit Ab Coaster exercise products.[24]

A Colorado court in *Two Moms and a Toy, LLC v. Intl Playthings, LLC*[25] ruled that Two Moms could not satisfy the competitive injury element where (a) it did not compete with defendant,[26] and (b) it had not alleged an *actual* competitive injury: "it has only asserted that it *could* lose or that it *could* have already lost potential licensees."[27] The court noted that several other courts had required (that the complaint plead) competition between the parties to support an assertion of competitive injury. The court also distinguished *Fasteners for Retail* on the basis that there, the parties were direct competitors in manufacturing.[28]

Presumption of Competitive Injury. Courts are divided on whether a presumption of "competitive injury" can arise under suitable conditions. A Washington court in *Ira Green, Inc. v. J.L. Darling Corp.* noted that "as previously interpreted in the context of a Lanham Act claim, the court imposes a general presumption of a competitive injury whenever the defendant and the plaintiff are direct competitors and defendant's misrepresentation has a tendency to mislead consumers."[29] An Oregon court noted that the presumption is

---

[23]*Greene v. Ab Coaster Holdings, Inc.*, 2012 WL 4442749, *13 (S.D. Ohio 2012).

[24]*Greene v. Ab Coaster Holdings, Inc.*, 2012 WL 4442749, *14 (S.D. Ohio 2012).

[25]*Two Moms and a Toy, LLC v. International Playthings, LLC*, 2012 WL 4510686, *3-4 (D. Colo. 2012).

[26]The *Two Moms* court noted Tenth Circuit authority that "competitive injury" under the Lanham Act requires a plaintiff to be a competitor of defendant for there to be competitive injury. *Two Moms and a Toy, LLC v. International Playthings, LLC*, 2012 WL 4510686, *3 (D. Colo. 2012) citing *Stanfield v. Osborne Industries, Inc.*, 52 F.3d 867, 873, 34 U.S.P.Q.2d 1456 (10th Cir. 1995). Accord, *Stauffer v. Brooks Bros., Inc.*, 2012 WL 6621374, *4 (S.D. N.Y. 2012).

[27]*Two Moms and a Toy, LLC v. International Playthings, LLC*, 2012 WL 4510686, *4 (D. Colo. 2012).

[28]*Two Moms and a Toy, LLC v. International Playthings, LLC*, 2012 WL 4510686, *3 n.5 (D. Colo. 2012).

[29]*Ira Green, Inc. v. J.L. Darling Corp.*, 2011 WL 6218146, *4 (W.D. Wash. 2011), citing *TrafficSchool.com, Inc. v. Edriver Inc.*, 653 F.3d 820,

rebuttable.[30] A Maryland court in *Introsan Dental Prods., Inc. v. Dentsply Tulsa Dental, LLC* approached the issue of a presumption, provided the plaintiff and defendant are competitors. However, no such relationship existed in that particular case.[31]

In contrast, the *Introsan* court ruled that even when the adverse parties are competitors, that fact alone may be insufficient to plausibly plead that the alleged mismarking resulted in a competitive injury.[32] Further, a Texas court in *WE-Flex* rejected the presumption of competitive injury, stating:

> FN 46. * * * The fact that the parties are in competition and may suffer an injury is not enough to satisfy the new statutory requirement; an injury is necessary.[33]

§ 9:7 Standing to sue for false marking

Even before the AIA enactment, various district courts had sought to limit *qui tam* litigation on the basis of lack of standing.[1] New subsection (b) changes the standing from "any person" to "[a] person who has suffered competitive injury as a result of a violation [of Section 292]."

Courts apply distinct kinds of "standing," namely, Constitutional (Article III) standing,[2] a judicially-imposed pruden-

---

99 U.S.P.Q.2d 1628, 2011-2 Trade Cas. (CCH) ¶ 77637 (9th Cir. 2011).

[30] *RB Rubber Products, Inc. v. ECORE Intern., Inc.*, 2012 WL 4068557, *9 (D. Or. 2012).

[31] *Introsan Dental Products, Inc. v. Dentsply Tulsa Dental, LLC*, 2012 WL 3011830, *4 (D. Md. 2012) (rejecting presumption due to absence of pleading facts that render it plausible that defendant could be considered a competitor of plaintiff).

[32] *Introsan Dental Products, Inc. v. Dentsply Tulsa Dental, LLC*, 2012 WL 3011830, *5 (D. Md. 2012).

[33] *We-Flex, LLC v. NBSP, Inc.*, 2012 WL 1440439, *7 n.46 (S.D. Tex. 2012).

[Section 9:7]

[1] *Stauffer v. Brooks Bros., Inc.*, 615 F. Supp. 2d 248, 254 (S.D. N.Y. 2009), judgment rev'd, 619 F.3d 1321, 96 U.S.P.Q.2d 1304 (Fed. Cir. 2010); *FLFMC, LLC v. Wham-O, Inc., United States v. WHAM-O, Inc.*, 2010 WL 3156162 (W.D. Pa. 2010), abrogated 444 Fed.Appx. 447.

[2] "Article III imposes constitutional standing, an 'irreducible [ ] minimum' requirement to sue in federal court, consisting of an injury-in-fact that is fairly traceable to an act of the defendant and that is likely redressed by a favorable judicial decision. *Lujan v. Defenders of Wildlife*, 504 U.S. 555, 560–61, 112 S. Ct. 2130, 119 L. Ed. 2d 351, 34 Env't. Rep.

tial standing,[3] and statutory standing.[4] In *Advanced Cartridge Technologies, LLC v. Lexmark Intl*, plaintiff "ACT" was one of many companies created by the same individual who invents and patents toner cartridge technology, including replacement computer chips. ACT acquired some patents and sued Lexmark for patent infringement and for false marking a few weeks after the acquisition. Dismissing the false marking claims, the court ruled that ACT had failed to plead Article III standing: "A plaintiff's initial obligation is to plead facts that confer Article III standing, beginning with an injury in fact that is 'concrete and particularized.' "[5]

Regarding prudential standing, the court explained that a claim for false marking should meet the same prudential standing requirement as unfair competition and anti-competitive acts:

> . . . Nothing in the America Invents Act "expressly negates" the prudential standing requirement, which therefore applies in some form. * * * For unfair competition and anti-competitive behavior, prudential standing serves mainly to deny a plaintiff standing to sue for a speculative or remote

---

Cas. (BNA) 1785, 22 Envtl. L. Rep. 20913 (1992)." *Advanced Cartridge Technologies, LLC v. Lexmark Intern., Inc.*, 2011 WL 6719725, *2 (M.D. Fla. 2011).

[3]"The judiciary imposes prudential standing, a limit to federal jurisdiction that preserves the 'properly limited[ ] role of the courts in a democratic society.' *Bennett v. Spear*, 520 U.S. 154, 162, 117 S. Ct. 1154, 137 L. Ed. 2d 281, 44 Env't. Rep. Cas. (BNA) 1161, 27 Envtl. L. Rep. 20824 (1997)." *Advanced Cartridge Technologies, LLC v. Lexmark Intern., Inc.*, 2011 WL 6719725, *2 (M.D. Fla. 2011).

[4]One court explained statutory standing as follows: "Congress can eliminate prudential standing (although prudential standing "applies [to a statute] unless it is expressly negated," 520 U.S. at 163), and, conversely, Congress can impose a requirement of statutory standing, a stricter standing requirement that is analogous to, and not neatly distinguishable from, the injury element of a legal claim. *Roberts v. Hamer*, 655 F.3d 578, 580–81 (6th Cir. 2011); *Alliance For Environmental Renewal, Inc. v. Pyramid Crossgates Co.*, 436 F.3d 82, 85–87, 61 Env't. Rep. Cas. (BNA) 1983 (2d Cir. 2006); *Abecassis v. Wyatt*, 704 F. Supp. 2d 623, 645 (S.D. Tex. 2010); *see also* William A. Fletcher, *The Structure of Standing,* 98 Yale L.J. 221 (1988)." *Advanced Cartridge Technologies, LLC v. Lexmark Intern., Inc.*, 2011 WL 6719725, *2 (M.D. Fla. 2011).

[5]*Advanced Cartridge Technologies, LLC v. Lexmark Intern., Inc.*, 2011 WL 6719725, *3 (M.D. Fla. 2011), citing *Lujan v. Defenders of Wildlife*, 504 U.S. 555, 560–61, 112 S. Ct. 2130, 119 L. Ed. 2d 351, 34 Env't. Rep. Cas. (BNA) 1785, 22 Envtl. L. Rep. 20913 (1992); *Dermer v. Miami-Dade County*, 599 F.3d 1217, 1220 (11th Cir. 2010); and *El Paso Natural Gas Co. v. F.E.R.C.*, 50 F.3d 23, 28, 134 O.G.R. 680 (D.C. Cir. 1995).

harm. *Natural Answers, Inc. v. SmithKline Beecham Corp.*, 529 F.3d 1325, 1330–32 (11th Cir. 2008) (false advertising); *Associated General Contractors of Cal., Inc. v. Cal. State Council of Carpenters,* 459 U.S. 519, 532–45, 103 S.Ct. 897, 74 L.Ed.2d 723 (1983) (antitrust); *Florida Seed Co., Inc. v. Monsanto Co.,* 105 F.3d 1372, 1374 (11th Cir. 1997) (same). A claim for false marking invites the same prudential limitation.[6]

The absence of a competitive injury "strongly disfavors" prudential standing, and a failure to compete directly with the defendant "remains a strong reason to deny prudential standing."[7] In this case, ACT lacked Article III standing and incurred no judicially cognizable injury.

As explained in the section *supra*, courts have determined the sufficiency of pleadings as to "competitive injury." Essentially the same question can be asked in the context whether the plaintiff pleaded injury in fact. Thus, in *Rogers v. Conair Corp.*,[8] defendant moved for judgment on the pleadings, arguing that Plaintiff had failed to allege the required competitive injury. The court addressed this from a standing perspective and explained that while Rogers pleaded loss of retail shelf space and sales, for example, no facts established a plausible causal connection between that loss and defendant's marking practices. The court explained the deficiency as follows:

> Plaintiff alleges that he "sells hair accessories in the Eastern District of Pennsylvania and elsewhere and is a competitor and licensor of products within the hair accessory marketplace."[FN33] He further alleges: "In marking its unpatented products with words or phrases claiming that its hair accessories are subject to pending patent or are patented, Conair has stifled competition, has acted for the purpose of deceiving the public and the citizens of the United States, and has made it more difficult for competitors (including Plaintiff) to obtain retail shelf space and sales for their competing products."[FN34] Finally, he alleges: "as a direct and proximate result of Conair's conduct, Plaintiff Mr. Rogers has suffered economic damages in the form of lost sales and competitive

---

[6]*Advanced Cartridge Technologies, LLC v. Lexmark Intern., Inc.*, 2011 WL 6719725, *3 (M.D. Fla. 2011).

[7]*Advanced Cartridge Technologies, LLC v. Lexmark Intern., Inc.*, 2011 WL 6719725, *4 (M.D. Fla. 2011). The court suggested that a cartridge re-manufacturer attempting to design and sell a toner cartridge that competes directly with a falsely marked Lexmark toner cartridge is perhaps a proper plaintiff. *Advanced Cartridge Technologies, LLC v. Lexmark Intern., Inc.*, 2011 WL 6719725, *5 (M.D. Fla. 2011).

[8]*Rogers v. Conair Corp.*, 2012 WL 1443905 (E.D. Pa. 2012).

disadvantage."FN35 These are the only allegations of the Complaint which support Plaintiff's claim that he has suffered a competitive injury.

FN33. Compl. at ¶ 3.

FN34. Compl. at ¶ 16.

FN35. Compl. at ¶ 17.

To establish standing under the Amendment, Plaintiff must allege a tangible economic loss caused by the illegal competitive means (i.e., the false patent marking).FN36 The Court agrees with Defendant that the Complaint "fails to allege any actual competitive injury to Rogers resulting from Conair's marking practices that goes beyond mere speculation and conclusory statements."FN37 While Plaintiff sets forth the legal conclusion that Conair's false marking practices led to limited shelf space for his products and loss of sales, he alleges no facts from which the Court can find a plausible causal connection between any difficulty Plaintiff experienced in obtaining retail shelf space or selling his product and Conair's marking practices.FN38 Accordingly, the Court finds that Plaintiff has failed to allege a competitive injury sufficient to establish standing to sue under the Amendment.

FN36. While the Third Circuit has not yet defined "competitive injury" in the patent marking context, this Court agrees with other district courts which have so interpreted the term. *See Advanced Cartridge Technologies, LLC v. Lexmark Intern., Inc.*, 2011 WL 6719725, *2, 4 (M.D. Fla. 2011), *Fisher-Price, Inc. v. Kids II, Inc.*, 2011 WL 6409665, *9 (W.D. N.Y. 2011).

FN37. Doc, No. 84 at 7.

FN38. *See Fisher-Price, Inc. v. Kids II, Inc.*, 2011 WL 6409665, *9-10 (W.D. N.Y. 2011) (finding competitor did not adequately allege that false markings had deterred or discouraged it from manufacturing or marketing competing products in the relevant market).

Without discussing different types of standing, in *Mikitiyanskiy v. Rowpar Pharma, Inc.,* a New York court dismissed a case for lack of standing and for plaintiff's inability to allege plausibly a violation of Section 282 after the AIA was enacted.[9]

§ 9:8 Standing—Declaratory judgment actions for no false marking

One party accused of false patent marking sought a declaratory judgment that no false marking violation oc-

[9]*Mikityanskiy v. Rowpar Pharmaceuticals, Inc.*, 2011 WL 6014216 (S.D. N.Y. 2011).

curred in *Adirondack Cookie Co., Inc. v. Monaco Baking Co.* Specifically, the plaintiff sought a declaration that its patent marking of the product in question did not give rise to liability under the "False Marking Statute" and that defendant lacked standing to bring a 35 U.S.C. § 292 claim against plaintiff because defendant had not suffered a competitive injury under § 292 as amended. The court ruled that even though defendant sent letters to plaintiff "discussing possible legal issues,"[1] the complaint failed to present an actual justiciable controversy, and the court lacked jurisdiction. Moreover, the court viewed the action as seeking a ruling on an anticipatory defense—an alleged lack of competitive injury. Even if the court had subject matter jurisdiction, it would decline to exercise it for that reason:

> Moreover, Plaintiff commenced this action seeking a declaration that Defendant did not suffer a competitive injury due to Plaintiff's actions. Essentially, Plaintiff is raising a defense to a claim that it anticipates Defendant will possibly bring at some unknown time in the future. As courts have repeatedly recognized, " '[t]he anticipation of defenses is not ordinarily a proper use of the declaratory judgment procedure,' " as " '[i]t deprives the plaintiff of his traditional choice of forum and timing, and it provokes a disorderly race to the courthouse.' " *Hanes Corp. v. Millard,* 531 F.2d 585, 592—93 (D.C.Cir.1976), *superceded by statute on other grounds; see also BASF Corp. v. Symington,* 50 F.3d 555, 559 (8th Cir.1995). As such, "numerous courts have refused to grant declaratory relief to a party who has come to court only to assert an anticipatory defense." *Veoh Networks, Inc. v. UMG Recordings, Inc.,* 522 F.Supp.2d 1265, 1271 (S.D.Cal.2007) (citing cases). Plaintiff is clearly asking the Court to rule on a defense it would present if Defendant ever brought suit under the False Marking Statute.
>
> Viewed collectively, the various considerations that guide the Court's exercise of its Declaratory Judgment Act discretion weigh in favor of denying relief in this case; and, therefore, the Court grants Defendant's motion to dismiss on this alternative basis.[2]

§ 9:9 Constitutional challenges to AIA § 16(b)

Prior to enactment of the AIA, some defendants had successfully urged that *qui tam* litigation under § 292 violated

---

[Section 9:8]

[1] *Adirondack Cookie Co. Inc. v. Monaco Baking Co.*, 2012 WL 1640565, *7 (N.D. N.Y. 2012).

[2] *Adirondack Cookie Co. Inc. v. Monaco Baking Co.*, 2012 WL 1640565, *8 (N.D. N.Y. 2012).

the Take Care Clause because the delegation of prosecutorial authority to private citizens lacked the "sufficient control" required to be given to the Executive Branch to fulfill its duties.[1] Most courts, however, rejected this attack.[2]

After the AIA was enacted, *qui tam* relators—particularly ones who had already filed suit—challenged the retroactive aspect of AIA § 16(b) on several constitutional grounds. Courts have rejected arguments that the retroactive effect of AIA § 16(b) in abolishing *qui tam* actions for false marking violates the Fifth Amendment,[3] and particularly its Due Process Clause[4] and its Takings Clause,[5] the Take Care Clause

---

[Section 9:9]

[1]*Rogers v. Tristar Products, Inc.*, 793 F. Supp. 2d 711, 99 U.S.P.Q.2d 1438 (E.D. Pa. 2011), decision vacated, appeal dismissed, 449 Fed. Appx. 921 (Fed. Cir. 2011); *Unique Product Solutions, Ltd. v. Hy-Grade Valve, Inc.*, 765 F. Supp. 2d 997, 98 U.S.P.Q.2d 1337 (N.D. Ohio 2011), reconsideration granted, order vacated, 813 F. Supp. 2d 854 (N.D. Ohio 2011), vacated and remanded, 462 Fed. Appx. 967 (Fed. Cir. 2012).

[2]See *Hollander v. Ranbaxy Laboratories Inc.*, 804 F. Supp. 2d 344 (E.D. Pa. 2011) (discussing cases); *Emmert Second Ltd. Partnership v. Marshalltown Co.*, 2011 WL 4025872 (W.D. Okla. 2011) (collecting cases).

[3]U.S. Constitution, Amend. V provides: "No person shall be held to answer for a capital, or otherwise infamous crime, unless on a presentment or indictment of a Grand Jury, except in cases arising in the land or naval forces, or in the Militia, when in actual service in time of War or public danger; nor shall any person be subject for the same offense to be twice put in jeopardy of life or limb; nor shall be compelled in any criminal case to be a witness against himself, nor be deprived of life, liberty, or property, without due process of law; nor shall private property be taken for public use, without just compensation."

[4]Due Process Clause: *Brooks v. Dunlop Mfg. Inc.*, 702 F.3d 624, 2012 WL 6200227 (Fed. Cir. 2012); *Rogers v. Tristar Products, Inc.*, 102 U.S.P.Q.2d 1722, 2012 WL 1660604, *3 (Fed. Cir. 2012); *Brule Research Associates Team, L.L.C. v. A.O. Smith Corp.*, 2012 WL 2087345 (E.D. Wis. 2012); *Cloverleaf Golf Course, Inc. v. Bayer Cropscience LP*, 2012 WL 3990735 (M.D. N.C. 2012); *Rogers v. Conair Corp.*, 2012 WL 1443905 (E.D. Pa. 2012); *U.S. ex rel. Heathcote Holdings Corp., Inc. v. Suncast Corp.*, 2012 WL 3042898 (N.D. Ill. 2012); *Seirus Innovative Accessories, Inc. v. Cabela's Inc.*, 100 U.S.P.Q.2d 1953, 2011 WL 6400630 (S.D. Cal. 2011); *Brooks v. Dunlop Mfg. Inc.*, 2011 WL 6140912 (N.D. Cal. 2011); *Public Patent Foundations Inc. v. McNeil-PPC, Inc.*, 2012 WL 527198 (S.D. N.Y. 2012); *Cloverleaf Golf Course, Inc. v. FMC Corp.*, 863 F. Supp. 2d 768 (S.D. Ill. 2012); *Brooks v. Dunlop Mfg. Inc.*, 2011 WL 6140912, *4 (N.D. Cal. 2011).

[5]Takings Clause: *Brooks v. Dunlop Mfg. Inc.*, 702 F.3d 624, 2012 WL 6200227 (Fed. Cir. 2012); *Rogers v. Tristar Products, Inc.*, 102 U.S.P.Q.2d 1722, 2012 WL 1660604, *2 (Fed. Cir. 2012); *Brule Research Associates Team, L.L.C. v. A.O. Smith Corp.*, 2012 WL 2087345 (E.D. Wis. 2012);

of Art. II, § 3,[6] the Appointments Clause (Art. II, § 2)[7] and the Patent Clause (Art. I, § 8, clause 8).[8] Another rejected attack alleged that the retroactivity provision usurps the President's pardon power (U.S. Const. Art. II, cl. 1) and thus violates the separation of powers.[9]

The Federal Circuit has rejected various constitutional attacks on the AIA provisions which retroactively remove standing in false marking *qui tam* actions. Recently, the Court remarked:

> In September 2011, Congress enacted the Leahy-Smith America Invents Act (AIA), which, among other changes, eliminated standing in false marking cases for third parties that have not suffered a competitive injury as a result of the false marking. The change was applied retroactively to pending false marking cases. As a result of the changes enacted by the AIA, the district court held that PubPat no longer had standing to pursue this case and dismissed the action.
>
> ***
>
> In [*Brooks v. Dunlop Mfg. Inc.*, 702 F.3d 624 (Fed. Cir. 2012)], this court held that Congress's retroactive application of the false marking provision of the AIA does not violate the Due Process Clause or the Intellectual Property Clause of the Constitution. *Brooks*, 702 F.3d at 625-26. This court has also held that the AIA's change to the false marking provision "appl[ies] to all cases, without exception, that are pending on, or commenced on or after, the date of the enactment" of the AIA. *Hall v. Bed Bath & Beyond, Inc.*, 705 F.3d 1357, 1373 (Fed. Cir. 2013) (quoting AIA, Pub. L. No. 112-29, § 16(b)(4), 125

Cloverleaf Golf Course, Inc. v. Bayer Cropscience LP, 2012 WL 3990735 (M.D. N.C. 2012); *Cloverleaf Golf Course, Inc. v. FMC Corp.*, 863 F. Supp. 2d 768 (S.D. Ill. 2012); *Slack v. Bon Aqua Intern., Inc.*, 2012 WL 1957589 (M.D. N.C. 2012), report and recommendation adopted, 2012 WL 2428255 (M.D. N.C. 2012); *Rogers v. Conair Corp.*, 2012 WL 1443905 (E.D. Pa. 2012); *Brooks v. Dunlop Mfg. Inc.*, 2011 WL 6140912, *5-6 (N.D. Cal. 2011); *Seirus Innovative Accessories, Inc. v. Cabela's Inc.*, 100 U.S.P.Q.2d 1953, 2011 WL 6400630 (S.D. Cal. 2011).

[6]"[The President] shall take Care that the Laws be faithfully executed . . . ." *FLFMC, LLC v. Wham-O, Inc.*, 444 Fed. Appx. 447, 100 U.S.P.Q.2d 1857 (Fed. Cir. 2011) (noting but not discussing the issue).

[7]*FLFMC, LLC v. Wham-O, Inc.*, 444 Fed. Appx. 447, 100 U.S.P.Q.2d 1857 (Fed. Cir. 2011) (noting but not discussing the issue).

[8]*Cloverleaf Golf Course, Inc. v. Bayer Cropscience LP*, 2012 WL 3990735 (M.D. N.C. 2012); *Cloverleaf Golf Course, Inc. v. FMC Corp.*, 863 F. Supp. 2d 768 (S.D. Ill. 2012).

[9]*Stauffer v. Brooks Bros., Inc.*, 2012 WL 6621374 (S.D. N.Y. 2012).

Stat. 284, 329 (2011)).[10]

Plaintiffs are not entitled to dismiss their *qui tam* claims without prejudice so that they might be reinstated in the event that a future suit against the United States in the Court of Federal Claims succeeds in proving that the retroactive effect of AIA § 16(b) is unconstitutional.[11]

§ 9:10 Preemption of state causes of action

False patent marking can be similar to various state causes of action, and generally courts have found no preemption of those other causes. In *Sukumar v. Nautilus, Inc.,*[1] Sukumar pleaded unfair/unlawful business practices under a California unfair competition law,[2] false advertising under the California false advertising law,[3] and unfair competition in violation of the Washington State Consumer Protection Act.[4] Rejecting claims of federal preemption, the court observed first that the America Invents Act contains no express preemption provision.[5] Second, the court ruled that the AIA does not show that Congress intended to occupy the field of false marking law completely, and there was no "field preemption."[6] Third, the court found no "conflict preemption."[7]

Even so, the patent law *does* preempt certain "claims of liability for publicizing a patent in the marketplace unless the

---

[10]*Public Patent Foundation, Inc. v McNeil-PPC, Inc. v. United States*, appeal no 12-1274, slip opin. at 2-3 (Fed. Cir. May 3, 2013) (non-precedential), pet'n. for cert. filed Aug. 1, 2013 (S.Ct.).

[11]*Hollander v. Ortho-McNeil-Janssen Pharmaceuticals, Inc.*, 2012 WL 85437 (E.D. Pa. 2012).

[Section 9:10]

[1]*Sukumar v. Nautilus, Inc.*, 829 F. Supp. 2d 386, 390 (W.D. Va. 2011).

[2]Cal. Bus. & Prof. Code 17200 to 17209 (West 2008).

[3]Cal. Bus. & Prof. Code 17500 (West 2008).

[4]Wash. Rev. Code. § 19.86.020 (2010).

[5]*Sukumar v. Nautilus, Inc.*, 829 F. Supp. 2d 386, 393, 398 (W.D. Va. 2011).

[6]*Sukumar v. Nautilus, Inc.*, 829 F. Supp. 2d 386, 393–96 (W.D. Va. 2011).

[7]*Sukumar v. Nautilus, Inc.*, 829 F. Supp. 2d 386, 396–99 (W.D. Va. 2011).

plaintiff can show that the patentholder acted in bad faith."[8] In *Sukumar*, however, the amended complaint adequately alleged bad faith on the part of the defendant in its patent marking.

---

[8]*Sukumar v. Nautilus, Inc.*, 829 F. Supp. 2d 386, 399 (W.D. Va. 2011), citing *Hunter Douglas, Inc. v. Harmonic Design, Inc.*, 153 F.3d 1318, 47 U.S.P.Q.2d 1769 (Fed. Cir. 1998) (overruled on other grounds by, Midwest Industries, Inc. v. Karavan Trailers, Inc., 175 F.3d 1356, 1359, 50 U.S.P.Q.2d 1672 (Fed. Cir. 1999)) and *Spotless Enterprises, Inc. v. Carlisle Plastics, Inc.*, 56 F. Supp. 2d 274, 284–85, 1999-2 Trade Cas. (CCH) ¶ 72620 (E.D. N.Y. 1999) ("[Federal Circuit cases] make it abundantly clear that state unfair competition claims based on a patentholder's good faith publication of his patent rights . . . cannot be successful").

Chapter 10

Enhanced Damages and Advice of Counsel

AIA § 17
35 U.S.C.A. § 298

§ 10:1 Background to new 35 U.S.C. § 298

Chapter 29 of the patent statute provides for damages, including enhanced damages. The previous statute does not explain when enhanced damages should be awarded and leaves this to the courts:

> **§ 284. Damages.**
>
> Upon finding for the claimant the court shall award the claimant damages adequate to compensate for the infringement but in no event less than a reasonable royalty for the use made of the invention by the infringer, together with interest and costs as fixed by the court.
>
> When the damages are not found by a jury, the court shall assess them. In either event the court may increase the damages up to three times the amount found or assessed. Increased damages under this paragraph shall not apply to provisional rights under section 154(d) of this title.

Courts determined that an award of increased damages

requires a showing of willful infringement. The award does not follow automatically, but a finding of willfulness *permits* enhanced damages to be awarded. The award is discretionary. "Trial courts have had statutory discretion to enhance damages for patent infringement since 1836."[1]

Whether an infringer acted willfully raises questions of the state of mind, and accused infringers seek to establish that they acted in good faith. To establish good faith, accused infringers turn to exculpatory opinions of counsel and assert reasonable reliance on advice from counsel.[2]

Conversely, plaintiffs have cited the failure to obtain an opinion of counsel (or acting contrary to the presumed advice of counsel) as evidence of intent to infringe willfully. Reliance on whether or how an alleged infringer was counseled, however, raises sensitive questions regarding the attorney-client privilege, and courts have had to address this issue.

In 1983, the Federal Circuit in *Underwater Devices Inc. v. Morrison-Knudsen Co., Inc.*[3] sustained a (fact) finding of willful infringement. The court also ruled that a potential infringer on actual notice of another's patent rights has an affirmative duty to exercise due care to ascertain whether he is infringing, including the duty to obtain competent legal advice from counsel.[4] In this case, the opinion was ruled to be inadequate, and "appellant clearly failed to exercise its affirmative duty . . . [T]he district court did not abuse its discretion in awarding treble damages."[5]

In 1985, the Federal Circuit in *Shatterproof Glass Corp. v.*

[Section 10:1]

[1] *In re Seagate Technology, LLC*, 497 F.3d 1360, 1368 n.3, 83 U.S.P.Q.2d 1865 (Fed. Cir. 2007).

[2] *In re Seagate Technology, LLC*, 497 F.3d 1360, 1369, 83 U.S.P.Q.2d 1865 (Fed. Cir. 2007).

[3] *Underwater Devices Inc. v. Morrison-Knudsen Co., Inc.*, 717 F.2d 1380, 219 U.S.P.Q. 569 (Fed. Cir. 1983) (overruled by, In re Seagate Technology, LLC, 497 F.3d 1360, 83 U.S.P.Q.2d 1865 (Fed. Cir. 2007)).

[4] *Underwater Devices Inc. v. Morrison-Knudsen Co., Inc.*, 717 F.2d 1380, 1389–90, 219 U.S.P.Q. 569 (Fed. Cir. 1983) (overruled by, In re Seagate Technology, LLC, 497 F.3d 1360, 83 U.S.P.Q.2d 1865 (Fed. Cir. 2007)).

[5] *Underwater Devices Inc. v. Morrison-Knudsen Co., Inc.*, 717 F.2d 1380, 1390, 219 U.S.P.Q. 569 (Fed. Cir. 1983) (overruled by, In re Seagate Technology, LLC, 497 F.3d 1360, 83 U.S.P.Q.2d 1865 (Fed. Cir. 2007)).

Libbey-Owens Ford Co.[6] ruled that a record devoid of any opinion of counsel could support negative inferences but nevertheless did not establish an abuse of discretion by the district court in declining to increase damages for willful infringement.

In 2004, an *en banc* Federal Circuit addressed the adverse inference rule in *Knorr-Bremse Systeme Fuer Nutzfahrzeuge GmbH v. Dana Corp.* and declared that "no adverse inference shall arise from invocation of the attorney-client and/or work product privilege."[7] In other words, a fact-finder could not infer that if the alleged infringer asserted the privilege, this is evidence that the advice given by counsel was against the client.

In 2007, the Federal Circuit in *In re Seagate Technology*[8] declared *en banc* that there is no duty to seek an opinion of counsel:

> Accordingly, we overrule the standard set out in *Underwater Devices*[9] and hold that proof of willful infringement permitting enhanced damages requires at least a showing of objective recklessness. Because we abandon the affirmative duty of due care, we also reemphasize that there is no affirmative obligation to obtain opinion of counsel.[10]

Whether the infringer sought an opinion of counsel had to be excluded from consideration in determining willfulness remained unsettled. In 2008, the Federal Circuit ruled in *Broadcom Corp. v. Qualcomm Inc.* that it was proper for a district court to instruct a jury that it may consider all circumstances, including whether Qualcomm obtained the advice of counsel, on the issue of willfulness.[11]

Turning to inducement of patent infringement, accused

---

[6]*Shatterproof Glass Corp. v. Libbey-Owens Ford Co.*, 758 F.2d 613, 628–29, 225 U.S.P.Q. 634 (Fed. Cir. 1985).

[7]*Knorr-Bremse Systeme Fuer Nutzfahrzeuge GmbH v. Dana Corp.*, 383 F.3d 1337, 1347, 72 U.S.P.Q.2d 1560, 65 Fed. R. Evid. Serv. 365 (Fed. Cir. 2004).

[8]*In re Seagate Technology, LLC*, 497 F.3d 1360, 83 U.S.P.Q.2d 1865 (Fed. Cir. 2007).

[9]*Underwater Devices Inc. v. Morrison-Knudsen Co., Inc.*, 717 F.2d 1380, 219 U.S.P.Q. 569 (Fed. Cir. 1983) (overruled by, In re Seagate Technology, LLC, 497 F.3d 1360, 83 U.S.P.Q.2d 1865 (Fed. Cir. 2007)).

[10]*In re Seagate Technology, LLC*, 497 F.3d 1360, 1371, 83 U.S.P.Q.2d 1865 (Fed. Cir. 2007).

[11]*Broadcom Corp. v. Qualcomm Inc.*, 543 F.3d 683, 699, 88 U.S.P.Q.2d 1641 (Fed. Cir. 2008).

"inducers" raise an argument similar to the good faith argument against willful infringement, namely, that they did not reasonably believe their actions would cause direct infringement.

§ 10:2 Congressional intent re advice of counsel[1]

The House Report explains that Congress specifically intended to uphold the attorney-client privilege and abrogate the Federal Circuit's decision in *Broadcom Corp. v. Qualcomm Inc.*:[2]

> *Advice of Counsel*
>
> The Act includes a new provision that bars courts and juries from drawing an adverse inference from an accused infringer's failure to obtain opinion of counsel as to infringement or his failure to waive privilege and disclose such an opinion. Section 298 of title 35 is designed to protect attorney-client privilege and to reduce pressure on accused infringers to obtain opinions of counsel for litigation purposes. It reflects a policy choice that the probative value of this type of evidence is outweighed by the harm that coercing a waiver of attorney-client privilege inflicts on the attorney-client relationship. Section 298 applies to findings of both willfulness and intent to induce infringement—and thus legislatively abrogates the Federal Circuit's decision in *Broadcom Corp. v. Qualcomm Inc.,* 543 F.3d 683, 699 (Fed. Cir. 2008).
>
> * * *

[Section 10:2]

[1]The Supreme Court cautions against relying on interpretations advanced in legislative statements that are not "anchored in the text of the statute." *Shannon v. U.S.*, 512 U.S. 573, 583, 114 S. Ct. 2419, 129 L. Ed. 2d 459 (1994), stating "[C]ourts have no authority to enforce [a] principl[e] gleaned solely from legislative history that has no statutory reference point." *Shannon,* 512 U.S. at 584, quoting *International Broth. of Elec. Workers, Local Union No. 474, AFL-CIO v. N.L.R.B.*, 814 F.2d 697, 712, 124 L.R.R.M. (BNA) 2993, 106 Lab. Cas. (CCH) P 12256 (D.C. Cir. 1987). The authoritative statement "is the statutory text, not the legislative history." *Exxon Mobil Corp. v. Allapattah Services, Inc.*, 545 U.S. 546, 568, 125 S. Ct. 2611, 162 L. Ed. 2d 502 (2005). However, lower courts have cited the legislative history of the AIA already in recent cases. E.g., *Rogers v. Tristar Products, Inc.*, 102 U.S.P.Q.2d 1722, 2012 WL 1660604, *2 (Fed. Cir. 2012) (non-precedential); *Byrne v. Wood, Herron & Evans, LLP*, 676 F.3d 1024, 1029, 102 U.S.P.Q.2d 1073 (Fed. Cir. 2012) (dissenting opin.).

[2]*Broadcom Corp. v. Qualcomm Inc.*, 543 F.3d 683, 699, 88 U.S.P.Q.2d 1641 (Fed. Cir. 2008)

Section 17. Advice of Counsel.

Section 17 creates a new § 298 of the Patent Act that states that the failure of an infringer to obtain the advice of counsel regarding any allegedly infringed patent, or the failure of the infringer to present such advice to the court or jury, may not be used to prove that the accused infringer willfully infringed the patent or that the infringer intended to induce infringement of the patent.[3]

§ 10:3 AIA provisions re advice of counsel

The America Invents Act in § 17 rejected the rule in *Broadcom* and added the following new provision to Chapter 29 of the patent statute:

New Statute (35 U.S.C. § 298)

§ 298. Advice of counsel

The failure of an infringer to obtain the advice of counsel with respect to any allegedly infringed patent, or the failure of the infringer to present such advice to the court or jury, may not be used to prove that the accused infringer willfully infringed the patent or that the infringer intended to induce infringement of the patent.

§ 10:4 Effective date of AIA provisions re advice of counsel

Congress did not make a specific provision for the effective date of this new provision. As such, the default effective date provision, AIA § 35, must apply. That default provision focuses on patent issuance dates and provides:

SEC. 35. EFFECTIVE DATE.

Except as otherwise provided in this Act, the provisions of this Act shall take effect upon the expiration of the 1-year period beginning on the date of the enactment of this Act and shall apply to any patent issued on or after that effective date.

As originally enacted, AIA § 35 made AIA § 17 applicable to all *patents* granted on or after September 16, 2012 (and inapplicable to patents granted before then). It makes more sense for § 17 to apply to all *civil actions* filed on or after September 16, 2012. Placing restrictions on the failure to obtain or present the advice of counsel on a per patent basis introduces new complexities in patent litigation, where a number of patents are often alleged to be infringed in any given case. Some of these may have issue dates on either

[3]H. R. Rep. No. 112-98, pt. 1, at 53, 80 (2011).

side of September 16, 2012. In such a case, different substantive law would apply to different patents in the same action.

Congress addressed this problem and passed H.R. 6621, a technical corrections bill, on January 1, 2013. Section 1(a) makes 35 U.S.C. § 298 applicable to any civil action commenced on or after the date of enactment of H.R. 6621.[1] While this corrects the problem on a going forward basis, the statute as written does not date back to September 16, 2012 and thus leaves a period of about fifteen (15) months where different versions of the law may apply in the same lawsuit, depending on the issue dates of the patents in suit.

§ 10:5 Discussion of new 35 U.S.C. § 298

New 35 U.S.C. § 298 expresses two prohibitions:

- First, the failure of an alleged infringer to present the advice of counsel as to an asserted patent cannot be used to prove that the alleged infringer acted willfully.
- Second, the failure of an alleged infringer to present the advice of counsel cannot be used to prove that the alleged infringer intended to induce infringement.

The first prohibition abrogates the Federal Circuit's decision in *Broadcom Corp. v. Qualcomm Inc.*, 543 F.3d 683, 699, 88 U.S.P.Q.2d 1641 (Fed. Cir. 2008). The second prohibition may not abrogate prior case law. It could be important alongside the Supreme Court ruling in *Global-Tech Appliances, Inc. v. SEB S.A.*,[1] where the Supreme Court ruled that willful blindness as to the existence of a patent can be used in showing induced infringement. Under the willful blindness test, possession of sufficient suggestions is deemed to be knowledge of the ultimate fact suggested. Courts will have to consider whether willful blindness is shown without being able to rely on adverse inferences from the failure to obtain or present the advice of counsel.

As of December 1, 2012, no federal case had yet mentioned

[Section 10:4]

[1]H.R. 6621 § 1(a) (2013) provides: "(a) Advice of Counsel— Notwithstanding section 35 of the Leahy-Smith America Invents Act (35 U.S.C.A. 1 note), section 298 of title 35, United States Code, shall apply to any civil action commenced on or after the date of the enactment of this Act."

[Section 10:5]

[1]*Global-Tech Appliances, Inc. v. SEB S.A.*, 131 S. Ct. 2060, 179 L. Ed. 2d 1167, 98 U.S.P.Q.2d 1665 (2011).

the new § 298.

Chapter 11

Venue for Review of USPTO Decisions

KeyCite®: Cases and other legal materials listed in KeyCite Scope can be researched through the KeyCite service on Westlaw®. Use KeyCite to check citations for form, parallel references, prior and later history, and comprehensive citator information, including citations to other decisions and secondary materials.

AIA § 9
15 U.S.C.A. § 1071(b)(4)
35 U.S.C.A. §§ 32, 145, 146, 154(b)(4)(A), 293

§ 11:1 Background to the venue changes

Various statutes provide for appellate review of USPTO decisions. Just prior to enactment of the AIA, the patent statute provided that the United States District Court for the District of Columbia is the venue for reviewing USPTO decisions relating to suspension of registered attorneys,[1] instituting civil actions to address the Director's denial of a

---

[Section 11:1]

[1]35 U.S.C.A. § 32 (2006): **"Suspension or Exclusion from Practice.** The Director may, after notice and opportunity for a hearing, suspend or exclude, either generally or in any particular case, from further practice before the Patent and Trademark Office, any person, agent, or attorney shown to be incompetent or disreputable, or guilty of gross misconduct, or who does not comply with the regulations established under section 2 (b)(2)(D) of this title, or who shall, by word, circular, letter, or advertising, with intent to defraud in any manner, deceive, mislead, or threaten any applicant or prospective applicant, or other person having immediate or prospective business before the Office. The reasons for any

patent application,[2] reviewing interference decisions,[3] and

---

such suspension or exclusion shall be duly recorded. The Director shall have the discretion to designate any attorney who is an officer or employee of the United States Patent and Trademark Office to conduct the hearing required by this section. The United States District Court for the District of Columbia, under such conditions and upon such proceedings as it by its rules determines, may review the action of the Director upon the petition of the person so refused recognition or so suspended or excluded."

[2]35 U.S.C.A. § 145 (2006): **Civil action to obtain patent** An applicant dissatisfied with the decision of the Board of Patent Appeals and Interferences in an appeal under section 134 (a) of this title may, unless appeal has been taken to the United States Court of Appeals for the Federal Circuit, have remedy by civil action against the Director in the United States District Court for the District of Columbia if commenced within such time after such decision, not less than sixty days, as the Director appoints. The court may adjudge that such applicant is entitled to receive a patent for his invention, as specified in any of his claims involved in the decision of the Board of Patent Appeals and Interferences, as the facts in the case may appear and such adjudication shall authorize the Director to issue such patent on compliance with the requirements of law. All the expenses of the proceedings shall be paid by the applicant.

[3]35 U.S.C.A. § 146 (2006): **"Civil action in case of interference.** Any party to an interference dissatisfied with the decision of the Board of Patent Appeals and Interferences on the interference, may have remedy by civil action, if commenced within such time after such decision, not less than sixty days, as the Director appoints or as provided in section 141 of this title, unless he has appealed to the United States Court of Appeals for the Federal Circuit, and such appeal is pending or has been decided. In such suits the record in the Patent and Trademark Office shall be admitted on motion of either party upon the terms and conditions as to costs, expenses, and the further cross-examination of the witnesses as the court imposes, without prejudice to the right of the parties to take further testimony. The testimony and exhibits of the record in the Patent and Trademark Office when admitted shall have the same effect as if originally taken and produced in the suit.

Such suit may be instituted against the party in interest as shown by the records of the Patent and Trademark Office at the time of the decision complained of, but any party in interest may become a party to the action. If there be adverse parties residing in a plurality of districts not embraced within the same state, or an adverse party residing in a foreign country, the United States District Court for the District of Columbia shall have jurisdiction and may issue summons against the adverse parties directed to the marshal of any district in which any adverse party resides. Summons against adverse parties residing in foreign countries may be served by publication or otherwise as the court directs. The Director shall not be a necessary party but he shall be notified of the filing of the suit by the clerk of the court in which it is filed and shall have the right to intervene. Judgment of the court in favor of the right of an applicant to a patent shall authorize the Director to issue such patent on the filing in the Patent and Trademark Office of a certified copy of the judgment and on compliance with the requirements of law."

reviewing decisions relating to patent term adjustments.[4] The statute also provides a venue to hear civil actions against foreign patentees.[5]

Likewise, just prior to enactment of the AIA, the trademark statute fixed the venue for judicial review of decisions of the Trademark Trial and Appeal Board.[6]

Because the USPTO moved out of the District of Columbia

---

[4]35 U.S.C.A. § 154(b)(4)(A) (2006): "**Contents and term of patent; provisional rights.** * * * (b) Adjustment of Patent Term.—* * * (B) * * * (4) **Appeal of patent term adjustment determination.**—(A) An applicant dissatisfied with a determination made by the Director under paragraph (3) shall have remedy by a civil action against the Director filed in the United States District Court for the District of Columbia within 180 days after the grant of the patent. Chapter 7 of title 5 shall apply to such action. Any final judgment resulting in a change to the period of adjustment of the patent term shall be served on the Director, and the Director shall thereafter alter the term of the patent to reflect such change. * * *"

[5]35 U.S.C.A. § 293 (2006): "**Nonresident patentee; service and notice.** Every patentee not residing in the United States may file in the Patent and Trademark Office a written designation stating the name and address of a person residing within the United States on whom may be served process or notice of proceedings affecting the patent or rights thereunder. If the person designated cannot be found at the address given in the last designation, or if no person has been designated, the United States District Court for the District of Columbia shall have jurisdiction and summons shall be served by publication or otherwise as the court directs. The court shall have the same jurisdiction to take any action respecting the patent or rights thereunder that it would have if the patentee were personally within the jurisdiction of the court."

[6]15 U.S.C.A. § 1071(b)(4) (2006): "**Appeal to courts** * * *(b) Civil action; persons entitled to; jurisdiction of court; status of Director; procedure. (1) Whenever a person authorized by subsection (a) of this section to appeal to the United States Court of Appeals for the Federal Circuit is dissatisfied with the decision of the Director or Trademark Trial and Appeal Board, said person may, unless appeal has been taken to said United States Court of Appeals for the Federal Circuit, have remedy by a civil action if commenced within such time after such decision, not less than sixty days, as the Director appoints or as provided in subsection (a) of this section. The court may adjudge that an applicant is entitled to a registration upon the application involved, that a registration involved should be canceled, or such other matter as the issues in the proceeding require, as the facts in the case may appear. Such adjudication shall authorize the Director to take any necessary action, upon compliance with the requirements of law. However, no final judgment shall be entered in favor of an applicant under section 1051 (b) of this title before the mark is registered, if such applicant cannot prevail without establishing constructive use pursuant to section 1057 (c) of this title.

(2) The Director shall not be made a party to an inter partes proceeding under this subsection, but he shall be notified of the filing of

many years ago, venue ought to have been moved also to the district court of the host jurisdiction. Leaving venue in the District Court for the District of Columbia burdened that court unnecessarily.

§ 11:2 Congressional intent re venue changes[1]

According to the House Committee Report, Congress intended that venue of actions addressed to USPTO deci-

---

the complaint by the clerk of the court in which it is filed and shall have the right to intervene in the action.

(3) In any case where there is no adverse party, a copy of the complaint shall be served on the Director, and, unless the court finds the expenses to be unreasonable, all the expenses of the proceeding shall be paid by the party bringing the case, whether the final decision is in favor of such party or not. In suits brought hereunder, the record in the Patent and Trademark Office shall be admitted on motion of any party, upon such terms and conditions as to costs, expenses, and the further cross-examination of the witnesses as the court imposes, without prejudice to the right of any party to take further testimony. The testimony and exhibits of the record in the Patent and Trademark Office, when admitted, shall have the same effect as if originally taken and produced in the suit.

(4) Where there is an adverse party, such suit may be instituted against the party in interest as shown by the records of the Patent and Trademark Office at the time of the decision complained of, but any party in interest may become a party to the action. If there be adverse parties residing in a plurality of districts not embraced within the same State, or an adverse party residing in a foreign country, the United States District Court for the District of Columbia shall have jurisdiction and may issue summons against the adverse parties directed to the marshal of any district in which any adverse party resides. Summons against adverse parties residing in foreign countries may be served by publication or otherwise as the court directs."

[Section 11:2]

[1]The Supreme Court cautions against relying on interpretations advanced in legislative statements that are not "anchored in the text of the statute." *Shannon v. U.S.*, 512 U.S. 573, 583, 114 S. Ct. 2419, 129 L. Ed. 2d 459 (1994), stating "[C]ourts have no authority to enforce [a] principl[e] gleaned solely from legislative history that has no statutory reference point." *Shannon,* 512 U.S. at 584, quoting *International Broth. of Elec. Workers, Local Union No. 474, AFL-CIO v. N.L.R.B.*, 814 F.2d 697, 712, 124 L.R.R.M. (BNA) 2993, 106 Lab. Cas. (CCH) P 12256 (D.C. Cir. 1987). The authoritative statement "is the statutory text, not the legislative history." *Exxon Mobil Corp. v. Allapattah Services, Inc.*, 545 U.S. 546, 568, 125 S. Ct. 2611, 162 L. Ed. 2d 502 (2005). However, lower courts have cited the legislative history of the AIA already in recent cases. E.g., *Rogers v. Tristar Products, Inc.*, 102 U.S.P.Q.2d 1722, 2012 WL 1660604, *2 (Fed. Cir. 2012) (non-precedential); *Byrne v. Wood, Herron & Evans, LLP*, 676 F.3d 1024, 1029, 102 U.S.P.Q.2d 1073 (Fed. Cir. 2012) (dissenting opin.).

sions be the U.S. District Court where the USPTO resides. The House Report states as follows:

> *Venue*
>
> In 1999, as part of the American Inventors Protection Act (AIPA), Congress established that as a general matter the venue of the USPTO is the district where it resides.[FN46] The USPTO currently resides in the Eastern District of Virginia. However, Congress inadvertently failed to make this change uniformly throughout the entire patent statute. As a result, certain sections of the patent statute (and one section of the trademark statute) continue to allow challenges to USPTO decisions to be brought in the District of Columbia, a place where the USPTO has not resided in decades.
>
> FN 46. *See* 35 U.S.C. Sec. 1(b).
>
> Because the USPTO no longer resides in the District of Columbia, the sections that authorize venue for litigation against the USPTO are consistently changed to reflect the venue where the USPTO currently resides.
>
> * * *
>
> *Section 9. Venue.*
>
> The venue for certain district court challenges of USPTO decisions is changed from the District of Columbia to the Eastern District of Virginia, the district where the USPTO resides.[2]

§ 11:3 The AIA amendment to the venue statutes

Section 9 of the America Invents Act provides as follows:

> **SEC. 9. VENUE.—**
>
> (a) TECHNICAL AMENDMENTS RELATING TO VENUE.— Sections 32, 145, 146, 154(b)(4)(A), and 293 of title 35, United States Code, and section 21(b)(4) of the Trademark Act of 1946 (15 U.S.C. 1071(b)(4)), are each amended by striking "United States District Court for the District of Columbia" each place that term appears and inserting "United States District Court for the Eastern District of Virginia".
>
> (b) EFFECTIVE DATE.— The amendments made by this section shall take effect on the date of the enactment of this Act and shall apply to any civil action commenced on or after that date.

§ 11:4 Discussion of venue changes

The America Invents Act in § 9 changes the venue of the federal court reviewing USPTO actions. It strikes "United States District Court for the District of Columbia" and re-

[2] H. R. Rep. No. 112-98, pt. 1, at 49, 77 (2011).

places it with "United States District Court for the Eastern District of Virginia," the district where the USPTO resides.

Although the USPTO will have a number of satellite offices in states other than Virginia, the AIA does not place venue where those satellite offices are located but instead where the USPTO main office is located. This should reduce any risk of inconsistent decisions and promote uniformity among the several offices akin to the way that the U.S. Court of Appeals for the Federal Circuit has appellate jurisdiction over appeals from all U.S. District Courts in patent cases.

This AIA section became effective on September 16, 2011 and applies to all civil actions commenced on or after that date. One civil action involving a patent term extension calculation was filed in the Eastern District of Virginia before that crossover date. Ruling on USPTO Director Kappos' motion to dismiss for lack of jurisdiction, the Virginia court explained that this venue change is prospective only, and the District Court for the District of Columbia has exclusive venue over complaints filed before September 16, 2011. Acting "in the interest of justice," the Virginia court transferred the case to the District of Columbia.[1] Courts have recognized that venue now resides in the district court for the Eastern District of Virginia for district court challenges of USPTO decisions.[2]

[Section 11:4]

[1]*Janssen Pharmaceutica, N.V. v. Kappos*, 844 F. Supp. 2d 707, 101 U.S.P.Q.2d 1924 (E.D. Va. 2012).

[2]See *Kappos v. Hyatt*, 132 S. Ct. 1690, 1694 n.1, 182 L. Ed. 2d 704, 102 U.S.P.Q.2d 1337 (2012); *Alberts v. Kappos*, 917 F. Supp. 2d 94, 104 n.2 (D.D.C. 2013); *SD3, LLC v. Dudas*, 2013 WL 3368873, at *10 n.6 (D.D.C. 2013); *Vosk Intern. Co. v. Zao Gruppa Predpriyatij Ost*, 2012 WL 1033535, at *2-4 (W.D. Wash. 2012) (review of TTAB decision; statute provides supplemental forum which is not exclusive); *Mama Cares Foundation v. Nutriset Societe Par Actions Cimplifiee*, 825 F. Supp. 2d 178, 184 n.2 (D.D.C. 2011).

Chapter 12

Jurisdiction

AIA § 19(a–c)
28 U.S.C.A. §§ 1295, 1338, New § 1454

§ 12:1 Background re jurisdiction

Patents are creatures of federal statute. They have attributes of personal property. 35 U.S.C. § 261 (1st para.). Congress wanted patent litigation to occur in federal courts, and it centralized the appellate review of patent cases in the U.S. Court of Appeals for the Federal Circuit.

The Supreme Court ruling *Holmes Group, Inc. v. Vornado Air Circulation Systems, Inc.*, 535 U.S. 826, 122 S. Ct. 1889, 153 L. Ed. 2d 13, 62 U.S.P.Q.2d 1801 (2002) ruled that the regional courts of appeal have appellate jurisdiction over a case if the case as originally filed did not plead a patent cause of action, regardless of whether one was pleaded by way of counterclaim.

§ 12:2 Congressional intent re jurisdiction statutes[1]

The House Report has two statements about the jurisdic-

[Section 12:2]

[1]The Supreme Court cautions against relying on interpretations advanced in legislative statements that are not "anchored in the text of

tional provisions:

Jurisdictional and procedural matters

a) State court jurisdiction and the US Court of Appeals for the Federal Circuit

The US district courts area [*sic*, are] given original jurisdiction to hear patent cases,[FN57] while the US Court of Appeals for the Federal Circuit adjudicates all patent appeals.[FN58] The Supreme Court ruled in 2002,[FN59] however, that patent counterclaims do not give the Federal Circuit appellate jurisdiction over a case.

The Act clarifies the jurisdiction of the US district courts and stipulates that the US Court of Appeals for the Federal Circuit has jurisdiction over appeals involving compulsory patent counterclaims. The legislative history of this provision, which we reaffirm and adopt as our own, appears in the Committee Report accompanying H.R. 2955 from the 109th Congress,[FN60] which the Committee reported favorably to the House on April 5, 2006.

FN 57. 28 U.S.C. § 1338.

FN 58. 28 U.S.C. § 1295.

FN 59. *Holmes Group, Inc. v. Vornado Air Circulation Systems, Inc.*, 535 U.S. 826, 122 S. Ct. 1889, 153 L. Ed. 2d 13, 62 U.S.P.Q.2d 1801 (2002).

FN 60. H. Rep. 109-405.

* * *

Section 19. Jurisdiction and procedural matters.

Subsection (a) through (d) enact the so-called *Holmes Group* fix (H.R. 2955, 109th Congress), which the House Judiciary Committee reported favorably in 2006. The Committee Report accompanying H.R. 2955 (House Rep. 109-407), which we reaffirm, explains the bill's reasons for abrogating *Holmes Group, Inc. v. Vornado Air Circulation Systems, Inc.*, 535 U.S. 826

---

the statute." *Shannon v. U.S.*, 512 U.S. 573, 583, 114 S. Ct. 2419, 129 L. Ed. 2d 459 (1994), stating "[C]ourts have no authority to enforce [a] principl[e] gleaned solely from legislative history that has no statutory reference point." *Shannon,* 512 U.S. at 584, quoting *International Broth. of Elec. Workers, Local Union No. 474, AFL-CIO v. N.L.R.B.*, 814 F.2d 697, 712, 124 L.R.R.M. (BNA) 2993, 106 Lab. Cas. (CCH) P 12256 (D.C. Cir. 1987). The authoritative statement "is the statutory text, not the legislative history." *Exxon Mobil Corp. v. Allapattah Services, Inc.*, 545 U.S. 546, 568, 125 S. Ct. 2611, 162 L. Ed. 2d 502 (2005). However, lower courts have cited the legislative history of the AIA already in recent cases. E.g., *Rogers v. Tristar Products, Inc.*, 102 U.S.P.Q.2d 1722, 2012 WL 1660604, *2 (Fed. Cir. 2012) (non-precedential); *Byrne v. Wood, Herron & Evans, LLP*, 676 F.3d 1024, 1029, 102 U.S.P.Q.2d 1073 (Fed. Cir. 2012) (dissenting opin.).

(2002), and more fully precluding state court jurisdiction over patent legal claims.

* * *

The changes set forth in Section 19 shall apply to any civil action commenced on or after the date of enactment of the Act.[2]

§ 12:3 AIA provisions re jurisdiction statutes

AIA § 19 amends or adds three jurisdictional provisions and has an effective date provision. AIA § 19(b) amends 28 U.S.C. § 1295(a)(1) concerning Federal Circuit jurisdiction as follows:

Revised 28 U.S.C. § 1295(a)(1)[1]

§ 1295. Jurisdiction of the United States Court of Appeals for the Federal Circuit

(a) The United States Court of Appeals for the Federal Circuit shall have exclusive jurisdiction ~~(1) of an appeal from a final decision of a district court of the United States, the United States District Court for the District of the Canal Zone, the District Court of Guam, the District Court of the Virgin Islands, or the District Court for the Northern Mariana Islands, if the jurisdiction of that court was based, in whole or in part, on section 1338 of this title, except that a case involving a claim arising under any Act of Congress relating to copyrights, exclusive rights in mask works, or trademarks and no other claims under section 1338(a) shall be governed by sections 1291, 1292, and 1294 of this title;~~ (1) of an appeal from a final decision of a district court of the United States, the District Court of Guam, the District Court of the Virgin Islands, or the District Court of the Northern Mariana Islands, in any civil action arising under, or in any civil action in which a party has asserted a compulsory counterclaim arising under, any Act of Congress relating to patents or plant variety protection;

* * *

(4) of an appeal from a decision of ~~(A) the Board of Patent Appeals and Interferences of the United States Patent and Trademark Office with respect to patent applications and interferences, at the instance of an applicant for a patent or any party to a patent interference, and any such appeal shall waive the right of such applicant or party to~~

---

[2]H. R. Rep. No. 112-98, pt. 1, at 54, 80 (2011).

[Section 12:3]

[1]Revised statutes are shown with underscoring for new language and strikethrough for deleted language.

~~proceed under section 145 or 146 of title 35;~~ (A) the Patent Trial and Appeal Board of the United States Patent and Trademark Office with respect to a patent application, derivation proceeding, reexamination, post-grant review, or inter partes review under title 35, at the instance of a party who exercised that party's right to participate in the applicable proceeding before or appeal to the Board, except that an applicant or a party to a derivation proceeding may also have remedy by civil action pursuant to section 145 or 146 of title 35; an appeal under this subparagraph of a decision of the Board with respect to an application or derivation proceeding shall waive the right of such applicant or party to proceed under section 145 or 146 of title 35;

AIA § 19(a) amends 28 U.S.C. § 1338(a) concerning state court jurisdiction:

Revised 28 U.S.C. § 1338(a)[2]

§ 1338. Patents, plant variety protection, copyrights, mask works, designs, trademarks, and unfair competition

(a) The district courts shall have original jurisdiction of any civil action arising under any Act of Congress relating to patents, plant variety protection, copyrights and trademarks. ~~Such jurisdiction shall be exclusive of the courts of the states in patent, plant variety protection and copyright cases.~~ No State court shall have jurisdiction over any claim for relief arising under any Act of Congress relating to patents, plant variety protection, or copyrights. For purposes of this subsection, the term "State" includes any State of the United States, the District of Columbia, the Commonwealth of Puerto Rico, the United States Virgin Islands, American Samoa, Guam, and the Northern Mariana Islands.

AIA § 19(c) adds a new section regarding removal jurisdiction in Title 28, United States Code, Chapter 89:

New 28 U.S.C. § 1454

§ 1454. Patent, plant variety protection, and copyright cases

(a) In General.— A civil action in which any party asserts a claim for relief arising under any Act of Congress relating to patents, plant variety protection, or copyrights may be removed to the district court of the United States for the district and division embracing the place where the action is pending.

(b) Special Rules.— The removal of an action under this

[2]Revised statutes are shown with underscoring for new language and strikethrough for deleted language.

section shall be made in accordance with section 1446, except that if the removal is based solely on this section—

(1) the action may be removed by any party; and

(2) the time limitations contained in section 1446(b) may be extended at any time for cause shown.

(c) CLARIFICATION OF JURISDICTION IN CERTAIN CASES.— The court to which a civil action is removed under this section is not precluded from hearing and determining any claim in the civil action because the State court from which the civil action is removed did not have jurisdiction over that claim.

(d) REMAND.— If a civil action is removed solely under this section, the district court—

(1) shall remand all claims that are neither a basis for removal under subsection (a) nor within the original or supplemental jurisdiction of the district court under any Act of Congress; and

(2) may, under the circumstances specified in section 1367(c), remand any claims within the supplemental jurisdiction of the district court under section 1367.

Regarding the effective date, AIA § 19(e) states as follows:

(e) EFFECTIVE DATE.— The amendments made by this section shall apply to any civil action commenced on or after the date of the enactment of this Act.

§ 12:4 Discussion re AIA changes to jurisdiction statutes

The changes by AIA § 19 regarding jurisdiction reinforce Congress' determination that patent cases, even if they arise by way of compulsory counterclaim, are to be heard by federal courts, and their appeals must be heard exclusively by the U.S. Court of Appeals for the Federal Circuit.[1] Thus, as to counterclaims, the AIA legislatively overruled the rule of *Holmes Group, Inc. v. Vornado Air Circulation Systems, Inc.*, 535 U.S. 826, 122 S. Ct. 1889, 153 L. Ed. 2d 13, 62 U.S.P.Q.2d 1801 (2002) where the claims of patent infringement raised as counterclaims did not confer appellate jurisdiction upon the Federal Circuit but rather regional circuit jurisdiction.

Regarding state court jurisdiction, the amendment to 28

[Section 12:4]

[1]*Serby v. First Alert, Inc.*, 2013 WL 1281561, at *8 n.2 (E.D. N.Y. 2013) (noting Congress' 2011 amendment to 28 U.S.C.A. § 1295(a)(1), which explicitly restored federal jurisdiction over cases containing patent law counterclaims).

U.S.C. § 1338(a) emphatically precludes state courts from exercising jurisdiction over patent cases. Specifically, 28 U.S.C. § 1338(a) is amended to clarify that state courts do not have jurisdiction over legal actions relating to patents, plant variety protection, or copyrights. The definition of "State" is new to § 1338(a).[2]

Regarding removal and remand, the AIA adds a new section to the removal section of the Judicial Code that allows patent issues in a state action to be removed to an appropriate United States District Court. It also provides that other State or supplementary matters to be remanded back to State court. Also addressed in the *Holmes Group* "fix," this new statute provides for removal of an action where patent or copyright-specific issues are pleaded by way of counterclaim, cross claim, or other third party action. The rules relating to how removal must be accomplished remain the same except that under the new provision, any party can seek removal (as opposed to being limited to "defendants"). Also, the otherwise jurisdictional time limitations for removal under 28 U.S.C. § 1446(b) may be extended for "cause shown."

This amendment does not have retroactive application but rather applies to any civil action commenced after September 16, 2011, as courts have indicated.[3]

---

[2]The revisions to § 1338(a) do not explicitly address whether state courts may exercise jurisdiction over suits claiming malpractice arising from the handling of a federal patent infringement suit where the state court will not be called upon to resolve "a substantial question of federal patent law." *Christianson v. Colt Industries Operating Corp.*, 486 U.S. 800, 108 S. Ct. 2166, 100 L. Ed. 2d 811, 7 U.S.P.Q.2d 1109, 1988-1 Trade Cas. (CCH) ¶ 68081, 11 Fed. R. Serv. 3d 452 (1988). Federal courts will have exclusive jurisdiction over such malpractice claims if resolving the "case within a case" would require addressing a substantial question of patent law. Stated differently, if the state court is required to retry an infringement case and evaluate the effects of evidence claimed to require a change in the underlying outcome, the matter belongs in federal court. *See, e.g., Air Measurement Technologies, Inc. v. Akin Gump Strauss Hauer & Feld, L.L.P.*, 504 F.3d 1262, 84 U.S.P.Q.2d 2002 (Fed. Cir. 2007) (disapproved of by, RX.com, Inc. v. O'Quinn, 766 F. Supp. 2d 790 (S.D. Tex. 2011)), and *Immunocept, LLC v. Fulbright & Jaworski, LLP*, 504 F.3d 1281, 85 U.S.P.Q.2d 1085 (Fed. Cir. 2007); See generally, *Byrne v. Wood, Herron & Evans, LLP*, 676 F.3d 1024, 102 U.S.P.Q.2d 1073 (Fed. Cir. 2012).

[3]*Nolen v. Lufkin Industries, Inc.*, 466 Fed. Appx. 895 (Fed. Cir. 2012) (patents); *Byrne v. Wood, Herron & Evans, LLP*, 450 Fed. Appx. 956, 961 n.3 (Fed. Cir. 2011), petition for cert. filed, 80 U.S.L.W. 3693, 81 U.S.L.W.

3032 (U.S. June 8, 2012); *Vosk Intern. Co. v. Zao Gruppa Predpriyatij Ost*, 2012 WL 1033535, *2 n.4 (W.D. Wash. 2012) (re trademarks).

Chapter 13

Joinder and Consolidation

AIA § 19(d)
New 35 U.S.C.A. § 299

§ 13:1 Background re joinder and consolidation

Prior to the AIA, Rule 20 of the Federal Rules of Civil Procedure governed the question of whether a patent owner may sue multiple alleged infringers in the same legal action. That rule states in relevant part:

Rule 20. Permissive Joinder of Parties

(a) Persons Who May Join or Be Joined

(1) Plaintiffs. Persons may join in one action as plaintiffs if:

(A) they assert any right to relief jointly, severally, or in the alternative with respect to or arising out of the same transaction, occurrence, or series of transactions or occurrences; and

(B) any question of law or fact common to all plaintiffs will arise in the action.

(2) Defendants. Persons . . . may be joined in one action as defendants if:

(A) any right to relief is asserted against them jointly, severally, or in the alternative with respect to or arising out of the same transaction, occurrence, or series of transactions or occurrences; and

(B) any question of law or fact common to all defendants will arise in the action.

(3) Extent of Relief. Neither a plaintiff nor a defendant need be interested in obtaining or defending against all the relief demanded. The court may grant judgment to one or more plaintiffs according to their rights, and against one or more defendants according to their liabilities.

(b) Protective Measures. The court may issue orders—including an order for separate trials—to protect a party against embarrassment, delay, expense, or other prejudice that arises from including a person against whom the party asserts no claim and who asserts no claim against the party.

This rule specifies the conditions for permissive joinder of parties for federal civil actions in general. ". . . [T]he central purpose of Rule 20 is to promote trial convenience and expedite the resolution of disputes, thereby eliminating unnecessary lawsuits."[1] If a misjoinder occurs, the court may sever any claim against a party, and it may add or drop a party at any time, as Rule 21 provides:

Rule 21. Misjoinder and Nonjoinder of Parties. Misjoinder of parties is not a ground for dismissing an action. On motion or on its own, the court may at any time, on just terms, add or drop a party. The court may also sever any claim against a party.

The Federal Rules of Civil Procedure also provide for consolidation or separate trials. Rule 42 states:

[Section 13:1]

[1] *Brandywine Communications Technologies, LLC. v. Verizon Communications, Inc.*, 2012 WL 527862, *1 (M.D. Fla. 2012) citing *Alexander v. Fulton County, Ga.*, 207 F.3d 1303, 1323, 82 Fair Empl. Prac. Cas. (BNA) 858, 78 Empl. Prac. Dec. (CCH) P 40046, 46 Fed. R. Serv. 3d 347 (11th Cir. 2000) (overruled on other grounds by, Manders v. Lee, 338 F.3d 1304 (11th Cir. 2003)).

Rule 42. Consolidation; Separate Trials

(a) Consolidation. If actions before the court involve a common question of law or fact, the court may:

(1) join for hearing or trial any or all matters at issue in the actions;

(2) consolidate the actions; or

(3) issue any other orders to avoid unnecessary cost or delay.

(b) Separate Trials. For convenience, to avoid prejudice, or to expedite and economize, the court may order a separate trial of one or more separate issues, claims, crossclaims, counterclaims, or third-party claims. When ordering a separate trial, the court must preserve any federal right to a jury trial.

Some plaintiffs join numerous defendants in a single patent infringement action when each defendant is alleged to infringe the patent(s)-in-suit. Trying common questions such as claim construction or validity together may result in judicial efficiency. Some defendants may not object to such joinder even when there is no claim for joint or several liability, or alternative liability, because those defendants can enter into a joint defense agreement, pool resources, allocate tasks, and achieve certain economies in defending the suit.

Nevertheless, many unrelated accused infringers do object to being joined. They may "not have a meaningful opportunity to present individualized defenses on issues such as infringement, willfulness, and damages because each defendant will have limited opportunities to present its own defense to the jury."[2] Congress noted that the joined defendants "sometimes number[ ] in the dozens," with "tenuous connections to the underlying disputes in patent infringement suits."[3]

§ 13:2 Congressional intent[1]

Congress expressed its intent in the House Report:

---

[2]*In re EMC Corp.*, 677 F.3d 1351, 1355, 102 U.S.P.Q.2d 1539, 82 Fed. R. Serv. 3d 456 (Fed. Cir. 2012).

[3]H. Rep. No. 112-98, at 54.

[Section 13:2]

[1]The Supreme Court cautions against relying on interpretations advanced in legislative statements that are not "anchored in the text of the statute." *Shannon v. U.S.*, 512 U.S. 573, 583, 114 S. Ct. 2419, 129 L. Ed. 2d 459 (1994), stating "[C]ourts have no authority to enforce [a] principl[e] gleaned solely from legislative history that has no statutory

b) *Joinder*

The Act also addresses problems occasioned by the joinder of defendants (sometimes numbering in the dozens) who have tenuous connections to the underlying disputes in patent infringement suits.

The Act amends chapter 29 of the Patent Act by creating a new § 299 that addresses joinder under Rule 20 and consolidation of trials under Rule 42. Pursuant to the provision, parties who are accused infringers in most patent suits may be joined as defendants or counterclaim defendants only if: (1) relief is asserted against the parties, jointly, severally, or in the alternative, arising out of the same transaction regarding the manufacture, use, or importation of the accused product or process; and (2) questions of fact common to all of the defendants will arise in the action. New 299 also clarifies that joinder will not be available if it based solely on allegations that a defendant has infringed the patent(s) in question.[FN61]

FN 61. Section 299 legislatively abrogates the construction of Rule 20(a) adopted in *MyMail, Ltd. v. America Online, Inc.*, 223 F.R.D. 455 (E.D. Tex. 2004); *Sprint Communications Co., L.P. v. Theglobe.com, Inc.*, 233 F.R.D. 615 (D. Kan. 2006); *Adrain v. Genetec Inc.*, 2009 WL 3063414 (E.D. Tex. 2009); *Better Educ., Inc. v. Einstruction Corp.*, 2010 WL 918307 (E.D. Tex. 2010); *Mannatech, Inc. v. Country Life, LLC*, 2010 WL 2944574 (N.D. Tex. 2010); *Alford Safety Services, Inc. v. Hot-Hed, Inc.*, 2010 WL 3418233 (E.D. La. 2010); and *Eolas Technologies, Inc. v. Adobe Systems, Inc.*, 2010 WL 3835762 (E.D. Tex. 2010)—effectively conforming these courts' jurisprudence to that followed by a majority of jurisdictions. *See generally Rudd v. Lux Products Corporation Emerson Climate Technologies Braeburn Systems, LLC*, 2011 WL 148052 (N.D. Ill. 2011).

* * *

Section 19. Jurisdiction and procedural matters.

* * * Subsection (e) creates a new § 299 of the Patent Act that addresses joinder of accused infringers in patent actions or trials not involving certain drugs and biologics. Parties ac-

---

reference point." *Shannon,* 512 U.S. at 584, quoting *International Broth. of Elec. Workers, Local Union No. 474, AFL-CIO v. N.L.R.B.*, 814 F.2d 697, 712, 124 L.R.R.M. (BNA) 2993, 106 Lab. Cas. (CCH) P 12256 (D.C. Cir. 1987). The authoritative statement "is the statutory text, not the legislative history." *Exxon Mobil Corp. v. Allapattah Services, Inc.*, 545 U.S. 546, 568, 125 S. Ct. 2611, 162 L. Ed. 2d 502 (2005). However, lower courts have cited the legislative history of the AIA already in recent cases. E.g., *Rogers v. Tristar Products, Inc.*, 102 U.S.P.Q.2d 1722, 2012 WL 1660604, *2 (Fed. Cir. 2012) (non-precedential); *Byrne v. Wood, Herron & Evans, LLP*, 676 F.3d 1024, 1029, 102 U.S.P.Q.2d 1073 (Fed. Cir. 2012) (dissenting opin.).

cused as defendants may be joined in one action as defendants or counterclaim defendants only if: (1) any right to relief is asserted against the parties jointly, severally, or in the alternative with respect to or arising out of the same transaction, occurrence, or series of transactions or occurrences relating to the making, using, importing into the United States, offering for sale, or selling of the same accused product or process; and (2) questions of fact common to all defendants or counterclaim defendants will arise in the action.

For purposes of subsection (e), accused infringers may not be joined based solely on allegations that they each have infringed the patent or patents in suit.

The changes set forth in Section 19 shall apply to any civil action commenced on or after the date of enactment of the Act.[2]

§ 13:3 America Invents Act changes to joinder and consolidation

Section 19(d) of the America Invents Act amended title 35 of the United States Code to include the following new Section 299 directed in name to joinder but also addressing consolidation for trial:

§ 299. Joinder of Parties

(a) JOINDER OF ACCUSED INFRINGERS.— With respect to any civil action arising under any Act of Congress relating to patents, other than an action or trial in which an act of infringement under section 271(e)(2) has been pled, parties that are accused infringers may be joined in one action as defendants or counterclaim defendants, or have their actions consolidated for trial, or counterclaim defendants[1] only if—

(1) any right to relief is asserted against the parties

---

[2]H.R. Rep. No. 112-98, pt. 1, at 54 to 55, 81 (2011).

[Section 13:3]

[1]The AIA contained an error of transcription with respect to counterclaim defendants. The language of § 299(a) repeats the phrase "*or counterclaim defendants*" at the end of the first paragraph without evident reason. The repetition does not appear in the House Report (June 1, 2011) articulation of proposed § 299, and the statute's precursor also does not include the phrase, "or have their actions consolidated for trial." H.R. Rep. No. 112-98, pt. 1, at 33. Likewise, the same report in its "Purpose and Summary" section does not include this error and states, "Pursuant to the provision, parties who are accused infringers in most patent suits may be joined as defendants or counterclaim defendants only if . . ." H.R. Rep. No. 112-98, pt. 1, at 54 to 55; accord p. 81. Thus, it appears that when the provision for consolidation for trial was added, the phrase "or counterclaim defendants" was inadvertently repeated. J. Matal's comprehensive history on this legislation reports that these three repeated words "are a scrivener's error that crept into the bill when it was engrossed after House pas-

jointly, severally, or in the alternative with respect to or arising out of the same transaction, occurrence, or series of transactions or occurrences relating to the making, using, importing into the United States, offering for sale, or selling of the same accused product or process; and

(2) questions of fact common to all defendants or counterclaim defendants will arise in the action.

(b) ALLEGATIONS INSUFFICIENT FOR JOINDER.— For purposes of this subsection, accused infringers may not be joined in one action as defendants or counterclaim defendants, or have their actions consolidated for trial, based solely on allegations that they each have infringed the patent or patents in suit.

(c) WAIVER.— A party that is an accused infringer may waive the limitations set forth in this section with respect to that party.

(d) CONFORMING AMENDMENT.— The table of sections for chapter 29 of title 35, United States Code, as amended by this Act is further amended by adding at the end the following new item: "299. Joinder of parties."

(e) EFFECTIVE DATE.— The amendments made by this section shall apply to any civil action commenced on or after the date of the enactment of this Act.

§ 13:4 Applicability—Generally

Section 299 is directed to all civil actions that "arise under" an Act of Congress relating to patents. However, certain Hatch-Waxman litigation is specifically excluded from § 299.[1] Hence, § 299 applies to other suits asserting patent infringement, as such suits are civil actions arising under the patent statute.

Section 299 applies to declaratory judgment actions also. It states specifically that it applies to the joinder of counter-

---

sage," citing "157 Cong. Rec. H4446 (daily ed. June 22, 2011) (text of manager's amendment." Matal, Guide to the Legislative History of the America Invents Act: Part II of II, *Federal Circuit Bar Journal,* Vol. 21, at 590, n. 332. H.R. 6621, § 1(c) made a technical correction by deleting the superfluous "or counterclaim defendants."

[Section 13:4]

[1]Section 299(a) exempts actions or trials where infringement under 35 U.S.C.A. § 271(e)(2) has been pled. Hence the new joinder provision does not apply to joinder of accused infringers in proceedings under the Hatch-Waxman Act regarding the artificial (but statutory) act of infringement caused by filing an abbreviated new drug application and the serving of a notice.

claim defendants.[2]

The Federal Circuit has yet to interpret § 299. However, one Federal Circuit ruling noted § 299 when applying pre-AIA law and is discussed below.[3] While not interpreting § 299 specifically, this ruling may have relevance because some of the language in § 299 overlaps the language of F.R. Civ. Proc. 20(a)(2) as to joint, several, or alternative relief and questions of fact common to all defendants. Until the Federal Circuit gives guidance on § 299 specifically, district courts interpreting § 299 should consider this earlier Federal Circuit analysis to the extent it addresses the same statutory language.[4]

§ 13:5 Effective date

The AIA directs that its provisions regarding joinder and consolidation in § 299 "apply to any civil action commenced on or after the date of enactment of this Act," *i.e.,* on or after September 16, 2011.

Courts agree that 35 U.S.C. § 299 is not retroactive.[1] Denying a request for reconsideration, one court ruled that the subsequent enactment of § 299, which is not retroactive, did

---

[2] 35 U.S.C.A. § 299(a) ("joined in one action as . . . counterclaim defendants"); *accord*, § 299(a)(2) and (b).

[3] *In re EMC Corp.*, 677 F.3d 1351, 1354, 102 U.S.P.Q.2d 1539, 82 Fed. R. Serv. 3d 456 (Fed. Cir. 2012), decided on petition for a writ of mandamus to the Eastern District of Texas to direct that court to sever and transfer several cases. Plaintiff charged defendants with offering a similar commercial online backup/storage service allegedly covered by method claims of plaintiff's patent. A magistrate judge found nothing improper in maintaining these claims in one action, as claim validity, claim construction, and the scope of the patents are common questions as to all defendants in the case. The magistrate judge ruled that the claims arose out of the same transaction, occurrence, or series of transactions or occurrences because the accused services were "not dramatically different." The district court adopted the magistrate's findings and conclusions. The Federal Circuit found that "not dramatically different" is the wrong standard. The standard to apply is explained in main text *infra.* For the case on remand, see *Oasis Research, LLC v. Carbonite, Inc.*, 2012 WL 3544881 (E.D. Tex. 2012).

[4] Note, however, that the Federal Circuit has cautioned that it has not ruled on the meaning of § 299. *In re EMC Corp.*, 677 F.3d 1351, 1360 n.4, 102 U.S.P.Q.2d 1539, 82 Fed. R. Serv. 3d 456 (Fed. Cir. 2012).

[Section 13:5]

[1] *In re EMC Corp.*, 677 F.3d 1351, 1356, 102 U.S.P.Q.2d 1539, 82 Fed. R. Serv. 3d 456 (Fed. Cir. 2012); *Ganas, LLC v. Sabre Holdings Corp.*, 2011 WL 8183246 (E.D. Tex. 2011).

not represent an intervening change in the law controlling that case.[2] Hence, the court did not need to reconsider its ruling.

The situation is more interesting when a case straddles the effective date of the statute, *i.e.*, where suit is filed *before* the effective date but a claim for relief, joining other parties, is raised in a pleading *after* that date. The statute does not speak directly to this limited situation. The two courts that faced this situation both applied § 299. However, the issue was not litigated in one case, and in the other, the court said it would reach the same outcome under either Rule 20 or § 299.[3]

§ 13:6 Required conditions for joinder or consolidation for trial

The first condition for joinder or consolidation for trial in patent cases is stated in § 299(a)(1). Subparagraph (1) borrows the wording of Rule 20(a)(2)(A), F. R. Civ. Proc. and then adds to it. The table below compares the relevant portions of Rule 20 and § 299 in parallel columns [emphasis added]:

Rule 20, F. R. Civ. Proc.	35 U.S.C. § 299
(2) Defendants. Persons . . . may be joined in one action as defendants if:	(a) JOINDER OF ACCUSED INFRINGERS.—. . . parties that are accused infringers may be joined in one action as defendants or counterclaim defendants, or have their actions consolidated for trial, or counterclaim defendants only if—

[2]*Softview LLC v. Apple Inc.*, 2011 WL 6100421 (D. Del. 2011).

[3]In *IpVenture, Inc. v. Acer, Inc.*, 2012 WL 3016958 (D. Del. 2012), a post-AIA amended complaint joined new defendants. The parties litigated whether Rule 20 or § 299 controls the joinder question. The court concluded, "I am inclined to think [§ 299] does apply. . ." but indicated that the outcome (granting severance) would result under either rule. In *Motorola Mobility, Inc. v. Tivo, Inc.*, 2012 WL 2935450 (E.D. Tex. 2012), a declaratory judgment action, Tivo filed counterclaims against Motorola and Time Warner Cable after the AIA was enacted. The district court did not discuss retroactivity but simply applied § 299.

Rule 20, F. R. Civ. Proc.	35 U.S.C. § 299
(A) any right to relief is asserted against them jointly, severally, or in the alternative with respect to or arising out of the same transaction, occurrence, or series of transactions or occurrences; and	(1) any right to relief is asserted against the parties jointly, severally, or in the alternative with respect to or arising out of the same transaction, occurrence, or series of transactions or occurrences *relating to the making, using, importing into the United States, offering for sale, or selling of the same accused product or process*; and
(B) any question of law or fact common to all defendants will arise in the action.	(2) questions of fact common to all defendants or counterclaim defendants will arise in the action.
	(b) ALLEGATIONS INSUFFICIENT FOR JOINDER.—For purposes of this subsection, accused infringers may not be joined in one action as defendants or counterclaim defendants, or have their actions consolidated for trial, based solely on allegations that they each have infringed the patent or patents in suit.

As can be seen in the right column of the table, the italicized portion of § 299(a)(1) has no corresponding language in Rule 20 and specifies the further limitation that the asserted rights must relate "to the making, using, importing into the United States, offering for sale, or selling of the same accused product or process."[1] This addition makes the requirements for joinder "more stringent" and "more difficult" than joinder under Rule 20.[2] With this addition (and that of § 299(b)), Congress intended to settle

[Section 13:6]

[1] *PerfectVision Mfg., Inc. v. PPC Broadband, Inc.*, 2013 WL 2553507, at *11 (E.D. Ark. 2013) (if different products are at issue, waiver of joinder protection would be required).

[2] *Motorola Mobility, Inc. v. Apple Inc.*, 2012 WL 3113932, *2, *4 (S.D.

divergent jurisprudence on the question of "arising out of the same transaction . . . ." The House Report affirmatively states in footnote 61 that § 299 abrogates the minority (more liberal) reading of the Rule 20(a) requirement, as quoted above in subsection 1 on "Congressional Intent."

The second condition for joinder or consolidation for trial—common questions of fact—is stated in § 299(a)(2). Compared to Rule 20(a)(2)(B), the new statute omits the word "any," adds the phrase "or counterclaim defendants," and omits the reference to common questions of law. The House Report indicates that one factor in the joinder/consolidation calculus is whether questions of fact common to all of the defendants will arise in the action, but the House Report does not explain why common questions of law were omitted.[3]

Section 299(b), entitled "Allegations Insufficient for Joinder," adds another limitation on both permissive joinder and consolidation for trial. Neither joinder nor consolidation for trial may occur based *solely* on allegations that each defendant (or counterclaim defendant) infringed. Rules 20, 21, and 42, Fed.R.Civ.P., contain no corresponding requirement, and hence this is further narrowing language.

§ 13:7 Specific applications—Joinder and severance of parties or claims

A district court has broad discretion whether to sever a claim under Rule 21.[1] Within that discretion, it must apply Federal Circuit law. In May 2012, the Federal Circuit speci-

---

Fla. 2012).

[3]Patent claim interpretation is one issue routinely characterized as an issue of law. See *Cybor Corp. v. FAS Technologies, Inc.*, 138 F.3d 1448, 1456, 46 U.S.P.Q.2d 1169 (Fed. Cir. 1998) (en banc).

[Section 13:7]

[1]*Body Science LLC v. Boston Scientific Corp.*, 846 F. Supp. 2d 980, 81 Fed. R. Serv. 3d 1094 (N.D. Ill. 2012) citing *Rice v. Sunrise Express, Inc.*, 209 F.3d 1008, 1016, 5 Wage & Hour Cas. 2d (BNA) 1770, 140 Lab. Cas. (CCH) P 34036, 46 Fed. R. Serv. 3d 929 (7th Cir. 2000); accord, *CyberFone Systems, LLC v. Cellco Partnership*, 2012 WL 1509504 (D. Del. 2012), citing *Walsh v. Miehle-Goss-Dexter, Inc.*, 378 F.2d 409 (3d Cir. 1967). The *CyberFone* court refused to sever a case having where the complaints did not allege joint infringement or any relationships or common activities among the individual defendants, stating that "all parties share the same discovery and motion deadlines, the cases will progress to trial on parallel tracks and the court will address in due course how trial will be managed." *GeoTag, Inc. v. Fred's, Inc.*, 2013 WL 2181166, at *1 (W.D. Tenn. 2013) (defendants previously severed from the Eastern

fied that because joinder in patent cases depends on an analysis of accused acts of infringement, its own law, rather than regional circuit law, applies to motions to sever.[2]

That independent actors are defendants has not by itself been a sufficient reason to refuse joinder under Rule 20, F.R. Civ. Proc.[3] Independent defendants have satisfied the transaction-or-occurrence test of Rule 20 when there was a logical relationship between the separate causes, and the logical relationship test was met if there is substantial evidentiary overlap in facts giving rise to the cause of action:

> The logical relationship test is satisfied if there is substantial evidentiary overlap in the facts giving rise to the cause of action against each defendant. In other words, the defendants' allegedly infringing acts, which give rise to the individual claims of infringement, must share an aggregate of operative facts.[4]
>
> * * *
>
> The sameness of the accused products is not enough to establish that claims of infringement arise from the "same transaction." Unless there is an actual link between the facts underlying each claim of infringement, independently developed products using differently sourced parts are not part of the same transaction, even if they are otherwise coincidentally identical.[5]

When analyzing motions—whether under Rule 20 or

District of Texas "pursuant to the America Invents Act"); *GeoTag, Inc. v. Circle K Stores, Inc.*, Case No. 2:11-cv-405, slip opin. at 4 (E.D. Tex. Aug. 14, 2012) ("The AIA establishes that 'accused infringers may not be joined in one action as defendants or counterclaim defendants, or have their actions consolidated for trial, based solely on allegations that they each have infringed the patent or patents in suit.' 35 U.S.C. § 299(b). The only commonality between the Defendants is that they each independently infringe the patent. This allegation is insufficient to establish joinder.").

[2]*In re EMC Corp.*, 677 F.3d 1351, 1354, 102 U.S.P.Q.2d 1539, 82 Fed. R. Serv. 3d 456 (Fed. Cir. 2012); *ChriMar Systems, Inc. v. Cisco Systems, Inc.*, 2013 WL 828220, at *2 (D. Del. 2013). Prior to this ruling, at least one district court asserted that regional law applied in the Tenth Circuit, but there was no prevailing rule in that Circuit for patent cases. *Genetic Technologies Ltd. v. Agilent Technologies, Inc.*, 2012 WL 1015355 (D. Colo. 2012).

[3]*In re EMC Corp.*, 677 F.3d 1351, 1356, 102 U.S.P.Q.2d 1539, 82 Fed. R. Serv. 3d 456 (Fed. Cir. 2012), citing *U.S. v. Mississippi*, 380 U.S. 128, 85 S. Ct. 808, 13 L. Ed. 2d 717 (1965).

[4]*In re EMC Corp.*, 677 F.3d 1351, 1358, 102 U.S.P.Q.2d 1539, 82 Fed. R. Serv. 3d 456 (Fed. Cir. 2012).

[5]*In re EMC Corp.*, 677 F.3d 1351, 1359, 102 U.S.P.Q.2d 1539, 82 Fed. R. Serv. 3d 456 (Fed. Cir. 2012).

§ 299—courts consider the facts alleged in the complaint, amended complaint, and other relevant pleadings in analyzing whether joinder is proper.[6] Accordingly, if multiple parties are joined in a complaint, facts sufficient to support that joinder need to be pleaded.

Whether a factual situation constitutes a "single transaction or occurrence" is determined on a case-by-case basis.[7]

The Federal Circuit outlined factors to consider on whether joinder is proper under Rule 20:

> In addition to finding that the same product or process is involved, to determine whether the joinder test is satisfied, pertinent factual considerations include whether the alleged acts of infringement occurred during the same time period, the existence of some relationship among the defendants, the use of identically sourced components, licensing or technology agreements between the defendants, overlap of the products' or processes' development and manufacture, and whether the case involves a claim for lost profits. The district court enjoys considerable discretion in weighing the relevant factors.[8]

The existence of a common question of law or fact, by itself, is "clearly insufficient" to justify joinder under Rule 20.[9] However, when common questions of law or fact were found and there was a logical relationship between the causes of action for each defendant, motions for severance have been denied.[10] Conversely, even when there was some commonal-

---

[6]See *Lantiq Deutschland GMBH v. Ralink Technology Corp.*, 2012 WL 1536070, *3 (N.D. Cal. 2012) (allegations in amended complaint not challenged that one defendant sells other defendant's product); *H-W Technology, L.C. v. Apple, Inc.*, 2012 WL 3072776, *4 (N.D. Tex. 2012), report and recommendation adopted, 2012 WL 3079088 (N.D. Tex. 2012) (". . . complaint . . . does not allege that Apple acted in concert with or in conspiracy with . . .") (severance recommended); *IpVenture, Inc. v. Acer, Inc.*, 2012 WL 3016958, *2 (D. Del. 2012).

[7]*Motorola Mobility, Inc. v. Apple Inc.*, 2012 WL 3113932, *3 (S.D. Fla. 2012); *Brandywine Communications Technologies, LLC v. Verizon Communications, Inc.*, 2012 WL 527536, *2 (M.D. Fla. 2012), report and recommendation adopted, 2012 WL 527862 (M.D. Fla. 2012).

[8]*In re EMC Corp.*, 677 F.3d 1351, 1359–1360, 102 U.S.P.Q.2d 1539, 82 Fed. R. Serv. 3d 456 (Fed. Cir. 2012), citing *U.S. v. Mississippi*, 380 U.S. 128, 85 S. Ct. 808, 13 L. Ed. 2d 717 (1965).

[9]E.g., *Ameranth, Inc. v. Pizza Hut, Inc.*, 2012 WL 3223694, *2 (S.D. Cal. 2012).

[10]See *Novartis Vaccines & Diagnostics, Inc. v. MedImmune, LLC*, 2012 WL 3150524 (D. Del. 2012) (expression vector manufactured by common source, even though defendants claimed post-acquisition modification); *Lantiq Deutschland GMBH v. Ralink Technology Corp.*, 2012 WL

ity, joinder can be improper and severance can be granted.[11]

§ 13:8 Specific topics

Some recurring topics are addressed below. In this discussion, cases applying pre-AIA law are often mentioned because in those rulings, the court specifically mentioned § 299.

"Any" Claim. District courts have interpreted § 299 so that complete commonality of *all* claims is not required to satisfy the requirements of § 299(a)(1), referring specifically to the word "any" in § 299(a)(1) ("[a]*ny* right to relief . . .").[1]

Under Rule 20, the right to relief that supported joinder may have been a non-patent claim for relief. Under § 299, the claim for relief that supports joinder (or consolidation for trial) must relate to making, using, importing into the U.S., offering for sale, or selling the same accused product or process. This language adopted in § 299 parallels 35 U.S.C. § 271(a) directed to (direct) patent infringement.

While language from § 271(a) was borrowed for the new § 299, language concerning indirect infringement under § 271(b) or (c) was not included, nor was language from § 271(f) or (g). Courts will eventually have to address whether parties charged with these other types of infringement can be properly joined in an action alleging direct infringement.

One interesting question is whether the joinder (or consolidation for trial) conditions must be met as to the pa-

---

1536070 (N.D. Cal. 2012) (allegations in amended complaint not challenged that one defendant sells other defendant's product).

[11]The court in *Motorola Mobility, Inc. v. Apple Inc.*, 2012 WL 3113932 (S.D. Fla. 2012) granted a motion to sever under the AIA even though both the parties accused of infringing Apple's patents, HTC and Motorola, both used the Android open source code operating systems in their cell phones. The court held, however, that the products are not the same even though both are downstream purchasers of the Android software, reasoning that neither company sells or distributes Android to the other. In *Mednovus, Inc. v. QinetiQ Group PLC*, 2012 WL 4513539 (C.D. Cal. 2012), the court severed the product distributors from a case against the product inventor and manufacturing entities.

[Section 13:8]

[1]*Motorola Mobility, Inc. v. Tivo, Inc.*, 2012 WL 2935450, *2 (E.D. Tex. 2012); *Omega Patents, LLC v. Skypatrol, LLC*, 2012 WL 2339320, *2 (S.D. Fla. 2012) (so long as joinder is appropriate for one or more claims, misjoinder does not result due to independent infringement claims against only one of the defendants).

tent causes of action, or, on the other hand, they can relate to other causes. As written, "any right to relief" that is asserted jointly, severally, or alternatively with respect to the same transaction or occurrence, or series thereof, relating to making, using, selling, etc. the same accused product or process may satisfy one prong of the test. While it is true that § 299(a) contemplates civil actions relating to patents, other causes of action can be part of a suit, and § 299(a)(1) does not state specifically that it is the *patent* cause of action that must meet this test. Courts will eventually have to rule on whether a non-patent claim that involves the manufacture or sale of the same accused product would support proper joinder or consolidation for trial under § 299.

Same Patent(s). Courts have not yet had occasion to address the argument that where multiple accused infringers violate the same patent(s), joinder under § 299 is proper. Many cases involve litigation over the same patent(s), and different courts applying pre-AIA law take different views over whether this supports permissive joinder under Rule 20.[2] The addition by the AIA of paragraph (b) in § 299 (allegations of infringement of same patent alone are insufficient to support joinder or consolidation for trial) aligns with the majority view,[3] and Congress specifically opted to abrogate the minority view.[4] Courts have agreed that § 299(a) "effectively codifies current law as it has been applied outside of the Eastern District of Texas"[5] (as to joinder). One court in a case involving the same patent denied a mo-

---

[2]*Compare*, *Rudd v. Lux Products Corporation Emerson Climate Technologies Braeburn Systems, LLC*, 2011 WL 148052, *2-3 (N.D. Ill. 2011) (a party fails to satisfy Rule 20(a)'s requirement of a common transaction or occurrence where unrelated defendants, based on different acts, are alleged to have infringed the same patent), FN2 citing cases, *with MyMail, Ltd. v. America Online, Inc.*, 223 F.R.D. 455 (E.D. Tex. 2004). See also, *Imperium (IP) Holdings, Inc. v. Apple Inc.*, 2012 WL 461775 (E.D. Tex. 2012), report and recommendation adopted, 2012 WL 461802 (E.D. Tex. 2012).

[3]See, e.g., *Brandywine Communications Technologies, LLC v. Verizon Communications, Inc.*, 2012 WL 527536, *1 (M.D. Fla. 2012), report and recommendation adopted, 2012 WL 527862, *1 (M.D. Fla. 2012) (first element of joinder test not satisfied when unrelated defendants are accused of independently infringing same patent).

[4]*Body Science LLC v. Boston Scientific Corp.*, 846 F. Supp. 2d 980, 988, 81 Fed. R. Serv. 3d 1094 (N.D. Ill. 2012) citing H.R. Rep. No. 112-98, pt. 1, at 55, n. 61 (2011), quoted *supra*. Accord, *Lektron, Inc. v. GE Lighting, Inc.*, 2012 WL 1085486 (N.D. Okla. 2012).

[5]*Medsquire LLC v. Quest Diagnostics, Inc.*, 2011 WL 7710203, *2

tion to consolidate for various pre-trial activities such as discovery, claim construction, and dispositive motions. The reasons for denial of the motion were an insufficient showing by the movant that judicial economy would be achieved, prejudice to one party, and confidentiality concerns.[6]

Same or Different Products. Joinder has been found proper under § 299 when one defendant "manufactures a product that allegedly infringes the patents in question and then provides the product to [another defendant] who reconfigures, modifies, and rebrands the same product—using information and documentation provided by [the first defendant]—for distribution under its own name."[7] However, joinder under Rule 20 has not been appropriate where different products or processes are involved in respects relevant to the patent.[8] Joinder under § 299 should be more rigorous[9] because the new statute specifically calls for parties who are selling *the same* accused product or process.[10] One district court referred to multiple defendants selling "extremely similar" accused products a "lame response" and noted that under the AIA, the same transaction requirement relates to "*the same accused product or process.*"[11] Another district court stated that § 299 "precludes complete joinder of cases involving different

(C.D. Cal. 2011) citing 157 Cong. Rec. S5429 (daily ed. Sept. 8, 2011). Cases from the Eastern District of Texas holding the minority view and mentioning but not applying the AIA provision on joinder include *Ganas, LLC v. Sabre Holdings Corp.*, 2011 WL 8183246 (E.D. Tex. 2011); *Imperium (IP) Holdings, Inc. v. Apple Inc.*, 2012 WL 461775 (E.D. Tex. 2012), report and recommendation adopted, 2012 WL 461802 (E.D. Tex. 2012); *Norman IP Holdings, LLC v. Lexmark Intern., Inc.*, 2012 WL 3307942 (E.D. Tex. 2012); and *Oasis Research, LLC v. Carbonite, Inc.*, 2012 WL 3544881 (E.D. Tex. 2012).

[6]*PB & J Software, LLC v. Acronis, Inc.*, 2012 WL 4815132 (E.D. Mo. 2012).

[7]*Omega Patents, LLC v. Skypatrol, LLC*, 2012 WL 2339320, *2 (S.D. Fla. 2012).

[8]*In re EMC Corp.*, 677 F.3d 1351, 1359, 102 U.S.P.Q.2d 1539, 82 Fed. R. Serv. 3d 456 (Fed. Cir. 2012).

[9]The court in *Motorola Mobility, Inc. v. Apple Inc.*, 2012 WL 3113932 (S.D. Fla. 2012) noted that the AIA adds a requirement to the Rule 20 first prong and hence joinder under the AIA is more stringent than under Rule 20.

[10]35 U.S.C.A. § 299(a)(1).

[11]*Pinpoint, Inc. v. Groupon, Inc.*, 2011 WL 6097738, *1 (N.D. Ill. 2011) (emphasis by the court).

accused products."[12]

Applying new § 299, a California court severed two distributor defendants from the manufacturer company and the originator (another entity) in *Mednovus, Inc. v. Qinetiq Group PLC*,[13] relying on the both the "same product" and "same transaction" requirements of § 299. Defendant QinetiQ developed and commercialized its own patented "Ferroguard" line of products. Defendant Metrasens was a spin-off of QinetiQ that was licensed to manufacture and sell Ferroguard products. Defendants ETS-Lindgren and Invivo were distributors of differing products in the Ferroguard product line. The court relied on these differing product sales in severing the distributors from the action. The court further ruled that the transactions were neither the same nor part of the same series. The court did not sever Metrasens from the case in view of the "close relationship" between it and QiniteQ.

Same Industry Standard. Cases arise from time to time where alleged infringers must comply with an industry standard, and patent holders have asserted that evidence thereof satisfies the "common transaction" question. Recent cases have rejected this reasoning.[14]

Joining Insignificant Parties for Venue. Additionally, joinder of an insignificant party for the mere purpose of establishing venue is said to be an impermissible form of forum-shopping.[15]

§ 13:9 Consolidation for pre-trial or trial

Consolidation is different from joinder, and different standards have been applied prior to the AIA.[1] District courts have enjoyed considerable discretion to consolidate cases for

---

[12] *Oplus Technologies, Ltd. v. Sears Holding Corp.*, 2012 WL 2400478, *3 (N.D. Ill. 2012).

[13] *Mednovus, Inc. v. QinetiQ Group PLC*, 2012 WL 4513539 (C.D. Cal. 2012).

[14] *Medsquire LLC v. Quest Diagnostics, Inc.*, 2011 WL 7710203, *2 (C.D. Cal. 2011) citing *WiAV Networks, LLC v. 3Com Corp.*, 2010 WL 3895047 (N.D. Cal. 2010) (both rejecting this argument).

[15] *Oplus Technologies, Ltd. v. Sears Holding Corp.*, 2012 WL 2400478, *3 (N.D. Ill. 2012).

[Section 13:9]

[1] Multidistrict litigation practice is addressed in a separate section *infra*.

discovery and for trial under Rule 42 where venue is proper and there is (only) a common question of law or fact.[2] Judicial economy is often cited as a reason to consolidate cases where joinder is improper.[3] In the past, consolidation was allowed even when joinder was not, provided that the requirements of Rule 42 were met.[4] Severing claims or defendants for failing the "transaction-or-occurrence" test but consolidating the severed actions was often the outcome of a motion to sever. Some courts called for "coordinated case management" as a form of "limited consolidation."[5] Other courts called for partial consolidation or consolidation through pre-trial without closing the door on consolidation for trial.[6] Prior to the AIA, consolidation was allowed even though the claims arose out of independent transactions.[7] Courts sometimes severed claims from one civil action, even if they were not misjoined, and consolidated them into other pending actions to promote efficiency, fairness, and judicial economy.[8] Courts also considered that prejudice, delay, judicial economy, and fundamental fairness can be factors weighing *against*

[2]*In re EMC Corp.*, 677 F.3d 1351, 1360, 102 U.S.P.Q.2d 1539, 82 Fed. R. Serv. 3d 456 (Fed. Cir. 2012).

[3]*Norman IP Holdings, LLC v. Lexmark Intern., Inc.*, 2012 WL 3307942 (E.D. Tex. 2012), *Oasis Research, LLC v. Carbonite, Inc.*, 2012 WL 3544881 (E.D. Tex. 2012) (citing *Norman* and *EMC*).

[4]E.g., *Norman IP Holdings, LLC v. Lexmark Intern., Inc.*, 2012 WL 3307942 (E.D. Tex. 2012), where District Judge Davis agreed that there was improper joinder under both the AIA provisions and Rule 20, F.R.Civ. Proc. Under both Rule 20 and new § 299, these unrelated defendants were improperly joined and had to be dismissed from the case or severed into their own cases. However, pointing out the limited resources of the court and the need for judicial efficiency and cost saving management procedures for the benefit of not only the court but also the parties and counsel, the court then consolidated all of the cases for pretrial proceedings. The court relied on the existence of common questions of law or fact among these multiple severed matters, citing *In re EMC Corp.*, 677 F.3d 1351, 1359, 102 U.S.P.Q.2d 1539, 82 Fed. R. Serv. 3d 456 (Fed. Cir. 2012).

[5]*Brandywine Communications Technologies, LLC v. Verizon Communications, Inc.*, 2012 WL 527536, *1 (M.D. Fla. 2012), report and recommendation adopted, 2012 WL 527862 (M.D. Fla. 2012).

[6]*Oasis Research, LLC v. Carbonite, Inc.*, 2012 WL 3544881 (E.D. Tex. 2012).

[7]*In re EMC Corp.*, 677 F.3d 1351, 1360, 102 U.S.P.Q.2d 1539, 82 Fed. R. Serv. 3d 456 (Fed. Cir. 2012) citing 9A Charles Alan Wright et al., *Federal Practice and Procedure* § 2382 (3d ed.2001).

[8]*Motorola Mobility, Inc. v. Tivo, Inc.*, 2012 WL 2935450, *2-3 (E.D. Tex. 2012).

consolidation.[9]

The addition of 35 U.S.C. § 299 requires a change in direction as to some consolidation practice in patent cases. Despite the title of § 299 ("Joinder of Parties"), the limitations of this section also extend to consolidation of actions *for trial*. Subsection (a) explicitly imposes the same restrictions on consolidation for trial as it does for joinder (". . . parties that are accused infringers may . . . have their actions consolidated for trial . . . only if . . .").

On the other hand, consolidation for *pre-trial* proceedings is not addressed in § 299.[10] For example, a court might consolidate claims for pretrial proceedings under Rule 42 but could not order consolidation for trial without satisfying the conditions of § 299. As noted above, common questions of *law* are not factors on which joinder or consolidation for trial may be predicated under § 299.

One recent Missouri case denied a motion for consolidation for pre-trial activities, claim construction, and dispositive motions.[11] The Court explained the standard to be met as follows:

> The party seeking consolidation has the burden of showing the commonality of factual and legal issues, and the Court must examine "the special underlying facts" with "close attention" before ordering consolidation. *In re Repetitive Stress Injury Litig.,* 11 F.3d 368, 373 (2d Cir.1993) (cited by *Furminator, Inc. v. Ontel Prods. Corp.,* No. 4:06-cv-1294 CAS, 2005 WL 3827522, *2 (E.D.Mo. Dec. 28, 2006)). The purpose of consolidation is to promote convenience and economy in administration. *Enterprise Bank v. Saettele,* 21 F.3d 233, 235 (8th Cir.1994). Consolidation is not appropriate if it "leads to inefficiency, inconvenience, or unfair prejudice to a party." *EEOC v. HBE Corp.,* 135 F.3d 543, 551 (8th Cir.1998).[12]

Plaintiff did not meet its burden, according to the court. As

---

[9]E.g., *Body Science LLC v. Boston Scientific Corp.*, 846 F. Supp. 2d 980, 990–91, 81 Fed. R. Serv. 3d 1094 (N.D. Ill. 2012) (consolidation denied where defendants are wholly different companies, over 76 accused products spanning different product categories, calling for different documents, technical drawings, and witnesses).

[10]*C.R. Bard, Inc. v. Medical Components, Inc.*, 2012 WL 3060105, *1 (D. Utah 2012) (". . . the America Invents Act remains silent on *pre* trial consolidation") [emphasis by the court].

[11]*PB & J Software, LLC v. Acronis, Inc.*, 2012 WL 4815132 (E.D. Mo. 2012).

[12]*PB & J Software, LLC v. Acronis, Inc.*, 2012 WL 4815132, *2 (E.D. Mo. 2012).

for claim construction, the plaintiff made no showing that the claims in each suit were the same, and judges in the other cases could easily be made aware of any prior rulings and choose to accept or reject them.[13] Also, the cases were at different stages, and prejudice would result. Finally, because the defendants were competitors, the court had confidentiality concerns.

§ 13:10 Multidistrict litigation

The Panel on Multidistrict Litigation operates pursuant to 28 U.S.C. § 1407 which provides, in part (a):

> (a) When civil actions involving one or more common questions of fact are pending in different districts, such actions may be transferred to any district for coordinated or consolidated pretrial proceedings. Such transfers shall be made by the judicial panel on multidistrict litigation authorized by this section upon its determination that transfers for such proceedings will be for the convenience of parties and witnesses and will promote the just and efficient conduct of such actions. Each action so transferred shall be remanded by the panel at or before the conclusion of such pretrial proceedings to the district from which it was transferred unless it shall have been previously terminated: *Provided, however*, That the panel may separate any claim, cross-claim, counter-claim, or third-party claim and remand any of such claims before the remainder of the action is remanded.

The joinder provision of the AIA does not limit the authority of the Judicial Panel on Multidistrict Litigation to transfer cases to a single district.[1] The Panel itself does not order pretrial consolidation. Instead, the Panel "centralizes" when it transfers . . .

> "civil actions involving one or more common questions of fact" that "are pending in different districts" to a single district "for coordinated or consolidated pretrial proceedings." [citation omitted] * * * [W]e do not order pretrial "consolidation" of the cases before us. That is done, if at all, in a district court, typically the MDL transferee court. We refrain from dictating the

---

[13] *PB & J Software, LLC v. Acronis, Inc.*, 2012 WL 4815132, *2 (E.D. Mo. 2012).

[Section 13:10]

[1] *Unified Messaging Solutions, LLC v. United Online, Inc.*, 2013 WL 1874211, at *6-7 (N.D. Ill. 2013); *In re: Bear Creek Technologies, Inc., ('722) Patent Litigation*, 858 F. Supp. 2d 1375 (U.S.J.P.M.L. 2012).

structure of an MDL's pretrial proceedings . . . .[2]

A transfer under § 1407 and the joinder requirement under § 299 use different standards. The § 1407 transfer requires civil actions pending in more than one district having "common questions of fact" for which a transfer will be "for the convenience of parties and witnesses" and "promote the just and efficient conduct of such actions." Joinder under 35 U.S.C. § 299 requires not only questions of fact common to all defendants but also that the claims "must arise out of the same transaction, occurrence, or series. . ." relating to the patent infringement.[3] Indeed, § 299 is silent as to § 1407.[4] "The plain meaning of the AIA's joinder provision simply does not implicate Section 1407 transfer, and the Act's terms do not contain sufficient ambiguity to imply such a meaning."[5]

The AIA's right to separate trials is to be taken into account when considering centralization of multiple actions:

> Respondents also argue that the AIA is incompatible with centralization. While we recently held that "the America Invents Act does not alter our authority to order pretrial centralization of this litigation," *see In re Bear Creek Techs., Inc., ('722) Patent Litig.,* __ F.Supp.2d. __, 2012 WL 1523340, *2 (J.P.M.L. May 2, 2012), respondents correctly note that the AIA's right to separate trials should be taken into account when making the decision to centralize a given litigation, inasmuch as the AIA is the new reality in patent litigation and its right to separate trials could impact the Panel's calculus regarding whether centralization benefits "the convenience of parties and witnesses" and "will promote the just and efficient conduct" of the litigation. 28 U.S.C. § 1407(a).
>
> While the AIA changed the landscape of patent litigation—particularly the filing of actions against multiple unrelated defendants and the right to a separate trial when defendants are only accused of violating the same patent—it does not follow that the mere possibility of factual disputes regarding a particular invalidity defense or the infringement of a particular product that might need to be presented to a jury (or juries) is sufficient to deny centralization of actions otherwise involving common factual questions. Nor should such a determina-

---

[2]*In re: Bear Creek Technologies, Inc., ('722) Patent Litigation*, 858 F. Supp. 2d 1375 (U.S.J.P.M.L. 2012).

[3]*In re: Bear Creek Technologies, Inc., ('722) Patent Litigation*, 858 F. Supp. 2d 1375 (U.S.J.P.M.L. 2012).

[4]*In re: Bear Creek Technologies, Inc., ('722) Patent Litigation*, 858 F. Supp. 2d 1375 (U.S.J.P.M.L. 2012).

[5]*In re: Bear Creek Technologies, Inc., ('722) Patent Litigation*, 858 F. Supp. 2d 1375 (U.S.J.P.M.L. 2012).

tion automatically trump the pretrial efficiencies (notably in having a single judge construe the patent's claims, as opposed to five judges in various districts) that can be gained from centralizing this litigation.[6]

The Panel on Multidistrict Litigation agreed that the rights of an alleged infringer under the joinder and consolidation provisions of the AIA may have a role in how a transferee judge conducts the MDL proceedings. For instance, the court may order a prompt remand after the common claims are construed and summary judgment is addressed on common invalidity grounds, if appropriate.[7]

§ 13:11 Waivability

Under § 299(c), the restraints on joinder and consolidation for trial are waivable by the affected party. This allows alleged infringers to stay in the same action if they so choose and take advantage of the efficiencies noted briefly above, along with other reasons why they may favor proceeding in this manner.

---

[6] *In re: Maxim Integrated Products, Inc., Patent Litigation*, 867 F. Supp. 2d 1333 (U.S.J.P.M.L. 2012).

[7] *In re: Maxim Integrated Products, Inc., Patent Litigation*, 867 F. Supp. 2d 1333 (U.S.J.P.M.L. 2012).

Chapter 14

Miscellaneous Enforcement Issues

AIA §§ 15(a), 20
35 U.S.C.A. § 282(b), 288

§ 14:1 Introduction

The AIA contains various other provisions that impact patent enforcement litigation.

§ 14:2 The best mode defense is eliminated

Part I of this book noted the changes to the best mode *requirement*. This chapter concerns the elimination of the best mode *defense*. The House Report indicates Congress' intent in these revisions:[1]

[Section 14:2]

[1]The Supreme Court cautions against relying on interpretations advanced in legislative statements that are not "anchored in the text of the statute." *Shannon v. U.S.*, 512 U.S. 573, 583, 114 S. Ct. 2419, 129 L. Ed. 2d 459 (1994), stating "[C]ourts have no authority to enforce [a] principl[e] gleaned solely from legislative history that has no statutory reference point." *Shannon,* 512 U.S. at 584, quoting *International Broth. of Elec. Workers, Local Union No. 474, AFL-CIO v. N.L.R.B.*, 814 F.2d 697, 712, 124 L.R.R.M. (BNA) 2993, 106 Lab. Cas. (CCH) P 12256 (D.C.

Best mode requirement

The Act amends § 282(b) to eliminate as a defense to patent infringement the patentee's failure to comply with the best mode requirement of 112. An applicant for a patent must disclose: (1) a written description of the invention; (2) a written description of the manner of making and using the invention, sufficient to enable one skilled in the art to make and use it (known as the "enablement requirement"); and (3) the best mode contemplated by the inventor of carrying out the invention.[FN53] The disclosures required of an applicant are part of the important tradeoff that underlies the patent laws: the grant of a limited-term monopoly in exchange for disclosure of the invention.

FN53. 35 U.S.C. Sec. 112. Section 112 also requires an applicant to disclose a written description of the invention and a written description of the manner of making and using the invention, sufficient to enable one skilled in the art to make and use it.

Under current law, the defense of patent invalidity is available for failure to comply with any requirement of § 112 (specification) or 251 (reissued patents). Further, a defendant in patent litigation may also allege an intentional nondisclosure of the best mode, with intent to deceive the Office, as a basis for an unenforceability defense. Many have argued in recent years that the best mode requirement, which is unique to American patent law, is counterproductive.[FN54] They argue that challenges to patents based on best mode are inherently subjective and not relevant by the time the patent is in litigation, because the best mode contemplated at the time of the invention may not be the best mode for practicing or using the invention years later.

FN54. Among those who have so argued are the National Academy of Sciences, the Biotechnology Industry Organization, the American Intellectual Property Law Association, the Intellectual Property Owners Association, and Pharmaceutical Research and Manufacturers of America.

In response to these concerns, the Act includes a provision that eliminates best mode as a basis for both invalidity and unenforceability defenses under § 282; other defenses are unaffected.

The AIA trends toward global harmonization by eliminat-

Cir. 1987). The authoritative statement "is the statutory text, not the legislative history." *Exxon Mobil Corp. v. Allapattah Services, Inc.*, 545 U.S. 546, 568, 125 S. Ct. 2611, 162 L. Ed. 2d 502 (2005). However, lower courts have cited the legislative history of the AIA already in recent cases. E.g., *Rogers v. Tristar Products, Inc.*, 102 U.S.P.Q.2d 1722, 2012 WL 1660604, *2 (Fed. Cir. 2012) (non-precedential); *Byrne v. Wood, Herron & Evans, LLP*, 676 F.3d 1024, 1029, 102 U.S.P.Q.2d 1073 (Fed. Cir. 2012) (dissenting opin.).

ing the best mode defense from litigation and USPTO challenges to patent validity but retaining the best mode requirement for patent applications. Section 282(b) is revised as follows:

Revised 35 U.S.C. § 282[2]

§ 282. Presumption of validity; defenses

* * *

(b) *DEFENSES*.— The following shall be defenses in any action involving the validity or infringement of a patent and shall be pleaded:

(1) Noninfringement, absence of liability for infringement or ~~unenforceability,~~ unenforceability.

(2) Invalidity of the patent or any claim in suit on any ground specified in part II ~~of this title~~ as a condition for ~~patentability,~~ patentability.

~~(3) Invalidity of the patent or any claim in suit for failure to comply with any requirement of sections 112 or 251 of this title,~~

(3) Invalidity of the patent or any claim in suit for failure to comply with—

(A) any requirement of section 112, except that the failure to disclose the best mode shall not be a basis on which any claim of a patent may be canceled or held invalid or otherwise unenforceable; or

(B) any requirement of section 251.

(4) Any other fact or act made a defense by this title.

As can be seen, until passage of the AIA, 35 U.S.C. § 282(b)(3) made the failure to observe *any requirement* of section 112 (or 251) a defense. However, as rewritten, subpart (b)(3) now specifically excepts the failure to disclose the best mode as a basis for challenging validity or unenforceability. This exception also applies to post-grant reviews, *inter partes* reviews, reexaminations, and other proceedings after September 16, 2011.

---

[2] Revised statutes are shown with underscoring for new language and strikethrough for deleted language.

§ 14:3 The deceptive intent defense is eliminated

The AIA eliminates a defense stated implicitly in 35 U.S.C. § 288. The AIA amendment is as follows:[1]

35 U.S.C. 288 Action for infringement of a patent containing an invalid claim.

Whenever~~, without deceptive intention,~~ a claim of a patent is invalid, an action may be maintained for the infringement of a claim of the patent which may be valid. The patentee shall recover no costs unless a disclaimer of the invalid claim has been entered at the Patent and Trademark Office before the commencement of the suit.

It would appear that a defense of deceptive intention on the part of the patent applicant is subsumed in the inequitable conduct defense that has been raised with disturbing frequency. There are no comments in the House Report concerning this deletion. Chapter 26 of this book discusses the AIA's removal of "deceptive intent" from several parts of the patent statute.

§ 14:4 The biotechnology composition of matter exception in § 282

Another defense that has been eliminated relates to Section 103. The discussion *supra* in Part I indicates that § 103(b) has been removed. The AIA makes a corresponding change to § 282(a), as follows:[1]

Revised Statute (35 U.S.C. § 282)

§ 282. Presumption of validity; defenses

(a) In general. A patent shall be presumed valid. Each claim of a patent (whether in independent, dependent, or multiple dependent form) shall be presumed valid independently of the validity of other claims; dependent or multiple dependent claims shall be presumed valid even though dependent upon an invalid claim. ~~Notwithstanding the preceding sentence, if a claim to a composition of matter is held invalid and that claim was the basis of a determination of nonobvious-~~

[Section 14:3]

[1]Revised statutes are shown with underscoring for new language and strikethrough for deleted language.

[Section 14:4]

[1]Revised statutes are shown with underscoring for new language and strikethrough for deleted language.

~~ness under section 103(b)(1), the process shall no longer be considered nonobvious solely on the basis of section 103(b)(1).~~ The burden of establishing invalidity of a patent or any claim thereof shall rest on the party asserting such invalidity.

Part III

USPTO TRIAL PROCEEDINGS

Chapter 15

PTAB Trial Practice

AIA §§ 3, 6, 7, 18
35 U.S.C.A. §§ 6, 135, 316, 326
37 C.F.R. Part 42

§ 15:1 The Patent Trial and Appeal Board and its rules—Generally

The House Report indicates Congressional intent in establishing the Patent Trial and Appeal Board:[1]

[Section 15:1]

[1]The Supreme Court cautions against relying on interpretations advanced in legislative statements that are not "anchored in the text of the statute." *Shannon v. U.S.*, 512 U.S. 573, 583, 114 S. Ct. 2419, 129 L. Ed. 2d 459 (1994), stating "[C]ourts have no authority to enforce [a] principl[e] gleaned solely from legislative history that has no statutory reference point." *Shannon*, 512 U.S. at 584, quoting *International Broth. of Elec. Workers, Local Union No. 474, AFL-CIO v. N.L.R.B.*, 814 F.2d 697, 712, 124 L.R.R.M. (BNA) 2993, 106 Lab. Cas. (CCH) P 12256 (D.C. Cir. 1987). The authoritative statement "is the statutory text, not the legislative history." *Exxon Mobil Corp. v. Allapattah Services, Inc.*, 545 U.S. 546, 568, 125 S. Ct. 2611, 162 L. Ed. 2d 502 (2005). However, lower courts have cited the legislative history of the AIA already in recent cases. E.g., *Rogers v. Tristar Products, Inc.*, 102 U.S.P.Q.2d 1722, 2012 WL 1660604, *2 (Fed. Cir. 2012) (non-precedential); *Byrne v. Wood, Herron &*

Patent Trial and Appeal Board.

The Act renames the Patent Board the "Patent Trial and Appeal Board" and sets forth its duties, which are expanded to include jurisdiction over the new post-grant review and derivation proceedings. This section strikes references to proceedings eliminated by the Act, including interference proceedings, and updates the various appeals statutes.

* * *

Section 7. Patent Trial and Appeal Board.

The Board of Patent Appeals and Interferences is replaced with the new Patent Trial and Appeal Board ("Board"). The Board is charged with (i) reviewing adverse decisions of examiners on applications and reexamination proceedings, (ii) conducting derivation proceedings, and (iii) conducting the post-grant review proceedings. This section also updates the various appeals statutes.[2]

Section 7 of the America Invents Act amends 35 U.S.C. § 6 to create the Patent Trial and Appeal Board ("PTAB"). This replaces the Board of Patent Appeal and Interferences. The duties of the new PTAB are set forth in 35 U.S.C. § 6(b), namely to (1) review adverse decisions of examiners upon applications for patents pursuant to 35 U.S.C. § 134(a); (2) review appeals of reexaminations pursuant to § 134(b); (3) conduct derivation proceedings pursuant to § 135; and (4) conduct *inter partes* reviews and post-grant reviews pursuant to Chapters 31 and 32. Each appeal, derivation proceeding, post-grant review and *inter partes* review must be heard by at least three members of the PTAB. 35 U.S.C. § 6(c).

In other words, in addition to having appellate jurisdiction over *ex parte* matters, the new PTAB has original jurisdiction over the four new contested cases ("trials"), namely:

- *inter partes* review ("IPR"),
- post-grant review ("PGR"),
- covered business method patent review ("CBM"), and
- derivation proceedings.[3]

The implementing legislation requires the Commissioner

Evans, LLP, 676 F.3d 1024, 1029, 102 U.S.P.Q.2d 1073 (Fed. Cir. 2012) (dissenting opin.).

[2]H. R. Rep. No. 112-98, pt. 1, pp. 48, 77 (2011).

[3]Ex parte reexaminations and reissues are not "trials" to be heard originally by the PTAB.

to set forth rules for the conduct of these proceedings.[4]

These proceedings are conducted with considerable speed and in accordance with a specific sequence from which the Board is reluctant to deviate. For example, it has rejected the suggestion of having an entire claim construction proceeding in advance of other scheduled events such as the post-institution response by the patent owner.[5]

The Board issues written rulings throughout the course of the pre-trial and trial proceedings, and it has posted several of its rulings as "Representative Orders, Decisions, and Notices" which are available on a dedicated portion of the PTAB web site.[6] A typical schedule is shown below:

---

[4]AIA § 6(a) specifies that 35 U.S.C.A. Chapter 31 will include § 316 for the "conduct of *inter partes* review" and specifying that "[t]he Director shall prescribe regulations . . ." that provide for filing the proceedings, setting forth standards, governing the proceedings, providing for protective orders, and so forth. AIA § 6(c) requires the Director to issue regulations to carry out Chapter 31 of Title 35 within one year after the date of enactment of the AIA. Similarly, AIA § 6(d) instituted post-grant reviews and added a new Chapter 32 to the patent statute. Section 326 thereof calls for the Director to prescribe regulations for such proceedings, and Section 6(f) requires the Director to issue regulations to carry out Chapter 32. AIA § 18 is directed to the "Transitional Program For Covered Business Method Patents," and § 18(a)(1) requires the Director to issue regulations establishing and implementing the transitional post-grant review proceeding for the review of the validity of covered business method patents. Finally, AIA § 3(i) calls for derivation proceedings under 35 U.S.C.A. § 135, and AIA Section 3(j) calls for the elimination of references to "interferences" from 35 U.S.C.A. §§ 134, 145, 146, 154, and 305.

[5]*CRS Advanced Technologies, Inc. v. Frontline Technologies, Inc.*, CBM2012-00005, Paper No. 31, p. 3 (PTAB Feb. 13, 2013).

[6]http://www.uspto.gov/ip/boards/bpai/representative_orders_and_opinions.jsp.

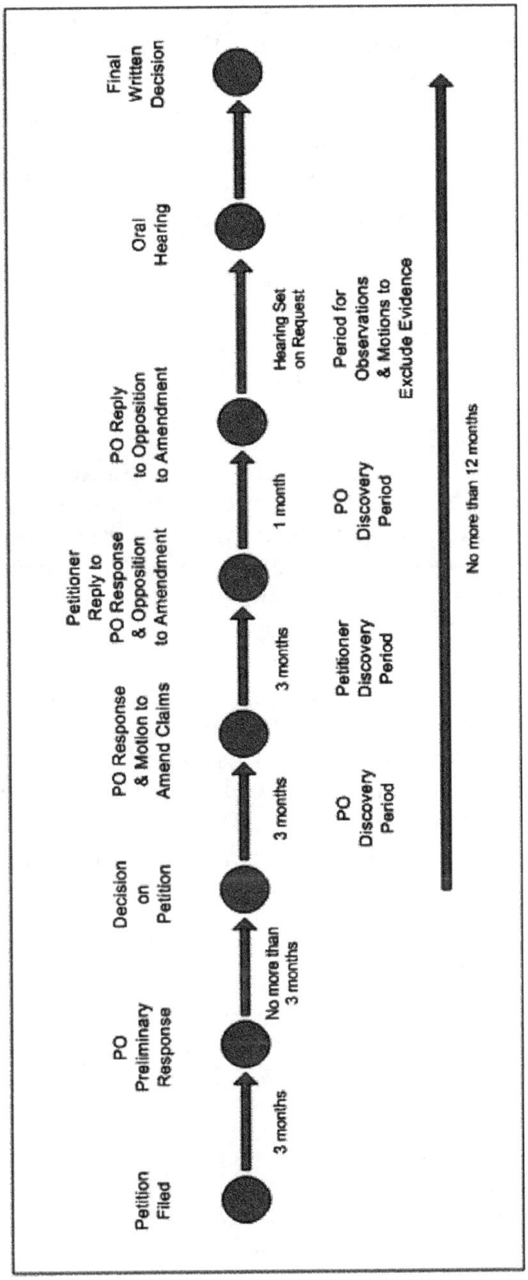

Pursuant to its authority, the USPTO set forth proposed rules and then final rules to govern these contested proceedings. These rules for contested cases appear generally at 37 C.F.R. Part 42, entitled "Trial Practice Before the Patent Trial and Appeal Board." Part 42 contains the following subparts:

- Subpart A, trial practice and procedure, §§ 42.1–42.80.
- Subpart B, *inter partes* review, §§ 42.100–42.123.
- Subpart C, post-grant review, §§ 42.200–42.224.
- Subpart D, transitional program for covered business method patents, §§ 42.300–42.304.
- Subpart E, derivation proceedings, §§ 42.400–42.412.

The USPTO also issued a "Trial Practice Guide" at 77 Fed. Reg. (No. 157) 48756 to 48773 (August 14, 2012). Some material appears in the Trial Practice Guide only. Thus the sources for rules and information on how these four contested cases are handled in the USPTO are the statutory revisions found in the AIA, the final rules and regulations set forth in 37 C.F.R., the Trial Practice Guide, and the comments to the final rules of the PTAB appearing at 77 Fed. Reg. (No. 157) 48612 to 48678 (August 14, 2012). The Trial Practice Guide and this chapter provide a general overview of the contested proceedings heard by the PTAB. Specific information about the four separate procedures is contained in subsequent chapters of this book. The Trial Practice Guide applies to *inter partes* review, post-grant review and covered business method patent review proceedings begun on or after September 16, 2012. It also applies to derivation proceedings commencing on or after March 16, 2013.[7]

There are a number of general rules to note. Parallel to Federal Rule of Civil Procedure 1, the "policy" rules set forth in 37 C.F.R. § 42.1 provide, "This part shall be construed to secure the just, speedy, and inexpensive resolution of every proceeding." 37 C.F.R. § 42.1(b). The Rules demand decorum and candor from all who appear before the PTAB (usually referred to as the "Board" in the rules), and the PTAB can—and likely will—impose sanctions pursuant to for improper behavior:

§ **42.1. Policy.** * * *

(c) *Decorum.* Every party must act with courtesy and decorum in all proceedings before the Board, including in interactions with other parties.

§ **42.11. Duty of candor.**

Parties and individuals involved in the proceeding have a duty of candor and good faith to the Office during the course of

[7]77 Fed. Reg. 48756 (August 14, 2012).

a proceeding.

§ 42.12. Sanctions.

(a) The Board may impose a sanction against a party for misconduct, including:

(1) Failure to comply with an applicable rule or order in the proceeding;

(2) Advancing a misleading or frivolous argument or request for relief;

(3) Misrepresentation of a fact;

(4) Engaging in dilatory tactics;

(5) Abuse of discovery;

(6) Abuse of process; or

(7) Any other improper use of the proceeding, including actions that harass or cause unnecessary delay or an unnecessary increase in the cost of the proceeding.

(b) Sanctions include entry of one or more of the following:

(1) An order holding facts to have been established in the proceeding;

(2) An order expunging or precluding a party from filing a paper;

(3) An order precluding a party from presenting or contesting a particular issue;

(4) An order precluding a party from requesting, obtaining, or opposing discovery;

(5) An order excluding evidence;

(6) An order providing for compensatory expenses, including attorney fees;

(7) An order requiring terminal disclaimer of patent term; or

(8) Judgment in the trial or dismissal of the petition.

It is highly advisable that counsel adhere strictly to the rules and the timetable set by the Board. Remember that the Board is charged by statute with reaching its final decision within 12 months, extendible for up to six further months for good cause. As such, counsel (or parties) who misrepresent facts or who are dilatory, abusive, or frivolous are exposed to sanctions. Even the simple "failure to comply with an applicable rule or order in the proceeding" can lead to sanctions. Given that estoppels attach to the outcome, and the proceeding cannot be terminated except by settlement, it is vitally important that counsel and parties understand and abide the rules that govern trial practice before the PTAB.

§ 15:2 PTAB "trials"—Generally

A "trial" before the PTAB is quite different from a "trial" in a civil action in state or federal court. In the PTAB, a "trial" is a defined term which means a contested case instituted by the Board based upon a petition. 37 C.F.R. § 42.2. The PTAB "trial" includes, but is not the same as, a "hearing," and § 42.2 defines "hearing" as "consideration of the trial."

§ 42.2. Definitions

Hearing means consideration of the trial.

Trial means a contested case instituted by the Board based upon a petition. A trial begins with a written decision notifying the petitioner and patent owner of the institution of the trial. The term *trial* specifically includes a derivation proceeding under 35 U.S.C. 135; an *inter partes* review under Chapter 31 of title 35, United States Code; a post-grant review under Chapter 32 of title 35, United States Code; and a transitional business-method review under section 18 of the Leahy-Smith America Invents Act. Patent interferences are administered under part 41 and not under part 42 of this title, and therefore are not trials.[1]

Thus, the PTAB "trial" is roughly equivalent to the generalist's term "litigation" or "lawsuit," connoting the entire process of the contested case from the time the Board issues a decision instituting the matter through the final disposition of the matter.

In federal court, a civil action is generally commenced by filing a complaint. The court does not decide whether it will call that a civil action or not, but in the PTAB, one has to request a "trial" by filing a petition. The events leading up to the decision whether to institute a PTAB trial are called the "Preliminary Proceeding." The following Rules give further relevant definitions:

§ 42.2. Definitions.

Petition is a request that a trial be instituted.

Petitioner means the party filing a petition requesting that a trial be instituted.

Preliminary Proceeding begins with the filing of a petition

[Section 15:2]

[1]37 C.F.R. § 42.2.

for instituting a trial and ends with a written decision as to whether a trial will be instituted.

Proceeding means a trial or preliminary proceeding.

If the PTAB grants the petition, it enters a notice of trial, and this entity "institutes" the trial:

§ 42.4. Notice of trial.

(a) *Institution of trial.* The Board institutes the trial on behalf of the Director.

(b) Notice of a trial will be sent to every party to the proceeding. The entry of the notice institutes the trial.

§ 42.4. Notice of trial.

(a)

(b)

§ 15:3 Starting a preliminary proceeding—The petition generally

The USPTO divides these four contested matters into segments. The first segment occurs before the "trial" and is called the "Preliminary Proceeding." It commences when a "Petitioner" files a "Petition" to commence a "Proceeding" and ends when the Board files a written decision on whether it will institute a trial. The following definitions in § 42.2 are applicable:

Petition is a request that a trial be instituted.

Petitioner means the party filing a petition requesting that a trial be instituted.

Preliminary Proceeding begins with the filing of a petition for instituting a trial and ends with a written decision as to whether a trial will be instituted.

Proceeding means a trial or preliminary proceeding.

The petitioner must file a petition meeting substantive requirements that are set forth in the statute and the rules of 37 C.F.R. Part 42. The petition should be quite unlike a complaint in federal court that usually contains only notice pleading. Instead, a PTAB petition should set forth the petitioner's case-in-chief, complete with all evidence in the form of exhibits along with testimony (also as exhibits). Typically, the petitioner will have been working on this for several months.

Form. All petitions must be double spaced on 8.5 by 11 inch paper and must use a 14 point font. Only certain items may have less than double spacing: claim charts, headings, tables of contents, tables of authorities, indices, signature blocks, and certificates of service. Margins must be one (1) inch or more on all sides.

A petition for instituting an *inter partes* review or a derivation proceeding is limited to 60 pages. A petition for instituting a post-grant review or covered business method patent review may have up to 80 pages.[1] The table of contents, table of authorities, certificate of service, or appendix of exhibits are not included in the page count.[2] A petitioner may seek to waive the page limits under 37 C.F.R. § 42.24(a)(2). The petitioner must provide a showing of how a waiver of the page limits is in the interests of justice. The proposed petition according to the motion must be attached. If the motion is not granted, the proposed petition may be expunged or returned.

Further matters of form are discussed in § 15:6 *infra*.

Content. The statute and specific rules set forth required showings in petitions, but the following general rule § 42.22 must also be followed for all petitions (and all motions):

§ 42.22. Content of petitions and motions.

(a) Each petition or motion must be filed as a separate paper and must include:

(1) A statement of the precise relief requested; and

(2) A full statement of the reasons for the relief requested, including a detailed explanation of the significance of the evidence including material facts, and the governing law, rules, and precedent.

(b) Relief requested. Where a rule in part 1 of this title ordinarily governs the relief sought, the petition or motion must make any showings required under that rule in addition to any showings required in this part.

(c) Statement of material facts. Each petition or motion may include a statement of material fact. Each material fact preferably shall be set forth as a separately numbered sentence with specific citations to the portions of the record that support the fact.

(d) The Board may order additional showings or explanations as a condition for authorizing a motion (*see* § 42.20(b)).

The specific petition requirements for the four trial types are discussed in subsequent chapters. However:

[Section 15:3]

[1]37 C.F.R. § 42.24(a).

[2]37 C.F.R. § 42.24(a).

- For *inter partes* review, see 35 U.S.C. § 312 and 37 C.F.R. § 42.104;
- For post-grant review, see 35 U.S.C. § 322 and 37 C.F.R. § 42.204;
- For review of a covered business method patent, see AIA § 18 and 37 C.F.R. § 304; and
- For a derivation proceeding, see 35 U.S.C. § 135 and 37 C.F.R. § 405.

The PTAB has cautioned against including content so voluminous and unfocused that it creates too much of a burden on the PTAB and the patent owner. Thus, in *Liberty Mutual Ins. Co. v. Progressive Casualty Ins. Co.*, CBM2012-00003, Paper No. 7 (PTAB Oct. 25, 2012), an expanded panel of nine PTAB judges set forth a "Redundant Grounds" order advising the petitioner that its 422 grounds of unpatentability over prior art, with an average of over 21 grounds per claim, was unacceptable due to multiple redundancies. The Board ordered the petitioner to notify the Board within seven days of which single group of grounds to maintain against each challenged claim. In a companion ruling by the three-member panel only, the Board rejected 196 of the alleged grounds even before the patent owner submitted a preliminary response, stating, "Petitioner has not advanced a credible rationale . . . [W]e regard Petitioner's stated reasoning . . . to be unsupported by the record and simply unpersuasive." *Liberty Mutual Ins. Co. v. Progressive Casualty Ins. Co.*, CBM2012-00003, Paper No. 8, pp. 11-12 (PTAB Oct. 25, 2012).

Fees. Petitions will be rejected absent payment of the appropriate filing fee. These fees are listed in 37 C.F.R. § 42.15.

§ 15:4 Mandatory notices—Real party in interest

Judgments in trials raise estoppels against the petitioner and real party in interest. 37 C.F.R. § 42.73(d). As such, and to assist the Board in identifying potential conflicts of interest,[1] the rules require disclosure of the real party in interest. It is one of the mandatory notices:

§ 42.8. Mandatory notices.

(a) Each notice listed in paragraph (b) of this section must

[Section 15:4]

[1]Trial Practice Guide, 77 Fed.Reg. 48756, 48759 (Aug. 14, 2012).

be filed with the Board:

(1) By the petitioner, as part of the petition;

(2) By the patent owner, or applicant in the case of derivation, within 21 days of service of the petition; or

(3) By either party, within 21 days of a change of the information listed in paragraph (b) of this section stated in an earlier paper.

(b) Each of the following notices must be filed:

(1) Real party-in-interest. Identify each real party-in-interest for the party.

(2) Related matters. Identify any other judicial or administrative matter that would affect, or be affected by, a decision in the proceeding.

(3) *Lead and back-up counsel.* If the party is represented by counsel, then counsel must be identified.

(4) Service information. Identify (if applicable):

(i) An electronic mail address;

(ii) A postal mailing address;

(iii) A hand-delivery address, if different than the postal mailing address;

(iv) A telephone number; and

(v) A facsimile number.

Identifying the real party in interest is the subject of some discussion in the Trial Practice Guide.[2] Identifying the real party in interest is not a new requirement: the USPTO and courts have required such statements for many years, and a body of law has developed and can be consulted.

The Trial Practice Guide indicates, "Whether a party who is not a named participant in a given proceeding nonetheless constitutes a 'real party-in-interest' or 'privy' is a highly fact-dependent question," that courts have avoided rigid definitions or recitals of necessary factors, and that the common law expression does not fit directly into the AIA trial context.[3] It explains that one purpose of binding real parties-in-interest to the outcome of proceedings is to "protect patent owners from harassment via successive petitions by the same or related parties." It also prevents parties from a "second bite at the apple." Further, it seeks "to protect the integrity of both the USPTO and Federal Courts by assuring that all

[2]Trial Practice Guide, 77 Fed.Reg. 48756, 48759 to 48760 (Aug. 14, 2012).

[3]Trial Practice Guide, 77 Fed.Reg. 48756, 48759 (Aug. 14, 2012).

issues are promptly raised and vetted."[4] The Guide then explains:

> The USPTO will apply traditional common-law principles with these goals in mind and parties will be well-served to factor in these considerations when determining whom to identify.
>
> Whether a party who is not a named participant in a given proceeding nevertheless constitutes a "real party-in-interest" or "privy" to that proceeding is a highly fact-dependent question. * * *
>
> . . . the "real party-in-interest" is the party that desires review of the patent. Thus, the "real party-in-interest" may be the petitioner itself, and/or it may be the party or parties at whose behest the petition has been filed.[5]

The Guide explains that for purposes of AIA trials, one need not be a "privy" in order to be regarded as a "real party-in-interest," that a party who funds, directs, and controls an IPR or PGR petition or proceeding constitutes a "real party-in-interest,"[6] and that less than complete funding and control may still suffice but "requires consideration of the pertinent facts."[7] It states:

> The Office has received requests to state whether particular facts will qualify a party as a "real party-in-interest" or "privy." Some fact combinations will generally justify applying the "real party-in-interest" or "privy" label. For example, a party that funds and directs and controls an IPR or PGR petition or proceeding constitutes a "real party-in-interest," even if that party is not a "privy" of the petitioner. But whether something less than complete funding and control suffices to justify similarly treating the party requires consideration of the pertinent facts. *See, e.g., Cal. Physicians,* 163 Cal.App.4th at 1523–25 (discussing the role of control in the "privy" analysis, and observing that "preclusion can apply even in the absence of such control"). *The Office will handle such questions on a case-by-case basis* taking into consideration how courts have viewed the terms. Similarly, while generally a party does not become a "real party-in-interest" or a "privy" of the petitioner merely through association with another party in an unrelated endeavor, slight alterations in the facts, as well as consideration of other facts, might result in a different conclusion. So, for example, if Trade Association X files an IPR petition, Party A does not become a "real party-in-interest" or a "privy" of the Association simply based on its membership in the Association.

---

[4]Trial Practice Guide, 77 Fed.Reg. 48756, 48759 (Aug. 14, 2012).

[5]Trial Practice Guide, 77 Fed.Reg. 48756, 48759 (Aug. 14, 2012).

[6]Trial Practice Guide, 77 Fed.Reg. 48756, 48760 (Aug. 14, 2012).

[7]Trial Practice Guide, 77 Fed.Reg. 48756, 48760 (Aug. 14, 2012).

> Similarly, if Party A is part of a Joint Defense Group with Party B in a patent infringement suit, and Party B files a PGR petition, Party A is not a "real party-in-interest" or a "privy" for the purposes of the PGR petition based solely on its participation in that Group. That is not to say that Party A's membership in Trade Association X, or the Joint Defense Group, in those scenarios is irrelevant to the determination; deeper consideration of the facts in the particular case is necessary to determine whether Party A is a "real party-in-interest" or a "privy" of the petitioner. Relevant factors include: Party A's relationship with the petitioner; Party A's relationship to the petition itself, including the nature and/or degree of involvement in the filing; and the nature of the entity filing the petition. In short, because rarely will one fact, standing alone, be determinative of the inquiry, the Office cannot prejudge the impact of a particular fact on whether a party is a "real party-in-interest" or "privy" of the petitioner.[8] [emphasis added]

Within the quoted passage, the statement that "The Office will handle such questions on a case-by-case basis" indicates a USPTO expectation that it will be involved in further determinations. Certainly these questions will arise in PTAB trials, but it is unlikely that the Board expects to receive requests for guidance from prospective petitioners (or others) about who to identify as a "real party-in-interest" in a hypothetical future proceeding or that any such request would be answered substantively, particularly in view of the ban on *ex parte* communications set forth in 37 C.F.R. § 42.5(d).[9] The rule on its face appears sufficiently broad to interdict contacts by non-parties. Hence, even if someone other than the prospective petitioner were to contemplate contacting the Board with a "real party-in-interest" question, § 42.5(d) by its literal terms is not confined to *ex parte* communications from only the parties but more generally prohibits *ex parte* communications.

Parties have challenged the completeness of real party in interest designations, but typically the PTAB has rejected the challenges, as occurred in the representative case of *Intellectual Ventures Management, LLC v. Xilinx, Inc.*, IPR2012-00018, 00019, 00020, and 00023 (PTAB January 24, 2013), where the patent owner Xilinx asserted that the

---

[8]Trial Practice Guide, 77 Fed.Reg. 48756, 48760 (Aug. 14, 2012).

[9]"(d) *Ex parte communications.* Communication regarding a specific proceeding with a Board member defined in 35 U.S.C.A. 6(a) is not permitted unless both parties have an opportunity to be involved in the communication."

petitioner IVM had failed to identify the other real parties in interest. One exhibit offered by Xilinx was a certificate of interested entities or persons filed by six defendants (including IVM) in a district court proceeding unrelated to the instant IPRs. That certificate named 63 entities who (i) purportedly had either a financial interest in the controversy or in a party to the proceeding, or (ii) who had a non-financial interest in the subject matter or in a party that could be affected substantially by the outcome of the proceeding. The Board rejected this challenge on the basis that the challenger, Xilinx, had not sufficiently shown the relevance of its exhibit. In particular, it had not shown that the considerations of whether a non-party is a real party in interest in an IPR are the same or similar to the considerations or requirements under the local civil rules and the Federal Rules of Civil Procedure. The Board declined to assume that the 63 listed entities should be named as real parties in interest in the pending IPRs. Xilinx provided insufficient evidence for the Board to conclude that IVM was not the only real party in interest in any of the four proceedings.[10]

The Office has not issued a rule on what to do when a petitioner has legitimate questions of who a petitioner or patent owner must identify as a "real party-in-interest."[11] A safe course of action would be for the filer—whether the petitioner or the patent owner—to consult applicable case law and apply it to the specific facts of the case and state the filing party's belief who it believes to be the real party or parties in interest and to explain the pertinent facts as to other candidates, thereby to allow the Board to reach its own determination. Moreover, this affords the Board the opportunity to avoid potential conflicts of interest.

In addition, a *joint* telephone conference with a member of

---

[10]*See also Ranbaxy Laboratories Ltd. v. Vertex Pharmaceuticals*, IPR 2013-00024, Paper No. 45, p. 4 (PTAB May 24, 2013) (any third party participation in the deposition of a petitioner's declarant might bind the third party even if not identified as a real party in interest); *Apple Inc. v. Achates Reference Publishing, Inc.*, IPR 2013-00080-00081, Paper No. 17, pp. 5-7 (PTAB Apr. 3, 2013) (indemnification clause not enough to create a real party-in-interest); *Innolux Corp. v. Semiconductor Energy Laboratory Co., Ltd.*, IPR 2013-00028, Paper No. 14, p. 8 (PTAB Mar. 21, 2013) (PTAB considers whether a party has exercised control or funding of a petition to determine if that petition is binding upon the party as a real party in interest).

[11]The Trial Practice Guide gives the name and telephone number of Michael Tierney, Lead Administrative Patent Judge of the PTAB as a contact "for further information." 77 Fed. Reg. 48760 (Aug. 14, 2012).

the Board over this issue would not constitute an *ex parte* communication and therefore would not violate 37 C.F.R. § 42.5(d).

Parenthetically, § 42.8 does not require a filer to identify the real party in interest for anyone else. By its terms, it calls for the filer to identify "each real party-in-interest *for the party*." [emphasis added] Hence, the petitioner need not identify who it believes to be the real party-in-interest for the patent owner, nor need the patent owner identify who it thinks the real party-in-interest is for the petitioner. On the other hand, the rule does not prohibit raising the question, so long as this is not a dilatory tactic, a frivolous argument, or an action to harass or cause unnecessary delay or unnecessary increase in cost of the proceeding which exposes the party to sanctions pursuant to § 42.12.

Related Matters. The second item required in the mandatory notice of 37 C.F.R. § 42.8(b) is the identity of all other judicial or administrative matters that would affect or be affected by a decision in the proceeding. Companion litigation should be identified. If there are other proceedings pending in the USPTO that would be affected, they must be disclosed also.

Counsel. The third item required in the mandatory notice is identification of counsel. This topic is the subject of the next section of this chapter.

Service Information and Service. The final item required in the mandatory notice concerns service information. The notice must identify, as applicable, one's email address, postal mailing address, hand delivery address (if different), telephone number, and facsimile number. This information will facilitate service of responsive papers.

Additionally, each petition must be served on the patent owner in the manner specified by 37 C.F.R. § 42.6(e), reproduced in the discussion below concerning matters of form. See also, §§ 42.105, 42.205, 42.406.

§ 15:5 Mandatory notices—Counsel in a PTAB trial

Another mandatory notice that is required by 37 C.F.R. 42.8 to be filed (1) by the petitioner as part of the petition, (2) by the patent owner or applicant (in the case of a derivation) within 21 days of service of the petition, and (3) by either party within 21 days of a change in such information that had been stated in an earlier paper is the identity of lead and back-up counsel. The USPTO provides rules on who may appear as counsel to a party before the PTAB:

§ 42.10. Counsel.

(a) If a party is represented by counsel, the party must designate a lead counsel and a back-up counsel who can conduct business on behalf of the lead counsel.

(b) A power of attorney must be filed with the designation of counsel, except the patent owner should not file an additional power of attorney if the designated counsel is already counsel of record in the subject patent or application.

(c) The Board may recognize counsel pro hac vice during a proceeding upon a showing of good cause, subject to the condition that lead counsel be a registered practitioner and to any other conditions as the Board may impose. For example, where the lead counsel is a registered practitioner, a motion to appear pro hac vice by counsel who is not a registered practitioner may be granted upon showing that counsel is an experienced litigating attorney and has an established familiarity with the subject matter at issue in the proceeding.

(d) A panel of the Board may disqualify counsel for cause after notice and opportunity for hearing. A decision to disqualify is not final for the purposes of judicial review until certified by the Chief Administrative Patent Judge.

(e) Counsel may not withdraw from a proceeding before the Board unless the Board authorizes such withdrawal.

Each party represented by counsel must appoint a lead counsel and a back-up counsel. Lead counsel must be registered to practice before the USPTO. *See* 37 C.F.R. § 42.10(c). Lead counsel is expected to participate in all hearings and conference calls with the Board and the back-up counsel may have such participation. "In addition, the role of back-up counsel is to conduct business with the Office on behalf of lead counsel when lead counsel is not available. Actions not conducted before the Office (*e.g.*, taking of deposition) may be conducted by lead or back-up counsel."[1] If the power of attorney designating counsel is already of record, no new one needs to be filed. 37 C.F.R. § 42.10(b).

Litigators may *apply* for appearance before the Board *pro hac vice*. 37 C.F.R. § 42.10(c). The rules call for a showing of good cause, and no *pro hac vice* counsel may appear *unless lead counsel is a registered practitioner*. 37 C.F.R. § 42.10(c). The Trial Practice Guide indicates that granting a motion

---

[Section 15:5]

[1]Trial Practice Guide, 77 Fed.Reg. 48756, 48758.

for counsel to appear *pro hac vice* is discretionary. The Board will take into account the specifics of the particular proceeding. The Guide notes that these proceedings can be technically complex and "it is expected that amendments to a patent will be sought."[2] Hence, non-PTO practitioners can often be unfamiliar with patent amendments. It is unclear whether a non-practitioner who is admitted *pro hac vice* can submit an amendment.

The PTAB has occasionally denied applications for pro hac vice admission. For example, in *SAP America, Inc. v Versata Development Group, Inc.*, CBM2012-00001, Paper No. 21 (PTAB Nov. 6, 2012), petitioner SAP supplied evidence that the attorney who sought to be admitted as *pro hac vice* counsel for patent owner Versata had engaged in a pattern of protective order violations in a companion civil action.[3]

---

[2]Trial Practice Guide, 77 Fed.Reg. 48756, 48758.

[3]Versata sought admission of its lead trial counsel in the companion civil suit where Versata asserted the patent against SAP. The counsel submitted a declaration noting that he is a member in good standing of the Texas bar and that no sanctions or contempt citations had ever been imposed against him by a court or administrative body. SAP opposed the admission on the basis that his participation could circumvent the district court's protective order. The Board learned during a conference call that SAP opposed Versata's reliance on expert witnesses who had received access to SAP's confidential information in the related litigation, further implicating the court's protective order. The Board then required the parties to supply additional information, including court rulings related to the protective order, its revisions, and any violations and enforcement of the order. While Versata supplied the Board with copies of the original and revised protective order, SAP supplied additional rulings concerning Versata's violation of the protective order where the same attorney at issue represented Versata at the hearing. The Board quoted from a court opinion supplied by only SAP:

> Pending before the Court is Defendant's motion to strike Versata's equitable claims as sanction for Versata's violation of the March 6, 2008 Protective Order and February 26, 2008 Order. (Dkt. No. 144.) The Court held an evidentiary hearing on this issue on May 14, 2009. *The Court finds that Versata breached the plain language of the Protective Order through a pattern of violations involving several members of its litigation team and discovery vendor.* Given Versata's violation of the Court's order, it is fair to stay the injunction the Court has issued in this case. As a result, the Court exercises its equitable discretion in a manner adverse to Versata and stays the injunction pending the disposition of any appeal.

SAP America, Inc. v Versata Development Group, Inc., CBM2012-00001, Paper No. 21, p. 4 (PTAB Nov. 6, 2012) [emphasis by the Board or the court]. The Board then remarked that neither Versata's submissions nor the attorney's declaration addressed (or even mentioned) the district court's finding of a pattern of protective order violations where the attorney was lead counsel.

Additionally, the Board can revoke a *pro hac vice* appearance in its discretion and will take into account various factors "including incompetence, unwillingness to abide by the Office's Rules of Professional Conduct, and incivility."[4]

§ 15:6 Form of the petition and other filings

Rules 42.6 and 42.24 set forth particular requirements for papers, including the original petition, filed with the PTAB in a trial.

§ 42.6. Filing of documents, including exhibits; service.

(a) *General format requirements.*

(1) Page size must be 8½ inch × 11 inch except in the case of exhibits that require a larger size in order to preserve details of the original.

(2) In documents, including affidavits, created for the proceeding:

(i) Markings must be in black or must otherwise provide an equivalent dark, high-contrast image;

(ii) Either a proportional or monospaced font may be used:

(A) The proportional font must be 14- point or larger, and

(B) The monospaced font must not contain more than four characters per centimeter (ten characters per inch);

(iii) Double spacing must be used except in claim charts, headings, tables of contents, tables of authorities, indices, signature blocks, and certificates of service. Block quotations may be 1.5 spaced, but must be indented from both the left and the right margins; and

(iv) Margins must be at least 2.5 centimeters (1 inch) on all sides.

(3) *Incorporation by reference; combined documents.* Arguments must not be incorporated by reference from one document into another document. Combined motions, oppositions, replies, or other combined documents are not permitted.

(4) *Signature; identification.* Documents must be signed in accordance with §§ 1.33 and 11.18(a) of this title, and should be identified by the trial number (where known).

(b) *Modes of filing.*

---

[4] Trial Practice Guide, 77 Fed.Reg. 48756, 48758.

(1) Electronic filing. Unless otherwise authorized, submissions are to be made to the Board electronically via the Internet according to the parameters established by the Board and published on the Web site of the Office.

(2)(i) *Filing by means other than electronic filing.* A document filed by means other than electronic filing must:

(A) Be accompanied by a motion requesting acceptance of the submission; and

(B) Identify a date of transmission where a party seeks a filing date other than the date of receipt at the Board.

(ii) Mailed correspondence shall be sent to:

Mail Stop PATENT BOARD,

Patent Trial and Appeal Board,

United States Patent and Trademark Office,

PO Box 1450,

Alexandria, Virginia 22313—1450.

(c) *Exhibits.* Each exhibit must be filed with the first document in which it is cited except as the Board may otherwise order.

(d) *Previously filed paper.* A document already in the record of the proceeding must not be filed again, not even as an exhibit or an appendix, without express Board authorization.

(e) *Service.*

(1) *Electronic or other mode.* Service may be made electronically upon agreement of the parties. Otherwise, service may be by EXPRESS MAIL® or by means at least as fast and reliable as EXPRESS MAIL®.

(2) *Simultaneous with filing.* Each document filed with the Board, if not previously served, must be served simultaneously on each opposing party.

(3) *Counsel of record.* If a party is represented by counsel of record in the proceeding, service must be on counsel.

(4) *Certificate of service.*

(i) Each document, other than an exhibit, must include a certificate of service at the end of that document. Any exhibit filed with the document may be included in the certification for the document.

(ii) For an exhibit filed separately, a transmittal letter incorporating the certificate of service must be filed. If more than one exhibit is filed at one time, a single letter should be used for all of the exhibits filed together. The letter must state the name and exhibit number for every exhibit filed with the letter.

(iii) The certificate of service must state:

(A) The date and manner of service; and

(B) The name and address of every person served.

§ 42.24. Page limits for petitions, motions, oppositions, and replies.

(a) *Petitions and motions.*

(1) The following page limits for petitions and motions apply and include any statement of material facts to be admitted or denied in support of the petition or motion. The page limit does not include a table of contents, a table of authorities, a certificate of service, or appendix of exhibits.

(i) Petition requesting *inter partes* review: 60 pages.

(ii) Petition requesting post-grant review: 80 pages.

(iii) Petition requesting covered business method patent review: 80 pages.

(iv) Petition requesting derivation proceeding: 60 pages.

(v) Motions: 15 pages.

(2) Petitions to institute a trial must comply with the stated page limits but may be accompanied by a motion to waive the page limits. The petitioner must show in the motion how a waiver of the page limits is in the interests of justice and must append a copy of proposed petition exceeding the page limit to the motion. If the motion is not granted, the proposed petition exceeding the page limit may be expunged or returned. Any other motion to waive page limits must be granted in advance of filing a motion, opposition, or reply for which the waiver is necessary.

(b) Patent owner responses and oppositions. The page limits set forth in this paragraph do not include a listing of facts which are admitted, denied, or cannot be admitted or denied.

(1) The page limits for a patent owner preliminary response to petition are the same as the page limits for the petition.

(2) The page limits for a patent owner response to petition are the same as the page limits for the petition.

(3) The page limits for oppositions are the same as those for corresponding motions.

(c) Replies. The following page limits for replies apply and include the required statement of facts in support of the reply. The page limits do not include a table of contents, a table of authorities, a listing of facts which are admitted, denied, or cannot be admitted or denied, a certificate of service, or appendix of exhibits.

(1) Replies to patent owner responses to petitions: 15 pages.

(2) Replies to oppositions: 5 pages.

As noted above, there are page limits for each type of petition, and the font size, pitch, and line spacing a party must use are dictated by the rule. The PTAB also has admonished parties against presenting their arguments within claim tables, which may be single-spaced, as this seeks to evade the page limitation.

As noted, the petition may contain a claim chart which includes arguments on anticipation, obviousness, or other issues permitted to be raised. In one case, the Board instituted IPR on some, but not all, of the challenged claims. The petitioner sought rehearing, and in denying the request, the Board explained that petitions must give clear guidance to the Board and the patent owner of what arguments are being made against which particular claims:

> MicroStrategy's position is misplaced. If done properly, we agree that it is not improper to eliminate redundant text. But it is improper to omit arguments from where they are expected, based on explicit caption in the petition, and locate them where they are not expected, without leaving an explanatory notation. It might even be acceptable if an argument presented elsewhere is accompanied by an indication that that argument also applies at a different location in the petition to another claim, but that is not the circumstance here. MicroStrategy has pointed to nothing in its petition, which provides notice to either Zillow as the patent owner or the Board, that the arguments it presented for claims 30 and 32 also are made with respect to claim 18.[1]

§ 15:7 Public availability; default protective order

In general, the public will have access to the record of proceedings:

> **§ 42.14. Public availability.**
>
> The record of a proceeding, including documents and things, shall be made available to the public, except as otherwise ordered. A party intending a document or thing to be sealed shall file a motion to seal concurrent with the filing of the document or thing to be sealed. The document or thing shall be provisionally sealed on receipt of the motion and remain so pending the outcome of the decision on the motion.

This rule provides that the Board can order certain evi-

[Section 15:6]

[1] *Microstrategy Inc. v. Zillow, Inc.*, IPR 2013-00034, Paper No. 23, page 3 (PTAB April 22, 2013).

dence not to be made available to the public.

A petitioner may provide confidential information in the petition and want to protect it against disclosure. This is addressed in 37 C.F.R. § 42.55 and the default protective order which is found in the Trial Practice Guide. The provisions in the Rules and the Trial Practice Guide come under the aegis of the statute where, *e.g.*, 35 U.S.C. § 316(a)(7) provides, with respect to *inter partes* review, "The Director shall prescribe regulations—providing for protective orders governing the exchange and submission of confidential information." 35 U.S.C. § 326(a)(7) provides similarly for post-grant review proceedings. Pursuant to this authority, 37 C.F.R. § 42.55 provides for a default protective order (subpart (a)), and another protective order other than the default protective order (subpart (b)), as follows:

§ 42.55. Confidential information in a petition.

A petitioner filing confidential information with a petition may, concurrent with the filing of the petition, file a motion to seal with a proposed protective order as to the confidential information. The institution of the requested trial will constitute a grant of the motion to seal unless otherwise ordered by the Board.

(a) *Default protective order*. Where a motion to seal requests entry of the default protective order set forth in the Office Patent Trial Practice Guide, the petitioner must file, but need not serve, the confidential information under seal. The patent owner may only access the filed sealed information prior to the institution of the trial by agreeing to the terms of the default protective order or obtaining relief from the Board.

(b) *Protective ordersother than default protective order*. Where a motion to seal requests entry of a protective order other than the default protective order, the petitioner must file, but need not serve, the confidential information under seal. The patent owner may only access the sealed confidential information prior to the institution of the trial by:

(1) agreeing to the terms of the protective order requested by the petitioner;

(2) agreeing to the terms of a protective order that the parties file jointly; or

(3) obtaining entry of a protective order (e.g., the default protective order).

The PTAB default protective order that is entered automatically upon the filing of a petition is a single-level protective order that allows access to "persons" who own the involved patent, parties, counsel of record, and in-house counsel. Provided they sign a prescribed acknowledgement, access to the confidential information can be given to retained experts and other employees or consultants. The burden is on anyone who opposes disclosure to employees, consultants, or others working for a party. The protective order requires maintaining confidential materials in a secure location. A party may file documents or information with the Board under seal along with a description of the sealed information and an explanation of why it is confidential and should not be made available to the public. The Trial Practice Guide provides as follows:

DEFAULT PROTECTIVE ORDER[1]

The following Standing Protective Order will be automatically entered into the proceeding upon the filing of a petition for review or institution of a derivation:

Standing Protective Order

This standing protective order governs the treatment and filing of confidential information, including documents and testimony.

1. Confidential information shall be clearly marked "PROTECTIVE ORDER MATERIAL."

2. Access to confidential information is limited to the following individuals who have executed the acknowledgment appended to this order:

(A) *Parties.* Persons who are owners of a patent involved in the proceeding and other persons who are named parties to the proceeding.

(B) *Party Representatives.* Representatives of record for a party in the proceeding.

(C) *Experts.* Retained experts of a party in the proceeding who further certify in the Acknowledgement that they are not a competitor to any party, or a consultant for, or employed by, such a competitor with respect to the subject matter of the proceeding.

(D) *In-house counsel.* In-house counsel of a party.

(E) *Other Employees of a Party.* Employees, consultants or other persons performing work for a party, other than in-house counsel and in-house counsel's support staff, who sign the Acknowledgement shall be extended access to confidential information only upon agreement of the parties or by order of the Board upon

---

[Section 15:7]

[1]Trial Practice Guide, 77 Fed.Reg. 48756, 48771 (Aug. 14, 2012).

a motion brought by the party seeking to disclose confidential information to that person. The party opposing disclosure to that person shall have the burden of proving that such person should be restricted from access to confidential information.

(F) *The Office.* Employees and representatives of the Office who have a need for access to the confidential information shall have such access without the requirement to sign an Acknowledgement. Such employees and representatives shall include the Director, members of the Board and their clerical staff, other support personnel, court reporters, and other persons acting on behalf of the Office.

(G) *Support Personnel.* Administrative assistants, clerical staff, court reporters and other support personnel of the foregoing persons who are reasonably necessary to assist those persons in the proceeding shall not be required to sign an Acknowledgement, but shall be informed of the terms and requirements of the Protective Order by the person they are supporting who receives confidential information.

3. Persons receiving confidential information shall use reasonable efforts to maintain the confidentiality of the information, including:

(A) Maintaining such information in a secure location to which persons not authorized to receive the information shall not have access;

(B) Otherwise using reasonable efforts to maintain the confidentiality of the information, which efforts shall be no less rigorous than those the recipient uses to maintain the confidentiality of information not received from the disclosing party;

(C) Ensuring that support personnel of the recipient who have access to the confidential information understand and abide by the obligation to maintain the confidentiality of information received that is designated as confidential; and

(D) Limiting the copying of confidential information to a reasonable number of copies needed for conduct of the proceeding and maintaining a record of the locations of such copies.

4. Persons receiving confidential information shall use the following procedures to maintain the confidentiality of the information:

(A) *Documents and Information Filed With the Board.*

(i) A party may file documents or information with the Board under seal, together with a non-confidential description of the nature of the confidential information that is under seal and the reasons why the information is confidential and should not be made available to the public. The submission shall be treated as confidential and remain under seal, unless, upon motion of a party and after a hearing on the issue, or *sua sponte,* the Board determines that the documents or information do not to qualify for confidential treatment.

(ii) Where confidentiality is alleged as to some but not all of the information submitted to the Board, the submitting party shall file confidential and non-confidential versions of its submission, together with a Motion to Seal the confidential version setting forth the reasons why the information redacted from the non-confidential version is confidential and should not be made available to the public. The nonconfidential version of the submission shall clearly indicate the locations of information that has been redacted. The confidential version of the submission shall be filed under seal. The redacted information shall remain under seal unless, upon motion of a party and after a hearing on the issue, or *sua sponte,* the Board determines that some or all of the redacted information does not qualify for confidential treatment.

(B) *Documents and Information Exchanged Among the Parties.* Information designated as confidential that is disclosed to another party during discovery or other proceedings before the Board shall be clearly marked as "PROTECTIVE ORDER MATERIAL" and shall be produced in a manner that maintains its confidentiality.

(j) *Standard Acknowledgement of Protective Order.* The following form may be used to acknowledge a protective order and gain access to information covered by the protective order:

[CAPTION]

Standard Acknowledgment for Access to Protective Order Material

I ____, affirm that I have read the Protective Order; that I will abide by its terms; that I will use the confidential information only in connection with this proceeding and for no other purpose; that I will only allow access to support staff who are reasonably necessary to assist me in this proceeding; that prior to any disclosure to such support staff I informed or will inform them of the requirements of the Protective Order; that I am personally responsible for the requirements of the terms of the Protective Order and I agree to submit to the jurisdiction of the Office and the United States District Court for the Eastern District of Virginia for purposes of enforcing the terms of the Protective Order and providing remedies for its breach.

[SIGNATURE]

The Board does not grant all motions to seal. Its representative decision in *Garmin Intl., Inc. v. Cuozzo Speed Technologies LLC*, IPR2012-00001, Paper No. 36 (PTAB April 5, 2013) provides the following guidance:

- There is a strong public policy for making all information filed in a quasi-judicial administrative proceeding open to the public, especially ones that affect the rights of the public. Under the statute, the default rule is that all papers filed in an IPR are open and available for access by the public.[2]
- Only "confidential information" can be protected from disclosure.[3]
- The standard for granting a motion to seal is "good cause."[4]
- A motion to seal requires a proposed protective order with a certification that the moving party has in good faith conferred or attempted to confer with the opposing party to seek agreement on the scope of the proposed order.[5]
- Mere references to how information was produced in a related district court proceeding is an insufficient showing of good cause.[6]

The Board partially granted the motion to seal where it would protect personal confidential information having no relevance to the proceeding and where "the public's interest in having access . . . is [no more than minimal]." The Board explained:

> Here, when determining whether Cuozzo has established good cause for sealing the evidence, we balance Cuozzo's needs in protecting the above-identified personal confidential infor-

---

[2] *Garmin Intl., Inc. v. Cuozzo Speed Technologies LLC*, IPR2012-00001, Paper No. 36, p. 3 (PTAB April 5, 2013).

[3] *Garmin Intl., Inc. v. Cuozzo Speed Technologies LLC*, IPR2012-00001, Paper No. 36, p. 3 (PTAB April 5, 2013).

[4] *Garmin Intl., Inc. v. Cuozzo Speed Technologies LLC*, IPR2012-00001, Paper No. 36, p. 4 (PTAB April 5, 2013).

[5] *Garmin Intl., Inc. v. Cuozzo Speed Technologies LLC*, IPR2012-00001, Paper No. 36, p. 4 (PTAB April 5, 2013).

[6] *Garmin Intl., Inc. v. Cuozzo Speed Technologies LLC*, IPR2012-00001, Paper No. 36, p. 4 (PTAB April 5, 2013).

mation and the public's interest in maintaining a complete and understandable file history of this *inter partes* review of the '074 patent. Based on our review as discussed above, we determine that there is good cause for protecting Exhibits B, K, L, and P by placing them under seal because the information is personal confidential and has little relevance to the merits of any substantive issue. We see little harm to the public's interest in restricting access to the information.[FN2]

FN2: To minimize cost, delay, and burden on the parties and Board, parties should not submit confidential personal information which clearly has little relevance to the merits of the case, such as account number on a check, social security number, and full driving record. Non-useful personal confidential information in a document should be redacted when the document is submitted and the submission should be accompanied by a paper noting the reasons for the redaction. Similarly, moving to seal information when that information is contained in a public document filed by the moving party also leads to inefficient use of resources and should be avoided.[7]

However, the Board denied the motion as to waived attorney-client privileged information which was submitted to the Board to show pre-filing conception and diligence toward constructive reduction to practice.

§ 15:8 Non-default protective orders

If a party is dissatisfied with the default protective order, it can request a different one. 37 C.F.R. § 42.55(b) speaks to this, as follows:

§ 42.55. Confidential information in a petition.

A petitioner filing confidential information with a petition may, concurrent with the filing of the petition, file a motion to seal with a proposed protective order as to the confidential information. The institution of the requested trial will constitute a grant of the motion to seal unless otherwise ordered by the Board.

(a) *Default protective order*. Where a motion to seal requests entry of the default protective order set forth in the Office Patent Trial Practice Guide, the petitioner must file, but need not serve, the confidential information under seal. The patent owner may only access the filed sealed information prior to the institution of the trial by agreeing to the terms of the default protective order or obtaining relief from the Board.

---

[7] *Garmin Intl., Inc. v. Cuozzo Speed Technologies LLC*, IPR2012-00001, Paper No. 36, p. 8 (PTAB April 5, 2013).

(b) *Protective orders other than default protective order.* Where a motion to seal requests entry of a protective order other than the default protective order, the petitioner must file, but need not serve, the confidential information under seal. The patent owner may only access the sealed confidential information prior to the institution of the trial by:

(1) agreeing to the terms of the protective order requested by the petitioner;

(2) agreeing to the terms of a protective order that the parties file jointly; or

(3) obtaining entry of a protective order (e.g., the default protective order).

The Trial Practice Guide provides for non-default protective orders, as follows:

APPENDIX B: Protective Order Guidelines (based on the trial rules).[1]

(a) *Purpose.* This document provides guidance on the procedures for filing of motions to seal and the entry of protective orders in proceedings before the Board. The protective order governs the protection of confidential information contained in documents, discovery, or testimony adduced, exchanged, or filed with the Board. The parties are encouraged to agree on the entry of a stipulated protective order. Absent such agreement, the default standing protective order will be automatically entered.

(b) *Timing; lifting or modification of the Protective Order.* The terms of a protective order take effect upon the filing of a Motion to Seal by a party, and remain in place until lifted or modified by the Board either on the motion of a party for good cause shown or *sua sponte* by the Board.

(c) *Protective Order to Govern Treatment of Confidential Information.* The terms of a protective order govern the treatment of the confidential portions of documents, testimony, and other information designated as confidential, as well as the filing of confidential documents or discussion of confidential information in any papers filed with the Board. The Board shall have the authority to enforce the terms of the Protective Order, to provide remedies for its breach, and to impose sanctions on a party and a party's representatives for any violations of its terms.

(d) *Contents.* The Protective Order shall include the following terms:

[Section 15:8]

[1]Trial Practice Guide, 77 Fed. Reg. (No. 157) 48756, 48769–48771 (Aug. 14, 2012).

(1) *Designation of Confidential Information.* The producing party shall have the obligation to clearly mark as "PROTECTIVE ORDER MATERIAL" any documents or information considered to be confidential under the Protective Order.

(2) *Persons Entitled to Access to Confidential Information.* A party receiving confidential information shall strictly restrict access to that information to the following individuals who first have signed and filed an Acknowledgement as provided herein:

(A) *Parties.* Persons who are owners of a patent involved in the proceeding and other persons who are named parties to the proceeding.

(B) *Party Representatives.* Representatives of record for a party in the proceeding.

(C) *Experts.* Retained experts of a party in the proceeding who further certify in the Acknowledgement that they are not a competitor to any party, or a consultant for, or employed by, such a competitor with respect to the subject matter of the proceeding.

(D) *In-house counsel.* In-house counsel of a party.

(E) *Other Employees of a Party.* Employees, consultants, or other persons performing work for a party, other than in-house counsel and in-house counsel's support staff, who sign the Acknowledgement, shall be extended access to confidential information only upon agreement of the parties or by order of the Board upon a motion brought by the party seeking to disclose confidential information to that person. The party opposing disclosure to that person shall have the burden of proving that such person should be restricted from access to confidential information.

(F) *The Office.* Employees and representatives of the U.S. Patent and Trademark Office who have a need for access to the confidential information shall have such access without the requirement to sign an Acknowledgement. Such employees and representatives shall include the Director, members of the Board and staff, other Office support personnel, court reporters, and other persons acting on behalf of the Office.

(G) *Support Personnel.* Administrative assistants, clerical staff, court reporters, and other support personnel of the foregoing persons who are reasonably necessary to assist those persons in the proceeding. Such support personnel shall not be required to sign an Acknowledgement, but shall be informed of the terms and requirements of the Protective Order by the person they are supporting who receives confidential information.

(3) *Protection of Confidential Information.* Persons receiving confidential information shall take reasonable care to maintain the confidentiality of that information, including:

(A) Maintaining such information in a secure location to which persons not authorized to receive the information shall not have access;

(B) Otherwise using reasonable efforts to maintain the confidentiality of the information, which efforts shall be no less rigorous than those the recipient uses to maintain the confidentiality of information not received from the disclosing party;

(C) Ensuring that support personnel of the recipient who have access to the confidential information understand and abide by the obligation to maintain the confidentiality of information received that is designated as confidential; and

(D) Limiting the copying of confidential information to a reasonable number of copies needed to conduct the proceeding and maintaining a record of the locations of such copies, which similarly must be kept secure.

(4) *Treatment of Confidential Information.* Persons receiving confidential information shall use the following procedures to maintain confidentiality of documents and other information—

(A) *Documents and Information Filed With the Board.*

(i) A party may file documents or information with the Board under seal, together with a non-confidential description of the nature of the confidential information that is under seal and the reasons why the information is confidential and should not be made available to the public. The submission shall be treated as confidential and remain under seal, unless upon motion of a party and after a hearing on the issue, or *sua sponte,* the Board determines that the documents or information do not qualify for confidential treatment.

(ii) Where confidentiality is alleged as to some but not all of the information submitted to the Board, the submitting party shall file confidential and non-confidential versions of its submission, together with a Motion to Seal the confidential version setting forth the reasons why the information redacted from the non-confidential version is confidential and should not be made publicly available. The non-confidential version of the submission shall clearly indicate the locations of information that has been redacted. The confidential version of the submission shall be filed under seal. The redacted information shall remain under seal, unless upon motion of a party and after a hearing on the issue, or *sua sponte,* the Board determines that some or all of the redacted information does not qualify for confidential treatment.

(B) *Documents and Information Exchanged Among the Parties.* Information designated as confidential that is disclosed to another party during discovery or other proceedings before the Board shall be clearly marked as "PROTECTIVE ORDER MATERIAL" and shall be produced in a manner that maintains its confidentiality.

(5) *Confidential Testimony.* Any person providing testimony in a proceeding may, on the record during the testimony, preliminarily designate the entirety of the person's testimony and all transcriptions thereof as confidential, pending further review. Within ten days of the receipt of the transcript of the testimony, that person, or that person's representative, shall advise the opposing party of those portions of the testimony to which a claim of confidentiality is to be maintained, and the reasons in support of that claim. Such portions shall be treated as confidential and maintained under seal in any filings to the Board unless, upon motion of a party and after a hearing on the issue, or *sua sponte,* the Board determines that some or all of the redacted information does not qualify for confidential treatment.

(6) *Other Restrictions Imposed By the Board.* In addition to the foregoing, the Board may, in its discretion, include other terms and conditions in a Protective Order it enters in any proceeding.

(7) *Requirement of Acknowledgement.* Any person receiving confidential information during a proceeding before the Board shall, prior to receipt of any confidential information, first sign an Acknowledgement, under penalty of perjury, stating the following:

(A) The person has read the Protective Order and understands its terms;

(B) The person agrees to be bound by the Protective Order and will abide by its terms;

(C) The person will use the confidential information only in connection with that proceeding and for no other purpose;

(D) The person shall only extend access to the confidential information to support personnel, such as administrative assistants, clerical staff, paralegals, and the like, who are reasonably necessary to assist him or her in the proceeding. The person shall inform such support personnel of the terms and requirements of the Protective Order prior to disclosure of any confidential information to such support personnel and shall be personally responsible for their compliance with the terms of the Protective Order; and

(E) The person agrees to submit to the jurisdiction of the Office for purposes of enforcing the terms of the Protective Order and providing remedies for its breach.

(e) *Filing of Executed Protective Order.* The party filing a Motion to Seal shall include with its supporting papers a copy of a proposed Protective Order, signed by the party or its representative of record, certifying that the party accepts and agrees to the terms of the Protective Order. Prior to the receipt of confidential information, any other party to the proceeding also shall file a copy of the proposed Protective Order, signed by the party or its representative of record, certifying that the party accepts and agrees to the terms of the proposed Protective Order. The proposed Protective Order shall remain in effect until superseded by a Protective Order entered by the Board.

(f) *Duty To Retain Acknowledgements.* Each party to the proceeding shall maintain a signed Acknowledgement from each person acting on its behalf who obtains access to confidential information after signing an Acknowledgement, as set forth herein, and shall produce such Acknowledgements to the Office upon request.

(g) *Motion to Seal.* A party may file an opposition to the motion that may include a request that the terms of the proposed Protective Order be modified including limiting the persons who are entitled to access under the Order. Any such opposition shall state with particularity the grounds for modifying the proposed Protective Order. The party seeking the modification shall have the burden of proving that such modifications are necessary. While the motion is pending, no disclosure of confidential information shall be made to the persons for whom disclosure is opposed, but the filing of the motion shall not preclude disclosure of the confidential information to persons for whom disclosure is not opposed and shall not toll the time for taking any action in the proceeding.

(h) *Other Proceedings.* Counsel for a party who receives confidential information in a proceeding will not be restricted by the Board from representing that party in any other proceeding or matter before the Office. Confidential information received in a proceeding, however, may not be used in any other Office proceeding in which the providing party is not also a party.

(i) *Disposal of Confidential Information.* Within one month after final termination of a proceeding, including any appeals, or within one month after the time for appeal has expired, each party shall assemble all copies of all confidential information it has received, including confidential information provided to its representatives and experts, and shall destroy the confidential information and provide a certification of destruction to the party who produced the confidential information.

§ 15:9 Initial handling of petitions at the PTAB; notice of filing date

In response to receiving a petition, a PTAB trial clerk reviews the documents and may accept or reject them. The petition can be rejected for various informalities, in which case the PTAB may issue a "Notice of Incomplete Petition" and allow the petitioner a limited time, *e.g.*, one month, within which to correct the informality.[1] On occasion, the PTAB may have a telephone conference with counsel for the petitioner concerning the informality and may in its discretion accept a telephonic correction.[2]

Once the petitioner cures the objection, the PTAB will issue a "Notice of Accepting Corrected Petition."[3]

When an acceptable petition is filed, the PTAB will issue a notice styled illustratively as a "Notice of Filing Date Accorded to Petition and Time for Filing Patent Owner Preliminary Response."[4] In such notice, the trial clerk will notify the patent owner of which administrative patent judge is assigned to manage the proceeding, when a preliminary response can be filed, if at all, and other preliminary matters such as when the patent owner mandatory notice informa-

[Section 15:9]

[1]E.g., *Innolux Corp. v. Semiconductor Energy Laboratory Co., Ltd.*, IPR 2013-00066, Paper No. 4, (PTAB Nov. 5, 2012) rejecting the petition because "Service was not properly made upon the Patent Owner."

[2]See *Liberty Mutual Insurance Company v. Progressive Casualty/BHGL*, CBM 2012-00002 (PTAB Sept. 21, 2012) ("On September 17, 2012, a conference called was held between Lead Trial Judge Michael P. Tierney and counsel for Petitioner . . . . The call was conducted to confirm the certification requirement under 37 C.F.R. § 42.304, as a review of the petition revealed that the certification was missing. During the call counsel was requested to certify that the petitioner is not barred or estopped from requesting the CBM proceeding. Counsel then confirmed that the petitioner is not barred or estopped from requesting this proceeding. The Board exercises its discretion and accepts the telephonic certification.").

[3]E.g., *Innolux Corp. v. Semiconductor Energy Laboratory Co., Ltd.*, IPR 2013-00066, Paper No. 5, (PTAB Dec. 4, 2012).

[4]E.g., *Innolux Corp. v. Semiconductor Energy Laboratory Co., Ltd.*, IPR 2013-00066, Paper No. 6, (PTAB Dec. 5, 2012).

tion must be filed, and procedures for seeking appearances *pro hac vice*, and filing in accordance with the Patent Review Processing System (PRPS).

§ 15:10 Patent owner's responses prior to institution of trial

The rules generally refer to the patent owner responses, but in the case of derivation proceedings, the respondent could be the owner of either an issued patent application or an application that has been published.[1] In the following discussions, "patent owner" should be understood to mean the owner of a published patent application or issued patent targeted in a petition for derivation proceeding.

A preliminary question is whether one has the right to respond to the USPTO. The rules include a provision speaking to whether the inventor may be excluded:

> **§ 42.9. Action by patent owner.**
>
> (a) *Entire interest.* An owner of the entire interest in an involved application or patent may act to the exclusion of the inventor (see § 3.71 of this title).
>
> (b) *Part interest.* An owner of a part interest in the subject patent may move to act to the exclusion of an inventor or a co-owner. The motion must show the inability or refusal of an inventor or co-owner to prosecute the proceeding or other cause why it is in the interests of justice to permit the owner of a part interest to act in the trial. In granting the motion, the Board may set conditions on the actions of the parties.

<u>Mandatory Notice (21 Days)</u>. After the filing of a petition, the patent owner has two filings to consider. The first one is mandatory: under § 42.8, the patent owner within 21 days of service of the petition must file the mandatory notice identifying: (1) each real party in interest; (2) all related judicial or administrative matters that would affect or be affected by a decision in the proceeding; (3) lead and backup counsel; and (4) service information. See §§ 15:4, 15:5 supra.

<u>Optional Preliminary Response (3 Months)</u>. The patent owner or other respondent has the right but not the obligation to file a preliminary response to the petition explaining that the proceeding ought not be commenced because the petition fails to meet one or more requirements of the statute.

[Section 15:10]

[1]"*Respondent* means a party other than the petitioner." 37 C.F.R. § 42.401.

E.g., 35 U.S.C. § 313.

The rules provide a three (3) month window for the patent owner to file the preliminary response, if it wishes, in response to a petition for *inter partes* review or post-grant review. The rules in §§ 42.107 and 42.207 set forth the metes and bounds of this filing. § 42.107 (regarding *inter partes* review) is typical and provides:

§ 42.107. Preliminary response to petition.

(a) The patent owner may file a preliminary response to the petition. The response is limited to setting forth the reasons why no *inter partes* review should be instituted under 35 U.S.C. 314. The response can include evidence except as provided in paragraph (c) of this section. The preliminary response is subject to the page limits under § 42.24.

(b) *Due date.* The preliminary response must be filed no later than three months after the date of a notice indicating that the request to institute an *inter partes* review has been granted a filing date. A patent owner may expedite the proceeding by filing an election to waive the patent owner preliminary response.

(c) *No new testimonial evidence.* The preliminary response shall not present new testimony evidence beyond that already of record, except as authorized by the Board.

(d) *No amendment.* The preliminary response shall not include any amendment.

(e) *Disclaim Patent Claims.* The patent owner may file a statutory disclaimer under 35 U.S.C. 253(a) in compliance with § 1.321(a) of this chapter, disclaiming one or more claims in the patent. No *inter partes* review will be instituted based on disclaimed claims.

As can be seen in part (e), the patent owner cannot yet amend claims at this time. However, it is allowed to disclaim claims. If all of the challenged claims are disclaimed, then no *inter partes* review nor post-grant review will be instituted. §§ 42.107(e), 42.207(e).

The patent owner may (a) file a preliminary response, (b) file a statement indicating that no preliminary response will be submitted, or (c) do nothing. A patent owner wishing to expedite the process can use option (b), which is specifically authorized by §§ 42.107(b) and 42.207(b). If the patent owner chooses to do nothing, the PTAB will wait for three months to pass before ruling on the petition.

In a preliminary response, the patent owner may challenge the petition in various ways. Here are some options:

1. The petitioner is barred by statute from pursuing the

review.[2]

2. The references relied upon in the petition are not in fact prior art.[3]
3. The references all lack a material limitation that is found in each of the independent claims that are challenged.[4]
4. The prior art teaches or suggests away from a combination that the petitioner advocates.[5]
5. The petitioner's claim interpretation is unreasonable.[6]
6. If the petition seeks post-grant review and raises 35 U.S.C. § 101 grounds, the patent owner may offer a brief explanation as to how the challenged claims are indeed directed to patent-eligible subject matter.[7]

Agreed Mandatory Initial Disclosures. If the parties agree to the content of the mandatory initial disclosures, the agreement must be filed by the time that the Preliminary Response is due, according to 37 C.F.R. § 42.51 (emphasis added):

§ 42.51. Discovery.

(a) *Mandatory initial disclosures.*

(1) With agreement. Parties may agree to mandatory discovery requiring the initial disclosures set forth in the Office Patent Trial Practice Guide.

(i) The parties must submit any agreement reached on initial disclosures by no later than the filing of the patent owner preliminary response or the expiration of the time period for filing such a response. The initial disclosures of the parties shall be filed as exhibits.

Page Limit. The length of the preliminary response is limited by § 42.24(b)(1) to the same page limit as the corresponding petition. Thus, for an *inter partes* proceeding or derivation proceeding, the preliminary response is limited to 60 pages. For a post-grant review or review of a covered business method patent, the limit is 80 pages. While the rule permits a motion by a *petitioner* to waive the page limits, no such leave is granted for the patent owner to request modify-

[2]Trial Practice Guide, 77 Fed. Reg. at 48764 (Aug. 14, 2012).

[3]Trial Practice Guide, 77 Fed. Reg. at 48764 (Aug. 14, 2012).

[4]Trial Practice Guide, 77 Fed. Reg. at 48764 (Aug. 14, 2012).

[5]Trial Practice Guide, 77 Fed. Reg. at 48764 (Aug. 14, 2012).

[6]Trial Practice Guide, 77 Fed. Reg. at 48764 (Aug. 14, 2012).

[7]Trial Practice Guide, 77 Fed. Reg. at 48764 (Aug. 14, 2012).

ing the page limits. Hopefully, if a petitioner succeeds in securing a waiver of the page limit or an extension of the limit, the Board will make some provision for the respondent in the Board's order.

§ 15:11 Ruling on the petition; institution of trial

Pursuant to statute, the Board has three (3) months to decide whether to institute the requested trial. These three months follow the patent owner's filing of a preliminary response or notice that none will be filed, or after the time has expired for a preliminary response.[1] For example, 35 U.S.C. § 314 provides:

> **§ 314. Institution of inter partes review**
>
> (a) THRESHOLD.— The Director may not authorize an inter partes review to be instituted unless the Director determines that the information presented in the petition filed under section 311 and any response filed under section 313 shows that there is a reasonable likelihood that the petitioner would prevail with respect to at least 1 of the claims challenged in the petition.
>
> (b) TIMING.— The Director shall determine whether to institute an inter partes review under this chapter pursuant to a petition filed under section 311 within 3 months after—
>
> (1) receiving a preliminary response to the petition under section 313; or
>
> (2) if no such preliminary response is filed, the last date on which such response may be filed.
>
> (c) NOTICE.— The Director shall notify the petitioner and patent owner, in writing, of the Director's determination under subsection (a), and shall make such notice available to the public as soon as is practicable. Such notice shall include the date on which the review shall commence.
>
> (d) NO APPEAL.— The determination by the Director whether to institute an inter partes review under this section shall be final and nonappealable.

[Section 15:11]

[1]However, sometimes the Board is so dissatisfied with one or more of the alleged grounds in the petition that it denies them even before the patent owner's time for preliminary response is due. In one ruling, the Board rejected 196 of 422 alleged grounds promulgated in the petition even before the patent owner submitted a preliminary response. The Board stated, "[W]e regard Petitioner's stated reasoning . . . to be unsupported by the record and simply unpersuasive." *Liberty Mutual Ins. Co. v. Progressive Casualty Ins. Co.*, CBM2012-00003, Paper No. 8, p. 12 (PTAB Oct. 25, 2012).

The PTAB applies the standard specified in the statute in deciding whether, and how, to grant the petition. Thus, for *inter partes* proceedings, the standard is whether there is "a reasonable likelihood that the petitioner would prevail with respect to at least 1 of the claims challenged in the petition." 35 U.S.C. § 314(a).[2]

For a post-grant review, the standard is the preponderance standard of whether it is more likely than not that a challenged claim is unpatentable. 35 U.S.C. § 324(a).

For review of a covered business method patent, the AIA adopts the standards of a post-grant review. AIA § 18(a).

For a derivation proceeding, the standard is whether the petition is supported by substantial evidence including at least one affidavit addressing communication of the derived invention and lack of authorization that, if unrebutted, would support a determination of derivation. This showing of communication must be corroborated. 37 C.F.R. § 42.405(c).

The Board has the ability to choose the issues and claims that it will hear in the trial.[3] The Trial Practice Guide indicates that . . .

> [I]n instituting a trial, the Board will narrow the issues for final decision by authorizing the trial to proceed only on the challenged claims for which the threshold standards for the proceeding have been met. Further, the Board will identify, on a claim-by-claim basis the grounds on which the trial will proceed. Any claim or issue not included in the authorization for review will not be part of the trial.[4]

Board rulings on whether, and how, to proceed or not with the requested proceeding are not subject to review. However, a party may request rehearing as to points believed to have been overlooked or misapprehended as set forth in 37 C.F.R. 42.71(c) and (d).

Despite statutory language declaring, "The determination

---

[2]A district court expressed the view that the new, "reasonable likelihood" standard for granting *inter partes* reexaminations, which is the same standard as that for *inter partes* review, is higher than the prior standard of whether the petition raises a substantial new question of patentability. *Pragmatus AV, LLC v. Facebook, Inc.*, 2011 WL 4802958, *3 n.1 (N.D. Cal. 2011).

[3]For example, in *Microstrategy Inc. v. Zillow, Inc.*, IPR 2013-00034, Paper No. 23 (PTAB April 22, 2013), the Board adhered to its decision not to address some of the challenged claims.

[4]77 Fed. Reg. at 48757 (August 14, 2012).

by the Director whether to institute . . . review under this section shall be final and nonappealable," 35 U.S.C.A. §§ 314(d), 324(e), courts have been asked to set aside the PTAB decision to institute. In *Versata Development Corp. v. Rea*, 2013 WL 4014649 (E.D. Va. 2013), the patent owner Versata had obtained judgments of infringement against SAP America, Inc. in companion litigation. SAP filed a petition for post grant review of the patent-in-suit as a "covered business method" patent. After the PTAB granted the petition and instituted trial, Versata sought a judicial interlocutory review under the Administrative Procedure Act of the PTAB decision to initiate review of the challenged patent. SAP intervened in the civil action. Granting motions to dismiss, the district court noted that the AIA itself directed that there be no judicial review of a decision to institute, so the court lacked subject matter jurisdiction.[5] Second, the decision to institute was not a final agency action subject to review under the APA, so the matter was not ripe anyway.[6] The proper avenue of review is an appeal to the Federal Circuit from the final, substantive agency action, as specified by the AIA:

> Congress's intent was to create a streamlined system while providing all parties with full access to judicial review. Accordingly, not only is the PTAB's decision to institute post-grant review not a "final agency action," adequate remedies also exist for Plaintiff to appeal the decision, namely an appeal to the Federal Circuit, at which time Versata may present arguments concerning the decision to initiate review and, if necessary, the prudence of reviewing this decision on an appeal from the substantive and final decision.[7]

If the Board grants the petition, in whole or in part, it issues a notice of trial.

§ **42.4. Notice of trial.**

(a) *Institution of trial.* The Board institutes the trial on behalf of the Director.

(b) Notice of a trial will be sent to every party to the proceeding. The entry of the notice institutes the trial.

(c) The Board may authorize additional modes of notice,

---

[5] *Versata Development Corp. v. Rea*, 2013 WL 4014649, *5-10 (E.D. Va. 2013).

[6] *Versata Development Corp. v. Rea*, 2013 WL 4014649, *10-14 (E.D. Va. 2013).

[7] *Versata Development Corp. v. Rea*, 2013 WL 4014649, *13 (E.D. Va. 2013).

including:

(1) Sending notice to another address associated with the party, or

(2) Publishing the notice in the Official Gazette of the United States Patent and Trademark Office or the Federal Register.

The Board will indicate, claim-by-claim, the grounds on which the trial will proceed.[8] Any claim or issue not in the document will not be part of the trial.[9]

§ 15:12 The scheduling order

Upon granting a petition, the Board enters a Scheduling Order which will set out due dates for the trial, "taking into account the complexity of the proceeding but insuring that the trial is completed within one year of institution."[1] The Trial Practice Guide sets out the following representative timeline that is reflective of a typical scheduling order:[2]

---

[8]Trial Practice Guide, 77 Fed. Reg. at 48757 (August 14, 2012).

[9]Trial Practice Guide, 77 Fed. Reg. at 48757 (August 14, 2012).

[Section 15:12]

[1]Trial Practice Guide, 77 Fed. Reg. at 48757 (August 14, 2012).

[2]Trial Practice Guide, 77 Fed. Reg. (No. 157) 48756, 48757 (Aug. 14, 2012).

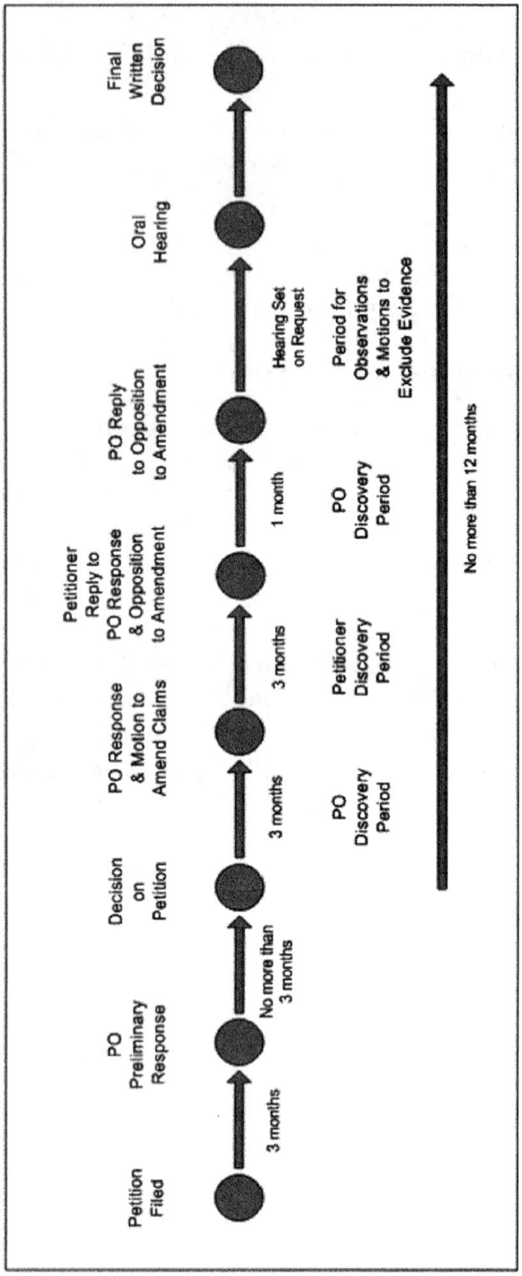

In this timeline, the bottom arrow that is labeled "No more than 12 months" constitutes the time for the "trial." The Trial Practice Guide sets forth two sample scheduling orders.

The first one applies to *Inter Partes* Review ("IPR"), Post-Grant Review ("PGR"), and Covered Business Method Patents ("CBM") Review. The second one is for Derivation Proceedings. These are, respectively, Appendices A-1 and A-2 to the Trial Practice Guide. The individual segments are discussed below.

Draft Scheduling Orders. In reviewing these draft scheduling orders, bear in mind that the Rules allow the parties to agree to change some of the dates but not the ultimate dates. The several due dates for an IPR, PGR, or CBM Review are discussed in other sections of this chapter, *infra*.

APPENDIX A—1: Scheduling Order for *Inter Partes* Review, Post-Grant Review, and Covered Business Method Patents Review (based on the trial rules).

A. DUE DATES

This order sets due dates for the parties to take action after institution of the proceeding. The parties may stipulate different dates for DUE DATES 1 through 5 (earlier or later, but no later than DUE DATE 6). A notice of the stipulation, specifically identifying the changed due dates, must be promptly filed. The parties may not stipulate an extension of DUE DATES 6—7.

In stipulating different times, the parties should consider the effect of the stipulation on times to object to evidence (§ 42.64(b)(1)), to supplement evidence (§ 42.64(b)(2)), to conduct cross-examination, and to draft papers depending on the evidence and cross-examination testimony (*see* section B, below).

1. DUE DATE 1

The patent owner is not required to file anything in response to the petition. The patent owner may file—

a. A patent owner's response to the petition, and

b. A motion to amend the patent.

Any response or amendment must be filed by DUE DATE 1. If the patent owner elects not to file anything, the patent owner must arrange a conference call with the parties and the Board.

2. DUE DATE 2

Any reply to the patent owner's response, and opposition to the motion to amend, filed by petitioner under § 42.23 must be filed by DUE DATE 2.

3. DUE DATE 3

The patent owner must file any reply to the petitioner's opposition to patent owner's motion to amend by DUE DATE 3.

4. DUE DATE 4

a. The petitioner must file any motion for an observation on the cross-examination testimony of a reply witness (*see* section C, below) by DUE DATE 4. § 42.20.

b. Each party must file any motion to exclude evidence (§ 42.64(c)) and any request for oral argument (§ 42.70(a)) by DUE DATE 4.

5. DUE DATE 5

a. The patent owner must file any reply to a petitioner observation on cross-examination testimony by DUE DATE 5.

b. Each party must file any opposition to a motion to exclude evidence by DUE DATE 5.

6. DUE DATE 6

Each party must file any reply for a motion to exclude evidence by DUE DATE 6.

B. CROSS—EXAMINATION

Except as the parties might otherwise agree, for each due date—

1. Cross-examination begins after any supplemental evidence is due. §§ 42.64(b) and 42.53(d)(2).

2. Cross-examination ends no later than a week before the filing date for any paper in which the cross-examination testimony is expected to be used. *Id.*

C. MOTION FOR OBSERVATION ON CROSS—EXAMINATION

A motion for observation on cross-examination provides the petitioner with a mechanism to draw the Board's attention to relevant cross-examination testimony of a reply witness, since no further substantive paper is permitted after the reply. The observation must be a concise statement of the relevance of the precisely identified testimony to a precisely identified argument or portion of an exhibit. Each observation should not exceed a single, short paragraph. The patent owner may respond to the observation. Any response must be equally concise and specific.

DUE DATE APPENDIX—IPR, PGR, CBM Patents	
DUE DATE 1: Patent owner's response to the petition. Patent owner's motion to amend the patent.	3 months.
DUE DATE 2: Petitioner's reply to patent owner response to petition. Petitioner's opposition to motion to amend.	3 months.
DUE DATE 3: Patent owner's reply to petitioner opposition.	1 month.

DUE DATE APPENDIX—IPR, PGR, CBM Patents	
DUE DATE 4: Petitioner's motion for observation regarding cross-examination of reply witness. Motion to exclude evidence. Request for oral argument.	3 weeks.
DUE DATE 5: Patent owner's response to observation. Opposition to motion to exclude.	2 weeks.
DUE DATE 6: Reply to opposition to motion to exclude.	1 week.
DUE DATE 7: Oral argument	Set on request.

APPENDIX A—2: Scheduling Order for Derivation Proceedings.

A. DUE DATES

This order sets due dates for the parties to take action in this proceeding. The parties may stipulate different dates for DUE DATES 1 through 5 (earlier or later, but not later than DUE DATE 6). A notice of the stipulation, specifically identifying the changed due dates, must be promptly filed. The parties may not stipulate an extension of DUE DATES 6—7.

In stipulating different times, the parties should consider the effect of the stipulation on times to object to evidence (§ 42.64(b)(1)), to supplement evidence (§ 42.64(b)(2)), to conduct cross-examination, and to draft papers depending on the evidence and cross-examination testimony (*see* section B, below).

1. DUE DATE 1

The respondent is not required to file anything in response to the petition. The respondent may file—

a. A response to the petition, and

b. A motion to amend, if authorized.

Any such response or motion to amend must be filed by DUE DATE 1. If the respondent elects not to file anything, the respondent must arrange a conference call with the parties and the Board.

2. DUE DATE 2

The petitioner must file any reply to the respondent's response and opposition to motion to amend by DUE DATE 2.

3. DUE DATE 3

The respondent must file any reply to the petitioner's opposition by DUE DATE 3.

4. DUE DATE 4

a. The petitioner must file any observation on the cross-examination testimony of a reply witness (*see* section C, below) by DUE DATE 4.

b. Each party must file any motion to exclude evidence (§ 42.64(c)) and any request for oral argument (§ 42.70(a)) by DUE DATE 4.

5. DUE DATE 5

a. The respondent must file any response to a petitioner observation on cross-examination testimony by DUE DATE 5.

b. Each party must file any opposition to a motion to exclude evidence by DUE DATE 5.

6. DUE DATE 6

Each party must file any reply for a motion to exclude evidence by DUE DATE 6.

B. CROSS—EXAMINATION

Except as the parties might otherwise agree, for each due date—

1. Cross-examination begins after any supplemental evidence is due. §§ 42.64(b) and 42.53(d)(2).

2. Cross-examination ends no later than a week before the filing date for any paper in which the cross-examination testimony is expected to be used. *Id.*

C. MOTION FOR OBSERVATION ON CROSS—EXAMINATION

A motion for observation on cross-examination provides the petitioner with a mechanism to draw the Board's attention to relevant cross-examination testimony of a reply witness, since no further substantive paper is permitted after the reply. The observation must be a concise statement of the relevance of the precisely identified testimony to a precisely identified argument or portion of an exhibit. Each observation should not exceed a single, short paragraph. The patent owner may respond to the observation. Any response must be equally concise and specific.

DUE DATE APPENDIX—Derivation Proceedings	
DUE DATE 1: Respondent response to the petition. Respondent motion to amend.	3 months.
DUE DATE 2: Petitioner reply to Respondent response to petition. Petitioner opposition to Respondent's motion to amend.	3 months.
DUE DATE 3: Respondent reply to petitioner opposition.	1 month.

DUE DATE APPENDIX—Derivation Proceedings	
DUE DATE 4: Petitioner motion for observation regarding cross-examination of reply witness. Motion to exclude. Request for oral argument.	3 weeks.
DUE DATE 5: Respondent response to observation. Opposition to motion to exclude.	2 weeks.
DUE DATE 6: Reply to opposition to motion to exclude.	1 week.
DUE DATE 7: Oral argument	Set on request.

§ 15:13 Objections to petition evidence

Objections to Evidence (10 Days). Before discussing the scheduling order, however, it is important to note that the chart shown above omits an important date that is set forth in § 42.64(b)(1):

> **§ 42.64. Objection; motion to exclude; motion in limine.**
>
> (a) *Deposition evidence.* * * *
>
> (b) *Other evidence.* For evidence other than deposition evidence:
>
> (1) *Objection.* Any objection to evidence submitted during a preliminary proceeding must be served within ten business days of the institution of the trial. Once a trial has been instituted, any objection must be served within five business days of service of evidence to which the objection is directed. The objection must identify the grounds for the objection with sufficient particularity to allow correction in the form of supplemental evidence.

Under this rule, the patent owner has only *ten business days* after institution of the trial to serve objections to non-deposition evidence.[1] Thereafter, the party relying on the objected-to evidence has ten business days to respond to the objection by serving supplemental evidence. § 42.64(b)(2).

[Section 15:13]

[1]Note also that under § 42.64(c), a party must file a motion to exclude evidence in order to preserve any objection.

See § 15:30 Evidence—Motions to Exclude.[2]

§ 15:14 Due date 1: the patent owner's discovery and motion period

Following a decision to institute a trial in an IPR, PGR, or CBM, the first due date is typically when the patent owner must file its response to the petition. Due Date 1 is typically up to three (3) months after the date of institution of trial. During this time, the patent owner may depose the petitioner's declarants, beginning as soon as the proceeding is instituted.[1] The patent owner should be considering its discovery plan while awaiting the Board's decision on whether to institute the trial.

Respondent's Discovery. A petition filed with the PTAB should be quite unlike a complaint in federal court that contains mere notice pleading. Instead, the petition should set forth the petitioner's case-in-chief, complete with all evi-

---

[2]One of the PTAB's representative decisions explains how a patent owner did not follow the procedure of 37 C.F.R. § 42.64 when, instead of *objecting* to the evidence, it sought to *exclude* some of the petitioner's evidence when filing its patent owner preliminary response. The Board ruled that an *objection* (not a motion) by a party to evidence submitted at that time must be served within ten business days of institution of trial. Thereafter, the proponent of the evidence may submit supplemental evidence within certain time limits, and then the objecting party may file a motion to exclude at the scheduled time, subject to rules applicable generally to motions. The Board explained:

> The objection to the evidence must identify the grounds for the objection with sufficient particularity to allow correction in the form of supplemental evidence. This process allows the party relying on the evidence to which an objection is timely served, the opportunity to correct, by serving supplemental evidence within so many days of the service of the objection. *See*, 37 CFR 42.64(b)(1) and (b)(2). If, upon receiving the supplemental evidence, the opposing party is still of the opinion that the evidence is inadmissible, the opposing party may file a motion to exclude such evidence. The time for filing a motion to exclude is typically several months into a trial. *See, e.g.*, 77 Fed. Reg. 157 (August 14, 2012) 48765 regarding Scheduling Order and Appendix A—Due Date 4.
>
> *** [A] request to exclude evidence [challenged as hearsay and not authenticated] is typically made by way of a motion to exclude. 37 CFR § 42.64(c). As stated above, motions to exclude are not authorized until much later during a trial, if a trial is instituted. Clearlamp's "motion to exclude" is premature and also prevents LKQ from correcting as permitted by the rules."

LKQ Corp. v. Clearlamp, LLC, IPR2013-00020, Paper No. 17, pp. 3-4 (PTAB March 5, 2013).

[Section 15:14]

[1]Trial Practice Guide, 77 Fed. Reg. (No. 157) 48756, 48757 (Aug. 14, 2012).

dence in the form of exhibits along with testimony (also as exhibits). Typically, the petitioner will have been working on this for several months. As soon as the patent owner or respondent receives the petition, it should begin analyzing it and planning what discovery is needed and what evidence to put before the Board in response to the petition. The respondent (patent owner) may have up to six months for this, as once the petition is filed, the respondent has only three months to file a preliminary response (if desired), following which the Board has up to three more months to rule on whether it will institute the requested proceeding and on what grounds. Accordingly, the respondent should be ready to proceed with discovery as soon as it becomes available. This first period is when the respondent (usually the patent owner) has the opportunity to take discovery.

Motion(s) to Amend. The IPR and PGR statutes ensure the patent owner of at least one opportunity to amend the patent. As should be understood from the discussion of how the PTAB has acted, practitioners should not assume that amendments may be made liberally. 35 U.S.C.A. § 316(d)(1) provides that in an IPR, the patent owner may file one motion to amend "the patent" in two ways. The first and simplest way allows the owner to "cancel any challenged patent claim." The second way allows the owner to "propose a reasonable number of substitute claims" for each challenged claim. The PGR statutory provisions are the same. § 326(d)(1). While the statute allows the owner to *propose* an amendment, in practice the Board has not been receptive to plenary amendments of claims, as discussed below. The deadline set by the Board for such an amendment is Due Date 1. In a requested IPR, PGR and CBM, the patent owner may file motions to amend the claims subject to the conditions set forth in 37 C.F.R. §§ 42.121 and 42.221. Motions require conferring with the Board prior to filing the motion. Having a conference call should not be understood to be the same as obtaining approval. In the case of a first motion to amend, while such a conference is required, the patent owner may file a first motion to amend without obtaining Board approval[2] (but not without a conference). During the conference call, or shortly following the call (via a written ruling), the panel will provide guidance to the patent owner and the petitioner regarding the motion, including how the filing of the motion will impact the schedule. It is possible that

[2]Trial Practice Guide, 77 Fed. Reg. 48756, 48766 (August 14, 2012).

adjusting the schedule and authorization to conduct additional discovery might be needed.[3]

A motion to amend must be accompanied by the proposed amendment, and the claims to be amended should be shown as substitute claims. The amendment should state for each claim whether it is original, cancelled, replaced by a proposed substitute, a proposed substitute for original claim X, or a proposed new claim.[4]

Under § 42.121(b), any motion to amend the claims must include a claim listing, show the changes clearly, and set forth the support and the original disclosure of the patent for each claim added or amended and show the support in any earlier-filed disclosure for each claim for which the benefit of an earlier filing date is sought.[5]

The Board takes the position that "A motion to amend is contingent upon the Board determining that the arguments made in a patent owner response are not persuasive."[6] Hence, the proposed amendment needs to distinguish the amended or new claims over the art, in addition to meeting the requirements stated above of showing support, etc.[7]

The PTAB cites two representative decisions on motions to amend: *Nichia Corp. v. Emcore Corp.* and *Idle Free Systems, Inc. v. Bergstrom, Inc.*[8] These cases provide the following guidance:

- The purpose of the advance telephone conference is to provide an opportunity to the patent owner to obtain guidance from the Board prior to filing a motion to amend.[9]
- Filing a motion to amend without having a conference call with the Board violates 37 C.F.R. § 42.121(a) and

[3]Trial Practice Guide, 77 Fed. Reg. 48756, 48766 (August 14, 2012).

[4]Trial Practice Guide, 77 Fed. Reg. 48756, 48766 (August 14, 2012).

[5]37 C.F.R. § 42.121(b).

[6]E.g., *Innolux Corp. v. Semiconductor Energy Laboratory Co., Ltd.*, IPR 2013-00066, Paper No. 24, p. 4 (PTAB July 18, 2013).

[7]37 C.F.R. § § 42.121, 42.221.

[8]*Nichia Corp. v. Emcore Corp.*, IPR 2012-00005, Paper No. 27 (PTAB June 3, 2013); *Idle Free Systems, Inc. v. Bergstrom, Inc.*, IPR 2012-00027, Paper No. 26 (PTAB June 11, 2013).

[9]*Nichia Corp. v. Emcore Corp.*, IPR 2012-00005, Paper No. 27, p. 2 (PTAB June 3, 2013).

exposes the motion to amend to dismissal.[10]

- The advance call promotes efficiency by directing the patent owner as to what the Board will accept as a reasonable number of substitute claims and ensuring that the amendment responds to a ground of unpatentability.[11]
- At the time of the advance call, the patent owner need not have a fully developed claim set.[12]
- The Board will not, absent special circumstances, allow a challenged claim to be replaced by more than one claim.[13]
- A patent owner cannot broaden a challenged claim in any respect when responding to a ground of alleged unpatentability and must instead only narrow the scope of a claim to be replaced by a substitute claim.[14]
- An IPR "is more adjudicatory than examinational." The Board does not regard a patent owner's desire for a new set of claims with a hierarchy of different scope as a "special circumstance" satisfactory to justify such relief. Instead, the patent owner can seek *ex parte* reexamination, relying on the Board's conclusion that the petitioner has shown a reasonable likelihood of success on one or more grounds of alleged unpatentability as raising the necessary substantial new question of patentability. A patent owner can seek a reissue patent in appropriate circumstances.[15]
- Adding features to dependent claims where the antecedent independent claim is also proposed to be amended calls for the patent owner to show meaningful reasons to establish "special circumstances" that justify

---

[10] *Idle Free Systems, Inc. v. Bergstrom, Inc.*, IPR 2012-00027, Paper No. 26, p. 2 (PTAB June 11, 2013) (motion dismissed but with leave to file a renewed motion within one week).

[11] *Nichia Corp. v. Emcore Corp.*, IPR 2012-00005, Paper No. 27, p. 2 (PTAB June 3, 2013).

[12] *Nichia Corp. v. Emcore Corp.*, IPR 2012-00005, Paper No. 27, pp. 2-3 (PTAB June 3, 2013).

[13] 35 U.S.C.A. § 316(d)(3): "Scope of Claims.—An amendment under this subsection may not enlarge the scope of the claims of the patent or introduce new matter"; *Idle Free Systems, Inc. v. Bergstrom, Inc.*, IPR 2012-00027, Paper No. 26, p. 5 (PTAB June 11, 2013).

[14] *Idle Free Systems, Inc. v. Bergstrom, Inc.*, IPR 2012-00027, Paper No. 26, pp. 4-5 (PTAB June 11, 2013).

[15] *Idle Free Systems, Inc. v. Bergstrom, Inc.*, IPR 2012-00027, Paper No. 26, p. 6 (PTAB June 11, 2013).

the addition of the additional features. One special circumstance would be showing a patentable distinction between *each* of the proposed substitute, amended, dependent claims. "Adding features for no meaningful reason is generally inconsistent with proposing a reasonable number of substitute claims, and also not responsive to an alleged ground of unpatentability."[16]

- The motion to amend must identify the written description support for a proposed substitute claim in the *original disclosure* of the patent (application). The Board looks to *Ariad Pharmaceuticals, Inc. v. Eli Lilly and Co.*, 598 F.3d 1336, 1351, 94 U.S.P.Q.2d 1161 (Fed. Cir. 2010) (en banc) for the written description test.[17]
- The original disclosure need not use identical language to the proposed claim language, but if it does not, " a mere citation to the original disclosure without any explanation as to why a person of ordinary skill in the art would have recognized that the inventor possessed the claimed subject matter as a whole may be . . . inadequate."[18]
- The contingency for entering the substitute claims must be stated clearly, without ambiguity. The Board regards as unclear an instruction stating simply that if claims 1-50 are found unpatentable, then substitute claims 51-100 should be entered. Instead, patent owners should adopt a claim-by-claim approach to the contingency of substitution that identifies "which claim for which claim and in what circumstance."[19]
- The patent owner, as the moving party asking to amend the claim, bears the burden of proof in establishing entitlement to the relief it requests.[20] The burden is *not* on the petitioner to show unpatentability of the proposed replacement or new claim, and the patent owner must show patentability over the prior art of record *and prior*

---

[16] *Idle Free Systems, Inc. v. Bergstrom, Inc.*, IPR 2012-00027, Paper No. 26, pp. 9-10 (PTAB June 11, 2013).

[17] *Nichia Corp. v. Emcore Corp.*, IPR 2012-00005, Paper No. 27, p. 3 (PTAB June 3, 2013).

[18] *Nichia Corp. v. Emcore Corp.*, IPR 2012-00005, Paper No. 27, p. 4 (PTAB June 3, 2013).

[19] *Idle Free Systems, Inc. v. Bergstrom, Inc.*, IPR 2012-00027, Paper No. 26, p. 10 (PTAB June 11, 2013).

[20] *Nichia Corp. v. Emcore Corp.*, IPR 2012-00005, Paper No. 27, p. 2 (PTAB June 3, 2013) citing 37 C.F.R. § 42.20(c).

art known to the patent owner.[21]

As of August 2013, there was no separate rule on the length of proposed amendments. As such, the general rule on motions (37 C.F.R. § 42.24(a)(v)) applies and allows 15 pages for motions. This is inclusive of the claim listing (although one case holds otherwise), all argument, and other remarks in the motion. In practice, the PTAB is not generally receptive to requests for additional pages in the motion to amend the patent. See, e.g., *Innolux Corp. v. Semiconductor Energy Laboratory Co., Ltd.*, IPR 2013-00066, Paper No. 24 (PTAB July 18, 2013) where the Board:

- Denied the patent owner's request for four (4) additional pages for its motion to amend in one proceeding and ten (10) additional pages for its motion in a companion IPR where there were numerous challenged independent claims, each of which was lengthy. Instead of allowing SEL to amend each challenged independent claim, "A single claim per motion to amend may be sufficient" where the same feature(s) would be added to each of the independent claims.
- Denied the patent owner's request to list the claims in a single spaced claim chart and to the contrary insisted on adherence to all PTAB format requirements, including double spacing.
- Denied the patent owner's request to place some of the arguments favoring amendment in its Patent Owner Response to the Petition (because a motion to amend claims is contingent on the arguments made in the Response being non-persuasive, and to avoid incorporating arguments from one document into another simply by reference).
- Declared that the patent owner's requests would "impede the goal to secure the just, speedy, and inexpensive resolution of [the IPRs]."

In the event that the patent owner later desires an additional motion to amend claims, §§ 42.121(c) or 42.221(c) are applicable and require Board authorization to file such additional motions. The Trial Practice Guide indicates that such an additional motion would typically be authorized if there were a joint request for the purposes of materially

---

[21] *Idle Free Systems, Inc. v. Bergstrom, Inc.*, IPR 2012-00027, Paper No. 26, p. 7 (PTAB June 11, 2013).

advancing a settlement.[22] Filing an additional motion to amend may be authorized upon a showing of good cause. In making such a "good cause" determination, the Board will consider as one of the factors whether a petitioner has submitted supplemental information after the time period set for filing a motion to amend. Additional evidence could be a good cause for allowing the patent owner to file an additional motion to amend the claims. The Board will also consider the time remaining for trial, the degree to which the additional evidence impacts patentability of the claims, and whether the additional evidence was known to the patent owner already.[23]

§ 15:15 Due date 2: petitioner's discovery, reply and opposition period

The second due date is illustratively three months after Due Date 1, *i.e.*, six months into the trial. This is the period for the petitioner's discovery. During this time, the petitioner can reply to the patent owner response to the petition and may file an opposition to any motion to amend the patent claims.

The petitioner requires no authorization to file an opposition to a motion to amend, and the petitioner may respond to any new issues that proposed substitute claims raise. This includes evidence responsive to the amendment.[1] This also includes submitting new (additional) expert declarations directed to the proposed substitute claims.

Also during this period, the petitioner may reply to the arguments raised in the patent owner's opposition. The reply must be confined to only the arguments raised in the corresponding opposition or patent owner response.[2] If the reply raises a new issue or belatedly presents evidence, the Board will not consider it and may return it.[3] The Board will not attempt to sort the proper aspects of the reply from the

[22] Trial Practice Guide, 77 Fed. Reg. 48756, 48766 (August 14, 2012).

[23] Trial Practice Guide, 77 Fed. Reg. 48756, 48766 (August 14, 2012).

[Section 15:15]

[1] 35 U.S.C.A. §§ 316(a) and 326(a).

[2] 37 C.F.R. § 42.23(b).

[3] Trial Practice Guide, 77 Fed. Reg. 48756, 48767 (Aug. 14, 2012).

improper ones.[4]

During this second period, the petitioner may take discovery.[5] Apart from the timed discovery, upon institution of trial, parties may automatically take discovery of information identified in the initial disclosures.[6] Thus, the rules and Scheduling Order provide a sequenced discovery process.[7]

§ 15:16 Due date 3: patent owner's further discovery period

Due Date 3 is illustratively one month after Due Date 2, *e.g.,* seven months after institution of the trial. During this term, the patent owner may have further discovery and reply to the petitioner's opposition to any motions that the patent owner will have filed. Again, replies must be confined strictly to the matters raised.

§ 15:17 Due date 4: various motion deadlines

Due Date 4 is illustratively set three weeks after Due Date 3, *e.g.,* nearly eight months after institution of the trial. By Due Date 4, the petitioner must file any motion for observation on the cross-examination testimony of a reply witness. A motion for observation on cross-examination must be calculated to draw the Board's attention to relevant cross-examination testimony of a reply witness. No further substantive paper is permitted after the reply. The observation must be a concise statement of the relevance of particularly identified testimony to a particularly identified argument or portion of an exhibit. Each observation should be confined to a single, short paragraph.[1]

Also by Due Date 4, motions to exclude evidence are due under § 42.64(c). "A motion to exclude evidence must be filed to preserve any objection. The motion must identify the objections in the record in order and must explain the

---

[4]Trial Practice Guide, 77 Fed. Reg. 48756, 48767 (Aug. 14, 2012).

[5]It is called the "Petition Discovery Period" in the USPTO's representative timeline. Trial Practice Guide, 77 Fed. Reg. 48756, 48757 (Aug. 14, 2012). See also 37 C.F.R. § 42.51.

[6]37 C.F.R. § 42.51(a)(1)(ii).

[7]Trial Practice Guide, 77 Fed. Reg. 48756, 48761 (Aug. 14, 2012).

[Section 15:17]

[1]Trial Practice Guide, 77 Fed. Reg. 48756, 48768 to 48769 (Aug. 14, 2012).

objections."[2]

If any party desires oral argument under § 42.70, a request must be submitted by Due Date 4. "A party may request oral argument on an issue raised in a paper at a time set by the Board. The request must be filed as a separate paper and must specify the issues to be argued."[3] In the event that a party wants to use demonstrative exhibits at the oral argument, they must be served on opposing counsel at least five business days before the oral argument, and they must be filed at the time of the oral argument or previously.[4] The term for Due Date 4 is typically three weeks.

§ 15:18 Due date 5: reply and opposition deadlines

Due Date 5 is illustratively two weeks after Due Date 4, *e.g.*, just over eight months after institution of the trial. By Due Date 5, the patent owner must file any reply to a petition or observation on cross-examination testimony. Also, each party must file oppositions to motions to exclude evidence.

§ 15:19 Due date 6: replies to motions to exclude evidence

Due Date 6 is typically a one week term and provides the time for replies to oppositions to motions to exclude. This is typically eight and one-half months after trial is instituted.

§ 15:20 Due date 7: oral argument

Due Date 7 is the oral argument which, as noted previously, must be requested under 37 C.F.R. § 42.70 and must be directed to issues that are specified in the request for oral argument. The applicable Trial Practice Rule provides as follows:

> **§ 42.70. Oral argument.**
>
> (a) *Request for oral argument.* A party may request oral argument on an issue raised in a paper at a time set by the Board. The request must be filed as a separate paper and must specify the issues to be argued.
>
> (b) Demonstrative exhibits must be served at least five business days before the oral argument and filed no later than

[2] 37 C.F.R. § 42.64(c).

[3] 37 C.F.R. § 42.70(a).

[4] 37 C.F.R. § 42.70(b).

the time of the oral argument.

The date of oral argument is set on request but must leave sufficient time for the Board to reach its final written decision twelve months after institution of trial.

§ 15:21 Discovery—Generally

Discovery in PTAB trial proceedings bears general similarities in *form* to discovery under the Federal Rules of Civil Procedure but is quite different in *scope* and *timing*. We begin with the statutory language concerning discovery. The AIA delegated responsibility to the USPTO Director to provide regulations for discovery via the following statutes, beginning first with *inter partes* review:

35 USC § 316 (2011)—Conduct of *inter partes* review

(a) Regulations.—The Director shall prescribe regulations—

***

(5) setting forth standards and procedures for discovery of relevant evidence, including that such discovery shall be limited to—

(A) the deposition of witnesses submitting affidavits or declarations; and

(B) what is otherwise necessary in the interest of justice;

(6) prescribing sanctions for abuse of discovery, abuse of process, or any other improper use of the proceeding, such as to harass or to cause unnecessary delay or an unnecessary increase in the cost of the proceeding;

(7) providing for protective orders governing the exchange and submission of confidential information;

***

(b) Considerations.—In prescribing regulations under this section, the Director shall consider the effect of any such regulation on the economy, the integrity of the patent system, the efficient administration of the Office, and the ability of the Office to timely complete proceedings instituted under this chapter.

For post grant reviews, the statute has parallel language to the IPR statute as to sanctions, protective orders, and "considerations," but the PGR statute does not state the same standard for obtaining discovery:

35 USC § 326 (2011)—Conduct of post-grant review

(a) Regulations.—The Director shall prescribe regulations—

***

(5) setting forth standards and procedures for discovery of relevant evidence, including that such discovery shall be limited to evidence directly related to factual assertions advanced by either party in the proceeding;

6) prescribing sanctions for abuse of discovery, abuse of process, or any other improper use of the proceeding, such as to harass or to cause unnecessary delay or an unnecessary increase in the cost of the proceeding;

(7) providing for protective orders governing the exchange and submission of confidential information;

***

(b) Considerations.—In prescribing regulations under this section, the Director shall consider the effect of any such regulation on the economy, the integrity of the patent system, the efficient administration of the Office, and the ability of the Office to timely complete proceedings instituted under this chapter.

Discovery is timed and sequenced by the Board rules. The rules for taking discovery in PTAB trials are set forth in 37 C.F.R. §§ 42.51 to 42.54 and 42.224. Further rules concerning *evidence* are discussed *infra*. Notably, however, § 42.63 speaks to the form of evidence and sets forth a requirement for exhibits. The rule specifies, "Evidence consists of affidavits, transcripts of depositions, documents, and things. All evidence must be filed in the form of an exhibit."

Parties are entitled to limited discovery to develop the evidence which they will submit as exhibits. Direct testimony is generally by way of affidavit or declaration, with cross-examination by deposition. Discovery can also include document production, interrogatories, and requests for admission. Discovery can be compelled, as the AIA authorizes parties to seek subpoenas under 35 U.S.C.A. § 24:

Congress's most recent amendment to the Patent Act further demonstrates that Congress intended for subpoenas under section 24 to be made available in those proceedings in which depositions are relied upon by the PTO. In 2011, Congress replaced inter partes reexamination with a new proceeding called inter partes review. *See* Leahy-Smith America Invents Act ("AIA"), Pub. L. No. 112-29, § 6(a), 125 Stat. 284, 299-304 (2011), *to be codified at* 35 U.S.C. §§ 311-319 (2013). The purpose of this reform was to "convert[ ] inter partes reexamination from an examinational to an adjudicative proceeding," and one of its touted "improvements" over the former proceeding is to allow the limited use of depositions. H.R.Rep. No. 112-98, pt. 1, at 46-47 (2011); *see* AIA § 6(a), 125 Stat. at 302, *to be codified at* § 316(a)(5)(A). In particular, Congress provided for depositions of affiants in the proceeding, and also authorized parties to "seek such discovery as the Patent Office determines is otherwise necessary in the interest of justice." *See* H.R.Rep. No. 112-98, pt. 1, at 47. In the course of implementing these mandates, the PTO has recognized that the AIA authorizes parties to seek section 24 subpoenas in the new proceedings. *See* 37 C.F.R. §§ 42.52-.53 (2013); *see also Office Patent Trial Practice Guide*, 77 Fed. Reg. 48,756, 48,761 (Aug. 14, 2012). Congress's actions in creating these inter partes review proceedings thus demonstrate that depositions and section 24 subpoenas go hand in hand.[1]

According to the rules adopted by the PTO, discovery generally falls into three categories:

- Mandatory initial disclosures,
- Routine discovery, and
- Additional discovery.

1. Discovery is limited to the mandatory initial disclosures as explained in § 42.51(a) and as otherwise authorized in the Trial Rules (Subpart A of Part 42).
2. All exhibits are to be served with the citing paper or testimony.
3. Direct, uncompelled testimony must in affidavit form.
4. Cross examination of affidavit testimony is permitted within the time periods set by the Board.
5. Parties are obligated to serve on the opponent information that is inconsistent with positions they are taking.
6. Parties may agree between themselves to have further discovery.
7. Compelled testimony or document production requires a motion that contains specific information.
8. If the testimony or production is outside the United States, then further information is required in the motion.
9. Uncompelled direct testimony can be taken anytime to support a petition, motion, opposition, or reply, but otherwise it can be taken only during a testimony period set by the Board.
10. Absent a stipulation by the parties or order by the Board, cross-examination is limited to seven (7) hours, redirect is limited to four (4) hours, and re-cross is limited to two (2) hours.

[Section 15:21]

[1] *Abbott Laboratories v. Cordis Corp.*, 710 F.3d 1318, 1326, 106 U.S.P. Q.2d 1227 (Fed. Cir. 2013).

11. Cross exam should ordinarily occur after supplemental evidence relating to the direct testimony has been filed, and more than a week before the filing date for a paper in which the cross exam testimony is expected to be used.
12. Pre-deposition notices are required. § 42.53(b)(3).
13. A notice of deposition must be filed 10 days or more before a deposition. For direct deposition testimony, the notice must not only give the time and place of the deposition and the address of the witness, but also a list of exhibits to be relied on during the deposition and a general description of the scope and nature of the testimony to be elicited.
14. Cross exam is limited to the scope of the direct testimony.
15. If a foreign language involving an interpreter will be used, the party calling the witness must initiate a Board conference at least 5 business days in advance of the deposition.
16. Objections as to content, form, or manner of taking the deposition are waived unless made on the record during the deposition and preserved by a timely motion to exclude.

Mandatory Initial Disclosures

Discovery begins with mandatory initial disclosures after the proceeding is declared. 37 C.F.R. § 42.51(a) addresses the mandatory initial disclosures. It should be noted again that agreements as to mandatory disclosures must be filed with the Board no later than the due date for the patent owner preliminary response.

§ 42.51. Discovery.

(a) *Mandatory initial disclosures.*

(1) *With agreement.* Parties may agree to mandatory discovery requiring the initial disclosures set forth in the Office Patent Trial Practice Guide.

(i) The parties must submit any agreement reached on initial disclosures by no later than the filing of the patent owner preliminary response or the expiration of the time period for filing such a response. The initial disclosures of the parties shall be filed as exhibits.

(ii) Upon the institution of a trial, parties may automatically take discovery of the information identified in the initial disclosures.

(2) *Without agreement.* Where the parties fail to agree to

the mandatory discovery set forth in paragraph (a)(1), a party may seek such discovery by motion.

* * *

The Trial Practice Guide contains a discussion on mandatory disclosures. The Trial Practice Guide explains that where the parties agree to the mandatory initial disclosures, two options are open. "Option 1" is modeled after F.R. Civ. Prov. Rule 26(a)(1)(A) and "Option 2" is more extensive:

Mandatory Disclosures:

Section 42.51(a) provides for mandatory initial disclosures, either by agreement (subparagraph (a)(1)) or, where the parties fail to reach an agreement, by motion, if granted (subparagraph (a)(2)). To proceed under § 42.51(a)(1), the parties must submit any agreement reached on initial disclosures no later than the filing of the patent owner's preliminary response, or by the expiration of the time period for filing such a response. *See* § 42.51(a)(1)(i).

Where the parties agree to mandatory initial disclosures under § 42.51(a)(1), two options are available as follows:

Option 1

This first option is modeled after Rule 26(a)(1)(A) of the Federal Rules of Civil Procedure, and requires disclosure of the following information:

(1) the name and, if known, the address and telephone number of each individual likely to have discoverable information—along with the subjects of that information—that the disclosing party may use to support its claims or defenses, unless the use would be solely for impeachment; and

(2) a copy—or a description by category and location—of all documents, electronically stored information, and tangible things that the disclosing party has in its possession, custody, or control and may use to support its claims or defenses, unless the use would be solely for impeachment.

Option 2

This second option is more extensive, and includes the following disclosures listed under both items I and II:

I. If the petition seeks cancellation of one or more claims in whole or part on the basis of the existence of an alleged prior non-published public disclosure, the petitioner will provide a statement:

(1) Identifying, to the extent known by the petitioner, the names and information sufficient to contact all persons other than those offering affidavits or declarations who are reasonably likely to know of the alleged

prior non-published public disclosure;

(2) indicating which of such persons are within the control of petitioner, or who have otherwise consented to appear for a testimony in connection with the proceeding;

(3) indicating which, if any, of such persons are represented by petitioner's counsel;

(4) identifying all documents and things within petitioner's possession, custody, or control referring to or relating to the alleged prior non-published public disclosure; and

(5) identifying all things relating to the alleged prior nonpublished public disclosure, including a complete description, photographs, the chemical analysis (if the chemical composition is in issue), and computer code (for computer-related subject matter), and their locations, and whether petitioner will produce such things for inspection, analysis, testing, and sampling.

II. If the petition seeks cancellation of one or more claims in whole or in part on the basis of the alleged obviousness of one or more of the claims, the petitioner will provide a statement:

(1) identifying, to the extent known by the petitioner, the names and information sufficient to contact all persons other than those offering affidavits or declarations who are reasonably likely to have information regarding the secondary indicia of non-obviousness;

(2) indicating which of such persons are within the control of petitioner, or have otherwise consented to appear for a testimony in connection with the proceeding;

(3) indicating which, if any, of such persons are represented by petitioner's counsel;

(4) identifying all documents and things within petitioner's possession, custody, or control referring to or relating to such secondary indicia of non-obviousness; and

(5) identifying all things relating to the secondary indicia of nonobviousness, including a complete description, photographs, the chemical analysis (if the chemical composition is in issue), and computer code (for computer-related subject matter), and their locations, and whether petitioner will produce such things for inspection, analysis, testing, and sampling.

Under § 42.51(a)(1)(ii), upon institution of a trial, the parties may automatically take discovery of the information identified in the initial disclosures. Accordingly, the initial disclosures of a party shall be filed as exhibits as soon as reasonably practicable to permit discovery related to that information. *See* § 42.51(a)(1)(i).[2]

Routine Discovery and Additional Discovery

The rules regarding discovery beyond mandatory initial disclosures are contained in 37 C.F.R. §§ 42.51-42.54 and 37 C.F.R. § 42.224 which provide as follows:

§ 42.51. Discovery.

(a) *Mandatory initial disclosures.*

* * *

(b) Limited discovery. A party is not entitled to discovery except as provided in paragraph (a) of this section, or as otherwise authorized in this subpart.

(1) Routine discovery. Except as the Board may otherwise order:

(i) Unless previously served or otherwise by agreement of the parties, any exhibit cited in a paper or in testimony must be served with the citing paper or testimony.

(ii) Cross examination of affidavit testimony is authorized within such time period as the Board may set.

(iii) Unless previously served, a party must serve relevant information that is inconsistent with a position advanced by the party during the proceeding concurrent with the filing of the documents or things that contains the inconsistency. This requirement does not make discoverable anything otherwise protected by legally recognized privileges such as attorney-client or attorney work product. This requirement extends to inventors, corporate officers, and persons involved in the preparation or filing of the documents or things.

(2) Additional discovery.

(i) The parties may agree to additional discovery between themselves. Where the parties fail to agree, a party may move for additional discovery. The moving party must show that such additional discovery is in the interests of justice, except in post-grant reviews where additional discovery is limited to evidence directly related to factual assertions advanced by either party in the proceeding (see § 42.224). The Board may specify conditions for such additional discovery.

(ii) When appropriate, a party may obtain production of documents and things during cross examination of an opponent's witness or during authorized compelled testimony under § 42.52.

[2]Trial Practice Guide, 77 Fed. Reg. 48756, 48763 to 48764 (Aug. 14, 2012) (formatting added).

(c) Production of documents. Except as otherwise ordered by the Board, a party producing documents and things shall either provide copies to the opposing party or make the documents and things available for inspection and copying at a reasonable time and location in the United States.

§ 42.52. Compelling testimony and production.

(a) *Authorization required.* A party seeking to compel testimony or production of documents or things must file a motion for authorization. The motion must describe the general relevance of the testimony, document, or thing, and must:

(1) In the case of testimony, identify the witness by name or title; and

(2) In the case of a document or thing, the general nature of the document or thing.

(b) *Outside the United States.* For testimony or production sought outside the United States, the motion must also:

(1) In the case of testimony.

(i) Identify the foreign country and explain why the party believes the witness can be compelled to testify in the foreign country, including a description of the procedures that will be used to compel the testimony in the foreign country and an estimate of the time it is expected to take to obtain the testimony; and

(ii) Demonstrate that the party has made reasonable efforts to secure the agreement of the witness to testify in the United States but has been unsuccessful in obtaining the agreement, even though the party has offered to pay the travel expenses of the witness to testify in the United States.

(2) In the case of production of a document or thing.

(i) Identify the foreign country and explain why the party believes production of the document or thing can be compelled in the foreign country, including a description of the procedures that will be used to compel production of the document or thing in the foreign country and an estimate of the time it is expected to take to obtain production of the document or thing; and

(ii) Demonstrate that the party has made reasonable efforts to obtain the agreement of the individual or entity having possession, custody, or control of the document or thing to produce the document or thing in the United States but has been unsuccessful in obtaining that agreement, even though the party has offered to pay the expenses of producing the document or thing in the United States.

§ 42.53. Taking testimony.

(a) *Form.* Uncompelled direct testimony must be submitted

in the form of an affidavit. All other testimony, including testimony compelled under 35 U.S.C. 24, must be in the form of a deposition transcript. Parties may agree to video-recorded testimony, but may not submit such testimony without prior authorization of the Board. In addition, the Board may authorize or require live or video-recorded testimony.

(b) *Time and location.*

(1) Uncompelled direct testimony may be taken at any time to support a petition, motion, opposition, or reply; otherwise, testimony may only be taken during a testimony period set by the Board.

(2) Except as the Board otherwise orders, during the testimony period, deposition testimony may be taken at any reasonable time and location within the United States before any disinterested official authorized to administer oaths at that location.

(3) Uncompelled deposition testimony outside the United States may only be taken upon agreement of the parties or as the Board specifically directs.

(c) *Duration.*

(1) Unless stipulated by the parties or ordered by the Board, direct examination, cross-examination, and redirect examination for compelled deposition testimony shall be subject to the following time limits: Seven hours for direct examination, four hours for cross-examination, and two hours for redirect examination.

(2) Unless stipulated by the parties or ordered by the Board, cross-examination, redirect examination, and re-cross examination for uncompelled direct deposition testimony shall be subject to the following time limits: Seven hours for cross-examination, four hours for redirect examination, and two hours for re-cross examination.

(d) *Notice of deposition.* (1) Prior to the taking of deposition testimony, all parties to the proceeding must agree on the time and place for taking testimony. If the parties cannot agree, the party seeking the testimony must initiate a conference with the Board to set a time and place.

(2) Cross-examination should ordinarily take place after any supplemental evidence relating to the direct testimony has been filed and more than a week before the filing date for any paper in which the cross-examination testimony is expected to be used. A party requesting cross-examination testimony of more than one witness may choose the order in which the witnesses are to be cross-examined.

(3) In the case of direct deposition testimony, at least three business days prior to the conference in paragraph (d)(1) of this section, or if there is no conference, at least ten

days prior to the deposition, the party seeking the direct testimony must serve:

(i) A list and copy of each document under the party's control and on which the party intends to rely; and

(ii) A list of, and proffer of reasonable access to, anything other than a document under the party's control and on which the party intends to rely.

(4) The party seeking the deposition must file a notice of the deposition at least ten business days before a deposition.

(5) Scope and content—

(i) For direct deposition testimony, the notice limits the scope of the testimony and must list:

(A) The time and place of the deposition;

(B) The name and address of the witness;

(C) A list of the exhibits to be relied upon during the deposition; and

(D) A general description of the scope and nature of the testimony to be elicited.

(ii) For cross-examination testimony, the scope of the examination is limited to the scope of the direct testimony.

(iii) The notice must list the time and place of the deposition.

(iv) Where an additional party seeks to take direct testimony of a third party witness at the time and place noticed in paragraph (d)(5) of this section, the additional party must provide a counter notice that lists the exhibits to be relied upon in the deposition and a general description of the scope and nature of the testimony to be elicited.

(6) Motion to quash—Objection to a defect in the notice is waived unless the objecting party promptly seeks authorization to file a motion to quash.

(e) Deposition in a foreign language. If an interpreter will be used during the deposition, the party calling the witness must initiate a conference with the Board at least five business days before the deposition.

(f) Manner of taking deposition testimony. (1) Before giving deposition testimony, each witness shall be duly sworn according to law by the officer before whom the deposition is to be taken. The officer must be authorized to take testimony under 35 U.S.C. 23.

(2) The testimony shall be taken with any questions and answers recorded in their regular order by the officer, or by some other disinterested person in the presence of the officer, unless the presence of the officer is waived on the record by agreement of all parties.

(3) Any exhibits used during the deposition must be

numbered as required by § 42.63(c), and must, if not previously served, be served at the deposition. Exhibits objected to shall be accepted pending a decision on the objection.

(4) All objections made at the time of the deposition to the qualifications of the officer taking the deposition, the manner of taking it, the evidence presented, the conduct of any party, and any other objection to the deposition shall be noted on the record by the officer.

(5) When the testimony has been transcribed, the witness shall read and sign (in the form of an affidavit) a transcript of the deposition unless:

(i) The parties otherwise agree in writing;

(ii) The parties waive reading and signature by the witness on the record at the deposition; or

(iii) The witness refuses to read or sign the transcript of the deposition.

(6) The officer shall prepare a certified transcript by attaching a certificate in the form of an affidavit signed and sealed by the officer to the transcript of the deposition. Unless the parties waive any of the following requirements, in which case the certificate shall so state, the certificate must state:

(i) The witness was duly sworn by the officer before commencement of testimony by the witness;

(ii) The transcript is a true record of the testimony given by the witness;

(iii) The name of the person who recorded the testimony, and if the officer did not record it, whether the testimony was recorded in the presence of the officer;

(iv) The presence or absence of any opponent;

(v) The place where the deposition was taken and the day and hour when the deposition began and ended;

(vi) The officer has no disqualifying interest, personal or financial, in a party; and

(vii) If a witness refuses to read or sign the transcript, the circumstances under which the witness refused.

(7) Except where the parties agree otherwise, the proponent of the testimony must arrange for providing a copy of the transcript to all other parties. The testimony must be filed by proponent as an exhibit.

(8) Any objection to the content, form, or manner of taking the deposition, including the qualifications of the officer, is waived unless made on the record during the deposition and preserved in a timely filed motion to exclude.

(g) Costs. Except as the Board may order or the parties

may agree in writing, the proponent of the direct testimony shall bear all costs associated with the testimony, including the reasonable costs associated with making the witness available for the cross-examination.

§ 42.54. Protective order.

(a) A party may file a motion to seal where the motion to seal contains a proposed protective order, such as the default protective order set forth in the Office Patent Trial Practice Guide. The motion must include a certification that the moving party has in good faith conferred or attempted to confer with other affected parties in an effort to resolve the dispute. The Board may, for good cause, issue an order to protect a party or person from disclosing confidential information, including, but not limited to, one or more of the following:

(1) Forbidding the disclosure or discovery;

(2) Specifying terms, including time and place, for the disclosure or discovery;

(3) Prescribing a discovery method other than the one selected by the party seeking discovery;

(4) Forbidding inquiry into certain matters, or limiting the scope of disclosure or discovery to certain matters;

(5) Designating the persons who may be present while the discovery is conducted;

(6) Requiring that a deposition be sealed and opened only by order of the Board;

(7) Requiring that a trade secret or other confidential research, development, or commercial information not be revealed or be revealed only in a specified way; and

(8) Requiring that the parties simultaneously file specified documents or information in sealed envelopes, to be opened as the Board directs.

(b) [Reserved].

After Institution of Post-Grant Review

***

§ 42.224 Discovery.

Notwithstanding the discovery provisions of subpart A:[3]

(a) Requests for additional discovery may be granted upon a showing of good cause as to why the discovery is needed; and

(b) Discovery is limited to evidence directly related to factual assertions advanced by either party in the proceeding.

The "good cause" standard for "Additional Discovery" for

[3]Subpart A of Part 42 is entitled "Trial Practice and Procedure."

PGRs (and therefore CBM reviews) differs (slightly) from the "interests of justice" standard for IPRs and derivation proceedings. The application of these standards is explained in the next sections.

The Trial Practice Guide supplements and explains the trial practice rules set forth in 37 C.F.R. Part 42. The portions of the Trial Practice Guide relevant to "routine discovery" and "additional discovery" state as follows:

> *F. Discovery*
>
> Discovery is a tool to develop a fair record and to aid the Board in assessing the credibility of witnesses. To streamline the proceedings, the rules and Scheduling Order provide a sequenced discovery process upon institution of the trial. Specifically, each party will be provided respective discovery periods, beginning with the patent owner. The sequenced discovery allows parties to conduct meaningful discovery before they are required to submit their respective motions and oppositions during the trial. Thus, discovery before the Board is focused on what the parties reasonably need to respond to the grounds raised by an opponent. In this way, the scope of the trial continually narrows.
>
> 1. *Routine Discovery*: Routine discovery includes: (1) Production of any exhibit cited in a paper or testimony; (2) the cross-examination of the other side's declarants; and (3) relevant information that is inconsistent with a position advanced during the proceeding. Routine discovery places the parties on a level playing field and streamlines the proceeding. Board authorization is not required to conduct routine discovery, although the Board will set the times for conducting this discovery in its Scheduling Order.
>
> (a) *Inconsistent Statements*: The following situations exemplify instances where disclosures of inconsistent statements are to be made. Example 1: where a petitioner relies upon an expert affidavit alleging that a method described in a patent cannot be carried out, the petitioner would be required to provide any non-privileged work undertaken by, or on behalf of, the petitioner that is inconsistent with the contentions in the expert's affidavit. Example 2: where a patent owner relies upon surprising and unexpected results to rebut an allegation of obviousness, the patent owner should provide the petitioner with non-privileged evidence that is inconsistent with the contention of unexpected properties.
>
> (b) *Witness Expenses*: The burden and expense of producing a witness for redirect or cross-examination should normally fall on the party presenting the witness. Thus, a party presenting a witness's testimony by affidavit should arrange to make the witness available for cross-examination. This applies to witnesses employed by a party as well as experts and non-

party witnesses. If there are associated expenses such as expert witness fees or travel, those should be borne by the party presenting the testimony. Should the witness's testimony be presented by transcript, the same rules apply, and the witness fees and expenses should be borne by the presenting party.

(c) *Document Translation*: All proceedings before the Board will be conducted in English. Translations therefore must be provided for: (1) Those documents produced in discovery under Sec. 42.51; and (2) all documents relied on, or otherwise used, during the proceedings. Unless accompanied by an English language translation, such documents in a language other than English will not be considered by the Board.

2. *Additional Discovery*: A request for additional discovery must be in the form of a motion, although the parties may agree to discovery amongst themselves. § 42.51(b)(2). The types of discovery available under the Federal Rules of Civil Procedure can be sought by the parties. The standard for granting such requests varies with the proceeding. An "interests of justice" standard applies in IPR and derivations, whereas the more liberal "good cause" standard applies in PGR and CBM. Id. An additional discovery request could be granted under either standard, for example, when a party raises an issue where the evidence on that issue is uniquely in the possession of the party that raised it.

3. *Compelled Testimony*: A party can request authorization to compel testimony under 35 U.S.C. 24. If a motion to compel testimony is granted, testimony may be (1) ex parte, subject to subsequent cross-examination, or (2) *inter partes*. *Therriault v. Garbe*, 53 USPQ2d 1179, 1184 (BPAI 1999). Prior to moving for or opposing compelled testimony, the parties should discuss which procedure is appropriate. See Appendix D for guidance on compelled testimony.

4. *Mandatory Initial Disclosures* ***

Recapitulating, discovery begins with mandatory initial disclosures under 37 C.F.R. § 42.41(a). Thereafter, "routine discovery" *as defined* may proceed. What is "routine" in federal district court litigation is quite different from what is "routine" in PTAB trials where "routine" means serving exhibits or testimony, cross examining declarants within the scheduled time period, and serving the opponent with inconsistent information concurrent with the filing of the underlying document. Counsel should note the requirement of § 42.51(b)(1)(iii) that "This requirement extends to inventors, corporate officers, and persons involved in the preparation or filing of the documents or things."

Anything beyond this narrow "routine discovery" is deemed "additional discovery" within the meaning of the rule. Parties may voluntarily agree to further "additional discovery." Absent agreement, a party who desires further discovery must move for such discovery and must show how the additional discovery meets the applicable standard. In IPRs and derivations, the standard is the restrictive "interests of justice" standard, and in PGRs and CBM reviews, it is the more liberal "good cause" standard.

§ 15:22 Discovery—"Interests of justice" standard

Discovery in PTAB trial proceedings bears general similarities in *form* to discovery under the Federal Rules of Civil Procedure but is quite different in *scope* and *timing*. The Board has declined requests for "additional discovery" (over and above the "routine discovery" mentioned in the Trial Practice Guide) unless the party seeking such discovery has a sound basis.

The Board ruling in *Garmin Intl, Inc. v. Cuozzo Speed Technologies LLC*, IPR2012-00001, Paper No. 26 (PTAB March 5, 2013) is a representative (and leading) decision that shows how the PTAB regulates discovery in an IPR under the "interests of justice" standard. A copy of this ruling is included as an Appendix to this book. This ruling is cited in subsequent IPR discovery rulings. As will be seen, this discovery is vastly more limited than federal courts routinely allow.

Some key points note from this ruling and its later representative decisions at the PTAB are:

- Routine Discovery. "Routine discovery" is narrowly directed to specific discovery known to the responding company to be inconsistent with a position it advanced. It is *not* broadly directed to any subject area where the movant hopes to discover something inconsistent.[1]
- Routine Discovery—Time for Serving. The time for serving the routinely discoverable information is concurrent with the time for serving the documents or things which contain the inconsistency—not before.[2]
- Routine Discovery—Test Protocols and Procedures; Samples. When one party prepares compositions

[Section 15:22]

[1] *Garmin Intl, Inc. v. Cuozzo Speed Technologies LLC*, IPR2012-00001, Paper No. 26, p. 4 (PTAB March 5, 2013).

[2] *Garmin Intl, Inc. v. Cuozzo Speed Technologies LLC*, IPR2012-00001, Paper No. 26, pp. 4, 13 (PTAB March 5, 2013).

disclosed in the prior art and tests the samples for the properties set forth in the claims, a request for the protocols and procedures is not "routine discovery," but it is "additional discovery" that the Board has granted in the interest of justice.[3] Neither are samples of the prepared compositions routine discovery, and in this instance, the Board denied the request for samples as additional discovery.[4]

- Additional Discovery Is Limited. The scope of "additional discovery" is limited in IPRs as compared to the scope of discovery allowed in district court litigation where the Federal Rules of Civil Procedure apply.[5] The reason for limited discovery is to lower costs, minimize complexity, and shorten the time required for resolving the dispute.[6]
- Fed. R. Civ. Proc. Inapplicable. The Federal Rules of Civil Procedure do not apply in *inter partes* reviews.[7]
- Burden of Proof. The moving party must show that the additional discovery is in the interest of justice.[8] Only what is necessary in the interest of justice is available "additional discovery" under the IPR statute and rules. This should be limited to minor discovery and special circumstances.[9] The burden is on the movant to demonstrate that the additional discovery is in the interest of

---

[3]*Corning Inc. v. DSM IP Assets B.V.*, IPR2013-00043, Paper No. 27, pp. 3-4 (PTAB June 21, 2013).

[4]*Corning Inc. v. DSM IP Assets B.V.*, IPR2013-00043, Paper No. 27, pp. 5-6 (PTAB June 21, 2013) (DSM failed to indicate which samples it wanted, which samples would take "several weeks to create," the quantity requested; which ones DSM would have trouble duplicating, or that the request would not unduly burden Corning).

[5]*Garmin Intl, Inc. v. Cuozzo Speed Technologies LLC*, IPR2012-00001, Paper No. 26, p. 5 (PTAB March 5, 2013).

[6]*Garmin Intl, Inc. v. Cuozzo Speed Technologies LLC*, IPR2012-00001, Paper No. 26, p. 5 (PTAB March 5, 2013); see also *Microsoft Corporation v. Proxyconn, Inc.*, IPR2012-00026 and IPR2013-00109, Paper No. 32, p. 3 (PTAB March 8, 2013).

[7]*Garmin Intl, Inc. v. Cuozzo Speed Technologies LLC*, IPR2012-00001, Paper No. 26, p. 13 (PTAB March 5, 2013).

[8]*Garmin Intl, Inc. v. Cuozzo Speed Technologies LLC*, IPR2012-00001, Paper No. 26, p. 5 (PTAB March 5, 2013).

[9]*Microsoft Corporation v. Proxyconn, Inc.*, IPR2012-00026 and IPR2013-00109, Paper No. 32, p. 3 (PTAB March 8, 2013).

justice.[10]

- Burden of Proof—Time for Showing. The interest of justice standard for granting additional discovery requires the showing of relevance to be made before the request for additional discovery is granted.[11]
- Speculation and Allegations Insufficient. Mere possibilities and allegations (that relevant or useful information will be discovered) are not enough to meet the "interests of justice" standard. The party moving for additional discovery must show that the requested information would be "useful." "Useful" means more than just relevant or admissible and instead means favorable in substantive value to the moving party.[12]
- "Likely to Lead to Admissible Evidence" Not the Standard. Stating that the discovery is likely to yield relevant, admissible evidence is similar to the district court litigation standard but is not the PTAB standard. The movant must show more. The mere possibility that something "useful" will be found is insufficient.[13]
- Discovery of Secondary Consideration Evidence. A threshold showing is required to meet the standard for evidence of secondary considerations.[14]
- Copying. In the case of alleged "copying," a threshold amount of evidence is required tending to show copying beyond mere speculation.[15]
- Commercial Success. In the case of alleging "commercial success," the movant must show (in the motion) a satisfactory nexus between the claimed invention and the discovery request. This includes accounting for the presence of other desirable features on the same units for

---

[10] *Microsoft Corporation v. Proxyconn, Inc.*, IPR2012-00026 and IPR2013-00109, Paper No. 32, p. 8 (PTAB March 8, 2013).

[11] *Microsoft Corporation v. Proxyconn, Inc.*, IPR2012-00026 and IPR2013-00109, Paper No. 32, p. 5 (PTAB March 8, 2013).

[12] *Garmin Intl, Inc. v. Cuozzo Speed Technologies LLC*, IPR2012-00001, Paper No. 26, p. 7 (PTAB March 5, 2013).

[13] *Garmin Intl, Inc. v. Cuozzo Speed Technologies LLC*, IPR2012-00001, Paper No. 26, pp. 7-8 (PTAB March 5, 2013).

[14] *Garmin Intl, Inc. v. Cuozzo Speed Technologies LLC*, IPR2012-00001, Paper No. 26, passim (PTAB March 5, 2013).

[15] *Garmin Intl, Inc. v. Cuozzo Speed Technologies LLC*, IPR2012-00001, Paper No. 26, p. 8 (PTAB March 5, 2013).

which discovery is sought.[16] The Board can require the movant to show in its motion how the discovery is relevant, *i.e.*, show that the commercial success derives from the feature in question as opposed to other economic and commercial factors unrelated to the quality of the patented subject matter.[17] The nexus requirement need not be conclusive at the motion stage but must contain some showing of relevance.[18]

- Failure of Others. When a patent owner alleges "failure by others," a motion for additional discovery must show a threshold amount of evidence tending to show that a skilled artisan with knowledge of the pertinent prior art had tried but failed to solve a problem at issue.[19]
- Long Felt, Unresolved Needs. In the case of "long felt but unresolved needs," the movant must explain why it needs discovery from the non-movant to establish the assertion.[20] The Board presumes that the movant can conduct its own market surveys and make its own comparisons.[21]
- File Histories. Requesting file histories from an opponent is improper when they are publicly available.[22]
- Litigation Positions. Asking for litigation positions is inappropriate because the Board already has a schedule in place. A party is not obligated to inform its opponent of its positions before that party is ready to present them.[23]
- Publicly Available Information. If the information requested is publicly available elsewhere, "additional

[16] *Garmin Intl, Inc. v. Cuozzo Speed Technologies LLC*, IPR2012-00001, Paper No. 26, p. 8 (PTAB March 5, 2013).

[17] *Microsoft Corporation v. Proxyconn, Inc.*, IPR2012-00026 and IPR2013-00109, Paper No. 32, pp. 3-5 (PTAB March 8, 2013).

[18] *Microsoft Corporation v. Proxyconn, Inc.*, IPR2012-00026 and IPR2013-00109, Paper No. 32, p. 5 (PTAB March 8, 2013).

[19] *Garmin Intl, Inc. v. Cuozzo Speed Technologies LLC*, IPR2012-00001, Paper No. 26, p. 9 (PTAB March 5, 2013).

[20] *Garmin Intl, Inc. v. Cuozzo Speed Technologies LLC*, IPR2012-00001, Paper No. 26, p. 14 (PTAB March 5, 2013).

[21] *Garmin Intl, Inc. v. Cuozzo Speed Technologies LLC*, IPR2012-00001, Paper No. 26, p. 14 (PTAB March 5, 2013).

[22] *Garmin Intl, Inc. v. Cuozzo Speed Technologies LLC*, IPR2012-00001, Paper No. 26, p. 14 (PTAB March 5, 2013).

[23] *Garmin Intl, Inc. v. Cuozzo Speed Technologies LLC*, IPR2012-00001, Paper No. 26, p. 13 (PTAB March 5, 2013).

discovery" is unnecessary to obtain it from the non-movant.[24] For example, pricing information would appear to be available publicly.[25]

- Movant Can Generate/Obtain Information On Its Own. If the movant can generate the information on its own, compelling its production from the opponent is not in the interest of justice. For example, if "long-felt need" is the issue, the movant must explain why it needs the additional discovery instead of simply conducting its own survey or otherwise generating its own data.[26]
- Instructions for Additional Discovery. The instructions for discovery must be easily understandable.[27]
- Burden. Requests for additional discovery must not be overly burdensome to answer.[28] They should be time-limited, precise, and focused.[29]
- Rule 30(b)(6) Depositions Improper. Requesting depositions in the style of Fed. R. Civ. Proc. 30(b)(6) are improper for the same reasons that document discovery of the same topics is improper.[30]
- Privilege Log. The Board *denied* a request for a privilege log of withheld information.[31]

§ 15:23 Discovery—"Good cause" standard

The "good cause" standard for additional discovery is

---

[24] *Garmin Intl, Inc. v. Cuozzo Speed Technologies LLC*, IPR2012-00001, Paper No. 26, p. 14 (PTAB March 5, 2013); *Microsoft Corporation v. Proxyconn, Inc.*, IPR2012-00026 and IPR2013-00109, Paper No. 32, p. 6 (PTAB March 8, 2013).

[25] *Microsoft Corporation v. Proxyconn, Inc.*, IPR2012-00026 and IPR2013-00109, Paper No. 32, p. 6 (PTAB March 8, 2013).

[26] *Garmin Intl, Inc. v. Cuozzo Speed Technologies LLC*, IPR2012-00001, Paper No. 26, p. 14 (PTAB March 5, 2013).

[27] *Garmin Intl, Inc. v. Cuozzo Speed Technologies LLC*, IPR2012-00001, Paper No. 26, pp. 6-7 (PTAB March 5, 2013).

[28] *Garmin Intl, Inc. v. Cuozzo Speed Technologies LLC*, IPR2012-00001, Paper No. 26, pp. 14-16 (PTAB March 5, 2013).

[29] *Microsoft Corporation v. Proxyconn, Inc.*, IPR2012-00026 and IPR2013-00109, Paper No. 32, p. 6 (PTAB March 8, 2013).

[30] *Garmin Intl, Inc. v. Cuozzo Speed Technologies LLC*, IPR2012-00001, Paper No. 26, p. 16 (PTAB March 5, 2013).

[31] *Corning Inc. v. DSM IP Assets B.V.*, IPR2013-00043, Paper No. 27, pp. 6-74 (PTAB June 21, 2013) (DSM provided no indication that it has evidence tending to show beyond speculation that something useful will be uncovered by such a request; no explanation of why this is not overly burdensome to Corning).

stated explicitly in 37 C.F.R. § 42.224. In a representative ruling in May 2013, the Board modified the five *Garmin* discovery factors for use under this standard in covered business method patent reviews:

Discovery Factors for Covered Business Method Patent Review

1. *More Than A Possibility And Mere Allegation—*

The mere possibility of finding something useful, and mere allegation that something useful will be found, are insufficient to establish a good cause showing. "Useful" means favorable in substantive value to a contention of the party moving for discovery. A good cause showing requires the moving party to provide a specific factual reason for expecting reasonably that the discovery will be "useful."

2. *Litigation Positions And Underlying Basis—*

Asking for the other party's litigation positions and the underlying basis for those positions is insufficient to demonstrate that the additional discovery is necessary for good cause. The Board has established rules for the presentation of arguments and evidence. There is a proper time and place for each party to make its presentation. A party may not attempt to alter the Board's trial procedures under the pretext of discovery.

3. *Ability To Generate Equivalent Information By Other Means—*

A party should not seek information that reasonably can be generated without a discovery request.

4. *Easily Understandable Instructions—*

Instructions and questions should be easily understandable. For example, ten pages of complex instructions for answering questions is prima facie unclear. Such instructions are counterproductive and tend to undermine the responder's ability to answer efficiently, accurately, and confidently.

5. *Requests Not Overly Burdensome To Answer—*

Requests must not be overly burdensome to answer, given the expedited nature of a covered-business method patent review. The burden includes financial burden, burden on human resources, and burden on meeting the time schedule of the trial. Requests should be sensible and responsibly tailored according to a genuine need.[1]

Key points to note from this representative ruling and other CBM (or PGR) rulings at the PTAB are as follows:

- Additional Discovery Standard for PGRs/CBMs: The interests of justice standard (applied in IPRs) is "slightly higher" than the good cause standard.[2]
- Additional Discovery Is Limited. The statutory provisions for IPRs, PGRs, and CBM reviews caution against overly broad discovery and are guided by the same considerations of efficient administration of the Office and the ability to complete the proceeding in timely fashion.[3] The Board notes the legislative history stating that regardless of the standards imposed, the PTO will be "conservative" in its grants of discovery.[4] The discovery rules must be construed to secure the just, speedy, and inexpensive resolution of every proceeding.[5]
- Burden of Proof. The moving party must show entitlement to the additional discovery.[6]
- Good Cause Standard. A good cause showing requires a specific factual reason for reasonably expecting the discovery will be "useful" (as defined).[7]
- Information Considered by Opposing Expert. The Board granted a request for production of documents and things that the opposing expert considered in preparing his declaration as filed in the instant proceeding

[Section 15:23]

[1] *Bloomberg Inc. et al. v. Markets-Alert Pty Ltd.*, CBM2013-00005, Paper No. 32, p. 5 (PTAB May 29, 2013). These factors had not been adopted yet when *SAP America, Inc. v. Versata Development Group, Inc.*, CBM2012-00001, Paper No. 24 (PTAB Nov. 15, 2012) was decided (granting limited additional discovery prior to the decision to institute).

[2] *Bloomberg Inc. et al. v. Markets-Alert Pty Ltd.*, CBM2013-00005, Paper No. 32, p. 3 (PTAB May 29, 2013).

[3] *Bloomberg Inc. et al. v. Markets-Alert Pty Ltd.*, CBM2013-00005, Paper No. 32, p. 3 (PTAB May 29, 2013).

[4] *Bloomberg Inc. et al. v. Markets-Alert Pty Ltd.*, CBM2013-00005, Paper No. 32, p. 3 (PTAB May 29, 2013).

[5] *Bloomberg Inc. et al. v. Markets-Alert Pty Ltd.*, CBM2013-00005, Paper No. 32, p. 4 (PTAB May 29, 2013).

[6] *Bloomberg Inc. et al. v. Markets-Alert Pty Ltd.*, CBM2013-00005, Paper No. 32, p. 4 (PTAB May 29, 2013).

[7] *Bloomberg Inc. et al. v. Markets-Alert Pty Ltd.*, CBM2013-00005, Paper No. 32, p. 5 (PTAB May 29, 2013).

because specific factual reasons were shown.[8]

- Speculation and Allegations Insufficient. The party moving for additional discovery must show that the requested information would be "useful." "Useful" means more than just relevant or admissible and instead means favorable in substantive value to the moving party.[9]
- Potential Probative Value Not the Standard. Stating that the discovery is likely to have probative value is not the PTAB standard. The mere possibility that something "useful" will be found is insufficient. The movant must show a specific factual reason or evidence.[10] Mere possibilities and allegations are not sufficient to meet the burden.
- Prior Art Known to Petitioner and Information It Considered. The Board was not persuaded by arguments that the patent owner needed to discover all the prior art known to the petitioner and all information it had considered. This discovery was deemed speculative.[11]
- Discovery of Secondary Consideration Evidence. A showing is required to meet the "good cause" standard for seeking evidence of secondary considerations. The arguments cannot be speculative and must be meaningful. Mere allegations that something "useful" will result are insufficient.[12]
- Copying. In the case of alleged "copying," the Board denied a motion for additional discovery where the mov-

---

[8] *Bloomberg Inc. et al. v. Markets-Alert Pty Ltd.*, CBM2013-00005, Paper No. 32, p. 6 (PTAB May 29, 2013) (request is specific and tailored narrowly, seeks information from only one individual rather than a whole company, relates to a single declaration, and the movant (Markets-Alert) provided specific examples; discovery granted only to the extent of the expert's recollection).

[9] *Bloomberg Inc. et al. v. Markets-Alert Pty Ltd.*, CBM2013-00005, Paper No. 32, p. 5 (PTAB May 29, 2013).

[10] *Bloomberg Inc. et al. v. Markets-Alert Pty Ltd.*, CBM2013-00005, Paper No. 32, p. 10 (PTAB May 29, 2013).

[11] *Bloomberg Inc. et al. v. Markets-Alert Pty Ltd.*, CBM2013-00005, Paper No. 32, pp. 7-8 (PTAB May 29, 2013) (insufficient factual reasons provided by movant; speculative usefulness; art deemed cumulative; no explanation of why patent owner's own prior art search and expert opinion would not suffice).

[12] *Bloomberg Inc. et al. v. Markets-Alert Pty Ltd.*, CBM2013-00005, Paper No. 32, p. 10 (PTAB May 29, 2013).

ant provided no evidence of copying or seeking a license.[13]

- Failure of Others. The Board denied a motion for additional discovery where the motion lacked a specific factual reason or credible evidence to show that anyone had tried but failed to solve a problem at issue.[14]
- Long Felt, Unresolved Needs. A movant must explain why it needs discovery to establish an assertion of "long felt but unresolved needs." For example, the movant can rely on its own analysis and independent analysts without a discovery request.[15]
- Movant Can Generate/Obtain Information On Its Own. If the movant can generate the information on its own, compelling its production from the opponent is not required. For example, if "long-felt need" is the issue, the movant must explain why it needs the additional discovery instead of simply conducting its own survey or otherwise generating its own data.[16]
- Instructions for Additional Discovery. The instructions for discovery must not be overly broad, not place an undue burden, and not cause unnecessary substantial delays.[17]
- Burden. Requests for additional discovery must not be overly burdensome to answer. They should be time-limited, precise, and focused. In one case, the Board rejected the request because, *inter alia*, the argument for discovery was not commensurate with the scope of the requests.[18]

§ 15:24 *[Reserved]*

§ 15:25 *[Reserved]*

---

[13]*Bloomberg Inc. et al. v. Markets-Alert Pty Ltd.*, CBM2013-00005, Paper No. 32, p. 11 (PTAB May 29, 2013).

[14]*Bloomberg Inc. et al. v. Markets-Alert Pty Ltd.*, CBM2013-00005, Paper No. 32, pp. 10-11 (PTAB May 29, 2013).

[15]*Bloomberg Inc. et al. v. Markets-Alert Pty Ltd.*, CBM2013-00005, Paper No. 32, p.11 (PTAB May 29, 2013).

[16]See, *Bloomberg Inc. et al. v. Markets-Alert Pty Ltd.*, CBM2013-00005, Paper No. 32, p.11 (PTAB May 29, 2013).

[17]*Bloomberg Inc. et al. v. Markets-Alert Pty Ltd.*, CBM2013-00005, Paper No. 32, p.11 (PTAB May 29, 2013).

[18]*Bloomberg Inc. et al. v. Markets-Alert Pty Ltd.*, CBM2013-00005, Paper No. 32, p. 9 (PTAB May 29, 2013).

§ 15:26 *[Reserved]*

§ 15:27 *[Reserved]*

§ 15:28 Motions

Early in the trial, the Board will have an initial conference with the parties. At least two days before the conference, the parties must submit a list of motions they expect to file. The PTAB provided guidance on the motions list in another representative ruling, explaining that the list's purpose is simply to provide the Board and opposing party adequate notice to prepare for the initial call and the proceeding. It is not an opportunity to set forth the motion itself, and it is improper to specify pages of facts, arguments, or scheduling.[1]

The schedule permits motions to be filed by the parties within certain prescribed times. For example, the patent owner may move to amend the claims during the first phase of the trial. Motions to exclude are necessary to preserve objections, as described herein and in the rules. See especially § 15:30.

The Trial Practice rules regarding motions are set forth below:

Petition and Motion Practice

§ 42.20. Generally.

(a) *Relief.* Relief, other than a petition requesting the institution of a trial, must be requested in the form of a motion.

(b) Prior authorization. A motion will not be entered without Board authorization. Authorization may be provided in an order of general applicability or during the proceeding.

(c) Burden of proof. The moving party has the burden of proof to establish that it is entitled to the requested relief.

(d) Briefing. The Board may order briefing on any issue involved in the trial.

§ 42.21. Notice of basis for relief.

(a) *Notice of request for relief.* The Board may require a party to file a notice stating the relief it requests and the basis for its entitlement to relief. A notice must include sufficient detail to place the Board and each opponent on notice of the precise relief requested. A notice is not evidence except as an admission by a party-opponent.

[Section 15:28]

[1] *CRS Advanced Technologies, Inc. v. Frontline Technologies, Inc.*, CBM2012-00005, Paper No. 31, p. 2 (PTAB Feb. 13, 2013).

(b) *Filing and service.* The Board may set the times and conditions for filing and serving notices required under this section. The Board may provide for the notice filed with the Board to be maintained in confidence for a limited time.

(c) *Effect.* If a notice under paragraph (a) of this section is required:

(1) A failure to state a sufficient basis for relief may result in a denial of the relief requested;

(2) A party will be limited to filing motions consistent with the notice; and

(3) Ambiguities in the notice will be construed against the party.

(d) Correction. A party may move to correct its notice. The motion should be filed promptly after the party becomes aware of the basis for the correction. A correction filed after the time set for filing notices will only be entered if entry would serve the interests of justice.

§ 42.23. Oppositions and replies.

(a) Oppositions and replies must comply with the content requirements for motions and must include a statement identifying material facts in dispute. Any material fact not specifically denied may be considered admitted.

(b) All arguments for the relief requested in a motion must be made in the motion. A reply may only respond to arguments raised in the corresponding opposition or patent owner response.

§ 42.25. Default filing times.

(a) A motion may only be filed according to a schedule set by the Board. The default times for acting are:

(1) An opposition is due one month after service of the motion; and

(2) A reply is due one month after service of the opposition.

(b) A party should seek relief promptly after the need for relief is identified. Delay in seeking relief may justify a denial of relief sought.

Parties will note the particular requirements of motion practice stated in these rules. They must also follow the requirements of form set forth above.

§ 15:29 Motions—For joinder

Different PTAB proceedings may be joined together. For example, 35 U.S.C.A. § 315(b) and (c) provide as follows with respect to *inter partes* reviews:

35 U.S.C. 315 Relation to other proceedings or actions

***

(b) Patent Owner's Action.—An inter partes review may not be instituted if the petition requesting the proceeding is filed more than 1 year after the date on which the petitioner, real party in interest, or privy of the petitioner is served with a complaint alleging infringement of the patent. *The time limitation set forth in the preceding sentence shall not apply to a request for joinder under subsection (c).*

(c) Joinder.—If the Director institutes an inter partes review, the Director, in his or her discretion, may join as a party to that inter partes review any person who properly files a petition under section 311 that the Director, after receiving a preliminary response under section 313 or the expiration of the time for filing such a response, determines warrants the institution of an inter partes review under section 314.

[emphasis added] With respect to joinder to a post grant review, the statute is similar but not identical to 35 U.S.C.A. § 315(c). See 35 U.S.C.A. § 325(c).[1]

The final rule adopted by the PTO regarding joinder in IPRs provides as follows:

37 C.F.R. § 42.122 Multiple proceedings and Joinder.

(a) *Multiple proceedings*. Where another matter involving the patent is before the Office, the Board may during the pendency of the *inter partes* review enter any appropriate order regarding the additional matter including providing for the stay, transfer, consolidation, or termination of any such matter.

(b) *Request for joinder*. Joinder may be requested by a patent owner or petitioner. Any request for joinder must be filed, as a motion under § 42.22, no later than one month after the institution date of any *inter partes* review for which joinder is requested. The time period set forth in § 42.101(b) shall not apply when the petition is accompanied by a request for joinder.

A parallel final rule regarding joinder for PGRs appears as

[Section 15:29]

[1]**35 U.S.C. 325 Relation to other proceedings or actions** *** "(c) Joinder.—If more than 1 petition for a post-grant review under this chapter is properly filed against the same patent and the Director determines that more than 1 of these petitions warrants the institution of a post-grant review under section 324, the Director may consolidate such reviews into a single post-grant review."

37 C.F.R. § 42.222:

§ 42.222 Multiple proceedings and Joinder.

(a) *Multiple proceedings*. Where another matter involving the patent is before the Office, the Board may during the pendency of the post-grant review enter any appropriate order regarding the additional matter including providing for the stay, transfer, consolidation, or termination of any such matter.

(b) *Request for joinder*. Joinder may be requested by a patent owner or petitioner. Any request for joinder must be filed, as a motion under § 42.22, no later than one month after the institution date of any post-grant review for which joinder is requested.

As can be seen from the rules, a request (motion) for joinder is timely *if filed within one month after an IPR or PGR has been granted*. Accordingly, prospective patent challengers need to be aware of the status of pending petitions by other challengers in respect of the same patent(s), as they have only one month to file a motion for joinder to the declared IPR or PGR.

Practitioners should also note the special dispensation from the one-year rule in the case of IPR petitions with respect to patents already being asserted in an infringement suit. "The time limitation set forth in the preceding sentence shall not apply to a request for joinder under subsection (c)." 35 U.S.C.A. § 315(b). The statute thus allows a joinder request to be filed outside the one-year limitation. This provision has been raised and discussed in litigation already.

In *Kyocera Corporation v. Softview LLC*, IPR2013-00004, Paper No. 15 (PTAB April 24, 2013), the Board approved the request of Apple Inc. to file a motion for joinder to two IPRs even though Apple had been served with a complaint more than one year prior alleging infringement of the challenged patent.[2]

In *Microsoft Corp. v. Proxyconn, Inc.*, IPR2013-00109,

[2]About 20 days after the PTAB declared IPR2013-00004 and IPR2013-00007 involving two patents being asserted against Apple in litigation, Apple requested a conference call with the PTAB four days later, indicating that Apple planned to file concurrent petitions for IPR and motions for joinder no later than one month after the two IPRs had been instituted. Apple explained that: (1) the Board had previously stayed reexamination proceedings initiated by Apple against the same patents involved in the IPRs; (2) the petitioner in the two IPRs relied upon a declaration of Apple's expert; (3) Apple would agree to shortened schedules; and (4) the number of new issues Apple might raise in its concurrent IPR

Paper No. 15 (PTAB Feb. 25, 2013), the Board granted Microsoft's motion to join the instant IPR with an earlier-filed one, IPR2012-00026, involving the same parties, the same challenged patent, and one of the same reference patents being applied as prior art. The patent owner did not object, and the Board found no discernible prejudice to the patent owner or the petitioner from the prospective joinder. Although Microsoft had been served with a complaint asserting infringement of the challenged patent more than a year before filing its second petition, "the one-year time bar does not apply to a request for joinder."[3] Absent joinder with the earlier IPR, Microsoft's second petition would be time-barred. Here, Microsoft filed its second petition together with its motion for joinder after learning that additional claims were being asserted by the patent owner in the pending, concurrent, district court litigation.

Joinder provides a basis for the PTAB to extend the time for final written decision of the IPR, as provided by 35 U.S.C.A. § 316:

35 USC § 316—Certificate of patentability, unpatentability, and claim cancellation

(a) Regulations.—The Director shall prescribe regulations—

***

(4) establishing and governing inter partes review under this chapter and the relationship of such review to other proceedings under this title;

***

(11) requiring that the final determination in an inter partes

---

petitions would be limited. The patent owner opposed Apple's request because in the infringement suit, Apple had been served with the complaint more than one year prior. Approving Apple's request to file a motion, the Board ruled that its decision to grant joinder is discretionary, and it construes the governing rules to "secure the just, speedy and inexpensive resolution of every proceeding." As Apple's petitions might raise new grounds of unpatentability, increase work, and increase costs, the Board reserved its decision on how it might rule but allowed Apple to file its motions, explain why joinder is appropriate, identify any new ground of unpatentability being raised, and explain how the impact on the schedule and costs of the current proceedings would be minimized. *Kyocera Corporation v. Softview LLC*, IPR2013-00004, Paper No. 15, pp. 3-4 (PTAB April 24, 2013).

[3] *Microsoft Corp. v. Proxyconn, Inc.*, IPR2013-00109, Paper No. 15, p. 4 (PTAB Feb. 25, 2013).

review be issued not later than 1 year after the date on which the Director notices the institution of a review under this chapter, except that the Director may, for good cause shown, extend the 1-year period by not more than 6 months, and may adjust the time periods in this paragraph in the case of joinder under section 315(c);[4]

(12) setting a time period for requesting joinder under section 315(c); ***

The PTAB noted this provision when granting the motion for joinder in *Microsoft Corp. v. Proxyconn, Inc.*, IPR2013-00109, Paper No. 15, p. 4 (PTAB Feb. 25, 2013).

§ 15:30 Evidence

All evidence to be presented to the Board must be in the form of an exhibit. If the evidence is not taken, sought, and filed in accordance with the Trial Practice Rules, then it is inadmissible. Subpart A contains several applicable trial practice rules. These are reproduced below along with some introductory comments:

1. Evidence not taken, sought, or filed in accordance with the Trial Rules (Subpart A of Part 42) is inadmissible.
2. The Federal Rules of Evidence apply, except for portions relating to criminal proceedings, juries, and other irrelevant matters.
3. Evidence consists of affidavits, transcripts of depositions, documents, and things.
4. All evidence must be filed in the form of an exhibit.
5. Translation is required with an attestation.
6. Petitioner's exhibits are numbered 1001-1999. Patent owner exhibits are numbered 2001-2999.
7. Objections to the admissibility of deposition evidence must be made on the record during the deposition. § 42.64.
8. Evidence to cure the objection must be provided during the deposition absent stipulation otherwise. § 42.64.
9. Objections to other evidence submitted before the institution of trial must be served within 10 business days of institution of trial. § 42.64.
10. Once trial is instituted, objections to evidence must be served within 5 business days of service of that

[4]See 35 U.S.C.A. § 326(a)(11) for a parallel provision related to post-grant reviews.

evidence. § 42.64.

11. A party may respond to an objection to evidence by submitting supplemental evidence within 10 business days of service of the objection. § 42.64.
12. A motion to exclude is necessary to preserve an objection to evidence. § 42.64.
13. The rules set forth specific requirements on expert testimony and technical test or data from a test. § 42.65.

The Trial Practice Rules in 37 C.F.R. regarding evidence are reproduced below:

§ 42.61. Admissibility.

(a) Evidence that is not taken, sought, or filed in accordance with this subpart is not admissible.

(b) Records of the Office. Certification is not necessary as a condition to admissibility when the evidence to be submitted is a record of the Office to which all parties have access.

(c) Specification and drawings. A specification or drawing of a United States patent application or patent is admissible as evidence only to prove what the specification or drawing describes. If there is data in the specification or a drawing upon which a party intends to rely to prove the truth of the data, an affidavit by an individual having first-hand knowledge of how the data was generated must be filed.

§ 42.62. Applicability of the Federal Rules of Evidence.

(a) *Generally.* Except as otherwise provided in this subpart, the Federal Rules of Evidence shall apply to a proceeding.

(b) *Exclusions.* Those portions of the Federal Rules of Evidence relating to criminal proceedings, juries, and other matters not relevant to proceedings under this subpart shall not apply.

(c) *Modifications in terminology.* Unless otherwise clear from context, the following terms of the Federal Rules of Evidence shall be construed as indicated:

Appellate court means United States Court of Appeals for the Federal Circuit.

Civil action, civil proceeding, and *action* mean a proceeding before the Board under part 42.

Courts of the United States, U.S. Magistrate, court, trial court, trier of fact, and *judge* mean Board.

Hearing means, as defined in Federal Rule of Evidence 804(a)(5), the time for taking testimony.

Judicial notice means official notice.

Trial or *hearing* in Federal Rule of Evidence 807 means

the time for taking testimony.

(d) In determining foreign law, the Board may consider any relevant material or source, including testimony, whether or not submitted by a party or admissible under the Federal Rules of Evidence.

§ 42.63. Form of evidence.

(a) *Exhibits required.* Evidence consists of affidavits, transcripts of depositions, documents, and things. All evidence must be filed in the form of an exhibit.

(b) *Translation required.* When a party relies on a document or is required to produce a document in a language other than English, a translation of the document into English and an affidavit attesting to the accuracy of the translation must be filed with the document.

(c) *Exhibit numbering.* Each party's exhibits must be uniquely numbered sequentially in a range the Board specifies. For the petitioner, the range is 1001–1999, and for the patent owner, the range is 2001–2999.

(d) *Exhibit format.* An exhibit must conform with the requirements for papers in § 42.6 and the requirements of this paragraph.

(1) Each exhibit must have an exhibit label.

(i) An exhibit filed with the petition must include the petitioner's name followed by a unique exhibit number.

(ii) For exhibits not filed with the petition, the exhibit label must include the party's name followed by a unique exhibit number, the names of the parties, and the trial number.

(2) When the exhibit is a paper:

(i) Each page must be uniquely numbered in sequence; and

(ii) The exhibit label must be affixed to the lower right corner of the first page of the exhibit without obscuring information on the first page or, if obscuring is unavoidable, affixed to a duplicate first page.

(e) *Exhibit list.* Each party must maintain an exhibit list with the exhibit number and a brief description of each exhibit. If the exhibit is not filed, the exhibit list should note that fact. A current exhibit list must be served whenever evidence is served and the current exhibit list must be filed when filing exhibits.

§ 42.64. Objection; motion to exclude; motion in limine.

(a) *Deposition evid*ence. An objection to the admissibility of deposition evidence must be made during the deposition. Evidence to cure the objection must be provided during the deposition, unless the parties to the deposition stipulate otherwise on the deposition record.

(b) *Other evidence.* For evidence other than deposition evidence:

(1) *Objection.* Any objection to evidence submitted during a preliminary proceeding must be served within ten business days of the institution of the trial. Once a trial has been instituted, any objection must be served within five business days of service of evidence to which the objection is directed. The objection must identify the grounds for the objection with sufficient particularity to allow correction in the form of supplemental evidence.

(2) *Supplemental evidence.* The party relying on evidence to which an objection is timely served may respond to the objection by serving supplemental evidence within ten business days of service of the objection.

(c) *Motion to exclude.* A motion to exclude evidence must be filed to preserve any objection. The motion must identify the objections in the record in order and must explain the objections. The motion may be filed without prior authorization from the Board.

§ 42.65. Expert testimony; tests and data.

(a) Expert testimony that does not disclose the underlying facts or data on which the opinion is based is entitled to little or no weight. Testimony on United States patent law or patent examination practice will not be admitted.

(b) If a party relies on a technical test or data from such a test, the party must provide an affidavit explaining:

(1) Why the test or data is being used;

(2) How the test was performed and the data was generated;

(3) How the data is used to determine a value;

(4) How the test is regarded in the relevant art; and

(5) Any other information necessary for the Board to evaluate the test and data.

§ 15:31 Evidence—Motions to exclude

As noted above, the PTAB has a specific procedure in 37 C.F.R. § 42.64 for moving to exclude evidence. One of the PTAB's representative decisions explains how a patent owner did not follow that procedure when it sought to exclude some of the petitioner's evidence on hearsay or authentication grounds when filing a patent owner preliminary response. *LKQ Corp. v. Clearlamp, LLC*, IPR2013-00020, Paper No. 17 (PTAB March 5, 2013). The evidence was submitted during the preliminary proceeding (that is, before trial was instituted). The Board ruled that an *objection* (not a motion) by a party to evidence submitted at that time must be served within ten business days of institution of trial. Thereafter, the proponent of the evidence may submit supplemental evidence within certain time limits and then the objecting party may file a motion to exclude at the scheduled time, subject to rules applicable generally to motions. The Board explained:

> The objection to the evidence must identify the grounds for the objection with sufficient particularity to allow correction in the form of supplemental evidence. This process allows the party relying on the evidence to which an objection is timely served, the opportunity to correct, by serving supplemental evidence within so many days of the service of the objection. *See*, 37 CFR 42.64(b)(1) and (b)(2). If, upon receiving the supplemental evidence, the opposing party is still of the opinion that the evidence is inadmissible, the opposing party may file a motion to exclude such evidence. The time for filing a motion to exclude is typically several months into a trial. *See, e.g.*, 77 Fed. Reg. 157 (August 14, 2012) 48765 regarding Scheduling Order and Appendix A—Due Date 4.
>
> *** [A] request to exclude evidence [challenged as hearsay and not authenticated] is typically made by way of a motion to exclude. 37 CFR § 42.64(c). As stated above, motions to exclude are not authorized until much later during a trial, if a trial is instituted. Clearlamp's "motion to exclude" is premature and also prevents LKQ from correcting as permitted by the rules.[1]

§ 15:32 Settlement

Parties are free to settle their disputes, and there can be a strong impetus to do so in light of the estoppels that attach upon issuance of a final written decision of the Board absent a settlement. The new and amended statutes §§ 317 (*inter partes* review) and 327 (post-grant review) speak to settlement of PTAB trials and indicate four important points:

1. A review shall be terminated as to a petitioner upon a joint request of the petitioner and the patent owner unless the PTAB already decided the merits.
2. As to that petitioner, if the review is terminated, there is no estoppel against that petitioner or its real party in interest or privy.
3. However, even if no petitioner remains in the review,

[Section 15:31]

[1] *LKQ Corp. v. Clearlamp, LLC*, IPR2013-00020, Paper No. 17, pp. 3-4 (PTAB March 5, 2013).

the PTAB can still proceed to final written decision, or it can terminate the review altogether.

4. Settlement agreements must be in writing and filed with the PTAB before termination of the review. All collateral agreements must also be filed.

The new statutes address settlement and provide as follows:

35 U.S.C. § 317. Settlement

(a) IN GENERAL.— An inter partes review instituted under this chapter shall be terminated with respect to any petitioner upon the joint request of the petitioner and the patent owner, unless the Office has decided the merits of the proceeding before the request for termination is filed. If the inter partes review is terminated with respect to a petitioner under this section, no estoppel under section 315(e) shall attach to the petitioner, or to the real party in interest or privy of the petitioner, on the basis of that petitioner's institution of that inter partes review. If no petitioner remains in the inter partes review, the Office may terminate the review or proceed to a final written decision under section 318(a).

(b) AGREEMENTS IN WRITING.— Any agreement or understanding between the patent owner and a petitioner, including any collateral agreements referred to in such agreement or understanding, made in connection with, or in contemplation of, the termination of an inter partes review under this section shall be in writing and a true copy of such agreement or understanding shall be filed in the Office before the termination of the inter partes review as between the parties. At the request of a party to the proceeding, the agreement or understanding shall be treated as business confidential information, shall be kept separate from the file of the involved patents, and shall be made available only to Federal Government agencies on written request, or to any person on a showing of good cause.

* * *

35 U.S.C. § 327. Settlement

(a) IN GENERAL.— A post-grant review instituted under this chapter shall be terminated with respect to any petitioner upon the joint request of the petitioner and the patent owner, unless the Office has decided the merits of the proceeding before the request for termination is filed. If the post-grant review is terminated with respect to a petitioner under this section, no estoppel under section 325(e) shall attach to the petitioner, or to the real party in interest or privy of the petitioner, on the basis of that petitioner's institution of that post-grant review. If no petitioner remains in the post-grant review, the Office may terminate the post-grant review or proceed to a final written decision under section 328(a).

(b) AGREEMENTS IN WRITING.— Any agreement or understanding between the patent owner and a petitioner, including any collateral agreements referred to in such agreement or understanding, made in connection with, or in contemplation of, the termination of a post-grant review under this section shall be in writing, and a true copy of such agreement or understanding shall be filed in the Office before the termination of the post-grant review as between the parties. At the request of a party to the proceeding, the agreement or understanding shall be treated as business confidential information, shall be kept separate from the file of the involved patents, and shall be made available only to Federal Government agencies on written request, or to any person on a showing of good cause.

In addition to the statutes, the following rule addresses settlement.

37 C.F.R. § 42.74. Settlement.

(a) *Board role.* The parties may agree to settle any issue in a proceeding, but the Board is not a party to the settlement and may independently determine any question of jurisdiction, patentability, or Office practice.

(b) *Agreements in writing.* Any agreement or understanding between the parties made in connection with, or in contemplation of, the termination of a proceeding shall be in writing and a true copy shall be filed with the Board before the termination of the trial.

(c) *Request to keep separate.* A party to a settlement may request that the settlement be treated as business confidential information and be kept separate from the files of an involved patent or application. The request must be filed with the settlement. If a timely request is filed, the settlement shall only be available:

(1) To a Government agency on written request to the Board; or

(2) To any other person upon written request to the Board to make the settlement agreement available, along with the fee specified in § 42.15(d) and on a showing of good cause.

Thus, under the Rule, a settlement agreement can be treated as business confidential information and kept separate from the files of the involved patent(s) or application(s). Provisions exist for the federal government to have access to the agreement, and others may seek access but must pay a fee and show "good cause." To file a confidential settlement agreement, the PTO PRPS system allows uploading the document with a restricted access status.[1]

The PTAB has generally accepted settlements and terminated trial proceedings. However, it has noted, "That termination of a proceeding is discretionary with the Board is confirmed by Rule 42.72 . . . At the same time, 'the Board is not a party to the settlement and may independently determine any question of jurisdiction, patentability, or Office practice.' 37 C.F.R. § 42.74(a)."[2]

§ 15:33 Decisions on motions and petitions; final decision

The Board sets the schedule so that it can deliver its final written decision twelve (12) months after trial is instituted. The Board will generally make intermediate rulings on motions or which dispose of portions of the trial. For example, a party can request judgment against itself at any time, and the adverse judgment might or might not dispose of the entire trial. The following Trial Practice Rule applies generally to decisions on petitions or motions:

[Section 15:32]

[1]The FAQs advise: "To file a confidential settlement agreement, select the appropriate case from the "My Docket" tab and click on "Upload Document." Enter the information for the document in the next screen. In the "Availability" field, enter "Parties and Board Only." Click on "Upload File" and then "Submit." The filer should also upload a request that the settlement agreement be treated as business confidential information and be kept separate from the files of the involved patent or application. *See* 37 C.F.R. § 42.74(c). The party should also mark the settlement agreement confidential." See http://www.uspto.gov/ip/boards/bpai/prps.jsp visited August 16, 2013 (FAQ G2). See also *International Business Machines Corp.v. Financial Systems Technology (Intellectual Property) Pty. Ltd.*, IPR2013-00078, Paper No. 7 (PTAB Feb. 8, 2013).

[2]*Macauto U.S.A. v. BOS GmbH & Kg*, IPR2012-00004, Paper No. 21, p. 2 (PTAB Feb. 4, 2013). In this case, the Board suspended proceedings for one week (after trial had been declared) to allow the parties to prepare the necessary documents for filing. In response to such filing, in Paper No. 23 (Feb. 20. 2013) the Board terminated the proceeding, noting that although trial had already been instituted, the conference call with the parties to discuss scheduling had not yet occurred and the case was in its early stages. "Under these circumstances the Board determines that it is appropriate to terminate the trial without rendering a final written decision. 37 C.F.R. § 42.72." Id. p. 2. The Board also allowed the settlement agreement to be maintained as "business confidential." See also, *International Business Machines Corporation v. Financial Systems Technology (Intellectual Property) Pty. Ltd.*, IPR2013-00078, Paper No. 11 (PTAB Feb. 12, 2013) (case in preliminary proceeding stage terminated; settlement agreement treated as business confidential information).

§ 42.71. Decision on petitions or motions.

(a) *Order of consideration.* The Board may take up petitions or motions for decisions in any order, may grant, deny, or dismiss any petition or motion, and may enter any appropriate order.

(b) *Interlocutory decisions.* A decision on a motion without a judgment is not final for the purposes of judicial review. If a decision is not a panel decision, the party may request that a panel rehear the decision. When rehearing a nonpanel decision, a panel will review the decision for an abuse of discretion. A panel decision on an issue will govern the trial.

(c) *Petition decisions.* A decision by the Board on whether to institute a trial is final and non-appealable. A party may request rehearing on a decision by the Board on whether to institute a trial pursuant to paragraph (d) of this section. When rehearing a decision on petition, a panel will review the decision for an abuse of discretion.

(d) *Rehearing.* A party dissatisfied with a decision may file a request for rehearing, without prior authorization from the Board. The burden of showing a decision should be modified lies with the party challenging the decision. The request must specifically identify all matters the party believes the Board misapprehended or overlooked, and the place where each matter was previously addressed in a motion, an opposition, or a reply. A request for rehearing does not toll times for taking action. Any request must be filed:

(1) Within 14 days of the entry of a non-final decision or a decision to institute a trial as to at least one ground of unpatentability asserted in the petition; or

(2) Within 30 days of the entry of a final decision or a decision not to institute a trial.

The Board may terminate the trial before rendering a final written decision if appropriate. Illustratively, a settlement may lead to a termination of trial. Termination is authorized by the following Trial Practice Rule:

§ 42.72. Termination of trial.

The Board may terminate a trial without rendering a final written decision, where appropriate, including where the trial is consolidated with another proceeding or pursuant to a joint request under 35 U.S.C. 317(a) or 327(a).

If the trial does not terminate but instead the Board issues a final written decision, estoppels attach to remaining parties (and the real party/parties in interest and privies) in accordance with the Trial Practice rules on judgment and the pertinent statute. The following Trial Practice Rules apply to the judgment and the certificate that the Board will issue upon the conclusion of the trial:

§ **42.73. Judgment.**

(a) A judgment, except in the case of a termination, disposes of all issues that were, or by motion reasonably could have been, raised and decided.

(b) *Request for adverse judgment.* A party may request judgment against itself at any time during a proceeding. Actions construed to be a request for adverse judgment include:

(1) Disclaimer of the involved application or patent;

(2) Cancellation or disclaimer of a claim such that the party has no remaining claim in the trial;

(3) Concession of unpatentability or derivation of the contested subject matter; and

(4) Abandonment of the contest.

(c) *Recommendation.* The judgment may include a recommendation for further action by an examiner or by the Director.

(d) *Estoppel.*

(1) *Petitioner other than in derivation proceeding.* A petitioner, or the real party in interest or privy of the petitioner, is estopped in the Office from requesting or maintaining a proceeding with respect to a claim for which it has obtained a final written decision on patentability in an *inter partes* review, post-grant review, or a covered business method patent review, on any ground that the petitioner raised or reasonably could have raised during the trial, except that estoppel shall not apply to a petitioner, or to the real party in interest or privy of the petitioner who has settled under 35 U.S.C. 317 or 327.

(2) *In a derivation,* the losing party who could have properly moved for relief on an issue, but did not so move, may not take action in the Office after the judgment that is inconsistent with that party's failure to move, except that a losing party shall not be estopped with respect to any contested subject matter for which that party was awarded a favorable judgment.

(3) *Patent applicant or owner.* A patent applicant or owner is precluded from taking action inconsistent with the adverse judgment, including obtaining in any patent:

(i) A claim that is not patentably distinct from a finally refused or canceled claim; or

(ii) An amendment of a specification or of a drawing that was denied during the trial proceeding, but this provision does not apply to an application or patent that has a different written description.

Certificate

§ **42.80. Certificate.**

After the Board issues a final written decision in an *inter partes* review, post-grant review, or covered business method patent review and the time for appeal has expired or any appeal has terminated, the Office will issue and publish a certificate canceling any claim of the patent finally determined to be unpatentable, confirming any claim of the patent determined to be patentable, and incorporating in the patent any new or amended claim determined to be patentable by operation of the certificate.

§ 15:34 Rehearing requests

Rehearing requests do not require prior authorization from the Board and are governed by Trial Practice Rule § 42.71(d):

(d) *Rehearing.* A party dissatisfied with a decision may file a request for rehearing, without prior authorization from the Board. The burden of showing a decision should be modified lies with the party challenging the decision. The request must specifically identify all matters the party believes the Board misapprehended or overlooked, and the place where each matter was previously addressed in a motion, an opposition, or a reply. A request for rehearing does not toll times for taking action. Any request must be filed:

(1) Within 14 days of the entry of a non-final decision or a decision to institute a trial as to at least one ground of unpatentability asserted in the petition; or

(2) Within 30 days of the entry of a final decision or a decision not to institute a trial.

§ 15:35 Expungement of confidential information

After final decision (or a decision denying the institution of a trial), information that is confidential and subject to a protective order would become public absent action by the parties. First, Trial Practice Rule 42.56 applies:

§ 42.56. Expungement of confidential information.

After denial of a petition to institute a trial or after final judgment in a trial, a party may file a motion to expunge confidential information from the record.

Further explanation about this rule is provided in the Trial Practice Guide:

6. *Expungement of Confidential Information:* Confidential information that is subject to a protective order ordinarily would become public 45 days after denial of a petition to institute a trial or 45 days after final judgment in a trial. There is an expectation that information will be made public where the existence of the information is referred to in a deci-

> sion to grant or deny a request to institute a review or is identified in a final written decision following a trial. A party seeking to maintain the confidentiality of information, however, may file a motion to expunge the information from the record prior to the information becoming public. § 42.56. The rule balances the needs of the parties to submit confidential information with the public interest in maintaining a complete and understandable file history for public notice purposes. The rule encourages parties to redact sensitive information, where possible, rather than seeking to seal entire documents.[1]

Even when a protective order has been entered, confidential information contained in the papers would become public if it is referred to in a decision, either to grant or deny a petition or in a final written decision.

A party may nevertheless move to expunge the information from the record prior to it becoming public. 37 C.F.R. § 42.56 authorizes such a motion.

§ 15:36 PTAB Statistics

On its website, the USPTO maintains statistics on AIA activity. It reported the following statistics as of August 2, 2013:

- It received 403 IPR petitions. Of these, almost 80 were in July 2013, over 60 in June, and over 40 in May. The number of filings is steadily increasing.
- It received 32 CBM review petitions. Of these, one was in July, seven in June, and three in May.

[Section 15:35]

[1]Trial Practice Guide, 77 Fed. Reg. 48756, 48761 (Aug. 14, 2012).

Chapter 16

Post-Grant Review

AIA § 6(d)
35 U.S.C.A. §§ 321–329
37 C.F.R. §§ 42.200–42.224

§ 16:1 Background and congressional intent[1]

The background to the adoption of the post-grant review procedure is covered extensively in the House Report,[2] pertinent portions of which are reproduced below. The general objectives are to provide a mechanism which is both less costly than litigation and allows a fairly comprehensive review of patentability issues in an issued U.S. patent. The two types of reexamination proceedings in the USPTO extant at the time of the AIA enactment had not met this need fully because they confined the scope of review to printed publications, including patent publications. This left other types of prior art or other types of challenges, *e.g.*, Section 101 and 112 issues, to be dealt with by courts or administrative agencies where patents are enforced. Moreover, reexamination proceedings often took several years at the USPTO, notwithstanding the statutory requirement for "special dispatch."[3]

The concept of allowing interested members of the public to mount a broad-based challenge to patent rights has already been used outside the U.S. For example, the European Patent Convention ("EPC") provides for oppositions to European patents. During the first nine months after a patent grant is mentioned in the *European Patent Bulletin*, third parties can challenge the patent on grounds that the invention lacks novelty, inventive step, enablement, etc. See EPC Articles 99 *et seq.* as amended by the Act revising the

---

[Section 16:1]

[1]The Supreme Court cautions against relying on interpretations advanced in legislative statements that are not "anchored in the text of the statute." *Shannon v. U.S.*, 512 U.S. 573, 583, 114 S. Ct. 2419, 129 L. Ed. 2d 459 (1994), stating "[C]ourts have no authority to enforce [a] principl[e] gleaned solely from legislative history that has no statutory reference point." *Shannon,* 512 U.S. at 584, quoting *International Broth. of Elec. Workers, Local Union No. 474, AFL-CIO v. N.L.R.B.*, 814 F.2d 697, 712, 124 L.R.R.M. (BNA) 2993, 106 Lab. Cas. (CCH) P 12256 (D.C. Cir. 1987). The authoritative statement "is the statutory text, not the legislative history." *Exxon Mobil Corp. v. Allapattah Services, Inc.*, 545 U.S. 546, 568, 125 S. Ct. 2611, 162 L. Ed. 2d 502 (2005). However, lower courts have cited the legislative history of the AIA already in recent cases. E.g., *Rogers v. Tristar Products, Inc.*, 102 U.S.P.Q.2d 1722, 2012 WL 1660604, *2 (Fed. Cir. 2012) (non-precedential); *Byrne v. Wood, Herron & Evans, LLP,* 676 F.3d 1024, 1029, 102 U.S.P.Q.2d 1073 (Fed. Cir. 2012) (dissenting opin.).

[2]H. R. Rep. No. 112-98, pt. 1 (2011).

[3]35 U.S.C.A. §§ 305, 314 (2002).

European Patent Convention of 29 November 2010.[4] Various countries, mainly civil code countries, also provide for invalidity proceedings that are conducted at the patent office rather than in court.

Relevant portions reflecting Congressional intent in adopting a post-grant provision are as follows:[5]

> *Post-grant review proceedings*
>
> The Act amends ex parte and *inter partes* reexamination and establishes a new **post-grant review** procedure. Under current law, there are two ways to challenge the validity and enforceability of a patent that has issued. The patent may be challenged in district court litigation or in a reexamination at the USPTO.
>
> Nearly 30 years ago, Congress created the administrative

[4]EPC Article 99 (Opposition) provides: "(1) Within nine months of the publication of the mention of the grant of the European patent in the European Patent Bulletin, any person may give notice to the European Patent Office of opposition to that patent, in accordance with the Implementing Regulations. Notice of opposition shall not be deemed to have been filed until the opposition fee has been paid."

EPC Art. 100 (Grounds for Opposition) provides, "Opposition may only be filed on the grounds that: (a) the subject-matter of the European patent is not patentable under Articles 52 to 57; (b) the European patent does not disclose the invention in a manner sufficiently clear and complete for it to be carried out by a person skilled in the art; (c) the subject-matter of the European patent extends beyond the content of the application as filed, or, if the patent was granted on a divisional application or on a new application filed under Article 61, beyond the content of the earlier application as filed."

EPC Art. 101 (Examination of the Opposition—Revocation or maintenance of the European patent) provides: "(1) If the opposition is admissible, the Opposition Division shall examine, in accordance with the Implementing Regulations, whether at least one ground for opposition under Article 100 prejudices the maintenance of the European patent. During this examination, the Opposition Division shall invite the parties, as often as necessary, to file observations on communications from another party or issued by itself.(2) If the Opposition Division is of the opinion that at least one ground for opposition prejudices the maintenance of the European patent, it shall revoke the patent. Otherwise, it shall reject the opposition. (3) If the Opposition Division is of the opinion that, taking into consideration the amendments made by the proprietor of the European patent during the opposition proceedings, the patent and the invention to which it relates (a)meet the requirements of this Convention, it shall decide to maintain the patent as amended, provided that the conditions laid down in the Implementing Regulations are fulfilled; (b) do not meet the requirements of this Convention, it shall revoke the patent."

[5]H. R. Rep. No. 112-98, pt. 1, pp. 45 to 48, 75 to 77 (2011), emphasis added *passim*.

"reexamination" process, through which the USPTO could review the validity of already-issued patents on the request of either the patent holder or a third party,[FN30] in the expectation that it would serve as an effective and efficient alternative to often costly and protracted district court litigation.[FN31] Reexamination requires the USPTO to review the patent in light of a substantial new question of patentability not presented during the original examination.[FN32] The initial reexamination statute had several limitations that later proved to make it a less viable alternative to litigation for evaluating patent validity than Congress intended. First, a reexamination request could only be based on prior art, and could not be based on prior public use or prior sales. Moreover, the requestor could not raise any challenge based on § 101 (utility, eligibility) or 112 (indefiniteness, enablement, written description, best mode). A third party alleging a patent is invalid, therefore, had fewer challenges it could raise in the proceeding and, therefore, may instead opt to risk infringement and litigate the validity of the patent in court. Second, in the original reexamination system, the third-party challenger had no role once the proceeding was initiated, while the patent holder had significant input throughout the entire process. Third, a challenger that lost at the USPTO under reexamination had no right to appeal an examiner's, or the Patent Board's, decision either administratively or in court. Restrictions such as these made reexamination a much less favored avenue to challenge questionable patents than litigation. Reexamination proceedings are also often costly, taking several years to complete,[FN33] and are first conducted by examiners and, if the patent is rejected, then by Patent Board judges. Thus, many patents must go through two rounds of administrative review (one by the examiner, and a second by the Patent Board) adding to the length of the proceeding.[FN34]

FN30. See 35 U.S.C. Sec. 301–307. A patent holder will typically request reexamination to bolster the patent in view of new prior art. A third party may request reexamination to challenge, and ultimately invalidate, the patent.

FN31. "Reexamination will permit efficient resolution of questions about the validity of issued patents without recourse to expensive and lengthy infringement litigation . . .. The reexamination of issued patents could be conducted with a fraction of the time and cost of formal legal proceedings and would help restore confidence in the effectiveness of our patent system . . .. It is anticipated that these measures provide a useful and necessary alternative for challengers and for patent owners to test the validity of United States patents in an efficient and relatively inexpensive manner." *See* H.R. Rep. No. 96-1307(I) at 3 (1980), reprinted in 1980 U.S.C.C.A.N. 6460, 6462–63.

FN32. *See* 35 U.S.C. Sec. 303.

FN33. *See Perspectives on Patents: Hearing Before the*

Subcomm. on Intellectual Prop. of the Senate Comm. on the Judiciary, 109th Cong. (2005) (statement of Jon W. Dudas, Undersecretary of Commerce for Intellectual Property, Director of the U.S. Patent and Trademark Office), explaining that "a large number of reexamination proceedings have been pending before the USPTO for more than 4 years," and questioning whether this amount of time is consistent with the statutory requirement that "[a]ll reexamination proceedings . . . will be conducted with special dispatch within the Office." *See also* 35 U.S.C. Sec. 305.

FN34. For several years, the standard practice at the USPTO was to assign the reexamination to the patent examiner who had originally examined that patent. In addition, the same third-party requester could file multiple, serial reexaminations based on the same "substantial new question of patentability," so long as the initial reexamination was not complete. More recently, the USPTO ended some of these procedures, and now reexaminations are handled by a Central Reexamination Unit (CRU), and subsequent serial reexamination, based on the same "substantial new question of patentability," is no longer permitted. *See, e.g.,* Manual of Patent Examining Procedure (MPEP) Sec. 2236 and 2240 (August 2006).

Congress has responded several times to criticisms of the reexamination system by making amendments to the process.[FN35] In 1999, Congress created a second reexamination procedure—called *inter partes* reexamination—that gave third-party challengers greater input throughout the proceeding by permitting them to respond to every pleading submitted by the patent holder.[FN36] Congress also eventually gave third-party challengers the right to appeal adverse decisions.[FN37]

FN35. *See e.g.,* 21st Century Dep't of Justice Appropriations Authorization Act, Pub. L. No. 107-273, Sec. 13105–06, 13202, 116 Stat. 1758, 1761 (2002) (effective Nov. 2, 2002); American Inventors Protection Act, Pub.L. 106-113, 113 Stat. 1536, 1501A et seq. (1999) (creating *inter partes* reexamination) (hereafter referred to as the "AIPA".

FN36. *See* 35 U.S.C. Sec. 311–318.

FN37. *See* 35 U.S.C. Sec. 315(b).

As part of the 1999 improvements to reexamination, Congress directed the USPTO to submit a report to Congress evaluating the *inter partes* reexamination process and making any recommendations for changes.[FN38] Initially, the USPTO projected that in the first year after the creation of *inter partes* reexamination, it would receive 400 such requests and it projected that by 2004 it would receive nearly 600.[FN39] No *inter partes* reexamination requests were actually filed in 2000 and only 27 such requests had been filed by 2004.[FN40] Over the 5-year period studied by the USPTO, it issued 900,000 patents and received only 53 requests for *inter partes* reexamination.[FN41]

FN38. AIPA, Pub. L. 106-113, Sec. 4606.

FN39. *See United States Patent and Trademark Office, Report to Congress on* Inter Partes *Reexamination* (2004) (hereinafter referred to as "*Report on Inter Partes Reexamination*"), at 4.

FN40. *See United States Patent and Trademark Office, Report to Congress on* Inter Partes *Reexamination* (2004) (hereinafter referred to as "*Report on Inter Partes Reexamination*"), at 5.

FN41. *See United States Patent and Trademark Office, Report to Congress on* Inter Partes *Reexamination* (2004) (hereinafter referred to as "*Report on Inter Partes Reexamination*"), at 5.

* * *

The Act also creates a new post-grant opposition procedure that can be utilized during the first 12 months after the grant of a patent or issue of a reissue patent. Unlike reexamination proceedings, which provide only a limited basis on which to consider whether a patent should have issued, the post-grant review proceeding permits a challenge on any ground related to invalidity under section 282. The intent of the post-grant review process is to enable early challenges to patents, while still protecting the rights of inventors and patent owners against new patent challenges unbounded in time and scope. The Committee believes that this new, early-stage process for challenging patent validity and its clear procedures for submission of art will make the patent system more efficient and improve the quality of patents and the patent system. This new, but time-limited, post-grant review procedure will provide a meaningful opportunity to improve patent quality and restore confidence in the presumption of validity that comes with issued patents in court.

In utilizing the post-grant review process, petitioners, real parties in interest, and their privies are precluded from improperly mounting multiple challenges to a patent or initiating challenges after filing a civil action challenging the validity [of] a claim in the patent. Further, a final decision in a post-grant review process will prevent the petitioner, a real party in interest, or its privy from challenging any patent claim on a ground that was raised in the post-grant review process. The post-grant review procedure is not intended, however, to inhibit patent owners from pursuing the various avenues of enforcement of their rights under a patent, and the amendment makes clear that the filing or institution of a post-grant review proceeding does not limit a patent owner from commencing such actions.

The Committee recognizes the importance of quiet title to

patent owners to ensure continued investment resources. While this amendment is intended to remove current disincentives to current administrative processes, the changes made by it are not to be used as tools for harassment or a means to prevent market entry through repeated litigation and administrative attacks on the validity of a patent. Doing so would frustrate the purpose of the section as providing quick and cost effective alternatives to litigation. Further, such activity would divert resources from the research and development of inventions. As such, the Committee intends for the USPTO to address potential abuses and current inefficiencies under its expanded procedural authority.

* * *

Section 6. ***Post-grant review*** *proceedings.*

Subsections (a) and (d) enact new chapters 31 and 32, which create adjudicative systems of **post-grant** and *inter partes* review. The parallel sections of these new chapters are as follows:

§§ 311 and 321. *Inter partes* review may be sought on the basis of patents and printed publications any time after a **post-grant review** is concluded or, if no such review is instituted, after the time for seeking such review has expired. **Post-grant review** may be sought on any invalidity ground during the first 12 months after a patent is issue[d] or reissued.[6]

§§ 312 and 322. Petitions for review shall explain the basis for seeking review, shall identify the petitioner's real parties in interest and privies, and shall be made publicly available as soon as is practicable.

§§ 313 and 323. Patent owners may file a response to a petition for [review] explaining why a review should not be instituted. §§ 314 and 324. *Inter partes* review shall not be instituted unless the information in the petition and response shows that there is a reasonable likelihood that a claim would be found invalid. **Post-grant review** shall not be instituted unless the information presented in the petition, if not rebutted, shows that it is more likely than not that a claim would be found invalid, or the petition raises a novel or unsettled legal question that is important to other patents or applications.

§§ 315 and 325.

(a) Review may not be instituted if the petitioner has previously filed a civil action challenging the validity of the patent. The petitioner may, however, file a declaratory-

[6]Comments in these later pages of the House Report contemplate an earlier draft of the bill. For example, the comment about section 321 is incorrect when referring to a 12 month period, as the AIA allows only 9 months to initiate a post-grant review. 35 U.S.C.A. § 321(c).

judgment action challenging the validity of one or more claims in the patent on or after the day that he files the review petition, but such action is automatically stayed until the patent owner countersues for infringement.

(b) *Inter partes* review must be sought by a party within 12 months of the date when the party is served with a complaint for infringement. If a patent owner sues for infringement within 3 months of the patent's issue, a pending petition for **post-grant review** or the institution of such a proceeding may not serve as a basis for staying the court's consideration of the patent owner's motion for a preliminary injunction.

(c) The Director may allow other petitioners to join an *inter partes* or **post-grant review**.

(d) The Director may consolidate multiple proceedings or matters concerning the same patent and decline requests for repeated proceedings on the same question.

(e) *Inter partes* and **post-grant petitioners** are estopped from raising in a subsequent Office proceeding any issue that they raised or reasonably could have raised in the *inter partes* or **post grant review**, and *inter partes* petitioners are also estopped from raising in civil litigation or an ITC proceeding any issue that they raised or could have raised in the *inter partes* review. **Post-grant petitioners** are only estopped from raising in civil litigation or ITC proceedings those issues that they actually raised in the **post-grant review**.

(f) **Post-grant review** may not be used to challenge claims in a reissue patent that are the same as or narrower than claims in the original patent if the time for seeking review of the original patent has lapsed.

§§ 316 and 326.

(a) The Director shall prescribe regulations that make the file in proceedings public; define standards for instituting reviews; allow submission of additional information; establish and govern review and its relationship to other proceedings; set a time limit for requesting joinder in *inter partes* review; set standards for discovery; prescribe sanctions for abuse of the proceedings; provide for protective orders for confidential information; allow the patent owner to file a response after an *inter partes* review has been instituted; allow the patent owner to amend the patent; provide either party with the right to an oral hearing; and set a 1-year time limit for completion of the proceeding, with a 6-month extension for good cause; and provide the petitioner with at least one opportunity to file written comments after the proceeding is instituted.

(b) In prescribing regulations, the Director shall consider the integrity of the patent system and the efficient operation of the Office.

(c) The Patent Trial and Appeal Board shall conduct review proceedings.

(d) The patent owner may submit one amendment with a reasonable number of substitute claims, and additional amendments either as agreed to by the parties for settlement, for good cause shown in **post-grant review**, or as prescribed in regulations by the Director in *inter partes* review.

(e) The challenger shall have the burden of providing unpatentability by a preponderance of the evidence.

§§ 317 and 327. Parties may agree to settle review proceedings, in which case estoppel shall not apply and a copy of the settlement agreement shall be filed in the Office.

§§ 318 and 328. The Patent Trial and Appeal Board shall issue a final written decision and a certificate cancelling, confirming, or incorporating claims.

§§ 319 and 329. A party dissatisfied with a final written decision may appeal to the U.S. Court of Appeals for the Federal Circuit.[7]

§ 16:2 The new statute—Post-grant review

Post-grant review ("PGR") is an entirely new procedure in U.S. patent practice intended to improve the quality of issued patents without invoking the federal court system. It allows a third party (not the patent owner) to initiate a review of the patent (or reissue patent) during its first nine (9) months of life. The scope of review is vastly more broad than has been available via reexaminations. The new statute provides as follows:

New Statute (Chapter 32, §§ 321–329)

CHAPTER 32. POST-GRANT REVIEW

Sec.
321. Post-grant review.
322. Petitions.
323. Preliminary response to petition.
324. Institution of post-grant review.
325. Relation to other proceedings or actions.
326. Conduct of post-grant review.
327. Settlement.

[7] H. R. Rep. No. 112-98, pt. 1, pp. 45 to 46, 75 to 77 (2011), emphasis added *passim*.

§ 321. Post-grant review

(a) IN GENERAL.— Subject to the provisions of this chapter, a person who is not the owner of a patent may file with the Office a petition to institute a post-grant review of the patent. The Director shall establish, by regulation, fees to be paid by the person requesting the review, in such amounts as the Director determines to be reasonable, considering the aggregate costs of the post-grant review.

(b) SCOPE.— A petitioner in a post-grant review may request to cancel as unpatentable 1 or more claims of a patent on any ground that could be raised under paragraph (2) or (3) of section 282(b) (relating to invalidity of the patent or any claim).

(c) FILING DEADLINE.— A petition for a post-grant review may only be filed not later than the date that is 9 months after the date of the grant of the patent or of the issuance of a reissue patent (as the case may be).

§ 322. Petitions

(a) REQUIREMENTS OF PETITION.— A petition filed under section 321 may be considered only if—

(1) the petition is accompanied by payment of the fee established by the Director under section 321;

(2) the petition identifies all real parties in interest;

(3) the petition identifies, in writing and with particularity, each claim challenged, the grounds on which the challenge to each claim is based, and the evidence that supports the grounds for the challenge to each claim, including—

(A) copies of patents and printed publications that the petitioner relies upon in support of the petition; and

(B) affidavits or declarations of supporting evidence and opinions, if the petitioner relies on other factual evidence or on expert opinions;

(4) the petition provides such other information as the Director may require by regulation; and

(5) the petitioner provides copies of any of the documents required under paragraphs (2), (3), and (4) to the patent owner or, if applicable, the designated representative of the patent owner.

(b) PUBLIC AVAILABILITY.— As soon as practicable after the receipt of a petition under section 321, the Director shall make the petition available to the public.

§ 323. Preliminary response to petition

If a post-grant review petition is filed under section 321, the patent owner shall have the right to file a preliminary response to the petition, within a time period set by the Director, that sets forth reasons why no post-grant review should be instituted based upon the failure of the petition to meet any requirement of this chapter.

§ 324. Institution of post-grant review

(a) THRESHOLD.— The Director may not authorize a post-grant review to be instituted unless the Director determines that the information presented in the petition filed under section 321, if such information is not rebutted, would demonstrate that it is more likely than not that at least 1 of the claims challenged in the petition is unpatentable.

(b) ADDITIONAL GROUNDS.— The determination required under subsection (a) may also be satisfied by a showing that the petition raises a novel or unsettled legal question that is important to other patents or patent applications.

(c) TIMING.— The Director shall determine whether to institute a post-grant review under this chapter pursuant to a petition filed under section 321 within 3 months after—

(1) receiving a preliminary response to the petition under section 323; or

(2) if no such preliminary response is filed, the last date on which such response may be filed.

(d) NOTICE.— The Director shall notify the petitioner and patent owner, in writing, of the Director's determination under subsection (a) or (b), and shall make such notice available to the public as soon as is practicable. Such notice shall include the date on which the review shall commence.

(e) NO APPEAL.— The determination by the Director whether to institute a post-grant review under this section shall be final and nonappealable.

§ 325. Relation to other proceedings or actions

(a) INFRINGER'S CIVIL ACTION.—

(1) POST-GRANT REVIEW BARRED BY CIVIL ACTION.— A post-grant review may not be instituted under this chapter if, before the date on which the petition for such a review is filed, the petitioner or real party in interest filed a civil action challenging the validity of a claim of the patent.

(2) STAY OF CIVIL ACTION.— If the petitioner or real party in interest files a civil action challenging the validity of a claim of the patent on or after the date on which the petitioner files a petition for post-grant review of the patent, that civil action shall be automatically stayed until either—

(A) the patent owner moves the court to lift the stay;

(B) the patent owner files a civil action or counterclaim alleging that the petitioner or real party in interest has infringed the patent; or

(C) the petitioner or real party in interest moves the court to dismiss the civil action.

(3) TREATMENT OF COUNTERCLAIM.— A counterclaim challenging the validity of a claim of a patent does not constitute a civil action challenging the validity of a claim of a patent for purposes of this subsection.

(b) PRELIMINARY INJUNCTIONS.— If a civil action alleging infringement of a patent is filed within 3 months after the date on which the patent is granted, the court may not stay its consideration of the patent owner's motion for a preliminary injunction against infringement of the patent on the basis that a petition for post-grant review has been filed under this chapter or that such a post-grant review has been instituted under this chapter.

(c) JOINDER.— If more than 1 petition for a post-grant review under this chapter is properly filed against the same patent and the Director determines that more than 1 of these petitions warrants the institution of a post-grant review under section 324, the Director may consolidate such reviews into a single post-grant review.

(d) MULTIPLE PROCEEDINGS.— Notwithstanding sections 135(a), 251, and 252, and chapter 30, during the pendency of any post-grant review under this chapter, if another proceeding or matter involving the patent is before the Office, the Director may determine the manner in which the post-grant review or other proceeding or matter may proceed, including providing for the stay, transfer, consolidation, or termination of any such matter or proceeding. In determining whether to institute or order a proceeding under this chapter, chapter 30, or chapter 31, the Director may take into account whether, and reject the petition or request because, the same or substantially the same prior art or arguments previously were presented to the Office.

(e) ESTOPPEL.—

(1) PROCEEDINGS BEFORE THE OFFICE.—The petitioner in a post-grant review of a claim in a patent under this chapter

that results in a final written decision under section 328(a), or the real party in interest or privy of the petitioner, may not request or maintain a proceeding before the Office with respect to that claim on any ground that the petitioner raised or reasonably could have raised during that post-grant review.

(2) CIVIL ACTIONS AND OTHER PROCEEDINGS.—The petitioner in a post-grant review of a claim in a patent under this chapter that results in a final written decision under section 328(a), or the real party in interest or privy of the petitioner, may not assert either in a civil action arising in whole or in part under section 1338 of title 28 or in a proceeding before the International Trade Commission under section 337 of the Tariff Act of 1930 that the claim is invalid on any ground that the petitioner raised or reasonably could have raised during that post-grant review.

(f) REISSUE PATENTS.— A post-grant review may not be instituted under this chapter if the petition requests cancellation of a claim in a reissue patent that is identical to or narrower than a claim in the original patent from which the reissue patent was issued, and the time limitations in section 321(c) would bar filing a petition for a post-grant review for such original patent.

§ 326. Conduct of post-grant review

(a) REGULATIONS.— The Director shall prescribe regulations—

(1) providing that the file of any proceeding under this chapter shall be made available to the public, except that any petition or document filed with the intent that it be sealed shall, if accompanied by a motion to seal, be treated as sealed pending the outcome of the ruling on the motion;

(2) setting forth the standards for the showing of sufficient grounds to institute a review under subsections (a) and (b) of section 324;

(3) establishing procedures for the submission of supplemental information after the petition is filed;

(4) establishing and governing a post-grant review under this chapter and the relationship of such review to other proceedings under this title;

(5) setting forth standards and procedures for discovery of relevant evidence, including that such discovery shall be limited to evidence directly related to factual assertions advanced by either party in the proceeding;

(6) prescribing sanctions for abuse of discovery, abuse of process, or any other improper use of the proceeding, such as to harass or to cause unnecessary delay or an unneces-

sary increase in the cost of the proceeding;

(7) providing for protective orders governing the exchange and submission of confidential information;

(8) providing for the filing by the patent owner of a response to the petition under section 323 after a post-grant review has been instituted, and requiring that the patent owner file with such response, through affidavits or declarations, any additional factual evidence and expert opinions on which the patent owner relies in support of the response;

(9) setting forth standards and procedures for allowing the patent owner to move to amend the patent under subsection (d) to cancel a challenged claim or propose a reasonable number of substitute claims, and ensuring that any information submitted by the patent owner in support of any amendment entered under subsection (d) is made available to the public as part of the prosecution history of the patent;

(10) providing either party with the right to an oral hearing as part of the proceeding;

(11) requiring that the final determination in any post-grant review be issued not later than 1 year after the date on which the Director notices the institution of a proceeding under this chapter, except that the Director may, for good cause shown, extend the 1-year period by not more than 6 months, and may adjust the time periods in this paragraph in the case of joinder under section 325(c); and

(12) providing the petitioner with at least 1 opportunity to file written comments within a time period established by the Director.

(b) Considerations.— In prescribing regulations under this section, the Director shall consider the effect of any such regulation on the economy, the integrity of the patent system, the efficient administration of the Office, and the ability of the Office to timely complete proceedings instituted under this chapter.

(c) Patent Trial and Appeal Board.— The Patent Trial and Appeal Board shall, in accordance with section 6, conduct each post-grant review instituted under this chapter.

(d) Amendment of the Patent.—

(1) In General.— During a post-grant review instituted under this chapter, the patent owner may file 1 motion to amend the patent in 1 or more of the following ways:

(A) Cancel any challenged patent claim.

(B) For each challenged claim, propose a reasonable number of substitute claims.

(2) Additional motions.— Additional motions to amend may be permitted upon the joint request of the petitioner and the patent owner to materially advance the settlement of a proceeding under section 327, or upon the request of the patent owner for good cause shown.

(3) Scope of Claims.— An amendment under this subsection may not enlarge the scope of the claims of the patent or introduce new matter.

(e) Evidentiary Standards.— In a post-grant review instituted under this chapter, the petitioner shall have the burden of proving a proposition of unpatentability by a preponderance of the evidence.

§ 327. Settlement

(a) In General.— A post-grant review instituted under this chapter shall be terminated with respect to any petitioner upon the joint request of the petitioner and the patent owner, unless the Office has decided the merits of the proceeding before the request for termination is filed. If the post-grant review is terminated with respect to a petitioner under this section, no estoppel under section 325(e) shall attach to the petitioner, or to the real party in interest or privy of the petitioner, on the basis of that petitioner's institution of that post-grant review. If no petitioner remains in the post-grant review, the Office may terminate the post-grant review or proceed to a final written decision under section 328(a).

(b) Agreements in Writing.— Any agreement or understanding between the patent owner and a petitioner, including any collateral agreements referred to in such agreement or understanding, made in connection with, or in contemplation of, the termination of a post-grant review under this section shall be in writing, and a true copy of such agreement or understanding shall be filed in the Office before the termination of the post-grant review as between the parties. At the request of a party to the proceeding, the agreement or understanding shall be treated as business confidential information, shall be kept separate from the file of the involved patents, and shall be made available only to Federal Government agencies on written request, or to any person on a showing of good cause.

§ 328. Decision of the Board

(a) Final Written Decision.— If a post-grant review is instituted and not dismissed under this chapter, the Patent Trial and Appeal Board shall issue a final written decision with respect to the patentability of any patent claim challenged by the petitioner and any new claim added under section 326(d).

(b) CERTIFICATE.— If the Patent Trial and Appeal Board issues a final written decision under subsection (a) and the time for appeal has expired or any appeal has terminated, the Director shall issue and publish a certificate canceling any claim of the patent finally determined to be unpatentable, confirming any claim of the patent determined to be patentable, and incorporating in the patent by operation of the certificate any new or amended claim determined to be patentable.

(c) INTERVENING RIGHTS.— Any proposed amended or new claim determined to be patentable and incorporated into a patent following a post-grant review under this chapter shall have the same effect as that specified in section 252 of this title for reissued patents on the right of any person who made, purchased, or used within the United States, or imported into the United States, anything patented by such proposed amended or new claim, or who made substantial preparation therefor, before the issuance of a certificate under subsection (b).

(d) DATA ON LENGTH OF REVIEW.— The Office shall make available to the public data describing the length of time between the institution of, and the issuance of a final written decision under subsection (a) for, each post-grant review.

§ 329. Appeal

A party dissatisfied with the final written decision of the Patent Trial and Appeal Board under section 328(a) may appeal the decision pursuant to sections 141 through 144. Any party to the post-grant review shall have the right to be a party to the appeal.

§ 16:3 Post-grant review procedures generally

A post-grant review is one of the four "trials" heard by the PTAB and as such is subject to the trial rules and procedures set forth in 37 C.F.R. §§ 42.1 to 42.80. The trial rules are covered in chapter 15. The Director also issued additional rules that are specific to post-grant review procedures, and these are set forth at §§ 42.200–42.224.

During a post-grant review, a claim of an unexpired patent is given its "broadest reasonable construction in light of the specification of the patent in which it appears."[1] One reason given by the USPTO for this broad construction is that the patent owner is entitled to amend the claims at least once during the proceeding.[2] This is unlike patent litigation in federal court where the patent claims cannot be amended. Because the patent owner has the opportunity to amend claims to distinguish over the prior art (or to address other problems), the Office believes this broad interpretation is fair to the patent owner.[3]

The PTAB will administer the post-grant review proceeding so that its pendency before the Board after the proceeding is instituted (which may take six months) is normally one year or less, but that pendency can be extended by up to six additional months for good cause shown. However, the Office anticipates that "extensions of the one year period are anticipated to be rare."[4] On the other hand, the schedule can also be lengthened in the case of a joinder with another proceeding.[5] This one-year term does not include any time for appeals, which would be added to the one year.

§ 16:4 Filing a petition for post-grant review

To obtain a post-grant review, one files a petition with the USPTO. The petition must meet certain requirements to avoid automatic rejection. These requirements are set forth in the statute and the rules adopted for post-grant proceedings. The following checklist may be helpful.

[Section 16:3]

[1]37 C.F.R. § 42.200(b).

[2]For an interesting discussion of why the broadest, reasonable interpretation is used and the standard of review, see *Flo Healthcare Solutions, LLC v. Kappos*, 697 F.3d 1367, 104 U.S.P.Q.2d 1834 (Fed. Cir. 2012) (additional views of Judge Plager and additional views of Judge Newman).

[3]77 Fed. Reg. 48680, 48690 (Aug. 14, 2012) ("Changes to Implement Inter Partes Review, Post-Grant Review Proceedings, and Transitional Program for Covered Business Method Patents; Final Rule), citing *In re Yamamoto*, 740 F.2d 1569, 1571-72, 222 U.S.P.Q. 934 (Fed. Cir. 1984); see also discussion at pp 48697–98. See also, *SAP America, Inc. v. Versata Development Group, Inc.*, CBM2012-00001, Final Written Decision, Paper No. --, pp. 7-19 (June 11, 2013) (ruling *inter alia* that the PTAB is not bound to apply a claim construction of a district court in enforcement litigation on the challenged patent).

[4]77 Fed. Reg. 48680, 48695 (Aug. 14, 2012).

[5]37 C.F.R. § 42.200(c).

Checklist for PGR Petition

- Certifications:
    - The patent is available for post grant review. § 42.204(a).[1]
    - The petitioner is not barred from challenging the claims on the grounds identified in the petition. § 42.101(a). The petitioner should certify that:
        - ☐ Neither the petitioner nor its real party in interest has filed a civil action challenging the validity of any claim of the patent. 35 U.S.C. § 325(a)(1), 37 C.F.R. § 42.201(a).
        - ☐ The PGR review period (1st nine months) has not expired. § 42.202(a).
    - The petitioner, real party-in-interest, and privy are not estopped from challenging the claims on the grounds identified in the petition. § 42.201(b); 42.204(a).
    - The petitioner is not the patent owner. 35 U.S.C. § 321(a), 37 C.F.R. § 42.201.
- Any USPTO limit on the number of PGRs for the year has not been exceeded. § 42.202(b).
- Include the proper filing fee. §§ 42.203, 42.15(b).
- Mandatory notices (§ 42.8) identifying:
    - each real party-in-interest for the petitioner,
    - all related judicial and administrative matters,
    - petitioner's lead and back-up counsel, and
    - the service information for petitioner.
- State the precise relief requested. § 42.22(a)(1), (b); see also § 42.204(b).
- Show all requirements of any rule in 37 C.F.R. Part 1 that ordinarily governs the relief sought (along with showings required in Part 42). § 42.22(b).
- Provide a full statement of the reasons for relief, including a detailed explanation of the significance of the evidence, including material facts, and the governing law, rules, and precedent. § 42.22(a)(2).
- Provide a statement of facts. § 42.22(c).
- For each challenged claim, state:
    - the claim itself. § 42.204(b)(1).

[Section 16:4]

[1]References in the check list are to 37 C.F.R. unless otherwise stated.

  - the specific statutory grounds under 35 U.S.C. §§ 282(b) or (3) on which the challenge is based. 35 U.S.C. § 321(b) (2011). § 42.204(b)(2).
  - how the challenged claim should be construed. § 42.204(b)(3).
  - how the construed claim is unpatentable under the specified grounds, including where each claim element is found in the prior art. If the basis for unpatentability is not prior art, identify the specific part of the claim that fails to comply with the statutory grounds and how the identified subject matter fails to comply with the statute. § 42.204(b)(4).
  - the exhibit number of the supporting evidence. § 42.204(b)(5).
- Provide copies of the evidence relied upon. § 42.6(c); 35 U.S.C. § 322(a)(5).
- Note format requirements, § 42.6, and citation format § 42.13.
- Page limit of 80 pages. § 42.24.
- Optional motion to waive page limits. § 42.24(a)(2).
- Certificate of service on correspondence address of record. § 42.6(e).
- Any duty of candor disclosures. § 42.11.
- Optional motion to seal. § 42.55.

* * *

As should be understood from the checklist above, the petitioner must show that it avoids three disqualifiers:

- The petitioner cannot be the owner of the patent;[2]
- The petitioner or real party in interest cannot have filed a civil action challenging the validity of any claim of the patent involved;[3] and
- The petitioner, real party-in-interest, or privy cannot be someone who is estopped from challenging the claims on the grounds identified in the petition.[4] (It is possible that some grounds of post-grant review will be estopped while others will not be estopped.)

The petition must certify affirmatively that the patent is

---

[2]35 U.S.C.A. § 321, 37 C.F.R. § 42.201.

[3]35 U.S.C.A. § 325, 37 C.F.R. § 42.201.

[4]37 C.F.R. § 42.201.

available for post-grant review and that the petitioner is neither barred nor estopped from challenging the claims on the grounds identified in the petition.[5] Omitting this information results in an incomplete petition.

The petition for post-grant review must be filed not later than nine (9) months after the original patent issue date or the date of issue of a reissue patent.[6]

If the PGR is directed to a reissue patent, the AIA provides that no petition may seek review of a claim that is the same as or narrower than a claim in the original patent on which the reissue patent was based, unless the petition is filed within nine months of the date of the grant of the original patent.[7] In other words, petitioners do not get a second opportunity to attack the patent merely because it has undergone reissue. If a claim is broadened (as permitted within two years of the original issue date), or is a new claim, then it can be challenged. If the claim is either narrower or an original claim that was issued in the original patent, post-grant review appears to be prohibited under 35 U.S.C. § 325(f) and 37 C.F.R. § 42.202(a).

The USPTO Director may limit the number of post-grant reviews that can be instituted during each of the first four years in which the post-grant procedure is in effect. Notices will be provided in the Official Gazette or Federal Register, and petitions filed after the stated limit has been reached will be treated as untimely.[8]

The petitioner is required to submit a fee without which no filing date will be given to the petition.[9] The fee was originally set at $35,800 for seeking review of between one and 20 claims, with a surcharge of $800 for each added claim.[10] The USPTO changed the fee arrangement so that substantial forfeitures are avoided.

37 C.F.R. § 42.204 sets forth the required contents of the petition. It begins by referring back to four provisions of the trial practice rules. These have been discussed *supra* in Chapter 15 directed to PTAB trials. Briefly, however, the pe-

---

[5] 37 C.F.R. § 42.204(a).

[6] 37 C.F.R. § 42.202(a).

[7] 35 U.S.C.A. § 325(f); 37 C.F.R. § 42.202(a).

[8] 37 C.F.R. § 42.202(b).

[9] 37 C.F.R. § 42.203.

[10] 37 C.F.R. §§ 42.203 and 42.15(b).

tition must meet a certain general format requirement.[11] A petition requesting a post-grant review is limited to 80 pages, but the page limit does not include the tables of contents or authorities, the certificate of service, nor the appendix of exhibits. 37 C.F.R. § 42.24(a).

Arguments cannot be incorporated by reference. Each document must indicate that it was served and include a certificate of service. The petition requires a mandatory notice set forth in 37 C.F.R. § 42.8 identifying each real party-in-interest for the party, identifying any related matters, identifying the lead counsel and back-up counsel, and specifying the service information.

Also, the petition must meet the 37 C.F.R. § 42.22 general requirements for all petitions and motions calling for, *inter alia*, a full statement of the reasons for relief requested and optionally a statement of individually numbered material facts.

The precise relief requested must be articulated in the petition, which must also identify, for each challenged claim: the claim itself; the specific statutory grounds under 35 U.S.C. § 282(b)(2) or (3) on which the challenge is based; how the challenged claim should be construed; how the construed claim is unpatentable under the specified grounds; and the exhibit number of the supporting evidence. With regard to the showing of unpatentability, to the extent the challenge is based on prior art, the petition must specify where each element of the claim can be found in the prior art. To the extent the challenge is not based on prior art, the petition must identify the specific part of the claim that fails to comply with the statutory grounds raised in the petition and state how the identified subject matter fails to comply with the statute.[12] The grounds that can be asserted include lack of novelty or obviousness over prior art, enablement, lack of written description, and indefiniteness, but not the best mode. The USPTO will also consider challenges based on 35 U.S.C. § 101 for patent eligibility, although the basis

[11]It must be on 8.5" x 11" paper, except for exhibits that require larger size to preserve details. If the typing uses a proportional font, it must be 14 point or larger, and if the typing uses a monospaced font, it cannot have more than 10 characters per inch or 4 characters per centimeter. The document must be double-spaced except for claim charts, headings, tables of contents and authorities, indices, signature blocks, and certificates of service. Block quotations may be 1.5 spacing.

[12]37 C.F.R. § 42.204(a).

for doing so is not explicit in 35 U.S.C. § 282.[13] The PTAB declared that § 101 challenges are within its jurisdiction.[14] It cited Supreme Court and Federal Circuit law for the proposition that 35 U.S.C.A. § 101 is a condition of patentability, and it noted that the AIA legislative history demonstrates that Congress intended the PTO to consider § 101 challenges in post-grant reviews. Also, it cited prior statements by the USPTO itself that § 101 challenges would be within the PTAB's jurisdiction in PGR proceedings.

The petition need not reiterate claim challenges individually. Grouping is permitted:

> The rules do not prohibit petitioners from grouping claims where the basis for the alleged unpatentability of the grouped claims is the same. When grouping claims, the petitioner must provide sufficient notice as to the merits of the challenge for

---

[13]35 U.S.C.A. § 321(b) sets out the scope of validity challenges in a post-grant review and specifies § 282(b)(2) and (3), omitting (b)(1) and (b)(4). In § 282(b), paragraph (1) is for non-infringement and unenforceability. Paragraph (2) refers to "invalidity . . . on any ground specified in Part II as a condition for patentability." Part II of Title 35 begins with Chapter 10, starting with § 100 and therefore includes the subject matter eligibility provisions. *However*, the language of § 282 explicitly refers to those portions of Part II that are "specified . . . *as a condition for patentability*." § 102 is entitled "*Conditions for patentability*; novelty," and § 103 is entitled "*Conditions for patentability*; non-obvious subject matter." [emphasis added] In contrast, § 100 is for "Definitions," and § 101 is for "Inventions patentable." Thus, neither of these §§ 100, 101 is specified as "conditions for patentability." Hence, the explicit wording of § 282(b)(2) and (3) appears to exclude § 101. If one were concerned that § 112 is *not* stated to be a "condition for patentability," that section is addressed by paragraph (b)(3) of § 282, which addresses §§ 112 and 251 explicitly. This wording therefore suggests that § 101 is not expressly contemplated by § 282(b)(2) or (3).

Paragraph (4) of § 282(b) says that defenses also include, "Any other fact or act made a defense by this title." While paragraph (4) may allow § 101 subject matter eligibility to be a defense in civil actions, 35 U.S.C.A. § 321(b) omits that paragraph from § 282 as "defenses" that can be used in a post-grant review. This seems like an anomaly because the reviews of covered business method ("CBM") patents is a species of post-grant review, and Congress specifically referred to the invalidity of many CBM patents under recent Supreme Court case law declaring claims in a CBM patent application ineligible subject matter. *Bilski v. Kappos*, 130 S. Ct. 3218, 177 L. Ed. 2d 792, 95 U.S.P.Q.2d 1001, 2010-1 U.S. Tax Cas. (CCH) P 50481 (2010).

[14]*SAP America, Inc. v. Versata Development Group, Inc.*, CBM 2012-00001, Paper No. --, pp. 32-36 (PTAB January 9, 2013).

each claim so challenged.[15]

The objective of the petitioner is to set forth sufficient evidence (and argument) that, if not rebutted, "would demonstrate that it is *more likely than not* that at least 1 of the claims challenged in the petition is unpatentable."[16] [emphasis added] Alternatively, even if the petition does not show likely unpatentability, the petition would nevertheless suffice if it raises a novel or unsettled legal question that is important to other patents or patent applications.[17]

The petition must be served in the manner specified by 37 C.F.R. § 42.205. This includes serving the patent owner at the correspondence address of record. The petitioner optionally may serve the petition and supporting evidence at any other known address for the patent owner which is likely to effect service.[18] The parties may agree to have service electronically if they desire. Service may be made by Express Mail® or other means at least as fast and reliable as Express Mail®. Personal service is not required but not forbidden.

If the USPTO receives a rule-compliant petition which is complete, shows valid service, and is accompanied by the filing fee, then the USPTO will grant it a filing date.[19] If the petition is incomplete, however, the filing date will be denied, and the Office will dismiss the petition unless the deficiency is corrected within one month of a notice of the incomplete petition or the expiration of the statutory deadline (nine months) in which to file the petition for post-grant review, whichever is *earlier*.[20]

§ 16:5 Patent owner preliminary response (three months after the petition)

The PTAB cannot immediately grant petitions that receive a filing date.[1] It will not act to institute a trial until the patent owner has had three months to submit a preliminary response to the petition or has submitted a waiver notifying

---

[15] 77 Fed. Reg. 48680, 48696 (Aug. 14, 2012).

[16] 35 U.S.C.A. § 324(a) (2011).

[17] 35 U.S.C.A. § 324(b) (2011).

[18] 37 C.F.R. § 42.205(a).

[19] 37 C.F.R. § 42.206.

[20] 37 C.F.R. § 42.206(b).

[Section 16:5]

[1] 35 U.S.C.A. § 324(c).

the PTAB that the patent owner intends not to submit a response.[2]

However, sometimes the Board is so dissatisfied with one or more of the alleged grounds in the petition that it denies them even before the patent owner's time for preliminary response is due. In one ruling involving a petition for a CBM review, the Board rejected 196 of 422 alleged grounds promulgated in the petition even before the patent owner submitted a preliminary response. The Board stated, "[W]e regard Petitioner's stated reasoning . . . to be unsupported by the record and simply unpersuasive." *Liberty Mutual Ins. Co. v. Progressive Casualty Ins. Co.*, CBM2012-00003, Paper No. 8, p. 12 (PTAB Oct. 25, 2012).

The patent owner's preliminary response is optional, and its content is limited to reasons why no post-grant review should be commenced under 35 U.S.C. § 324. The patent owner's preliminary response is allowed to include evidence other than new testimonial evidence, which cannot be included unless authorized by the Board.[3] The preliminary response has a page limitation equal to the page limit for the petition. Since the page limit for a post-grant review petition is 80 pages, the patent owner is entitled to file a preliminary response of (up to) 80 pages.[4]

While the preliminary response is prohibited from amending the patent,[5] the patent owner may file a statutory disclaimer that disclaims one or more claims of the patent. In such event, no post-grant review will be instituted with respect to the disclaimed claims.[6] If the patent owner were willing to disclaim all of the challenged claims, it can prevent the proceeding from being instituted.

§ 16:6 Institution of post-grant review: beginning of "trial"

After the Board receives the preliminary response to the petition or a waiver of a preliminary response, or after three months have transpired during which time the patent owner might have filed a preliminary response, the Board has three months to rule on the petition. This three month term for

---

[2]37 C.F.R. § 42.207(b).

[3]37 C.F.R. § 42.207(a) and (c).

[4]37 C.F.R. § 42.224(d)(1).

[5]37 C.F.R. § 42.207(d).

[6]37 C.F.R. § 42.207(e).

decision is mandated by statute.[1] The statute does not require the Board to wait until the end of its permitted time. There would be no reason why the Board could not *reject* a petition in whole or in part even before the time expires for a patent owner's preliminary response if the Board decides that the petition lacks sufficient merit to meet the burden of proof, even if unrebutted. That dismissal would not be unfair to the patent owner. It would be unfair, however, for the Board to *grant* a petition prior to the patent owner time to submit its preliminary response. However, the procedure chosen by Congress says that the ruling by the Board will be "after" the preliminary response of the patent owner is received or its time for filing expires.[2]

The standard for instituting the post-grant review is whether the information in the petition, if unrebutted, would demonstrate that it is more likely than not that at least one claim identified in the petition is unpatentable.[3] The Board will consider any patent owner preliminary response that has been timely filed.[4]

If the Board institutes a post-grant review, it may select some of the challenged claims and reject others, and it may select all or some of the grounds of unpatentability for any claim it has selected.[5] The Board is free to accept all, some, or none of the claims, and all, some, or none of the grounds.

Alternatively, a showing that the petition raises a novel or unsettled legal question which is important to other patents or patent applications will be sufficient to institute a post-grant review.[6]

If the Board decides to proceed with post-grant review, it will notify the petitioner and patent owner in writing and make the notice available to the public. The notice will include the date on which the review will commence.[7] The Director's determination whether to institute a post-grant

---

[Section 16:6]

[1] 35 U.S.C.A. § 324(c).

[2] 35 U.S.C.A. § 324(c).

[3] 35 U.S.C.A. § 324(a); 37 C.F.R. § 42.208(c).

[4] 37 C.F.R. § 42.208(c).

[5] 37 C.F.R. § 42.208(a).

[6] 35 U.S.C.A. § 324(b); 37 C.F.R. § 42.208(d).

[7] 35 U.S.C.A. § 324(d).

review is final and non-appealable.[8] Although the ruling is final and not appealable, the petitioner may request rehearing without any prior authorization from the Board. The petitioner bears the burden of showing that the decision should be modified and must specifically identify all the matters the petitioner believes the Board misapprehended or overlooked and the place where each matter was previously addressed. The time within which a request for rehearing must be filed is 30 days after the final decision to institute or not institute a trial.[9] The standard of review is abuse of discretion.[10]

The ruling on the petition marks the end of the preliminary period and, if the petition is granted, the beginning of "trial" at the PTAB.

§ 16:7 Trial proceedings; initial conference call (1 month)

After a trial is instituted by granting the petition for post-grant review, the Board will have a conference call within about one month to discuss the Scheduling Order and any motions that the parties might anticipate filing during the trial. The Board expects a list of proposed motions to be filed no later than two business days before the conference call. An accurate list of motions is needed to provide adequate notice for preparation for the call and planning for the proceeding.[1]

The proceedings after institution comport with the general rules set forth in the chapter on PTAB trials. That is, the general rules pertaining to trial practice and procedures set forth at 37 C.F.R. §§ 42.1 to 42.80 apply, along with the Trial Practice Guide.

---

[8]35 U.S.C.A. § 324(e); 37 C.F.R. § 42.71(c). For judicial requests to review a PTAB decision to institute, see *Versata Development Corp. v. Rea*, 2013 WL 4014649 (E.D. Va. 2013), discussed *supra* in § 15:12 (district court lacked subject matter jurisdiction and the PTAB decision to institute was not a final agency action subject to review under the APA; proper avenue of review is appeal to the Federal Circuit from the final, substantive agency action, as specified by the AIA.).

[9]37 C.F.R. § 42.71(c) and (d).

[10]37 C.F.R. § 42.71(c).

[Section 16:7]

[1]Trial Practice Guide, 77 Fed. Reg. 48756, 48765 (August 14, 2012).

§ 16:8 Patent owner response and amendment (3 months after trial commences)

The patent owner is entitled as a matter of right to file a response to the petition after the post-grant review has been instituted. In the response, the patent owner may address any ground not already denied. The response constitutes an opposition subject to the page limits of § 42.24 which in the case of a post-grant review is 80 pages. Absent a contrary date in the Board order instituting the post-grant review, the default date for the patent owner response is three months after the date of institution.[1]

The patent owner may seek to amend the patent within the due date provided in the Board order instituting the post-grant review. Absent a specified date, the patent owner desiring to amend the patent must file a motion to amend within the time specified for filing the patent owner response, typically three months. Additionally, the patent owner may not file a motion to amend without having first conferred with the Board.[2] Parties must remember that communications with the Board must be with the other party present, as *ex parte* communications are strictly prohibited.[3]

The motion to amend claims can be denied for several reasons. For example, if the amendment does not respond to a ground of unpatentability involved in the trial, the Board may deny the motion to amend.[4] Likewise, if the amendment seeks to enlarge the claim scope or introduce new matter, the motion can be denied.[5] The patent owner may move to cancel a challenged claim or propose "a reasonable number of substitute claims." The Office presumes that only one substitute claim would be needed to replace a challenged claim, although this presumption can be rebutted by the patent owner demonstrating the need to include more than one replacement claim.[6]

The motion to amend claims must conform to a specified format. It must include a claim listing, show each change

---

[Section 16:8]

[1] 37 C.F.R. § 42.220.

[2] 37 C.F.R. § 42.221(a).

[3] 37 C.F.R. § 42.5(d).

[4] 37 C.F.R. § 42.221(a)(2).

[5] 37 C.F.R. § 42.221(a)(2).

[6] 37 C.F.R. § 42.221(a)(3).

clearly, and show the support in the original disclosure of the patent for each claim that is added or amended. If the benefit of an earlier filing date is sought, the motion must show the support in the earlier-filed disclosure for the claim.[7]

Additional motions to amend the claims cannot be filed by the patent owner without prior authorization from the Board. Such authorization may be given where, for example, the petitioner and the patent owner jointly request the amendment in order to materially advance a settlement.[8] Otherwise, the motion must demonstrate good cause. The Office has explained that it will not be favorably disposed to such motions if they jeopardize the ability of the Office to complete the proceeding on time:

> In considering whether good cause is shown, the Board will take into account how the filing of such motions would impact the timely completion of the proceeding and the additional burden placed on the petitioner. Specifically, belated motions to amend may cause the integrity and efficiency of the review to suffer as the petitioner may be required to devote significant time and resources on claims that are of constantly changing scope. Furthermore, due to time constraints, motions to amend late in the process may not provide a petitioner a full and fair opportunity to respond to the newly presented subject matter. In determining whether to authorize such an additional motion to amend, the Board will consider whether a petitioner has submitted supplemental information after the time period set for filing a motion to amend in § 42.221(a)(1). Similarly, a motion to amend may be permitted upon a joint request of the petitioner and the patent owner to advance settlement where the motion does not jeopardize the ability of the Office to complete the proceeding timely. [*sic*, in timely fashion (?)][9]

§ 16:9 Multiple proceedings and joinder

During the pendency of the proceeding, the involved patent may also become the subject, or may previously have become the subject, of another proceeding. The USPTO seeks efficient processing of these matters and has authorized the Board to stay, transfer, consolidate, or terminate any such

[7] 37 C.F.R. § 42.221(b).

[8] 37 C.F.R. § 42.221(c).

[9] 77 Fed. Reg. 48680, 48693 (Aug. 14, 2012).

other matter involving the same patent.[1] Additionally, either the petitioner or the patent owner may request joinder of another matter with the post-grant review, provided, however, that the request for joinder be filed by motion within one month after instituting any post-grant review for which joinder is requested.[2]

§ 16:10 Submitting supplemental information

By motion, a party may supplement its submission to the Board with "supplemental information." Supplemental information usually responds to an objection by the opponent to evidence a party has submitted. The rules require that any request for approval to file a motion to submit supplemental information must be made within one month of the date the trial is instituted. Further, the supplemental information must be relevant to a claim for which the trial has been instituted. Before the PTAB, a motion will generally not be entered without prior authorization of the Board.[1] There are exceptions when it is impractical to seek Board authorization. There are motions also where authorization is automatically granted without conferring with the Board, including requests for rehearing, observations on cross-examination, and motions to exclude evidence. Typically, however, an authorization for a motion is obtained during an initial conference call which generally occurs within one month of the institution of the IPR, PGR, CBM or derivation proceeding.[2]

If the supplemental information cannot be timely filed, a party may offer a late submission of supplemental information.[3] The party seeking to submit supplemental information after the first month of the trial must request authorization to file a motion to submit the information, and the motion must show why the supplemental information reasonably could not have been obtained earlier. Further, the motion to submit must explain that consideration of the supplemental information would be in the interests of

---

[Section 16:9]

[1] 37 C.F.R. § 42.222(a).

[2] 37 C.F.R. § 42.222(b).

[Section 16:10]

[1] 37 C.F.R. § 42.20(b).

[2] Trial Practice Guide, 77 Fed. Reg. 48756, 48763.

[3] 37 C.F.R. § 42.223(b).

justice.[4] In the event that a party seeks to submit supplemental information that is *not* relevant to a claim for which the trial has been instituted, the party must request authorization to file such a motion to submit the information. Again, the motion must show why the supplemental information reasonably could not have been obtained earlier and that supplementation would be in the interests of justice.[5]

§ 16:11 Discovery and trial procedure

The general trial rules set forth in 37 C.F.R. Part 42 (Trial Practice Before the PTAB), Subpart A (Trial Practice and Procedure; §§ 42.1 to 42.80) apply to the post-grant review proceeding. However, the rules specific to post-grant review provide a modification. Regardless of anything provided in Subpart A: (1) requests for additional discovery require a showing of good cause why that discovery is needed, and (2) discovery is limited to evidence *directly related* to factual assertions of either party in the proceeding.[1]

At trial, the petitioner has the burden to prove unpatentability by a preponderance of the evidence.[2]

§ 16:12 Relationship to civil litigation

A patent challenger has to make an election. The challenger can either file a declaratory judgment action seeking a declaration of patent invalidity, provided that there is a "case or controversy," or (regardless of "case or controversy") can petition for a post-grant review, but not both. These are mutually exclusive.[1] If a patent challenger or real party in interest filed a civil action challenging the validity of any claim before seeking post-grant review, then post-grant review is barred by the statute.[2] Conversely, if the petitioner or real party in interest who has filed a petition to institute a post-grant review subsequently files a civil action challenging validity of a claim, the civil action must be automatically

[4] 37 C.F.R. § 42.223(b).

[5] 37 C.F.R. § 42.223(c).

[Section 16:11]

[1] 37 C.F.R. § 42.224.

[2] 35 U.S.C.A. § 325(a)(1).

[Section 16:12]

[1] 35 U.S.C.A. § 326(e).

[2] 35 U.S.C.A. § 325(a)(1).

stayed until any of three events occur:

- the patent owner moves the court to lift the stay;
- the patent owner files a civil action or counterclaim alleging that the petitioner or real party in interest has infringed the patent, or
- the petitioner or real party in interest moves the court to dismiss the civil action.[3]

As to the first bullet point, this protects the patent owner by disallowing the petitioner from forcing the patent owner to defend both a (potential) post-grant review and a civil action. If the patent owner, however, decides to accede to the civil action (where he can counterclaim for infringement), it can move the court to lift the stay. This is under the control of the patent owner, not the petitioner.

The second bullet point also relies on action by the patent owner. If the patent owner files an infringement suit or counterclaim after a petitioner has sought a post-grant review, there is no automatic stay of the patent owner's suit, and if the petitioner had also filed a declaratory judgment action for invalidity which was automatically stayed, that stay will be terminated. Hence, the patent owner can opt to await the outcome of the petition for a post-grant review before allowing the automatic stay of litigation to be lifted, or the patent owner can move forward with civil litigation forthwith and not take advantage of the protection of the statute.

The third bullet point concerns action by the petitioner rather than the patent owner. Here, the petitioner (or real party in interest) can move the court to dismiss its own suit. The automatic stay is lifted for consideration of that motion.

Filing a counterclaim challenging the validity of a claim of an asserted patent does not constitute a civil action for purposes of § 325.[4]

The statute prevents a patent challenger from eluding a preliminary injunction simply by seeking a post-grant review. Under 35 U.S.C. § 325(b), if the patent owner sues for infringement within three (3) months of the date of the patent grant and moves for a preliminary injunction, the court cannot stay its consideration of that motion on the

[3]35 U.S.C.A. § 325(a)(2). Curiously, the statute does not indicate that the civil action ban would be lifted if the USPTO declines to commence a post-grant review.

[4]35 U.S.C.A. § 325(a)(3).

basis of the filing of a petition for or initiation of a post-grant review proceeding. The statute does not state explicitly that the *motion* for a preliminary injunction must be filed within the three months—only that the *lawsuit* must be filed during that time. As a practical matter, however, plaintiffs who seek preliminary injunctions cannot delay in filing them, else they risk denial of the motion on the basis that the matter lacks the urgency which courts require for granting extraordinary relief. Parenthetically, the statute does not say that the defendant must be the post-grant review petitioner. Instead, § 325(b) refers simply to "a petition" without identifying the petitioner. Whether the petitioner is the defendant or a third party, if the infringement suit is filed within three months of the patent grant, the court cannot rely on any post-grant review petition to stay its consideration of a preliminary injunction motion.

A patent owner should take advantage of the protection of this statute by preparing a potential enforcement action in which preliminary injunctive relief is contemplated when it pays the issue fee or even earlier, *e.g.,* upon receiving its notice of allowance or notice of allowability of specific claims in the application.

§ 16:13 Estoppels

35 U.S.C. § 325(e) and 37 C.F.R. § 42.73(d)(1) provide for various estoppels. Where a final written decision occurs under § 328(a), the petitioner, the real party in interest, and anyone "privy of" the petitioner is estopped from requesting or maintaining any USPTO proceeding challenging that same claim on any ground that the petitioner raised or reasonably could have raised during the post-grant review.[1] In other words, once one petitions and obtains a post-grant review, all issues that were raised and which reasonably

---

[Section 16:13]

[1] 37 C.F.R. § 42.73(d)(1). *See also Ranbaxy Laboratories Ltd. v. Vertex Pharmaceuticals*, IPR 2013-00024 (Paper No. 45, p. 4, May 24, 2013) (third party participation in the deposition of a petitioner's declarant might bind the third party even if not identified as a real party in interest); *Apple Inc. v. Achates Reference Publishing, Inc.*, IPR 2013-00080-00081 (Paper No. 17, pp. 5-7, Apr. 3, 2013) (indemnification clause not enough to create a real party-in-interest); *Innolux Corp. v. Semiconductor Energy Laboratory Co., Ltd.*, IPR 2013-00028 (Paper No. 14, p. 8, Mar. 21, 2013) (PTAB considers whether a party has exercised control or funding of a petition to determine if that petition is binding upon the party as a real party in interest).

could have been raised as to the challenged patent claims are barred from being raised in another post-grant review or other USPTO proceeding, *e.g.*, a reexamination, by that same petitioner and various related entities. Whether the estoppel would apply to other claims not in the post grant review trial is not perfectly clear under the statute. At present, the scope of these estoppels awaits judicial explication.

A similar estoppel applies in civil actions. Following a post-grant review, the petitioner and the real party in interest are barred from asserting, in a civil action or an ITC proceeding, invalidity of a patent claim in the post-grant review on any ground that the petitioner raised or could reasonably have raised.[2] The scope of the defenses under § 282(b)(2) and (3) is quite large. Until courts determine the metes and bounds of what the petitioner could "reasonably have raised," post-grant reviews directed to only a narrow scope of issues may be dangerous for an unsuccessful petitioner. The estoppel as to a petitioner can be avoided by a settlement under the conditions specified in § 327(a).

Estoppels apply against the patent owner also. The statute at § 325 concerns estoppels binding the petitioner and the real party in interest. It does not address the patent owner. However, such estoppels are addressed in the rules, particularly 37 C.F.R. § 42.73(d)(3). The patent owner is estopped against obtaining certain claims or making certain amendments:

> (3) *Patent applicant or owner.* A patent applicant or owner is precluded from taking action inconsistent with the adverse judgment, including obtaining in any patent:
>
> (i) A claim that is not patentably distinct from a finally refused or canceled claim; or
>
> (ii) An amendment of a specification or of a drawing that was denied during the trial proceeding, but this provision does not apply to an application or patent that has a different written description.

§ 16:14 Settlements

35 U.S.C. § 327 provides a mechanism for the petitioner and the patent owner to settle the matter before the PTAB decides the merits of the proceeding. Should the parties come to a mutually acceptable resolution, they must reduce their agreement to writing and file a true copy of it with the Office before the termination of the post-grant review. At a party's

[2] 35 U.S.C.A. § 325(e)

request, the agreement or understanding will be treated as business confidential information, kept separate from the patent file, and made available only to federal government agencies upon written request or to any person on a showing of good cause. Good cause is not defined. The parties may jointly request termination of the post-grant review upon settlement, unless a decision on the merits has been reached. Under § 327(a), the post-grant review "shall be terminated with respect to the petitioner" upon a joint request of the petitioner and the patent owner. This does not mean that the post-grant review necessarily terminates, as the PTAB "may terminate the post-grant review or proceed to a final written decision under § 328(a)" if no petitioner remains in the post-grant review.[1] How the PTAB handles this remains to be seen.

In any event, the statute and applicable USPTO rules indicate that a settlement prevents estoppels against the petitioner.[2]

§ 16:15 USPTO certificate and intervening rights

Under § 328, final decisions of the Board must be in writing. Upon expiration of the time for or completion of any appeal, the Director will issue a certificate either cancelling or confirming any challenged claim.

Under § 328(c), any amended or new claim determined to be patentable and incorporated into the patent gives rise to intervening rights:[1]

> (c) INTERVENING RIGHTS.—Any proposed amended or new claim determined to be patentable and incorporated into a patent following a post-grant review under this chapter shall have the same effect as that specified in section 252 of this title for reissued patents on the right of any person who made, purchased, or used within the United States, or imported into

[Section 16:14]

[1] 77 Fed. Reg. 48680, 48686 (Aug. 14, 2012); see 35 U.S.C.A. § 327(a).

[2] 35 U.S.C.A. § 327(a); 37 C.F.R. § 42.73(d)(1).

[Section 16:15]

[1] See *Marine Polymer Technologies, Inc. v. HemCon, Inc.*, 672 F.3d 1350, 102 U.S.P.Q.2d 1161 (Fed. Cir. 2012) (*en banc*) where a sharply divided Court ruled that intervening rights do not arise without writing a new claim or changing the words of the claim, even if claim scope changed during reexamination as a result of the cancelation of dependent claims which, when present, required the parent claim to be interpreted broadly enough to permit the features of the dependent claims.

the United States, anything patented by such proposed amended or new claim, or who made substantial preparation therefor, before the issuance of a certificate under subsection (b).

§ 16:16 Rehearing and judicial review

Any party dissatisfied with a decision of the Board may request rehearing.[1]

Also, pursuant to 35 U.S.C. § 329, a dissatisfied party may appeal the Board's decision in accordance with 35 U.S.C. §§ 141 to 144. The appeal lies to only the U.S. Court of Appeals for the Federal Circuit. There is no right to a *de novo* hearing in the district court. Every party has the right to be a party to the appeal.[2] It is not necessary to have requested rehearing from the Board in order to appeal to the Federal Circuit.

§ 16:17 Effective dates

The AIA provides a specific effective date provision for post-grant reviews:

AIA Sec. 6(f)(1)–(f)(2)(f)(2)

(f) REGULATIONS AND EFFECTIVE DATE.—

* * *

(2) APPLICABILITY.—

(A) IN GENERAL.— The amendments made by subsection (d) [AIA Sec. 6(d)] shall take effect upon the expiration of the 1-year period beginning on the date of the enactment of this Act and, except as provided in section 18 and in paragraph (3), shall apply only to patents described in section 3(n)(1).[1]

(B) LIMITATION.— The Director may impose a limit on the number of post-grant reviews that may be instituted under chapter 32 of title 35, United States Code, during each of the first 4 1-year periods in which the amendments made by subsection (d) are in effect.

Commencement. Pursuant to subsection 6(f) of the AIA, the post-grant review procedure became available on

---

[Section 16:16]

[1]37 C.F.R. § 42.71(c) & (d).

[2]35 U.S.C.A. § 329.

[Section 16:17]

[1]As explained in Chapter 1, these are patents issued under the new first-inventor-to-file regime.

September 16, 2012 for covered business method patents and on March 16, 2013 for patents issuing under the first-inventor-to-file regime.[2]

Limitation. By statute, the USPTO may limit the number of post-grant reviews for four years. While the AIA authorizes the Director to limit the number of PGR petitions, the Office does not plan to limit the number of petitions at this time. If the Director decides to place a limit at a later time, the Office will provide advance notice to the public in the Office's Official Gazette or Federal Register. See 37 C.F.R. § 42.202(b).

---

[2] 77 Fed. Reg. 48680, 48687 (Aug. 14, 2012).

Chapter 17

Review of Covered Business Method Patents

AIA § 18
37 C.F.R. §§ 42.300–42.3

§ 17:1 Background and congressional intent[1]

[Section 17:1]

[1]The Supreme Court cautions against relying on interpretations advanced in legislative statements that are not "anchored in the text of the statute." *Shannon v. U.S.*, 512 U.S. 573, 583, 114 S. Ct. 2419, 129 L. Ed. 2d 459 (1994), stating "[C]ourts have no authority to enforce [a] principl[e] gleaned solely from legislative history that has no statutory reference point." *Shannon,* 512 U.S. at 584, quoting *International Broth. of Elec. Workers, Local Union No. 474, AFL-CIO v. N.L.R.B.*, 814 F.2d

Congressional concerns arose over business method patents after the Federal Circuit sustained a financial business method patent in *State Street Bank & Trust Co. v. Signature Financial Group, Inc*, 149 F.3d 1368, 47 U.S.P.Q.2d 1596 (Fed. Cir. 1998) (abrogated by, *In re Bilski*, 545 F.3d 943, 88 U.S.P.Q.2d 1385, 2008-2 U.S. Tax Cas. (CCH) P 50621 (Fed. Cir. 2008)). This was a financial patent involving a mutual funds system. It used "means-plus-function" claims. The district court ruled that the claims were non-statutory, but the Federal Circuit reversed, holding that the transformation of data representing discrete dollar amounts by a machine constitutes a practical application of a mathematical algorithm because it produces a useful, concrete and tangible result and thus satisfies 35 U.S.C. § 101.

Congress feared that the USPTO had been issuing patents that covered business methods already in place in the U.S. financial industry. Prior art records at the USPTO were thought to be incomplete, and examiners were allowing patents in which Congress placed far less confidence than patents directed to historical technologies. When Congress passed the American Inventor Protection Act of 1999 ("AIPA"), it included a "prior inventor" defense to infringement cases that were based on financial business method patents. The AIPA added 35 U.S.C. § 273, which stated:

> It is not patent infringement for a prior user to continue to use certain subject matter even if someone later obtains patent protection covering it, if certain conditions are met.

Congress expanded on this defense in AIA Section 5(c), restating and enlarging 35 U.S.C. § 273 as the prior user defense. That legislation is treated in a separate chapter of this volume.

In addition to Congress, the Supreme Court also questioned the eligibility of business method patents and took up *Bilski v. Kappos*, 130 S. Ct. 3218, 177 L. Ed. 2d 792, 95 U.S.P.Q.2d 1001, 2010-1 U.S. Tax Cas. (CCH) P 50481 (2010)

697, 712, 124 L.R.R.M. (BNA) 2993, 106 Lab. Cas. (CCH) P 12256 (D.C. Cir. 1987). The authoritative statement "is the statutory text, not the legislative history." *Exxon Mobil Corp. v. Allapattah Services, Inc.*, 545 U.S. 546, 568, 125 S. Ct. 2611, 162 L. Ed. 2d 502 (2005). However, lower courts have cited the legislative history of the AIA already in recent cases. E.g., *Rogers v. Tristar Products, Inc.*, 102 U.S.P.Q.2d 1722, 2012 WL 1660604, *2 (Fed. Cir. 2012) (non-precedential); *Byrne v. Wood, Herron & Evans, LLP*, 676 F.3d 1024, 1029, 102 U.S.P.Q.2d 1073 (Fed. Cir. 2012) (dissenting opin).

to review a patent application claiming a (business) method of hedging risk in commodity markets. The Court concluded that Mr. Bilski's appealed claims concerned subject matter ineligible for patenting. The Court voiced skepticism regarding the patentability of most business method patents, with at least one of the Justices wanting a categorical rule against such patents. That view did not form a majority, however, and the Court did not announce a categorical rule against business method patents.

Congress stepped in again, noting the Supreme Court holding that the *Bilski* claims were ineligible subject matter and supposing that the USPTO had already issued patents that would not pass muster under the rule of *Bilski* yet would burden the financial and banking industry.

Two sources of Congressional intent are the House Report and some extension remarks in the Federal Register by one of the bill sponsors. The House Report contains the following relevant comments:[2]

> *Transitional program for covered business method patents*
>
> A number of patent observers believe the issuance of poor business-method patents during the late 1990's through the early 2000's led to the patent "troll" lawsuits that compelled the Committee to launch the patent reform project 6 years ago. At the time, the USPTO lacked a sufficient number of examiners with expertise in the relevant art area. Compounding this problem, there was a dearth of available prior art to assist examiners as they reviewed business method applications. Critics also note that most countries do not grant patents for business methods.
>
> The Act responds to the problem by creating a transitional program 1 year after enactment of the bill to implement a provisional post-grant proceeding for review of the validity of any business method patent. In contrast to the era of the late 1990's-early 2000's, examiners will review the best prior art available. A petition to initiate a review will not be granted unless the petitioner is first sued for infringement or is accused of infringement. The program otherwise generally functions on the same terms as other post-grant proceedings initiated pursuant to the bill. Any party may request a stay of a civil action if a related post-grant proceeding is granted. The program sunsets after 10 years, which ensures that patent holders cannot delay filing a lawsuit over a shorter time period to avoid reevaluation under the transitional program.
>
> * * *

---

[2]H. R. Rep. No. 112-98, pt. 1, pp. 54, 80 to 81 (2011).

Section 18. Transitional program for covered business method patents.

Section 18 creates a transitional program to allow post-grant review of the validity of business method patents.

Under subsection (a), the Director is authorized to establish regulations governing the use of the new proceeding, which will be modeled after post-grant review as set forth in Section 6 (new Chapter 32 of the Patent Act). The proceeding is limited in certain respects. A petition cannot be accepted unless the petitioner or his real party in interest has been sued for infringement of the patent or has been charged with infringement. Nor can the petitioner or his real party in interest later assert invalidity before the ITC or a Federal court on a ground that was considered and resulted in a written decision by the agency in the course of a transitional proceeding.

The program takes effect 1 year following the date of enactment and applies to any covered business method patent issued before, on, or after the effective date, with the exception of a patent that satisfies the requirements of § 321(c) of the Patent Act as set forth in Section 6 of the bill. The program sunsets after 10 years.

Subsection (b) addresses requests for a stay of a civil action alleging infringement under § 281 of the Patent Act. A US district court shall decide to grant a stay based on prescribed criteria: (A) whether a stay (or denial thereof) will simplify the issues in question and streamline the trial; (B) whether discovery is complete and whether a trial date has been set; (C) whether a stay (or a denial thereof) would unduly prejudice the non-moving party or present a clear tactical advantage for the moving party; and (D) whether a stay (or the denial thereof) will reduce the burden of litigation on the parties and on the court. A party may seek an interlocutory appeal of the US district court's decision, which the Federal Circuit shall review to ensure consistent application of established precedent, and such review may be de novo.

Subsection (c) deems that in an action for infringement under § 281 of a covered business method patent, an automated teller machine ("ATM") shall not be considered a regular and established place of business for purposes of the patent venue statute.

Subsection (d) defines "covered business method patent" as one that claims a method or corresponding apparatus for performing data processing or other operations used in the practice, administration, or management of a financial product or service, except that it does not include patents for technological inventions.

Finally, subsection (e) clarifies that nothing in Section 18 shall be construed as amending or interpreting categories of patent-eligible subject matter under § 101 of the Patent Act.[3]

On June 22, 2012, H.R. 1249 sponsor Representative Lamar Smith provided the following "extension remarks":

Section 18 (H.R. 1249)—Business Method Patent Transitional Program

The proceeding would create a cheap and speedy alternative to litigation—allowing parties to resolve these disputes rather than spend millions of dollars that litigation now costs. In the process, the proceeding would also prevent nuisance or extortion litigation settlements.

Business methods were generally not patentable in the United States before the late 1990s, and generally are not patentable elsewhere in the world, but the Federal Circuit (in what was an activist decision) created a new class of patents in its 1998 *State Street* decision.

In its 2010 decision in *Bilski v. Kapoos* [*sic*], the U.S. Supreme Court clamped down on the patenting of business methods and other patents of poor quality.

It is likely that most if not all the business method patents that were issued after *State Street* are now invalid under *Bilski*. There is no sense in allowing expensive litigation over patents that are no longer valid.

This provision is strongly supported by community banks, credit unions and other institutions that are an important source of lending to homeowners and small businesses. Money spent litigating over invalid business-method patents, or paying nuisance settlements, cannot be loaned to Americans to purchase new homes and start new businesses.

Resolving the validity of these patents in civil litigation typically costs about $5-to- $10 million per patent. Resolving the validity of these patents through the bill's administrative proceeding costs much less.

Moreover, the proceeding allows business-method patents to be reviewed by the experts at the Patent Office under the correct (*Bilski*) standard.

To use this proceeding, a challenger must make an up-front showing to the PTO of evidence that the business-method patent is more likely than not invalid. This is a high standard. Only the worst patents, which probably never should have been issued, will be eligible for review in this proceeding.

Additionally any argument about this provision and Constitutionality is simply a red herring. Congress has the authority to create administrative proceedings to review the validity of existing patents. We have done it before and we will be doing it in the future.

---

[3]H. R. Rep. No. 112-98, pt. 1, pp. 54, 80 to 81 (2011).

This issue has been litigated and rejected by the courts, when Congress created ex parte reexam in 1980. Ex parte reexam was applied to all existing patents when that system was created. In *Patlex Corp. v. Mossinghoff*, the Federal Circuit rejected the argument that applying a new system of administrative review to existing patents is a taking. The same logic applies to this provision.

Never in the history of U.S. patent law has it been held, after a patent claim was determined to be invalid because it covered unprotectable subject matter, that the owner of the patent was nevertheless entitled to compensation on the basis of that invalid claim.

This section only creates a new mechanism for reviewing the validity of business-method patents. It does not alter the substantive law governing the validity of those patents. Under settled precedent, the transitional review program is absolutely constitutional.

It is wrong and offensive for this provision to be referred to as a bail-out. The program does not give one cent to any private party and the costs of the proceeding are required to be fully recouped through the fee charged for initiating the proceeding. It is a necessary program to allow the PTO to fix mistakes that occurred in light of an activist judicial decision in the 1998 *State Street* decision that created this new patentable subject matter without Congress' approval.

This bill will provide the patent office with a fast, precise vehicle to review low quality business method patents, which the Supreme Court has acknowledged are often abstract and overly broad. And it bears repeating that defendants cannot even start this program unless they can persuade a panel of judges at the outset of the proceeding that it is more likely than not that the patent is invalid. This is a high threshold, which requires the challenger to present his best evidence and arguments at the outset. Very few patents that undergo this review are likely to be valid patents.

Specifically, the bill's provision applies to patents that describe a series of steps used to conduct every day business applications in the financial products and retail service space. These are patents that can be and have been asserted against all types of businesses— from community banks and credit unions to retailers like Walmart, Bed Bath & Beyond, Best Buy, J.C. Penney, Staples and Office Max to other companies like Dr. Pepper Snapple Group, UPS, Hilton, AT&T, Facebook, Frito-Lay, Google, Marriott, Walt Disney, Delta Airlines and YouTube.

This provision is not tied to one industry or sector of the economy—it affects everyone. For example, this program would allow the Patent Office to decide whether to review patents for business methods related to:

Printing ads at the bottom of billing statements

Buying something online and picking it up in the store

Re-ordering checks online

Converting a [*sic*] IRA to a Roth IRA

Getting a text message when you use your credit card

Those who argue that this provision is a Wall Street bailout are just plain wrong. This is about questionable patents and the frivolous litigation that results from them. This provision is important legal reform, supported by the U.S. Chamber of Commerce and is important for American job creators.[4]

§ 17:2 The new statute—Review of business method patents

The AIA does not say whether business method patents are statutory or not. Instead, Congress simply provided for a transitional program of post-grant review ("PGR") of such patents in AIA § 18. The transitional program was not designated for codification and provides as follows:

AIA Sec. 18(a)

SEC. 18. TRANSITIONAL PROGRAM FOR COVERED BUSINESS METHOD PATENTS.

(a) TRANSITIONAL PROGRAM.—

(1) ESTABLISHMENT.— Not later than the date that is 1 year after the date of the enactment of this Act, the Director shall issue regulations establishing and implementing a transitional post-grant review proceeding for review of the validity of covered business method patents. The transitional proceeding implemented pursuant to this subsection shall be regarded as, and shall employ the standards and procedures of, a post-grant review under chapter 32 of title 35, United States Code, subject to the following:

(A) Section 321(c) of title 35, United States Code, and subsections (b), (e)(2), and (f) of section 325 of such title shall not apply to a transitional proceeding.

(B) A person may not file a petition for a transitional proceeding with respect to a covered business method patent unless the person or the person's real party in interest or privy has been sued for infringement of the patent or has been charged with infringement under that patent.

(C) A petitioner in a transitional proceeding who challenges the validity of 1 or more claims in a covered business method patent on a ground raised under section 102 or 103 of title 35, United States Code, as in effect on the day before the effective date set forth in section 3(n)(1),

[4]157 Cong. Rec. E1192-85 (daily ed. June 23, 2011).

may support such ground only on the basis of—

(i) prior art that is described by section 102(a) of such title of such title (as in effect on the day before such effective date); or

(ii) prior art that—

(I) discloses the invention more than 1 year before the date of the application for patent in the United States; and

(II) would be described by section 102(a) of such title (as in effect on the day before the effective date set forth in section 3(n)(1)) if the disclosure had been made by another before the invention thereof by the applicant for patent.

(D) The petitioner in a transitional proceeding that results in a final written decision under section 328(a) of title 35, United States Code, with respect to a claim in a covered business method patent, or the petitioner's real party in interest, may not assert, either in a civil action arising in whole or in part under section 1338 of title 28, United States Code, or in a proceeding before the International Trade Commission under section 337 of the Tariff Act of 1930 (19 U.S.C. 1337), that the claim is invalid on any ground that the petitioner raised during that transitional proceeding.

(E) The Director may institute a transitional proceeding only for a patent that is a covered business method patent.

(2) EFFECTIVE DATE.— The regulations issued under paragraph (1) shall take effect upon the expiration of the 1-year period beginning on the date of the enactment of this Act and shall apply to any covered business method patent issued before, on, or after that effective date, except that the regulations shall not apply to a patent described in section 6(f)(2)(A) of this Act during the period in which a petition for post-grant review of that patent would satisfy the requirements of section 321(c) of title 35, United States Code.

(3) SUNSET.—

(A) IN GENERAL.— This subsection, and the regulations issued under this subsection, are repealed effective upon the expiration of the 8-year period beginning on the date that the regulations issued under to [sic] paragraph (1) take effect.

(B) APPLICABILITY.— Notwithstanding subparagraph (A), this subsection and the regulations issued under this subsection shall continue to apply, after the date of the repeal under subparagraph (A), to any petition for a transitional proceeding that is filed before the date of such repeal.

(b) REQUEST FOR STAY.—

(1) IN GENERAL.—If a party seeks a stay of a civil action alleging infringement of a patent under section 281 of title 35, United States Code, relating to a transitional proceeding for that patent, the court shall decide whether to enter a stay based on—

(A) whether a stay, or the denial thereof, will simplify the issues in question and streamline the trial;

(B) whether discovery is complete and whether a trial date has been set;

(C) whether a stay, or the denial thereof, would unduly prejudice the nonmoving party or present a clear tactical advantage for the moving party; and

(D) whether a stay, or the denial thereof, will reduce the burden of litigation on the parties and on the court.

(2) REVIEW.— A party may take an immediate interlocutory appeal from a district court's decision under paragraph (1). The United States Court of Appeals for the Federal Circuit shall review the district court's decision to ensure consistent application of established precedent, and such review may be de novo.

(c) ATM EXEMPTION FOR VENUE PURPOSES.— In an action for infringement under section 281 of title 35, United States Code, of a covered business method patent, an automated teller machine shall not be deemed to be a regular and established place of business for purposes of section 1400(b) of title 28, United States Code.

(d) DEFINITION.—

(1) IN GENERAL.— For purposes of this section, the term "covered business method patent" means a patent that claims a method or corresponding apparatus for performing data processing or other operations used in the practice, administration, or management of a financial product or service, except that the term does not include patents for technological inventions.

(2) REGULATIONS.— To assist in implementing the transitional proceeding authorized by this subsection, the Director shall issue regulations for determining whether a patent is for a technological invention.

(e) RULE OF CONSTRUCTION.— Nothing in this section shall be construed as amending or interpreting categories of patent-eligible subject matter set forth under section 101 of title 35, United States Code.

§ 17:3 Introduction to the statute

This legislation is somewhat unique from other portions of

the AIA, perhaps because Congress was addressing a unique problem. Section 18 creates another trial proceeding heard by the PTAB: this trial is a post-grant review (PGR) directed to a specific kind of patent under specific conditions. It is a PGR for a "Covered Business Method" and thus is referred to by the USPTO documents as a "CBM" review.

Congress required more preconditions for instituting a CBM proceeding than a routine PGR. These are similar to the conditions normally required for raising a "case or controversy" sufficient to sustain declaratory judgment subject matter jurisdiction in federal court. The specific requirements are discussed below in the section on filing a petition.

Congress also set forth specific directives to federal courts when they are deciding motions to stay litigation in view of a CBM proceeding. It provided for immediate interlocutory appeal also. Further, Congress commented on venue for litigation involving CBM patents. The section below (§ 17:10) on the Effect on Civil Litigation addresses these aspects of the legislation.

The provisions for CBM review are temporary. Under the AIA, they expire on Sept. 15, 2020:

> (3) Sunset.—
>
> (A) In General.— This subsection, and the regulations issued under this subsection, are repealed effective upon the expiration of the 8-year period beginning on the date that the regulations issued under to paragraph (1) take effect.
>
> (B) Applicability.— Notwithstanding subparagraph (A), this subsection and the regulations issued under this subsection shall continue to apply, after the date of the repeal under subparagraph (A), to any petition for a transitional proceeding that is filed before the date of such repeal.

After Sept. 15, 2020, no new petitions for CBM review will be accepted. However, the statute and rules adopted before then will continue to apply to any petition filed before Sept. 16, 2020.

§ 17:4 Patents eligible for CBM review

CBM review became available on September 16, 2012 for all CBM patents, whenever issued.[1] "The Director may institute a transitional proceeding only for a patent that is a covered business method patent."[2] Not all business method patents are "covered" business method patents eligible for CBM review. The statute partially defines the eligible patents as concerning "a financial product or service":

> (1) IN GENERAL.— For purposes of this section, the term "covered business method patent" means a patent that claims a method or corresponding apparatus for performing data processing or other operations used in the practice, administration, or management of a financial product or service, except that the term does not include patents for technological inventions.[3]

Thus, AIA Section 18(d)(1) places several conditions on the eligible patents:

- The patent must claim a method or apparatus;
- The claim must be "for performing data processing or other operations";
- The use must be for "practice, administration, or management";
- The use must be with respect to "a financial product or service"; and
- A patent for a "technological invention" is ineligible. The AIA does not define the term but delegates authority to the USPTO to define it.[4]

The USPTO adopted rules for CBM review at Part 42, Subpart D (37 C.F.R. §§ 42.300 to 42.301). These adopt the AIA statutory definition of a "covered business method" and explain factors, without defining them, involved in deciding whether a claim is for a "technological invention" as follows:

[Section 17:4]

[1] AIA § 18(a)(2) (2011).

[2] AIA § 18(a)(1)(E) (2011).

[3] AIA § 18(d)(1) (2011).

[4] AIA § 18(d)(2) (2011). Interestingly, the rejection by the examiner being reviewed in *Bilski v. Kappos*, 130 S. Ct. 3218, 177 L. Ed. 2d 792, 95 U.S.P.Q.2d 1001, 2010-1 U.S. Tax Cas. (CCH) P 50481 (2010) was based on a "technological arts" test that did not exist in patent law at that time. *Bilski,* 130 S. Ct. at 3224. The Board of Patent Appeals and Interferences rejected the technological arts test but affirmed the rejection under the machine or transformation test. *Bilski,* 130 S. Ct. at 3224.

§ 42.301. Definitions.

In addition to the definitions in § 42.2, the following definitions apply to proceedings under this subpart D:

(a) *Covered business method patent* means a patent that claims a method or corresponding apparatus for performing data processing or other operations used in the practice, administration, or management of a financial product or service, except that the term does not include patents for technological inventions.

(b) *Technological invention.* In determining whether a patent is for a technological invention solely for purposes of the Transitional Program for Covered Business Methods (section 42.301(a)), the following will be considered on a case-by-case basis:

whether the claimed subject matter as a whole recites a technological feature that is novel and unobvious over the prior art; and solves a technical problem using a technical solution.[5]

Accordingly, patents directed to technological inventions are ineligible for CBM review. Whether a patent qualifies as a technological invention depends on whether its claims recite a technological feature that is novel and nonobvious and whether it solves a technical problem using a technical solution. The determination is based on the *claimed* subject matter, and this determination is solely for purposes of considering a CBM review. AIA § 18(e) specifically indicates that these provisions cannot be construed as amending or construing Section 35 U.S.C. § 101.[6]

The scope of "financial product or service" may be imprecise. In adopting this final rule, the USPTO offered this comment:

The definition set forth in § 42.301(a) for covered business method patent adopts the definition for covered business method patent provided in section 18(d)(1) of the AIA. In administering the program, the Office will consider the legislative intent and history behind the public law definition and the transitional program itself. For example, the legislative history explains that the definition of covered business method patent was drafted to encompass patents "claiming activities that are financial in nature, incidental to a financial activity

[5]37 C.F.R. § 42.301.

[6]AIA § 18(e) provides, "RULE OF CONSTRUCTION.—Nothing in this section shall be construed as amending or interpreting categories of patent-eligible subject matter set forth under section 101 of title 35, United States Code."

> or complementary to a financial activity." 157 Cong. Rec. S5432 (daily ed. Sept. 8, 2011) (statement of Sen. Schumer). This remark tends to support the notion that "financial product or service" should be interpreted broadly.[7]

The USPTO offered these comments relating to its definition of a "technological invention":

> The definition is consistent with the legislative history of the AIA. *See, e.g.,* 157 Cong. Rec. S1364 (daily ed. Mar. 8, 2011) (statement of Sen. Schumer) ("The 'patents for technological inventions' exception only excludes those patents whose novelty turns on a technological innovation over the prior art and are concerned with a technical problem which is solved with a technical solution and which requires the claims to state the technical features which the inventor desires to protect."); 157 Cong. Rec. H4497 (daily ed. June 23, 2011) (statement of Rep. Smith) ("Patents for technological inventions are those patents whose novelty turns on a technological innovation over the prior art and are concerned with a technical problem which is solved with a technical solution."); 157 Cong. Rec. S5428 (daily ed. Sept. 8, 2011) (statement of Sen. Coburn) ("Patents for technological inventions are those patents whose novelty turns on a technological innovation over the prior art and are concerned with a technical problem which is solved with a technical solution.").[8]

Some hypothetical examples illustrate how the statute and rules may be applied:

Example 1: A patent legitimately recites a technological feature in its claims. However, that feature is known to the prior art, and it is used for performing a covered business method (as defined). The exclusion should not apply, and the patent may be a CBM patent.

Example 2: A patent discloses and claims a software application for a business process. The claims are directed to hedging risk in purchasing and reselling a commodity such as coal, natural gas, or oil. This patent appears to be a CBM patent, as it contains no claim for an apparent technological invention and it relates to the practice, administration, or management of a financial service.

Example 3: A patent discloses and claims software or architecture for a video game. This appears not to be a "financial product or service," so this patent would not be eligible for CBM review.

Example 4: The patent meets all the stated requirements

---

[7] 77 Fed. Reg. 48734, 48735 (Aug. 14, 2012).

[8] 77 Fed. Reg. 48734, 48735 (Aug. 14, 2012).

but issued under the first-inventor-to-file regime starting March 16, 2013. This will be a CBM patent, as the statute embraces FITF patents and first-to-invent patents alike.

If a patent includes one claim that falls within the definition of a CBM patent (claim), then the entire patent is (theoretically) exposed to CBM review, as the USPTO explained in its rulemaking.[9]

Reissue patents. Among several provisions in the AIA contrasting CBM review with regular PGR, one provision concerns eligible patents and more specifically, eligible claims. AIA § 18(a)(1)(A) mandates that 35 U.S.C. § 325(f) does not apply to CBM proceedings. That provision is the limitation on challenging reissue patent claims that are identical to or narrower than a claim in the original patent.

Whether the challenged patent met the definition of a "covered business method patent" was disputed in the very first CBM proceeding, *SAP America, Inc. v. Versata Development Group, Inc.*, CBM 2012-00001, involving U.S. Patent 6,553,350. SAP's '350 patent related to pricing of products or services for various customers. Financial products or services were not mentioned in the specification or claims, according to Versata. However, the PTAB ruled that the statute does not require explicit recitation in the claims of "financial product" or "financial service," that it is enough for the patent to be "financial" that it relates to monetary matters, and that:

> Versata's '350 patent claims methods and products for determining a price and that these claims, which are complementary to a financial activity and relate to monetary matters, are considered financial products and services under § 18(d)(1).[10]

§ 17:5 Restrictions on who is eligible to file a petition

To be eligible to file a petition for CBM review, a petitioner, its real party in interest, or a privy of the petitioner must have either: (1) been sued for infringement of the patent, or (2) been charged with infringement of the patent. "Charged with infringement" is such that the petitioner would have

---

[9] "A patent having one or more claims directed to a covered business method is a covered business method patent for purposes of the review, even if the patent includes additional claims." 77 Fed. Reg. 48734, 48736 (Aug. 14, 2012).

[10] *SAP America, Inc. v. Versata Development Group, Inc.*, CBM 2012-00001, Paper No. 36, p. 23 (PTAB January 9, 2013).

standing to file a declaratory judgment action in federal court, and that the dispute is "real and substantial" regarding infringement of a CBM patent.[1] This suggests that licensees in good standing may be unable to seek CBM review absent a charge of infringement.

In addition, one cannot file an acceptable petition if he, his real party in interest, or his privy is estopped from challenging the claims on the grounds stated in the petition.[2]

§ 17:6 Restrictions on when a petition is timely

The USPTO rule adopts a nine month ban on filing a petition for CBM.[1] This is based on the effective date provision for CBM transitional proceedings stated in AIA § 18(a)(2). Understanding that section requires considering a series of other statutory provisions. To begin:

> AIA § 18(a)(2). EFFECTIVE DATE.—The regulations issued under paragraph (1) shall take effect upon the expiration of the 1-year period beginning on the date of the enactment of this Act and shall apply to any covered business method patent issued before, on, or after that effective date, except that the regulations shall not apply to a patent described in section 6(f)(2)(A) of this Act during the period in which a petition for post-grant review of that patent would satisfy the requirements of section 321(c) of title 35, United States Code.

The relevant portion is the "except that" clause, which refers to AIA § 6(f)(2)(A). Thus, AIA § 18(a)(2) tells us that the CBM proceeding is effective beginning on September 16, 2012 except with respect to patents contemplated by AIA § 6(f)(2)(A). As to those patents, the CBM proceeding shall not apply for the period in which a petition for PGR meets the requirements of 35 U.S.C. § 321(c). § 321(c) indicates that the time period is nine months.[2] The patents contemplated by AIA § 6(f)(2)(A)[3] are patents described in AIA § 3(n)(1). Section 3(n)(1) relates to FITF patents.

[Section 17:5]

[1]37 C.F.R. § 42.302(a).

[2]37 C.F.R. § 42.302(b).

[Section 17:6]

[1]37 C.F.R. § 42.303.

[2]"A petition for a post-grant review may only be filed not later than the date that is 9 months after the date of the grant of the patent or of the issuance of a reissue patent (as the case may be)." 35 U.S.C.A. § 321(c).

[3]AIA § 6(f)(2)(A) provides: "IN GENERAL.—The amendments made

Summing this up, a petition seeking CBM review can be filed anytime except during the initial nine (9) month period after issuance of a first-inventor-to-file patent. This is the period when a petition to institute PGR is timely under 35 U.S.C. § 321(c).

During these initial nine months, a prospective petitioner could file a petition seeking a PGR or could wait for nine months and file a petition for CBM. The filing fee is the same, but there are some differences, for example in the scope of the estoppels, which are more extensive for PGR than they are for CBM proceedings.

With respect to a non-FITF patent, *i.e.,* a patent with no claim having an effective filing date on or after March 16, 2013, a CBM petition can be filed at any time.[4] The nine month restriction does not apply.

§ 17:7 Content of a petition for CBM review

The rule specific to the content of a petition seeking CBM review is 37 C.F.R. § 42.304. This rule does not itself call for the petitioner to "certify" any facts but instead calls for the petitioner to "demonstrate" facts. The following checklist may be helpful in preparing a petition for CMB Review:

Checklist for CBM Review Petition

- Show that the challenged patent is a "covered business method patent" as defined in § 42.301. § 42.304(a).[1]
- Certify that the petitioner, its real party in interest, or its privy has been sued for infringement of the patent or charged with its infringement. §§ 42.304(a), 43.302(a).
- Certify that the petitioner, real party-in-interest, and privy are not estopped from challenging the claims on the grounds identified in the petition. § 42.302(b).
- Certify that the PRG time period has expired (if the pa-

---

by subsection (d) shall take effect upon the expiration of the 1-year period beginning on the date of the enactment of this Act and, except as provided in section 18 and in paragraph (3), shall apply only to patents described in section 3(n)(1)."

[4]See USPTO "Reference Guide to Statutory Provisions and Final Rules Effective on September 16, 2012," slide 213. Available at http://www.uspto.gov/aia_implementation/120910-aia-reference-guide-to-statutory-provisions-and-final-rules.pdf, visited Oct. 27, 2012.

[Section 17:7]

[1]References in the check list are to 37 C.F.R. unless otherwise stated.

tent is a first-inventor-to-file patent). § 42.303
- Include the proper filing fee. §§ 42.203, 42.15(b).
- Include mandatory notices (§ 42.8) identifying:
  - each real party-in-interest for the petitioner,
  - all related judicial and administrative matters,
  - petitioner's lead and back-up counsel, and
  - the service information for petitioner.
- State the precise relief requested. § 42.22(a)(1), (b).
- Show all requirements of any rule in 37 C.F.R. Part 1 that ordinarily governs the relief sought (along with showings required in Part 42). § 42.22(b).
- Provide a full statement of the reasons for relief, including a detailed explanation of the significance of the evidence, including material facts, and the governing law, rules, and precedent. § 42.22(a)(2).
- Provide a statement of facts. § 42.22(c).
- For each challenged claim, state:
  - the claim itself. § 42.304(b)(1).
  - the specific statutory grounds under 35 U.S.C. §§ 282(b) or (3), as modified by AIA § 18(a)(1)(C) on which the challenge is based. § 42.304(b)(2).
  - how the challenged claim should be construed. § 42.304(b)(3).
  - how the construed claim is unpatentable under the specified grounds, including where each claim element is found in the prior art. If the grounds for unpatentability is not prior art, identify the specific part of the claim that fails to comply with the statutory grounds and how the identified subject matter fails to comply with the statute. § 42.304(b)(4).
  - the exhibit number of the supporting evidence. § 42.304(b)(5).
- Copies of the evidence relied upon. § 42.6(c).
- Format requirements., § 42.6, and citation format § 42.13.
- Page limit of 80 pages. § 42.24.
  - Optional motion to waive page limits. § 42.24(a)(2).
- Certificate of service on correspondence address of record. § 42.6(e).
- Duty of candor disclosures. § 42.11.
- Optional motion to seal. § 42.55.

* * *

A petition for CBM review falls under the general trial rules of the PTAB as it seeks institution of a trial proceeding. The notices required by Part 42, subparts A (Trial Practice and Procedure) and C (Post-Grant Review) are required for CBM review also.[2]

The petition must request judgment against one or more claims of a CBM patent.

The petition must meet several requirements, starting with the following:

- 37 C.F.R. § 42.6 (format, exhibits, and service),[3]
- 37 C.F.R. § 42.8 (mandatory notices of real party in interest, related matters, lead and backup counsel, etc.),[4]
- 37 C.F.R. § 42.22 (general requirements of petition contents),[5] and
- 37 C.F.R. § 42.24 (page limits).[6] The page limit for a petition for CBM review is 80 pages.

The rule next states several further specific requirements. This includes demonstrating proper standing.[7] Standing includes two parts: (a) showing that the patent is a CBM patent as explained in § 17:3, and (b) showing that the petitioner meets the eligibility requirements as explained in § 17:4.

The petition must identify the challenge properly.[8] Also, the petition must identify the precise relief requested *for each challenged claim.* This requires identifying the claim, the statutory ground under 35 U.S.C. § 282(b), paragraphs 2 or 3, as modified by AIA § 18(a)(1)(C). Paragraph (2) of § 282(b) mentions grounds specified in the patent statute, Part II (35 U.S.C. § 100 et seq.). Paragraph (3) identifies the Section 112 defenses other than best mode as a basis or invalidity for unenforceability. AIA § 18(a)(1)(C) specifies the prior art on which a petition may rely. This is discussed more fully in a section below.

The petition must explain how the claim is to be

[2]37 C.F.R. § 42.304 (first paragraph).

[3]37 C.F.R. § 42.304 (first paragraph).

[4]37 C.F.R. § 42.304 (first paragraph).

[5]37 C.F.R. § 42.304 (first paragraph).

[6]37 C.F.R. § 42.304 (first paragraph).

[7]37 C.F.R. § 42.304 (a).

[8]37 C.F.R. § 42.304 (b).

construed.[9] All claims of unexpired patents involved in CBM review are required to be given the broadest reasonable construction in light of the specification in which it appears.[10] If the claim contains a means-plus-function claim element, the petition must identify the specific portions of the specification that describe the structure, material, or acts corresponding to each claimed function.[11]

Additionally, the petition must explain how the claim as construed is unpatentable under the identified statutory grounds.[12] To the extent the grounds are based on prior art, the petition must show where each claim element is found in the prior art.[13] For other grounds, the petition must identify the specific part of the claim that does not comply with the identified statutory grounds and state how the identified subject matter fails to comply with the patent statute.[14] Thus a CBM review may challenge patent validity on the basis of subject matter ineligibility, as in, *e.g.*, *Bilski v. Kappos.* The PTAB ruled very early that § 101 challenges are within its jurisdiction.[15] It cited Supreme Court law and Federal Circuit for the proposition that 35 U.S.C.A. § 101 is a condition of patentability, and it noted that the AIA legislative history demonstrates that Congress intended the PTO to consider § 101 challenges in post-grant reviews. Also, it cited prior statements by the USPTO itself that § 101 challenges would be within the PTAB's jurisdiction in PGR proceedings.

The petition must identify exhibit numbers of supporting evidence.[16] The petition must explain how the exhibit, including specific portions, is relevant to support the challenge. The failure to provide these explanations may result in the

---

[9] 37 C.F.R. § 42.304(b)(3).

[10] 37 C.F.R. § 42.300(b). For an interesting discussion of why the broadest, reasonable interpretation is used and the standard of review, see *Flo Healthcare Solutions, LLC v. Kappos*, 697 F.3d 1367, 104 U.S.P. Q.2d 1834 (Fed. Cir. 2012) (additional views of Judge Plager and additional views of Judge Newman).

[11] 37 C.F.R. § 42.304(b)(3).

[12] 37 C.F.R. § 42.304(b)(4).

[13] 37 C.F.R. § 42.304(b)(4).

[14] 37 C.F.R. § 42.304(b)(4).

[15] *SAP America, Inc. v. Versata Development Group, Inc.*, CBM 2012-00001, Paper No. 36, pp. 32-36 (PTAB Jan. 9, 2013).

[16] 37 C.F.R. § 42.304(b)(5).

Board excluding the evidence or giving it no weight.[17]

In the event that the petitioner files a motion to correct clerical or typographic errors in the petition, granting such a motion will not change the filing date of the petition.[18]

§ 17:8 Prior art against "first-to-invent" patents

A CBM review is a PGR allowing a very broad spectrum of challenges against the subject patent. Some of those bases concern invalidity over prior art. As noted above, AIA § 18(a)(1)(C) modifies the scope of the prior art that can be employed in certain situations. If the petitioner is challenging a patent issued under the "first-to-invent" regime, then AIA § 18(a)(1)(C) applies to the extent that the challenge asserts former § 102 or former § 103. The AIA expresses this with reference to the patent statute as it exists on the day before the AIA effective date for FITF inventions. The AIA provides:

AIA § 18(a)(1)(C)

> (C) A petitioner in a transitional proceeding who challenges the validity of 1 or more claims in a covered business method patent on a ground raised under section 102 or 103 of title 35, United States Code, as in effect on the day before the effective date set forth in section 3(n)(1),[1] may support such ground only on the basis of—
>
> (i) prior art that is described by section 102(a) of such title of such title [*sic*] (as in effect on the day before such effective date); or
>
> (ii) prior art that—
>
> (I) discloses the invention more than 1 year before the date of the application for patent in the United States; and
>
> (II) would be described by section 102(a) of such title (as in effect on the day before the effective date set forth in section 3(n)(1)) if the disclosure had been made by another before the invention thereof by the applicant for patent.

Although the USPTO did not issue any rules explicating

[17] 37 C.F.R. § 42.304(b)(5).

[18] 37 C.F.R. § 42.304(c).

[Section 17:8]

[1] AIA Sec. 3(n)(1) addresses patents having a claim with an effective filing date on or after March 16, 2013 and are thus subject to the AIA's first-inventor-to-file provisions.

this section of the statute, it did offer the following comment explaining AIA § 18(a)(1)(C):

> Section 18(a)(1)(C) of the AIA further provides that limited prior art shall apply for those challenged covered business method patents granted under first-to-invent provisions. Specifically, section 18(a)(1)(C) provides that a petitioner in a transitional proceeding who challenges the validity of 1 or more claims in a covered business method patent on a ground raised under section 102 or 103 of title 35, United States Code, as in effect on the day before the effective date set forth in section 3(n)(1), may support such ground only on the basis of prior art that is described by section 102(a) of such title (as in effect on the day before such effective date); or prior art that discloses the invention more than 1 year before the date of the application for patent in the United States; and would be described by section 102(a) of such title (as in effect on the day before the effective date set forth in section 3(n)(1)) if the disclosure had been made by another before the invention thereof by the applicant for patent.[2]

Effectively, AIA § 18(a)(1)(C) says that if the CBM patent is not a FITF patent but instead is a first-to-invent patent and is challenged on the basis of prior art, the only prior art that can be applied is specified in subparts (i) and (ii). Under AIA § 18(a)(1)(C)(i), such prior art arises under the old § 102(a). Prior art under AIA § 18(a)(1)(C)(ii) must meet the requirements of paragraphs I and II. Paragraph I requires the prior art to have disclosed the invention more than one year before the date of the application for [the involved CBM] patent in the United States. It is similar to former § 102(b), which raised insuperable prior art for purposes of denying novelty. Paragraph (II) defines a *sui generis* class of prior art. It would be § 102(a)[3] prior art if it had been made by another before the invention thereof by the applicant for the patent.

These restrictions do *not* exclude on sale activities or public uses of the claimed invention. It appears to exclude prior art under at least 35 U.S.C. § 102(f) and (g).

§ 17:9 CBM proceedings

A CBM review is a PGR, and the AIA specifies that it

[2] 77 Fed. Reg. 48680, 48687 (Aug. 14, 2012).

[3] Former 35 U.S.C.A. § 102(a) reads: "§ 102 (a). The invention was known or used by others in this country, or patented or described in a printed publication in this or a foreign country, before the invention thereof by the applicant for the patent."

"shall employ the standards and procedures of . . . a post-grant review" subject to certain exclusions. See the prior chapters on PTAB trials and PGR for a detailed description of how these proceed.

The USPTO rules for CBM review specify that the proceeding will be administered so that its pendency before the PTAB, after institution of the proceeding, will normally not exceed one year, and that term can be extended for good cause by the Chief Administrative Patent Judge.[1]

Accordingly, one initiates the proceeding by filing a petition, submitting a fee, and completing the requirements for a PGR except as otherwise stated. The patent owner has three months for filing a preliminary response, and then the PTAB has three months within which to decide whether to institute the trial or not. If trial is declared, the Trial Rules and Trial Practice Guide apply, as specified in the chapters *supra*. Appeals go to the Federal Circuit. Any party dissatisfied with the ultimate ruling may appeal.

Though the decision of the PTAB to institute a post-grant review "shall be final and nonappealable," 35 U.S.C.A. § 324(e), one patent owner asked a district court to set aside the PTAB decision to institute a CBM review. In *Versata Development Corp. v. Rea*, 2013 WL 4014649 (E.D. Va. 2013), the patent owner Versata had obtained judgments of infringement against SAP America, Inc. in companion litigation. On the first day that CBM review petitions could be filed at the PTO, September 16, 2012 (exactly one year after the AIA became law), SAP filed a petition for post grant review of the patent-in-suit as a "covered business method" patent. After the PTAB granted the petition and instituted trial, Versata sought a judicial interlocutory review under the Administrative Procedure Act of the PTAB decision to initiate review of the challenged patent. SAP intervened in the civil action. Granting motions to dismiss, the district court ruled that the AIA itself directed that there be no judicial review of a decision to institute, so the court lacked subject matter jurisdiction.[2] Second, the decision to institute was not a final agency action subject to review under the

[Section 17:9]

[1]37 C.F.R. § 42.300(c).

[2]*Versata Development Corp. v. Rea*, 2013 WL 4014649 (E.D. Va. 2013).

APA, so the matter was not ripe anyway.[3] The proper avenue of review is an appeal to the Federal Circuit from an eventual final, substantive agency action, as specified by the AIA:

> Congress's intent was to create a streamlined system while providing all parties with full access to judicial review. Accordingly, not only is the PTAB's decision to institute post-grant review not a "final agency action," adequate remedies also exist for Plaintiff to appeal the decision, namely an appeal to the Federal Circuit, at which time Versata may present arguments concerning the decision to initiate review and, if necessary, the prudence of reviewing this decision on an appeal from the substantive and final decision.[4]

§ 17:10 Effect on civil litigation

The AIA includes provisions for CBM review that address venue for civil litigation, stays, estoppels, and injunctions. Estoppels are addressed in the next section.

Venue. With respect to venue, several banks have automated teller machines (ATMs) in several states and conduct business via those ATMs. AIA § 18(c) declares that ATM machines cannot be a "regular and established place of business for purposes of section 1400(b) of title 28, United States Code."[1]

Stay of litigation. A patent challenger will often seek to stay federal court litigation on the basis that the patent-in-suit is undergoing a review process at the USPTO. The AIA specifically speaks to such motions for stays. While the AIA does not mandate a stay one way or the other, it does set forth factors on which the district court must base its decision.[2] In addition, the AIA permits interlocutory appeals to the Federal Circuit, which may review stay orders under

---

[3] *Versata Development Corp. v. Rea*, 2013 WL 4014649 (E.D. Va. 2013).

[4] *Versata Development Corp. v. Rea*, 2013 WL 4014649 (E.D. Va. 2013).

[Section 17:10]

[1] 28 U.S.C.A. § 1400(b) provides: "Any civil action for patent infringement may be brought in the judicial district where the defendant resides, or where the defendant has committed acts of infringement and has a regular and established place of business."

[2] These factors "closely resemble the stay analysis courts have applied in assessing a motion to stay pending *inter partes* or *ex parte* reexamination by the [PTO]. . . . The substantial difference between the test set forth in § 18(b)(1) and that employed by courts in the ordinary pa-

a *de novo* reviews standard. Under this provision of the AIA, whether the interlocutory appeal can proceed is not within the discretion of the trial court. The AIA provides:

AIA Sec.18(b)

18(b) REQUEST FOR STAY.—

(1) IN GENERAL.— If a party seeks a stay of a civil action alleging infringement of a patent under section 281 of title 35, United States Code, relating to a transitional proceeding for that patent, the court shall decide whether to enter a stay based on—

(A) whether a stay, or the denial thereof, will simplify the issues in question and streamline the trial;

(B) whether discovery is complete and whether a trial date has been set;

(C) whether a stay, or the denial thereof, would unduly prejudice the nonmoving party or present a clear tactical advantage for the moving party; and

(D) whether a stay, or the denial thereof, will reduce the burden of litigation on the parties and on the court.

(2) REVIEW.— A party may take an immediate interlocutory appeal from a district court's decision under paragraph (1). The United States Court of Appeals for the Federal Circuit shall review the district court's decision to ensure consistent application of established precedent, and such review may be de novo.

Preliminary Injunctions. The AIA includes a provision at 35 U.S.C. § 325(b) mandating that a patent owner who files infringement litigation within three months of the issue date of its patent-in-suit cannot have its motion for a preliminary injunction stayed on account of a PGR petition at the USPTO.[3] This provision is affirmatively excluded with re-

---

tent reexamination context is the inclusion of [the] fourth factor" as defined in § 18(b)(1)(D). *Market-Alerts Pty. Ltd. v. Bloomberg Finance L.P.*, 922 F. Supp. 2d 486 (D. Del. 2013). *See also Sightsound Technologies, LLC v. Apple, Inc.*, 2013 WL 2457284, at *3 (W.D. Pa. 2013) (holding that the relevant stay provisions of the AIA apply when the petition for review is filed).

[3]35 U.S.C.A. § 325(b) provides: "Preliminary Injunctions.—If a civil action alleging infringement of a patent is filed within 3 months after the date on which the patent is granted, the court may not stay its consideration of the patent owner's motion for a preliminary injunction against infringement of the patent on the basis that a petition for post-grant review has been filed under this chapter or that such a post-grant review has been instituted under this chapter."

spect to CBM review by AIA § 18(a)(1)(A).[4] In other words, even if the patent owner files a suit within three months, if the defendant (or anyone else) seeks a CBM review, that *could* be used to support a motion to deny a preliminary injunction. On the other hand, with respect to FITF patents, a petition for CBM review cannot be filed within the first three months of a patent issue date anyway, and must wait for nine months to transpire, as explained in § 17:5 and specified in 37 C.F.R. § 42.303.

§ 17:11 Estoppels

Congress made the estoppels less restrictive for CBM reviews than for PGR. The relevant provision, AIA § 18(a)(1)(D), refers only to matters that the petitioner raised; it does not estop the petitioner against matters that *reasonably could have been raised.* This concerns estoppels in civil litigation only, not estoppel at the USPTO, which is the same estoppel that arises from a PGR. The CBM estoppel provision reads as follows:

AIA Sec.18(a)(1)(D)

> (D) The petitioner in a transitional proceeding that results in a final written decision under section 328(a) of title 35, United States Code, with respect to a claim in a covered business method patent, or the petitioner's real party in interest, may not assert, either in a civil action arising in whole or in part under section 1338 of title 28, United States Code, or in a proceeding before the International Trade Commission under section 337 of the Tariff Act of 1930 (19 U.S.C. 1337), that the claim is invalid on any ground that the petitioner raised during that transitional proceeding.

As can be seen, this provision speaks to estoppel in federal court litigation arising under 28 U.S.C. § 1338 and ITC proceedings under 19 U.S.C. § 1337. This estoppel provision is silent as to the estoppel effects at the USPTO.

The AIA specifically excludes the PGR estoppel provisions for civil actions (stated in 35 U.S.C. § 325(e)(2)) from the CBM procedure:

New Statute (AIA Sec. 18 (a)(1)(A))

> (A) Section 321(c) of title 35, United States Code, and

[4]AIA § 18(a)(1)(A) states: "Section 321(c) of title 35, United States Code, and subsections (b), (e)(2), and (f) of section 325 of such title shall not apply to a transitional proceeding."

subsections (b), (e)(2), and (f) of section 325 of such title shall not apply to a transitional proceeding.

However, this leaves the estoppel provisions of 35 U.S.C. § 325(e)(1) in full force with respect to CBM reviews. For convenience, both subparts of Section 325(e) are shown below:

§ 325(e) Estoppel.—

(1) Proceedings Before the Office.— The petitioner in a post-grant review of a claim in a patent under this chapter that results in a final written decision under section 328(a), or the real party in interest or privy of the petitioner, may not request or maintain a proceeding before the Office with respect to that claim on any ground that the petitioner raised or reasonably could have raised during that post-grant review.

(2) Civil Actions and Other Proceedings.— The petitioner in a post-grant review of a claim in a patent under this chapter that results in a final written decision under section 328(a), or the real party in interest or privy of the petitioner, may not assert either in a civil action arising in whole or in part under section 1338 of title 28 or in a proceeding before the International Trade Commission under section 337 of the Tariff Act of 1930 that the claim is invalid on any ground that the petitioner raised or reasonably could have raised during that post-grant review.

Because CBM review is a PGR, and because § AIA 18(a)(1) provides that PGR standards and procedures apply to CBM review except as otherwise stated, ("[t]he transitional proceeding implemented pursuant to this subsection shall be regarded as, and shall employ the standards and procedures of, a post-grant review . . . subject to the following . . ."), the full estoppel applies against the CBM review petitioner in subsequent USPTO proceedings.

§ 17:12 PTAB statistics re CBM reviews

On its website, the USPTO maintains statistics on AIA activity.[1] It reported that as of October 17, 2013, it had received 71 CBM review petitions. Almost 70% of all AIA petitions were in the electrical and computer arts, followed by mechanical (14%), chemical (9%), bio/pharma (7%), and

[Section 17:12]

[1] http://www.uspto.gov/aia_implementation/statistics.jsp (visited August 22, 2013).

design patents (1%).

Chapter 18

Inter Partes Review

AIA § 6(a–c)
35 U.S.C.A. §§ 311–319
37 C.F.R. §§ 42.100–42.123

§ 18:1 Background and congressional intent[1]

The background to the enactment of the *inter partes* review procedure is discussed in the House Report,[2] pertinent portions of which are reproduced below. The general objectives are to provide a mechanism which is less costly than federal court litigation and allows a time-predictable review of patentability issues pertaining to an issued U.S. patent. The two types of reexamination proceedings in the USPTO extant at the time of the AIA enactment had not met this need fully. Reexamination proceedings often took several years at the USPTO, notwithstanding the statutory requirement for "special dispatch."[3]

To address these problems, Congress created the post-grant review procedure, covered in Chapter 16, which is a broad scope (but not plenary) adversarial proceeding tried at the USPTO's new PTAB. Also, the AIA replaced *inter partes* reexaminations with *inter partes* review, which is to be conducted much more quickly than its predecessor. This chapter addresses the *inter partes* review. The changes to the now-superseded *inter partes* reexamination are covered in Chapter 23 ("Reexaminations").

Relevant portions reflecting Congressional intent in adopting the *inter partes* review provisions are as follows:[4]

[Section 18:1]

[1]The Supreme Court cautions against relying on interpretations advanced in legislative statements that are not "anchored in the text of the statute." *Shannon v. U.S.*, 512 U.S. 573, 583, 114 S. Ct. 2419, 129 L. Ed. 2d 459 (1994), stating "[C]ourts have no authority to enforce [a] principl[e] gleaned solely from legislative history that has no statutory reference point." Shannon, 512 U.S. at 584, quoting *International Broth. of Elec. Workers, Local Union No. 474, AFL-CIO v. N.L.R.B.*, 814 F.2d 697, 712, 124 L.R.R.M. (BNA) 2993, 106 Lab. Cas. (CCH) P 12256 (D.C. Cir. 1987). The authoritative statement "is the statutory text, not the legislative history." *Exxon Mobil Corp. v. Allapattah Services, Inc.*, 545 U.S. 546, 568, 125 S. Ct. 2611, 162 L. Ed. 2d 502 (2005). However, lower courts have cited the legislative history of the AIA already in recent cases. E.g., *Rogers v. Tristar Products, Inc.*, 102 U.S.P.Q.2d 1722, 2012 WL 1660604, *2 (Fed. Cir. 2012) (non-precedential); *Byrne v. Wood, Herron & Evans, LLP*, 676 F.3d 1024, 1029, 102 U.S.P.Q.2d 1073 (Fed. Cir. 2012) (dissenting opin.).

[2]H. R. Rep. No. 112-98, pt. 1 (2011).

[3]35 U.S.C.A. §§ 305, 314 (2002).

[4]H. R. Rep. No. 112-98, pt. 1, pp. 45 to 48, 75 to 77 (2011).

Post-grant review proceedings

The Act amends *ex parte* and *inter partes* reexamination and establishes a new post-grant review procedure. Under current law, there are two ways to challenge the validity and enforceability of a patent that has issued. The patent may be challenged in district court litigation or in a reexamination at the USPTO.

Nearly 30 years ago, Congress created the administrative "reexamination" process, through which the USPTO could review the validity of already-issued patents on the request of either the patent holder or a third party,[FN30] in the expectation that it would serve as an effective and efficient alternative to often costly and protracted district court litigation.[FN31] Reexamination requires the USPTO to review the patent in light of a substantial new question of patentability not presented during the original examination.[FN32] The initial reexamination statute had several limitations that later proved to make it a less viable alternative to litigation for evaluating patent validity than Congress intended. First, a reexamination request could only be based on prior art, and could not be based on prior public use or prior sales. Moreover, the requestor could not raise any challenge based on § 101 (utility, eligibility) or 112 (indefiniteness, enablement, written description, best mode). A third party alleging a patent is invalid, therefore, had fewer challenges it could raise in the proceeding and, therefore, may instead opt to risk infringement and litigate the validity of the patent in court. Second, in the original reexamination system, the third-party challenger had no role once the proceeding was initiated, while the patent holder had significant input throughout the entire process. Third, a challenger that lost at the USPTO under reexamination had no right to appeal an examiner's, or the Patent Board's, decision either administratively or in court. Restrictions such as these made reexamination a much less favored avenue to challenge questionable patents than litigation. Reexamination proceedings are also often costly, taking several years to complete,[FN33] and are first conducted by examiners and, if the patent is rejected, then by Patent Board judges. Thus, many patents must go through two rounds of administrative review (one by the examiner, and a second by the Patent Board) adding to the length of the proceeding.[FN34]

FN30. See 35 U.S.C. Sec. 301–307. A patent holder will typically request reexamination to bolster the patent in view of new prior art. A third party may request reexamination to challenge, and ultimately invalidate, the patent.

FN31. "Reexamination will permit efficient resolution of questions about the validity of issued patents without recourse to expensive and lengthy infringement litigation . . .. The reexamination of issued patents could be conducted with a fraction of the time and cost of formal legal proceedings and would help restore confidence in the effectiveness of our patent system . . .. It is anticipated that these measures provide a useful and necessary alternative for challengers and for patent owners to test the validity of United States patents in an efficient and relatively inexpensive manner." *See* H.R. Rep. No. 96-1307(I) at 3 (1980), reprinted in 1980 U.S.C.C.A.N. 6460, 6462–63.

FN32. *See* 35 U.S.C. Sec. 303.

FN33. *See Perspectives on Patents: Hearing Before the Subcomm. on Intellectual Prop. of the Senate Comm. on the Judiciary,* 109th Cong. (2005) (statement of Jon W. Dudas, Undersecretary of Commerce for Intellectual Property, Director of the U.S. Patent and Trademark Office), explaining that "a large number of reexamination proceedings have been pending before the USPTO for more than 4 years," and questioning whether this amount of time is consistent with the statutory requirement that "[a]ll reexamination proceedings . . . will be conducted with special dispatch within the Office." *See also* 35 U.S.C. Sec. 305.

FN34. For several years, the standard practice at the USPTO was to assign the reexamination to the patent examiner who had originally examined that patent. In addition, the same third-party requester could file multiple, serial reexaminations based on the same "substantial new question of patentability," so long as the initial reexamination was not complete. More recently, the USPTO ended some of these procedures, and now reexaminations are handled by a Central Reexamination Unit (CRU), and subsequent serial reexamination, based on the same "substantial new question of patentability," is no longer permitted. *See, e.g.,* Manual of Patent Examining Procedure (MPEP) Sec. 2236 and 2240 (August 2006).

Congress has responded several times to criticisms of the reexamination system by making amendments to the process.[FN35] In 1999, Congress created a second reexamination procedure—called *inter partes* reexamination—that gave third-party challengers greater input throughout the proceeding by permitting them to respond to every pleading submitted by the patent holder.[FN36] Congress also eventually gave third-party challengers the right to appeal adverse decisions.[FN37]

FN35. *See e.g.,* 21st Century Dep't of Justice Appropriations Authorization Act, Pub. L. No. 107-273, Sec. 13105–06, 13202, 116 Stat. 1758, 1761 (2002) (effective Nov. 2, 2002); American Inventors Protection Act, Pub.L. 106-113, 113 Stat. 1536, 1501A et seq. (1999) (creating *inter partes* reexamination) (hereafter referred to as the "AIPA").

FN36. *See* 35 U.S.C. Sec. 311 to 318.

See 35 U.S.C. Sec. 315(b).

As part of the 1999 improvements to reexamination,

Congress directed the USPTO to submit a report to Congress evaluating the *inter partes* reexamination process and making any recommendations for changes.[FN38] Initially, the USPTO projected that in the first year after the creation of *inter partes* reexamination, it would receive 400 such requests and it projected that by 2004 it would receive nearly 600.[FN39] No *inter partes* reexamination requests were actually filed in 2000 and only 27 such requests had been filed by 2004.[FN40] Over the 5-year period studied by the USPTO, it issued 900,000 patents and received only 53 requests for *inter partes* reexamination.[FN41]

FN38. AIPA, Pub. L. 106-113, Sec. 4606.

FN39. *See United States Patent and Trademark Office, Report to Congress on* Inter Partes *Reexamination* (2004) (hereinafter referred to as *"Report on Inter Partes Reexamination"*), at 4.

FN40. *See United States Patent and Trademark Office, Report to Congress on* Inter Partes *Reexamination* (2004) (hereinafter referred to as *"Report on Inter Partes Reexamination"*), at 5.

FN41. *See United States Patent and Trademark Office, Report to Congress on* Inter Partes *Reexamination* (2004) (hereinafter referred to as *"Report on Inter Partes Reexamination"*), at 5.

The Act expands the category of documents that may be cited in a reexamination proceeding to include written statements of the patent owner that have been filed in a proceeding before a Federal court or the USPTO regarding the scope of claims. This addition will counteract the ability of patent owners to offer differing interpretations of prior art in different proceedings. These written statements, which include documents, pleadings or evidence from proceedings that address the patent owner's statements, shall not be considered for any purpose other than to determine the proper meaning of the claims that are the subject of the request in a proceeding. Specifically, the Committee does not intend these statements to be a basis for the institution of a reexamination proceeding. Reexaminations will continue to be available only on the basis of "patents or printed publications."[FN42]

FN42. The scope of "patent and printed publication" prior art in the amended section 301 is intended to be coextensive with these terms in current section 102 of the title 35. Further, amendments made by Section 2 of the Act, which expand and contract the definition of certain other forms of prior art, are not intended to change the particular "patent or printed publication" prior art, which will continue to be the sole basis for initiating reexamination proceedings.

The Act also amends the *ex parte* reexamination procedure to allow the Director to institute a reexamination on the Director's own initiative if a substantial new question of patentability is raised by patents or publications.

The Act converts *inter partes* reexamination from an examinational to an adjudicative proceeding, and renames the proceeding "*inter partes* review."[5] The Act also makes the following improvements to this proceeding:

- **"Reasonable likelihood of success" for instituting *inter partes* review.** The threshold for initiating an *inter partes* review is elevated from "significant [*sic*][6] new question of patentability"—a standard that currently allows 95% of all requests to be granted—to a standard requiring petitioners to present information showing that their challenge has a reasonable likelihood of success. Satisfaction of the new threshold will be assessed based on the information presented both in the petition for the proceeding and in the patent owner's response to the petition.[7]
- **"Reasonably could have raised" estoppel applied to subsequent administrative proceedings.** A party that uses *inter partes* review is estopped from raising in a subsequent PTO proceeding (such as an *ex parte* reexamination or *inter partes* review) any issue that it raised or reasonably could have raised in the *inter partes* review.
- **Repeal of the 1999 limit.** The limit on challenging patents issued before 1999 in *inter partes* reexamination is eliminated; all patents can be challenged in *inter partes* review.
- **Preponderance burden.** Petitioners bear the burden of proving that a patent is invalid by a preponderance of the evidence in *inter partes* review.
- **Time limits during litigation.** Parties who want to use *inter partes* review during litigation are required to seek a proceeding within 12 months of being served with a complaint alleging infringement of the patent, and are barred from seeking or maintaining an *inter partes* review if they file an action for a declaratory judgment that the patent is invalid.

---

[5]*Star Envirotech, Inc. v. Redline Detection, LLC*, 2013 WL 1716068, at *1 (C.D. Cal. 2013) (noting that the AIA "revised and streamlined the *inter partes* reexamination process and renamed it the inter partes review process.").

[6]The patent statute did not call for a "significant" new question of patentability but instead for a "substantial" new question of patentability for both ex parte and inter partes reexaminations. 35 U.S.C.A. §§ 303, 313 (2006).

[7]A district court noted that the new, "reasonable likelihood" standard for granting inter partes reexaminations (which is the same standard as that for inter partes review, is higher than the prior standard of whether the petition raises a substantial new question of patentability. *Pragmatus AV, LLC v. Facebook, Inc.*, 2011 WL 4802958, *3 n.1 (N.D. Cal. 2011).

- **Discovery.** Parties may depose witnesses submitting affidavits or declarations and seek such discovery as the Patent Office determines is otherwise necessary in the interest of justice.
- **12- to 18-month deadline.** *Inter partes* review must be completed within 1 year of when the proceeding is instituted, except that the Office can extend this deadline by 6 months for good cause.
- **Oral hearing.** Each party has the right to request an oral hearing as part of an *inter partes* review.
- **Three-judge panels.** *Inter partes* reviews will be conducted before a panel of three Administrative Patent Judges. Decisions will be appealed directly to the Federal Circuit.

* * *

Section 6. Post-grant review proceedings.

Subsections (a) and (d) enact new chapters 31 and 32, which create adjudicative systems of post-grant and *inter partes* review. The parallel sections of these new chapters are as follows:

§§ 311 and 321. *Inter partes* review may be sought on the basis of patents and printed publications any time after a post-grant review is concluded or, if no such review is instituted, after the time for seeking such review has expired. Post-grant review may be sought on any invalidity ground during the first 12 months after a patent is issue[d] or reissued.

§§ 312 and 322. Petitions for review shall explain the basis for seeking review, shall identify the petitioner's real parties in interest and privies, and shall be made publicly available as soon as is practicable.

§§ 313 and 323. Patent owners may file a response to a petition for reviewing [*sic,* review] explaining why a review should not be instituted. §§ 314 and 324. *Inter partes* review shall not be instituted unless the information in the petition and response shows that there is a reasonable likelihood that a claim would be found invalid. Post-grant review shall not be instituted unless the information presented in the petition, if not rebutted, shows that it is more likely than not that a claim would be found invalid, or the petition raises a novel or unsettled legal question that is important to other patents or applications.

§§ 315 and 325. (a) Review may not be instituted if the petitioner has previously filed a civil action challenging the validity of the patent. The petitioner may, however, file a declaratory-judgment action challenging the validity of one or more claims in the patent on or after the day that he files the review petition, but such action is automatically stayed until the patent owner countersues for infringement.

(b) *Inter partes* review must be sought by a party within 12 months of the date when the party is served with a complaint for infringement. If a patent owner sues for infringement within 3 months of the patent's issue, a pending petition for post-grant review or the institution of such a proceeding may not serve as a basis for staying the court's consideration of the patent owner's motion for a preliminary injunction.

(c) The Director may allow other petitioners to join an *inter partes* or post-grant review.

(d) The Director may consolidate multiple proceedings or matters concerning the same patent and decline requests for repeated proceedings on the same question.

(e) *Inter partes* and post-grant petitioners are estopped from raising in a subsequent Office proceeding any issue that they raised or reasonably could have raised in the *inter partes* or post grant review, and *inter partes* petitioners are also estopped from raising in civil litigation or an ITC proceeding any issue that they raised or could have raised in the *inter partes* review. Post-grant petitioners are only estopped from raising in civil litigation or ITC proceedings those issues that they actually raised in the post-grant review.

(f) Post-grant review may not be used to challenge claims in a reissue patent that are the same as or narrower than claims in the original patent if the time for seeking review of the original patent has lapsed.

§§ 316 and 326. (a) The Director shall prescribe regulations that make the file in proceedings public; define standards for instituting reviews; allow submission of additional information; establish and govern review and its relationship to other proceedings; set a time limit for requesting joinder in *inter partes* review; set standards for discovery; prescribe sanctions for abuse of the proceedings; provide for protective orders for confidential information; allow the patent owner to file a response after an *inter partes* review has been instituted; allow the patent owner to amend the patent; provide either party with the right to an oral hearing; and set a 1-year time limit for completion of the proceeding, with a 6-month extension for good cause; and provide the petitioner with at least one opportunity to file written comments after the proceeding is instituted.

(b) In prescribing regulations, the Director shall consider the integrity of the patent system and the efficient operation of the Office.

(c) The Patent Trial and Appeal Board shall conduct review proceedings.

(d) The patent owner may submit one amendment with a reasonable number of substitute claims, and additional amendments either as agreed to by the parties for settlement, for good cause shown in post-grant review, or as prescribed in regulations by the Director in *inter partes* review.

(e) The challenger shall have the burden of providing [*sic*, proving] unpatentability by a preponderance of the evidence.

§§ 317 and 327. Parties may agree to settle review proceedings, in which case estoppel shall not apply and a copy of the settlement agreement shall be filed in the Office.

§§ 318 and 328. The Patent Trial and Appeal Board shall issue a final written decision and a certificate cancelling, confirming, or incorporating claims.

§§ 319 and 329. A party dissatisfied with a final written decision may appeal to the U.S. Court of Appeals for the Federal Circuit.

Subsections (b) and (e) of section 5 make technical and conforming amendments.

Subsections (c) and (f) require the Director to issue regulations implementing the new reviews within 1 year, and create transition provisions for proceedings pending between the enactment of the Act and the full implementation of the new reviews.[8]

§ 18:2 The new statute: *inter partes* review replaces *inter partes* reexamination

Section 6 of the AIA replaces the *inter partes* reexamination provisions, rewriting 35 U.S.C. Chapter 31 to read as follows.[1]

CHAPTER 31. INTER PARTES REVIEW

§ 311. Inter partes review

(a) IN GENERAL.— Subject to the provisions of this chapter, a person who is not the owner of a patent may file with the Office a petition to institute an inter partes review of the patent. The Director shall establish, by regulation, fees to be paid by the person requesting the review, in such amounts as the Director determines to be reasonable, considering the aggregate costs of the review.

(b) SCOPE.— A petitioner in an inter partes review may request to cancel as unpatentable 1 or more claims of a patent only on a ground that could be raised under section

---

[8]H. R. Rep. No. 112-98, pt. 1, pp. 45 to 48, 75 to 77 (2011).

[Section 18:2]

[1]AIA § 6 also provided several transitional provisions that were in place from September 16, 2011 through September 15, 2012 for the inter partes reexamination. The primary change was a change in the threshold for granting reexamination, which changed from a substantial new question of patentability to the new IPR standard of "a reasonable likelihood that the requester would prevail with respect to at least 1 of the claims challenged in the request . . ." 35 U.S.C.A. § 312 (transitional provision).

102 or 103 and only on the basis of prior art consisting of patents or printed publications.

(c) FILING DEADLINE.[2]— A petition for inter partes review shall be filed after the later of either—

(1) the date that is 9 months after the grant of a patent or issuance of a reissue of a patent;[3] or

(2) if a post-grant review is instituted under chapter 32, the date of the termination of such post-grant review.

§ 312. Petitions

(a) REQUIREMENTS OF PETITION.— A petition filed under section 311 may be considered only if—

(1) the petition is accompanied by payment of the fee established by the Director under section 311;

(2) the petition identifies all real parties in interest;

(3) the petition identifies, in writing and with particularity, each claim challenged, the grounds on which the challenge to each claim is based, and the evidence that supports the grounds for the challenge to each claim, including—

(A) copies of patents and printed publications that the petitioner relies upon in support of the petition; and

(B) affidavits or declarations of supporting evidence and opinions, if the petitioner relies on expert opinions;

(4) the petition provides such other information as the Director may require by regulation; and

(5) the petitioner provides copies of any of the documents required under paragraphs (2), (3), and (4) to the patent owner or, if applicable, the designated representative of the patent owner.

(b) PUBLIC AVAILABILITY.— As soon as practicable after the receipt of a petition under section 311, the Director shall make the petition available to the public.

§ 313. Preliminary response to petition

---

[2]H.R. 6621, § 1(d)(1) amended the patent statute to state that 35 U.S.C.A. § 311(c) does not apply to petitions to institute inter partes proceedings of patents not described in AIA § 3(n)(1), *i.e.*, are not first-inventor-to-file patents. As such, for first-to-invent patents, there would be no wait before filing a petition seeking IPR. This eliminates the nine-month "dead zone" that would otherwise exist for non-FITF patents. *Inter partes* review can commence forthwith against patents issued after September 16, 2011, provided they are not FITF patents.

[3]H.R. 6621, § 1(d)(2) amended § 311(c) of the patent statute to strike "or issuance of a reissue of a patent." The statute as thus amended allows *inter partes* review immediately for reissue patents, without a nine-month wait.

If an inter partes review petition is filed under section 311, the patent owner shall have the right to file a preliminary response to the petition, within a time period set by the Director, that sets forth reasons why no inter partes review should be instituted based upon the failure of the petition to meet any requirement of this chapter.

§ 314. Institution of inter partes review

(a) THRESHOLD.— The Director may not authorize an inter partes review to be instituted unless the Director determines that the information presented in the petition filed under section 311 and any response filed under section 313 shows that there is a reasonable likelihood that the petitioner would prevail with respect to at least 1 of the claims challenged in the petition.

(b) TIMING.— The Director shall determine whether to institute an inter partes review under this chapter pursuant to a petition filed under section 311 within 3 months after—

(1) receiving a preliminary response to the petition under section 313; or

(2) if no such preliminary response is filed, the last date on which such response may be filed.

(c) NOTICE.— The Director shall notify the petitioner and patent owner, in writing, of the Director's determination under subsection (a), and shall make such notice available to the public as soon as is practicable. Such notice shall include the date on which the review shall commence.

(d) NO APPEAL.— The determination by the Director whether to institute an inter partes review under this section shall be final and nonappealable.

§ 315. Relation to other proceedings or actions

(a) INFRINGER'S CIVIL ACTION.—

(1) INTER PARTES REVIEW BARRED BY CIVIL ACTION.— An inter partes review may not be instituted if, before the date on which the petition for such a review is filed, the petitioner or real party in interest filed a civil action challenging the validity of a claim of the patent.

(2) STAY OF CIVIL ACTION.— If the petitioner or real party in interest files a civil action challenging the validity of a claim of the patent on or after the date on which the petitioner files a petition for inter partes review of the patent, that civil action shall be automatically stayed until either—

(A) the patent owner moves the court to lift the stay;

(B) the patent owner files a civil action or counterclaim

alleging that the petitioner or real party in interest has infringed the patent; or

(C) the petitioner or real party in interest moves the court to dismiss the civil action.

(3) TREATMENT OF COUNTERCLAIM.— A counterclaim challenging the validity of a claim of a patent does not constitute a civil action challenging the validity of a claim of a patent for purposes of this subsection.

(b) PATENT OWNER'S ACTION.— An inter partes review may not be instituted if the petition requesting the proceeding is filed more than 1 year after the date on which the petitioner, real party in interest, or privy of the petitioner is served with a complaint alleging infringement of the patent. The time limitation set forth in the preceding sentence shall not apply to a request for joinder under subsection (c).

(c) JOINDER.— If the Director institutes an inter partes review, the Director, in his or her discretion, may join as a party to that inter partes review any person who properly files a petition under section 311 that the Director, after receiving a preliminary response under section 313 or the expiration of the time for filing such a response, determines warrants the institution of an inter partes review under section 314.

(d) MULTIPLE PROCEEDINGS.— Notwithstanding sections 135(a), 251, and 252, and chapter 30, during the pendency of an inter partes review, if another proceeding or matter involving the patent is before the Office, the Director may determine the manner in which the inter partes review or other proceeding or matter may proceed, including providing for stay, transfer, consolidation, or termination of any such matter or proceeding.

(e) ESTOPPEL.—

(1) PROCEEDINGS BEFORE THE OFFICE.— The petitioner in an inter partes review of a claim in a patent under this chapter that results in a final written decision under section 318(a), or the real party in interest or privy of the petitioner, may not request or maintain a proceeding before the Office with respect to that claim on any ground that the petitioner raised or reasonably could have raised during that inter partes review.

(2) CIVIL ACTIONS AND OTHER PROCEEDINGS.— The petitioner in an inter partes review of a claim in a patent under this chapter that results in a final written decision under section 318(a), or the real party in interest or privy of the petitioner, may not assert either in a civil action arising in

whole or in part under section 1338 of title 28 or in a proceeding before the International Trade Commission under section 337 of the Tariff Act of 1930 that the claim is invalid on any ground that the petitioner raised or reasonably could have raised during that inter partes review.

§ 316. Conduct of inter partes review

(a) REGULATIONS.— The Director shall prescribe regulations—

(1) providing that the file of any proceeding under this chapter shall be made available to the public, except that any petition or document filed with the intent that it be sealed shall, if accompanied by a motion to seal, be treated as sealed pending the outcome of the ruling on the motion;

(2) setting forth the standards for the showing of sufficient grounds to institute a review under section 314(a);

(3) establishing procedures for the submission of supplemental information after the petition is filed;

(4) establishing and governing inter partes review under this chapter and the relationship of such review to other proceedings under this title;

(5) setting forth standards and procedures for discovery of relevant evidence, including that such discovery shall be limited to—

(A) the deposition of witnesses submitting affidavits or declarations; and

(B) what is otherwise necessary in the interest of justice;

(6) prescribing sanctions for abuse of discovery, abuse of process, or any other improper use of the proceeding, such as to harass or to cause unnecessary delay or an unnecessary increase in the cost of the proceeding;

(7) providing for protective orders governing the exchange and submission of confidential information;

(8) providing for the filing by the patent owner of a response to the petition under section 313 after an inter partes review has been instituted, and requiring that the patent owner file with such response, through affidavits or declarations, any additional factual evidence and expert opinions on which the patent owner relies in support of the response;

(9) setting forth standards and procedures for allowing the patent owner to move to amend the patent under subsection (d) to cancel a challenged claim or propose a reasonable number of substitute claims, and ensuring that any information submitted by the patent owner in support of any amendment entered under subsection (d) is made available to the public as part of the prosecution history of the patent;

(10) providing either party with the right to an oral hearing as part of the proceeding;

(11) requiring that the final determination in an inter partes review be issued not later than 1 year after the date on which the Director notices the institution of a review under this chapter, except that the Director may, for good cause shown, extend the 1-year period by not more than 6 months, and may adjust the time periods in this paragraph in the case of joinder under section 315(c);

(12) setting a time period for requesting joinder under section 315(c); and

(13) providing the petitioner with at least 1 opportunity to file written comments within a time period established by the Director.

(b) CONSIDERATIONS.— In prescribing regulations under this section, the Director shall consider the effect of any such regulation on the economy, the integrity of the patent system, the efficient administration of the Office, and the ability of the Office to timely complete proceedings instituted under this chapter.

(c) PATENT TRIAL AND APPEAL BOARD.— The Patent Trial and Appeal Board shall, in accordance with section 6, conduct each inter partes review instituted under this chapter.

(d) AMENDMENT OF THE PATENT.—

(1) IN GENERAL.—During an inter partes review instituted under this chapter, the patent owner may file 1 motion to amend the patent in 1 or more of the following ways:

(A) Cancel any challenged patent claim.

(B) For each challenged claim, propose a reasonable number of substitute claims.

(2) ADDITIONAL MOTIONS.— Additional motions to amend may be permitted upon the joint request of the petitioner and the patent owner to materially advance the settlement of a proceeding under section 317, or as permitted by regulations prescribed by the Director.

(3) SCOPE OF CLAIMS.— An amendment under this subsection may not enlarge the scope of the claims of the patent or introduce new matter.

(e) EVIDENTIARY STANDARDS.— In an inter partes review instituted under this chapter, the petitioner shall have the burden of proving a proposition of unpatentability by a preponderance of the evidence.

§ 317. Settlement

(a) IN GENERAL.— An inter partes review instituted

under this chapter shall be terminated with respect to any petitioner upon the joint request of the petitioner and the patent owner, unless the Office has decided the merits of the proceeding before the request for termination is filed. If the inter partes review is terminated with respect to a petitioner under this section, no estoppel under section 315(e) shall attach to the petitioner, or to the real party in interest or privy of the petitioner, on the basis of that petitioner's institution of that inter partes review. If no petitioner remains in the inter partes review, the Office may terminate the review or proceed to a final written decision under section 318(a).

(b) AGREEMENTS IN WRITING.— Any agreement or understanding between the patent owner and a petitioner, including any collateral agreements referred to in such agreement or understanding, made in connection with, or in contemplation of, the termination of an inter partes review under this section shall be in writing and a true copy of such agreement or understanding shall be filed in the Office before the termination of the inter partes review as between the parties. At the request of a party to the proceeding, the agreement or understanding shall be treated as business confidential information, shall be kept separate from the file of the involved patents, and shall be made available only to Federal Government agencies on written request, or to any person on a showing of good cause.

§ 318. Decision of the Board

(a) FINAL WRITTEN DECISION.— If an inter partes review is instituted and not dismissed under this chapter, the Patent Trial and Appeal Board shall issue a final written decision with respect to the patentability of any patent claim challenged by the petitioner and any new claim added under section 316(d).

(b) CERTIFICATE.— If the Patent Trial and Appeal Board issues a final written decision under subsection (a) and the time for appeal has expired or any appeal has terminated, the Director shall issue and publish a certificate canceling any claim of the patent finally determined to be unpatentable, confirming any claim of the patent determined to be patentable, and incorporating in the patent by operation of the certificate any new or amended claim determined to be patentable.

(c) INTERVENING RIGHTS.— Any proposed amended or new claim determined to be patentable and incorporated into a patent following an inter partes review under this chapter shall have the same effect as that specified in section 252 for reissued patents on the right of any person who made, purchased, or used within the United States, or imported into the United States, anything patented by such proposed amended or new claim, or who made substantial preparation therefor, before the issuance of a certificate under subsection (b).

(d) DATA ON LENGTH OF REVIEW.— The Office shall make available to the public data describing the length of time between the institution of, and the issuance of a final written decision under subsection (a) for, each inter partes review.

§ 319. Appeal

A party dissatisfied with the final written decision of the Patent Trial and Appeal Board under section 318(a) may appeal the decision pursuant to sections 141 through 144. Any party to the inter partes review shall have the right to be a party to the appeal.

§ 18:3 *Inter partes* review procedures generally

An *inter partes* post review is one of the four "trials" heard by the PTAB and as such is subject to the trial rules and procedures set forth in 37 C.F.R. §§ 42.1 to 42.80. The trial rules are covered in Chapter 15. The Director also issued additional rules that are specific to *inter partes* review procedures, and these are set forth at §§ 42.100 to 42.123.

During *inter partes* review, a claim of an unexpired patent is given its "broadest reasonable construction in light of the specification of the patent in which it appears."[1] One reason given by the USPTO for this broad construction is that the patent owner is entitled to amend the claims at least once during the proceeding.[2] This is unlike patent litigation in federal court where the patent claims cannot be amended.

[Section 18:3]

[1]37 C.F.R. § 42.100(b).

[2]For an interesting discussion of why the broadest, reasonable interpretation is used and the standard of review, see *Flo Healthcare Solutions, LLC v. Kappos*, 697 F.3d 1367, 104 U.S.P.Q.2d 1834 (Fed. Cir. 2012) (additional views of Judge Plager and additional views of Judge Newman). See also, *SAP America, Inc. v. Versata Development Group, Inc.*, CBM2012-00001, Final Written Decision, pp. 7-19 (PTAB June 11, 2013) (ruling *inter alia* that the PTAB is not bound to apply a claim construction of a district court determined in enforcement litigation on the challenged patent).

Because the patent owner has the opportunity to amend claims to distinguish over the prior art (or to address other problems), the Office believes this broad interpretation is fair to the patent owner.[3] As will be seen, the right to amend is fairly constrained, however, by the applicable rules and the PTAB policy on page limits.

The PTAB will administer the *inter partes* review proceeding so that its pendency before the Board after the proceeding is instituted (which may take six months) is normally one year or less, but that pendency can be extended by up to six additional months for good cause shown.[4] However, the Office anticipates that "extensions of the one year period are anticipated to be rare."[5] On the other hand, the schedule can also be lengthened in the case of a joinder with another proceeding.[6] This one-year term does not include any time for appeals, which would be added to the one year.

Inter partes reviews cannot begin until after the term for a post-grant review expires.[7]

§ 18:4 Filing a petition for *inter partes* review

To obtain an *inter partes* review, one files a petition with the USPTO. The petition must meet certain requirements to avoid automatic rejection. These requirements are set forth in the statute and the rules adopted for *inter partes* proceedings. The following petition checklist may be helpful:

Checklist for IPR Petition

- Certifications:
  - The patent is available for *inter partes* review. § 42.104(a).[1]
  - The petitioner is not barred from challenging the

[3]77 Fed. Reg. 48680, 48688 (Aug. 14, 2012) ("Changes to Implement Inter Partes Review, Post-Grant Review Proceedings, and Transitional Program for Covered Business Method Patents; Final Rule), citing *In re Yamamoto*, 740 F.2d 1569, 1571–72, 222 U.S.P.Q. 934 (Fed. Cir. 1984); see also discussion at pp. 48697–98.

[4]37 C.F.R. § 42.100(c).

[5]77 Fed. Reg. 48680, 48695 (Aug. 14, 2012).

[6]37 C.F.R. § 42.100(c).

[7]35 U.S.C.A. § 311(c); 37 C.F.R. § 42.102(a).

[Section 18:4]

[1]References are to 37 C.F.R. unless otherwise stated.

claims on the grounds identified in the petition. § 42.101(a). A petitioner needs to certify that:

- ☐ Neither the petitioner nor its real party in interest filed a civil action challenging the validity of any claim of the patent. 35 U.S.C. § 315(a)(1), 37 C.F.R. § 42.101(a).
- ☐ If the challenged patent is an FITF patent, the PGR review period (1st nine months) has ended, and any PGR that was commenced against any of the patents for which IPR is sought has terminated. § 42.102(a).[2]
- ☐ None of the petitioner, the real party in interest, and privies of the petitioner was served more than 1 year ago with a complaint for infringement on the challenged patent. § 42.102(b); 35 U.S.C. § 315(b).

  - The petitioner, real party-in-interest, and privy are not estopped from challenging the claims on the grounds identified in the petition. § 42.101(c); § 42.104(a).
  - The petitioner is not the patent owner. 35 U.S.C. § 311(a), 37 C.F.R. § 42.101.
- Any limit on the number of IPRs for the year has not been exceeded. § 42.102(b).
- Include the proper filing fee. §§ 42.103, 42.15(b).
- Include the mandatory notices (§ 42.8) identifying:
  - each real party-in-interest for the petitioner,
  - all related judicial and administrative matters,
  - petitioner's lead and back-up counsel, and
  - the service information for petitioner.
- State the precise relief requested. § 42.22(a)(1), (b). See also § 42.104(b).
- Show all requirements of any rule in 37 C.F.R. Part 1 that ordinarily governs the relief sought (along with showings required in Part 42). § 42.22(b).

---

[2] H.R. 6621, § 1(d)(1) amended the patent statute to state that 35 U.S.C.A. § 311(c) does not apply to petitions to institute *inter partes* proceedings of patents not described in AIA § 3(n)(1), *i.e.*, are not first-inventor-to-file patents. As such, for first-to-invent patents, there would be no wait before filing a petition seeking IPR. This eliminates the nine-month "dead zone" that would otherwise exist for non-FITF patents. *Inter partes* review can commence forthwith against patents issued after September 16, 2011, provided they are not FITF patents.

- Provide a full statement of the reasons for relief, including a detailed explanation of the significance of the evidence, including material facts, and the governing law, rules, and precedent. § 42.22(a)(2).
- Provide a statement of facts. § 42.22(c).
- For each challenged claim, state:
  - the claim itself. § 42.104(b)(1).
  - the specific statutory grounds under 35 U.S.C. §§ 102(b) or 103 on which the challenge is based; the only prior art that can be considered are patents or other printed publications. 35 U.S.C. § 311(b) (2011). § 42.104(b)(2).
  - how the challenged claim should be construed. § 42.104(b)(3).
  - how the construed claim is unpatentable under the specified grounds, including where each claim element is found in the prior art. § 42.104(b)(4).
  - the exhibit number of the supporting evidence. § 42.104(b)(5).
- Copies of the evidence relied upon. § 42.6(c); 35 U.S.C. § 312(a)(5).
- Format and citation requirements. §§ 42.6, 42.13.
- Page limit of 60 pages. § 42.24.
  - Optional motion to waive page limits. § 42.24(a)(2).
- Certificate of service on correspondence address of record. § 42.6(e).
- Duty of candor disclosures. § 42.11.
- Optional motion to seal. § 42.55.

* * *

The petition must certify affirmatively that the patent is available for *inter partes* review and that the petitioner is neither barred nor estopped from challenging the claims on the grounds identified in the petition.[2] Omitting this information results in an incomplete petition.

The statute limits the right to file a petition. One limitation concerns prior civil actions. A petitioner can be barred by a prior civil action under 35 U.S.C.A. § 315(a), which provides in pertinent part:

---

[2]37 C.F.R. § 42.104(a).

35 USC § 315—Relation to other proceedings or actions

(a) Infringer's Civil Action.—

(1) Inter partes review barred by civil action.—An inter partes review may not be instituted if, before the date on which the petition for such a review is filed, the petitioner or real party in interest filed a civil action challenging the validity of a claim of the patent.

***

(3) Treatment of counterclaim.—A counterclaim challenging the validity of a claim of a patent does not constitute a civil action challenging the validity of a claim of a patent for purposes of this subsection.

However, a petitioner was *not* estopped under this statute where it had earlier sued the exclusive licensee of the patent for a declaration of no infringement (not a declaration of invalidity) and had, after receiving a counterclaim in that civil suit, raised an affirmative defense of invalidity. In other words, the petitioner had never asserted an independent claim of invalidity of this patent in a civil action and the petitioner still had standing to seek an IPR.[3]

Another limitation concerns timeliness. Turning to the relationship of the IPR to a patent owner's civil action, 35 U.S.C.A. § 315(b), provides:

(b) Patent Owner's Action.—An inter partes review may not be instituted if the petition requesting the proceeding is filed more than 1 year after the date on which the petitioner, real party in interest, or privy of the petitioner is served with a complaint alleging infringement of the patent. The time limitation set forth in the preceding sentence shall not apply to a request for joinder under subsection (c).

Under this statute, the PTAB cannot institute *inter partes* review based on a petition filed more than one year after the date on which the petitioner, real party in interest, or privy of the petitioner is "served with a complaint" alleging infringement.[4] After that one year period, that petitioner is barred from filing a petition seeking IPR of that patent. The PTO final rules require the petition to state that the petitioner is neither barred nor estopped from requesting IPR on the grounds identified in the petition, so the petition

[3] *Ariosa Diagnostics v. Isis Innovation Limited*, IPR2012-00022, Paper No. 20 (PTAB Feb. 12, 2013).

[4] 35 U.S.C.A. § 315(b); 37 C.F.R. § 42.101(b).

should address the one year requirement.

The beginning of the one year term has been litigated. In one case, the PTAB decided that "served with a complaint" calls for service of a summons along with the complaint, and receipt of a copy of a complaint without a summons does not start the one-year clock.[5]

The time for filing an IPR petition depends on whether the challenged patent is a first-inventor-to-file (FITF) patent. If it is an FITF patent, then the petition for *inter partes* review must be filed at least nine (9) months *after* the original patent issue date or the date of issue of a reissue patent, or, if a post-grant review is instituted, then after the date of termination of that proceeding.[6] However, if the challenged patent is not an FITF patent, then the nine-month waiting period does not apply.[7]

The USPTO Director may limit the number of *inter partes* reviews that can be instituted during each of the first four years in which the *inter partes* procedure is in effect. Notices will be provided in the Official Gazette or Federal Register, and petitions filed after the stated limit has been reached will be treated as untimely.[8]

The petitioner is required to submit a fee without which no filing date will be given to the petition.[9] The PTO rules as originally adopted set a fee of $27,200 for seeking review of between one and 20 claims, with a surcharge of $600.00 for

---

[5] *Motorola Mobility LLC v. Arnouse*, IPR 2013-00010, Paper No. 20 (PTAB Jan. 30, 2013) (the one year time period of § 315(b) affords defendants an opportunity to fully analyze the patent claims but does not create an open-ended process; rejecting the contention that the one-year period would begin to run even before the petitioner is a defendant); *Larson Archery Co. v. Mathews, Inc.*, 2013 WL 139472, at *2 (D. Utah 2013) (stating that the AIA" streamlined the *inter partes* reexamination process and shortened the duration of reexamination proceedings").

[6] 37 C.F.R. § 42.102(a).

[7] H.R. 6621, Pub. L. 112–274 (2013), § 1(d)(1) amended the patent statute to state that 35 U.S.C.A. § 311(c) does not apply to petitions to institute *inter partes* proceedings of patents not described in AIA § 3(n)(1), *i.e.*, are not first-inventor-to-file patents. As such, for first-to-invent patents, there would be no wait before filing a petition seeking IPR. This eliminates the nine-month "dead zone" that would otherwise exist for non-FITF patents. *Inter partes* review can commence forthwith against patents issued after September 16, 2011, provided they are not FITF patents.

[8] 37 C.F.R. § 42.102(b).

[9] 37 C.F.R. § 42.103.

each added claim.[10] Even if no IPR is declared, no refund of the fee was given. The PTO revised its fee schedule to replace the large single fee with smaller fees due at progressive stages of an IPR, thus giving some relief to unsuccessful IPR petitioners. Under the current rule (37 C.F.R. § 42.15(a)), the petitioner pays two separate fees with the petition. The first fee is the request fee, which as of August 2013 was $9,000 plus $200 for each challenged claim in excess of 20. The second fee is the trial fee, which as of that same date was $14,000 plus $400 for each challenged claim in excess of 15. The second fee is refundable if no *inter partes* review is instituted.

37 C.F.R. § 42.104 sets forth the required contents of the petition. It begins by referring back to four provisions of the trial practice rules. These have been discussed *supra* in Chapter 15 directed to PTAB trials. Briefly, however, the petition must meet a certain general format requirement.[11] A petition requesting an *inter partes* review is limited to 60 pages, but the page limit does not include the statement of material facts, the tables of contents or authorities, the certificate of service, nor the appendix of exhibits.

Arguments cannot be incorporated by reference. Each document must indicate that it was served and include a certificate of service. The petition requires a mandatory notice set forth in 37 C.F.R. § 42.8 identifying each real party-in-interest for the party, any related matters, the lead counsel and back-up counsel, and specifying the service information.

Also, the petition must meet the 37 C.F.R. § 42.22 general requirements for all petitions and motions calling for, *inter alia*, a full statement of the reasons for relief requested and optionally a statement of individually numbered material facts.

The petition must state the precise relief requested. It must also identify, for each challenged claim: the claim itself; the specific statutory grounds under 35 U.S.C. §§ 102(b) or 103 on which the challenge is based; how the challenged

[10]37 C.F.R. §§ 42.103 and 42.15(a).

[11]It must be on 8.5" x 11" paper, except for exhibits that require larger size to preserve details. If the typing uses a proportional font, it must be 14 point or larger, and if the typing uses a monospaced font, it cannot have more than 10 characters per inch or 4 characters per centimeter. The document must be double-spaced except for claim charts, headings, tables of contents and authorities, indices, signature blocks, and certificates of service. Block quotations may be 1.5 spacing.

claim should be construed; how the construed claim is unpatentable under the specified grounds; and the exhibit number of the supporting evidence. The petition must specify where each element of the claim can be found in the prior art.[12] The grounds that can be asserted for invalidating a claim are only lack of novelty or obviousness over prior art patents or other printed publications.[13] The petitioner must provide copies of the art with the petition.[14]

The petition need not reiterate claim challenges individually. Grouping is permitted:

> The rules do not prohibit petitioners from grouping claims where the basis for the alleged unpatentability of the grouped claims is the same. When grouping claims, the petitioner must provide sufficient notice as to the merits of the challenge for each claim so challenged.[15]

The objective of the petitioner is to meet the threshold requirement by setting forth sufficient information to show that "there is a reasonable likelihood that the petitioner would prevail with respect to at least 1 of the claims challenged in the petition."[16] The alternative test available in post-grant reviews is inapplicable for *inter partes* reviews. (That inapplicable test is whether the petition raises a novel or unsettled legal question that is important to other patents or patent applications.[17])

The petition must be served in the manner specified by 37 C.F.R. § 42.205. This includes serving the patent owner at the correspondence address of record. The petitioner optionally may serve the petition and supporting evidence at any other known address for the patent owner which is likely to effect service.[18] The parties may agree to effect service electronically if they desire. Service may be made by Express Mail® or other means at least as fast and reliable as Express Mail®. Personal service is not required but not forbidden.[19]

If the USPTO receives a rule-compliant petition which is

---

[12] 37 C.F.R. § 42.104(a).

[13] 35 U.S.C.A. § 311(b) (2011).

[14] 35 U.S.C.A. § 312(a)(5) (2011); 37 C.F.R. § 42.6(c).

[15] 77 Fed. Reg. 48680, 48696 (Aug. 14, 2012).

[16] 35 U.S.C.A. § 314(a) (2011).

[17] 35 U.S.C.A. § 324(b) (2011).

[18] 37 C.F.R. § 42.105(a).

[19] See *Innolux Corp. v. Semiconductor Energy Laboratory Co., Ltd.*, IPR 2013-00066, Paper No. 4, (PTAB Nov. 5, 2012) rejecting the petition

complete, shows valid service, and is accompanied by the filing fee, then the USPTO will grant it a filing date.[20] If the petition is incomplete, however, the filing date will be denied, and the Office will dismiss the petition unless the deficiency is not corrected within one month of a notice of the incomplete petition.[21]

§ 18:5 Patent owner preliminary response (3 months after the petition)[1]

The PTAB cannot immediately grant petitions that receive a filing date.[2] It will not act to institute a trial until the patent owner has had three months to submit a preliminary response to the petition or has submitted a waiver notifying the PTAB that the patent owner intends not to submit a response.[3]

Sometimes, the Board is dissatisfied with one or more of the alleged grounds that it denies them even before the patent owner's time for preliminary response is due. In one ruling involving a petition for a CBM review, the Board rejected 196 of the 422 alleged grounds even before the patent owner submitted a preliminary response, stating, "[W]e regard Petitioner's stated reasoning . . . to be unsupported by the record and simply unpersuasive." *Liberty Mutual Ins. Co. v. Progressive Casualty Ins. Co.*, CBM2012-00003, Paper No. 8, p. 12 (PTAB Oct. 25, 2012).

The preliminary response is optional, and its content is limited to reasons why no *inter partes* review should be commenced under 35 U.S.C. § 314.[4] The patent owner's preliminary response is allowed to include evidence other than new testimonial evidence, which cannot be included unless authorized by the Board.[5] However, the USPTO has indicated that patent owners can submit testimony in a preliminary

---

because "Service was not properly made upon the Patent Owner."

[20] 37 C.F.R. § 42.106.

[21] 37 C.F.R. § 42.106(b).

[Section 18:5]

[1] Before the three months, the respondent must file its mandatory notices. These are due 21 days after service of the petition. 37 C.F.R. § 42.8.

[2] 35 U.S.C.A. § 314(b).

[3] 37 C.F.R. § 42.107(b).

[4] 37 C.F.R. § 42.107(a).

[5] 37 C.F.R. § 42.107(a) and (c).

response in appropriate circumstances:

> In addition to documentary evidence, patent owners may provide testimonial evidence in a preliminary response where the interests of justice so require, *e.g.*, to demonstrate that petitioner's real party in interest is estopped from challenging patent claims. *See* Practice Guide, Section II.C.[6]

The preliminary response has a page limitation equal to the page limit for the petition. Since the page limit for an *inter partes* review petition is 60 pages, the patent owner is entitled to file a preliminary response of 60 pages.[7]

The ability of the patent owner to file a preliminary response before any substantive review of the petition by the USPTO is new. Under the now-superseded *inter partes* reexamination procedure, the patent owner was prohibited from filing anything until after the USPTO had issued a first Office Action on the merits.[8] This new procedural development of a patent owner's preliminary response should speed up the process.

While the preliminary response is prohibited from amending the patent,[9] the patent owner may file a statutory disclaimer that disclaims one or more claims of the patent. In such event, no *inter partes* review will be instituted with respect to the disclaimed claims.[10] If the patent owner were willing to disclaim all of the challenged claims, it can prevent the proceeding from being instituted.

§ 18:6 Institution of *inter partes* review: beginning of "trial"

After the Board receives the preliminary response to the petition or a waiver of a preliminary response, or after three months have transpired during which time the patent owner

[6]See USPTO "Reference Guide to Statutory Provisions and Final Rules Effective on September 16, 2012," slide 216. Available at http://www.uspto.gov/aia_implementation/120910-aia-reference-guide-to-statutory-provisions-and-final-rules.pdf, visited Oct. 27, 2012.

[7]37 C.F.R. § 42.24(b)(1).

[8]37 C.F.R. § 1.939 provided: "Unauthorized papers in inter partes reexamination. (a) If an unauthorized paper is filed by any party at any time during the inter partes reexamination proceeding it will not be considered and may be returned. (b) Unless otherwise authorized, no paper shall be filed prior to the initial Office action on the merits of the inter partes reexamination."

[9]37 C.F.R. § 42.107(d).

[10]37 C.F.R. § 42.107(e).

might have filed a preliminary response, the Board has three months to rule on the petition. This three month term for decision is the maximum allowed by statute.[1] The statute does not require the Board to wait until the end of its permitted time. In practice, the PTAB has issued its decisions on whether to institute the proceeding without using the whole three months within which it must act, and instead the PTAB often issues its ruling six to eight weeks after the patent owner's preliminary response. Conceptually, there would be no reason why the Board could not *reject* a petition even before the time expires for a patent owner's preliminary response if the Board decides that the petition lacks sufficient merit to meet the burden of proof, even if unrebutted. That dismissal would not be unfair to the patent owner. It would be unfair, however, for the Board to *grant* a petition prior to the patent owner time to submit its preliminary response. However, the procedure chosen by Congress specifies that the ruling by the Board will be "after" the preliminary response of the patent owner is received or its time for filing expires.[2]

The standard for instituting the *inter partes r*eview is whether "there is a reasonable likelihood that the petitioner would prevail with respect to at least 1 of the claims challenged in the petition."[3] The Board will consider any patent owner preliminary response that has been timely filed.[4]

The "reasonable likelihood" standard is the subject of some characterizations. Statements in the legislative history or by legislators call this an elevated standard. Addressing this issue, the USPTO has stated, "A 'reasonable likelihood' requirement is a lower threshold than a 'more likely than not' requirement."[5] The Office still uses the "substantial new question of patentability" threshold for *ex parte* reexamination, as mandated by 35 U.S.C. § 303. Upon enactment, AIA § 6(c)(3) transitional provisions changed the standard for *inter partes* reexamination from that substantial new question of patentability to be the same as the current standard

---

[Section 18:6]

[1] 35 U.S.C.A. § 314(c).

[2] 35 U.S.C.A. § 314(c).

[3] 35 U.S.C.A. § 314(a); 37 C.F.R. § 42.108(c).

[4] 37 C.F.R. § 42.108(c).

[5] 77 Fed. Reg. 48680, 48702 (Aug. 14, 2012).

for *inter partes* review.[6]

If the Board institutes an *inter partes* review, it may select some of the challenged claims and reject others, and it may select all or some of the grounds of unpatentability for any claim it has selected.[7] The Board is free to accept all, some, or none of the claims, and all, some, or none of the grounds. The Board can deny any (or all) of the grounds at any time prior to institution of the review.[8]

If the Board decides to proceed with *inter partes* review, it will notify the petitioner and patent owner in writing and make the notice available to the public. The notice will include the date on which the review will commence.[9] Typically, the decision to institute is a detailed written opinion by the judges of the PTAB panel assigned to the petition. The decision reviews the issues, performs a claim interpretation, and indicates (preliminary) findings sufficient to meet the standard for commencing IPR. For example, one early IPR decision included the following paragraph after discussing each of the references alleged to anticipate one or more of the challenged claims:

> Turning first to Petitioner's anticipation contentions, the Board is persuaded by the analysis of each of Perlman (EX1003), Yohe (EX1005), and Santos (EX1004) set forth in the Petition and supporting materials, including Appendix A, that there is a reasonable likelihood that Petitioner will prevail on those contentions as to claims 1 and 3. As to Perlman, the "digital digests" required by the claims are met by the "unique, fixed-length digest 'signature' whose contents are substantially less than those of the [data base]." Perlman col. 4, ll.13-20. In Yohe, this limitation is met by the "signature" generated through the MD5 or CRC protocols. Yohe col.11, ll.56-63, col.13, ll.30-39. In Santos, the compressor module calculates fixed-size "fingerprints" from packet data of arbitrary size. Santos 7-8. Similarly, Petitioner has established a reasonable likelihood that the other claim limitations are met by these references. *See* EX1001, App. A 2-11. In summary, we

---

[6]A district court noted that the new, "reasonable likelihood" standard for granting inter partes reexaminations (which is the same standard as that for inter partes review, is higher than the prior standard of whether the petition raises a substantial new question of patentability. *Pragmatus AV, LLC v. Facebook, Inc.*, 2011 WL 4802958, *3 n.1 (N.D. Cal. 2011). *See also Evolve Composites, Inc. v. Diversitech Corp.*, 2013 WL 958828, at *1 n.1 (N.D. Ga. 2013).

[7]37 C.F.R. § 42.108(a).

[8]37 C.F.R. § 42.108(b).

[9]35 U.S.C.A. § 314(c).

> determine that Petitioner has met the threshold standard of demonstrating a reasonable likelihood of prevailing on the issue of whether these claims are anticipated by any one of Perlman, Yohe, or Santos.[10]

Likewise, when the Board accepts a proposed assertion of unpatentability due to obviousness, it explains its reasoning. The following is an example from the same case quoted immediately above:

> This independent system claim is similar to claim 1 with one significant difference: in claim 10 the receiver/computer includes means for storing the digital digest received from the network "in its permanent storage memory." Petitioner recognizes that Perlman uses non-permanent memory (RAM) for its cache. Pet. 9. *Also see* EX1007, Long Decl. 13. Petitioner points out that Perlman is not limited to this embodiment. Pet. 9. Nevertheless, in the absence of a specific disclosure of a permanent memory as claimed, we are not persuaded that Petitioner has sufficiently demonstrated that there is a reasonable likelihood of prevailing on the assertion that Perlman anticipates claim 10. *See* infra. However, for the reasons stated above we conclude that Petitioner has sufficiently demonstrated that there is a reasonable likelihood of prevailing on the contention that claim 10 is unpatentable over the combination of Perlman and Yohe. As there is evidence that Yohe discloses use of permanent memory (disc) for cache storage (EX1007, Long Decl. 13) and at least a rational basis for combining the references (*id.* at 11-18) there is at least a reasonable likelihood of Petitioner prevailing on the assertion that claim 10 would have been obvious over the Perlman/Yohe combination.[11]

The Director's determination whether to institute an *inter partes* review is final and non-appealable.[12] Although the petition is final and not appealable, the petitioner may request rehearing without any prior authorization from the Board. The petitioner bears the burden of showing that the decision should be modified and must specifically identify all the matters the petitioner believes the Board misapprehended or overlooked and the place where each matter was previously addressed. The time within which a request for rehearing must be filed is 30 days after the final decision to institute or

---

[10] *Microsoft Corp. v. Proxyconn, Inc.*, IPR 2012-00026, Paper No. 17, p. 18 (PTAB Dec. 21, 2012).

[11] *Microsoft Corp. v. Proxyconn, Inc.*, IPR 2012-00026, Paper No. 17, pp. 19-20 (PTAB Dec. 21, 2012).

[12] 35 U.S.C.A. § 314(d); 37 C.F.R. § 42.71(c).

not institute a trial.[13] The standard of review is abuse of discretion.[14]

The ruling on the petition marks the end of the preliminary period and, if the petition is granted to any extent, the beginning of "trial" at the PTAB.

§ 18:7 Trial proceedings; initial conference call (1 month)

After a trial is instituted by granting the petition for *inter partes* review, the Board will have a conference call within about one month to discuss the Scheduling Order and any motions that the parties might anticipate filing during the trial. The Board expects a list of proposed motions to be filed no later than two business days before the conference call. An accurate list of motions is needed to provide adequate notice for preparation for the call and planning for the proceeding.[1]

The proceedings after institution comport with the general rules set forth in the chapter on PTAB trials. That is, the general rules pertaining to trial practice and procedures set forth at 37 C.F.R. §§ 42.1 to 42.80 apply along with the Trial Practice Guide.

§ 18:8 Patent owner response and amendment (3 months after trial commences)

The patent owner is entitled as a matter of right to file a response to the petition after the *inter partes* review has been instituted. In the response, the patent owner may address any ground not already denied. The response constitutes an opposition subject to the page limits of § 42.24 which in the case of an *inter partes* review is 60 pages. Absent a contrary date in the Board order instituting the review, the default date for the patent owner response is three months after the date of institution.[1]

The patent owner may seek to amend the patent within the due date provided in the Board order instituting the

---

[13] 37 C.F.R. § 42.71(c) and (d).

[14] 37 C.F.R. § 42.71(c).

[Section 18:7]

[1] Trial Practice Guide, 77 Fed. Reg. 48756, 48765 (August 14, 2012).

[Section 18:8]

[1] 37 C.F.R. § 42.120(b).

review. Absent a specified date, the patent owner desiring to amend the patent must file a motion to amend within the time specified for filing the patent owner response, typically three months. Additionally, the patent owner may not file a motion to amend without having first conferred with the Board.[2] Parties must remember that communications with the Board must be with the other party present, as *ex parte* communications are strictly prohibited.[3]

The motion to amend claims can be denied for several reasons. For example, if the amendment does not respond to a ground of unpatentability involved in the trial, the Board may deny the motion to amend.[4] Likewise, if the amendment seeks to enlarge the claim scope or introduce new matter, the motion can be denied.[5] The patent owner may move to cancel a challenged claim or propose "a reasonable number of substitute claims." The Office presumes that only one substitute claim would be needed to replace a challenged claim, although this presumption can be rebutted by the patent owner demonstrating the need to include more than one replacement claim.[6]

The motion to amend claims must conform to a specified format. It must include a claim listing, show each change clearly, and show the support in the original disclosure of the patent for each claim that is added or amended. If the benefit of an earlier filing date is sought, the motion must show the support in the earlier-filed disclosure for the claim.[7]

A more detailed treatment of patent owner motions to amend, including a discussion of PTAB guiding decisions on such motions, appears *supra* at § 15:13.

Additional motions to amend the claims cannot be filed by the patent owner without prior authorization from the Board. Such authorization may be given where, for example, the petitioner and the patent owner jointly request the amendment in order to materially advance a settlement.[8] Otherwise, the motion must demonstrate good cause. The Office has explained that it will not be favorably disposed to

---

[2] 37 C.F.R. § 42.1221(a).

[3] 37 C.F.R. § 42.5(d).

[4] 37 C.F.R. § 42.121(a)(2).

[5] 37 C.F.R. § 42.121(a)(2).

[6] 37 C.F.R. § 42.121(a)(3).

[7] 37 C.F.R. § 42.121(b).

[8] 37 C.F.R. § 42.121(c).

such motions if they jeopardize the ability of the Office to complete the proceeding on time:

> In considering whether good cause is shown, the Board will take into account how the filing of such motions would impact the timely completion of the proceeding and the additional burden placed on the petitioner. Specifically, belated motions to amend may cause the integrity and efficiency of the review to suffer as the petitioner may be required to devote significant time and resources on claims that are of constantly changing scope. Furthermore, due to time constraints, motions to amend late in the process may not provide a petitioner a full and fair opportunity to respond to the newly presented subject matter. In determining whether to authorize such an additional motion to amend, the Board will consider whether a petitioner has submitted supplemental information after the time period set for filing a motion to amend in § 42.121(a)(1). Similarly, motions to amend may be permitted upon a joint request of the petitioner and the patent owner to advance settlement where the motion does not jeopardize the ability of the Office to complete the proceeding timely. [*sic*, in timely fashion (?)][9]

§ 18:9 Multiple proceedings and joinder

During the pendency of the proceeding, the involved patent may also become the subject, or may previously have become the subject, of another proceeding. The USPTO seeks efficient processing of these matters and has authorized the Board to stay, transfer, consolidate, or terminate any such other matter involving the same patent.[1] The Board has, however, declined to stay examination of different applications related to the patent challenged in an IPR.[2] Additionally, either the petitioner or the patent owner may request

[9] 77 Fed. Reg. 48680, 48690 (Aug. 14, 2012).

[Section 18:9]

[1] 37 C.F.R. § 42.122(a). *See also, e.g., Denso Corp. v. Beacon Navigation GMBH*, IPR 2013-00027 (Paper No. 11, p. 2, Feb. 1, 2013) (ordering stay of *ex parte* reexamination while IPR was pending where the proceedings were directed to overlapping patent claims); *Lumondi Inc. d/b/a Luminox Watch Co. v. Lennon Imager Technologies LLC*, IPR2013-00432, Paper No. 7 (PTAB Aug. 6, 2013) (staying *ex parte* reexamination while IPR was pending over same claims).

[2] *Chi Mei Innolux Corp. v. Semiconductor Energy Laboratory Co., Ltd.*, IPR2013-0028, Paper No. 8 (PTAB Nov. 28, 2012) (denying motion to suspend or take jurisdiction over pending applications that are progeny of the patent challenged in the IPR; Board declines to be gatekeeper for all papers filed in ex parte examinations; no showing the claims are patentably indistinct from the challenged claims; examiner can suspend applica-

joinder of another matter with the *inter partes* review, provided, however, that the request for joinder be filed by motion within one month after instituting any *inter partes* review for which joinder is requested.[3] See § 15:28 for a detailed discussion of motions for joinder.

§ 18:10 Submitting supplemental information

By motion, a party may supplement its submission to the Board with "supplemental information." The rules require that any request for approval to file a motion to submit supplemental information must be made within one month of the date the trial is instituted. Further, the supplemental information must be relevant to a claim for which the trial has been instituted. Before the PTAB, a motion will generally not be entered without prior authorization of the Board.[1] There are exceptions when it is impractical to seek Board authorization. There are motions also where authorization is automatically granted without conferring with the Board, including requests for rehearing, observations on cross-examination, and motions to exclude evidence. Typically, however, an authorization for a motion is obtained during an initial conference call which generally occurs within one month of the institution of the IPR, PGR, CBM, or derivation proceeding.[2]

If the supplemental information cannot be timely filed, a party may offer a late submission of supplemental information.[3] The party seeking to submit supplemental information after the first month of the trial must request authorization to file a motion to submit the information, and the motion must show why the supplemental information reasonably could not have been obtained earlier. Further, the motion to submit must explain that consideration of the supplemental information would be in the interests of justice.[4] In the event that a party seeks to submit supplemental information that is *not* relevant to a claim for which the

---

tions pending outcome of IPR if examiner decides the claims are patentably indistinct).

[3]37 C.F.R. § 42.122(b).

[Section 18:10]

[1]37 C.F.R. § 42.20(b).

[2]Trial Practice Guide, 77 Fed. Reg. 48756, 48763.

[3]37 C.F.R. § 42.123(b).

[4]37 C.F.R. § 42.123(b).

trial has been instituted, the party must request authorization to file such a motion to submit the information. Again, the motion must show why the supplemental information reasonably could not have been obtained earlier and that supplementation would be in the interests of justice.[5]

§ 18:11 Discovery and trial procedure

The general trial rules set forth in Part 42 (Trial Practice Before the PTAB), Subpart A (Trial Practice and Procedure; §§ 42.1–42.80) apply to the *inter partes* review proceeding.

At trial, the petitioner has the burden to prove unpatentability by a preponderance of the evidence.[1]

§ 18:12 Relationship to civil litigation—Automatic stays

A prospective patent challenger who has *not* been sued for infringement of the patent in question has to elect the forum in which to challenge the patent. The challenger can either file a declaratory judgment action seeking a declaration of patent invalidity, provided that there is a "case or controversy," or it can petition for an *inter partes* review, but not both. These are mutually exclusive.[1] If a patent challenger or real party in interest filed a civil action challenging the validity of any claim before seeking *inter partes* review, then *inter partes* review is barred by the statute.[2] Conversely, if the petitioner or real party in interest who has filed a petition to institute an *inter partes* review subsequently files a civil action challenging validity of a claim, the civil action must be automatically stayed until any of three events occur:

- the patent owner moves the court to lift the stay;
- the patent owner files a civil action or counterclaim alleging that the petitioner or real party in interest has infringed the patent, or
- the petitioner or real party in interest moves the court

[5]37 C.F.R. § 42.123(c).

[Section 18:11]

[1]35 U.S.C.A. § 316(e).

[Section 18:12]

[1]35 U.S.C.A. § 315(a)(1).

[2]35 U.S.C.A. § 315(a)(1).

to dismiss the civil action.[3]

As to the first bullet point, this protects the patent owner by disallowing the petitioner from forcing the patent owner to defend both a (potential) *inter partes* review and a civil action. If the patent owner, however, decides to accede to the civil action (where he can counterclaim for infringement), he can move the court to lift the stay. This is under the control of the patent owner, not the petitioner.

The second bullet point also relies on action by the patent owner. If the patent owner files an infringement suit or counterclaim after a petitioner has sought an *inter partes* review, there is no automatic stay of the patent owner's suit, and if the petitioner had also filed a declaratory judgment action for invalidity which was automatically stayed, that stay is terminated. Hence, the patent owner can opt to await the outcome of the petition for an *inter partes* review before allowing the automatic stay of litigation to be lifted, or the patent owner can move forward with civil litigation forthwith and not take advantage of the protection of the statute.

The third bullet point concerns action by the petitioner rather than the patent owner. Here, the petitioner (or real party in interest) can move the court to dismiss its own suit. The automatic stay is lifted for consideration of that motion.

Filing a counterclaim challenging the validity of a claim of an asserted patent does not constitute a civil action for purposes of § 315.[4]

§ 18:13 Relationship to civil litigation—Permissive stays

It has been common for defendants charged with patent infringement to seek reexamination of the asserted patent(s) and move the court for a stay pending reexamination. Considerable jurisprudence developed with respect to such motions. Many of the same factors are involved when the USPTO proceeding is an IPR rather than a reexamination, and courts faced with motions to stay pending the outcome of an IPR have adopted the framework used for considering

[3]35 U.S.C.A. § 315(a)(2). Curiously, the statute does not indicate that the civil action ban would be lifted if the USPTO declines to commence a post-grant review.

[4]35 U.S.C.A. § 315(a)(3).

stays pending reexamination.[1] "Three significant factors in deciding whether to stay an action are: "(1) whether discovery is complete and whether a trial date has been set; (2) whether a stay will simplify the issues in question and trial of the case; and (3) whether a stay would unduly prejudice or present a clear tactical disadvantage to the nonmoving party."[2]

A patent challenger who has been sued for infringement in a civil action has one year after service of the complaint, 35 U.S.C.A. § 315(b), within which to file a petition (after September 16, 2012) seeking IPR.[3] The challenger may *also* counterclaim against the validity of the asserted patent. A challenger who petitions the USPTO to declare an IPR will often seek a stay of the civil action. The majority of courts facing such motions find that the automatic stay provisions of 35 U.S.C.A. § 315(a) do not apply to this situation and that granting the stay is discretionary.[4] Courts have denied such stays when the USPTO has not yet reached a decision

---

[Section 18:13]

[1]*Semiconductor Energy Laboratory Co., Ltd. v. Chimei Innolux Corp.*, 2012 WL 7170593, at *1 n.1 (C.D. Cal. 2012) ("The Court sees no reason why the three factor assessment would not still be relevant [to the new *inter partes* review proceeding]."); *Universal Electronics, Inc. v. Universal Remote Control, Inc.*, 2013 WL 1876459, at *2 (C.D. Cal. 2013).

[2]*Universal Electronics, Inc. v. Universal Remote Control, Inc.*, 2013 WL 1876459, at *2 (C.D. Cal. 2013) citing *Aten Intern. Co., Ltd v. Emine Technology Co., Ltd.*, 2010 WL 1462110, at *6 (C.D. Cal. 2010) (quoting *Telemac Corp. v. Teledigital, Inc.*, 450 F. Supp. 2d 1107, 1111 (N.D. Cal. 2006)); see also *Nippon Steel & Sumito Metal Corp. v. POSCO*, 2013 WL 1867042 (D.N.J. 2013) (denying stay after reexaminations granted).

[3]A patent challenger, real party in interest, or privy of the challenger is barred by 35 U.S.C.A. § 315(b) from filing for *inter partes* review where that party has been served with a complaint alleging infringement of the patent more than one year before filing the petition. The opening of the one year period begins once process is *served* pursuant to Rule 4 of the Federal Rules of Civil Procedure and not with a mere receipt by the patentee of a courtesy copy of the complaint. *Motorola Mobility LLC v. Arnouse*, IPR 2013-0010, Paper No. 20, pp. 2-5 (PTAB Jan. 30, 2013).

[4]See *Medichem, S.A. v. Rolabo, S.L.*, 353 F.3d 928, 936, 69 U.S.P.Q.2d 1283 (Fed. Cir. 2003) stating that a stay of district court proceedings pending the outcome of parallel proceedings at the USPTO is discretionary to the court. *But see Cellectis S.A. v. Precision Biosciences*, 883 F. Supp. 2d 526, 533 (D. Del. 2012) (dictum) (court is mandated to stay litigation in favor of inter partes review unless a stay would not serve the interests of justice).

on whether to institute the IPR,[5] or where the court has already invested significant time in the case, such as by having ruled on claim construction.[6] Indeed, some courts have denied the stay motion even after IPR has been instituted,[7] while other courts have granted stays where the IPR has already been granted.[8]

Interestingly, some courts have granted stays when the patent-in-suit is being challenged in an IPR brought by an unrelated party, even when the PTAB has not yet decided whether to institute IPR.[9]

§ 18:14 Estoppels

Just as the superseded *inter partes* reexamination statute provided for estoppels,[1] so too does the new IPR statute and applicable rule. 35 U.S.C. § 315(e) and 37 C.F.R. § 42.73(d)(1)

---

[5]*Automatic Mfg. Systems, Inc. v. Primera Technology, Inc.*, 2013 WL 1969247, at *3 (M.D. Fla. 2013) (denying motion for stay as premature until PTAB decides whether to institute IPR and announce its scope); *Universal Electronics, Inc. v. Universal Remote Control, Inc.*, 2013 WL 1876459 (C.D. Cal. 2013).

[6]*Universal Electronics, Inc. v. Universal Remote Control, Inc.*, 2013 WL 1876459 (C.D. Cal. 2013).

[7]*ImageVision.Net, Inc. v. Internet Payment Exchange, Inc.*, 2013 WL 1743854, at *2 (D. Del. 2013) (applying traditional three-factor test to determine that stay is not appropriate).

[8]*Regents of University of Michigan v. St. Jude Medical, Inc.*, 2013 WL 2393340, at *2 (E.D. Mich. 2013); see also *Smart Modular Technologies, Inc. v. Netlist, Inc.*, 2013 WL 2384342, at *3 (E.D. Cal. 2013) (denying preliminary injunction motion and granting defendant's motion for stay where reexamination had been ordered and claims had been rejected).

[9]See *e-Watch v. FLIR Systems*, Case No. 4-13-00638 (S.D. Texas, August 8, 2013) and *e-Watch v. ACTi Corp.*, Case No. 5-12-cv-00695, Report and Recommendation (W.D. Texas, August 9, 2013). Here, a defendant in a third lawsuit (*e-Watch v. Mobotix Corp.*, Case No. 5-12-cv-00492, (W.D. Texas)) petitioned for IPR and the other courts granted stays based on the petition.

[Section 18:14]

[1]*Mikkelsen Graphic Engineering, Inc. v. Zund America, Inc.*, 2013 WL 4269406, at *8 (Fed. Cir. 2013) (non-precedential): "Section 315(c) provided that in a civil suit, third-party requestors would be 'estopped from asserting . . . the invalidity of any claim finally determined to be valid and patentable *on any ground which the third-party requester raised or could have raised during the inter partes reexamination proceedings.* This subsection does not prevent the assertion of invalidity based on newly discovered prior art unavailable to the third-party requester and the Patent and Trademark Office at the time of the inter partes reexamination proceedings.' 35 U.S.C. § 315(c) (2006) (emphasis added).

provide for various estoppels. Where a final written decision occurs under § 318(a), the petitioner, the real party in interest, and anyone "privy of" the petitioner is estopped from requesting or maintaining any USPTO proceeding challenging that same claim on any ground that the petitioner raised or reasonably could have raised during the *inter partes* review.[2] In other words, once one petitions and obtains an *inter partes* review, all issues that were raised and which reasonably could have been raised as to the challenged patent claims are barred from being raised in another *inter partes* review or other USPTO proceeding, *e.g.*, a reexamination, by that same petitioner and various related entities. Whether the estoppel would apply to other claims not in the review is not perfectly clear under the statute.

A similar estoppel applies in civil actions. Following an *inter partes* review, the petitioner, the real party in interest, and any privy of the petitioner are barred from asserting, in a civil action or an ITC proceeding, invalidity of a patent claim in the *inter partes* review on any ground that the petitioner raised or could reasonably have raised.[3] Until courts determine the metes and bounds of what the petitioner could "reasonably have raised," some uncertainty will remain in just what will be estopped. In may be noted that the prior *inter partes* reexamination statute contained an express exclusion from the estoppel ("newly discovered prior art unavailable to the third-party requester and the Patent and Trademark Office at the time of the inter partes reexamination proceedings;" 35 U.S.C.A. § 315(c) (2006)), but this exclusion has not been reiterated in the new statute, § 315(e) (2011). How courts treat this change remains to be seen. The estoppel as to a petitioner can be avoided by a settlement

---

Section 315 was superseded by the statute that created inter partes review. *See* Leahy-Smith America Invents Act, Pub.L. No. 112-29, § 6(a), 125 Stat. 284, 299-304 (2011), *codified at* 35 U.S.C. §§ 311-319."

[2]35 U.S.C.A. § 315(e); 37 C.F.R. § 42.73(d)(1). *See also Ranbaxy Laboratories Ltd. v. Vertex Pharmaceuticals*, IPR2013-00024 (Paper No. 45, p. 4, May 24, 2013) (any third party participation in the deposition of a petitioner's declarant might bind the third party even if not identified as a real party in interest); *Apple Inc. v. Achates Reference Publishing, Inc.*, IPR 2013-00080-00081 (Paper No. 17, p. 5-7, Apr. 3, 2013) (indemnification clause not enough to create a real party-in-interest); *Innolux Corp. v. Semiconductor Energy Laboratory Co., Ltd.*, IPR2013-00028 (Paper No. 14, p. 8, Mar. 21, 2013) (PTAB considers whether a party has exercised control or funding of a petition to determine if that petition is binding upon the party as a real party in interest).

[3]35 U.S.C.A. § 325(e).

under the conditions specified in § 317(a).

The patent owner also faces estoppels. The statute at § 315 concerns estoppels binding the petitioner and the real party in interest. It does not address the patent owner. However, such estoppels are addressed in the rules, particularly 37 C.F.R. § 42.73(d)(3). The patent owner is estopped also against obtaining certain claims or making certain amendments:

> (3) *Patent applicant or owner*. A patent applicant or owner is precluded from taking action inconsistent with the adverse judgment, including obtaining in any patent:
>
> (i) A claim that is not patentably distinct from a finally refused or canceled claim; or
>
> (ii) An amendment of a specification or of a drawing that was denied during the trial proceeding, but this provision does not apply to an application or patent that has a different written description.

§ 18:15 Settlements

35 U.S.C. § 317 provides a mechanism for the petitioner and the patent owner to settle the matter before the PTAB decides the merits of the proceeding. Should the parties reach a mutually acceptable resolution, they must reduce their agreement to writing and file a true copy of it with the Office before the termination of the review. At a party's request, the agreement or understanding will be treated as business confidential information, kept separate from the patent file, and made available only to federal government agencies upon written request or to any person on a showing of good cause. Good cause is not defined. The parties may jointly request termination of the proceeding upon settlement, unless a decision on the merits has been reached. Under § 317(a), the *inter partes* review "shall be terminated with respect to the petitioner upon the joint request of the petitioner and the patent owner, unless the Office has decided the merits of the proceeding before the request for termination." The *inter partes* review might not terminate, as the PTAB has discretion over this. It "may terminate the *inter partes* review or proceed to a final written decision under § 318(a)" if no petitioner remains in the *inter partes*

review.[1] How the PTAB handles this remains to be seen.

In any event, a settlement prevents estoppels against the petitioner. "If the inter partes review is terminated with respect to a petitioner under this section, no estoppel under section 315(e) shall attach to the petitioner, or to the real party in interest or privy of the petitioner, on the basis of that petitioner's institution of that inter partes review."[2]

§ 18:16 USPTO certificate and intervening rights

Under § 318, final decisions of the Board must be in writing. Upon expiration of the time for or completion of any appeal, the Director will issue a certificate either cancelling or confirming any challenged claim.

Under § 318(c), any amended or new claim determined to be patentable and incorporated into the patent gives rise to intervening rights:[1]

> (c) INTERVENING RIGHTS.— Any proposed amended or new claim determined to be patentable and incorporated into a patent following an inter partes eview under this chapter shall have the same effect as that specified in section 252 for reissued patents on the right of any person who made, purchased, or used within the United States, or imported into the United States, anything patented by such proposed amended or new claim, or who made substantial preparation therefor, before the issuance of a certificate under subsection (b).

§ 18:17 Rehearing and judicial review

Any party dissatisfied with a decision of the Board may request rehearing.[1] Also, pursuant to 35 U.S.C. § 319, a dissatisfied party may appeal the Board's final written decision

---

[Section 18:15]

[1]77 Fed. Reg. 48680, 48686 (Aug. 14, 2012); see 35 U.S.C.A. § 327(a).

[2]35 U.S.C.A. § 317(a); accord, 37 C.F.R. § 42.73(d)(1).

[Section 18:16]

[1]See *Marine Polymer Technologies, Inc. v. HemCon, Inc.*, 672 F.3d 1350, 102 U.S.P.Q.2d 1161 (Fed. Cir. 2012) (en banc) where a sharply divided Court ruled that intervening rights do not arise without writing a new claim or changing the words of the claim, even if claim scope changed during reexamination as a result of the cancelation of dependent claims which, when present, required the parent claim to be interpreted broadly enough to permit the features of the dependent claims.

[Section 18:17]

[1]37 C.F.R. § 42.71(c) & (d).

in accordance with 35 U.S.C. §§ 141 to 144. The appeal lies to only the U.S. Court of Appeals for the Federal Circuit. There is no right to a *de novo* hearing in the district court. Every party has the right to be a party to the appeal.[2] It is not necessary to have requested a rehearing from the Board in order to appeal to the Federal Circuit.

§ 18:18 Effective dates

Inter partes reviews became available on September 16, 2012—one year after the signature of the AIA into law.[1] At that time, the USPTO also stopped accepting requests for *inter partes* reexamination.

§ 18:19 PTAB Statistics

On its website, the USPTO maintains statistics on AIA activity.[1] As of October 17, 2013, the PTAB had received 577 IPR petitions. The data show that monthly filings are increasing—over 40 in May 2013, over 60 in June, and almost 80 in July. From October 2012 through April 2013, the PTAB received 20-40 new petitions per month. Nearly 70% of the AIA petitions have been in the electrical and computer arts.

---

[2] 35 U.S.C.A. § 319.

[Section 18:18]

[1] AIA § 6(c)(2) (2011).

[Section 18:19]

[1] http://www.uspto.gov/aia_implementation/statistics.jsp (visited August 22, 2013).

Chapter 19

Derivation Proceedings Replace Interferences

AIA § 3(h, i)
35 U.S.C.A. § 135

§ 19:1 Background

Section 135 of the 1952 patent statute is directed to interferences. Its language was "largely a restatement of the old statute with minor changes in language . . .."[1] The interference procedure is unique on the world stage because

[Section 19:1]

[1]P.J. Federico, Commentary on the New Patent Act, 35 U.S.C.A. (West 1954), p. 37.

only the U.S. had a first to invent system. In the U.S., the question of who filed the first patent application at the Patent Office first was simply one data point because the first person to file may not be the first person to invent, and under the 1952 statute, the first person to *invent* was entitled to the patent. An "interference" contest seeks to determine which of two (or more) proclaimed inventors was first to invent.

Section 135 interference contests were referred to in Section 102(g) of the 1952 statute. It indicates that a person is not entitled to a patent if another inventor establishes, in an interference conducted under Section 135 or Section 291 (interferences between patents), that another inventor made the invention before the applicant and did not abandon, suppress, or conceal it, within the extent permitted, so long as that proof was permitted by Section 104. Section 102(g) provided secondly that the applicant would be denied a patent if, before the applicant's invention, the invention was made in the U.S. by another inventor who had not abandoned, suppressed, or concealed it. Section 102(g) provided additionally that in determining priority of invention, the respective dates of conception and reduction to practice of the invention were to be considered along with the reasonable diligence of an inventor who was first to conceive but last to reduce the invention to practice, from a time prior to conception by the other inventor.[2] These provisions were designed to ensure that the patent right would be granted to the first person to invent the subject matter claimed in a patent, but they led to considerable disputes that were time-consuming and costly to resolve. The Section 135 being superseded by the AIA provided as follows:

Old Statute (35 U.S.C. § 135(a)).

(a) Whenever an application is made for a patent which, in the opinion of the Director, would interfere with any pending application, or with any unexpired patent, an interference may be declared and the Director shall give notice of such declaration to the applicants, or applicant and patentee, as the case may be. The Board of Patent Appeals and Interferences shall determine questions of priority of the inventions and may determine questions of patentability. Any final decision, if adverse to the claim of an applicant, shall constitute the final refusal by the Patent and Trademark Office of the claims involved, and the Director may issue a patent to the applicant

[2] 35 U.S.C.A. § 102(g).

who is adjudged the prior inventor. A final judgment adverse to a patentee from which no appeal or other review has been or can be taken or had shall constitute cancellation of the claims involved in the patent, and notice of such cancellation shall be endorsed on copies of the patent distributed after such cancellation by the Patent and Trademark Office.

(b) (1) A claim which is the same as, or for the same or substantially the same subject matter as, a claim of an issued patent may not be made in any application unless such a claim is made prior to one year from the date on which the patent was granted.

(2) A claim which is the same as, or for the same or substantially the same subject matter as, a claim of an application published under section 122(b) of this title may be made in an application filed after the application is published only if the claim is made before 1 year after the date on which the application is published.

(c) Any agreement or understanding between parties to an interference, including any collateral agreements referred to therein, made in connection with or in contemplation of the termination of the interference, shall be in writing and a true copy thereof filed in the Patent and Trademark Office before the termination of the interference as between the said parties to the agreement or understanding. If any party filing the same so requests, the copy shall be kept separate from the file of the interference, and made available only to Government agencies on written request, or to any person on a showing of good cause. Failure to file the copy of such agreement or understanding shall render permanently unenforceable such agreement or understanding and any patent of such parties involved in the interference or any patent subsequently issued on any application of such parties so involved. The Director may, however, on a showing of good cause for failure to file within the time prescribed, permit the filing of the agreement or understanding during the six-month period subsequent to the termination of the interference as between the parties to the agreement or understanding. The Director shall give notice to the parties or their attorneys of record, a reasonable time prior to said termination, of the filing requirement of this section. If the Director gives such notice at a later time, irrespective of the right to file such agreement or understanding within the six-month period on a showing of good cause, the parties may file such agreement or understanding within sixty days of the receipt of such notice. Any discretionary action of the Director under this subsection shall be reviewable under section 10 of the Administrative Procedure Act.

(d) Parties to a patent interference, within such time as may be specified by the Director by regulation, may determine such contest or any aspect thereof by arbitration. Such arbitra-

> tion shall be governed by the provisions of title 9 to the extent such title is not inconsistent with this section. The parties shall give notice of any arbitration award to the Director, and such award shall, as between the parties to the arbitration, be dispositive of the issues to which it relates. The arbitration award shall be unenforceable until such notice is given. Nothing in this subsection shall preclude the Director from determining patentability of the invention involved in the interference.

The administration of this interference has been very complex. A bar of specialist IP practitioners developed, along with a considerable jurisprudence. The cost of an interference proceeding rivaled the cost of infringement litigation and typically took years to complete. It was hard to predict the outcome because, among other things, the rules for interference practice were not especially conducive to the admission of all relevant evidence. Practitioners in the U.S. whose clients owned pending applications or unexpired patents that became embroiled in an interference (at the behest of an adverse patent applicant) had to explain to those clients that this proceeding is unique to the U.S. patent system and is a consequence of the first to invent approach mandated by Congress. Unfortunately, because an interference contest typically took several years, the issuance of pending applications that became involved in an interference was delayed and, if the interference involved an already issued patent, a cloud remained over the issued patent during the years that the interference contest was pending. Sometimes the cloud overshadowed much of the remaining life of the issued patent.

Additionally, under the prior system in the U.S. where patents were granted for a term of 17 years from the date of issuance, involving a patent application in an interference extended long into the future the prospective issue date of one's patent application, presuming that the applicant would emerge from the interference with some claims intact. In some cases (if not many), this made the patent application even more valuable because industry would be developing during these added years.

Some practitioners used interferences very aggressively. They would seek to "provoke" (a term of art) an interference against an issued patent belonging to a major business company. A frequent response by the target was that the applicant "could not make the count." This meant that the patent specification of the applicant could not adequately support (under 35 U.S.C. § 112) the specific subject matter which the applicant tried to "copy" into his claims. While this might end the interference contest, however, it became a Pyrrhic victory because the applicant would then simply remove the narrow language in the proposed claim which the PTO had ruled the applicant could not support, leaving broadened language in its place. When the applicant's patent issued, it tended to dominate the target patents with which interference had been sought, generally leaving the aggressor with a licensing opportunity, assuming that the target company practiced its own patent.

Abandoning the first-to-invent system would obviate the need to determine priority of invention. In seeking to modernize the patent statute, Congress wanted to bring the U.S. patent system closer to international standards and practices which are based on the priority of patent application *filing* rather than priority of invention.

In shifting from a first to invent system to a first inventor to file system, Congress still wanted to protect inventors from derivation so that a genuine inventor would not be deprived a patent simply because someone else learned of the invention and won the race to a patent office. Congress intended to provide relief for such a situation, and while it was no longer needed to determine questions of priority of invention, Congress did make provision for determining whether one applicant or patent owner had in fact derived the subject matter from another person. Under the AIA (and the U.S. Constitution), one must still be an "inventor" to obtain a patent, however, and to the extent one has copied or derived from another, one is not an "inventor." This explains why derivation proceedings are a proper replacement for interferences.

§ 19:2 Congressional intent[1]

The House Report explains that interferences are relevant

[Section 19:2]

[1]The Supreme Court cautions against relying on interpretations advanced in legislative statements that are not "anchored in the text of the statute." *Shannon v. U.S.*, 512 U.S. 573, 583, 114 S. Ct. 2419, 129 L. Ed. 2d 459 (1994), stating "[C]ourts have no authority to enforce [a] principl[e] gleaned solely from legislative history that has no statutory reference point." Shannon, 512 U.S. at 584, quoting *International Broth. of Elec. Workers, Local Union No. 474, AFL-CIO v. N.L.R.B.*, 814 F.2d 697, 712, 124 L.R.R.M. (BNA) 2993, 106 Lab. Cas. (CCH) P 12256 (D.C. Cir. 1987). The authoritative statement "is the statutory text, not the

in a "first to invent" system:[2]

First Inventor to File

The "America Invents Act" creates a new "first-inventor-to-file" system. Every industrialized nation other than the United States uses a patent priority system commonly referred to as "first-to-file." In a first-to-file system, when more than one application claiming the same invention is filed, the priority of a right to a patent is based on the earlier-filed application. The United States, by contrast, currently uses a "first-to-invent" system, in which priority is established through a proceeding to determine which applicant actually invented the claimed invention first. Differences between the two systems arise in large part from the date that is most relevant to each respective system. In a first-to-file system, the filing date of the application is most relevant; the filing date of an application is an objective date, simple to determine, for it is listed on the face of the patent. In contrast, in a first-to-invent system, the date the invention claimed in the application was actually invented is the determinative date. Unlike the objective date of filing, the date someone invents something is often uncertain, and, when disputed, typically requires corroborating evidence as part of an adjudication.

There are significant, practical differences between the two systems. Among them is the ease of determining the right to a claimed invention in the instance in which two different people file patent applications for the same invention. In a first-to-file system, the application with the earlier filing date prevails and will be awarded the patent, if one issues. In the first-to-invent system, a lengthy, complex and costly administrative proceeding (called an "interference proceeding") must be conducted at the United States Patent and Trademark Office ("USPTO") to determine who actually invented first. Interference proceedings can take years to complete (even if there is no appeal to the United States Court of Appeals for the Federal Circuit), cost hundreds of thousands of dollars, and require extensive discovery. In addition, because it is always possible that an applicant could be involved in an interference proceeding, companies must maintain extensive recording and document retention systems in case they are later required to prove the date they invented the claimed invention.

Another important difference between the two systems is

---

legislative history." *Exxon Mobil Corp. v. Allapattah Services, Inc.*, 545 U.S. 546, 568, 125 S. Ct. 2611, 162 L. Ed. 2d 502 (2005). However, lower courts have cited the legislative history of the AIA already in recent cases. E.g., *Rogers v. Tristar Products, Inc.*, 102 U.S.P.Q.2d 1722, 2012 WL 1660604, *2 (Fed. Cir. 2012) (non-precedential); *Byrne v. Wood, Herron & Evans, LLP*, 676 F.3d 1024, 1029, 102 U.S.P.Q.2d 1073 (Fed. Cir. 2012) (dissenting opin.).

[2]H.R. Rep. No. 112-98, pt. 1, at 40 to 42, 48, 73 to 74 (2011).

that in some first-to-file systems, prior art can include the inventor's own disclosure of his invention prior to the filing date of his application. Such systems do not provide the inventor any grace period during which time he is allowed to publish his invention without fear of its later being used against him as prior art. The Committee heard from universities and small inventors, in particular, about the importance of maintaining that grace period in our system. They argued that the grace period affords the necessary time to prepare and file applications, and in some instances, to obtain the necessary funding that enables the inventor to prepare adequately the application. In addition, the grace period benefits the public by encouraging early disclosure of new inventions, regardless of whether an application may later be filed for a patent on it.

Numerous organizations, institutions, and companies have advocated that the U.S. adopt a first-to-file system similar to those used in the rest of the world. The National Academy of Sciences made a similar recommendation after an extensive study of the patent system. When the United States patent system was first adopted, inventors did not typically file in other countries. It is now common for inventors and companies to file for protection in several countries at the same time. Thus, United States applicants, who also want to file abroad, are forced to follow and comply with two different filing systems. Maintaining a filing system so different from the rest of the world disadvantages United States applicants who, in most instances, also file in other countries. A change is long overdue.

Drawing on the best aspects of the two existing systems, the America Invents Act creates a new "first-inventor-to-file" system. This new system provides patent applicants in the United States the efficiency benefits of the first-to-file systems used in the rest of the world by moving the U.S. system much closer to a first-to-file system and making the filing date that which is most relevant in determining whether an application is patentable. The new system continues, however, to provide inventors the benefit of the 1-year grace period. As part of the transition to a simpler, more efficient first-inventor-to-file system, this provision eliminates costly, complex interference proceedings, because priority will be based on the first application. A new administrative proceeding—called a "derivation" proceeding—is created to ensure that the first person to file the application is actually a true inventor. This new proceeding will ensure that a person will not be able to obtain a patent for the invention that he did not actually invent. If a dispute arises as to which of two applicants is a true inventor (as opposed to who invented it first), it will be resolved through an administrative proceeding by the Patent Board.

* * *

Patent Trial and Appeal Board.

The Act renames the Patent Board the "Patent Trial and Appeal Board" and sets forth its duties, which are expanded to include jurisdiction over the new post-grant review and derivation proceedings. This section strikes references to proceedings eliminated by the Act, including interference proceedings, and updates the various appeals statutes.

* * *

Subsections (h), (i) & (j)-Repeals interference proceeding and makes conforming changes to § 291. Amends § 135(a) and provides for a "derivation proceeding," designed to determine the inventor with the right to file an application on a claimed invention. An applicant requesting a derivation proceeding must set forth the basis for finding that an earlier applicant derived the claimed invention and without authorization filed an application claiming such invention. The request must be filed within 1 year of the date of first publication of an application for a claim that is substantially the same as the claimed invention. The Patent Trial and Appeal Board (the "Board") shall determine the right to patent and issue a final decision thereon. Decisions of the Board may be appealed to the Federal Circuit, or to district court pursuant to § 146.[3]

§ 19:3 The new statute re derivation proceedings and derived patents

New Statute (35 U.S.C. § 135 as amended by H.R. 6621 (2013))

§ 135. Derivation proceedings.[1]

(a) INSTITUTION OF PROCEEDING—

[3] H.R. Rep. No. 112-98, pt. 1, at 40 to 42, 48, 73 to 74 (2011).

[Section 19:3]

[1] As originally enacted in 2011, § 135(a) provided as follows: "(a) INSTITUTION OF PROCEEDING.—An applicant for patent may file a petition to institute a derivation proceeding in the Office. The petition shall set forth with particularity the basis for finding that an inventor named in an earlier application derived the claimed invention from an inventor named in the petitioner's application and, without authorization, the earlier application claiming such invention was filed. Any such petition may be filed only within the 1-year period beginning on the date of the first publication of a claim to an invention that is the same or substantially the same as the earlier application's claim to the invention, shall be made under oath, and shall be supported by substantial evidence. Whenever the Director determines that a petition filed under this subsection demonstrates that the standards for instituting a derivation proceeding are met, the Director may institute a derivation proceeding. The determination by the Director whether to institute a derivation proceeding shall be final and nonappealable." H.R. 6621 replaced this entire

(1) IN GENERAL—An applicant for patent may file a petition with respect to an invention to institute a derivation proceeding in the Office. The petition shall set forth with particularity the basis for finding that an individual named in an earlier application as the inventor or a joint inventor derived such invention from an individual named in the petitioner's application as the inventor or a joint inventor and, without authorization, the earlier application claiming such invention was filed. Whenever the Director determines that a petition filed under this subsection demonstrates that the standards for instituting a derivation proceeding are met, the Director may institute a derivation proceeding.

(2) TIME FOR FILING—A petition under this section with respect to an invention that is the same or substantially the same invention as a claim contained in a patent issued on an earlier application, or contained in an earlier application when published or deemed published under section 122(b), may not be filed unless such petition is filed during the 1-year period following the date on which the patent containing such claim was granted or the earlier application containing such claim was published, whichever is earlier.

(3) EARLIER APPLICATION—For purposes of this section, an application shall not be deemed to be an earlier application with respect to an invention, relative to another application, unless a claim to the invention was or could have been made in such application having an effective filing date that is earlier than the effective filing date of any claim to the invention that was or could have been made in such other application.

(4) NO APPEAL—A determination by the Director whether to institute a derivation proceeding under paragraph (1) shall be final and not appealable.[2]

(b) DETERMINATION BY PATENT TRIAL AND APPEAL BOARD.—In a derivation proceeding instituted under subsection (a), the Patent Trial and Appeal Board shall determine whether an inventor named in the earlier application derived the claimed invention from an inventor named in the petitioner's application and, without authorization, the earlier application claiming such invention was filed. In appropriate circumstances, the Patent Trial and Appeal Board may correct the naming of the inventor in any application or patent at issue. The Director shall prescribe regulations setting forth standards for the conduct of derivation proceedings, including requiring parties to provide sufficient evidence to prove and rebut a claim of derivation.

(c) DEFERRAL OF DECISION.—The Patent Trial and Appeal

---

paragraph with new text having subparts (1)-(4) shown in the main text.

[2]This amendment to § 135(a) by H.R. 6621 (2013) is to be effective "as if included in the amendment made by section 3(i) of the Leahy-Smith America Invents Act."

Board may defer action on a petition for a derivation proceeding until the expiration of the 3-month period beginning on the date on which the Director issues a patent that includes the claimed invention that is the subject of the petition. The Patent Trial and Appeal Board also may defer action on a petition for a derivation proceeding, or stay the proceeding after it has been instituted, until the termination of a proceeding under chapter 30, 31, or 32 involving the patent of the earlier applicant.

(d) Effect of Final Decision.—The final decision of the Patent Trial and Appeal Board, if adverse to claims in an application for patent, shall constitute the final refusal by the Office on those claims. The final decision of the Patent Trial and Appeal Board, if adverse to claims in a patent, shall, if no appeal or other review of the decision has been or can be taken or had, constitute cancellation of those claims, and notice of such cancellation shall be endorsed on copies of the patent distributed after such cancellation.

(e) Settlement.—Parties to a proceeding instituted under subsection (a) may terminate the proceeding by filing a written statement reflecting the agreement of the parties as to the correct inventors[3] of the claimed invention in dispute. Unless the Patent Trial and Appeal Board finds the agreement to be inconsistent with the evidence of record, if any, it shall take action consistent with the agreement. Any written settlement or understanding of the parties shall be filed with the Director. At the request of a party to the proceeding, the agreement or understanding shall be treated as business confidential information, shall be kept separate from the file of the involved patents or applications, and shall be made available only to Government agencies on written request, or to any person on a showing of good cause.

(f) Arbitration.—Parties to a proceeding instituted under subsection (a) may, within such time as may be specified by the Director by regulation, determine such contest or any aspect thereof by arbitration. Such arbitration shall be governed by the provisions of title 9, to the extent such title is not inconsistent with this section. The parties shall give notice of any arbitration award to the Director, and such award shall, as between the parties to the arbitration, be dispositive of the issues to which it relates. The arbitration award shall be unenforceable until such notice is given. Nothing in this subsection shall preclude the Director from determining the patentability of the claimed inventions involved in the proceeding.

Section 3(h) of the AIA also rewrites 35 U.S.C. § 291 so that now it refers to "derived patents" rather than "interfering patents." The new Section 291 provides as follows:

[3]H.R. 6621, § 1(e) (2013) changes "inventors" to "inventor."

New Statute (35 U.S.C. § 291)

§ 291. Derived Patents

(a) IN GENERAL—The owner of a patent may have relief by civil action against the owner of another patent that claims the same invention and has an earlier effective filing date, if the invention claimed in such other patent was derived from the inventor of the invention claimed in the patent owned by the person seeking relief under this section.

(b) FILING LIMITATION—An action under this section may be filed only before the end of the 1-year period beginning on the date of the issuance of the first patent containing a claim to the allegedly derived invention and naming an individual alleged to have derived such invention as the inventor or joint inventor.

§ 19:4 Derivation proceedings—Generally

Derivation proceedings are not completely new. In an interference contest conducted under Section 135 of the Patent Act of 1952 and the preceding similar provisions of the prior patent statutes, parties could establish that one party derived the subject matter from the other.

The derivation proceeding is one of the four trial proceedings to be conducted before the PTAB and is therefore required to use the procedures set forth in Part 42, Subpart A of the USPTO regulations.[1] Generally, while the issue of derivation is the primary focus, just as with interference contests the Board may authorize (or direct) the parties to address patentability issues that arise during the course of the proceeding.[2]

§ 19:5 Filing a petition

The requirements for instituting a derivation trial are set forth in Part 42, Subpart E (§§ 42.400–412) and 35 U.S.C. § 135 (2011). The following checklist may be helpful when preparing a petition for a derivation proceeding.

Checklist for Derivation Petition

- Show that petitioner is an applicant for patent.

[Section 19:4]

[1]37 C.F.R. § 42.400(a).

[2]37 C.F.R. § 42.400(b).

§§ 42.402, 42.405(a)(1).[1]

- Show that the petition is filed within 1 year of first publication. § 42.403.[2]
- The proper filing fee. §§ 42.404, 42.15.
- Mandatory notice (§ 42.8) identifying:
  - each real party-in-interest for the petitioner,
  - all related judicial and administrative matters,
  - petitioner's lead and back-up counsel, and
  - the service information for petitioner.
- Provide sufficient information to identify the adverse application or patent for which the petitioner seeks a derivation proceeding. § 42.405(b)(1).
- State the precise relief requested. § 42.22(a)(1), (b).
- Show all requirements of any rule in 37 C.F.R. Part 1 that ordinarily governs the relief sought (along with showings required in Part 42). § 42.22(b).
- Provide a full statement of the reasons for relief, including a detailed explanation of the significance of the evidence, including material facts, and the governing law, rules, and precedent. § 42.22(a)(2).
- Provide a statement of facts. § 42.22(c).
- Show that petitioner has at least one claim that is:
  - the same (or substantially the same) as respondent's claimed invention; and
  - the same (or substantially the same) as the invention disclosed to the respondent. § 42.405(a)(2).
- Demonstrate that an adverse claim of the respondent was derived from an inventor named in the petitioner's application and that such inventor did not authorize the filing of the respondent's application ("the earliest application claiming such invention"). § 42.405(b)(2).
- For each of the respondent's claims to the derived invention:
  - show why the claimed invention is the same (or substantially the same) as the invention disclosed to the respondent. § 42.405(b)(3).
  - Indicate how the claim should be construed.

[Section 19:5]

[1]References in the check list are to 37 C.F.R. unless otherwise stated.

[2]The USPTO position is that the one year period is measured from the first publication of an adversely-held, derived claim.

§ 42.405(b)(3).

- Provide "substantial evidence" including at least one affidavit addressing communication of the derived invention and lack of authorization that, if unrebutted, would support a determination of derivation. § 42.405(c).
- Show corroboration of the communication. § 42.405(c).
- Provide copies of the evidence relied upon. § 42.6(c).
- Format and citation requirements. §§ 42.6, 42.13.
- Page limit of 60 pages. § 42.24.
    - Optional motion to waive page limits. § 42.24(a)(2).
- Certificate of service on correspondence address of record. § 42.6(e).
- Duty of candor disclosures. § 42.11.
- Optional motion to seal. § 42.55.

* * *

<u>Only Applicants Can Petition.</u> A derivation proceeding is a "trial" which one seeks to commence by filing a petition. Only a patent applicant may file a petition for a derivation proceeding.[3] The owner of an already-issued patent who believes that an application is pending which claims subject matter derived from an inventor of the patent owner's patent *cannot* seek to institute a derivation proceeding at the PTAB but instead must await issuance of the adverse application and then institute a civil action under 35 U.S.C. § 291 which is directed to "derived patents." Alternatively, the patent owner could file a reissue application and then, being a "patent applicant," could petition for institution of a derivation proceeding under the rules.

<u>Petition Deadline</u>. The time for filing a petition for institution of a derivation proceeding is the subject of 37 C.F.R. § 42.403 which provides as follows:

§ 42.403. Time for filing.

A petition for a derivation proceeding must be filed within the one-year period beginning on the date of the first publication of a claim to an invention that is the same or substantially the same as the earlier application's claim to the allegedly derived invention.

This rule is almost identical in language to 35 U.S.C. § 135(a) (2011). The USPTO believes that the timing requirement in the statute contains ambiguity and this entitles the

[3] 37 C.F.R. § 42.402.

Office to declare a reasonable meaning of the statute. The USPTO interprets the statute so that the timing of the process is similar to the clear provision made in 35 U.S.C. § 291 (2011) and in the former 35 U.S.C. § 135. In both of these statutes, the person who believes there is interference has a one year period from the issue date or the publication date of the adverse patent or patent application, as the case may be, within which to copy claims or commence a civil action seeking a contest between the two. This is a sensible way of proceeding.

It appeared, however, that revision to § 135(a) (2011) was needed if that is the process that Congress truly intended. Indeed, one may wonder why Congress did not use language in § 135 corresponding to language in § 291(b) where Congress said that "an action under [Section 291] may be filed only before the end of the 1-year period beginning on the date of the issuance of the first patent containing a claim to the allegedly derived information and naming an individual alleged to have derived such invention as the inventor or joint inventor." When Congress revised § 135, however, instead of using language parallel to § 291 (2011), Congress stated that the "petition may be filed only within the 1 year period beginning on the date of the first publication of a claim to an invention that is the same or substantially the same *as the earlier application's claim to the invention . . .*" [emphasis added] The italicized language does not appear in § 291 and left something to be desired.[4]

Ultimately, Congress made a technical correction via H.R. 6621 (2013) and removed the problem. The text shown above in § 19:3 is the corrected text and clarifies in § 135(a)(2) that the petition is due within one year of the grant date or publication date, whichever is earlier, of the earlier application.

[4]When the new statute and 37 C.F.R. § 42.403 refer to the date of first publication of a claim that is the same or substantially the same as the earlier application's claim to the allegedly derived invention, this means that the earlier application contains the claim to the allegedly derived invention. As such, this statute and rule presume that the deriver files the first application. The statute and rule then talk about a 1 year period commencing on the date of first publication of a claim, i.e., another claim presumably belonging to the true inventor, to an invention that is the same or substantially the same as the (deriver's) claim. Under this (literal) reading, the true inventor could not file a petition to institute a derivation proceeding until the true inventor's own application is published, and he may file a petition only within one year thereafter. This is contrary to the USPTO interpretation which is that the one year period begins with the publication of the earlier application, not the later one.

Filing Fee. The next requirement for obtaining a filing date for a petition is to send the proper derivation fee to the USPTO. The current fee is $400.[5]

Petitioner's Claims. The petitioner must be a proper petitioner, meet the time requirement, and pay the specified filing fee, as just discussed. In addition, the petition filed by the petitioner must meet the several requirements of § 42.405 specifying the contents of a proper petition, as follows:

> **§ 42.405 Content of petition.**
>
> (a) *Grounds for standing.* The petition must:
>
> (1) Demonstrate compliance with §§ 42.402 and 42.403; and
>
> (2) Show that the petitioner has at least one claim that is:
>
> (i) The same or substantially the same as the respondent's claimed invention; and
>
> (ii) The same or substantially the same as the invention disclosed to the respondent.
>
> (b) In addition to the requirements of § § 42.8 and 42.22, the petition must:
>
> (1) Provide sufficient information to identify the application or patent for which the petitioner seeks a derivation proceeding;
>
> (2) Demonstrate that a claimed invention was derived from an inventor named in the petitioner's application, and that the inventor from whom the invention was derived did not authorize the filing of the earliest application claiming such invention; and
>
> (3) For each of the respondent's claims to the derived invention,
>
> (i) Show why the claimed invention is the same or substantially the same as the invention disclosed to the respondent, and
>
> (ii) Identify how the claim is to be construed. Where the claim to be construed contains a means-plus-function or step-plus-function limitation as permitted under 35 U.S.C. 112(f), the construction of the claim must identify the specific portions of the specification that describe the structure, material, or acts corresponding to each claimed function.***

Under § 42.405(a)(2), the petitioner must show that it has at least one claim that is "(i) the same or substantially the same as the respondent's claimed invention, and (ii) the same or substantially the same as the invention disclosed to the respondent." Note that unlike the prior trial rules which call

[5]37 C.F.R § 42.404; § 42.15(c).

for this petition to "certify" certain facts, this portion of the rule calls for the petitioner to "show" facts.[6] Accordingly, the petition must "show" that the patent application of the petitioner has at least one claim that is the same or substantially the same as the respondent's "claimed invention." The AIA defines "claimed invention" in new 35 U.S.C. § 100(j) as "the subject matter defined by a claim in a patent or an application for a patent." Thus, when the rule calls for the petition to show that the petitioner has a claim that is the same or substantially the same as the respondent's claimed invention, that means that the petition must show that a claim in the respondent's patent or application is the same or substantially the same as a claim in the petitioner's application.

The next requirement is that the petition must show that the claim in the petitioner's application is the same or substantially the same as the invention disclosed to the respondent.[7] This seems logical in that the derivation proceeding is to show that the respondent derived subject matter, *i.e.,* a claim or claims, from the applicant. If the respondent does not have a claim which is (substantially) the same as the invention disclosed to the respondent, that suggests that the respondent obtained the subject matter on its own or via another route, but not from the petitioner. It may well be the case that the respondent invented the same claimed subject matter that the petitioner invented but the petitioner did not communicate the invention to the alleged deriver (the respondent). Under § 42.405(a)(2)(ii), the petition is insufficient where it fails to disclose that the respondent's claim is the same or substantially the same as the invention disclosed to the respondent.

<u>The Respondent's Claims and Acts.</u> Turning to § 42.405(b), the first requirement is that the petition must provide sufficient information to identify the application or patent for

---

[6]37 C.F.R § 42.204 relating to post-grant review petitions calls for the petitioner to "certify" certain facts regarding standing. 37 C.F.R § 42.104(a) relating to inter partes review likewise calls for the petitioner to "certify" certain grounds for standing. In contrast, § 42.304 relating to the petition in the covered business method patent review simply calls for the petitioner to "demonstrate" certain facts regarding standing. The language of § 42.405 relating to derivation proceeding petitions calls for the petitioner to "demonstrate" or "show" in these initial portions of the petition requirements. A later portion of this particular rule calls for an affidavit and corroboration.

[7]37 C.F.R § 42.405(a)(2)(ii).

which the petitioner seeks a derivation proceeding. The rule relieves the USPTO of any burden of having to search for applications or patents which a petitioner thinks may have been derived but for which the petitioner has no concrete identifying information. The burden here is on the petitioner to give sufficient information to identify the application which is to be the subject of the derivation proceeding.

The next requirement is that the petition must "demonstrate" three things: (1) that a claimed invention was derived from an inventor named in the petitioner's application; (2) that such inventor from whom the invention was derived did not authorize the filing of the "earliest application claiming such invention," *i.e.*, the respondent's earlier application; and (3) for each of the respondent's claims directed to the derived invention, the petition must show why that claimed invention is the same or substantially the same as the invention disclosed to the respondent. The language of the rule leaves open the possibility that the disclosure of the petitioner's invention may have been indirect—it may have come from someone other than the inventor or joint inventor of the petitioner. For instance, it could have come from illicit or improper means via someone other than one of the true inventors.

Claim Construction. Another requirement of the petition is to indicate how each claim of the respondent to be involved in the derivation proceeding should be construed. Like the other rules, if the language uses means-plus-function or step-plus-function limitations as permitted under 35 U.S.C. § 112(f), the construction of the claim in the petition must identify the specific portions of the specification describing the structure, material, or acts corresponding to each claimed function. During a derivation proceeding, "a claim of an application or unexpired patent will be given its broadest reasonable construction in light of the specification of the patent in which it appears. This means that the words of the claim will be given their plain meaning unless the plain meaning is inconsistent with the specification."[8]

Sufficiency of Showing. The 2011 statute requires the

---

[8]77 Fed. Reg. 56068, 56075 (September 11, 2012) citing *In re Zletz*, 893 F.2d 319, 321, 13 U.S.P.Q.2d 1320 (Fed. Cir. 1989). For an interesting discussion of why the broadest, reasonable interpretation is used and the standard of review, see *Flo Healthcare Solutions, LLC v. Kappos*, 697 F.3d 1367, 104 U.S.P.Q.2d 1834 (Fed. Cir. 2012) (additional views of Judge Plager and additional views of Judge Newman).

derivation petition to be under oath and be supported by substantial evidence. The USPTO rules speak to the sufficiency of the petitioner's showing. The exact language of the rule is as follows:

> § 42.405(c) *Sufficiency of showing.* A derivation showing is not sufficient unless it is supported by substantial evidence, including at least one affidavit addressing communication of the derived invention and lack of authorization that, if unrebutted, would support a determination of derivation. The showing of communication must be corroborated.

Thus, the petitioner's showings must be supported by at least one affidavit that must address: (1) communication of the derived invention, and (2) lack of authorization. These showings must be of such quality that, if unrebutted, they would support a determination of derivation. The rule maintains the long-time requirement of corroboration as to the communication.

Averring the communication on information and belief, with corroboration to be obtained during discovery, may prove to be insufficient. The statement, "The showing of communication must be corroborated," is directed to the contents for the *petition* and suggests that corroboration needs to be demonstrated in the petition papers themselves rather than something to be discovered after institution of trial. It remains to be seen how the PTAB will construe this and how rigorous the showings must be to be accepted by the Board.[9]

The showing of derivation requires both earlier conception as well as communication of the conception.[10] Hence, the requirement for demonstrating the derivation carries with it a requirement for corroborating the earlier conception.[11]

With regard to the quality or amount of corroboration, "whether a petition makes a sufficient showing of derivation will be decided on a case-by-case basis. * * * The Board expects to apply a 'rule of reason' when [assessing] sufficiency of corroboration."[12]

The PTO has announced that "documentary evidence alone

[9]If the showings are not accepted, then the applicant should have the opportunity after a patent issues (assuming that it is not rejected over the allegedly derived application) to file a civil action under 35 U.S.C.A. § 291 concerning derived patents.

[10]77 Fed. Reg. 56068, 56075 (September 11, 2012).

[11]77 Fed. Reg. 56068, 56074 (September 11, 2012) citing 37 C.F.R. § 42.405(c).

[12]77 Fed. Reg. 56068, 56076 (September 11, 2012).

is not sufficient" with regard to the showings of § 42.405(b) concerning the fact of derivation and the lack of authorization.[13] Indeed, the Office encourages petitioners "to set forth their entire case and supporting evidence in their petitions, lest the petitioner risk a determination by the Board not to institute the derivation proceeding."[14]

The USPTO has commented on the sufficiency of the evidence, calling for substantial evidence. Answering frequently asked questions, the USPTO lists the following:

> Question DER4: What is the standard for instituting a derivation proceeding *** ?
>
> A derivation may be instituted where the petition sets forth a basis for finding that the inventor named in an earlier application derived the claimed invention and there is substantial evidence to support the allegations raised in the petition. ***[15]

Service. The next requirement of the petitioner is to demonstrate that the petition and supporting evidence have been served on the respondent at the correspondence address of record for the earlier application or the subject patent.[16] The petitioner may also serve the petition and supporting evidence on the respondent at any other address known to the petitioner that is likely to effect service. Further, the parties may agree that service by Express Mail® or some means at least as fast as Express Mail® will be sufficient.[17] Additionally, personal service is not required.[18]

Format. The petition must meet the format requirements of 37 C.F.R. § 42.6 and is limited to 60 pages.[19]

Mandatory Notices. The petition must also include the mandatory notices identifying the real party-in-interest, all related judicial or administrative matters that would affect or be affected by a decision in the proposed derivation proceeding, the lead and back-up counsel, and the service information, all as specified by 37 C.F.R. § 42.8.

Incomplete Petition. If the USPTO receives a rule-

---

[13] 77 Fed. Reg. 56068, 56074 (September 11, 2012).

[14] 77 Fed. Reg. 56068, 56074 (September 11, 2012).

[15] http://www.uspto.gov/aia_implementation/faqs_derivation_proceedings.jsp (visited December 29, 2012).

[16] 37 C.F.R § 42.406.

[17] 37 C.F.R § 42.406.

[18] 37 C.F.R § 42.406.

[19] 37 C.F.R § 42.24.

compliant petition which is complete, shows valid service, is accompanied by the filing fee and is properly served, then the USPTO will grant it a filing date.[20] However, if the petition is incomplete in any fashion, it will not receive a filing date and the USPTO will dismiss the petition unless the deficiency is corrected within one month from the date of notice of an incomplete petition or the date of expiration of the statutory deadline, whichever date is earlier.[21]

§ 19:6 The respondent's responses

Mandatory Notices. A respondent who is served with a petition seeking a derivation proceeding has to comply with the mandatory notice provision of 37 C.F.R. § 42.8 which requires the patent owner or applicant in the case of a derivation to submit the mandatory notice within 21 days of service of the petition. The respondent's notice must, as is the case for the petitioner, identify the real party-in-interest for the respondent, all related judicial and administrative matters that would affect or be affected by a decision in the proposed derivation proceeding, identify lead and back-up counsel, and provide the service information listed in § 42.8.

Preliminary Response. It is unclear whether the respondent has the right to file a preliminary response. The post-grant review and *inter partes* review rules both specify that a patent owner may submit a preliminary response, and its deadline is three months after the date of notice indicating that a filing date has been granted to the petition.[1] However, the rules for derivation proceedings do not contain any particular provision for submitting a preliminary response or the time within which it can be filed. Presumably, the Board will issue a schedule upon receipt of the petition, and the schedule will indicate a due date for a respondent's preliminary response. The page limit on any preliminary response would be the same page limit as the petition, i.e., 60 pages.

§ 19:7 Institution of a derivation proceeding

The rules specific to *inter partes* review and post-grant review indicate specifically that it is the *Board* that decides

[20] 37 C.F.R § 42.407.

[21] 37 C.F.R § 42.407(b).

[Section 19:6]

[1] 37 C.F.R. §§ 42.107, 42.207.

whether to institute the review proceeding.[1] In the case of derivation proceedings, however, the rules authorize an administrative patent judge to institute the proceeding on behalf of the Director.[2]

Additionally, once declared or subsequent to the petition, the petitioner has the right to suggest the addition of a patent or application to the derivation proceeding. The rule requires that this additional derivation proceeding request or suggestion must be supported by the showings required under § 42.405 and an explanation of why the suggestion could not have been made in the original petition.[3] For instance, in the time between the petition was filed and the time for making an additional proceeding request, an additional patent or publication may come to light that contains an additional derived claim by the original respondent. Also, another party may be found to have derived. The rules permit the re-declaration or reinstitution of the derivation proceeding to include further respondents.

§ 19:8 After institution of derivation proceeding

The derivation proceeding is administered in accordance with the trial rules and the Trial Practice Guide as explained in Chapter 15. The Part 42, Subpart E specific rules concerning derivation proceedings speak to only a few additional issues.

Settlements. First, § 42.409 indicates that an agreement or understanding under 35 U.S.C. § 135(e) is a settlement for purposes of 37 C.F.R. § 42.74.[1] Section 42.74 is in the general trial rules and addresses the topic of settlements in general. That rule provides as follows:

> **§ 42.74. Settlement.**
>
> (a) *Board role.* The parties may agree to settle any issue in a proceeding, but the Board is not a party to the settlement and may independently determine any question of jurisdiction, patentability, or Office practice.

[Section 19:7]

[1] 37 C.F.R. § 42.108(a) (". . . the Board may authorize the review to proceed . . ."); 37 C.F.R. § 42.208 (re post-grant reviews) (same).

[2] 37 C.F.R. § 42.408(a).

[3] 37 C.F.R. § 42.408(b).

[Section 19:8]

[1] 37 C.F.R. § 42.409.

(b) *Agreements in writing.* Any agreement or understanding between the parties made in connection with, or in contemplation of, the termination of a proceeding shall be in writing and a true copy shall be filed with the Board before the termination of the trial.

(c) *Request to keep separate.* A party to a settlement may request that the settlement be treated as business confidential information and be kept separate from the files of an involved patent or application. The request must be filed with the settlement. If a timely request is filed, the settlement shall only be available:

(1) To a Government agency on written request to the Board; or

(2) To any other person upon written request to the Board to make the settlement agreement available, along with the fee specified in § 42.15(d) and on a showing of good cause.

Arbitration. Rule § 42.410 addresses arbitration and confirms that the parties may resort to binding arbitration to determine any issue. The Office is not a party to the arbitration and not bound by it. The rule makes it clear that the Board will not set a time for or otherwise modify the proceeding for an arbitration unless (1) the arbitration is to be conducted in accordance with Title 9 of the United States Code, (2) the parties notify the Board in writing of their intent to arbitrate, and (3) the agreement to arbitrate meets certain requirements. Those requirements simply are that the agreement be in writing, that it specifies the issues to be arbitrated, names the arbitrators or a date not more than 30 days after the agreement is executed for selecting the arbitrator, provides that the arbitrator award will be binding on all of the parties and judgment can be entered by the Board, provides that a copy of the agreement will be filed within 20 days after execution, and provides that the arbitration will be completed within the time that the Board sets.[2] The parties remain solely responsible for selecting the arbitrator and the conduct of the arbitration. Further, to the extent that the arbitration does not resolve some issues, the Board may determine the issues.[3] The Board will not consider the arbitration award unless it is binding on the parties, is in writing, and states in a clear and definite manner each issue that was arbitrated and the disposition of each issue. Further, it must be filed within 20 days of the

[2] 37 C.F.R. § 42.410(b).

[3] 37 C.F.R. § 42.410(d).

award itself.[4] Once the award is filed, the parties to the award may not take actions inconsistent with it, and if the award is dispositive of the subject matter for any party, the Board may enter judgment as to that party.[5]

Common Ownership. In the event that a derivation proceeding is instituted between an application and another patent or application that are commonly owned, the Board may decline to institute a derivation proceeding or, if one has already been instituted, the Board may issue a judgment in it.[6]

Public Availability. Finally, § 42.412 speaks to the public availability of Board records in derivations. The rule provides as follows:

> **§ 42.412. Public availability of Board records.**
>
> (a) *Publication.* (1) *Generally.* Any Board decision is available for public inspection without a party's permission if rendered in a file open to the public pursuant to § 1.11 of this chapter or inan application that has been published in accordance with §§ 1.211 to 1.221 of this chapter. The Office may independently publish any Board decision that is available for public inspection.
>
> (2) *Determination of special circumstances.* Any Board decision not publishable under paragraph (a)(1) of this section may be published or made available for public inspection if the Director believes that special circumstances warrant publication and a party does not petition within two months after being notified of the intention to make the decision public, objecting in writing on the ground that the decision discloses the objecting party's trade secret or other confidential information and stating with specificity that such information is not otherwise publicly available.
>
> (b) *Record of proceeding.* (1) The record of a Board proceeding is available to the public, unless a patent application not otherwise available to the public is involved.
>
> (2) Notwithstanding paragraph (b)(1) of this section, after a final Board decision in or judgment in a Board proceeding, the record of the Board proceeding will be made available to the public if any involved file is or becomes open to the public under § 1.11 of this chapter or an involved application is or becomes published under §§ 1.211 to 1.221 of this chapter.

Any Board decision becomes available for public inspection

---

[4]37 C.F.R. § 42.410(e).

[5]37 C.F.R. § 42.410(f).

[6]37 C.F.R. § 42.411.

even without the permission of a party, provided that the decision is in an open file under 37 C.F.R. § 1.11 or in accordance with 37 C.F.R. §§ 1.211 to 1.221. Section 1.11 states, among other things, that the file of any interference or trial before the PTAB is open to the public except for the prohibitions in §§ 41.6(b), 42.14, or 42.410(b) (relating to arbitrations).[7]

However, there may be certain special circumstances regarding a Board decision that is not publishable under § 42.412(a)(1). As to those, the USPTO may publish them or make them available for inspection if the Director believes that special circumstances warrant such publication and if a party does not petition within two months of notice of the PTO's intent to make the decision public.

Further, the record of proceedings before the Board is available to the public except for cases involving a patent application not otherwise available to the public.[8] Even in such cases, however, after a final Board decision or judgment in a Board proceeding, the record of the Board will be made available publicly if any involved file is open to the public under § 1.11 or becomes open to the public under that section, or if an involved application is or becomes published under §§ 1.211 through 1.221.

§ 19:9 Derivation actions between owners of issued patents

The AIA revises 35 U.S.C. § 291 so that it no longer refers to interferences between patents but instead addresses the problem where the invention claimed in one patent is (allegedly) derived from an inventor in another patent. Section 291(a) authorizes relief by civil action (in the courts) against the owner of the derived patent having an earlier effective filing date and claiming the same invention. However, such civil action cannot be filed except during the period of one year following the issuance date of the first patent containing a claim to the derived invention and naming an individual who allegedly derived the invention. Thus, a one year window is provided.

§ 19:10 Effective date

The changes to §§ 135 and 291 are stated in AIA § 3, which

---

[7] 37 C.F.R. § 41.6(b).

[8] 37 C.F.R. § 42.412(b).

has its own effective date provision at § 3(n). That provision has been discussed *supra*. The derivation proceeding comes into operation with the first inventor to file system on March 16, 2013.

§ 19:11 Statistics

As of October 17, 2013, the PTAB had received only one derivation petition. It was received in the third quarter of the PTO fiscal year, and had not yet declared whether to institute the trial.

Part IV

USPTO NON-TRIAL SUBMISSIONS OF ART OR INFORMATION; REEXAMINATIONS

Chapter 20

Pre-Issuance Submissions

KeyCite®: Cases and other legal materials listed in KeyCite Scope can be researched through the KeyCite service on Westlaw®. Use KeyCite to check citations for form, parallel references, prior and later history, and comprehensive citator information, including citations to other decisions and secondary materials.

AIA § 8
35 U.S.C.A. § 122

§ 20:1 Background

Pending patent applications are confidential.[1] 35 U.S.C. § 122(a) requires the USPTO to keep applications in confidence and not provide information about them except: (1) as authorized by the owner; (2) unless necessary to carry out the provisions of an Act of Congress; or (3) in special circumstances determined by the Director. However, after 18 months, utility patent applications are published pursuant to § 122(b), subject to exceptions listed in § 122.

Until the AIA, the USPTO provided three routes for third parties to call information to its attention regarding patent applications:

1. art citations by third parties under 37 C.F.R. § 1.99;[2]
2. protests under 37 C.F.R. § 1.291; and
3. public use proceedings under 37 C.F.R. § 1.292.

Art Citations. 37 C.F.R. § 1.99 permitted art citations unaccompanied by any explanation:

37 C.F.R. § 1.99. Third-party submission in published application.

(a) A submission by a member of the public of patents or publications relevant to a pending published application may be entered in the application file if the submission complies with the requirements of this section and the application is still pending when the submission and application file are brought before the examiner.

(b) A submission under this section must identify the application to which it is directed by application number and include:

(1) The fee set forth in § 1.17(p);

(2) A list of the patents or publications submitted for consideration by the Office, including the date of publication of each patent or publication;

(3) A copy of each listed patent or publication in written form or at least the pertinent portions; and

(4) An English language translation of all the necessary and pertinent parts of any non-English language patent or

---

[Section 20:1]

[1]See 35 U.S.C.A. § 122 ("Confidential status of applications; publication of patent applications.").

[2]See also, Manual of Patent Examining Procedure § 1134 ("Third Party Inquiries and Correspondence in a Published Application.").

publication in written form relied upon.

(c) The submission under this section must be served upon the applicant in accordance with § 1.248.

(d) A submission under this section shall not include any explanation of the patents or publications, or any other information. The Office will not enter such explanation or information if included in a submission under this section. A submission under this section is also limited to ten total patents or publications.

(e) A submission under this section must be filed within two months from the date of publication of the application (§ 1.215(a)) or prior to the mailing of a notice of allowance (§ 1.311), whichever is earlier. Any submission under this section not filed within this period is permitted only when the patents or publications could not have been submitted to the Office earlier, and must also be accompanied by the processing fee set forth in § 1.17(i). A submission by a member of the public to a pending published application that does not comply with the requirements of this section will not be entered.

(f) A member of the public may include a self-addressed postcard with a submission to receive an acknowledgment by the Office that the submission has been received. A member of the public filing a submission under this section will not receive any communications from the Office relating to the submission other than the return of a self-addressed postcard. In the absence of a request by the Office, an applicant has no duty to, and need not, reply to a submission under this section.[3] [emphasis added]

While this rule permitted the submission of various art by third parties only in the form of a patent or publication, the third party submitter was precluded by subsection (d) from giving any explanations. In particular, the third party could *not* explain why it chose the art or its relevancy to the application. Not only did such restrictions decrease the value of the information to the examiner, but they also deterred such submissions. A third party in possession of strong prior art references would feel considerable reluctance to submit them for USPTO consideration without having the opportunity to explain the value of the references and how they can be used to reject one or more pending claims. Since the Examiner might not recognize the importance of the reference or understand it in the same way as the third party

[3] 37 C.F.R. § 1.99 was deleted and replaced by § 1.290 in the USPTO rulemaking that implements the Preissuance Submissions portion of the AIA. 77 Fed. Reg. 42150, 42173 (July17, 2012).

(or its expert) understands it, the application could easily issue over the reference. If the eventual patent owner were to seek to license or enforce the resulting patent, the fact that this especially relevant reference was "of record" would create difficulty for the third party, whose potentially best prior art would be shadowed by a presumption of validity. Hence, this pre-AIA procedure available to third parties under 37 C.F.R. 1.99 for citing art against pending applications was not very conducive to obtaining disclosures of relevant prior art.

Public Protests. The second procedure was the public protest specified by 37 C.F.R. § 1.291, which provided as follows:

37 C.F.R. § 1.291. Protests by the public against pending applications.

(a) A protest may be filed by a member of the public against a pending application, and it will be matched with the application file if it adequately identifies the patent application. A protest submitted within the time frame of paragraph (b) of this section, which is not matched, or not matched in a timely manner to permit review by the examiner during prosecution, due to inadequate identification, may not be entered and may be returned to the protestor where practical, or, if return is not practical, discarded.

(b) The protest will be entered into the record of the application if, in addition to complying with paragraph (c) of this section, the protest has been served upon the applicant in accordance with § 1.248, or filed with the Office in duplicate in the event service is not possible; and, except for paragraph (b)(1) of this section, the protest was filed prior to the date the application was published under § 1.211, or a notice of allowance under § 1.311 was mailed, whichever occurs first.

(1) If a protest is accompanied by the written consent of the applicant, the protest will be considered if the protest is matched with the application in time to permit review during prosecution.

(2) A statement must accompany a protest that it is the first protest submitted in the application by the real party in interest who is submitting the protest; or the protest must comply with paragraph (c)(5) of this section. This section does not apply to the first protest filed in an application.

(c) In addition to compliance with paragraphs (a) and (b) of this section, a protest must include:

(1) A listing of the patents, publications, or other information relied upon;

(2) A concise explanation of the relevance of each item listed pursuant to paragraph (c)(1) of this section;

(3) A copy of each listed patent, publication, or other item of information in written form, or at least the pertinent portions thereof;

(4) An English language translation of all the necessary and pertinent parts of any non-English language patent, publication, or other item of information relied upon; and

(5) If it is a second or subsequent protest by the same real party in interest, an explanation as to why the issue(s) raised in the second or subsequent protest are significantly different than those raised earlier and why the significantly different issue(s) were not presented earlier, and a processing fee under § 1.17(i) must be submitted.

(d) A member of the public filing a protest in an application under this section will not receive any communication from the Office relating to the protest, other than the return of a self-addressed postcard which the member of the public may include with the protest in order to receive an acknowledgment by the Office that the protest has been received. The limited involvement of the member of the public filing a protest pursuant to this section ends with the filing of the protest, and no further submission on behalf of the protestor will be considered, unless the submission is made pursuant to paragraph (c)(5) of this section.

(e) Where a protest raising inequitable conduct issues satisfies the provisions of this section for entry, it will be entered into the application file, generally without comment on the inequitable conduct issues raised in it.

(f) In the absence of a request by the Office, an applicant has no duty to, and need not, reply to a protest.

(g) Protests that fail to comply with paragraphs (b) or (c) of this section may not be entered, and if not entered, will be returned to the protestor, or discarded, at the option of the Office.[4]

As can be seen in 37 C.F.R. § 291(c)(2), the public protest procedure allowed the protester to state "a concise explanation of the relevance of each item listed . . . ." However, the protest had to be filed either before a notice of allowance was issued or before publication of the application. It could be considered after publication only if the applicant gave written consent. This mechanism was generally unwieldy because third parties usually do not know other inventors' patent application serial numbers and filing dates prior to

[4]69 Fed. Reg. 56544 (Sept. 21, 2004).

publication of the application. Third parties could try to identify the application in question in other ways, but if the USPTO could not match the protest with the application, it was returned or discarded.[5]

Public Use Proceedings. The final way that information from the interested party could be considered was via a public use under 37 C.F.R. § 1.292 which provided:

§ 1.292. Public use proceedings.

(a) When a petition for the institution of public use proceedings, supported by affidavits or declarations is found, on reference to the examiner, to make a prima facie showing that the invention claimed in an application believed to be on file had been in public use or on sale more than one year before the filing of the application, a hearing may be had before the Director to determine whether a public use proceeding should be instituted. If instituted, the Director may designate an appropriate official to conduct the public use proceeding, including the setting of times for taking testimony, which shall be taken as provided by part 41, subpart D, of this title. The petitioner will be heard in the proceedings but after decision therein will not be heard further in the prosecution of the application for patent.

(b) The petition and accompanying papers, or a notice that such a petition has been filed, shall be entered in the application file if:

(1) The petition is accompanied by the fee set forth in § 1.17(j);

(2) The petition is served on the applicant in accordance with § 1.248, or filed with the Office in duplicate in the event service is not possible; and

(3) The petition is submitted prior to the date the application was published or the mailing of a notice of allowance under § 1.311, whichever occurs first.

(c) A petition for institution of public use proceedings shall not be filed by a party to an interference as to an application involved in the interference. Public use and on sale issues in an interference shall be raised by a motion under § 41.121(a)(1) of this title.[6]

The document required to be filed by § 1.292 was due either before the publication date or the mailing of a notice of

[5] 37 C.F.R. § 291(a) (2004).

[6] 42 Fed. Reg. 5595, Jan. 28, 1977, as amended at 49 Fed. Reg. 48454, Dec. 12, 1984; 61 Fed. Reg. 42807, Aug. 19, 1996; 65 Fed. Reg. 57060, Sept. 20, 2000; 69 Fed. Reg. 50000, Aug. 12, 2004.

allowance. If the submission established a prima facie showing that the invention had been in public use or on sale more than one year before the filing date of the application, then the Director could institute a public use proceeding. This procedure has hardly ever been used.

In sum, the mechanisms available to third parties to assist the USPTO in locating relevant art were generally unsatisfactory.

§ 20:2 Congressional intent[1]

The House Report contains two comments about preissuance submissions:

> *Preissuance submissions by third parties*
>
> After an application is published, members of the public—most likely, a competitor or someone else familiar with the patented invention's field—may realize they have information relevant to a pending application. The relevant information may include prior art that would prohibit the pending application from issuing as a patent. Current USPTO rules permit the submission of such prior art by third parties only if it is in the form of a patent or publication,[FN43] but the submitter is precluded from explaining why the prior art was submitted or what its relevancy to the application might be.[FN44] Such restrictions decrease the value of the information to the examiner and may, as a result, deter such submissions.[FN45]
>
> FN 43. *See* 35 C.F.R. Sec. 1.99.
>
> FN 44. *See* 35 C.F.R. Sec. 1.99(d) ("A submission under this section shall not include any explanation of the patents or publications, or any other information.").

[Section 20:2]

[1]The Supreme Court cautions against relying on interpretations advanced in legislative statements that are not "anchored in the text of the statute." *Shannon v. U.S.*, 512 U.S. 573, 583, 114 S. Ct. 2419, 129 L. Ed. 2d 459 (1994), stating "[C]ourts have no authority to enforce [a] principl[e] gleaned solely from legislative history that has no statutory reference point." Shannon, 512 U.S. at 584, quoting *International Broth. of Elec. Workers, Local Union No. 474, AFL-CIO v. N.L.R.B.*, 814 F.2d 697, 712, 124 L.R.R.M. (BNA) 2993, 106 Lab. Cas. (CCH) P 12256 (D.C. Cir. 1987). The authoritative statement "is the statutory text, not the legislative history." *Exxon Mobil Corp. v. Allapattah Services, Inc.*, 545 U.S. 546, 568, 125 S. Ct. 2611, 162 L. Ed. 2d 502 (2005). However, lower courts have cited the legislative history of the AIA already in recent cases. E.g., *Rogers v. Tristar Products, Inc.*, 102 U.S.P.Q.2d 1722, 2012 WL 1660604, *2 (Fed. Cir. 2012) (non-precedential); *Byrne v. Wood, Herron & Evans, LLP*, 676 F.3d 1024, 1029, 102 U.S.P.Q.2d 1073 (Fed. Cir. 2012) (dissenting opin.).

FN 45. *See Perspectives on Patents: Hearing Before the Subcomm. on Intellectual Prop. of the Senate Comm. on the Judiciary,* 109th Cong. (2005) (statement of David Simon, Chief Patent Counsel, Intel Corporation).

The Act improves the process by which third parties submit relevant information to the UPSTO by permitting those third parties to make statements concerning the relevance of the patents, patent applications, and other printed publications that they bring to the USPTO's attention.

* * *

Section 8. Preissuance submissions by third parties.

This section amends § 122 to create a mechanism for third parties to submit timely pre-issuance information relevant to the examination of the application, including a concise statement of the relevance of the submission.[2]

§ 20:3 The amended statute

AIA § 8(a) amends 35 U.S.C. § 122 by adding a new subsection (e) to the end of that statute. Further, AIA § 8(b) provides an effective date. These provide as follows:

New Statute (35 U.S.C. § 122(e))

(e) PREISSUANCE SUBMISSIONS BY THIRD PARTIES.—

(1) IN GENERAL.— Any third party may submit for consideration and inclusion in the record of a patent application, any patent, published patent application, or other printed publication of potential relevance to the examination of the application, if such submission is made in writing before the earlier of—

(A) the date a notice of allowance under section 151 is given or mailed in the application for patent; or

(B) the later of—

(i) 6 months after the date on which the application for patent is first published under section 122 by the Office, or

(ii) the date of the first rejection under section 132 of any claim by the examiner during the examination of the application for patent.

(2) OTHER REQUIREMENTS.— Any submission under paragraph (1) shall—

(A) set forth a concise description of the asserted relevance of each submitted document;

(B) be accompanied by such fee as the Director may prescribe; and

[2]H. R. Rep. No. 112-98, pt. 1, at 48–49, 77 (2011).

(C) include a statement by the person making such submission affirming that the submission was made in compliance with this section.

New Statute (AIA Sec. 8(b))

(b) EFFECTIVE DATE.— The amendments made by this section shall take effect upon the expiration of the 1-year period beginning on the date of the enactment of this Act and shall apply to any patent application filed before, on, or after that effective date.

§ 20:4 New rule 1.290 for third party preissuance submissions

The USPTO withdrew 37 C.F.R. §§ 1.99 and 1.292 and replaced them with a new C.F.R. § 1.290 for preissuance submissions against applications on file.

37 CFR § 1.290. Submissions by third parties in applications.

(a) A third party may submit, for consideration and entry in the record of a patent application, any patents, published patent applications, or other printed publications of potential relevance to the examination of the application if the submission is made in accordance with 35 U.S.C. 122(e) and this section. A third-party submission may not be entered or considered by the Office if any part of the submission is not in compliance with 35 U.S.C. 122(e) and this section.

(b) Any third-party submission under this section must be filed prior to the earlier of:

(1) The date a notice of allowance under § 1.311 is given or mailed in the application; or

(2) The later of:

(i) Six months after the date on which the application is first published by the Office under 35 U.S.C. 122(b) and § 1.211, or

(ii) The date the first rejection under § 1.104 of any claim by the examiner is given or mailed during the examination of the application.

(c) Any third-party submission under this section must be made in writing.

(d) Any third-party submission under this section must include:

(1) A document list identifying the documents, or portions of documents, being submitted in accordance with paragraph (e) of this section;

(2) A concise description of the asserted relevance of each item identified in the document list;

(3) A legible copy of each item identified in the document list, other than U.S. patents and U.S. patent application publications;

(4) An English language translation of any non-English language item identified in the document list; and

(5) A statement by the party making the submission that:

(i) The party is not an individual who has a duty to disclose information with respect to the application under § 1.56; and

(ii) The submission complies with the requirements of 35 U.S.C. 122(e) and this section.

(e) The document list required by paragraph (d)(1) of this section must include a heading that identifies the list as a third-party submission under § 1.290, identify on each page of the list the application number of the application in which the submission is being filed, list U.S. patents and U.S. patent application publications in a separate section from other items, and identify each:

(1) U.S. patent by patent number, first named inventor, and issue date;

(2) U.S. patent application publication by patent application publication number, first named inventor, and publication date;

(3) Foreign patent or published foreign patent application by the country or patent office that issued the patent or published the application; the applicant, patentee, or first named inventor; an appropriate document number; and the publication date indicated on the patent or published application; and

(4) Non-patent publication by author (if any), title, pages being submitted, publication date, and, where available, publisher and place of publication. If no publication date is known, the third party must provide evidence of publication.

(f) Any third-party submission under this section must be accompanied by the fee set forth in § 1.17(p) for every ten items or fraction thereof identified in the document list.

(g) The fee otherwise required by paragraph (f) of this section is not required for a submission listing three or fewer total items that is accompanied by a statement by the party making the submission that, to the knowledge of the person signing the statement after making reasonable inquiry, the submission is the first and only submission under 35 U.S.C. 122(e) filed in the application by the party or a party in privity with the party.

(h) In the absence of a request by the Office, an applicant need not reply to a submission under this section.

(i) The provisions of § 1.8 do not apply to the time periods set forth in this section.

§ 20:5 Filing a preissuance submission under the new rule

Under the amended statute and the final rules adopted by the USPTO, a preissuance submission calls for the following:

- A document list;
- A description of relevance to the application in question;
- A legible copy of each item, except U.S. patents and published U.S. patent applications;
- An English translation of each non-English language item in the document list;
- A statement by the submitting party that the party does *not* have a duty to disclose with respect to the pending application under § 1.56 and that the submission complies with 35 U.S.C. § 122(e) and 37 C.F.R. § 1.290;
- A fee (currently $180).

The "application" contemplated by the statute is understood by the USPTO to mean any non-provisional utility, design, or plant application, or a continuation thereof.[1] The USPTO will not accept a preissuance submission under § 1.290 against a reissue patent application because the statute specifically says this is for *preissuance* submissions.[2] For the same reason, the USPTO will not accept such submissions in reexamination proceedings[3] or against issued patents.[4] Also, the "application" contemplated by the statute and the rule need *not* be a live, "pending" application but could instead be an abandoned application.[5] Section 20:6 *infra* discusses the time for filing such a submission.

The new § 122(e) and the rule allow a third party—not anyone "involved" in the application to such an extent that he has a duty to disclose—to submit *only* the following items for USPTO consideration:

[Section 20:5]

[1] 77 Fed. Reg. 42150 (July 17, 2012).

[2] 77 Fed. Reg. 42150, 42151 (July 17, 2012).

[3] 77 Fed. Reg. 42150, 42151 (July 17, 2012).

[4] 77 Fed. Reg. 42150, 42154 (July 17, 2012).

[5] 77 Fed. Reg. 42150, 42152 (July 17, 2012).

- Any patent;
- Any published patent application;
- Any other printed publication of potential relevance.[6]

The submission does not need to aver that the documents constitute prior art, and the statute has no such requirement.[7]

Business with the USPTO is normally conducted in writing. As such, and pursuant to the statute, all preissuance submissions must be in writing.[8] The USPTO has developed a dedicated web-based interface for electronic filing of § 1.291 submissions.[9] The USPTO strongly encourages use of the web interface.[10]

Unlike the former rule of 37 C.F.R. § 1.99, but like § 1.291(c)(2), the submitting third party must provide a concise description of the asserted relevance of each submitted document.[11] This is a major improvement over the earlier practice. The USPTO notes that a description of relevance differs from arguments against patentability, which the USPTO now allows under § 1.291.[12] The USPTO suggests "a narrative description or a claim chart."[13] However, setting forth a "concise description" does not go so far as to permit the submitter to propose rejections or set forth arguments against an applicant's reply to an Office Action.[14] The "best practice" suggested by the USPTO is to point out the relevant pages or lines of the document. Verbose descriptions are discouraged in light of the statutory requirement that the description be "concise."[15]

The fee that is required is for each 10 items of art.[16] Note however the three for free provision of 37 C.F.R. § 1.290(g).

The submitting party must provide a statement that its

---

[6]35 U.S.C.A. § 122(e)(1) (2011); 37 C.F.R. § 1.290(a).

[7]77 Fed. Reg. 42150, 42154 (July 17, 2012).

[8]35 U.S.C.A. § 122(e)(1) (2011); 37 C.F.R. § 1.290(c).

[9]77 Fed. Reg. 42150, 42151 (July 17, 2012).

[10]77 Fed. Reg. 42150, 42152 (July 17, 2012).

[11]35 U.S.C.A. § 122(e)(2)(A) (2011); 37 C.F.R. § 1.290(d)(2).

[12]77 Fed. Reg. 42150, 42151 (July 17, 2012).

[13]77 Fed. Reg. 42150, 42156 (July 17, 2012).

[14]77 Fed. Reg. 42150, 42156 (July 17, 2012).

[15]77 Fed. Reg. 42150, 42156 (July 17, 2012).

[16]37 C.F.R. § 1.290(f); 77 Fed. Reg. 42150, 42157 (July 17, 2012).

submission is being made in compliance with the statute.[17]

Interestingly, the statute does not contain a specific provision for identifying the real party in interest behind the submission. Also, there is no requirement of service on the applicant.[18]

This provision became effective on September 16, 2012 and applies to all applications regardless of filing date.

§ 20:6 The timing requirement

The timing requirement for a preissuance submission is specific. The third party submission must be made before the earlier of:

(a) the date a notice of allowance is issued, or
(b) the later of:
  (i) six months after the date the application is first published, or
  (ii) the date of the first rejection by the examiner under § 132 of any claim.[1]

In other words, the amended statute grants a third party a time-limited right to submit documents to the USPTO relevant to the claims of an application. The statute and rule are silent on when the window opens but they are specific about when the window closes. Theoretically, a third party could offer a submission the day after the filing date, as long as the third party can identify the application number.[2] Unless a third party is privy to the patent application serial number, the filing details generally are not disclosed until publication. The USPTO understands "publication" to mean publication by the USPTO.[3] Regardless of how early a third party can submit the citations, the window closes using these corollary rules:

Corollary 1: Once a notice of allowance issues, no preissu-

---

[17] 35 U.S.C.A. § 122(e)(2)(C) (2011).

[18] 77 Fed. Reg. 42150, 42152 (July 17, 2012).

[Section 20:6]

[1] 35 U.S.C.A. § 122(e)(1)(A) to (B) (2011).

[2] This requirement of stating the application serial number appears to be stated only in 37 C.F.R. § 1.290(e) concerning the contents of the document list. That provision requires that each page of the list identify "the application number of the application in which the submission is being filed. . ."

[3] 77 Fed. Reg. 42150, 42155 (July 17, 2012).

ance submission is timely.

Corollary 2: Subject to Corollary 1, once a publication of the application occurs, the third party has six months to file a submission, even if there has been an Office Action rejecting claims.

Corollary 3: Subject to Corollary 1, if there has not yet been an Office Action rejecting claims, even if six months go by after publication, a submission is timely up until the USPTO issues the *first* rejection of any claim.[4]

Corollary 4: If the USPTO rejects any claim before six months after the application is published, the submission is timely until the six months expire, unless a Notice of Allowance issues.

An interesting application of the timing requirements of the statute and rule involves an abandoned application. Note that neither the statute nor the rule specifies that the application must be a "*pending*" or "live" application. That means it can be abandoned, perhaps for failure to respond to an Office Action that rejects claims. A preissuance submission under § 1.290 can still be filed, either while the application is abandoned or after revival. If the application revives, the § 1.290 submission must be filed before mailing of a Notice of Allowance or, if none, within six months after publication of the application.[5]

The amended statute grants any third party the absolute right to submit documents falling within the specified categories during the permitted period, thus providing a means for interested parties to challenge a patent application during the preissuance stage. Consent of the applicant is not required.

Practitioners should note that § 1.290(i) excludes § 1.290 submissions from the benefit of a certificate of mailing or fax transmission.[6] Simply mailing the papers within the allowed time and including a certificate of mailing will not ensure that the submission is timely. If the papers reach the USPTO too late, the certificate will not be effective. The papers can be delivered by hand, by mail, by Express Mail, or prefer-

---

[4]The statute and rule do not reference the date of an "Office Action" but rather a "first rejection under § 1.104." Hence, a restriction requirement does not count, nor other communications short of a rejection of a claim.

[5]77 Fed. Reg. 42150, 42152 to 42153 (July 17, 2012).

[6]See 37 C.F.R. § 1.8 (July 17, 2012).

ably filed electronically.[7]

§ 20:7 Subsequent handling of § 1.290 submissions

Regardless of the submission method, third party submissions are not entered automatically into the electronic image file wrapper of an application; they are not automatically made of record. Before entry into the record, they will be reviewed by the Office to ensure compliance with the statute and the rule.[1]

Pursuant to § 1.290(h), an applicant need not respond to a § 1.290 submission by a third party.

§ 20:8 Protests under 35 U.S.C. § 122(c) and 37 C.F.R. § 1.291 survive

The USPTO withdrew 37 C.F.R. § 1.292 regarding public use proceedings[1] and made some changes to 37 C.F.R. § 1.291 concerning protests by the public against pending applications. As amended, and including the unchanged sections, the public protest rule provides as follows (new provisions underscored):

> **§ 1.291. Protests by the public against pending applications.**
>
> (a) A protest may be filed by a member of the public against a pending application, and it will be matched with the application file if it adequately identifies the patent application. A protest submitted within the time frame of paragraph (b) of this section, which is not matched, or not matched in a timely manner to permit review by the examiner during prosecution, due to inadequate identification, may not be entered and may be returned to the protestor where practical, or, if return is not practical, discarded.
>
> <u>(b) The protest will be entered into the record of the application if, in addition to complying with paragraph (c) of this section, the protest has been served upon the applicant in accordance with § 1.248, or filed with the Office in duplicate in</u>

[7] 77 Fed. Reg. 42150, 42152 (July 17, 2012).

[Section 20:7]

[1] 77 Fed. Reg. 42150, 42152 (July 17, 2012).

[Section 20:8]

[1] The USPTO final rules of July 17, 2012 eliminate this section relating to public use proceedings. 77 Fed. Reg. at 42174. The USPTO deems it unnecessary in view of the new post-grant review procedure where public use can be raised. 77 Fed. Reg. 42150.

the event service is not possible; and, except for paragraph (b)(1) of this section, the protest was filed prior to the date the application was published under § 1.211, or the date a notice of allowance under § 1.311 was given or mailed, whichever occurs first:

(1) If a protest is accompanied by the written consent of the applicant, the protest will be considered if the protest is filed prior to the date a notice of allowance under § 1.311 is given or mailed in the application.

(2) A statement must accompany a protest that it is the first protest submitted in the application by the real party in interest who is submitting the protest; or the protest must comply with paragraph (c)(5) of this section. This section does not apply to the first protest filed in an application.

(c) In addition to compliance with paragraphs (a) and (b) of this section, a protest must include:

(1) An information list of the documents, portions of documents, or other information being submitted, where each:

(i) U.S. patent is identified by patent number, first named inventor, and issue date;

(ii) U.S. patent application publication is identified by patent application publication number, first named inventor, and publication date;

(iii) Foreign patent or published foreign patent application is identified by the country or patent office that issued the patent or published the application; an appropriate document number; the applicant, patentee, or first named inventor; and the publication date indicated on the patent or published application;

(iv) Non-patent publication is identified by author (if any), title, pages being submitted, publication date, and, where available, publisher and place of publication; and

(v) Item of other information is identified by date, if known.

(2) A concise explanation of the relevance of each item identified in the information list pursuant to paragraph (c)(1) of this section;

(3) A legible copy of each item identified in the information list, other than U.S. patents and U.S. patent application publications;

(4) An English language translation of any non-English language item identified in the information list; and

(5) If it is a second or subsequent protest by the same real party in interest, an explanation as to why the issue(s) raised in the second or subsequent protest are significantly

different than those raised earlier and why the significantly different issue(s) were not presented earlier, and a processing fee under § 1.17(i) must be submitted.

(d) A member of the public filing a protest in an application under this section will not receive any communication from the Office relating to the protest, other than the return of a self-addressed postcard which the member of the public may include with the protest in order to receive an acknowledgment by the Office that the protest has been received. The limited involvement of the member of the public filing a protest pursuant to this section ends with the filing of the protest, and no further submission on behalf of the protestor will be considered, unless the submission is made pursuant to paragraph (c)(5) of this section.

(e) Where a protest raising inequitable conduct issues satisfies the provisions of this section for entry, it will be entered into the application file, generally without comment on the inequitable conduct issues raised in it.

(f) In the absence of a request by the Office, an applicant need not reply to a protest.

(g) Protests that fail to comply with paragraphs (b) or (c) of this section may not be entered, and if not entered, will be returned to the protestor, or discarded, at the option of the Office.

37 C.F.R. § 1.291 was amended to improve clarity and consistency with the new statute and new § 1.290. One should note that § 1.291(c)(1) does not refer to a "document list" but rather an "information list" and that this subsection indicates that "other information" beyond documents can be submitted.

§ 20:9 USPTO statistics re pre-issuance submissions

On its website, the USPTO maintains statistics on AIA activity.[1] It reported that as of August 30, 2013, it had received 935 preissuance submissions. Following the part-month in September 2012, the mean number of submissions is over 80 per month.

[Section 20:9]

[1] http://www.uspto.gov/aia_implementation/statistics.jsp (visited October 21, 2013).

Chapter 21

Post-Issuance Submissions

AIA § 6(g)
35 U.S.C.A. § 301

§ 21:1 Background

The provision allowing the citation of art with respect to an issued patent appears in Chapter 30 of the patent statute as codified. Chapter 30 begins with 35 U.S.C. § 301 (Citation of Prior Art) and then contains the statutory provisions for *ex parte* reexamination at §§ 302–307. Section 301 provides authority for any person at any time to cite to the USPTO material falling within the definition of prior art which that person believes to be relevant to the patentability of any claim of a particular patent. Former § 301 reads:

Old Statute (35 U.S.C. § 301)

§ 301. Citation of prior art.

Any person at any time may cite to the Office in writing prior art consisting of patents or printed publications which that person believes to have a bearing on the patentability of any claim of a particular patent. If the person explains in writing the pertinency and manner of applying such prior art

> to at least one claim of the patent, the citation of such prior art and the explanation thereof will become a part of the official file of the patent. At the written request of the person citing the prior art, his or her identity will be excluded from the patent file and kept confidential.

To implement § 301, the USPTO adopted 37 C.F.R. § 501, which provided as follows:

> **37 CFR § 501. Citation of prior art in patent files.**
>
> (a) At any time during the period of enforceability of a patent, any person may cite, to the Office in writing, prior art consisting of patents or printed publications which that person states to be pertinent and applicable to the patent and believes to have a bearing on the patentability of any claim of the patent. If the citation is made by the patent owner, the explanation of pertinency and applicability may include an explanation of how the claims differ from the prior art. Such citations shall be entered in the patent file except as set forth in §§ 1.502 and 1.902.
>
> (b) If the person making the citation wishes his or her identity to be excluded from the patent file and kept confidential, the citation papers must be submitted without any identification of the person making the submission.
>
> (c) Citation of patents or printed publications by the public in patent files should either: (1) Reflect that a copy of the same has been mailed to the patent owner at the address as provided for in § 1.33(c); or in the event service is not possible (2) Be filed with the Office in duplicate.[1]

There are reasons someone might offer a submission of prior art, assuming the submission is successfully entered into the official record of the patent.

First, in future litigation or prospective litigation, anyone examining the file history would see the prior art cited via § 301. This could be useful in limiting or invalidating the claims.

Second, the material submitted via § 301 is usable in a reexamination proceeding. Section 305, directed to "Conduct of reexamination proceedings," included this statement:

> In any reexamination proceeding under this chapter, the patent owner will be permitted to propose any amendment to his patent and a new claim or claims thereto, in order to distin-

---

[Section 21:1]

[1]46 FR 29185, May 29, 1981, effective July 1, 1981; para. (a) revised, 65 FR 76756, Dec. 7, 2000, effective Feb. 5, 2001.

guish the invention as claimed from the prior art cited under the provisions of section 301 of this title, or in response to a decision adverse to the patentability of a claim of a patent.

A third potential reason for citing art via § 301 is that the Director might initiate reexamination on his own initiative pursuant to § 304, and art of record may be considered.

§ 21:2 Congressional intent[1]

Two passages in the House Report bear on post-issue submissions. The passage at pp. 45–46 comes under the title of "Post-grant review proceedings" but generally indicates the reasoning of Congress in making its changes to post-issue citations within the overall framework of the old and new procedures:

> Nearly 30 years ago, Congress created the administrative "reexamination" process, through which the USPTO could review the validity of already-issued patents on the request of either the patent holder or a third party,[FN30] in the expectation that it would serve as an effective and efficient alternative to often costly and protracted district court litigation.[FN31]
>
> FN 30. See 35 U.S.C. Sec. 301–307. A patent holder will typically request reexamination to bolster the patent in view of new prior art. A third party may request reexamination to challenge, and ultimately invalidate, the patent.
>
> FN 31. "Reexamination will permit efficient resolution of questions about the validity of issued patents without recourse to expensive and lengthy infringement litigation . . .. The reexamination of issued patents could be conducted with a fraction of the time and cost of formal legal proceedings and would help restore confidence in the effectiveness

---

[Section 21:2]

[1]The Supreme Court cautions against relying on interpretations advanced in legislative statements that are not "anchored in the text of the statute." *Shannon v. U.S.*, 512 U.S. 573, 583, 114 S. Ct. 2419, 129 L. Ed. 2d 459 (1994), stating "[C]ourts have no authority to enforce [a] principl[e] gleaned solely from legislative history that has no statutory reference point." Shannon, 512 U.S. at 584, quoting *International Broth. of Elec. Workers, Local Union No. 474, AFL-CIO v. N.L.R.B.*, 814 F.2d 697, 712, 124 L.R.R.M. (BNA) 2993, 106 Lab. Cas. (CCH) P 12256 (D.C. Cir. 1987). The authoritative statement "is the statutory text, not the legislative history." *Exxon Mobil Corp. v. Allapattah Services, Inc.*, 545 U.S. 546, 568, 125 S. Ct. 2611, 162 L. Ed. 2d 502 (2005). However, lower courts have cited the legislative history of the AIA already in recent cases. E.g., *Rogers v. Tristar Products, Inc.*, 102 U.S.P.Q.2d 1722, 2012 WL 1660604, *2 (Fed. Cir. 2012) (non-precedential); *Byrne v. Wood, Herron & Evans, LLP*, 676 F.3d 1024, 1029, 102 U.S.P.Q.2d 1073 (Fed. Cir. 2012) (dissenting opin.).

of our patent system . . .. It is anticipated that these measures provide a useful and necessary alternative for challengers and for patent owners to test the validity of United States patents in an efficient and relatively inexpensive manner." *See* H.R. Rep. No. 96-1307(I) at 3 (1980), reprinted in 1980 U.S.C.C.A.N. 6460, 6462–63.

* * *

The [America Invents] Act expands the category of documents that may be cited in a reexamination proceeding to include written statements of the patent owner that have been filed in a proceeding before a Federal court or the USPTO regarding the scope of claims. This addition will counteract the ability of patent owners to offer differing interpretations of prior art in different proceedings. These written statements, which include documents, pleadings or evidence from proceedings that address the patent owner's statements, shall not be considered for any purpose other than to determine the proper meaning of the claims that are the subject of the request in a proceeding. Specifically, the Committee does not intend these statements to be a basis for the institution of a reexamination proceeding. Reexaminations will continue to be available only on the basis of "patents or printed publications."[FN42]

FN 42. The scope of "patent and printed publication" prior art in the amended section 301 is intended to be coextensive with these terms in current section 102 of the title 35. Further, amendments made by Section 2 of the Act, which expand and contract the definition of certain other forms of prior art, are not intended to change the particular "patent or printed publication" prior art, which will continue to be the sole basis for initiating reexamination proceedings.[2]

* * *

Subsection (g) amends § 301 to include written statements of the patent owner filed in a proceedings before a Federal court or the Office as citable prior art. The section is further amended to provide rules for submitting such statements and the limitations on their use.[3]

§ 21:3 The amended statute regarding post-issue submissions

The AIA expanded § 301 to allow for certain written statements to be cited to the USPTO, as follows:

New Statute (35 U.S.C. § 301)

§ 301. Citation of prior art and written statements

(a) IN GENERAL.—Any person at any time may cite to the Of-

---

[2]H.R. Rep. No. 112-98, pt. 1, at 45 to 46 (2011).

[3]H.R. Rep. No. 112-98, pt. 1, at 77 (2011).

fice in writing—

(1) prior art consisting of patents or printed publications which that person believes to have a bearing on the patentability of any claim of a particular patent; or

(2) statements of the patent owner filed in a proceeding before a Federal court or the Office in which the patent owner took a position on the scope of any claim of a particular patent.

(b) OFFICIAL FILE.—If the person citing prior art or written statements pursuant to subsection (a) explains in writing the pertinence and manner of applying the prior art or written statements to at least 1 claim of the patent, the citation of the prior art or written statements and the explanation thereof shall become a part of the official file of the patent.

(c) ADDITIONAL INFORMATION.—A party that submits a written statement pursuant to subsection (a)(2) shall include any other documents, pleadings, or evidence from the proceeding in which the statement was filed that addresses the written statement.

(d) LIMITATIONS.—A written statement submitted pursuant to subsection (a)(2), and additional information submitted pursuant to subsection (c), shall not be considered by the Office for any purpose other than to determine the proper meaning of a patent claim in a proceeding that is ordered or instituted pursuant to section 304, 314, or 324. If any such written statement or additional information is subject to an applicable protective order, such statement or information shall be redacted to exclude information that is subject to that order.

(e) CONFIDENTIALITY.—Upon the written request of the person citing prior art or written statements pursuant to subsection (a), that person's identity shall be excluded from the patent file and kept confidential.

New Statute (AIA Sec. 6(g)(3))

EFFECTIVE DATE.—The amendments made by this subsection [AIA 6(g)] shall take effect upon the expiration of the 1-year period beginning on the date of the enactment of this Act and shall apply to any patent issued before, on, or after that effective date.

§ 21:4 New regulation 37 C.F.R. § 1.501

To implement the revised statute § 301, the USPTO issued the following 37 C.F.R. § 1.501:

§ 1.501. Citation of prior art and written statements in patent files.

(a) *Information content of submission*: At any time during the period of enforceability of a patent, any person may file a written submission with the Office under this section, which is directed to the following information:

(1) Prior art consisting of patents or printed publications which the person making the submission believes to have a bearing on the patentability of any claim of the patent; or

(2) Statements of the patent owner filed by the patent owner in a proceeding before a Federal court or the Office in which the patent owner took a position on the scope of any claim of the patent. Any statement submitted under this paragraph must be accompanied by any other documents, pleadings, or evidence from the proceeding in which the statement was filed that address the written statement, and such statement and accompanying information under this paragraph must be submitted in redacted form to exclude information subject to an applicable protective order.

(3) Submissions under paragraph (a)(2) of this section must identify:

(i) The forum and proceeding in which patent owner filed each statement;

(ii) The specific papers and portions of the papers submitted that contain the statements; and

(iii) How each statement submitted is a statement in which patent owner took a position on the scope of any claim in the patent.

(b) *Explanation*: A submission pursuant to paragraph (a) of this section:

(1) Must include an explanation in writing of the pertinence and manner of applying any prior art submitted under paragraph (a)(1) of this section and any written statement and accompanying information submitted under paragraph (a)(2) of this section to at least one claim of the patent, in order for the submission to become a part of the official file of the patent; and

(2) May, if the submission is made by the patent owner, include an explanation of how the claims differ from any prior art submitted under paragraph (a)(1) of this section or any written statements and accompanying information submitted under paragraph (a)(2) of this section.

(c) *Reexamination pending*: If a reexamination proceeding has been requested and is pending for the patent in which the submission is filed, entry of the submission into the official file of the patent is subject to the provisions of §§ 1.502 and 1.902.

(d) *Identity*: If the person making the submission wishes his or her identity to be excluded from the patent file and kept confidential, the submission papers must be submitted anonymously without any identification of the person making the submission.

(e) *Certificate of Service*: A submission under this section by a person other than the patent owner must include a certification that a copy of the submission was served in its entirety upon patent owner at the address as provided for in § 1.33 (c). A submission by a person other than the patent owner that fails to include proper proof of service as required by § 1.248(b) will not be entered into the patent file.

§ 21:5 Filing a post-issue citation of art or information

35 U.S.C. § 301 and 37 C.F.R. § 1.501 took effect on Sept. 16, 2012, one year after the enactment of the AIA.

The most significant change made by the AIA to § 301 is that the statute as amended permits anyone to submit written statements that were filed by the patent owner in federal court or the USPTO, where such written statements took a position on the scope of any claim in the patent. One major concern is over positions taken with respect to the prior art in different proceedings. "Permitting submission of these claim scope statements is intended to limit a patent owner's ability to put forward different positions with respect to the prior art in different proceedings on the same patent."[1]

The person who offers a submission under these rules may be the patent owner, the inventor, a related company, a licensee, a competitor, a rival inventor, an adversary, or a member of the general public. The statute and rule place no restriction on who the submitter may be.

The submission can be done anonymously,[2] as previously allowed.

The submission itself is relatively straightforward. It requires:

- In the case of prior art, a copy of the patents and printed publications which the submitter believes have a bearing on the patentability of any claim of the patent;
- In the case of patent owner statements, a proper identification of where the statements are from (forum and proceeding);
- Identification of the specific papers being submitted;
- Submission of related papers required by the rule for completeness ("other documents, pleadings, or evidence from the proceeding in which the statement was filed

[Section 21:5]

[1] 77 Fed. Reg. 46615, 46617 (Aug. 6, 2012).

[2] 35 U.S.C.A. § 301(e) (2011); 37 C.F.R. § 501(d).

that address the written statement . . .");

- An explanation of how each submitted statement is a statement by the patent owner concerning the scope of any claim in the patent;
- A written explanation of the pertinence and manner of applying, to at least one claim, any prior art that is being submitted and any information being submitted; and
- A certificate of service.

Additionally, a statement submitted by the patent owner may include an explanation of how the claims differ from any prior art submitted under 37 C.F.R. § 1.501(a)(1) or any written statements under paragraph (a)(2).

While the revised § 301 retains the limitation that the only prior art to be submitted is patents and printed publications, now it also allows citations of statements made by a patent owner in a proceeding before a federal court[3] or the USPTO in which the patent owner took a position on the scope of any claim of a particular patent. The party submitting a written statement filed by the patent owner *must* include any other documents, pleadings, or evidence from the proceeding in which the statement is filed that address the written statement.[4] If any of the information is confidential or otherwise protected by the terms of a protective order, then redaction is proper.

Patent owner statements submitted under 35 U.S.C. § 301 regarding claim scope *cannot* be considered when the USPTO is determining whether to order *ex parte* reexamination under 35 U.S.C. § 303. In making that determination, the USPTO uses the broadest reasonable interpretation consistent with the specification, except in the case of an expired patent.[5] However, after a reexamination commences, the USPTO intends to consider submitted patent owner statements about claim scope "to the fullest extent possible when determining the scope of any claims of the patent which are subject to reexamination."[6]

---

[3]The Office interprets "Federal court" to include the United States Court of International Trade, but to exclude the United States International Trade Commission, which is a federal agency. 77 Fed. Reg. 46615, 46617 (Aug. 6, 2012).

[4]35 U.S.C.A. § 301(c) (2011); 37 C.F.R. § 501(a)(2).

[5]77 Fed. Reg. 46615, 46618 (Aug. 6, 2012).

[6]77 Fed. Reg. 46615, 46618 (Aug. 6, 2012).

§ 21:6 USPTO use of a post-issue submission

The statute dictates that if the filing conditions are met, then the prior art or written statements will become part of the official file of the patent.[1]

It is not wholly clear how the Office will proceed or how courts will regard this USPTO use, as the claim interpretation that usually applies in Office proceedings is the broadest, reasonable interpretation.[2] That is not the claim interpretation that courts apply in patent litigation where some of the patent owner statements may have been made. However, if the Director determines that a different standard should apply in a post-patent USPTO proceeding over a patent, courts might sustain that, particularly in light of the statutory authority in 35 U.S.C. § 301(d) that "[a] written statement submitted pursuant to subsection (a)(2), and additional information submitted pursuant to subsection (c), shall not be considered by the Office for any purpose other than to determine the proper meaning of a patent claim in a proceeding that is ordered or instituted pursuant to section 304, 314, or 324 . . ." It is interesting to note that the USPTO might apply one claim interpretation when deciding whether to grant a reexamination request and a different one during the proceeding.

[Section 21:6]

[1]35 U.S.C.A. § 301(b) (2011).

[2]For an interesting discussion of why the broadest, reasonable interpretation is used and the standard of review, see *Flo Healthcare Solutions, LLC v. Kappos*, 697 F.3d 1367, 104 U.S.P.Q.2d 1834 (Fed. Cir. 2012) (additional views of Judge Plager and additional views of Judge Newman).

Chapter 22

Supplemental Examination

AIA § 12
35 U.S.C.A. § 257

§ 22:1 Background

Before passage of the AIA, the patent statute contained various provisions allowing the USPTO to consider or reconsider its grant of a patent when a patent owner becomes aware of new facts concerning prior art.

The primary route for such post-grant consideration of prior art has been the reexamination provisions where the patentability of issued claims could, within limits, be addressed by a patent owner using 35 U.S.C. Chapter 30, directed to "Prior Art Citations To Office and Ex Parte Reexamination Of Patents." This chapter permits a patent owner who becomes aware of further prior art in the form of a patent or other published document to submit a request for *ex parte* reexamination. If the new prior art raises a substantial new question of patentability, the request would be approved, and the patent owner can address the resulting issues of patentability. Two notable limitations of *ex parte* reexamination are: (1) the prior art that can be considered is limited to issued patents and other published documents; and (2) reexamination does not address the duty to disclose information material to patentability nor the applicant's duty of good faith and candor in dealing with the USPTO.

Another but less effective procedure includes the reissue provision of 35 U.S.C. § 251, which provides that whenever a patent is, through error (but without deceptive intent),[1] deemed wholly or partly inoperative or invalid by reason of a defective specification or by reason of a claim scope being too broad or too narrow, the reissue process can be initiated. The reissue process is not designed to address issues regarding the patentability of originally issued claims or the enforceability of the patent. Instead, it focuses on the correction of errors in the specification, drawings, and claims. It has been used often to add new claims and to amend (or cancel) already-issued claims.

As a result, issues of patentability in light of newly-discovered non-documentary prior art, incorrect information, or the like could be resolved only in federal court litigation. That process, however, suffers from other limitations and disadvantages. First, and most obviously, it requires an adverse party. Federal courts have jurisdiction over patents granted by the USPTO, but not without a "case or controversy." The patent statute does not provide for suing the USPTO Director in a civil action to consider prior art or other information. Second, when there is a bona fide adversary and a genuine case or controversy, the complainant demands relief from the court in the form of a declaration of rights, an injunction, or money damages. Further, patent litigation is costly, and its outcome always includes a measure of unpredictability due to such factors as credibility issues, jury issues, evidentiary rulings, and the risk that the entire patent will be ruled unenforceable due to conduct that (a) the patent owner might not even know about yet, and (b) that might be confined to one or more claims that are utterly irrelevant to the supposed infringement. Compounding this,

---

[Section 22:1]

[1]AIA § 20(d) and (e) deleted reference to deceptive intent from 35 U.S.C.A. § 251 and many other sections of the statute.

a patent owner can sometimes be liable for an opponent's attorney fees. These factors can dissuade patent owners from pursuing infringers when issues of enforceability threaten the patent.

§ 22:2 Congressional intent[1]

The intent of Congress in providing for supplemental examination is reflected in various sources. First, the House Committee Report includes these statements:

> *Supplemental examination*
>
> Patents are unenforceable and invalid if they are obtained through fraud. This concept is addressed in the "inequitable conduct" defense, which allows a defendant in an infringement suit to plead that the plaintiff patent-holder would not have received a patent but for misrepresentations made to the USPTO. Inequitable conduct requires proof of materiality as well as intent to deceive. These standards require courts and litigants to invest time and resources in determining the patent-holder's state of mind or intent when developing the invention and submitting the application. Critics of the inequitable conduct defense, including the National Academies and the Federal Trade Commission, argue that our patent system is hampered by provisions that require courts to divine the difficult-to-prove subjective intent of individuals in patent disputes. And most defendants reflexively plead inequitable conduct as a defense to infringement, prompting the Federal Circuit to label the practice a "plague" on the patent system.
>
> The Act addresses the inequitable conduct doctrine by authorizing supplemental examination of a patent to correct errors or omissions in proceedings before the Office. Under

---

[Section 22:2]

[1]The Supreme Court cautions against relying on interpretations advanced in legislative statements that are not "anchored in the text of the statute." *Shannon v. U.S.*, 512 U.S. 573, 583, 114 S. Ct. 2419, 129 L. Ed. 2d 459 (1994), stating "[C]ourts have no authority to enforce [a] principl[e] gleaned solely from legislative history that has no statutory reference point." Shannon, 512 U.S. at 584, quoting *International Broth. of Elec. Workers, Local Union No. 474, AFL-CIO v. N.L.R.B.*, 814 F.2d 697, 712, 124 L.R.R.M. (BNA) 2993, 106 Lab. Cas. (CCH) P 12256 (D.C. Cir. 1987). The authoritative statement "is the statutory text, not the legislative history." *Exxon Mobil Corp. v. Allapattah Services, Inc.*, 545 U.S. 546, 568, 125 S. Ct. 2611, 162 L. Ed. 2d 502 (2005). However, lower courts have cited the legislative history of the AIA already in recent cases. E.g., *Rogers v. Tristar Products, Inc.*, 102 U.S.P.Q.2d 1722, 2012 WL 1660604, *2 (Fed. Cir. 2012) (non-precedential); *Byrne v. Wood, Herron & Evans, LLP*, 676 F.3d 1024, 1029, 102 U.S.P.Q.2d 1073 (Fed. Cir. 2012) (dissenting opin.).

this new procedure, information that was not considered or was inadequately considered or was incorrect can be presented to the Office. If the Office determines that the information does not present a substantial new question of patentability or that the patent is still valid, that information cannot later be used to hold the patent unenforceable or invalid on the basis for an inequitable-conduct attack in civil litigation.

* * *

Section 12. Supplemental examination.

This section authorizes a new § 257 of the Patent Act that addresses the "supplemental examination" of a patent to correct errors or omissions in proceedings before the Office. Information that was not considered or was inadequately considered or was incorrect can be presented to the Office.

Under new subsection (a) of § 257, the Director must initially determine whether a petitioner's request for supplemental examination of one or more items in the request raises a new question of patentability. The Director must make this determination within 3 months of receiving a request for supplemental examination.

Under new subsection (b), if the Director issues a certificate affirming that this threshold is met, a reexamination shall be ordered and will be conducted according to the procedures under Chapter 30 of the Patent Act (*ex parte* reexamination).

New Subsection (c) of § 257 stipulates that a patent cannot be held unenforceable on the basis of conduct relating to information that had not been considered, was inadequately considered, or was incorrect in a prior examination if the information was considered, reconsidered, or corrected during the supplemental examination. Challengers may still argue in court that the Office's conclusion in supplemental examination was erroneous and that the information renders the patent invalid, but the information cannot be used to render the patent invalid or unenforceable on the basis of inequitable conduct.

New subsection (c) also enumerates three exceptions to these terms: (1) prior allegations involving certain new drug applications (21 USC § 355(j)); (2) patent enforcement actions before the International Trade Commission or a US district court, unless the supplemental examination was concluded before the date on which the action is brought; and (3) instances in which fraud on the USPTO was practiced or attempted.

New subsection (d) of § 257 authorizes the Director to establish fees, by regulation, to help defray the cost of a supplemental examination, in addition to those charged pursuant to Chapter 30.

Finally, new subsection (e) clarifies that nothing in Section 12 limits the application of criminal or antitrust laws or the ability of the USPTO Director to investigate and sanction persons or their representatives for misconduct before the

Office.[2]

Another expression of Congressional intent includes the following statement of Representative Lamar Smith:[3]

AMERICA INVENTS ACT
SPEECH OF
HON. LAMAR SMITH
OF TEXAS
IN THE HOUSE OF REPRESENTATIVES
Wednesday, June 22, 2011

The House in Committee of the Whole House on the State of the Union had under consideration the bill (H.R. 1249) to amend title 35, United States Code, to provide for patent reform:

Mr. SMITH of Texas. Madam Chair, I submit: (1) Manager's Statement on Supplemental Examination; * * *

CHAIRMAN'S FLOOR REMARKS/MANAGER'S STATEMENT: SUPPLEMENTAL EXAMINATION IN H.R. 1249

Mr. Speaker, this bill also contains a very important new administrative proceeding available to patent owners, to help improve the quality of issued patents. This new "Supplemental Examination" procedure encourages the voluntary and proactive disclosure of information that may be relevant to patent prosecution for the Office to consider, reconsider, or correct. The voluntary disclosure by patentees serves to strengthen valid patents, while narrowing or eliminating patents or claims that should not have been issued. Both of these outcomes promote investment in innovation by removing uncertainty about the scope, validity or enforceability of patents, and thus the use of this new proceeding by patent owners is to be encouraged. Subparagraph (C) relating to Supplemental Examination is intended to address the circumstance where, during the course of a supplemental examination or reexamination proceeding ordered under this section, a court or administrative agency advises the PTO that it has made a determination that a fraud on the Office may have been committed in connection with the patent that is the subject of the supplemental examination. In such a circumstance, subparagraph (C) provides that, in addition to any other actions the Director is authorized to take, including the cancellation of any claims found to be invalid under section 307 as a result of the reexamination ordered under this section, the Director shall also refer the matter to the Attorney

[2]H.R. Rep. No. 112-98, pt. 1, at 50, 78 (2011).

[3]Congressional Record, Vol. 157, Number 91, pp. E1182.

General. As such, this provision is not intended to impose any obligation on the PTO beyond those it already undertakes, or require it to investigate or prosecute any such potential fraud. Subparagraph (C) is neither an investigative nor an adjudicative provision, and, as such, is not intended to expand the authority or obligation of the PTO to investigate or adjudicate allegations of fraud lodged by private parties.

Further, any referral under this subjection is not meant to relieve the Director from his obligation to conclude the supplemental examination or reexamination proceeding ordered under this section. It is important for the process to proceed through conclusion of reexamination, so that any claims that are invalid can be properly cancelled. The decision to make referrals under subsection (c) is not meant to be delegated to examiners or other agents of the PTO, but rather is a determination that should only be made by the Director himself or herself. Supplemental Examination has the potential to play a powerful role in improving patent quality and boosting investment in innovation, economic growth, and job creation. The Director should implement this new authority in a way that maximizes this potential.

§ 22:3 The new statute for supplemental examination

Congress added a new procedure to Patent Office practice that is an alternative to patent infringement litigation, is conducted expeditiously and *ex parte* at the USPTO, and is a less risky way to resolve the problems addressed above. AIA § 12 added the following new provision to the patent statute:

New Statute (35 U.S.C. § 257)

§ 257. Supplemental examinations to consider, reconsider, or correct information

(a) REQUEST FOR SUPPLEMENTAL EXAMINATION.— A patent owner may request supplemental examination of a patent in the Office to consider, reconsider, or correct information believed to be relevant to the patent, in accordance with such requirements as the Director may establish. Within 3 months after the date a request for supplemental examination meeting the requirements of this section is received, the Director shall conduct the supplemental examination and shall conclude such examination by issuing a certificate indicating whether the information presented in the request raises a substantial new question of patentability.

(b) REEXAMINATION ORDERED.— If the certificate issued under subsection (a) indicates that a substantial new question of patentability is raised by 1 or more items of information in the request, the Director shall order reexamination of the patent. The reexamination shall be conducted according to procedures established by chapter 30, except that the patent owner shall not have the right to file a statement pursuant to section 304. During the reexamination, the Director shall address each substantial new question of patentability identified during the supplemental examination, notwithstanding the limitations in chapter 30 relating to patents and printed publication or any other provision of such chapter.

(c) EFFECT.—

(1) IN GENERAL.— A patent shall not be held unenforceable on the basis of conduct relating to information that had not been considered, was inadequately considered, or was incorrect in a prior examination of the patent if the information was considered, reconsidered, or corrected during a supplemental examination of the patent. The making of a request under subsection (a), or the absence thereof, shall not be relevant to enforceability of the patent under section 282.

(2) EXCEPTIONS.—

(A) PRIOR ALLEGATIONS.— Paragraph (1) shall not apply to an allegation pled with particularity in a civil action, or set forth with particularity in a notice received by the patent owner under section 505(j)(2)(B)(iv)(II) of the Federal Food, Drug, and Cosmetic Act (21 U.S.C. 355(j)(2)(B)(iv)(II)), before the date of a supplemental examination request under subsection (a) to consider, reconsider, or correct information forming the basis for the allegation.

(B) PATENT ENFORCEMENT ACTIONS.— In an action brought under section 337(a) of the Tariff Act of 1930 (19 U.S.C. 1337(a)), or section 281 of this title, paragraph (1) shall not apply to any defense raised in the action that is based upon information that was considered, reconsidered, or corrected pursuant to a supplemental examination request under subsection (a), unless the supplemental examination, and any reexamination ordered pursuant to the request, are concluded before the date on which the action is brought.

(d) FEES AND REGULATIONS.—

(1) FEES.— The Director shall, by regulation, establish fees for the submission of a request for supplemental examination of a patent, and to consider each item of information submitted in the request. If reexamination is ordered under subsection (b), fees established and applicable to ex parte reexamination proceedings under chapter 30 shall be paid, in addition to fees applicable to supplemental examination.

(2) REGULATIONS.— The Director shall issue regulations governing the form, content, and other requirements of requests for supplemental examination, and establishing procedures for reviewing information submitted in such

requests.[1]

(e) Fraud.— If the Director becomes aware, during the course of a supplemental examination or reexamination proceeding ordered under this section, that a material fraud on the Office may have been committed in connection with the patent that is the subject of the supplemental examination, then in addition to any other actions the Director is authorized to take, including the cancellation of any claims found to be invalid under section 307 as a result of a reexamination ordered under this section, the Director shall also refer the matter to the Attorney General for such further action as the Attorney General may deem appropriate. Any such referral shall be treated as confidential, shall not be included in the file of the patent, and shall not be disclosed to the public unless the United States charges a person with a criminal offense in connection with such referral.

(f) Rule of Construction.— Nothing in this section shall be construed—

(1) to preclude the imposition of sanctions based upon criminal or antitrust laws (including section 1001(a) of title 18, the first section of the Clayton Act, and section 5 of the Federal Trade Commission Act to the extent that section relates to unfair methods of competition);

(2) to limit the authority of the Director to investigate issues of possible misconduct and impose sanctions for misconduct in connection with matters or proceedings before the Office; or

(3) to limit the authority of the Director to issue regulations under chapter 3 relating to sanctions for misconduct by representatives practicing before the Office.

* * *

AIA Sec. 12(c)

(c) Effective Date.— The amendments made by this section shall take effect upon the expiration of the 1-year period beginning on the date of the enactment of this Act and shall apply to any patent issued before, on, or after that effective date.

§ 22:4 General overview of supplemental examination

Unlike prior reexaminations, supplemental examination is relatively unfettered as to what can be raised. Matters can

[Section 22:3]

[1]The USPTO final rules concerning supplemental examination are found in 37 C.F.R. Part 1, Subpart E, which comprises §§ 1.601–1.625.

include but are not limited to situations where an error has occurred. The prior art, potential prior art, or other information that may be tendered to the USPTO can be anything the patent owner wants to submit. Unlike reexamination, the art is not limited to issued patents and other published documents. The new statute permits patent owners to request a supplemental examination, which will follow essentially the reexamination procedure, in order to consider, reconsider, or correct ***any information*** believed to be relevant to the patentability of the patent. For example, information relating to "offers for sale," "public disclosures," or "public uses" could be considered, just as information about such events in an Information Disclosure Statement would be considered during original examination.

The Supplemental Examination is a short, three-month procedure in which the USPTO determines whether any submitted information raises a substantial new question of patentability. Whichever way the determination comes out, a corresponding certificate is issued by the USPTO. If a substantial new question is found, the patent automatically enters *ex parte* reexamination.

Importantly, invoking a supplemental examination allows a patent owner to preempt issues of inequitable conduct that could otherwise be raised by prospective patent challengers. As such, questions about action or inaction during prosecution are removed from any inequitable conduct determination.

Under AIA Section 12(c), the effective date of supplemental examination occurred on September 16, 2012, one year after enactment. Since then, all patents existing on, issued on or issued thereafter may be subjected to requests for supplemental examination.

§ 22:5 Requesting supplemental examination

Under 35 U.S.C. § 257(a), a patent owner may request supplemental examination "to consider, reconsider, or correct information believed to be relevant to the patent."[1] The requester must be the owner or owners of the entire right,

[Section 22:5]

[1]35 U.S.C.A. § 257(a). "REQUEST FOR SUPPLEMENTAL EXAMINATION.—A patent owner may request supplemental examination of a patent in the Office to consider, reconsider, or correct information believed to be relevant to the patent, in accordance with such require-

title, and interest in the patent.[2] This means that a mere licensee lacks standing to file such a request. Indeed, no one except the patent owner may file any paper or otherwise participate in the supplemental examination.[3] The patent owner may file the request any time during the enforceability period of the patent.[4]

A request for supplemental examination may include no more than twelve (12) items of "information" that the owner believes are relevant. If there are more than 12 items, multiple requests may be submitted to accommodate them.[5] Audio and video materials may be considered as an "item" if converted to text form.[6] The specific contents of a request are set forth in 37 C.F.R. § 1.610(b):

§ 1.610. Content of request for supplemental examination.

* * *

---

ments as the Director may establish. * * *"

[2]37 C.F.R. § 1.601(a) "A request for supplemental examination of a patent must be filed by the owner(s) of the entire right, title, and interest in the patent."

[3]37 C.F.R. § 1.601(b) "Any party other than the patent owner (i.e., any third party) is prohibited from filing papers or otherwise participating in any manner in a supplemental examination proceeding."

[4]37 C.F.R. § 1.601(c) "A request for supplemental examination of a patent may be filed at any time during the period of enforceability of the patent."

[5]37 C.F.R. § 1.605 provides: "(a) Each request for supplemental examination may include no more than twelve items of information believed to be relevant to the patent. More than one request for supplemental examination of the same patent may be filed at any time during the period of enforceability of the patent. (b) An item of information includes a document submitted as part of the request that contains information, believed to be relevant to the patent, that the patent owner requests the Office to consider, reconsider, or correct. If the information to be considered, reconsidered, or corrected is not, at least in part, contained within or based on any document submitted as part of the request, the discussion within the body of the request relative to the information will be considered as an item of information. (c) An item of information must be in writing in accordance with § 1.2. To be considered, any audio or video recording must be submitted in the form of a written transcript. (d) If one item of information is combined in the request with one or more additional items of information, each item of information of the combination may be separately counted. Exceptions include the combination of a non-English language document and its translation, and the combination of a document that is over 50 pages in length and its summary pursuant to § 1.610(b)(8)."

[6]37 C.F.R. § 1.605(c).

(b) A request for supplemental examination must include:

(1) An identification of the number of the patent for which supplemental examination is requested.

(2) A list of the items of information that are requested to be considered, reconsidered, or corrected. Where appropriate, the list must meet the requirements of § 1.98(b).

(3) A list identifying any other prior or concurrent post-patent Office proceedings involving the patent for which supplemental examination is being requested, including an identification of the type of proceeding, the identifying number of any such proceeding (*e.g.,* a control number or reissue application number), and the filing date of any such proceeding.

(4) An identification of each claim of the patent for which supplemental examination is requested.

(5) A separate, detailed explanation of the relevance and manner of applying each item of information to each claim of the patent for which supplemental examination is requested.

(6) A copy of the patent for which supplemental examination is requested and a copy of any disclaimer or certificate issued for the patent.

(7) A copy of each item of information listed in paragraph (b)(2) of this section, accompanied by a written English translation of all of the necessary and pertinent parts of any non-English language item of information. The patent owner is not required to submit copies of items of information that form part of the discussion within the body of the request as specified in § 1.605(b), or copies of U.S. patents and U.S. patent application publications.

(8) A summary of the relevant portions of any submitted document, other than the request, that is over 50 pages in length. The summary must include citations to the particular pages containing the relevant portions.

(9) An identification of the owner(s) of the entire right, title, and interest in the patent requested to be examined, and a submission by the patent owner in compliance with § 3.73(c) of this chapter establishing the entirety of the ownership in the patent requested to be examined.

(c) The request may also include:

(1) A cover sheet itemizing each component submitted as part of the request;

(2) A table of contents for the request;

(3) An explanation of how the claims patentably distinguish over the items of information; and

(4) An explanation of why each item of information submitted with the request does or does not raise a substantial new question of patentability.

With one major exception, the contents of a request for supplemental examination are not dramatically different from a request for reexamination. The major exception is that the requester is *not* required to assert that the submitted materials raise a substantial new question of patentability. Indeed, the requester is permitted (but not required) to explain why any item submitted does, or does not, raise such a question.[7] However, the requester is required to submit a "separate, detailed explanation of the relevance and manner of applying each item of information to each claim of the patent for which supplemental examination is requested."[8]

The format of papers filed in a supplemental examination request is specified in 37 C.F.R. § 1.615 which (1) calls for papers to comply with 37 C.F.R. § 1.52, and (2) permits redaction of court documents and non-patent literature.

The requester must submit the fee for a supplemental examination specified in § 1.20(k)(1), which is currently $5,140. In addition, the requester must also include the fee for *ex parte* reexamination specified in § 1.20(k)(1), which is currently $16,120.[9] The reexamination fee is refundable if the USPTO decides not to institute a reexamination proceeding.[10] Extra fees are payable for documents of excess size.[11]

If the request does not comply with the rules, the USPTO has discretion under 37 C.F.R. § 1.610(d) not to assign a filing date to the request.[12] However, if it decides not to assign a filing date, the Office will permit the requester to submit a

[7] 37 C.F.R. § 1.610(c)(4).

[8] 37 C.F.R. § 1.610(b)(5).

[9] 37 C.F.R. §§ 1.610, 1.20(k).

[10] 37 C.F.R. § 1.26(c)(3).

[11] 37 C.F.R. § 1.20(k)(iii).

[12] 37 C.F.R. § 1.610(d) provides, "The filing date of a request for supplemental examination will not be granted if the request is not in compliance with §§ 1.605, 1.615, and this section, subject to the discretion of the Office. If the Office determines that the request, as originally submitted, is not entitled to a filing date, the patent owner will be so notified and will be given an opportunity to complete the request within a specified time. If the patent owner does not timely comply with the notice, the request for supplemental examination will not be granted a filing date and the fee for reexamination as set forth in § 1.20(k)(2) will be refunded.

corrected request, which if compliant will be granted a filing date corresponding to when the corrected request is received by the Office.[13]

§ 22:6 USPTO determination re a substantial new question of patentability

Under 35 U.S.C. § 257(a), the USPTO must evaluate the request for supplemental examination and issue a certificate within three months of receiving a proper request.[1] 37 C.F.R. § 1.620 confirms that the Office will determine within three months of the filing date whether a substantial new question of patentability affecting *any claim* is raised by any of the items. The determination is based on the claims in effect at the time of the determination.[2]

The rules prevent extraneous or new issues from arising during the three months when the Office is making its determination. Accordingly, no unauthorized or improper papers may be filed during the supplemental proceeding. If one is submitted, it will not become part of the official file and will not be considered.[3] No amendment may be filed dur-

---

If the patent owner timely files a corrected request in response to the notice that properly addresses all of the defects set forth in the notice and that otherwise complies with all of the requirements of §§ 1.605, 1.615, and this section, the filing date of the supplemental examination request will be the receipt date of the corrected request."

[13]37 C.F.R. § 1.610(d).

[Section 22:6]

[1]35 U.S.C.A. § 257(a). "REQUEST FOR SUPPLEMENTAL EXAMINATION.—* * * Within 3 months after the date a request for supplemental examination meeting the requirements of this section is received, the Director shall conduct the supplemental examination and shall conclude such examination by issuing a certificate indicating whether the information presented in the request raises a substantial new question of patentability."

[2]37 C.F.R. § 620(a): "(a) Within three months after the filing date of a request for supplemental examination, the Office will determine whether a substantial new question of patentability affecting any claim of the patent is raised by any of the items of information presented in the request. The determination will generally be limited to a review of the item(s) of information identified in the request as applied to the identified claim(s) of the patent. The determination will be based on the claims in effect at the time of the determination and will become a part of the official record of the patent."

[3]37 C.F.R. § 620(c).

ing this time,[4] and interviews are prohibited.[5]

Likewise, if a petition is filed involving the patent, the USPTO *may* hold action on such petition or other paper in abeyance until after the supplemental examination is concluded by the electronic issuance of a supplemental examination certificate.[6] In this vein, if the patent owner discovers a previously-filed or a concurrent post-patent proceeding in the USPTO, the owner must notify the USPTO in a minimal filing that is limited to "notifying the Office of the post-patent Office proceeding, if such notice has not been previously provided with the request. The notice shall be limited to an identification of the post-patent Office proceeding, including the type of proceeding, the identifying number of any such proceeding (e.g., a control number or reissue application number), and the filing date of any such proceeding, without any discussion of the issues of the current supplemental examination proceeding or of the identified post-patent Office proceeding(s)."[7]

The supplemental examination process is able to preempt issues of inequitable conduct, as explained below, but Congress and the USPTO are very concerned with fraud. The statute speaks to issues of fraud as follows, *requiring* the USPTO to refer the matter to the Attorney General:

> § 257(e) Fraud.— If the Director becomes aware, during the course of a supplemental examination or reexamination proceeding ordered under this section, that a material fraud on the Office may have been committed in connection with the patent that is the subject of the supplemental examination, then in addition to any other actions the Director is authorized to take, including the cancellation of any claims found to be invalid under section 307 as a result of a reexamination ordered under this section, the Director shall also refer the matter to the Attorney General for such further action as the Attorney General may deem appropriate. Any such referral shall be treated as confidential, shall not be included in the file of the patent, and shall not be disclosed to the public unless the United States charges a person with a criminal offense in connection with such referral.

The corresponding regulation, 37 C.F.R. § 1.620, confirms that if the Office becomes aware of material fraud during the

[4]37 C.F.R. § 620(f).

[5]37 C.F.R. § 620(e).

[6]37 C.F.R. § 620(b).

[7]37 C.F.R. § 620(d).

course of the supplemental examination or an ensuing reexamination, then it will continue the proceeding and refer the matter to the Attorney General.

§ 22:7 Conclusion of supplemental examination

The supplemental examination concludes when the USPTO determines whether there is, or is not, a substantial new question of patentability and issues a certificate of supplemental examination. If the Director concludes that a substantial new question of patentability is raised, then under 35 U.S.C. § 257(b) the patent enters *ex parte* reexamination (for which the requester has prepaid):

> § 257(b) REEXAMINATION ORDERED.— If the certificate issued under subsection (a) indicates that a substantial new question of patentability is raised by 1 or more items of information in the request, the Director shall order reexamination of the patent. The reexamination shall be conducted according to procedures established by chapter 30, except that the patent owner shall not have the right to file a statement pursuant to section 304. During the reexamination, the Director shall address each substantial new question of patentability identified during the supplemental examination, notwithstanding the limitations in chapter 30 relating to patents and printed publication or any other provision of such chapter.

The corresponding rule at the USPTO indicates that the Office will issue a "supplemental examination certificate," whether the Office finds a substantial new question of patentability or not, and the certificate will state the finding. The rule also indicates that if one is found, the patent directly enters *ex parte* reexamination, but the patent owner cannot file a patent owner's statement:[1]

37 CFR § 1.625. Conclusion of supplemental examina-

[Section 22:7]

[1]35 U.S.C.A. 304. Reexamination order by Director. "If, in a determination made under the provisions of subsection 303(a) of this title, the Director finds that a substantial new question of patentability affecting any claim of a patent is raised, the determination will include an order for reexamination of the patent for resolution of the question. The patent owner will be given a reasonable period, not less than two months from the date a copy of the determination is given or mailed to him, within which he may file a statement on such question, including any amendment to his patent and new claim or claims he may wish to propose, for consideration in the reexamination. If the patent owner files such a statement, he promptly will serve a copy of it on the person who has requested reexamination under the provisions of section 302 of this title. Within a period of two months from the date of service, that person may file and

tion; publication of supplemental examination certificate; procedure after conclusion.

(a) A supplemental examination proceeding will conclude with the electronic issuance of a supplemental examination certificate. The supplemental examination certificate will indicate the result of the determination whether any of the items of information presented in the request raised a substantial new question of patentability.

(b) If the supplemental examination certificate states that a substantial new question of patentability is raised by one or more items of information in the request, *ex parte* reexamination of the patent will be ordered under 35 U.S.C. 257. Upon the conclusion of the *ex parte* reexamination proceeding, an *ex parte* reexamination certificate, which will include a statement specifying that *ex parte* reexamination was ordered under 35 U.S.C. 257, will be published. The electronically issued supplemental examination certificate will remain as part of the public record of the patent.

(c) If the supplemental examination certificate indicates that no substantial new question of patentability is raised by any of the items of information in the request, and *ex parte* reexamination is not ordered under 35 U.S.C. 257, the electronically issued supplemental examination certificate will be published in due course. The fee for reexamination ordered as a result of supplemental examination, as set forth in § 1.20(k)(2), will be refunded in accordance with § 1.26(c).

(d) Any *ex parte* reexamination ordered under 35 U.S.C. 257 will be conducted in accordance with §§ 1.530 through 1.570, which govern *ex parte* reexamination, except that:

(1) The patent owner will not have the right to file a statement pursuant to § 1.530, and the order will not set a time period within which to file such a statement;

(2) Reexamination of any claim of the patent may be conducted on the basis of any item of information as set forth in § 1.605, and is not limited to patents and printed publications or to subject matter that has been added or deleted during the reexamination proceeding, notwithstanding § 1.552(a);

(3) Issues in addition to those raised by patents and printed publications, and by subject matter added or deleted during a reexamination proceeding, may be considered and resolved, notwithstanding § 1.552(c); and

---

have considered in the reexamination a reply to any statement filed by the patent owner. That person promptly will serve on the patent owner a copy of any reply filed."

(4) Information material to patentability will be defined by § 1.56(b), notwithstanding § 1.555(b).

§ 22:8 Benefits of supplemental examination

A patent owner could simply request *ex parte* reexamination, but the scope of the resulting procedure would be restricted to patents and printed publications, and the outcome would not preempt any inequitable conduct issues. The reason a patent owner would incur the added expense of requesting supplemental examination is to allow consideration of the broadest possible prior art and to overcome issues of potential inequitable conduct. The statute prohibits a finding of unenforceability on the basis of conduct that was "considered, reconsidered, or corrected during a supplemental reexamination":

35 U.S.C. § 257(c) EFFECT.—

(1) IN GENERAL.— A patent shall not be held unenforceable on the basis of conduct relating to information that had not been considered, was inadequately considered, or was incorrect in a prior examination of the patent if the information was considered, reconsidered, or corrected during a supplemental examination of the patent. The making of a request under subsection (a), or the absence thereof, shall not be relevant to enforceability of the patent under section 282.

(2) EXCEPTIONS.—

(A) PRIOR ALLEGATIONS.— Paragraph (1) shall not apply to an allegation pled with particularity in a civil action, or set forth with particularity in a notice received by the patent owner under section 505(j)(2)(B)(iv)(II) of the Federal Food, Drug, and Cosmetic Act (21 U.S.C. 355(j)(2)(B)(iv)(II)), before the date of a supplemental examination request under subsection (a) to consider, reconsider, or correct information forming the basis for the allegation.

(B) PATENT ENFORCEMENT ACTIONS.— In an action brought under section 337(a) of the Tariff Act of 1930 (19 U.S.C. 1337(a)), or section 281 of this title, paragraph (1) shall not apply to any defense raised in the action that is based upon information that was considered, reconsidered, or corrected pursuant to a supplemental examination request under subsection (a), unless the supplemental examination, and any reexamination ordered pursuant to the request, are concluded before the date on which the action is brought.

New § 257(c) stipulates that a patent cannot be held *unen-*

forceable on the basis of conduct relating to information that had not been considered, was inadequately considered, or was incorrect in a prior examination if the information was considered, reconsidered, or corrected during the supplemental examination.

In addition, even the *making of a request* for supplemental examination "shall not be relevant to enforceability of the patent under section 282." 35 U.S.C. § 257(c). Hence, the statute offers a safe harbor for patent owners who are forthcoming with issues of potential inequitable conduct or invalidity.

The safe harbor is not without limits, however. Patent challengers can always assert invalidity despite the USPTO's validity conclusion. They may challenge validity in court, arguing that the USPTO conclusion in the supplemental examination proceeding (and reexamination) was erroneous.

Further, § 257(c) contains some exceptions concerning inequitable conduct. First, supplemental examination cannot be used to preempt allegations that had already been pleaded in a previously-filed civil action. A patent owner cannot be charged with inequitable conduct in court and then seek to extinguish that liability by requesting supplemental examination. Second, it cannot be used against allegations set forth with particularity in a notice received by the patent owner under Section 505(j)(2)(B)(iv)(II) of the Federal Food, Drug and Cosmetic Act (21 U.S.C. § 355(j)). Third, supplemental examination cannot apply to any defense raised in a patent enforcement action before the International Trade Commission or a U.S. district court action under 35 U.S.C. § 281, unless the supplemental examination was concluded before the date on which the action is brought.

The first exception addresses a problem that could arise in Hatch-Waxman litigation where the filer of an abbreviated new drug application (ANDA) details an inequitable conduct charge in a Paragraph IV notice. Supplemental examination cannot be used to purge the then-live allegation. Another exception applies more broadly to allegations before the ITC or a district court to prevent then-live allegations from being addressed in an ex parte fashion.

Apart from the significant costs involved, the new statute can be used by proactive patent owners who contemplate enforcement of patents but who have become aware of information that was not previously considered, inadequately considered, or was incorrect in a prior examination. This new procedure provides a basis for broad consideration by the USPTO of prior art, or potential prior art, of all types. Invalidity can be assessed by the USPTO rather than in a judicial setting where there is an adversary. In addition, issues of inequitable conduct (but not fraud) are taken off the table if timely raised in a supplemental examination request. On the negative side, once a patent enters reexamination, the presumption of validity is inapplicable at the USPTO, and the USPTO does not have to prove invalidity to a "clear and convincing" standard—only a preponderance standard.

§ 22:9 USPTO statistics re supplemental examinations

On its website, the USPTO maintains statistics on AIA activity.[1] It reported that as of August 30, 2013, it had received 40 requests for supplemental examination.

[Section 22:9]

[1] http://www.uspto.gov/aia_implementation/statistics.jsp (visited October 20, 2013).

Chapter 23

Reexaminations (*Inter Partes* and *Ex Parte*)

AIA § 6
35 U.S.C.A. §§ 303, 306, 312, 313

§ 23:1 Reexaminations generally

Prior to enactment of the AIA, two forms of patent reexamination were available, *ex parte* reexamination and *inter partes* reexamination. Under both, the threshold question was whether the petitioner had raised a substantial, new question of patentability ("SNQ") as to any claim.

The AIA replaced *inter partes* reexamination with *inter partes* review, using a different threshold standard, "a reasonable likelihood that the requester would prevail with respect to at least 1 of the claims challenged in the petition."[1] The new *inter partes* review procedure is the subject of a separate chapter in Part III directed to USPTO Trial

---

[Section 23:1]

[1]35 U.S.C.A. § 314(a) (2011).

Proceedings.

In creating *inter partes* review, Congress made provisions to wind down *inter partes* reexaminations and enacted various transition provisions.

With respect to *ex parte* reexamination, Congress made some changes that harmonize the existing procedure with other features of the AIA, most notably the estoppel provisions.

§ 23:2 Congressional intent[1]

The following passages from the House Report address reexaminations:

> *Post-grant review proceedings*
>
> The Act amends ex parte and inter partes reexamination and establishes a new post-grant review procedure. Under current law, there are two ways to challenge the validity and enforceability of a patent that has issued. The patent may be challenged in district court litigation or in a reexamination at the USPTO.
>
> Nearly 30 years ago, Congress created the administrative "reexamination" process, through which the USPTO could review the validity of already-issued patents on the request of either the patent holder or a third party,[FN30] in the expectation that it would serve as an effective and efficient alternative to often costly and protracted district court litigation.[FN31] Reexamination requires the USPTO to review the patent in light of a substantial new question of patentability not presented during the original examination.[FN32] The initial reexamination statute had several limitations that later

[Section 23:2]

[1]The Supreme Court cautions against relying on interpretations advanced in legislative statements that are not "anchored in the text of the statute." *Shannon v. U.S.*, 512 U.S. 573, 583, 114 S. Ct. 2419, 129 L. Ed. 2d 459 (1994), stating "[C]ourts have no authority to enforce [a] principl[e] gleaned solely from legislative history that has no statutory reference point." Shannon, 512 U.S. at 584, quoting *International Broth. of Elec. Workers, Local Union No. 474, AFL-CIO v. N.L.R.B.*, 814 F.2d 697, 712, 124 L.R.R.M. (BNA) 2993, 106 Lab. Cas. (CCH) P 12256 (D.C. Cir. 1987). The authoritative statement "is the statutory text, not the legislative history." *Exxon Mobil Corp. v. Allapattah Services, Inc.*, 545 U.S. 546, 568, 125 S. Ct. 2611, 162 L. Ed. 2d 502 (2005). However, lower courts have cited the legislative history of the AIA already in recent cases. E.g., *Rogers v. Tristar Products, Inc.*, 102 U.S.P.Q.2d 1722, 2012 WL 1660604, *2 (Fed. Cir. 2012) (non-precedential); *Byrne v. Wood, Herron & Evans, LLP*, 676 F.3d 1024, 1029, 102 U.S.P.Q.2d 1073 (Fed. Cir. 2012) (dissenting opin.).

proved to make it a less viable alternative to litigation for evaluating patent validity than Congress intended. First, a reexamination request could only be based on prior art, and could not be based on prior public use or prior sales. Moreover, the requestor could not raise any challenge based on § 101 (utility, eligibility) or 112 (indefiniteness, enablement, written description, best mode). A third party alleging a patent is invalid, therefore, had fewer challenges it could raise in the proceeding and, therefore, may instead opt to risk infringement and litigate the validity of the patent in court. Second, in the original reexamination system, the third-party challenger had no role once the proceeding was initiated, while the patent holder had significant input throughout the entire process. Third, a challenger that lost at the USPTO under reexamination had no right to appeal an examiner's, or the Patent Board's, decision either administratively or in court. Restrictions such as these made reexamination a much less favored avenue to challenge questionable patents than litigation. Reexamination proceedings are also often costly, taking several years to complete,[FN33] and are first conducted by examiners and, if the patent is rejected, then by Patent Board judges. Thus, many patents must go through two rounds of administrative review (one by the examiner, and a second by the Patent Board) adding to the length of the proceeding.[FN34]

FN 30. See 35 U.S.C. Sec. 301–307. A patent holder will typically request reexamination to bolster the patent in view of new prior art. A third party may request reexamination to challenge, and ultimately invalidate, the patent.

FN 31. "Reexamination will permit efficient resolution of questions about the validity of issued patents without recourse to expensive and lengthy infringement litigation . . .. The reexamination of issued patents could be conducted with a fraction of the time and cost of formal legal proceedings and would help restore confidence in the effectiveness of our patent system . . .. It is anticipated that these measures provide a useful and necessary alternative for challengers and for patent owners to test the validity of United States patents in an efficient and relatively inexpensive manner." *See* H.R. Rep. No. 96-1307(I) at 3 (1980), reprinted in 1980 U.S.C.C.A.N. 6460, 6462–63.

FN 32. *See* 35 U.S.C. Sec. 303.

FN 33. *See Perspectives on Patents: Hearing Before the Subcomm. on Intellectual Prop. of the Senate Comm. on the Judiciary,* 109th Cong. (2005) (statement of Jon W. Dudas, Undersecretary of Commerce for Intellectual Property, Director of the U.S. Patent and Trademark Office), explaining that "a large number of reexamination proceedings have been pending before the USPTO for more than 4 years," and questioning whether this amount of time is consistent with the statutory requirement that "[a]ll reexamination proceedings . . . will be conducted with special dispatch within the

Office." *See also* 35 U.S.C. Sec. 305.

FN 34. For several years, the standard practice at the USPTO was to assign the reexamination to the patent examiner who had originally examined that patent. In addition, the same third-party requester could file multiple, serial reexaminations based on the same "substantial new question of patentability," so long as the initial reexamination was not complete. More recently, the USPTO ended some of these procedures, and now reexaminations are handled by a Central Reexamination Unit (CRU), and subsequent serial reexamination, based on the same "substantial new question of patentability," is no longer permitted. *See, e.g.,* Manual of Patent Examining Procedure (MPEP) Sec. 2236 and 2240 (August 2006).

Congress has responded several times to criticisms of the reexamination system by making amendments to the process.[FN35] In 1999, Congress created a second reexamination procedure—called *inter partes* reexamination—that gave third-party challengers greater input throughout the proceeding by permitting them to respond to every pleading submitted by the patent holder.[FN36] Congress also eventually gave third-party challengers the right to appeal adverse decisions.[FN37]

FN 35. *See e.g.,* 21st Century Dep't of Justice Appropriations Authorization Act, Pub. L. No. 107-273, Sec. 13105–06, 13202, 116 Stat. 1758, 1761 (2002) (effective Nov. 2, 2002); American Inventors Protection Act, Pub.L. 106-113, 113 Stat. 1536, 1501A et seq. (1999) (creating *inter partes* reexamination) (hereafter referred to as the "AIPA".

FN 36. *See* 35 U.S.C. Sec. 311–318.

FN 37. *See* 35 U.S.C. Sec. 315(b).

As part of the 1999 improvements to reexamination, Congress directed the USPTO to submit a report to Congress evaluating the *inter partes* reexamination process and making any recommendations for changes.[FN38] Initially, the USPTO projected that in the first year after the creation of *inter partes* reexamination, it would receive 400 such requests and it projected that by 2004 it would receive nearly 600.[FN39] No *inter partes* reexamination requests were actually filed in 2000 and only 27 such requests had been filed by 2004.[FN40] Over the 5-year period studied by the USPTO, it issued 900,000 patents and received only 53 requests for *inter partes* reexamination.[FN41]

FN 38. AIPA, Pub. L. 106-113, Sec. 4606.

FN 39. *See United States Patent and Trademark Office, Report to Congress on* Inter Partes *Reexamination* (2004) (hereinafter referred to as "*Report on Inter Partes Reexamination*"), at 4.

FN 40. *See United States Patent and Trademark Office, Report to Congress on* Inter Partes *Reexamination* (2004) (hereinafter referred to as *"Report on Inter Partes Reexamination"*), at 5.

FN 41. *See United States Patent and Trademark Office, Report to Congress on* Inter Partes *Reexamination* (2004) (hereinafter referred to as *"Report on Inter Partes Reexamination"*), at 5.

The Act expands the category of documents that may be cited in a reexamination proceeding to include written statements of the patent owner that have been filed in a proceeding before a Federal court or the USPTO regarding the scope of claims. This addition will counteract the ability of patent owners to offer differing interpretations of prior art in different proceedings. These written statements, which include documents, pleadings or evidence from proceedings that address the patent owner's statements, shall not be considered for any purpose other than to determine the proper meaning of the claims that are the subject of the request in a proceeding. Specifically, the Committee does not intend these statements to be a basis for the institution of a reexamination proceeding. Reexaminations will continue to be available only on the basis of "patents or printed publications."[FN42]

FN 42. The scope of "patent and printed publication" prior art in the amended section 301 is intended to be coextensive with these terms in current section 102 of the title 35. Further, amendments made by Section 2 of the Act, which expand and contract the definition of certain other forms of prior art, are not intended to change the particular "patent or printed publication" prior art, which will continue to be the sole basis for initiating reexamination proceedings.

The Act also amends the *ex parte* reexamination procedure to allow the Director to institute a reexamination on the Director's own initiative if a substantial new question of patentability is raised by patents or publications.

The Act converts inter partes reexamination from an examinational to an adjudicative proceeding, and renames the proceeding *"inter partes* review." The Act also makes the following improvements to this proceeding:

- **"Reasonable likelihood of success" for instituting inter partes review.** The threshold for initiating an *inter partes* review is elevated from "significant [*sic*][2] new question of patentability"—a standard that currently allows 95% of all requests to be granted—to a standard requiring petitioners to present information showing that their challenge has a reasonable likelihood of success. Satisfaction of the new threshold will be assessed based on the informa-

[2]The patent statute did not call for a "significant" new question of patentability but instead for a "substantial" new question of patentability for both ex parte and inter partes reexaminations. 35 U.S.C.A. §§ 303, 313 (2006).

tion presented both in the petition for the proceeding and in the patent owner's response to the petition.

- **"Reasonably could have raised" estoppel applied to subsequent administrative proceedings.** A party that uses *inter partes* review is estopped from raising in a subsequent PTO proceeding (such as an *ex parte* reexamination or *inter partes* review) any issue that it raised or reasonably could have raised in the *inter partes* review.

* * *

Subsection (h) amends § 303 to provide that the Director may determine whether to initiate reexamination on the Director's own initiative based on citations by any person other than the owner of the patent under section 301 or 302. Also, § 306 is amended to conform to the changes made by § 4605 of the American Inventors Protection Act of 1999, Public Law 106–113, to §§ 134 and 141 of title 35.[3]

§ 23:3 AIA provisions re *inter partes* reexamination statute

AIA § 6(a) propounds the new statutes for *inter partes* review (35 U.S.C. §§ 311 to 319). AIA § 6(b) provides a conforming amendment relating to the table of chapters. AIA § 6(c) is directed to "Regulations and Effective Date" regarding *inter partes* reviews.

Subpart (3) of AIA § 6(c) concerns the transition provisions for *inter partes* reexaminations. These provisions endured for only one year, until *inter partes* review became available. The AIA transition provided the following transition provisions in 35 U.S.C. §§ 312 and 313.

Revised 35 U.S.C. § 312 (transitional)[1]

35 U.S.C. § 312. Determination of issue by Director (Transitional Provision)

(a) Rexamination.— Not later than 3 months after the filing of a request for inter partes reexamination under section 311, the Director shall determine whether the information presented in the request shows that there is a reasonable likelihood that the requester would prevail with respect to at least 1 of the claims challenged in the request ~~a substantial new question of patentability affecting any claim of the patent concerned is raised by the request~~, with or without consider-

[3] H. R. Rep. No. 112-98, pt. 1, pp. 45 to 47, 77 (2011).

[Section 23:3]

[1] In this markup, strikethrough indicates text being removed from the statute, and underscoring indicates text being added to the statute.

ation of other patents or printed publications. A showing that there is a reasonable likelihood that the requester would prevail with respect to at least 1 of the claims challenged in the request The existence of a substantial new question of patentability is not precluded by the fact that a patent or printed publication was previously cited by or to the Office or considered by the Office.

(b) Record.— A record of the Director's determination under subsection (a) shall be placed in the official file of the patent, and a copy shall be promptly given or mailed to the owner of record of the patent and to the third-party requester.

(c) Final Decision.— A determination by the Director under subsection (a) shall be final and non-appealable. Upon a determination that the showing required by subsection (a) has not been made, ~~no substantial new question of patentability has been raised,~~ the Director may refund a portion of the inter partes reexamination fee required under **section 311**.

35 U.S.C. § 313. Inter Partes reexamination order by Director (Transitional Provision)

If, in a determination made under section 312(a), the Director finds that it has been shown that there is a reasonable likelihood that the requester would prevail with respect to at least 1 of the claims challenged in the request ~~a substantial new question of patentability affecting a claim of a patent is raised~~, the determination shall include an order for inter partes reexamination of the patent for resolution of the question. The order may be accompanied by the initial action of the Patent and Trademark Office on the merits of the inter partes reexamination conducted in accordance with section 314.

The AIA also provided the following concerning the effective date of these changes and the continued applicability of prior provisions during the transition period:

New statute (AIA § 6(c)(3))

6(B) APPLICATION.— The amendments made by this paragraph—

(i) shall take effect on the date of the enactment of this Act; and

(ii) shall apply to requests for inter partes reexamination that are filed on or after such date of enactment, but before the effective date set forth in paragraph (2)(A) of this subsection.

(C) CONTINUED APPLICABILITY OF PRIOR PROVISIONS.— The provisions of chapter 31 of title 35, United States Code, as amended by this paragraph, shall continue to apply to requests for inter partes reexamination that are filed before the effective date set forth in paragraph

(2)(A) as if subsection (a) had not been enacted.

§ 23:4 New USPTO rules re *inter partes* reexamination

The USPTO amended the following rules pertaining to *inter partes* reexamination:

§ 1.913. Persons eligible to file, and time for filing, a request for inter partes reexamination.

(a) Except as provided for in § 1.907 and in paragraph (b) of this section, any person other than the patent owner or its privies may, at any time during the period of enforceability of a patent which issued from an original application filed in the United States on or after November 29, 1999, file a request for inter partes reexamination by the Office of any claim of the patent on the basis of prior art patents or printed publications cited under § 1.501.

(b) **Any request for an inter partes reexamination submitted on or after September 16, 2012, will not be accorded a filing date, and any such request will not be granted.** [emphasis added]

§ 1.915. Content of request for inter partes reexamination.

* * * * *

(b) * * *

(2) A citation of the patents and printed publications which are presented to provide a **showing that there is a reasonable likelihood that the requester will prevail** with respect to at least one of the claims challenged in the request.

(3) A statement pointing out, based on the cited patents and printed publications, each **showing of a reasonable likelihood that the requester will prevail** with respect to at least one of the claims challenged in the request, and a detailed explanation of the pertinency and manner of applying the patents and printed publications to every claim for which reexamination is requested.

* * * * *

§ 1.923. Examiner's determination on the request for inter partes reexamination.

Within three months following the filing date of a request for inter partes reexamination under § 1.915, **the examiner will consider the request** and determine whether or not the request and the prior art establish a **reasonable likelihood that the requester will prevail** with respect to at least one of the claims challenged in the request. The examiner's determination will be based on the claims in effect at the time of the determination, will become a part of the official file of the patent, and will be mailed to the patent owner at the address as provided for in § 1.33(c) and to the third party requester. If the examiner determines that the request has not established a reasonable likelihood that the requester will prevail with respect to at least one of the challenged claims, the examiner shall refuse the request and shall not order inter partes reexamination.

§ 1.927. Petition to review refusal to order *inter partes* reexamination.

The third party requester may seek review by a petition to the Director under § 1.181 within one month of the mailing date of the examiner's determination refusing to order inter partes reexamination. Any such petition must comply with § 1.181(b). If no petition is timely filed or if the decision on petition affirms that **a reasonable likelihood that the requester will prevail** with respect to at least one of the claims challenged in the request has not been established, the determination shall be final and nonappealable.

§ 1.931. Order for *inter partes* reexamination.

(a) If it is found that there is a **reasonable likelihood that the requester will prevail** with respect to at least one of the claims challenged in the request, the determination will include an order for inter partes reexamination of the patent for resolution of the question of whether the requester will prevail.

§ 1.937. Conduct of *inter partes* reexamination.

* * * * *

(a) All *inter partes* reexamination proceedings, including any appeals to the Patent Trial and Appeal Board, will be conducted with special dispatch within the Office, unless the Director makes a determination that there is good cause for suspending the reexamination proceeding.

* * *

(d) A petition in an *inter partes* reexamination proceeding must be accompanied by the fee set forth in § 1.20(c)(6), except for petitions under § 1.956 to extend the period for response by a patent owner, petitions under § 1.958 to accept a delayed response by a patent owner, petitions under § 1.78 to accept an unintentionally delayed benefit claim, and petitions under § 1.530(l) for correction of inventorship in a reexamination proceeding.

[emphasis added]

The rules address the transition period from September 16, 2011 to September 15, 2012. Before September 16, 2011, the prior rules apply.

For petitions filed during the transition period, the petitioner must establish a reasonable likelihood of prevailing as to at least one claim as it then exists. Most of the changes in the rules concern the change from the former "substantial new question of patentability" standard to the new "reasonable likelihood" standard.

Second, under § 1.913(b), a petition for *inter partes* reexamination that is filed after the transition period, *i.e.*, on or after September 16, 2012, will be denied a filing date. As of that date, no new petitions for such reexamination can be accepted, and petitioners must seek *inter partes* review before the Patent Trial and Appeal Board ("PTAB").

Third, under § 1.923, an *inter partes* reexamination petition during the transition period is considered by the examiner (not the PTAB). If the reexamination is declared, it will proceed as before, with "special dispatch," with *appeal* to the PTAB.

Regarding the new threshold (standard) that must be met, there is disagreement on where that standard is set. The House Report indicates that it is *elevated* above the old SNQ standard.[1] The USPTO Road Show and other documents suggest that it is lower.

§ 23:5 AIA provisions re *ex parte* reexamination Statute

The AIA does not extinguish *ex parte* reexamination. The changes to the statutes for *ex parte* reexamination are minor. AIA § 6(h) expands the art available for consideration by the Director in determining whether to initiate a reexamination on his own initiative. Before the AIA, the Director was able

---

[Section 23:4]

[1]The House Report comments, "The threshold for initiating an inter partes review is elevated from 'significant [sic] new question of patentability'—a standard that currently allows 95% of all requests to be granted—to a standard requiring petitioners to present information showing that their challenge has a reasonable likelihood of success. Satisfaction of the new threshold will be assessed based on the information presented both in the petition for the proceeding and in the patent owner's response to the petition." H. R. Rep. No. 112-98, pt. 1, at 47 (2011). Note, however, that the patent statute did not call for a "significant" new question of patentability but instead for a "substantial" new question of patentability for both ex parte and inter partes reexaminations. 35 U.S.C.A. §§ 303, 313 (2006).

to consider material from § 301, but after the AIA amendment, the Director is also allowed to consider material submitted under § 302 in this determination.

The AIA also removes the reference to 35 U.S.C. § 145 for commencing a civil action for review of a decision by the Board on appeal from an examiner's ruling in a reexamination. The AIA amends 35 U.S.C. § 303 as follows:[1]

Revised 35 U.S.C. §§ 303, 306

Sec. 303. Determination of issue by Director

(a) Within three months following the filing of a request for reexamination under the provisions of section 302 ~~of this title~~, the Director will determine whether a substantial new question of patentability affecting any claim of the patent concerned is raised by the request, with or without consideration of other patents or printed publications. On his own initiative, and any time, the Director may determine whether a substantial new question of patentability is raised by patents and publications discovered by him or cited under the provisions of section 301 or 302 ~~section 301 of this title~~. The existence of a substantial new question of patentability is not precluded by the fact that a patent or printed publication was previously cited by or to the Office or considered by the Office.

(b) A record of the Director's determination under subsection (a) of this section will be placed in the official file of the patent, and a copy promptly will be given or mailed to the owner of record of the patent and to the person requesting reexamination, if any.

(c) A determination by the Director pursuant to subsection (a) of this section that no substantial new question of patentability has been raised will be final and nonappealable. Upon such a determination, the Director may refund a portion of the reexamination fee required under section 302 ~~of this title~~.

Sec. 306. Appeal

The patent owner involved in a reexamination proceeding under this chapter may appeal under the provisions of section 134 ~~of this title~~, and may seek court review under the provisions of sections 141 to 144 145 of this title, with respect to any decision adverse to the patentability of any original or proposed amended or new claim of the patent.[2][3]

New statute (AIA § 6(h))

6(h) REEXAMINATION.—

[Section 23:5]

[1]In this markup, strikethrough indicates text being removed from the statute, and underscoring indicates text being added to the statute.

[2]35 U.S.C.A. Sections 141 to 144 address appeal to the U.S. Court of Appeals for the Federal Circuit from a Board ruling under Section 134.

(1) DETERMINATION BY DIRECTOR.—

* * *

(B) EFFECTIVE DATE.—The amendment made by this paragraph shall take effect upon the expiration of the 1-year period beginning on the date of the enactment of this Act and shall apply to any patent issued before, on, or after that effective date.

(2) APPEAL.—

* * *

(B) EFFECTIVE DATE.—The amendment made by this paragraph shall take effect on the date of the enactment of this Act and shall apply to any appeal of a reexamination before the Board of Patent Appeals and Interferences or the Patent Trial and Appeal Board that is pending on, or brought on or after, the date of the enactment of this Act.

§ 23:6 New USPTO rules re *ex parte* reexamination

The USPTO revised its rules for *ex parte* reexamination. The rules as amended provide as follow:

§ 1.510. Request for *ex parte* reexamination.

(a) Any person may, at any time during the period of enforceability of a patent, file a request for an *ex parte* reexamination by the Office of any claim of the patent on the basis of prior art patents or printed publications cited under § 1.501, unless prohibited by 35 U.S.C. 315(e)(1) or 35 U.S.C. 325(e)(1). The request must be accompanied by the fee for requesting reexamination set in § 1.20(c)(1).

(b) * * *

(2) An identification of every claim for which reexamination is requested, and a detailed explanation of the pertinency and manner of applying the cited prior art to every claim for which reexamination is requested. For each statement of the patent owner and accompanying information submitted pursuant to § 1.501(a)(2) which is relied upon in the detailed explanation, the request must explain how that statement is being used to determine the proper meaning of a patent claim in connection with the prior art applied to that claim and how each relevant claim is being interpreted. If appropriate, the party requesting reexamination may also point out how claims distinguish over cited prior art.

---

[3] 35 USC 144. "Decision on appeal. The United States Court of Appeals for the Federal Circuit shall review the decision from which an appeal is taken on the record before the Patent and Trademark Office. Upon its determination the court shall issue to the Director its mandate and opinion, which shall be entered of record in the Patent and Trademark Office and shall govern the further proceedings in the case."

* * * * *

(6) A certification by the third party requester that the statutory estoppel provisions of 35 U.S.C. 315(e)(1) or 35 U.S.C. 325(e)(1) do not prohibit the requester from filing the ex parte reexamination request.

* * * * *

§ 1.515. Determination of the request for *ex parte* reexamination.

(a) Within three months following the filing date of a request for an ex parte reexamination, an examiner will consider the request and determine whether or not a substantial new question of patentability affecting any claim of the patent is raised by the request and the prior art cited therein, with or without consideration of other patents or printed publications. A statement and any accompanying information submitted pursuant to § 1.501(a)(2) will not be considered by the examiner when making a determination on the request. The examiner's determination will be based on the claims in effect at the time of the determination, will become a part of the official file of the patent, and will be given or mailed to the patent owner at the address provided for in § 1.33(c) and to the person requesting reexamination.

* * * * *

§ 1.530. Statement by patent owner in *ex parte* reexamination; amendment by patent owner in *ex parte* or *inter partes* reexamination; inventorship change in *ex parte* or *inter partes* reexamination.

* * * * *

(l) * * *

(1) When it appears in a patent being reexamined that the correct inventor or inventors were not named, the Director may, on petition of all the parties set forth in § 1.324(b)(1) and (b)(2), including the assignees, and satisfactory proof of the facts and payment of the fee set forth in § 1.20(b), or on order of a court before which such matter is called in question, include in the reexamination certificate to be issued under § 1.570 or § 1.997 an amendment naming only the actual inventor or inventors. The petition must be submitted as part of the reexamination proceeding and must satisfy the requirements of § 1.324.

* * * * *

§ 1.550. Conduct of ex parte reexamination proceedings.

* * * * *

(i) A petition in an *ex parte* reexamination proceeding must be accompanied by the fee set forth in § 1.20(c)(6), except for petitions under paragraph (c) of this section to extend the period for response by a patent owner, petitions under paragraph (e) of this section to accept a delayed response by a patent owner, petitions under § 1.78 to accept an unintentionally delayed benefit claim, and petitions under § 1.530(l) for correction of inventorship in a reexamination proceeding.

§ 1.552. Scope of reexamination in ex parte reexamination proceedings.

* * * * *

(d) Any statement of the patent owner and any accompanying information submitted pursuant to § 1.501(a)(2) which is of record in the patent being reexamined (which includes any reexamination files for the patent) may be used after a reexamination proceeding has been ordered to determine the proper meaning of a patent claim when applying patents or printed publications.

The final rules revise Section 1.510(a) in light of the estoppel limitations of 35 U.S.C. §§ 315(e)(1) and 325(e)(1) which limit the ability to seek *ex parte* reexamination.

Section 1.510(b) outlines the required contents of a request for reexamination. Subsection (b)(2) is rewritten to require the reexamination request to address in detail how each patent owner statement submitted under § 1.501(a)(2) (and relied upon in the request's detailed explanation) is being used to determine the proper claim meaning in connection with the prior art being applied to that claim. The request must also state how each relevant claim is being interpreted.

Section 1.510(b)(6) is new and calls for a certification that the third party requester is not subject to the statutory estoppels of post grant review or *inter partes* review.

Section 515 is amended to comport with the new statutory requirement of 35 U.S.C. § 301(d) prohibiting the use of patent owner statements about claim scope from being used initially, when determining whether to grant the reexamination request. The USPTO comments incident to announcing this final rule explain:

> Thus, a patent owner claim scope statement will not be considered when making the determination of whether to order *ex parte* reexamination under 35 U.S.C. 303. *See also* H.R. Rep. No. 112-98, Part 1, at page 46 (2011). In making the § 1.515(a) determination of whether to order *ex parte* reexamination, the Office will give the claims the broadest reasonable interpretation consistent with the specification, except in the case of an expired patent. *See Ex parte Papst-Motoren,* 1

> USPQ2d 1655 (Bd. Pat. App. & Inter. 1986); *In re Yamamoto,* 740 F.2d 1569 (Fed. Cir. 1984); *see also Manual of Patent Examining Procedure* § 2258 I.(G) (8th ed. 2001) (Rev. 8, July 2010) (MPEP). If reexamination is ordered, the patent owner statements submitted pursuant to 35 U.S.C. 301(a)(2) will be considered to the fullest extent possible when determining the scope of any claims of the patent which are subject to reexamination.[1] [emphasis added]

Correspondingly, 37 C.F.R. § 1.552 addresses using patent owner statements *after* a reexamination proceeding has commenced.

In short, patent owner statements cannot be used before reexamination is declared. After a declaration, however, such statements can be used "to determine the proper meaning of a patent claim when applying patents or printed publications."[2]

The new fee specified by 37 C.F.R. § 1.20 for requesting *ex parte* reexamination is $17,750. Refunds are ruled by 37 C.F.R. § 1.26. Subpart (c)(1) provides that if the Office decides not to grant the request for reexamination, the filing fee paid by the requester will be refunded, less the fee set forth in (newly-added) 37 C.F.R. § 1.20(c)(7), *i.e.,* $4,320.

[Section 23:6]

[1]77 Fed. Reg. 46615, 46618 (August 6, 2012).

[2]37 C.F.R. § 1.552.

Part V

MISCELLANEOUS PROVISIONS

Chapter 24

Assignee Filing and Inventor's Oath

AIA § 4
35 U.S.C.A. §§ 115, 118

§ 24:1 Background

Since 1790, U.S. patent applications have been filed by the inventor or his representative. The inventor has had to attest to a belief of being the original and first inventor of the subject matter. Only when the inventor refuses to sign or cannot be found has the U.S. patent statute permitted a patent application to be filed by an assignee or other entity showing the proper interest in the invention. In this respect, the U.S. has been unlike other countries where patents are granted upon applications that often are filed by the employer or assignee of the inventor. Indeed, Patent Cooperation Treaty forms for filing a patent application have allowed the inventor's employer-assignee to be the applicant with respect to member states other than the U.S., but in the U.S. the applicant had to be the inventor(s). In this respect, the U.S. is out of step.

The relevant portions of the U.S. patent statute at the time the AIA was enacted were 35 U.S.C. Sections 115 and 118:

Old Statute (35 U.S.C. § 115) (superseded)

35 U.S.C. 115. Oath of applicant.

The applicant shall make oath that he believes himself to be the original and first inventor of the process, machine, manufacture, or composition of matter, or improvement thereof, for which he solicits a patent; and shall state of what country he is a citizen. Such oath may be made before any person within the United States authorized by law to administer oaths, or, when made in a foreign country, before any diplomatic or consular officer of the United States authorized to administer oaths, or before any officer having an official seal and authorized to administer oaths in the foreign country in which the applicant may be, whose authority is proved by certificate of a diplomatic or consular officer of the United States, or apostille of an official designated by a foreign country which, by treaty or convention, accords like effect to apostilles of designated officials in the United States. Such oath is valid if it complies with the laws of the state or country where made. When the application is made as provided in this title by a person other than the inventor, the oath may be so varied in form that it can be made by him. For purposes of this section, a consular officer shall include any United States citizen serving overseas, authorized to perform notarial functions pursuant to section 1750 of the Revised Statutes, as amended (22 U.S.C. 4221).

Old Statute (35 U.S.C. § 118) (pre-revision)

35 U.S.C. 118. Filing by other than inventor.

Whenever an inventor refuses to execute an application for patent, or cannot be found or reached after diligent effort, a person to whom the inventor has assigned or agreed in writing to assign the invention or who otherwise shows sufficient proprietary interest in the matter justifying such action, may make application for patent on behalf of and as agent for the inventor on proof of the pertinent facts and a showing that such action is necessary to preserve the rights of the parties or to prevent irreparable damage; and the Director may grant a patent to such inventor upon such notice to him as the Director deems sufficient, and on compliance with such regulations as he prescribes.

§ 24:2 Congressional intent[1]

The House Report includes two relevant passages that indicate Congress' intent in the revisions to these statutory provisions:

Inventor's oath or declaration

The U.S. patent system, when first adopted in 1790, contemplated that individual inventors would file their own patent applications, or would have a patent practitioner do so on their behalf. It has become increasingly common for patent applications to be assigned to corporate entities, most commonly the employer of the inventor.[FN22] In fact, many employment contracts require employees to assign their inventions to their employer.[FN23]

FN 22. *See* John R. Allison & Mark A. Lemley, *The Growing Complexity of the United States Patent System,* 82 B.U. L. Rev. 77, 97 (2002) (study showing that approximately 85% of the patents issued between 1996–98 were assigned by inventors to corporations; an increase from 79% during the period between 1976–78).

FN 23. See Jerry C. Liu, *Overview of Patent Ownership Considerations in Joint Technology Development,* 2005 Syracuse Sci. & Tech. L. Rep. 1 (2005).

Current law still reflects the antiquated notion that it is the inventor who files the application, not the company-assignee. For example, every inventor must sign an oath as part of the

[Section 24:2]

[1]The Supreme Court cautions against relying on interpretations advanced in legislative statements that are not "anchored in the text of the statute." *Shannon v. U.S.*, 512 U.S. 573, 583, 114 S. Ct. 2419, 129 L. Ed. 2d 459 (1994), stating "[C]ourts have no authority to enforce [a] principl[e] gleaned solely from legislative history that has no statutory reference point." Shannon, 512 U.S. at 584, quoting *International Broth. of Elec. Workers, Local Union No. 474, AFL-CIO v. N.L.R.B.*, 814 F.2d 697, 712, 124 L.R.R.M. (BNA) 2993, 106 Lab. Cas. (CCH) P 12256 (D.C. Cir. 1987). The authoritative statement "is the statutory text, not the legislative history." *Exxon Mobil Corp. v. Allapattah Services, Inc.*, 545 U.S. 546, 568, 125 S. Ct. 2611, 162 L. Ed. 2d 502 (2005). However, lower courts have cited the legislative history of the AIA already in recent cases. E.g., *Rogers v. Tristar Products, Inc.*, 102 U.S.P.Q.2d 1722, 2012 WL 1660604, *2 (Fed. Cir. 2012) (non-precedential); *Byrne v. Wood, Herron & Evans, LLP*, 676 F.3d 1024, 1029, 102 U.S.P.Q.2d 1073 (Fed. Cir. 2012) (dissenting opin.).

patent application stating that the inventor believes he or she is the true inventor of the invention claimed in the application.[FN24] By the time an application is eventually filed, however, the applicant filing as an assignee may have difficulty locating and obtaining every inventor's signature for the statutorily required oath. Although the USPTO has adopted certain regulations to allow filing of an application when the inventor's signature is unobtainable,[FN25] many have advocated that the statute be modernized to facilitate the filing of applications by assignees.[FN26]

FN 24. 35 U.S.C. Sec. 115.

FN 25. *See* 37 C.F.R. Sec. 1.47, which permits an applicant to petition the Director of the USPTO to have the application accepted without every inventor's signature in limited circumstances, e.g., when the inventor cannot be found or refuses to participate in the application.

FN 26. *See Perspectives on Patents: Harmonization and Other Matters: Hearing Before the Subcomm. on Intellectual Prop. of the Senate Comm. on the Judiciary,* 109th Cong. (2005) (statement of David Beier, Senior Vice President of Global Government Affairs, Amgen).

The Act updates the patent system by facilitating the process by which an assignee may file and prosecute patent applications. It provides similar flexibility for a person to whom the inventor is obligated to assign, but has not assigned, rights to the invention (the "obligated assignee").

Section 115 of title 35 is amended to allow a substitute statement to be submitted in lieu of an inventor's oath when either the inventor (i) is unable to submit an oath, or (ii) is both unwilling to do so and under an obligation to assign the invention. If an error is discovered, the statement may later be corrected. A savings clause is included to prevent an invalidity or unenforceability challenge to the patent based on failure to comply with these requirements, provided that any error has been remedied. Willful false statements remain punishable, however, under Federal criminal laws.[FN27]

FN 27. *See* 18 U.S.C. Sec. 1001.

Section 118 of title 35 is also amended to make it easier for an assignee to file a patent application. The amendment now allows obligated assignees—entities to which the inventor is obligated to assign the application—to file applications, as well. It also allows a person who has a sufficient proprietary interest in the invention to file an application to preserve that person's rights and those of the inventor.

* * *

Section 4. Inventor's oath or declaration.

The section streamlines the requirement that the inventor submit an oath as part of a patent application, and makes it easier for patent owners to file applications.

Subsection (a)—Section 115 is amended to permit an applicant to submit a substitute statement in lieu of the inventor's oath or declaration in certain circumstances, including if the inventor is (i) unable to do so, or (ii) unwilling to do so and is under an obligation to assign the invention. A savings clause provides that failure to comply with the requirements of this section will not be a basis for invalidity or unenforceability of the patent if the failure is remedied by a supplemental and corrected statement. False substitute statements are subject to the same penalties as false oaths and declarations.

Subsection (b)—Section 118 is amended to allow the person to whom the inventor has assigned (or is under an obligation to assign) the invention to file a patent application. A person who otherwise shows sufficient proprietary interest in the invention may file a patent application as an agent of the inventor to preserve the rights of the parties.[2]

§ 24:3 The amended and new statutes

Section 4(b)(1) of the AIA amends 35 U.S.C. § 118 to allow assignee filing and replaces § 115 completely with an extensive new § 115, as follows:[1]

Revised Statute (35 U.S.C. § 118)

§ 118. Filing by other than inventor

~~Whenever an inventor refuses to execute an application for patent, or cannot be found or reached after diligent effort, a~~ A person to whom the inventor has assigned or is under an obligation to assign the invention may make an application for patent. A person ~~or~~ who otherwise shows sufficient proprietary interest in the matter ~~justifying such action~~ may make an application for patent on behalf of and as agent for the inventor on proof of the pertinent facts and a showing that such action is appropriate to preserve the rights of the parties ~~or to prevent irreparable damage; and the Director may grant a patent to such inventor upon such notice to him as the Director deems sufficient, and on compliance with such regulations as he prescribes.~~. If the Director grants a patent on an application filed under this section by a person other than the inventor, the patent shall be granted to the real party in interest and upon such notice to the inventor as the Director considers to be sufficient.

[2]H. R. Rep. No. 112-98, pt. 1, pp. 43 to 44, 74 (2011).

[Section 24:3]

[1]H.R. Rep. No. 112-98, pt. 1, pp. 55, 82 (2011).

New Statute (35 U.S.C. § 115 as amended by H.R. 6621 (2013))

§ 115. Inventor's oath or declaration

(a) NAMING THE INVENTOR; INVENTOR'S OATH OR DECLARATION.—An application for patent that is filed under section 111(a) or commences the national stage under section 371 shall include, or be amended to include, the name of the inventor for any invention claimed in the application. Except as otherwise provided in this section, each individual who is the inventor or a joint inventor of a claimed invention in an application for patent shall execute an oath or declaration in connection with the application.

(b) REQUIRED STATEMENTS.—An oath or declaration under subsection (a) shall contain statements that—

(1) the application was made or was authorized to be made by the affiant or declarant; and

(2) such individual believes himself or herself to be the original inventor or an original joint inventor of a claimed invention in the application.

(c) ADDITIONAL REQUIREMENTS.—The Director may specify additional information relating to the inventor and the invention that is required to be included in an oath or declaration under subsection (a).

(d) SUBSTITUTE STATEMENT.—

(1) IN GENERAL.—In lieu of executing an oath or declaration under subsection (a), the applicant for patent may provide a substitute statement under the circumstances described in paragraph (2) and such additional circumstances that the Director may specify by regulation.

(2) PERMITTED CIRCUMSTANCES.—A substitute statement under paragraph (1) is permitted with respect to any individual who—

(A) is unable to file the oath or declaration under subsection (a) because the individual—

(i) is deceased;

(ii) is under legal incapacity; or

(iii) cannot be found or reached after diligent effort; or

(B) is under an obligation to assign the invention but has refused to make the oath or declaration required under subsection (a).

(3) CONTENTS.—A substitute statement under this subsection shall—

(A) identify the individual with respect to whom the statement applies;

(B) set forth the circumstances representing the permitted basis for the filing of the substitute statement in lieu of the oath or declaration under subsection (a); and

(C) contain any additional information, including any showing, required by the Director.

(e) MAKING REQUIRED STATEMENTS IN ASSIGNMENT OF RECORD.—An individual who is under an obligation of assignment of an application for patent may include the required statements under subsections (b) and (c) in the assignment executed by the individual, in lieu of filing such statements separately.

(f) TIME FOR FILING.—The applicant for patent shall provide each required oath or declaration under subsection (a), substitute statement under subsection (d), or recorded assignment meeting the requirements of subsection (e) no later than the date on which the issue fee for the patent is paid.[2]

(g) EARLIER-FILED APPLICATION CONTAINING REQUIRED STATEMENTS OR SUBSTITUTE STATEMENT.—

(1) EXCEPTION.—The requirements under this section shall not apply to an individual with respect to an application for patent in which the individual is named as the inventor or a joint inventor and who claims the benefit under section 120, 121, or 365(c) of the filing of an earlier-filed application, if—

(A) an oath or declaration meeting the requirements of subsection (a) was executed by the individual and was filed in connection with the earlier-filed application;

(B) a substitute statement meeting the requirements of subsection (d) was filed in connection with the earlier filed application with respect to the individual; or

(C) an assignment meeting the requirements of subsection (e) was executed with respect to the earlier-filed application by the individual and was recorded in connection with the earlier-filed application.

(2) COPIES OF OATHS, DECLARATIONS, STATEMENTS, OR ASSIGNMENTS.—Notwithstanding paragraph (1), the Director may require that a copy of the executed oath or declaration, the substitute statement, or the assignment filed in connection with the earlier-filed application be included in the later-filed application.

(h) SUPPLEMENTAL AND CORRECTED STATEMENTS; FILING ADDITIONAL STATEMENTS.—

(1) IN GENERAL.—Any person making a statement required under this section may withdraw, replace, or otherwise correct the statement at any time. If a change is made in the

[2]As originally written in the AIA, § 115(f) provided, "(f) TIME FOR FILING.—A notice of allowance under section 151 may be provided to an applicant for patent only if the applicant for patent has filed each required oath or declaration under subsection (a) or has filed a substitute statement under subsection (d) or recorded an assignment meeting the requirements of subsection (e)." H.R. 6621, § 1(f) (2013) repealed that section and replaced it with the language set forth in the main text for § 115(f).

naming of the inventor requiring the filing of 1 or more additional statements under this section, the Director shall establish regulations under which such additional statements may be filed.

(2) SUPPLEMENTAL STATEMENTS NOT REQUIRED.—If an individual has executed an oath or declaration meeting the requirements of subsection (a) or an assignment meeting the requirements of subsection (e) with respect to an application for patent, the Director may not thereafter require that individual to make any additional oath, declaration, or other statement equivalent to those required by this section in connection with the application for patent or any patent issuing thereon.

(3) SAVINGS CLAUSE.—A patent shall not be invalid or unenforceable based upon the failure to comply with a requirement under this section if the failure is remedied as provided under paragraph (1).

(i) ACKNOWLEDGMENT OF PENALTIES.—Any declaration or statement filed pursuant to this section shall contain an acknowledgment that any willful false statement made in such declaration or statement is punishable under section 1001 of title 18 by fine or imprisonment of not more than 5 years, or both.

§ 24:4 The new and amended regulations

The USPTO issued revised regulations concerning the oath and application. It also updated the regulation on inventorship. The following 37 C.F.R. Sections are relevant:

1.41 Inventorship;
1.42 Applicant for patent;
1.43 Application for patent by a legal representative of a deceased or legally incapacitated inventor;
1.45 Application for patent by joint inventors;
1.46 Application for patent by an assignee, obligated assignee, or a person who otherwise shows sufficient proprietary interest in the matter;
1.55 Claim for foreign priority;
1.63 Inventor's oath or declaration;
1.64 Substitute statement in lieu of an oath or declaration;
1.67 Supplemental oath or declaration; and
1.76 Application data sheet.

§ 1.41. Inventorship.

(a) An application must include, or be amended to include, the name of the inventor for any invention claimed in the application.

(b) The inventorship of a nonprovisional application under

35 U.S.C. 111(a) is the inventor or joint inventors set forth in the application data sheet in accordance with § 1.76 filed before or concurrently with the inventor's oath or declaration. If an application data sheet is not filed before or concurrently with the inventor's oath or declaration, the inventorship is the inventor or joint inventors set forth in the inventor's oath or declaration, except as provided for in §§ 1.53(d)(4) and 1.63(d). Once an application data sheet or the inventor's oath or declaration is filed in a nonprovisional application, any correction of inventorship must be pursuant to § 1.48. If neither an application data sheet nor the inventor's oath or declaration is filed during the pendency of a nonprovisional application, the inventorship is the inventor or joint inventors set forth in the application papers filed pursuant to § 1.53(b), unless the applicant files a paper, including the processing fee set forth in § 1.17(i), supplying the name or names of the inventor or joint inventors.

(c) The inventorship of a provisional application is the inventor or joint inventors set forth in the cover sheet as prescribed by § 1.51(c)(1). Once a cover sheet as prescribed by § 1.51(c)(1) is filed in a provisional application, any correction of inventorship must be pursuant to § 1.48. If a cover sheet as prescribed by § 1.51(c)(1) is not filed during the pendency of a provisional application, the inventorship is the inventor or joint inventors set forth in the application papers filed pursuant to § 1.53(c), unless applicant files a paper including the processing fee set forth in § 1.17(q), supplying the name or names of the inventor or joint inventors.

(d) In a nonprovisional application under 35 U.S.C. 111(a) filed without an application data sheet or the inventor's oath or declaration, or in a provisional application filed without a cover sheet as prescribed by § 1.51(c)(1), the name and residence of each person believed to be an actual inventor should be provided when the application papers pursuant to § 1.53(b) or § 1.53(c) are filed.

(e) The inventorship of an international application entering the national stage under 35 U.S.C. 371 is the inventor or joint inventors set forth in the application data sheet in accordance with § 1.76 filed with the initial submission under 35 U.S.C. 371. Unless the initial submission under 35 U.S.C. 371 is accompanied by an application data sheet in accordance with § 1.76 setting forth the inventor or joint inventors, the inventorship is the inventor or joint inventors set forth in the international application, which includes any change effected under PCT Rule 92 *bis*.

§ 1.42. Applicant for patent.

(a) The word "applicant" when used in this title refers to the inventor or all of the joint inventors, or to the person applying for a patent as provided in §§ 1.43, 1.45, or 1.46.

(b) If a person is applying for a patent as provided in § 1.46, the word "applicant" refers to the assignee, the person to whom the inventor is under an obligation to assign the invention, or the person who otherwise shows sufficient proprietary interest in the matter, who is applying for a patent under § 1.46 and not the inventor.

(c) If fewer than all joint inventors are applying for a patent as provided in § 1.45, the phrase "the applicant" means the joint inventors who are applying for the patent without the omitted inventor(s).

(d) Any person having authority may deliver an application and fees to the Office on behalf of the applicant. However, an oath or declaration, or substitute statement in lieu of an oath or declaration, may be executed only in accordance with § 1.63 or 1.64, a correspondence address may be provided only in accordance with § 1.33(a), and amendments and other papers must be signed in accordance with § 1.33(b).

(e) The Office may require additional information where there is a question concerning ownership or interest in an application, and a showing may be required from the person filing the application that the filing was authorized where such authorization comes into question.

§ 1.43. Application for patent by a legal representative of a deceased or legally incapacitated inventor.

If an inventor is deceased or under legal incapacity, the legal representative of the inventor may make an application for patent on behalf of the inventor. If an inventor dies during the time intervening between the filing of the application and the granting of a patent thereon, the letters patent may be issued to the legal representative upon proper intervention. See § 1.64 concerning the execution of a substitute statement by a legal representative in lieu of an oath or declaration.

§ 1.45. Application for patent by joint inventors.

(a) Joint inventors must apply for a patent jointly, and each must make an inventor's oath or declaration as required by § 1.63, except as provided for in § 1.64. If a joint inventor refuses to join in an application for patent or cannot be found or reached after diligent effort, the other joint inventor or inventors may make the application for patent on behalf of themselves and the omitted inventor. See § 1.64 concerning the execution of a substitute statement by the other joint inventor or inventors in lieu of an oath or declaration.

(b) Inventors may apply for a patent jointly even though:

(1) They did not physically work together or at the same time;

(2) Each inventor did not make the same type or amount of contribution; or

(3) Each inventor did not make a contribution to the subject matter of every claim of the application.

(c) If multiple inventors are named in a nonprovisional application, each named inventor must have made a contribution, individually or jointly, to the subject matter of at least one claim of the application and the application will be considered to be a joint application under 35 U.S.C. 116. If multiple inventors are named in a provisional application, each named inventor must have made a contribution, individually or jointly, to the subject matter disclosed in the provisional application and the provisional application will be considered to be a joint application under 35 U.S.C. 116.

§ 1.46. Application for patent by an assignee, obligated assignee, or a person who otherwise shows sufficient proprietary interest in the matter.

(a) A person to whom the inventor has assigned or is under an obligation to assign the invention may make an application for patent. A person who otherwise shows sufficient proprietary interest in the matter may make an application for patent on behalf of and as agent for the inventor on proof of the pertinent facts and a showing that such action is appropriate to preserve the rights of the parties.

(b) If an application under 35 U.S.C. 111 is made by a person other than the inventor under paragraph (a) of this section, the application must contain an application data sheet under § 1.76 specifying in the applicant information section (§ 1.76(b)(7)) the assignee, person to whom the inventor is under an obligation to assign the invention, or person who otherwise shows sufficient proprietary interest in the matter. If the application is the national stage of an international application, the person who is identified in the international stage as an applicant for the United States is the person specified as the original applicant for the national stage.

(1) If the applicant is the assignee or a person to whom the inventor is under an obligation to assign the invention, documentary evidence of ownership (e.g., assignment for an assignee, employment agreement for a person to whom the inventor is under an obligation to assign the invention) should be recorded as provided for in part 3 of this chapter no later than the date the issue fee is paid in the application.

(2) If the applicant is a person who otherwise shows sufficient proprietary interest in the matter, such applicant must submit a petition including:

(i) The fee set forth in § 1.17(g);

(ii) A showing that such person has sufficient proprietary interest in the matter; and

(iii) A statement that making the application for patent by a person who otherwise shows sufficient proprietary interest in the matter on behalf of and as agent for the inventor is appropriate to preserve the rights of the parties.

(c) Any request to correct or update the name of the applicant after an applicant has been specified under paragraph (b) of this section must include an application data sheet under § 1.76 specifying the correct or updated name of the applicant in the applicant information section (§ 1.76(b)(7)). Any request to change the applicant after an original applicant has been specified under paragraph (b) of this section must include an application data sheet under § 1.76 specifying the applicant in the applicant information section (§ 1.76(b)(7)) and comply with §§ 3.71 and 3.73 of this title.

(d) Even if the whole or a part interest in the invention or in the patent to be issued is assigned or obligated to be assigned, an oath or declaration must be executed by the actual inventor or each actual joint inventor, except as provided for in § 1.64. *See* § 1.64 concerning the execution of a substitute statement by an assignee, person to whom the inventor is under an obligation to assign the invention, or a person who otherwise shows sufficient proprietary interest in the matter.

(e) If a patent is granted on an application filed under this section by a person other than the inventor, the patent shall be granted to the real party in interest. Otherwise, the patent may be issued to the assignee or jointly to the inventor and the assignee as provided in § 3.81. Where a real party in interest has filed an application under § 1.46, the applicant shall notify the Office of any change in the real party in interest no later than payment of the issue fee. The Office will treat the absence of such a notice as an indication that there has been no change in the real party in interest.

(f) The Office may publish notice of the filing of the application by a person who otherwise shows sufficient proprietary interest in the *Official Gazette*.

§ 1.47. [Removed and Reserved]

§ 1.55. Claim for foreign priority.

(a) * * **** [unchanged language: An applicant in a nonprovisional application may claim the benefit of the filing date of one or more prior foreign applications under the conditions specified in 35 U.S.C. 119(a) through (d) and (f), 172, and 365(a) and (b).]

(1) (i) In an original application filed under 35 U.S.C. 111(a), the claim for foreign priority must be presented in an application data sheet (§ 1.76(b)(6)) during the pen-

dency of the application, and within the later of four months from the actual filing date of the application or sixteen months from the filing date of the prior foreign application. This time period is not extendable. The claim must identify the foreign application for which priority is claimed, as well as any foreign application for the same subject matter and having a filing date before that of the application for which priority is claimed, by specifying the application number, country (or intellectual property authority), day, month, and year of its filing. The time periods in this paragraph do not apply in an application under 35 U.S.C. 111(a) if the application is:

* * * * *

(c) Unless such claim is accepted in accordance with the provisions of this paragraph, any claim for priority under 35 U.S.C. 119(a)–(d) or 365(a) not presented in an application data sheet (§ 1.76(b)(6)) within the time period provided by paragraph (a) of this section is considered to have been waived. If a claim for priority under 35 U.S.C. 119(a)–(d) or 365(a) is presented after the time period provided by paragraph (a) of this section, the claim may be accepted if the claim identifying the prior foreign application by specifying its application number, country (or intellectual property authority), and the day, month, and year of its filing was unintentionally delayed. A petition to accept a delayed claim for priority under 35 U.S.C. 119(a)–(d) or 365(a) must be accompanied by:

* * * * *

(d) (1) * * *

(ii) The foreign application is identified in an application data sheet (§ 1.76(b)(6)); and

* * * * *

§ 1.63. Inventor's oath or declaration.

(a) The inventor, or each individual who is a joint inventor of a claimed invention, in an application for patent must execute an oath or declaration directed to the application, except as provided for in § 1.64. An oath or declaration under this section must:

(1) Identify the inventor or joint inventor executing the oath or declaration by his or her legal name;

(2) Identify the application to which it is directed;

(3) Include a statement that the person executing the oath or declaration believes the named inventor or joint inventor to be the original inventor or an original joint inventor of a claimed invention in the application for which the oath or declaration is being submitted; and

(4) State that the application was made or was authorized to be made by the person executing the oath or

declaration.

(b) Unless the following information is supplied in an application data sheet in accordance with § 1.76, the oath or declaration must also identify:

(1) Each inventor by his or her legal name; and

(2) A mailing address where the inventor customarily receives mail, and residence, if an inventor lives at a location which is different from where the inventor customarily receives mail, for each inventor.

(c) A person may not execute an oath or declaration for an application unless that person has reviewed and understands the contents of the application, including the claims, and is aware of the duty to disclose to the Office all information known to the person to be material to patentability as defined in § 1.56. There is no minimum age for a person to be qualified to execute an oath or declaration, but the person must be competent to execute, i.e., understand, the document that the person is executing.

(d) (1) A newly executed oath or declaration under § 1.63, or substitute statement under § 1.64, is not required under § 1.51(b)(2) and § 1.53(f) or § 1.497 for an inventor in a continuing application that claims the benefit under 35 U.S.C. 120, 121, or 365(c) in compliance with § 1.78 of an earlier-filed application, provided that an oath or declaration in compliance with this section, or substitute statement under § 1.64, was executed by or with respect to such inventor and was filed in the earlier-filed application, and a copy of such oath, declaration, or substitute statement showing the signature or an indication thereon that it was executed, is submitted in the continuing application.

(2) The inventorship of a continuing application filed under 35 U.S.C. 111(a) is the inventor or joint inventors specified in the application data sheet filed before or concurrently with the copy of the inventor's oath or declaration from the earlier-filed application. If an application data sheet is not filed before or concurrently with the copy of the inventor's oath or declaration from the earlier-filed application, the inventorship is the inventorship set forth in the copy of the inventor's oath or declaration from the earlier-filed application, unless it is accompanied by a statement signed pursuant to § 1.33(b) stating the name of each inventor in the continuing application.

(3) Any new joint inventor named in the continuing application must provide an oath or declaration in compliance with this section, except as provided for in § 1.64.

(e) (1) An assignment may also serve as an oath or declaration required by this section if the assignment as executed:

(i) Includes the information and statements required

under paragraphs (a) and (b) of this section; and

(ii) A copy of the assignment is recorded as provided for in part 3 of this chapter.

(2) Any reference to an oath or declaration under this section includes an assignment as provided for in this paragraph.

(f) With respect to an application naming only one inventor, any reference to the inventor's oath or declaration in this chapter includes a substitute statement executed under § 1.64. With respect to an application naming more than one inventor, any reference to the inventor's oath or declaration in this chapter means the oaths, declarations, or substitute statements that have been collectively executed by or with respect to all of the joint inventors, unless otherwise clear from the context.

(g) An oath or declaration under this section, including the statement provided for in paragraph (e) of this section, must be executed (i.e., signed) in accordance either with § 1.66 or with an acknowledgment that any willful false statement made in such declaration or statement is punishable under 18 U.S.C. 1001 by fine or imprisonment of not more than five (5) years, or both.

(h) An oath or declaration filed at any time pursuant to 35 U.S.C. 115(h)(1) will be placed in the file record of the application or patent, but may not necessarily be reviewed by the Office. Any request for correction of the named inventorship must comply with § 1.48 in an application and § 1.324 in a patent.

§ 1.64. Substitute statement in lieu of an oath or declaration.

(a) An applicant under § 1.43, 1.45 or 1.46 may execute a substitute statement in lieu of an oath or declaration under § 1.63 if the inventor is deceased, is under a legal incapacity, has refused to execute the oath or declaration under § 1.63, or cannot be found or reached after diligent effort.

(b) A substitute statement under this section must:

(1) Comply with the requirements of § 1.63(a), identifying the inventor or joint inventor with respect to whom a substitute statement in lieu of an oath or declaration is executed, and stating upon information and belief the facts which such inventor is required to state; (2) Identify the person executing the substitute statement and the relationship of such person to the inventor or joint inventor with respect to whom the substitute statement is executed, and unless such information is supplied in an application data sheet in accordance with § 1.76, the residence and mailing address of the person signing the substitute statement;

(3) Identify the circumstances permitting the person to execute the substitute statement in lieu of an oath or declaration under § 1.63, namely whether the inventor is deceased, is under a legal incapacity, cannot be found or reached after a diligent effort was made, or has refused to execute the oath or declaration under § 1.63; and

(4) Unless the following information is supplied in an application data sheet in accordance with § 1.76, also identify:

(i) Each inventor by his or her legal name; and

(ii) The last known mailing address where the inventor customarily receives mail, and last known residence, if an inventor lives at a location which is different from where the inventor customarily receives mail, for each inventor who is not deceased or under a legal incapacity.

(c) A person may not execute a substitute statement provided for in this section for an application unless that person has reviewed and understands the contents of the application, including the claims, and is aware of the duty to disclose to the Office all information known to the person to be material to patentability as defined in § 1.56.

(d) Any reference to an inventor's oath or declaration includes a substitute statement provided for in this section.

(e) A substitute statement under this section must contain an acknowledgment that any willful false statement made in such statement is punishable under section 1001 of title 18 by fine or imprisonment of not more than 5 years, or both.

(f) A nonsigning inventor or legal representative may subsequently join in the application by submitting an oath or declaration under § 1.63. The submission of an oath or declaration by a nonsigning inventor or legal representative in an application filed under § 1.43, 1.45 or 1.46 will not permit the nonsigning inventor or legal representative to revoke or grant a power of attorney.

§ 1.67. Supplemental oath or declaration.

(a) The applicant may submit an inventor's oath or declaration meeting the requirements of § 1.63, § 1.64, or § 1.162 to correct any deficiencies or inaccuracies present in an earlier-filed inventor's oath or declaration. Deficiencies or inaccuracies due to the failure to meet the requirements of § 1.63(b) in an oath or declaration may be corrected with an application data sheet in accordance with § 1.76, except that any correction of inventorship must be pursuant to § 1.48.

(b) A supplemental inventor's oath or declaration under this section must be executed by the person whose inventor's oath or declaration is being withdrawn, replaced, or otherwise corrected. (c) The Office will not require a person who has executed an oath or declaration in compliance with 35 U.S.C. 115

and § 1.63 or 1.162 for an application to provide an additional inventor's oath or declaration for the application.

(d) No new matter may be introduced into a nonprovisional application after its filing date even if an inventor's oath or declaration is filed to correct deficiencies or inaccuracies present in the earlier-filed inventor's oath or declaration.

§ 1.76. Application data sheet.

(a) *Application data sheet*: An application data sheet is a sheet or sheets, that may be submitted in a provisional application under 35 U.S.C. 111(b), a nonprovisional application under 35 U.S.C. 111(a), or a national stage application under 35 U.S.C. 371, and must be submitted when required by § 1.55 or 1.78 to claim priority to or the benefit of a prior-filed application under 35 U.S.C. 119, 120, 121, or 365. An application data sheet must be titled "Application Data Sheet." An application data sheet must contain all of the section headings listed in paragraph (b) of this section, except as provided in paragraph (c)(2) of this section, with any appropriate data for each section heading. If an application data sheet is provided, the application data sheet is part of the application for which it has been submitted.

(b) * * * [unchanged language: *Bibliographic data.* Bibliographic data as used in paragraph (a) of this section includes:]

(1) *Inventor information.* This information includes the legal name, residence, and mailing address of the inventor or each joint inventor. * * * * *

(2) *Correspondence information.* This information includes the correspondence address, which may be indicated by reference to a customer number, to which correspondence is to be directed (*see* § 1.33(a)).]

(3) *Application information.* This information includes the title of the invention, the total number of drawing sheets, a suggested drawing figure for publication (in a nonprovisional application), any docket number assigned to the application, the type of application (*e.g.,* utility, plant, design, reissue, provisional), whether the application discloses any significant part of the subject matter of an application under a secrecy order pursuant to § 5.2 of this chapter (*see* § 5.2(c)), and, for plant applications, the Latin name of the genus and species of the plant claimed, as well as the variety denomination.

(4) * * * [unchanged language: *Representative information.* This information includes the registration number of each practitioner having a power of attorney or authorization of agent in the application (preferably by reference to a customer number). Providing this information in the application data sheet does not constitute a power of at-

torney or authorization of agent in the application (see § 1.34(b)).]

(5) *Domestic benefit information.* This information includes the application number, the filing date, the status (including patent number if available), and relationship of each application for which a benefit is claimed under 35 U.S.C. 119(e), 120, 121, or 365(c). Providing this information in the application data sheet constitutes the specific reference required by 35 U.S.C. 119(e) or 120, and § 1.78(a)(2) or § 1.78(a)(5).

(6) * * * [unchanged language: Foreign priority information. This information includes the application number, country, and filing date of each foreign application for which priority is claimed, as well as any foreign application having a filing date before that of the application for which priority is claimed. Providing this information in the application data sheet constitutes the claim for priority as required by 35 U.S.C. 119(b) and § 1.55(a).]

(7) *Applicant information:* This information includes the name (either natural person or juristic entity) and address of the legal representative, assignee, person to whom the inventor is under an obligation to assign the invention, or person who otherwise shows sufficient proprietary interest in the matter who is the applicant under § 1.43 or § 1.46. Providing assignment information in the application data sheet does not substitute for compliance with any requirement of part 3 of this chapter to have an assignment recorded by the Office.

(c) *Correcting and updating an application data sheet.* (1) Information in a previously submitted application data sheet, inventor's oath or declaration under § 1.63, § 1.64 or § 1.67, or otherwise of record, may be corrected or updated until payment of the issue fee by a new application data sheet providing corrected or updated information, except that inventorship changes must comply with the requirements of § 1.48, foreign priority and domestic benefit information changes must comply with §§ 1.55 and 1.78, and correspondence address changes are governed by § 1.33(a).

(2) An application data sheet providing corrected or updated information may include all of the sections listed in paragraph (b) of this section or only those sections containing changed or updated information. The application data sheet must include the section headings listed in paragraph (b) of this section for each section included in the application data sheet, and must identify the information that is being changed, with underlining for insertions, and strike-through or brackets for text removed, except that identification of information being changed is not required for an application data sheet included with an initial submission under 35

U.S.C. 371.

(d) Inconsistencies between application data sheet and other documents. For inconsistencies between information that is supplied by both an application data sheet under this section and other documents:

(1) The most recent submission will govern with respect to inconsistencies as between the information provided in an application data sheet, a designation of a correspondence address, or by the inventor's oath or declaration, except that:

(i) The most recent application data sheet will govern with respect to foreign priority (§ 1.55) or domestic benefit (§ 1.78) claims; and

(ii) The naming of the inventorship is governed by § 1.41 and changes to inventorship or the names of the inventors is governed by § 1.48.

(2) The information in the application data sheet will govern when the inconsistent information is supplied at the same time by a designation of correspondence address or the inventor's oath or declaration.

(3) The Office will capture bibliographic information from the application data sheet. The Office will generally not review the inventor's oath or declaration to determine if the bibliographic information contained therein is consistent with the bibliographic information provided in an application data sheet. Incorrect bibliographic information contained in an application data sheet may be corrected as provided in paragraph (c)(1) of this section.

(e) *Signature requirement.* An application data sheet must be signed in compliance with § 1.33(b). An unsigned application data sheet will be treated only as a transmittal letter.

§ 24:5 Practice—The applicant

According to the revised practice under the new and revised statutes and regulations effective on September 16, 2012, the "applicant" no longer means only the inventor(s). It includes the person applying for a patent under 37 C.F.R. §§ 1.43, 1.45, or 1.46.[1] The applicant can be an assignee, person to whom the inventor is obligated to assign, or a person who has sufficient proprietary interest in the claimed

[Section 24:5]

[1] 37 C.F.R. § 1.42(a).

invention.[2] Each inventor must still be named,[3] but the patent, if granted, will be awarded to the real party in interest, on such notice to the inventor(s) as the Director deems sufficient.[4] A party with less than the entire right, title, and interest cannot apply for the patent on its own.[5]

If the applicant is neither the inventor nor the assignee of the entire right, title, and interest but nevertheless believes itself to have a sufficient proprietary interest in the matter, such applicant must submit a petition that includes: the fee set forth in 37 C.F.R. § 1.17(g) ($200); a showing that such applicant has a sufficient proprietary interest; and a statement that making the application is appropriate to preserve the rights of the parties.[6] Persons with a sufficient proprietary interest are not confined to instances in which an inventor or inventors refused to execute the application or could not be found despite diligent effort.

§ 24:6 Practice—The name of the inventor

Applicants may name the inventor by either a signed application data sheet under § 1.76 or an executed inventor oath or declaration. Once the names of the inventors are provided by a signed application data sheet or signed inventor oath or declaration, a change in sequence or a correction as to inventorship requires proceeding under § 1.48, other than in a reissue application, with a corresponding change in the application data sheet as required by § 1.46(c). These changes illustratively include the addition or deletion of an inventor name, a correction or updating of the name of the inventor, such as correcting a misspelling or a name change, or changing the order of the names as the applicant desires the names to be printed on the face of the patent. As of November 2012, it appears that 37 C.F.R. § 1.48 still requires amendment because it refers to errors in inventorship occurring "without deceptive intention." As discussed in Chapter 26 below, deceptive intent has been stripped from the patent

[2] 37 C.F.R. § 1.42(b), 1.46.

[3] 35 U.S.C.A. § 115 (2011), 37 C.F.R. § 1.63(e).

[4] 35 U.S.C.A. § 118 (2011).

[5] See USPTO "Reference Guide to Statutory Provisions and Final Rules Effective on September 16, 2012," slide 11. Available at http://www.uspto.gov/aia_implementation/120910-aia-reference-guide-to-statutory-provisions-and-final-rules.pdf, visited Oct. 27, 2012.

[6] 37 C.F.R. § 1.46(b)(2).

statute by the America Invents Act.

§ 24:7 Practice—The oath or declaration

For each inventor, the application must have an oath or declaration executed by the inventor, a substitute statement[1] with respect to the inventor, or an assignment that contains the statements required for an oath/declaration by the inventor.[2] The oath or declaration requires the inventor to swear or declare to being an "original" inventor of the application and attesting to being the "first" inventor is no longer required.[3] The oath or declaration must state that the application was made or authorized to be made by the person executing the oath or declaration.[4]

The penalty clause in the inventor oath or declaration has changed. It now requires acknowledgement that any willful false statement is punishable under § 1001 of Title 18 by fine or imprisonment of not more than five years, or both.[5] However, under the new practice, there is no requirement to state in the oath or declaration that all statements are true and that all statements made on information and belief are believed to be true.

The inventor or other person executing the oath or declaration is no longer required to acknowledge in writing the duty of disclosure under § 1.56 or that such person has reviewed and understands the contents of the application. Nevertheless, 37 C.F.R. § 1.63(c) requires that such person "has reviewed and understands the contents of the application, including the claims, and is aware of the duty to disclose to the Office all information known to the person to be material to patentability as defined in § 1.56." In other words, the person need not aver the statements in the oath or declaration *itself*, but must be aware of these requirements when signing the oath or declaration.

The submission of an inventor oath or declaration may be

[Section 24:7]

[1]A "substitute statement" is a document that an applicant may file in lieu of an oath or declaration on behalf of the inventor under circumstances permitted in 35 U.S.C.A. § 115(d).

[2]35 U.S.C.A. § 115(a) (2011).

[3]37 C.F.R. § 1.63(a)(3).

[4]37 C.F.R. § 1.63(a)(4).

[5]35 U.S.C.A. § 115(i), 37 C.F.R. § 1.63(g).

postponed "until the application is otherwise in condition for allowance under the conditions specified in paragraphs (f)(3)(i) and (f)(3)(ii) of this section."[6] However, this is subject to the provisos that the application is an original application, not a reissue application, and that an application data sheet under § 1.76 had earlier been submitted identifying each inventor by legal name and providing a mailing address where mail is customarily received and residence address for each inventor. Another condition is that Application Data Sheet (ADS) has been signed.[7] Note, however, that H.R. 6621 (2013) repealed 35 U.S.C. § 115(f) as set forth in the AIA and made the due date for the required oath(s) or declaration(s) the date when the issue fee is paid, stating: (f) Time for Filing—The applicant for patent shall provide each required oath or declaration under subsection (a), substitute statement under subsection (d), or recorded assignment meeting the requirements of subsection (e) no later than the date on which the issue fee for the patent is paid.

An applicant who uses the delayed submission of an inventor oath or declaration is required to pay a surcharge as specified in 35 U.S.C. §§ 111(a)(3) and 371(d). The USPTO cannot issue a Notice of Allowance without the proper inventor oath or declaration.

The ADS must identify each inventor properly (legal name) and provide a mailing address and residence for each named inventor. A statement of citizenship is no longer required.

An oath or declaration is still required prior to examination for a reissue application. If the oath or declaration is not provided when the application is filed, then a surcharge applies.

Continuation applications have to comply with the new oath/declaration requirements.[8]

---

[6]37 C.F.R. § 1.53(f)(3).

[7]"An unsigned application data sheet will be treated only as a transmittal letter." 37 C.F.R. § 1.76(e).

[8]37 C.F.R. §§ 1.63(d)(1): "A newly executed oath or declaration under § 1.63, or substitute statement under § 1.64, is not required under § 1.51(b)(2) and § 1.53(f) or § 1.497 for an inventor in a continuing application that claims the benefit under 35 U.S.C.A. 120, 121, or 365(c) in compliance with § 1.78 of an earlier-filed application, provided that an oath or declaration in compliance with this section, or substitute statement under § 1.64, was executed by or with respect to such inventor and was filed in the earlier-filed application, and a copy of such oath, declaration, or substitute statement showing the signature or an indication thereon that

§ 24:8 Practice—Substitute statements

The regulations delineate particular instances when a substitute statement can be submitted in lieu of an oath or declaration. These strict requirements allow an applicant under 37 C.F.R. §§ 1.43, 1.45 or 1.46 to execute a substitute statement in lieu of an oath or declaration under § 1.63 under four conditions, namely, if the inventor: (a) is deceased, (b) is under a legal incapacity, (c) has refused to execute the oath or declaration under § 1.63, or (d) cannot be found or reached after diligent effort.[1]

§ 24:9 Practice—Priority claims

Priority claims belong in the Application Data Sheet. This is the sole effective location for priority claims. Placing them in the specification is insufficient,[1] and failure to place the priority claim in the ADS could be deemed as a waiver. "For applications entering the national stage under 35 U.S.C. 371, foreign priority claims are not required to be set forth in the ADS. Foreign priority claims in these applications must have been timely made in the international phase in the PCT request form or in a notice from applicant."[2]

§ 24:10 Practice—Application data sheet

The application data sheet specified by 37 C.F.R. § 1.76 is now a critical document to original patent applications that are filed under 35 U.S.C. § 111. Any application submitted under § 111 by an assignee, an obligated assignee, or a person who otherwise shows sufficient interest in the subject matter must include an application data sheet which specifies certain information about the applicant. Among other things, this must include the name of the assignee, the person to whom the inventor is under an obligation to assign the invention, or the person who otherwise shows sufficient proprietary interest in the matter who is the applicant under

---

it was executed, is submitted in the continuing application." [emphasis added]

[Section 24:8]

[1]37 C.F.R. § 1.64(a).

[Section 24:9]

[1]See 37 C.F.R. §§ 1.76(a)(5); 1.55(a)(1)(i) and (c).

[2]See http://www.uspto.gov/aia_implementation/inventors-oath-or-declaration-quick-reference-guide.pdf, at p. 2 (visited Nov. 4, 2012).

§ 1.43 or § 1.46.[1] Providing assignment information in the application data sheet is not a substitute for complying with the requirements of Part 3 of the Rules to have an assignment recorded by the Office.[2]

Despite the change in practice where an assignee (or others) may file an application for a patent, the USPTO will continue to use the name of the first-named inventor when identifying patent applications.[3]

In the event of a change in the name of the applicant, such as a correction or update, after the application has been originally filed, a substitute application data sheet is required and must specify the correct or updated name of the applicant in the applicant information section.[4]

In the event that the application is sold, the applicant information will change, and a new application data sheet is required. Note that this also requires compliance with 37 C.F.R. § 3.71(b).

§ 24:11 Practice—USPTO recommendations

In addition to the USPTO "Quick Reference Guide,"[1] some best practice recommendations from the USPTO are as follows:[2]

1. For every application, submit a signed ADS identifying the inventors and assignee and stating the earlier filing date claims (domestic and foreign).
2. Re-execute a new oath or declaration in each "child" application filed after September 16, 2012.
3. Submit a combined assignment/statement on the same day to avoid a surcharge.
4. If a PCT application was filed before September 16, 2012, do not use the new inventor declaration form in

[Section 24:10]

[1]37 C.F.R. § 1.76(b)(7).

[2]37 C.F.R. § 1.76(b)(7).

[3]See 37 C.F.R. § 1.5.

[4]37 C.F.R. § 1.46(c).

[Section 24:11]

[1]See http://www.uspto.gov/aia_implementation/inventors-oath-or-declaration-quick-reference-guide.pdf.

[2]See Janet Gongola (Patent Reform Coordinator, USPTO) presentation, "The America Invents Act: Best Practices and Pitfalls for Newly-Effective Provisions," Nov. 2, 2012.

an application entering the national stage after that date.

5. Do not submit papers signed by a corporation or other juristic entity.
6. As with the prior practice, do *not* make any substantive changes to an application after the inventor's oath or declaration has been executed.
7. Use USPTO forms available at http://www.uspto.gov/forms for the oath or declaration, substitute statement, power of attorney, and application data sheet.

Chapter 25

PTO Fee Setting and Fees

AIA §§ 10, 11
35 U.S.C.A. § 41

§ 25:1 Background and congressional intent[1]

This chapter addresses PTO fee setting and fees. Questions of fee diversion and PTO funding are addressed in the next chapter.

[Section 25:1]

[1]The Supreme Court cautions against relying on interpretations advanced in legislative statements that are not "anchored in the text of the statute." *Shannon v. U.S.*, 512 U.S. 573, 583, 114 S. Ct. 2419, 129 L. Ed. 2d 459 (1994), stating "[C]ourts have no authority to enforce [a] principl[e] gleaned solely from legislative history that has no statutory reference point." Shannon, 512 U.S. at 584, quoting *International Broth. of Elec. Workers, Local Union No. 474, AFL-CIO v. N.L.R.B.*, 814 F.2d 697, 712, 124 L.R.R.M. (BNA) 2993, 106 Lab. Cas. (CCH) P 12256 (D.C. Cir. 1987). The authoritative statement "is the statutory text, not the legislative history." *Exxon Mobil Corp. v. Allapattah Services, Inc.*, 545 U.S. 546, 568, 125 S. Ct. 2611, 162 L. Ed. 2d 502 (2005). However, lower courts have cited the legislative history of the AIA already in recent cases. E.g., *Rogers v. Tristar Products, Inc.*, 102 U.S.P.Q.2d 1722, 2012 WL 1660604, *2 (Fed. Cir. 2012) (non-precedential); *Byrne v. Wood, Herron & Evans, LLP*, 676 F.3d 1024, 1029, 102 U.S.P.Q.2d 1073 (Fed. Cir. 2012) (dissenting opin.).

The House Report speaks to the issues of PTO fee setting authority and fees:

Fee-setting authority

a) Agency fee setting authority

Although the USPTO has had the ability to set certain fees by regulation, most fees (*e.g.*, filing fee, issuance fee, maintenance fees) are set by Congress. History has shown that such a scheme does not allow the USPTO to respond promptly to the challenges that confront it. The USPTO has argued for years that it must have fee-setting authority to administer properly the agency and its growing workload.

The Act allows the USPTO to set or adjust all of its fees, including those related to patents and trademarks, so long as they do no more than reasonably compensate the USPTO for the services performed. Prior to setting such fees, the Director must give notice to, and receive input from, the Patent or Trademark Public Advisory Committee (PPAC or TPAC). The Director may also reduce fees for any given fiscal year, but only after consultation with the PPAC or TPAC. The Act details the procedures for how the Director shall consult with the PPAC and TPAC, including providing for public hearings and the dissemination to the public of any recommendations made by either Committee. Fees shall be prescribed by rule. Any proposed fee change shall be published in the Federal Register and include the specific rationale and purpose for the proposed change. The Director must seek public comments for no less than 45 days. The Director must also notify Congress of any final decision regarding proposed fees. Congress shall have no more than 45 days to consider and comment on any proposed fee, but no proposed fee shall be effective prior to the expiration of this 45-day period.

b) "Microentity" defined

As part of the ongoing effort to nurture U.S. innovation, Congress has long recognized that certain groups, including independent inventors, small business concerns, and non-profit organizations (collectively referred to as "small business entities") should not bear the same financial burden for filing patent applications as larger corporate interests. The current statute provides for a significant reduction in certain fees for small business entities. The Committee was made aware, however, that there is likely a benefit to describing—and then accommodating—a group of inventors who are even smaller, in order to ensure that the USPTO can tailor its requirements, and its assistance, to the people with very little capital, and just a few inventions, as they are starting out.

This section of the Act defines this even smaller group—the micro-entity—that includes only truly independent inventors. The Committee expects that the USPTO will make accommodations under its authority in recognition of the special status of micro-entities.

* * *

Section 10. Fee-setting authority.

This section gives the Director rulemaking authority to set or adjust any fee under §§ 41 and 376, and section 1113 of title 15, provided that such fee amounts are set to reasonably compensate the USPTO for the services performed. The Director may also reduce such fees. The Director shall consult with the patent and trademark advisory committees as provided for in this section. Any proposal for a change in fees (including the rationale, purpose, and possible expectations or benefits that will result) shall be published in the Federal Register and shall seek public comment for a period of not less than 45 days. The Director shall notify Congress of any final proposed fee change and Congress shall have up to 45 days to consider and comment before any proposed fee change becomes effective.

Rules of construction are provided.

Section 11. Fees for patent services.

The Act includes the current patent fee schedule in the text. This schedule represents a reference point for any future adjustments to the fee schedule by the Director.[2]

§ 25:2 The amended statutes

AIA Section 10 addresses the USPTO fee-setting authority. AIA Section 11 addresses fees for patent services. These statutes, along with 35 U.S.C. § 41 (post-revisions), provide as follows:

New Statute (AIA Sec.10)

SEC. 10. FEE SETTING AUTHORITY

(a) FEE SETTING.—

(1) IN GENERAL.— The Director may set or adjust by rule any fee established, authorized, or charged under title 35, United States Code, or the Trademark Act of 1946 (15 U.S.C. 1051 et seq.), for any services performed by or materials furnished by, the Office, subject to paragraph (2).

(2) FEES TO RECOVER COSTS.— Fees may be set or adjusted under paragraph (1) only to recover the aggregate estimated costs to the Office for processing, activities, services, and materials relating to patents (in the case of patent fees) and trademarks (in the case of trademark fees), including

[2]H. R. Rep. No. 112-98, pt. 1, pp. 49 to 51, 78 to 79 (2011) (footnotes omitted).

administrative costs of the Office with respect to such patent or trademark fees (as the case may be).

(b) SMALL AND MICRO ENTITIES.— The fees set or adjusted under subsection (a) for filing, searching, examining, issuing, appealing, and maintaining patent applications and patents shall be reduced by 50 percent with respect to the application of such fees to any small entity that qualifies for reduced fees under section 41(h)(1) of title 35, United States Code, and shall be reduced by 75 percent with respect to the application of such fees to any micro entity as defined in section 123 of that title (as added by subsection (g) of this section).

(c) REDUCTION OF FEES IN CERTAIN FISCAL YEARS.— In each fiscal year, the Director—

(1) shall consult with the Patent Public Advisory Committee and the Trademark Public Advisory Committee on the advisability of reducing any fees described in subsection (a); and

(2) after the consultation required under paragraph (1), may reduce such fees.

(d) ROLE OF THE PUBLIC ADVISORY COMMITTEE.— The Director shall—

(1) not less than 45 days before publishing any proposed fee under subsection (a) in the Federal Register, submit the proposed fee to the Patent Public Advisory Committee or the Trademark Public Advisory Committee, or both, as appropriate;

(2) (A) provide the relevant advisory committee described in paragraph (1) a 30-day period following the submission of any proposed fee, in which to deliberate, consider, and comment on such proposal;

(B) require that, during that 30-day period, the relevant advisory committee hold a public hearing relating to such proposal; and

(C) assist the relevant advisory committee in carrying out that public hearing, including by offering the use of the resources of the Office to notify and promote the hearing to the public and interested stakeholders;

(3) require the relevant advisory committee to make available to the public a written report setting forth in detail the comments, advice, and recommendations of the committee regarding the proposed fee; and

(4) consider and analyze any comments, advice, or recommendations received from the relevant advisory committee before setting or adjusting (as the case may be) the fee.

(e) PUBLICATION IN THE FEDERAL REGISTER.—

(1) PUBLICATION AND RATIONALE.— The Director shall—

(A) publish any proposed fee change under this section

in the Federal Register;

(B) include, in such publication, the specific rationale and purpose for the proposal, including the possible expectations or benefits resulting from the proposed change; and

(C) notify, through the Chair and Ranking Member of the Committees on the Judiciary of the Senate and the House of Representatives, the Congress of the proposed change not later than the date on which the proposed change is published under subparagraph (A).

(2) PUBLIC COMMENT PERIOD.— The Director shall, in the publication under paragraph (1), provide the public a period of not less than 45 days in which to submit comments on the proposed change in fees.

(3) PUBLICATION OF FINAL RULE.— The final rule setting or adjusting a fee under this section shall be published in the Federal Register and in the Official Gazette of the Patent and Trademark Office.

(4) CONGRESSIONAL COMMENT PERIOD.— A fee set or adjusted under subsection (a) may not become effective—

(A) before the end of the 45-day period beginning on the day after the date on which the Director publishes the final rule adjusting or setting the fee under paragraph (3); or

(B) if a law is enacted disapproving such fee.

(5) RULE OF CONSTRUCTION.— Rules prescribed under this section shall not diminish—

(A) the rights of an applicant for a patent under title 35, United States Code, or for a mark under the Trademark Act of 1946; or

(B) any rights under a ratified treaty.

(f) RETENTION OF AUTHORITY.— The Director retains the authority under subsection (a) to set or adjust fees only during such period as the Patent and Trademark Office remains an agency within the Department of Commerce.

(g) MICRO ENTITY DEFINED.—

(1) IN GENERAL.— Chapter 11 of title 35, United States Code, is amended by adding at the end the following new section:

"§ 123. Micro entity defined

"(a) IN GENERAL.— For purposes of this title, the term 'micro entity' means an applicant who makes a certification that the applicant—

"(1) qualifies as a small entity, as defined in regulations issued by the Director;

"(2) has not been named as an inventor on more than 4

previously filed patent applications, other than applications filed in another country, provisional applications under section 111(b), or international applications filed under the treaty defined in section 351(a) for which the basic national fee under section 41(a) was not paid;

"(3) did not, in the calendar year preceding the calendar year in which the applicable fee is being paid, have a gross income, as defined in section 61(a) of the Internal Revenue Code of 1986, exceeding 3 times the median household income for that preceding calendar year, as most recently reported by the Bureau of the Census; and

"(4) has not assigned, granted, or conveyed, and is not under an obligation by contract or law to assign, grant, or convey, a license or other ownership interest in the application concerned to an entity that, in the calendar year preceding the calendar year in which the applicable fee is being paid, had a gross income, as defined in section 61(a) of the Internal Revenue Code of 1986, exceeding 3 times the median household income for that preceding calendar year, as most recently reported by the Bureau of the Census.

"(b) Applications Resulting From Prior Employment.— An applicant is not considered to be named on a previously filed application for purposes of subsection (a)(2) if the applicant has assigned, or is under an obligation by contract or law to assign, all ownership rights in the application as the result of the applicant's previous employment.

"(c) Foreign Currency Exchange Rate.— If an applicant's or entity's gross income in the preceding calendar year is not in United States dollars, the average currency exchange rate, as reported by the Internal Revenue Service, during that calendar year shall be used to determine whether the applicant's or entity's gross income exceeds the threshold specified in paragraphs (3) or (4) of subsection (a).

"(d) Institutions of Higher Education.— For purposes of this section, a micro entity shall include an applicant who certifies that—

"(1) the applicant's employer, from which the applicant obtains the majority of the applicant's income, is an institution of higher education as defined in section 101(a) of the Higher Education Act of 1965 (20 U.S.C. 1001(a)); or

"(2) the applicant has assigned, granted, conveyed, or is under an obligation by contract or law, to assign, grant, or convey, a license or other ownership interest in the particular applications to such an institution of higher education.

"(e) Director's Authority.— In addition to the limits imposed by this section, the Director may, in the Director's discretion, impose income limits, annual filing limits, or other limits on who may qualify as a micro entity pursuant to this section if the Director determines that such additional limits are reasonably necessary to avoid an undue impact on other patent applicants or owners or are otherwise reasonably necessary and appropriate. At least 3 months before any limits proposed to be imposed pursuant to this subsection take effect, the Director shall inform the Committee on the Judiciary of the House of Representatives and the Committee on the Judiciary of the Senate of any such proposed limits."

(2) Conforming Amendment.— Chapter 11 of title 35, United States Code, is amended by adding at the end the following new item:

"123. Micro entity defined."

(h) Electronic Filing Incentive.—

(1) In General.— Notwithstanding any other provision of this section, an additional fee of $400 shall be established for each application for an original patent, except for a design, plant, or provisional application, that is not filed by electronic means as prescribed by the Director. The fee established by this subsection shall be reduced by 50 percent for small entities that qualify for reduced fees under section 41(h)(1) of title 35, United States Code. All fees paid under this subsection shall be deposited in the Treasury as an offsetting receipt that shall not be available for obligation or expenditure.

(2) Effective Date.— This subsection shall take effect upon the expiration of the 60-day period beginning on the date of the enactment of this Act.

(i) Effective Date; Sunset.—

(1) Effective Date.— Except as provided in subsection (h), this section and the amendments made by this section shall take effect on the date of the enactment of this Act.

(2) Sunset.— The authority of the Director to set or adjust any fee under subsection (a) shall terminate upon the expiration of the 7-year period beginning on the date of the enactment of this Act.

(3) Prior Regulations Not Affected.— The termination of authority under this subsection shall not affect any regulations issued under this section before the effective date of such termination or any rulemaking proceeding for the issuance of regulations under this section that is pending on such date.

AIA Sec. 11 (Revising 35 U.S.C. § 41)[1]

SEC. 11. FEES FOR PATENT SERVICES.

(a) General Patent Services.— Subsections (a) and (b) of section 41 of title 35, United States Code, are amended to read as follows:

"(a) General Fees.— The Director shall charge the following fees:

"(1) Filing and Basic National Fees.—

"(A) On filing each application for an original patent, except for design, plant, or provisional applications, $330.

"(B) On filing each application for an original design patent, $220.

"(C) On filing each application for an original plant patent, $220.

"(D) On filing each provisional application for an original patent, $220.

"(E) On filing each application for the reissue of a patent, $330.

"(F) The basic national fee for each international application filed under the treaty defined in section 351(a) entering the national stage under section 371, $330.

"(G) In addition, excluding any sequence listing or computer program listing filed in an electronic medium as prescribed by the Director, for any application the specification and drawings of which exceed 100 sheets of paper (or equivalent as prescribed by the Director if filed in an electronic medium), $270 for each additional 50 sheets of paper (or equivalent as prescribed by the Director if filed in an electronic medium) or fraction thereof.

"(2) Excess Claim Fees.—

"(A) In General.— In addition to the fee specified in paragraph (1)—

"(i) on filing or on presentation at any other time, $220 for each claim in independent form in excess of 3;

"(ii) on filing or on presentation at any other time, $52 for each claim (whether dependent or independent) in excess of 20; and

"(iii) for each application containing a multiple de-

[Section 25:2]

[1]All of 35 U.S.C.A. § 41(a), (b), (d), and (h) are replaced by the text set forth above. § 41(g) is removed. The full text of § 41 post-revision is shown in the main text below AIA § 11.

pendent claim, $390.

"(B) Multiple Dependent Claims.— For the purpose of computing fees under subparagraph (A), a multiple dependent claim referred to in section 112 or any claim depending therefrom shall be considered as separate dependent claims in accordance with the number of claims to which reference is made.

"(C) Refunds; Errors in Payment.— The Director may by regulation provide for a refund of any part of the fee specified in subparagraph (A) for any claim that is canceled before an examination on the merits, as prescribed by the Director, has been made of the application under section 131. Errors in payment of the additional fees under this paragraph may be rectified in accordance with regulations prescribed by the Director.

"(3) Examination Fees.—

"(A) In General.—

"(i) For examination of each application for an original patent, except for design, plant, provisional, or international applications, $220.

"(ii) For examination of each application for an original design patent, $140.

"(iii) For examination of each application for an original plant patent, $170.

"(iv) For examination of the national stage of each international application, $220.

"(v) For examination of each application for the reissue of a patent, $650.

"(B) Applicability of Other Fee Provisions.— The provisions of paragraphs (3) and (4) of section 111(a) relating to the payment of the fee for filing the application shall apply to the payment of the fee specified in subparagraph (A) with respect to an application filed under section 111(a). The provisions of section 371(d) relating to the payment of the national fee shall apply to the payment of the fee specified in subparagraph (A) with respect to an international application.

"(4) Issue Fees.—

"(A) For issuing each original patent, except for design or plant patents, $1,510.

"(B) For issuing each original design patent, $860.

"(C) For issuing each original plant patent, $1,190.

"(D) For issuing each reissue patent, $1,510.

"(5) Disclaimer Fee.— On filing each disclaimer, $140.

"(6) Appeal Fees.—

"(A) On filing an appeal from the examiner to the Patent Trial and Appeal Board, $540.

"(B) In addition, on filing a brief in support of the appeal, $540, and on requesting an oral hearing in the appeal before the Patent Trial and Appeal Board, $1,080.

"(7) REVIVAL FEES.— On filing each petition for the revival of an unintentionally abandoned application for a patent, for the unintentionally delayed payment of the fee for issuing each patent, or for an unintentionally delayed response by the patent owner in any reexamination proceeding, $1,620, unless the petition is filed under section 133 or 151, in which case the fee shall be $540.

"(8) EXTENSION FEES.— For petitions for 1-month extensions of time to take actions required by the Director in an application—

"(A) on filing a first petition, $130;

"(B) on filing a second petition, $360; and

"(C) on filing a third or subsequent petition, $620.

"(b) MAINTENANCE FEES.—

"(1) IN GENERAL.— The Director shall charge the following fees for maintaining in force all patents based on applications filed on or after December 12, 1980:

"(A) Three years and 6 months after grant, $980.

"(B) Seven years and 6 months after grant, $2,480.

"(C) Eleven years and 6 months after grant, $4,110.

"(2) GRACE PERIOD; SURCHARGE.— Unless payment of the applicable maintenance fee under paragraph (1) is received in the Office on or before the date the fee is due or within a grace period of 6 months thereafter, the patent shall expire as of the end of such grace period. The Director may require the payment of a surcharge as a condition of accepting within such 6-month grace period the payment of an applicable maintenance fee.

"(3) NO MAINTENANCE FEE FOR DESIGN OR PLANT PATENT.— No fee may be established for maintaining a design or plant patent in force."

(b) DELAYS IN PAYMENT.— Subsection (c) of section 41 of title 35, United States Code, is amended—

(1) by striking "(c)(1) The Director" and inserting:

"(c) DELAYS IN PAYMENT OF MAINTENANCE FEES.—

"(1) ACCEPTANCE.— The Director"; and

(2) by striking "(2) A patent" and inserting:

"(2) EFFECT OF RIGHTS ON OTHERS. —A patent".

(c) PATENT SEARCH FEES.— Subsection (d) of section 41 of title 35, United States Code, is amended to read as follows:

"(d) PATENT SEARCH AND OTHER FEES.—

"(1) PATENT SEARCH FEES.—

"(A) In General.— The Director shall charge the fees specified under subparagraph (B) for the search of each application for a patent, except for provisional applications. The Director shall adjust the fees charged under this paragraph to ensure that the fees recover an amount not to exceed the estimated average cost to the Office of searching applications for patent by Office personnel.

"(B) Specific Fees.— The fees referred to in subparagraph (A) are—

"(i) $540 for each application for an original patent, except for design, plant, provisional, or international applications;

"(ii) $100 for each application for an original design patent;

"(iii) $330 for each application for an original plant patent;

"(iv) $540 for the national stage of each international application; and

"(v) $540 for each application for the reissue of a patent.

"(C) Applicability of Other Provisions.— The provisions of paragraphs (3) and (4) of section 111(a) relating to the payment of the fee for filing the application shall apply to the payment of the fee specified in this paragraph with respect to an application filed under section 111(a). The provisions of section 371(d) relating to the payment of the national fee shall apply to the payment of the fee specified in this paragraph with respect to an international application.

"(D) Refunds.— The Director may by regulation provide for a refund of any part of the fee specified in this paragraph for any applicant who files a written declaration of express abandonment as prescribed by the Director before an examination has been made of the application under section 131.

"(2) Other Fees.—

"(A) In General.— The Director shall establish fees for all other processing, services, or materials relating to patents not specified in this section to recover the estimated average cost to the Office of such processing, services, or materials, except that the Director shall charge the following fees for the following services:

"(i) For recording a document affecting title, $40 per property.

"(ii) For each photocopy, $.25 per page.

"(iii) For each black and white copy of a patent, $3.

"(B) Copies for Libraries.— The yearly fee for

providing a library specified in section 12 with uncertified printed copies of the specifications and drawings for all patents in that year shall be $50.".

(d) FEES FOR SMALL ENTITIES.— Subsection (h) of section 41 of title 35, United States Code, is amended to read as follows:

"(h) FEES FOR SMALL ENTITIES.—

"(1) REDUCTIONS IN FEES.— Subject to paragraph (3), fees charged under subsections (a), (b), and (d)(1) shall be reduced by 50 percent with respect to their application to any small business concern as defined under section 3 of the Small Business Act, and to any independent inventor or nonprofit organization as defined in regulations issued by the Director.

"(2) SURCHARGES AND OTHER FEES.— With respect to its application to any entity described in paragraph (1), any surcharge or fee charged under subsection (c) or (d) shall not be higher than the surcharge or fee required of any other entity under the same or substantially similar circumstances.

"(3) REDUCTION FOR ELECTRONIC FILING.— The fee charged under subsection (a)(1)(A) shall be reduced by 75 percent with respect to its application to any entity to which paragraph (1) applies, if the application is filed by electronic means as prescribed by the Director.

(e) TECHNICAL AMENDMENTS.— Section 41 of title 35, United States Code, is amended—

(1) in subsection (e), in the first sentence, by striking "The Director" and inserting "WAIVER OF FEES; COPIES REGARDING NOTICE.—The Director";

(2) in subsection (f), by striking "The fees" and inserting "ADJUSTMENT OF FEES.—The fees";

(3) by repealing subsection (g); and

(4) in subsection (i)—

(A) by striking "(i)(1) The Director" and inserting the following:

"(i) ELECTRONIC PATENT AND TRADEMARK DATA.—

"(1) MAINTENANCE OF COLLECTIONS.— The Director";

(B) by striking "(2) The Director" and inserting the following:

"(2) AVAILABILITY OF AUTOMATED SEARCH SYSTEMS.— The Director";

(C) by striking "(3) The Director" and inserting the following:

"(3) ACCESS FEES.— The Director"; and

(D) by striking "(4) The Director" and inserting the

following:

"(4) ANNUAL REPORT TO CONGRESS.— The Director".

(f) ADJUSTMENT OF TRADEMARK FEES.— Section 802(a) of division B of the Consolidated Appropriations Act, 2005 (Public Law 108-447) is amended—

(1) in the first sentence, by striking "During fiscal years 2005, 2006, and 2007,", and inserting "Until such time as the Director sets or adjusts the fees otherwise,"; and

(2) in the second sentence, by striking "During fiscal years 2005, 2006, and 2007, the" and inserting "The".

(g) EFFECTIVE DATE, APPLICABILITY, AND TRANSITION PROVISIONS.— Section 803(a) of division B of the Consolidated Appropriations Act, 2005 (Public Law 108-447) is amended by striking "and shall apply only with respect to the remaining portion of fiscal year 2005 and fiscal year 2006".

(h) PRIORITIZED EXAMINATION FEE.—

(1) IN GENERAL.—

(A) FEE.—

(i) PRIORITIZED EXAMINATION FEE.— A fee of $4,800 shall be established for filing a request, pursuant to section 2(b)(2)(G) of title 35, United States Code, for prioritized examination of a nonprovisional application for an original utility or plant patent.

(ii) ADDITIONAL FEES.— In addition to the prioritized examination fee under clause (i), the fees due on an application for which prioritized examination is being sought are the filing, search, and examination fees (including any applicable excess claims and application size fees), processing fee, and publication fee for that application.

(B) REGULATIONS; LIMITATIONS.—

(i) REGULATIONS.— The Director may by regulation prescribe conditions for acceptance of a request under subparagraph (A) and a limit on the number of filings for prioritized examination that may be accepted.

(ii) LIMITATION ON CLAIMS.— Until regulations are prescribed under clause (i), no application for which prioritized examination is requested may contain or be amended to contain more than 4 independent claims or more than 30 total claims.

(iii) LIMITATION ON TOTAL NUMBER OF REQUESTS.— The Director may not accept in any fiscal year more than 10,000 requests for prioritization until regulations are prescribed under this subparagraph setting another limit.

(2) REDUCTION IN FEES FOR SMALL ENTITIES.— The Direc-

tor shall reduce fees for providing prioritized examination of nonprovisional applications for original utility and plant patents by 50 percent for small entities that qualify for reduced fees under section 41(h)(1) of title 35, United States Code.

(3) DEPOSIT OF FEES.— All fees paid under this subsection shall be credited to the United States Patent and Trademark Office Appropriation Account, shall remain available until expended, and may be used only for the purposes specified in section 42(c)(3)(A) of title 35, United States Code.

(4) EFFECTIVE DATE AND TERMINATION.—

(A) EFFECTIVE DATE.— This subsection shall take effect on the date that is 10 days after the date of the enactment of this Act.

(B) TERMINATION.— The fee imposed under paragraph (1)(A)(i), and the reduced fee under paragraph (2), shall terminate on the effective date of the setting or adjustment of the fee under paragraph (1)(A)(i) pursuant to the exercise of the authority under section 10 for the first time with respect to that fee.

(i) APPROPRIATION ACCOUNT TRANSITION FEES.—

(1) SURCHARGE.—

(A) IN GENERAL.— There shall be a surcharge of 15 percent, rounded by standard arithmetic rules, on all fees charged or authorized by subsections (a), (b), and (d)(1) of section 41, and section 132(b), of title 35, United States Code. Any surcharge imposed under this subsection is, and shall be construed to be, separate from and in addition to any other surcharge imposed under this Act or any other provision of law.

(B) DEPOSIT OF AMOUNTS.— Amounts collected pursuant to the surcharge imposed under subparagraph (A) shall be credited to the United States Patent and Trademark Appropriation Account, shall remain available until expended, and may be used only for the purposes specified in section 42(c)(3)(A) of title 35, United States Code.

(2) EFFECTIVE DATE AND TERMINATION OF SURCHARGE.— The surcharge provided for in paragraph (1)—

(A) shall take effect on the date that is 10 days after the date of the enactment of this Act; and

(B) shall terminate, with respect to a fee to which paragraph (1)(A) applies, on the effective date of the setting or adjustment of that fee pursuant to the exercise of the authority under section 10 for the first time with respect to that fee.

(j) EFFECTIVE DATE.— Except as otherwise provided in this section, this section and the amendments made by this section shall take effect on the date of the enactment of this Act.

35 U.S.C. § 41 (after AIA revision)

§ 41. Patent fees; patent and trademark search systems

(a) General Fees.— The Director shall charge the following fees:

(1) Filing and basic national fees.—

(A) On filing each application for an original patent, except for design, plant, or provisional applications, $330.

(B) On filing each application for an original design patent, $220.

(C) On filing each application for an original plant patent, $220.

(D) On filing each provisional application for an original patent, $220.

(E) On filing each application for the reissue of a patent, $330.

(F) The basic national fee for each international application filed under the treaty defined in section 351 (a) entering the national stage under section 371, $330.

(G) In addition, excluding any sequence listing or computer program listing filed in an electronic medium as prescribed by the Director, for any application the specification and drawings of which exceed 100 sheets of paper (or equivalent as prescribed by the Director if filed in an electronic medium), $270 for each additional 50 sheets of paper (or equivalent as prescribed by the Director if filed in an electronic medium) or fraction thereof.

(2) Excess claims fees.—

(A) In general.— In addition to the fee specified in paragraph (1)—

(i) on filing or on presentation at any other time, $220 for each claim in independent form in excess of 3;

(ii) on filing or on presentation at any other time, $52 for each claim (whether dependent or independent) in excess of 20; and

(iii) for each application containing a multiple dependent claim, $390.

(B) Multiple dependent claims.— For the purpose of computing fees under subparagraph (A), a multiple dependent claim referred to in section 112 or any claim depending therefrom shall be considered as separate dependent claims in accordance with the number of claims to which reference is made.

(C) Refunds; errors in payment.— The Director may by

regulation provide for a refund of any part of the fee specified in subparagraph (A) for any claim that is canceled before an examination on the merits, as prescribed by the Director, has been made of the application under section 131. Errors in payment of the additional fees under this paragraph may be rectified in accordance with regulations prescribed by the Director.

(3) Examination fees.—

(A) In general.—

(i) For examination of each application for an original patent, except for design, plant, provisional, or international applications, $220.

(ii) For examination of each application for an original design patent, $140.

(iii) For examination of each application for an original plant patent, $170.

(iv) For examination of the national stage of each international application, $220.

(v) For examination of each application for the reissue of a patent, $650.

(B) Applicability of other fee provisions.— The provisions of paragraphs (3) and (4) of section 111 (a) relating to the payment of the fee for filing the application shall apply to the payment of the fee specified in subparagraph (A) with respect to an application filed under section 111 (a). The provisions of section 371 (d) relating to the payment of the national fee shall apply to the payment of the fee specified in subparagraph (A) with respect to an international application.

(4) Issue fees.—

(A) For issuing each original patent, except for design or plant patents, $1,510.

(B) For issuing each original design patent, $860.

(C) For issuing each original plant patent, $1,190.

(D) For issuing each reissue patent, $1,510.

(5) Disclaimer fee.— On filing each disclaimer, $140.

(6) Appeal fees.—

(A) On filing an appeal from the examiner to the Patent Trial and Appeal Board, $540.

(B) In addition, on filing a brief in support of the appeal, $540, and on requesting an oral hearing in the appeal before the Patent Trial and Appeal Board, $1,080.

(7) Revival fees.— On filing each petition for the revival of an unintentionally abandoned application for a patent, for the unintentionally delayed payment of the fee for issuing

each patent, or for an unintentionally delayed response by the patent owner in any reexamination proceeding, $1,620, unless the petition is filed under section 133 or 151, in which case the fee shall be $540.

(8) Extension fees.— For petitions for 1-month extensions of time to take actions required by the Director in an application—

(A) on filing a first petition, $130;

(B) on filing a second petition, $360; and

(C) on filing a third or subsequent petition, $620.

(b) Maintenance Fees.—

(1) In general.— The Director shall charge the following fees for maintaining in force all patents based on applications filed on or after December 12, 1980:

(A) Three years and 6 months after grant, $980.

(B) Seven years and 6 months after grant, $2,480.

(C) Eleven years and 6 months after grant, $4,110.

(2) Grace period; surcharge.— Unless payment of the applicable maintenance fee under paragraph (1) is received in the Office on or before the date the fee is due or within a grace period of 6 months thereafter, the patent shall expire as of the end of such grace period. The Director may require the payment of a surcharge as a condition of accepting within such 6-month grace period the payment of an applicable maintenance fee.

(3) No maintenance fee for design or plant patent.— No fee may be established for maintaining a design or plant patent in force.

(c) Delays in Payment of Maintenance Fees.—

(1) Acceptance.— The Director may accept the payment of any maintenance fee required by subsection (b) of this section which is made within twenty-four months after the six-month grace period if the delay is shown to the satisfaction of the Director to have been unintentional, or at any time after the six-month grace period if the delay is shown to the satisfaction of the Director to have been unavoidable. The Director may require the payment of a surcharge as a condition of accepting payment of any maintenance fee after the six-month grace period. If the Director accepts payment of a maintenance fee after the six-month grace period, the patent shall be considered as not having expired at the end of the grace period.

(2) Effect on rights of others.— A patent, the term of which has been maintained as a result of the acceptance of a payment of a maintenance fee under this subsection, shall

not abridge or affect the right of any person or that person's successors in business who made, purchased, offered to sell, or used anything protected by the patent within the United States, or imported anything protected by the patent into the United States after the 6-month grace period but prior to the acceptance of a maintenance fee under this subsection, to continue the use of, to offer for sale, or to sell to others to be used, offered for sale, or sold, the specific thing so made, purchased, offered for sale, used, or imported. The court before which such matter is in question may provide for the continued manufacture, use, offer for sale, or sale of the thing made, purchased, offered for sale, or used within the United States, or imported into the United States, as specified, or for the manufacture, use, offer for sale, or sale in the United States of which substantial preparation was made after the 6-month grace period but before the acceptance of a maintenance fee under this subsection, and the court may also provide for the continued practice of any process that is practiced, or for the practice of which substantial preparation was made, after the 6-month grace period but before the acceptance of a maintenance fee under this subsection, to the extent and under such terms as the court deems equitable for the protection of investments made or business commenced after the 6-month grace period but before the acceptance of a maintenance fee under this subsection.

(d) Patent Search and Other Fees.—

(1) Patent search fees.—

(A) In general.— The Director shall charge the fees specified under subparagraph (B) for the search of each application for a patent, except for provisional applications. The Director shall adjust the fees charged under this paragraph to ensure that the fees recover an amount not to exceed the estimated average cost to the Office of searching applications for patent by Office personnel.

(B) Specific fees.— The fees referred to in subparagraph (A) are—

(i) $540 for each application for an original patent, except for design, plant, provisional, or international applications;

(ii) $100 for each application for an original design patent;

(iii) $330 for each application for an original plant patent;

(iv) $540 for the national stage of each international application; and

(v) $540 for each application for the reissue of a

patent.

(C) Applicability of other provisions.— The provisions of paragraphs (3) and (4) of section 111 (a) relating to the payment of the fee for filing the application shall apply to the payment of the fee specified in this paragraph with respect to an application filed under section 111 (a). The provisions of section 371 (d) relating to the payment of the national fee shall apply to the payment of the fee specified in this paragraph with respect to an international application.

(D) Refunds.— The Director may by regulation provide for a refund of any part of the fee specified in this paragraph for any applicant who files a written declaration of express abandonment as prescribed by the Director before an examination has been made of the application under section 131.

(2) Other fees.—

(A) In general.— The Director shall establish fees for all other processing, services, or materials relating to patents not specified in this section to recover the estimated average cost to the Office of such processing, services, or materials, except that the Director shall charge the following fees for the following services:

(i) For recording a document affecting title, $40 per property.

(ii) For each photocopy, $.25 per page.

(iii) For each black and white copy of a patent, $3.

(B) Copies for libraries.— The yearly fee for providing a library specified in section 12 with uncertified printed copies of the specifications and drawings for all patents in that year shall be $50.

(e) Waiver of Fees; Copies Regarding Notice.— The Director may waive the payment of any fee for any service or material related to patents in connection with an occasional or incidental request made by a department or agency of the Government, or any officer thereof. The Director may provide any applicant issued a notice under section 132 with a copy of the specifications and drawings for all patents referred to in that notice without charge.

(f) Adjustment of Fees.— The fees established in subsections (a) and (b) of this section may be adjusted by the Director on October 1, 1992, and every year thereafter, to reflect any fluctuations occurring during the previous 12 months in the Consumer Price Index, as determined by the Secretary of Labor. Changes of less than 1 per centum may be ignored.

[(g) Repealed. Pub. L. 112-29, § 11(e)(3), Sept. 16, 2011, 125 Stat. 323.]

(h) Fees for Small Entities.—

(1) Reductions in fees.— Subject to paragraph (3), fees charged under subsections (a), (b), and (d)(1) shall be reduced by 50 percent with respect to their application to any small business concern as defined under section 3 of the Small Business Act, and to any independent inventor or nonprofit organization as defined in regulations issued by the Director.

(2) Surcharges and other fees.— With respect to its application to any entity described in paragraph (1), any surcharge or fee charged under subsection (c) or (d) shall not be higher than the surcharge or fee required of any other entity under the same or substantially similar circumstances.

(3) Reduction for electronic filing.— The fee charged under subsection (a)(1)(A) shall be reduced by 75 percent with respect to its application to any entity to which paragraph (1) applies, if the application is filed by electronic means as prescribed by the Director.

(i) Electronic Patent and Trademark Data.—

(1) Maintenance of collections.— The Director shall maintain, for use by the public, paper, microform, or electronic collections of United States patents, foreign patent documents, and United States trademark registrations arranged to permit search for and retrieval of information. The Director may not impose fees directly for the use of such collections, or for the use of the public patent or trademark search rooms or libraries.

(2) Availability of automated search systems.— The Director shall provide for the full deployment of the automated search systems of the Patent and Trademark Office so that such systems are available for use by the public, and shall assure full access by the public to, and dissemination of, patent and trademark information, using a variety of automated methods, including electronic bulletin boards and remote access by users to mass storage and retrieval systems.

(3) Access fees.— The Director may establish reasonable fees for access by the public to the automated search systems of the Patent and Trademark Office. If such fees are established, a limited amount of free access shall be made available to users of the systems for purposes of education and training. The Director may waive the payment by an individual of fees authorized by this subsection upon a showing of need or hardship, and if such a waiver is in the public interest.

(4) Annual report to congress.— The Director shall submit to the Congress an annual report on the automated search systems of the Patent and Trademark Office and the access

by the public to such systems. The Director shall also publish such report in the Federal Register. The Director shall provide an opportunity for the submission of comments by interested persons on each such report.

§ 25:3 Discussion of AIA Section 10 fee setting

Fee Adjustments. The revisions to the patent statute sections dealing with fee setting give the USPTO authority to adjust its fees so that it can recover aggregated estimated costs relating to processing patents and trademark registrations, etc. Before changing fees, however, the statute calls for a committee comment period involving a Patent Public Advisory Committee or a Trademark Public Advisory Committee, or both, as appropriate. These committees have a 30 day period to comment. They will hold a public hearing relating to the proposal and report to the Office its comments, findings, and recommendations. The Director then must publish any proposed fee changes in the Federal Register, allowing at least 45 days for the public to comment. Only after this period can the Director issue a final rule. At that point, Congress has 45 days to legislate against the proposed fee. Only after this period does the fee or adjusted fee become effective.

Small Entities. AIA § 10 preserves the small entity status that entitles qualifying patent applicants to a 50% fee reduction in filing, searching, examining, issuing, appealing and maintaining patent applications and patents.

Micro Entities. AIA § 10 adds a definition at 35 U.S.C. § 123 of a new category of applicant, the "micro entity," which receives even greater fee reductions than "small entities"—a 75% reduction. To be qualified as a "micro entity," the applicant must certify that it:

- qualifies as a small entity as defined in the regulations;
- has not been named as an inventor on more than four previously filed patent applications, other than applications filed in another country, provisional applications, or international applications filed under § 351(a) for which the basic national fee under § 41(a) was not paid;
- did not, in the calendar year preceding the calendar year in which the applicable fee is being paid, have a gross income, as defined in § 61(a) of the Internal Revenue Code exceeding 3 times the median household income for that preceding calendar year as most recently reported by the Bureau of the Census; and

- has not assigned, granted or conveyed, and is not under an obligation by contract or law to assign, grant or convey a license or other ownership interest in the application concerned to an entity that, in the calendar year preceding the calendar year in which the applicable fee is being paid, had a gross income exceeding 3 times the median household income for that preceding calendar year.

An applicant that meets this micro entity definition is entitled to a 75% reduction in fees for filing, searching, examining, issuing, appealing, and maintaining patent applications and patents.

In addition to the limits imposed by the micro entity definition, the Director may exercise discretion to impose income limits, annual filing limits, or other limits on who may qualify as a micro entity if the Director determines that such additional limits are reasonably necessary to avoid an undue hardship or impact on other patent applicants or owners or are otherwise reasonably necessary and appropriate.

Electronic Filing Fee Incentive. AIA § 10 provides an incentive to use electronic filing for applications. Failure to use electronic filing results in an additional fee of $400.00 for each application for an original patent other than a design, plant, or provisional application that is not filed by electronic means as prescribed by the Director. This fee is likewise subject to a 50% reduction for an applicant who qualifies as a small entity.

Sunset. The Director's authority to set or adjust fees under this section terminates after seven years following enactment.

§ 25:4 Discussion of AIA Section 11 fees

AIA § 11 amends 35 U.S.C. § 41(a) and (b) to increase the fees for various patent services. The fees set forth in 35 U.S.C. § 41 are determined by Congress and are subject to adjustment as discussed above with respect to AIA § 10.

1. Most fees are increased slightly or moderately. Some increases are substantial either in absolute dollars or in comparison to the prior fee specified by 35 U.S.C. § 41.
2. The fee for independent claims in excess of 3 increases to $220. § 41(a)(2).
3. The fee for claims in excess of 20 increases to $52. § 41(a)(2).
4. The appeal fee increases (appeal brief) to $540, and the

fee for requesting oral argument before the Board increases to $1,080. § 41(a)(6).

5. The maintenance fees increase moderately, but the 12-year maintenance fee increases substantially to $4,110. § 41(b).
6. Small entities can receive a 75% reduction in original, nonprovisional, utility patent application filing fees if they file electronically. § 41(h).
7. AIA § 11(h) provides for a prioritized examination fee of $4,800. The regulations also establish a reduced fee for small entities to request prioritized examination. This accelerated examination is discussed in Chapter 29.
8. AIA § 11(i) adds a surcharge of 15% as "account transition fees" for the fees specified in 35 U.S.C. §§ 41(a), (b), (d)(1), and 132(b). These fees take effect 10 days after enactment under AIA section 11(i)(2)(A) and terminate with the USPTO setting the respective fee through its new fee-setting provisions.

Chapter 26

Fee Diversion-PTO Funding

KeyCite®: Cases and other legal materials listed in KeyCite Scope can be researched through the KeyCite service on Westlaw®. Use KeyCite to check citations for form, parallel references, prior and later history, and comprehensive citator information, including citations to other decisions and secondary materials.

AIA § 22
35 U.S.C.A. § 42

§ 26:1 Background and congressional intent[1]

The USPTO has suffered a chronic diversion of the fees it collects and which it needs to perform its assigned functions.

In 2011, the USPTO Director wrote to Senator Coburn indicating that about $80 million in fees paid into the

[Section 26:1]

[1]The Supreme Court cautions against relying on interpretations advanced in legislative statements that are not "anchored in the text of the statute." *Shannon v. U.S.*, 512 U.S. 573, 583, 114 S. Ct. 2419, 129 L. Ed. 2d 459 (1994), stating "[C]ourts have no authority to enforce [a] principl[e] gleaned solely from legislative history that has no statutory reference point." Shannon, 512 U.S. at 584, quoting *International Broth. of Elec. Workers, Local Union No. 474, AFL-CIO v. N.L.R.B.*, 814 F.2d 697, 712, 124 L.R.R.M. (BNA) 2993, 106 Lab. Cas. (CCH) P 12256 (D.C. Cir. 1987). The authoritative statement "is the statutory text, not the legislative history." *Exxon Mobil Corp. v. Allapattah Services, Inc.*, 545 U.S. 546, 568, 125 S. Ct. 2611, 162 L. Ed. 2d 502 (2005). However, lower courts have cited the legislative history of the AIA already in recent cases. E.g., *Rogers v. Tristar Products, Inc.*, 102 U.S.P.Q.2d 1722, 2012 WL 1660604, *2 (Fed. Cir. 2012) (non-precedential); *Byrne v. Wood, Herron & Evans, LLP*, 676 F.3d 1024, 1029, 102 U.S.P.Q.2d 1073 (Fed. Cir. 2012) (dissenting opin.).

USPTO in that fiscal year would not be available to the USPTO to perform the corresponding services. Senator Coburn had sought to include a provision for a revolving fund for USPTO use, but the House leadership opposed it.[2] The proposed revolving fund was removed from the bill, but in exchange, the bill was amended to ensure that monies added to the Reserve Fund would remain available to the USPTO until they were expended.

Congress spoke to the issue in its House Report as follows.

Patent and Trademark Office funding

The USPTO is a fee-funded agency. The revenue it collects from fees imposed on inventors and trademark filers is deposited in a special USPTO appropriations account in the Treasury. To obtain funding for its operations, the agency must request the revenue back from congressional appropriators. Since the early 1990's, however, more than $800 million has been diverted from the agency and spent on non-USPTO initiatives.

The Committee believes the USPTO could operate more efficiently and productively if the agency had full access to all of its fee-generated revenue. The House bill therefore creates a USPTO revolving fund within the Treasury that allows the agency to keep all of the funds it raises until expended.

The provision also requires the Director to submit an annual spending plan as well as an annual year-end report to the House and Senate Appropriations and Judiciary Committees.

* * *

Section 22. Patent and Trademark Office funding.

Subsections (a) defines the "United State Patent and Trademark Office Public Enterprise Fund" ("the Fund") that replaces the existing "Patent and Trademark Office Appropriation Account."

Subsection (b) clarifies the USPTO Director's authority under the new Fund to collect all patent and trademark user fee revenue, which shall be available to the agency until expended. This change shall take effect on the later of October 1, 2011, or the first day of the first fiscal year that begins after the date of the enactment of the Act.

Subsection (c) establishes the Fund as a revolving fund in the US Treasury. Any amounts in the Fund shall be available

---

[2]See generally J. Matal, "A Guide to the Legislative History of the America Invents Act (Part II of II)," 21 *Federal Circuit Bar J.* 435, 646 (2011).

for use by the Director without fiscal year limitation. Patent and trademark fees deposited in the Fund shall be recorded as offsetting receipts. Amounts deposited in the Fund shall be available, without fiscal year limitation, to cover all expenses determined in the discretion of the Director to be ordinary and reasonable.

Subsection (d) requires the Director, not later than 60 days after the end of each fiscal year, to submit a report to Congress that summarizes the USPTO operations for the preceding fiscal year, details the operating plan of the agency, describes its long-term modernization plans as well as any progress made toward modernization efforts in the previous fiscal year, and includes the results of the most recent audit as carried out by subsection (f).

Not later than 30 days after the beginning of each fiscal year, subsection (e) instructs the Director to notify the Committees on Appropriations of both houses of Congress of the plan for the obligation and expenditure of the total amount of the funds for that fiscal year under Public Law 109-108.

Subsection (f) mandates that the Director annually shall provide for an independent audit of the financial statement of the USPTO.

Subsection (g) requires the Director to prepare and submit to the President an annual "business-type" budget for the Fund as the President prescribes by regulation for the Federal Budget.[3]

§ 26:2 The amended statute

AIA § 22 amends 35 U.S.C. § 42 as follows:[1]

Revised Statute (35 U.S.C. § 42)

42. Patent and Trademark Office Funding.

(a) All fees for services performed by or materials furnished by the Patent and Trademark Office will be payable to the Director.

(b) All fees paid to the Director and all appropriations for defraying the costs of the activities of the Patent and Trademark Office will be credited to the Patent and Trademark Office Appropriation Account in the Treasury of the United States.

(1) To the extent and in the amounts provided in advance in appropriations Acts, fees authorized in this title or any other Act to be charged or established by the Director shall

[3] H. R. Rep. No. 112-98, pt. 1, pp. 55, 82 (2011).

[Section 26:2]

[1] In this markup, strikethrough indicates text being removed from the statute, and underscoring indicates text being added to the statute.

be collected by and shall, subject to paragraph (3), be available to the Director to carry out the activities of the Patent and Trademark Office. ~~All fees available to the Director under section 31 of the Trademark Act of 1946 shall be used only for the processing of trademark registrations and for other activities, services, and materials relating to trademarks and to cover a proportionate share of the administrative costs of the Patent and Trademark Office.~~

(2) There is established in the Treasury a Patent and Trademark Fee Reserve Fund. If fee collections by the Patent and Trademark Office for a fiscal year exceed the amount appropriated to the Office for that fiscal year, fees collected in excess of the appropriated amount shall be deposited in the Patent and Trademark Fee Reserve Fund. To the extent and in the amounts provided in appropriations Acts, amounts in the Fund shall be made available until expended only for obligation and expenditure by the Office in accordance with paragraph (3).

(3)(A) Any fees that are collected under sections 41, 42, and 376,[2] and any surcharges on such fees, may only be used for expenses of the Office relating to the processing of patent applications and for other activities, services, and materials relating to patents and to cover a share of the administrative costs of the Office relating to patents.[3]

(B) Any fees that are collected under section 31 of the Trademark Act of 1946, and any surcharges on such fees, may only be used for expenses of the Office relating to the processing of trademark registrations and for other activities, services, and materials relating to trademarks and to cover a share of the administrative costs of the Office relating to trademarks.

(d) The Director may refund any fee paid by mistake or any amount paid in excess of that required.

(e) The Secretary of Commerce shall, on the day each year on which the President submits the annual budget to the Congress, provide to the Committees on the Judiciary of the Senate and the House of Representatives—

(1) a list of patent and trademark fee collections by the Patent and Trademark Office during the preceding fiscal year;

(2) a list of activities of the Patent and Trademark Office

[2] H.R. 6621, § 1(j)(A) (2013) struck "sections 41, 42, and 376" and inserted "this title." in its place.

[3] H.R. 6621, § 1(j)(B) (2013) struck "cover a share of the administrative costs of the Office relating to patents" and replaced it with "a proportionate share of the administrative costs of the Office."

during the preceding fiscal year which were supported by patent fee expenditures, trademark fee expenditures, and appropriations;

(3) budget plans for significant programs, projects, and activities of the Office, including out-year funding estimates;

(4) any proposed disposition of surplus fees by the Office; and

(5) such other information as the committees consider necessary.

AIA Sec. 22(b)

(b) Effective Date—The amendments made by this section shall take effect on October 1, 2011.

§ 26:3 Discussion of revisions to 35 U.S.C. § 42

The revision to 35 U.S.C. § 42 made in AIA § 22 sets up a "Patent and Trademark Fee Reserve Fund" within the United States Treasury. The operative language suggests that to the extent USPTO fee collections during a fiscal year surpass the amount appropriated to the USPTO for that fiscal year, such excess fees will be deposited in the Reserve Fund. The last sentence of subsection (c)(2) indicates that these monies can be spent "only for obligation and expenditure by the Office in accordance with paragraph (3)." Accordingly, subsection (c)(2) appears to insulate the USPTO monies from being diverted elsewhere.

Subsection (c)(3) affirms that fees collected under 35 U.S.C. §§ 41, 42 and 376, along with surcharges on those fees, may be used only for expenses of the USPTO relating to processing patent applications and other specified activities relating to patents and a share of administrative costs of the USPTO relating to patents. Subsection 3(b) speaks similarly with respect to the trademark fees.

Under the revised statute, monies in the Reserve Fund will be made available to the USPTO until expended. However, this mechanism does not to authorize the USPTO to access the Reserve Fund on an as-needed basis, like a revolving fund, but only via appropriations acts of Congress. The revision to § 42(c) attempts to avoid fee diversion but the ultimate benefit to the USPTO will be based on acts of Congress appropriating funds for USPTO use. Under § 42(c), the USPTO must appear before Congressional appropriators in order to receive appropriations.

Chapter 27

Removal of Deceptive Intent From Statute

AIA § 20
35 U.S.C.A. §§ 116, 184, 185, 251, 253, 256, 288

§ 27:1 Background and congressional intent[1]

Several provisions of the patent statute required showing

[Section 27:1]

[1]The Supreme Court cautions against relying on interpretations advanced in legislative statements that are not "anchored in the text of the statute." *Shannon v. U.S.*, 512 U.S. 573, 583, 114 S. Ct. 2419, 129 L. Ed. 2d 459 (1994), stating "[C]ourts have no authority to enforce [a] principl[e] gleaned solely from legislative history that has no statutory reference point." Shannon, 512 U.S. at 584, quoting *International Broth. of Elec. Workers, Local Union No. 474, AFL-CIO v. N.L.R.B.*, 814 F.2d 697, 712, 124 L.R.R.M. (BNA) 2993, 106 Lab. Cas. (CCH) P 12256 (D.C. Cir. 1987). The authoritative statement "is the statutory text, not the legislative history." *Exxon Mobil Corp. v. Allapattah Services, Inc.*, 545 U.S. 546, 568, 125 S. Ct. 2611, 162 L. Ed. 2d 502 (2005). However, lower courts have cited the legislative history of the AIA already in recent cases. E.g., *Rogers v. Tristar Products, Inc.*, 102 U.S.P.Q.2d 1722, 2012 WL 1660604, *2 (Fed. Cir. 2012) (non-precedential); *Byrne v. Wood, Herron & Evans, LLP*, 676 F.3d 1024, 1029, 102 U.S.P.Q.2d 1073 (Fed. Cir. 2012) (dissenting opin.).

a lack of deceptive intent, for example to correct errors. The subjective intent of the inventor was relevant. Section 256 is typical:

§ 256. Correction of named inventor.

Whenever through error a person is named in an issued patent as the inventor, or through error an inventor is not named in an issued patent and such error arose without any deceptive intention on his part, the Director may, on application of all the parties and assignees, with proof of the facts and such other requirements as may be imposed, issued a certificate correcting such error. The error of omitting inventors or naming persons who are not inventors shall not invalidate the patent in which such error occurred if it can be corrected as provided in this section. The court before which such matter is called in question may order correction of the patent on notice and hearing of all parties concerned and the Director shall issue a certificate accordingly. [emphasis added]

There is no discussion in the House Report about this topic.[2] Nevertheless, the following explanation by Senator Kyl gives insight to the changes intended here:

[Section 20] of the bill has been modified by reinserting language that eliminates various deceptive-intent requirements that relate to correcting the naming of the inventor or a joint inventor, obtaining a retroactive foreign filing license, seeking section 251 reissue, or enforcing remaining valid claims if a claim is invalidated. See generally *Kearney & Trecker Corp. v. Giddings & Lewis, Inc.*, 452 F.2d 579, 596, 7th Cir. 1971. These changes were first proposed in section 5 of the original Patent Reform Act of 2005, H.R. 2795, 109th Congress, and have been advocated by universities and their technology-transfer offices. For reasons that are not entirely clear, subsequent bills maintained this section and its addition of substructure and titles to the affected code sections, but struck the substantive part of the section—i.e., its elimination of the deceptive-intent requirements.

Eliminating the various deceptive-intent requirements moves the U.S. patent system away from the 19th century model that focused on the patent owner's subjective intent, and towards a more objective-evidence-based system that will be much cheaper to litigate and more efficient to administer.[3]

According to Sen. Kyl's statement, Congress had intended to remove the deceptive intent requirements as far back as the (draft) Patent Reform Act of 2005. However, for unclear

---

[2]H. R. Rep. No. 112-98, pt. 1 (2011).

[3]157 Cong. Rec. S1378 (daily ed. Mar. 8, 2011) (statement of Sen. Kyl).

reasons, the substance of those reforms was lost, though the titles and substructures had been maintained in subsequent iterations of patent reform bills. Congress believed that these changes will advance the U.S. patent system beyond a 19th Century model and make the system less expensive to litigate and easier to administer.

§ 27:2 The AIA eliminates all deceptive intent requirements from the patent statute

In general, the AIA removed "deceptive intention" from seven sections of the patent statute. The revisions to these sections are shown below:[1]

§ 116. Inventors

(a) Joint Inventions— When an invention is made by two or more persons jointly, they shall apply for patent jointly and each make the required oath, except as otherwise provided in this title. Inventors may apply for a patent jointly even though (1) they did not physically work together or at the same time, (2) each did not make the same type or amount of contribution, or (3) each did not make a contribution to the subject matter of every claim of the patent.

(b) Omitted Inventor— If a joint inventor refuses to join in an application for patent or cannot be found or reached after diligent effort, the application may be made by the other inventor on behalf of himself and the omitted inventor. The Director, on proof of the pertinent facts and after such notice to the omitted inventor as he prescribes, may grant a patent to the inventor making the application, subject to the same rights which the omitted inventor would have had if he had been joined. The omitted inventor may subsequently join in the application.

(c) Correction of Errors in Application— Whenever through error a person is named in an application for patent as the inventor, or through error an inventor is not named in an application, ~~and such error arose without any deceptive intention on his part,~~ the Director may permit the application to be amended accordingly, under such terms as he prescribes.

§ 184. Filing of application in foreign country

(a) Filing in Foreign Country.— Except when authorized by a license obtained from the Commissioner of Patents a person shall not file or cause or authorize to be filed in any foreign country prior to six months after filing in the United States an application for patent or for the registration of a

---

[Section 27:2]

[1]H.R. Rep. No. 112-98, pt. 1, pp. 55, 82 (2011).

utility model, industrial design, or model in respect of an invention made in this country. A license shall not be granted with respect to an invention subject to an order issued by the Commissioner of Patents pursuant to section 181 of this title without the concurrence of the head of the departments and the chief officers of the agencies who caused the order to be issued. The license may be granted retroactively where an application has been filed abroad through error ~~and without deceptive intent~~ and the application does not disclose an invention within the scope of section 181 of this title.

§ 185. Patent barred for filing without license

Notwithstanding any other provisions of law any person, and his successors, assigns, or legal representatives, shall not receive a United States patent for an invention if that person, or his successors, assigns, or legal representatives shall, without procuring the license prescribed in section 184 ~~of this title~~, have made, or consented to or assisted another's making, application in a foreign country for a patent or for the registration of a utility model, industrial design, or model in respect of the invention. A United States patent issued to such person, his successors, assigns, or legal representatives shall be invalid, unless the failure to procure such license was through error ~~and without deceptive intent~~, and the patent does not disclose subject matter within the scope of section 181 ~~of this title~~.

§ 251. Reissue of defective patents

Whenever any patent is, through error ~~without any deceptive intention~~, deemed wholly or partly inoperative or invalid, by reason of a defective specification or drawing, or by reason of the patentee claiming more or less than he had a right to claim in the patent, the Director shall, on the surrender of such patent and the payment of the fee required by law, reissue the patent for the invention disclosed in the original patent, and in accordance with a new and amended application, for the unexpired part of the term of the original patent. No new matter shall be introduced into the application for reissue.

§ 253. Disclaimer

~~Whenever, without any deceptive intention~~, (a) In general.—Whenever a claim of a patent is invalid the remaining claims shall not thereby be rendered invalid. A patentee, whether of the whole or any sectional interest therein, may, on payment of the fee required by law, make disclaimer of any complete claim, stating therein the extent of his interest in such patent. Such disclaimer shall be in writing, and recorded in the Patent and Trademark Office; and it shall thereafter be considered as part of the original patent to the extent of the interest possessed by the disclaimant and by those claiming under him.

~~In like manner~~ (b) Additional disclaimer or dedication.—any patentee or applicant may disclaim or dedicate to the public the entire term, or any terminal part of the term, of the patent granted or to be granted.

§ 256. Correction of named inventor.

~~Whenever~~ (a) Correction.—Whenever through error a person is named in an issued patent as the inventor, or through error an inventor is not named in an issued patent ~~and such error arose without any deceptive intention on his part~~, the Director may, on application of all the parties and assignees, with proof of the facts and such other requirements as may be imposed, issued a certificate correcting such error.

~~The error~~ (b) Patent valid if error corrected.—The error of omitting inventors or naming persons who are not inventors shall not invalidate the patent in which such error occurred if it can be corrected as provided in this section. The court before which such matter is called in question may order correction of the patent on notice and hearing of all parties concerned and the Director shall issue a certificate accordingly.

§ 288. Action for infringement of a patent containing an invalid claim

Whenever~~, without deceptive intention,~~ a claim of a patent is invalid, an action may be maintained for the infringement of a claim of the patent which may be valid. The patentee shall recover no costs unless a disclaimer of the invalid claim has been entered at the Patent and Trademark Office before the commencement of the suit.

§ 27:3 Discussion of AIA amendments re error and deceptive intent

These changes by the AIA will simplify and allow smoother administration of the patent statute and generally relieve the USPTO of having to determine whether errors occurred without deceptive intent.[1] They also bring the U.S. statute closer to the patent statutes of major foreign countries.

Under the new derivation statute (35 U.S.C. § 135), the Board has the right to change the inventorship of a derived patent application. This is despite any deceptive intention of the deriver. Outside of a new derivation contest, however, changing inventorship to remedy a misappropriated invention has been problematic. As the misappropriator (or

---

[Section 27:3]

[1]Note however that "deceptive" was not removed from Section 297 dealing with deceptive invention promotion.

deriver) filed a patent application with a false declaration or oath declaring himself to be the true and original inventor, this raised a bar against the true inventor (whose work had been misappropriated) having the USPTO or a court change the inventorship on the incorrect application. The application was tainted with deceptive intent and therefore beyond the reach of the remedial provisions of the patent statute. Thus, in *Bemis v. Chevron Research Co.*, 599 F.2d 910, 203 U.S.P.Q. 123 (9th Cir. 1979), the Ninth Circuit ruled that 35 U.S.C. § 256 (providing for issuance of a certificate when the patent is issued with improper joinder or nonjoinder of inventors) was intended to remedy only *innocent* errors and did not provide a basis for requiring the Commissioner of Patents to issue a corrected patent to the plaintiff showing that he, and not the defendant, was the true inventor. A different result may be available under the statutes as amended by the AIA.[2]

---

[2]One lingering problem may be that the derived application may be tainted with inequitable conduct.

Chapter 28

Satellite Offices

AIA §§ 23–24
35 U.S.C.A. § 1

§ 28:1 Background and congressional intent[1]

The USPTO has had the authority but not the mandate to establish satellite offices. This authority is conferred in 35 U.S.C. § 1, as follows:

35 U.S.C. 1. Establishment.

[Section 28:1]

[1]The Supreme Court cautions against relying on interpretations advanced in legislative statements that are not "anchored in the text of the statute." *Shannon v. U.S.*, 512 U.S. 573, 583, 114 S. Ct. 2419, 129 L. Ed. 2d 459 (1994), stating "[C]ourts have no authority to enforce [a] principl[e] gleaned solely from legislative history that has no statutory reference point." Shannon, 512 U.S. at 584, quoting *International Broth. of Elec. Workers, Local Union No. 474, AFL-CIO v. N.L.R.B.*, 814 F.2d 697, 712, 124 L.R.R.M. (BNA) 2993, 106 Lab. Cas. (CCH) P 12256 (D.C. Cir. 1987). The authoritative statement "is the statutory text, not the legislative history." *Exxon Mobil Corp. v. Allapattah Services, Inc.*, 545 U.S. 546, 568, 125 S. Ct. 2611, 162 L. Ed. 2d 502 (2005). However, lower courts have cited the legislative history of the AIA already in recent cases. E.g., *Rogers v. Tristar Products, Inc.*, 102 U.S.P.Q.2d 1722, 2012 WL 1660604, *2 (Fed. Cir. 2012) (non-precedential); *Byrne v. Wood, Herron & Evans, LLP*, 676 F.3d 1024, 1029, 102 U.S.P.Q.2d 1073 (Fed. Cir. 2012) (dissenting opin.).

* * *

(b) OFFICES.- The United States Patent and Trademark Office shall maintain its principal office in the metropolitan Washington, D.C., area, for the service of process and papers and for the purpose of carrying out its functions. The United States Patent and Trademark Office shall be deemed, for purposes of venue in civil actions, to be a resident of the district in which its principal office is located, except where jurisdiction is otherwise provided by law. The United States Patent and Trademark Office may establish satellite offices in such other places in the United States as it considers necessary and appropriate in the conduct of its business.

In the AIA, Congress directed the USPTO to establish satellite offices. Its intent is stated in the House Report, as follows:

Satellite offices

The USPTO is conducting a pilot to create and operate a new satellite office located in Detroit. The bill requires the Director to establish three other satellite offices within a 3-year window, subject to available resources. The legislation includes criteria that must be invoked when selecting the new sites.

Designation of Detroit satellite office

The House and Senate bills contain a provision that designates the PTO satellite office in Detroit as the "Elijah J. McCoy United States Patent and Trademark Office." Elijah McCoy was an African-Canadian inventor who spent much of his life in Michigan and earned 57 US patents. His work on an automatic lubricator to oil railroad steam engines gave rise to the expression, "the real McCoy."

* * *

Section 23. Satellite offices.

Pursuant to subsection (a), and subject to available resources, the Director shall establish three or more satellite offices in the United States to carry out the responsibilities of the USPTO. The Director has 3 years after the date of enactment of the Act to complete the task.

Subject (b) enumerates the purposes of the satellite offices, including efforts to increase outreach activities, enhance patent examiner retention, and improve the quality of patent examination.

Subsection (c) details the required considerations the Director must invoke in selecting each location. Among the criteria are geographic diversity among the offices and reliance upon previous evaluations.

Not later than three fiscal years after the date of enactment of the Act, Subsection (d) requires the Director to submit a report to Congress on the rationale of the Director in selecting the location of any satellite office, the progress in establishing any satellite offices so selected, and whether the operation of any existing satellite office is achieving the purposes set forth in subsection (b).

Section 24. Designation of the Detroit satellite office.

Section 24 designates the USPTO satellite office to be located in Detroit, Michigan, as the "Elijah J. McCoy United States Patent and Trademark Office."[2]

Other Congressional history contains the following statement about Elijah McCoy, the namesake of the new Detroit satellite office:

> [Elijah McCoy's] parents escaped slavery and fled across the border to Canada. After training as an apprentice in Scotland, he came to Ypsilanti, Michigan and set up a home-based invention shop.
>
> Over the course of his brilliant life, Elijah McCoy secured more than 50 patents, but he is best known for his inventions that revolutionized how our heavy-duty machinery, including locomotives, function today. In July of 1872, he invented the automatic lubricator, a device that kept steam engines working properly so trains could run faster and longer without stopping for service.
>
> His invention was incredibly effective and many tried to copy his idea, but nobody could match McCoy's idea. Machinists started asking if the engines were using the "real McCoy" technology, and people still use that phrase today when they want the best quality product.[3]

§ 28:2 AIA provisions re satellite offices

Sections 23 and 24 of the AIA are not codified into 35 U.S.C., and they provide as follows:

AIA Sec. 23

SEC. 23. SATELLITE OFFICES.

(a) ESTABLISHMENT.— Subject to available resources, the Director shall, by not later than the date that is 3 years after the date of the enactment of this Act, establish 3 or more satellite offices in the United States to carry out the responsibilities of the Office.

(b) PURPOSES.— The purposes of the satellite offices established under subsection (a) are to—

(1) increase outreach activities to better connect patent

[2] H. R. Rep. No. 112-98, pt. 1, pp. 55 to 56, 82 to 83 (2011).

[3] 157 Cong. Rec. S1183 to S1184 (daily ed. Mar. 3, 2011).

filers and innovators with the Office;

(2) enhance patent examiner retention;

(3) improve recruitment of patent examiners;

(4) decrease the number of patent applications waiting for examination; and

(5) improve the quality of patent examination.

(c) REQUIRED CONSIDERATIONS.—

(1) In General.— In selecting the location of each satellite office to be established under subsection (a), the Director—

(A) shall ensure geographic diversity among the offices, including by ensuring that such offices are established in different States and regions throughout the Nation;

(B) may rely upon any previous evaluations by the Office of potential locales for satellite offices, including any evaluations prepared as part of the Office's Nationwide Workforce Program that resulted in the 2010 selection of Detroit, Michigan, as the first satellite office of the Office;

(C) shall evaluate and consider the extent to which the purposes of satellite offices listed under subsection (b) will be achieved;

(D) shall consider the availability of scientific and technically knowledgeable personnel in the region from which to draw new patent examiners at minimal recruitment cost; and

(E) shall consider the economic impact to the region.

(2) OPEN SELECTION PROCESS.— Nothing in paragraph (1) shall constrain the Office to only consider its evaluations in selecting the Detroit, Michigan, satellite office.

(d) REPORT TO CONGRESS.— Not later than the end of the third fiscal year that begins after the date of the enactment of this Act, the Director shall submit a report to Congress on—

(1) the rationale of the Director in selecting the location of any satellite office required under subsection (a), including an explanation of how the selected location will achieve the purposes of satellite offices listed under subsection (b) and how the required considerations listed under subsection (c) were met;

(2) the progress of the Director in establishing all such satellite offices; and

(3) whether the operation of existing satellite offices is achieving the purposes under subsection (b).

AIA Sec. 24

SEC. 24. DESIGNATION OF DETROIT SATELLITE OFFICE.

(a) DESIGNATION.— The satellite office of the United States

Patent and Trademark Office to be located in Detroit, Michigan, shall be known and designated as the "Elijah J. McCoy United States Patent and Trademark Office".

(b) REFERENCES.— Any reference in a law, map, regulation, document, paper, or other record of the United States to the satellite office of the United States Patent and Trademark Office to be located in Detroit, Michigan, referred to in subsection (a) shall be deemed to be a reference to the "Elijah J. McCoy United States Patent and Trademark Office".

§ 28:3 Discussion of satellite office provisions

AIA § 23 called on the USPTO to establish three or more satellite offices within 3 years after the date of enactment of the AIA. Section 23 explains the purposes for the establishment of the satellite offices and sets forth a series of considerations for use in selecting the location of each satellite office. The purposes identified for establishing these satellite offices include the following: (1) to better connect patent filers and innovators with the USPTO; (2) to enhance patent examiner retention; (3) to improve recruitment of patent examiners; (4) to decrease the number of patent applications waiting for examination; and (5) to improve the quality of patent examination. The AIA also set forth considerations that the Director is required to follow.[1]

The establishment provision does not explicitly state that the *examining* function will occur at satellite offices. Instead, the operative language is "to carry out the [unspecified] responsibilities of the Office." Even so, the language of Section 23(b) (especially concerning patent examiner recruitment and retention) suggests very strongly that examination will occur at satellite offices and not just ministerial activities. The Director could also place entire examining groups in dif-

---

[Section 28:3]

[1]Some of these considerations include (1) insuring that geographic diversity exists among the various offices and that such offices are established in different states and different regions throughout the United States; (2) considering the availability of scientific and technically knowledgeable personnel in the region from which to draw new patent examiners at minimum recruitment costs; and (3) considering the economic impact to the region selected. The Director may also rely upon any previous evaluations by the USPTO of potential locales for satellite offices including the 2010 selection of Detroit, Michigan as the first satellite office to be established. In this regard, Section 24 of the revised statute specifically identifies Detroit as the location of the first satellite office and that this office shall be known and designated as the "Elijah J. McCoy United States Patent and Trademark Office."

ferent cities.

On July 2, 2012, the USPTO issued a press release entitled, "U.S. Commerce Department Four Regional U.S. Patent Offices that Will Speed Up the Patent Process and Help American Businesses Innovate, Grow, and Create Jobs." The four regional offices are Detroit, Michigan (to open July 13, 2012); Dallas, Texas; Denver, Colorado; and "Silicon Valley," California. These new offices "will help the USPTO attract talented IP experts throughout the country who will work closely with entrepreneurs to process patent applications, reduce the backlog of unexamined patents, and speed up the overall process, allowing businesses to move their innovation to market more quickly, and giving them more room to create new jobs." The press release also indicated, "the USPTO also seeks to identify and maximize the unique regional strengths of all four offices to further reduce the backlog of patent applications and appeals."

The USPTO exceeded the minimum requirement of three new satellite offices and has instead identified four—one for each time zone. In referring to "regional strengths," one may presume that this contemplates electronics and semiconductor manufacturing in Silicon Valley and may also contemplate biotechnology there. The Detroit, Michigan site would seem to correlate best with strengths in the mechanical arts. Obviously each city will have inventions from all technologies, but there can be regional strengths from one city to the other in terms of concentrations of the technology practiced there.

Chapter 29

Prioritized Examination & Priority Examination for Important Technologies

AIA §§ 11(h), 25
35 U.S.C.A. § 2(b)

§ 29:1 Background

Examiners are generally required to examine pending nonprovisional patent applications assigned to them in date order. The applicable regulation is 37 C.F.R. § 1.102, which explains that only when there are special conditions may an application be examined out of turn. The USPTO's *Manual of Patent Examining Procedure* ("MPEP") explains the general sequential examination rule as follows:

> **708. Order of Examination.**
>
> Nonprovisional applications filed in the U.S. Patent and Trademark Office and accepted as complete applications are assigned for examination to the respective examining Technology Centers (TCs) having the classes of inventions to which the applications relate. Nonprovisional applications shall be

taken up for examination by the examiner to whom they have been assigned in the order in which they have been filed except for those applications in which examination has been advanced pursuant to 37 CFR 1.102.

The USPTO provided two ways to advance an application out of turn. One way required no fees while the other did. The various no-fee bases included: (1) applicant's advanced age or poor health; (2) the invention will materially enhance the quality of the environment; (3) the invention will materially contribute to the development or conservation of energy resources; or (4) the invention will materially contribute to countering terrorism.[1]

A change in practice became effective on August 25, 2006. For applications filed on or after that date, unless a petition to make special was based on an applicant's health, age or the Patent Prosecution Highway (PPH) pilot program, it had to comply with extensive requirements set forth in MPEP § 708.02(a)(I). These requirements called for a more complex petition than had earlier been required, and this significantly increased the costs for an applicant wanting to advance the prosecution of an application.

§ 29:2 Congressional intent[1]

The House Report contains two passages about priority examination, as follows:

[Section 29:1]

[1]37 C.F.R. § 1.102(b) (2004).

[Section 29:2]

[1]The Supreme Court cautions against relying on interpretations advanced in legislative statements that are not "anchored in the text of the statute." *Shannon v. U.S.*, 512 U.S. 573, 583, 114 S. Ct. 2419, 129 L. Ed. 2d 459 (1994), stating "[C]ourts have no authority to enforce [a] principl[e] gleaned solely from legislative history that has no statutory reference point." Id. at 584, quoting *International Broth. of Elec. Workers, Local Union No. 474, AFL-CIO v. N.L.R.B.*, 814 F.2d 697, 712, 124 L.R.R.M. (BNA) 2993, 106 Lab. Cas. (CCH) P 12256 (D.C. Cir. 1987). The authoritative statement "is the statutory text, not the legislative history." *Exxon Mobil Corp. v. Allapattah Services, Inc.*, 545 U.S. 546, 568, 125 S. Ct. 2611, 162 L. Ed. 2d 502 (2005). However, lower courts have cited the legislative history of the AIA already in recent cases. E.g., *Rogers v. Tristar Products, Inc.*, 102 U.S.P.Q.2d 1722, 2012 WL 1660604, *2 (Fed. Cir. 2012) (non-precedential); *Byrne v. Wood, Herron & Evans, LLP*, 676 F.3d 1024, 1029, 102 U.S.P.Q.2d 1073 (Fed. Cir. 2012) (dissenting opin.).

Priority examination for technologies important to American competitiveness

The Act stipulates that the USPTO may promulgate regulations, not inconsistent with law, that prioritize examination of applications for products, processes, or technologies that are important to the national economy or national competitiveness. This may be done without recovering the aggregate extra cost of providing the prioritization.

* * *

Section 26. Priority examination for technologies important to American competitiveness.

Section 26 amends § 2(b)(2) of the Patent Act by permitting the USPTO to prioritize the examination of applications for products, processes, or technologies that are important to the national economy or national competitiveness without recovering the aggregate extra cost of providing such prioritization.[2]

§ 29:3 The amended statutes re accelerated examination

AIA § 25 provides a statutory basis in 35 U.S.C. § 2 permitting the Director to give priority to some applications for important technologies without recovering the aggregate extra cost. The revision is shown below, followed by the non-codified portions of AIA § 25:[1]

Revised Statute (35 U.S.C. § 2(b))

§ 2. Powers and duties

* * *

(b) Specific Powers—The Office—

* * *

(2) may establish regulations, not inconsistent with law, which—

* * *

(G) may, subject to any conditions prescribed by the Director and at the request of the patent applicant, provide for prioritization of examination of applications for products, processes, or technologies that are important to the national economy or national competitiveness without recovering the aggregate extra cost of providing such prioritization, notwithstanding section 41 or any

---

[2]H. R. Rep. No. 112-98, pt. 1, pp. 56, 83 (2011).

[Section 29:3]

[1]In this markup, strikethrough indicates text being removed from the statute, and underscoring indicates text being added to the statute.

other provision of law;* * *

AIA § 11(h)

(h) PRIORITIZED EXAMINATION FEE.—

(1) IN GENERAL.—

(A) FEE.—

(i) PRIORITIZED EXAMINATION FEE.— A fee of $4,800 shall be established for filing a request, pursuant to section 2(b)(2)(G) of title 35, United States Code, for prioritized examination of a nonprovisional application for an original utility or plant patent.

(ii) ADDITIONAL FEES.— In addition to the prioritized examination fee under clause (i), the fees due on an application for which prioritized examination is being sought are the filing, search, and examination fees (including any applicable excess claims and application size fees), processing fee, and publication fee for that application.

(B) REGULATIONS; LIMITATIONS.—

(i) REGULATIONS.— The Director may by regulation prescribe conditions for acceptance of a request under subparagraph (A) and a limit on the number of filings for prioritized examination that may be accepted.

(ii) LIMITATION ON CLAIMS.— Until regulations are prescribed under clause (i), no application for which prioritized examination is requested may contain or be amended to contain more than 4 independent claims or more than 30 total claims.

(iii) LIMITATION ON TOTAL NUMBER OF REQUESTS.— The Director may not accept in any fiscal year more than 10,000 requests for prioritization until regulations are prescribed under this subparagraph setting another limit.

§ 29:4 Non-fee based revised accelerated examination provisions

The AIA provides for "prioritized" examination (based on the applicant paying a fee) and "priority examination" which is based on national interests and does not require a fee.

With respect to non-fee advancement, the USPTO may advance the examination of applications for products, processes, or technologies that are important to the national economy or national competitiveness. Although USPTO previously had the right to advance applications out of turn for various reasons, this provides statutory authority for a specified genre of patent applications. Importantly, the AIA revision to 35 U.S.C. § 2 authorizes the Director to make these advancements without having to recover the added costs from the applicants. The revised Section 2 mentions 35 U.S.C. § 41, which is the statutory provision for patent fees.

Priority examination became effective on Sept. 16, 2012, twelve months after the enactment of the AIA. No final rules have been adopted for priority examination, and the MPEP appears not to address "priority examination."

§ 29:5 Fee-based accelerated examination provisions

Immediately prior to enactment of the AIA, the patent statute did not include a provision for an applicant to obtain advancement of an application simply upon paying a fee. Under the new, fee-based advancement, an applicant does not need to explain that there is infringement, perform a pre-examination search, or meet any conditions beyond paying the fee.

An applicant may want to accelerate prosecution to have a patent issue prior to when it would normally be published. This would make it harder to mount a post grant review because the challenger would not have the advantage of the lead time given by the normal publication of the application after 18 months. Instead, the first time that a challenger may know of the patent application is when it issues as a patent.

Another reason to advance prosecution is because the patent term is measured from the effective filing date. The time spent waiting in the queue before an application is taken up for examination normally does not normally result in added patent term. Accordingly, paying the fee for prioritized examination would ordinarily provide a longer effective patent coverage, assuming that the application in fact results in the issuance of a patent.

§ 29:6 Fee-based accelerated examination—Conditions

The AIA in Section 11(h) places *initial* conditions on fee-based petitions for advancing applications. It specifies that the Director may prescribe regulations, and *until regulations are prescribed,* there would be three conditions: (1) the application to be advanced cannot have more than four (4) independent claims before or after amendment; (2) the application cannot have more than 30 total claims before or after amendment; and (3) the USPTO could not accept more than 10,000 requests for prioritization in any fiscal year.[1]

Interestingly, AIA § 11(h)(1)(A) specifically mentions other fees, including "applicable excess claims." As such, the statute would permit the Director to advance applications upon payment of a fee even when they include excess claims.

The statute specifies a fee of $4,800. Whether this amount is regarded as large or small depends on the context. For a small inventor on a routine invention, it might represent a significant surcharge beyond the initial charges for drafting and filing the application. For an established entity filing applications each of which costs several tens of thousands of dollars to prepare and file, or which are to protect hundreds of millions of dollars invested in research and development of a new drug, for instance, the added cost should not be a substantial deterrent to occasional use. The amount may be significant enough to deter routine use on *all* applications of heavy filers.

The USPTO did adopt regulations. The fees are specified in 37 C.F.R. § 1.17, giving relief to small entities:

New 37 C.F.R. 1.17(c)

§ 1.17. Patent application and reexamination processing fees.

* * *

(c) For filing a request for prioritized examination under § 1.102(e):

By a small entity (§ 1.27(a))	$2,400.00
By other than a small entity	$4,800.00

The substantive regulations for fee-based advancement do not change the initial claim limits specified in the statute: four independent claims and 30 total claims:

Revised 37 CFR § 1.102

§ 1.102. Advancement of examination.

(a) Applications will not be advanced out of turn for examination or for further action except as provided by this part, or upon order of the Director to expedite the business of the Office, or upon filing of a request under paragraph (b) or (e) of this section or upon filing a petition or request under para-

[Section 29:6]

[1]AIA § 11(b)(1)(B).

graph (c) or (d) of this section with a showing which, in the opinion of the Director, will justify so advancing it.

* * *

(e) A request for prioritized examination under this paragraph must comply with the requirements of this paragraph and be accompanied by the prioritized examination fee set forth in Sec. 1.17(c), the processing fee set forth in Sec. 1.17(i), and if not already paid, the publication fee set forth in Sec. 1.18(d). An application for which prioritized examination has been requested may not contain or be amended to contain more than four independent claims, more than thirty total claims, or any multiple dependent claim. Prioritized examination under this paragraph will not be accorded to international applications that have not entered the national stage under 35 U.S.C. 371, design applications, reissue applications, provisional applications, or reexamination proceedings. A request for prioritized examination must also comply with the requirements of paragraph (e)(1) or paragraph (e)(2) of this section.

(1) A request for prioritized examination may be filed with an original utility or plant nonprovisional application under 35 U.S.C. 111(a) that is complete as defined by Sec. 1.51(b), with any fees due under Sec. 1.16 paid on filing. If the application is a utility application, it must be filed via the Office's electronic filing system. The request for prioritized examination in compliance with this paragraph must be present upon filing of the application.

(2) A request for prioritized examination may be filed with or after a request for continued examination in compliance with Sec.1.114. If the application is a utility application, the request must be filed via the Office's electronic filing system. The request must be filed before the mailing of the first Office action after the filing of the request for continued examination under Sec. 1.114. Only a single such request for prioritized examination under this paragraph may be granted in an application.

* * *

The rule *prohibits* fee-based prioritized examination for the following applications:

- international applications that have not entered the national stage under Section 371;[2]
- design applications;

[2]"However, an applicant who has filed an international application may participate in the prioritized examination program by filing a by-pass continuation under 35 U.S.C.A. 111(a) rather than entering the national stage under 35 U.S.C.A. 371." 76 Fed. Reg. 59050, 59052 (Sept. 23, 2011).

- reissue applications;
- provisional applications;
- reexamination applications;
- applications with more than 4 independent claims;
- applications with more than 30 total claims; and
- applications containing any multiple dependent claim.

Importantly, for an original utility patent application, the request for prioritized examination must be submitted with the application when filed. The USPTO provides a form for requesting prioritized examination.[3] The application must be complete as defined by 35 U.S.C. § 111(a) and 37 C.F.R. § 1.51(b), and fees due under 37 C.F.R. § 1.16 must be paid on filing. In other words, these require a specification as required by § 112, including at least one claim, a drawing when necessary, an oath or declaration, and the prescribed filing fee, search fee, examination fee, and application size fee. The original utility application seeking prioritized examination *must* be filed electronically via the EFS.

However, the rule also allows a request for prioritized examination to be filed later, with a request for continued examination (RCE) or thereafter. Again, in the case of a utility application, the request must be filed via the EFS. One limitation is that the request has to be filed prior to the date of mailing the first Office Action that follows the RCE. Further, an applicant may request prioritized examination in this way (with or after an RCE) only once for that application.

The prioritized examination is Track One of the Three-Track examination process of the USPTO. The following USPTO comments illuminate the process and explain that the USPTO goal is to reach a final disposition of a prioritized application within 12 months of the grant of prioritized status. This means that it is not just the initial examination that is advanced but all aspects of prosecution up until final disposition:

> Under prioritized examination, an application will be accorded special status and placed on the examiner's special docket throughout its entire course of prosecution before the examiner until a final disposition is reached in the application. The goal for handling applications under prioritized examination is to on average provide a final disposition within twelve months of prioritized status being granted. The final disposition for the twelve-month goal means that within twelve months from the date prioritized status has been granted that

[3] http://www.uspto.gov/forms/sb0424.pdf.

one of the following occur: (1) Mailing of a notice of allowance; (2) mailing of a final Office action; (3) filing of a notice of appeal; (4) completion of examination as defined in 37 C.F.R. 41.102; (5) filing of a request for continued examination; or (6) abandonment of the application. An application under prioritized examination, however, would not be accorded special status throughout its entire course of appeal or interference before the BPAI, or after the filing of a request for continued examination.[4]

Nevertheless, under prioritized examination, the time for an applicant to respond to an Office Action remains the same as in regular prosecution. This differs from the Accelerated Examination program where the time for reply to an Office Action is one month, with no extensions.[5] Under prioritized examination, an applicant will continue to have a shortened statutory period of three months.

Various acts will result in termination of the prioritized examination. This occurs when an applicant petitions for a time extension to respond or files an amendment that results in more than four independent claims, more than 30 total claims, or any multiply dependent claim.[6] When this happens, the application is removed from the examiner's special docket and placed in the regular docket in accordance with its stage of prosecution.[7] The USPTO will not refund the prioritized examination fee upon these events because they do not represent payment of the fee by mistake or in an amount exceeding the required amount.[8]

When a final rejection is mailed, this terminates the prioritized examination, and the applicant may then amend claims without restriction as to the number of claims, subject to the normal rules concerning after-final prosecution.[9]

Further details of the procedure are available in the comments accompanying the final rule published in the Federal Register on September 23, 2011, at 76 Fed. Reg. 59050. Prioritized examination became available on Sept. 26, 2011 and appears to be very well received. As reported in Director Kappos' public blog, as of January 3, 2012, 1,694 "Track One" petitions had been submitted to the USPTO. Twenty

[4] 76 Fed. Reg. 59050, 59051 (Sept. 23, 2011).

[5] 76 Fed. Reg. 59050, 59051 (Sept. 23, 2011).

[6] 76 Fed. Reg. 59050, 59051 (Sept. 23, 2011).

[7] 76 Fed. Reg. 59050, 59051 (Sept. 23, 2011).

[8] 76 Fed. Reg. 59050, 59051 (Sept. 23, 2011).

[9] 76 Fed. Reg. 59050, 59051 (Sept. 23, 2011).

three (23) allowances had already been mailed.[10] Other USPTO statistics show that in fiscal year 2012, the USPTO received 5,036 requests for prioritized examination; it granted 4,239 and dismissed 268 of those requests, and 529 remained pending.[11]

---

[10]See http://www.uspto.gov/blog/director/entry/uspto_track_i_the_agency, visited November 4, 2012.

[11]See http://www.uspto.gov/patents/init_events/Track_One.jsp, visited November 4, 2012.

Chapter 30

Patent Term Extension Calculation

AIA § 37
35 U.S.C.A. § 156(d)

§ 30:1 Background and congressional intent[1]

Since 1984, patent owners were able to extend the patent term by the amount of time that the patented product was subject to federal regulatory approval without which the product could not be marketed or sold. Under 35 U.S.C. § 156

[Section 30:1]

[1]The Supreme Court cautions against relying on interpretations advanced in legislative statements that are not "anchored in the text of the statute." *Shannon v. U.S.*, 512 U.S. 573, 583, 114 S. Ct. 2419, 129 L. Ed. 2d 459 (1994), stating "[C]ourts have no authority to enforce [a] principl[e] gleaned solely from legislative history that has no statutory reference point." Shannon, 512 U.S. at 584, quoting *International Broth. of Elec. Workers, Local Union No. 474, AFL-CIO v. N.L.R.B.*, 814 F.2d 697, 712, 124 L.R.R.M. (BNA) 2993, 106 Lab. Cas. (CCH) P 12256 (D.C. Cir. 1987). The authoritative statement "is the statutory text, not the legislative history." *Exxon Mobil Corp. v. Allapattah Services, Inc.*, 545 U.S. 546, 568, 125 S. Ct. 2611, 162 L. Ed. 2d 502 (2005). However, lower courts have cited the legislative history of the AIA already in recent cases. E.g., *Rogers v. Tristar Products, Inc.*, 102 U.S.P.Q.2d 1722, 2012 WL 1660604, *2 (Fed. Cir. 2012) (non-precedential); *Byrne v. Wood, Herron & Evans, LLP*, 676 F.3d 1024, 1029, 102 U.S.P.Q.2d 1073 (Fed. Cir. 2012) (dissenting opin.).

("Extension of patent term") the patent owner could seek the extension of time from the USPTO but only within a 60-day window which began on the day the product received permission from the regulatory body (not the USPTO).

One situation arose where the USPTO denied as untimely an application for a patent term extension on a major drug patent. The amount at issue (the estimated value of the 4.5 years of extension) was well beyond one billion dollars, and the patent owner could not recover that amount from insurance or by legal action against the law firm that handled the patent. The amount was too large. Representative Conyers added an amendment to the patent reform bill giving relief. Representative Lamar Smith, co-sponsor of the Act, opposed the amendment. This part of the bill received sharp criticism, and legislators referred to "ferocious lobbying," "an egregious example," and a "shameless special interest provision" favoring a prominent law firm and its client.[2]

The House Report includes the following statements about this provision:

> *Calculation of 60-day period for application of patent term extension*
>
> The USPTO has inconsistently applied "counting" rules that are imposed on patent holders who must submit documents to the agency within statutory time periods for consideration of additional patent term under § 156 of the Patent Act. The Act clarifies that the agency should impose a "business-day" construction for application to 156, consistent with recent case law on the matter.[FN62]
>
> FN 62. *Medicines Co. v. Kappos*, 731 F. Supp. 2d 470, 96 U.S.P.Q.2d 1732 (E.D. Va. 2010).
>
> *Section 27.*[3] *Calculation of 60-day period for application of patent term extension.*
>
> Subsection (a) clarifies USPTO "counting" rules that are used to determine whether an applicant has submitted an application to the agency in a timely manner under § 156(d)(1) of the Patent Act. If the application is transmitted after 4:30 pm, EST, on a business day, or is transmitted on a day that is not a business day, the product addressed by the application shall be deemed to receive "permission" on the next business day. "Business day" means any Monday, Tuesday, Wednesday,

---

[2]See generally J. Matal, "A Guide to the Legislative History of the America Invents Act (Part II of II)," 21 Federal Circuit Bar J. 435, 647–653 (2011).

[3]This later became AIA § 37.

Thursday, or Friday, excluding any legal holiday under 5 USC § 6103.

Subsection (b) states that subsection (a) shall apply to any application for extension of term under § 156 of the Patent Act that is pending on, filed after, or as to which a decision regarding the application is subject judicial review on, the date of enactment of the Act.[4]

§ 30:2 The amended statute

AIA § 37 is entitled, "Calculation of 60-Day Period for Application for Patent Term Extension." It appends a provision to 35 U.S.C. § 156(d), as follows:[1]

Amended Statute 35 U.S.C. § 156(d)

(d) (1) To obtain an extension of the term of a patent under this section, the owner of record of the patent or its agent shall submit an application to the Director. Except as provided in paragraph (5), such an application may only be submitted within the sixty-day period beginning on the date the product received permission under the provision of law under which the applicable regulatory review period occurred for commercial marketing or use. The application shall contain—

(A) the identity of the approved product and the Federal statute under which regulatory review occurred;

(B) the identity of the patent for which an extension is being sought and the identity of each claim of such patent;

(C) information to enable the Director to determine under subsections (a) and (b) the eligibility of a patent for extension and the rights that will be derived from the extension and information to enable the Director and the Secretary of Health and Human Services or the Secretary of Agriculture to determine the period of the extension under subsection (g);

(D) a brief description of the activities undertaken by the applicant during the applicable regulatory review period with respect to the approved product and the significant dates applicable to such activities; and

(E) such patent or other information as the Director may require.

<u>For purposes of determining the date on which a product receives permission under the second sentence of this</u>

---

[4]H. R. Rep. No. 112-98, pt. 1, pp. 56, 83 (2011).

[Section 30:2]

[1]In this markup, strikethrough indicates text being removed from the statute, and underscoring indicates text being added to the statute.

paragraph, if such permission is transmitted after 4:30 P.M., Eastern Time, on a business day, or is transmitted on a day that is not a business day, the product shall be deemed to receive such permission on the next business day. For purposes of the preceding sentence, the term "business day" means any Monday, Tuesday, Wednesday, Thursday, or Friday, excluding any legal holiday under section 6103 of title 5.

AIA Sec. 37(b)

(b) Applicability. The amendment made by subsection (a) shall apply to any application for extension of a patent term under section 156 of title 35, United States Code, that is pending on, that is filed after, or as to which a decision regarding the application is subject to judicial review on, the date of the enactment of this Act.

§ 30:3 Discussion of patent term extension provisions

AIA § 37(a) clarifies the beginning of the 60-day window during which a patent owner may apply for a patent term extension. This provision is used in the case of patents for, *inter alia*, pharmaceuticals, medical devices, food products and color additives. As amended, 35 U.S.C. § 156(d)(1) provides that if regulatory approval is transmitted to the patentee after 4:30 PM Eastern Time on a business day, or is transmitted on a day that is not a business day (i.e., Saturday or Sunday or a federal holiday), the product shall be deemed to have received approval on the next business day that is not a legal holiday.

AIA § 37(b) states the applicability of this amendment and provides for limited retroactivity. In particular, this provision applies to extension applications that were pending, filed after, or as to which a decision under § 156 remains subject to judicial review on the date of enactment of the AIA, *i.e.*, Sept. 16, 2011. Hence, this retroactive feature appears to be calculated to address a late patent term extension filing by The Medicines Company that was in litigation when the AIA was enacted.[1]

Also on the related topic of patent terms, H.R. 6621, § 1(h) (2013) makes changes to 35 U.S.C. § 154(b) "Adjustment of patent term." This was not covered in the AIA, but H.R. 6621 provides technical corrections to the AIA and amends

---

[Section 30:3]

[1]H. R. Rep. No. 112-98, pt. 1, at 56 (2011).

the patent statute as well, in particular § 154(b). Section 1(h) permits the USPTO to advise applicants of the final patent term adjustment ("PTA") when it grants the patent. It also sets a condition precedent before an applicant or patentee files suit to correct the patent term by requiring an applicant to exhaust administrative remedies first. The revision requires the applicant to have received the Director's decision on reconsideration before appealing the patent term adjustment determination to the district court.

Chapter 31

Other AIA Provisions and PTO Programs

AIA §§ 3, 13, 21, 26–34

§ 31:1 Background

The AIA includes several further provisions that have not been discussed in separate respective chapters. These AIA provisions are presented below along with their corresponding House Report comments.[1]

§ 31:2 Funding agreements (AIA § 3(g)(7)(A, B); § 13(a); § 20(i)(2))

The AIA amends 35 U.S.C. § 202 concerning patent rights in inventions made with federal assistance. The House Report refers to government-owned, contractor-operated facilities ("GOCOs") and comments on these changes:

> *Funding agreements*
>
> The Patent and Trademark Amendments Act of 1980 (commonly referred to as the Bayh-Dole Act) granted universities, other non-profit organizations, and small businesses the right to title to inventions developed using Federal funds. In 1984, Congress amended the law to ensure that universities and small businesses operating at Government facilities (GOCOs) reaped the benefits of Bayh-Dole by giving them the right to elect title to a subject invention. The 1984 Act permitted GOCOs to retain the balance of any royalties or income earned from licensing inventions, up to 5 percent of the annual budget of the facility, for further research, development, and related activities. If the balance exceeds 5 percent of the facility's annual budget, however, 75 percent of the excess is recouped by the Government, with the remaining 25 percent of the excess also retained by the GOCO for further research, development, and related activities.
>
> The Senate Judiciary Committee considered testimony that the requirement to repay the government 75 percent of the excess on royalty payments may be causing a disincentive for universities and small business operating under the GOCO provisions to commercialize products. Based on these concerns,

---

[Section 31:1]

[1]The Supreme Court cautions against relying on interpretations advanced in legislative statements that are not "anchored in the text of the statute." *Shannon v. U.S.*, 512 U.S. 573, 583, 114 S. Ct. 2419, 129 L. Ed. 2d 459 (1994), stating "[C]ourts have no authority to enforce [a] principl[e] gleaned solely from legislative history that has no statutory reference point." Shannon, 512 U.S. at 584, quoting *International Broth. of Elec. Workers, Local Union No. 474, AFL-CIO v. N.L.R.B.*, 814 F.2d 697, 712, 124 L.R.R.M. (BNA) 2993, 106 Lab. Cas. (CCH) P 12256 (D.C. Cir. 1987). The authoritative statement "is the statutory text, not the legislative history." *Exxon Mobil Corp. v. Allapattah Services, Inc.*, 545 U.S. 546, 568, 125 S. Ct. 2611, 162 L. Ed. 2d 502 (2005). However, lower courts have cited the legislative history of the AIA already in recent cases. E.g., *Rogers v. Tristar Products, Inc.*, 102 U.S.P.Q.2d 1722, 2012 WL 1660604, *2 (Fed. Cir. 2012) (non-precedential); *Byrne v. Wood, Herron & Evans, LLP*, 676 F.3d 1024, 1029, 102 U.S.P.Q.2d 1073 (Fed. Cir. 2012) (dissenting opin.).

the Act maintains the essence of the agreement GOCOs made with the taxpayers when they received funding that they would reimburse the taxpayer if they are sufficiently successful in commercializing a product invented with taxpayer dollars, but which reduces the burden on universities and small businesses, thereby encouraging commercialization. Pursuant to the Act, instead of reimbursing 75% of the excess to the Government, the GOCO will retain 85 percent for further research, development, and related activities and reimburse the Government 15 percent.

* * *

Section 13. Funding agreements.

Clause (i) of § 202(c)(7)(E) is amended to permit a nonprofit organization that has a funding agreement for the operation of a Government- owned-contractor-operated facility to retain 85%, rather than 25% under current law, of licensing royalties in excess of the amount equal to 5% of the annual budget of the facility.[1]

The AIA amended 35 U.S.C. § 202 to make some technical changes, but the substantive change relating to the funding appears in § 202(c)(7) as follows:

Revised 35 U.S.C. § 202(c)(7)

§ 202(c). Each funding agreement with a small business firm or nonprofit organization shall contain appropriate provisions to effectuate the following:

* * *

(7) In the case of a nonprofit organization,

(A) a prohibition upon the assignment of rights to a subject invention in the United States without the approval of the Federal agency, except where such assignment is made to an organization which has as one of its primary functions the management of inventions (provided that such assignee shall be subject to the same provisions as the contractor);

(B) a requirement that the contractor share royalties with the inventor;

(C) except with respect to a funding agreement for the operation of a Government-owned-contractor-operated facility, a requirement that the balance of any royalties or income earned by the contractor with respect to subject inventions, after payment of expenses (including payments to inventors) incidental to the

[Section 31:2]

[1]H. R. Rep. No. 112-98, pt. 1, pp. 51, 79 (2011) (citations omitted).

administration of subject inventions, be utilized for the support of scientific research or education;

(D) a requirement that, ~~except where it proves infeasible after a reasonable inquiry, in the licensing of subject inventions shall be given to small business firms; and~~ except where it is determined to be infeasible following a reasonable inquiry, a preference in the licensing of subject inventions shall be given to small business firms; and

(E) with respect to a funding agreement for the operation of a Government-owned-contractor-operated facility, requirements

(i) that after payment of patenting costs, licensing costs, payments to inventors, and other expenses incidental to the administration of subject inventions, 100 percent of the balance of any royalties or income earned and retained by the contractor during any fiscal year up to an amount equal to 5 percent of the annual budget of the facility, shall be used by the contractor for scientific research, development, and education consistent with the research and development mission and objectives of the facility, including activities that increase the licensing potential of other inventions of the facility; provided that if said balance exceeds 5 percent of the annual budget of the facility, that ~~75 percent~~ 15 percent of such excess shall be paid to the Treasury of the United States and the remaining ~~25 percent~~ 85 percent shall be used for the same purposes ~~as described above in this clause (D);~~ described above in this clause; and

(ii) that, to the extent it provides the most effective technology transfer, the licensing of subject inventions shall be administered by contractor employees on location at the facility.

* * *

§ 31:3 Travel expenses; payment of administrative law judges (AIA § 21)

The House Report indicates as follows regarding Congressional intent:

Travel expenses and payment of administrative judges

The USPTO Director is authorized to conduct programs or exchanges pertaining to intellectual property law and protection "domestically and throughout the world." The House bill clarifies that this authority includes expending funds to cover the subsistence and travel expenses of non-Federal employees who attend these programs.

The House bill also clarifies that the Director may fix the pay for administrative patent judges and administrative trademark judges under the new Patent Trial and Appeal Board set forth in Section 6 of the bill.

* * *

Section 21. Travel expenses and payment of administrative judges.

Subsection (a) authorizes the USPTO to expend funds to cover the subsistence and travel-related expenses of non-Federal employees attending intellectual property programs hosted by the agency.

Subsection (b) authorizes the Director to fix the rate of basic pay for administrative patent and trademark judges at a rate not greater than that payable for level III of the Executive Pay Schedule under 5 USC § 5314.[1]

Section 21 of the AIA amends 35 U.S.C. §§ 2 and 3 to allow the USPTO Director to reimburse travel-related expenses of non-federal employees attending specific types of programs, and it modifies the provisions regarding the compensation of administrative patent judges. The relevant portions of the amended patent statute are as follows:[2]

Revised 35 U.S.C. § 2(b)(11)

35 U.S.C. 2. Powers and duties.

* * *

(b) SPECIFIC POWERS.- The Office—

* * *

(11) may conduct programs, studies, or exchanges of items or services regarding domestic and international intellectual property law and the effectiveness of intellectual property protection domestically and throughout the world, and the Office is authorized to expend funds to cover the subsistence expenses and travel-related expenses, including per diem, lodging costs, and transportation costs, of persons attending such programs who are not Federal employees;

Revised 35 U.S.C. § 3(b)(11)

3(b) Officers and Employees of the Office.—

(6) Administrative patent judges and administrative trademark judges.—The Director may fix the rate of basic

---

[Section 31:3]

[1] H. R. Rep. No. 112-98, pt. 1, pp. 55, 82 (2011) (citations omitted).

[2] In this markup, strikethrough indicates text being removed from the statute, and underscoring indicates text being added to the statute.

pay for the administrative patent judges appointed pursuant to section 6 and the administrative trademark judges appointed pursuant to section 17 of the Trademark Act of 1946 (15 U.S.C. 1067) at not greater than the rate of basic pay payable for level III of the Executive Schedule under section 5314 of title 5. The payment of a rate of basic pay under this paragraph shall not be subject to the pay limitation under section 5306(e) or 5373 of title 5.

The effective date of these changes of AIA § 21 was originally covered by AIA § 35. However, a change occurred with H.R. 6611 (2013) which provided in section 1(g) that such changes shall be in effect from September 16, 2011:

(g) Travel Expenses and Payment of Administrative Judges-Notwithstanding section 35 of the Leahy-Smith America Invents Act (35 U.S.C. 1 note), the amendments made by section 21 of the Leahy-Smith America Invents Act (Public Law 112-29; 125 Stat. 335) shall be effective as of September 16, 2011.

§ 31:4 Study on AIA implementation (AIA § 26)

The House Report comments on a study on the implementation of the AIA that AIA § 26 directs the USPTO Director to conduct:

Study on implementation

The Act requires the USPTO Director to conduct a study regarding the implementation of the legislation and on such other aspects of Federal patent policies and practices with respect to patent rights, innovation in the United States, competitiveness of US markets, access by small business to capital and investment, and such other issues as the Director deems appropriate. The study must be completed within 4 years and the results submitted to the House and Senate Committees on the Judiciary.

* * *

Section 28. Study on implementation.

Subsection (a) requires the Director to conduct a study on the manner in which the Act is being implemented by the USPTO, along with a review of patent policies and practices of the Federal Government with respect to patent rights, US innovation, access by small business to capital, and other issues as the Director deems appropriate.

Subsection (b) stipulates that the Director shall submit the results of the study along with his recommendations for any changes to the Senate and House Judiciary Committees not later than 4 years after the date of enactment of the Act.[1]

The statutory provision in the AIA is as follows:

AIA § 26

AIA SEC. 26. STUDY ON IMPLEMENTATION.

(a) PTO Study- The Director shall conduct a study on the manner in which this Act and the amendments made by this Act are being implemented by the Office, and on such other aspects of the patent policies and practices of the Federal Government with respect to patent rights, innovation in the United States, competitiveness of United States markets, access by small businesses to capital for investment, and such other issues, as the Director considers appropriate.

(b) Report to Congress- The Director shall, not later than the date that is 4 years after the date of the enactment of this Act, submit to the Committees on the Judiciary of the House of Representatives and the Senate a report on the results of the study conducted under subsection (a), including recommendations for any changes to laws and regulations that the Director considers appropriate.

The USPTO is to report the results of this study by September 16, 2015. As of this writing, the USPTO had not completed the report. As of November 5, 2012, the USPTO website reported the status of this study as follows:

Implementation of AIA.

Congress requires USPTO to study how the Act is being implemented by the Office as well as other aspects of the Federal Government's patent policies and practices, including their effect on innovation, competitiveness in the U.S., and access to capital for small business investment. Within four years of enactment of the AIA, i.e., by September 16, 2015, the USPTO must report to Congress on the results of this study, including any recommendations for changing patent laws and regulations.

Additional information is forthcoming.[2]

§ 31:5 Study on genetic testing (AIA § 27)

AIA § 27 was added as part of the House floor manager's amendment and calls for the USPTO Director to conduct a

[Section 31:4]

[1]H. R. Rep. No. 112-98, pt. 1, pp. 56, 83–84 (2011).

[2]http://www.uspto.gov/aia_implementation/aia_studies_reports.jsp#heading-9.

study concerning genetic testing and patents.[1] The main advocate for this provision was concerned with "ways to remove barriers for patient access to second opinions on genetic testing on patented genes."[2] She urged that this "study would address questions about the current effects such patents have on patient outcomes and how best to provide truly independent, confirmatory tests."[3] The AIA provides as follows:

New AIA § 27

AIA SEC. 27. STUDY ON GENETIC TESTING.

(a) In General- The Director shall conduct a study on effective ways to provide independent, confirming genetic diagnostic test activity where gene patents and exclusive licensing for primary genetic diagnostic tests exist.

(b) Items Included in Study- The study shall include an examination of at least the following:

(1) The impact that the current lack of independent second opinion testing has had on the ability to provide the highest level of medical care to patients and recipients of genetic diagnostic testing, and on inhibiting innovation to existing testing and diagnoses.

(2) The effect that providing independent second opinion genetic diagnostic testing would have on the existing patent and license holders of an exclusive genetic test.

(3) The impact that current exclusive licensing and patents on genetic testing activity has on the practice of medicine, including but not limited to: the interpretation of testing results and performance of testing procedures.

(4) The role that cost and insurance coverage have on access to and provision of genetic diagnostic tests.

(c) Confirming Genetic Diagnostic Test Activity Defined- For purposes of this section, the term 'confirming genetic diagnostic test activity' means the performance of a genetic diagnostic test, by a genetic diagnostic test provider, on an individual solely for the purpose of providing the individual with an independent confirmation of results obtained from another test provider's prior performance of the test on the individual.

(d) Report- Not later than 9 months after the date of enact-

[Section 31:5]

[1]See generally J. Matal, "A Guide to the Legislative History of the America Invents Act (Part I of II)," 21 Federal Circuit Bar J. 435, 507–508 (2011).

[2]157 Cong. Rec. H4433 (daily ed. June 22, 2011).

[3]157 Cong. Rec. H4433 (daily ed. June 22, 2011).

ment of this Act, the Director shall report to the Committee on the Judiciary of the Senate and the Committee on the Judiciary of the House of Representatives on the findings of the study and provide recommendations for establishing the availability of such independent confirming genetic diagnostic test activity.

The USPTO was to have reported the results of this study by June 16, 2012. It held public hearings in February and March 2012. As of November 5, 2012, the USPTO had not completed the report. The USPTO website reports that the Office requested more time to complete the study due to its complexity:

On August 28, 2012, the Department of Commerce sent a letter to the House and Senate Judiciary Committee leadership updating them on the status of the genetic testing report. The letter stated in part: "Given the complexity and diversity of the opinions, comments and suggestions provided by interested parties, and the important policy considerations involved, we believe that further review, discussion and analysis are required before a final report can be submitted to Congress." To that end, the USPTO plans to organize an additional public hearing in late Fall 2012, review the comments received during the last year, and then finalize its recommendations to Congress.[4]

§ 31:6 The patent ombudsman program (AIA § 28)

The House Report comments on a patent ombudsman program at the USPTO Director:

Patent Ombudsman Program for small business concerns

The Act requires the USPTO Director to establish a Patent Ombudsman Program to provide support and services regarding patent filings to small business concerns. The authorization is subject to available resources.

* * *

Section 25. Patent Ombudsman Program for small business concerns.

Section 25 states that, using available resources, the Director shall establish and maintain in the USPTO a Patent Ombudsman Program, whose staff shall provide support and services

[4] http://www.uspto.gov/aia_implementation/aia_studies_reports.jsp#heading-3, visited November 12, 2012.

relating to patent filings to small business concerns.[1]

The AIA provides as follows:

SEC. 28. PATENT OMBUDSMAN PROGRAM FOR SMALL BUSINESS CONCERNS.

Using available resources, the Director shall establish and maintain in the Office a Patent Ombudsman Program. The duties of the Program's staff shall include providing support and services relating to patent filings to small business concerns and independent inventors.

The USPTO issued a relatively short report on the Patent Ombudsman Program which is reproduced below. As will be noted, the USPTO already had an ombudsman program and used it in creating a "Program for Small Business Concerns":

AMERICA INVENTS ACT

Section 29: Patent Ombudsman Program for Small Business Concerns

Section 28 of the Leahy-Smith America Invents Act (AIA), Pub.L. 112-29 (2010), requires the United States Patent and Trademark Office (USPTO) to establish and maintain a Patent Ombudsman Program for Small Business Concerns using its existing resources. The AIA specifies that the program provide support and services relating to patent filings for small business concerns and independent inventors. In accordance with the AIA, the USPTO has established such a program to be known as the Program for Small Business Concerns.

More specifically, the USPTO has combined the efforts of the existing Office of Innovation Development and the existing Patents Ombudsman Program to form the new Program for Small Business Concerns. This new Small Business Concerns program will serve the needs of small businesses and independent inventors, while still offering an ombudsman service to all patent applicants. The new Small Business Concerns program offers a full range of services at all stages of the patent process, including before an application is filed, while an application is pending at the USPTO, and after a patent has issued.

The Office of Innovation Development provides users with resources before the filing of an application and after a patent has been granted. In contrast, the Patents Ombudsman Program helps users who have already filed an application and need assistance advancing the prosecution of that application. A dedicated web page for the AIA Small Business

[Section 31:6]

[1]H. R. Rep. No. 112-98, pt. 1, pp. 56, 83 (2011).

Concerns Program is under construction and when completed will act as a central location for relevant information and to channel queries to the appropriate area such as Office of Innovation Development and the Patents Ombudsman Program. A general overview of the Office of Innovation Development and the Patents Ombudsman Program follows.

Office of Innovation Development

The Office of Innovation Development (OID) provides users with a wide-range of practical information on how to file a patent application, scam prevention, pro se and pro bono programs, educational materials, and outreach events. OID also provides the small business community with customized information about the intellectual property system.

OID works directly with independent inventor organizations across the country to assist them with their various needs and is in the process of establishing the same types of relationships with organizations, both within the Federal Government and the private sector, that assist small businesses. Close communication with these organizations will benefit small businesses and allow them to have better access to information and assistance from the USPTO.

Additionally, OID recently partnered with the National Institute of Science and Technology Manufacturing Extension Partnership to develop the IP Awareness Assessment Tool, which was launched in a beta version in the spring of 2012. This tool helps small businesses and inventors assess their intellectual property awareness and learn what steps they should take to protect these valuable assets. The tool is currently located on numerous government agency websites, including BusinessUSA, and has been introduced at small business conferences.

To view OID's website, please visit **http://www.uspto.gov/inventors/index.jsp**. OID also can be contacted by telephone at 571-272-8877 and by email at mailto:independentinventor@uspto.gov.

Patents Ombudsman Program

The Patents Ombudsman Program can assist pro se patent applicants, attorneys, and agents with application-processing issues, particularly those with concerns about advancement of prosecution. The majority of patent applications filed with the USPTO proceed through the examination process in accordance with established USPTO procedures. However, in some situations, patent applicants, attorneys, and agents have felt that examination has stalled and that their efforts to move their applications forward through normal channels have not been effective (e.g., the examiner not appear to address a new argument or amendment, and the applicant cannot reach the examiner and Supervisory Patent Examiner after a reasonable period of time). The Patents Ombudsman Program is a vehicle for assistance in these circumstances.

For those applications in which the normal process has gone awry and after all other procedural avenues have been used but failed to provide the needed assistance, the Patents Ombudsman Program Representative may be contacted for an application-processing issue that the applicant has been unable to resolve. The Program is not designed to circumvent normal communication between pro se applicants or applicants' representatives and examiners or Supervisory Patent Examiners, and it is not intended to supersede the authority of the examiners or Supervisory Patent Examiners. Rather, the Patents Ombudsman Program is intended to: (i) facilitate complaint-handling for pro se applicants and applicants' representatives whose applications have stalled in the pre-examination and examination processes; (ii) track complaints to ensure each is handled within ten business days; (iii) provide feedback and early warning alerts to USPTO management regarding training needs based on complaint trends; (iv) build a database of frequently asked questions accessible by the public that tracks commonly seen problems and effective resolutions; and (v) engage in outreach efforts to the intellectual property community.

To view the Patents Ombudsman Program's website, please visit http://www.uspto.gov/patents/ombudsman.jsp. The Patents Ombudsman Program also can be contacted via telephone at 571-272-5555 or 855-559-8589, or by email at mail to: mailto:ombudsmanprogram@uspto.gov.[2]

§ 31:7 Studying the diversity of applicants (AIA § 29)

Representative Gwen Moore offered the amendment adding § 29 to the AIA. She explained that the amendment was in the interests of "understanding the nature and scope of the underrepresentation of minority communities in intellectual property."[1] The statute provides:

New AIA § 29

AIA § 29. ESTABLISHMENT OF METHODS FOR STUDYING THE DIVERSITY OF APPLICANTS.

The Director shall, not later than the end of the 6-month period beginning on the date of the enactment of this Act, establish methods for studying the diversity of patent applicants,

---

[2]http://www.uspto.gov/aia_implementation/120910-aia-ombudsman-white-paper.pdf, visited Nov. 5, 2012.

[Section 31:7]

[1]See generally J. Matal, "A Guide to the Legislative History of the America Invents Act (Part I of II)," 21 Federal Circuit Bar J. 435, 509 (2011), citing 157 Cong. Rec. H4484 (daily ed. June 23, 2011).

including those applicants who are minorities, women, or veterans. The Director shall not use the results of such study to provide any preferential treatment to patent applicants.

USPTO Report. The USPTO issued the following brief report on methodology, which is available on the USPTO website:

AMERICA INVENTS ACT

Section 29: Establishment of methods for studying the diversity of applicants.

Section 29 of the Leahy-Smith America Invents Act (the Act), Pub.L. 112-29 (2010), requires that the "Director [of the USPTO] shall, not later than the end of the 6-month period beginning on the date of the enactment of this Act, establish methods for studying the diversity of patent applicants, including those applicants who are minorities, women, or veterans." This statement outlines the methodology the USPTO will follow in order to allow the study of important issues related to applicant diversity.

At the outset, the Agency's method for discovering more about how the USPTO is serving diverse communities must respect the interests of individuals and organizations in protecting private information. The method we have chosen underscores our sensitivity to this issue, and therefore takes an iterative, careful approach to collecting potentially sensitive information from USPTO applicants.

Accordingly, the USPTO is pursuing the following method to develop a basis for studying the diversity of patent applicants:

(1) The USPTO is concluding a memorandum of agreement (MOA) with the U.S. Census Bureau providing for a cooperative program in which information currently collected by the USPTO will be provided to the Center for Economic Studies (CES) at Census, allowing CES employees to attempt to match these data to existing diversity information, such as race, gender, veteran status, age, economic status, education, and geography (for individuals), as well as to diversity information such as revenues, number of employees, and geography (for companies). The USPTO will use the proper process to modify the use of the existing information collection under the Paperwork Reduction Act and Privacy Act. Because sensitive Census information concerning diversity characteristics is protected under Title 13, once the USPTO information becomes comingled with Census data, it is also protected under Title 13 and cannot become public. Therefore, the planned outcome of this matching program will be tabulations that CES will deliver to the USPTO. These tabulations will consist only of aggregated information concerning the diversity of patent applicants by group, with no diversity information on any specific

applicant provided to the USPTO. After conducting the matching, Census will consult with the USPTO on the accuracy and reliability of the statistics that CES was able to provide using existing USPTO information, including any bias that may have been introduced by any inability to adequately match the data, and offer suggestions as to what modeling may be used, or what additional data may be necessary, to accomplish a more accurate match and better outcomes.

(2) The USPTO also plans to publish a Request for Information (RFI) in the Federal Register asking the public to comment on several questions associated with the collection of private information. The USPTO recognizes from the outset that the Census MOA described above includes only U.S. individuals and organizations, yet over fifty percent of U.S. patent applications originate outside the US. We may also find that given the limited information that the USPTO currently collects about applicants, the match to Census Title 13 data may be inadequate to provide a robust picture of diversity even for U.S. applicants. The RFI will therefore ask the public to comment on several questions, including whether, and to what extent, the USPTO should consider collecting personal identifying information to enable the Agency to conduct better matching, analytics, and studies with the Census Bureau, as well as the desirability of possible other approaches to better reach the pool of non-U.S. applicants.

(3) After the USPTO has collected information both from the RFI and the first match with Census data described above, the USPTO will decide whether, and under what restrictions, it may need to take further steps to ensure that it is able to accurately describe patent applicant diversity information consistent with Section 29 of the Act. We expect that the USPTO will be able to make such a determination not later than November 2012. The USPTO will then publicly announce what decision has been made, and whether any further process is necessary.

The USPTO is committed to responding adequately to the concerns of Congress and the increasing need in the innovation economy to analyze and understand how the various parts of the Federal Government are responding to the needs of innovators. The method we have established takes important preliminary steps toward this end, while also carefully considering the possible public concerns about collecting and using sensitive diversity information, thus protecting public confidence that the USPTO is treating all inventors seeking patent protection fairly and equally.[2]

§ 31:8 Sense of congress re small businesses and inventors (AIA § 30)

Congress expressed its concern over developing new

[2]http://www.uspto.gov/aia_implementation/20120316-diversity_of_applicant_methodology.pdf, visited Nov. 5, 2012.

technologies, spurring growth, and creating jobs, including protecting small businesses and inventors from depredation by others. It therefore included the following § 30 in the AIA expressing Congress' expectations:

AIA § 30

AIA § 30. SENSE OF CONGRESS.

It is the sense of Congress that the patent system should promote industries to continue to develop new technologies that spur growth and create jobs across the country which includes protecting the rights of small businesses and inventors from predatory behavior that could result in the cutting off of innovation.

§ 31:9 Study on international patent protection for small business (AIA § 31)

Congress made several provisions for small businesses, such as reduced fees, the creation of the micro entity, the ombudsman program, etc. In AIA § 31, Congress directed the USPTO Director to consult with the Administrator of the Small Business Administration and the Secretary of Commerce to conduct a study about the assisting small businesses with regard to seeking international patent protection. Such protection can be expensive, particularly with annual maintenance fees in various jurisdictions. AIA § 31 provides as follows:

AIA § 31. USPTO STUDY ON INTERNATIONAL PATENT PROTECTIONS FOR SMALL BUSINESSES.

(a) Study Required- The Director, in consultation with the Secretary of Commerce and the Administrator of the Small Business Administration, shall, using the existing resources of the Office, carry out a study—

(1) to determine how the Office, in coordination with other Federal departments and agencies, can best help small businesses with international patent protection; and

(2) whether, in order to help small businesses pay for the costs of filing, maintaining, and enforcing international patent applications, there should be established either—

(A) a revolving fund loan program to make loans to small businesses to defray the costs of such applications, maintenance, and enforcement and related technical assistance; or

(B) a grant program to defray the costs of such applications, maintenance, and enforcement and related technical assistance.

(b) Report- Not later than 120 days after the date of the enactment of this Act, the Director shall issue a report to the Congress containing—

(1) all findings and determinations made in carrying out the study required under subsection (a);

(2) a statement of whether the determination was made that—

(A) a revolving fund loan program described under subsection (a)(2)(A) should be established;

(B) a grant program described under subsection (a)(2)(B) should be established; or

(C) neither such program should be established; and

(3) any legislative recommendations the Director may have developed in carrying out such study.

USPTO Report. The USPTO completed the study and produced a 33-page report, *International Patent Protections for Small Businesses* (January 2012) which is available via the USPTO website. The report stated, *inter alia*:

There is too little evidence upon which to base sound policy in this area: Neither the academic research nor public comment offered sufficient evidence to determine relative advantages, if any, of the U.S. government employing a loan versus a grant program to help defray the expenses of small businesses seeking international patent protection. Given the lack of data, USPTO does not recommend a program of taxpayer-funded financial assistance to support small business foreign patenting at this time. However, it would be useful and informative as a next step for the USPTO, the SBA, and other allied agencies to collect more information.[1]

§ 31:10 Pro bono program (AIA § 32)

Congress included Section 32 of the AIA to promote pro bono programs around the country to assist independent inventors and small businesses who were financially under-resourced. The House Report states Congress' intent as follows:

Pro bono program

The Committee acknowledges the importance of individuals and small businesses to the patent system and our national

---

[Section 31:9]

[1]International Patent Protections for Small Businesses, p. 3, http://www.uspto.gov/aia_implementation/20120113-ippr_report.pdf visited Nov. 5, 2012.

culture of innovation. Consistent with this sentiment, the Act requires the USPTO Director to support intellectual property law associations across the United States to establish pro bono programs to assist under-resourced independent inventors and businesses.

Section 29. Pro bono program.

Section 29 requires the Director to work with and support intellectual law associations across the country to establish pro bono programs to assist financially under-resourced independent inventors and small businesses.[1]

This statute is not codified in 35 U.S.C. and provides as follows:

AIA § 32. PRO BONO PROGRAM.

(a) In General- The Director shall work with and support intellectual property law associations across the country in the establishment of pro bono programs designed to assist financially under-resourced independent inventors and small businesses.

(b) Effective Date- This section shall take effect on the date of the enactment of this Act.

The USPTO began a pro bono program and reports the following on its website:

Pro Bono Program

The AIA directs the USPTO to work with intellectual property law associations across the country in order to establish pro bono programs for financially under-resourced inventors and small businesses. A pilot program in Minnesota was launched in June of 2010 to provide legal services to help such individuals and businesses obtain solid patent protection. Using the Minnesota pilot program as a model, the USPTO has contacted numerous law associations across the country to assist in putting together additional pro bono programs. As a result five new regional pro bono programs will open their doors during the second half of 2012. The five new pro bono programs include Denver, California, Texas, Washington DC metropolitan area, including Maryland and Virginia, and New York City metropolitan area, including northern New Jersey and Connecticut. Look for at least ten additional regional programs to open their doors in 2013. Also be on the lookout for a single entry point for anyone interested in pro bono assistance, which should be ready for applicants in July. Notice will be posted on the USPTO website providing additional in-

---

[Section 31:10]

[1]H. R. Rep. No. 112-98, pt. 1, p. 56, 84 (2011).

formation about the progress of each of these exciting steps forward.

Eligibility and acceptance to any regional pro bono program will be determined by an initial screening process. The screening will look at the individual's or small business' knowledge of the patent system, the potential patentability an invention and income qualifications. The knowledge requirement can be shown through a filing receipt for a pending patent application or through a certificate of completion for a general knowledge course provided at **https://uspto.connectsolutions.com/certificationpackage/.** The ability to show an invention's patentability can be shown through a patent search for similar prior art. The qualification of income limit is determined by each regional program. Please visit **http://www.uspto.gov/inventors/proseprobono/index.jsp** for additional information as it becomes available.[2]

§ 31:11 Study on patent litigation by non-practicing entities (AIA § 34)

The House Report mentions a study on patent litigation but does not explain Congressional intent. It states merely, "Subsection (o)—Contains a study of patent litigation and its effect on the patent system."[1] The text of AIA § 34 is fairly self-explanatory on the scope of the mandated study and provides as follows:

AIA § 34. STUDY OF PATENT LITIGATION

(a) GAO Study- The Comptroller General of the United States shall conduct a study of the consequences of litigation by non-practicing entities, or by patent assertion entities, related to patent claims made under title 35, United States Code, and regulations authorized by that title.

(b) Contents of Study- The study conducted under this section shall include the following:

(1) The annual volume of litigation described in subsection (a) over the 20-year period ending on the date of the enactment of this Act.

(2) The volume of cases comprising such litigation that are found to be without merit after judicial review.

(3) The impacts of such litigation on the time required to resolve patent claims.

(4) The estimated costs, including the estimated cost of

---

[2]See, http://www.uspto.gov/aia_implementation/programs.jsp, visited November 5, 2012.

[Section 31:11]

[1]H. R. Rep. No. 112-98, pt. 1, p. 74 (2011).

defense, associated with such litigation for patent holders, patent licensors, patent licensees, and inventors, and for users of alternate or competing innovations.

(5) The economic impact of such litigation on the economy of the United States, including the impact on inventors, job creation, employers, employees, and consumers.

(6) The benefit to commerce, if any, supplied by non-practicing entities or patent assertion entities that prosecute such litigation.

(c) Report to Congress- The Comptroller General shall, not later than the date that is 1 year after the date of the enactment of this Act, submit to the Committee on the Judiciary of the House of Representatives and the Committee on the Judiciary of the Senate a report on the results of the study required under this section, including recommendations for any changes to laws and regulations that will minimize any negative impact of patent litigation that was the subject of such study.

The USPTO as of November 5, 2012 had not completed the report, which was due on Sept. 16, 2012. The status of the USPTO efforts as of that date were reported on its website as follows:

Patent Litigation

Congress requires the Government Accountability Office (GAO) to study the consequences of patent litigation by non-practicing entities (NPEs) or patent assertion entities (PAEs) in consultation with the USPTO. This study will include the volume of litigation in the 20 years before enactment of the AIA, the volume of cases which are found to be without merit after judicial review, the impact of litigation on the time to resolve patent claims, the costs with such litigation, its economic impact on the U.S. economy and job creation, and any benefits created by NPEs or PAEs. Within one year from the date of enactment of the AIA, i.e., by September 16, 2012, the GAO must report to Congress the results of this study, including recommendations to minimize any negative impact of such patent litigation.

Additional information is forthcoming.[2]

§ 31:12 Budgetary effects (AIA § 36)

The House Report mentions budgetary effects but does not explain Congressional intent. It states merely, "*Budgetary effects.* The House bill retains a Senate provision that refer-

---

[2] http://www.uspto.gov/aia_implementation/aia_studies_reports.jsp#heading-5, visited November 5, 2012.

ences a CBO PAYGO score in *The Congressional Record.*"[1] It further states, "Section 31 references text from S. 23 regarding the budgetary effects of the Act as it pertains to PAYGO compliance."[2]

The text of AIA § 36 is fairly explanatory on the scope of the mandated study, and provides as follows:

AIA § 36. BUDGETARY EFFECTS.

The budgetary effects of this Act, for the purpose of complying with the Statutory Pay-As-You-Go Act of 2010, shall be determined by reference to the latest statement titled 'Budgetary Effects of PAYGO Legislation' for this Act, submitted for printing in the Congressional Record by the Chairman of the House Budget Committee, provided that such statement has been submitted prior to the vote on passage.

[Section 31:12]

[1]H. R. Rep. No. 112-98, pt. 1, p. 57 (2011). "CBO PAYGO" stands for the Congressional Budget Office PAYGO program wherein the federal government pays for expenditures with funds that are currently available, not borrowed. See generally the Budget Enforcement Act of 1990, Pub. L. 101-508, title XIII; 104 Stat. 1388-573.

[2]H. R. Rep. No. 112-98, pt. 1, p. 84 (2011).

Chapter 32

Effective Dates

AIA § 35

§ 32:1 Background and congressional intent[1]

The House Report contains only cursory comments on the effective date provisions:

Effective date

Except as otherwise provided, the provisions of the bill take

[Section 32:1]

[1]The Supreme Court cautions against relying on interpretations advanced in legislative statements that are not "anchored in the text of the statute." *Shannon v. U.S.*, 512 U.S. 573, 583, 114 S. Ct. 2419, 129 L. Ed. 2d 459 (1994), stating "[C]ourts have no authority to enforce [a] principl[e] gleaned solely from legislative history that has no statutory reference point." Shannon, 512 U.S. at 584, quoting *International Broth. of Elec. Workers, Local Union No. 474, AFL-CIO v. N.L.R.B.*, 814 F.2d 697, 712, 124 L.R.R.M. (BNA) 2993, 106 Lab. Cas. (CCH) P 12256 (D.C. Cir. 1987). The authoritative statement "is the statutory text, not the legislative history." *Exxon Mobil Corp. v. Allapattah Services, Inc.*, 545 U.S. 546, 568, 125 S. Ct. 2611, 162 L. Ed. 2d 502 (2005). However, lower courts have cited the legislative history of the AIA already in recent cases. E.g., *Rogers v. Tristar Products, Inc.*, 102 U.S.P.Q.2d 1722, 2012 WL 1660604, *2 (Fed. Cir. 2012) (non-precedential); *Byrne v. Wood, Herron & Evans, LLP*, 676 F.3d 1024, 1029, 102 U.S.P.Q.2d 1073 (Fed. Cir. 2012) (dissenting opin.).

effect 1 year following the date of enactment and shall apply to any patent issued on or after that date.

Section 30. Effective date.

Except as otherwise provided, this Act takes effect 12 months after the date of enactment and applies to any patent issued on or after that effective date.[2]

§ 32:2 The AIA effective date provision

New Statute (AIA Sec. 35))

AIA § 35. EFFECTIVE DATE.

Except as otherwise provided in this Act, the provisions of this Act shall take effect upon the expiration of the 1-year period beginning on the date of the enactment of this Act and shall apply to any patent issued on or after that effective date.

§ 32:3 Table of AIA effective dates

AIA § 35 defines the default effective date of the Act as one year following passage of the Act. The AIA was signed by the President on September 16, 2011. Therefore, unless otherwise specified, each AIA provision has an effective date of September 16, 2012.

Nevertheless, the AIA contains many provisions specifying another effective date. Those AIA sections having specified effective dates other than the default effective date are summarized below:

Section	Subject	Relative Effective Date	Specific Effective Date (if known)	Special Rules
Default	Effective Date	1 year after enactment	Sept. 16, 2012	Patents issued on or after effective date.
3(e)	Repeal of Statutory Invention Registrations	18 months after enactment	March 16, 2013	
3(k)	Extended Statute of Limitations for 35 U.S.C. § 32	Date of enactment	Sept. 16, 2011	Not extended retroactively.
Other 3	First-to-invent	18 months after enactment	March 16, 2013	Generally not retroactive.
4	Inventor's Oath or Declaration	1 year after enactment	Sept. 16, 2012	Not retroactive.
5	Prior user rights	Date of enactment	Sept. 16, 2011	Not retroactive.

[2]H. R. Rep. No. 112-98, pt. 1, 57, 84 (2011).

Section	Subject	Relative Effective Date	Specific Effective Date (if known)	Special Rules
6(a)	*Inter partes* Review	1 year after enactment	Sept. 16, 2012	Possible limits on number of *inter partes* reviews.
6(c)	35 U.S.C. § 312: *inter partes* reexamination	Date of enactment	Sept. 16, 2011	Change in standard to grant review.
6(d)	Post-grant Review	1 year after enactment	Sept. 16, 2012	Transition provisions.
6(g)	Citation of prior art and written statements	1 year after enactment	Sept. 16, 2012	All patents issued before, on, or after the date.
6(h)(1)	Decision to grant reexamination	1 year after enactment	Sept. 16, 2012	All patents issued before, on, or after the date.
6(h)(2)	Appeal of reexamination	Date of enactment	Sept. 16, 2011	All patents issued before, on, or after the date.
7	Patent trial and appeal board	1 year after enactment	Sept. 16, 2012	No.
8	Preissuance submissions	1 year after enactment	Sept. 16, 2012	All patent applications filed before, on, or after the date.
9	Venue	Date of enactment	Sept. 16, 2011	No.
10(h)	Electronic filing incentive	60 days after enactment	Nov. 15, 2011	No.
Other 10	Fee Setting Authority	Date of enactment	Sept. 16, 2011	No.
11(h)	Prioritized examination fee	10 days after enactment	Sept. 26, 2011	No.
11(i)	15% fee increase	10 days after enactment	Sept. 26, 2011	No.
Other 11	Fees for patent services	Date of enactment	Sept. 16, 2011	No.
12	Supplemental Examination	1 year after enactment	Sept. 16, 2012	All patents issued before, on, or after the date.
13	Funding Agreements	Date of enactment	Sept. 16, 2011	All patents issued before, on, or after the date.

Section	Subject	Relative Effective Date	Specific Effective Date (if known)	Special Rules
14	Tax Strategies deemed to be in prior art	Date of the enactment	Sept. 16, 2011	All patent applications pending on, or filed on or after the date, and to any patent that is issued on or after the date.
15	Best Mode	Date of enactment	Sept. 16, 2011	All actions commenced on or after the date.
16(a)	Virtual Marking	Date of enactment	Sept. 16, 2011	Applies to all actions pending on or commenced on or after the date.
16(b)	False Marking	Date of enactment	Sept. 16, 2011	Applies to all actions pending on or commenced on or after the date.
18(a)(1)	Post-grant review of business method patents	1 year after enactment	Sept. 16, 2012	any covered business method patent issued before, on, or after that effective date, except for those eligible for standard post-grant review.
19	Jurisdiction and Joinder	Date of enactment	Sept. 16, 2011	Applies to all actions commenced on or after the date.
20	Technical amendments	1 year after enactment	Sept. 16, 2012	Proceedings commenced on or after the date.
22	USPTO funding	October 1, 2011	Oct. 1, 2011	No.
32	Pro Bono Program	Date of enactment	Sept. 16, 2011	No.
33(a)	Human Organisms	Date of enactment	Sept. 16, 2011	Any patent application pending on or filed on or after the effective date. No retroactive effect on issued patents.

Section	Subject	Relative Effective Date	Specific Effective Date (if known)	Special Rules
37	Patent Term Extension	Date of enactment	Sept. 16, 2011	Any patent term extension request pending on, filed after, or subject to judicial review on, the date.

APPENDICES

APPENDIX 1

House Report Excerpts

The following is reproduced from House Committee Report 112-98 submitted by Mr. Smith, from the Committee on the Judiciary.

* * *

PURPOSE AND SUMMARY

The Constitution explicitly grants Congress the power to "promote the progress of science and useful arts, by securing for limited times to . . . inventors the exclusive right to their respective . . . discoveries."[1] Congress has responded by authorizing patents to issue to inventors of new and useful inventions or improvements on inventions.[2] The patent law thus accomplishes two objectives, consistent with the authorization granted by the Constitution: first, it encourages inventors by granting them limited, but exclusive rights to their inventions; second, in exchange for the grant of those exclusive rights, the patent law requires disclosure of the invention and terminates the monopoly after a period of years.[3] This disclosure and limited time benefits both society and future inventors by making the details of the invention available to the public immediately, and the right to make use of that invention after the expiration of 20 years from the date the patent application was filed.

Congress has not enacted comprehensive patent law

---

[1]U.S. Const. Art. 1, Sec. 8.

[2]See 35 U.S.C. Sec. 101.

[3]See Perspectives on Patents: Post-Grant Review Procedures and Other Litigation Reforms: Hearing before the Subcomm. on Intellectual Prop. of the Senate Comm. on the Judiciary, 109th Cong. (2006) (statement of Nathan P. Myhrvold, Chief Executive Officer, Intellectual Ventures); Perspectives on Patents: Hearing before the Subcomm. on Intellectual Prop. of the Senate Comm. on the Judiciary, 109th Cong. (2005) (statement of Dean Kamen, President, DEKA Research and Development Corp.).

reform in nearly 60 years.[4] The object of the patent law today must remain true to the constitutional command, but its form needs to change, both to correct flaws in the system that have become unbearable, and to accommodate changes in the economy and the litigation practices in the patent realm. The need to update our patent laws has been meticulously documented in 15 hearings before the Committee or its Subcommittee on Courts, the Internet, and Intellectual Property, as well as eight hearings before the United States Senate Committee on the Judiciary. In addition, these legislative findings are augmented by the Federal Trade Commission and the National Academy of Sciences,[5] both of which published authoritative reports on patent reform, and a plethora of academic commentary.[6]

While Congress has considered patent reform legislation over the last four Congresses, the need to modernize our patent laws has found expression in the courts, as well. The Supreme Court has reversed the Federal Circuit in six of the patent-related cases that it has heard since the beginning of the 109th Congress.[7] The Court's decisions have moved in

---

[4]The last major revision of the patent laws was the Patent Act of 1952, P.L. 82-593.

[5]The National Academy of Sciences (NAS), and the Federal Trade Commission (FTC) conducted multi-year studies on the patent system and its need for reform. See National Research Council of the National Academies, A Patent System for the 21st Century (2004) (hereinafter 'NAS Report'); and Federal Trade Comm'n, To Promote Innovation: The Proper Balance of Competition and Patent Law and Policy (2003) (hereinafter 'FTC Report').

[6]See, e.g., Mark A. Lemley and Carl Shapiro, Patent Holdup and Royalty Stacking, 85 Tex. L. Rev. 1991 (2007); Donald S. Chisum, Reforming Patent Law Reform, 4 J. Marshall Rev. Intell. Prop. L. 336 (2005); Gerald J. Mossinghoff, The First-to-Invent Rule in the U.S. Patent System has Provided no Advantage to Small Entities, 87 JPTOS 514 (2005); Joseph Farrell & Robert P. Merges, Incentives to Challenge and Defend Patents: Why Litigation Won't Reliably Fix Patent Office Errors and Why Administrative Patent Review Might Help, 19 Berkeley Tech. L.J. 943, 958 (2004); see also Adam B. Jaffe & Josh Lerner, Innovation and Its Discontents: How Our Broken Patent System is Endangering Innovation and Progress, and What to Do About It (2004); Kevin G. Rivette & David Kline, Rembrandts in the Attic, Unlocking the Hidden Value of Patents (2000).

[7]See *Bilski v. Kappos*, __ U.S. __, 130 S.Ct. 3218 (2010) (reversing the Federal Circuit and holding that the machine-or-transformation test is not the sole test for determining the patent eligibility of a process); *Quanta Computer, Inc. v. LG Elecs. Inc.*, 553 U.S. 617 (2008) (reversing the Federal Circuit and holding that patent exhaustion applies to method

the direction of improving patent quality and making the determination of patent validity more efficient. The decisions reflect a growing sense that questionable patents are too easily obtained and are too difficult to challenge.[8] Recent decisions by the Federal Circuit reflect a similar trend in response to these concerns.[9] But the courts are constrained in their decisions by the text of the statutes at issue. It is time for Congress to act.

The voices heard during the debate over changes to the patent law have been diverse and their proposals have been far from uniform. They have focused the Committee's attention on the value of harmonizing our system for granting patents with the best parts of other major patent systems throughout the industrialized world for the benefit of U.S. patent holders; improving patent quality and providing a more efficient system for challenging patents that should not have issued; and reducing unwarranted litigation costs and inconsistent damage awards.

The purpose of the "America Invents Act," as reported by the Committee on the Judiciary, is to ensure that the patent system in the 21st century reflects the constitutional imperative. Congress must promote innovation by granting inventors temporally limited monopolies on their inventions in a manner that ultimately benefits the public through the disclosure of the invention to the public. The legislation is

---

patents when the essential or inventive feature of the invention is embodied in the product); *Microsoft Corp. v. AT&T Corp.*, 550 U.S. 437 (2007) (reversing the Federal Circuit and limiting the extraterritorial reach of section 271(f), which imposes liability on a party which supplies from the U.S. components of a patented invention for combination outside the U.S.); *KSR Int'l Co. v. Teleflex Inc.*, 550 U.S. 398 (2007) (reversing the Federal Circuit and strengthening the standard for determining when an invention is obvious under section 103); *MedImmune, Inc. v. Genentech, Inc.*, 549 U.S. 118 (2007) (reversing the Federal Circuit and holding that the threat of a private enforcement action is sufficient to confirm standing under the Constitution); *eBay Inc. v. MercExchange, L.L.C.*, 547 U.S. 388 (2006) (reversing the Federal Circuit and holding that the generally applicable four-factor test for injunctive relief applies to disputes in patent cases).

[8]See generally Patent Reform in the 111th Congress: Legislation and Recent Court Decisions, Senate Judiciary Committee, 111th Cong. (2009) (statement of Professor Mark A. Lemley, Stanford Law School).

[9]See, e.g., *In re Seagate Tech., LLC*, 497 F.3d 1360 (Fed. Cir. 2007) (holding that willful infringement requires at least a demonstration of objectively reckless behavior and removing any affirmative obligation to obtain an opinion of counsel letter to combat an allegation of willful infringement).

designed to establish a more efficient and streamlined patent system that will improve patent quality and limit unnecessary and counterproductive litigation costs.

If the United States is to maintain its competitive edge in the global economy, it needs a system that will support and reward all innovators with high quality patents. The Committee has taken testimony from and its members have held meetings with interested parties that have different and often conflicting perspectives on the patent system. The Committee has taken all of those views into consideration, and drafted and then amended the "America Invents Act" to balance the competing interests. The legislation ordered reported by the Committee on a vote of 32-3 is a consensus approach that will modernize the United States patent system in significant respects.

BACKGROUND AND NEED FOR THE LEGISLATION

First Inventor to File

The "America Invents Act" creates a new "first-inventor-to-file" system. Every industrialized nation other than the United States uses a patent priority system commonly referred to as "first-to-file." In a first-to-file system, when more than one application claiming the same invention is filed, the priority of a right to a patent is based on the earlier-filed application. The United States, by contrast, currently uses a "first-to-invent" system, in which priority is established through a proceeding to determine which applicant actually invented the claimed invention first. Differences between the two systems arise in large part from the date that is most relevant to each respective system. In a first-to-file system, the filing date of the application is most relevant;[10] the filing date of an application is an objective date, simple to determine, for it is listed on the face of the patent. In contrast, in a first-to-invent system, the date the invention claimed in the application was actually invented is the determinative date. Unlike the objective date of filing, the date someone invents something is often uncertain, and, when disputed, typically requires corroborating evidence as part of an adjudication.

There are significant, practical differences between the

[10]When the term 'filing date' is used herein, it is also meant to include, when appropriate, the effective filing date, i.e., the earliest date the claim in an application-claims priority.

two systems. Among them is the ease of determining the right to a claimed invention in the instance in which two different people file patent applications for the same invention. In a first-to-file system, the application with the earlier filing date prevails and will be awarded the patent, if one issues. In the first-to-invent system, a lengthy, complex and costly administrative proceeding (called an "interference proceeding") must be conducted at the United States Patent and Trademark Office ("USPTO") to determine who actually invented first.[11] Interference proceedings can take years to complete (even if there is no appeal to the United States Court of Appeals for the Federal Circuit), cost hundreds of thousands of dollars, and require extensive discovery.[12] In addition, because it is always possible that an applicant could be involved in an interference proceeding, companies must maintain extensive recording and document retention systems in case they are later required to prove the date they invented the claimed invention.

Another important difference between the two systems is that in some first-to-file systems, prior art can include the inventor's own disclosure of his invention prior to the filing date of his application. Such systems do not provide the inventor any grace period during which time he is allowed to publish his invention without fear of its later being used against him as prior art. The Committee heard from universities and small inventors, in particular, about the importance of maintaining that grace period in our system.[13] They argued that the grace period affords the necessary time to prepare and file applications, and in some instances, to obtain the necessary funding that enables the inventor to prepare adequately the application. In addition, the grace period benefits the public by encouraging early disclosure of

---

[11]See 35 U.S.C. Sec. 135.

[12]See, e.g., Robert W. Pritchard, The Future is Now—The Case for Patent Harmonization, 20 N.C. J. Int'l L. & Com. Reg. 291, 313 (1995).

[13]See, e.g., Perspectives on Patents: Harmonization and Other Matters: Hearing Before the Subcomm. on Intellectual Prop. of the Senate Comm. on the Judiciary, 109th Cong. (2005) (statement of Charles E. Phelps, Provost, University of Rochester, on behalf of the Association of American Universities); Patent Law Reform: Injunctions and Damages: Hearing Before the Subcomm. on Intellectual Prop. of the Senate Comm. on the Judiciary, 109th Cong. (2005) (statement of Carl Gulbrandsen, Managing Director, Wisconsin Alumni Research Foundation (WARF)); Perspective on Patents: Hearing Before the Subcomm. on Intellectual Prop. of the Senate Comm. on the Judiciary, 109th Cong. (2005) (statement of William Parker, Diffraction, Ltd.).

new inventions, regardless of whether an application may later be filed for a patent on it.

Numerous organizations, institutions, and companies have advocated that the U.S. adopt a first-to-file system similar to those used in the rest of the world.[14] The National Academy of Sciences made a similar recommendation after an extensive study of the patent system.[15] When the United States patent system was first adopted, inventors did not typically file in other countries. It is now common for inventors and companies to file for protection in several countries at the same time.[16] Thus, United States applicants, who also want to file abroad, are forced to follow and comply with two different filing systems. Maintaining a filing system so different from the rest of the world disadvantages United States applicants who, in most instances, also file in other

[14]See, e.g., Perspectives on Patents: Harmonization and Other Matters: Hearing Before the Subcomm. on Intellectual Prop. of the Senate Comm. on the Judiciary, 109th Cong. (2005) (statement of Gerald J. Mossinghoff, Former Assistant Secretary of Commerce and Commissioner of Patents and Trademarks); Perspectives on Patents: Harmonization and Other Matters: Hearing Before the Subcomm. on Intellectual Prop. of the Senate Comm. on the Judiciary, 109th Cong. (2005) (statement of Q. Todd Dickinson, Former Under Secretary of Commerce for Intellectual Property and Director of the United States Patent and Trademark Office); Patent Law Reform: Injunctions and Damages: Hearing Before the Subcomm. on Intellectual Prop. of the Senate Comm. on the Judiciary, 109th Cong. (2005) (statement of Jeffrey P. Kushan, Partner, Sidley Austin Brown & Wood, LLP); Patent Law Reform: Injunctions and Damages: Hearing Before the Subcomm. on Intellectual Prop. of the Senate Comm. on the Judiciary, 109th Cong. (2005) (statement of Mark A. Lemley, Professor, Stanford Law School); Perspectives on Patents: Hearing Before the Subcomm. on Intellectual Prop. of the Senate Comm. on the Judiciary, 109th Cong. (2005) (statement of Robert A. Armitage, Senior Vice President and General Patent Counsel, Eli Lilly and Company); Perspectives on Patents: Hearing Before the Subcomm. on Intellectual Prop. of the Senate Comm. on the Judiciary, 109th Cong. (2005) (statement of Michael K. Kirk, Executive Director, American Intellectual Property Law Association).

[15]See NAS Report at 124; see also Perspectives on Patents: Hearing Before the Subcomm. on Intellectual Prop. of the Senate Comm. on the Judiciary, 109th Cong. (2005) (statement of Richard C. Levin, Yale University).

[16]See Perspectives on Patents: Harmonization and Other Matters: Hearing Before the Subcomm. on Intellectual Prop. of the Senate Comm. on the Judiciary, 109th Cong. (2005) (statement of Gerald J. Mossinghoff, Former Assistant Secretary of Commerce and Commissioner of Patents and Trademarks).

countries.[17] A change is long overdue.[18]

Drawing on the best aspects of the two existing systems, the America Invents Act creates a new "first-inventor-to-file" system. This new system provides patent applicants in the United States the efficiency benefits of the first-to-file systems used in the rest of the world by moving the U.S. system much closer to a first-to-file system and making the filing date that which is most relevant in determining whether an application is patentable. The new system continues, however, to provide inventors the benefit of the 1-year grace period. As part of the transition to a simpler, more efficient first-inventor-to-file system, this provision eliminates costly, complex interference proceedings, because priority will be based on the first application. A new administrative proceeding—called a "derivation" proceeding—is created to ensure that the first person to file the application is actually a true inventor. This new proceeding will ensure that a person will not be able to obtain a patent for the invention that he did not actually invent. If a dispute arises as to which of two applicants is a true inventor (as opposed to who invented it first), it will be resolved through an administrative proceeding by the Patent Board. The Act also simplifies how prior art is determined, provides more certainty, and reduces the cost associated with filing and

---

[17]See Perspectives on Patents: Hearing Before the Subcomm. on Intellectual Prop. of the Senate Comm. on the Judiciary, 109th Cong. (2005) (statement of Richard C. Levin, President, Yale University, and Mark B. Meyers, Visiting Executive Professor, Management Department at the Wharton Business School, University of Pennsylvania), estimating that it costs as much as $750,000 to $1 million to obtain worldwide patent protection on an important invention, and the lack of harmonization regarding filing systems adds unnecessary cost and delay.

[18]The NAS recommended changing the U.S. to a first-to-file system, while maintaining a grace period. See NAS Report at 124–27. See also Patent Reform in the 111th Congress: Legislation and Recent Court Decisions: Hearing Before the Senate Comm. on the Judiciary, 111th Cong. (2009) (statement of Steven Appleton, Chairman and Chief Executive Officer, Micron Technologies, Inc.); Patent Reform in the 111th Congress: Legislation and Recent Court Decisions: Hearing Before the Senate Comm. on the Judiciary, 111th Cong. (2009) (statement of Philip S. Johnson, Chief Patent Counsel, Johnson & Johnson); Patent Reform in the 111th Congress: Legislation and Recent Court Decisions: Hearing Before the Senate Comm. on the Judiciary, 111th Cong. (2009) (statement of Herbert C. Wamsley, Executive Director, Intellectual Property Owners Association); Patent Reform in the 111th Congress: Legislation and Recent Court Decisions: Hearing Before the Senate Comm. on the Judiciary, 111th Cong. (2009) (statement of Mark A. Lemley, Professor, Stanford Law School).

litigating patents.

The Act maintains a 1-year grace period for U.S. applicants. Applicants' own publication or disclosure that occurs within 1 year prior to filing will not act as prior art against their applications. Similarly, disclosure by others during that time based on information obtained (directly or indirectly) from the inventor will not constitute prior art. This 1-year grace period should continue to give U.S. applicants the time they need to prepare and file their applications.

This provision also, and necessarily, modifies the prior-art sections of the patent law. Prior art will be measured from the filing date of the application and will typically include all art that publicly exists prior to the filing date, other than disclosures by the inventor within 1 year of filing. Prior art also will no longer have any geographic limitations. Thus, in section 102 the "in this country" limitation as applied to "public use" and "on sale" is removed, and the phrase "available to the public" is added to clarify the broad scope of relevant prior art, as well as to emphasize the fact that it must be publicly accessible. Prior art based on earlier-filed United States applications is maintained,[19] as is current law's grace period, which will apply to all actions by the patent owner during the year prior to filing that would otherwise create § 102(a) prior art.[20] Sections (and subsections) of the existing statute are renumbered, modified, or deleted consistent with converting to a first-inventor-to-file system.[21] Finally, the intent behind the CREATE Act to promote joint research activities is preserved by including a prior art exception for subject matter invented by parties to a joint research agreement. The Act also provides that its enactment of new section 102(c) of title 35 is done with the same intent to promote joint research activities that was expressed in the Cooperative Research and Technology Enhancement Act of 2004 (Public Law 108-453), and that section 102(c) shall be administered in a manner consistent with such intent.

Inventor's oath or declaration

The U.S. patent system, when first adopted in 1790,

---

[19]Compare current Sec. 102(e) with new 102(a)(2).

[20]See generally 157 Cong. Rec. S.1496 to S.1497 (daily ed. March 9, 2011), S. 1370 to 1371 (daily ed. March 8, 2011).

[21]The Committee does not intend a substantive change by replacing the word 'negatived' in section 103 of title 35 with "negated."

contemplated that individual inventors would file their own patent applications, or would have a patent practitioner do so on their behalf. It has become increasingly common for patent applications to be assigned to corporate entities, most commonly the employer of the inventor.[22] In fact, many employment contracts require employees to assign their inventions to their employer.[23]

Current law still reflects the antiquated notion that it is the inventor who files the application, not the company-assignee. For example, every inventor must sign an oath as part of the patent application stating that the inventor believes he or she is the true inventor of the invention claimed in the application.[24] By the time an application is eventually filed, however, the applicant filing as an assignee may have difficulty locating and obtaining every inventor's signature for the statutorily required oath. Although the USPTO has adopted certain regulations to allow filing of an application when the inventor's signature is unobtainable,[25] many have advocated that the statute be modernized to facilitate the filing of applications by assignees.[26]

The Act updates the patent system by facilitating the process by which an assignee may file and prosecute patent applications. It provides similar flexibility for a person to whom the inventor is obligated to assign, but has not assigned, rights to the invention (the "obligated assignee").

Section 115 of title 35 is amended to allow a substitute statement to be submitted in lieu of an inventor's oath when either the inventor (i) is unable to submit an oath, or (ii) is

---

[22]See John R. Allison & Mark A. Lemley, The Growing Complexity of the United States Patent System, 82 B.U. L. Rev. 77, 97 (2002) (study showing that approximately 85% of the patents issued between 1996–98 were assigned by inventors to corporations; an increase from 79% during the period between 1976–78).

[23]See Jerry C. Liu, Overview of Patent Ownership Considerations in Joint Technology Development, 2005 Syracuse Sci. & Tech. L. Rep. 1 (2005).

[24]35 U.S.C. Sec. 115.

[25]See 37 C.F.R. Sec. 1.47, which permits an applicant to petition the Director of the USPTO to have the application accepted without every inventor's signature in limited circumstances, e.g., when the inventor cannot be found or refuses to participate in the application.

[26]See Perspectives on Patents: Harmonization and Other Matters: Hearing Before the Subcomm. on Intellectual Prop. of the Senate Comm. on the Judiciary, 109th Cong. (2005) (statement of David Beier, Senior Vice President of Global Government Affairs, Amgen).

both unwilling to do so and under an obligation to assign the invention. If an error is discovered, the statement may later be corrected. A savings clause is included to prevent an invalidity or unenforceability challenge to the patent based on failure to comply with these requirements, provided that any error has been remedied. Willful false statements remain punishable, however, under Federal criminal laws.[27]

Section 118 of title 35 is also amended to make it easier for an assignee to file a patent application. The amendment now allows obligated assignees—entities to which the inventor is obligated to assign the application—to file applications, as well. It also allows a person who has a sufficient proprietary interest in the invention to file an application to preserve that person's rights and those of the inventor.

Defense to infringement based on earlier inventor

Under current law, "prior user rights" may offer a defense to patent infringement when the patent in question is a "business method patent"[28] and its inventor uses the invention, but never files a patent application for it.[29] If the same invention is later patented by another party, the prior user may not be liable for infringement to the new patent holder, although all others may be.

Many counties [*sic*] include a more expansive prior-user rights regime within their first-to-file system. In the United States, this is particularly important to high-tech businesses that prefer not to patent every process or method that is part of their commercial operations. The Act responds to this point by revising US law as follows: First, the prior-use defense may be asserted against any patent (not just method patents), provided the person asserting the defense reduced the subject matter of the patent to practice and commercially used the subject matter at least 1 year before the effective filing date of the patent. Second, the defense cannot be asserted if the subject matter was derived from the patent holder or persons in privity with the patent holder. And third, the defense cannot be asserted unless the prior user both reduced the subject matter of the patent to practice and commercially used it at least 1 year before the effective filing date of the patent or the date that the patentee publicly

[27]See 18 U.S.C. Sec. 1001.

[28]35 U.S.C. Sec. 273(a)(3) states: 'The term 'method' means a method of doing or conducting business.

[29]See 35 U.S.C. Sec. 273.

disclosed the invention and invoked the § 102(b) grace period, whichever is earlier.

This narrow expansion of prior-user rights balances the interests of patent holders, including universities, against the legitimate concerns of businesses that want to avoid infringement suits relating to processes that they developed and used prior to another party acquiring related patents.

Post-grant review proceedings

The Act amends ex parte and inter partes reexamination and establishes a new post-grant review procedure. Under current law, there are two ways to challenge the validity and enforceability of a patent that has issued. The patent may be challenged in district court litigation or in a reexamination at the USPTO.

Nearly 30 years ago, Congress created the administrative "reexamination" process, through which the USPTO could review the validity of already-issued patents on the request of either the patent holder or a third party,[30] in the expectation that it would serve as an effective and efficient alternative to often costly and protracted district court litigation.[31] Reexamination requires the USPTO to review the patent in light of a substantial new question of patentability not presented during the original examination.[32] The initial reexamination statute had several limitations that later proved to make it a less viable alternative to litigation for evaluating patent validity than Congress intended. First, a reexamination request could only be based on prior art, and could not be based on prior public use or prior sales. Moreover, the requestor could not raise any challenge based on § 101 (utility, eligibility) or 112 (indefiniteness, enablement,

[30]See 35 U.S.C. Sec. 301 to 307. A patent holder will typically request reexamination to bolster the patent in view of new prior art. A third party may request reexamination to challenge, and ultimately invalidate, the patent.

[31]"Reexamination will permit efficient resolution of questions about the validity of issued patents without recourse to expensive and lengthy infringement litigation . . .. The reexamination of issued patents could be conducted with a fraction of the time and cost of formal legal proceedings and would help restore confidence in the effectiveness of our patent system . . .. It is anticipated that these measures provide a useful and necessary alternative for challengers and for patent owners to test the validity of United States patents in an efficient and relatively inexpensive manner." See H.R. Rep. No. 96-1307(I) at 3 (1980), reprinted in 1980 U.S.C.C.A.N. 6460, 6462–63.

[32]See 35 U.S.C. Sec. 303.

written description, best mode). A third party alleging a patent is invalid, therefore, had fewer challenges it could raise in the proceeding and, therefore, may instead opt to risk infringement and litigate the validity of the patent in court. Second, in the original reexamination system, the third-party challenger had no role once the proceeding was initiated, while the patent holder had significant input throughout the entire process. Third, a challenger that lost at the USPTO under reexamination had no right to appeal an examiner's, or the Patent Board's, decision either administratively or in court. Restrictions such as these made reexamination a much less favored avenue to challenge questionable patents than litigation. Reexamination proceedings are also often costly, taking several years to complete,[33] and are first conducted by examiners and, if the patent is rejected, then by Patent Board judges. Thus, many patents must go through two rounds of administrative review (one by the examiner, and a second by the Patent Board) adding to the length of the proceeding.[34]

Congress has responded several times to criticisms of the reexamination system by making amendments to the process.[35] In 1999, Congress created a second reexamination procedure—called inter partes reexamination—that gave

---

[33]See Perspectives on Patents: Hearing Before the Subcomm. on Intellectual Prop. of the Senate Comm. on the Judiciary, 109th Cong. (2005) (statement of Jon W. Dudas, Undersecretary of Commerce for Intellectual Property, Director of the U.S. Patent and Trademark Office), explaining that "a large number of reexamination proceedings have been pending before the USPTO for more than 4 years," and questioning whether this amount of time is consistent with the statutory requirement that "[a]ll reexamination proceedings . . . will be conducted with special dispatch within the Office." See also 35 U.S.C. Sec. 305.

[34]For several years, the standard practice at the USPTO was to assign the reexamination to the patent examiner who had originally examined that patent. In addition, the same third-party requester could file multiple, serial reexaminations based on the same "substantial new question of patentability," so long as the initial reexamination was not complete. More recently, the USPTO ended some of these procedures, and now reexaminations are handled by a Central Reexamination Unit (CRU), and subsequent serial reexamination, based on the same "substantial new question of patentability," is no longer permitted. See, e.g., Manual of Patent Examining Procedure (MPEP) Sec. 2236 and 2240 (August 2006).

[35]See e.g., 21st Century Dep't of Justice Appropriations Authorization Act, Pub. L. No. 107-273, Sec. 13105 to 13106, 13202, 116 Stat. 1758, 1761 (2002) (effective Nov. 2, 2002); American Inventors Protection Act, Pub.L. 106-113, 113 Stat. 1536, 1501A et seq. (1999) (creating inter partes reexamination) (hereafter referred to as the "AIPA".

third-party challengers greater input throughout the proceeding by permitting them to respond to every pleading submitted by the patent holder.[36] Congress also eventually gave third-party challengers the right to appeal adverse decisions.[37]

As part of the 1999 improvements to reexamination, Congress directed the USPTO to submit a report to Congress evaluating the inter partes reexamination process and making any recommendations for changes.[38] Initially, the USPTO projected that in the first year after the creation of inter partes reexamination, it would receive 400 such requests and it projected that by 2004 it would receive nearly 600.[39] No inter partes reexamination requests were actually filed in 2000 and only 27 such requests had been filed by 2004.[40] Over the 5-year period studied by the USPTO, it issued 900,000 patents and received only 53 requests for inter partes reexamination.[41]

The Act expands the category of documents that may be cited in a reexamination proceeding to include written statements of the patent owner that have been filed in a proceeding before a Federal court or the USPTO regarding the scope of claims. This addition will counteract the ability of patent owners to offer differing interpretations of prior art in different proceedings. These written statements, which include documents, pleadings or evidence from proceedings that address the patent owner's statements, shall not be considered for any purpose other than to determine the proper meaning of the claims that are the subject of the request in a proceeding. Specifically, the Committee does not intend these statements to be a basis for the institution of a reexamination proceeding. Reexaminations will continue to be available only on the basis of "patents or printed publications."[42]

The Act also amends the ex parte reexamination proce-

---

[36]See 35 U.S.C. Sec. 311 to 318.

[37]See 35 U.S.C. Sec. 315(b).

[38]AIPA, Pub. L. 106-113, Sec. 4606.

[39]See United States Patent and Trademark Office, Report to Congress on Inter Partes Reexamination (2004) (hereinafter referred to as "Report on Inter Partes Reexamination"), at 4.

[40]Id. at 5.

[41]Id.

[42]The scope of "patent and printed publication" prior art in the amended section 301 is intended to be coextensive with these terms in current section 102 of the title 35. Further, amendments made by Section

dure to allow the Director to institute a reexamination on the Director's own initiative if a substantial new question of patentability is raised by patents or publications.

The Act converts inter partes reexamination from an examinational to an adjudicative proceeding, and renames the proceeding "inter partes review." The Act also makes the following improvements to this pro-ceeding:

- **"Reasonable likelihood of success" for instituting inter partes review.** The threshold for initiating an inter partes review is elevated from "significant new question of patentability"—a standard that currently allows 95% of all requests to be granted—to a standard requiring petitioners to present information showing that their challenge has a reasonable likelihood of success. Satisfaction of the new threshold will be assessed based on the information presented both in the petition for the proceeding and in the patent owner's response to the petition.
- **"Reasonably could have raised" estoppel applied to subsequent administrative proceedings.** A party that uses inter partes review is estopped from raising in a subsequent PTO proceeding (such as an ex parte reexamination or inter partes review) any issue that it raised or reasonably could have raised in the inter partes review.
- **Repeal of the 1999 limit.** The limit on challenging patents issued before 1999 in inter partes reexamination is eliminated; all patents can be challenged in inter partes review.
- **Preponderance burden.** Petitioners bear the burden of proving that a patent is invalid by a preponderance of the evidence in inter partes review.
- **Time limits during litigation.** Parties who want to use inter partes review during litigation are required to seek a proceeding within 12 months of being served with a complaint alleging infringement of the patent, and are barred from seeking or maintaining an inter partes review if they file an action for a declaratory judgment that the patent is invalid.
- **Discovery.** Parties may depose witnesses submitting

---

2 of the Act, which expand and contract the definition of certain other forms of prior art, are not intended to change the particular "patent or printed publication" prior art, which will continue to be the sole basis for initiating reexamination proceedings.

affidavits or declarations and seek such discovery as the Patent Office determines is otherwise necessary in the interest of justice.

- **12- to 18-month deadline.** Inter partes review must be completed within 1 year of when the proceeding is instituted, except that the Office can extend this deadline by 6 months for good cause.
- **Oral hearing.** Each party has the right to request an oral hearing as part of an inter partes review.
- **Three-judge panels.** Inter partes reviews will be conducted before a panel of three Administrative Patent Judges. Decisions will be appealed directly to the Federal Circuit.

The Act also creates a new post-grant opposition procedure that can be utilized during the first 12 months after the grant of a patent or issue of a reissue patent. Unlike reexamination proceedings, which provide only a limited basis on which to consider whether a patent should have issued, the post-grant review proceeding permits a challenge on any ground related to invalidity under section 282. The intent of the post-grant review process is to enable early challenges to patents, while still protecting the rights of inventors and patent owners against new patent challenges unbounded in time and scope. The Committee believes that this new, early-stage process for challenging patent validity and its clear procedures for submission of art will make the patent system more efficient and improve the quality of patents and the patent system. This new, but time-limited, post-grant review procedure will provide a meaningful opportunity to improve patent quality and restore confidence in the presumption of validity that comes with issued patents in court.

In utilizing the post-grant review process, petitioners, real parties in interest, and their privies are precluded from improperly mounting multiple challenges to a patent or initiating challenges after filing a civil action challenging the validity [of] a claim in the patent. Further, a final decision in a post-grant review process will prevent the petitioner, a real party in interest, or its privy from challenging any patent claim on a ground that was raised in the post-grant review process. The post-grant review procedure is not intended, however, to inhibit patent owners from pursuing the various avenues of enforcement of their rights under a patent, and the amendment makes clear that the filing or institution of a post-grant review proceeding does not limit a patent owner from commencing such actions.

The Committee recognizes the importance of quiet title to patent owners to ensure continued investment resources. While this amendment is intended to remove current disincentives to current administrative processes, the changes made by it are not to be used as tools for harassment or a means to prevent market entry through repeated litigation and administrative attacks on the validity of a patent. Doing so would frustrate the purpose of the section as providing quick and cost effective alternatives to litigation. Further, such activity would divert resources from the research and development of inventions. As such, the Committee intends for the USPTO to address potential abuses and current inefficiencies under its expanded procedural authority.

Patent Trial and Appeal Board.

The Act renames the Patent Board the "Patent Trial and Appeal Board" and sets forth its duties, which are expanded to include jurisdiction over the new post-grant review and derivation proceedings. This section strikes references to proceedings eliminated by the Act, including interference proceedings, and updates the various appeals statutes.

Preissuance submissions by third parties

After an application is published, members of the public—most likely, a competitor or someone else familiar with the patented invention's field—may realize they have information relevant to a pending application. The relevant information may include prior art that would prohibit the pending application from issuing as a patent. Current USPTO rules permit the submission of such prior art by third parties only if it is in the form of a patent or publication,[43] but the submitter is precluded from explaining why the prior art was submitted or what its relevancy to the application might be.[44] Such restrictions decrease the value of the information to the examiner and may, as a result, deter such submissions.[45]

The Act improves the process by which third parties

---

[43]See 35 C.F.R. Sec. 1.99.

[44]See 35 C.F.R. Sec. 1.99(d) ("A submission under this section shall not include any explanation of the patents or publications, or any other information.").

[45]See Perspectives on Patents: Hearing Before the Subcomm. on Intellectual Prop. of the Senate Comm. on the Judiciary, 109th Cong. (2005)

submit relevant information to the UPSTO by permitting those third parties to make statements concerning the relevance of the patents, patent applications, and other printed publications that they bring to the USPTO's attention.

Venue

In 1999, as part of the American Inventors Protection Act (AIPA), Congress established that as a general matter the venue of the USPTO is the district where it resides.[46] The USPTO currently resides in the Eastern District of Virginia. However, Congress inadvertently failed to make this change uniformly throughout the entire patent statute. As a result, certain sections of the patent statute (and one section of the trademark statute) continue to allow challenges to USPTO decisions to be brought in the District of Columbia, a place where the USPTO has not resided in decades.

Because the USPTO no longer resides in the District of Columbia, the sections that authorize venue for litigation against the USPTO are consistently changed to reflect the venue where the USPTO currently resides.

Fee-setting authority

a) Agency fee setting authority

Although the USPTO has had the ability to set certain fees by regulation, most fees (*e.g.*, filing fee, issuance fee, maintenance fees) are set by Congress.[47] History has shown that such a scheme does not allow the USPTO to respond promptly to the challenges that confront it. The USPTO has argued for years that it must have fee-setting authority to administer properly the agency and its growing workload.

The Act allows the USPTO to set or adjust all of its fees, including those related to patents and trademarks, so long as they do no more than reasonably compensate the USPTO for the services performed. Prior to setting such fees, the Director must give notice to, and receive input from, the Patent or Trademark Public Advisory Committee (PPAC or TPAC). The Director may also reduce fees for any given fiscal year, but only after consultation with the PPAC or TPAC. The Act details the procedures for how the Director shall

(statement of David Simon, Chief Patent Counsel, Intel Corporation).

[46]See 35 U.S.C. Sec. 1(b).

[47]See, e.g., 35 U.S.C. Sec. 41.

consult with the PPAC and TPAC, including providing for public hearings and the dissemination to the public of any recommendations made by either Committee. Fees shall be prescribed by rule. Any proposed fee change shall be published in the Federal Register and include the specific rationale and purpose for the proposed change. The Director must seek public comments for no less than 45 days. The Director must also notify Congress of any final deci-sion regarding proposed fees. Congress shall have no more than 45 days to consider and comment on any proposed fee, but no proposed fee shall be effective prior to the expiration of this 45-day period.

b) "Microentity" defined

As part of the ongoing effort to nurture U.S. innovation, Congress has long recognized that certain groups, including independent inventors, small business concerns, and non-profit organizations (collectively referred to as "small business entities") should not bear the same financial burden for filing patent applications as larger corporate interests. The current statute provides for a significant reduction in certain fees for small business entities.[48] The Committee was made aware, however, that there is likely a benefit to describing—and then accommodating—a group of inventors who are even smaller, in order to ensure that the USPTO can tailor its requirements, and its assistance, to the people with very little capital, and just a few inventions, as they are starting out.

This section of the Act defines this even smaller group—the micro-entity—that includes only truly independent inventors. The Committee expects that the USPTO will make accommodations under its authority in recognition of the special status of micro-entities.

Supplemental examination

Patents are unenforceable and invalid if they are obtained through fraud. This concept is addressed in the "inequitable conduct" defense, which allows a defendant in an infringement suit to plead that the plaintiff patent-holder would not have received a patent but for misrepresentations made to the USPTO. Inequitable conduct requires proof of materiality as well as intent to deceive. These standards require courts and litigants to invest time and resources in determin-

---

[48]See 35 U.S.C. Sec. 41(h).

ing the patent-holder's state of mind or intent when developing the invention and submitting the application. Critics of the inequitable conduct defense, including the National Academies and the Federal Trade Commission, argue that our patent system is hampered by provisions that require courts to divine the difficult-to-prove subjective intent of individuals in patent disputes. And most defendants reflexively plead inequitable conduct as a defense to infringement, prompting the Federal Circuit to label the practice a "plague" on the patent system.

The Act addresses the inequitable conduct doctrine by authorizing supplemental examination of a patent to correct errors or omissions in proceedings before the Office. Under this new procedure, information that was not considered or was inadequately considered or was incorrect can be presented to the Office. If the Office determines that the information does not present a substantial new question of patentability or that the patent is still valid, that information cannot later be used to hold the patent unenforceable or invalid on the basis for an inequitable-conduct attack in civil litigation.

Funding agreements

The Patent and Trademark Amendments Act of 1980 (commonly referred to as the Bayh-Dole Act)[49] granted universities, other non-profit organizations, and small businesses the right to title to inventions developed using Federal funds. In 1984, Congress amended the law to ensure that universities and small businesses operating at Government facilities (GOCOs) reaped the benefits of Bayh-Dole by giving them the right to elect title to a subject invention.[50] The 1984 Act permitted GOCOs to retain the balance of any royalties or income earned from licensing inventions, up to 5 percent of the annual budget of the facility, for further research, development, and related activities. If the balance exceeds 5 percent of the facility's annual budget, however, 75 percent of the excess is recouped by the Government, with the remaining 25 percent of the excess also retained by the GOCO for further research, development, and related activities.[51]

The Senate Judiciary Committee considered testimony

[49] P.L. 96-517.

[50] P.L. 98-620, Sec. 501.

[51] 35 U.S.C. Sec. 202(c)(7).

that the requirement to repay the government 75 percent of the excess on royalty payments may be causing a disincentive for universities and small business operating under the GOCO provisions to commercialize products.[52] Based on these concerns, the Act maintains the essence of the agreement GOCOs made with the taxpayers when they received funding that they would reimburse the taxpayer if they are sufficiently successful in commercializing a product invented with taxpayer dollars, but which reduces the burden on universities and small businesses, thereby encouraging commercialization. Pursuant to the Act, instead of reimbursing 75% of the excess to the Government, the GOCO will retain 85 percent for further research, development, and related activities and reimburse the Government 15 percent.

Tax strategies deemed within the prior art

In recent years, the numbers of patents on tax-strategies have increased. Critics assert that it is not fair to permit patents on techniques used to satisfy a government mandate, such as compliance with the Internal Revenue Code.

Tax preparers, lawyers, and planners have a long history of sharing their knowledge regarding how to file returns, plan estates, and advise clients. The ability to interpret the tax law and implement such interpretations should remain in the public domain, available to all taxpayers and their advisors.

The Act mandates that tax strategies are deemed "insufficient to differentiate a claimed invention from the prior art." In other words, any future tax strategy will be considered indistinguishable from all other publicly available information that is relevant to a patent's claim of originality. Under the Act, however, protection (an exclusion) is made available for software that enables individuals to file their income tax returns or that assists them with managing their finances. The exclusion does not apply to that part of the software related to a tax strategy.

Best mode requirement

The Act amends § 282(b) to eliminate as a defense to patent infringement the patentee's failure to comply with the best mode requirement of 112. An applicant for a patent

[52]See The Role of Federally-Funded University Research in the Patent System: Hearing Before the Senate Comm. on the Judiciary, 110th Cong. (2008) (statement of Dr. Elizabeth Hoffman, Executive Vice President and Provost, Iowa State University).

must disclose: (1) a written description of the invention; (2) a written description of the manner of making and using the invention, sufficient to enable one skilled in the art to make and use it (known as the "enablement requirement"); and (3) the best mode contemplated by the inventor of carrying out the invention.[53] The disclosures required of an applicant are part of the important tradeoff that underlies the patent laws: the grant of a limited-term monopoly in exchange for disclosure of the invention.

Under current law, the defense of patent invalidity is available for failure to comply with any requirement of § 112 (specification) or 251 (reissued patents). Further, a defendant in patent litigation may also allege an intentional nondisclosure of the best mode, with intent to deceive the Office, as a basis for an unenforceability defense. Many have argued in recent years that the best mode requirement, which is unique to American patent law, is counterproductive.[54] They argue that challenges to patents based on best mode are inherently subjective and not relevant by the time the patent is in litigation, because the best mode contemplated at the time of the invention may not be the best mode for practicing or using the invention years later.

In response to these concerns, the Act includes a provision that eliminates best mode as a basis for both invalidity and unenforceability defenses under § 282; other defenses are unaffected.

Marking

a) Virtual Marking

In general, for patented "articles," a patent holder must give an alleged infringer notice of the claimed infringement, and the infringer must continue to infringe, before the patent holder may succeed in a suit for damages.[55] Actual notice requires the affirmative communication of infringement to the defendant, which may include the filing of a lawsuit.

[53]35 U.S.C. Sec. 112. Section 112 also requires an applicant to disclose a written description of the invention and a written description of the manner of making and using the invention, sufficient to enable one skilled in the art to make and use it.

[54]Among those who have so argued are the National Academy of Sciences, the Biotechnology Industry Organization, the American Intellectual Property Law Association, the Intellectual Property Owners Association, and Pharmaceutical Research and Manufacturers of America.

[55]See 35 U.S.C. Sec. 287.

Constructive notice is possible by "marking" any patented article that the patent holder (or its licensee) makes, uses, sells or imports.[56] Failure to appropriately mark an article can preclude the recovery of damages until notice is effective.

The Act permits patent holders to "virtually mark" a product by providing the address of a publicly available website that associates the patented article with the number of the patent. The burden will remain on the patent holder to demonstrate that the marking was effective. This amendment will save costs for pro-ducers of products that include technology on which a patent issues after the product is on the market, and will facilitate effective marking on smaller products.

b) False marking

The Federal Circuit's recent decision in *Forest Group, Inc. v. Bon Tool Co.*, 590 F.3d 1295 (Fed. Cir. 2009), which held that section 292's $500 fine is assessed for each product that is falsely marked, has created a surge in false-marking qui tam litigation. Though one might assume that section 292 actions are targeted at parties that assert fictitious patents in order to deter competitors, such a scenario is almost wholly unknown to false-marking litigation. False-marking suits are almost always based on allegations that a valid patent that did cover the product has expired, but the manufacturer continued to sell products stamped with the patent; or that an existing patent used to mark products is invalid or unenforceable; or that an existing and valid patent's claims should not be construed to cover the product in question.

Indeed, a recent survey of such suits found that a large majority involved valid patents that covered the products in question but had simply expired. For many products, it is difficult and expensive to change a mold or other means by which a product is marked as patented, and marked products continue to circulate in commerce for some period after the patent expires. It is doubtful that the Congress that originally enacted this section anticipated that it would force manufacturers to immediately remove marked products from commerce once the patent expired, given that the expense to manufacturers of doing so will generally greatly outweigh any conceivable harm of allowing such products to continue to circulate in commerce.

To address the recent surge in litigation, the bill replaces

---

[56] See 35 U.S.C. Sec. 287.

the qui tam remedy for false marking with a new action that allows a party that has suffered a competitive injury as a result of such marking to seek compensatory damages. The United States would be allowed to seek the $500-per-article fine, and competitors may recover in relation to actual injuries that they have suffered as a result of false marking, but the bill would eliminate litigation brought by unrelated, private third parties.

Advice of Counsel

The Act includes a new provision that bars courts and juries from drawing an adverse inference from an accused infringer's failure to obtain opinion of counsel as to infringement or his failure to waive privilege and disclose such an opinion. Section 298 of title 35 is designed to protect attorney-client privilege and to reduce pressure on accused infringers to obtain opinions of counsel for litigation purposes. It reflects a policy choice that the probative value of this type of evidence is outweighed by the harm that coercing a waiver of attorney-client privilege inflicts on the attorney-client relationship. Section 298 applies to findings of both willfulness and intent to induce infringement—and thus legislatively abrogates the Federal Circuit's decision in *Broadcom Corp. v. Qualcomm Inc.*, 543 F.3d 683, 699 (Fed. Cir. 2008).

Transitional program for covered business method patents

A number of patent observers believe the issuance of poor business-method patents during the late 1990's through the early 2000's led to the patent "troll" lawsuits that compelled the Committee to launch the patent reform project 6 years ago. At the time, the USPTO lacked a sufficient number of examiners with expertise in the relevant art area. Compounding this problem, there was a dearth of available prior art to assist examiners as they reviewed business method applications. Critics also note that most countries do not grant patents for business methods.

The Act responds to the problem by creating a transitional program 1 year after enactment of the bill to implement a provisional post-grant proceeding for review of the validity of any business method patent. In contrast to the era of the late 1990's-early 2000's, examiners will review the best prior art available. A petition to initiate a review will not be granted unless the petitioner is first sued for infringement or is accused of infringement. The program otherwise generally functions on the same terms as other post-grant proceedings initiated pursuant to the bill. Any party may request a stay of a civil action if a related post-grant proceeding is granted. The program sunsets after 10 years, which ensures that patent holders cannot delay filing a lawsuit over a shorter time period to avoid reevaluation under the transitional program.

Jurisdictional and procedural matters

a) State court jurisdiction and the US Court of Appeals for the Federal Circuit

The US district courts area given original jurisdiction to hear patent cases,[57] while the US Court of Appeals for the Federal Circuit adjudicates all patent appeals.[58] The Supreme Court ruled in 2002,[59] however, that patent counterclaims do not give the Federal Circuit appellate jurisdiction over a case.

The Act clarifies the jurisdiction of the US district courts and stipulates that the US Court of Appeals for the Federal Circuit has jurisdiction over appeals involving compulsory patent counterclaims. The legislative history of this provision, which we reaffirm and adopt as our own, appears in the Committee Report accompanying H.R. 2955 from the 109th Congress,[60] which the Committee reported favorably to the House on April 5, 2006.

b) Joinder

The Act also addresses problems occasioned by the joinder of defendants (sometimes numbering in the dozens) who have tenuous connections to the underlying disputes in patent infringement suits.

The Act amends chapter 29 of the Patent Act by creating a new § 299 that addresses joinder under Rule 20 and consolidation of trials under Rule 42. Pursuant to the provision, parties who are accused infringers in most patent suits may be joined as defendants or counterclaim defendants only if: (1) relief is asserted against the parties, jointly, severally, or

[57] 28 U.S.C. Sec. 1338.

[58] 28 U.S.C. Sec. 1295.

[59] *Holmes Group, Inc., v. Vornado Air Circulation Systems, Inc.*, 535 U.S. 826 (2002).

[60] H. Rep. 109-405.

in the alternative, arising out of the same transaction regarding the manufacture, use, or importation of the accused product or process; and (2) questions of fact common to all of the defendants will arise in the action. New 299 also clarifies that joinder will not be available if it based solely on allegations that a defendant has infringed the patent(s) in question.[61]

Technical amendments

The Act contains technical amendments to improve the organization of the patent statute.

Travel expenses and payment of administrative judges

The USPTO Director is authorized to conduct programs or exchanges pertaining to intellectual property law and protection "domestically and throughout the world." The House bill clarifies that this authority includes expending funds to cover the subsistence and travel expenses of non-Federal employees who attend these programs.

The House bill also clarifies that the Director may fix the pay for administrative patent judges and administrative trademark judges under the new Patent Trial and Appeal Board set forth in Section 6 of the bill.

Patent and Trademark Office funding

The USPTO is a fee-funded agency. The revenue it collects from fees imposed on inventors and trademark filers is deposited in a special USPTO appropriations account in the Treasury. To obtain funding for its operations, the agency must request the revenue back from congressional appropriators. Since the early 1990's, however, more than $800 million has been diverted from the agency and spent on non-USPTO initiatives.

The Committee believes the USPTO could operate more

---

[61]Section 299 legislatively abrogates the construction of Rule 20(a) adopted in *MyMail, Ltd. v. America Online, Inc.*, 223 F.R.D. 455 (E.D. Tex. 2004); *Sprint Communications Co. v. Theglobe.com, Inc.*, 233 F.R.D. 615 (D. Kan. 2006); *Adrain v. Genetec Inc.*, 2009 WL 3063414 (E.D. Tex. 2009); *Better Educ. Inc. v. Einstruction Corp.*, 2010 WL 918307 (E.D. Tex. March 10, 2010); *Mannatech, Inc. v. Country Life, LLC*, 2010 WL 2944574 (N.D. Tex. July 26, 2010); *Alford Safety Services, Inc., v. Hot-Hed, Inc.*, 2010 WL 3418233 (E.D. La. August 24, 2010); and *Eolas Technologies, Inc. v. Adobe Systems, Inc.*, 2010 WL 3835762 (E.D. Tex. September 28, 2010)—effectively conforming these courts' jurisprudence to that followed by a majority of jurisdictions. See generally *Rudd v. Lux Products Corp.*, 2011 WL 148052 (N.D. Ill. January 12, 2011).

efficiently and productively if the agency had full access to all of its fee-generated revenue. The House bill therefore creates a USPTO revolving fund within the Treasury that allows the agency to keep all of the funds it raises until expended.

The provision also requires the Director to submit an annual spending plan as well as an annual year-end report to the House and Senate Appropriations and Judiciary Committees.

Satellite offices

The USPTO is conducting a pilot to create and operate a new satellite office located in Detroit. The bill requires the Director to establish three other satellite offices within a 3-year window, subject to available resources. The legislation includes criteria that must be invoked when selecting the new sites.

Designation of Detroit satellite office

The House and Senate bills contain a provision that designates the PTO satellite office in Detroit as the "Elijah J. McCoy United States Patent and Trademark Office." Elijah McCoy was an African-Canadian inventor who spent much of his life in Michigan and earned 57 US patents. His work on an automatic lubricator to oil railroad steam engines gave rise to the expression, "the real McCoy."

Patent Ombudsman Program for small business concerns

The Act requires the USPTO Director to establish a Patent Ombudsman Program to provide support and services regarding patent filings to small business concerns. The authorization is subject to available resources.

Priority examination for technologies important to American competitiveness

The Act stipulates that the USPTO may promulgate regulations, not inconsistent with law, that prioritize examination of applications for products, processes, or technologies that are important to the national economy or national competitiveness. This may be done without recovering the aggregate extra cost of providing the prioritization.

Calculation of 60-day period for application of patent term extension

The USPTO has inconsistently applied "counting" rules that are imposed on patent holders who must submit documents to the agency within statutory time periods for consideration of additional patent term under § 156 of the Patent Act. The Act clarifies that the agency should impose a "business-day" construction for application to 156, consistent with recent case law on the matter.[62]

Study on implementation

The Act requires the USPTO Director to conduct a study regarding the implementation of the legislation and on such other aspects of Federal patent policies and practices with respect to patent rights, innovation in the United States, competitiveness of US markets, access by small business to capital and investment, and such other issues as the Director deems appropriate. The study must be completed within 4 years and the results submitted to the House and Senate Committees on the Judiciary.

Pro bono program

The Committee acknowledges the importance of individuals and small businesses to the patent system and our national culture of innovation. Consistent with this sentiment, the Act requires the USPTO Director to support intellectual property law associations across the United States to establish pro bono programs to assist under-resourced independent inventors and businesses.

Effective date

Except as otherwise provided, the provisions of the bill take effect 1 year following the date of enactment and shall apply to any patent issued on or after that date.

Budgetary effects

The House bill retains a Senate provision that references a CBO PAYGO score in *The Congressional Record.*

Hearings

The Committee's Subcommittee on Intellectual Property, Competition, and the Internet held 1 day of hearings on H.R. 1249. The hearing took place on March 30, 2011. Testimony was received from the Honorable David Kappos, Under Secretary of Commerce for Intellectual Property and Director of the United States Patent and Trademark Office; Steve Bartlett, President and CEO of The Financial Services

---

[62] *The Medicines Co. v. Kappos*, 731 F. Supp. 2d 470 (E.D. Va. 2010).

Roundtable; Steven Miller, President and General Counsel (Intellectual Property) for Procter & Gamble; Mark Chandler, Senior Vice President, General Counsel, and Secretary for Cisco; and John Vaughn, Executive Vice President of the Association of American Universities.

The Subcommittee also conducted three separate but related hearings on January 25, 2011 ("How an Improved US Patent and Trademark Office Can Create Jobs," Serial No. 112-6), February 11, 2011 ("Crossing the Finish Line on Patent Reform—What Can and Should be Done," Serial No. 112-8), and March 10, 2011 ("Review of Recent Judicial Decisions on Patent Law," Serial No. 112-20).

Given that the bill is a 6-year work in progress, the legislative record should also reflect that the Subcommittee conducted related hearings on patent reform in the 109th through 111th Congresses. These hearings include the following: "H.R. 2795, the 'Patent Reform Act of 2005' " (June 19, 2005); "Committee Print Regarding Patent Quality Improvement (Part I)" (April 20, 2005, Serial No. 109-11); "Committee Print Regarding Patent Quality Improvement (Part II)" (April 28, 2005, Serial No. 109-11); "Review of US Patent and Trademark Office Operations" (September 8, 2005, Serial No. 109-48); "Patent Quality Enhancement in the Information-Based Economy" (April 5, 2006, Serial No. 109-99); "Patent Harmonization" (April 26, 2006, Serial No. 109-100); "Patent Trolls: Fact or Fiction?" (June 15, 2006, Serial No. 109-104); "Oversight Hearing on the US Patent and Trademark Office" (February 27, 2008, Serial No. 110-115); "The 'Patent Reform Act of 2007' " (April 26, 2007, Serial No. 110-65); "H.R. 1260, The 'Patent Reform Act of 2009' " (April 30, 2009, Serial No. 111-92); and "The US Patent and Trademark Office" (May 5, 2010, Serial No. 111-135).

Finally, the United States Senate Committee on the Judiciary devoted substantial process to patent reform over the same time period. Beginning in 2005, the Senate Judiciary Committee conducted eight hearings on the subject and reported separate bills in the 110th (S. 1145), 111th (S. 515), and 112th (S. 23) Congresses. The full Senate passed S. 23 on March 8, 2011, by a vote of 95-5. H.R. 1249 is substantially similar to S. 23.

* * *

Section-by-Section

Section 1. Short title; table of contents.

This Act may be cited as the "America Invents Act."

Section 2. Definitions.

Section 2 defines the following terms: "Director," "Office," "Patent Public Advisory Committee," "Trademark Act of 1946," and "Trademark Public Advisory Committee."

Section 3. First inventor to file.

Subsection (a)—§ 100 is amended to include definitions for additional terms, including "effective filing date."

Subsection (b)—§ 102 is amended to make an invention's priority date its effective filing date. This change moves the United States to the first-to-file system. New section 102(b) preserves the grace period, ensuring that during the year prior to filing, an invention will not be rendered unpatentable based on any of the inventor's own disclosures, or any disclosure made by any party after the inventor has disclosed his invention to the public. Section 102(c) recodifies the CREATE Act, and section 102(d) defines the effective filing date of a patent or application that is cited as prior art to a claimed invention.

Subsection (c)—§ 103 is amended consistent with moving to a first-to-file system. Existing subsection (a) is amended slightly; subsection (b) is deleted because it is no longer needed; subsection (c), which is the CREATE Act, has been moved to § 102.

Subsection (d)—Repeals § 104 (Inventions Made Abroad).

Subsection (e)—Repeals § 157 (Statutory Invention Registration).

Subsection (f)—Amends § 120 related to filing dates to conform with the CREATE Act.

Subsection (g)—Makes various conforming amendments.

Subsections (h), (i) & (j)—Repeals interference proceeding and makes conforming changes to § 291. Amends § 135(a) and provides for a "derivation proceeding," designed to determine the inventor with the right to file an application on a claimed invention. An applicant requesting a derivation proceeding must set forth the basis for finding that an earlier applicant derived the claimed invention and without authorization filed an application claiming such invention. The request must be filed within 1 year of the date of first publication of an application for a claim that is substantially the same as the claimed invention. The Patent Trial and Appeal Board (the "Board") shall determine the right to patent and issue a final decision thereon. Decisions of the Board may be appealed to the Federal Circuit, or to district court pursuant to § 146.

Subsection (k)—Paragraph (1) amends § 32 of the Patent Act ("suspension or exclusion from practice") by placing time limitations on the commencement of a proceeding. Paragraph (2) imposes a reporting requirement on the Director regarding instances of misconduct before the agency and how they were addressed.

Subsection (l)—Contains a provision for a study regarding first-to- file to be conducted by the Small Business Administration and the USPTO.

Subsection (m)—Requires a study of prior user rights.

Subsection (n)—Contains an effective date provision.

Subsection (o)—Contains a study of patent litigation and its effect on the patent system.

Subsection (p)—Sets forth the sense of Congress that the first-to-file system promotes the purposes of Article I, section 8, clause 8, of the US Constitution.

Subsection (q)—Sets forth the sense of Congress that the first-to-file system promotes harmonization of the US and other patent systems.

Section 4. Inventor's oath or declaration.

The section streamlines the requirement that the inventor submit an oath as part of a patent application, and makes it easier for patent owners to file applications.

Subsection (a)—Section 115 is amended to permit an applicant to submit a substitute statement in lieu of the inventor's oath or declaration in certain circumstances, including if the inventor is (i) unable to do so, or (ii) unwilling to do so and is under an obligation to assign the invention. A savings clause provides that failure to comply with the requirements of this section will not be a basis for invalidity or unenforceability of the patent if the failure is remedied by a supplemental and corrected statement. False substitute statements are subject to the same penalties as false oaths and declarations.

Subsection (b)—Section 118 is amended to allow the person to whom the inventor has assigned (or is under an obligation to assign) the invention to file a patent application. A person who otherwise shows sufficient proprietary interest in the invention may file a patent application as an agent of the inventor to preserve the rights of the parties.

Section 5. Defense to infringement based on earlier inventor.

Section 5 amends § 273 of the Patent Act, which addresses prior user rights, as follows:

The prior-use defense may be asserted against any patent (not just methods), provided the person asserting the defense reduced the subject matter of the patent to practice and commercially used the subject matter at least 1 year before the effective filing date of the patent. However, the defense cannot be asserted if the subject matter was derived from the patent holder or persons in privity with the patent holder. Nor can the defense be asserted unless the prior user both reduced the subject matter of the patent to practice and commercially used it at least 1 year before the effective filing date of the patent or the date that the patentee publicly disclosed the invention and invoked the § 102(b) grace period, whichever is earlier.

Section 5 also clarifies that a person may not assert the defense if the subject matter of the patent on which the defense is based was developed pursuant to a funding agreement under Chapter 18 of the Patent Act (patent rights in inventions made with Federal assistance) or by a university or a technology transfer organization affiliated with a university that did not receive private business funding in support of the patent's development.

Finally, Section 5 states that the defense may only be asserted by the person who performed or caused the performance of the acts necessary to establish the defense, as well as any other entity that controls, is controlled by, or is under common control with such person; and except for any transfer to the patent owner, the right to assert the defense cannot be licensed or assigned or transferred to another person except as an ancillary and subordinate part of a good faith assignment or transfer for other reasons of the entire enterprise or line of [business] to which the defense relates.

Section 6. Post-grant review proceedings.

Subsections (a) and (d) enact new chapters 31 and 32, which create adjudicative systems of post-grant and inter partes review. The parallel sections of these new chapters are as follows:

§§ 311 and 321. Inter partes review may be sought on the basis of patents and printed publications any time after a post-grant review is concluded or, if no such review is instituted, after the time for seeking such review has expired. Post-grant review may be sought on any invalidity ground during the first 12 months after a patent is issue or reissued.

§§ 312 and 322. Petitions for review shall explain the basis for seeking review, shall identify the petitioner's real parties in interest and privies, and shall be made publicly available as soon as is practicable.

§§ 313 and 323. Patent owners may file a response to a petition for reviewing explaining why a review should not be instituted. §§ 314 and 324. Inter partes review shall not be instituted unless the information in the petition and response shows that there is a reasonable likelihood that a claim would be found invalid. Post-grant review shall not be instituted unless the information presented in the petition, if not rebutted, shows that it is more likely than not that a claim would be found invalid, or the petition raises a novel or unsettled legal question that is important to other patents or applications.

§§ 315 and 325. (a) Review may not be instituted if the petitioner has previously filed a civil action challenging the validity of the patent. The petitioner may, however, file a declaratory- judgment action challenging the validity of one or more claims in the patent on or after the day that he files the review petition, but such action is automatically stayed until the patent owner countersues for infringement.

(b) Inter partes review must be sought by a party within 12 months of the date when the party is served with a complaint for infringement. If a patent owner sues for infringement within 3 months of the patent's issue, a pending petition for postgrant review or the institution of such a proceeding may not serve as a basis for staying the court's consideration of the patent owner's motion for a preliminary injunction.

(c) The Director may allow other petitioners to join an inter partes or post-grant review.

(d) The Director may consolidate multiple proceedings or matters concerning the same patent and decline requests for repeated proceedings on the same question.

(e) Inter partes and post-grant petitioners are estopped from raising in a subsequent Office proceeding any issue that they raised or reasonably could have raised in the inter partes or post grant review, and inter partes petitioners are also estopped from raising in civil litigation or an ITC proceeding any issue that they raised or could have raised in the inter partes review. Post-grant petitioners are only estopped from raising in civil litigation or ITC proceedings those issues that they actually raised in the post-grant review.

(f) Post-grant review may not be used to challenge claims in a reissue patent that are the same as or narrower than claims in the original patent if the time for seeking review of the original patent has lapsed.

§§ 316 and 326. (a) The Director shall prescribe regulations that make the file in proceedings public; define standards for instituting reviews; allow submission of additional information; establish and govern review and its relationship to other proceedings; set a time limit for requesting joinder in inter partes review; set standards for discovery; prescribe sanctions for abuse of the proceedings; provide for protective orders for confidential information; allow the patent owner to file a response after an inter partes review has been instituted; allow the patent owner to amend the patent; provide either party with the right to an oral hearing; and set a 1-year time limit for completion of the proceeding, with a 6-month extension for good cause; and provide the petitioner with at least one opportunity to file written comments after the proceeding is instituted.

(b) In prescribing regulations, the Director shall consider the integrity of the patent system and the efficient operation of the Office.

(c) The Patent Trial and Appeal Board shall conduct review proceedings.

(d) The patent owner may submit one amendment with a reasonable number of substitute claims, and additional amendments either as agreed to by the parties for settlement, for good cause shown in post-grant review, or as prescribed in regulations by the Director in inter partes review.

(e) The challenger shall have the burden of providing unpatentability by a preponderance of the evidence.

§§ 317 and 327. Parties may agree to settle review proceedings, in which case estoppel shall not apply and a copy of the settlement agreement shall be filed in the Office.

§§ 318 and 328. The Patent Trial and Appeal Board shall issue a final written decision and a certificate cancelling, confirming, or incorporating claims.

§§ 319 and 329. A party dissatisfied with a final written decision may appeal to the U.S. Court of Appeals for the Federal Circuit.

Subsections (b) and (e) of section 5 make technical and conforming amendments.

Subsections (c) and (f) require the Director to issue regulations implementing the new reviews within 1 year, and create transition provisions for proceedings pending between the enactment of the Act and the full implementation of the new reviews.

Subsection (g) amends § 301 to include written statements of the patent owner filed in a proceedings before a Federal court or the Office as citable prior art. The section is further amended to provide rules for submitting such statements and the limitations on their use.

Subsection (h) amends § 303 to provide that the Director may determine whether to initiate reexamination on the Director's own initiative based on citations by any person other than the owner of the patent under section 301 or 302. Also, § 306 is amended to conform to the changes made by § 4605 of the American Inventors Protection Act of 1999, Public Law 10-113, to §§ 134 and 141 of title 35.

Section 7. Patent Trial and Appeal Board.

The Board of Patent Appeals and Interferences is replaced with the new Patent Trial and Appeal Board ("Board"). The Board is charged with (i) reviewing adverse decisions of examiners on applications and reexamination proceedings, (ii) conducting derivation proceedings, and (iii) conducting the post-grant review proceedings. This section also updates the various appeals statutes.

Section 8. Preissuance submissions by third parties.

This section amends § 122 to create a mechanism for third parties to submit timely pre-issuance information relevant to the examination of the application, including a concise statement of the relevance of the submission.

Section 9. Venue.

The venue for certain district court challenges of USPTO decisions is changed from the District of Columbia to the Eastern District of Virginia, the district where the USPTO resides.

Section 10. Fee-setting authority.

This section gives the Director rulemaking authority to set or adjust any fee under §§ 41 and 376, and section 1113 of title 15, provided that such fee amounts are set to reasonably compensate the USPTO for the services performed. The Director may also reduce such fees. The Director shall consult with the patent and trademark advisory committees as provided for in this section. Any proposal for a change in fees (including the rationale, purpose, and possible expectations or benefits that will result) shall be published in the Federal Register and shall seek public comment for a period of not less than 45 days. The Director shall notify Congress of any final proposed fee change and Congress shall have up to 45 days to consider and comment before any proposed fee change becomes effective.

Rules of construction are provided.

Section 11. Fees for patent services.

The Act includes the current patent fee schedule in the

text. This schedule represents a reference point for any future adjustments to the fee schedule by the Director.

Section 12. Supplemental examination.

This section authorizes a new § 257 of the Patent Act that addresses the "supplemental examination" of a patent to correct errors or omissions in proceedings before the Office. Information that was not considered or was inadequately considered or was incorrect can be presented to the Office.

Under new subsection (a) of § 257, the Director must initially determine whether a petitioner's request for supplemental examination of one or more items in the request raises a new question of patentability. The Director must make this determination within 3 months of receiving a request for supplemental examination.

Under new subsection (b), if the Director issues a certificate affirming that this threshold is met, a reexamination shall be ordered and will be conducted according to the procedures under Chapter 30 of the Patent Act (ex parte reexamination).

New Subsection (c) of § 257 stipulates that a patent cannot be held unenforceable on the basis of conduct relating to information that had not been considered, was inadequately considered, or was incorrect in a prior examination if the information was considered, reconsidered, or corrected during the supplemental examination. Challengers may still argue in court that the Office's conclusion in supplemental examination was erroneous and that the information renders the patent invalid, but the information cannot be used to render the patent invalid or unenforceable on the basis of inequitable conduct.

New subsection (c) also enumerates three exceptions to these terms: (1) prior allegations involving certain new drug applications (21 U.S.C. § 355(j)); (2) patent enforcement actions before the International Trade Commission or a US district court, unless the supplemental examination was concluded before the date on which the action is brought; and (3) instances in which fraud on the USPTO was practiced or attempted.

New subsection (d) of § 257 authorizes the Director to establish fees, by regulation, to help defray the cost of a supplemental examination, in addition to those charged pursuant to Chapter 30.

Finally, new subsection (e) clarifies that nothing in Section 12 limits the application of criminal or antitrust laws or the ability of the USPTO Director to investigate and sanction persons or their representatives for misconduct before the Office.

Section 13. Funding agreements.

Clause (i) of § 202(c)(7)(E) is amended to permit a non-profit organization that has a funding agreement for the operation of a Government- owned-contractor-operated facility to retain 85%, rather than 25% under current law, of licensing royalties in excess of the amount equal to 5% of the annual budget of the facility.

Section 14. Tax strategies deemed within the prior art.

This section provides that strategies for reducing, avoiding, or deferring tax liability shall be deemed insufficient to differentiate an invention from the prior art. In other words, applicants will no longer be able to rely on the novelty or non-obviousness of a tax strategy embodied in their claims in order to distinguish their claims from the prior art under the statutory novelty and non-obviousness requirements of those provisions.

Under the provision, the term "tax liability" refers to any liability for a tax under any Federal, State, or local law, or law of any foreign jurisdiction, including any statute, rule, regulation, or ordinance that levies, imposes, or assesses such tax liability.

The provision is directed to tax strategies, which are a subset of business methods, and is not intended to deny patent protection for an invention that consists of tax preparation software or other tools used solely to enter data on tax or information returns or any other filing required by a tax authority. Thus, a software program that is novel and non-obvious as software would not be affected by this section even though the software is used for a tax purpose. A prior-art software program, however, could not overcome the section 102 and 103 hurdles by implementing a novel and non-obvious strategy for reducing, avoiding, or deferring taxes.

There may be situations in which some aspects of an invention are separable from the tax strategy. In this case, any claim that encompasses a tax strategy will be subject to the provision and the novelty or non-obviousness of the tax strategy will be deemed insufficient to differentiate that claim from the prior art. However, any claim that does not involve a tax strategy would not be within the scope of the provision. In such a case, if the invention includes claims that are separable from the tax strategy, such claims could, if otherwise enforceable, be enforced.

Inventions that fall within the scope of the provision include those especially suitable for use with tax-favored structures that must meet certain requirements, such as employee benefit plans, tax-exempt organizations, or any other entities that must be structured or operated in a particular manner to obtain certain tax consequences. Thus, the provision applies if the effect of an invention is to aid in satisfying the qualification requirements for the desired tax-favored entity status, to take advantage of the specific tax benefits offered in a tax-favored structure, or to allow for tax reduction, avoidance, or deferral not otherwise automatically available in such entity or structure.

In general, the USPTO may seek advice and assistance from Treasury and the IRS to better recognize tax strategies. Such consultations should help ensure that patents do not infringe on the ability of others to interpret the tax law and that implementing such interpretations remains in the public domain, available to all taxpayers and their advisors.

Section 15. Best Mode Requirement.

This section amends § 282(b) by removing the failure to disclose the best mode under section 112 as a basis for canceling or holding either invalid or unenforceable a patent claim.

Section 16. Marking.

Subsection (a) addresses virtual marking. The provision allows a patent holder to satisfy the requirements of § 287 of the Patent Act by affixing to a patented article the word "patent" or the abbreviation "pat." together with an Internet address that the public can access free of charge to determine the status of the patent. The USPTO is also instructed to submit a report to Congress on the effectiveness of virtual marking that is due no later than 3 years after the date of enactment.

Subsection (b) addresses false marking in the following ways: (1) Only the United States may sue for the qui tam penalty under the subsection. (2) A person who has suffered a competitive injury as a result of a violation may still bring a civil action in US district court for compensatory damages. (3) Persons or companies otherwise liable under § 292 (the false marking statute) are protected during a 3-year window beginning on the date the patent at issue expires. Beyond the 3-year window, persons or companies are also protected if they place the word "patent" or "patented", the abbreviation "pat.", or the patent number either on the article or through an Internet posting, consistent with the amendments in subsection (a).

Section 17. Advice of Counsel.

Section 17 creates a new § 298 of the Patent Act that states that the failure of an infringer to obtain the advice of counsel regarding any allegedly infringed patent, or the failure of the infringer to present such advice to the court or jury, may not be used to prove that the accused infringer willfully infringed the patent or that the infringer intended to induce infringement of the patent.

Section 18. Transitional program for covered business method patents.

Section 18 creates a transitional program to allow post-grant review of the validity of business method patents.

Under subsection (a), the Director is authorized to establish regulations governing the use of the new proceeding, which will be modeled after post-grant review as set forth in Section 6 (new Chapter 32 of the Patent Act). The proceeding is limited in certain respects. A petition cannot be accepted unless the petitioner or his real party in interest has been sued for infringement of the patent or has been charged with infringement. Nor can the petitioner or his real party in interest later assert invalidity before the ITC or a Federal court on a ground that was considered and resulted in a written decision by the agency in the course of a transitional proceeding.

The program takes effect 1 year following the date of enactment and applies to any covered business method patent issued before, on, or after the effective date, with the exception of a patent that satisfies the requirements of § 321(c) of the Patent Act as set forth in Section 6 of the bill. The program sunsets after 10 years.

Subsection (b) addresses requests for a stay of a civil action alleging infringement under § 281 of the Patent Act. A US district court shall decide to grant a stay based on prescribed criteria: (A) whether a stay (or denial thereof) will simplify the issues in question and streamline the trial; (B) whether discovery is complete and whether a trial date has been set; (C) whether a stay (or a denial thereof) would unduly prejudice the non-moving party or present a clear tactical advantage for the moving party; and (D) whether a stay (or the denial thereof) will reduce the burden of litigation on the parties and on the court. A party may seek an interlocutory appeal of the US district court's decision, which the Federal Circuit shall review to ensure consistent application of established precedent, and such review may be de novo.

Subsection (c) deems that in an action for infringement under § 281 of a covered business method patent, an automated teller machine ("ATM") shall not be considered a regular and established place of business for purposes of the patent venue statute.

Subsection (d) defines "covered business method patent" as one that claims a method or corresponding apparatus for performing data processing or other operations used in the practice, administration, or management of a financial product or service, except that it does not include patents for technological inventions.

Finally, subsection (e) clarifies that nothing in Section 18 shall be construed as amending or interpreting categories of patent-eligible subject matter under § 101 of the Patent Act.

Section 19. Jurisdiction and procedural matters.

Subsection (a) through (d) enact the so-called Holmes Group fix (H.R. 2955, 109th Congress), which the House Judiciary Committee reported favorably in 2006. The Committee Report accompanying H.R. 2955 (House Rep. 109-407), which we reaffirm, explains the bill's reasons for abrogating *Holmes Group, Inc. v. Vornado Air Circulation Systems, Inc.*, 535 U.S. 826 (2002), and more fully precluding state court jurisdiction over patent legal claims.

Subsection (e) creates a new § 299 of the Patent Act that addresses joinder of accused infringers in patent actions or trials not involving certain drugs and biologics. Parties accused as defendants may be joined in one action as defendants or counterclaim defendants only if: (1) any right to relief is asserted against the parties jointly, severally, or in the alternative with respect to or arising out of the same transaction, occurrence, or series of transactions or occurrences relating to the making, using, importing into the United States, offering for sale, or selling of the same accused product or process; and (2) questions of fact common to all defendants or counterclaim defendants will arise in the action.

For purposes of subsection (e), accused infringers may not be joined based solely on allegations that they each have infringed the patent or patents in suit.

The changes set forth in Section 19 shall apply to any civil action commenced on or after the date of enactment of the Act.

Section 20. Technical amendments.

This section sets forth technical amendments consistent with this Act.

Section 21. Travel expenses and payment of administrative judges.

Subsection (a) authorizes the USPTO to expend funds to cover the subsistence and travel-related expenses of non-Federal employees attending intellectual property programs hosted by the agency.

Subsection (b) authorizes the Director to fix the rate of basic pay for administrative patent and trademark judges at a rate not greater than that payable for level III of the Executive Pay Schedule under 5 U.S.C. § 5314.

Section 22. Patent and Trademark Office funding.

Subsections (a) defines the "United State Patent and Trademark Office Public Enterprise Fund" ("the Fund") that replaces the existing "Patent and Trademark Office Appropriation Account."

Subsection (b) clarifies the USPTO Director's authority under the new Fund to collect all patent and trademark user fee revenue, which shall be available to the agency until expended. This change shall take effect on the later of October 1, 2011, or the first day of the first fiscal year that begins after the date of the enactment of the Act.

Subsection (c) establishes the Fund as a revolving fund in the US Treasury. Any amounts in the Fund shall be available for use by the Director without fiscal year limitation. Patent and trademark fees deposited in the Fund shall be recorded as offsetting receipts. Amounts deposited in the Fund shall be available, without fiscal year limitation, to cover all expenses determined in the discretion of the Director to be ordinary and reasonable.

Subsection (d) requires the Director, not later than 60 days after the end of each fiscal year, to submit a report to Congress that summarizes the USPTO operations for the preceding fiscal year, details the operating plan of the agency, describes its long-term modernization plans as well as any progress made toward modernization efforts in the previous fiscal year, and includes the results of the most recent audit as carried out by subsection (f).

Not later than 30 days after the beginning of each fiscal year, subsection (e) instructs the Director to notify the Committees on Appropriations of both houses of Congress of the plan for the obligation and expenditure of the total amount of the funds for that fiscal year under Public Law 109-108.

Subsection (f) mandates that the Director annually shall provide for an independent audit of the financial statement of the USPTO.

Subsection (g) requires the Director to prepare and submit to the President an annual "business-type" budget for the Fund as the President prescribes by regulation for the Federal Budget.

Section 23. Satellite offices.

Pursuant to subsection (a), and subject to available resources, the Director shall establish three or more satellite offices in the United States to carry out the responsibilities of the USPTO. The Director has 3 years after the date of enactment of the Act to complete the task.

Subject (b) enumerates the purposes of the satellite offices, including efforts to increase outreach activities, enhance patent examiner retention, and improve the quality of patent examination.

Subsection (c) details the required considerations the Director must invoke in selecting each location. Among the criteria are geographic diversity among the offices and reliance upon previous evaluations.

Not later than three fiscal years after the date of enactment of the Act, Subsection (d) requires the Director to submit a report to Congress on the rationale of the Director in selecting the location of any satellite office, the progress in establishing any satellite offices so selected, and whether the operation of any existing satellite office is achieving the purposes set forth in subsection (b).

Section 24. Designation of the Detroit satellite office.

Section 24 designates the USPTO satellite office to be located in Detroit, Michigan, as the "Elijah J. McCoy United States Patent and Trademark Office."

Section 25. Patent Ombudsman Program for small business concerns.

Section 25 states that, using available resources, the Director shall establish and maintain in the USPTO a Patent Ombudsman Program, whose staff shall provide support and services relating to patent filings to small business concerns.

Section 26. Priority examination for technologies important to American competitiveness.

Section 26 amends § 2(b)(2) of the Patent Act by permitting the USPTO to prioritize the examination of applications for products, processes, or technologies that are important to the national economy or national competitiveness without recovering the aggregate extra cost of providing such prioritization.

Section 27. Calculation of 60-day period for application of patent term extension.

Subsection (a) clarifies USPTO "counting" rules that are used to determine whether an applicant has submitted an application to the agency in a timely manner under § 156(d)(1) of the Patent Act. If the application is transmitted after 4:30 pm, EST, on a business day, or is transmitted on a day that is not a business day, the product addressed by the application shall be deemed to receive "permission" on the next business day. "Business day" means any Monday, Tuesday, Wednesday, Thursday, or Friday, excluding any legal holiday under 5 U.S.C. § 6103.

Subsection (b) states that subsection (a) shall apply to any application for extension of term under § 156 of the Patent Act that is pending on, filed after, or as to which a decision regarding the application is subject judicial review on, the date of enactment of the Act.

Section 28. Study on implementation.

Subsection (a) requires the Director to conduct a study on the manner in which the Act is being implemented by the USPTO, along with a review of patent policies and practices of the Federal

Government with respect to patent rights, US innovation, access by small business to capital, and other issues as the Director deems appropriate.

Subsection (b) stipulates that the Director shall submit the results of the study along with his recommendations for any changes to the Senate and House Judiciary Committees not later than 4 years after the date of enactment of the Act.

Section 29. Pro bono program.

Section 29 requires the Director to work with and support intellectual law associations across the country to establish pro bono programs to assist financially under-resourced independent inventors and small businesses.

Section 30. Effective date.

Except as otherwise provided, this Act takes effect 12 months after the date of enactment and applies to any patent issued on or after that effective date.

Section 31. Budgetary effects.

Section 31 references text from S. 23 regarding the budgetary effects of the Act as it pertains to PAYGO compliance.

APPENDIX 2

The Leahy-Smith America Invents Act

One Hundred Twelfth Congress of the United States of America

AT THE FIRST SESSION

Begun and held at the City of Washington on Wednesday, the fifth day of January, two thousand and eleven

An Act

To amend title 35, United States Code, to provide for patent reform.

Be it enacted by the Senate and House of Representatives of the United States of America in Congress assembled,

SECTION 1. SHORT TITLE; TABLE OF CONTENTS.

(a) SHORT TITLE.—This Act may be cited as the "Leahy-Smith America Invents Act".

(b) TABLE OF CONTENTS.—The table of contents for this Act is as follows:

SEC. 2. DEFINITIONS.

In this Act:

(1) DIRECTOR.—The term "Director" means the Under Secretary of Commerce for Intellectual Property and Director of the United States Patent and Trademark Office.

(2) Office.—The term "Office" means the United States Patent and Trademark Office.

(3) Patent public advisory committee.—The term "Patent Public Advisory Committee" means the Patent Public Advisory Committee established under section 5(a) of title 35, United States Code.

(4) Trademark act of 1946.—The term "Trademark Act of 1946" means the Act entitled "An Act to provide for the registration and protection of trademarks used in commerce, to carry out the provisions of certain international conventions, and for other purposes", approved July 5, 1946 (15 U.S.C. 1051 et seq.) (commonly referred to as the "Trademark Act of 1946" or the "Lanham Act").

(5) Trademark public advisory committee.—The term "Trademark Public Advisory Committee" means the Trademark Public Advisory Committee established under section 5(a) of title 35, United States Code.

SEC. 3. FIRST INVENTOR TO FILE.

(a) Definitions.—Section 100 of title 35, United States Code, is amended—

(1) in subsection (e), by striking "or inter partes reexamination under section 311"; and

(2) by adding at the end the following:

"(f) The term 'inventor' means the individual or, if a joint invention, the individuals collectively who invented or discovered the subject matter of the invention.

"(g) The terms 'joint inventor' and 'coinventor' mean any 1 of the individuals who invented or discovered the subject matter of a joint invention.

"(h) The term 'joint research agreement' means a written contract, grant, or cooperative agreement entered into by 2 or more persons or entities for the performance of experimental, developmental, or research work in the field of the claimed invention.

"(i)(1) The term 'effective filing date' for a claimed invention in a patent or application for patent means—

"(A) if subparagraph (B) does not apply, the actual filing date of the patent or the application for the patent containing a claim to the invention; or

"(B) the filing date of the earliest application for which the patent or application is entitled, as to such invention, to a right of priority under section 119, 365(a), or 365(b) or to the benefit of an earlier filing date under section 120, 121, or 365(c).

"(2) The effective filing date for a claimed invention in an application for reissue or reissued patent shall be determined by deeming the claim to the invention to have been contained in the patent for which reissue was sought.

"(j) The term 'claimed invention' means the subject matter defined by a claim in a patent or an application for a patent.".

(b) Conditions for Patentability.—

(1) In general.—Section 102 of title 35, United States Code, is amended to read as follows:

"§ 102. Conditions for patentability; novelty

"(a) Novelty; Prior Art.—A person shall be entitled to a patent unless—

H. R. 1249—3

"(1) the claimed invention was patented, described in a printed publication, or in public use, on sale, or otherwise available to the public before the effective filing date of the claimed invention; or

"(2) the claimed invention was described in a patent issued under section 151, or in an application for patent published or deemed published under section 122(b), in which the patent or application, as the case may be, names another inventor and was effectively filed before the effective filing date of the claimed invention.

"(b) EXCEPTIONS.—

"(1) DISCLOSURES MADE 1 YEAR OR LESS BEFORE THE EFFECTIVE FILING DATE OF THE CLAIMED INVENTION.—A disclosure made 1 year or less before the effective filing date of a claimed invention shall not be prior art to the claimed invention under subsection (a)(1) if—

"(A) the disclosure was made by the inventor or joint inventor or by another who obtained the subject matter disclosed directly or indirectly from the inventor or a joint inventor; or

"(B) the subject matter disclosed had, before such disclosure, been publicly disclosed by the inventor or a joint inventor or another who obtained the subject matter disclosed directly or indirectly from the inventor or a joint inventor.

"(2) DISCLOSURES APPEARING IN APPLICATIONS AND PATENTS.—A disclosure shall not be prior art to a claimed invention under subsection (a)(2) if—

"(A) the subject matter disclosed was obtained directly or indirectly from the inventor or a joint inventor;

"(B) the subject matter disclosed had, before such subject matter was effectively filed under subsection (a)(2), been publicly disclosed by the inventor or a joint inventor or another who obtained the subject matter disclosed directly or indirectly from the inventor or a joint inventor; or

"(C) the subject matter disclosed and the claimed invention, not later than the effective filing date of the claimed invention, were owned by the same person or subject to an obligation of assignment to the same person.

"(c) COMMON OWNERSHIP UNDER JOINT RESEARCH AGREEMENTS.—Subject matter disclosed and a claimed invention shall be deemed to have been owned by the same person or subject to an obligation of assignment to the same person in applying the provisions of subsection (b)(2)(C) if—

"(1) the subject matter disclosed was developed and the claimed invention was made by, or on behalf of, 1 or more parties to a joint research agreement that was in effect on or before the effective filing date of the claimed invention;

"(2) the claimed invention was made as a result of activities undertaken within the scope of the joint research agreement; and

"(3) the application for patent for the claimed invention discloses or is amended to disclose the names of the parties to the joint research agreement.

"(d) PATENTS AND PUBLISHED APPLICATIONS EFFECTIVE AS PRIOR ART.—For purposes of determining whether a patent or

H. R. 1249—4

application for patent is prior art to a claimed invention under subsection (a)(2), such patent or application shall be considered to have been effectively filed, with respect to any subject matter described in the patent or application—

"(1) if paragraph (2) does not apply, as of the actual filing date of the patent or the application for patent; or

"(2) if the patent or application for patent is entitled to claim a right of priority under section 119, 365(a), or 365(b), or to claim the benefit of an earlier filing date under section 120, 121, or 365(c), based upon 1 or more prior filed applications for patent, as of the filing date of the earliest such application that describes the subject matter.".

(2) CONTINUITY OF INTENT UNDER THE CREATE ACT.—The enactment of section 102(c) of title 35, United States Code, under paragraph (1) of this subsection is done with the same intent to promote joint research activities that was expressed, including in the legislative history, through the enactment of the Cooperative Research and Technology Enhancement Act of 2004 (Public Law 108–453; the "CREATE Act"), the amendments of which are stricken by subsection (c) of this section. The United States Patent and Trademark Office shall administer section 102(c) of title 35, United States Code, in a manner consistent with the legislative history of the CREATE Act that was relevant to its administration by the United States Patent and Trademark Office.

(3) CONFORMING AMENDMENT.—The item relating to section 102 in the table of sections for chapter 10 of title 35, United States Code, is amended to read as follows:

"102. Conditions for patentability; novelty.".

(c) CONDITIONS FOR PATENTABILITY; NONOBVIOUS SUBJECT MATTER.—Section 103 of title 35, United States Code, is amended to read as follows:

"§ 103. Conditions for patentability; non-obvious subject matter

"A patent for a claimed invention may not be obtained, notwithstanding that the claimed invention is not identically disclosed as set forth in section 102, if the differences between the claimed invention and the prior art are such that the claimed invention as a whole would have been obvious before the effective filing date of the claimed invention to a person having ordinary skill in the art to which the claimed invention pertains. Patentability shall not be negated by the manner in which the invention was made.".

(d) REPEAL OF REQUIREMENTS FOR INVENTIONS MADE ABROAD.—Section 104 of title 35, United States Code, and the item relating to that section in the table of sections for chapter 10 of title 35, United States Code, are repealed.

(e) REPEAL OF STATUTORY INVENTION REGISTRATION.—

(1) IN GENERAL.—Section 157 of title 35, United States Code, and the item relating to that section in the table of sections for chapter 14 of title 35, United States Code, are repealed.

(2) REMOVAL OF CROSS REFERENCES.—Section 111(b)(8) of title 35, United States Code, is amended by striking "sections 115, 131, 135, and 157" and inserting "sections 131 and 135".

H. R. 1249—5

(3) EFFECTIVE DATE.—The amendments made by this subsection shall take effect upon the expiration of the 18-month period beginning on the date of the enactment of this Act, and shall apply to any request for a statutory invention registration filed on or after that effective date.

(f) EARLIER FILING DATE FOR INVENTOR AND JOINT INVENTOR.—Section 120 of title 35, United States Code, is amended by striking "which is filed by an inventor or inventors named" and inserting "which names an inventor or joint inventor".

(g) CONFORMING AMENDMENTS.—

(1) RIGHT OF PRIORITY.—Section 172 of title 35, United States Code, is amended by striking "and the time specified in section 102(d)".

(2) LIMITATION ON REMEDIES.—Section 287(c)(4) of title 35, United States Code, is amended by striking "the earliest effective filing date of which is prior to" and inserting "which has an effective filing date before".

(3) INTERNATIONAL APPLICATION DESIGNATING THE UNITED STATES: EFFECT.—Section 363 of title 35, United States Code, is amended by striking "except as otherwise provided in section 102(e) of this title".

(4) PUBLICATION OF INTERNATIONAL APPLICATION: EFFECT.—Section 374 of title 35, United States Code, is amended by striking "sections 102(e) and 154(d)" and inserting "section 154(d)".

(5) PATENT ISSUED ON INTERNATIONAL APPLICATION: EFFECT.—The second sentence of section 375(a) of title 35, United States Code, is amended by striking "Subject to section 102(e) of this title, such" and inserting "Such".

(6) LIMIT ON RIGHT OF PRIORITY.—Section 119(a) of title 35, United States Code, is amended by striking "; but no patent shall be granted" and all that follows through "one year prior to such filing".

(7) INVENTIONS MADE WITH FEDERAL ASSISTANCE.—Section 202(c) of title 35, United States Code, is amended—

(A) in paragraph (2)—

(i) by striking "publication, on sale, or public use," and all that follows through "obtained in the United States" and inserting "the 1-year period referred to in section 102(b) would end before the end of that 2-year period"; and

(ii) by striking "prior to the end of the statutory" and inserting "before the end of that 1-year"; and

(B) in paragraph (3), by striking "any statutory bar date that may occur under this title due to publication, on sale, or public use" and inserting "the expiration of the 1-year period referred to in section 102(b)".

(h) DERIVED PATENTS.—

(1) IN GENERAL.—Section 291 of title 35, United States Code, is amended to read as follows:

"§ 291. Derived Patents

"(a) IN GENERAL.—The owner of a patent may have relief by civil action against the owner of another patent that claims the same invention and has an earlier effective filing date, if the invention claimed in such other patent was derived from the inventor of the invention claimed in the patent owned by the person seeking relief under this section.

"(b) FILING LIMITATION.—An action under this section may be filed only before the end of the 1-year period beginning on the date of the issuance of the first patent containing a claim to the allegedly derived invention and naming an individual alleged to have derived such invention as the inventor or joint inventor.".

(2) CONFORMING AMENDMENT.—The item relating to section 291 in the table of sections for chapter 29 of title 35, United States Code, is amended to read as follows:

"291. Derived patents.".

(i) DERIVATION PROCEEDINGS.—Section 135 of title 35, United States Code, is amended to read as follows:

"§ 135. Derivation proceedings

"(a) INSTITUTION OF PROCEEDING.—An applicant for patent may file a petition to institute a derivation proceeding in the Office. The petition shall set forth with particularity the basis for finding that an inventor named in an earlier application derived the claimed invention from an inventor named in the petitioner's application and, without authorization, the earlier application claiming such invention was filed. Any such petition may be filed only within the 1-year period beginning on the date of the first publication of a claim to an invention that is the same or substantially the same as the earlier application's claim to the invention, shall be made under oath, and shall be supported by substantial evidence. Whenever the Director determines that a petition filed under this subsection demonstrates that the standards for instituting a derivation proceeding are met, the Director may institute a derivation proceeding. The determination by the Director whether to institute a derivation proceeding shall be final and nonappealable.

"(b) DETERMINATION BY PATENT TRIAL AND APPEAL BOARD.—In a derivation proceeding instituted under subsection (a), the Patent Trial and Appeal Board shall determine whether an inventor named in the earlier application derived the claimed invention from an inventor named in the petitioner's application and, without authorization, the earlier application claiming such invention was filed. In appropriate circumstances, the Patent Trial and Appeal Board may correct the naming of the inventor in any application or patent at issue. The Director shall prescribe regulations setting forth standards for the conduct of derivation proceedings, including requiring parties to provide sufficient evidence to prove and rebut a claim of derivation.

"(c) DEFERRAL OF DECISION.—The Patent Trial and Appeal Board may defer action on a petition for a derivation proceeding until the expiration of the 3-month period beginning on the date on which the Director issues a patent that includes the claimed invention that is the subject of the petition. The Patent Trial and Appeal Board also may defer action on a petition for a derivation proceeding, or stay the proceeding after it has been instituted, until the termination of a proceeding under chapter 30, 31, or 32 involving the patent of the earlier applicant.

"(d) EFFECT OF FINAL DECISION.—The final decision of the Patent Trial and Appeal Board, if adverse to claims in an application for patent, shall constitute the final refusal by the Office on those claims. The final decision of the Patent Trial and Appeal

H. R. 1249—7

Board, if adverse to claims in a patent, shall, if no appeal or other review of the decision has been or can be taken or had, constitute cancellation of those claims, and notice of such cancellation shall be endorsed on copies of the patent distributed after such cancellation.

"(e) SETTLEMENT.—Parties to a proceeding instituted under subsection (a) may terminate the proceeding by filing a written statement reflecting the agreement of the parties as to the correct inventors of the claimed invention in dispute. Unless the Patent Trial and Appeal Board finds the agreement to be inconsistent with the evidence of record, if any, it shall take action consistent with the agreement. Any written settlement or understanding of the parties shall be filed with the Director. At the request of a party to the proceeding, the agreement or understanding shall be treated as business confidential information, shall be kept separate from the file of the involved patents or applications, and shall be made available only to Government agencies on written request, or to any person on a showing of good cause.

"(f) ARBITRATION.—Parties to a proceeding instituted under subsection (a) may, within such time as may be specified by the Director by regulation, determine such contest or any aspect thereof by arbitration. Such arbitration shall be governed by the provisions of title 9, to the extent such title is not inconsistent with this section. The parties shall give notice of any arbitration award to the Director, and such award shall, as between the parties to the arbitration, be dispositive of the issues to which it relates. The arbitration award shall be unenforceable until such notice is given. Nothing in this subsection shall preclude the Director from determining the patentability of the claimed inventions involved in the proceeding.".

(j) ELIMINATION OF REFERENCES TO INTERFERENCES.—(1) Sections 134, 145, 146, 154, and 305 of title 35, United States Code, are each amended by striking "Board of Patent Appeals and Interferences" each place it appears and inserting "Patent Trial and Appeal Board".

(2)(A) Section 146 of title 35, United States Code, is amended—

(i) by striking "an interference" and inserting "a derivation proceeding"; and

(ii) by striking "the interference" and inserting "the derivation proceeding".

(B) The subparagraph heading for section 154(b)(1)(C) of title 35, United States Code, is amended to read as follows:

"(C) GUARANTEE OF ADJUSTMENTS FOR DELAYS DUE TO DERIVATION PROCEEDINGS, SECRECY ORDERS, AND APPEALS.—".

(3) The section heading for section 134 of title 35, United States Code, is amended to read as follows:

"§ 134. Appeal to the Patent Trial and Appeal Board".

(4) The section heading for section 146 of title 35, United States Code, is amended to read as follows:

H. R. 1249—8

"§ 146. Civil action in case of derivation proceeding".

(5) The items relating to sections 134 and 135 in the table of sections for chapter 12 of title 35, United States Code, are amended to read as follows:

"134. Appeal to the Patent Trial and Appeal Board.
"135. Derivation proceedings.".

(6) The item relating to section 146 in the table of sections for chapter 13 of title 35, United States Code, is amended to read as follows:

"146. Civil action in case of derivation proceeding.".

(k) STATUTE OF LIMITATIONS.—

(1) IN GENERAL.—Section 32 of title 35, United States Code, is amended by inserting between the third and fourth sentences the following: "A proceeding under this section shall be commenced not later than the earlier of either the date that is 10 years after the date on which the misconduct forming the basis for the proceeding occurred, or 1 year after the date on which the misconduct forming the basis for the proceeding is made known to an officer or employee of the Office as prescribed in the regulations established under section 2(b)(2)(D).".

(2) REPORT TO CONGRESS.—The Director shall provide on a biennial basis to the Judiciary Committees of the Senate and House of Representatives a report providing a short description of incidents made known to an officer or employee of the Office as prescribed in the regulations established under section 2(b)(2)(D) of title 35, United States Code, that reflect substantial evidence of misconduct before the Office but for which the Office was barred from commencing a proceeding under section 32 of title 35, United States Code, by the time limitation established by the fourth sentence of that section.

(3) EFFECTIVE DATE.—The amendment made by paragraph (1) shall apply in any case in which the time period for instituting a proceeding under section 32 of title 35, United States Code, had not lapsed before the date of the enactment of this Act.

(l) SMALL BUSINESS STUDY.—

(1) DEFINITIONS.—In this subsection—

(A) the term "Chief Counsel" means the Chief Counsel for Advocacy of the Small Business Administration;

(B) the term "General Counsel" means the General Counsel of the United States Patent and Trademark Office; and

(C) the term "small business concern" has the meaning given that term under section 3 of the Small Business Act (15 U.S.C. 632).

(2) STUDY.—

(A) IN GENERAL.—The Chief Counsel, in consultation with the General Counsel, shall conduct a study of the effects of eliminating the use of dates of invention in determining whether an applicant is entitled to a patent under title 35, United States Code.

(B) AREAS OF STUDY.—The study conducted under subparagraph (A) shall include examination of the effects of eliminating the use of invention dates, including examining—

(i) how the change would affect the ability of small business concerns to obtain patents and their costs of obtaining patents;

(ii) whether the change would create, mitigate, or exacerbate any disadvantages for applicants for patents that are small business concerns relative to applicants for patents that are not small business concerns, and whether the change would create any advantages for applicants for patents that are small business concerns relative to applicants for patents that are not small business concerns;

(iii) the cost savings and other potential benefits to small business concerns of the change; and

(iv) the feasibility and costs and benefits to small business concerns of alternative means of determining whether an applicant is entitled to a patent under title 35, United States Code.

(3) REPORT.—Not later than the date that is 1 year after the date of the enactment of this Act, the Chief Counsel shall submit to the Committee on Small Business and Entrepreneurship and the Committee on the Judiciary of the Senate and the Committee on Small Business and the Committee on the Judiciary of the House of Representatives a report on the results of the study under paragraph (2).

(m) REPORT ON PRIOR USER RIGHTS.—

(1) IN GENERAL.—Not later than the end of the 4-month period beginning on the date of the enactment of this Act, the Director shall report, to the Committee on the Judiciary of the Senate and the Committee on the Judiciary of the House of Representatives, the findings and recommendations of the Director on the operation of prior user rights in selected countries in the industrialized world. The report shall include the following:

(A) A comparison between patent laws of the United States and the laws of other industrialized countries, including members of the European Union and Japan, Canada, and Australia.

(B) An analysis of the effect of prior user rights on innovation rates in the selected countries.

(C) An analysis of the correlation, if any, between prior user rights and start-up enterprises and the ability to attract venture capital to start new companies.

(D) An analysis of the effect of prior user rights, if any, on small businesses, universities, and individual inventors.

(E) An analysis of legal and constitutional issues, if any, that arise from placing trade secret law in patent law.

(F) An analysis of whether the change to a first-to-file patent system creates a particular need for prior user rights.

(2) CONSULTATION WITH OTHER AGENCIES.—In preparing the report required under paragraph (1), the Director shall consult with the United States Trade Representative, the Secretary of State, and the Attorney General.

H. R. 1249—10

(n) EFFECTIVE DATE.—

(1) IN GENERAL.—Except as otherwise provided in this section, the amendments made by this section shall take effect upon the expiration of the 18-month period beginning on the date of the enactment of this Act, and shall apply to any application for patent, and to any patent issuing thereon, that contains or contained at any time—

(A) a claim to a claimed invention that has an effective filing date as defined in section 100(i) of title 35, United States Code, that is on or after the effective date described in this paragraph; or

(B) a specific reference under section 120, 121, or 365(c) of title 35, United States Code, to any patent or application that contains or contained at any time such a claim.

(2) INTERFERING PATENTS.—The provisions of sections 102(g), 135, and 291 of title 35, United States Code, as in effect on the day before the effective date set forth in paragraph (1) of this subsection, shall apply to each claim of an application for patent, and any patent issued thereon, for which the amendments made by this section also apply, if such application or patent contains or contained at any time—

(A) a claim to an invention having an effective filing date as defined in section 100(i) of title 35, United States Code, that occurs before the effective date set forth in paragraph (1) of this subsection; or

(B) a specific reference under section 120, 121, or 365(c) of title 35, United States Code, to any patent or application that contains or contained at any time such a claim.

(o) SENSE OF CONGRESS.—It is the sense of the Congress that converting the United States patent system from "first to invent" to a system of "first inventor to file" will promote the progress of science and the useful arts by securing for limited times to inventors the exclusive rights to their discoveries and provide inventors with greater certainty regarding the scope of protection provided by the grant of exclusive rights to their discoveries.

(p) SENSE OF CONGRESS.—It is the sense of the Congress that converting the United States patent system from "first to invent" to a system of "first inventor to file" will improve the United States patent system and promote harmonization of the United States patent system with the patent systems commonly used in nearly all other countries throughout the world with whom the United States conducts trade and thereby promote greater international uniformity and certainty in the procedures used for securing the exclusive rights of inventors to their discoveries.

SEC. 4. INVENTOR'S OATH OR DECLARATION.

(a) INVENTOR'S OATH OR DECLARATION.—

(1) IN GENERAL.—Section 115 of title 35, United States Code, is amended to read as follows:

"§ 115. Inventor's oath or declaration

"(a) NAMING THE INVENTOR; INVENTOR'S OATH OR DECLARATION.—An application for patent that is filed under section 111(a) or commences the national stage under section 371 shall include, or be amended to include, the name of the inventor for any invention claimed in the application. Except as otherwise provided in this section, each individual who is the inventor or a joint inventor

H. R. 1249—11

of a claimed invention in an application for patent shall execute an oath or declaration in connection with the application.

"(b) REQUIRED STATEMENTS.—An oath or declaration under subsection (a) shall contain statements that—

"(1) the application was made or was authorized to be made by the affiant or declarant; and

"(2) such individual believes himself or herself to be the original inventor or an original joint inventor of a claimed invention in the application.

"(c) ADDITIONAL REQUIREMENTS.—The Director may specify additional information relating to the inventor and the invention that is required to be included in an oath or declaration under subsection (a).

"(d) SUBSTITUTE STATEMENT.—

"(1) IN GENERAL.—In lieu of executing an oath or declaration under subsection (a), the applicant for patent may provide a substitute statement under the circumstances described in paragraph (2) and such additional circumstances that the Director may specify by regulation.

"(2) PERMITTED CIRCUMSTANCES.—A substitute statement under paragraph (1) is permitted with respect to any individual who—

"(A) is unable to file the oath or declaration under subsection (a) because the individual—

"(i) is deceased;

"(ii) is under legal incapacity; or

"(iii) cannot be found or reached after diligent effort; or

"(B) is under an obligation to assign the invention but has refused to make the oath or declaration required under subsection (a).

"(3) CONTENTS.—A substitute statement under this subsection shall—

"(A) identify the individual with respect to whom the statement applies;

"(B) set forth the circumstances representing the permitted basis for the filing of the substitute statement in lieu of the oath or declaration under subsection (a); and

"(C) contain any additional information, including any showing, required by the Director.

"(e) MAKING REQUIRED STATEMENTS IN ASSIGNMENT OF RECORD.—An individual who is under an obligation of assignment of an application for patent may include the required statements under subsections (b) and (c) in the assignment executed by the individual, in lieu of filing such statements separately.

"(f) TIME FOR FILING.—A notice of allowance under section 151 may be provided to an applicant for patent only if the applicant for patent has filed each required oath or declaration under subsection (a) or has filed a substitute statement under subsection (d) or recorded an assignment meeting the requirements of subsection (e).

"(g) EARLIER-FILED APPLICATION CONTAINING REQUIRED STATEMENTS OR SUBSTITUTE STATEMENT.—

"(1) EXCEPTION.—The requirements under this section shall not apply to an individual with respect to an application for patent in which the individual is named as the inventor or a joint inventor and who claims the benefit under section 120, 121, or 365(c) of the filing of an earlier-filed application, if—

"(A) an oath or declaration meeting the requirements of subsection (a) was executed by the individual and was filed in connection with the earlier-filed application;

"(B) a substitute statement meeting the requirements of subsection (d) was filed in connection with the earlier filed application with respect to the individual; or

"(C) an assignment meeting the requirements of subsection (e) was executed with respect to the earlier-filed application by the individual and was recorded in connection with the earlier-filed application.

"(2) COPIES OF OATHS, DECLARATIONS, STATEMENTS, OR ASSIGNMENTS.—Notwithstanding paragraph (1), the Director may require that a copy of the executed oath or declaration, the substitute statement, or the assignment filed in connection with the earlier-filed application be included in the later-filed application.

"(h) SUPPLEMENTAL AND CORRECTED STATEMENTS; FILING ADDITIONAL STATEMENTS.—

"(1) IN GENERAL.—Any person making a statement required under this section may withdraw, replace, or otherwise correct the statement at any time. If a change is made in the naming of the inventor requiring the filing of 1 or more additional statements under this section, the Director shall establish regulations under which such additional statements may be filed.

"(2) SUPPLEMENTAL STATEMENTS NOT REQUIRED.—If an individual has executed an oath or declaration meeting the requirements of subsection (a) or an assignment meeting the requirements of subsection (e) with respect to an application for patent, the Director may not thereafter require that individual to make any additional oath, declaration, or other statement equivalent to those required by this section in connection with the application for patent or any patent issuing thereon.

"(3) SAVINGS CLAUSE.—A patent shall not be invalid or unenforceable based upon the failure to comply with a requirement under this section if the failure is remedied as provided under paragraph (1).

"(i) ACKNOWLEDGMENT OF PENALTIES.—Any declaration or statement filed pursuant to this section shall contain an acknowledgment that any willful false statement made in such declaration or statement is punishable under section 1001 of title 18 by fine or imprisonment of not more than 5 years, or both.".

(2) RELATIONSHIP TO DIVISIONAL APPLICATIONS.—Section 121 of title 35, United States Code, is amended by striking "If a divisional application" and all that follows through "inventor.".

(3) REQUIREMENTS FOR NONPROVISIONAL APPLICATIONS.—Section 111(a) of title 35, United States Code, is amended—

(A) in paragraph (2)(C), by striking "by the applicant" and inserting "or declaration";

(B) in the heading for paragraph (3), by inserting "OR DECLARATION" after "AND OATH"; and

(C) by inserting "or declaration" after "and oath" each place it appears.

H. R. 1249—13

(4) CONFORMING AMENDMENT.—The item relating to section 115 in the table of sections for chapter 11 of title 35, United States Code, is amended to read as follows:

"115. Inventor's oath or declaration.".

(b) FILING BY OTHER THAN INVENTOR.—

(1) IN GENERAL.—Section 118 of title 35, United States Code, is amended to read as follows:

"§ 118. Filing by other than inventor

"A person to whom the inventor has assigned or is under an obligation to assign the invention may make an application for patent. A person who otherwise shows sufficient proprietary interest in the matter may make an application for patent on behalf of and as agent for the inventor on proof of the pertinent facts and a showing that such action is appropriate to preserve the rights of the parties. If the Director grants a patent on an application filed under this section by a person other than the inventor, the patent shall be granted to the real party in interest and upon such notice to the inventor as the Director considers to be sufficient.".

(2) CONFORMING AMENDMENT.—Section 251 of title 35, United States Code, is amended in the third undesignated paragraph by inserting "or the application for the original patent was filed by the assignee of the entire interest" after "claims of the original patent".

(c) SPECIFICATION.—Section 112 of title 35, United States Code, is amended—

(1) in the first undesignated paragraph—

(A) by striking "The specification" and inserting "(a) IN GENERAL.—The specification"; and

(B) by striking "of carrying out his invention" and inserting "or joint inventor of carrying out the invention";

(2) in the second undesignated paragraph—

(A) by striking "The specification" and inserting "(b) CONCLUSION.—The specification"; and

(B) by striking "applicant regards as his invention" and inserting "inventor or a joint inventor regards as the invention";

(3) in the third undesignated paragraph, by striking "A claim" and inserting "(c) FORM.—A claim";

(4) in the fourth undesignated paragraph, by striking "Subject to the following paragraph," and inserting "(d) REFERENCE IN DEPENDENT FORMS.—Subject to subsection (e),";

(5) in the fifth undesignated paragraph, by striking "A claim" and inserting "(e) REFERENCE IN MULTIPLE DEPENDENT FORM.—A claim"; and

(6) in the last undesignated paragraph, by striking "An element" and inserting "(f) ELEMENT IN CLAIM FOR A COMBINATION.—An element".

(d) CONFORMING AMENDMENTS.—

(1) Sections 111(b)(1)(A) of title 35, United States Code, is amended by striking "the first paragraph of section 112 of this title" and inserting "section 112(a)".

(2) Section 111(b)(2) of title 35, United States Code, is amended by striking "the second through fifth paragraphs of

section 112," and inserting "subsections (b) through (e) of section 112,".

(e) EFFECTIVE DATE.—The amendments made by this section shall take effect upon the expiration of the 1-year period beginning on the date of the enactment of this Act and shall apply to any patent application that is filed on or after that effective date.

SEC. 5. DEFENSE TO INFRINGEMENT BASED ON PRIOR COMMERCIAL USE.

(a) IN GENERAL.—Section 273 of title 35, United States Code, is amended to read as follows:

"§ 273. Defense to infringement based on prior commercial use

"(a) IN GENERAL.—A person shall be entitled to a defense under section 282(b) with respect to subject matter consisting of a process, or consisting of a machine, manufacture, or composition of matter used in a manufacturing or other commercial process, that would otherwise infringe a claimed invention being asserted against the person if—

"(1) such person, acting in good faith, commercially used the subject matter in the United States, either in connection with an internal commercial use or an actual arm's length sale or other arm's length commercial transfer of a useful end result of such commercial use; and

"(2) such commercial use occurred at least 1 year before the earlier of either—

"(A) the effective filing date of the claimed invention; or

"(B) the date on which the claimed invention was disclosed to the public in a manner that qualified for the exception from prior art under section 102(b).

"(b) BURDEN OF PROOF.—A person asserting a defense under this section shall have the burden of establishing the defense by clear and convincing evidence.

"(c) ADDITIONAL COMMERCIAL USES.—

"(1) PREMARKETING REGULATORY REVIEW.—Subject matter for which commercial marketing or use is subject to a premarketing regulatory review period during which the safety or efficacy of the subject matter is established, including any period specified in section 156(g), shall be deemed to be commercially used for purposes of subsection (a)(1) during such regulatory review period.

"(2) NONPROFIT LABORATORY USE.—A use of subject matter by a nonprofit research laboratory or other nonprofit entity, such as a university or hospital, for which the public is the intended beneficiary, shall be deemed to be a commercial use for purposes of subsection (a)(1), except that a defense under this section may be asserted pursuant to this paragraph only for continued and noncommercial use by and in the laboratory or other nonprofit entity.

"(d) EXHAUSTION OF RIGHTS.—Notwithstanding subsection (e)(1), the sale or other disposition of a useful end result by a person entitled to assert a defense under this section in connection with a patent with respect to that useful end result shall exhaust the patent owner's rights under the patent to the extent that such rights would have been exhausted had such sale or other disposition been made by the patent owner.

"(e) LIMITATIONS AND EXCEPTIONS.—

"(1) PERSONAL DEFENSE.—

"(A) IN GENERAL.—A defense under this section may be asserted only by the person who performed or directed the performance of the commercial use described in subsection (a), or by an entity that controls, is controlled by, or is under common control with such person.

"(B) TRANSFER OF RIGHT.—Except for any transfer to the patent owner, the right to assert a defense under this section shall not be licensed or assigned or transferred to another person except as an ancillary and subordinate part of a good-faith assignment or transfer for other reasons of the entire enterprise or line of business to which the defense relates.

"(C) RESTRICTION ON SITES.—A defense under this section, when acquired by a person as part of an assignment or transfer described in subparagraph (B), may only be asserted for uses at sites where the subject matter that would otherwise infringe a claimed invention is in use before the later of the effective filing date of the claimed invention or the date of the assignment or transfer of such enterprise or line of business.

"(2) DERIVATION.—A person may not assert a defense under this section if the subject matter on which the defense is based was derived from the patentee or persons in privity with the patentee.

"(3) NOT A GENERAL LICENSE.—The defense asserted by a person under this section is not a general license under all claims of the patent at issue, but extends only to the specific subject matter for which it has been established that a commercial use that qualifies under this section occurred, except that the defense shall also extend to variations in the quantity or volume of use of the claimed subject matter, and to improvements in the claimed subject matter that do not infringe additional specifically claimed subject matter of the patent.

"(4) ABANDONMENT OF USE.—A person who has abandoned commercial use (that qualifies under this section) of subject matter may not rely on activities performed before the date of such abandonment in establishing a defense under this section with respect to actions taken on or after the date of such abandonment.

"(5) UNIVERSITY EXCEPTION.—

"(A) IN GENERAL.—A person commercially using subject matter to which subsection (a) applies may not assert a defense under this section if the claimed invention with respect to which the defense is asserted was, at the time the invention was made, owned or subject to an obligation of assignment to either an institution of higher education (as defined in section 101(a) of the Higher Education Act of 1965 (20 U.S.C. 1001(a)), or a technology transfer organization whose primary purpose is to facilitate the commercialization of technologies developed by one or more such institutions of higher education.

"(B) EXCEPTION.—Subparagraph (A) shall not apply if any of the activities required to reduce to practice the subject matter of the claimed invention could not have been undertaken using funds provided by the Federal Government.

"(f) UNREASONABLE ASSERTION OF DEFENSE.—If the defense under this section is pleaded by a person who is found to infringe the patent and who subsequently fails to demonstrate a reasonable basis for asserting the defense, the court shall find the case exceptional for the purpose of awarding attorney fees under section 285.

"(g) INVALIDITY.—A patent shall not be deemed to be invalid under section 102 or 103 solely because a defense is raised or established under this section.".

(b) CONFORMING AMENDMENT.—The item relating to section 273 in the table of sections for chapter 28 of title 35, United States Code, is amended to read as follows:

"273. Defense to infringement based on prior commercial use.".

(c) EFFECTIVE DATE.—The amendments made by this section shall apply to any patent issued on or after the date of the enactment of this Act.

SEC. 6. POST-GRANT REVIEW PROCEEDINGS.

(a) INTER PARTES REVIEW.—Chapter 31 of title 35, United States Code, is amended to read as follows:

"CHAPTER 31—INTER PARTES REVIEW

"Sec.
"311. Inter partes review.
"312. Petitions.
"313. Preliminary response to petition.
"314. Institution of inter partes review.
"315. Relation to other proceedings or actions.
"316. Conduct of inter partes review.
"317. Settlement.
"318. Decision of the Board.
"319. Appeal.

"§ 311. Inter partes review

"(a) IN GENERAL.—Subject to the provisions of this chapter, a person who is not the owner of a patent may file with the Office a petition to institute an inter partes review of the patent. The Director shall establish, by regulation, fees to be paid by the person requesting the review, in such amounts as the Director determines to be reasonable, considering the aggregate costs of the review.

"(b) SCOPE.—A petitioner in an inter partes review may request to cancel as unpatentable 1 or more claims of a patent only on a ground that could be raised under section 102 or 103 and only on the basis of prior art consisting of patents or printed publications.

"(c) FILING DEADLINE.—A petition for inter partes review shall be filed after the later of either—

"(1) the date that is 9 months after the grant of a patent or issuance of a reissue of a patent; or

"(2) if a post-grant review is instituted under chapter 32, the date of the termination of such post-grant review.

H. R. 1249—17

"§ 312. Petitions

"(a) REQUIREMENTS OF PETITION.—A petition filed under section 311 may be considered only if—

"(1) the petition is accompanied by payment of the fee established by the Director under section 311;

"(2) the petition identifies all real parties in interest;

"(3) the petition identifies, in writing and with particularity, each claim challenged, the grounds on which the challenge to each claim is based, and the evidence that supports the grounds for the challenge to each claim, including—

"(A) copies of patents and printed publications that the petitioner relies upon in support of the petition; and

"(B) affidavits or declarations of supporting evidence and opinions, if the petitioner relies on expert opinions;

"(4) the petition provides such other information as the Director may require by regulation; and

"(5) the petitioner provides copies of any of the documents required under paragraphs (2), (3), and (4) to the patent owner or, if applicable, the designated representative of the patent owner.

"(b) PUBLIC AVAILABILITY.—As soon as practicable after the receipt of a petition under section 311, the Director shall make the petition available to the public.

"§ 313. Preliminary response to petition

"If an inter partes review petition is filed under section 311, the patent owner shall have the right to file a preliminary response to the petition, within a time period set by the Director, that sets forth reasons why no inter partes review should be instituted based upon the failure of the petition to meet any requirement of this chapter.

"§ 314. Institution of inter partes review

"(a) THRESHOLD.—The Director may not authorize an inter partes review to be instituted unless the Director determines that the information presented in the petition filed under section 311 and any response filed under section 313 shows that there is a reasonable likelihood that the petitioner would prevail with respect to at least 1 of the claims challenged in the petition.

"(b) TIMING.—The Director shall determine whether to institute an inter partes review under this chapter pursuant to a petition filed under section 311 within 3 months after—

"(1) receiving a preliminary response to the petition under section 313; or

"(2) if no such preliminary response is filed, the last date on which such response may be filed.

"(c) NOTICE.—The Director shall notify the petitioner and patent owner, in writing, of the Director's determination under subsection (a), and shall make such notice available to the public as soon as is practicable. Such notice shall include the date on which the review shall commence.

"(d) NO APPEAL.—The determination by the Director whether to institute an inter partes review under this section shall be final and nonappealable.

"§ 315. Relation to other proceedings or actions

"(a) INFRINGER'S CIVIL ACTION.—

H. R. 1249—18

"(1) INTER PARTES REVIEW BARRED BY CIVIL ACTION.—An inter partes review may not be instituted if, before the date on which the petition for such a review is filed, the petitioner or real party in interest filed a civil action challenging the validity of a claim of the patent.

"(2) STAY OF CIVIL ACTION.—If the petitioner or real party in interest files a civil action challenging the validity of a claim of the patent on or after the date on which the petitioner files a petition for inter partes review of the patent, that civil action shall be automatically stayed until either—

"(A) the patent owner moves the court to lift the stay;

"(B) the patent owner files a civil action or counterclaim alleging that the petitioner or real party in interest has infringed the patent; or

"(C) the petitioner or real party in interest moves the court to dismiss the civil action.

"(3) TREATMENT OF COUNTERCLAIM.—A counterclaim challenging the validity of a claim of a patent does not constitute a civil action challenging the validity of a claim of a patent for purposes of this subsection.

"(b) PATENT OWNER'S ACTION.—An inter partes review may not be instituted if the petition requesting the proceeding is filed more than 1 year after the date on which the petitioner, real party in interest, or privy of the petitioner is served with a complaint alleging infringement of the patent. The time limitation set forth in the preceding sentence shall not apply to a request for joinder under subsection (c).

"(c) JOINDER.—If the Director institutes an inter partes review, the Director, in his or her discretion, may join as a party to that inter partes review any person who properly files a petition under section 311 that the Director, after receiving a preliminary response under section 313 or the expiration of the time for filing such a response, determines warrants the institution of an inter partes review under section 314.

"(d) MULTIPLE PROCEEDINGS.—Notwithstanding sections 135(a), 251, and 252, and chapter 30, during the pendency of an inter partes review, if another proceeding or matter involving the patent is before the Office, the Director may determine the manner in which the inter partes review or other proceeding or matter may proceed, including providing for stay, transfer, consolidation, or termination of any such matter or proceeding.

"(e) ESTOPPEL.—

"(1) PROCEEDINGS BEFORE THE OFFICE.—The petitioner in an inter partes review of a claim in a patent under this chapter that results in a final written decision under section 318(a), or the real party in interest or privy of the petitioner, may not request or maintain a proceeding before the Office with respect to that claim on any ground that the petitioner raised or reasonably could have raised during that inter partes review.

"(2) CIVIL ACTIONS AND OTHER PROCEEDINGS.—The petitioner in an inter partes review of a claim in a patent under this chapter that results in a final written decision under section 318(a), or the real party in interest or privy of the petitioner, may not assert either in a civil action arising in whole or in part under section 1338 of title 28 or in a proceeding before the International Trade Commission under section 337 of the Tariff Act of 1930 that the claim is invalid on any ground that the petitioner raised or reasonably could have raised during that inter partes review.

"§ 316. Conduct of inter partes review

"(a) REGULATIONS.—The Director shall prescribe regulations—

"(1) providing that the file of any proceeding under this chapter shall be made available to the public, except that any petition or document filed with the intent that it be sealed shall, if accompanied by a motion to seal, be treated as sealed pending the outcome of the ruling on the motion;

"(2) setting forth the standards for the showing of sufficient grounds to institute a review under section 314(a);

"(3) establishing procedures for the submission of supplemental information after the petition is filed;

"(4) establishing and governing inter partes review under this chapter and the relationship of such review to other proceedings under this title;

"(5) setting forth standards and procedures for discovery of relevant evidence, including that such discovery shall be limited to—

"(A) the deposition of witnesses submitting affidavits or declarations; and

"(B) what is otherwise necessary in the interest of justice;

"(6) prescribing sanctions for abuse of discovery, abuse of process, or any other improper use of the proceeding, such as to harass or to cause unnecessary delay or an unnecessary increase in the cost of the proceeding;

"(7) providing for protective orders governing the exchange and submission of confidential information;

"(8) providing for the filing by the patent owner of a response to the petition under section 313 after an inter partes review has been instituted, and requiring that the patent owner file with such response, through affidavits or declarations, any additional factual evidence and expert opinions on which the patent owner relies in support of the response;

"(9) setting forth standards and procedures for allowing the patent owner to move to amend the patent under subsection (d) to cancel a challenged claim or propose a reasonable number of substitute claims, and ensuring that any information submitted by the patent owner in support of any amendment entered under subsection (d) is made available to the public as part of the prosecution history of the patent;

"(10) providing either party with the right to an oral hearing as part of the proceeding;

"(11) requiring that the final determination in an inter partes review be issued not later than 1 year after the date on which the Director notices the institution of a review under this chapter, except that the Director may, for good cause shown, extend the 1-year period by not more than 6 months, and may adjust the time periods in this paragraph in the case of joinder under section 315(c);

"(12) setting a time period for requesting joinder under section 315(c); and

"(13) providing the petitioner with at least 1 opportunity to file written comments within a time period established by the Director.

"(b) CONSIDERATIONS.—In prescribing regulations under this section, the Director shall consider the effect of any such regulation on the economy, the integrity of the patent system, the efficient administration of the Office, and the ability of the Office to timely complete proceedings instituted under this chapter.

"(c) PATENT TRIAL AND APPEAL BOARD.—The Patent Trial and Appeal Board shall, in accordance with section 6, conduct each inter partes review instituted under this chapter.

"(d) AMENDMENT OF THE PATENT.—

"(1) IN GENERAL.—During an inter partes review instituted under this chapter, the patent owner may file 1 motion to amend the patent in 1 or more of the following ways:

"(A) Cancel any challenged patent claim.

"(B) For each challenged claim, propose a reasonable number of substitute claims.

"(2) ADDITIONAL MOTIONS.—Additional motions to amend may be permitted upon the joint request of the petitioner and the patent owner to materially advance the settlement of a proceeding under section 317, or as permitted by regulations prescribed by the Director.

"(3) SCOPE OF CLAIMS.—An amendment under this subsection may not enlarge the scope of the claims of the patent or introduce new matter.

"(e) EVIDENTIARY STANDARDS.—In an inter partes review instituted under this chapter, the petitioner shall have the burden of proving a proposition of unpatentability by a preponderance of the evidence.

"§ 317. Settlement

"(a) IN GENERAL.—An inter partes review instituted under this chapter shall be terminated with respect to any petitioner upon the joint request of the petitioner and the patent owner, unless the Office has decided the merits of the proceeding before the request for termination is filed. If the inter partes review is terminated with respect to a petitioner under this section, no estoppel under section 315(e) shall attach to the petitioner, or to the real party in interest or privy of the petitioner, on the basis of that petitioner's institution of that inter partes review. If no petitioner remains in the inter partes review, the Office may terminate the review or proceed to a final written decision under section 318(a).

"(b) AGREEMENTS IN WRITING.—Any agreement or understanding between the patent owner and a petitioner, including any collateral agreements referred to in such agreement or understanding, made in connection with, or in contemplation of, the termination of an inter partes review under this section shall be in writing and a true copy of such agreement or understanding shall be filed in the Office before the termination of the inter partes review as between the parties. At the request of a party to the proceeding, the agreement or understanding shall be treated as business confidential information, shall be kept separate from the file of the involved patents, and shall be made available only to Federal Government agencies on written request, or to any person on a showing of good cause.

"§ 318. Decision of the Board

"(a) FINAL WRITTEN DECISION.—If an inter partes review is instituted and not dismissed under this chapter, the Patent Trial and Appeal Board shall issue a final written decision with respect to the patentability of any patent claim challenged by the petitioner and any new claim added under section 316(d).

"(b) CERTIFICATE.—If the Patent Trial and Appeal Board issues a final written decision under subsection (a) and the time for appeal has expired or any appeal has terminated, the Director shall issue and publish a certificate canceling any claim of the patent finally determined to be unpatentable, confirming any claim of the patent determined to be patentable, and incorporating in the patent by operation of the certificate any new or amended claim determined to be patentable.

"(c) INTERVENING RIGHTS.—Any proposed amended or new claim determined to be patentable and incorporated into a patent following an inter partes review under this chapter shall have the same effect as that specified in section 252 for reissued patents on the right of any person who made, purchased, or used within the United States, or imported into the United States, anything patented by such proposed amended or new claim, or who made substantial preparation therefor, before the issuance of a certificate under subsection (b).

"(d) DATA ON LENGTH OF REVIEW.—The Office shall make available to the public data describing the length of time between the institution of, and the issuance of a final written decision under subsection (a) for, each inter partes review.

"§ 319. Appeal

"A party dissatisfied with the final written decision of the Patent Trial and Appeal Board under section 318(a) may appeal the decision pursuant to sections 141 through 144. Any party to the inter partes review shall have the right to be a party to the appeal.".

(b) CONFORMING AMENDMENT.—The table of chapters for part III of title 35, United States Code, is amended by striking the item relating to chapter 31 and inserting the following:

"31. Inter Partes Review .... 311".

(c) REGULATIONS AND EFFECTIVE DATE.—

(1) REGULATIONS.—The Director shall, not later than the date that is 1 year after the date of the enactment of this Act, issue regulations to carry out chapter 31 of title 35, United States Code, as amended by subsection (a) of this section.

(2) APPLICABILITY.—

(A) IN GENERAL.—The amendments made by subsection (a) shall take effect upon the expiration of the 1-year period beginning on the date of the enactment of this Act and shall apply to any patent issued before, on, or after that effective date.

(B) GRADUATED IMPLEMENTATION.—The Director may impose a limit on the number of inter partes reviews that may be instituted under chapter 31 of title 35, United States Code, during each of the first 4 1-year periods in which the amendments made by subsection (a) are in effect, if such number in each year equals or exceeds the number of inter partes reexaminations that are ordered under chapter 31 of title 35, United States Code, in the last fiscal year ending before the effective date of the amendments made by subsection (a).

(3) TRANSITION.—

H. R. 1249—22

(A) IN GENERAL.—Chapter 31 of title 35, United States Code, is amended—

(i) in section 312—

(I) in subsection (a)—

(aa) in the first sentence, by striking "a substantial new question of patentability affecting any claim of the patent concerned is raised by the request," and inserting "the information presented in the request shows that there is a reasonable likelihood that the requester would prevail with respect to at least 1 of the claims challenged in the request,"; and

(bb) in the second sentence, by striking "The existence of a substantial new question of patentability" and inserting "A showing that there is a reasonable likelihood that the requester would prevail with respect to at least 1 of the claims challenged in the request"; and

(II) in subsection (c), in the second sentence, by striking "no substantial new question of patentability has been raised," and inserting "the showing required by subsection (a) has not been made,"; and

(ii) in section 313, by striking "a substantial new question of patentability affecting a claim of the patent is raised" and inserting "it has been shown that there is a reasonable likelihood that the requester would prevail with respect to at least 1 of the claims challenged in the request".

(B) APPLICATION.—The amendments made by this paragraph—

(i) shall take effect on the date of the enactment of this Act; and

(ii) shall apply to requests for inter partes reexamination that are filed on or after such date of enactment, but before the effective date set forth in paragraph (2)(A) of this subsection.

(C) CONTINUED APPLICABILITY OF PRIOR PROVISIONS.—The provisions of chapter 31 of title 35, United States Code, as amended by this paragraph, shall continue to apply to requests for inter partes reexamination that are filed before the effective date set forth in paragraph (2)(A) as if subsection (a) had not been enacted.

(d) POST-GRANT REVIEW.—Part III of title 35, United States Code, is amended by adding at the end the following:

"CHAPTER 32—POST-GRANT REVIEW

"§ 321. Post-grant review

"(a) IN GENERAL.—Subject to the provisions of this chapter, a person who is not the owner of a patent may file with the Office a petition to institute a post-grant review of the patent. The Director shall establish, by regulation, fees to be paid by the person requesting the review, in such amounts as the Director determines to be reasonable, considering the aggregate costs of the post-grant review.

"(b) SCOPE.—A petitioner in a post-grant review may request to cancel as unpatentable 1 or more claims of a patent on any ground that could be raised under paragraph (2) or (3) of section 282(b) (relating to invalidity of the patent or any claim).

"(c) FILING DEADLINE.—A petition for a post-grant review may only be filed not later than the date that is 9 months after the date of the grant of the patent or of the issuance of a reissue patent (as the case may be).

"§ 322. Petitions

"(a) REQUIREMENTS OF PETITION.—A petition filed under section 321 may be considered only if—

"(1) the petition is accompanied by payment of the fee established by the Director under section 321;

"(2) the petition identifies all real parties in interest;

"(3) the petition identifies, in writing and with particularity, each claim challenged, the grounds on which the challenge to each claim is based, and the evidence that supports the grounds for the challenge to each claim, including—

"(A) copies of patents and printed publications that the petitioner relies upon in support of the petition; and

"(B) affidavits or declarations of supporting evidence and opinions, if the petitioner relies on other factual evidence or on expert opinions;

"(4) the petition provides such other information as the Director may require by regulation; and

"(5) the petitioner provides copies of any of the documents required under paragraphs (2), (3), and (4) to the patent owner or, if applicable, the designated representative of the patent owner.

"(b) PUBLIC AVAILABILITY.—As soon as practicable after the receipt of a petition under section 321, the Director shall make the petition available to the public.

"§ 323. Preliminary response to petition

"If a post-grant review petition is filed under section 321, the patent owner shall have the right to file a preliminary response to the petition, within a time period set by the Director, that sets forth reasons why no post-grant review should be instituted based upon the failure of the petition to meet any requirement of this chapter.

"§ 324. Institution of post-grant review

"(a) THRESHOLD.—The Director may not authorize a post-grant review to be instituted unless the Director determines that the information presented in the petition filed under section 321, if such information is not rebutted, would demonstrate that it is more likely than not that at least 1 of the claims challenged in the petition is unpatentable.

H. R. 1249—24

"(b) ADDITIONAL GROUNDS.—The determination required under subsection (a) may also be satisfied by a showing that the petition raises a novel or unsettled legal question that is important to other patents or patent applications.

"(c) TIMING.—The Director shall determine whether to institute a post-grant review under this chapter pursuant to a petition filed under section 321 within 3 months after—

"(1) receiving a preliminary response to the petition under section 323; or

"(2) if no such preliminary response is filed, the last date on which such response may be filed.

"(d) NOTICE.—The Director shall notify the petitioner and patent owner, in writing, of the Director's determination under subsection (a) or (b), and shall make such notice available to the public as soon as is practicable. Such notice shall include the date on which the review shall commence.

"(e) NO APPEAL.—The determination by the Director whether to institute a post-grant review under this section shall be final and nonappealable.

"§ 325. Relation to other proceedings or actions

"(a) INFRINGER'S CIVIL ACTION.—

"(1) POST-GRANT REVIEW BARRED BY CIVIL ACTION.—A post-grant review may not be instituted under this chapter if, before the date on which the petition for such a review is filed, the petitioner or real party in interest filed a civil action challenging the validity of a claim of the patent.

"(2) STAY OF CIVIL ACTION.—If the petitioner or real party in interest files a civil action challenging the validity of a claim of the patent on or after the date on which the petitioner files a petition for post-grant review of the patent, that civil action shall be automatically stayed until either—

"(A) the patent owner moves the court to lift the stay;

"(B) the patent owner files a civil action or counterclaim alleging that the petitioner or real party in interest has infringed the patent; or

"(C) the petitioner or real party in interest moves the court to dismiss the civil action.

"(3) TREATMENT OF COUNTERCLAIM.—A counterclaim challenging the validity of a claim of a patent does not constitute a civil action challenging the validity of a claim of a patent for purposes of this subsection.

"(b) PRELIMINARY INJUNCTIONS.—If a civil action alleging infringement of a patent is filed within 3 months after the date on which the patent is granted, the court may not stay its consideration of the patent owner's motion for a preliminary injunction against infringement of the patent on the basis that a petition for post-grant review has been filed under this chapter or that such a post-grant review has been instituted under this chapter.

"(c) JOINDER.—If more than 1 petition for a post-grant review under this chapter is properly filed against the same patent and the Director determines that more than 1 of these petitions warrants the institution of a post-grant review under section 324, the Director may consolidate such reviews into a single post-grant review.

"(d) MULTIPLE PROCEEDINGS.—Notwithstanding sections 135(a), 251, and 252, and chapter 30, during the pendency of any post-

H. R. 1249—25

grant review under this chapter, if another proceeding or matter involving the patent is before the Office, the Director may determine the manner in which the post-grant review or other proceeding or matter may proceed, including providing for the stay, transfer, consolidation, or termination of any such matter or proceeding. In determining whether to institute or order a proceeding under this chapter, chapter 30, or chapter 31, the Director may take into account whether, and reject the petition or request because, the same or substantially the same prior art or arguments previously were presented to the Office.

"(e) ESTOPPEL.—

"(1) PROCEEDINGS BEFORE THE OFFICE.—The petitioner in a post-grant review of a claim in a patent under this chapter that results in a final written decision under section 328(a), or the real party in interest or privy of the petitioner, may not request or maintain a proceeding before the Office with respect to that claim on any ground that the petitioner raised or reasonably could have raised during that post-grant review.

"(2) CIVIL ACTIONS AND OTHER PROCEEDINGS.—The petitioner in a post-grant review of a claim in a patent under this chapter that results in a final written decision under section 328(a), or the real party in interest or privy of the petitioner, may not assert either in a civil action arising in whole or in part under section 1338 of title 28 or in a proceeding before the International Trade Commission under section 337 of the Tariff Act of 1930 that the claim is invalid on any ground that the petitioner raised or reasonably could have raised during that post-grant review.

"(f) REISSUE PATENTS.—A post-grant review may not be instituted under this chapter if the petition requests cancellation of a claim in a reissue patent that is identical to or narrower than a claim in the original patent from which the reissue patent was issued, and the time limitations in section 321(c) would bar filing a petition for a post-grant review for such original patent.

"§ 326. Conduct of post-grant review

"(a) REGULATIONS.—The Director shall prescribe regulations—

"(1) providing that the file of any proceeding under this chapter shall be made available to the public, except that any petition or document filed with the intent that it be sealed shall, if accompanied by a motion to seal, be treated as sealed pending the outcome of the ruling on the motion;

"(2) setting forth the standards for the showing of sufficient grounds to institute a review under subsections (a) and (b) of section 324;

"(3) establishing procedures for the submission of supplemental information after the petition is filed;

"(4) establishing and governing a post-grant review under this chapter and the relationship of such review to other proceedings under this title;

"(5) setting forth standards and procedures for discovery of relevant evidence, including that such discovery shall be limited to evidence directly related to factual assertions advanced by either party in the proceeding;

"(6) prescribing sanctions for abuse of discovery, abuse of process, or any other improper use of the proceeding, such as to harass or to cause unnecessary delay or an unnecessary increase in the cost of the proceeding;

"(7) providing for protective orders governing the exchange and submission of confidential information;

"(8) providing for the filing by the patent owner of a response to the petition under section 323 after a post-grant review has been instituted, and requiring that the patent owner file with such response, through affidavits or declarations, any additional factual evidence and expert opinions on which the patent owner relies in support of the response;

"(9) setting forth standards and procedures for allowing the patent owner to move to amend the patent under subsection (d) to cancel a challenged claim or propose a reasonable number of substitute claims, and ensuring that any information submitted by the patent owner in support of any amendment entered under subsection (d) is made available to the public as part of the prosecution history of the patent;

"(10) providing either party with the right to an oral hearing as part of the proceeding;

"(11) requiring that the final determination in any post-grant review be issued not later than 1 year after the date on which the Director notices the institution of a proceeding under this chapter, except that the Director may, for good cause shown, extend the 1-year period by not more than 6 months, and may adjust the time periods in this paragraph in the case of joinder under section 325(c); and

"(12) providing the petitioner with at least 1 opportunity to file written comments within a time period established by the Director.

"(b) CONSIDERATIONS.—In prescribing regulations under this section, the Director shall consider the effect of any such regulation on the economy, the integrity of the patent system, the efficient administration of the Office, and the ability of the Office to timely complete proceedings instituted under this chapter.

"(c) PATENT TRIAL AND APPEAL BOARD.—The Patent Trial and Appeal Board shall, in accordance with section 6, conduct each post-grant review instituted under this chapter.

"(d) AMENDMENT OF THE PATENT.—

"(1) IN GENERAL.—During a post-grant review instituted under this chapter, the patent owner may file 1 motion to amend the patent in 1 or more of the following ways:

"(A) Cancel any challenged patent claim.

"(B) For each challenged claim, propose a reasonable number of substitute claims.

"(2) ADDITIONAL MOTIONS.—Additional motions to amend may be permitted upon the joint request of the petitioner and the patent owner to materially advance the settlement of a proceeding under section 327, or upon the request of the patent owner for good cause shown.

"(3) SCOPE OF CLAIMS.—An amendment under this subsection may not enlarge the scope of the claims of the patent or introduce new matter.

"(e) EVIDENTIARY STANDARDS.—In a post-grant review instituted under this chapter, the petitioner shall have the burden of proving a proposition of unpatentability by a preponderance of the evidence.

"§ 327. Settlement

"(a) IN GENERAL.—A post-grant review instituted under this chapter shall be terminated with respect to any petitioner upon the joint request of the petitioner and the patent owner, unless the Office has decided the merits of the proceeding before the request for termination is filed. If the post-grant review is terminated with respect to a petitioner under this section, no estoppel under section 325(e) shall attach to the petitioner, or to the real party in interest or privy of the petitioner, on the basis of that petitioner's institution of that post-grant review. If no petitioner remains in the post-grant review, the Office may terminate the post-grant review or proceed to a final written decision under section 328(a).

"(b) AGREEMENTS IN WRITING.—Any agreement or understanding between the patent owner and a petitioner, including any collateral agreements referred to in such agreement or understanding, made in connection with, or in contemplation of, the termination of a post-grant review under this section shall be in writing, and a true copy of such agreement or understanding shall be filed in the Office before the termination of the post-grant review as between the parties. At the request of a party to the proceeding, the agreement or understanding shall be treated as business confidential information, shall be kept separate from the file of the involved patents, and shall be made available only to Federal Government agencies on written request, or to any person on a showing of good cause.

"§ 328. Decision of the Board

"(a) FINAL WRITTEN DECISION.—If a post-grant review is instituted and not dismissed under this chapter, the Patent Trial and Appeal Board shall issue a final written decision with respect to the patentability of any patent claim challenged by the petitioner and any new claim added under section 326(d).

"(b) CERTIFICATE.—If the Patent Trial and Appeal Board issues a final written decision under subsection (a) and the time for appeal has expired or any appeal has terminated, the Director shall issue and publish a certificate canceling any claim of the patent finally determined to be unpatentable, confirming any claim of the patent determined to be patentable, and incorporating in the patent by operation of the certificate any new or amended claim determined to be patentable.

"(c) INTERVENING RIGHTS.—Any proposed amended or new claim determined to be patentable and incorporated into a patent following a post-grant review under this chapter shall have the same effect as that specified in section 252 of this title for reissued patents on the right of any person who made, purchased, or used within the United States, or imported into the United States, anything patented by such proposed amended or new claim, or who made substantial preparation therefor, before the issuance of a certificate under subsection (b).

"(d) DATA ON LENGTH OF REVIEW.—The Office shall make available to the public data describing the length of time between the institution of, and the issuance of a final written decision under subsection (a) for, each post-grant review.

"§ 329. Appeal

"A party dissatisfied with the final written decision of the Patent Trial and Appeal Board under section 328(a) may appeal the decision pursuant to sections 141 through 144. Any party to the post-grant review shall have the right to be a party to the appeal.".

(e) CONFORMING AMENDMENT.—The table of chapters for part III of title 35, United States Code, is amended by adding at the end the following:

"32. Post-Grant Review .... 321".

(f) REGULATIONS AND EFFECTIVE DATE.—

(1) REGULATIONS.—The Director shall, not later than the date that is 1 year after the date of the enactment of this Act, issue regulations to carry out chapter 32 of title 35, United States Code, as added by subsection (d) of this section.

(2) APPLICABILITY.—

(A) IN GENERAL.—The amendments made by subsection (d) shall take effect upon the expiration of the 1-year period beginning on the date of the enactment of this Act and, except as provided in section 18 and in paragraph (3), shall apply only to patents described in section 3(n)(1).

(B) LIMITATION.—The Director may impose a limit on the number of post-grant reviews that may be instituted under chapter 32 of title 35, United States Code, during each of the first 4 1-year periods in which the amendments made by subsection (d) are in effect.

(3) PENDING INTERFERENCES.—

(A) PROCEDURES IN GENERAL.—The Director shall determine, and include in the regulations issued under paragraph (1), the procedures under which an interference commenced before the effective date set forth in paragraph (2)(A) is to proceed, including whether such interference—

(i) is to be dismissed without prejudice to the filing of a petition for a post-grant review under chapter 32 of title 35, United States Code; or

(ii) is to proceed as if this Act had not been enacted.

(B) PROCEEDINGS BY PATENT TRIAL AND APPEAL BOARD.—For purposes of an interference that is commenced before the effective date set forth in paragraph (2)(A), the Director may deem the Patent Trial and Appeal Board to be the Board of Patent Appeals and Interferences, and may allow the Patent Trial and Appeal Board to conduct any further proceedings in that interference.

(C) APPEALS.—The authorization to appeal or have remedy from derivation proceedings in sections 141(d) and 146 of title 35, United States Code, as amended by this Act, and the jurisdiction to entertain appeals from derivation proceedings in section 1295(a)(4)(A) of title 28, United States Code, as amended by this Act, shall be deemed to extend to any final decision in an interference that is commenced before the effective date set forth in paragraph (2)(A) of this subsection and that is not dismissed pursuant to this paragraph.

(g) CITATION OF PRIOR ART AND WRITTEN STATEMENTS.—

(1) IN GENERAL.—Section 301 of title 35, United States Code, is amended to read as follows:

H. R. 1249—29

"§ 301. Citation of prior art and written statements

"(a) IN GENERAL.—Any person at any time may cite to the Office in writing—

"(1) prior art consisting of patents or printed publications which that person believes to have a bearing on the patentability of any claim of a particular patent; or

"(2) statements of the patent owner filed in a proceeding before a Federal court or the Office in which the patent owner took a position on the scope of any claim of a particular patent.

"(b) OFFICIAL FILE.—If the person citing prior art or written statements pursuant to subsection (a) explains in writing the pertinence and manner of applying the prior art or written statements to at least 1 claim of the patent, the citation of the prior art or written statements and the explanation thereof shall become a part of the official file of the patent.

"(c) ADDITIONAL INFORMATION.—A party that submits a written statement pursuant to subsection (a)(2) shall include any other documents, pleadings, or evidence from the proceeding in which the statement was filed that addresses the written statement.

"(d) LIMITATIONS.—A written statement submitted pursuant to subsection (a)(2), and additional information submitted pursuant to subsection (c), shall not be considered by the Office for any purpose other than to determine the proper meaning of a patent claim in a proceeding that is ordered or instituted pursuant to section 304, 314, or 324. If any such written statement or additional information is subject to an applicable protective order, such statement or information shall be redacted to exclude information that is subject to that order.

"(e) CONFIDENTIALITY.—Upon the written request of the person citing prior art or written statements pursuant to subsection (a), that person's identity shall be excluded from the patent file and kept confidential.".

(2) CONFORMING AMENDMENT.—The item relating to section 301 in the table of sections for chapter 30 of title 35, United States Code, is amended to read as follows:

"301. Citation of prior art and written statements.".

(3) EFFECTIVE DATE.—The amendments made by this subsection shall take effect upon the expiration of the 1-year period beginning on the date of the enactment of this Act and shall apply to any patent issued before, on, or after that effective date.

(h) REEXAMINATION.—

(1) DETERMINATION BY DIRECTOR.—

(A) IN GENERAL.—Section 303(a) of title 35, United States Code, is amended by striking "section 301 of this title" and inserting "section 301 or 302".

(B) EFFECTIVE DATE.—The amendment made by this paragraph shall take effect upon the expiration of the 1-year period beginning on the date of the enactment of this Act and shall apply to any patent issued before, on, or after that effective date.

(2) APPEAL.—

(A) IN GENERAL.—Section 306 of title 35, United States Code, is amended by striking "145" and inserting "144".

(B) EFFECTIVE DATE.—The amendment made by this paragraph shall take effect on the date of the enactment of this Act and shall apply to any appeal of a reexamination before the Board of Patent Appeals and Interferences or the Patent Trial and Appeal Board that is pending on, or brought on or after, the date of the enactment of this Act.

SEC. 7. PATENT TRIAL AND APPEAL BOARD.

(a) COMPOSITION AND DUTIES.—

(1) IN GENERAL.—Section 6 of title 35, United States Code, is amended to read as follows:

"§ 6. Patent Trial and Appeal Board

"(a) IN GENERAL.—There shall be in the Office a Patent Trial and Appeal Board. The Director, the Deputy Director, the Commissioner for Patents, the Commissioner for Trademarks, and the administrative patent judges shall constitute the Patent Trial and Appeal Board. The administrative patent judges shall be persons of competent legal knowledge and scientific ability who are appointed by the Secretary, in consultation with the Director. Any reference in any Federal law, Executive order, rule, regulation, or delegation of authority, or any document of or pertaining to the Board of Patent Appeals and Interferences is deemed to refer to the Patent Trial and Appeal Board.

"(b) DUTIES.—The Patent Trial and Appeal Board shall—

"(1) on written appeal of an applicant, review adverse decisions of examiners upon applications for patents pursuant to section 134(a);

"(2) review appeals of reexaminations pursuant to section 134(b);

"(3) conduct derivation proceedings pursuant to section 135; and

"(4) conduct inter partes reviews and post-grant reviews pursuant to chapters 31 and 32.

"(c) 3-MEMBER PANELS.—Each appeal, derivation proceeding, post-grant review, and inter partes review shall be heard by at least 3 members of the Patent Trial and Appeal Board, who shall be designated by the Director. Only the Patent Trial and Appeal Board may grant rehearings.

"(d) TREATMENT OF PRIOR APPOINTMENTS.—The Secretary of Commerce may, in the Secretary's discretion, deem the appointment of an administrative patent judge who, before the date of the enactment of this subsection, held office pursuant to an appointment by the Director to take effect on the date on which the Director initially appointed the administrative patent judge. It shall be a defense to a challenge to the appointment of an administrative patent judge on the basis of the judge's having been originally appointed by the Director that the administrative patent judge so appointed was acting as a de facto officer.".

(2) CONFORMING AMENDMENT.—The item relating to section 6 in the table of sections for chapter 1 of title 35, United States Code, is amended to read as follows:

"6. Patent Trial and Appeal Board.".

(b) ADMINISTRATIVE APPEALS.—Section 134 of title 35, United States Code, is amended—

(1) in subsection (b), by striking "any reexamination proceeding" and inserting "a reexamination"; and

H. R. 1249—31

(2) by striking subsection (c).

(c) CIRCUIT APPEALS.—

(1) IN GENERAL.—Section 141 of title 35, United States Code, is amended to read as follows:

"§ 141. Appeal to Court of Appeals for the Federal Circuit

"(a) EXAMINATIONS.—An applicant who is dissatisfied with the final decision in an appeal to the Patent Trial and Appeal Board under section 134(a) may appeal the Board's decision to the United States Court of Appeals for the Federal Circuit. By filing such an appeal, the applicant waives his or her right to proceed under section 145.

"(b) REEXAMINATIONS.—A patent owner who is dissatisfied with the final decision in an appeal of a reexamination to the Patent Trial and Appeal Board under section 134(b) may appeal the Board's decision only to the United States Court of Appeals for the Federal Circuit.

"(c) POST-GRANT AND INTER PARTES REVIEWS.—A party to an inter partes review or a post-grant review who is dissatisfied with the final written decision of the Patent Trial and Appeal Board under section 318(a) or 328(a) (as the case may be) may appeal the Board's decision only to the United States Court of Appeals for the Federal Circuit.

"(d) DERIVATION PROCEEDINGS.—A party to a derivation proceeding who is dissatisfied with the final decision of the Patent Trial and Appeal Board in the proceeding may appeal the decision to the United States Court of Appeals for the Federal Circuit, but such appeal shall be dismissed if any adverse party to such derivation proceeding, within 20 days after the appellant has filed notice of appeal in accordance with section 142, files notice with the Director that the party elects to have all further proceedings conducted as provided in section 146. If the appellant does not, within 30 days after the filing of such notice by the adverse party, file a civil action under section 146, the Board's decision shall govern the further proceedings in the case.".

(2) JURISDICTION.—Section 1295(a)(4)(A) of title 28, United States Code, is amended to read as follows:

"(A) the Patent Trial and Appeal Board of the United States Patent and Trademark Office with respect to a patent application, derivation proceeding, reexamination, post-grant review, or inter partes review under title 35, at the instance of a party who exercised that party's right to participate in the applicable proceeding before or appeal to the Board, except that an applicant or a party to a derivation proceeding may also have remedy by civil action pursuant to section 145 or 146 of title 35; an appeal under this subparagraph of a decision of the Board with respect to an application or derivation proceeding shall waive the right of such applicant or party to proceed under section 145 or 146 of title 35;".

(3) PROCEEDINGS ON APPEAL.—Section 143 of title 35, United States Code, is amended—

(A) by striking the third sentence and inserting the following: "In an ex parte case, the Director shall submit to the court in writing the grounds for the decision of the Patent and Trademark Office, addressing all of the issues raised in the appeal. The Director shall have the

H. R. 1249—32

right to intervene in an appeal from a decision entered by the Patent Trial and Appeal Board in a derivation proceeding under section 135 or in an inter partes or post-grant review under chapter 31 or 32."; and

(B) by striking the last sentence.

(d) CONFORMING AMENDMENTS.—

(1) ATOMIC ENERGY ACT OF 1954.—Section 152 of the Atomic Energy Act of 1954 (42 U.S.C. 2182) is amended in the third undesignated paragraph—

(A) by striking "Board of Patent Appeals and Interferences" each place it appears and inserting "Patent Trial and Appeal Board"; and

(B) by inserting "and derivation" after "established for interference".

(2) TITLE 51.—Section 20135 of title 51, United States Code, is amended—

(A) in subsections (e) and (f), by striking "Board of Patent Appeals and Interferences" each place it appears and inserting "Patent Trial and Appeal Board"; and

(B) in subsection (e), by inserting "and derivation" after "established for interference".

(e) EFFECTIVE DATE.—The amendments made by this section shall take effect upon the expiration of the 1-year period beginning on the date of the enactment of this Act and shall apply to proceedings commenced on or after that effective date, except that—

(1) the extension of jurisdiction to the United States Court of Appeals for the Federal Circuit to entertain appeals of decisions of the Patent Trial and Appeal Board in reexaminations under the amendment made by subsection (c)(2) shall be deemed to take effect on the date of the enactment of this Act and shall extend to any decision of the Board of Patent Appeals and Interferences with respect to a reexamination that is entered before, on, or after the date of the enactment of this Act;

(2) the provisions of sections 6, 134, and 141 of title 35, United States Code, as in effect on the day before the effective date of the amendments made by this section shall continue to apply to inter partes reexaminations that are requested under section 311 of such title before such effective date;

(3) the Patent Trial and Appeal Board may be deemed to be the Board of Patent Appeals and Interferences for purposes of appeals of inter partes reexaminations that are requested under section 311 of title 35, United States Code, before the effective date of the amendments made by this section; and

(4) the Director's right under the fourth sentence of section 143 of title 35, United States Code, as amended by subsection (c)(3) of this section, to intervene in an appeal from a decision entered by the Patent Trial and Appeal Board shall be deemed to extend to inter partes reexaminations that are requested under section 311 of such title before the effective date of the amendments made by this section.

SEC. 8. PREISSUANCE SUBMISSIONS BY THIRD PARTIES.

(a) IN GENERAL.—Section 122 of title 35, United States Code, is amended by adding at the end the following:

"(e) PREISSUANCE SUBMISSIONS BY THIRD PARTIES.—

"(1) IN GENERAL.—Any third party may submit for consideration and inclusion in the record of a patent application, any patent, published patent application, or other printed publication of potential relevance to the examination of the application, if such submission is made in writing before the earlier of—

"(A) the date a notice of allowance under section 151 is given or mailed in the application for patent; or

"(B) the later of—

"(i) 6 months after the date on which the application for patent is first published under section 122 by the Office, or

"(ii) the date of the first rejection under section 132 of any claim by the examiner during the examination of the application for patent.

"(2) OTHER REQUIREMENTS.—Any submission under paragraph (1) shall—

"(A) set forth a concise description of the asserted relevance of each submitted document;

"(B) be accompanied by such fee as the Director may prescribe; and

"(C) include a statement by the person making such submission affirming that the submission was made in compliance with this section.".

(b) EFFECTIVE DATE.—The amendments made by this section shall take effect upon the expiration of the 1-year period beginning on the date of the enactment of this Act and shall apply to any patent application filed before, on, or after that effective date.

SEC. 9. VENUE.

(a) TECHNICAL AMENDMENTS RELATING TO VENUE.—Sections 32, 145, 146, 154(b)(4)(A), and 293 of title 35, United States Code, and section 21(b)(4) of the Trademark Act of 1946 (15 U.S.C. 1071(b)(4)), are each amended by striking "United States District Court for the District of Columbia" each place that term appears and inserting "United States District Court for the Eastern District of Virginia".

(b) EFFECTIVE DATE.—The amendments made by this section shall take effect on the date of the enactment of this Act and shall apply to any civil action commenced on or after that date.

SEC. 10. FEE SETTING AUTHORITY.

(a) FEE SETTING.—

(1) IN GENERAL.—The Director may set or adjust by rule any fee established, authorized, or charged under title 35, United States Code, or the Trademark Act of 1946 (15 U.S.C. 1051 et seq.), for any services performed by or materials furnished by, the Office, subject to paragraph (2).

(2) FEES TO RECOVER COSTS.—Fees may be set or adjusted under paragraph (1) only to recover the aggregate estimated costs to the Office for processing, activities, services, and materials relating to patents (in the case of patent fees) and trademarks (in the case of trademark fees), including administrative costs of the Office with respect to such patent or trademark fees (as the case may be).

(b) SMALL AND MICRO ENTITIES.—The fees set or adjusted under subsection (a) for filing, searching, examining, issuing, appealing, and maintaining patent applications and patents shall be reduced by 50 percent with respect to the application of such fees to any small entity that qualifies for reduced fees under section 41(h)(1) of title 35, United States Code, and shall be reduced by 75 percent with respect to the application of such fees to any micro entity as defined in section 123 of that title (as added by subsection (g) of this section).

(c) REDUCTION OF FEES IN CERTAIN FISCAL YEARS.—In each fiscal year, the Director—

(1) shall consult with the Patent Public Advisory Committee and the Trademark Public Advisory Committee on the advisability of reducing any fees described in subsection (a); and

(2) after the consultation required under paragraph (1), may reduce such fees.

(d) ROLE OF THE PUBLIC ADVISORY COMMITTEE.—The Director shall—

(1) not less than 45 days before publishing any proposed fee under subsection (a) in the Federal Register, submit the proposed fee to the Patent Public Advisory Committee or the Trademark Public Advisory Committee, or both, as appropriate;

(2)(A) provide the relevant advisory committee described in paragraph (1) a 30-day period following the submission of any proposed fee, in which to deliberate, consider, and comment on such proposal;

(B) require that, during that 30-day period, the relevant advisory committee hold a public hearing relating to such proposal; and

(C) assist the relevant advisory committee in carrying out that public hearing, including by offering the use of the resources of the Office to notify and promote the hearing to the public and interested stakeholders;

(3) require the relevant advisory committee to make available to the public a written report setting forth in detail the comments, advice, and recommendations of the committee regarding the proposed fee; and

(4) consider and analyze any comments, advice, or recommendations received from the relevant advisory committee before setting or adjusting (as the case may be) the fee.

(e) PUBLICATION IN THE FEDERAL REGISTER.—

(1) PUBLICATION AND RATIONALE.—The Director shall—

(A) publish any proposed fee change under this section in the Federal Register;

(B) include, in such publication, the specific rationale and purpose for the proposal, including the possible expectations or benefits resulting from the proposed change; and

(C) notify, through the Chair and Ranking Member of the Committees on the Judiciary of the Senate and the House of Representatives, the Congress of the proposed change not later than the date on which the proposed change is published under subparagraph (A).

(2) PUBLIC COMMENT PERIOD.—The Director shall, in the publication under paragraph (1), provide the public a period of not less than 45 days in which to submit comments on the proposed change in fees.

(3) PUBLICATION OF FINAL RULE.—The final rule setting or adjusting a fee under this section shall be published in

the Federal Register and in the Official Gazette of the Patent and Trademark Office.

(4) CONGRESSIONAL COMMENT PERIOD.—A fee set or adjusted under subsection (a) may not become effective—

(A) before the end of the 45-day period beginning on the day after the date on which the Director publishes the final rule adjusting or setting the fee under paragraph (3); or

(B) if a law is enacted disapproving such fee.

(5) RULE OF CONSTRUCTION.—Rules prescribed under this section shall not diminish—

(A) the rights of an applicant for a patent under title 35, United States Code, or for a mark under the Trademark Act of 1946; or

(B) any rights under a ratified treaty.

(f) RETENTION OF AUTHORITY.—The Director retains the authority under subsection (a) to set or adjust fees only during such period as the Patent and Trademark Office remains an agency within the Department of Commerce.

(g) MICRO ENTITY DEFINED.—

(1) IN GENERAL.—Chapter 11 of title 35, United States Code, is amended by adding at the end the following new section:

"§ 123. Micro entity defined

"(a) IN GENERAL.—For purposes of this title, the term 'micro entity' means an applicant who makes a certification that the applicant—

"(1) qualifies as a small entity, as defined in regulations issued by the Director;

"(2) has not been named as an inventor on more than 4 previously filed patent applications, other than applications filed in another country, provisional applications under section 111(b), or international applications filed under the treaty defined in section 351(a) for which the basic national fee under section 41(a) was not paid;

"(3) did not, in the calendar year preceding the calendar year in which the applicable fee is being paid, have a gross income, as defined in section 61(a) of the Internal Revenue Code of 1986, exceeding 3 times the median household income for that preceding calendar year, as most recently reported by the Bureau of the Census; and

"(4) has not assigned, granted, or conveyed, and is not under an obligation by contract or law to assign, grant, or convey, a license or other ownership interest in the application concerned to an entity that, in the calendar year preceding the calendar year in which the applicable fee is being paid, had a gross income, as defined in section 61(a) of the Internal Revenue Code of 1986, exceeding 3 times the median household income for that preceding calendar year, as most recently reported by the Bureau of the Census.

"(b) APPLICATIONS RESULTING FROM PRIOR EMPLOYMENT.—An applicant is not considered to be named on a previously filed application for purposes of subsection (a)(2) if the applicant has assigned, or is under an obligation by contract or law to assign, all ownership rights in the application as the result of the applicant's previous employment.

H. R. 1249—36

"(c) FOREIGN CURRENCY EXCHANGE RATE.—If an applicant's or entity's gross income in the preceding calendar year is not in United States dollars, the average currency exchange rate, as reported by the Internal Revenue Service, during that calendar year shall be used to determine whether the applicant's or entity's gross income exceeds the threshold specified in paragraphs (3) or (4) of subsection (a).

"(d) INSTITUTIONS OF HIGHER EDUCATION.—For purposes of this section, a micro entity shall include an applicant who certifies that—

"(1) the applicant's employer, from which the applicant obtains the majority of the applicant's income, is an institution of higher education as defined in section 101(a) of the Higher Education Act of 1965 (20 U.S.C. 1001(a)); or

"(2) the applicant has assigned, granted, conveyed, or is under an obligation by contract or law, to assign, grant, or convey, a license or other ownership interest in the particular applications to such an institution of higher education.

"(e) DIRECTOR'S AUTHORITY.—In addition to the limits imposed by this section, the Director may, in the Director's discretion, impose income limits, annual filing limits, or other limits on who may qualify as a micro entity pursuant to this section if the Director determines that such additional limits are reasonably necessary to avoid an undue impact on other patent applicants or owners or are otherwise reasonably necessary and appropriate. At least 3 months before any limits proposed to be imposed pursuant to this subsection take effect, the Director shall inform the Committee on the Judiciary of the House of Representatives and the Committee on the Judiciary of the Senate of any such proposed limits.".

(2) CONFORMING AMENDMENT.—Chapter 11 of title 35, United States Code, is amended by adding at the end the following new item:

"123. Micro entity defined.".

(h) ELECTRONIC FILING INCENTIVE.—

(1) IN GENERAL.—Notwithstanding any other provision of this section, an additional fee of $400 shall be established for each application for an original patent, except for a design, plant, or provisional application, that is not filed by electronic means as prescribed by the Director. The fee established by this subsection shall be reduced by 50 percent for small entities that qualify for reduced fees under section 41(h)(1) of title 35, United States Code. All fees paid under this subsection shall be deposited in the Treasury as an offsetting receipt that shall not be available for obligation or expenditure.

(2) EFFECTIVE DATE.—This subsection shall take effect upon the expiration of the 60-day period beginning on the date of the enactment of this Act.

(i) EFFECTIVE DATE; SUNSET.—

(1) EFFECTIVE DATE.—Except as provided in subsection (h), this section and the amendments made by this section shall take effect on the date of the enactment of this Act.

(2) SUNSET.—The authority of the Director to set or adjust any fee under subsection (a) shall terminate upon the expiration of the 7-year period beginning on the date of the enactment of this Act.

(3) PRIOR REGULATIONS NOT AFFECTED.—The termination of authority under this subsection shall not affect any regulations issued under this section before the effective date of such termination or any rulemaking proceeding for the issuance of regulations under this section that is pending on such date.

SEC. 11. FEES FOR PATENT SERVICES.

(a) GENERAL PATENT SERVICES.—Subsections (a) and (b) of section 41 of title 35, United States Code, are amended to read as follows:

"(a) GENERAL FEES.—The Director shall charge the following fees:

"(1) FILING AND BASIC NATIONAL FEES.—

"(A) On filing each application for an original patent, except for design, plant, or provisional applications, $330.

"(B) On filing each application for an original design patent, $220.

"(C) On filing each application for an original plant patent, $220.

"(D) On filing each provisional application for an original patent, $220.

"(E) On filing each application for the reissue of a patent, $330.

"(F) The basic national fee for each international application filed under the treaty defined in section 351(a) entering the national stage under section 371, $330.

"(G) In addition, excluding any sequence listing or computer program listing filed in an electronic medium as prescribed by the Director, for any application the specification and drawings of which exceed 100 sheets of paper (or equivalent as prescribed by the Director if filed in an electronic medium), $270 for each additional 50 sheets of paper (or equivalent as prescribed by the Director if filed in an electronic medium) or fraction thereof.

"(2) EXCESS CLAIMS FEES.—

"(A) IN GENERAL.—In addition to the fee specified in paragraph (1)—

"(i) on filing or on presentation at any other time, $220 for each claim in independent form in excess of 3;

"(ii) on filing or on presentation at any other time, $52 for each claim (whether dependent or independent) in excess of 20; and

"(iii) for each application containing a multiple dependent claim, $390.

"(B) MULTIPLE DEPENDENT CLAIMS.—For the purpose of computing fees under subparagraph (A), a multiple dependent claim referred to in section 112 or any claim depending therefrom shall be considered as separate dependent claims in accordance with the number of claims to which reference is made.

"(C) REFUNDS; ERRORS IN PAYMENT.—The Director may by regulation provide for a refund of any part of the fee specified in subparagraph (A) for any claim that is canceled before an examination on the merits, as prescribed by the Director, has been made of the application under section 131. Errors in payment of the additional fees under this paragraph may be rectified in accordance with regulations prescribed by the Director.

"(3) EXAMINATION FEES.—

"(A) IN GENERAL.—

"(i) For examination of each application for an original patent, except for design, plant, provisional, or international applications, $220.

"(ii) For examination of each application for an original design patent, $140.

"(iii) For examination of each application for an original plant patent, $170.

"(iv) For examination of the national stage of each international application, $220.

"(v) For examination of each application for the reissue of a patent, $650.

"(B) APPLICABILITY OF OTHER FEE PROVISIONS.—The provisions of paragraphs (3) and (4) of section 111(a) relating to the payment of the fee for filing the application shall apply to the payment of the fee specified in subparagraph (A) with respect to an application filed under section 111(a). The provisions of section 371(d) relating to the payment of the national fee shall apply to the payment of the fee specified in subparagraph (A) with respect to an international application.

"(4) ISSUE FEES.—

"(A) For issuing each original patent, except for design or plant patents, $1,510.

"(B) For issuing each original design patent, $860.

"(C) For issuing each original plant patent, $1,190.

"(D) For issuing each reissue patent, $1,510.

"(5) DISCLAIMER FEE.—On filing each disclaimer, $140.

"(6) APPEAL FEES.—

"(A) On filing an appeal from the examiner to the Patent Trial and Appeal Board, $540.

"(B) In addition, on filing a brief in support of the appeal, $540, and on requesting an oral hearing in the appeal before the Patent Trial and Appeal Board, $1,080.

"(7) REVIVAL FEES.—On filing each petition for the revival of an unintentionally abandoned application for a patent, for the unintentionally delayed payment of the fee for issuing each patent, or for an unintentionally delayed response by the patent owner in any reexamination proceeding, $1,620, unless the petition is filed under section 133 or 151, in which case the fee shall be $540.

"(8) EXTENSION FEES.—For petitions for 1-month extensions of time to take actions required by the Director in an application—

"(A) on filing a first petition, $130;

"(B) on filing a second petition, $360; and

"(C) on filing a third or subsequent petition, $620.

"(b) MAINTENANCE FEES.—

"(1) IN GENERAL.—The Director shall charge the following fees for maintaining in force all patents based on applications filed on or after December 12, 1980:

"(A) Three years and 6 months after grant, $980.

"(B) Seven years and 6 months after grant, $2,480.

"(C) Eleven years and 6 months after grant, $4,110.

"(2) GRACE PERIOD; SURCHARGE.—Unless payment of the applicable maintenance fee under paragraph (1) is received in the Office on or before the date the fee is due or within a grace period of 6 months thereafter, the patent shall expire as of the end of such grace period. The Director may require the payment of a surcharge as a condition of accepting within such 6-month grace period the payment of an applicable maintenance fee.

"(3) NO MAINTENANCE FEE FOR DESIGN OR PLANT PATENT.—No fee may be established for maintaining a design or plant patent in force.".

(b) DELAYS IN PAYMENT.—Subsection (c) of section 41 of title 35, United States Code, is amended—

(1) by striking "(c)(1) The Director" and inserting:

"(c) DELAYS IN PAYMENT OF MAINTENANCE FEES.—

"(1) ACCEPTANCE.—The Director"; and

(2) by striking "(2) A patent" and inserting:

"(2) EFFECT ON RIGHTS OF OTHERS.—A patent".

(c) PATENT SEARCH FEES.—Subsection (d) of section 41 of title 35, United States Code, is amended to read as follows:

"(d) PATENT SEARCH AND OTHER FEES.—

"(1) PATENT SEARCH FEES.—

"(A) IN GENERAL.—The Director shall charge the fees specified under subparagraph (B) for the search of each application for a patent, except for provisional applications. The Director shall adjust the fees charged under this paragraph to ensure that the fees recover an amount not to exceed the estimated average cost to the Office of searching applications for patent by Office personnel.

"(B) SPECIFIC FEES.—The fees referred to in subparagraph (A) are—

"(i) $540 for each application for an original patent, except for design, plant, provisional, or international applications;

"(ii) $100 for each application for an original design patent;

"(iii) $330 for each application for an original plant patent;

"(iv) $540 for the national stage of each international application; and

"(v) $540 for each application for the reissue of a patent.

"(C) APPLICABILITY OF OTHER PROVISIONS.—The provisions of paragraphs (3) and (4) of section 111(a) relating to the payment of the fee for filing the application shall apply to the payment of the fee specified in this paragraph with respect to an application filed under section 111(a). The provisions of section 371(d) relating to the payment of the national fee shall apply to the payment of the fee specified in this paragraph with respect to an international application.

"(D) REFUNDS.—The Director may by regulation provide for a refund of any part of the fee specified in this paragraph for any applicant who files a written declaration of express abandonment as prescribed by the Director before an examination has been made of the application under section 131.

"(2) OTHER FEES.—

"(A) IN GENERAL.—The Director shall establish fees for all other processing, services, or materials relating to patents not specified in this section to recover the estimated average cost to the Office of such processing, services, or materials, except that the Director shall charge the following fees for the following services:

"(i) For recording a document affecting title, $40 per property.

"(ii) For each photocopy, $.25 per page.

"(iii) For each black and white copy of a patent, $3.

"(B) COPIES FOR LIBRARIES.—The yearly fee for providing a library specified in section 12 with uncertified printed copies of the specifications and drawings for all patents in that year shall be $50.".

(d) FEES FOR SMALL ENTITIES.—Subsection (h) of section 41 of title 35, United States Code, is amended to read as follows:

"(h) FEES FOR SMALL ENTITIES.—

"(1) REDUCTIONS IN FEES.—Subject to paragraph (3), fees charged under subsections (a), (b), and (d)(1) shall be reduced by 50 percent with respect to their application to any small business concern as defined under section 3 of the Small Business Act, and to any independent inventor or nonprofit organization as defined in regulations issued by the Director.

"(2) SURCHARGES AND OTHER FEES.—With respect to its application to any entity described in paragraph (1), any surcharge or fee charged under subsection (c) or (d) shall not be higher than the surcharge or fee required of any other entity under the same or substantially similar circumstances.

"(3) REDUCTION FOR ELECTRONIC FILING.—The fee charged under subsection (a)(1)(A) shall be reduced by 75 percent with respect to its application to any entity to which paragraph (1) applies, if the application is filed by electronic means as prescribed by the Director.".

(e) TECHNICAL AMENDMENTS.—Section 41 of title 35, United States Code, is amended—

(1) in subsection (e), in the first sentence, by striking "The Director" and inserting "WAIVER OF FEES; COPIES REGARDING NOTICE.—The Director";

(2) in subsection (f), by striking "The fees" and inserting "ADJUSTMENT OF FEES.—The fees";

(3) by repealing subsection (g); and

(4) in subsection (i)—

(A) by striking "(i)(1) The Director" and inserting the following:

"(i) ELECTRONIC PATENT AND TRADEMARK DATA.—

"(1) MAINTENANCE OF COLLECTIONS.—The Director";

(B) by striking "(2) The Director" and inserting the following:

"(2) AVAILABILITY OF AUTOMATED SEARCH SYSTEMS.—The Director";

(C) by striking "(3) The Director" and inserting the following:

"(3) ACCESS FEES.—The Director"; and

(D) by striking "(4) The Director" and inserting the following:

H. R. 1249—41

"(4) ANNUAL REPORT TO CONGRESS.—The Director".

(f) ADJUSTMENT OF TRADEMARK FEES.—Section 802(a) of division B of the Consolidated Appropriations Act, 2005 (Public Law 108–447) is amended—

(1) in the first sentence, by striking "During fiscal years 2005, 2006, and 2007,", and inserting "Until such time as the Director sets or adjusts the fees otherwise,"; and

(2) in the second sentence, by striking "During fiscal years 2005, 2006, and 2007, the" and inserting "The".

(g) EFFECTIVE DATE, APPLICABILITY, AND TRANSITION PROVISIONS.—Section 803(a) of division B of the Consolidated Appropriations Act, 2005 (Public Law 108–447) is amended by striking "and shall apply only with respect to the remaining portion of fiscal year 2005 and fiscal year 2006".

(h) PRIORITIZED EXAMINATION FEE.—

(1) IN GENERAL.—

(A) FEE.—

(i) PRIORITIZED EXAMINATION FEE.—A fee of $4,800 shall be established for filing a request, pursuant to section 2(b)(2)(G) of title 35, United States Code, for prioritized examination of a nonprovisional application for an original utility or plant patent.

(ii) ADDITIONAL FEES.—In addition to the prioritized examination fee under clause (i), the fees due on an application for which prioritized examination is being sought are the filing, search, and examination fees (including any applicable excess claims and application size fees), processing fee, and publication fee for that application.

(B) REGULATIONS; LIMITATIONS.—

(i) REGULATIONS.—The Director may by regulation prescribe conditions for acceptance of a request under subparagraph (A) and a limit on the number of filings for prioritized examination that may be accepted.

(ii) LIMITATION ON CLAIMS.— Until regulations are prescribed under clause (i), no application for which prioritized examination is requested may contain or be amended to contain more than 4 independent claims or more than 30 total claims.

(iii) LIMITATION ON TOTAL NUMBER OF REQUESTS.—The Director may not accept in any fiscal year more than 10,000 requests for prioritization until regulations are prescribed under this subparagraph setting another limit.

(2) REDUCTION IN FEES FOR SMALL ENTITIES.—The Director shall reduce fees for providing prioritized examination of nonprovisional applications for original utility and plant patents by 50 percent for small entities that qualify for reduced fees under section 41(h)(1) of title 35, United States Code.

(3) DEPOSIT OF FEES.—All fees paid under this subsection shall be credited to the United States Patent and Trademark Office Appropriation Account, shall remain available until expended, and may be used only for the purposes specified in section 42(c)(3)(A) of title 35, United States Code.

(4) EFFECTIVE DATE AND TERMINATION.—

(A) EFFECTIVE DATE.—This subsection shall take effect on the date that is 10 days after the date of the enactment of this Act.

(B) TERMINATION.—The fee imposed under paragraph (1)(A)(i), and the reduced fee under paragraph (2), shall terminate on the effective date of the setting or adjustment of the fee under paragraph (1)(A)(i) pursuant to the exercise of the authority under section 10 for the first time with respect to that fee.

(i) APPROPRIATION ACCOUNT TRANSITION FEES.—

(1) SURCHARGE.—

(A) IN GENERAL.—There shall be a surcharge of 15 percent, rounded by standard arithmetic rules, on all fees charged or authorized by subsections (a), (b), and (d)(1) of section 41, and section 132(b), of title 35, United States Code. Any surcharge imposed under this subsection is, and shall be construed to be, separate from and in addition to any other surcharge imposed under this Act or any other provision of law.

(B) DEPOSIT OF AMOUNTS.—Amounts collected pursuant to the surcharge imposed under subparagraph (A) shall be credited to the United States Patent and Trademark Appropriation Account, shall remain available until expended, and may be used only for the purposes specified in section 42(c)(3)(A) of title 35, United States Code.

(2) EFFECTIVE DATE AND TERMINATION OF SURCHARGE.—The surcharge provided for in paragraph (1)—

(A) shall take effect on the date that is 10 days after the date of the enactment of this Act; and

(B) shall terminate, with respect to a fee to which paragraph (1)(A) applies, on the effective date of the setting or adjustment of that fee pursuant to the exercise of the authority under section 10 for the first time with respect to that fee.

(j) EFFECTIVE DATE.—Except as otherwise provided in this section, this section and the amendments made by this section shall take effect on the date of the enactment of this Act.

SEC. 12. SUPPLEMENTAL EXAMINATION.

(a) IN GENERAL.—Chapter 25 of title 35, United States Code, is amended by adding at the end the following:

"§ 257. Supplemental examinations to consider, reconsider, or correct information

"(a) REQUEST FOR SUPPLEMENTAL EXAMINATION.—A patent owner may request supplemental examination of a patent in the Office to consider, reconsider, or correct information believed to be relevant to the patent, in accordance with such requirements as the Director may establish. Within 3 months after the date a request for supplemental examination meeting the requirements of this section is received, the Director shall conduct the supplemental examination and shall conclude such examination by issuing a certificate indicating whether the information presented in the request raises a substantial new question of patentability.

"(b) REEXAMINATION ORDERED.—If the certificate issued under subsection (a) indicates that a substantial new question of patentability is raised by 1 or more items of information in the request, the Director shall order reexamination of the patent. The reexamination shall be conducted according to procedures established by chapter 30, except that the patent owner shall not have the right to file a statement pursuant to section 304. During the reexamination, the Director shall address each substantial new question of patentability identified during the supplemental examination, notwithstanding the limitations in chapter 30 relating to patents and printed publication or any other provision of such chapter.

"(c) EFFECT.—

"(1) IN GENERAL.—A patent shall not be held unenforceable on the basis of conduct relating to information that had not been considered, was inadequately considered, or was incorrect in a prior examination of the patent if the information was considered, reconsidered, or corrected during a supplemental examination of the patent. The making of a request under subsection (a), or the absence thereof, shall not be relevant to enforceability of the patent under section 282.

"(2) EXCEPTIONS.—

"(A) PRIOR ALLEGATIONS.—Paragraph (1) shall not apply to an allegation pled with particularity in a civil action, or set forth with particularity in a notice received by the patent owner under section 505(j)(2)(B)(iv)(II) of the Federal Food, Drug, and Cosmetic Act (21 U.S.C. 355(j)(2)(B)(iv)(II)), before the date of a supplemental examination request under subsection (a) to consider, reconsider, or correct information forming the basis for the allegation.

"(B) PATENT ENFORCEMENT ACTIONS.—In an action brought under section 337(a) of the Tariff Act of 1930 (19 U.S.C. 1337(a)), or section 281 of this title, paragraph (1) shall not apply to any defense raised in the action that is based upon information that was considered, reconsidered, or corrected pursuant to a supplemental examination request under subsection (a), unless the supplemental examination, and any reexamination ordered pursuant to the request, are concluded before the date on which the action is brought.

"(d) FEES AND REGULATIONS.—

"(1) FEES.—The Director shall, by regulation, establish fees for the submission of a request for supplemental examination of a patent, and to consider each item of information submitted in the request. If reexamination is ordered under subsection (b), fees established and applicable to ex parte reexamination proceedings under chapter 30 shall be paid, in addition to fees applicable to supplemental examination.

"(2) REGULATIONS.—The Director shall issue regulations governing the form, content, and other requirements of requests for supplemental examination, and establishing procedures for reviewing information submitted in such requests.

"(e) FRAUD.—If the Director becomes aware, during the course of a supplemental examination or reexamination proceeding ordered under this section, that a material fraud on the Office may have been committed in connection with the patent that is the subject of the supplemental examination, then in addition to any other actions the Director is authorized to take, including the cancellation of any claims found to be invalid under section 307 as a result of a reexamination ordered under this section, the Director shall also refer the matter to the Attorney General for such further action as the Attorney General may deem appropriate. Any such referral shall be treated as confidential, shall not be included in the file of the patent, and shall not be disclosed to the public unless the United States charges a person with a criminal offense in connection with such referral.

"(f) RULE OF CONSTRUCTION.—Nothing in this section shall be construed—

"(1) to preclude the imposition of sanctions based upon criminal or antitrust laws (including section 1001(a) of title 18, the first section of the Clayton Act, and section 5 of the Federal Trade Commission Act to the extent that section relates to unfair methods of competition);

"(2) to limit the authority of the Director to investigate issues of possible misconduct and impose sanctions for misconduct in connection with matters or proceedings before the Office; or

"(3) to limit the authority of the Director to issue regulations under chapter 3 relating to sanctions for misconduct by representatives practicing before the Office.".

(b) CONFORMING AMENDMENT.—The table of sections for chapter 25 of title 35, United States Code, is amended by adding at the end the following new item:

"257. Supplemental examinations to consider, reconsider, or correct information.".

(c) EFFECTIVE DATE.—The amendments made by this section shall take effect upon the expiration of the 1-year period beginning on the date of the enactment of this Act and shall apply to any patent issued before, on, or after that effective date.

SEC. 13. FUNDING AGREEMENTS.

(a) IN GENERAL.—Section 202(c)(7)(E)(i) of title 35, United States Code, is amended—

(1) by striking "75 percent" and inserting "15 percent";

(2) by striking "25 percent" and inserting "85 percent"; and

(3) by striking "as described above in this clause (D);" and inserting "described above in this clause;".

(b) EFFECTIVE DATE.—The amendments made by this section shall take effect on the date of the enactment of this Act and shall apply to any patent issued before, on, or after that date.

SEC. 14. TAX STRATEGIES DEEMED WITHIN THE PRIOR ART.

(a) IN GENERAL.—For purposes of evaluating an invention under section 102 or 103 of title 35, United States Code, any strategy for reducing, avoiding, or deferring tax liability, whether known or unknown at the time of the invention or application for patent, shall be deemed insufficient to differentiate a claimed invention from the prior art.

(b) DEFINITION.—For purposes of this section, the term "tax liability" refers to any liability for a tax under any Federal, State, or local law, or the law of any foreign jurisdiction, including any statute, rule, regulation, or ordinance that levies, imposes, or assesses such tax liability.

(c) EXCLUSIONS.—This section does not apply to that part of an invention that—

(1) is a method, apparatus, technology, computer program product, or system, that is used solely for preparing a tax

or information return or other tax filing, including one that records, transmits, transfers, or organizes data related to such filing; or

(2) is a method, apparatus, technology, computer program product, or system used solely for financial management, to the extent that it is severable from any tax strategy or does not limit the use of any tax strategy by any taxpayer or tax advisor.

(d) RULE OF CONSTRUCTION.—Nothing in this section shall be construed to imply that other business methods are patentable or that other business method patents are valid.

(e) EFFECTIVE DATE; APPLICABILITY.—This section shall take effect on the date of the enactment of this Act and shall apply to any patent application that is pending on, or filed on or after, that date, and to any patent that is issued on or after that date.

SEC. 15. BEST MODE REQUIREMENT.

(a) IN GENERAL.—Section 282 of title 35, United States Code, is amended in the second undesignated paragraph by striking paragraph (3) and inserting the following:

"(3) Invalidity of the patent or any claim in suit for failure to comply with—

"(A) any requirement of section 112, except that the failure to disclose the best mode shall not be a basis on which any claim of a patent may be canceled or held invalid or otherwise unenforceable; or

"(B) any requirement of section 251.".

(b) CONFORMING AMENDMENT.—Sections 119(e)(1) and 120 of title 35, United States Code, are each amended by striking "the first paragraph of section 112 of this title" and inserting "section 112(a) (other than the requirement to disclose the best mode)".

(c) EFFECTIVE DATE.—The amendments made by this section shall take effect upon the date of the enactment of this Act and shall apply to proceedings commenced on or after that date.

SEC. 16. MARKING.

(a) VIRTUAL MARKING.—

(1) IN GENERAL.—Section 287(a) of title 35, United States Code, is amended by striking "or when," and inserting "or by fixing thereon the word 'patent' or the abbreviation 'pat.' together with an address of a posting on the Internet, accessible to the public without charge for accessing the address, that associates the patented article with the number of the patent, or when,".

(2) EFFECTIVE DATE.—The amendment made by this subsection shall apply to any case that is pending on, or commenced on or after, the date of the enactment of this Act.

(3) REPORT.—Not later than the date that is 3 years after the date of the enactment of this Act, the Director shall submit a report to Congress that provides—

(A) an analysis of the effectiveness of "virtual marking", as provided in the amendment made by paragraph (1) of this subsection, as an alternative to the physical marking of articles;

(B) an analysis of whether such virtual marking has limited or improved the ability of the general public to access information about patents;

(C) an analysis of the legal issues, if any, that arise from such virtual marking; and

(D) an analysis of the deficiencies, if any, of such virtual marking.

(b) FALSE MARKING.—

(1) CIVIL PENALTY.—Section 292(a) of title 35, United States, Code, is amended by adding at the end the following: "Only the United States may sue for the penalty authorized by this subsection.".

(2) CIVIL ACTION FOR DAMAGES.—Subsection (b) of section 292 of title 35, United States Code, is amended to read as follows:

"(b) A person who has suffered a competitive injury as a result of a violation of this section may file a civil action in a district court of the United States for recovery of damages adequate to compensate for the injury.".

(3) EXPIRED PATENTS.—Section 292 of title 35, United States Code, is amended by adding at the end the following:

"(c) The marking of a product, in a manner described in subsection (a), with matter relating to a patent that covered that product but has expired is not a violation of this section.".

(4) EFFECTIVE DATE.—The amendments made by this subsection shall apply to all cases, without exception, that are pending on, or commenced on or after, the date of the enactment of this Act.

SEC. 17. ADVICE OF COUNSEL.

(a) IN GENERAL.—Chapter 29 of title 35, United States Code, is amended by adding at the end the following:

"§ 298. Advice of counsel

"The failure of an infringer to obtain the advice of counsel with respect to any allegedly infringed patent, or the failure of the infringer to present such advice to the court or jury, may not be used to prove that the accused infringer willfully infringed the patent or that the infringer intended to induce infringement of the patent.".

(b) CONFORMING AMENDMENT.—The table of sections for chapter 29 of title 35, United States Code, is amended by adding at the end the following:

"298. Advice of counsel.".

SEC. 18. TRANSITIONAL PROGRAM FOR COVERED BUSINESS METHOD PATENTS.

(a) TRANSITIONAL PROGRAM.—

(1) ESTABLISHMENT.—Not later than the date that is 1 year after the date of the enactment of this Act, the Director shall issue regulations establishing and implementing a transitional post-grant review proceeding for review of the validity of covered business method patents. The transitional proceeding implemented pursuant to this subsection shall be regarded as, and shall employ the standards and procedures of, a post-grant review under chapter 32 of title 35, United States Code, subject to the following:

(A) Section 321(c) of title 35, United States Code, and subsections (b), (e)(2), and (f) of section 325 of such title shall not apply to a transitional proceeding.

(B) A person may not file a petition for a transitional proceeding with respect to a covered business method patent unless the person or the person's real party in interest or privy has been sued for infringement of the patent or has been charged with infringement under that patent.

(C) A petitioner in a transitional proceeding who challenges the validity of 1 or more claims in a covered business method patent on a ground raised under section 102 or 103 of title 35, United States Code, as in effect on the day before the effective date set forth in section 3(n)(1), may support such ground only on the basis of—

(i) prior art that is described by section 102(a) of such title of such title (as in effect on the day before such effective date); or

(ii) prior art that—

(I) discloses the invention more than 1 year before the date of the application for patent in the United States; and

(II) would be described by section 102(a) of such title (as in effect on the day before the effective date set forth in section 3(n)(1)) if the disclosure had been made by another before the invention thereof by the applicant for patent.

(D) The petitioner in a transitional proceeding that results in a final written decision under section 328(a) of title 35, United States Code, with respect to a claim in a covered business method patent, or the petitioner's real party in interest, may not assert, either in a civil action arising in whole or in part under section 1338 of title 28, United States Code, or in a proceeding before the International Trade Commission under section 337 of the Tariff Act of 1930 (19 U.S.C. 1337), that the claim is invalid on any ground that the petitioner raised during that transitional proceeding.

(E) The Director may institute a transitional proceeding only for a patent that is a covered business method patent.

(2) EFFECTIVE DATE.—The regulations issued under paragraph (1) shall take effect upon the expiration of the 1-year period beginning on the date of the enactment of this Act and shall apply to any covered business method patent issued before, on, or after that effective date, except that the regulations shall not apply to a patent described in section 6(f)(2)(A) of this Act during the period in which a petition for post-grant review of that patent would satisfy the requirements of section 321(c) of title 35, United States Code.

(3) SUNSET.—

(A) IN GENERAL.—This subsection, and the regulations issued under this subsection, are repealed effective upon the expiration of the 8-year period beginning on the date that the regulations issued under to paragraph (1) take effect.

(B) APPLICABILITY.—Notwithstanding subparagraph (A), this subsection and the regulations issued under this subsection shall continue to apply, after the date of the repeal under subparagraph (A), to any petition for a transitional proceeding that is filed before the date of such repeal.

(b) REQUEST FOR STAY.—

(1) IN GENERAL.—If a party seeks a stay of a civil action alleging infringement of a patent under section 281 of title 35, United States Code, relating to a transitional proceeding for that patent, the court shall decide whether to enter a stay based on—

(A) whether a stay, or the denial thereof, will simplify the issues in question and streamline the trial;

(B) whether discovery is complete and whether a trial date has been set;

(C) whether a stay, or the denial thereof, would unduly prejudice the nonmoving party or present a clear tactical advantage for the moving party; and

(D) whether a stay, or the denial thereof, will reduce the burden of litigation on the parties and on the court.

(2) REVIEW.—A party may take an immediate interlocutory appeal from a district court's decision under paragraph (1). The United States Court of Appeals for the Federal Circuit shall review the district court's decision to ensure consistent application of established precedent, and such review may be de novo.

(c) ATM EXEMPTION FOR VENUE PURPOSES.—In an action for infringement under section 281 of title 35, United States Code, of a covered business method patent, an automated teller machine shall not be deemed to be a regular and established place of business for purposes of section 1400(b) of title 28, United States Code.

(d) DEFINITION.—

(1) IN GENERAL.—For purposes of this section, the term "covered business method patent" means a patent that claims a method or corresponding apparatus for performing data processing or other operations used in the practice, administration, or management of a financial product or service, except that the term does not include patents for technological inventions.

(2) REGULATIONS.—To assist in implementing the transitional proceeding authorized by this subsection, the Director shall issue regulations for determining whether a patent is for a technological invention.

(e) RULE OF CONSTRUCTION.—Nothing in this section shall be construed as amending or interpreting categories of patent-eligible subject matter set forth under section 101 of title 35, United States Code.

SEC. 19. JURISDICTION AND PROCEDURAL MATTERS.

(a) STATE COURT JURISDICTION.—Section 1338(a) of title 28, United States Code, is amended by striking the second sentence and inserting the following: "No State court shall have jurisdiction over any claim for relief arising under any Act of Congress relating to patents, plant variety protection, or copyrights. For purposes of this subsection, the term 'State' includes any State of the United States, the District of Columbia, the Commonwealth of Puerto Rico, the United States Virgin Islands, American Samoa, Guam, and the Northern Mariana Islands.".

(b) COURT OF APPEALS FOR THE FEDERAL CIRCUIT.—Section 1295(a)(1) of title 28, United States Code, is amended to read as follows:

"(1) of an appeal from a final decision of a district court of the United States, the District Court of Guam, the District Court of the Virgin Islands, or the District Court of the Northern Mariana Islands, in any civil action arising under, or in any civil action in which a party has asserted a compulsory counterclaim arising under, any Act of Congress relating to patents or plant variety protection;".

(c) REMOVAL.—

(1) IN GENERAL.—Chapter 89 of title 28, United States Code, is amended by adding at the end the following new section:

"§ 1454. Patent, plant variety protection, and copyright cases

"(a) IN GENERAL.—A civil action in which any party asserts a claim for relief arising under any Act of Congress relating to patents, plant variety protection, or copyrights may be removed to the district court of the United States for the district and division embracing the place where the action is pending.

"(b) SPECIAL RULES.—The removal of an action under this section shall be made in accordance with section 1446, except that if the removal is based solely on this section—

"(1) the action may be removed by any party; and

"(2) the time limitations contained in section 1446(b) may be extended at any time for cause shown.

"(c) CLARIFICATION OF JURISDICTION IN CERTAIN CASES.—The court to which a civil action is removed under this section is not precluded from hearing and determining any claim in the civil action because the State court from which the civil action is removed did not have jurisdiction over that claim.

"(d) REMAND.—If a civil action is removed solely under this section, the district court—

"(1) shall remand all claims that are neither a basis for removal under subsection (a) nor within the original or supplemental jurisdiction of the district court under any Act of Congress; and

"(2) may, under the circumstances specified in section 1367(c), remand any claims within the supplemental jurisdiction of the district court under section 1367.".

(2) CONFORMING AMENDMENT.—The table of sections for chapter 89 of title 28, United States Code, is amended by adding at the end the following new item:

"1454. Patent, plant variety protection, and copyright cases.".

(d) PROCEDURAL MATTERS IN PATENT CASES.—

(1) JOINDER OF PARTIES AND STAY OF ACTIONS.—Chapter 29 of title 35, United States Code, as amended by this Act, is further amended by adding at the end the following new section:

"§ 299. Joinder of parties

"(a) JOINDER OF ACCUSED INFRINGERS.—With respect to any civil action arising under any Act of Congress relating to patents, other than an action or trial in which an act of infringement under section 271(e)(2) has been pled, parties that are accused infringers may be joined in one action as defendants or counterclaim defendants, or have their actions consolidated for trial, or counterclaim defendants only if—

"(1) any right to relief is asserted against the parties jointly, severally, or in the alternative with respect to or arising out of the same transaction, occurrence, or series of transactions or occurrences relating to the making, using, importing into the United States, offering for sale, or selling of the same accused product or process; and

"(2) questions of fact common to all defendants or counterclaim defendants will arise in the action.

"(b) Allegations Insufficient for Joinder.—For purposes of this subsection, accused infringers may not be joined in one action as defendants or counterclaim defendants, or have their actions consolidated for trial, based solely on allegations that they each have infringed the patent or patents in suit.

"(c) Waiver.—A party that is an accused infringer may waive the limitations set forth in this section with respect to that party.".

(2) Conforming amendment.—The table of sections for chapter 29 of title 35, United States Code, as amended by this Act, is further amended by adding at the end the following new item:

"299. Joinder of parties.".

(e) Effective Date.—The amendments made by this section shall apply to any civil action commenced on or after the date of the enactment of this Act.

SEC. 20. TECHNICAL AMENDMENTS.

(a) Joint Inventions.—Section 116 of title 35, United States Code, is amended—

(1) in the first undesignated paragraph, by striking "When" and inserting "(a) Joint Inventions.—When";

(2) in the second undesignated paragraph, by striking "If a joint inventor" and inserting "(b) Omitted Inventor.—If a joint inventor"; and

(3) in the third undesignated paragraph—

(A) by striking "Whenever" and inserting "(c) Correction of Errors in Application.—Whenever"; and

(B) by striking "and such error arose without any deceptive intention on his part,".

(b) Filing of Application in Foreign Country.—Section 184 of title 35, United States Code, is amended—

(1) in the first undesignated paragraph—

(A) by striking "Except when" and inserting "(a) Filing in Foreign Country.—Except when"; and

(B) by striking "and without deceptive intent";

(2) in the second undesignated paragraph, by striking "The term" and inserting "(b) Application.—The term"; and

(3) in the third undesignated paragraph, by striking "The scope" and inserting "(c) Subsequent Modifications, Amendments, and Supplements.—The scope".

(c) Filing Without a License.—Section 185 of title 35, United States Code, is amended by striking "and without deceptive intent".

(d) Reissue of Defective Patents.—Section 251 of title 35, United States Code, is amended—

(1) in the first undesignated paragraph—

(A) by striking "Whenever" and inserting "(a) In General.—Whenever"; and

(B) by striking "without any deceptive intention";

(2) in the second undesignated paragraph, by striking "The Director" and inserting "(b) MULTIPLE REISSUED PATENTS.—The Director";

(3) in the third undesignated paragraph, by striking "The provisions" and inserting "(c) APPLICABILITY OF THIS TITLE.—The provisions"; and

(4) in the last undesignated paragraph, by striking "No reissued patent" and inserting "(d) REISSUE PATENT ENLARGING SCOPE OF CLAIMS.—No reissued patent".

(e) EFFECT OF REISSUE.—Section 253 of title 35, United States Code, is amended—

(1) in the first undesignated paragraph, by striking "Whenever, without any deceptive intention," and inserting "(a) IN GENERAL.—Whenever"; and

(2) in the second undesignated paragraph, by striking "In like manner" and inserting "(b) ADDITIONAL DISCLAIMER OR DEDICATION.—In the manner set forth in subsection (a),".

(f) CORRECTION OF NAMED INVENTOR.—Section 256 of title 35, United States Code, is amended—

(1) in the first undesignated paragraph—

(A) by striking "Whenever" and inserting "(a) CORRECTION.—Whenever"; and

(B) by striking "and such error arose without any deceptive intention on his part"; and

(2) in the second undesignated paragraph, by striking "The error" and inserting "(b) PATENT VALID IF ERROR CORRECTED.—The error".

(g) PRESUMPTION OF VALIDITY.—Section 282 of title 35, United States Code, is amended—

(1) in the first undesignated paragraph—

(A) by striking "A patent" and inserting "(a) IN GENERAL.—A patent"; and

(B) by striking the third sentence;

(2) in the second undesignated paragraph—

(A) by striking "The following" and inserting "(b) DEFENSES.—The following";

(B) in paragraph (1), by striking "uneforceability," and inserting "unenforceability."; and

(C) in paragraph (2), by striking "patentability," and inserting "patentability." ; and

(3) in the third undesignated paragraph—

(A) by striking "In actions involving the validity or infringement of a patent" and inserting "(c) NOTICE OF ACTIONS; ACTIONS DURING EXTENSION OF PATENT TERM.—In an action involving the validity or infringement of a patent"; and

(B) by striking "Claims Court" and inserting "Court of Federal Claims".

(h) ACTION FOR INFRINGEMENT.—Section 288 of title 35, United States Code, is amended by striking ", without deceptive intention,".

(i) REVISER'S NOTES.—

(1) Section 3(e)(2) of title 35, United States Code, is amended by striking "this Act," and inserting "that Act,".

(2) Section 202 of title 35, United States Code, is amended—

(A) in subsection (b)(3), by striking "the section 203(b)" and inserting "section 203(b)"; and

(B) in subsection (c)(7)(D), by striking "except where it proves" and all that follows through "small business firms; and" and inserting: "except where it is determined to be infeasible following a reasonable inquiry, a preference in the licensing of subject inventions shall be given to small business firms; and".

(3) Section 209(d)(1) of title 35, United States Code, is amended by striking "nontransferrable" and inserting "nontransferable".

(4) Section 287(c)(2)(G) of title 35, United States Code, is amended by striking "any state" and inserting "any State".

(5) Section 371(b) of title 35, United States Code, is amended by striking "of the treaty" and inserting "of the treaty.".

(j) UNNECESSARY REFERENCES.—

(1) IN GENERAL.—Title 35, United States Code, is amended by striking "of this title" each place that term appears.

(2) EXCEPTION.—The amendment made by paragraph (1) shall not apply to the use of such term in the following sections of title 35, United States Code:

(A) Section 1(c).

(B) Section 101.

(C) Subsections (a) and (b) of section 105.

(D) The first instance of the use of such term in section 111(b)(8).

(E) Section 161.

(F) Section 164.

(G) Section 171.

(H) Section 251(c), as so designated by this section.

(I) Section 261.

(J) Subsections (g) and (h) of section 271.

(K) Section 287(b)(1).

(L) Section 289.

(M) The first instance of the use of such term in section 375(a).

(k) ADDITIONAL TECHNICAL AMENDMENTS.—Sections 155 and 155A of title 35, United States Code, and the items relating to those sections in the table of sections for chapter 14 of such title, are repealed.

(l) EFFECTIVE DATE.—The amendments made by this section shall take effect upon the expiration of the 1-year period beginning on the date of the enactment of this Act and shall apply to proceedings commenced on or after that effective date.

SEC. 21. TRAVEL EXPENSES AND PAYMENT OF ADMINISTRATIVE JUDGES.

(a) AUTHORITY TO COVER CERTAIN TRAVEL RELATED EXPENSES.—Section 2(b)(11) of title 35, United States Code, is amended by inserting ", and the Office is authorized to expend funds to cover the subsistence expenses and travel-related expenses, including per diem, lodging costs, and transportation costs, of persons attending such programs who are not Federal employees" after "world".

H. R. 1249—53

(b) PAYMENT OF ADMINISTRATIVE JUDGES.—Section 3(b) of title 35, United States Code, is amended by adding at the end the following:

"(6) ADMINISTRATIVE PATENT JUDGES AND ADMINISTRATIVE TRADEMARK JUDGES.—The Director may fix the rate of basic pay for the administrative patent judges appointed pursuant to section 6 and the administrative trademark judges appointed pursuant to section 17 of the Trademark Act of 1946 (15 U.S.C. 1067) at not greater than the rate of basic pay payable for level III of the Executive Schedule under section 5314 of title 5. The payment of a rate of basic pay under this paragraph shall not be subject to the pay limitation under section 5306(e) or 5373 of title 5.".

SEC. 22. PATENT AND TRADEMARK OFFICE FUNDING.

(a) IN GENERAL.—Section 42(c) of title 35, United States Code, is amended—

(1) by striking "(c)" and inserting "(c)(1)";

(2) in the first sentence, by striking "shall be available" and inserting "shall, subject to paragraph (3), be available";

(3) by striking the second sentence; and

(4) by adding at the end the following:

"(2) There is established in the Treasury a Patent and Trademark Fee Reserve Fund. If fee collections by the Patent and Trademark Office for a fiscal year exceed the amount appropriated to the Office for that fiscal year, fees collected in excess of the appropriated amount shall be deposited in the Patent and Trademark Fee Reserve Fund. To the extent and in the amounts provided in appropriations Acts, amounts in the Fund shall be made available until expended only for obligation and expenditure by the Office in accordance with paragraph (3).

"(3)(A) Any fees that are collected under sections 41, 42, and 376, and any surcharges on such fees, may only be used for expenses of the Office relating to the processing of patent applications and for other activities, services, and materials relating to patents and to cover a share of the administrative costs of the Office relating to patents.

"(B) Any fees that are collected under section 31 of the Trademark Act of 1946, and any surcharges on such fees, may only be used for expenses of the Office relating to the processing of trademark registrations and for other activities, services, and materials relating to trademarks and to cover a share of the administrative costs of the Office relating to trademarks.".

(b) EFFECTIVE DATE.—The amendments made by this section shall take effect on October 1, 2011.

SEC. 23. SATELLITE OFFICES.

(a) ESTABLISHMENT.—Subject to available resources, the Director shall, by not later than the date that is 3 years after the date of the enactment of this Act, establish 3 or more satellite offices in the United States to carry out the responsibilities of the Office.

(b) PURPOSES.—The purposes of the satellite offices established under subsection (a) are to—

(1) increase outreach activities to better connect patent filers and innovators with the Office;

(2) enhance patent examiner retention;

(3) improve recruitment of patent examiners;

H. R. 1249—54

(4) decrease the number of patent applications waiting for examination; and

(5) improve the quality of patent examination.

(c) REQUIRED CONSIDERATIONS.—

(1) IN GENERAL.—In selecting the location of each satellite office to be established under subsection (a), the Director—

(A) shall ensure geographic diversity among the offices, including by ensuring that such offices are established in different States and regions throughout the Nation;

(B) may rely upon any previous evaluations by the Office of potential locales for satellite offices, including any evaluations prepared as part of the Office's Nationwide Workforce Program that resulted in the 2010 selection of Detroit, Michigan, as the first satellite office of the Office;

(C) shall evaluate and consider the extent to which the purposes of satellite offices listed under subsection (b) will be achieved;

(D) shall consider the availability of scientific and technically knowledgeable personnel in the region from which to draw new patent examiners at minimal recruitment cost; and

(E) shall consider the economic impact to the region.

(2) OPEN SELECTION PROCESS.—Nothing in paragraph (1) shall constrain the Office to only consider its evaluations in selecting the Detroit, Michigan, satellite office.

(d) REPORT TO CONGRESS.—Not later than the end of the third fiscal year that begins after the date of the enactment of this Act, the Director shall submit a report to Congress on—

(1) the rationale of the Director in selecting the location of any satellite office required under subsection (a), including an explanation of how the selected location will achieve the purposes of satellite offices listed under subsection (b) and how the required considerations listed under subsection (c) were met;

(2) the progress of the Director in establishing all such satellite offices; and

(3) whether the operation of existing satellite offices is achieving the purposes under subsection (b).

SEC. 24. DESIGNATION OF DETROIT SATELLITE OFFICE.

(a) DESIGNATION.—The satellite office of the United States Patent and Trademark Office to be located in Detroit, Michigan, shall be known and designated as the "Elijah J. McCoy United States Patent and Trademark Office".

(b) REFERENCES.—Any reference in a law, map, regulation, document, paper, or other record of the United States to the satellite office of the United States Patent and Trademark Office to be located in Detroit, Michigan, referred to in subsection (a) shall be deemed to be a reference to the "Elijah J. McCoy United States Patent and Trademark Office".

SEC. 25. PRIORITY EXAMINATION FOR IMPORTANT TECHNOLOGIES.

Section 2(b)(2) of title 35, United States Code, is amended—

(1) in subparagraph (E), by striking "and" after the semicolon;

(2) in subparagraph (F), by inserting "and" after the semicolon; and

(3) by adding at the end the following:

"(G) may, subject to any conditions prescribed by the Director and at the request of the patent applicant, provide for prioritization of examination of applications for products, processes, or technologies that are important to the national economy or national competitiveness without recovering the aggregate extra cost of providing such prioritization, notwithstanding section 41 or any other provision of law;".

SEC. 26. STUDY ON IMPLEMENTATION.

(a) PTO STUDY.—The Director shall conduct a study on the manner in which this Act and the amendments made by this Act are being implemented by the Office, and on such other aspects of the patent policies and practices of the Federal Government with respect to patent rights, innovation in the United States, competitiveness of United States markets, access by small businesses to capital for investment, and such other issues, as the Director considers appropriate.

(b) REPORT TO CONGRESS.—The Director shall, not later than the date that is 4 years after the date of the enactment of this Act, submit to the Committees on the Judiciary of the House of Representatives and the Senate a report on the results of the study conducted under subsection (a), including recommendations for any changes to laws and regulations that the Director considers appropriate.

SEC. 27. STUDY ON GENETIC TESTING.

(a) IN GENERAL.—The Director shall conduct a study on effective ways to provide independent, confirming genetic diagnostic test activity where gene patents and exclusive licensing for primary genetic diagnostic tests exist.

(b) ITEMS INCLUDED IN STUDY.—The study shall include an examination of at least the following:

(1) The impact that the current lack of independent second opinion testing has had on the ability to provide the highest level of medical care to patients and recipients of genetic diagnostic testing, and on inhibiting innovation to existing testing and diagnoses.

(2) The effect that providing independent second opinion genetic diagnostic testing would have on the existing patent and license holders of an exclusive genetic test.

(3) The impact that current exclusive licensing and patents on genetic testing activity has on the practice of medicine, including but not limited to: the interpretation of testing results and performance of testing procedures.

(4) The role that cost and insurance coverage have on access to and provision of genetic diagnostic tests.

(c) CONFIRMING GENETIC DIAGNOSTIC TEST ACTIVITY DEFINED.—For purposes of this section, the term "confirming genetic diagnostic test activity" means the performance of a genetic diagnostic test, by a genetic diagnostic test provider, on an individual solely for the purpose of providing the individual with an independent confirmation of results obtained from another test provider's prior performance of the test on the individual.

(d) REPORT.—Not later than 9 months after the date of enactment of this Act, the Director shall report to the Committee on the Judiciary of the Senate and the Committee on the Judiciary of the House of Representatives on the findings of the study and provide recommendations for establishing the availability of such independent confirming genetic diagnostic test activity.

SEC. 28. PATENT OMBUDSMAN PROGRAM FOR SMALL BUSINESS CONCERNS.

Using available resources, the Director shall establish and maintain in the Office a Patent Ombudsman Program. The duties of the Program's staff shall include providing support and services relating to patent filings to small business concerns and independent inventors.

SEC. 29. ESTABLISHMENT OF METHODS FOR STUDYING THE DIVERSITY OF APPLICANTS.

The Director shall, not later than the end of the 6-month period beginning on the date of the enactment of this Act, establish methods for studying the diversity of patent applicants, including those applicants who are minorities, women, or veterans. The Director shall not use the results of such study to provide any preferential treatment to patent applicants.

SEC. 30. SENSE OF CONGRESS.

It is the sense of Congress that the patent system should promote industries to continue to develop new technologies that spur growth and create jobs across the country which includes protecting the rights of small businesses and inventors from predatory behavior that could result in the cutting off of innovation.

SEC. 31. USPTO STUDY ON INTERNATIONAL PATENT PROTECTIONS FOR SMALL BUSINESSES.

(a) STUDY REQUIRED.—The Director, in consultation with the Secretary of Commerce and the Administrator of the Small Business Administration, shall, using the existing resources of the Office, carry out a study—

(1) to determine how the Office, in coordination with other Federal departments and agencies, can best help small businesses with international patent protection; and

(2) whether, in order to help small businesses pay for the costs of filing, maintaining, and enforcing international patent applications, there should be established either—

(A) a revolving fund loan program to make loans to small businesses to defray the costs of such applications, maintenance, and enforcement and related technical assistance; or

(B) a grant program to defray the costs of such applications, maintenance, and enforcement and related technical assistance.

(b) REPORT.—Not later than 120 days after the date of the enactment of this Act, the Director shall issue a report to the Congress containing—

(1) all findings and determinations made in carrying out the study required under subsection (a);

(2) a statement of whether the determination was made that—

(A) a revolving fund loan program described under subsection (a)(2)(A) should be established;

(B) a grant program described under subsection (a)(2)(B) should be established; or

(C) neither such program should be established; and

(3) any legislative recommendations the Director may have developed in carrying out such study.

SEC. 32. PRO BONO PROGRAM.

(a) IN GENERAL.—The Director shall work with and support intellectual property law associations across the country in the establishment of pro bono programs designed to assist financially under-resourced independent inventors and small businesses.

(b) EFFECTIVE DATE.—This section shall take effect on the date of the enactment of this Act.

SEC. 33. LIMITATION ON ISSUANCE OF PATENTS.

(a) LIMITATION.—Notwithstanding any other provision of law, no patent may issue on a claim directed to or encompassing a human organism.

(b) EFFECTIVE DATE.—

(1) IN GENERAL.—Subsection (a) shall apply to any application for patent that is pending on, or filed on or after, the date of the enactment of this Act.

(2) PRIOR APPLICATIONS.—Subsection (a) shall not affect the validity of any patent issued on an application to which paragraph (1) does not apply.

SEC. 34. STUDY OF PATENT LITIGATION.

(a) GAO STUDY.—The Comptroller General of the United States shall conduct a study of the consequences of litigation by non-practicing entities, or by patent assertion entities, related to patent claims made under title 35, United States Code, and regulations authorized by that title.

(b) CONTENTS OF STUDY.—The study conducted under this section shall include the following:

(1) The annual volume of litigation described in subsection (a) over the 20-year period ending on the date of the enactment of this Act.

(2) The volume of cases comprising such litigation that are found to be without merit after judicial review.

(3) The impacts of such litigation on the time required to resolve patent claims.

(4) The estimated costs, including the estimated cost of defense, associated with such litigation for patent holders, patent licensors, patent licensees, and inventors, and for users of alternate or competing innovations.

(5) The economic impact of such litigation on the economy of the United States, including the impact on inventors, job creation, employers, employees, and consumers.

(6) The benefit to commerce, if any, supplied by non-practicing entities or patent assertion entities that prosecute such litigation.

(c) REPORT TO CONGRESS.—The Comptroller General shall, not later than the date that is 1 year after the date of the enactment of this Act, submit to the Committee on the Judiciary of the House of Representatives and the Committee on the Judiciary of the Senate a report on the results of the study required under this section, including recommendations for any changes to laws and regulations that will minimize any negative impact of patent litigation that was the subject of such study.

SEC. 35. EFFECTIVE DATE.

Except as otherwise provided in this Act, the provisions of this Act shall take effect upon the expiration of the 1-year period beginning on the date of the enactment of this Act and shall apply to any patent issued on or after that effective date.

SEC. 36. BUDGETARY EFFECTS.

The budgetary effects of this Act, for the purpose of complying with the Statutory Pay-As-You-Go Act of 2010, shall be determined by reference to the latest statement titled "Budgetary Effects of PAYGO Legislation" for this Act, submitted for printing in the Congressional Record by the Chairman of the House Budget Committee, provided that such statement has been submitted prior to the vote on passage.

SEC. 37. CALCULATION OF 60-DAY PERIOD FOR APPLICATION OF PATENT TERM EXTENSION.

(a) IN GENERAL.—Section 156(d)(1) of title 35, United States Code, is amended by adding at the end the following flush sentence: "For purposes of determining the date on which a product receives permission under the second sentence of this paragraph, if such permission is transmitted after 4:30 P.M., Eastern Time, on a business day, or is transmitted on a day that is not a business day, the product shall be deemed to receive such permission on the next business day. For purposes of the preceding sentence, the term 'business day' means any Monday, Tuesday, Wednesday, Thursday, or Friday, excluding any legal holiday under section 6103 of title 5.".

(b) APPLICABILITY.—The amendment made by subsection (a) shall apply to any application for extension of a patent term under section 156 of title 35, United States Code, that is pending on, that is filed after, or as to which a decision regarding the application is subject to judicial review on, the date of the enactment of this Act.

Speaker of the House of Representatives.

Vice President of the United States and
President of the Senate.

APPENDIX 3

Final USPTO Rules Added for the America Invents Act[1]

(through April 3, 2013)

Contents:

---

[1]For a full compilation of 37 C.F.R., see www.ecfr.gov. Note, however, that it may not be current.

* * *

PART 1— RULES OF PRACTICE IN PATENT CASES

Authority: 35 U.S.C. 2(b)(2).

Subpart A— General Provisions

§ 1.1. Addresses for non-trademark correspondence with the United States Patent and Trademark Office.

* * * * *

(a) * * *

(1) * * *

(ii) *Patent Trial and Appeal Board.* See § 41.10 or § 42.6 of this title. Notices of appeal, appeal briefs, reply briefs, requests for oral hearing, as well as all other correspondence in an application or a patent involved in an appeal to the Board for which an address is not otherwise specified, should be addressed as set out in paragraph (a)(1)(i) of this section.

* * * * *

(e) *Patent term extension.* All applications for extension of patent term under 35 U.S.C. 156 and any communications relating thereto intended for the United States Patent and Trademark Office should be additionally marked "Mail Stop Hatch-Waxman PTE." When appropriate, the communication should also be marked to the attention of a particular individual, as where a decision has been rendered.

* * * * *

§ 1.4. Nature of correspondence and signature

requirements.

(a) * * *

(2) Correspondence in and relating to a particular application or other proceeding in the Office. See particularly the rules relating to the filing, processing, or other proceedings of national applications in subpart B, §§ 1.31 to 1.378; of international applications in subpart C, §§ 1.401 to 1.499; of ex parte reexaminations of patents in subpart D, §§ 1.501 to 1.570; of extension of patent term in subpart F, §§ 1.710 to 1.785; of *inter partes* reexaminations of patents in subpart H, §§ 1.902 to 1.997; and of the Patent Trial and Appeal Board in parts 41 and 42 of this title.

* * *

(4) Certifications—(i) Section 11.18 certifications. The presentation to the Office (whether by signing, filing, submitting, or later advocating) of any paper by a party, whether a practitioner or non-practitioner, constitutes a certification under § 11.18(b) of this subchapter. Violations of § 11.18(b)(2) of this subchapter by a party, whether a practitioner or non-practitioner, may result in the imposition of sanctions under § 11.18(c) of this subchapter. Any practitioner violating § 11.18(b) of this subchapter may also be subject to disciplinary action. See § 11.18(d) of this subchapter.

* * * * *

(e) The following correspondence must be submitted with an original handwritten signature personally signed in permanent dark ink or its equivalent:

(1) Correspondence requiring a person's signature and relating to registration to practice before the Patent and Trademark Office in patent cases, enrollment and disciplinary investigations, or disciplinary proceedings; and

(2) Payments by credit cards where the payment is not being made via the Office's electronic filing systems.

* * * * *

§ 1.5. Identification of patent, patent application, or patent-related proceeding.

(a) No correspondence relating to an application should be filed prior to receipt of the application number from the Patent and Trademark Office. When a letter directed to the Patent and Trademark Office concerns a previously filed application for a patent, it must identify on the top page in a conspicuous location, the application number (consisting of the series code and the serial number; *e.g.*, 07/123,456), or the serial number and filing date assigned to that application by the Patent and Trademark Office, or the international application number of the international application. Any correspondence not containing such identification will be returned to the sender where a return address is available. The returned correspondence will be accompanied with a cover letter which will indicate to the sender that if the returned correspondence is resubmitted to the Patent and Trademark Office within two weeks of the mail date on the cover letter, the original date of receipt of the correspondence will be considered by the Patent and Trademark Office as the date of receipt of the correspondence. Applicants may use either the Certificate of Mailing or Transmission procedure under § 1.8 or the Express Mail procedure under § 1.10 for resubmissions of returned correspondence if they desire to have the benefit of the date of deposit in the United States Postal Service. If the returned correspondence is not resubmitted within the two-week period, the date of receipt of the resubmission will be considered to be the date of receipt of the correspondence. The two-week period to resubmit the returned correspondence will not be extended. In addition to the application number, all letters directed to the Patent and Trademark Office concerning applications for patent should also state the name of the first listed inventor, the title of the invention, the date of filing the same, and, if known, the group art unit or other unit within the Patent and Trademark Office responsible for considering the letter and the name of the examiner or other person to which it has been assigned.

* * * * *

§ 1.6. Receipt of correspondence.

* * * * *

(d) * * *

(3) Correspondence which cannot receive the benefit of the certificate of mailing or transmission as specified in § 1.8(a)(2)(i)(A) through (D), (F), and (I), and § 1.8(a)(2)(iii)(A), except that a continued prosecution application under § 1.53(d) may be transmitted to the Office by facsimile; * * * * *

* * * * *

(c) Correspondence relating to a trial proceeding before

the Patent Trial and Appeal Board (part 42 of this title) are governed by § 42.6 of this title.

§ 1.6. Receipt of correspondence.

* * * * *

(d) Facsimile transmission. Except in the cases enumerated below, correspondence, including authorizations to charge a deposit account, may be transmitted by facsimile. The receipt date accorded to the correspondence will be the date on which the complete transmission is received in the United States Patent and Trademark Office, unless that date is a Saturday, Sunday, or Federal holiday within the District of Columbia. See paragraph (a)(3) of this section. To facilitate proper processing, each transmission session should be limited to correspondence to be filed in a single application or other proceeding before the United States Patent and Trademark Office. The application number of a patent application, the control number of a reexamination proceeding, the interference number of an interference proceeding, the trial number of a trial proceeding before the Board, or the patent number of a patent should be entered as a part of the sender's identification on a facsimile cover sheet. Facsimile transmissions are not permitted and, if submitted, will not be accorded a date of receipt in the following situations:

* * * * *

(9) In contested cases and trials before the Patent Trial and Appeal Board, except as the Board may expressly authorize.

* * * * *

§ 1.8. Certificate of mailing or transmission.

(a) * * *

(2) * * *

(i) * * *

(B) Papers filed in trials before the Patent Trial and Appeal Board, which are governed by § 42.6(b) of this title;

(C) Papers filed in contested cases before the Patent Trial and Appeal Board, which are governed by § 41.106 (f) of this title;

* * * * *

(G) The filing of a written declaration of abandonment under § 1.138;

(H) The filing of a submission under § 1.217 for

publication of a redacted copy of an application;

(I) The filing of a third-party submission under § 1.290; and

(J) The calculation of any period of adjustment, as specified in § 1.703(f).

§ 1.9. Definitions.

(a) (1) A national application as used in this chapter means a U.S. application for patent which was either filed in the Office under 35 U.S.C. 111, or an international application filed under the Patent Cooperation Treaty in which the basic national fee under 35 U.S.C. 41(a)(1)(F) has been paid.

(2) A provisional application as used in this chapter means a U.S. national application for patent filed in the Office under 35 U.S.C. 111(b).

(3) A nonprovisional application as used in this chapter means a U.S. national application for patent which was either filed in the Office under 35 U.S.C. 111(a), or an international application filed under the Patent Cooperation Treaty in which the basic national fee under 35 U.S.C. 41(a)(1)(F) has been paid.

(b) An international application as used in this chapter means an international application for patent filed under the Patent Cooperation Treaty prior to entering national processing at the Designated Office stage.

* * * * *

(d) (1) The term inventor or inventorship as used in this chapter means the individual or, if a joint invention, the individuals collectively who invented or discovered the subject matter of the invention.

(2) The term joint inventor or coinventor as used in this chapter means any one of the individuals who invented or discovered the subject matter of a joint invention.

(e) The term joint research agreement as used in this chapter means a written contract, grant, or cooperative agreement entered into by two or more persons or entities for the performance of experimental, developmental, or research work in the field of the claimed invention.

(f) The term claimed invention as used in this chapter means the subject matter defined by a claim in a patent or an application for a patent.

(g) For definitions in Patent Trial and Appeal Board proceedings, see parts 41 and 42 of this title.

* * * * *

§ 1.11. Files open to the public.

* * * * *

(e) Except as prohibited in § 41.6(b), § 42.14 or § 42.410(b), the file of any interference or trial before the Patent Trial and Appeal Board is open to public inspection and copies of the file may be obtained upon payment of the fee therefor.

§ 1.12. Assignment records open to public inspection.

* * * * *

(b) Assignment records, digests, and indexes relating to any pending or abandoned patent application, which is open to the public pursuant to § 1.11 or for which copies or access may be supplied pursuant to § 1.14, are available to the public. Copies of any assignment records, digests, and indexes that are not available to the public shall be obtainable only upon written authority of an inventor, the applicant, the assignee or an assignee of an undivided part interest, or a patent practitioner of record, or upon a showing that the person seeking such information is a bona fide prospective or actual purchaser, mortgagee, or licensee of such application, unless it shall be necessary to the proper conduct of business before the Office or as provided in this part.

(c) * * *

(2) Include written authority granting access to the member of the public to the particular assignment records from an inventor, the applicant, the assignee or an assignee of an undivided part interest, or a patent practitioner of record.

* * * * *

§ 1.14. Patent applications preserved in confidence.

* * * * *

(c) *Power to inspect a pending or abandoned application.* Access to an application may be provided to any person if the application file is available, and the application contains written authority (e.g., a power to inspect) granting access to such person. The written authority must be signed by:

(1) The applicant;

(2) A patent practitioner of record;

(3) The assignee or an assignee of an undivided part interest;

(4) The inventor or a joint inventor; or

(5) A registered attorney or agent named in the papers accompanying the application papers filed under § 1.53 or the national stage documents filed under § 1.495, if a power of attorney has not been appointed under § 1.32.

* * * * *

(f) *Notice to inventor of the filing of an application.* The Office may publish notice in the *Official Gazette* as to the filing of an application on behalf of an inventor by a person who otherwise shows sufficient proprietary interest in the matter.

* * * * *

§ 1.16. National application filing, search, and examination fees.

* * * * *

(a) Basic fee for filing each application under 35 U.S.C. 111 for an original patent, except design, plant, or provisional applications:

By a micro entity (§ 1.29)	$70.00
By a small entity (§ 1.27(a))	140.00
By a small entity (§ 1.27(a)) if the application is submitted in compliance with the Office electronic filing system (§ 1.27(b)(2))	70.00
By other than a small or micro entity	280.00

(b) Basic fee for filing each application for an original design patent:

By a micro entity (§ 1.29)	$45.00
By a small entity (§ 1.27(a))	90.00
By other than a small or micro entity	180.00

(c) Basic fee for filing each application for an original plant patent:

By a micro entity (§ 1.29)	$45.00
By a small entity (§ 1.27(a))	90.00

By other than a small or micro entity	180.00

(d) Basic fee for filing each provisional application:

By a micro entity (§ 1.29)	$65.00
By a small entity (§ 1.27(a))	130.00
By other than a small or micro entity	260.00

(e) Basic fee for filing each application for the reissue of a patent:

By a micro entity (§ 1.29)	$70.00
By a small entity (§ 1.27(a))	140.00
By other than a small or micro entity	280.00

(f) Surcharge for filing any of the basic filing fee, the search fee, the examination fee, or the oath or declaration on a date later than the filing date of the application, except provisional applications:

By a micro entity (§ 1.29)	$35.00
By a small entity (§ 1.27(a))	70.00
By other than a small or micro entity	140.00

(g) Surcharge for filing the basic filing fee or cover sheet (§ 1.51(c)(1)) on a date later than the filing date of the provisional application:

By a micro entity (§ 1.29)	$15.00
By a small entity (§ 1.27(a))	30.00
By other than a small or micro entity	60.00

(h) In addition to the basic filing fee in an application, other than a provisional application, for filing or later presentation at any other time of excess of 3:

By a micro entity (§ 1.29)	$105.00
By a small entity (§ 1.27(a))	210.00
By other than a small or micro entity	420.00

(i) In addition to the basic filing fee in an application, other than a provisional application, for filing or later presentation at any other time of each claim (whether dependent or independent) in excess of 20 (note that § 1.75(c) indicates how multiple dependent claims are considered for fee calculation purposes):

By a micro entity (§ 1.29)	$20.00
By a small entity (§ 1.27(a))	40.00
By other than a small or micro entity	80.00

(j) In addition to the basic filing fee in an application, other than a provisional application, that contains, or is amended to contain, a multiple dependent claim, per application:

By a micro entity (§ 1.29)	$195.00
By a small entity (§ 1.27(a))	390.00
By other than a small or micro entity	780.00

(k) Search fee for each application filed under 35 U.S.C. 111 for an original patent, except design, plant, or provisional applications:

By a micro entity (§ 1.29)	$150.00
By a small entity (§ 1.27(a))	300.00
By other than a small or micro entity	600.00

(l) Search fee for each application for an original design patent:

By a micro entity (§ 1.29)	$30.00
By a small entity (§ 1.27(a))	60.00
By other than a small or micro entity	120.00

(m) Search fee for each application for an original plant patent:

By a micro entity (§ 1.29)	$95.00
By a small entity (§ 1.27(a))	190.00
By other than a small or micro entity	380.00

(n) Search fee for each application for the reissue of a patent:

By a micro entity (§ 1.29)	$150.00
By a small entity (§ 1.27(a))	300.00
By other than a small or micro entity	600.00

(o) Examination fee for each application filed under 35 U.S.C. 111 for an original patent, except design, plant, or provisional applications:

By a micro entity (§ 1.29)	$180.00
By a small entity (§ 1.27(a))	360.00
By other than a small or micro entity	720.00

(p) Examination fee for each application for an original design patent:

By a micro entity (§ 1.29)	$115.00
By a small entity (§ 1.27(a))	230.00
By other than a small or micro entity	460.00

(q) Examination fee for each application for an original plant patent:

By a micro entity (§ 1.29)	$145.00
By a small entity (§ 1.27(a))	290.00
By other than a small or micro entity	580.00

(r) Examination fee for each application for the reissue of a patent:

By a micro entity (§ 1.29)	$540.00
By a small entity (§ 1.27(a))	1,080.00
By other than a small or micro entity	2,160.00

(s) Application size fee for any application filed under 35 U.S.C. 111 for the specification and drawings which exceed 100 sheets of paper, for each additional 50 sheets or fraction thereof:

By a micro entity (§ 1.29)	$100.00

By a small entity (§ 1.27(a))	200.00
By other than a small or micro entity	400.00

* * * * *

§ 1.17. Patent application and reexamination processing fees.

(a) Extension fees pursuant to § 1.136(a):

(1) For reply within first month:

By a micro entity (§ 1.29)	$50.00
By a small entity (§ 1.27(a))	100.00
By other than a small or micro entity	200.00

(2) For reply within second month:

By a micro entity (§ 1.29)	$150.00
By a small entity (§ 1.27(a))	300.00
By other than a small or micro entity	600.00

(3) For reply within third month:

By a micro entity (§ 1.29)	$350.00
By a small entity (§ 1.27(a))	700.00
By other than a small or micro entity	1,400.00

(4) For reply within fourth month:

By a micro entity (§ 1.29)	$550.00
By a small entity (§ 1.27(a))	1,100.00
By other than a small or micro entity	2,200.00

(5) For reply within fifth month:

By a micro entity (§ 1.29)	$750.00
By a small entity (§ 1.27(a))	1,500.00
By other than a small or micro entity	3,000.00

(b) For fees in proceedings before the Patent Trial and Appeal Board, see § 41.20 of this title.

(c) For filing a request for prioritized examination under § 1.102(e):

By a micro entity (§ 1.29)	$1,000.00
By a small entity (§ 1.27(a))	2,000.00
By other than a small or micro entity	4,000.00

(d) For correction of inventorship in an application after the first action on the merits:

By a micro entity (§ 1.29)	$150.00
By a small entity (§ 1.27(a))	300.00
By other than a small or micro entity	600.00

(e) To request continued examination pursuant to § 1.114:

(1) For filing a first request for continued examination pursuant to § 1.114 in an application:

By a micro entity (§ 1.29)	$300.00
By a small entity (§ 1.27(a))	600.00
By other than a small or micro entity	1,200.00

(2) For filing a second or subsequent request for continued examination pursuant to § 1.114 in an application:

By a micro entity (§ 1.29)	$425.00
By a small entity (§ 1.27(a))	850.00
By other than a small or micro entity	1,700.00

(f) For filing a petition under one of the following sections which refers to this paragraph:

By a micro entity (§ 1.29)	$100.00
By a small entity (§ 1.27(a))	200.00
By other than a small or micro entity	400.00

§ 1.36(a)—for revocation of a power of attorney by fewer than all of the applicants.

§ 1.53(e)—to accord a filing date.

§ 1.57(a)—to accord a filing date.

§ 1.182—for decision on a question not specifically provided for.

§ 1.183—to suspend the rules.

§ 1.378(e)—for reconsideration of decision on petition refusing to accept delayed payment of maintenance fee in an expired patent.

§ 1.741(b)—to accord a filing date to an application under § 1.740 for extension of a patent term.

* * * * *

(g) For filing a petition under one of the following sections which refers to this paragraph:

By a micro entity (§ 1.29)	$50.00
By a small entity (§ 1.27(a))	100.00
By other than a small or micro entity	200.00

§ 1.12—for access to an assignment record.

§ 1.14—for access to an application.

§ 1.46—for filing an application on behalf of an inventor by a person who otherwise shows sufficient proprietary interest in the matter.

§ 1.47—for filing by other than all the inventors or a person not the inventor.

§ 1.55(f)—for filing a belated certified copy of a foreign application.

§ 1.59—for expungement of information.

§ 1.103(a)—to suspend action in an application.

§ 1.136(b)—for review of a request for extension of time when the provisions of § 1.136(a) are not available.

§ 1.295—for review of refusal to publish a statutory invention registration.

§ 1.296—to withdraw a request for publication of a statutory invention registration filed on or after the date the notice of intent to publish issued.

§ 1.377—for review of decision refusing to accept and record payment of a maintenance fee filed prior to expiration of a patent.

§ 1.550(c)—for patent owner requests for extension of time in *ex parte* reexamination proceedings.
§ 1.956—for patent owner requests for extension of time in *inter partes* reexamination proceedings.
§ 5.12—for expedited handling of a foreign filing license.
§ 5.15—for changing the scope of a license.
§ 5.25—for retroactive license.

* * *(**h**) For filing a petition under one of the following sections which refers to this paragraph:

By a micro entity (§ 1.29)	$35.00
By a small entity (§ 1.27(a))	70.00
By other than a small or micro entity	140.00

§ 1.19(g)—to request documents in a form other than provided in this part.
§ 1.84—for accepting color drawings or photographs.
§ 1.91—for entry of a model or exhibit.
§ 1.102(d)—to make an application special.
§ 1.138(c)—to expressly abandon an application to avoid publication.
§ 1.313—to withdraw an application from issue.
§ 1.314—to defer issuance of a patent.

(**i**) Processing fees:

(1) for taking action under one of the following sections which refers to this paragraph:

By a micro entity (§ 1.29)	$35.00
By a small entity (§ 1.27(a))	70.00
By other than a small or micro entity	140.00

§ 1.28(c)(3)—for processing a non-itemized fee deficiency based on an error in small entity status.
§ 1.41—for supplying the name or names of the inventor or inventors after the filing date without an oath or declaration as prescribed by § 1.63, except in provisional applications.

§ 1.48—for correcting inventorship, except in provisional applications.

§ 1.52(d)—for processing a nonprovisional application filed with a specification in a language other than English.

§ 1.53(b)(3)—to convert a provisional application filed under § 1.53(c) into a nonprovisional application under § 1.53(b).

§ 1.55—for entry of late priority papers.

§ 1.71(g)(2)—for processing a belated amendment under § 1.71(g).

§ 1.99(e)—for processing a belated submission under § 1.99.

§ 1.102(e)—for requesting prioritized examination of an application.

§ 1.103(b)—for requesting limited suspension of action, continued prosecution application for a design patent (§ 1.53(d)).

§ 1.103(c)—for requesting limited suspension of action, request for continued examination (§ 1.114).

§ 1.103(d)—for requesting deferred examination of an application.

§ 1.291(c)(5)—for processing a second or subsequent protest by the same real party in interest.

§ 1.497(d)—for filing an oath or declaration pursuant to 35 U.S.C. 371(c)(4) naming an inventive entity different from the inventive entity set forth in the international stage.

§ 3.81—for a patent to issue to assignee, assignment submitted after payment of the issue fee.

(2) For taking action under one of the following sections which refers to this paragraph:

By other than a small or micro entity $130.00

§ 1.217—for processing a redacted copy of a paper submitted in the file of an application in which a redacted copy was submitted for the patent application publication.

§ 1.221—for requesting voluntary publication or republication of an application.

(i) Processing fee for taking action under one of the following sections which refers to this paragraph: $130.00

§ 1.28(c)(3)—for processing a non-itemized fee deficiency based on an error in small entity status.
§ 1.41(b)—for supplying the name or names of the inventor or joint inventors in an application without either an application data sheet or the inventor's oath or declaration, except in provisional applications.
§ 1.48—for correcting inventorship, except in provisional applications.
§ 1.52(d)—for processing a nonprovisional application filed with a specification in a language other than English.
§ 1.53(c)(3)—to convert a provisional application filed under § 1.53(c) into a nonprovisional application under § 1.53(b).
§ 1.55—for entry of a priority claim or certified copy of a foreign application after payment of the issue fee.
§ 1.71(g)(2)—for processing a belated amendment under § 1.71(g).
§ 1.103(b)—for requesting limited suspension of action, continued prosecution application for a design patent (§ 1.53(d)).
§ 1.103(c)—for requesting limited suspension of action, request for continued examination (§ 1.114).
§ 1.103(d)—for requesting deferred examination of an application.
§ 1.217—for processing a redacted copy of a paper submitted in the file of an application in which a redacted copy was submitted for the patent application publication.
§ 1.221—for requesting voluntary publication or republication of an application.
§ 1.291(c)(5)—for processing a second or subsequent protest by the same real party in interest.
§ 3.81—for a patent to issue to assignee, assignment submitted after payment of the issue fee.

* * *

(k) For filing a request for expedited examination under § 1.155(a):

By a micro entity (§ 1.29)	$225.00
By a small entity (§ 1.27(a))	450.00
By other than a small or micro entity	900.00

(l) For filing a petition for the revival of an unavoidably abandoned application under 35 U.S.C. 111, 133, 364, or 371, for the unavoidably delayed payment of the issue fee under 35 U.S.C. 151, or for the revival of an unavoidably terminated reexamination proceeding under 35 U.S.C. 133 (§ 1.137(a)):

By a micro entity (§ 1.29)	$160.00
By a small entity (§ 1.27(a))	320.00
By other than a small or micro entity	640.00

(m) For filing a petition for the revival of an unintentionally abandoned application, for the unintentionally delayed payment of the fee for issuing a patent, or for the revival of an unintentionally terminated reexamination proceeding under 35 U.S.C. 41(a)(7) (§ 1.137(b)):

By a micro entity (§ 1.29)	$475.00
By a small entity (§ 1.27(a))	950.00
By other than a small or micro entity	1,900.00

(n) [removed and reserved]

(o) [removed and reserved]

(p) For an information disclosure statement under § 1.97(c) or (d) or for the document fee for a submission under § 1.290

By a micro entity (§ 1.29)	$45.00
By a small entity (§ 1.27(a))	90.00
By other than a small or micro entity	180.00

§ 1.12—for access to an assignment record.

§ 1.14—for access to an application.

§ 1.28(c)(3)—for processing a non-itemized fee deficiency based on an error in small entity status.

§ 1.41(b)—for supplying the name or names of the inventor or joint inventors in an application without either an application data sheet or the inventor's oath or declaration, except in provisional applications.

§ 1.46—for filing an application on behalf of an inventor by a person who otherwise shows sufficient proprietary interest in the matter.

§ 1.48—for correcting inventorship, except in provisional applications.

§ 1.52(d)—for processing a nonprovisional application filed with a specification in a language other than English.

§ 1.53(b)(3)—to convert a provisional application filed under § 1.53(c) into a nonprovisional application under § 1.53(b).§ 1.53(c)(3)—to convert a provisional application filed under § 1.53(c) into a nonprovisional application under § 1.53(b).

§ 1.55—for entry of late priority papers.

§ 1.59—for expungement of information.

§ 1.71(g)(2)—for processing a belated amendment under § 1.71(g).

§ 1.99(e)—for processing a belated submission under § 1.99.

§ 1.102(e)—for requesting prioritized examination of an application.

§ 1.103(a)—to suspend action in an application.

§ 1.103(b)—for requesting limited suspension of action, continued prosecution application for a design patent (§ 1.53(d)).

§ 1.103(c)—for requesting limited suspension of action, request for continued examination (§ 1.114).

§ 1.103(d)—for requesting deferred examination of an application.

§ 1.136(b)—for review of a request for extension for extension of time when the provisions of § 1.136(a) are not available.

§ 1.217—for processing a redacted copy of a paper submitted in the file of an application in which a redacted copy was submitted for the patent application publication.

§ 1.221—for requesting voluntary publication or republication of an application.

§ 1.291(c)(5)—for processing a second or subsequent protest by the same real party in interest.

§ 1.295—for review of refusal to publish a statutory invention registration.

§ 1.296—to withdraw a request for publication of a statutory invention registration filed on or after the date the notice of intent to publish issued.

§ 1.377—for review of decision refusing to accept and record payment of a maintenance fee filed prior to expiration of a patent.

§ 1.497(d)—for filing an oath or declaration pursuant to 35 U.S.C. 371(c)(4) naming an inventive entity different from the inventive entity set forth in the international stage.

§ 1.550(c)—for patent owner requests for extension of time in ex *parte* reexamination proceedings.

§ 1.956—for patent owner requests for extension of time in *inter partes* reexamination proceedings.

* * * * *

§ 3.81—for a patent to issue to assignee, assignment submitted after payment of the issue fee.

* * * * *

§ 5.12—for expedited handling of a foreign filing license.

§ 5.15—for changing the scope of a license.

§ 5.25—for retroactive license.

(q) Processing fee for taking action under one of the following sections which refers to this paragraph: $50.00.

§ 1.41—to supply the name or names of the inventor or inventors after the filing date without a cover sheet as prescribed by § 1.51(c)(1) in a provisional application.

§ 1.48—for correction of inventorship in a provisional application.

§ 1.53(c)(2)—to convert a nonprovisional application filed under § 1.53(b) to a provisional application under § 1.53(c).

(r) For entry of a submission after final rejection under § 1.129(a):

By a micro entity (§ 1.29)	$210.00
By a small entity (§ 1.27(a))	420.00
By other than a small or micro entity	840.00

(s) For each additional invention requested to be examined under § 1.129(b):

By a micro entity (§ 1.29)	$210.00
By a small entity (§ 1.27(a))	420.00
By other than a small or micro entity	840.00

(t) For the acceptance of an unintentionally delayed claim for priority under 35 U.S.C. 119, 120, 121, or 365(a) or (c) (§§ 1.55 and 1.78) or for filing a request for the restoration of the right of priority under § 1.452:

By a micro entity (§ 1.29)	$355.00
By a small entity (§ 1.27(a))	710.00
By other than a small or micro entity	1,420.00

§ 1.18. Patent post allowance (including issue) fees.

(a) Issue fee for issuing each original patent, except a design or plant patent, or for issuing each reissue patent:

(1) For an issue fee paid on or after January 1, 2014:

By a micro entity (§ 1.29)	$240.00
By a small entity (§ 1.27(a))	480.00
By other than a small or micro entity	960.00

(2) For an issue fee paid before January 1, 2014:

By a micro entity (§ 1.29)	$445.00

By a small entity (§ 1.27(a))	890.00
By other than a small or micro entity	1,780.00

(b) Issue fee for issuing an original design patent:

(1) For an issue fee paid on or after January 1, 2014:

By a micro entity (§ 1.29)	$140.00
By a small entity (§ 1.27(a))	280.00
By other than a small or micro entity	560.00

(2) For an issue fee paid before January 1, 2014:

By a micro entity (§ 1.29)	$255.00
By a small entity (§ 1.27(a))	510.00
By other than a small or micro entity	1,020.00

(c) Issue fee for issuing an original plant patent:

(1) For an issue fee paid on or after January 1, 2014:

By a micro entity (§ 1.29)	$190.00
By a small entity (§ 1.27(a))	380.00
By other than a small or micro entity	760.00

(2) For an issue fee paid before January 1, 2014:

By a micro entity (§ 1.29)	$350.00
By a small entity (§ 1.27(a))	700.00
By other than a small or micro entity	1,400.00

(d)

(1) Publication fee on or after January 1, 2014 ..... $0.00

(2) Publication fee before January 1, 2014 ... 300.00

(3) Republication fee (§ 1.221(a)) 300.00

(e) For filing an application for patent term adjustment under § 1.705: $200.00.

(f) For filing a request for reinstatement of all or part of the term reduced pursuant to § 1.704(b) in an application for patent term adjustment under§ 1.705: $400.00.

§ 1.19. Document supply fees.

The United States Patent and Trademark Office will supply copies of the following patent-related documents upon payment of the fees indicated. Paper copies will be in black and white unless the original document is in color, a color copy is requested and the fee for a color copy is paid.

(a) Uncertified copies of patent application publications and patents:

(1) Printed copy of the paper portion of a patent application publication or patent including a design patent, statutory invention registration, or defensive publication document. Service includes preparation of copies by the Office within two to three business days and delivery by United States Postal Service; and preparation of copies by the Office within one business day of receipt and delivery to an Office Box or by electronic means (e.g., facsimile, electronic mail): $3.00.

(2) Printed copy of a plant patent in color: $15.00.

(3) Color copy of a patent (other than a plant patent) or statutory invention registration containing a color drawing: $25.00.

(b) Copies of Office documents to be provided in paper, or in electronic form, as determined by the Director (for other patent-related materials see § 1.21(k)):

(1) Copy of a patent application as filed, or a patent-related file wrapper and contents, stored in paper in a paper file wrapper, in an image format in an image file wrapper, or if color documents, stored in paper in an Artifact Folder:

(i) If provided on paper:

(A) Application as filed: $20.00.

(B) File wrapper and contents of 400 or fewer pages: $200.00.

(C) Additional fee for each additional 100 pages or portion thereof of file wrapper and contents: $40.00.

(D) Individual application documents, other than application as filed, per document: $25.00.

(ii) If provided on compact disc or other physical electronic medium in single order:

(A) Application as filed: $20.00.

(B) File wrapper and contents, first physical

electronic medium: $55.00.

(C) Additional fee for each continuing physical electronic medium in the single order of paragraph (b)(1)(ii)(B) of this section: $15.00.

(iii) If provided electronically (e.g., by electronic transmission) other than on a physical electronic medium as specified in paragraph (b)(1)(ii) of this section:

(A) Application as filed: $20.00.

(B) File wrapper and contents: $55.00.

(iv) If provided to a foreign intellectual property office pursuant to a priority document exchange agreement (*see* § 1.14 (h)(1)): $0.00.

(2) Copy of patent-related file wrapper contents that were submitted and are stored on compact disc or other electronic form (e.g., compact discs stored in an Artifact Folder), other than as available in paragraph (b)(1) of this section:

(i) If provided on compact disc or other physical electronic medium in a single order:

(A) First physical electronic medium in a single order: $55.00.

(B) Additional fee for each continuing physical electronic medium in the single order of this paragraph (b)(2)(i): $15.00.

(ii) If provided electronically other than on a physical electronic medium per order: $55.00.

(3) Copy of Office records, except copies available under paragraph (b)(1) or (2) of this section: $25.00.

(4) For assignment records, abstract of title and certification, per patent: $25.00.

(c) Library service (35 U.S.C. 13): For providing to libraries copies of all patents issued annually, per annum: $50.00.

(d) For list of all United States patents and statutory invention registrations in a subclass: $3.00.

(e) Uncertified statement as to status of the payment of maintenance fees due on a patent or expiration of a patent: $10.00.

(f) Uncertified copy of a non-United States patent document, per document: $25.00.

(g) Petitions for documents in a form other than that

provided by this part, or in a form other than that generally provided by the Director, will be decided in accordance with the merits of each situation. Any petition seeking a decision under this section must be accompanied by the petition fee set forth in § 1.17(h) and, if the petition is granted, the documents will be provided at cost.

§ 1.20. Post issuance fees.

(a) For providing a certificate of correction for applicant's mistake (§ 1.323): $100.00.

(b) Processing fee for correcting inventorship in a patent (§ 1.324): $130.00.

(c) In reexamination proceedings:

(1) For filing a request for *ex parte* reexamination (§ 1.510(a)):

By a micro entity (§ 1.29)	$3,000.00
By a small entity (§ 1.27(a))	6,000.00
By other than a small or micro entity	12,000.00

(2) [Reserved]

(3) For filing with a request for reexamination or later presentation at any other time of each claim in independent form in excess of 3 and also in excess of the number of claims in independent form in the patent under reexamination:

By a micro entity (§ 1.29)	$105.00
By a small entity (§ 1.27(a))	210.00
By other than a small or micro entity	420.00

(4) For filing with a request for reexamination or later presentation at any other time of each claim (whether dependent or independent) in excess of 20 and also in excess of the number of claims in the patent under reexamination (note that § 1.75(c) indicates how multiple dependent claims are considered for fee calculation purposes):

By a micro entity (§ 1.29)	$20.00
By a small entity (§ 1.27(a))	40.00
By other than a small or micro entity	80.00

(5) If the excess claims fees required by paragraphs (c)(3) and (4) of this section are not paid with the request for reexamination or on later presentation of the claims for which the excess claims fees are due, the fees required by paragraphs (c)(3) and (4) must be paid or the claims canceled by amendment prior to the expiration of the time period set for reply by the Office in any notice of fee deficiency in order to avoid abandonment.

(6) For filing a petition in a reexamination proceeding, except for those specifically enumerated in §§ 1.550(i) and 1.937(d):

By a micro entity (§ 1.29)	$485.00
By a small entity (§ 1.27(a))	970.00
By other than a small or micro entity	1,940.00

(7) For a refused request for *ex parte* reexamination under § 1.510 (included in the request for *ex parte* reexamination fee at § 1.20(c)(1)):

By a micro entity (§ 1.29)	$900.00
By a small entity (§ 1.27(a))	1,800.00
By other than a small or micro entity	3,600.00

(d) For filing each statutory disclaimer (§ 1.321):

By other than a small or micro entity	$160.00

(e) For maintaining an original or reissue patent, except a design or plant patent, based on an application filed on or after December 12, 1980, in force beyond four years, the fee being due by three years and six months after the original grant:

By a micro entity (§ 1.29)	$400.00
By a small entity (§ 1.27(a))	800.00
By other than a small or micro entity	1,600.00

(f) For maintaining an original or reissue patent, except a design or plant patent, based on an application filed on or after December 12, 1980, in force beyond eight years, the fee being due by seven years and six months after the original grant:

By a micro entity (§ 1.29)	$900.00
By a small entity (§ 1.27(a))	1,800.00
By other than a small or micro entity	3,600.00

(g) For maintaining an original or reissue patent, except a design or plant patent, based on an application filed on or after December 12, 1980, in force beyond twelve years, the fee being due by eleven years and six months after the original grant:

By a micro entity (§ 1.29)	$1,850.00
By a small entity (§ 1.27(a))	3,700.00
By other than a small or micro entity	7,400.00

(h) Surcharge for paying a maintenance fee during the six-month grace period following the expiration of three years and six months, seven years and six months, and eleven years and six months after the date of the original grant of a patent based on an application filed on or after December 12, 1980:

(1) By a micro entity (§ 1.29)	$40.00
(2) By a small entity (§ 1.27(a))	80.00
(3) By other than a small or micro entity	160.00

(i) Surcharge for accepting a maintenance fee after expiration of a patent for non-timely payment of a maintenance fee where the delay in payment is shown to the satisfaction of the Director to have been—

(1) Unavoidable:

By a micro entity (§ 1.29)	$175.00
By a small entity (§ 1.27(a))	350.00
By other than a small or micro entity	700.00

(2) Unintentional:

By a micro entity (§ 1.29)	$410.00
By a small entity (§ 1.27(a))	820.00

By other than a small or micro entity	1,640.00

(j) For filing an application for extension of the term of a patent

(1) Application for extension under § 1.740: $1,120.00.

(2) Initial application for interim extension under § 1.790: $420.00.

(3) Subsequent application for interim extension under § 1.790: $220.00.

(k) In supplemental examination proceedings:

(1) For processing and treating a request for supplemental examination:

By a micro entity (§ 1.29)	$1,100.00
By a small entity (§ 1.27(a))	2,200.00
By other than a small or micro entity	4,400.00

(2) For *ex parte* reexamination ordered as a result of a supplemental examination proceeding:

By a micro entity (§ 1.29)	$3,025.00
By a small entity (§ 1.27(a))	6,050.00
By other than a small or micro entity	12,100.00

(3) For processing and treating, in a supplemental examination proceeding, a non-patent document over 20 sheets in length, per document:

(i) Between 21 and 50 sheets:

By a micro entity (§ 1.29)	$45.00
By a small entity (§ 1.27(a))	90.00
By other than a small or micro entity	180.00

(ii) For each additional 50 sheets or a fraction thereof:

By a micro entity (§ 1.29)	$70.00
By a small entity (§ 1.27(a))	140.00
By other than a small or micro entity	280.00

* * * * *

§ 1.21. Miscellaneous fees and charges.

* * * * *

(a) Registration of attorneys and agents:

(1) For admission to examination for registration to practice:

(i) Application Fee (non-refundable): $40.00.

(ii) Registration examination fee.

(A) For test administration by commercial entity: $200.00.

(B) For test administration by the USPTO: $450.00.

(2) On registration to practice or grant of limited recognition under § 11.9(b) or (c): $100.00.

(3) [Reserved]

(4) For certificate of good standing as an attorney or agent: $10.00.

(i) Suitable for framing: $20.00.

(ii) [Reserved]

(5) For review of decision:

(i) By the Director of Enrollment and Discipline under § 11.2(c): $130.00.

(ii) Of the Director of Enrollment and Discipline under § 11.2(d): $130.00.

(6) [Reserved]

(7)–(8) [Reserved]

(9) (i) Delinquency fee: $50.00.

(ii) Administrative reinstatement fee: $100.00.

(10) On application by a person for recognition or registration after disbarment or suspension on ethical grounds, or resignation pending disciplinary proceedings in any other jurisdiction; on application by a person for recognition or registration who is asserting rehabilitation from prior conduct that resulted in an adverse decision in the Office regarding the person's moral character; and on application by a person for recognition or registration after being convicted of a felony or crime involving moral turpitude or breach of fiduciary duty; on petition for reinstatement by a person excluded or

suspended on ethical grounds, or excluded on consent from practice before the Office: $1,600.00.

* * * * *

(e) International type search reports:

For preparing an international type search report of an international type search made at the time of the first action on the merits in a national patent application: $40.00.

(g) Self-service copy charge, per page: $0.25.

(h) For recording each assignment, agreement, or other paper relating to the property in a patent or application, per property:

(1) If submitted electronically, on or after January 1, 2014: $0.00.

(2) If not submitted electronically: $40.00.

(i) Publication in Official Gazette: For publication in the Official Gazette of a notice of the availability of an application or a patent for licensing or sale: Each application or patent: $25.00.

(j) Labor charges for services, per hour or fraction thereof: $40.00.

(k) For items and services that the Director finds may be supplied, for which fees are not specified by statute or by this part, such charges as may be determined by the Director with respect to each such item or service: Actual cost.

* * * * *

(n) For handling an application in which proceedings are terminated pursuant to § 1.53(e): $130.00.

§ 1.26. Refunds.

* * * * *

(c) If the Director decides not to institute a reexamination proceeding in response to a request for reexamination or supplemental examination, fees paid with the request for reexamination or supplemental examination will be refunded or returned in accordance with paragraphs (c)(1) through (c)(3) of this section. The reexamination requester or the patent owner who requested a supplemental examination proceeding, as appropriate, should indicate the form in which any refund should be made (*e.g.*, by check, electronic funds transfer, credit to a deposit account). Generally, refunds will be issued in the form that the original payment was provided.

(1) For an *ex parte* reexamination request, the *ex parte* reexamination filing fee paid by the reexamination requester, less the fee set forth in § 1.20(c)(7), will be refunded to the requester if the Director decides not to institute an *ex parte* reexamination proceeding.

(2) For an *inter partes* reexamination request, a refund of $7,970 will be made to the reexamination requester if the Director decides not to institute an *inter partes* reexamination proceeding.

(3) For a supplemental examination request, the fee for reexamination ordered as a result of supplemental examination, as set forth in § 1.20(k)(2), will be returned to the patent owner who requested the supplemental examination proceeding if the Director decides not to institute a reexamination proceeding.

§ 1.27. Definition of small entities and establishing status as a small entity to permit payment of small entity fees; when a determination of entitlement to small entity status and notification of loss of entitlement to small entity status are required; fraud on the Office.

* * * * *

(c) * * *

(2) *Parties who can sign the written assertion.* The written assertion can be signed by:

(i) The applicant (§ 1.42 or § 1.421);

(ii) A patent practitioner of record or a practitioner acting in a representative capacity under § 1.34;

(iii) The inventor or a joint inventor, if the inventor is the applicant; or

(iv) The assignee.

* * * * *

§ 1.29. Micro entity status.

(a) To establish micro entity status under this paragraph, the applicant must certify that:

(1) The applicant qualifies as a small entity as defined in § 1.27;

(2) Neither the applicant nor the inventor nor a joint inventor has been named as the inventor or a joint inventor on more than four previously filed patent applications, other than applications filed in another

country, provisional applications under 35 U.S.C. 111(b), or international applications for which the basic national fee under 35 U.S.C. 41(a) was not paid;

(3) Neither the applicant nor the inventor nor a joint inventor, in the calendar year preceding the calendar year in which the applicable fee is being paid, had a gross income, as defined in section 61(a) of the Internal Revenue Code of 1986 (26 U.S.C. 61(a)), exceeding three times the median household income for that preceding calendar year, as most recently reported by the Bureau of the Census; and

(4) Neither the applicant nor the inventor nor a joint inventor has assigned, granted, or conveyed, nor is under an obligation by contract or law to assign, grant, or convey, a license or other ownership interest in the application concerned to an entity that, in the calendar year preceding the calendar year in which the applicable fee is being paid, had a gross income, as defined in section 61(a) of the Internal Revenue Code of 1986, exceeding three times the median household income for that preceding calendar year, as most recently reported by the Bureau of the Census.

(b) An applicant, inventor, or joint inventor is not considered to be named on a previously filed application for purposes of paragraph (a)(2) of this section if the applicant, inventor, or joint inventor has assigned, or is under an obligation by contract or law to assign, all ownership rights in the application as the result of the applicant's, inventor's, or joint inventor's previous employment.

(c) If an applicant's, inventor's, joint inventor's, or entity's gross income in the preceding calendar year is not in United States dollars, the average currency exchange rate, as reported by the Internal Revenue Service, during that calendar year shall be used to determine whether the applicant's, inventor's, joint inventor's, or entity's gross income exceeds the threshold specified in paragraph (a)(3) or (4) of this section.

(d) To establish micro entity status under this paragraph, the applicant must certify that:

(1) The applicant qualifies as a small entity as defined in § 1.27; and

(2) (i) The applicant's employer, from which the applicant obtains the majority of the applicant's income,

is an institution of higher education as defined in section 101(a) of the Higher Education Act of 1965 (20 U.S.C. 1001(a)); or

(ii) The applicant has assigned, granted, conveyed, or is under an obligation by contract or law, to assign, grant, or convey, a license or other ownership interest in the particular application to such an institution of higher education.

(e) Micro entity status is established in an application by filing a micro entity certification in writing complying with the requirements of either paragraph (a) or paragraph (d) of this section and signed in compliance with § 1.33(b). Status as a micro entity must be specifically established in each related, continuing and reissue application in which status is appropriate and desired. Status as a micro entity in one application or patent does not affect the status of any other application or patent, regardless of the relationship of the applications or patents. The refiling of an application under § 1.53 as a continuation, divisional, or continuation-in-part application (including a continued prosecution application under § 1.53(d)), or the filing of a reissue application, requires a new certification of entitlement to micro entity status for the continuing or reissue application.

(f) A fee may be paid in the micro entity amount only if it is submitted with, or subsequent to, the submission of a certification of entitlement to micro entity status.

(g) A certification of entitlement to micro entity status need only be filed once in an application or patent. Micro entity status, once established, remains in effect until changed pursuant to paragraph (i) of this section. However, a fee may be paid in the micro entity amount only if status as a micro entity as defined in paragraph (a) or (d) of this section is appropriate on the date the fee is being paid. Where an assignment of rights or an obligation to assign rights to other parties who are micro entities occurs subsequent to the filing of a certification of entitlement to micro entity status, a second certification of entitlement to micro entity status is not required.

(h) Prior to submitting a certification of entitlement to micro entity status in an application, including a related, continuing, or reissue application, a determination of such entitlement should be made pursuant to the requirements of this section. It should be determined that each applicant qualifies for micro entity status under paragraph (a) or (d) of this section, and that any other party holding rights in the invention qualifies for small entity status under § 1.27. The Office will generally not question certification of entitlement to micro entity status that is made in accordance with the requirements of this section.

(i) Notification of a loss of entitlement to micro entity status must be filed in the application or patent prior to paying, or at the time of paying, any fee after the date on which status as a micro entity as defined in paragraph (a) or (d) of this section is no longer appropriate. The notification that micro entity status is no longer appropriate must be signed by a party identified in § 1.33(b). Payment of a fee in other than the micro entity amount is not sufficient notification that micro entity status is no longer appropriate. A notification that micro entity status is no longer appropriate will not be treated as a notification that small entity status is also no longer appropriate unless it also contains a notification of loss of entitlement to small entity status under § 1.27(f)(2). Once a notification of a loss of entitlement to micro entity status is filed in the application or patent, a new certification of entitlement to micro entity status is required to again obtain micro entity status.

(j) Any attempt to fraudulently establish status as a micro entity, or pay fees as a micro entity, shall be considered as a fraud practiced or attempted on the Office. Improperly, and with intent to deceive, establishing status as a micro entity, or paying fees as a micro entity, shall be considered as a fraud practiced or attempted on the Office.

(k) If status as a micro entity is established in good faith in an application or patent, and fees as a micro entity are paid in good faith in the application or patent, and it is later discovered that such micro entity status either was established in error, or that the Office was not notified of a loss of entitlement to micro entity status as required by paragraph (i) of this section through error, the error will be excused upon compliance with the separate submission and itemization requirements of paragraph (k)(1) of this section and the deficiency payment requirement of paragraph (k)(2) of this section.

(1) Any paper submitted under this paragraph must be limited to the deficiency payment (all fees paid in error) required for a single application or patent. Where more than one application or patent is involved, separate submissions of deficiency payments are required for each application or patent (see § 1.4(b)). The paper must contain an itemization of the total deficiency payment

for the single application or patent and include the following information:

(i) Each particular type of fee that was erroneously paid as a micro entity, (*e.g.*, basic statutory filing fee, two-month extension of time fee) along with the current fee amount for a small or nonsmall entity, as applicable;

(ii) The micro entity fee actually paid, and the date on which it was paid;

(iii) The deficiency owed amount (for each fee erroneously paid); and

(iv) The total deficiency payment owed, which is the sum or total of the individual deficiency owed amounts as set forth in paragraph (k)(2) of this section.

(2) The deficiency owed, resulting from the previous erroneous payment of micro entity fees, must be paid. The deficiency owed for each previous fee erroneously paid as a micro entity is the difference between the current fee amount for a small entity or non-small entity, as applicable, on the date the deficiency is paid in full and the amount of the previous erroneous micro entity fee payment. The total deficiency payment owed is the sum of the individual deficiency owed amounts for each fee amount previously and erroneously paid as a micro entity.

(3) If the requirements of paragraphs (k)(1) and (2) of this section are not complied with, such failure will either be treated at the option of the Office as an authorization for the Office to process the deficiency payment and charge the processing fee set forth in § 1.17(i), or result in a requirement for compliance within a one-month time period that is not extendable under § 1.136(a) to avoid the return of the fee deficiency payment.

(4) Any deficiency payment (based on a previous erroneous payment of a micro entity fee) submitted under this paragraph will be treated as a notification of a loss of entitlement to micro entity status under paragraph (i) of this section, but payment of a deficiency based upon the difference between the current fee amount for a small entity and the amount of the previous erroneous micro entity fee payment will not be treated as an assertion of small entity status under § 1.27(c). Once a defi-

ciency payment is submitted under this paragraph, a written assertion of small entity status under § 1.27(c)(1) is required to obtain small entity status.

Subpart B— National Processing Provisions

§ 1.31. Applicant may be represented by one or more patent practitioners or joint inventors.

An applicant for patent may file and prosecute the applicant's own case, or the applicant may give power of attorney so as to be represented by one or more patent practitioners or joint inventors, except that a juristic entity (*e.g.*, organizational assignee) must be represented by a patent practitioner even if the juristic entity is the applicant. The Office cannot aid in the selection of a patent practitioner.

§ 1.32. Power of attorney.

(a) * * *

(2) *Power of attorney* means a written document by which a principal authorizes one or more patent practitioners or joint inventors to act on the principal's behalf.

(3) *Principal* means the applicant (§ 1.42) for an application for patent and the patent owner for a patent, including a patent in a supplemental examination or reexamination proceeding. The principal executes a power of attorney designating one or more patent practitioners or joint inventors to act on the principal's behalf.

(4) *Revocation* means the cancellation by the principal of the authority previously given to a patent practitioner or joint inventor to act on the principal's behalf.

* * * * *

(6) *Patent practitioner of record* means a patent practitioner who has been granted a power of attorney in an application, patent, or other proceeding in compliance with paragraph (b) of this section. The phrases practitioner of record and attorney or agent of record also mean a patent practitioner who has been granted a power of attorney in an application, patent, or other proceeding in compliance with paragraph (b) of this section.

(b) A power of attorney must:

(1) Be in writing;

(2) Name one or more representatives in compliance with paragraph (c) of this section;

(3) Give the representative power to act on behalf of the principal; and

(4) Be signed by the applicant for patent (§ 1.42) or the patent owner. A patent owner who was not the applicant under § 1.46 must appoint any power of attorney in compliance with §§ 3.71 and 3.73 of this chapter.

* * * * *

(d) A power of attorney from a prior national application for which benefit is claimed under 35 U.S.C. 120, 121, or 365(c) in a continuing application may have effect in the continuing application if a copy of the power of attorney from the prior application is filed in the continuing application unless:

(1) The power of attorney was granted by the inventor; and

(2) The continuing application names an inventor who was not named as an inventor in the prior application.

(e) If the power of attorney was granted by the originally named inventive entity, and an added inventor pursuant to § 1.48 does not provide a power of attorney consistent with the power of attorney granted by the originally named inventive entity, the addition of the inventor results in the loss of that power of attorney upon grant of the § 1.48 request. This provision does not preclude a practitioner from acting pursuant to § 1.34, if applicable.

§ 1.33. Correspondence respecting patent applications, patent reexamination proceedings, and other proceedings.

(a) *Correspondence address and daytime telephone number.* When filing an application, a correspondence address must be set forth in either an application data sheet (§ 1.76), or elsewhere, in a clearly identifiable manner, in any paper submitted with an application filing. If no correspondence address is specified, the Office may treat the mailing address of the first named inventor (if provided, *see* §§ 1.76(b)(1) and 1.63(b)(2)) as the correspondence address. The Office will direct, or otherwise make available, all notices, official letters, and other communications relating to the application to the person associated with the correspondence address. For correspondence submitted via the Office's electronic filing system, however, an electronic acknowledgment receipt will be sent to the submitter. The Office will generally not engage in double correspondence with an applicant and a patent practitioner, or with more than one patent practitioner except as deemed necessary by the Director. If more than one correspondence address is specified, the Office will select one of the specified addresses for use as the correspondence address and, if given, may select the address associated with a Customer Number over a typed correspondence address. For the party to whom correspondence is to be addressed, a daytime telephone number should be supplied in a clearly identifiable manner and may be changed by any party who may change the correspondence address. The correspondence address may be changed by the parties set forth in paragraph (b)(1) or (b)(3) of this section. Prior to the appointment of any power of attorney under § 1.32(b), the correspondence address may also be changed by any patent practitioner named in the application transmittal papers who acts in a representative capacity under the provisions of § 1.34.

(b) *Amendments* and *other papers*. Amendments and other papers, except for written assertions pursuant to § 1.27(c)(2)(iii) or (c)(2)(iv), filed in the application must be signed by:

(1) A patent practitioner of record;

(2) A patent practitioner not of record who acts in a representative capacity under the provisions of § 1.34; or

(3) The applicant (§ 1.42). Unless otherwise specified, all papers submitted on behalf of a juristic entity must be signed by a patent practitioner.

* * * * *

(f) Where application papers from a prior application are used in a continuing application and the correspondence address was changed during the prosecution of the prior application, an application data sheet or separate paper identifying the correspondence address to be used for the continuing application must be submitted. Otherwise, the Office may not recognize the change of correspondence address effected during the prosecution of the prior application.

(g) A patent practitioner acting in a representative capacity whose correspondence address is the correspondence address of record in an application may change the correspondence address after the patent has issued, provided that the change of correspondence address is accompanied by a statement that notice has been given to the patentee or owner.

§ 1.36. Revocation of power of attorney; withdrawal of patent attorney or agent.

(a) A power of attorney, pursuant to § 1.32(b), may be revoked at any stage in the proceedings of a case by the applicant or patent owner. A power of attorney to the patent practitioners associated with a Customer Number will be treated as a request to revoke any powers of attorney previously given. Fewer than all of the applicants (or fewer than all patent owners in a supplemental examination or reexamination proceeding) may revoke the power of attorney only upon a showing of sufficient cause, and payment of the petition fee set forth in § 1.17(f). A patent practitioner will be notified of the revocation of the power of attorney. Where power of attorney is given to the patent practitioners associated with a Customer Number (§ 1.32(c)(2)), the practitioners so appointed will also be notified of the revocation of the power of attorney when the power of attorney to all of the practitioners associated with the Customer Number is revoked. The notice of revocation will be mailed to the correspondence address for the application (§ 1.33) in effect before the revocation. An assignment will not of itself operate as a revocation of a power previously given, but the assignee may become the applicant under § 1.46(c) and revoke any previous power of attorney and grant a power of attorney as provided in § 1.32(b).

(b) A registered patent attorney or patent agent who has been given a power of attorney pursuant to § 1.32(b) may withdraw as attorney or agent of record upon application to and approval by the Director. The applicant or patent owner will be notified of the withdrawal of the registered patent attorney or patent agent. Where power of attorney is given to the patent practitioners associated with a Customer Number, a request to delete all of the patent practitioners associated with the Customer Number may not be granted if an applicant has given power of attorney to the patent practitioners associated with the Customer Number in an application that has an Office action to which a reply is due, but insufficient time remains for the applicant to file a reply. See § 41.5 of this title for withdrawal during proceedings before the Patent Trial and Appeal Board.

* * * * *

§ 1.41. Inventorship.

(a) An application must include, or be amended to include, the name of the inventor for any invention claimed in the application.

(b) The inventorship of a nonprovisional application under 35 U.S.C. 111(a) is the inventor or joint inventors set forth in the application data sheet in accordance with § 1.76 filed before or concurrently with the inventor's oath or declaration. If an application data sheet is not filed before or concurrently with the inventor's oath or declaration, the inventorship is the inventor or joint inventors set forth in the inventor's oath or declaration, except as provided for in §§ 1.53(d)(4) and 1.63(d). Once an application data sheet or the inventor's oath or declaration is filed in a nonprovisional application, any correction of inventorship must be pursuant to § 1.48. If neither an application data sheet nor the inventor's oath or declaration is filed during the pendency of a nonprovisional application, the inventorship is the inventor or joint inventors set forth in the application papers filed pursuant to § 1.53(b), unless the applicant files a paper, including the processing fee set forth in § 1.17(i), supplying the name or names of the inventor or joint inventors.

(c) The inventorship of a provisional application is the inventor or joint inventors set forth in the cover sheet as prescribed by § 1.51(c)(1). Once a cover sheet as prescribed by § 1.51(c)(1) is filed in a provisional application, any correction of inventorship must be pursuant to § 1.48. If a cover sheet as prescribed by § 1.51(c)(1) is not filed during the pendency of a provisional application, the inventorship is the inventor or joint inventors set forth in the application papers filed pursuant to § 1.53(c), unless applicant files a paper including the processing fee set forth in § 1.17(q), supplying the name or names of the inventor or joint inventors.

(d) In a nonprovisional application under 35 U.S.C. 111(a) filed without an application data sheet or the inventor's oath or declaration, or in a provisional application filed without a cover sheet as prescribed by § 1.51(c)(1), the name and residence of each person believed to be an actual inventor should be provided when the application papers pursuant to § 1.53(b) or § 1.53(c) are filed.

(e) The inventorship of an international application entering the national stage under 35 U.S.C. 371 is the inventor or joint inventors set forth in the application data sheet in accordance with § 1.76 filed with the initial submission under 35 U.S.C. 371. Unless the initial submission under 35 U.S.C. 371 is accompanied by an application data sheet in accordance with § 1.76 setting forth the inventor or joint inventors, the inventorship is the inventor or joint inventors set forth in the international application, which includes any change effected under PCT Rule 92 *bis*.

§ 1.42. Applicant for patent.

(a) The word "applicant" when used in this title refers to the inventor or all of the joint inventors, or to the person applying for a patent as provided in §§ 1.43, 1.45, or 1.46.

(b) If a person is applying for a patent as provided in § 1.46, the word "applicant" refers to the assignee, the person to whom the inventor is under an obligation to assign the invention, or the person who otherwise shows sufficient proprietary interest in the matter, who is applying for a patent under § 1.46 and not the inventor.

(c) If fewer than all joint inventors are applying for a patent as provided in § 1.45, the phrase "the applicant" means the joint inventors who are applying for the patent without the omitted inventor(s).

(d) Any person having authority may deliver an application and fees to the Office on behalf of the applicant. However, an oath or declaration, or substitute statement in lieu of an oath or declaration, may be executed only in accordance with § 1.63 or 1.64, a correspondence address may be provided only in accordance with § 1.33(a), and amendments and other papers must be signed in accordance with § 1.33(b).

(e) The Office may require additional information where there is a question concerning ownership or interest in an application, and a showing may be required from the person filing the application that the filing was authorized where such authorization comes into question.

§ 1.43. Application for patent by a legal representative of a deceased or legally incapacitated inventor.

If an inventor is deceased or under legal incapacity, the legal representative of the inventor may make an application for patent on behalf of the inventor. If an inventor dies during the time intervening between the filing of the application and the granting of a patent thereon, the letters patent may be issued to the legal representative upon proper intervention. See § 1.64 concerning the execution of a substitute statement by a legal representative in lieu of an oath or declaration.

§ 1.45. Application for patent by joint inventors.

(a) Joint inventors must apply for a patent jointly, and each must make an inventor's oath or declaration as required by § 1.63, except as provided for in § 1.64. If a joint inventor refuses to join in an application for patent or cannot be found or reached after diligent effort, the other joint inventor or inventors may make the application for patent on behalf of themselves and the omitted inventor. See § 1.64 concerning the execution of a substitute statement by the other joint inventor or inventors in lieu of an oath or declaration.

(b) Inventors may apply for a patent jointly even though:

(1) They did not physically work together or at the same time;

(2) Each inventor did not make the same type or amount of contribution; or

(3) Each inventor did not make a contribution to the subject matter of every claim of the application.

(c) If multiple inventors are named in a nonprovisional application, each named inventor must have made a contribution, individually or jointly, to the subject matter of at least one claim of the application and the application will be considered to be a joint application under 35 U.S.C. 116. If multiple inventors are named in a provisional application, each named inventor must have made a contribution, individually or jointly, to the subject matter disclosed in the provisional application and the provisional application will be considered to be a joint application under 35 U.S.C. 116.

§ 1.46. Application for patent by an assignee, obligated assignee, or a person who otherwise shows sufficient proprietary interest in the matter.

(a) A person to whom the inventor has assigned or is under an obligation to assign the invention may make an application for patent. A person who otherwise shows sufficient proprietary interest in the matter may make an application for patent on behalf of and as agent for the inventor on proof of the pertinent facts and a showing that such action is appropriate to preserve the rights of the parties.

(b) If an application under 35 U.S.C. 111 is made by a person other than the inventor under paragraph (a) of this section, the application must contain an application data sheet under § 1.76 specifying in the applicant information section (§ 1.76(b)(7)) the assignee, person to whom the inventor is under an obligation to assign the invention, or person who otherwise shows sufficient proprietary interest in the matter. If the application is the national stage of an international application, the person who is identified in the international stage as an applicant for the United States is the person specified as the original applicant for the national stage.

(1) If the applicant is the assignee or a person to whom the inventor is under an obligation to assign the invention, documentary evidence of ownership (e.g., assignment for an assignee, employment agreement for a person to whom the inventor is under an obligation to assign the invention) should be recorded as provided for in part 3 of this chapter no later than the date the issue fee is paid in the application.

(2) If the applicant is a person who otherwise shows sufficient proprietary interest in the matter, such applicant must submit a petition including:

(i) The fee set forth in § 1.17(g);

(ii) A showing that such person has sufficient proprietary interest in the matter; and

(iii) A statement that making the application for patent by a person who otherwise shows sufficient proprietary interest in the matter on behalf of and as agent for the inventor is appropriate to preserve the rights of the parties.

(c) Any request to correct or update the name of the applicant after an applicant has been specified under paragraph (b) of this section must include an application data sheet under § 1.76 specifying the correct or updated name of the applicant in the applicant information section (§ 1.76(b)(7)). Any request to change the applicant after an original applicant has been specified under paragraph (b) of this section must include an application data sheet under § 1.76 specifying the applicant in the applicant information section (§ 1.76(b)(7)) and comply with §§ 3.71 and 3.73 of this title.

(d) Even if the whole or a part interest in the invention or in the patent to be issued is assigned or obligated to be assigned, an oath or declaration must be executed by the actual inventor or each actual joint inventor, except as provided for in § 1.64. *See* § 1.64 concerning the execution of a substitute statement by an assignee, person to whom the inventor is under an obligation to assign the invention, or a person who otherwise shows sufficient proprietary interest in the matter.

(e) If a patent is granted on an application filed under this section by a person other than the inventor, the patent shall be granted to the real party in interest. Otherwise, the patent may be issued to the assignee or jointly to the inventor and the assignee as provided in § 3.81. Where a real party in interest has filed an application under § 1.46, the applicant shall notify the Office of any change in the real party in interest no later than payment of the issue fee. The Office will treat the absence of such a notice as an indication that there has been no change in the real party in interest.

(f) The Office may publish notice of the filing of the application by a person who otherwise shows sufficient proprietary interest in the *Official Gazette.*

§ 1.47. [Removed and Reserved]

§ 1.48. Correction of inventorship pursuant to 35 U.S.C. 116 or correction of the name or order of names in a patent application, other than a reissue application.

(a) *Nonprovisional application:* Any request to correct or change the inventorship once the inventorship has been established under § 1.41 must include:

(1) An application data sheet in accordance with § 1.76 that identifies each inventor by his or her legal name; and

(2) The processing fee set forth in § 1.17(i).

(b) *Inventor's oath or declaration for added inventor*: An oath or declaration as required by § 1.63, or a substitute statement in compliance with § 1.64, will be required for any actual inventor who has not yet executed such an oath or declaration.

(c) Any request to correct or change the inventorship under paragraph (a) of this section filed after the Office action on the merits has been given or mailed in the application must also be accompanied by the fee set forth in § 1.17(d), unless the request is accompanied by a statement that the request to correct or change the inventorship is due solely to the cancelation of claims in the application.

(d) *Provisional application.* Once a cover sheet as prescribed by § 1.51(c)(1) is filed in a provisional application, any request to correct or change the inventorship must include:

(1) A request, signed by a party set forth in § 1.33(b), to correct the inventorship that identifies each inventor by his or her legal name; and

(2) The processing fee set forth in § 1.17(q).

(e) *Additional information may be required.* The Office may require such other information as may be deemed appropriate under the particular circumstances surrounding the correction of inventorship.

(f) *Correcting or updating the name of an inventor:* Any request to correct or update the name of the inventor or a joint inventor, or the order of the names of joint inventors, in a nonprovisional application must include:

(1) An application data sheet in accordance with § 1.76 that identifies each inventor by his or her legal name in the desired order; and

(2) The processing fee set forth in § 1.17(i).

(g) Reissue applications not covered. The provisions of this section do not apply to reissue applications. See §§ 1.171 and 1.175 for correction of inventorship in a patent via a reissue application.

(h) *Correction of inventorship in patent.* See § 1.324 for correction of inventorship in a patent.

(i) Correction of inventorship in an interference or contested case before the Patent Trial and Appeal Board. In an interference under part 41, subpart D, of this title, a request for correction of inventorship in an application must be in the form of a motion under § 41.121(a)(2) of this title. In a contested case under part 42, subpart D, of this title, a request for correction of inventorship in an application must be in the form of a motion under § 42.22 of this title. The motion under § 41.121(a)(2) or 42.22 of this title must comply with the requirements of paragraph (a) of this section.

§ 1.51. General requisites of an application.

* * * * *

(b) * * *

(2) The inventor's oath or declaration, *see* §§ 1.63 and 1.64;

(c) * * *

(2) A specification as prescribed by 35 U.S.C. 112(a), see § 1.71;

* * * * *

§ 1.52. Language, paper, writing, margins, compact disc specifications.

* * * * *

(b) The application (specification, including the claims, drawings, and the inventor's oath or declaration) or supplemental examination or reexamination proceeding and any amendments or corrections to the application or reexamination proceeding.

* * * * *

(c) Interlineation, erasure, cancellation, or other alteration of the application papers may be made before or after the signing of the inventor's oath or declaration referring to those application papers, provided that the statements in the inventor's oath or declaration pursuant to § 1.63 remain applicable to those application papers. A substitute specification (§ 1.125) may be required if the application papers do not comply with paragraphs (a) and (b) of this section.

(d) A nonprovisional or provisional application under 35 U.S.C. 111 may be in a language other than English.

(1) *Nonprovisional application.* If a nonprovisional application under 35 U.S.C. 111(a) is filed in a language other than English, an English language translation of the non-English language application, a statement that the translation is accurate, and the processing fee set forth in § 1.17(i) are required. If these items are not filed with the application, the applicant will be notified and given a period of time within which they must be filed in order to avoid abandonment.

(2) *Provisional application.* If a provisional application under 35 U.S.C. 111(b) is filed in a language other than English, an English language translation of the non-English language provisional application will not be required in the provisional application. *See* § 1.78(a) for the requirements for claiming the benefit of such provisional application in a nonprovisional application.

* * * * *

§ 1.53. Application number, filing date, and completion of application.

* * * * *

(b) *Application filing requirements—Nonprovisional application.* The filing date of an application for patent filed under this section, except for a provisional application under paragraph (c) of this section or a continued prosecution application under paragraph (d) of this section, is the date on which a specification as prescribed by 35 U.S.C. 112 containing a description pursuant to § 1.71 and at least one claim pursuant to § 1.75, and any drawing required by § 1.81(a) are filed in the Patent and Trademark Office. No new matter may be introduced into an application after its filing date. A continuing application, which may be a continuation, divisional, or continuation-in-part application, may be filed under the conditions specified in 35 U.S.C. 120, 121, or 365(c) and § 1.78(c) and (d).

(c) *Application filing requirements—Provisional application.* The filing date of a provisional application is the date on which a specification as prescribed by 35 U.S.C. 112(a), and any drawing required by § 1.81(a) are filed in the Patent and Trademark Office. No amendment, other than to make the provisional application comply with the patent statute and all applicable regulations, may be made to the provisional application after the filing date of the provisional application.

* * * * *

(ii) Payment of the issue fee on the application filed under paragraph (b) of this section; or (iii) Expiration of twelve months after the filing date of the application filed under paragraph (b) of this section.

(3) A provisional application filed under paragraph (c) of this section may be converted to a nonprovisional application filed under paragraph (b) of this section and accorded the original filing date of the provisional application. The conversion of a provisional application to a nonprovisional application will not result in either the refund of any fee properly paid in the provisional application or the application of any such fee to the filing fee, or any other fee, for the nonprovisional application. Conversion of a provisional application to a nonprovisional application under this paragraph will result in the term of any patent to issue from the application being measured from at least the filing date of the provisional application for which conversion is requested. Thus, applicants should consider avoiding this adverse patent term impact by filing a nonprovisional application claiming the benefit of the provisional application under 35 U.S.C. 119(e) (rather than convert-

ing the provisional application into a nonprovisional application pursuant to this paragraph). A request to convert a provisional application to a nonprovisional application must be accompanied by the fee set forth in § 1.17(i) and an amendment including at least one claim as prescribed by 35 U.S.C. 112(b), unless the provisional application under paragraph (c) of this section otherwise contains at least one claim as prescribed by 35 U.S.C. 112(b). The nonprovisional application resulting from conversion of a provisional application must also include the filing fee, search fee, and examination fee for a nonprovisional application, the inventor's oath or declaration, and the surcharge required by § 1.16(f) if either the basic filing fee for a nonprovisional application or the inventor's oath or declaration was not present on the filing date accorded the resulting nonprovisional application (*i.e.,* the filing date of the original provisional application). A request to convert a provisional application to a nonprovisional application must also be filed prior to the earliest of:

* * * * *

(4) A provisional application is not entitled to the right of priority under 35 U.S.C. 119 or 365(a) or § 1.55, or to the benefit of an earlier filing date under 35 U.S.C. 120, 121, or 365(c) or § 1.78 of any other application. No claim for priority under 35 U.S.C. 119(e) or § 1.78(a) may be made in a design application based on a provisional application. The requirements of §§ 1.821 through 1.825 regarding application disclosures containing nucleotide and/or amino acid sequences are not mandatory for provisional applications.

(d) * * *

(2) * * *

(iv) Includes the request for an application under this paragraph, will utilize the file jacket and contents of the prior application, including the specification, drawings and the inventor's oath or declaration from the prior application, to constitute the new application, and will be assigned the application number of the prior application for identification purposes; and

* * * * *

(f) Completion of application subsequent to filing—Nonprovisional (including continued prosecution or reissue) application.

(1) If an application which has been accorded a filing date pursuant to paragraph (b) or (d) of this section does not include the basic filing fee, the search fee, or the examination fee, or if an application which has been accorded a filing date pursuant to paragraph (b) of this section does not include the inventor's oath or declaration (§ 1.63, § 1.64, § 1.162 or § 1.175), and the applicant has provided a correspondence address (§ 1.33(a)), the applicant will be notified and given a period of time within which to pay the basic filing fee, search fee, and examination fee, and pay the surcharge if required by § 1.16(f) to avoid abandonment.

(2) If an application which has been accorded a filing date pursuant to paragraph (b) of this section does not include the basic filing fee, the search fee, the examination fee, or the inventor's oath or declaration, and the applicant has not provided a correspondence address (§ 1.33(a)), the applicant has two months from the filing date of the application within which to pay the basic filing fee, search fee, and examination fee, and pay the surcharge required by § 1.16(f) to avoid abandonment.

(3) The inventor's oath or declaration in an application under § 1.53(b) must also be filed within the period specified in paragraph (f)(1) or (f)(2) of this section, except that the filing of the inventor's oath or declaration may be postponed until the application is otherwise in condition for allowance under the conditions specified in paragraphs (f)(3)(i) and (f)(3)(ii) of this section. (i) The application must be an original (non-reissue) application that contains an application data sheet in accordance with § 1.76 identifying:

(A) Each inventor by his or her legal name;

(B) A mailing address where the inventor customarily receives mail, and residence, if an inventor lives at a location which is different from where the inventor customarily receives mail, for each inventor.

(ii) The applicant must file an oath or declaration in compliance with § 1.63, or a substitute statement in compliance with § 1.64, executed by or with respect to each actual inventor no later than the expiration of the time period set in the "Notice of Allowability" to avoid abandonment, when the applicant is notified in a "Notice of Allowability" that an application is otherwise in condition for allowance. The time period set in a "Notice of Allowability" is not extendable. *See* § 1.136(c). The Office may dispense with the notice provided for in paragraph (f)(1) of this section if an oath or declaration under § 1.63, or a substitute statement under § 1.64, executed by or with respect to each actual inventor has been filed before the application is in condition for allowance.

(4) If the excess claims fees required by § 1.16(h) and (i) and multiple dependent claim fee required by § 1.16(j) are not paid on filing or on later presentation of the claims for which the excess claims or multiple dependent claim fees are due, the fees required by § 1.16(h), (i) and (j) must be paid or the claims canceled by amendment prior to the expiration of the time period set for reply by the Office in any notice of fee deficiency. If the application size fee required by § 1.16(s) (if any) is not paid on filing or on later presentation of the amendment necessitating a fee or additional fee under § 1.16(s), the fee required by § 1.16(s) must be paid prior to the expiration of the time period set for reply by the Office in any notice of fee deficiency in order to avoid abandonment.

(5) This paragraph applies to continuation or divisional applications under paragraphs (b) or (d) of this section and to continuation-in-part applications under paragraph (b) of this section. *See* § 1.63(d) concerning the submission of a copy of the inventor's oath or declaration from the prior application for a continuing application under paragraph (b) of this section.

(6) If applicant does not pay the basic filing fee during the pendency of the application, the Office may dispose of the application.

* * * * *

(h) *Subsequent treatment of application—Nonprovisional (including continued prosecution) application.* An application for a patent filed under paragraphs (b) or (d) of this section will not be placed on the files for examination until all its required parts, complying with the rules relating thereto, are received, except that the inventor's oath or declaration may be filed when the application is otherwise in condition for allowance pursuant to paragraph (f)(3) of this section and minor informalities may be waived subject to subsequent correction whenever required.

* * * * *

§ 1.55. Claim for foreign priority.

(a) *In general.* An applicant in a nonprovisional application may claim priority to one or more prior foreign applications under the conditions specified in 35 U.S.C. 119(a) through (d) and (f), 172, and 365(a) and (b) and this section.

(b) *Time for filing subsequent application.* The nonprovisional application must be filed not later than twelve months (six months in the case of a design application) after the date on which the foreign application was filed, or be entitled to claim the benefit under 35 U.S.C. 120, 121, or 365(c) of an application that was filed not later than twelve months (six months in the case of a design application) after the date on which the foreign application was filed. The twelve-month period is subject to 35 U.S.C. 21(b) (and § 1.7(a)) and PCT Rule 80.5, and the six-month period is subject to 35 U.S.C. 21(b) (and § 1.7(a)).

(c) *Time for filing priority claim and certified copy of foreign application in an application entering the national stage under 35 U.S.C. 371.* In an international application entering the national stage under 35 U.S.C. 371, the claim for priority must be made and a certified copy of the foreign application must be filed within the time limit set forth in the PCT and the Regulations under the PCT.

(d) *Time for filing priority claim in an application filed under 35 U.S.C. 111(a).* In an original application filed under 35 U.S.C. 111(a), the claim for priority must be filed within the later of four months from the actual filing date of the application or sixteen months from the filing date of the prior foreign application. The claim for priority must be presented in an application data sheet (§ 1.76(b)(6)), and must identify the foreign application for which priority is claimed, by specifying the application number, country (or intellectual property authority), day, month, and year of its filing. The time period in this paragraph does not apply in a design application.

(e) *Delayed priority claim in an application filed under 35 U.S.C. 111(a).* Unless such claim is accepted in accordance with the provisions of this paragraph, any claim for priority under 35 U.S.C. 119(a) through (d) or (f) or 365(a) in an original application filed under 35 U.S.C. 111(a) not presented in an application data sheet (§ 1.76(b)(6)) within the time period provided by paragraph (d) of this section is considered to have been waived. If a claim for priority is presented after the time period provided by paragraph (d) of this section, the claim may be accepted if the priority claim was unintentionally delayed. A petition to accept a delayed claim for priority under 35 U.S.C. 119(a) through (d) or (f) or 365(a) must be accompanied by:

(1) The priority claim under 35 U.S.C. 119(a) through (d) or (f) or 365(a) in an application data sheet (§ 1.76(b)(6)), identifying the foreign application for which priority is claimed, by specifying the application number, country (or intellectual property authority), day, month, and year of its filing, unless previously submitted;

(2) A certified copy of the foreign application if required by paragraph (f) of this section, unless previously submitted;

(3) The surcharge set forth in § 1.17(t); and

(4) A statement that the entire delay between the date the priority claim was due under paragraph (d) of this section and the date the priority claim was filed was unintentional. The Director may require additional information where there is a question whether the delay was unintentional.

(f) *Time for filing certified copy of foreign application in an application filed under 35 U.S.C. 111(a).* In an original application filed under 35 U.S.C. 111(a), a certified copy of the foreign application must be filed within the later of four months from the actual filing date of the application or sixteen months from the filing date of the prior foreign application, except as provided in paragraphs (h) and (i) of this section. If a certified copy of the foreign application is not filed within the later of four months from the actual filing date of the application or sixteen months from the filing date of the prior foreign application, and the exceptions in paragraphs (h) and (i) of this section are not applicable, the certified copy of the foreign application must be accompanied by a petition including a showing of good and sufficient cause for the delay and the petition fee set forth in § 1.17(g). The time period in this paragraph does not apply in a design application.

(g) *Requirement for filing priority claim, certified copy of foreign application, and translation in any application.*

(1) The claim for priority and the certified copy of the foreign application specified in 35 U.S.C. 119(b) or PCT Rule 17 must, in any event, be filed within the pendency of the application and before the patent is granted. If the claim for priority or the certified copy of the foreign application is filed after the date the issue fee is paid, it

must also be accompanied by the processing fee set forth in § 1.17(i), but the patent will not include the priority claim unless corrected by a certificate of correction under 35 U.S.C. 255 and § 1.323.

(2) The Office may require that the claim for priority and the certified copy of the foreign application be filed earlier than otherwise provided in this section:

(i) When the application is involved in an interference (see § 41.202 of this title) or derivation (see part 42 of this title) proceeding;

(ii) When necessary to overcome the date of a reference relied upon by the examiner; or

(iii) When deemed necessary by the examiner.

(3) An English language translation of a non-English language foreign application is not required except:

(i) When the application is involved in an interference (see § 41.202 of this title) or derivation (see part 42 of this title) proceeding;

(ii) When necessary to overcome the date of a reference relied upon by the examiner; or

(iii) When specifically required by the examiner.

(4) If an English language translation of a non-English language foreign application is required, it must be filed together with a statement that the translation of the certified copy is accurate.

(h) *Foreign intellectual property office participating in a priority document exchange agreement.* The requirement in paragraphs (c), (f), and (g) for a certified copy of the foreign application to be filed within the time limit set forth therein will be considered satisfied if:

(1) The foreign application was filed in a foreign intellectual property office participating with the Office in a bilateral or multilateral priority document exchange agreement (participating foreign intellectual property office), or a copy of the foreign application was filed in an application subsequently filed in a participating foreign intellectual property office that permits the Office to obtain such a copy;

(2) The claim for priority is presented in an application data sheet (§ 1.76(b)(6)), identifying the foreign application for which priority is claimed, by specifying the application number, country (or intellectual property authority), day, month, and year of its filing, and the ap-

plicant provides the information necessary for the participating foreign intellectual property office to provide the Office with access to the foreign application;

(3) The copy of the foreign application is received by the Office from the participating foreign intellectual property office, or a certified copy of the foreign application is filed, within the period specified in paragraph (g)(1) of this section; and

(4) The applicant files a request in a separate document that the Office obtain a copy of the foreign application from a participating intellectual property office that permits the Office to obtain such a copy if the foreign application was not filed in a participating foreign intellectual property office but a copy of the foreign application was filed in an application subsequently filed in a participating foreign intellectual property office that permits the Office to obtain such a copy. The request must identify the participating intellectual property office and the subsequent application by the application number, day, month, and year of its filing in which a copy of the foreign application was filed. The request must be filed within the later of sixteen months from the filing date of the prior foreign application or four months from the actual filing date of an application under 35 U.S.C. 111(a), within four months from the later of the date of commencement (§ 1.491(a)) or the date of the initial submission under 35 U.S.C. 371 in an application entering the national stage under 35 U.S.C. 371, or with a petition under paragraph (e) of this section.

(i) *Interim copy.* The requirement in paragraph (f) for a certified copy of the foreign application to be filed within the time limit set forth therein will be considered satisfied if:

(1) A copy of the original foreign application clearly labeled as "Interim Copy," including the specification, and any drawings or claims upon which it is based, is filed in the Office together with a separate cover sheet identifying the foreign application by specifying the application number, country (or intellectual property authority), day, month, and year of its filing, and stating that the copy filed in the Office is a true copy of the original application as filed in the foreign country (or intellectual property authority);

(2) The copy of the foreign application and separate cover sheet is filed within the later of sixteen months from the filing date of the prior foreign application or four months from the actual filing date of an application under 35 U.S.C. 111(a), or with a petition under paragraph (e) of this section; and

(3) A certified copy of the foreign application is filed within the period specified in paragraph (g)(1) of this section.

(j) *Requirements for certain applications filed on or after March 16, 2013.* If a nonprovisional application filed on or after March 16, 2013, claims priority to a foreign application filed prior to March 16, 2013, and also contains, or contained at any time, a claim to a claimed invention that has an effective filing date on or after March 16, 2013, the applicant must provide a statement to that effect within the later of four months from the actual filing date of the nonprovisional application, four months from the date of entry into the national stage as set forth in § 1.491 in an international application, sixteen months from the filing date of the prior filed foreign application, or the date that a first claim to a claimed invention that has an effective filing date on or after March 16, 2013, is presented in the nonprovisional application. An applicant is not required to provide such a statement if the applicant reasonably believes on the basis of information already known to the individuals designated in § 1.56(c) that the nonprovisional application does not, and did not at any time, contain a claim to a claimed invention that has an effective filing date on or after March 16, 2013.

(k) *Inventor's certificates.* An applicant in a nonprovisional application may under certain circumstances claim priority on the basis of one or more applications for an inventor's certificate in a country granting both inventor's certificates and patents. To claim the right of priority on the basis of an application for an inventor's certificate in such a country under 35 U.S.C. 119(d), the applicant when submitting a claim for such right as specified in this section, must include an affidavit or declaration. The affidavit or declaration must include a specific statement that, upon an investigation, he or she is satisfied that to the best of his or her knowledge, the applicant, when filing the application for the inventor's certificate, had the option to file an application for either a patent or an inventor's certificate as to the subject matter of the identified claim or claims forming the basis for the claim of priority.

(l) *Time periods not extendable.* The time periods set forth in this section are not extendable.

§ 1.56. Duty to disclose information material to patentability.

* * * * *

(c) * * *

(3) Every other person who is substantively involved in the preparation or prosecution of the application and who is associated with the inventor, the applicant, an assignee, or anyone to whom there is an obligation to assign the application.

* * * * *

§ 1.57. Incorporation by reference.

* * * * *

(c) * * *

(1) Provide a written description of the claimed invention, and of the manner and process of making and using it, in such full, clear, concise, and exact terms as to enable any person skilled in the art to which it pertains, or with which it is most nearly connected, to make and use the same, and set forth the best mode contemplated by the inventor of carrying out the invention as required by 35 U.S.C. 112(a);

(2) Describe the claimed invention in terms that particularly point out and distinctly claim the invention as required by 35 U.S.C. 112(b); or

(3) Describe the structure, material, or acts that correspond to a claimed means or step for performing a specified function as required by 35 U.S.C. 112(f).

* * * * *

§ 1.59. Expungement of information or copy of papers in application file.

(a) (1) Information in an application will not be expunged, except as provided in paragraph (b) of this section or § 41.7(a) or § 42.7(a) of this title.)

(2) Information forming part of the original disclosure (*i.e.*, written specification including the claims, drawings, and any preliminary amendment present on the filing date of the application) will not be expunged from the application file.

* * * * *

§ 1.63. Inventor's oath or declaration.

(a) The inventor, or each individual who is a joint inventor of a claimed invention, in an application for patent must execute an oath or declaration directed to the application, except as provided for in § 1.64. An oath or declaration under this section must:

(1) Identify the inventor or joint inventor executing the oath or declaration by his or her legal name;

(2) Identify the application to which it is directed;

(3) Include a statement that the person executing the oath or declaration believes the named inventor or joint inventor to be the original inventor or an original joint inventor of a claimed invention in the application for which the oath or declaration is being submitted; and

(4) State that the application was made or was authorized to be made by the person executing the oath or declaration.

(b) Unless the following information is supplied in an application data sheet in accordance with § 1.76, the oath or declaration must also identify:

(1) Each inventor by his or her legal name; and

(2) A mailing address where the inventor customarily receives mail, and residence, if an inventor lives at a location which is different from where the inventor customarily receives mail, for each inventor.

(c) A person may not execute an oath or declaration for an application unless that person has reviewed and understands the contents of the application, including the claims, and is aware of the duty to disclose to the Office all information known to the person to be material to patentability as defined in § 1.56. There is no minimum age for a person to be qualified to execute an oath or declaration, but the person must be competent to execute, i.e., understand, the document that the person is executing.

(d) (1) A newly executed oath or declaration under § 1.63, or substitute statement under § 1.64, is not required under § 1.51(b)(2) and § 1.53(f) or § 1.497 for an inventor in a continuing application that claims the benefit under 35 U.S.C. 120, 121, or 365(c) in compliance with § 1.78 of an earlier-filed application, provided that an oath or declaration in compliance with this section, or substitute statement under § 1.64, was executed by or with respect to such inventor and was filed in the earlier-filed application, and a copy of such oath, declaration, or substitute statement showing the signature or an indication thereon that it was executed, is submitted in the continuing application.

(2) The inventorship of a continuing application filed under 35 U.S.C. 111(a) is the inventor or joint inventors specified in the application data sheet filed before or concurrently with the copy of the inventor's oath or declaration from the earlier-filed application. If an application data sheet is not filed before or concurrently with the copy of the inventor's oath or declaration from the earlier-filed application, the inventorship is the inventorship set forth in the copy of the inventor's oath or declaration from the earlier-filed application, unless it is accompanied by a statement signed pursuant to § 1.33(b) stating the name of each inventor in the continuing application.

(3) Any new joint inventor named in the continuing application must provide an oath or declaration in compliance with this section, except as provided for in § 1.64.

(e) (1) An assignment may also serve as an oath or declaration required by this section if the assignment as executed:

(i) Includes the information and statements required under paragraphs (a) and (b) of this section; and

(ii) A copy of the assignment is recorded as provided for in part 3 of this chapter.

(2) Any reference to an oath or declaration under this section includes an assignment as provided for in this paragraph.

(f) With respect to an application naming only one inventor, any reference to the inventor's oath or declaration in this chapter includes a substitute statement executed under § 1.64. With respect to an application naming more than one inventor, any reference to the inventor's oath or declaration in this chapter means the oaths, declarations, or substitute statements that have been collectively executed by or with respect to all of the joint inventors, unless otherwise clear from the context.

(g) An oath or declaration under this section, including the statement provided for in paragraph (e) of this section, must be executed (i.e., signed) in accordance either with § 1.66 or with an acknowledgment that any willful false statement made in such declaration or statement is punishable under 18 U.S.C. 1001 by fine or imprisonment of not more than five (5) years, or both.

(h) An oath or declaration filed at any time pursuant to 35 U.S.C. 115(h)(1) will be placed in the file record of the application or patent, but may not necessarily be reviewed by the Office. Any request for correction of the named inventorship must comply with § 1.48 in an application and § 1.324 in a patent.

§ 1.64. Substitute statement in lieu of an oath or declaration.

(a) An applicant under § 1.43, 1.45 or 1.46 may execute a substitute statement in lieu of an oath or declaration under § 1.63 if the inventor is deceased, is under a legal incapacity, has refused to execute the oath or declaration under § 1.63, or cannot be found or reached after diligent effort.

(b) A substitute statement under this section must:

(1) Comply with the requirements of § 1.63(a), identifying the inventor or joint inventor with respect to whom a substitute statement in lieu of an oath or declaration is executed, and stating upon information and belief the facts which such inventor is required to state;

(2) Identify the person executing the substitute statement and the relationship of such person to the inventor or joint inventor with respect to whom the substitute statement is executed, and unless such information is supplied in an application data sheet in accordance with § 1.76, the residence and mailing address of the person signing the substitute statement;

(3) Identify the circumstances permitting the person to execute the substitute statement in lieu of an oath or declaration under § 1.63, namely whether the inventor is deceased, is under a legal incapacity, cannot be found or reached after a diligent effort was made, or has refused to execute the oath or declaration under § 1.63; and

(4) Unless the following information is supplied in an application data sheet in accordance with § 1.76, also identify:

(i) Each inventor by his or her legal name; and

(ii) The last known mailing address where the inventor customarily receives mail, and last known residence, if an inventor lives at a location which is different from where the inventor customarily receives mail, for each inventor who is not deceased or under a legal incapacity.

(c) A person may not execute a substitute statement provided for in this section for an application unless that person has reviewed and understands the contents of the application, including the claims, and is aware of the duty to disclose to the Office all information known to the person to be material to patentability as defined in § 1.56.

(d) Any reference to an inventor's oath or declaration includes a substitute statement provided for in this section.

(e) A substitute statement under this section must contain an acknowledgment that any willful false statement made in such statement is punishable under section 1001 of title 18 by fine or imprisonment of not more than 5 years, or both.

(f) A nonsigning inventor or legal representative may subsequently join in the application by submitting an oath or declaration under § 1.63. The submission of an oath or declaration by a nonsigning inventor or legal representative in an application filed under § 1.43, 1.45 or 1.46 will not permit the nonsigning inventor or legal representative to revoke or grant a power of attorney.

§ 1.66. Statements under oath.

An oath or affirmation may be made before any person within the United States authorized by law to administer oaths. An oath made in a foreign country may be made before any diplomatic or consular officer of the United States authorized to administer oaths, or before any officer having an official seal and authorized to administer oaths in the foreign country in which the applicant may be, whose authority shall be proved by a certificate of a diplomatic or consular officer of the United States, or by an apostille of an official designated by a foreign country which, by treaty or convention, accords like effect to apostilles of designated officials in the United States. The oath shall be attested in all cases in this and other countries, by the proper official seal of the officer before whom the oath or affirmation is made. Such oath or affirmation shall be valid as to execution if it complies with the laws of the State or country where made. When the person before whom the oath or affirmation is made in this country is not provided with a seal, his official character shall be established by competent evidence, as by a certificate from a clerk of a court of record or other proper officer having a seal.

§ 1.67. Supplemental oath or declaration.

(a) The applicant may submit an inventor's oath or declaration meeting the requirements of § 1.63, § 1.64, or § 1.162 to correct any deficiencies or inaccuracies present in an earlier-filed inventor's oath or declaration. Deficiencies or inaccuracies due to the failure to meet the requirements of § 1.63(b) in an oath or declaration may be corrected with an application data sheet in accordance with § 1.76, except that any correction of inventorship must be pursuant to § 1.48.

(b) A supplemental inventor's oath or declaration under this section must be executed by the person whose inventor's oath or declaration is being withdrawn, replaced, or otherwise corrected. (c) The Office will not require a person who has executed an oath or declaration in compliance with 35 U.S.C. 115 and § 1.63 or 1.162 for an application to provide an additional inventor's oath or declaration for the application.

(d) No new matter may be introduced into a nonprovisional application after its filing date even if an inventor's oath or declaration is filed to correct deficiencies or inaccuracies present in the earlier-filed inventor's oath or declaration.

§ 1.71. Detailed description and specification of the invention.

* * * * *

(g) (1) The specification may disclose or be amended to disclose the names of the parties to a joint research agreement as defined in § 1.9(e).

* * * * *

§ 1.76. Application data sheet.

(a) *Application data sheet*: An application data sheet is a sheet or sheets, that may be submitted in a provisional application under 35 U.S.C. 111(b), a nonprovisional application under 35 U.S.C. 111(a), or a national stage application under 35 U.S.C. 371, and must be submitted when required by § 1.55 or 1.78 to claim priority to or the benefit of a prior-filed application under 35 U.S.C. 119, 120, 121, or 365. An application data sheet must be titled "Application Data Sheet." An application data sheet must contain all of the section headings listed in paragraph (b) of this section, except as provided in paragraph (c)(2) of this section, with any appropriate data for each section heading. If an application data sheet is provided, the application data sheet is part of the application for which it has been submitted.

(b) * * *

(1) *Inventor information.* This information includes the legal name, residence, and mailing address of the inventor or each joint inventor. * * * * *

(3) *Application information.* This information includes the title of the invention, the total number of drawing sheets, a suggested drawing figure for publication (in a nonprovisional application), any docket number assigned to the application, the type of application (*e.g.*, utility, plant, design, reissue, provisional), whether the application discloses any significant part of the subject matter of an application under a secrecy order pursuant to § 5.2 of this chapter (*see* § 5.2(c)), and, for plant applications, the Latin name of the genus and species of the plant claimed, as well as the variety denomination.

* * * * *

(5) *Domestic benefit information.* This information includes the application number, the filing date, the status (including patent number if available), and relationship of each application for which a benefit is claimed under 35 U.S.C. 119(e), 120, 121, or 365(c). Providing this information in the application data sheet constitutes the specific reference required by 35 U.S.C. 119(e) or 120, and § 1.78.

(6) *Foreign priority information.* This information includes the application number, country, and filing date of each foreign application for which priority is claimed. Providing this information in the application data sheet constitutes the claim for priority as required by 35 U.S.C. 119(b) and § 1.55.

* * * * *

(7) *Applicant information:* This information includes the name (either natural person or juristic entity) and address of the legal representative, assignee, person to whom the inventor is under an obligation to assign the invention, or person who otherwise shows sufficient proprietary interest in the matter who is the applicant under § 1.43 or § 1.46. Providing assignment information in the application data sheet does not substitute for compliance with any requirement of part 3 of this

chapter to have an assignment recorded by the Office.

(c) *Correcting and updating an application data sheet.* (1) Information in a previously submitted application data sheet, inventor's oath or declaration under § 1.63, § 1.64 or § 1.67, or otherwise of record, may be corrected or updated until payment of the issue fee by a new application data sheet providing corrected or updated information, except that inventorship changes must comply with the requirements of § 1.48, foreign priority and domestic benefit information changes must comply with §§ 1.55 and 1.78, and correspondence address changes are governed by § 1.33(a).

(2) An application data sheet providing corrected or updated information may include all of the sections listed in paragraph (b) of this section or only those sections containing changed or updated information. The application data sheet must include the section headings listed in paragraph (b) of this section for each section included in the application data sheet, and must identify the information that is being changed, with underlining for insertions, and strike-through or brackets for text removed, except that identification of information being changed is not required for an application data sheet included with an initial submission under 35 U.S.C. 371.

(d) Inconsistencies between application data sheet and other documents. For inconsistencies between information that is supplied by both an application data sheet under this section and other documents:

(1) The most recent submission will govern with respect to inconsistencies as between the information provided in an application data sheet, a designation of a correspondence address, or by the inventor's oath or declaration, except that:

(i) The most recent application data sheet will govern with respect to foreign priority (§ 1.55) or domestic benefit (§ 1.78) claims; and

(ii) The naming of the inventorship is governed by § 1.41 and changes to inventorship or the names of the inventors is governed by § 1.48.

(2) The information in the application data sheet will govern when the inconsistent information is supplied at the same time by a designation of correspondence address or the inventor's oath or declaration.

(3) The Office will capture bibliographic information

from the application data sheet. The Office will generally not review the inventor's oath or declaration to determine if the bibliographic information contained therein is consistent with the bibliographic information provided in an application data sheet. Incorrect bibliographic information contained in an application data sheet may be corrected as provided in paragraph (c)(1) of this section.

(e) *Signature requirement.* An application data sheet must be signed in compliance with § 1.33(b). An unsigned application data sheet will be treated only as a transmittal letter.

§ 1.77. Arrangement of application elements.

* * * * *

(b) * * *

(2) Cross-reference to related applications.

* * * * *

(6) Statement regarding prior disclosures by the inventor or a joint inventor.

* * * * *

§ 1.78. Claiming benefit of earlier filing date and cross-references to other applications.

(a) *Claims under 35 U.S.C. 119(e) for the benefit of a prior-filed provisional application.* An applicant in a nonprovisional application, other than for a design patent, or an international application designating the United States of America may claim the benefit of one or more prior-filed provisional applications under the conditions set forth in 35 U.S.C. 119(e) and this section.

(1) The nonprovisional application or international application designating the United States of America must be filed not later than twelve months after the date on which the provisional application was filed, or be entitled to claim the benefit under 35 U.S.C. 120, 121, or 365(c) of an application that was filed not later than twelve months after the date on which the provisional application was filed. This twelvemonth period is subject to 35 U.S.C. 21(b) (and § 1.7(a)).

(2) Each prior-filed provisional application must name the inventor or a joint inventor named in the later—filed application as the inventor or a joint inventor. In addition, each priorfiled provisional application must be entitled to a filing date as set forth in § 1.53(c), and

the basic filing fee set forth in § 1.16(d) must have been paid for such provisional application within the time period set forth in § 1.53(g).

(3) Any nonprovisional application or international application designating the United States of America that claims the benefit of one or more prior-filed provisional applications must contain, or be amended to contain, a reference to each such prior-filed provisional application, identifying it by the provisional application number (consisting of series code and serial number). If the later-filed application is a nonprovisional application, the reference required by this paragraph must be included in an application data sheet (§ 1.76(b)(5)).

(4) The reference required by paragraph (a)(3) of this section must be submitted during the pendency of the later-filed application. If the later-filed application is an application filed under 35 U.S.C. 111(a), this reference must also be submitted within the later of four months from the actual filing date of the later-filed application or sixteen months from the filing date of the prior-filed provisional application. If the later-filed application is a nonprovisional application entering the national stage from an international application under 35 U.S.C. 371, this reference must also be submitted within the later of four months from the date on which the national stage commenced under 35 U.S.C. 371(b) or (f) in the laterfiled international application or sixteen months from the filing date of the prior-filed provisional application. Except as provided in paragraph (b) of this section, failure to timely submit the reference is considered a waiver of any benefit under 35 U.S.C. 119(e) of the prior-filed provisional application.

(5) If the prior-filed provisional application was filed in a language other than English and both an English language translation of the prior-filed provisional application and a statement that the translation is accurate were not previously filed in the prior-filed provisional application, the applicant will be notified and given a period of time within which to file, in the prior filed provisional application, the translation and the statement. If the notice is mailed in a pending nonprovisional application, a timely reply to such a notice must include the filing in the nonprovisional application of either a confirmation that the translation and statement

were filed in the provisional application, or an application data sheet eliminating the reference under paragraph (a)(3) of this section to the prior-filed provisional application, or the nonprovisional application will be abandoned. The translation and statement may be filed in the provisional application, even if the provisional application has become abandoned.

(6) If a nonprovisional application filed on or after March 16, 2013, claims the benefit of the filing date of a provisional application filed prior to March 16, 2013, and also contains, or contained at any time, a claim to a claimed invention that has an effective filing date on or after March 16, 2013, the applicant must provide a statement to that effect within the later of four months from the actual filing date of the nonprovisional application, four months from the date of entry into the national stage as set forth in § 1.491 in an international application, sixteen months from the filing date of the prior filed provisional application, or the date that a first claim to a claimed invention that has an effective filing date on or after March 16, 2013, is presented in the nonprovisional application. An applicant is not required to provide such a statement if the applicant reasonably believes on the basis of information already known to the individuals designated in § 1.56(c) that the nonprovisional application does not, and did not at any time, contain a claim to a claimed invention that has an effective filing date on or after March 16, 2013.

(b) *Delayed claims under 35 U.S.C. 119(e) for the benefit of a prior-filed provisional application.* If the reference required by 35 U.S.C. 119(e) and paragraph (a)(3) of this section is presented in a nonprovisional application after the time period provided by paragraph (a)(4) of this section, the claim under 35 U.S.C. 119(e) for the benefit of a prior-filed provisional application may be accepted if submitted during the pendency of the later-filed application and if the reference identifying the prior-filed application by provisional application number was unintentionally delayed. A petition to accept an unintentionally delayed claim under 35 U.S.C. 119(e) for the benefit of a prior-filed provisional application must be accompanied by:

(1) The reference required by 35 U.S.C. 119(e) and paragraph (a)(3) of this section to the prior-filed provisional application, unless previously submitted;

(2) The surcharge set forth in § 1.17(t); and

(3) A statement that the entire delay between the date the benefit claim was due under paragraph (a)(4) of this section and the date the benefit claim was filed was unintentional. The Director may require additional information where there is a question whether the delay was unintentional.

(c) *Claims under 35 U.S.C. 120, 121, or 365(c) for the benefit of a prior-filed nonprovisional or international application.* An applicant in a nonprovisional application (including an international application entering the national stage under 35 U.S.C. 371) or an international application designating the United States of America may claim the benefit of one or more prior-filed copending nonprovisional applications or international applications designating the United States of America under the conditions set forth in 35 U.S.C. 120, 121, or 365(c) and this section.

(1) Each prior-filed application must name the inventor or a joint inventor named in the later-filed application as the inventor or a joint inventor. In addition, each prior-filed application must either be:

(i) An international application entitled to a filing date in accordance with PCT Article 11 and designating the United States of America; or

(ii) A nonprovisional application under 35 U.S.C. 111(a) that is entitled to a filing date as set forth in § 1.53(b) or (d) for which the basic filing fee set forth in § 1.16 has been paid within the pendency of the application.

(2) Except for a continued prosecution application filed under § 1.53(d), any nonprovisional application, or international application designating the United States of America, that claims the benefit of one or more priorfiled nonprovisional applications or international applications designating the United States of America must contain or be amended to contain a reference to each such prior-filed application, identifying it by application number (consisting of the series code and serial number) or international application number and international filing date. If the later-filed application is a nonprovisional application, the reference required by this paragraph must be included in an application data sheet (§ 1.76(b)(5)). The reference also must identify the

relationship of the applications, namely, whether the later-filed application is a continuation, divisional, or continuation-in-part of the prior-filed nonprovisional application or international application.

(3) The reference required by 35 U.S.C. 120 and paragraph (c)(2) of this section must be submitted during the pendency of the later-filed application. If the later-filed application is an application filed under 35 U.S.C. 111(a), this reference must also be submitted within the later of four months from the actual filing date of the later-filed application or sixteen months from the filing date of the prior-filed application. If the later-filed application is a nonprovisional application entering the national stage from an international application under 35 U.S.C. 371, this reference must also be submitted within the later of four months from the date on which the national stage commenced under 35 U.S.C. 371(b) or (f) in the later-filed international application or sixteen months from the filing date of the prior-filed application. Except as provided in paragraph (d) of this section, failure to timely submit the reference required by 35 U.S.C. 120 and paragraph (c)(2) of this section is considered a waiver of any benefit under 35 U.S.C. 120, 121, or 365(c) to the prior-filed application. The time periods in this paragraph do not apply in a design application.

(4) The request for a continued prosecution application under § 1.53(d) is the specific reference required by 35 U.S.C. 120 to the prior-filed application. The identification of an application by application number under this section is the identification of every application assigned that application number necessary for a specific reference required by 35 U.S.C. 120 to every such application assigned that application number.

(5) Cross-references to other related applications may be made when appropriate (see § 1.14), but crossreferences to applications for which a benefit is not claimed under title 35, United States Code, must not be included in an application data sheet (§ 1.76(b)(5)).

(6) If a nonprovisional application filed on or after March 16, 2013, claims the benefit of the filing date of a nonprovisional application or an international application designating the United States of America filed prior to March 16, 2013, and also contains, or contained at

any time, a claim to a claimed invention that has an effective filing date on or after March 16, 2013, the applicant must provide a statement to that effect within the later of four months from the actual filing date of the later-filed application, four months from the date of entry into the national stage as set forth in § 1.491 in an international application, sixteen months from the filing date of the prior-filed application, or the date that a first claim to a claimed invention that has an effective filing date on or after March 16, 2013, is presented in the later-filed application. An applicant is not required to provide such a statement if either:

(i) The application claims the benefit of a nonprovisional application in which a statement under § 1.55(j), paragraph (a)(6) of this section, or this paragraph that the application contains, or contained at any time, a claim to a claimed invention that has an effective filing date on or after March 16, 2013 has been filed; or

(ii) The applicant reasonably believes on the basis of information already known to the individuals designated in § 1.56(c) that the later filed application does not, and did not at any time, contain a claim to a claimed invention that has an effective filing date on or after March 16, 2013.

(d) *Delayed claims under 35 U.S.C. 120, 121, or 365(c) for the benefit of a prior-filed nonprovisional application or international application.* If the reference required by 35 U.S.C. 120 and paragraph (c)(2) of this section is presented after the time period provided by paragraph (c)(3) of this section, the claim under 35 U.S.C. 120, 121, or 365(c) for the benefit of a prior-filed copending nonprovisional application or international application designating the United States of America may be accepted if the reference identifying the prior-filed application by application number or international application number and international filing date was unintentionally delayed. A petition to accept an unintentionally delayed claim under 35 U.S.C. 120, 121, or 365(c) for the benefit of a prior-filed application must be accompanied by:

(1) The reference required by 35 U.S.C. 120 and paragraph (c)(2) of this section to the prior-filed application, unless previously submitted;

(2) The surcharge set forth in § 1.17(t); and

(3) A statement that the entire delay between the date the benefit claim was due under paragraph (c)(3) of

this section and the date the benefit claim was filed was unintentional. The Director may require additional information where there is a question whether the delay was unintentional.

(e) *Applications containing patentably indistinct claims.* Where two or more applications filed by the same applicant contain patentably indistinct claims, elimination of such claims from all but one application may be required in the absence of good and sufficient reason for their retention during pendency in more than one application.

(f) *Applications or patents under reexamination naming different inventors and containing patentably indistinct claims.* If an application or a patent under reexamination and at least one other application naming different inventors are owned by the same person and contain patentably indistinct claims, and there is no statement of record indicating that the claimed inventions were commonly owned or subject to an obligation of assignment to the same person on the effective filing date (as defined in § 1.109), or on the date of the invention, as applicable, of the later claimed invention, the Office may require the applicant to state whether the claimed inventions were commonly owned or subject to an obligation of assignment to the same person on such date. Even if the claimed inventions were commonly owned, or subject to an obligation of assignment to the same person on the effective filing date (as defined in § 1.109), or on the date of the invention, as applicable, of the later claimed invention, the patentably indistinct claims may be rejected under the doctrine of double patenting in view of such commonly owned or assigned applications or patents under reexamination.

(g) *Time periods not extendable.* The time periods set forth in this section are not extendable.

§ 1.81. Drawings required in patent application.

(a) The applicant for a patent is required to furnish a drawing of the invention where necessary for the understanding of the subject matter sought to be patented; this drawing, or a high quality copy thereof, must be filed with the application. Since corrections are the responsibility of the applicant, the original drawing(s) should be retained by the applicant for any necessary future correction.

* * * * *

§ 1.84. Standards for drawings.

(a) * * *

(2) *Color.* On rare occasions, color drawings may be

necessary as the only practical medium by which to disclose the subject matter sought to be patented in a utility or design patent application. The color drawings must be of sufficient quality such that all details in the drawings are reproducible in black and white in the printed patent. Color drawings are not permitted in international applications (see PCT Rule 11.13), or in an application, or copy thereof, submitted under the Office electronic filing system. The Office will accept color drawings in utility or design patent applications only after granting a petition filed under this paragraph explaining why the color drawings are necessary. Any such petition must include the following:

* * * * *

Sec. 1.102. Advancement of examination.

(a) Applications will not be advanced out of turn for examination or for further action except as provided by this part, or upon order of the Director to expedite the business of the Office, or upon filing of a request under paragraph (b) or (e) of this section or upon filing a petition or request under paragraph (c) or (d) of this section with a showing which, in the opinion of the Director, will justify so advancing it.

* * * * *

* * * * *

(e) A request for prioritized examination under this paragraph must comply with the requirements of this paragraph and be accompanied by the prioritized examination fee set forth in Sec. 1.17(c), the processing fee set forth in Sec. 1.17(i), and if not already paid, the publication fee set forth in Sec.1.18(d). An application for which prioritized examination has been requested may not contain or be amended to contain more than four independent claims, more than thirty total claims, or any multiple dependent claim. Prioritized examination under this paragraph will not be accorded to international applications that have not entered the national stage under 35 U.S.C. 371, design applications, reissue applications, provisional applications, or reexamination proceedings. A request for prioritized examination must also comply with the requirements of paragraph (e)(1) or paragraph (e)(2) of this section.

(1) A request for prioritized examination may be filed with an original utility or plant nonprovisional application under 35 U.S.C. 111(a) that is complete as defined

by Sec. 1.51(b), with any fees due under Sec. 1.16 paid on filing. If the application is a utility application, it must be filed via the Office's electronic filing system. The request for prioritized examination in compliance with this paragraph must be present upon filing of the application.

(2) A request for prioritized examination may be filed with or after a request for continued examination in compliance with Sec. 1.114. If the application is a utility application, the request must be filed via the Office's electronic filing system. The request must be filed before the mailing of the first Office action after the filing of the request for continued examination under Sec. 1.114. Only a single such request for prioritized examination under this paragraph may be granted in an application.

*****

Section 1.103 is amended by removing paragraph (g).

§ 1.104. Nature of examination.

(c) * * *

(4) (i) Subject matter which would otherwise qualify as prior art under 35 U.S.C. 102(a)(2) and a claimed invention will be treated as commonly owned for purposes of 35 U.S.C. 102(b)(2)(C) if the applicant or patent owner provides a statement to the effect that the subject matter and the claimed invention, not later than the effective filing date of the claimed invention, were owned by the same person or subject to an obligation of assignment to the same person.

(ii) Subject matter which would otherwise qualify as prior art under 35 U.S.C. 102(a)(2) and a claimed invention will be treated as commonly owned for purposes of 35 U.S.C. 102(b)(2)(C) on the basis of a joint research agreement under 35 U.S.C. 102(c) if:

(A) The applicant or patent owner provides a statement to the effect that the subject matter was developed and the claimed invention was made by or on behalf of one or more parties to a joint research agreement, within the meaning of 35 U.S.C. 100(h) and § 1.9(e), that was in effect on or before the effective filing date of the claimed invention, and the claimed invention was made as a result of activities undertaken within the scope of the joint research agreement; and

(B) The application for patent for the claimed invention discloses or is amended to disclose the names of the parties to the joint research agreement.

(5)(i) Subject matter which qualifies as prior art under 35 U.S.C. 102(e), (f), or (g) in effect prior to March 16, 2013, and a claimed invention in an application filed on or after November 29, 1999, or any patent issuing thereon, in an application filed before November 29, 1999, but pending on December 10, 2004, or any patent issuing thereon, or in any patent granted on or after December 10, 2004, will be treated as commonly owned for purposes of 35 U.S.C. 103(c) in effect prior to March 16, 2013, if the applicant or patent owner provides a statement to the effect that the subject matter and the claimed invention, at the time the claimed invention was made, were owned by the same person or subject to an obligation of assignment to the same person.

(ii) Subject matter which qualifies as prior art under 35 U.S.C. 102(e), (f), or (g) in effect prior to March 16, 2013, and a claimed invention in an application pending on or after December 10, 2004, or in any patent granted on or after December 10, 2004, will be treated as commonly owned for purposes of 35 U.S.C. 103(c) in effect prior to March 16, 2013, on the basis of a joint research agreement under 35 U.S.C. 103(c)(2) in effect prior to March 16, 2013, if:

(A) The applicant or patent owner provides a statement to the effect that the subject matter and the claimed invention were made by or on behalf of the parties to a joint research agreement, within the meaning of 35 U.S.C. 100(h) and § 1.9(e), which was in effect on or before the date the claimed invention was made, and that the claimed invention was made as a result of activities undertaken within the scope of the joint research agreement; and

(B) The application for patent for the claimed invention discloses or is amended to disclose the names of the parties to the joint research agreement.

(6) Patents issued prior to December 10, 2004, from applications filed prior to November 29, 1999, are subject to 35 U.S.C. 103(c) in effect on November 28, 1999.

* * * * *

§ 1.109. Effective filing date of a claimed invention under the Leahy-Smith America Invents

Act.

(a) The effective filing date for a claimed invention in a patent or application for patent, other than in a reissue application or reissued patent, is the earliest of:

(1) The actual filing date of the patent or the application for the patent containing a claim to the invention; or

(2) The filing date of the earliest application for which the patent or application is entitled, as to such invention, to a right of priority or the benefit of an earlier filing date under 35 U.S.C. 119, 120, 121, or 365.

(b) The effective filing date for a claimed invention in a reissue application or a reissued patent is determined by deeming the claim to the invention to have been contained in the patent for which reissue was sought.

§ 1.110. Inventorship and ownership of the subject matter of individual claims.

When one or more joint inventors are named in an application or patent, the Office may require an applicant or patentee to identify the inventorship and ownership or obligation to assign ownership, of each claimed invention on its effective filing date (as defined in § 1.109) or on its date of invention, as applicable, when necessary for purposes of an Office proceeding. The Office may also require an applicant or patentee to identify the invention dates of the subject matter of each claim when necessary for purposes of an Office proceeding.

§ 1.130. Affidavit or declaration of attribution or prior public disclosure under the Leahy-Smith America Invents Act.

(a) *Affidavit or declaration of attribution.* When any claim of an application or a patent under reexamination is rejected, the applicant or patent owner may submit an appropriate affidavit or declaration to disqualify a disclosure as prior art by establishing that the disclosure was made by the inventor or a joint inventor, or the subject matter disclosed was obtained directly or indirectly from the inventor or a joint inventor.

(b) *Affidavit or declaration of prior public disclosure.* When any claim of an application or a patent under reexamination is rejected, the applicant or patent owner may submit an appropriate affidavit or declaration to disqualify a disclosure as prior art by establishing that the subject matter disclosed had, before such disclosure was made or before such subject matter was effectively filed, been publicly disclosed by the inventor or a joint inventor or another who obtained the subject matter disclosed directly or indirectly from the inventor or a joint inventor. An affidavit or declaration under this paragraph must identify the subject matter publicly disclosed and provide the date such subject matter was publicly disclosed by the inventor or a joint inventor or another who obtained the subject matter disclosed directly or indirectly from the inventor or a joint inventor.

(1) If the subject matter publicly disclosed on that date was in a printed publication, the affidavit or declaration must be accompanied by a copy of the printed publication.

(2) If the subject matter publicly disclosed on that date was not in a printed publication, the affidavit or declaration must describe the subject matter with sufficient detail and particularity to determine what subject matter had been publicly disclosed on that date by the inventor or a joint inventor or another who obtained the subject matter disclosed directly or indirectly from the inventor or a joint inventor.

(c) *When this section is not available.* The provisions of this section are not available if the rejection is based upon a disclosure made more than one year before the effective filing date of the claimed invention. The provisions of this section may not be available if the rejection is based upon a U.S. patent or U.S. patent application publication of a patented or pending application naming another inventor, the patent or pending application claims an invention that is the same or substantially the same as the applicant's or patent owner's claimed invention, and the affidavit or declaration contends that an inventor named in the U.S. patent or U.S. patent application publication derived the claimed invention from the inventor or a joint inventor named in the application or patent, in which case an applicant or a patent owner may file a petition for a derivation proceeding pursuant to § 42.401 *et seq.* of this title.

(d) *Applications and patents to which this section is applicable.* The provisions of this section apply to any application for patent, and to any patent issuing thereon, that contains, or contained at any time:

(1) A claim to a claimed invention that has an effective filing date as defined in 35 U.S.C. 100(i) that is on or after March 16, 2013; or

(2) A specific reference under 35 U.S.C. 120, 121, or 365(c) to any patent or application that contains, or contained at any time, a claim to a claimed invention that has an effective filing date as defined in 35 U.S.C. 100(i) that is on or after March 16, 2013.

§ 1.131. Affidavit or declaration of prior invention or to disqualify commonly owned patent or published application as prior art.

(a) When any claim of an application or a patent under reexamination is rejected, the inventor of the subject matter of the rejected claim, the owner of the patent under reexamination, or the party qualified under § 1.42 or § 1.46, may submit an appropriate oath or declaration to establish invention of the subject matter of the rejected claim prior to the effective date of the reference or activity on which the rejection is based. The effective date of a U.S. patent, U.S. patent application publication, or international application publication under PCT Article 21(2) is the earlier of its publication date or the date that it is effective as a reference under 35 U.S.C. 102(e) as in effect on March 15, 2013. Prior invention may not be established under this section in any country other than the United States, a NAFTA country, or a WTO member country. Prior invention may not be established under this section before December 8, 1993, in a NAFTA country other than the United States, or before January 1, 1996, in a WTO member country other than a NAFTA country. Prior invention may not be established under this section if either:

(1) The rejection is based upon a U.S. patent or U.S. patent application publication of a pending or patented application naming another inventor which claims interfering subject matter as defined in § 41.203(a) of this title, in which case an applicant may suggest an interference pursuant to § 41.202(a) of this title; or

(2) The rejection is based upon a statutory bar.

(b) The showing of facts for an oath or declaration under paragraph (a) of this section shall be such, in character and weight, as to establish reduction to practice prior to the effective date of the reference, or conception of the invention prior to the effective date of the reference coupled with due diligence from prior to said date to a subsequent reduction to practice or to the filing of the application. Original exhibits of drawings or records, or photocopies thereof, must accompany and form part of the affidavit or declaration or their absence must be satisfactorily explained.

(c) When any claim of an application or a patent under reexamination is rejected under 35 U.S.C. 103 as in effect on March 15, 2013, on a U.S. patent or U.S. patent application publication which is not prior art under 35 U.S.C. 102(b) as in effect on March 15, 2013, and the inventions defined by the claims in the application or patent under reexamination and by the claims in the patent or published application are not identical but are not patentably distinct, and the inventions are owned by the same party, the applicant or owner of the patent under reexamination may disqualify the patent or patent application publication as prior art. The patent or patent application publication can be disqualified as prior art by submission of:

(1) A terminal disclaimer in accordance with § 1.321(c); and

(2) An oath or declaration stating that the application or patent under reexamination and patent or published application are currently owned by the same party, and that the inventor named in the application or patent under reexamination is the prior inventor under 35 U.S.C. 104 as in effect on March 15, 2013.

(d) The provisions of this section apply to any application for patent, and to any patent issuing thereon, that contains, or contained at any time:

(1) A claim to an invention that has an effective filing date as defined in 35 U.S.C. 100(i) that is before March 16, 2013; or

(2) A specific reference under 35 U.S.C. 120, 121, or 365(c) to any patent or application that contains, or contained at any time, a claim to an invention that has an effective filing date as defined in 35 U.S.C. 100(i) that is before March 16, 2013.

(e) In an application for patent to which the provisions of § 1.130 apply, and to any patent issuing thereon, the provisions of this section are applicable only with respect to a rejection under 35 U.S.C. 102(g) as in effect on March 15, 2013.

§ 1.136. Extensions of time.

(a) (1) * * *

(iv) The reply is to a decision by the Patent Trial and Appeal Board pursuant to § 1.304 or to § 41.50 or § 41.52 of this title; or

(v) The application is involved in a contested case (§ 41.101(a) of this title) or a derivation proceeding (§ 42.4(b) of this title).

(2) The date on which the petition and the fee have been filed is the date for purposes of determining the period of extension and the corresponding amount of the fee. The expiration of the time period is determined by the amount of the fee paid. A reply must be filed prior to the expiration of the period of extension to avoid abandonment of the application (§ 1.135), but in no situation may an applicant reply later than the maximum time period set by statute, or be granted an extension of time under paragraph (b) of this section when the provisions of this paragraph are available. See § 1.304 for extensions of time to appeal to the U.S. Court of Appeals for the Federal Circuit or to commence a civil action; § 1.550(c) for extensions of time in ex parte reexamination proceedings, § 1.956 for extensions of time in inter partes reexamination proceedings; §§ 41.4(a) and 41.121(a)(3) of this title for extensions of time in contested cases before the Patent Trial and Appeal Board; and § 42.5(c) of this title for extensions of time in trials before the Patent Trial and Appeal Board.

* * * * *

(b) When a reply cannot be filed within the time period set for such reply and the provisions of paragraph (a) of this section are not available, the period for reply will be extended only for sufficient cause and for a reasonable time specified. Any request for an extension of time under this paragraph must be filed on or before the day on which such reply is due, but the mere filing of such a request will not effect any extension under this paragraph. In no situation can any extension carry the date on which reply is due beyond the maximum time period set by statute. See § 1.304 for extensions of time to appeal to the U.S. Court of Appeals for the Federal Circuit or to commence a civil action; § 1.550(c) for extensions of time in ex parte reexamination proceedings; § 1.956 for extensions of time in inter partes reexamination proceedings; §§ 41.4(a) and 41.121(a)(3) of this title for extensions of time in contested cases before the Patent Trial and Appeal Board; and § 42.5(c) of this title for extensions of time in trials before the Patent Trial and Appeal Board. Any request under this section must be accompanied by the petition fee set forth in § 1.17(g).

(c) * * *

(1) The period for submitting the inventor's oath or declaration;

* * * * *

§ 1.153. Title, description and claim, oath or declaration.

* * * * *

(b) The inventor's oath or declaration must comply with the requirements of § 1.63, or comply with the requirements of § 1.64 for a substitute statement.

§ 1.154. Arrangement of application elements in a design application.

(a) * * *

(6) The inventor's oath or declaration (*see* § 1.153(b)).

* * * * *

§ 1.162. Applicant, oath or declaration.

The inventor named for a plant patent application must be the person who has invented or discovered and asexually reproduced the new and distinct variety of plant for which a patent is sought. The inventor's oath or declaration, in addition to the averments required by § 1.63 or § 1.64, must state that the inventor has asexually reproduced the plant. Where the plant is a newly found plant, the inventor's oath or declaration must also state that it was found in a cultivated area.

§ 1.163. Specification and arrangement of application elements in a plant application.

* * * * *

(b) * * *

(6) The inventor's oath or declaration (§ 1.162).

* * * * *

§ 1.172. Reissue applicant.

(a) The reissue applicant is the original patentee, or the current patent owner if there has been an assignment. A reissue application must be accompanied by the written consent of all assignees, if any, currently owning an undivided interest in the patent. All assignees consenting to the reissue must establish their ownership in the patent by filing in the reissue application a submission in accordance with the provisions of § 3.73(c) of this chapter.

(b) A reissue will be granted to the original patentee,

his legal representatives or assigns as the interest may appear.

§ 1.175. Inventor's oath or declaration for a reissue application.

(a) The inventor's oath or declaration for a reissue application, in addition to complying with the requirements of § 1.63, § 1.64, or § 1.67, must also specifically identify at least one error pursuant to 35 U.S.C. 251 being relied upon as the basis for reissue and state that the applicant believes the original patent to be wholly or partly inoperative or invalid by reason of a defective specification or drawing, or by reason of the patentee claiming more or less than the patentee had the right to claim in the patent.

(b) If the reissue application seeks to enlarge the scope of the claims of the patent (a basis for the reissue is the patentee claiming less than the patentee had the right to claim in the patent), the inventor's oath or declaration for a reissue application must identify a claim that the application seeks to broaden. A claim is a broadened claim if the claim is broadened in any respect.

(c) The inventor, or each individual who is a joint inventor of a claimed invention, in a reissue application must execute an oath or declaration for the reissue application, except as provided for in § 1.64, and except that the inventor's oath or declaration for a reissue application may be signed by the assignee of the entire interest if:

(1) The application does not seek to enlarge the scope of the claims of the original patent; or

(2) The application for the original patent was filed under § 1.46 by the assignee of the entire interest.

(d) If errors previously identified in the inventor's oath or declaration for a reissue application pursuant to paragraph (a) of this section are no longer being relied upon as the basis for reissue, the applicant must identify an error being relied upon as the basis for reissue.

(e) The inventor's oath or declaration for a reissue application required by paragraph (a) of this section may be submitted under the provisions of § 1.53(f), except that the provisions of § 1.53(f)(3) do not apply to a reissue application.

(f) (1) The requirement for the inventor's oath or declaration for a continuing reissue application that claims the benefit under 35 U.S.C. 120, 121, or 365(c) in compliance with § 1.78 of an earlier-filed reissue application may be satisfied by a copy of the inventor's oath or declaration from the earlier-filed reissue application, provided that:

(i) The inventor, or each individual who is a joint inventor of a claimed invention, in the reissue application executed an inventor's oath or declaration for the earlier-filed reissue application, except as provided for in § 1.64;

(ii) The continuing reissue application does not seek to enlarge the scope of the claims of the original patent; or

(iii) The application for the original patent was filed under § 1.46 by the assignee of the entire interest.

(2) If all errors identified in the inventor's oath or declaration from the earlier-filed reissue application are no longer being relied upon as the basis for reissue, the applicant must identify an error being relied upon as the basis for reissue.

(g) An oath or declaration filed at any time pursuant to 35 U.S.C. 115(h)(1), will be placed in the file record of the reissue application, but may not necessarily be reviewed by the Office.

*****

§ 1.178. Original patent; continuing duty of applicant.

* * * * *

(b) In any reissue application before the Office, the applicant must call to the attention of the Office any prior or concurrent proceedings in which the patent (for which reissue is requested) is or was involved, such as interferences or trials before the Patent Trial and Appeal Board, reissues, reexaminations, or litigations and the results of such proceedings (see also § 1.173(a)(1)).

§ 1.181. Petition to the Director.

(a) * * *

(1) From any action or requirement of any examiner in the ex parte prosecution of an application, or in ex parte or inter partes prosecution of a reexamination proceeding which is not subject to appeal to the Patent Trial and Appeal Board or to the court;

* * * * *

(3) To invoke the supervisory authority of the Director in appropriate circumstances. For petitions involving action of the Patent Trial and Appeal Board, see § 41.3

of this title.

* * * * *

§ 1.191. Appeal to Patent Trial and Appeal Board.

Appeals to the Patent Trial and Appeal Board under 35 U.S.C. 134(a) and (b) are conducted according to part 41 of this title.

§ 1.198. Reopening after a final decision of the Patent Trial and Appeal Board.

When a decision by the Patent Trial and Appeal Board on appeal has become final for judicial review, prosecution of the proceeding before the primary examiner will not be reopened or reconsidered by the primary examiner except under the provisions of § 1.114 or § 41.50 of this title without the written authority of the Director, and then only for the consideration of matters not already adjudicated, sufficient cause being shown.

§ 1.211. Publication of applications.

* * * * *

(c) An application filed under 35 U.S.C. 111(a) will not be published until it includes the basic filing fee (§ 1.16(a) or § 1.16(c)) and any English translation required by § 1.52(d). The Office may delay publishing any application until it includes any application size fee required by the Office under § 1.16(s) or § 1.492(j), a specification having papers in compliance with § 1.52 and an abstract (§ 1.72(b)), drawings in compliance with § 1.84, a sequence listing in compliance with §§ 1.821 through 1.825 (if applicable), and the inventor's oath or declaration or application data sheet containing the information specified in § 1.63(b).

* * * * *

§ 1.215. Patent application publication.

(a) The publication of an application under 35 U.S.C. 122(b) shall include a patent application publication. The date of publication shall be indicated on the patent application publication. The patent application publication will be based upon the specification and drawings deposited on the filing date of the application, as well as the application data sheet and/or the inventor's oath or declaration. The patent application publication may also be based upon amendments to the specification (other than the abstract or the claims) that are reflected in a substitute specification under § 1.125(b), amendments to the abstract under § 1.121(b), amendments to the claims that are reflected in a complete claim listing under § 1.121(c), and amendments to the drawings under § 1.121(d), provided that such substitute specification or amendment is submitted in sufficient time to be entered into the Office file wrapper of the application before technical preparations for publication of the application have begun. Technical preparations for publication of an application generally begin four months prior to the projected date of publication. The patent application publication of an application that has entered the national stage under 35 U.S.C. 371 may also include amendments made during the international stage. *See* paragraph (c) of this section for publication of an application based upon a copy of the application submitted via the Office electronic filing system.

(b) The patent application publication will include the name of the assignee, person to whom the inventor is under an obligation to assign the invention, or person who otherwise shows sufficient proprietary interest in the matter if that information is provided in the application data sheet in an application filed under § 1.46. Assignee information may be included on the patent application publication in other applications if the assignee information is provided in an application data sheet submitted in sufficient time to be entered into the Office file wrapper of the application before technical preparations for publication of the application have begun. Providing assignee information in the application data sheet does not substitute for compliance with any requirement of part 3 of this chapter to have an assignment recorded by the Office.

(c) At applicant's option, the patent application publication will be based upon the copy of the application (specification, drawings, and the application data sheet and/or the inventor's oath or declaration) as amended, provided that applicant supplies such a copy in compliance with the Office electronic filing system requirements within one month of the mailing date of the first Office communication that includes a confirmation number for the application, or fourteen months of the earliest filing date for which a benefit is sought under title 35, United States Code, whichever is later.

* * * * *

§ 1.248. Service of papers; manner of service; proof of service in cases other than interferences and trials.

* * * * *

(c) See § 41.106(e) or § 42.6(e) of this title for service of papers in contested cases or trials before the Patent Trial and Appeal Board.

PREISSUANCE SUBMISSIONS AND PROTESTS BY THIRD PARTIES

§ 1.290. Submissions by third parties in applications.

(a) A third party may submit, for consideration and entry in the record of a patent application, any patents, published patent applications, or other printed publications of potential relevance to the examination of the application if the submission is made in accordance with 35 U.S.C. 122(e) and this section. A third-party submission may not be entered or considered by the Office if any part of the submission is not in compliance with 35 U.S.C. 122(e) and this section.

(b) Any third-party submission under this section must be filed prior to the earlier of:

(1) The date a notice of allowance under § 1.311 is given or mailed in the application; or

(2) The later of:

(i) Six months after the date on which the application is first published by the Office under 35 U.S.C. 122(b) and § 1.211, or

(ii) The date the first rejection under § 1.104 of any claim by the examiner is given or mailed during the examination of the application.

(c) Any third-party submission under this section must be made in writing.

(d) Any third-party submission under this section must include:

(1) A document list identifying the documents, or portions of documents, being submitted in accordance with paragraph (e) of this section;

(2) A concise description of the asserted relevance of each item identified in the document list;

(3) A legible copy of each item identified in the document list, other than U.S. patents and U.S. patent application publications;

(4) An English language translation of any non-English language item identified in the document list; and

(5) A statement by the party making the submission

that:

(i) The party is not an individual who has a duty to disclose information with respect to the application under § 1.56; and

(ii) The submission complies with the requirements of 35 U.S.C. 122(e) and this section.

(e) The document list required by paragraph (d)(1) of this section must include a heading that identifies the list as a third-party submission under § 1.290, identify on each page of the list the application number of the application in which the submission is being filed, list U.S. patents and U.S. patent application publications in a separate section from other items, and identify each:

(1) U.S. patent by patent number, first named inventor, and issue date;

(2) U.S. patent application publication by patent application publication number, first named inventor, and publication date;

(3) Foreign patent or published foreign patent application by the country or patent office that issued the patent or published the application; the applicant, patentee, or first named inventor; an appropriate document number; and the publication date indicated on the patent or published application; and

(4) Non-patent publication by author (if any), title, pages being submitted, publication date, and, where available, publisher and place of publication. If no publication date is known, the third party must provide evidence of publication.

(f) Any third-party submission under this section must be accompanied by the fee set forth in § 1.17(p) for every ten items or fraction thereof identified in the document list.

(g) The fee otherwise required by paragraph (f) of this section is not required for a submission listing three or fewer total items that is accompanied by a statement by the party making the submission that, to the knowledge of the person signing the statement after making reasonable inquiry, the submission is the first and only submission under 35 U.S.C. 122(e) filed in the application by the party or a party in privity with the party.

(h) In the absence of a request by the Office, an applicant need not reply to a submission under this section.

(i) The provisions of § 1.8 do not apply to the time

periods set forth in this section.

§ 1.291. Protests by the public against pending applications.

* * * * *

(b) The protest will be entered into the record of the application if, in addition to complying with paragraph (c) of this section, the protest has been served upon the applicant in accordance with § 1.248, or filed with the Office in duplicate in the event service is not possible; and, except for paragraph (b)(1) of this section, the protest was filed prior to the date the application was published under § 1.211, or the date a notice of allowance under § 1.311 was given or mailed, whichever occurs first:

(1) If a protest is accompanied by the written consent of the applicant, the protest will be considered if the protest is filed prior to the date a notice of allowance under § 1.311 is given or mailed in the application.

* * * * *

(c) * * *

(1) An information list of the documents, portions of documents, or other information being submitted, where each:

(i) U.S. patent is identified by patent number, first named inventor, and issue date;

(ii) U.S. patent application publication is identified by patent application publication number, first named inventor, and publication date;

(iii) Foreign patent or published foreign patent application is identified by the country or patent office that issued the patent or published the application; an appropriate document number; the applicant, patentee, or first named inventor; and the publication date indicated on the patent or published application;

(iv) Non-patent publication is identified by author (if any), title, pages being submitted, publication date, and, where available, publisher and place of publication; and

(v) Item of other information is identified by date, if known.

(2) A concise explanation of the relevance of each item identified in the information list pursuant to paragraph (c)(1) of this section;

(3) A legible copy of each item identified in the infor-

mation list, other than U.S. patents and U.S. patent application publications;

(4) An English language translation of any non-English language item identified in the information list; and

* * * * *

(f) In the absence of a request by the Office, an applicant need not reply to a protest.

* * * * *

§ 1.292. [Removed and reserved]

§ 1.293. [Removed and reserved]

§ 1.294. [Removed and reserved]

§ 1.295. [Removed and reserved]

§ 1.296. [Removed and reserved]

§ 1.297. [Removed and reserved]

§ 1.301. [Removed and reserved]

§ 1.302. [Removed and reserved]

§ 1.303. [Removed and reserved]

§ 1.304. [Removed and reserved]

§ 1.313. Withdrawal from issue.

* * * * *

(b) * * *

(4) For an interference or derivation proceeding.

* * * * *

§ 1.321. Statutory disclaimers, including terminal disclaimers.

* * * * *

(b) An applicant may disclaim or dedicate to the public the entire term, or any terminal part of the term, of a patent to be granted. Such terminal disclaimer is binding upon the grantee and its successors or assigns. The terminal disclaimer, to be recorded in the Patent and Trademark Office, must:

(1) Be signed by the applicant or an attorney or agent of record;

(2) Specify the portion of the term of the patent being disclaimed;

(3) State the present extent of applicant's ownership

interest in the patent to be granted; and

(4) Be accompanied by the fee set forth in § 1.20(d).

* * * * *

(d) A terminal disclaimer, when filed in a patent application or in a reexamination proceeding to obviate double patenting based upon a patent or application that is not commonly owned but was disqualified as prior art as set forth in either § 1.104(c)(4)(ii) or (c)(5)(ii) as the result of activities undertaken within the scope of a joint research agreement, must:

* * * * *

§ 1.322. Certificate of correction of Office mistake.

(a) * * *

(3) If the request relates to a patent involved in an interference or trial before the Patent Trial and Appeal Board, the request must comply with the requirements of this section and be accompanied by a motion under § 41.121(a)(2), § 41.121(a)(3), or § 42.20 of this title.

§ 1.323. Certificate of correction of applicant's mistake.

The Office may issue a certificate of correction under the conditions specified in 35 U.S.C. 255 at the request of the patentee or the patentee's assignee, upon payment of the fee set forth in § 1.20(a). If the request relates to a patent involved in an interference or trial before the Patent Trial and Appeal Board, the request must comply with the requirements of this section and be accompanied by a motion under § 41.121(a)(2), § 41.121(a)(3) or § 42.20 of this title.

§ 1.324. Correction of inventorship in patent, pursuant to 35 U.S.C. 256.

(a) Whenever through error a person is named in an issued patent as the inventor, or an inventor is not named in an issued patent, the Director, pursuant to 35 U.S.C. 256, may, on application of all the parties and assignees, or on order of a court before which such matter is called in question, issue a certificate naming only the actual inventor or inventors.

(b) Any request to correct inventorship of a patent pursuant to paragraph (a) of this section must be accompanied by:

(1) A statement from each person who is being added as an inventor and each person who is currently named

as an inventor either agreeing to the change of inventorship or stating that he or she has no disagreement in regard to the requested change;

(2) A statement from all assignees of the parties submitting a statement under paragraph (b)(1) of this section agreeing to the change of inventorship in the patent, which statement must comply with the requirements of § 3.73(c) of this chapter; and

(3) The fee set forth in § 1.20(b).

(c) For correction of inventorship in an application, see § 1.48.

(d) In an interference under part 41, subpart D, of this title, a request for correction of inventorship in a patent must be in the form of a motion under § 41.121(a)(2) of this title. In a contested case under part 42, subpart D, of this title, a request for correction of inventorship in a patent must be in the form of a motion under § 42.22 of this title. The motion under § 41.121(a)(2) or § 42.22 of this title must comply with the requirements of this section.

Subpart C— International Processing Provisions

* * *

§ 1.414. The United States Patent and Trademark Office as a Designated Office or Elected Office.

* * * * *

(c) * * *

(2) National stage processing for international applications entering the national stage under 35 U.S.C. 371.

§ 1.421. Applicant for international application.

(a) Only residents or nationals of the United States of America may file international applications in the United States Receiving Office. If an international application does not include an applicant who is indicated as being a resident or national of the United States of America, and at least one applicant:

(1) Has indicated a residence or nationality in a PCT Contracting State, or

(2) Has no residence or nationality indicated, applicant will be so notified and, if the international application includes a fee amount equivalent to that required by § 1.445(a)(4), the international application

will be forwarded for processing to the International Bureau acting as a Receiving Office (see also § 1.412(c)(6)).

(b) Although the United States Receiving Office will accept international applications filed by any applicant who is a resident or national of the United States of America for international processing, for the purposes of the designation of the United States, an international application will be accepted by the Patent and Trademark Office for the national stage only if the applicant is the inventor or other person as provided in § 1.422 or § 1.424. Joint inventors must jointly apply for an international application.

(c) A registered attorney or agent of the applicant may sign the international application Request and file the international application for the applicant. A separate power of attorney from each applicant may be required.

(d) Any indication of different applicants for the purpose of different Designated Offices must be shown on the Request portion of the international application.

(e) Requests for changes in the indications concerning the applicant, agent, or common representative of an international application shall be made in accordance with PCT Rule 92bis and may be required to be signed by all applicants.

(f) Requests for withdrawals of the international application, designations, priority claims, the Demand, or elections shall be made in accordance with PCT Rule 90*bis* and must be signed by all applicants. A separate power of attorney from the applicants will be required for the purposes of any request for a withdrawal in accordance with PCT Rule 90*bis* which is not signed by all applicants.

§ 1.422. Legal representative as applicant in an international application.

If an inventor is deceased or under legal incapacity, the legal representative of the inventor may be an applicant in an international application which designates the United States of America.

§ 1.423. [Removed and Reserved]

§ 1.424. Assignee, obligated assignee, or person having sufficient proprietary interest as applicant in an international application.

(a) A person to whom the inventor has assigned or is under an obligation to assign the invention may be an applicant in an international application which designates the United States of America. A person who otherwise shows sufficient proprietary interest in the matter may be an applicant in an international application which designates the United States of America on proof of the pertinent facts and a showing that such action is appropriate to preserve the rights of the parties.

(b) Neither any showing required under paragraph (a) of this section nor documentary evidence of ownership or proprietary interest will be required or considered by the Office in the international stage, but will be required in the national stage in accordance with the conditions and requirements of § 1.46.

§ 1.431. International application requirements.

* * * * *

(b) * * *

(3) * * *

(iii) The name of the applicant, as prescribed (note §§ 1.421, 1.422, and 1.424);

* * * * *

§ 1.445. International application filing, processing and search fees.

(a) The following fees and charges for international applications are established by law or by the Director under the authority of 35 U.S.C. 376:

(1) * * *

(i) A basic portion:

(A) For a transmittal fee paid on or after January 1, 2014:

By a micro entity (§ 1.29)	$60.00
By a small entity (§ 1.27(a))	120.00
By other than a small or micro entity	240.00

(B) For a transmittal fee paid before January 1, 2014: $240.00.

* * * * *

(2) A search fee (*see* 35 U.S.C. 361(d) and PCT Rule 16):

(i) For a search fee paid on or after January 1, 2014:

By a micro entity (§ 1.29)	$520.00
By a small entity (§ 1.27(a))	1,040.00
By other than a small or micro entity	2,080.00

(ii) For a search fee paid before January 1, 2014: $2,080.00.

(3) A supplemental search fee when required, per additional invention:

(i) For a supplemental search fee paid on or after January 1, 2014:

By a micro entity (§ 1.29)	$520.00
By a small entity (§ 1.27(a))	1,040.00
By other than a small or micro entity	2,080.00

(ii) For a supplemental search fee paid before January 1, 2014: $2,080.00.

(4) A fee equivalent to the transmittal fee in paragraph (a)(1) of this section that would apply if the USPTO was the Receiving Office for transmittal of an international application to the International Bureau for processing in its capacity as a Receiving Office (PCT Rule 19.4):

(i) For a fee equivalent to the transmittal fee in paragraph (a)(1) of this section filed on or after January 1, 2014:

By a micro entity (§ 1.29)	$60.00
By a small entity (§ 1.27(a))	120.00
By other than a small or micro entity	240.00

(ii) For a fee equivalent to the transmittal fee in paragraph (a)(1) of this section filed before January 1, 2014 .... 240.00

(b) The international filing fee shall be as prescribed in PCT Rule 15.

§ 1.482. International preliminary examination fees.

(a) The following fees and charges for international preliminary examination are established by the Director under the authority of 35 U.S.C. 376:

(1) The following preliminary examination fee is due on filing the Demand:

(i) If an international search fee as set forth in § 1.445(a)(2) has been paid on the international application to the United States Patent and Trademark Office as an International Searching Authority:

(A) For an international search fee filed on or after January 1, 2014:

By a micro entity (§ 1.29)	$150.00
By a small entity (§ 1.27(a))	300.00
By other than a small or micro entity	600.00

(B) For an international search fee filed before January 1, 2014: $600.00.

(ii) If the International Searching Authority for the international application was an authority other than the United States Patent and Trademark Office:

(A) For an international search fee filed on or after January 1, 2014:

By a micro entity (§ 1.29)	$190.00
By a small entity (§ 1.27(a))	380.00
By other than a small or micro entity	760.00

(B) For an international search fee filed before January 1, 2014: $750.00.

(2) An additional preliminary examination fee when required, per additional invention:

(i) For an additional preliminary examination fee filed on or after January 1, 2014:

By a micro entity (§ 1.29)	$150.00
By a small entity (§ 1.27(a))	300.00
By other than a small or micro entity	600.00
examination fee filed before January 1, 2014:	$600.00.

(b) The handling fee is due on filing the Demand and shall be prescribed in PCT Rule 57.

§ 1.491. National stage commencement, entry, and fulfillment.

* * * * *

(b) An international application enters the national stage when the applicant has filed the documents and fees required by 35 U.S.C. 371(c)(1) and (c)(2) within the period set in § 1.495.

(c) An international application fulfills the requirements of 35 U.S.C. 371 when the national stage has commenced under 35 U.S.C. 371(b) or (f) and all applicable requirements of 35 U.S.C. 371 have been satisfied.

§ 1.492. National stage fees.

The following fees and charges are established for international applications entering the national stage under 35 U.S.C. 371:

(a) The basic national fee for an international application entering the national stage under 35 U.S.C. 371:

By a micro entity (§ 1.29)	$70.00
By a small entity (§ 1.27(a))	140.00
By other than a small or micro entity	280.00

(b) Search fee for an international application entering the national stage under 35 U.S.C. 371:

(1) If an international preliminary examination report on the international application prepared by the United States International Preliminary Examining Authority or a written opinion on the international application prepared by the United States International Searching Authority states that the criteria of novelty, inventive step (non-obviousness), and industrial applicability, as defined in PCT Article 33(1) to (4) have been satisfied for all of the claims presented in the application entering the national stage:

By a micro entity (§ 1.29)	$0.00
By a small entity (§ 1.27(a))	0.00
By other than a small or micro entity	0.00

(2) If the search fee as set forth in § 1.445(a)(2) has been paid on the international application to the United States Patent and Trademark Office as an International Searching Authority:

By a micro entity (§ 1.29)	$30.00

By a small entity (§ 1.27(a))	60.00
By other than a small or micro entity	120.00

(3) If an international search report on the international application has been prepared by an International Searching Authority other than the United States International Searching Authority and is provided, or has been previously communicated by the International Bureau, to the Office:

By a micro entity (§ 1.29)	$120.00
By a small entity (§ 1.27(a))	240.00
By other than a small or micro entity	480.00

(4) In all situations not provided for in paragraphs (b)(1), (2), or (3) of this section:

By a micro entity (§ 1.29)	$150.00
By a small entity (§ 1.27(a))	300.00
By other than a small or micro entity	600.00

(c) The examination fee for an international application entering the national stage under 35 U.S.C. 371:

(1) If an international preliminary examination report on the international application prepared by the United States International Preliminary Examining Authority or a written opinion on the international application prepared by the United States International Searching Authority states that the criteria of novelty, inventive step (non-obviousness), and industrial applicability, as defined in PCT Article 33 (1) to (4) have been satisfied for all of the claims presented in the application entering the national stage:

By a micro entity (§ 1.29)	$0.00
By a small entity (§ 1.27(a))	0.00
By other than a small or micro entity	0.00

(2) In all situations not provided for in paragraph (c)(1) of this section:

By a micro entity (§ 1.29)	$180.00.
By a small entity (§ 1.27(a))	$360.00
By other than a small or micro entity	720.00

(d) In addition to the basic national fee, for filing or on later presentation at any other time of each claim in independent form in excess of 3:

By a micro entity (§ 1.29)	$105.00
By a small entity (§ 1.27(a))	210.00
By other than a small or micro entity	420.00

(e) In addition to the basic national fee, for filing or on later presentation at any other time of each claim (whether dependent or independent) in excess of 20 (note that § 1.75(c) indicates how multiple dependent claims are considered for fee calculation purposes):

By a micro entity (§ 1.29)	$20.00
By a small entity (§ 1.27(a))	40.00
By other than a small or micro entity	80.00

(f) In addition to the basic national fee, if the application contains, or is amended to contain, a multiple dependent claim, per application:

By a micro entity (§ 1.29)	$195.00
By a small entity (§ 1.27(a))	390.00
By other than a small or micro entity	780.00

(g) If the excess claims fees required by paragraphs (d) and (e) of this section and multiple dependent claim fee required by paragraph (f) of this section are not paid with the basic national fee or on later presentation of the claims for which excess claims or multiple dependent claim fees are due, the fees required by paragraphs (d), (e), and (f) of this section must be paid or the claims canceled by amendment prior to the expiration of the time period set for reply by the Office in any notice of fee deficiency in order to avoid abandonment.

(h) Surcharge for filing any of the search fee, the examination fee, or the oath or declaration after the date of the commencement of the national stage (§ 1.491(a)) pursuant to § 1.495(c):

By a micro entity (§ 1.29)	$35.00
By a small entity (§ 1.27(a))	70.00
By other than a small or micro entity	140.00

(i) For filing an English translation of an international application or any annexes to an international preliminary examination report later than thirty months after the priority date (§ 1.495(c) and (e)):

By a micro entity (§ 1.29)	$35.00
By a small entity (§ 1.27(a))	70.00
By other than a small or micro entity	140.00

(j) Application size fee for any international application, the specification and drawings of which exceed 100 sheets of paper, for each additional 50 sheets or fraction thereof:

By a micro entity (§ 1.29)	$100.00
By a small entity (§ 1.27(a))	200.00
By other than a small or micro entity	400.00

§ 1.495. Entering the national stage in the United States of America.

(a) The applicant in an international application must fulfill the requirements of 35 U.S.C. 371 within the time periods set forth in paragraphs (b) and (c) of this section in order to prevent the abandonment of the international application as to the United States of America. The thirty month time period set forth in paragraphs (b), (c), (d), (e) and (h) of this section may not be extended.

* * * * *

(c) (1) If applicant complies with paragraph (b) of this section before expiration of thirty months from the priority date, the Office will notify the applicant if he or she has omitted any of:

(i) A translation of the international application, as filed, into the English language, if it was originally filed in another language and if any English language translation of the publication of the international application previously submitted under 35 U.S.C. 154(d) (§ 1.417) is not also a translation of the international application as filed (35 U.S.C. 371(c)(2));

(ii) The inventor's oath or declaration (35 U.S.C. 371(c)(4) and § 1.497), if a declaration of inventorship in compliance with § 1.63 has not been previously submitted in the international application under PCT Rule 4.17(iv) within the time limits provided for in PCT Rule 26ter.1;

(iii) The search fee set forth in § 1.492(b);

(iv) The examination fee set forth in § 1.492(c); and

(v) Any application size fee required by § 1.492(j).

(2) A notice under paragraph (c)(1) of this section will set a time period within which applicant must provide any omitted translation, search fee set forth in § 1.492(b), examination fee set forth in § 1.492(c), and any application size fee required by § 1.492(j) in order to avoid abandonment of the application.

(3) The inventor's oath or declaration must also be filed within the period specified in paragraph (c)(2) of this section, except that the filing of the inventor's oath or declaration may be postponed until the application is otherwise in condition for allowance under the conditions specified in paragraphs (c)(3)(i) through (c)(3)(iii) of this section.

(i) The application contains an application data sheet in accordance with § 1.76 filed prior to the expiration of the time period set in any notice under paragraph (c)(1) identifying:

(A) Each inventor by his or her legal name;

(B) A mailing address where the inventor customarily receives mail, and residence, if an inventor lives at a location which is different from where the inventor customarily receives mail, for each inventor.

(ii) The applicant must file an oath or declaration in compliance with § 1.63, or substitute statement in compliance with § 1.64, executed by or with respect to each actual inventor no later than the expiration of the time period set in the "Notice of Allowability" to avoid abandonment, when the applicant is notified in a "Notice of Allowability" that an application is otherwise in condition for allowance. The time period set in a "Notice of Allowability" is not extendable. *See*

§ 1.136(c). The Office may dispense with the notice provided for in paragraph (c)(1) of this section if an oath or declaration under § 1.63, or substitute statement under § 1.64, executed by or with respect to each actual inventor has been filed before the application is in condition for allowance.

(iii) An international application in which the basic national fee under 35 U.S.C. 41(a)(1)(F) has been paid and for which an application data sheet in accordance with § 1.76 has been filed may be treated as complying with 35 U.S.C. 371 for purposes of eighteen month publication under 35 U.S.C. 122(b) and § 1.211 et seq.

(4) The payment of the processing fee set forth in § 1.492(i) is required for acceptance of an English translation later than the expiration of thirty months after the priority date. The payment of the surcharge set forth in § 1.492(h) is required for acceptance of any of the search fee, the examination fee, or the inventor's oath or declaration after the date of the commencement of the national stage (§ 1.491(a)).

(5) A "Sequence Listing" need not be translated if the "Sequence Listing" complies with PCT Rule 12.1(d) and the description complies with PCT Rule 5.2(b).

* * * * *

(g) The documents and fees submitted under paragraphs (b) and (c) of this section must be identified as a submission to enter the national stage under 35 U.S.C. 371. If the documents and fees contain conflicting indications as between an application under 35 U.S.C. 111 and a submission to enter the national stage under 35 U.S.C. 371, the documents and fees will be treated as a submission to enter the national stage under 35 U.S.C. 371.

(h) An international application becomes abandoned as to the United States thirty months from the priority date if the requirements of paragraph (b) of this section have not been complied with within thirty months from the priority date.

§ 1.496. Examination of international applications in the national stage.

National stage applications having paid therein the search fee as set forth in § 1.492(b)(1) and examination fee as set forth in § 1.492(c)(1) may be amended subsequent to the date of commencement of national stage processing only to the extent necessary to eliminate objections as to form or to cancel rejected claims. Such national stage applications will be advanced out of turn for examination.

§ 1.497. Inventor's oath or declaration under 35 U.S.C. 371(c)(4).

(a) When an applicant of an international application desires to enter the national stage under 35 U.S.C. 371 pursuant to § 1.495, and a declaration in compliance with § 1.63 has not been previously submitted in the international application under PCT Rule 4.17(iv) within the time limits provided for in PCT Rule 26ter.1, the applicant must file the inventor's oath or declaration. The inventor, or each individual who is a joint inventor of a claimed invention, in an application for patent must execute an oath or declaration in accordance with the conditions and requirements of § 1.63, except as provided for in § 1.64.

(b) An oath or declaration under § 1.63 will be accepted as complying with 35 U.S.C. 371(c)(4) if it complies with the requirements of §§ 1.63(a), (c) and (g). A substitute statement under § 1.64 will be accepted as complying with 35 U.S.C. 371(c)(4) if it complies with the requirements of §§ 1.64(b)(1), (c) and (e) and identifies the person executing the substitute statement. If a newly executed inventor's oath or declaration under § 1.63 or substitute statement under § 1.64 is not required pursuant to § 1.63(d), submission of the copy of the previously executed oath, declaration, or substitute statement under § 1.63(d)(1) is required to comply with 35 U.S.C. 371(c)(4).

(c) If an oath or declaration under § 1.63, or substitute statement under § 1.64, meeting the requirements of § 1.497(b) does not also meet the requirements of § 1.63 or § 1.64, an oath, declaration, substitute statement, or application data sheet in accordance with § 1.76 to comply with § 1.63 or § 1.64 will be required.

Subpart D— Ex Parte Reexamination of Patents

§ 1.501. Citation of prior art and written statements in patent files.

(a) *Information content of submission*: At any time during the period of enforceability of a patent, any person may file a written submission with the Office under this section, which is directed to the following information:

(1) Prior art consisting of patents or printed publications which the person making the submission believes to have a bearing on the patentability of any claim of the patent; or

(2) Statements of the patent owner filed by the patent owner in a proceeding before a Federal court or the Office in which the patent owner took a position on the scope of any claim of the patent. Any statement submitted under this paragraph must be accompanied by any other documents, pleadings, or evidence from the proceeding in which the statement was filed that address the written statement, and such statement and accompanying information under this paragraph must be submitted in redacted form to exclude information subject to an applicable protective order.

(3) Submissions under paragraph (a)(2) of this section must identify:

(i) The forum and proceeding in which patent owner filed each statement;

(ii) The specific papers and portions of the papers submitted that contain the statements; and

(iii) How each statement submitted is a statement in which patent owner took a position on the scope of any claim in the patent.

(b) *Explanation*: A submission pursuant to paragraph (a) of this section:

(1) Must include an explanation in writing of the pertinence and manner of applying any prior art submitted under paragraph (a)(1) of this section and any written statement and accompanying information submitted under paragraph (a)(2) of this section to at least one claim of the patent, in order for the submission to become a part of the official file of the patent; and

(2) May, if the submission is made by the patent owner, include an explanation of how the claims differ from any prior art submitted under paragraph (a)(1) of this section or any written statements and accompanying information submitted under paragraph (a)(2) of this section.

(c) *Reexamination pending*: If a reexamination proceeding has been requested and is pending for the patent in which the submission is filed, entry of the submission into the official file of the patent is subject to the provisions of §§ 1.502 and 1.902.

(d) *Identity*: If the person making the submission wishes his or her identity to be excluded from the patent file and kept confidential, the submission papers must be submitted anonymously without any identification of the person making the submission.

(e) *Certificate of Service*: A submission under this section by a person other than the patent owner must include a certification that a copy of the submission was served in its entirety upon patent owner at the address as provided for in § 1.33 (c). A submission by a person other than the patent owner that fails to include proper proof of service as required by § 1.248(b) will not be entered into the patent file.

§ 1.510. Request for ex parte reexamination.

(a) Any person may, at any time during the period of enforceability of a patent, file a request for an ex parte reexamination by the Office of any claim of the patent on the basis of prior art patents or printed publications cited under § 1.501, unless prohibited by 35 U.S.C. 315(e)(1) or 35 U.S.C. 325(e)(1). The request must be accompanied by the fee for requesting reexamination set in § 1.20(c)(1).

(b) * * *

(2) An identification of every claim for which reexamination is requested, and a detailed explanation of the pertinency and manner of applying the cited prior art to every claim for which reexamination is requested. For each statement of the patent owner and accompanying information submitted pursuant to § 1.501(a)(2) which is relied upon in the detailed explanation, the request must explain how that statement is being used to determine the proper meaning of a patent claim in connection with the prior art applied to that claim and how each relevant claim is being interpreted. If appropriate, the party requesting reexamination may also point out how claims distinguish over cited prior art.

* * * * *

(6) A certification by the third party requester that the statutory estoppel provisions of 35 U.S.C. 315(e)(1) or 35 U.S.C. 325(e)(1) do not prohibit the requester from filing the ex parte reexamination request.

* * * * *

§ 1.515. Determination of the request for ex parte reexamination.

(a) Within three months following the filing date of a request for an ex parte reexamination, an examiner will consider the request and determine whether or not a substantial new question of patentability affecting any claim of the patent is raised by the request and the prior art cited therein, with or without consideration of other patents or printed publications. A statement and any accompanying information submitted pursuant to § 1.501(a)(2) will not be considered by the examiner when making a determination on the request. The examiner's determination will be based on the claims in effect at the time of the determination, will become a part of the official file of the patent, and will be given or mailed to the patent owner at the address provided for in § 1.33(c) and to the person requesting reexamination.

* * * * *

§ 1.530. Statement by patent owner in *ex parte* reexamination; amendment by patent owner in *ex parte* or *inter partes* reexamination; inventorship change in *ex parte* or *inter partes* reexamination.

* * * * *

(l) * * *

(1) When it appears in a patent being reexamined that the correct inventor or inventors were not named, the Director may, on petition of all the parties set forth in § 1.324(b)(1) and (b)(2), including the assignees, and satisfactory proof of the facts and payment of the fee set forth in § 1.20(b), or on order of a court before which such matter is called in question, include in the reexamination certificate to be issued under § 1.570 or § 1.997 an amendment naming only the actual inventor or inventors. The petition must be submitted as part of the reexamination proceeding and must satisfy the requirements of § 1.324.

* * * * *

§ 1.550. Conduct of ex parte reexamination proceedings.

* * * * *

(i) A petition in an *ex parte* reexamination proceeding must be accompanied by the fee set forth in § 1.20(c)(6), except for petitions under paragraph (c) of this section to extend the period for response by a patent owner, petitions under paragraph (e) of this section to accept a delayed response by a patent owner, petitions under § 1.78 to accept an unintentionally delayed benefit claim, and petitions under § 1.530(l) for correction of inventorship in a reexamination proceeding.

§ 1.552. Scope of reexamination in ex parte reexamination proceedings.

* * * * *

(d) Any statement of the patent owner and any accompanying information submitted pursuant to § 1.501(a)(2) which is of record in the patent being reexamined (which includes any reexamination files for the patent) may be used after a reexamination proceeding has been ordered to determine the proper meaning of a patent claim when applying patents or printed publications.

Subpart E— Supplemental Examination of Patents

Sec.

§ 1.601. Filing of papers in supplemental examination.

(a) A request for supplemental examination of a patent must be filed by the owner(s) of the entire right, title, and interest in the patent.

(b) Any party other than the patent owner (*i.e.,* any third party) is prohibited from filing papers or otherwise participating in any manner in a supplemental examination proceeding.

(c) A request for supplemental examination of a patent may be filed at any time during the period of enforceability of the patent.

§ 1.605. Items of information.

(a) Each request for supplemental examination may include no more than twelve items of information believed to be relevant to the patent. More than one request for supplemental examination of the same patent may be filed at any time during the period of enforceability of the patent.

(b) An item of information includes a document submitted as part of the request that contains information, believed to be relevant to the patent, that the patent owner requests the Office to consider, reconsider, or correct. If the information to be considered, reconsidered, or corrected is not, at least in part, contained within or based on any document submitted as part of the request, the discussion within the body of the request relative to the information will be considered as an item of information.

(c) An item of information must be in writing in accordance with § 1.2. To be considered, any audio or video recording must be submitted in the form of a written transcript.

(d) If one item of information is combined in the request with one or more additional items of information, each item of information of the combination may be separately counted. Exceptions include the combination of a non-English language document and its translation, and the combination of a document that is over 50 pages in length and its summary pursuant to § 1.610(b)(8).

§ 1.610. Content of request for supplemental examination.

(a) A request for supplemental examination must be accompanied by the fee for filing a request for supplemental examination as set forth in § 1.20(k)(1), the fee for reexamination ordered as a result of a supplemental examination proceeding as set forth in § 1.20(k)(2), and any applicable document size fees as set forth in § 1.20(k)(3).

(b) A request for supplemental examination must include:

(1) An identification of the number of the patent for which supplemental examination is requested.

(2) A list of the items of information that are requested to be considered, reconsidered, or corrected. Where appropriate, the list must meet the requirements of § 1.98(b).

(3) A list identifying any other prior or concurrent post-patent Office proceedings involving the patent for which supplemental examination is being requested, including an identification of the type of proceeding, the identifying number of any such proceeding (*e.g.*, a control number or reissue application number), and the filing date of any such proceeding.

(4) An identification of each claim of the patent for which supplemental examination is requested.

(5) A separate, detailed explanation of the relevance and manner of applying each item of information to each claim of the patent for which supplemental examination is requested.

(6) A copy of the patent for which supplemental examination is requested and a copy of any disclaimer or certificate issued for the patent.

(7) A copy of each item of information listed in paragraph (b)(2) of this section, accompanied by a written English translation of all of the necessary and pertinent parts of any non-English language item of information. The patent owner is not required to submit copies of items of information that form part of the discussion within the body of the request as specified in § 1.605(b), or copies of U.S. patents and U.S. patent application publications.

(8) A summary of the relevant portions of any submitted document, other than the request, that is over 50 pages in length. The summary must include citations to the particular pages containing the relevant portions.

(9) An identification of the owner(s) of the entire right, title, and interest in the patent requested to be examined, and a submission by the patent owner in compliance with § 3.73(c) of this chapter establishing the entirety of the ownership in the patent requested to be examined.

(c) The request may also include:

(1) A cover sheet itemizing each component submitted as part of the request;

(2) A table of contents for the request;

(3) An explanation of how the claims patentably distinguish over the items of information; and

(4) An explanation of why each item of information submitted with the request does or does not raise a substantial new question of patentability.

(d) The filing date of a request for supplemental examination will not be granted if the request is not in compliance with §§ 1.605, 1.615, and this section, subject to the discretion of the Office. If the Office determines that the request, as originally submitted, is not entitled to a filing date, the patent owner will be so notified and will be given an opportunity to complete the request within a specified time. If the patent owner does not timely comply with the notice, the request for supplemental examination will not be granted a filing date and the fee for reexamination as set forth in § 1.20(k)(2) will be refunded. If the patent owner timely files a corrected request in response to the notice that properly addresses all of the defects set forth in the notice and that otherwise complies with all of the requirements of §§ 1.605, 1.615, and this section, the filing date of the supplemental examination request will be the receipt date of the corrected request.

§ 1.615. Format of papers filed in a supplemental examination proceeding.

(a) All papers submitted in a supplemental examination proceeding must be formatted in accordance with § 1.52.

(b) Court documents and non-patent literature may be redacted, but must otherwise be identical both in content and in format to the original documents, and, if a court document, to the document submitted in court, and must not otherwise be reduced in size or modified, particularly in terms of font type, font size, line spacing, and margins. Patents, patent application publications, and third-party-generated affidavits or declarations must not be reduced in size or otherwise modified in the manner described in this paragraph.

§ 1.620. Conduct of supplemental examination proceeding.

(a) Within three months after the filing date of a request for supplemental examination, the Office will determine whether a substantial new question of patentability affecting any claim of the patent is raised by any of the items of information presented in the request. The determination will generally be limited to a review of the item(s) of information identified in the request as applied to the identified claim(s) of the patent. The determination will be based on the claims in effect at the time of the determination and will become a part of the official record of the patent.

(b) The Office may hold in abeyance action on any petition or other paper filed in a supplemental examination proceeding until after the proceeding is concluded by the electronic issuance of the supplemental examination certificate as set forth in § 1.625.

(c) If an unauthorized or otherwise improper paper is filed in a supplemental examination proceeding, it will not be entered into the official file or considered, or if inadvertently entered, it will be expunged.

(d) The patent owner must, as soon as possible upon the discovery of any other prior or concurrent post-patent Office proceeding involving the patent for which the current supplemental examination is requested, file a paper limited to notifying the Office of the post- patent Office proceeding, if such notice has not been previously provided with the request. The notice shall be limited to an identification of the post-patent Office proceeding, including the type of proceeding, the identifying number of any such proceeding (*e.g.*, a control number or reissue application number), and the filing date of any such proceeding, without any discussion of the issues of the current supplemental examination proceeding or of the identified post-patent Office proceeding(s).

(e) Interviews are prohibited in a supplemental examination proceeding.

(f) No amendment may be filed in a supplemental examination proceeding.

(g) If the Office becomes aware, during the course of supplemental examination or of any reexamination ordered under 35 U.S.C. 257 as a result of the supplemental examination proceeding, that a material fraud on the Office may have been committed in connection with the patent requested to be examined, the supplemental examination proceeding or any reexamination proceeding ordered under 35 U.S.C. 257 will continue, and the matter will be referred to the U.S. Attorney General in accordance with 35 U.S.C. 257(e).

§ 1.625. Conclusion of supplemental examination; publication of supplemental examination certificate; procedure after conclusion.

(a) A supplemental examination proceeding will conclude with the electronic issuance of a supplemental examination certificate. The supplemental examination certificate will indicate the result of the determination whether any of the items of information presented in the request raised a substantial new question of patentability.

(b) If the supplemental examination certificate states that a substantial new question of patentability is raised by one or more items of information in the request, *ex parte* reexamination of the patent will be ordered under 35 U.S.C. 257. Upon the conclusion of the *ex parte* reexamination proceeding, an *ex parte* reexamination certificate, which will include a statement specifying that *ex parte* reexamination was ordered under 35 U.S.C. 257, will be published. The electronically issued supplemental examination certificate will remain as part of the public record of the patent.

(c) If the supplemental examination certificate indicates that no substantial new question of patentability is raised by any of the items of information in the request, and *ex parte* reexamination is not ordered under 35 U.S.C. 257, the electronically issued supplemental examination certificate will be published in due course. The fee for reexamination ordered as a result of supplemental examination, as set forth in § 1.20(k)(2), will be refunded in accordance with § 1.26(c).

(d) Any *ex parte* reexamination ordered under 35 U.S.C. 257 will be conducted in accordance with §§ 1.530 through 1.570, which govern *ex parte* reexamination, except that:

(1) The patent owner will not have the right to file a statement pursuant to § 1.530, and the order will not set a time period within which to file such a statement;

(2) Reexamination of any claim of the patent may be conducted on the basis of any item of information as set forth in § 1.605, and is not limited to patents and printed publications or to subject matter that has been added or deleted during the reexamination proceeding, notwithstanding § 1.552(a);

(3) Issues in addition to those raised by patents and printed publications, and by subject matter added or deleted during a reexamination proceeding, may be considered and resolved, notwithstanding § 1.552(c); and

(4) Information material to patentability will be defined by § 1.56(b), notwithstanding § 1.555(b).

Subpart F Adjustment and Extension of Patent Term

§ 1.701. Extension of patent term due to examination delay under the Uruguay Round Agreements Act (original applications, other than designs, filed on or after June 8, 1995, and before May 29, 2000).

(a) * * *

(1) Interference or derivation proceedings under 35 U.S.C. 135(a); and/or

* * * * *

(3) Appellate review by the Patent Trial and Appeal Board or by a Federal court under 35 U.S.C. 141 or 145, if the patent was issued pursuant to a decision in the review reversing an adverse determination of patentability and if the patent is not subject to a terminal disclaimer due to the issuance of another patent claiming subject matter that is not patentably distinct from that under appellate review. If an application is remanded by a panel of the Patent Trial and Appeal Board and the remand is the last action by a panel of the Patent Trial and Appeal Board prior to the mailing of a notice of allowance under 35 U.S.C. 151 in the application, the remand shall be considered a decision in the review reversing an adverse determination of patentability as that phrase is used in 35 U.S.C. 154(b)(2) as amended by section 532(a) of the Uruguay Round Agreements Act, Public Law 103-465, 108 Stat. 4809, 4983–85 (1994), and a final decision in favor of the applicant under paragraph (c)(3) of this section. A remand by a panel of the Patent Trial and Appeal Board shall not be considered a decision in the review reversing an adverse determination of patentability as provided in this paragraph if there is filed a request for continued examination under 35 U.S.C. 132(b) that was not first preceded by the mailing, after such remand, of at least one of an action under 35 U.S.C. 132 or a notice of allowance under 35 U.S.C. 151.

(c) (1) * * *

(i) With respect to each interference or derivation proceeding in which the application was involved, the number of days, if any, in the period beginning on the date the interference or derivation proceeding was instituted to involve the application in the interference or derivation proceeding and ending on the date that the interference or derivation proceeding was terminated with respect to the application; and

(ii) The number of days, if any, in the period beginning on the date prosecution in the application was suspended by the Patent and Trademark Office due to interference or derivation proceedings under 35 U.S.C. 135(a) not involving the application and ending on the date of the termination of the suspension.

(2) * * *

(iii) The number of days, if any, in the period beginning on the date applicant was notified that an interference or derivation proceeding would be instituted but for the secrecy order and ending on the date the secrecy order and any renewal thereof was removed; and

* * * * *

(3) The period of delay under paragraph (a)(3) of this section is the sum of the number of days, if any, in the period beginning on the date on which an appeal to the Patent Trial and Appeal Board was filed under 35 U.S.C. 134 and ending on the date of a final decision in favor of the applicant by the Patent Trial and Appeal Board or by a Federal court in an appeal under 35 U.S.C. 141 or a civil action under 35 U.S.C. 145.

* * * * *

§ 1.702. Grounds for adjustment of patent term due to examination delay under the Patent Term Guarantee Act of 1999 (original applications, other than designs, filed on or after May 29, 2000).

(a) * * *

(1) Mail at least one of a notification under 35 U.S.C. 132 or a notice of allowance under 35 U.S.C. 151 not later than fourteen months after the date on which the application was filed under 35 U.S.C. 111(a) or the date the national stage commenced under 35 U.S.C. 371(b) or (f) in an international application;

* * *

(3) Act on an application not later than four months after the date of a decision by the Patent Trial and Appeal Board under 35 U.S.C. 134 or 135 or a decision by a Federal court under 35 U.S.C. 141, 145, or 146 where at least one allowable claim remains in the application; or

* * * * *

(b) *Three-year pendency.* * * *

(2) Any time consumed by an interference or derivation proceeding under 35 U.S.C. 135(a);

* * * * *

(4) Any time consumed by review by the Patent Trial and Appeal Board or a Federal court; or

* * * * *

(c) Delays caused by interference and derivation

proceedings. Subject to the provisions of 35 U.S.C. 154(b) and this subpart, the term of an original patent shall be adjusted if the issuance of the patent was delayed due to interference or derivation proceedings under 35 U.S.C. 135(a).

* * * * *

(e) Delays caused by successful appellate review. Subject to the provisions of 35 U.S.C. 154(b) and this subpart, the term of an original patent shall be adjusted if the issuance of the patent was delayed due to review by the Patent Trial and Appeal Board under 35 U.S.C. 134 or by a Federal court under 35 U.S.C. 141 or 145, if the patent was issued under a decision in the review reversing an adverse determination of patentability. If an application is remanded by a panel of the Patent Trial and Appeal Board and the remand is the last action by a panel of the Patent Trial and Appeal Board prior to the mailing of a notice of allowance under 35 U.S.C. 151 in the application, the remand shall be considered a decision by the Patent Trial and Appeal Board as that phrase is used in 35 U.S.C. 154(b)(1)(A)(iii), a decision in the review reversing an adverse determination of patentability as that phrase is used in 35 U.S.C. 154(b)(1)(C)(iii), and a final decision in favor of the applicant under § 1.703(e). A remand by a panel of the Patent Trial and Appeal Board shall not be considered a decision in the review reversing an adverse determination of patentability as provided in this paragraph if there is filed a request for continued examination under 35 U.S.C. 132(b) that was not first preceded by the mailing, after such remand, of at least one of an action under 35 U.S.C. 132 or a notice of allowance under 35 U.S.C. 151.

* * * * *

§ 1.703. Period of adjustment of patent term due to examination delay.

(a) * * *

(1) The number of days, if any, in the period beginning on the day after the date that is fourteen months after the date on which the application was filed under 35 U.S.C. 111(a) or the date the national stage commenced under 35 U.S.C. 371(b) or (f) in an international application and ending on the date of mailing of either an action under 35 U.S.C. 132, or a notice of allowance under 35 U.S.C. 151, whichever occurs first;

* * *

(5) The number of days, if any, in the period beginning on the day after the date that is four months after the date of a final decision by the Patent Trial and Appeal Board or by a Federal court in an appeal under 35 U.S.C. 141 or a civil action under 35 U.S.C. 145 or 146 where at least one allowable claim remains in the application and ending on the date of mailing of either an action under 35 U.S.C. 132 or a notice of allowance under 35 U.S.C. 151, whichever occurs first; and

* * * * *

(b) * * *

(2) (i) The number of days, if any, in the period beginning on the date an interference or derivation proceeding was instituted to involve the application in the interference or derivation proceeding under 35 U.S.C. 135(a) and ending on the date that the interference or derivation proceeding was terminated with respect to the application; and

(ii) The number of days, if any, in the period beginning on the date prosecution in the application was suspended by the Office due to interference or derivation proceedings under 35 U.S.C. 135(a) not involving the application and ending on the date of the termination of the suspension;

(3) * * *

(iii) The number of days, if any, in the period beginning on the date applicant was notified that an interference or derivation proceeding under 35 U.S.C. 135(a) would be instituted but for the secrecy order and ending on the date the secrecy order was removed; and

* * * * *

(c) * * *

(1) The number of days, if any, in the period beginning on the date an interference or derivation proceeding was instituted to involve the application in the interference or derivation proceeding under 35 U.S.C. 135(a) and ending on the date that the interference or derivation proceeding was terminated with respect to the application; and

(2) The number of days, if any, in the period beginning on the date prosecution in the application was suspended by the Office due to interference or derivation

proceedings under 35 U.S.C. 135(a) not involving the application and ending on the date of the termination of the suspension.

(d) * * *

(3) The number of days, if any, in the period beginning on the date applicant was notified that an interference or derivation proceeding under 35 U.S.C. 135(a) would be instituted but for the secrecy order and ending on the date the secrecy order was removed; and

* * * * *

§ 1.704. Reduction of period of adjustment of patent term.

* * * * *

(c) * * *

(9) Submission of an amendment or other paper after a decision by the Patent Trial and Appeal Board, other than a decision designated as containing a new ground of rejection under § 41.50 (b) of this title or statement under § 41.50(c) of this title, or a decision by a Federal court, less than one month before the mailing of an Office action under 35 U.S.C. 132 or notice of allowance under 35 U.S.C. 151 that requires the mailing of a supplemental Office action or supplemental notice of allowance, in which case the period of adjustment set forth in § 1.703 shall be reduced by the lesser of:

* * * *

(e) The submission of a request under § 1.705(c) for reinstatement of reduced patent term adjustment will not be considered a failure to engage in reasonable efforts to conclude prosecution (processing or examination) of the application under paragraph (c)(10) of this section.

* * * * *

§ 1.705. Patent term adjustment determination.

(a) The patent will include notification of any patent term adjustment under 35 U.S.C. 154(b).

(b) Any request for reconsideration of the patent term adjustment indicated on the patent must be by way of an application for patent term adjustment filed no later than two months from the date the patent was granted. This two-month time period may be extended under the provisions of § 1.136(a). An application for patent term adjustment reduced pursuant to § 1.704(b) for failing to reply to a rejection, objection, argument, or other request within three months of the date of mailing of the Office communication notifying the applicant of the rejection, objection, argument, or other request must be filed prior to the issuance of the patent. This time period is not extendable. Any request for reinstatement of all or part of the period of adjustment reduced pursuant to § 1.704(b) under this paragraph must also be accompanied under this section must be accompanied by:

* * * * *

(c) Any request for reinstatement of all or part of the period of adjustment reduced pursuant to § 1.704(b) for failing to reply to a rejection, objection, argument, or other request within three months of the date of mailing of the Office communication notifying the applicant of the rejection, objection, argument, or other request must be filed prior to the issuance of the patent. This time period is not extendable. Any request for reinstatement of all or part of the period of adjustment reduced pursuant to § 1.704(b) under this paragraph must also be accompanied by:

* * * * *

§ 1.730. Applicant for extension of patent term; signature requirements.

* * * * *

(b) * * *

(1) The patent owner in compliance with § 3.73(c) of this chapter; or * * * * *

Subpart H— Inter Partes Reexamination of Patents That Issued From an Original Application Filed in the United States on or After November 29, 1999

§ 1.913. Persons eligible to file, and time for filing, a request for inter partes reexamination.

(a) Except as provided for in § 1.907 and in paragraph (b) of this section, any person other than the patent owner or its privies may, at any time during the period of enforceability of a patent which issued from an original application filed in the United States on or after November 29, 1999, file a request for inter partes reexamination by the Office of any claim of the patent on the basis of prior art patents or printed publications cited under § 1.501.

(b) Any request for an inter partes reexamination submitted on or after September 16, 2012, will not be accorded a filing date, and any such request will not be granted.

§ 1.915. Content of request for inter partes reexamination.

* * * * *

(b) * * *

(2) A citation of the patents and printed publications which are presented to provide a showing that there is a reasonable likelihood that the requester will prevail with respect to at least one of the claims challenged in the request.

(3) A statement pointing out, based on the cited patents and printed publications, each showing of a reasonable likelihood that the requester will prevail with respect to at least one of the claims challenged in the request, and a detailed explanation of the pertinency and manner of applying the patents and printed publications to every claim for which reexamination is requested.

* * * * *

§ 1.923. Examiner's determination on the request for inter partes reexamination.

Within three months following the filing date of a request for inter partes reexamination under § 1.915, the examiner will consider the request and determine whether or not the request and the prior art establish a reasonable likelihood that the requester will prevail with respect to at least one of the claims challenged in the request. The examiner's determination will be based on the claims in effect at the time of the determination, will become a part of the official file of the patent, and will be mailed to the patent owner at the address as provided for in § 1.33(c) and to the third party requester. If the examiner determines that the request has not established a reasonable likelihood that the requester will prevail with respect to at least one of the challenged claims, the examiner shall refuse the request and shall not order inter partes reexamination.

§ 1.927. Petition to review refusal to order inter partes reexamination.

The third party requester may seek review by a petition to the Director under § 1.181 within one month of the mailing date of the examiner's determination refusing to order inter partes reexamination. Any such petition must comply with § 1.181(b). If no petition is timely filed or if the decision on petition affirms that a reasonable likelihood that the requester will prevail with respect to at least one of the claims challenged in the request has not been established, the determination shall be final and nonappealable.

§ 1.931. Order for inter partes reexamination.

(a) If it is found that there is a reasonable likelihood that the requester will prevail with respect to at least one of the claims challenged in the request, the determination will include an order for inter partes reexamination of the patent for resolution of the question of whether the requester will prevail.

§ 1.937. Conduct of *inter partes* reexamination.

* * * * *

(a) All *inter partes* reexamination proceedings, including any appeals to the Patent Trial and Appeal Board, will be conducted with special dispatch within the Office, unless the Director makes a determination that there is good cause for suspending the reexamination proceeding.

* * *

(d) A petition in an *inter partes* reexamination proceeding must be accompanied by the fee set forth in § 1.20(c)(6), except for petitions under § 1.956 to extend the period for response by a patent owner, petitions under § 1.958 to accept a delayed response by a patent owner, petitions under § 1.78 to accept an unintentionally delayed benefit claim, and petitions under § 1.530(l) for correction of inventorship in a reexamination proceeding.

Appeal to the Patent Trial and Appeal Board in Inter Partes Reexamination

§ 1.959. Appeal in *inter partes* reexamination.

Appeals to the Patent Trial and Appeal Board under 35 U.S.C. 134(c) are conducted according to part 41 of this title.

§ 1.979. Return of Jurisdiction from the Patent Trial and Appeal Board; termination of appeal proceedings.

(a) Jurisdiction over an *inter partes* reexamination proceeding passes to the examiner after a decision by the Patent Trial and Appeal Board upon transmittal of the file to the examiner, subject to each appellant's right of appeal or other review, for such further action as the condition of the *inter partes* reexamination proceeding may require, to carry into effect the decision of the Patent Trial and Appeal Board.

(b) Upon judgment in the appeal before the Patent Trial and Appeal Board, if no further appeal has been taken (§ 1.983), the prosecution in the *inter partes* reexamination proceeding will be terminated and the Director will issue and publish a certificate under § 1.997 concluding the proceeding. If an appeal to the U.S. Court of Appeals for the Federal Circuit has been filed, that appeal is considered terminated when the mandate is issued by the Court.

§ 1.981. Reopening after a final decision of the Patent Trial and Appeal Board.

When a decision by the Patent Trial and Appeal Board on appeal has become final for judicial review, prosecution of the *inter partes* reexamination proceeding will not be reopened or reconsidered by the primary examiner except under the provisions of § 41.77 of this title without the written authority of the Director, and then only for the consideration of matters not already adjudicated, sufficient cause being shown.

§ 1.983. Appeal to the United States Court of Appeals for the Federal Circuit in inter partes reexamination.

(a) The patent owner or third party requester in an *inter partes* reexamination proceeding who is a party to an appeal to the Patent Trial and Appeal Board and who is dissatisfied with the decision of the Patent Trial and Appeal Board may, subject to § 41.81, appeal to the U.S. Court of Appeals for the Federal Circuit and may be a party to any appeal thereto taken from a reexamination decision of the Patent Trial and Appeal Board.

* * * * *

(c) If the patent owner has filed a notice of appeal to the U.S. Court of Appeals for the Federal Circuit, the third party requester may cross appeal to the U.S. Court of Appeals for the Federal Circuit if also dissatisfied with the decision of the Patent Trial and Appeal Board.

(d) If the third party requester has filed a notice of appeal to the U.S. Court of Appeals for the Federal Circuit, the patent owner may cross appeal to the U.S. Court of Appeals for the Federal Circuit if also dissatisfied with the decision of the Patent Trial and Appeal Board.

* * * * *

(f) Notwithstanding any provision of the rules, in any reexamination proceeding commenced prior to November 2, 2002, the third party requester is precluded from appealing and cross appealing any decision of the Patent

Trial and Appeal Board to the U.S. Court of Appeals for the Federal Circuit, and the third party requester is precluded from participating in any appeal taken by the patent owner to the U.S. Court of Appeals for the Federal Circuit.

§ 1.985. Notification of prior or concurrent proceedings in inter partes reexamination.

(a) In any *inter partes* reexamination proceeding, the patent owner shall call the attention of the Office to any prior or concurrent proceedings in which the patent is or was involved, including but not limited to interference or trial before the Patent Trial and Appeal Board, reissue, reexamination, or litigation and the results of such proceedings.

(b) Notwithstanding any provision of the rules, any person at any time may file a paper in an *inter partes* reexamination proceeding notifying the Office of a prior or concurrent proceeding in which the same patent is or was involved, including but not limited to interference or trial before the Patent Trial and Appeal Board, reissue, reexamination, or litigation and the results of such proceedings. Such paper must be limited to merely providing notice of the other proceeding without discussion of issues of the current *inter partes* reexamination proceeding.

§ 1.993. Suspension of concurrent interference and inter partes reexamination proceeding.

If a patent in the process of *inter partes* reexamination is or becomes involved in an interference or trial before the Patent Trial and Appeal Board, the Director may suspend the *inter partes* reexamination, interference, or trial. The Director will not consider a request to suspend an interference or trial unless a motion under § 41.121(a)(3) of this title to suspend the interference or trial has been presented to, and denied by, an administrative patent judge and the request is filed within ten (10) days of a decision by an administrative patent judge denying the motion for suspension or such other time as the administrative patent judge may set.

PART 3— ASSIGNMENT, RECORDING AND RIGHTS OF ASSIGNEE

Authority: 15 U.S.C. 1123; 35 U.S.C. 2(b)(2).

§ 3.31. Cover sheet content.

* * * * *

(h) The assignment cover sheet required by § 3.28 must

contain a conspicuous indication of an intent to utilize the assignment as the required oath or declaration under § 1.63 of this chapter.

§ 3.71. Prosecution by assignee.

(a) *Patents—conducting of prosecution.* One or more assignees as defined in paragraph (b) of this section may conduct prosecution of a national patent application as the applicant under § 1.46 of this title, or conduct prosecution of a supplemental examination or reexamination proceeding, to the exclusion of the inventor or previous applicant or patent owner. Conflicts between purported assignees are handled in accordance with § 3.73(c)(3).

(b) Patents—assignee(s) who can prosecute. The assignee(s) who may conduct either the prosecution of a national application for patent as the applicant under § 1.46 of this title or a supplemental examination or reexamination proceeding are:

(1) A single assignee. An assignee of the entire right, title and interest in the application or patent, or

(2) Partial assignee(s) together or with inventor(s). All partial assignees, or all partial assignees and inventors who have not assigned their right, title and interest in the application or patent, who together own the entire right, title and interest in the application or patent. A partial assignee is any assignee having less than the entire right, title and interest in the application or patent. The word "assignee" as used in this chapter means with respect to patent matters the single assignee of the entire right, title and interest in the application or patent if there is such a single assignee, or all of the partial assignees, or all of the partial assignee and inventors who have not assigned their interest in the application or patent, who together own the entire right, title and interest in the application or patent.

(c) Patents—Becoming of record. An assignee becomes of record as the applicant in a national patent application under § 1.46 of this title, and in a supplemental examination or reexamination proceeding, by filing a statement in compliance with § 3.73(c) that is signed by a party who is authorized to act on behalf of the assignee.

* * * * *

§ 3.73. Establishing right of assignee to take action.

(a) The original applicant is presumed to be the owner

of an application for an original patent, and any patent that may issue therefrom, unless there is an assignment. The original applicant is presumed to be the owner of a trademark application or registration, unless there is an assignment.

(b) In order to request or take action in a trademark matter, the assignee must establish its ownership of the trademark property of paragraph (a) of this section to the satisfaction of the Director. The establishment of ownership by the assignee may be combined with the paper that requests or takes the action. Ownership is established by submitting to the Office a signed statement identifying the assignee, accompanied by either:

(1) Documentary evidence of a chain of title from the original owner to the assignee (e.g., copy of an executed assignment). The documents submitted to establish ownership may be required to be recorded pursuant to § 3.11 in the assignment records of the Office as a condition to permitting the assignee to take action in a matter pending before the Office; or

(2) A statement specifying where documentary evidence of a chain of title from the original owner to the assignee is recorded in the assignment records of the Office (e.g., reel and frame number).

(c) (1) In order to request or take action in a patent matter, an assignee who is not the original applicant must establish its ownership of the patent property of paragraph (a) of this section to the satisfaction of the Director. The establishment of ownership by the assignee may be combined with the paper that requests or takes the action. Ownership is established by submitting to the Office a signed statement identifying the assignee, accompanied by either:

(i) Documentary evidence of a chain of title from the original owner to the assignee (e.g., copy of an executed assignment). The submission of the documentary evidence must be accompanied by a statement affirming that the documentary evidence of the chain of title from the original owner to the assignee was or concurrently is being submitted for recordation pursuant to § 3.11; or

(ii) A statement specifying where documentary evidence of a chain of title from the original owner to the assignee is recorded in the assignment records of the Office (e.g., reel and frame number).

(2) If the submission is by an assignee of less than the entire right, title and interest (*e.g.,* more than one assignee exists) the Office may refuse to accept the submission as an establishment of ownership unless:

(i) Each assignee establishes the extent (by percentage) of its ownership interest, so as to account for the entire right, title and interest in the application or patent by all parties including inventors; or

(ii) Each assignee submits a statement identifying the parties including inventors who together own the entire right, title and interest and stating that all the identified parties own the entire right, title and interest.

(3) If two or more purported assignees file conflicting statements under paragraph (c)(1) of this section, the Director will determine which, if any, purported assignee will be permitted to control prosecution of the application.

(d) The submission establishing ownership under paragraph (b) or (c) of this section must show that the person signing the submission is a person authorized to act on behalf of the assignee by:

(1) Including a statement that the person signing the submission is authorized to act on behalf of the assignee;

(2) Being signed by a person having apparent authority to sign on behalf of the assignee; or

(3) For patent matters only, being signed by a practitioner of record.

PART 5— SECRECY OF CERTAIN INVENTIONS AND LICENSES TO EXPORT AND FILE APPLICATIONS IN FOREIGN COUNTRIES

Authority: 35 U.S.C. 2(b)(2), 41, 181–188, as amended by the Patent Law Foreign Filing Amendments Act of 1988, Pub. L. 100-418, 102 Stat. 1567; the Arms Export Control Act, as amended, 22 U.S.C. 2751 et seq.; the Atomic Energy Act of 1954, as amended, 42 U.S.C. 2011 et seq.; the Nuclear Non Proliferation Act of 1978, 22 U.S.C. 3201 et seq.; and the delegations in the regulations under these Acts to the Director (15 CFR 370.10(j), 22 CFR 125.04, and 10 CFR 810.7).

§ 5.3. Prosecution of application under secrecy orders; withholding patent.

* * * * *

(b) An interference or derivation will not be instituted involving a national application under secrecy order. An applicant whose application is under secrecy order may suggest an interference (§ 41.202(a) of this title), but the Office will not act on the request while the application remains under a secrecy order.

* * * * *

§ 5.25. Petition for retroactive license.

(a) * * *

(3) * * *

(iii) An explanation of why the material was filed abroad through error without the required license under § 5.11 first having been obtained, and

* * * * *

(b) The explanation in paragraph (a) of this section must include a showing of facts rather than a mere allegation of action through error. The showing of facts as to the nature of the error should include statements by those persons having personal knowledge of the acts regarding filing in a foreign country and should be accompanied by copies of any necessary supporting documents such as letters of transmittal or instructions for filing. The acts which are alleged to constitute error should cover the period leading up to and including each of the proscribed foreign filings.

* * * * *

PART 10— REPRESENTATION OF OTHERS BEFORE THE PATENT AND TRADEMARK OFFICE

Authority: 5 U.S.C. 500, 15 U.S.C. 1123; 35 U.S.C. 2(b)(2), 31, 32, 41.

§ 10.1. Definitions.

* * * * *

(s) A proceeding before the Office includes an application, a reexamination, a protest, a public use proceeding, a patent interference, a trial before the Patent Trial and Appeal Board, an inter partes trademark proceeding, or any other proceeding which is pending before the Office.

* * * * *

§ 10.23. Misconduct.

* * * * *

(c) * * *

(11) [Reserved]

* * * * *

PART 11— REPRESENTATION OF OTHERS

BEFORE THE UNITED STATES PATENT AND TRADEMARK OFFICE

Authority: 5 U.S.C. 500, 15 U.S.C. 1123, 35 U.S.C. 2(b)(2), 32, 41.

§ 11.1. Definitions.

* * * * *

Grievance means a written submission from any source received by the OED Director that presents possible grounds for discipline of a specified practitioner.

§ 11.5. Register of attorneys and agents in patent matters; practice before the office.

* * * * *

(b) * * *

(1) *Practice before the Office in patent matters.* Practice before the Office in patent matters includes, but is not limited to, preparing and prosecuting any patent application, consulting with or giving advice to a client in contemplation of filing a patent application or other document with the Office, drafting the specification or claims of a patent application; drafting an amendment or reply to a communication from the Office that may require written argument to establish the patentability of a claimed invention; drafting a reply to a communication from the Office regarding a patent application; and drafting a communication for a public use, interference, reexamination proceeding, petition, appeal to or any other proceeding before the Patent Trial and Appeal Board, or other proceeding. Registration to practice before the Office in patent cases sanctions the performance of those services which are reasonably necessary and incident to the preparation and prosecution of patent applications or other proceeding before the Office involving a patent application or patent in which the practitioner is authorized to participate. The services include:

* * * * *

§ 11.6. Registration of attorneys and agents.

* * * * *

(d) *Patent Trial and Appeal Board matters.* For action by a person who is not registered in a proceeding before the Patent Trial and Appeal Board, see § 41.5(a) or § 42.10(c) of this title.

* * * * *

§ 11.10. Restrictions on practice in patent matters.

* * * * *

(b) * * *

(3) * * *

(iii) Particular patent or patent application means any patent or patent application, including, but not limited to, a provisional, substitute, international, continuation, divisional, continuation-in-part, or reissue patent application, as well as any protest, reexamination, petition, appeal, interference, or trial proceeding based on the patent or patent application.

* * * * *

§ 11.22. [Amended]

Section 11.22 is amended by removing and reserving paragraph (c).

§ 11.34. Complaint.

* * * * *

(d) Time for filing a complaint. A complaint shall be filed within one year after the date on which the OED Director receives a grievance forming the basis of the complaint. No complaint shall be filed more than ten years after the date on which the misconduct forming the basis for the proceeding occurred.

(e) Tolling agreements. The one-year period for filing a complaint under paragraph (d) of this section shall be tolled if the involved practitioner and the OED Director agree in writing to such tolling.

§ 11.58. Duties of disciplined or resigned practitioner, or practitioner on disability inactive status.

* * * * *

(b) * * *

(1) * * *

(i) File a notice of withdrawal as of the effective date of the exclusion, suspension, acceptance of resignation, or transfer to disability inactive status in each pending patent and trademark application, each pending reexamination and interference or trial proceeding, and every other matter pending in the Office, together with a copy of the notices sent pursuant to paragraphs (b) and (c) of this section;

* * * * *

PART 41— PRACTICE BEFORE THE PATENT

TRIAL AND APPEAL BOARD

Authority: 35 U.S.C. 2(b)(2), 3(a)(2)(A), 21, 23, 32, 41, 132, 133, 134, 135, 306, and 315.

§ 41.1. Policy.

(a) Scope. Part 41 governs appeals and interferences before the Patent Trial and Appeal Board. Sections 1.1 to 1.36 and 1.181 to 1.183 of this title also apply to practice before the Board, as do other sections of part 1 of this title that are incorporated by reference into part 41.

§ 41.2. Definitions.

* * * * *

Board means the Patent Trial and Appeal Board and includes:

* * * * *

§ 41.9. Action by owner.

(a) *Entire interest.* An owner of the entire interest in an application or patent involved in a Board proceeding may act in the proceeding to the exclusion of the inventor (*see* §§ 3.71 and 3.73 of this title).

* * * * *

§ 41.10. Correspondence addresses.

Except as the Board may otherwise direct,

(a) *Appeals.* Correspondence in an application or a patent involved in an appeal (subparts B and C of this part) during the period beginning when an appeal docketing notice is issued and ending when a decision has been rendered by the Board, as well as any request for rehearing of a decision by the Board, shall be mailed to: Patent Trial and Appeal Board, United States Patent and Trademark Office, PO Box 1450, Alexandria, Virginia 22313-1450. Notices of appeal, appeal briefs, reply briefs, requests for oral hearing, as well as all other correspondence in an application or a patent involved in an appeal to the Board for which an address is not otherwise specified, should be addressed as set out in § 1.1(a)(1)(i) of this title.

(b) *Interferences.* Mailed correspondence in interference (subpart D of this part) shall be sent to Mail Stop INTERFERENCE, Patent Trial and Appeal Board, United States Patent and Trademark Office, PO Box 1450, Alexandria, Virginia 22313-1450.

(c) *Trial Proceedings.* Correspondence in trial proceedings (part 42 of this title) are governed by § 42.6(b) of this title.

§ 41.20. Fees.

(a) *Petition fee.* The fee for filing a petition under this part is: $400.00.

(b) *Appeal fees.* (1) For filing a notice of appeal from the examiner to the Patent Trial and Appeal Board:

By a micro entity (§ 1.29)	$200.00
By a small entity (§ 1.27(a))	400.00
By other than a small or micro entity	800.00

(2) (i) For filing a brief in support of an appeal in an application or *ex parte* reexamination proceeding: $0.00.

(ii) In addition to the fee for filing a notice of appeal, for filing a brief in support of an appeal in an *inter partes* reexamination proceeding:

By a micro entity (§ 1.29)	$500.00
By a small entity (§ 1.27(a))	1,000.00
By other than a small or micro entity	2,000.00

(3) For filing a request for an oral hearing before the Board in an appeal under 35 U.S.C. 134:

By a micro entity (§ 1.29)	$325.00
By a small entity (§ 1.27(a))	650.00
By other than a small or micro entity	1,300.00

(4) In addition to the fee for filing a notice of appeal, for forwarding an appeal in an application or *ex parte* reexamination proceeding to the Board:

By a micro entity (§ 1.29)	$500.00
By a small entity (§ 1.27(a))	1,000.00
By other than a small or micro entity	2,000.00

§ 41.30. Definitions.

* * * * *

Proceeding means either a national application for a patent, an application for reissue of a patent, an ex parte reexamination proceeding, or a trial before the Patent Trial and Appeal Board. Appeal to the Board in an *inter partes* reexamination proceeding is controlled by subpart C of this part.

* * * * *

§ 41.37. Appeal brief.

(a) *Timing.* Appellant must file a brief under this section within two months from the date of filing the notice of appeal under § 41.31. The appeal brief fee in an application or *ex parte* reexamination proceeding is $0.00, but if the appeal results in an examiner's answer, the appeal forwarding fee set forth in § 41.20(b)(4) must be paid within the time period specified in § 41.48 to avoid dismissal of an appeal.

(b) *Failure to file a brief.* On failure to file the brief within the period specified in paragraph (a) of this section, the appeal will stand dismissed.

(c) * * *

(1) * * *

(ii) *Related appeals, interferences, and trials.* A statement identifying by application, patent, appeal, interference, or trial number all other prior and pending appeals, interferences, trials before the Board, or judicial proceedings (collectively, "related cases") which satisfy all of the following conditions: involve an application or patent owned by the appellant or assignee, are known to appellant, the appellant's legal representative, or assignee, and may be related to, directly affect or be directly affected by or have a bearing on the Board's decision in the pending appeal, except that such statement is not required if there are no such related cases. If an appeal brief does not contain a statement of related cases, the Office may assume that there are no such related cases.

(iii) *Summary of claimed subject matter.* A concise explanation of the subject matter defined in each of the rejected independent claims, which shall refer to the specification in the Record by page and line number or by paragraph number, and to the drawing, if any, by reference characters. For each rejected independent claim, and for each dependent claim argued separately under the provisions of paragraph (c)(1)(iv) of this section, if the claim contains a means plus function or step plus function recitation as permitted by 35 U.S.C. 112(f), then the concise explanation must identify the structure, material, or acts described in the specification in the Record as corresponding to each claimed function with reference to the specification in the Record by page and line number or by paragraph number, and to the drawing, if any, by reference characters. Reference to the patent application publication does not satisfy the requirements of this paragraph.

§ 41.45. Appeal forwarding fee.

(a) *Timing.* Appellant in an application or *ex parte* reexamination proceeding must pay the fee set forth in § 41.20(b)(4) within the later of two months from the date of either the examiner's answer, or a decision refusing to grant a petition under § 1.181 of this chapter to designate a new ground of rejection in an examiner's answer.

(b) *Failure to pay appeal forwarding fee.* On failure to fee set forth in § 41.20(b)(4) within the period specified in paragraph (a) of this section, the appeal will stand dismissed.

(c) *Extensions of time.* Extensions of time under § 1.136(a) of this title for patent applications are not applicable to the time period set forth in this section. *See* § 1.136(b) of this title for extensions of time to reply for patent applications and § 1.550(c) of this title for extensions of time to reply for *ex parte* reexamination proceedings.

§ 41.67. Appellant's brief.

* * * * *

(c) (1) * * *

(ii) *Related appeals, interferences, and trials.* A statement identifying by application, patent, appeal, interference, or trial number all other prior and pending appeals, interferences, trials before the Board, or judicial proceedings known to appellant, the appellant's legal representative, or assignee which may be related to, directly affect or be directly affected by or have a bearing on the Board's decision in the pending appeal. Copies of any decisions rendered by a court or the Board in any proceeding identified under this paragraph must be included in an appendix as required by paragraph (c)(1)(xi) of this section.

* * * * *

(v) *Summary of claimed subject matter.* A concise explanation of the subject matter defined in each of the independent claims involved in the appeal, which shall refer to the specification by column and line number, and to the drawing(s), if any, by reference characters. For each independent claim involved in the appeal and for each dependent claim argued separately under the provisions of paragraph (c)(1)(vii) of this section, every means plus function and step plus function as permitted by 35 U.S.C. 112(f), must be identified and the structure, material, or acts described in the specification as corresponding to each claimed function must be set forth with reference to the specification by page and line number, and to the drawing, if any, by reference characters.

§ 41.68. Respondent's brief.

* * * * *

(b) (1) * * *

(ii) *Related Appeals, Interferences, and trials.* A statement identifying by application, patent, appeal, interference, or trial number all other prior and pending appeals, interferences or judicial proceedings known to respondent, the respondent's legal representative, or assignee which may be related to, directly affect or be directly affected by or have a bearing on the Board's decision in the pending appeal. Copies of any decisions rendered by a court or the Board in any proceeding identified under this paragraph must be included in an appendix as required by paragraph (b)(1)(ix) of this section.

§ 41.77. Decisions and other actions by the Board.

(a) The Patent Trial and Appeal Board, in its decision, may affirm or reverse each decision of the examiner on all issues raised on each appealed claim, or remand the reexamination proceeding to the examiner for further consideration. The reversal of the examiner's determination not to make a rejection proposed by the third party requester constitutes a decision adverse to the patentability of the claims which are subject to that proposed rejection which will be set forth in the decision of the Patent Trial and Appeal Board as a new ground of rejection under paragraph (b) of this section. The affirmance of the rejection of a claim on any of the grounds specified constitutes a general affirmance of the decision of the examiner on that claim, except as to any ground specifically reversed.

* * * * *

§ 41.110. Filing claim information.

(b) * * *

(2) For each involved claim that contains a means-plus-function or step-plus- function limitation in the form permitted under 35 U.S.C. 112(f), file an annotated copy of the claim indicating in bold face between braces ({ }) the specific portions of the specification that describe the structure, material, or acts corresponding to each claimed function.

§ 41.201. Definitions.

* * * * *

Threshold issue * * *

(2) * * *

(ii) Unpatentability for lack of written description under 35 U.S.C. 112(a) of an involved application claim where the applicant suggested, or could have suggested, an interference under § 41.202(a).

§ 41.202. Suggesting an interference.

* * * * *

(b) *Patentee.* A patentee cannot suggest an interference under this section but may, to the extent permitted under § 1.291 of this title, alert the examiner of an application claiming interfering subject matter to the possibility of an interference.

* * * * *

PART 42— TRIAL PRACTICE BEFORE THE PATENT TRIAL AND APPEAL BOARD

Subpart A—Trial Practice and Procedure

General

42.1 Policy.
42.2 Definitions.
42.3 Jurisdiction.
42.4 Notice of trial.
42.5 Conduct of the proceeding.
42.6 Filing of documents, including exhibits; service.
42.7 Management of the record.
42.8 Mandatory notices.
42.9 Action by patent owner.
42.10 Counsel.

42.11 Duty of candor.
42.12 Sanctions.
42.13 Citation of authority.
42.14 Public availability.

Fees

42.15 Fees.

Petition and Motion Practice

42.20 Generally.
42.21 Notice of basis for relief.
42.22 Content of petitions and motions.
42.23 Oppositions and replies.
42.24 Page limits for petitions, motions, oppositions and replies.
42.25 Default filing times.

Testimony and Production

42.51 Discovery.
42.52 Compelling testimony and production.
42.53 Taking testimony.
42.54 Protective order.
42.55 Confidential information in a petition.
42.56 Expungement of confidential information.
42.61 Admissibility.
42.62 Applicability of the Federal Rules of Evidence.
42.63 Form of evidence.
42.64 Objection; motion to exclude; motion in limine.
42.65 Expert testimony; tests and data.

Oral Argument, Decision, and Settlement

42.70 Oral argument.
42.71 Decision on petitions or motions.
42.72 Termination of trial.
42.73 Judgment.
42.74 Settlement.

Certificate

42.80 Certificate.

Subpart D—Transitional Program for Covered Business Method Patents

Subpart E—Derivation

General

Instituting Derivation Proceeding

After Institution of Derivation Proceeding

Authority: 35 U.S.C. 2(b)(2), 6, 21, 23, 41, 135, 311, 312, 316, 321–326 and Leahy-Smith America Invents Act, Pub. L. 112-29, sections 6(c), 6(f) and 18, 125 Stat. 284, 304, 311, and 329 (2011).

Subpart A— Trial Practice and Procedure

General

§ 42.1. Policy.

(a) *Scope.* Part 42 governs proceedings before the Patent Trial and Appeal Board. Sections 1.4, 1.7, 1.14, 1.16, 1.22, 1.23, 1.25, 1.26, 1.32, 1.34, and 1.36 of this chapter also apply to proceedings before the Board, as do other sections of part 1 of this chapter that are incorporated by reference into this part.

(b) *Construction.* This part shall be construed to secure the just, speedy, and inexpensive resolution of every proceeding.

(c) *Decorum.* Every party must act with courtesy and decorum in all proceedings before the Board, including in interactions with other parties.

(d) *Evidentiary standard.* The default evidentiary standard is a preponderance of the evidence.

§ 42.2. Definitions.

The following definitions apply to this part:

Affidavit means affidavit or declaration under § 1.68 of this chapter. A transcript of an *ex parte* deposition or a declaration under 28 U.S.C. 1746 may be used as an affidavit.

Board means the Patent Trial and Appeal Board. Board means a panel of the Board, or a member or employee acting with the authority of the Board, including:

(1) For petition decisions and interlocutory decisions, a Board member or employee acting with the authority of the Board.

(2) For final written decisions under 35 U.S.C. 135(d), 318(a), and 328(a), a panel of the Board.

Business day means a day other than a Saturday, Sunday, or Federal holiday within the District of Columbia.

Confidential information means trade secret or other confidential research, development, or commercial information.

Final means final for the purpose of judicial review to the extent available. A decision is final only if it disposes of all necessary issues with regard to the party seeking judicial review, and does not indicate that further action is required.

Hearing means consideration of the trial.

Involved means an application, patent, or claim that

is the subject of the proceeding.

Judgment means a final written decision by the Board, or a termination of a proceeding.

Motion means a request for relief other than by petition.

Office means the United States Patent and Trademark Office.

Panel means at least three members of the Board.

Party means at least the petitioner and the patent owner and, in a derivation proceeding, any applicant or assignee of the involved application.

Petition is a request that a trial be instituted.

Petitioner means the party filing a petition requesting that a trial be instituted.

Preliminary Proceeding begins with the filing of a petition for instituting a trial and ends with a written decision as to whether a trial will be instituted.

Proceeding means a trial or preliminary proceeding.

Rehearing means reconsideration.

Trial means a contested case instituted by the Board based upon a petition. A trial begins with a written decision notifying the petitioner and patent owner of the institution of the trial. The term trial specifically includes a derivation proceeding under 35 U.S.C. 135; an *inter partes* review under Chapter 31 of title 35, United States Code; a post-grant review under Chapter 32 of title 35, United States Code; and a transitional business-method review under section 18 of the Leahy-Smith America Invents Act. Patent interferences are administered under part 41 and not under part 42 of this title, and therefore are not trials.

§ 42.3. Jurisdiction.

(a) The Board may exercise exclusive jurisdiction within the Office over every involved application and patent during the proceeding, as the Board may order.

(b) A petition to institute a trial must be filed with the Board consistent with any time period required by statute.

§ 42.4. Notice of trial.

(a) *Institution of trial.* The Board institutes the trial on behalf of the Director.

(b) Notice of a trial will be sent to every party to the proceeding. The entry of the notice institutes the trial.

(c) The Board may authorize additional modes of notice, including:

(1) Sending notice to another address associated with the party, or

(2) Publishing the notice in the Official Gazette of the United States Patent and Trademark Office or the Federal Register.

§ 42.5. Conduct of the proceeding.

(a) The Board may determine a proper course of conduct in a proceeding for any situation not specifically covered by this part and may enter non-final orders to administer the proceeding.

(b) The Board may waive or suspend a requirement of parts 1, 41, and 42 and may place conditions on the waiver or suspension.

(c) *Times.* (1) *Setting times.* The Board may set times by order. Times set by rule are default and may be modified by order. Any modification of times will take any applicable statutory pendency goal into account.

(2) *Extension of time.* A request for an extension of time must be supported by a showing of good cause.

(3) *Late action.* A late action will be excused on a showing of good cause or upon a Board decision that consideration on the merits would be in the interests of justice.

(d) *Ex parte communications.* Communication regarding a specific proceeding with a Board member defined in 35 U.S.C. 6(a) is not permitted unless both parties have an opportunity to be involved in the communication.

§ 42.6. Filing of documents, including exhibits; service.

(a) *General format requirements.* (1) Page size must be 81/2 inch × 11 inch except in the case of exhibits that require a larger size in order to preserve details of the original.

(2) In documents, including affidavits, created for the proceeding:

(i) Markings must be in black or must otherwise provide an equivalent dark, high-contrast image;

(ii) Either a proportional or monospaced font may be used:

(A) The proportional font must be 14- point or

larger, and

(B) The monospaced font must not contain more than four characters per centimeter (ten characters per inch);

(iii) Double spacing must be used except in claim charts, headings, tables of contents, tables of authorities, indices, signature blocks, and certificates of service. Block quotations may be 1.5 spaced, but must be indented from both the left and the right margins; and

(iv) Margins must be at least 2.5 centimeters (1 inch) on all sides.

(3) *Incorporation by reference; combined documents.* Arguments must not be incorporated by reference from one document into another document. Combined motions, oppositions, replies, or other combined documents are not permitted.

(4) *Signature; identification.* Documents must be signed in accordance with §§ 1.33 and 11.18(a) of this title, and should be identified by the trial number (where known).

(b) *Modes of filing.* (1) Electronic filing. Unless otherwise authorized, submissions are to be made to the Board electronically via the Internet according to the parameters established by the Board and published on the Web site of the Office.

(2) (i) *Filing by means other than electronic filing.* A document filed by means other than electronic filing must:

(A) Be accompanied by a motion requesting acceptance of the submission; and

(B) Identify a date of transmission where a party seeks a filing date other than the date of receipt at the Board.

(ii) Mailed correspondence shall be sent to: Mail Stop PATENT BOARD, Patent Trial and Appeal Board, United States Patent and Trademark Office, PO Box 1450, Alexandria, Virginia 22313-1450.

(c) *Exhibits.* Each exhibit must be filed with the first document in which it is cited except as the Board may otherwise order.

(d) *Previously filed paper.* A document already in the record of the proceeding must not be filed again, not even as an exhibit or an appendix, without express Board authorization.

(e) *Service.* (1) *Electronic or other mode.* Service may be made electronically upon agreement of the parties. Otherwise, service may be by EXPRESS MAIL® or by means at least as fast and reliable as EXPRESS MAIL®.

(2) *Simultaneous with filing.* Each document filed with the Board, if not previously served, must be served simultaneously on each opposing party.

(3) *Counsel of record.* If a party is represented by counsel of record in the proceeding, service must be on counsel.

(4) *Certificate of service.* (i) Each document, other than an exhibit, must include a certificate of service at the end of that document. Any exhibit filed with the document may be included in the certification for the document.

(ii) For an exhibit filed separately, a transmittal letter incorporating the certificate of service must be filed. If more than one exhibit is filed at one time, a single letter should be used for all of the exhibits filed together. The letter must state the name and exhibit number for every exhibit filed with the letter.

(iii) The certificate of service must state:

(A) The date and manner of service; and

(B) The name and address of every person served.

§ 42.7. Management of the record.

(a) The Board may expunge any paper directed to a proceeding or filed while an application or patent is under the jurisdiction of the Board that is not authorized under this part or in a Board order or that is filed contrary to a Board order.

(b) The Board may vacate or hold in abeyance any non-Board action directed to a proceeding while an application or patent is under the jurisdiction of the Board unless the action was authorized by the Board.

§ 42.8. Mandatory notices.

(a) Each notice listed in paragraph (b) of this section must be filed with the Board:

(1) By the petitioner, as part of the petition;

(2) By the patent owner, or applicant in the case of derivation, within 21 days of service of the petition; or

(3) By either party, within 21 days of a change of the

information listed in paragraph (b) of this section stated in an earlier paper.

(b) Each of the following notices must be filed:

(1) Real party-in-interest. Identify each real party-in-interest for the party.

(2) Related matters. Identify any other judicial or administrative matter that would affect, or be affected by, a decision in the proceeding.

(3) *Lead and back-up counsel.* If the party is represented by counsel, then counsel must be identified.

(4) Service information. Identify (if applicable):

(i) An electronic mail address;

(ii) A postal mailing address;

(iii) A hand-delivery address, if different than the postal mailing address;

(iv) A telephone number; and

(v) A facsimile number.

§ 42.9. Action by patent owner.

(a) *Entire interest.* An owner of the entire interest in an involved application or patent may act to the exclusion of the inventor (see § 3.71 of this title).

(b) *Part interest.* An owner of a part interest in the subject patent may move to act to the exclusion of an inventor or a co-owner. The motion must show the inability or refusal of an inventor or co-owner to prosecute the proceeding or other cause why it is in the interests of justice to permit the owner of a part interest to act in the trial. In granting the motion, the Board may set conditions on the actions of the parties.

§ 42.10. Counsel.

(a) If a party is represented by counsel, the party must designate a lead counsel and a back-up counsel who can conduct business on behalf of the lead counsel.

(b) A power of attorney must be filed with the designation of counsel, except the patent owner should not file an additional power of attorney if the designated counsel is already counsel of record in the subject patent or application.

(c) The Board may recognize counsel *pro hac vice* during a proceeding upon a showing of good cause, subject to the condition that lead counsel be a registered practitioner and to any other conditions as the Board may impose. For example, where the lead counsel is a registered practitioner, a motion to appear *pro hac vice* by counsel who is not a registered practitioner may be granted upon showing that counsel is an experienced litigating attorney and has an established familiarity with the subject matter at issue in the proceeding.

(d) A panel of the Board may disqualify counsel for cause after notice and opportunity for hearing. A decision to disqualify is not final for the purposes of judicial review until certified by the Chief Administrative Patent Judge.

(e) Counsel may not withdraw from a proceeding before the Board unless the Board authorizes such withdrawal.

§ 42.11. Duty of candor.

Parties and individuals involved in the proceeding have a duty of candor and good faith to the Office during the course of a proceeding.

§ 42.12. Sanctions.

(a) The Board may impose a sanction against a party for misconduct, including:

(1) Failure to comply with an applicable rule or order in the proceeding;

(2) Advancing a misleading or frivolous argument or request for relief;

(3) Misrepresentation of a fact;

(4) Engaging in dilatory tactics;

(5) Abuse of discovery;

(6) Abuse of process; or

(7) Any other improper use of the proceeding, including actions that harass or cause unnecessary delay or an unnecessary increase in the cost of the proceeding.

(b) Sanctions include entry of one or more of the following:

(1) An order holding facts to have been established in the proceeding;

(2) An order expunging or precluding a party from filing a paper;

(3) An order precluding a party from presenting or contesting a particular issue;

(4) An order precluding a party from requesting, obtaining, or opposing discovery;

(5) An order excluding evidence;

(6) An order providing for compensatory expenses, including attorney fees;

(7) An order requiring terminal disclaimer of patent term; or

(8) Judgment in the trial or dismissal of the petition.

§ 42.13. Citation of authority.

(a) For any United States Supreme Court decision, citation to the United States Reports is preferred.

(b) For any decision other than a United States Supreme Court decision, citation to the West Reporter System is preferred.

(c) Citations to authority must include pinpoint citations whenever a specific holding or portion of an authority is invoked.

(d) Non-binding authority should be used sparingly. If the authority is not an authority of the Office and is not reproduced in the United States Reports or the West Reporter System, a copy of the authority should be provided.

§ 42.14. Public availability.

The record of a proceeding, including documents and things, shall be made available to the public, except as otherwise ordered. A party intending a document or thing to be sealed shall file a motion to seal concurrent with the filing of the document or thing to be sealed. The document or thing shall be provisionally sealed on receipt of the motion and remain so pending the outcome of the decision on the motion.

Fees

§ 42.15. Fees.

(a) On filing a petition for *inter partes* review of a patent, payment of the following fees are due:

(1) *Inter Partes* Review request fee: $9,000.00.

(2) *Inter Partes* Review Post- Institution fee: $14,000.00.

(3) In addition to the *Inter Partes* Review request fee, for requesting review of each claim in excess of 20: $200.00.

(4) In addition to the *Inter Partes* Post- Institution request fee, for requesting review of each claim in excess of 15: $400.00.

(b) On filing a petition for post-grant review or covered business method patent review of a patent, payment of the following fees are due:

(1) Post-Grant or Covered Business Method Patent Review request fee: $12,000.00.

(2) Post-Grant or Covered Business Method Patent Review Post-Institution fee: $18,000.00.

(3) In addition to the Post-Grant or Covered Business Method Patent Review request fee, for requesting review of each claim in excess of 20: $250.00.

(4) In addition to the Post-Grant or Covered Business Method Patent Review request fee Post-Institution request fee, for requesting review of each claim in excess of 15: $550.00.

(c) On the filing of a petition for a derivation proceeding, payment of the following fees is due:

(1) Derivation petition fee: $400.00.

(d) Any request requiring payment of a fee under this part, including a written request to make a settlement agreement available: $400.00.

Petition and Motion Practice

§ 42.20. Generally.

(a) *Relief.* Relief, other than a petition requesting the institution of a trial, must be requested in the form of a motion.

(b) Prior authorization. A motion will not be entered without Board authorization. Authorization may be provided in an order of general applicability or during the proceeding.

(c) Burden of proof. The moving party has the burden of proof to establish that it is entitled to the requested relief.

(d) Briefing. The Board may order briefing on any issue involved in the trial.

§ 42.21. Notice of basis for relief.

(a) *Notice of request for relief.* The Board may require a party to file a notice stating the relief it requests and the basis for its entitlement to relief. A notice must include sufficient detail to place the Board and each opponent on notice of the precise relief requested. A notice is not evidence except as an admission by a party-opponent.

(b) *Filing and service.* The Board may set the times and

conditions for filing and serving notices required under this section. The Board may provide for the notice filed with the Board to be maintained in confidence for a limited time.

(c) *Effect.* If a notice under paragraph (a) of this section is required:

(1) A failure to state a sufficient basis for relief may result in a denial of the relief requested;

(2) A party will be limited to filing motions consistent with the notice; and

(3) Ambiguities in the notice will be construed against the party.

(d) Correction. A party may move to correct its notice. The motion should be filed promptly after the party becomes aware of the basis for the correction. A correction filed after the time set for filing notices will only be entered if entry would serve the interests of justice.

§ 42.22. Content of petitions and motions.

(a) Each petition or motion must be filed as a separate paper and must include:

(1) A statement of the precise relief requested; and

(2) A full statement of the reasons for the relief requested, including a detailed explanation of the significance of the evidence including material facts, and the governing law, rules, and precedent.

(b) Relief requested. Where a rule in part 1 of this title ordinarily governs the relief sought, the petition or motion must make any showings required under that rule in addition to any showings required in this part.

(c) Statement of material facts. Each petition or motion may include a statement of material fact. Each material fact preferably shall be set forth as a separately numbered sentence with specific citations to the portions of the record that support the fact.

(d) The Board may order additional showings or explanations as a condition for authorizing a motion (*see* § 42.20(b)).

§ 42.23. Oppositions and replies.

(a) Oppositions and replies must comply with the content requirements for motions and must include a statement identifying material facts in dispute. Any material fact not specifically denied may be considered admitted.

(b) All arguments for the relief requested in a motion must be made in the motion. A reply may only respond to arguments raised in the corresponding opposition or patent owner response.

§ 42.24. Page limits for petitions, motions, oppositions, and replies.

(a) *Petitions and motions.* (1) The following page limits for petitions and motions apply and include any statement of material facts to be admitted or denied in support of the petition or motion. The page limit does not include a table of contents, a table of authorities, a certificate of service, or appendix of exhibits.

(i) Petition requesting *inter partes* review: 60 pages.

(ii) Petition requesting post-grant review: 80 pages.

(iii) Petition requesting covered business method patent review: 80 pages.

(iv) Petition requesting derivation proceeding: 60 pages.

(v) Motions: 15 pages.

(2) Petitions to institute a trial must comply with the stated page limits but may be accompanied by a motion to waive the page limits. The petitioner must show in the motion how a waiver of the page limits is in the interests of justice and must append a copy of proposed petition exceeding the page limit to the motion. If the motion is not granted, the proposed petition exceeding the page limit may be expunged or returned. Any other motion to waive page limits must be granted in advance of filing a motion, opposition, or reply for which the waiver is necessary.

(b) *Patent owner responses and oppositions.* The page limits set forth in this paragraph do not include a listing of facts which are admitted, denied, or cannot be admitted or denied.

(1) The page limits for a patent owner preliminary response to petition are the same as the page limits for the petition.

(2) The page limits for a patent owner response to petition are the same as the page limits for the petition.

(3) The page limits for oppositions are the same as those for corresponding motions.

(c) Replies. The following page limits for replies apply and include the required statement of facts in support of the reply. The page limits do not include a table of contents, a table of authorities, a listing of facts which are admitted, denied, or cannot be admitted or denied, a certificate of service, or appendix of exhibits.

(1) Replies to patent owner responses to petitions: 15 pages.

(2) Replies to oppositions: 5 pages.

§ 42.25. Default filing times.

(a) A motion may only be filed according to a schedule set by the Board. The default times for acting are:

(1) An opposition is due one month after service of the motion; and

(2) A reply is due one month after service of the opposition.

(b) A party should seek relief promptly after the need for relief is identified. Delay in seeking relief may justify a denial of relief sought.

Testimony and Production

§ 42.51. Discovery.

(a) *Mandatory initial disclosures.*

(1) With agreement. Parties may agree to mandatory discovery requiring the initial disclosures set forth in the Office Patent Trial Practice Guide.

(i) The parties must submit any agreement reached on initial disclosures by no later than the filing of the patent owner preliminary response or the expiration of the time period for filing such a response. The initial disclosures of the parties shall be filed as exhibits.

(ii) Upon the institution of a trial, parties may automatically take discovery of the information identified in the initial disclosures.

(2) Without agreement. Where the parties fail to agree to the mandatory discovery set forth in paragraph (a)(1), a party may seek such discovery by motion.

(b) Limited discovery. A party is not entitled to discovery except as provided in paragraph (a) of this section, or as otherwise authorized in this subpart.

(1) Routine discovery. Except as the Board may otherwise order:

(i) Unless previously served or otherwise by agreement of the parties, any exhibit cited in a paper or in testimony must be served with the citing paper or testimony.

(ii) Cross examination of affidavit testimony is authorized within such time period as the Board may set.

(iii) Unless previously served, a party must serve relevant information that is inconsistent with a position advanced by the party during the proceeding concurrent with the filing of the documents or things that contains the inconsistency. This requirement does not make discoverable anything otherwise protected by legally recognized privileges such as attorney-client or attorney work product. This requirement extends to inventors, corporate officers, and persons involved in the preparation or filing of the documents or things.

(2) Additional discovery. (i) The parties may agree to additional discovery between themselves. Where the parties fail to agree, a party may move for additional discovery. The moving party must show that such additional discovery is in the interests of justice, except in post-grant reviews where additional discovery is limited to evidence directly related to factual assertions advanced by either party in the proceeding (see § 42.224). The Board may specify conditions for such additional discovery.

(ii) When appropriate, a party may obtain production of documents and things during cross examination of an opponent's witness or during authorized compelled testimony under § 42.52.

(c) Production of documents. Except as otherwise ordered by the Board, a party producing documents and things shall either provide copies to the opposing party or make the documents and things available for inspection and copying at a reasonable time and location in the United States.

§ 42.52. Compelling testimony and production.

(a) *Authorization* required. A party seeking to compel testimony or production of documents or things must file a motion for authorization. The motion must describe the general relevance of the testimony, document, or thing, and must:

(1) In the case of testimony, identify the witness by name or title; and

(2) In the case of a document or thing, the general

nature of the document or thing.

(b) Outside the United States. For testimony or production sought outside the United States, the motion must also:

(1) In the case of testimony. (i) Identify the foreign country and explain why the party believes the witness can be compelled to testify in the foreign country, including a description of the procedures that will be used to compel the testimony in the foreign country and an estimate of the time it is expected to take to obtain the testimony; and

(ii) Demonstrate that the party has made reasonable efforts to secure the agreement of the witness to testify in the United States but has been unsuccessful in obtaining the agreement, even though the party has offered to pay the travel expenses of the witness to testify in the United States.

(2) In the case of production of a document or thing. (i) Identify the foreign country and explain why the party believes production of the document or thing can be compelled in the foreign country, including a description of the procedures that will be used to compel production of the document or thing in the foreign country and an estimate of the time it is expected to take to obtain production of the document or thing; and

(ii) Demonstrate that the party has made reasonable efforts to obtain the agreement of the individual or entity having possession, custody, or control of the document or thing to produce the document or thing in the United States but has been unsuccessful in obtaining that agreement, even though the party has offered to pay the expenses of producing the document or thing in the United States.

§ 42.53. Taking testimony.

(a) *Form.* Uncompelled direct testimony must be submitted in the form of an affidavit. All other testimony, including testimony compelled under 35 U.S.C. 24, must be in the form of a deposition transcript. Parties may agree to video-recorded testimony, but may not submit such testimony without prior authorization of the Board. In addition, the Board may authorize or require live or video-recorded testimony.

(b) *Time and location.* (1) Uncompelled direct testimony may be taken at any time to support a petition, motion, opposition, or reply; otherwise, testimony may only be taken during a testimony period set by the Board.

(2) Except as the Board otherwise orders, during the testimony period, deposition testimony may be taken at any reasonable time and location within the United States before any disinterested official authorized to administer oaths at that location.

(3) Uncompelled deposition testimony outside the United States may only be taken upon agreement of the parties or as the Board specifically directs.

(c) *Duration.* (1) Unless stipulated by the parties or ordered by the Board, direct examination, cross-examination, and redirect examination for compelled deposition testimony shall be subject to the following time limits: Seven hours for direct examination, four hours for cross-examination, and two hours for redirect examination.

(2) Unless stipulated by the parties or ordered by the Board, cross-examination, redirect examination, and re-cross examination for uncompelled direct deposition testimony shall be subject to the following time limits: Seven hours for cross-examination, four hours for redirect examination, and two hours for re-cross examination.

(d) *Notice of deposition.* (1) Prior to the taking of deposition testimony, all parties to the proceeding must agree on the time and place for taking testimony. If the parties cannot agree, the party seeking the testimony must initiate a conference with the Board to set a time and place.

(2) Cross-examination should ordinarily take place after any supplemental evidence relating to the direct testimony has been filed and more than a week before the filing date for any paper in which the cross-examination testimony is expected to be used. A party requesting cross-examination testimony of more than one witness may choose the order in which the witnesses are to be cross-examined.

(3) In the case of direct deposition testimony, at least three business days prior to the conference in paragraph (d)(1) of this section, or if there is no conference, at least ten days prior to the deposition, the party seeking the direct testimony must serve:

(i) A list and copy of each document under the

party's control and on which the party intends to rely; and

(ii) A list of, and proffer of reasonable access to, anything other than a document under the party's control and on which the party intends to rely.

(4) The party seeking the deposition must file a notice of the deposition at least ten business days before a deposition.

(5) Scope and content— (i) For direct deposition testimony, the notice limits the scope of the testimony and must list:

(A) The time and place of the deposition;

(B) The name and address of the witness;

(C) A list of the exhibits to be relied upon during the deposition; and

(D) A general description of the scope and nature of the testimony to be elicited.

(ii) For cross-examination testimony, the scope of the examination is limited to the scope of the direct testimony.

(iii) The notice must list the time and place of the deposition.

(iv) Where an additional party seeks to take direct testimony of a third party witness at the time and place noticed in paragraph (d)(5) of this section, the additional party must provide a counter notice that lists the exhibits to be relied upon in the deposition and a general description of the scope and nature of the testimony to be elicited.

(6) Motion to quash—Objection to a defect in the notice is waived unless the objecting party promptly seeks authorization to file a motion to quash.

(e) Deposition in a foreign language. If an interpreter will be used during the deposition, the party calling the witness must initiate a conference with the Board at least five business days before the deposition.

(f) Manner of taking deposition testimony. (1) Beforc giving deposition testimony, each witness shall be duly sworn according to law by the officer before whom the deposition is to be taken. The officer must be authorized to take testimony under 35 U.S.C. 23.

(2) The testimony shall be taken with any questions and answers recorded in their regular order by the of-

ficer, or by some other disinterested person in the presence of the officer, unless the presence of the officer is waived on the record by agreement of all parties.

(3) Any exhibits used during the deposition must be numbered as required by § 42.63(c), and must, if not previously served, be served at the deposition. Exhibits objected to shall be accepted pending a decision on the objection.

(4) All objections made at the time of the deposition to the qualifications of the officer taking the deposition, the manner of taking it, the evidence presented, the conduct of any party, and any other objection to the deposition shall be noted on the record by the officer.

(5) When the testimony has been transcribed, the witness shall read and sign (in the form of an affidavit) a transcript of the deposition unless:

(i) The parties otherwise agree in writing;

(ii) The parties waive reading and signature by the witness on the record at the deposition; or

(iii) The witness refuses to read or sign the transcript of the deposition.

(6) The officer shall prepare a certified transcript by attaching a certificate in the form of an affidavit signed and sealed by the officer to the transcript of the deposition. Unless the parties waive any of the following requirements, in which case the certificate shall so state, the certificate must state:

(i) The witness was duly sworn by the officer before commencement of testimony by the witness;

(ii) The transcript is a true record of the testimony given by the witness;

(iii) The name of the person who recorded the testimony, and if the officer did not record it, whether the testimony was recorded in the presence of the officer;

(iv) The presence or absence of any opponent;

(v) The place where the deposition was taken and the day and hour when the deposition began and ended;

(vi) The officer has no disqualifying interest, personal or financial, in a party; and

(vii) If a witness refuses to read or sign the

transcript, the circumstances under which the witness refused.

(7) Except where the parties agree otherwise, the proponent of the testimony must arrange for providing a copy of the transcript to all other parties. The testimony must be filed by proponent as an exhibit.

(8) Any objection to the content, form, or manner of taking the deposition, including the qualifications of the officer, is waived unless made on the record during the deposition and preserved in a timely filed motion to exclude.

(g) Costs. Except as the Board may order or the parties may agree in writing, the proponent of the direct testimony shall bear all costs associated with the testimony, including the reasonable costs associated with making the witness available for the cross-examination.

§ 42.54. Protective order.

(a) A party may file a motion to seal where the motion to seal contains a proposed protective order, such as the default protective order set forth in the Office Patent Trial Practice Guide. The motion must include a certification that the moving party has in good faith conferred or attempted to confer with other affected parties in an effort to resolve the dispute. The Board may, for good cause, issue an order to protect a party or person from disclosing confidential information, including, but not limited to, one or more of the following:

(1) Forbidding the disclosure or discovery;

(2) Specifying terms, including time and place, for the disclosure or discovery;

(3) Prescribing a discovery method other than the one selected by the party seeking discovery;

(4) Forbidding inquiry into certain matters, or limiting the scope of disclosure or discovery to certain matters;

(5) Designating the persons who may be present while the discovery is conducted;

(6) Requiring that a deposition be sealed and opened only by order of the Board;

(7) Requiring that a trade secret or other confidential research, development, or commercial information not be revealed or be revealed only in a specified way; and

(8) Requiring that the parties simultaneously file

specified documents or information in sealed envelopes, to be opened as the Board directs.

(b) [Reserved].

§ 42.55. Confidential information in a petition.

A petitioner filing confidential information with a petition may, concurrent with the filing of the petition, file a motion to seal with a proposed protective order as to the confidential information. The institution of the requested trial will constitute a grant of the motion to seal unless otherwise ordered by the Board.

(a) Default protective order. Where a motion to seal requests entry of the default protective order set forth in the Office Patent Trial Practice Guide, the petitioner must file, but need not serve, the confidential information under seal. The patent owner may only access the filed sealed information prior to the institution of the trial by agreeing to the terms of the default protective order or obtaining relief from the Board.

(b) *Protective* orders other than default protective order. Where a motion to seal requests entry of a protective order other than the default protective order, the petitioner must file, but need not serve, the confidential information under seal. The patent owner may only access the sealed confidential information prior to the institution of the trial by:

(1) agreeing to the terms of the protective order requested by the petitioner;

(2) agreeing to the terms of a protective order that the parties file jointly; or

(3) obtaining entry of a protective order (e.g., the default protective order).

§ 42.56. Expungement of confidential information.

After denial of a petition to institute a trial or after final judgment in a trial, a party may file a motion to expunge confidential information from the record.

§ 42.61. Admissibility.

(a) Evidence that is not taken, sought, or filed in accordance with this subpart is not admissible.

(b) Records of the Office. Certification is not necessary as a condition to admissibility when the evidence to be submitted is a record of the Office to which all parties have access.

(c) Specification and drawings. A specification or drawing of a United States patent application or patent is admissible as evidence only to prove what the specification or drawing describes. If there is data in the specification or a drawing upon which a party intends to rely to prove the truth of the data, an affidavit by an individual having first-hand knowledge of how the data was generated must be filed.

§ 42.62. Applicability of the Federal rules of evidence.

(a) *Generally.* Except as otherwise provided in this subpart, the Federal Rules of Evidence shall apply to a proceeding.

(b) *Exclusions.* Those portions of the Federal Rules of Evidence relating to criminal proceedings, juries, and other matters not relevant to proceedings under this subpart shall not apply.

(c) *Modifications in terminology.* Unless otherwise clear from context, the following terms of the Federal Rules of Evidence shall be construed as indicated:

Appellate court means United States Court of Appeals for the Federal Circuit.

Civil action, civil proceeding, and *action* mean a proceeding before the Board under part 42.

Courts of the United States, U.S. Magistrate, court, trial court, trier of fact, and *judge* mean Board.

Hearing means, as defined in Federal Rule of Evidence 804(a)(5), the time for taking testimony.

Judicial notice means official notice.

Trial or *hearing* in Federal Rule of Evidence 807 means the time for taking testimony.

(d) In determining foreign law, the Board may consider any relevant material or source, including testimony, whether or not submitted by a party or admissible under the Federal Rules of Evidence.

§ 42.63. Form of evidence.

(a) *Exhibits required.* Evidence consists of affidavits, transcripts of depositions, documents, and things. All evidence must be filed in the form of an exhibit.

(b) *Translation required.* When a party relies on a document or is required to produce a document in a language other than English, a translation of the document into English and an affidavit attesting to the accuracy of the translation must be filed with the document.

(c) *Exhibit numbering.* Each party's exhibits must be uniquely numbered sequentially in a range the Board specifies. For the petitioner, the range is 1001-1999, and for the patent owner, the range is 2001-2999.

(d) *Exhibit format.* An exhibit must conform with the requirements for papers in § 42.6 and the requirements of this paragraph.

(1) Each exhibit must have an exhibit label.

(i) An exhibit filed with the petition must include the petitioner's name followed by a unique exhibit number.

(ii) For exhibits not filed with the petition, the exhibit label must include the party's name followed by a unique exhibit number, the names of the parties, and the trial number.

(2) When the exhibit is a paper:

(i) Each page must be uniquely numbered in sequence; and

(ii) The exhibit label must be affixed to the lower right corner of the first page of the exhibit without obscuring information on the first page or, if obscuring is unavoidable, affixed to a duplicate first page.

(e) *Exhibit list.* Each party must maintain an exhibit list with the exhibit number and a brief description of each exhibit. If the exhibit is not filed, the exhibit list should note that fact. A current exhibit list must be served whenever evidence is served and the current exhibit list must be filed when filing exhibits.

§ 42.64. Objection; motion to exclude; motion in limine.

(a) *Deposition evidence.* An objection to the admissibility of deposition evidence must be made during the deposition. Evidence to cure the objection must be provided during the deposition, unless the parties to the deposition stipulate otherwise on the deposition record.

(b) *Other evidence.* For evidence other than deposition evidence:

(1) *Objection.* Any objection to evidence submitted during a preliminary proceeding must be served within ten business days of the institution of the trial. Once a trial has been instituted, any objection must be served within five business days of service of evidence to which the objection is directed. The objection must identify the

grounds for the objection with sufficient particularity to allow correction in the form of supplemental evidence.

(2) *Supplemental evidence.* The party relying on evidence to which an objection is timely served may respond to the objection by serving supplemental evidence within ten business days of service of the objection.

(c) *Motion to exclude.* A motion to exclude evidence must be filed to preserve any objection. The motion must identify the objections in the record in order and must explain the objections. The motion may be filed without prior authorization from the Board.

§ 42.65. Expert testimony; tests and data.

(a) Expert testimony that does not disclose the underlying facts or data on which the opinion is based is entitled to little or no weight. Testimony on United States patent law or patent examination practice will not be admitted.

(b) If a party relies on a technical test or data from such a test, the party must provide an affidavit explaining:

(1) Why the test or data is being used;

(2) How the test was performed and the data was generated;

(3) How the data is used to determine a value;

(4) How the test is regarded in the relevant art; and

(5) Any other information necessary for the Board to evaluate the test and data.

Oral Argument, Decision, and Settlement

§ 42.70. Oral argument.

(a) *Request for oral argument.* A party may request oral argument on an issue raised in a paper at a time set by the Board. The request must be filed as a separate paper and must specify the issues to be argued.

(b) Demonstrative exhibits must be served at least five business days before the oral argument and filed no later than the time of the oral argument.

§ 42.71. Decision on petitions or motions.

(a) *Order of consideration.* The Board may take up petitions or motions for decisions in any order, may grant, deny, or dismiss any petition or motion, and may enter any appropriate order.

(b) *Interlocutory decisions.* A decision on a motion without a judgment is not final for the purposes of judicial review. If a decision is not a panel decision, the party may request that a panel rehear the decision. When rehearing a nonpanel decision, a panel will review the decision for an abuse of discretion. A panel decision on an issue will govern the trial.

(c) *Petition decisions.* A decision by the Board on whether to institute a trial is final and non-appealable. A party may request rehearing on a decision by the Board on whether to institute a trial pursuant to paragraph (d) of this section. When rehearing a decision on petition, a panel will review the decision for an abuse of discretion.

(d) *Rehearing.* A party dissatisfied with a decision may file a request for rehearing, without prior authorization from the Board. The burden of showing a decision should be modified lies with the party challenging the decision. The request must specifically identify all matters the party believes the Board misapprehended or overlooked, and the place where each matter was previously addressed in a motion, an opposition, or a reply. A request for rehearing does not toll times for taking action. Any request must be filed:

(1) Within 14 days of the entry of a non-final decision or a decision to institute a trial as to at least one ground of unpatentability asserted in the petition; or

(2) Within 30 days of the entry of a final decision or a decision not to institute a trial.

§ 42.72. Termination of trial.

The Board may terminate a trial without rendering a final written decision, where appropriate, including where the trial is consolidated with another proceeding or pursuant to a joint request under 35 U.S.C. 317(a) or 327(a).

§ 42.73. Judgment.

(a) A judgment, except in the case of a termination, disposes of all issues that were, or by motion reasonably could have been, raised and decided.

(b) *Request for adverse judgment.* A party may request judgment against itself at any time during a proceeding. Actions construed to be a request for adverse judgment include:

(1) Disclaimer of the involved application or patent;

(2) Cancellation or disclaimer of a claim such that the party has no remaining claim in the trial;

(3) Concession of unpatentability or derivation of the

contested subject matter; and

(4) Abandonment of the contest.

(c) *Recommendation.* The judgment may include a recommendation for further action by an examiner or by the Director.

(d) *Estoppel.* (1) *Petitioner other than in derivation proceeding.* A petitioner, or the real party in interest or privy of the petitioner, is estopped in the Office from requesting or maintaining a proceeding with respect to a claim for which it has obtained a final written decision on patentability in an *inter partes* review, post-grant review, or a covered business method patent review, on any ground that the petitioner raised or reasonably could have raised during the trial, except that estoppel shall not apply to a petitioner, or to the real party in interest or privy of the petitioner who has settled under 35 U.S.C. 317 or 327.

(2) *In a derivation,* the losing party who could have properly moved for relief on an issue, but did not so move, may not take action in the Office after the judgment that is inconsistent with that party's failure to move, except that a losing party shall not be estopped with respect to any contested subject matter for which that party was awarded a favorable judgment.

(3) *Patent applicant or owner.* A patent applicant or owner is precluded from taking action inconsistent with the adverse judgment, including obtaining in any patent:

(i) A claim that is not patentably distinct from a finally refused or canceled claim; or

(ii) An amendment of a specification or of a drawing that was denied during the trial proceeding, but this provision does not apply to an application or patent that has a different written description.

§ 42.74. Settlement.

(a) *Board role.* The parties may agree to settle any issue in a proceeding, but the Board is not a party to the settlement and may independently determine any question of jurisdiction, patentability, or Office practice.

(b) *Agreements in writing.* Any agreement or understanding between the parties made in connection with, or in contemplation of, the termination of a proceeding shall be in writing and a true copy shall be filed with the Board before the termination of the trial.

(c) *Request to keep separate.* A party to a settlement may request that the settlement be treated as business confidential information and be kept separate from the files of an involved patent or application. The request must be filed with the settlement. If a timely request is filed, the settlement shall only be available:

(1) To a Government agency on written request to the Board; or

(2) To any other person upon written request to the Board to make the settlement agreement available, along with the fee specified in § 42.15(d) and on a showing of good cause.

Certificate

§ 42.80. Certificate.

After the Board issues a final written decision in an *inter partes* review, post-grant review, or covered business method patent review and the time for appeal has expired or any appeal has terminated, the Office will issue and publish a certificate canceling any claim of the patent finally determined to be unpatentable, confirming any claim of the patent determined to be patentable, and incorporating in the patent any new or amended claim determined to be patentable by operation of the certificate.

Subpart B— Inter Partes Review

Sec.

General

Instituting *Inter partes* Review

After Institution of *Inter partes* Review

§ 42.100. Procedure; pendency.

(a) An *inter partes* review is a trial subject to the procedures set forth in subpart A of this part.

(b) A claim in an unexpired patent shall be given its broadest reasonable construction in light of the specification of the patent in which it appears.

(c) An *inter partes* review proceeding shall be administered such that pendency before the Board after institution is normally no more than one year. The time can be extended by up to six months for good cause by the Chief Administrative Patent Judge, or adjusted by the Board in the case of joinder.

§ 42.101. Who may petition for inter partes review.

A person who is not the owner of a patent may file with the Office a petition to institute an *inter partes* review of the patent unless:

(a) Before the date on which the petition for review is filed, the petitioner or real party-in-interest filed a civil action challenging the validity of a claim of the patent;

(b) The petition requesting the proceeding is filed more than one year after the date on which the petitioner, the petitioner's real party-in-interest, or a privy of the petitioner is served with a complaint alleging infringement of the patent; or

(c) The petitioner, the petitioner's real party-in-interest, or a privy of the petitioner is estopped from challenging the claims on the grounds identified in the petition.

§ 42.102. Time for filing.

(a) A petition for inter partes review of a patent must be filed after the later of the following dates, where applicable:

(1) If the patent is a patent described in section 3(n)(1) of the Leahy-Smith America Invents Act, the date that is nine months after the date of the grant of the patent;

(2) If the patent is a patent that is not described in section 3(n)(1) of the Leahy-Smith American Invents

Act, the date of the grant of the patent; or

(3) If a post-grant review is instituted as set forth in subpart C of this part, the date of the termination of such post-grant review.

(b) The Director may impose a limit on the number of *inter partes* reviews that may be instituted during each of the first four one-year periods in which the amendment made to chapter 31 of title 35, United States Code, is in effect by providing notice in the Office's Official Gazette or Federal Register. Petitions filed after an established limit has been reached will be deemed untimely.

§ 42.103. Inter partes review fee.

(a) An *inter partes* review fee set forth in § 42.15(a) must accompany the petition.

(b) No filing date will be accorded to the petition until full payment is received.

§ 42.104. Content of petition.

In addition to the requirements of §§ 42.6, 42.8, 42.22, and 42.24, the petition must set forth:

(a) *Grounds for standing.* The petitioner must certify that the patent for which review is sought is available for *inter partes* review and that the petitioner is not barred or estopped from requesting an *inter partes* review challenging the patent claims on the grounds identified in the petition.

(b) *Identification of challenge.* Provide a statement of the precise relief requested for each claim challenged. The statement must identify the following:

(1) The claim;

(2) The specific statutory grounds under 35 U.S.C. 102 or 103 on which the challenge to the claim is based and the patents or printed publications relied upon for each ground;

(3) How the challenged claim is to be construed. Where the claim to be construed contains a means-plus-function or step-plus-function limitation as permitted under 35 U.S.C. 112(f), the construction of the claim must identify the specific portions of the specification that describe the structure, material, or acts corresponding to each claimed function;

(4) How the construed claim is unpatentable under the statutory grounds identified in paragraph (b)(2) of this section. The petition must specify where each ele-

ment of the claim is found in the prior art patents or printed publications relied upon; and

(5) The exhibit number of the supporting evidence relied upon to support the challenge and the relevance of the evidence to the challenge raised, including identifying specific portions of the evidence that support the challenge. The Board may exclude or give no weight to the evidence where a party has failed to state its relevance or to identify specific portions of the evidence that support the challenge.

(c) A motion may be filed that seeks to correct a clerical or typographical mistake in the petition. The grant of such a motion does not change the filing date of the petition.

§ 42.105. Service of petition.

In addition to the requirements of § 42.6, the petitioner must serve the petition and exhibits relied upon in the petition as follows:

(a) The petition and supporting evidence must be served on the patent owner at the correspondence address of record for the subject patent. The petitioner may additionally serve the petition and supporting evidence on the patent owner at any other address known to the petitioner as likely to effect service.

(b) Upon agreement of the parties, service may be made electronically. Service may be by EXPRESS MAIL® or by means at least as fast and reliable as EXPRESS MAIL®. Personal service is not required.

§ 42.106. Filing date.

(a) Complete petition. A petition to institute *inter partes* review will not be accorded a filing date until the petition satisfies all of the following requirements:

(1) Complies with § 42.104;

(2) Effects service of the petition on the correspondence address of record as provided in § 42.105(a); and

(3) Is accompanied by the fee to institute required in § 42.15(a).

(b) *Incomplete petition.* Where a party files an incomplete petition, no filing date will be accorded, and the Office will dismiss the petition if the deficiency in the petition is not corrected within one month from the notice of an incomplete petition.

§ 42.107. Preliminary response to petition.

(a) The patent owner may file a preliminary response

to the petition. The response is limited to setting forth the reasons why no *inter partes* review should be instituted under 35 U.S.C. 314. The response can include evidence except as provided in paragraph (c) of this section. The preliminary response is subject to the page limits under § 42.24.

(b) *Due date.* The preliminary response must be filed no later than three months after the date of a notice indicating that the request to institute an *inter partes* review has been granted a filing date. A patent owner may expedite the proceeding by filing an election to waive the patent owner preliminary response.

(c) *No new testimonial evidence.* The preliminary response shall not present new testimony evidence beyond that already of record, except as authorized by the Board.

(d) *No amendment.* The preliminary response shall not include any amendment.

(e) *Disclaim Patent Claims.* The patent owner may file a statutory disclaimer under 35 U.S.C. 253(a) in compliance with § 1.321(a) of this chapter, disclaiming one or more claims in the patent. No *inter partes* review will be instituted based on disclaimed claims.

Instituting Inter Partes Review

§ 42.108. Institution of inter partes review.

(a) When instituting *inter partes* review, the Board may authorize the review to proceed on all or some of the challenged claims and on all or some of the grounds of unpatentability asserted for each claim.

(b) At any time prior to institution of *inter partes* review, the Board may deny some or all grounds for unpatentability for some or all of the challenged claims. Denial of a ground is a Board decision not to institute *inter partes* review on that ground.

(c) *Sufficient grounds. Inter partes* review shall not be instituted for a ground of unpatentability unless the Board decides that the petition supporting the ground would demonstrate that there is a reasonable likelihood that at least one of the claims challenged in the petition is unpatentable. The Board's decision will take into account a patent owner preliminary response where such a response is filed.

After Institution of Inter Partes Review

§ 42.120. Patent owner response.

(a) *Scope.* A patent owner may file a response to the petition addressing any ground for unpatentability not already denied. A patent owner response is filed as an opposition and is subject to the page limits provided in § 42.24.

(b) *Due date for response.* If no time for filing a patent owner response to a petition is provided in a Board order, the default date for filing a patent owner response is three months from the date the *inter partes* review was instituted.

§ 42.121. Amendment of the patent.

(a) Motion to amend. A patent owner may file one motion to amend a patent, but only after conferring with the Board.

(1) *Due date.* Unless a due date is provided in a Board order, a motion to amend must be filed no later than the filing of a patent owner response.

(2) *Scope.* A motion to amend may be denied where:

(i) The amendment does not respond to a ground of unpatentability involved in the trial; or

(ii) The amendment seeks to enlarge the scope of the claims of the patent or introduce new subject matter.

(3) A reasonable number of substitute claims. A motion to amend may cancel a challenged claim or propose a reasonable number of substitute claims. The presumption is that only one substitute claim would be needed to replace each challenged claim, and it may be rebutted by a demonstration of need.

(b) *Content.* A motion to amend claims must include a claim listing, show the changes clearly, and set forth:

(1) The support in the original disclosure of the patent for each claim that is added or amended; and

(2) The support in an earlier-filed disclosure for each claim for which benefit of the filing date of the earlier filed disclosure is sought.

(c) *Additional motion to amend.* In addition to the requirements set forth in paragraphs (a) and (b) of this section, any additional motion to amend may not be filed without Board authorization. An additional motion to amend may be authorized when there is a good cause showing or a joint request of the petitioner and the patent owner to materially advance a settlement. In determining whether to authorize such an additional motion to amend, the Board will consider whether a petitioner has submitted supplemental information after the time period set for filing a motion to amend in paragraph (a)(1) of this section.

§ 42.122. Multiple proceedings and Joinder.

(a) *Multiple proceedings.* Where another matter involving the patent is before the Office, the Board may during the pendency of the *inter partes* review enter any appropriate order regarding the additional matter including providing for the stay, transfer, consolidation, or termination of any such matter.

(b) *Request for joinder.* Joinder may be requested by a patent owner or petitioner. Any request for joinder must be filed, as a motion under § 42.22, no later than one month after the institution date of any *inter partes* review for which joinder is requested. The time period set forth in § 42.101(b) shall not apply when the petition is accompanied by a request for joinder.

§ 42.123. Filing of supplemental information.

(a) *Motion to submit supplemental information.* Once a trial has been instituted, a party may file a motion to submit supplemental information in accordance with the following requirements:

(1) A request for the authorization to file a motion to submit supplemental information is made within one month of the date the trial is instituted.

(2) The supplemental information must be relevant to a claim for which the trial has been instituted.

(b) *Late submission of supplemental information.* A party seeking to submit supplemental information more than one month after the date the trial is instituted, must request authorization to file a motion to submit the information. The motion to submit supplemental information must show why the supplemental information reasonably could not have been obtained earlier, and that consideration of the supplemental information would be in the interests-of-justice.

(c) *Other supplemental information.* A party seeking to submit supplemental information not relevant to a claim for which the trial has been instituted must request authorization to file a motion to submit the information. The motion must show why the supplemental information reasonably could not have been obtained earlier, and that consideration of the supplemental information would be in the interests-of-justice.

Subpart C— Post-Grant Review

§ 42.200. Procedure; pendency.

(a) A post-grant review is a trial subject to the procedures set forth in subpart A of this part.

(b) A claim in an unexpired patent shall be given its broadest reasonable construction in light of the specification of the patent in which it appears.

(c) A post-grant review proceeding shall be administered such that pendency before the Board after institution is normally no more than one year. The time can be extended by up to six months for good cause by the Chief Administrative Patent Judge, or adjusted by the Board in the case of joinder.

(d) Interferences commenced before September 16, 2012, shall proceed under part 41 of this chapter except as the Chief Administrative Patent Judge, acting on behalf of the Director, may otherwise order in the interests-of-justice.

§ 42.201. Who may petition for a post-grant review.

A person who is not the owner of a patent may file with the Office a petition to institute a post-grant review of the patent unless:

(a) Before the date on which the petition for review is filed, the petitioner or real party-in-interest filed a civil action challenging the validity of a claim of the patent; or

(b) The petitioner, the petitioner's real party-in-interest, or a privy of the petitioner is estopped from challenging the claims on the grounds identified in the petition.

§ 42.202. Time for filing.

(a) A petition for a post-grant review of a patent must be filed no later than the date that is nine months after the date of the grant of a patent or of the issuance of a reissue patent. A petition, however, may not request a post-grant review for a claim in a reissue patent that is identical to or narrower than a claim in the original patent from which the reissue patent was issued unless the petition is filed not later than the date that is nine months after the date of the grant of the original patent.

(b) The Director may impose a limit on the number of post-grant reviews that may be instituted during each of the first four one-year periods in which 35 U.S.C. 321 is in effect by providing notice in the Office's Official Gazette or Federal Register. Petitions filed after an established limit has been reached will be deemed untimely.

§ 42.203. Post-grant review fee.

(a) A post-grant review fee set forth in § 42.15(b) must accompany the petition.

(b) No filing date will be accorded to the petition until full payment is received.

§ 42.204. Content of petition.

In addition to the requirements of §§ 42.6, 42.8, 42.22, and 42.24, the petition must set forth:

(a) *Grounds for standing.* The petitioner must certify that the patent for which review is sought is available for post-grant review and that the petitioner is not barred or estopped from requesting a post-grant review challenging the patent claims on the grounds identified in the petition.

(b) *Identification of challenge.* Provide a statement of the precise relief requested for each claim challenged. The statement must identify the following:

(1) The claim;

(2) The specific statutory grounds permitted under 35 U.S.C. 282(b)(2) or (3) on which the challenge to the claim is based;

(3) How the challenged claim is to be construed. Where the claim to be construed contains a means-plus-function or step-plus-function limitation as permitted under 35 U.S.C. 112(f), the construction of the claim must identify the specific portions of the specification that describe the structure, material, or acts corresponding to each claimed function;

(4) How the construed claim is unpatentable under the statutory grounds identified in paragraph (b)(2) of this section. Where the grounds for unpatentability are based on prior art, the petition must specify where each element of the claim is found in the prior art. For all other grounds of unpatentability, the petition must identify the specific part of the claim that fails to comply with the statutory grounds raised and state how the identified subject matter fails to comply with the statute; and

(5) The exhibit number of the supporting evidence relied upon to support the challenge and the relevance of the evidence to the challenge raised, including identifying specific portions of the evidence that support the challenge. The Board may exclude or give no weight to the evidence where a party has failed to state its relevance or to identify specific portions of the evidence that support the challenge.

(c) A motion may be filed that seeks to correct a clerical or typographical mistake in the petition. The grant of such a motion does not change the filing date of the petition.

§ 42.205. Service of petition.

In addition to the requirements of § 42.6, the petitioner must serve the petition and exhibits relied upon in the petition as follows:

(a) The petition and supporting evidence must be served on the patent owner at the correspondence address of record for the subject patent. The petitioner may additionally serve the petition and supporting evidence on the patent owner at any other address known to the petitioner as likely to effect service.

(b) Upon agreement of the parties, service may be made electronically. Service may be by EXPRESS MAIL® or by means at least as fast and reliable as EXPRESS MAIL®.

Personal service is not required.

§ 42.206. Filing date.

(a) *Complete petition.* A petition to institute a post-grant review will not be accorded a filing date until the petition satisfies all of the following requirements:

(1) Complies with § 42.204 or § 42.304, as the case may be,

(2) Effects service of the petition on the correspondence address of record as provided in § 42.205(a); and

(3) Is accompanied by the filing fee in § 42.15(b).

(b) *Incomplete petition.* Where a party files an incomplete petition, no filing date will be accorded and the Office will dismiss the request if the deficiency in the petition is not corrected within the earlier of either one month from the notice of an incomplete petition, or the expiration of the statutory deadline in which to file a petition for post-grant review.

§ 42.207. Preliminary response to petition.

(a) The patent owner may file a preliminary response to the petition. The response is limited to setting forth the reasons why no post-grant review should be instituted under 35 U.S.C. 324. The response can include evidence except as provided in paragraph (c) of this section. The preliminary response is subject to the page limits under § 42.24.

(b) *Due date.* The preliminary response must be filed no later than three months after the date of a notice indicating that the request to institute a post-grant review has been granted a filing date. A patent owner may expedite the proceeding by filing an election to waive the patent owner preliminary response.

(c) *No new testimonial evidence.* The preliminary response shall not present new testimony evidence beyond that already of record, except as authorized by the Board.

(d) *No amendment.* The preliminary response shall not include any amendment.

(e) *Disclaim Patent Claims.* The patent owner may file a statutory disclaimer under 35 U.S.C. 253(a) in compliance with § 1.321(a), disclaiming one or more claims in the patent. No post-grant review will be instituted based on disclaimed claims.

Instituting Post-Grant Review

§ 42.208. Institution of post-grant review.

(a) When instituting post-grant review, the Board may authorize the review to proceed on all or some of the challenged claims and on all or some of the grounds of unpatentability asserted for each claim.

(b) At any time prior to institution of post-grant review, the Board may deny some or all grounds for unpatentability for some or all of the challenged claims. Denial of a ground is a Board decision not to institute post-grant review on that ground.

(c) *Sufficient grounds.* Post-grant review shall not be instituted for a ground of unpatentability, unless the Board decides that the petition supporting the ground would, if unrebutted, demonstrate that it is more likely than not that at least one of the claims challenged in the petition is unpatentable. The Board's decision will take into account a patent owner preliminary response where such a response is filed.

(d) *Additional grounds.* Sufficient grounds under § 42.208(c) may be a showing that the petition raises a novel or unsettled legal question that is important to other patents or patent applications.

After Institution of Post-Grant Review

§ 42.220. Patent owner response.

(a) *Scope.* A patent owner may file a response to the petition addressing any ground for unpatentability not already denied. A patent owner response is filed as an opposition and is subject to the page limits provided in § 42.24.

(b) *Due date for response.* If no date for filing a patent owner response to a petition is provided in a Board order, the default date for filing a patent owner response is three months from the date the post-grant review is instituted.

§ 42.221. Amendment of the patent.

(a) *Motion to amend.* A patent owner may file one motion to amend a patent, but only after conferring with the Board.

(1) *Due date.* Unless a due date is provided in a Board order, a motion to amend must be filed no later than the filing of a patent owner response.

(2) *Scope.* A motion to amend may be denied where:

(i) The amendment does not respond to a ground of unpatentability involved in the trial; or

(ii) The amendment seeks to enlarge the scope of

the claims of the patent or introduce new subject matter.

(3) *A reasonable number of substitute claims.* A motion to amend may cancel a challenged claim or propose a reasonable number of substitute claims. The presumption is that only one substitute claim would be needed to replace each challenged claim, and it may be rebutted by a demonstration of need.

(b) *Content.* A motion to amend claims must include a claim listing, show the changes clearly, and set forth:

(1) The support in the original disclosure of the patent for each claim that is added or amended; and

(2) The support in an earlier-filed disclosure for each claim for which benefit of the filing date of the earlier filed disclosure is sought.

(c) *Additional motion to amend.* In addition to the requirements set forth in paragraphs (a) and (b) of this section, any additional motion to amend may not be filed without Board authorization. An additional motion to amend may be authorized when there is a good cause showing or a joint request of the petitioner and the patent owner to materially advance a settlement. In determining whether to authorize such an additional motion to amend, the Board will consider whether a petitioner has submitted supplemental information after the time period set for filing a motion to amend in paragraph (a)(1) of this section.

§ 42.222. Multiple proceedings and Joinder.

(a) *Multiple proceedings.* Where another matter involving the patent is before the Office, the Board may during the pendency of the post-grant review enter any appropriate order regarding the additional matter including providing for the stay, transfer, consolidation, or termination of any such matter.

(b) *Request for joinder.* Joinder may be requested by a patent owner or petitioner. Any request for joinder must be filed, as a motion under § 42.22, no later than one month after the institution date of any post-grant review for which joinder is requested.

§ 42.223. Filing of supplemental information.

(a) *Motion to submit supplemental information.* Once a trial has been instituted, a party may file a motion to submit supplemental information in accordance with the following requirements:

(1) A request for the authorization to file a motion to

submit supplemental information is made within one month of the date the trial is instituted.

(2) The supplemental information must be relevant to a claim for which the trial has been instituted.

(b) *Late submission of supplemental information.* A party seeking to submit supplemental information more than one month after the date the trial is instituted, must request authorization to file a motion to submit the information. The motion to submit supplemental information must show why the supplemental information reasonably could not have been obtained earlier, and that consideration of the supplemental information would be in the interests-of-justice.

(c) *Other supplemental information.* A party seeking to submit supplemental information not relevant to a claim for which the trial has been instituted must request authorization to file a motion to submit the information. The motion must show why the supplemental information reasonably could not have been obtained earlier, and that consideration of the supplemental information would be in the interests-of-justice.

§ 42.224. Discovery.

Notwithstanding the discovery provisions of subpart A:

(a) Requests for additional discovery may be granted upon a showing of good cause as to why the discovery is needed; and

(b) Discovery is limited to evidence directly related to factual assertions advanced by either party in the proceeding.

Subpart D— Transitional Program for Covered Business Method Patents

Sec.

§ 42.300. Procedure; pendency.

(a) A covered business method patent review is a trial subject to the procedures set forth in subpart A of this part and is also subject to the post-grant review procedures set forth in subpart C except for §§ 42.200, 42.201, 42.202, and 42.204.

(b) A claim in an unexpired patent shall be given its broadest reasonable construction in light of the specification of the patent in which it appears.

(c) A covered business method patent review proceeding shall be administered such that pendency before the Board after institution is normally no more than one year. The time can be extended by up to six months for good cause by the Chief Administrative Patent Judge.

(d) The rules in this subpart are applicable until September 15, 2020, except that the rules shall continue to apply to any petition for a covered business method patent review filed before the date of repeal.

§ 42.301. Definitions.

In addition to the definitions in § 42.2, the following definitions apply to proceedings under this subpart D:

(a) *Covered business method patent* means a patent that claims a method or corresponding apparatus for performing data processing or other operations used in the practice, administration, or management of a financial product or service, except that the term does not include patents for technological inventions.

(b) *Technological invention.* In determining whether a patent is for a technological invention solely for purposes of the Transitional Program for Covered Business Methods (section 42.301(a)), the following will be considered on a case-by-case basis:

whether the claimed subject matter as a whole recites a technological feature that is novel and unobvious over the prior art; and solves a technical problem using a technical solution.

§ 42.302. Who may petition for a covered business method patent review.

(a) A petitioner may not file with the Office a petition to institute a covered business method patent review of the patent unless the petitioner, the petitioner's real party-in-interest, or a privy of the petitioner has been sued for infringement of the patent or has been charged with infringement under that patent. Charged with infringement means a real and substantial controversy regarding infringement of a covered business method patent exists such that the petitioner would have standing to bring a declaratory judgment action in Federal court.

(b) A petitioner may not file a petition to institute a

covered business method patent review of the patent where the petitioner, the petitioner's real party-in-interest, or a privy of the petitioner is estopped from challenging the claims on the grounds identified in the petition.

§ 42.303. Time for filing.

A petition requesting a covered business method patent review may be filed any time except during the period in which a petition for a post-grant review of the patent would satisfy the requirements of 35 U.S.C. 321(c).

§ 42.304. Content of petition.

In addition to any other notices required by subparts A and C of this part, a petition must request judgment against one or more claims of a patent identified by patent number. In addition to the requirements of §§ 42.6, 42.8, 42.22, and 42.24 the petition must set forth:

(a) *Grounds for standing.* The petitioner must demonstrate that the patent for which review is sought is a covered business method patent, and that the petitioner meets the eligibility requirements of § 42.302.

(b) *Identification of challenge.* Provide a statement of the precise relief requested for each claim challenged. The statement must identify the following:

(1) The claim;

(2) The specific statutory grounds permitted under paragraph (2) or (3) of 35 U.S.C. 282(b), except as modified by section 18(a)(1)(C) of the Leahy-Smith America Invents Act (Pub. L. 112-29, 125 Stat. 284 (2011)), on which the challenge to the claim is based;

(3) How the challenged claim is to be construed. Where the claim to be construed contains a means-plus-function or step-plus-function limitation as permitted under 35 U.S.C. 112(f), the construction of the claim must identify the specific portions of the specification that describe the structure, material, or acts corresponding to each claimed function;

(4) How the construed claim is unpatentable under the statutory grounds identified in paragraph (b)(2) of this section. Where the grounds for unpatentability are based on prior art, the petition must specify where each element of the claim is found in the prior art. For all other grounds of unpatentability, the petition must identify the specific part of the claim that fails to comply with the statutory grounds raised and state how the

identified subject matter fails to comply with the statute; and

(5) The exhibit number of supporting evidence relied upon to support the challenge and the relevance of the evidence to the challenge raised, including identifying specific portions of the evidence that support the challenge. The Board may exclude or give no weight to the evidence where a party has failed to state its relevance or to identify specific portions of the evidence that support the challenge.

(c) A motion may be filed that seeks to correct a clerical or typographical mistake in the petition. The grant of such a motion does not change the filing date of the petition.

Subpart E— Derivation

Sec.

General

Instituting Derivation Proceeding

After Institution of Derivation Proceeding

Subpart E—Derivation

General

§ 42.400. Procedure; pendency

(a) A derivation proceeding is a trial subject to the

procedures set forth in subpart A of this part.

(b) The Board may for good cause authorize or direct the parties to address patentability issues that arise in the course of the derivation proceeding.

§ 42.401. Definitions.

In addition to the definitions in § 42.2, the following definitions apply to proceedings under this subpart:

Agreement or *understanding under 35 U.S.C. 135(e)* means settlement for the purposes of § 42.74.

Applicant includes a reissue applicant.

Application includes both an application for an original patent and an application for a reissued patent.

First publication means either a patent or an application publication under 35 U.S.C. 122(b), including a publication of an international application designating the United States as provided by 35 U.S.C. 374.

Petitioner means a patent applicant who petitions for a determination that another party named in an earlier-filed patent application allegedly derived a claimed invention from an inventor named in the petitioner's application and filed the earlier application without authorization.

Respondent means a party other than the petitioner.

Same or substantially the same means patentably indistinct.

§ 42.402. Who may file a petition for a derivation proceeding.

An applicant for patent may file a petition to institute a derivation proceeding in the Office.

§ 42.403. Time for filing.

A petition for a derivation proceeding must be filed within the one-year period beginning on the date of the first publication of a claim to an invention that is the same or substantially the same as the earlier application's claim to the allegedly derived invention.

§ 42.404. Derivation fee.

(a) A derivation fee set forth in § 42.15(c) must accompany the petition.

(b) No filing date will be accorded to the petition until payment is complete.

§ 42.405. Content of petition.

(a) *Grounds for standing.* The petition must:

(1) Demonstrate compliance with §§ 42.402 and

42.403; and

(2) Show that the petitioner has at least one claim that is:

(i) The same or substantially the same as the respondent's claimed invention; and

(ii) The same or substantially the same as the invention disclosed to the respondent.

(b) In addition to the requirements of §§ 42.8 and 42.22, the petition must:

(1) Provide sufficient information to identify the application or patent for which the petitioner seeks a derivation proceeding;

(2) Demonstrate that a claimed invention was derived from an inventor named in the petitioner's application, and that the inventor from whom the invention was derived did not authorize the filing of the earliest application claiming such invention; and

(3) For each of the respondent's claims to the derived invention,

(i) Show why the claimed invention is the same or substantially the same as the invention disclosed to the respondent, and

(ii) Identify how the claim is to be construed. Where the claim to be construed contains a means-plus-function or step-plus-function limitation as permitted under 35 U.S.C. 112(f), the construction of the claim must identify the specific portions of the specification that describe the structure, material, or acts corresponding to each claimed function.

(c) *Sufficiency of showing.* A derivation showing is not sufficient unless it is supported by substantial evidence, including at least one affidavit addressing communication of the derived invention and lack of authorization that, if unrebutted, would support a determination of derivation. The showing of communication must be corroborated.

§ 42.406. Service of petition.

In addition to the requirements of § 42.6, the petitioner must serve the petition and exhibits relied upon in the petition as follows:

(a) The petition and supporting evidence must be served on the respondent at the correspondence address of record for the earlier application or subject patent. The petitioner may additionally serve the petition and supporting evidence on the respondent at any other address known to the petitioner as likely to effect service.

(b) Upon agreement of the parties, service may be made electronically. Service may be by EXPRESS MAIL® or by means at least as fast and reliable as EXPRESS MAIL®. Personal service is not required.

§ 42.407. Filing date.

(a) *Complete petition.* A petition to institute a derivation proceeding will not be accorded a filing date until the petition satisfies all of the following requirements:

(1) Complies with §§ 42.404 and 42.405, and

(2) Service of the petition on the correspondence address of record as provided in § 42.406.

(b) *Incomplete petition.* Where the petitioner files an incomplete petition, no filing date will be accorded, and the Office will dismiss the petition if the deficiency in the petition is not corrected within the earlier of either one month from notice of the incomplete petition, or the expiration of the statutory deadline in which to file a petition for derivation.

Instituting Derivation Proceeding

§ 42.408. Institution of derivation proceeding.

(a) An administrative patent judge institutes, and may as necessary reinstitute, the derivation proceeding on behalf of the Director.

(b) *Additional derivation proceeding.* The petitioner may suggest the addition of a patent or application to the derivation proceeding. The suggestion should make the showings required under § 42.405 and explain why the suggestion could not have been made in the original petition.

After Institution of Derivation Proceeding

§ 42.409. Settlement agreements.

An agreement or understanding under 35 U.S.C. 135(e) is a settlement for the purposes of § 42.74.

§ 42.410. Arbitration.

(a) Parties may resort to binding arbitration to determine any issue. The Office is not a party to the arbitration. The Board is not bound by, and may independently determine, any question of patentability.

(b) The Board will not set a time for, or otherwise

modify the proceeding for, an arbitration unless:

(1) It is to be conducted according to Title 9 of the United States Code;

(2) The parties notify the Board in writing of their intention to arbitrate;

(3) The agreement to arbitrate:

(i) Is in writing;

(ii) Specifies the issues to be arbitrated;

(iii) Names the arbitrator, or provides a date not more than 30 days after the execution of the agreement for the selection of the arbitrator;

(iv) Provides that the arbitrator's award shall be binding on the parties and that judgment thereon can be entered by the Board;

(v) Provides that a copy of the agreement is filed within 20 days after its execution; and

(vi) Provides that the arbitration is completed within the time the Board sets.

(c) The parties are solely responsible for the selection of the arbitrator and the conduct of the arbitration.

(d) The Board may determine issues the arbitration does not resolve.

(e) The Board will not consider the arbitration award unless it:

(1) Is binding on the parties;

(2) Is in writing;

(3) States in a clear and definite manner each issue arbitrated and the disposition of each issue; and

(4) Is filed within 20 days of the date of the award.

(f) Once the award is filed, the parties to the award may not take actions inconsistent with the award. If the award is dispositive of the contested subject matter for a party, the Board may enter judgment as to that party.

§ 42.411. Common interests in the invention.

The Board may decline to institute, or if already instituted the Board may issue judgment in, a derivation proceeding between an application and a patent or another application that are commonly owned.

§ 42.412. Public availability of Board records.

(a) *Publication.* (1) *Generally.* Any Board decision is available for public inspection without a party's permission if rendered in a file open to the public pursuant to § 1.11 of this chapter or in an application that has been published in accordance with §§ 1.211 to 1.221 of this chapter. The Office may independently publish any Board decision that is available for public inspection.

(2) *Determination of special circumstances.* Any Board decision not publishable under paragraph (a)(1) of this section may be published or made available for public inspection if the Director believes that special circumstances warrant publication and a party does not petition within two months after being notified of the intention to make the decision public, objecting in writing on the ground that the decision discloses the objecting party's trade secret or other confidential information and stating with specificity that such information is not otherwise publicly available.

(b) *Record of proceeding.* (1) The record of a Board proceeding is available to the public, unless a patent application not otherwise available to the public is involved.

(2) Notwithstanding paragraph (b)(1) of this section, after a final Board decision in or judgment in a Board proceeding, the record of the Board proceeding will be made available to the public if any involved file is or becomes open to the public under § 1.11 of this chapter or an involved application is or becomes published under §§ 1.211 to 1.221 of this chapter.

PART 90— JUDICIAL REVIEW OF PATENT TRIAL AND APPEAL BOARD DECISIONS

Sec.

Authority: 35 U.S.C. 2(b)(2).

§ 90.1. Scope.

The provisions herein govern judicial review for Patent Trial and Appeal Board decisions under chapter 13 of title 35, United States Code. Judicial review of decisions arising out of *inter partes* reexamination proceedings that are requested under 35 U.S.C. 311, and where available, judicial review of decisions arising out of interferences declared pursuant to 35 U.S.C. 135 continue to be governed by the pertinent regulations in effect on July 1, 2012.

§ 90.2. Notice; service.

(a) *For an appeal under 35 U.S.C. 141.*

(1) In all appeals, the notice of appeal required by 35 U.S.C. 142 must be filed with the Director of the United States Patent and Trademark Office as provided in § 104.2 of this title. A copy of the notice of appeal must also be filed with the Patent Trial and Appeal Board in the appropriate manner provided in § 41.10(a), 41.10(b), or 42.6(b).

(2) In all appeals, the party initiating the appeal must comply with the requirements of the Federal Rules of Appellate Procedure and Rules for the United States Court of Appeals for the Federal Circuit, including:

(i) Serving the requisite number of copies on the Court; and

(ii) Paying the requisite fee for the appeal.

(3) *Additional requirements.* (i) In appeals arising out of an ex parte reexamination proceeding ordered pursuant to § 1.525, notice of the appeal must be served as provided in § 1.550(f) of this title.

(ii) In appeals arising out of an *inter partes* review, a post-grant review, a covered business method patent review, or a derivation proceeding, notice of the appeal must provide sufficient information to allow the Director to determine whether to exercise the right to intervene in the appeal pursuant to 35 U.S.C. 143, and it must be served as provided in § 42.6(e) of this title.

(b) For a notice of election under 35 U.S.C. 141(d) to proceed under 35 U.S.C. 146.

(1) Pursuant to 35 U.S.C. 141(d), if an adverse party elects to have all further review proceedings conducted under 35 U.S.C. 146 instead of under 35 U.S.C. 141, that party must file a notice of election with the United States Patent and Trademark Office as provided in § 104.2.

(2) A copy of the notice of election must also be filed with the Patent Trial and Appeal Board in the manner provided in § 42.6(b).

(3) A copy of the notice of election must also be served where necessary pursuant to § 42.6(e).

(c) *For a civil action under 35 U.S.C. 146.* The party initiating an action under 35 U.S.C. 146 must file a copy of the complaint no later than five business days after filing the complaint in district court with the Patent Trial and Appeal Board in the manner provided in § 42.6(b), and the Office of the Solicitor pursuant to § 104.2. Failure to comply with this requirement can result in further action within the United States Patent and Trademark Office consistent with the final Board decision.

§ 90.3. Time for appeal or civil action.

(a) *Filing deadline.* (1) *For an appeal under 35 U.S.C. 141.* The notice of appeal filed pursuant to 35 U.S.C. 142 must be filed with the Director of the United States Patent and Trademark Office no later than sixty-three (63) days after the date of the final Board decision. Any notice of cross-appeal is controlled by Rule 4(a)(3) of the Federal Rules of Appellate Procedure, and any other requirement imposed by the Rules of the United States Court of Appeals for the Federal Circuit.

(2) *For a notice of election under 35 U.S.C. 141(d).* The time for filing a notice of election under 35 U.S.C. 141(d) is governed by 35 U.S.C. 141(d).

(3) *For a civil action under 35 U.S.C. 145 or 146.*

(i) A civil action must be commenced no later than sixty-three (63) days after the date of the final Board decision.

(ii) The time for commencing a civil action pursuant to a notice of election under 35 U.S.C. 141(d) is governed by 35 U.S.C. 141(d).

(b) *Time computation.* (1) Rehearing. A timely request for rehearing will reset the time for appeal or civil action to no later than sixty-three (63) days after action on the request. Any subsequent request for rehearing from the same party in the same proceeding will not reset the time for seeking judicial review, unless the additional request is permitted by order of the Board.

(2) *Holidays.* If the last day for filing an appeal or civil action falls on a Federal holiday in the District of Columbia, the time is extended pursuant to 35 U.S.C. 21(b).

(c) *Extension of time.* (1) The Director, or his designee, may extend the time for filing an appeal, or commencing a civil action, upon written request if:

(i) Requested before the expiration of the period for

filing an appeal or commencing a civil action, and upon a showing of good cause; or

(ii) Requested after the expiration of the period for filing an appeal of commencing a civil action, and upon a showing that the failure to act was the result of excusable neglect. 3

(2) The request must be filed as provided in § 104.2 of this title.

APPENDIX 4

Requirement For a Disclosure of The Best Mode

UNITED STATES PATENT AND TRADEMARK OFFICE

Commissioner for Patents
United States Patent and Trademark Office
P.O. Box 1450
Alexandria, VA 22313-1450
www.uspto.gov

MEMORANDUM

DATE: **September 20, 2011**

TO: Patent Examining Corps

FROM: Robert W. Bahr
Senior Patent Counsel
Acting Associate Commissioner
for Patent Examination Policy

SUBJECT: **Requirement for a Disclosure of the Best Mode**

35 U.S.C. § 112, first paragraph, provides that the specification of a patent application must include the following: (1) a written description of the invention; (2) the manner and process of making and using the invention (the enablement requirement); and (3) the best mode contemplated by the inventor of carrying out his invention. *See* MPEP 2161; *see also Ariad v. Elli Lilly,* 598 F.3d 1336, 1344 (Fed. Cir. 2010).

Section 15 of the Leahy-Smith America Invents Act does not eliminate the requirement in 35 U.S.C. § 112, first paragraph,[1] for a disclosure of the best mode, but does amend 35 U.S.C. § 282 (the provisions that sets forth defenses in a patent validity or infringement proceeding) to provide that the failure to disclose the best mode shall not be a basis on which any claim of a patent may be canceled or held invalid or otherwise unenforceable. As this change is applicable only in patent validity or infringement proceedings, it does not alter current patent examining practices set forth in MPEP 2165 for evaluation of an application for compliance with the best mode requirement of 35 U.S.C. § 112.

For an invention claimed in a later-filed application to receive the benefit of the filing date of an earlier-filed application, 35 U.S.C. §§ 119(e) and 120[2] require that the invention claimed in the later-filed application be disclosed in the earlier-filed application in the manner provided by 35 U.S.C. § 112, first paragraph. Section 15 of the Leahy-Smith America Invents Act also amends 35 U.S.C. §§ 119(e) and 120 to modify this requirement such that the disclosure in the earlier-filed application must be made in the manner provided by 35 U.S.C. § 112, first paragraph, "other than the requirement to disclose the best mode." This change should not noticeably impact patent examining procedure. MPEP 201.08 provides that there is no need to determine whether the earlier-filed application contains a disclosure of the invention claimed in the later-filed application in compliance with 35 U.S.C. § 112, first paragraph, unless the filing date of the earlier-filed application is actually necessary (*e.g.*, to overcome a reference). Examiners should

[1] The Leahy-Smith America Invents Act also redesignates 35 U.S.C. § 112, first through sixth paragraphs, as 35 U.S.C. § 112(a) through (f), respectively. This amendment, however, does not take effect until September 16, 2012.
[2] The provisions for claiming the benefit of a provisional application and a nonprovisional application, respectively.

consult with their supervisors if it appears that an earlier-filed application does not disclose the best mode for carrying out a claimed invention and the filing date of the earlier-filed application is actually necessary.

This provision took effect on September 16, 2011.

APPENDIX 5

Claims Directed To Or Encompassing a Human Organism

UNITED STATES PATENT AND TRADEMARK OFFICE

Commissioner for Patents
United States Patent and Trademark Office
P.O. Box 1450
Alexandria, VA 22313-1450
www.uspto.gov

MEMORANDUM

DATE: **September 20, 2011**

TO: Patent Examining Corps

FROM: Robert W. Bahr
Senior Patent Counsel
Acting Associate Commissioner
for Patent Examination Policy

SUBJECT: **Claims Directed to or Encompassing a Human Organism**

Section 33(a) of the Leahy-Smith America Invents Act states: "Notwithstanding any other provision of law, no patent may issue on a claim directed to or encompassing a human organism."

This provision of the Leahy-Smith America Invents Act does not change existing law or long-standing USPTO policy that a claim encompassing a human being is not patentable. *See Animals - Patentability*, 1077 *Off. Gaz. Pat. Office* 24 (April 21, 1987) (indicating that human organisms are excluded from the scope of patentable subject matter under 35 U.S.C. 101). This long-standing policy is reflected in MPEP § 2105, which currently provides that:

> If the broadest reasonable interpretation of the claimed invention as a whole encompasses a human being, then a rejection under 35 U.S.C. 101 must be made indicating that the claimed invention is directed to nonstatutory subject matter.

Thus, section 33(a) of the Leahy-Smith America Invents Act codifies existing USPTO policy that human organisms are not patent-eligible subject matter.

The USPTO is providing a new form paragraph (7.04.01) for use in rejecting claim(s) directed to or encompassing a human organism to reflect that such claim(s) are not permitted under either 35 U.S.C. 101 or section 33(a) of the America Invents Act.

Form Paragraph

7.04.01 Human Organism

Section 33(a) of the America Invents Act reads as follows:

> Notwithstanding any other provision of law, no patent may issue on a claim directed to or encompassing a human organism.

Claim [1] rejected under 35 U.S.C. 101 and section 33(a) of the America Invents Act as being directed to or encompassing a human organism. *See also Animals - Patentability*, 1077 *Off. Gaz. Pat. Office* 24 (April 21, 1987) (indicating that human organisms are excluded from the scope of patentable subject matter under 35 U.S.C. 101). **[2]**

Examiner Notes

1. This paragraph must be preceded by form paragraph 7.04 which quotes 35 U.S.C. 101.

2. In bracket [1], pluralize "Claim" if necessary, insert claim number(s), and insert "is" or "are" as appropriate.

3. In bracket [2], explain why the claim is interpreted to read on a human organism.

APPENDIX 6

Tax Strategies Are Deemed To Be Within the Prior Art

UNITED STATES PATENT AND TRADEMARK OFFICE

Commissioner for Patents
United States Patent and Trademark Office
P.O. Box 1450
Alexandria, VA 22313-1450
www.uspto.gov

MEMORANDUM

DATE: **September 20, 2011**

TO: Patent Examining Corps

FROM: Robert W. Bahr
Acting Associate Commissioner
for Patent Examination Policy

SUBJECT: **Tax Strategies Are Deemed To Be Within the Prior Art**

Section 14 of the Leahy-Smith America Invents Act, enacted on September 16, 2011, provides that for purposes of evaluating an invention for novelty and nonobviousness under 35 U.S.C. §§ 102 and 103, any strategy for reducing, avoiding, or deferring tax liability (hereinafter, "tax strategy"), whether known or unknown at the time of the invention or application for patent, shall be deemed insufficient to differentiate a claimed invention from the prior art. As a result, applicants will no longer be able to rely on the novelty or non-obviousness of a tax strategy embodied in their claims to distinguish them from the prior art. Section 14 aims to keep the ability to interpret the tax law and to implement such interpretation in the public domain, available to all taxpayers and their advisors.

The term ''tax liability'' is defined for purposes of this provision as referring to any liability for a tax under any Federal, State, or local law, or the law of any foreign jurisdiction, including any statute, rule, regulation, or ordinance that levies, imposes, or assesses such tax liability.

There are two exclusions to this provision. The first is that the provision does not apply to that part of an invention that is a method, apparatus, technology, computer program product, or system, that is used solely for preparing a tax or information return or other tax filing, including one that records, transmits, transfers, or organizes data related to such filing.

The second is that the provision does not apply to that part of an invention that is a method, apparatus, technology, computer program product, or system, that is used solely for financial management, to the extent that it is severable from any tax strategy or does not limit the use of any tax strategy by any taxpayer or tax advisor.

This provision took effect on September 16, 2011, and applies to any patent application that is pending on, or filed on or after, September 16, 2011, and to any patent issued on or after September 16, 2011. Accordingly, this provision will apply in a reexamination or other post-grant proceeding only to patents issued on or after September 16, 2011.

Examination Guidance for Claims Relating to Tax Strategies:

1. Construe the claim in accordance with MPEP 2111 *et seq.*
2. Analyze the claim for compliance with 35 U.S.C. §§ 101 and 112 in accordance with current guidance, which is unaffected by this provision.
3. Identify any limitations relating to a tax strategy, as defined above (note the listed exclusions).
   a. Inventions that fall within the scope of Section 14 of the Leahy-Smith America Invents Act include those tax strategies especially suitable for use with tax-favored structures that must meet certain requirements, such as employee benefit plans, tax-exempt organizations, or other entities that must be structured or operated in a particular manner to obtain certain tax consequences.
   b. Thus, Section 14 applies if the effect of an invention is to aid in satisfying the qualification requirements for a desired tax-favored entity status, to take advantage of the specific tax benefits offered in a tax-favored structure, or to allow for tax reduction, avoidance, or deferral not otherwise automatically available in such entity or structure.
4. Evaluate the claim in view of the prior art under 35 U.S.C. §§ 102 and 103, treating any limitations relating to a tax strategy as being within the prior art, and not as a patentable difference between the claim and the prior art. This approach is analogous to the treatment of printed matter limitations in a claim as discussed at MPEP 2112.01 (III).

Examples Directed to Computer-Implemented Methods:

A computer-implemented method that is deemed novel and non-obvious would not be affected by this provision even if used for a tax purpose. For example, a novel and non-obvious computer-implemented method for manipulating data would not be affected by this provision, even if the method organized data for a future tax filing. However, the presence of limitations relating to a tax strategy would not cause a claim that is otherwise within the prior art to become novel or non-obvious over the prior art.

Thus, for purposes of applying art to a software-related invention under §§ 102 and 103, claim limitations that are directed solely to enabling individuals to file their income tax returns or assisting them with managing their finances should be given patentable weight, but by contrast, claim limitations directed to a tax strategy should not be given patentable weight.

Form Paragraph

(New) ¶ 7.06. Claim Limitation Relating to a Tax Strategy Deemed To Be Within the Prior Art under 35 U.S.C. 102 and/or 103.

Claim limitation "**[1]**" has been interpreted as a strategy for reducing, avoiding, or deferring tax liability ("tax strategy") pursuant to Section 14 of the Leahy-Smith America Invents Act. Accordingly, this claim limitation is being treated as being within the prior art and is insufficient to differentiate the invention of claim **[2]** from the prior art.

Examiner Note:

1. In bracket 1, recite the claim limitation that relates to a tax strategy. For more information see the memorandum *Tax Strategies Are Deemed To Be Within the Prior Art* issued by Robert W. Bahr on September XX, 2011.
2. In bracket 2, insert claim number(s), pluralize "claim" as appropriate.

APPENDIX 7

HR 6621 as Passed by Congress

One Hundred Twelfth Congress

of the

United States of America

AT THE SECOND SESSION

Begun and held at the City of Washington on Tuesday, the third day of January, two thousand and twelve

An Act

To correct and improve certain provisions of the Leahy-Smith America Invents Act and title 35, United States Code.

Be it enacted by the Senate and House of Representatives of the United States of America in Congress assembled,

SECTION 1. TECHNICAL CORRECTIONS.

(a) Advice of Counsel. Notwithstanding section 35 of the Leahy-Smith America Invents Act (35 U.S.C. 1 note), section 298 of title 35, United States Code, shall apply to any civil action commenced on or after the date of the enactment of this Act.

(b) Transitional Program for Covered Business Method Patents. Section 18 of the Leahy-Smith America Invents Act (35 U.S.C. 321 note) is amended—

(1) in subsection (a)(1)(C)(i), by striking 'of such title' the second place it appears; and

(2) in subsection (d)(2), by striking 'subsection' and inserting 'section'.

(c) Joinder of Parties. Section 299(a) of title 35, United States Code, is amended in the matter preceding paragraph (1) by striking 'or counterclaim defendants only if' and inserting 'only if'.

(d) Dead Zones.—

(1) Inter partes review. Section 311(c) of title 35, United States Code, shall not apply to a petition to institute an inter partes review of a patent that is not a patent described

in section 3(n)(1) of the Leahy-Smith America Invents Act (35 U.S.C. 100 note).

(2) Reissue. Section 311(c)(1) of title 35, United States Code, is amended by striking 'or issuance of a reissue of a patent'.

(e) Correct Inventor.—

(1) In general. Section 135(e) of title 35, United States Code, as amended by section 3(i) of the Leahy-Smith America Invents Act, is amended by striking 'correct inventors' and inserting 'correct inventor'.

(2) Effective date. The amendment made by paragraph (1) shall be effective as if included in the amendment made by section 3(i) of the Leahy-Smith America Invents Act.

(f) Inventor's Oath or Declaration. Section 115 of title 35, United States Code, as amended by section 4 of the Leahy-Smith America Invents Act, is amended—

(1) by striking subsection (f) and inserting the following:

'(f) Time for Filing. The applicant for patent shall provide each required oath or declaration under subsection (a), substitute statement under subsection (d), or recorded assignment meeting the requirements of subsection (e) no later than the date on which the issue fee for the patent is paid.'; and

(2) in subsection (g)(1), by striking 'who claims' and inserting 'that claims'.

(g) Travel Expenses and Payment of Administrative Judges. Notwithstanding section 35 of the Leahy-Smith America Invents Act (35 U.S.C. 1 note), the amendments made by section 21 of the Leahy-Smith America Invents Act (Public Law 112-29; 125 Stat. 335) shall be effective as of September 16, 2011.

(h) Patent Term Adjustments. Section 154(b) of title 35, United States Code, is amended—

(1) in paragraph (1)—

(A) in subparagraph (A)(i)(II), by striking 'on which an international application fulfilled the requirements of section 371 of this title' and inserting 'of commencement of the national stage under section 371 in an international application'; and

(B) in subparagraph (B), in the matter preceding clause (i), by striking 'the application in the United States' and inserting 'the application under section 111(a) in the United States or, in the case of an international application, the date of commencement of the national stage under section 371 in the international application';

(2) in paragraph (3)(B)(i), by striking 'with the written notice of allowance of the application under section 151' and inserting 'no later than the date of issuance of the patent'; and

(3) in paragraph (4)(A)—

(A) by striking 'a determination made by the Director under paragraph (3) shall have remedy' and inserting 'the Director's decision on the applicant's request for reconsideration under paragraph (3)(B)(ii) shall have exclusive remedy'; and

(B) by striking 'the grant of the patent' and inserting 'the date of the Director's decision on the applicant's request for reconsideration'.

(i) Improper Applicant. Section 373 of title 35, United States Code, and the item relating to that section in the table of sections for chapter 37 of such title, are repealed.

(j) Financial Management Clarifications. Section 42(c)(3) of title 35, United States Code, is amended—

(1) in subparagraph (A)—

(A) by striking 'sections 41, 42, and 376,' and inserting 'this title,'; and

(B) by striking 'a share of the administrative costs of the Office relating to patents' and inserting 'a proportionate share of the administrative costs of the Office'; and

(2) in subparagraph (B), by striking 'a share of the administrative costs of the Office relating to trademarks' and inserting 'a proportionate share of the administrative costs of the Office'.

(k) Derivation Proceedings.—

(1) In general. Section 135(a) of title 35, United States Code, as amended by section 3(i) of the Leahy-Smith America Invents Act, is amended to read as follows:

'(a) Institution of Proceeding.—

'(1) In general. An applicant for patent may file a petition with respect to an invention to institute a derivation pro-ceeding in the Office. The petition shall set forth with particularity the basis for finding that an individual named in an earlier application as the inventor or a joint inventor derived such invention from an individual named in the peti-tioner's application as the inventor or a joint inventor and, without authorization, the earlier application claiming such invention was filed. Whenever the Director determines that a petition filed under this subsection demonstrates that the standards for instituting a derivation proceeding are met, the Director may institute a derivation proceeding.

'(2) Time for filing. A petition under this section with respect to an invention that is the same or substantially the same invention as a claim contained in a patent issued on an earlier application, or contained in an earlier application when published or deemed published under section 122(b), may not be filed unless such petition is filed during the 1-year period following the date on which the patent containing such claim was granted or the earlier application containing such claim was published, whichever is earlier.

'(3) Earlier application. For purposes of this section, an application shall not be deemed to be an earlier application with respect to an invention, relative to another application, unless a claim to the invention was or could have been made in such application having an effective filing date that is earlier than the effective filing date of any claim to the invention that was or could have been made in such other application.

'(4) No appeal. A determination by the Director whether to institute a derivation proceeding under paragraph (1) shall be final and not appealable.'.

(2) Effective date. The amendment made by paragraph (1) shall be effective as if included in the amendment made by section 3(i) of the Leahy-Smith America Invents Act.

(3) Review of interference decisions. The provisions of sections 6 and 141 of title 35, United States Code, and section 1295(a)(4)(A) of title 28, United States Code, as in effect on September 15, 2012, shall apply to interference pro-ceedings that are declared after September 15, 2012, under section 135 of title 35, United States Code, as in effect before the effective date under section 3(n) of the Leahy-Smith America Invents Act. The Patent Trial and Appeal Board may be deemed to be the Board of Patent Appeals and Interferences for purposes of such interference pro-ceedings.

(l) Patent and Trademark Public Advisory Committees.—

(1) In general. Section 5(a) of title 35, United States Code, is amended—

(A) in paragraph (1), by striking 'Members of' and all that follows through 'such appointments.' and inserting the following: 'In each year, 3 members shall be appointed to each Advisory Committee for 3-year terms that shall begin on December 1 of that year. Any vacancy on an Advisory Committee shall be filled within 90 days after it occurs. A new member who is appointed to fill a vacancy shall be appointed to serve for the remainder of the predecessor's term.';

(B) by striking paragraph (2) and inserting the following:

'(2) Chair. The Secretary of Commerce, in consultation with the Director, shall designate a Chair and Vice Chair of each Advisory Committee from among the members appointed under paragraph (1). If the Chair resigns before the completion of his or her term, or is otherwise unable to exercise the functions of the Chair, the Vice Chair shall exercise the functions of the Chair.'; and

(C) by striking paragraph (3).

(2) Transition.—

(A) In general. The Secretary of Commerce shall, in the Secretary's discretion, determine the time and manner in which the amendments made by paragraph (1) shall take effect, except that, in each year following the year in which this Act is enacted, 3 members shall be appointed to each Advisory Committee (to which such amendments apply) for 3-year terms that begin on December 1 of that year, in accordance with section 5(a) of title 35, United States Code, as amended by paragraph (1) of this subsection.

(B) Deemed termination of terms. In order to implement the amendments made by paragraph (1), the Secretary of Commerce may determine that the term of an existing member of an Advisory Committee under section 5 of title 35, United States Code, shall be deemed to terminate on December 1 of a year beginning after the date of the enactment of this Act, regardless of whether December 1 is before or after the date on which such member's term would terminate if this Act had not been enacted.

(m) Clerical Amendment. Section 123(a) of title 35, United States Code, is amended in the matter preceding paragraph (1) by inserting 'of this title' after 'For purposes'.

(n) Effective Date. Except as otherwise provided in this Act, the amendments made by this Act shall take effect on the date of enactment of this Act, and shall apply to proceedings commenced on or after such date of enactment.

Speaker of the House of Representatives.

Vice President of the United States and

President of the Senate.

APPENDIX 8

PTAB Representative Decision on Additional Discovery in an IPR

mailto:Trial@uspto.gov
571-272-7822

Paper No. 26
Entered March 5, 2013

UNITED STATES PATENT AND TRADEMARK OFFICE

BEFORE THE PATENT TRIAL AND APPEAL BOARD

GARMIN INTERNATIONAL, INC. ET AL.

Petitioner

v.

CUOZZO SPEED TECHNOLOGIES LLC

Patent Owner

Case IPR2012-00001

Patent 6,778,074

Before JAMESON LEE, MICHAEL P. TIERNEY, and JOSIAH C. COCKS, *Administrative Patent Judges.*

LEE, *Administrative Patent Judge.*

DECISION

On Motion For Additional Discovery

37 C.F.R. §§ 42.20 and 42.51(b)(2)

INTRODUCTION

The patent owner ("Cuozzo") has filed a motion for additional discovery. (Paper 21). Petitioner ("Garmin") has opposed. (Paper 22). Cuozzo has replied. (Paper 25). * * * For reasons discussed below, Cuozzo's motion for additional discovery is *denied.*

Prior to filing of the discovery motion, a conference call was held on February 14, 2013, during which time Cuozzo presented a proposed set of discovery requests and was advised by the Board of five (5) factors which are important in determining what constitutes discovery satisfying the "necessary in the interest of justice" standard under 35 U.S.C. § 316(a)(5). (Paper 20). The Board appreciates the effort expended by Cuozzo in:

1. reducing the number of interrogatories from nineteen to nine;
2. reducing the number of document requests from twenty to ten;
3. shortening instructions for answering interrogatories from nine pages in length to two pages; and
4. shortening the instructions for producing documents from eight pages to two.

Cuozzo's motion also requests what amounts to the equivalent of a district court litigation deposition of a corporate entity under Fed. R. Civ. P. 30(b)(6) on topics covered by the interrogatories and document requests, for information "that may not be recorded in documents or revealed in interrogatory responses." (Paper 21, 8:14 to 9:2).

We have considered every item of the discovery request. In its request, Cuozzo disagrees with the Board's non-final interpretation of the term "integrally attached" in instituting this *inter partes* review. For purposes of this decision on Cuozzo's motion for discovery, we employ Cuozzo's interpretation, recognizing that all discussions below apply under either our non-final interpretation or Cuozzo's proposed interpretation and that the outcome would be no different.

For reasons discussed below, Cuozzo's motion for additional discovery is *denied.*

DISCUSSION

A. Routine Discovery

First, we address Cuozzo's attempt to label all of its document requests and interrogatories as "Routine Discovery" under 37 C.F.R. §§ 41.51(b)(1)(i) and 41.51(b)(1)(iii). In that regard, it is noted that the Board's authorization is not required for Cuozzo to conduct routine discovery. *Office Patent Trial Practice Guide*, 77 Fed. Reg. 48756, 48761 (Aug. 14, 2012).

Under 37 C.F.R. § 41.51(b)(1)(i), "[u]nless previously served or otherwise by agreement of the parties, any exhibit cited in a paper or in testimony must be served with the citing paper or testimony." Under 37 C.F.R. § 41.51(b)(1)(iii), "[u]nless previously served, a party must serve relevant information that is inconsistent with a position advanced by the party during the proceeding concurrent with the filing of the documents or things that contains the inconsistency" [privileged information excepted].

Cuozzo construes 37 C.F.R. § 41.51(b)(1)(i) as including the file histories of prior art patents relied on by Garmin in its petition for review. That interpretation is unreasonably broad. It is sufficient that Garmin provides copies of the patents relied on in its petition since Garmin did not rely on the file histories of those patents. Cuozzo may independently obtain the file histories of the cited prior art patents if it so desires, through the Patent Application Information Retrieval (PAIR) System available on the USPTO Web site (www.uspto.gov/patents/ebc) or other commercial services.

Cuozzo construes 37 C.F.R. § 41.51(b)(1)(iii) as including discovery requests "tailored to target information inconsistent with positions Garmin has taken in its Petition." (Paper 21, 7:5-6). The language appears to be in line with the applicable rule by use of narrow terms such as "tailored," "target," and "inconsistent with positions Garmin has taken." In actuality, however, Cuozzo is not referencing information known to Garmin to be inconsistent with positions taken in the petition. Rather, Cuozzo casts a wide net directed to broad classes of information which may not include anything inconsistent with positions taken by Garmin.

Routine discovery under 37 C.F.R. § 41.51(b)(1)(iii) is narrowly directed to specific information known to the responding party to be inconsistent with a position advanced by that party in the proceeding, and not broadly directed to any subject area in general within which the requesting party hopes to discover such inconsistent information. Cuozzo's attempt to label very broad discovery requests as narrowly tailored routine discovery is misplaced.

Also, under 37 C.F.R. § 41.51(b)(1)(iii), the time for serving such routinely discoverable inconsistent information is concurrent with the filing of documents or things that contains the inconsistency. Nothing in Cuozzo's motion persuades us that Garmin has failed to comply with "routine discovery" under 37 C.F.R. § 41.51(b)(1)(iii), under our construction of the rule provision as discussed above. However, to assist in alleviating any concern, we will in the order section of this decision ask each party to confirm that up to now in this *inter partes* review it has produced all information covered by 37 C.F.R. § 41.51(b)(1)(iii) as routine discovery.

B. Additional Discovery

Under the Leahy-Smith America Invents Act, discovery is available for the deposition of witnesses submitting affidavits or declarations and for "what is otherwise necessary in the interest of justice." 35 U.S.C. § 316(a)(5); *see also* 37 C.F.R. § 42.51(b)(2) ("The moving party must show that such additional discovery is in the interests of justice . . . ."). That is significantly different from the scope of discovery generally available under the Federal Rules of Civil Procedure.

Congressional debate for the Leahy-Smith America Invents Act indicates that discovery standards under that legislation for *inter partes* review are identical to the standards in the original patent reform bill introduced by Senator Kyl in 2008. 157 Cong. Rec. S1375-76 (daily ed. Mar. 8, 2011). During introduction of the 2008 bill, Senator Kyl commented on the discovery standard for *inter partes* review, noting that it "restricts additional discovery to particular limited situations, such as minor discovery that PTO finds to be routinely useful, or to discovery that is justified by the special circumstances of the case." 154 Cong. Rec. S9988 (daily ed. Sept. 27, 2008) (statement of Sen. Kyl). Senator Kyl further commented that "[g]iven the time deadlines imposed on these proceedings, it is anticipated that, regardless of the standards imposed in [sections 316 and 326], PTO will be conservative in its grants of discovery." *Id.* at 9988–89.

Thus, in *inter partes* review, discovery is limited as compared to that available in district court litigation. Limited discovery lowers the cost, minimizes the complexity, and shortens the period required for dispute resolution. There is a one-year statutory deadline for completion of *inter partes* review, subject to limited exceptions. 35 U.S.C. § 316(a)(11); *see also* 37 C.F.R. § 42.100(c). What constitutes permissible discovery must be considered with that constraint in mind.

The statutory standard is "necessary in the interest of justice." 35 U.S.C. § 316(a)(5). We have previously advised Cuozzo, in an order authorizing the filing of a motion for additional discovery, that the following factors are important (Paper 20, 2-3):

1. More Than A Possibility And Mere Allegation— The mere possibility of finding something useful, and mere allegation that something useful will be found, are insufficient to demonstrate that the requested discovery is necessary in the interest of justice. The party requesting discovery should already be in possession of evidence tending to show beyond speculation that in fact something useful will be uncovered.

2. Litigation Positions And Underlying Basis—Asking for the other party's litigation positions and the underlying basis for those positions is not necessary in the interest of justice. The Board has established rules for the presentation of arguments and evidence. There is a proper time and place for each party to make its presentation. A party may not attempt to alter the Board's trial procedures under the pretext of discovery.

3. Ability To Generate Equivalent Information By Other Means—Information a party can reasonably figure out or assemble without a discovery request would not be in the interest of justice to have produced by the other party. In that connection, the Board would want to know the ability of the requesting party to generate the requested information without need of discovery.

4. Easily Understandable Instructions—The questions should be easily understandable. For example, ten pages of complex instructions for answering questions is prima facie unclear. Such instructions are counter-productive and tend to undermine the responder's ability to answer efficiently, accurately, and confidently.

5. Requests Not Overly Burdensome To Answer— The requests must not be overly burdensome to answer, given the expedited nature of *Inter Partes* Review. The burden includes financial burden, burden on human resources, and burden on meeting the time schedule of *Inter Partes* Review. Requests should be sensible and responsibly tailored according to a genuine need.

Factor (1)—More Than a Possibility and Mere Allegation

Critically undermining all aspects of the discovery motion is Cuozzo's misunderstanding of above-identified Factor (1). The essence of Factor (1) is unambiguously expressed by its language, *i.e.*, the requester of information should already be in possession of a threshold amount of evidence or reasoning tending to show beyond speculation that something useful will be uncovered. "Useful" in that context does not mean merely "relevant" and/or "admissible." In the context of Factor (1), "useful" means favorable in substantive value to a contention of the party moving for discovery. In the conference call held on February 14, 2013, we explained that meaning, in contrast to "relevant" and "admissible" to counsel for each party.

In its motion, Cuozzo re-wrote Factor (1) as "Likely to Yield Relevant, Admissible Evidence." (Paper 21, 9–11). The rewritten factor is incorrect, is very similar to the standard of discovery applicable in district court litigation, and is in sharp contrast to what Factor (1) means. We reiterate that in the context of Factor (1), "useful" means favorable in substantive value to a contention of the party moving for discovery. That notion is missing entirely from Cuozzo's rewritten factor.

The vast majority of Cuozzo's requested items relate to its potential assertion of secondary considerations of nonobviousness such as long-felt but unresolved need, failure of others, commercial success, and copying by others. Yet, conspicuously absent from Cuozzo's motion is a threshold amount of evidence or reasoning tending to show beyond speculation that the information to be discovered will be "useful" to Cuozzo. For instance, Cuozzo offered no evidence or sufficient reasoning tending to show beyond speculation that Garmin copied Cuozzo's invention, that Garmin had attempted but failed to develop a device having the features of Cuozzo's claimed invention, that Garmin achieved commercial success "because of" any inventive feature recited in Cuozzo's claims under review, or that Garmin recognized that there was a long-felt but unresolved need in the art for a feature implemented by Cuozzo's claimed invention. Note this language in Factor (1) above: "The mere possibility of finding something useful, and mere allegation that something useful will be found, are insufficient to demonstrate that the requested discovery is necessary in the interest of justice."

With regard to Cuozzo's potential assertion of commercial success as a secondary consideration of nonobviousness, there is an insufficient showing of nexus between the claimed invention and Cuozzo's discovery requests. Cuozzo has not made a sufficient threshold showing that the requested sales and pricing information are for units the sales of which are due to an inventive feature claimed by Cuozzo. Cuozzo has not accounted for the presence of other desirable features implemented on the same units for which sales and pricing information are requested. Cuozzo has not even represented that the units for which sales and pricing information are requested do not embody significant and desirable features not recited in Cuozzo's claims under review. Garmin in its opposition represents that the "speed limit alert feature" is but only one out of numerous features provided in Garmin's navigational devices. (Paper 22, 12). We note, in particular, that although the claims under review require a global positioning system receiver, none requires that global positioning system receiver to provide assistance in vehicle navigation. Thus, if Garmin's devices are navigational devices and if navigational assistance is a substantial and desirable feature, Cuozzo's requests lack critical nexus with its claimed invention. At least Interrogatory Nos. 3–7 and Request for Document Nos. 3, 4, 6, and 8 are adversely affected thereby.

With regard to Cuozzo's potential assertion of failure by others as secondary consideration of nonobviousness, we note that an allegation of failure by others is not evidence of nonobviousness unless it is shown that widespread efforts of skilled workers having knowledge of the prior art had failed to find a solution to the problem. *In re Allen*, 324 F.2d 993, 997 (CCPA 1963). Any failure by Garmin alone does not establish widespread failure by skilled workers in the art attempting to solve the same problem. Absent in Cuozzo's motion is a threshold amount of evidence tending to show that any skilled artisan having knowledge of the pertinent prior art had tried but failed to solve a problem related to speed limit alert indication. And even assuming that there are others who have tried but failed to solve a speed limit alert indication problem, Cuozzo has not set forth a threshold amount of evidence tending to show that Garmin itself had also tried but failed to solve that problem. At least Interrogatory No. 9 is adversely affected thereby Cuozzo speculates that Garmin charged an unusual premium for its navigation units on the basis of the "speed limit alert feature." (Paper 21, 11). Cuozzo requests information to substantiate that speculation. For instance, Request for Production No. 3 states: "License, settlement, co-development, or technology transfer agreements directly related to the speed limit alert feature." Request for Production No. 4 states: "To the extent the speed limit alert feature is discussed or addressed in them, Agreements between You and any customer, supplier, reseller, or distributor (including JVC Kenwood and Chrysler and excluding End-User License Agreements)." Request for Production No. 6 states: "Market analysis, market projections, projections, or roadmap Documents discussing Your decision to develop and commercialize the speed limit alert feature in Garmin products." Request for Production No. 8 states: "Documents sufficient to show the incremental commercial value of the speed limit alert feature included in Garmin's Personal Navigation Devices . . . ." Interrogatory Nos. 3-5 are similar.

However, Cuozzo has not presented a threshold amount of evidence or reasoning tending to show beyond speculation that Garmin was able to charge or demand a premium in the sense of unusual high price specifically for or on account of the "speed limit alert feature."

Request for Production No. 9 states: "Documents relating to the '074 patent, the inventor Guisseppe [sic] Cuozzo, or discussions YOU had with Mr. Cuozzo about his invention." Request for Production No. 10 states: "The file history for U.S. Patent No. 8,258,878 [Garmin's own patent on a navigation device], any agreements relating to it, and Documents discussing the '074 [Cuozzo's patent under review] or Guiseppe [*sic*] Cuozzo in connection with the '978 patent." Interrogatory Nos. 1, 7, and 8 are directed to Garmin's own technical development and introduction of a "speed alert/warning feature."

Presumably, Request for Production Nos. 9 and 10 and Interrogatory Nos. 1, 7, and 8 pertain to Cuozzo's potential assertion of copying by Garmin as a secondary consideration of nonobviousness. However, Cuozzo failed to present a threshold amount of evidence or reasoning tending to show beyond speculation that Garmin copied from Cuozzo. Accompanying the motion is a declaration of Cuozzo's sole inventor Giuseppe A. Cuozzo. (Ex. 2006). Paragraphs 3 and 4 of that declaration are reproduced below:

> 3. After my patent issued, I contacted Garmin by telephone because I noticed Garmin was selling a navigation device with a speed limit warning function. I asked to speak to someone in Garmin product development and eventually was contacted by a Garmin lawyer. I gave the number of my patent to the Garmin representative.
>
> 4. The Garmin lawyer told me that my claims did not cover Garmin's navigation devices because, according to the Garmin lawyer, my patent covered a system built in to the vehicle and their devices did not have a gauge cluster.

The above-quoted testimony establishes, at best, only that a Garmin lawyer had evaluated Cuozzo's patent and determined that Garmin's devices did not infringe. It does not even establish that Garmin was aware of Cuozzo's patent prior to making its navigation devices having a "speed limit alert feature." Even assuming infringement of Cuozzo's claims under review by Garmin's devices which is a matter we do not determine, that is not evidence of copying. Garmin might well have independently conceived of and developed the invention.

Under Federal Circuit jurisprudence, not every competing product that arguably falls within the scope of a patent is evidence of copying, because otherwise every infringement suit would automatically confirm the nonobviousness of the patent. *Wyers v. Master Lock Co.*, 616 F.3d 1231 (Fed. Cir. 2010); *Iron Grip Barbell Co. v. USA Sports, Inc.*, 392 F.3d 1317, 1325 (Fed. Cir. 2004). Copying as objective evidence of nonobviousness requires evidence of effort to replicate a specific product. *Wyers*, 616 F.3d at 1246; *Iron Grip Barbell Co.*, 392 F.3d at 1325. As we have stated above, Cuozzo failed to present a threshold amount of evidence or reasoning tending to show beyond speculation that Garmin copied from Cuozzo.

With regard to Cuozzo's potential assertion of long-felt but unresolved need as secondary consideration of nonobviousness, Cuozzo has not set forth a threshold amount of evidence or reasoning tending to show that Garmin recognized that there had been a long-felt but unresolved need with regard to a speed limit alert indicator. At least Interrogatory Nos. 1, 2, 5, and 7-9, and Request for Document Nos. 3, 4, and 6 are adversely affected thereby.

On page 1 of the motion, Cuozzo states generally that it seeks to discover the identity of Garmin's privies. In that regard, Interrogatory No. 6 states: "If any non-Garmin entity owns or has an interest in the speed limit alert technology or intellectual property, please identify the entities and Describe their respective interest." The motion does not explain for what purpose Cuozzo seeks the identity of Garmin's privies and a description of their respective interests. It is thus unknown in what manner Cuozzo expects the answer to the interrogatory to be "useful" in this review. During the telephone conference conducted on February 14, 2013, we already advised counsel for Cuozzo that the Federal Rules of Civil Procedure do not apply in inter parte[s] review and that Cuozzo must apply the rules for *inter partes* review regarding joinder of another party including a privy.

Factor (2)—Litigation Positions and Underlying Basis

Consideration of Factor (2) weighs against granting Cuozzo's Request for Production No. 5, which reads: "Documents You intend to rely upon at trial or have provided or intend to provide to an expert witness or declarant." In Factor (2), we indicate that asking for the other party's litigation positions and the underlying basis for those positions is not necessary in the interest of justice. Also in Factor (2), we indicate that the Board has established rules for the presentation of arguments and evidence and that there is a proper time and place for each party to make its presentation, and that a party may not attempt to alter the Board's trial procedures under the pretext of discovery. If and when Garmin presents affidavit or declaration testimony to support any position it maintains, Cuozzo has an opportunity to cross-examine the affiant or declarant with regard to the basis of the testimony. Garmin is not obligated to keep Cuozzo informed of its positions on substantive issues before Garmin is ready to present them in this review.

Factor (3)—Ability to Generate Equivalent Information by Other Means

With regard to Cuozzo's potential assertion of long-felt but unresolved need as secondary consideration of nonobviousness, and whether Garmin charged an unusual premium for the "speed limit alert feature," the discovery requests also fail Factor (3)—Ability to Generate Equivalent Information by Other Means. Cuozzo has not adequately explained why it needs Garmin's views to establish what Cuozzo believes had been a long-felt but unresolved need with regard to speed limit indicators. Cuozzo can rely on its own analysis of the state of the art or on the opinions of independent analysts. With regard to the price differential between Garmin products with and without the "speed limit alert feature," Cuozzo can conduct its own market survey and make its own comparison. Further applying Factor (3), we note that Garmin need not produce the file histories of prior art references relied upon by Garmin in its petition, which is the subject of Request for Production No. 7, or the file history for Patent 8,258,978, which is the subject of Request for Production No. 10.

Factor (4)—Easily Understandable Instructions

Factor (4) concerns easily understandable instructions. We have considered the two-page instructions for interrogatories and the two-page instructions for document requests and conclude that the instructions are easily understandable.

Factor (5)—Not Overly Burdensome to Answer

In Factor (5), we consider whether the requests are overly burdensome to answer, given the one-year statutory deadline for *inter partes* review. The burden includes financial burden, burden on human resources, and burden on meeting the time schedule of this review. Requests should be sensible and responsibly tailored according to a genuine need. As is explained with sufficient specificity in Garmin's opposition, compliance with the discovery request (except for production of several file histories) requires a very significant expenditure of human and financial resources. Even if Garmin suspects that no document meets a particular request, it is legally obligated to make a diligent search for information. The opposition notes that Garmin has millions of pages of engineering documents that potentially have to be searched to determine if any contain a reference to the "speed limit alert feature." The opposition also notes that responding to Interrogatories 3 and 4 will likely require 20–30 hours of time to compute the information on a product-by-product basis because of the manner in which Garmin maintains its financial data. (Paper 22, 8).

Garmin's estimate is that responding to the document requests could require approximately 75-125 labor hours and cost $22,500–$37,500 dollars, that responding to the interrogatories could require approximately 50–75 labor hours and cost $15,00[0]-$22,500 dollars, and that the cost of producing one or more persons to testify at a deposition could require approximately 50–75 labor hours and cost $15,000–$22,500 dollars. (*Id.* at 8–9). The total cost estimate is $52,500 to $82,500.

The burden imposed on all parties for meeting the time schedule of this *inter partes* review is also a consideration under Factor (5). Garmin filed its petition on September 16, 2012. Cuozzo waived its right to file a preliminary response. We instituted review on January 9, 2013. Cuozzo first requested authorization to file a motion for discovery on February 14, 2013. We cannot conclude on these facts that Cuozzo unduly delayed its request for additional discovery.

In considering whether the requests are responsibly tailored according to a genuine need under Factor (5), however, we identify Document Request No. 1 as failing in that regard. It reads as follows: "Documents and Things You considered in preparing Your responses to patent owner's Interrogatories." The undue breadth of such a request is self-evident. It suffices to say only that the documents and things need not contain anything useful or even relevant. The more thoughtful and diligent the respondent is in answering the interrogatories by considering the "potential" relevance of more items, the more items need to be produced regardless of usefulness and relevance. There is no valid reason for such an all-encompassing demand.

The Request for Deposition in the Manner of Fed R. Civ. P. 30(b)(6)

Cuozzo requests deposing a representative of Garmin under Fed. R. Civ. P 30(b)(6), on many of the same topics addressed by its Interrogatory Nos. 1–9 and request for Documents 1–10. Thus, all of the problems and deficiencies discussed above with respect to interrogatories and document production requests equally apply to the deposition request where the subject areas overlap.

CONCLUSION

For reasons discussed above, we conclude that Cuozzo's motion has not met the "necessary in the interest of justice" standard for any one of the requested items of discovery in its proposed Interrogatory Nos. 1–9, proposed Request for

Document Production Nos. 1–10, and proposed deposition of a Garmin representative pursuant to Federal Rule of Civil Procedure 30(b)(6).

ORDER

It is **ORDERED** that Cuozzo's motion for additional discovery is *denied*; and

FURTHER ORDERED that each party shall, within five days of the date of this communication file a paper to confirm whether it has, up to March 4, 2013, complied with the requirements of routine discovery under 37 C.F.R § 41.51(b)(1)(iii).

Table of Laws and Rules

UNITED STATES CONSTITUTION

AMERICA INVENTS ACT

AMERICA INVENTS ACT—Continued

FEDERAL FOOD, DRUG AND COSMETIC ACT

INTERNAL REVENUE CODE

PATENT ACT

UNITED STATES CODE ANNOTATED

UNITED STATES CODE ANNOTATED—Continued

UNITED STATES CODE ANNOTATED—Continued

CODE OF FEDERAL REGULATIONS

CODE OF FEDERAL REGULATIONS—Continued

CODE OF FEDERAL REGULATIONS—Continued

FEDERAL RULES OF CIVIL PROCEDURE

FEDERAL REGISTER

CALIFORNIA BUSINESS AND PROFESSIONS CODE

WASHINGTON REVISED CODE

Table of Cases

E

F

G

H

I

J

K

L

R

V

W

Y

Z

Index